TABLE OF CONTENTS

COLLECTOR'S EDITION

Fruits Basket 10

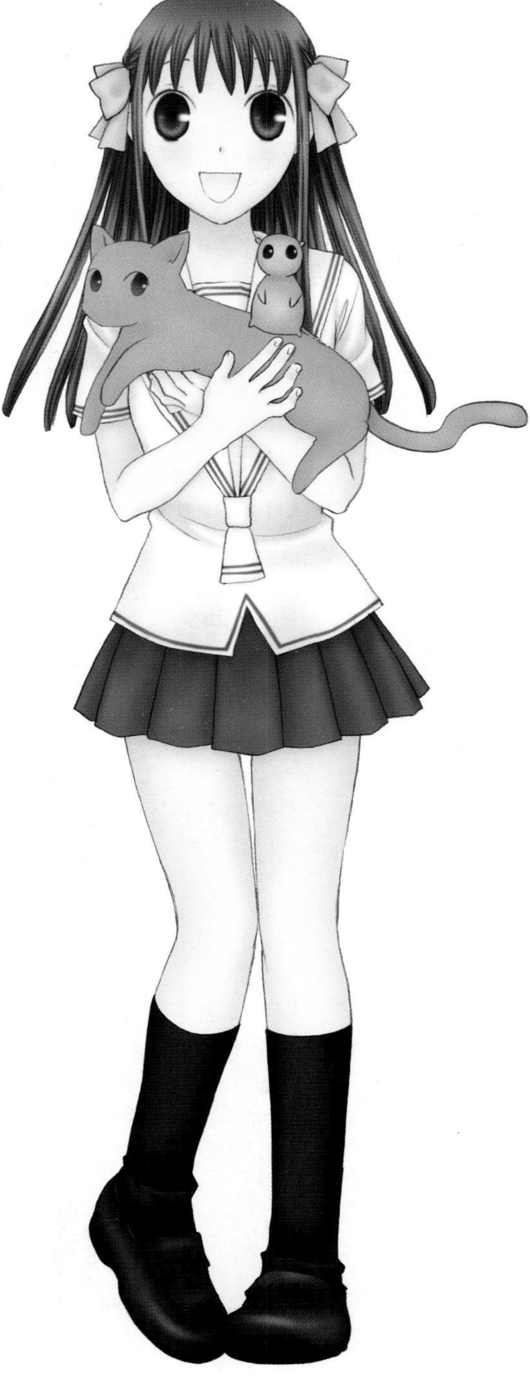

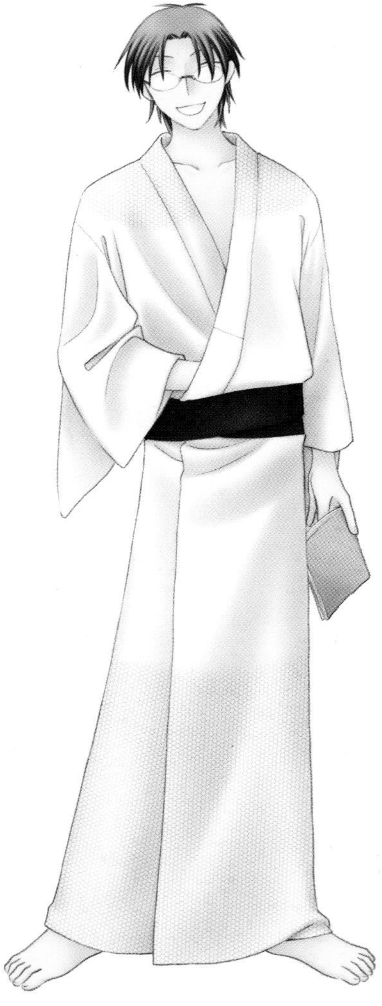

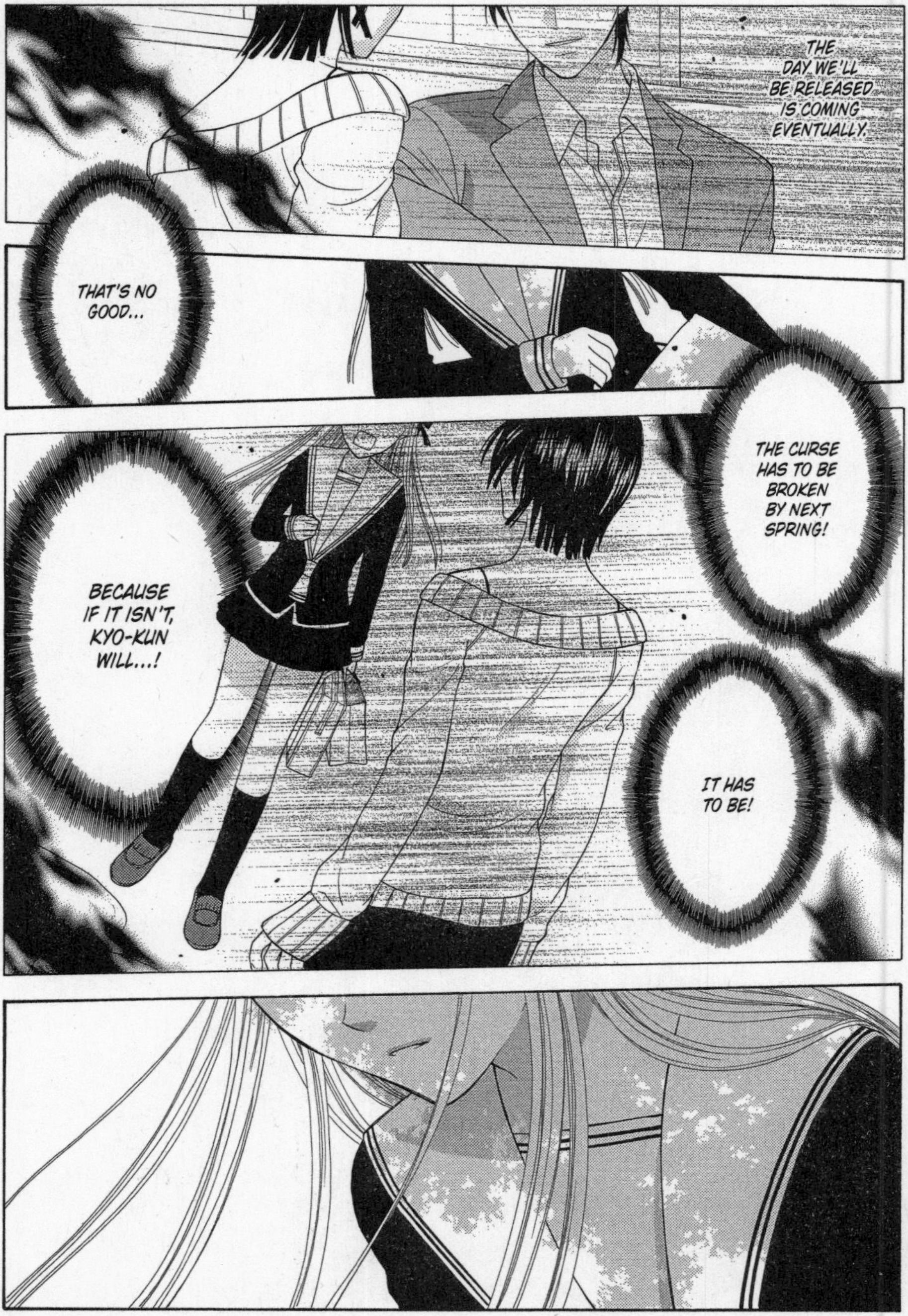
THE DAY WE'LL BE RELEASED IS COMING EVENTUALLY.
THAT'S NO GOOD...
THE CURSE HAS TO BE BROKEN BY NEXT SPRING!
IT HAS TO BE!
BECAUSE IF IT ISN'T, KYO-KUN WILL...!

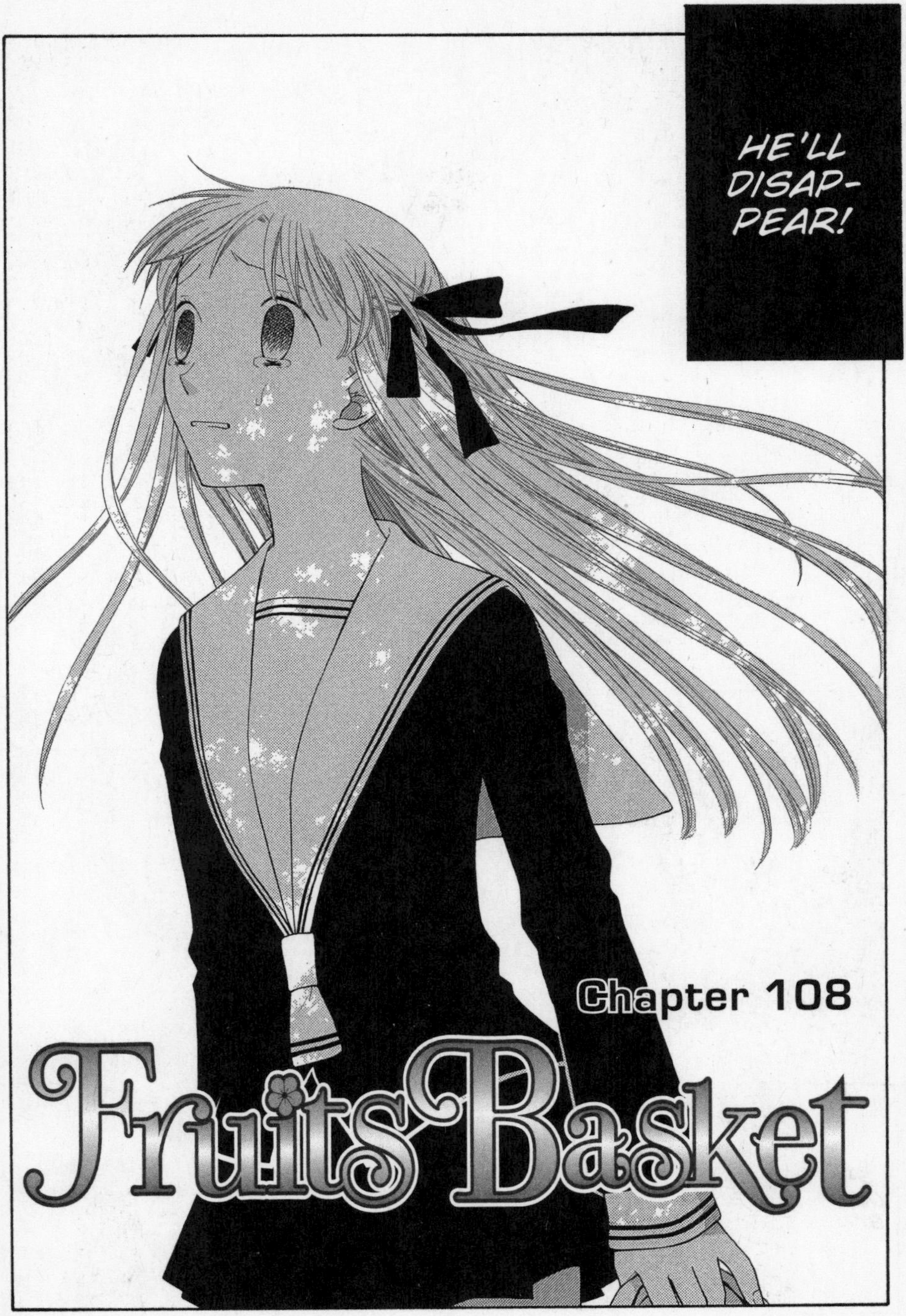
HE'LL DISAP- PEAR!
Chapter 108
Fruits Basket

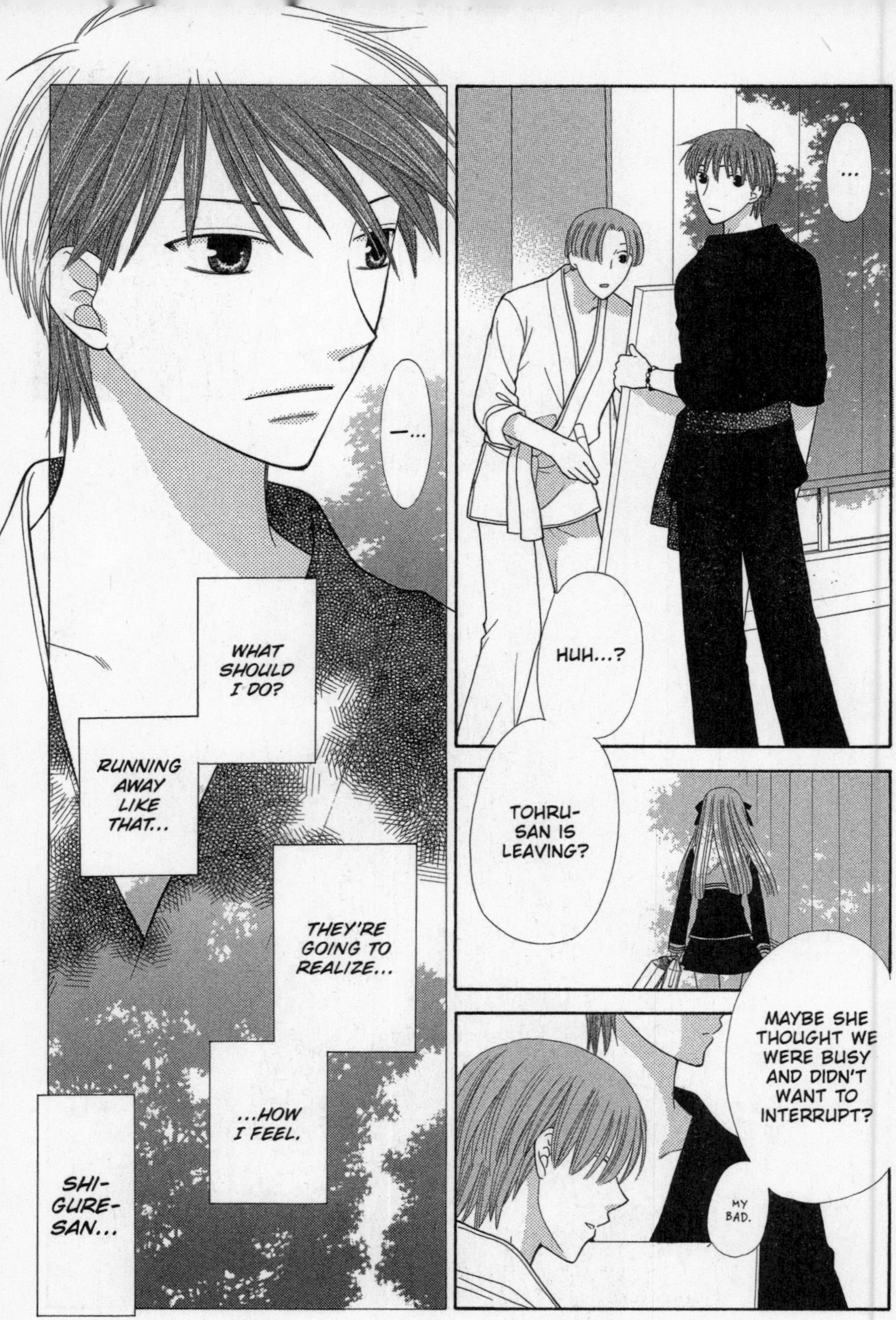
...
HUH...?
TOHRU-SAN IS LEAVING?
MAYBE SHE THOUGHT WE WERE BUSY AND DIDN'T WANT TO INTERRUPT?
MY BAD.
—...
WHAT SHOULD I DO?
RUNNING AWAY LIKE THAT...
THEY'RE GOING TO REALIZE...
...HOW I FEEL.
SHI-GURE-SAN...

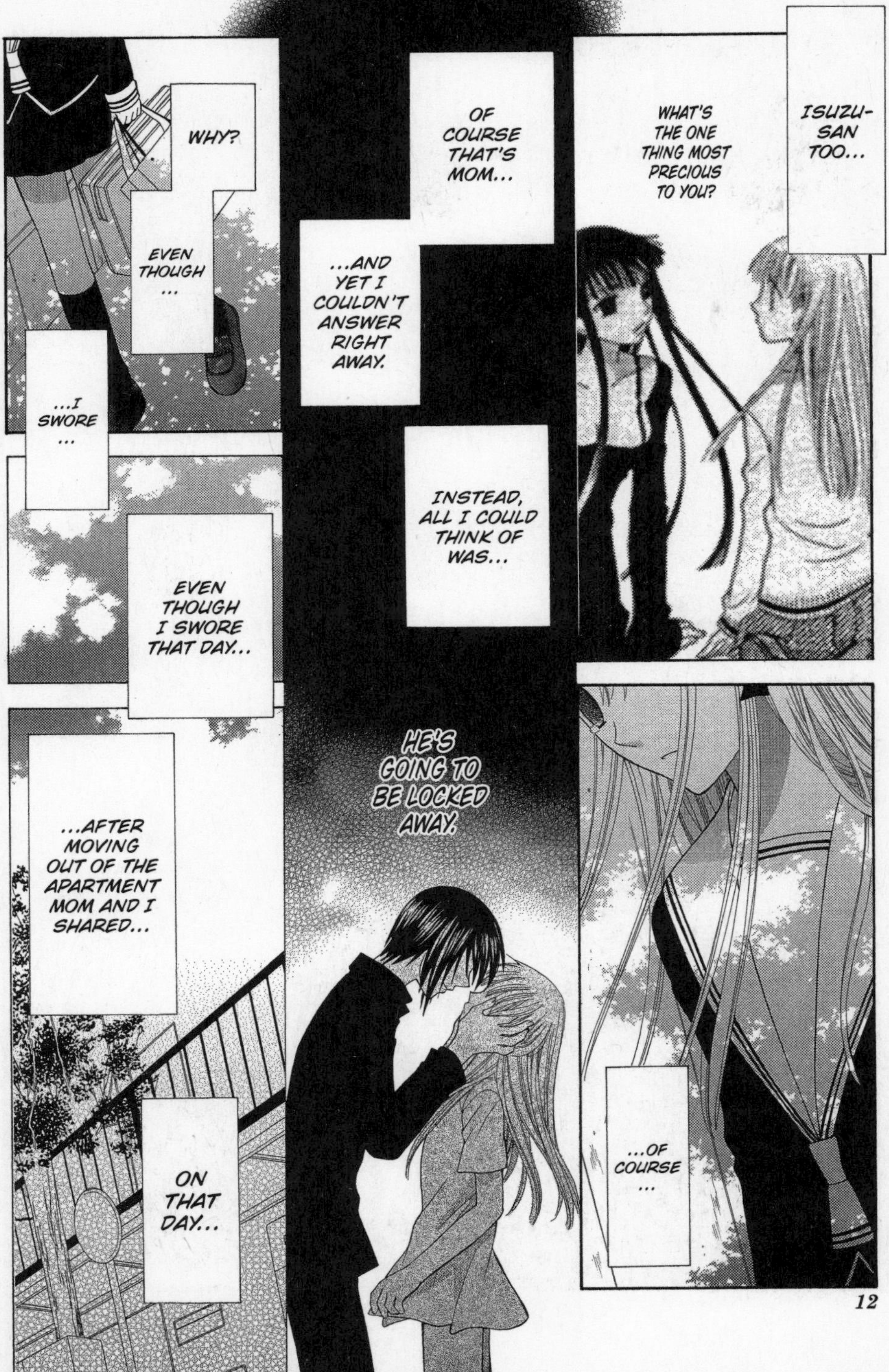
ISUZU-SAN TOO...
WHAT'S THE ONE THING MOST PRECIOUS TO YOU?
...OF COURSE...
OF COURSE THAT'S MOM...
...AND YET I COULDN'T ANSWER RIGHT AWAY.
INSTEAD, ALL I COULD THINK OF WAS...
HE'S GOING TO BE LOCKED AWAY.
WHY?
EVEN THOUGH...
...I SWORE...
EVEN THOUGH I SWORE THAT DAY...
...AFTER MOVING OUT OF THE APARTMENT MOM AND I SHARED...
ON THAT DAY...

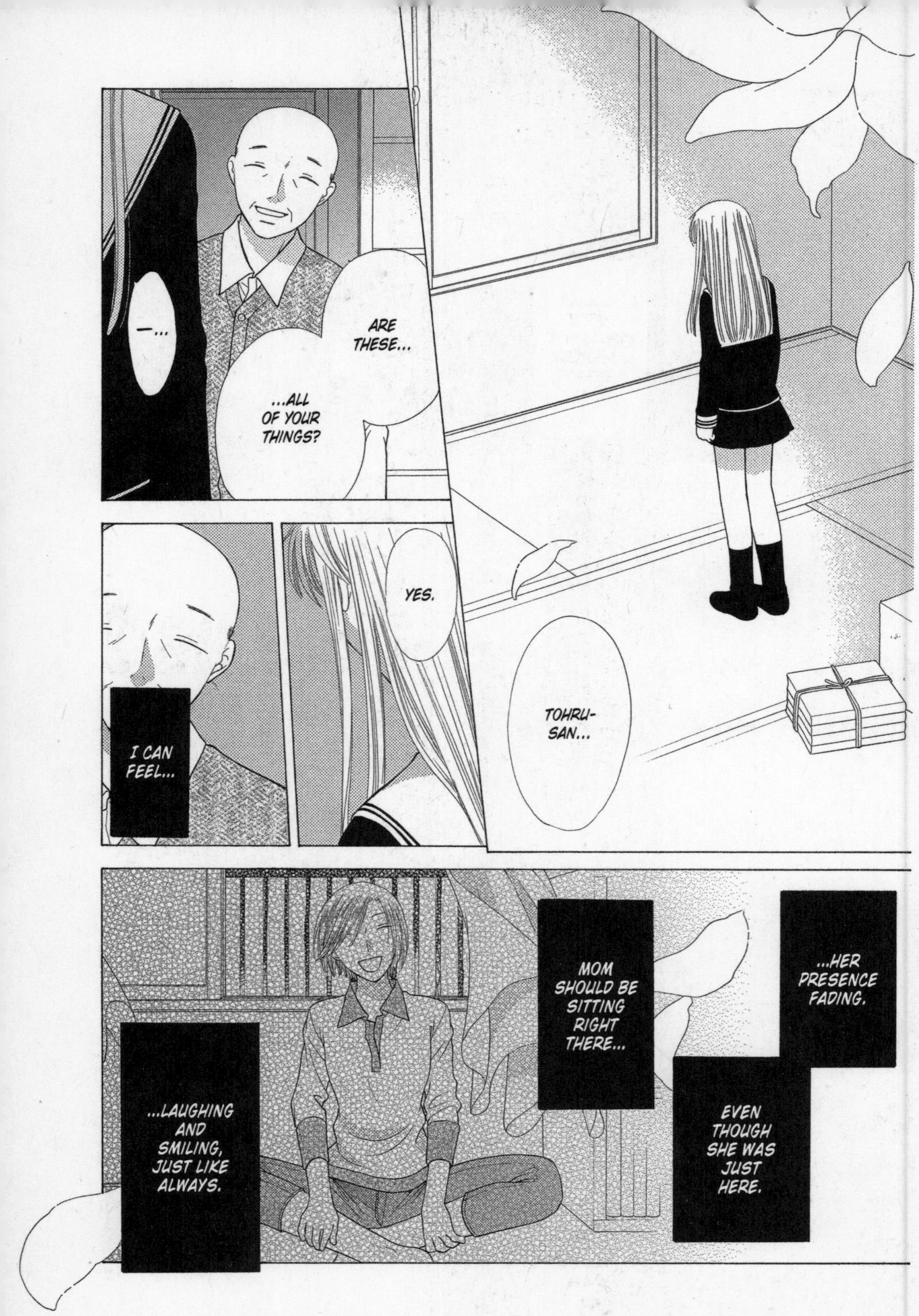
TOHRU-SAN...
ARE THESE...
...ALL OF YOUR THINGS?
—...
YES.
I CAN FEEL...
...HER PRESENCE FADING.
EVEN THOUGH SHE WAS JUST HERE.
MOM SHOULD BE SITTING RIGHT THERE...
...LAUGHING AND SMILING, JUST LIKE ALWAYS.

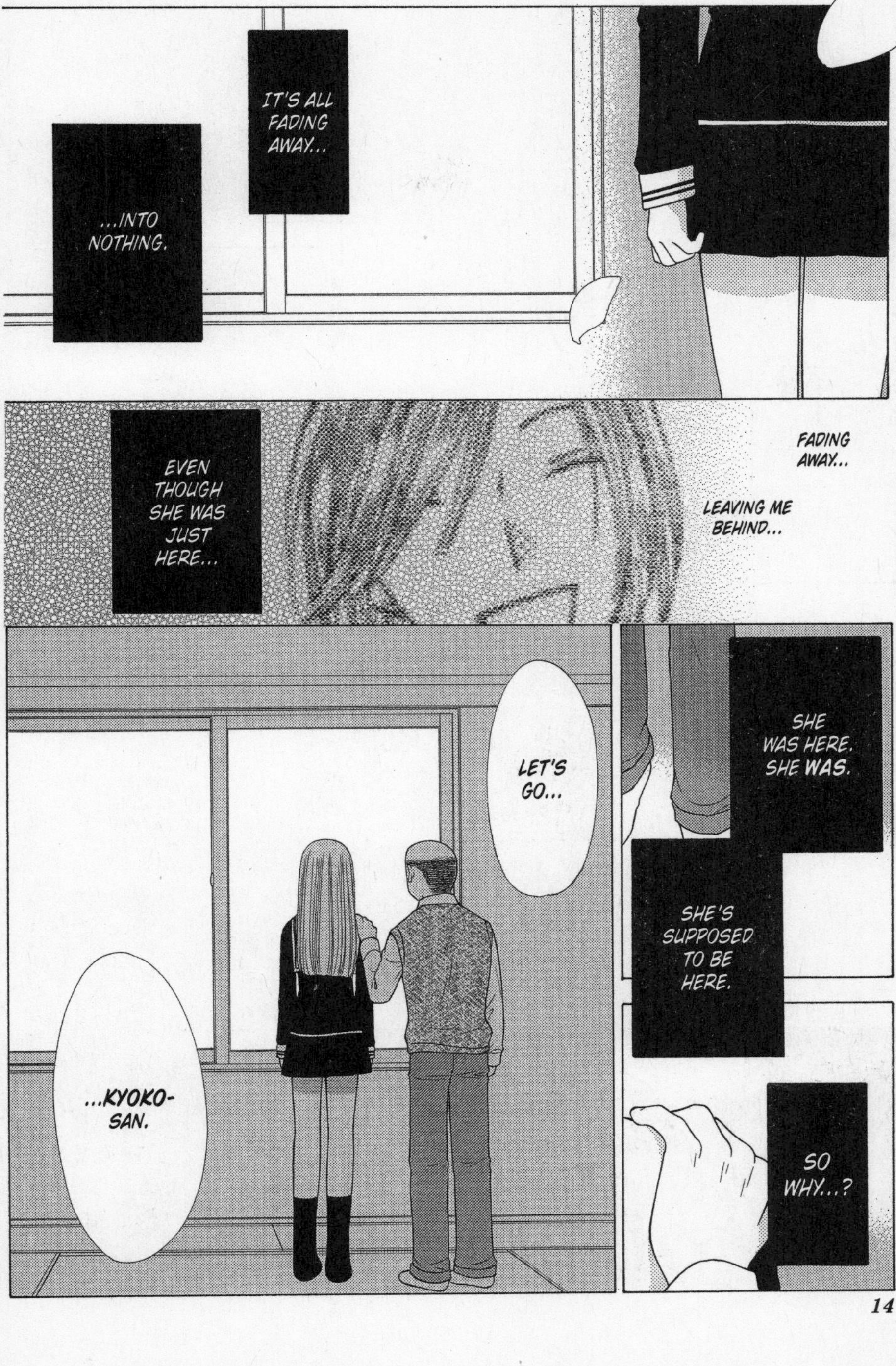
IT'S ALL FADING AWAY...
...INTO NOTHING.
FADING AWAY...
LEAVING ME BEHIND...
EVEN THOUGH SHE WAS JUST HERE...
SHE WAS HERE. SHE WAS.
SHE'S SUPPOSED TO BE HERE.
SO WHY...?
LET'S GO...
...KYOKO-SAN.

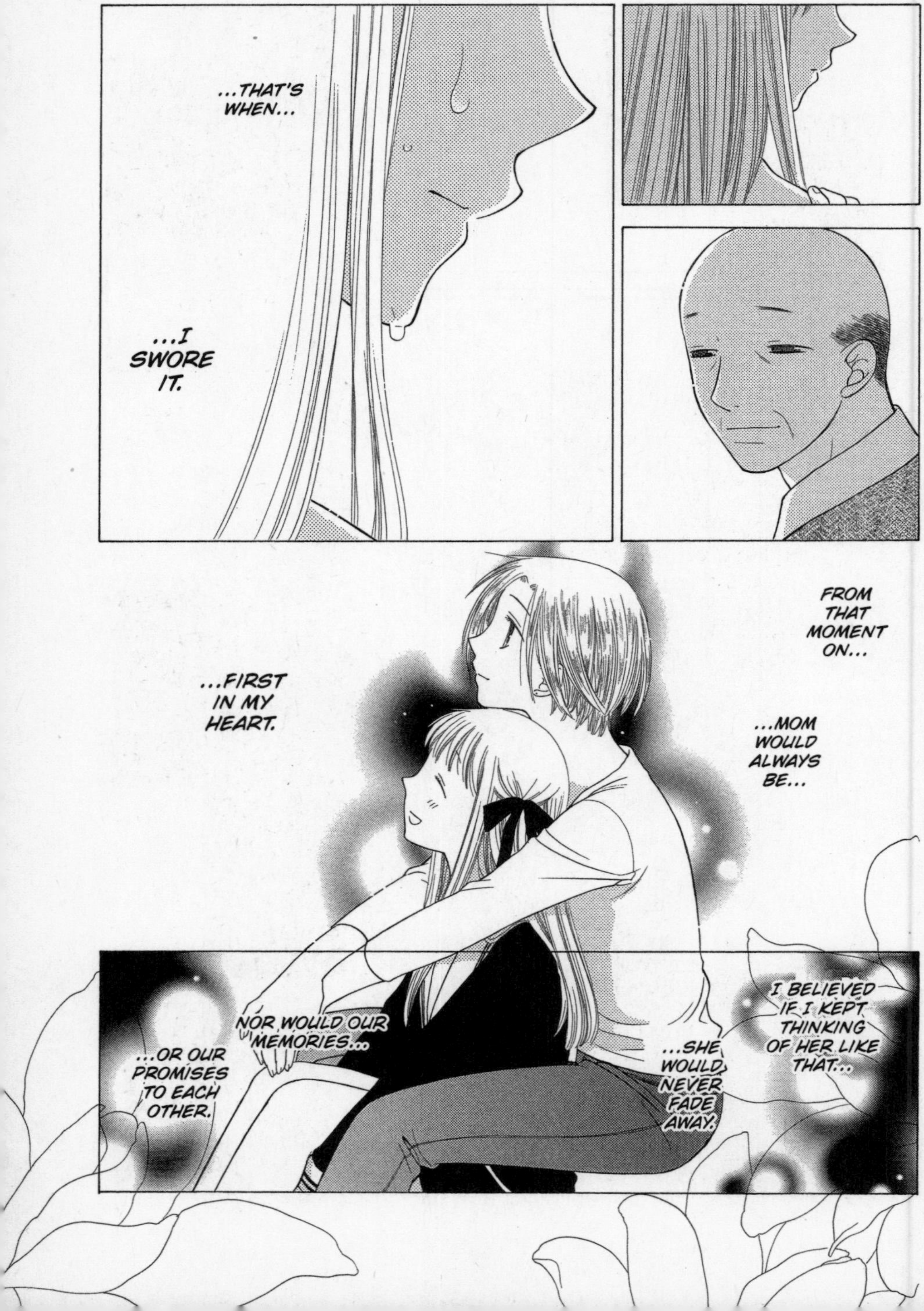
...THAT'S WHEN...
...I SWORE IT.
FROM THAT MOMENT ON...
...MOM WOULD ALWAYS BE...
...FIRST IN MY HEART.
I BELIEVED IF I KEPT THINKING OF HER LIKE THAT...
...SHE WOULD NEVER FADE AWAY.
NOR WOULD OUR MEMORIES...
...OR OUR PROMISES TO EACH OTHER.

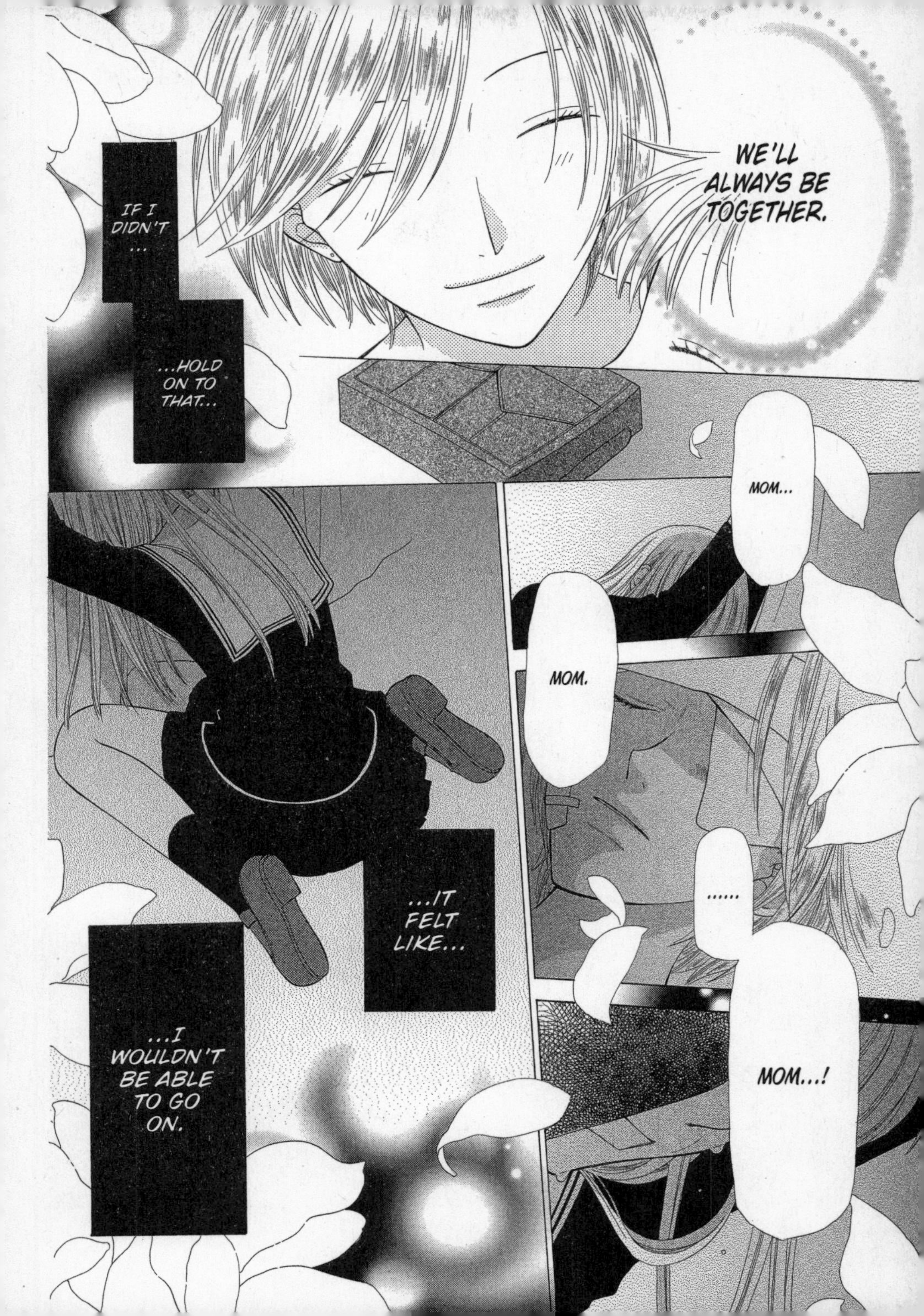
WE'LL ALWAYS BE TOGETHER.
IF I DIDN'T ...
...HOLD ON TO THAT...
MOM...
MOM.
......
MOM...!
...IT FELT LIKE...
...I WOULDN'T BE ABLE TO GO ON.

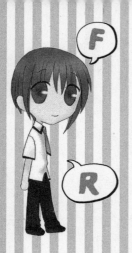

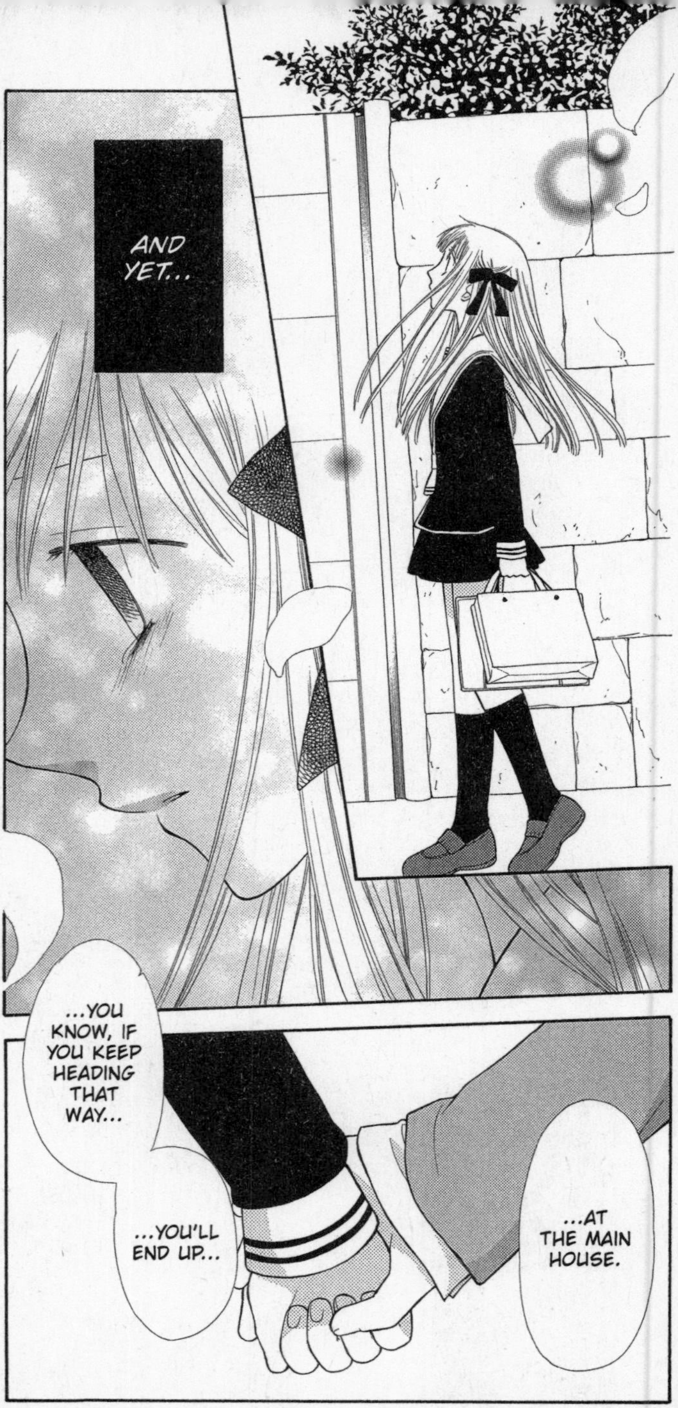
AND YET...
...YOU KNOW, IF YOU KEEP HEADING THAT WAY...
...YOU'LL END UP...
...AT THE MAIN HOUSE.

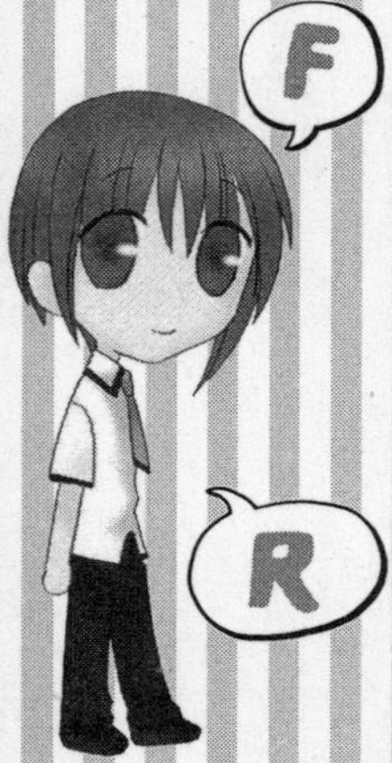
F
R

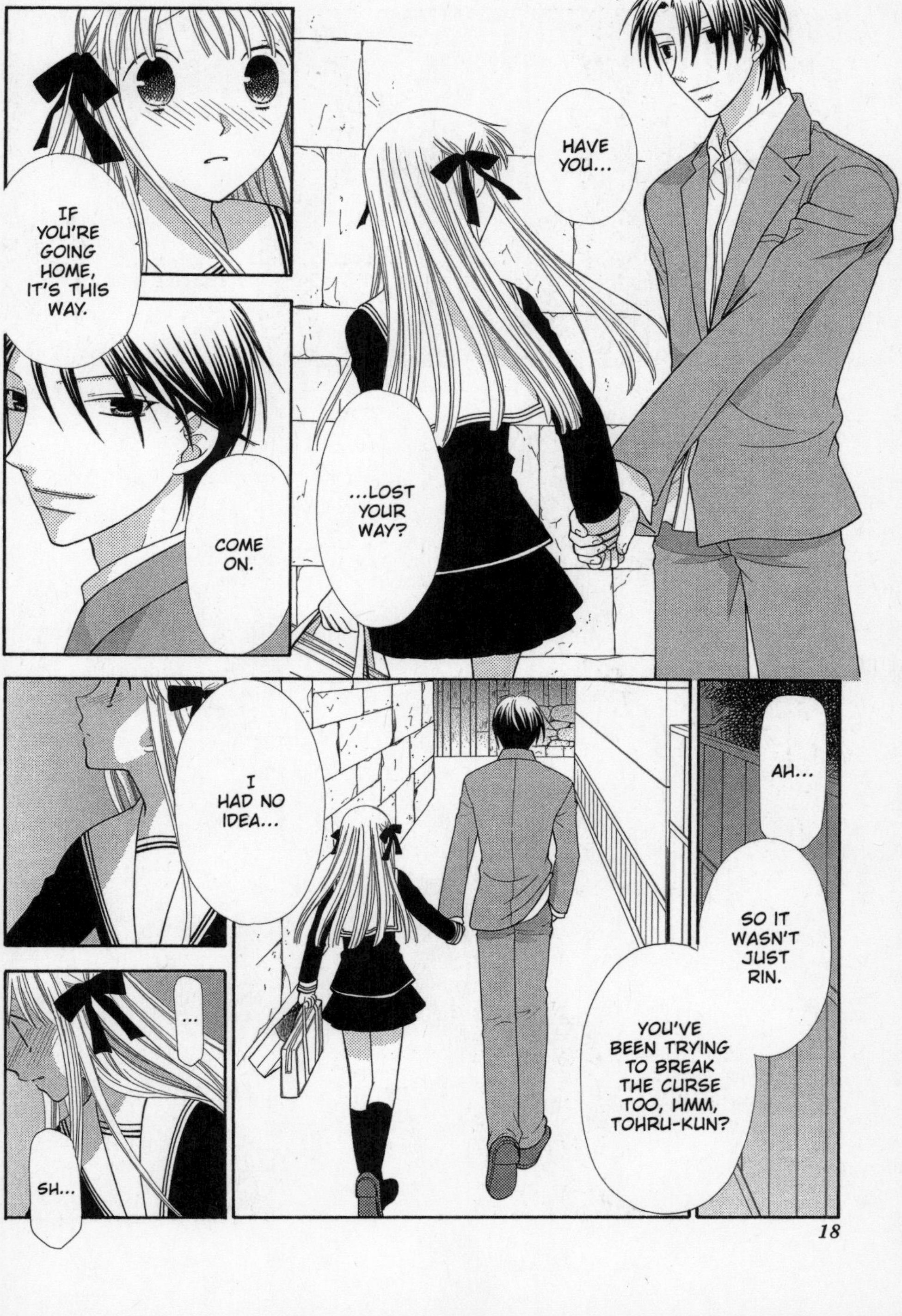
HAVE YOU...
...LOST YOUR WAY?
IF YOU'RE GOING HOME, IT'S THIS WAY.
COME ON.
AH...
SO IT WASN'T JUST RIN.
YOU'VE BEEN TRYING TO BREAK THE CURSE TOO, HMM, TOHRU-KUN?
I HAD NO IDEA...
...
SH...

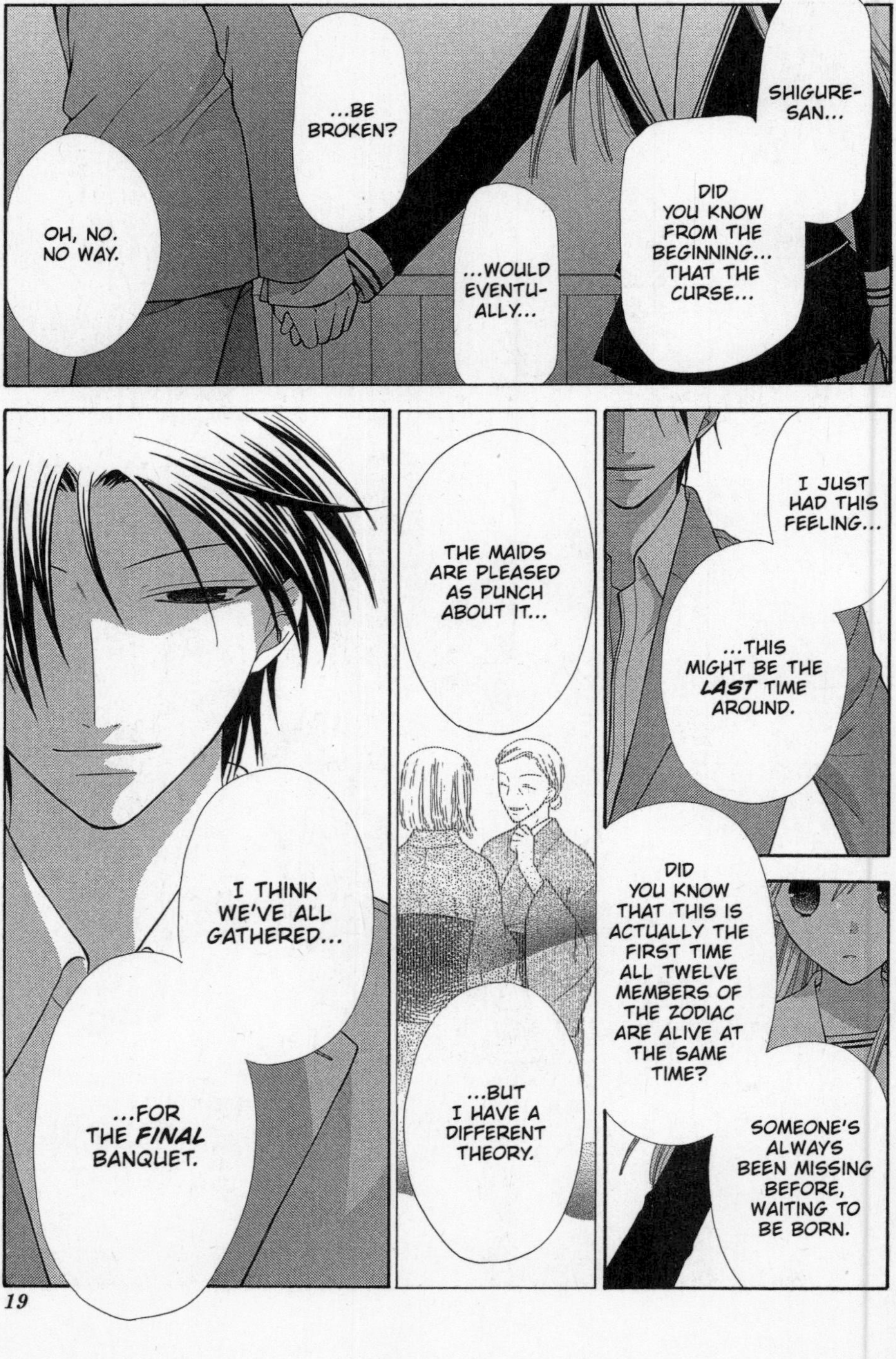
SHIGURE-SAN...
DID YOU KNOW FROM THE BEGINNING... THAT THE CURSE...
...WOULD EVENTU-ALLY...
...BE BROKEN?
OH, NO. NO WAY.
I JUST HAD THIS FEELING...
...THIS MIGHT BE THE *LAST* TIME AROUND.
DID YOU KNOW THAT THIS IS ACTUALLY THE FIRST TIME ALL TWELVE MEMBERS OF THE ZODIAC ARE ALIVE AT THE SAME TIME?
SOMEONE'S ALWAYS BEEN MISSING BEFORE, WAITING TO BE BORN.
THE MAIDS ARE PLEASED AS PUNCH ABOUT IT...
...BUT I HAVE A DIFFERENT THEORY.
I THINK WE'VE ALL GATHERED...
...FOR THE *FINAL* BANQUET.

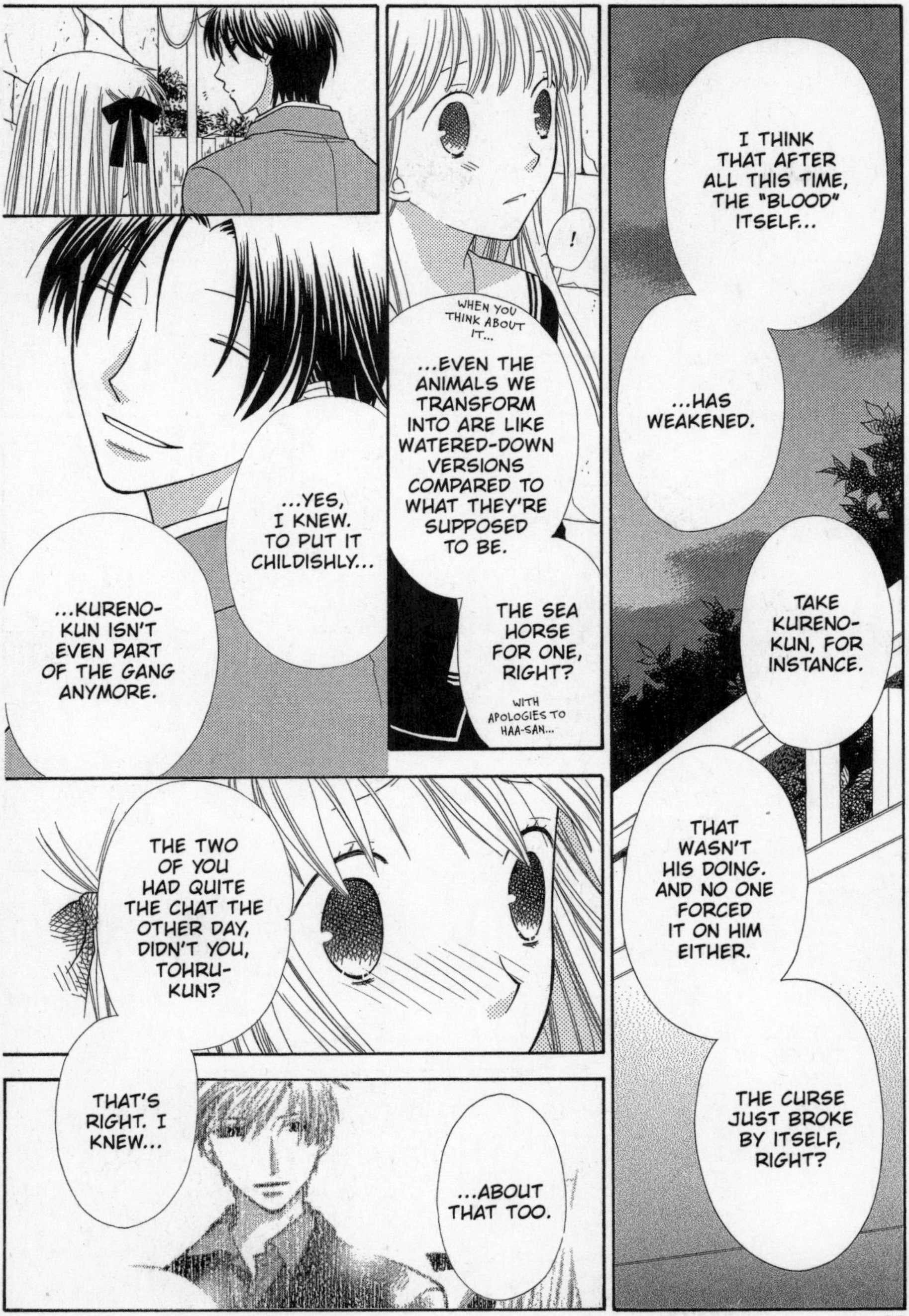
I THINK THAT AFTER ALL THIS TIME, THE "BLOOD" ITSELF...
...HAS WEAKENED.
!
WHEN YOU THINK ABOUT IT...
...EVEN THE ANIMALS WE TRANSFORM INTO ARE LIKE WATERED-DOWN VERSIONS COMPARED TO WHAT THEY'RE SUPPOSED TO BE.
THE SEA HORSE FOR ONE, RIGHT?
WITH APOLOGIES TO HAA-SAN...
TAKE KURENO-KUN, FOR INSTANCE.
THAT WASN'T HIS DOING. AND NO ONE FORCED IT ON HIM EITHER.
THE CURSE JUST BROKE BY ITSELF, RIGHT?
...YES, I KNEW. TO PUT IT CHILDISHLY...
...KURENO-KUN ISN'T EVEN PART OF THE GANG ANYMORE.
THE TWO OF YOU HAD QUITE THE CHAT THE OTHER DAY, DIDN'T YOU, TOHRU-KUN?
THAT'S RIGHT. I KNEW...
...ABOUT THAT TOO.

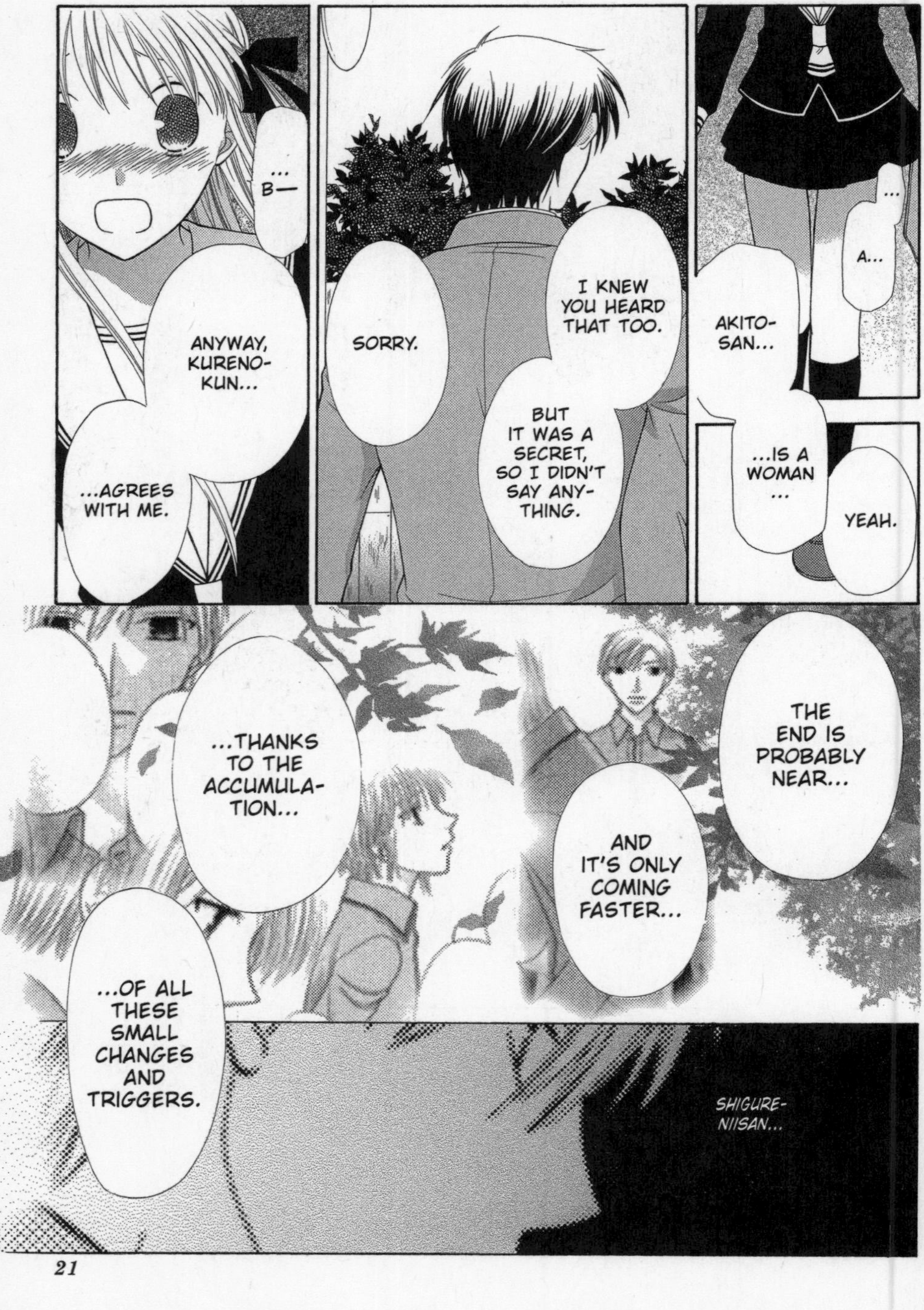
...
A...
AKITO-SAN...
...IS A WOMAN...
YEAH.
I KNEW YOU HEARD THAT TOO.
BUT IT WAS A SECRET, SO I DIDN'T SAY ANY-THING.
SORRY.
... B—
ANYWAY, KURENO-KUN...
...AGREES WITH ME.
THE END IS PROBABLY NEAR...
AND IT'S ONLY COMING FASTER...
...THANKS TO THE ACCUMULA-TION...
...OF ALL THESE SMALL CHANGES AND TRIGGERS.
SHIGURE-NIISAN...

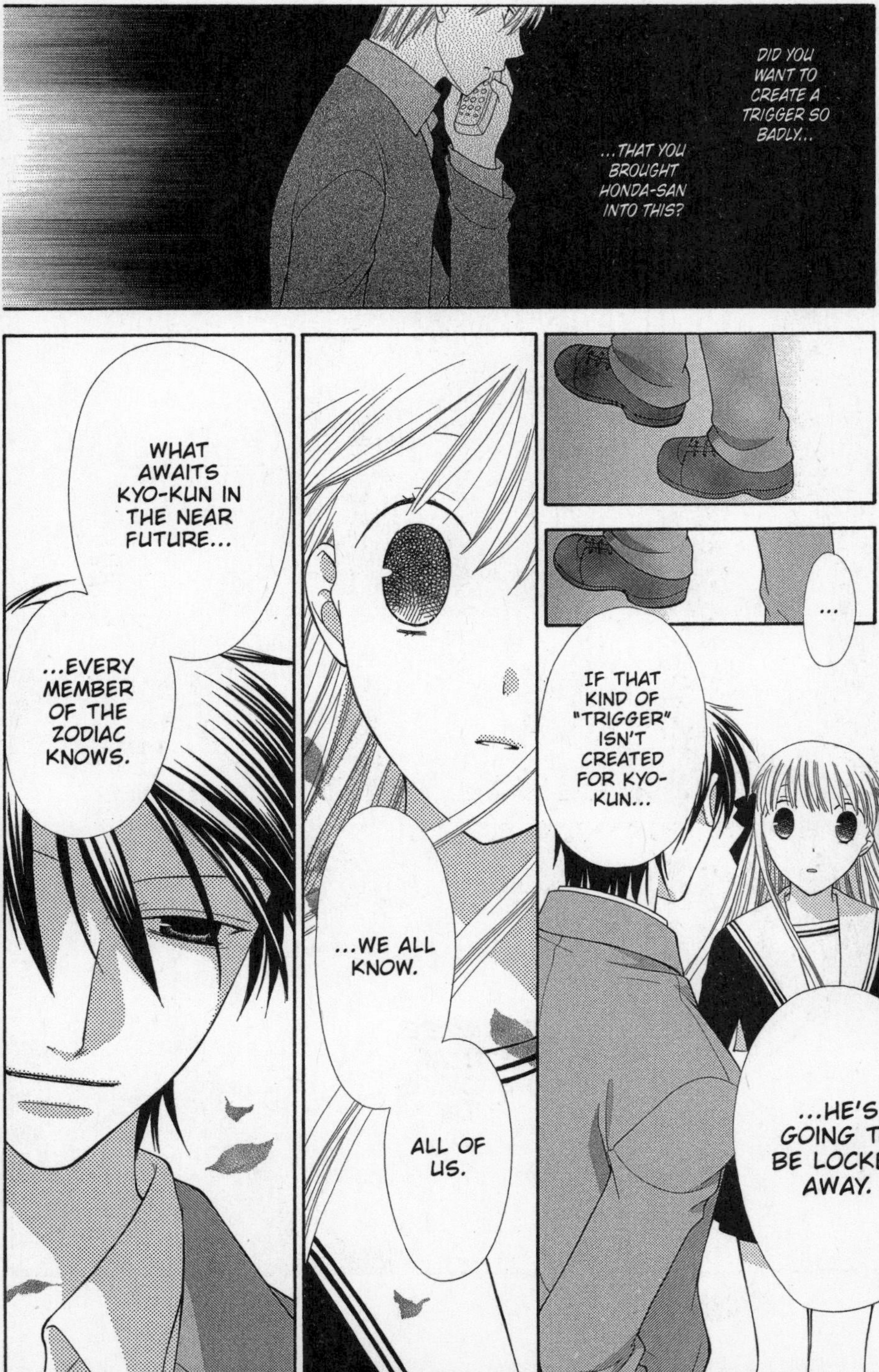
DID YOU WANT TO CREATE A TRIGGER SO BADLY...
...THAT YOU BROUGHT HONDA-SAN INTO THIS?
...
IF THAT KIND OF "TRIGGER" ISN'T CREATED FOR KYO-KUN...
...HE'S GOING TO BE LOCKED AWAY.
...WE ALL KNOW.
ALL OF US.
WHAT AWAITS KYO-KUN IN THE NEAR FUTURE...
...EVERY MEMBER OF THE ZODIAC KNOWS.

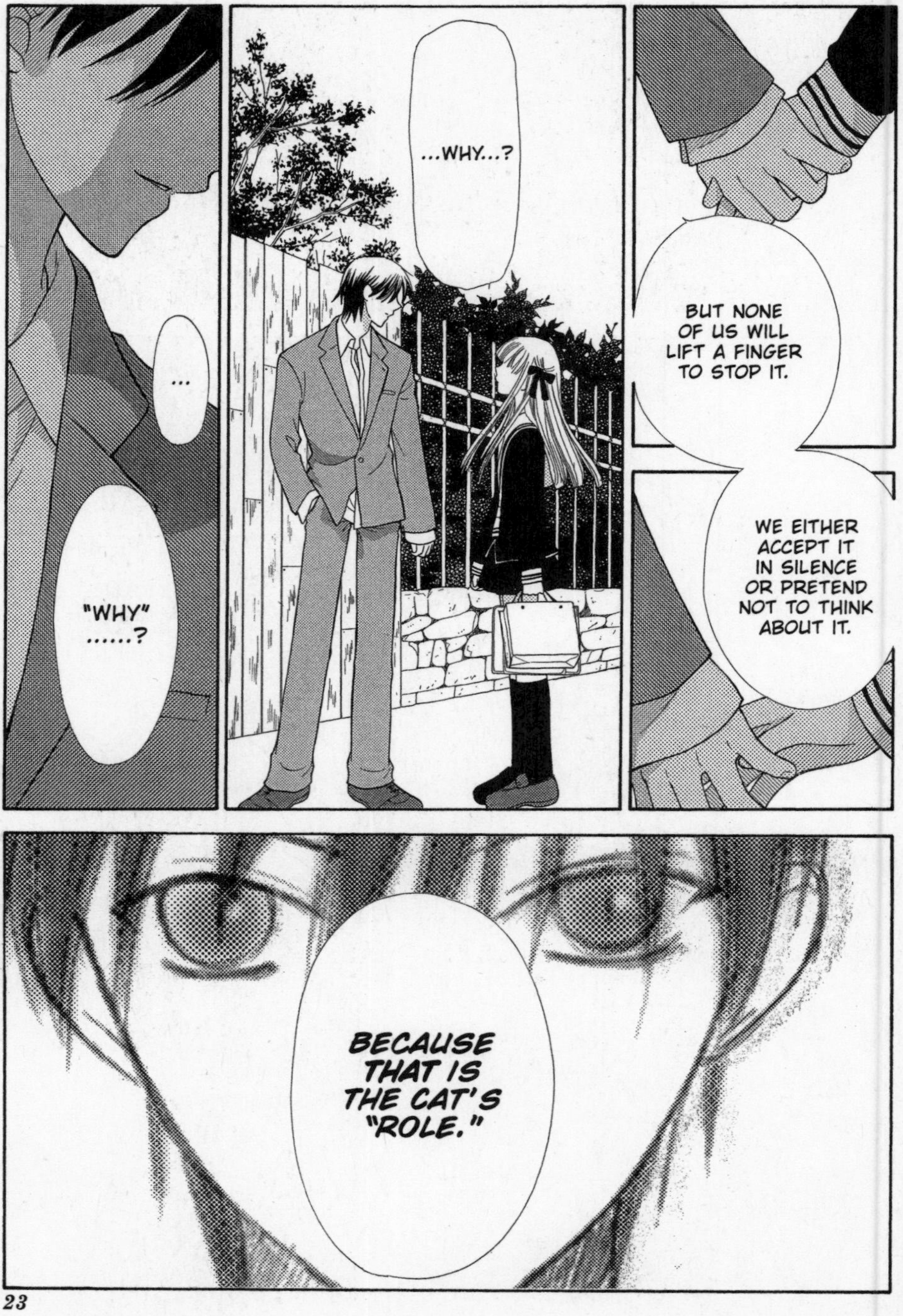
BUT NONE OF US WILL LIFT A FINGER TO STOP IT.
WE EITHER ACCEPT IT IN SILENCE OR PRETEND NOT TO THINK ABOUT IT.
...WHY...?
...
"WHY" ......?
BECAUSE THAT IS THE CAT'S "ROLE."

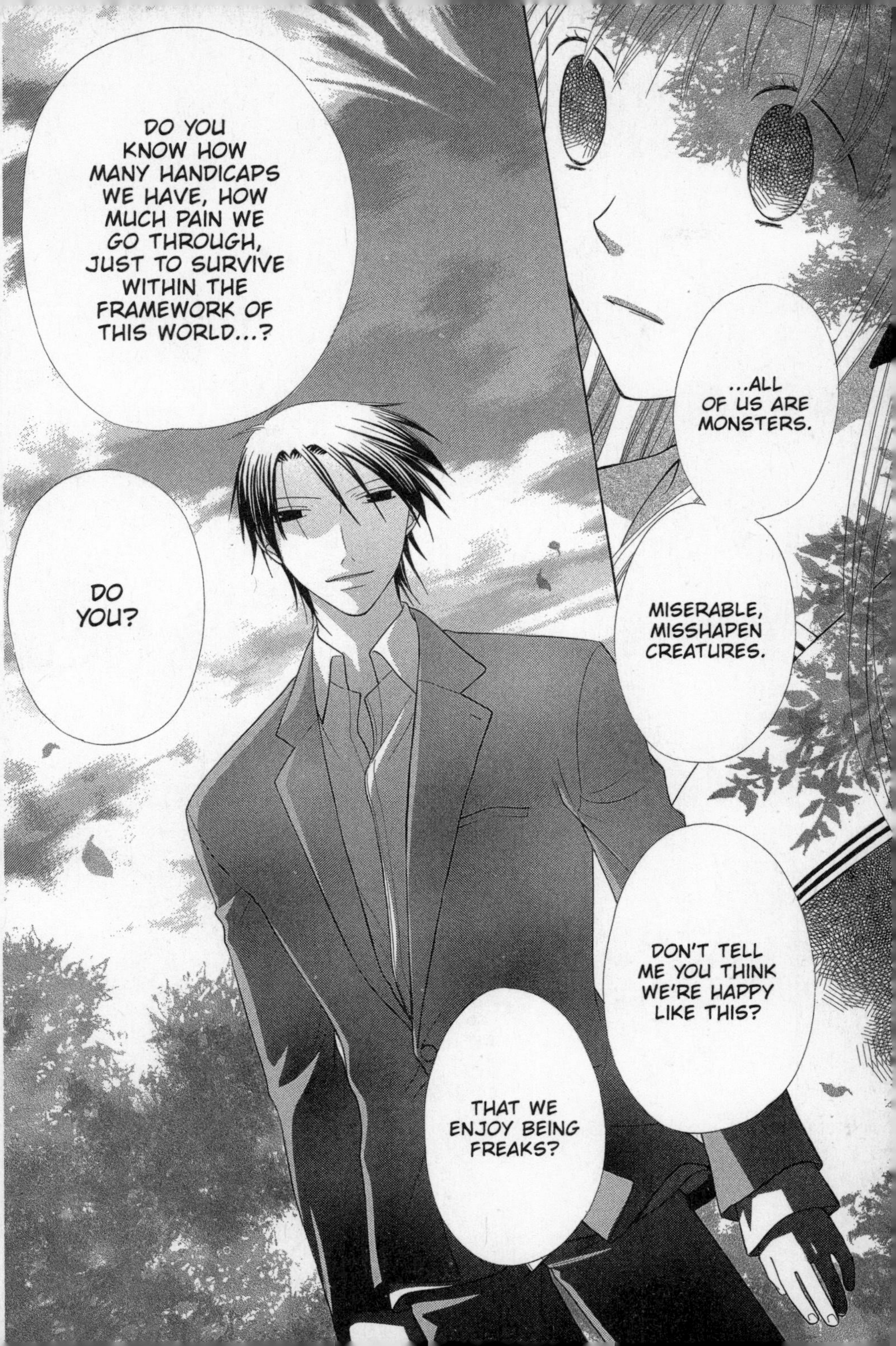
DO YOU KNOW HOW MANY HANDICAPS WE HAVE, HOW MUCH PAIN WE GO THROUGH, JUST TO SURVIVE WITHIN THE FRAMEWORK OF THIS WORLD...?
DO YOU?
...ALL OF US ARE MONSTERS.
MISERABLE, MISSHAPEN CREATURES.
DON'T TELL ME YOU THINK WE'RE HAPPY LIKE THIS?
THAT WE ENJOY BEING FREAKS?

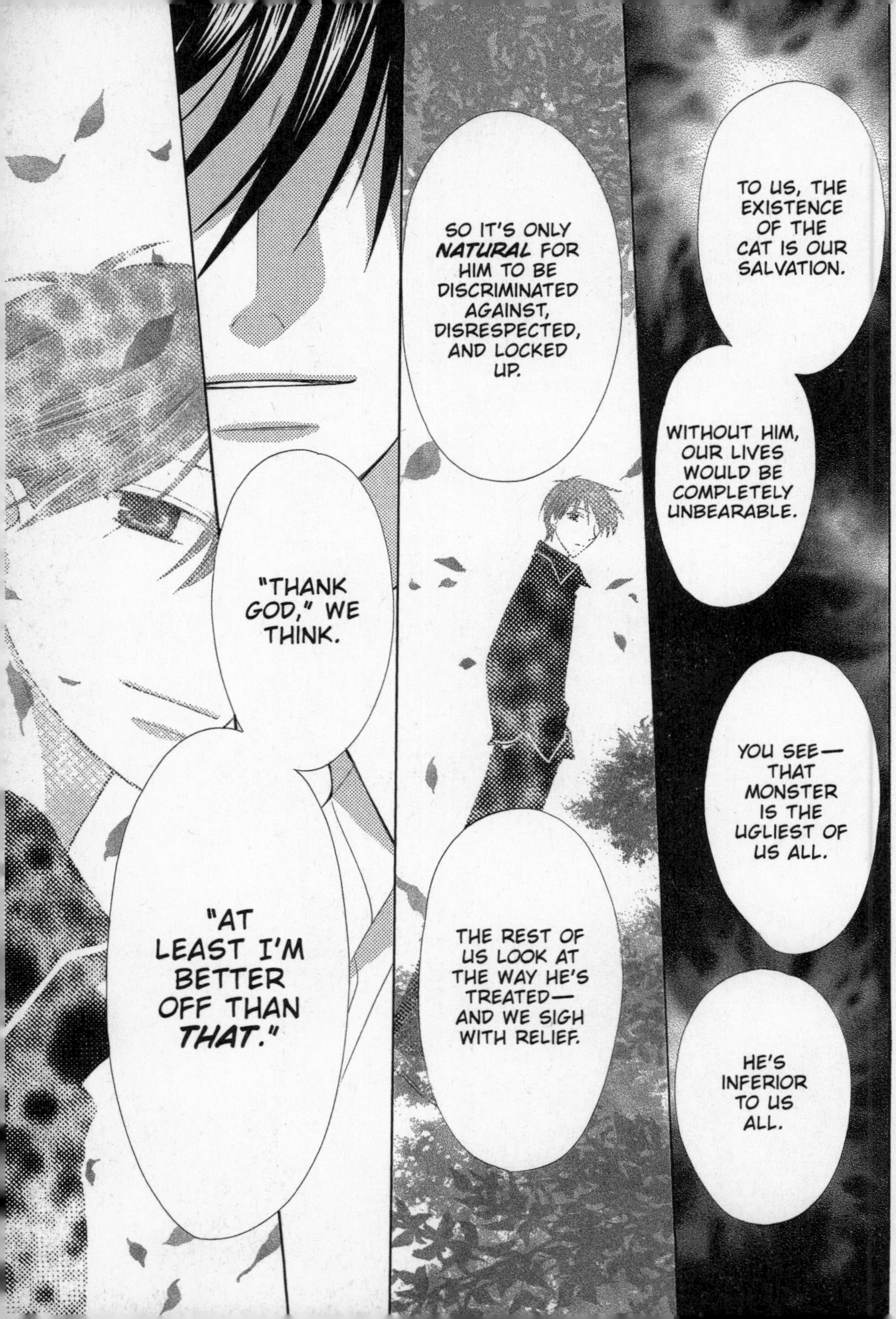
TO US, THE EXISTENCE OF THE CAT IS OUR SALVATION.
WITHOUT HIM, OUR LIVES WOULD BE COMPLETELY UNBEARABLE.
YOU SEE— THAT MONSTER IS THE UGLIEST OF US ALL.
HE'S INFERIOR TO US ALL.
SO IT'S ONLY *NATURAL* FOR HIM TO BE DISCRIMINATED AGAINST, DISRESPECTED, AND LOCKED UP.
THE REST OF US LOOK AT THE WAY HE'S TREATED— AND WE SIGH WITH RELIEF.
"THANK GOD," WE THINK.
"AT LEAST I'M BETTER OFF THAN *THAT*."

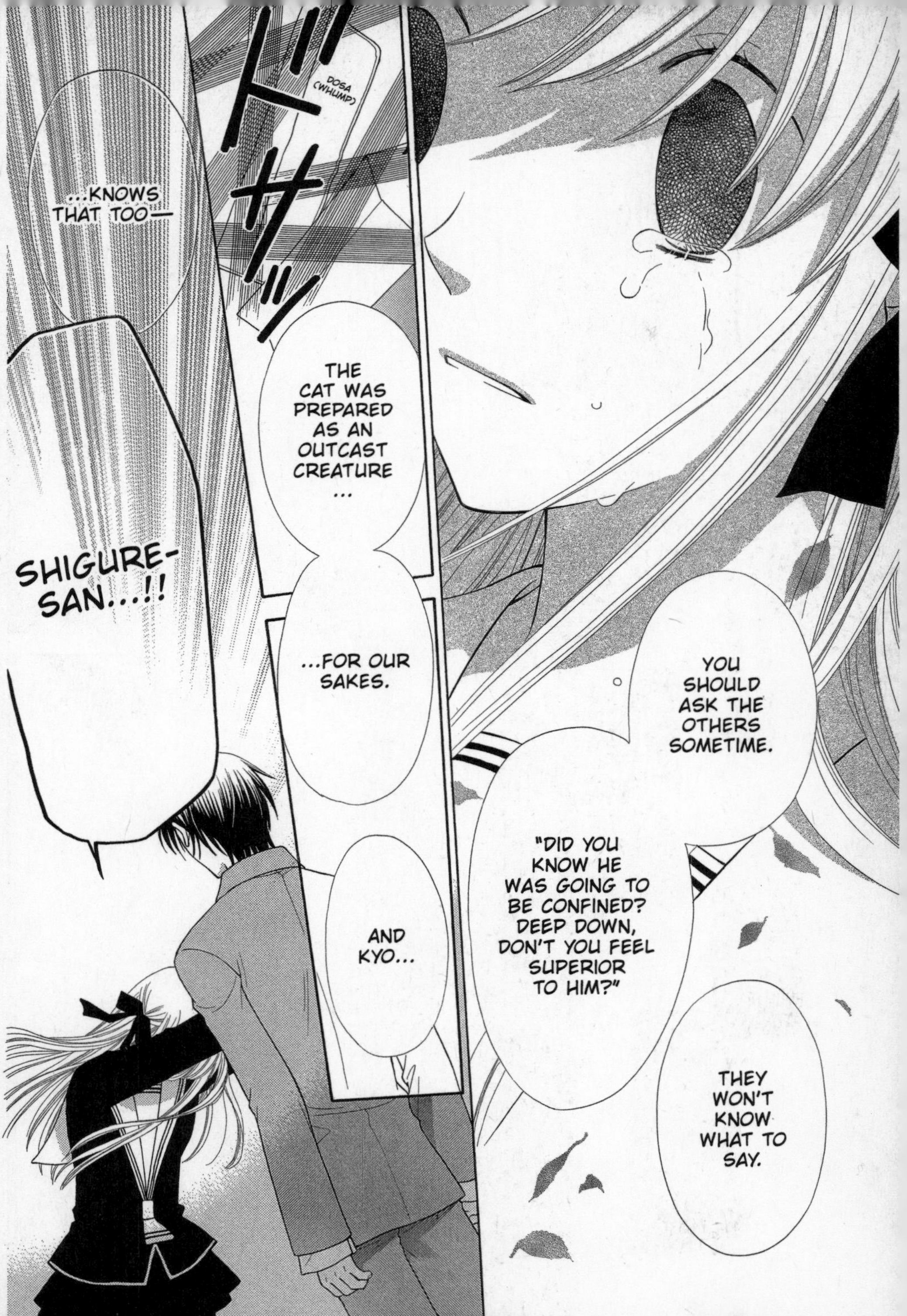
YOU SHOULD ASK THE OTHERS SOMETIME.
"DID YOU KNOW HE WAS GOING TO BE CONFINED? DEEP DOWN, DON'T YOU FEEL SUPERIOR TO HIM?"
THEY WON'T KNOW WHAT TO SAY.
DOSA (WHUMP)
THE CAT WAS PREPARED AS AN OUTCAST CREATURE ...
...FOR OUR SAKES.
AND KYO...
...KNOWS THAT TOO—
SHIGURE-SAN...!!

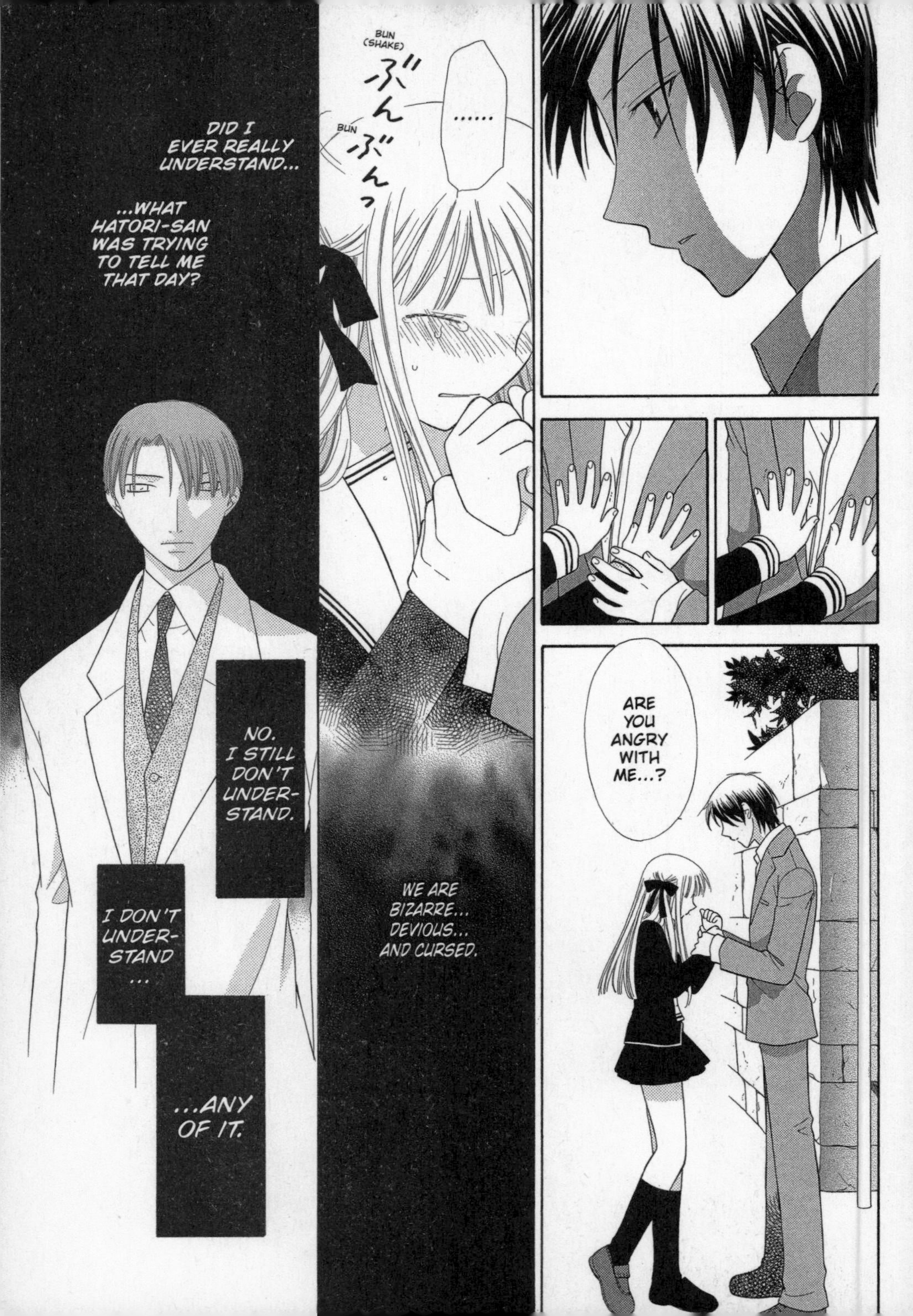
ARE YOU ANGRY WITH ME...?
BUN (SHAKE)
ぶんぶんっ
BUN
......
WE ARE BIZARRE... DEVIOUS... AND CURSED.
DID I EVER REALLY UNDERSTAND...
...WHAT HATORI-SAN WAS TRYING TO TELL ME THAT DAY?
NO. I STILL DON'T UNDER-STAND.
I DON'T UNDER-STAND ...
...ANY OF IT.

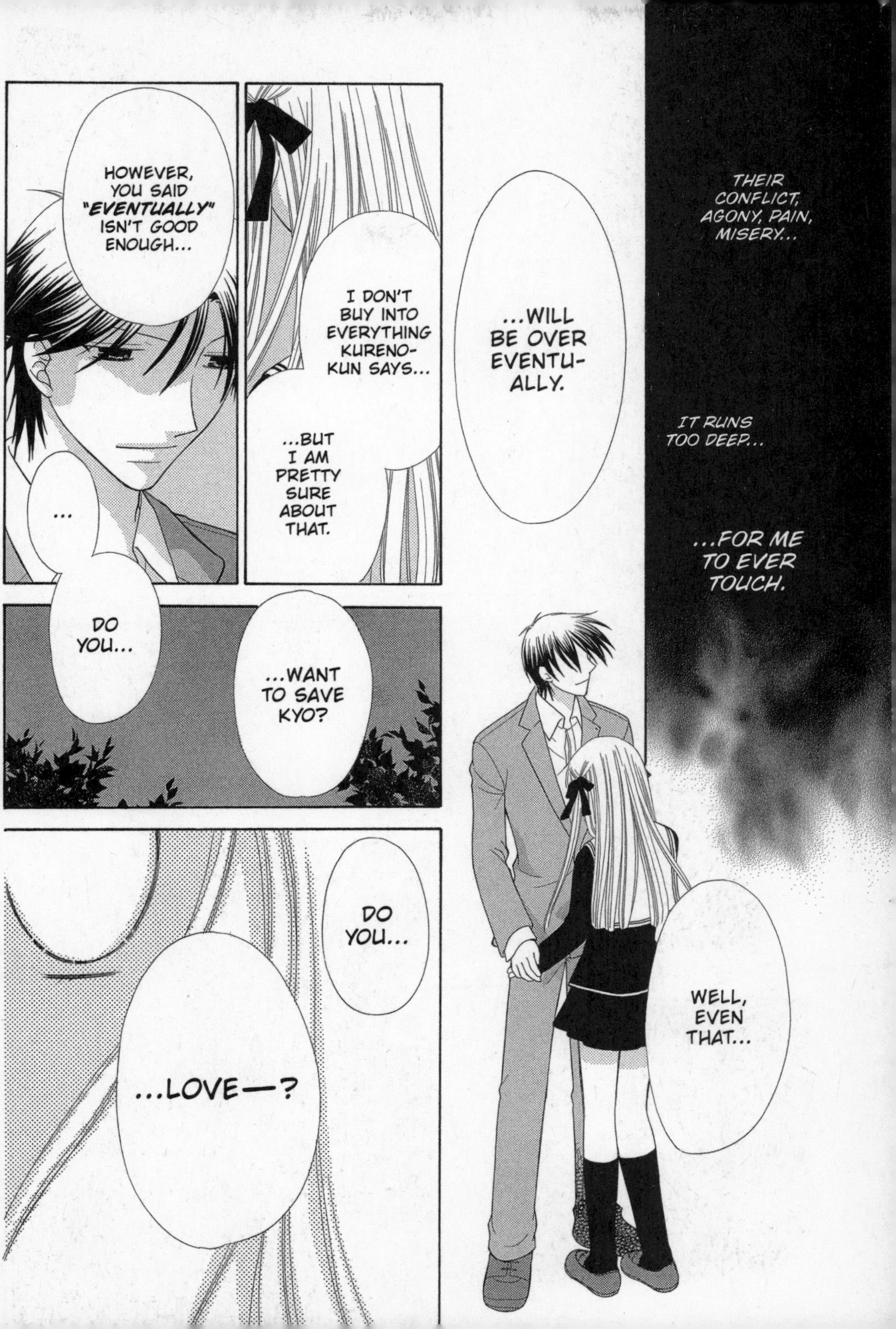
THEIR CONFLICT, AGONY, PAIN, MISERY...
IT RUNS TOO DEEP...
...FOR ME TO EVER TOUCH.
WELL, EVEN THAT...
...WILL BE OVER EVENTU-ALLY.
I DON'T BUY INTO EVERYTHING KURENO-KUN SAYS...
...BUT I AM PRETTY SURE ABOUT THAT.
HOWEVER, YOU SAID "EVENTUALLY" ISN'T GOOD ENOUGH...
...
DO YOU...
...WANT TO SAVE KYO?
DO YOU...
...LOVE—?

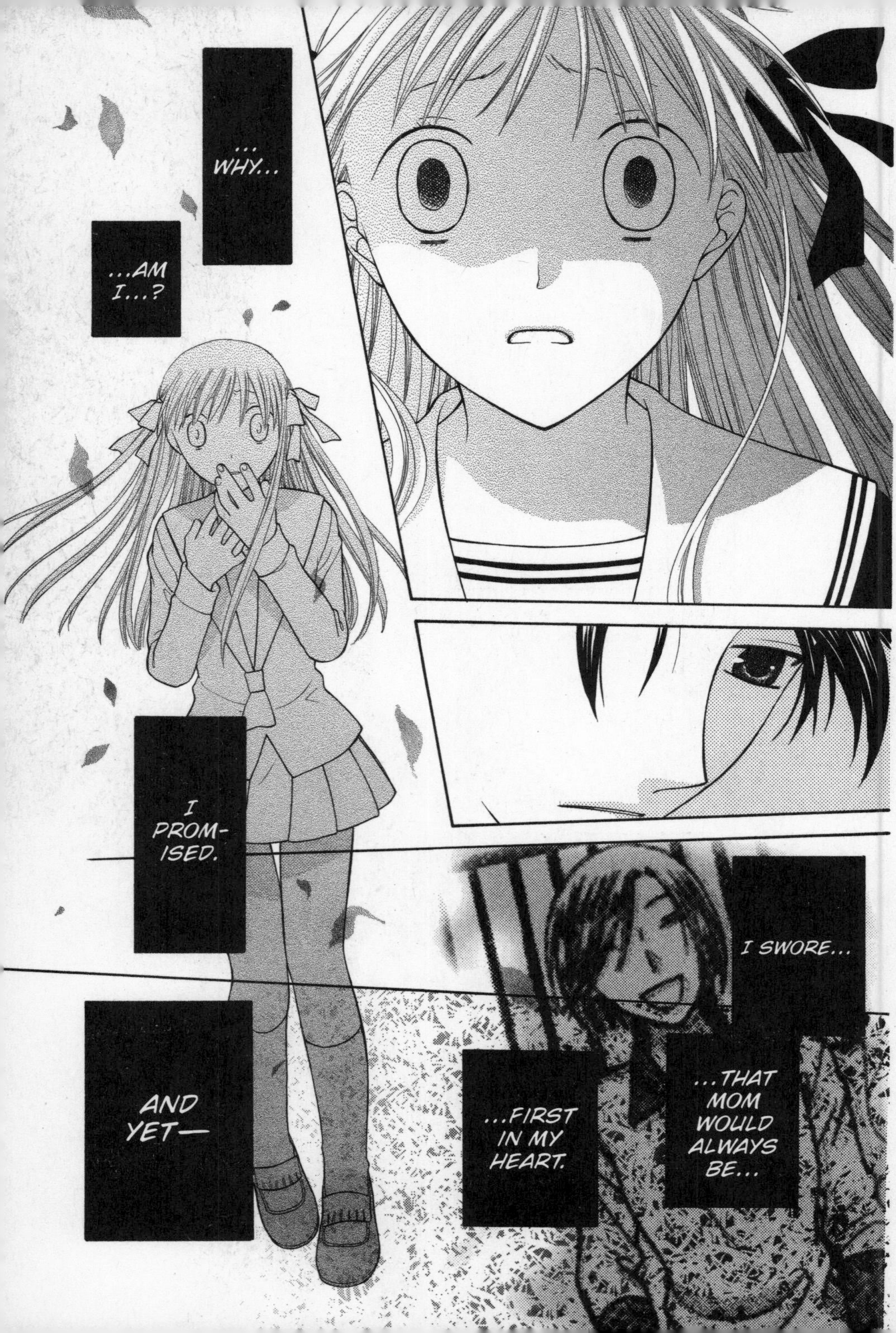
I SWORE...
...THAT MOM WOULD ALWAYS BE...
...FIRST IN MY HEART.
...WHY...
...AM I...?
I PROM-ISED.
AND YET—

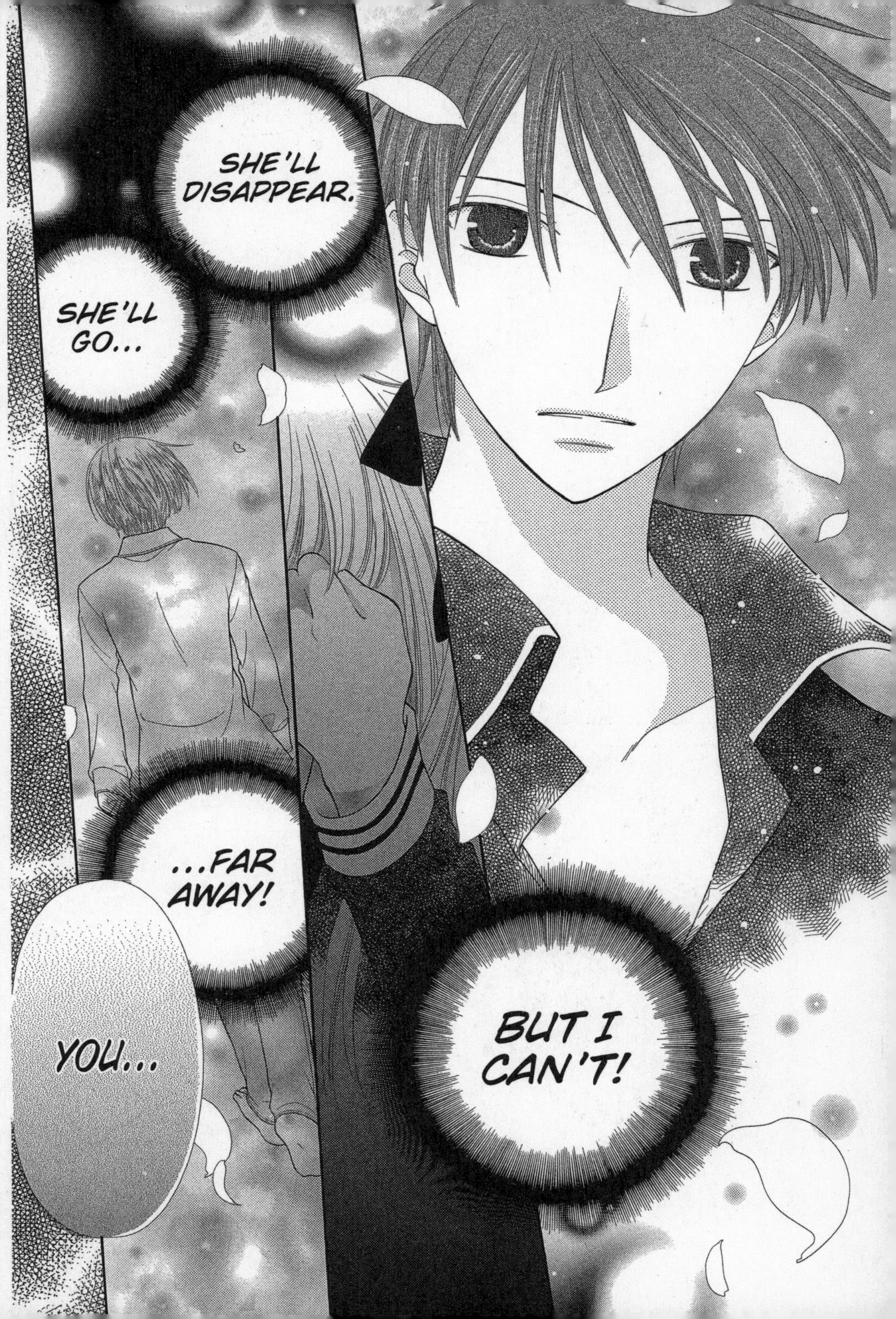
SHE'LL DISAPPEAR.
SHE'LL GO...
...FAR AWAY!
BUT I CAN'T!
YOU...

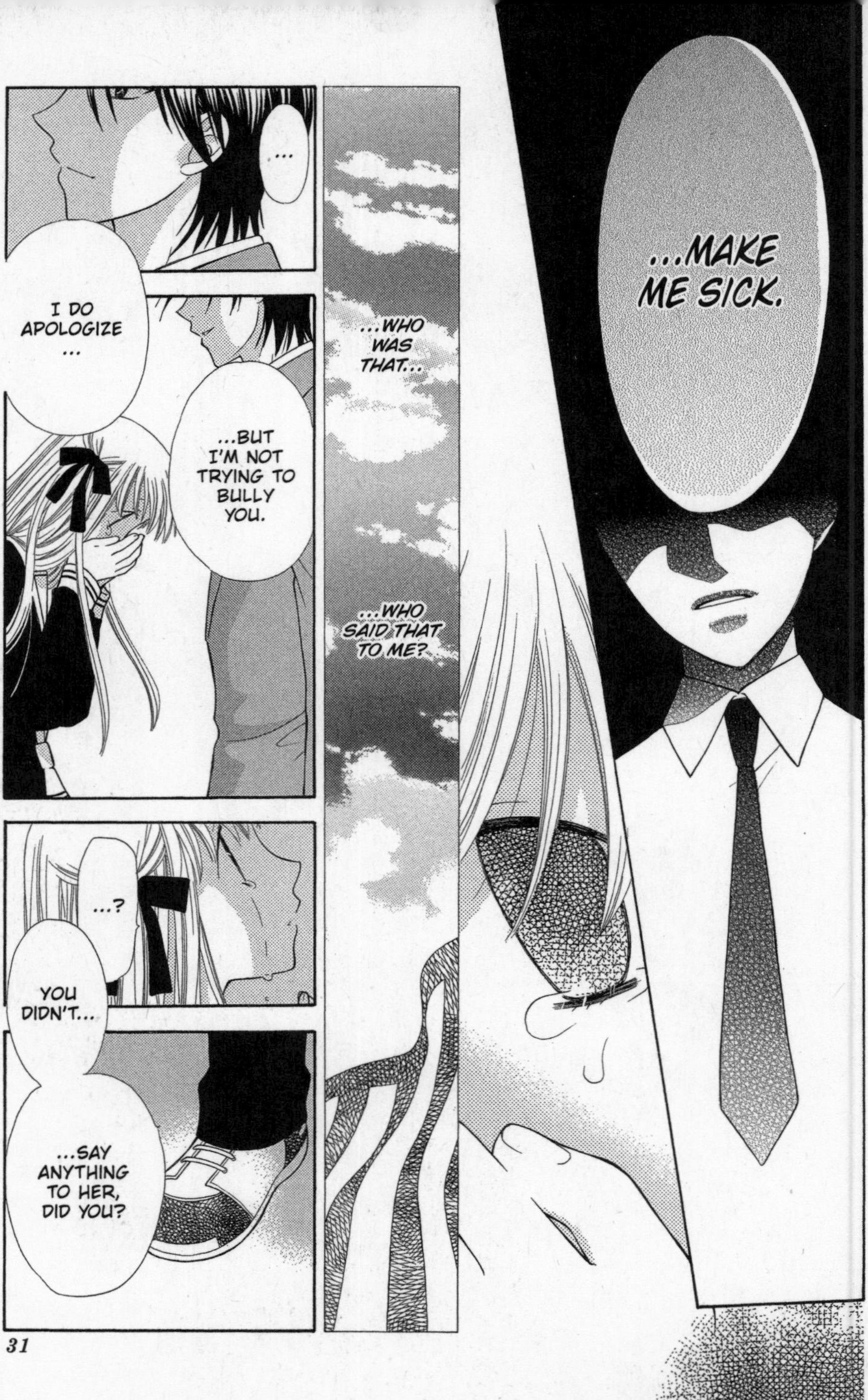
...MAKE ME SICK.
...WHO WAS THAT...
...WHO SAID THAT TO ME?
...
I DO APOLOGIZE ...
...BUT I'M NOT TRYING TO BULLY YOU.
...?
YOU DIDN'T...
...SAY ANYTHING TO HER, DID YOU?

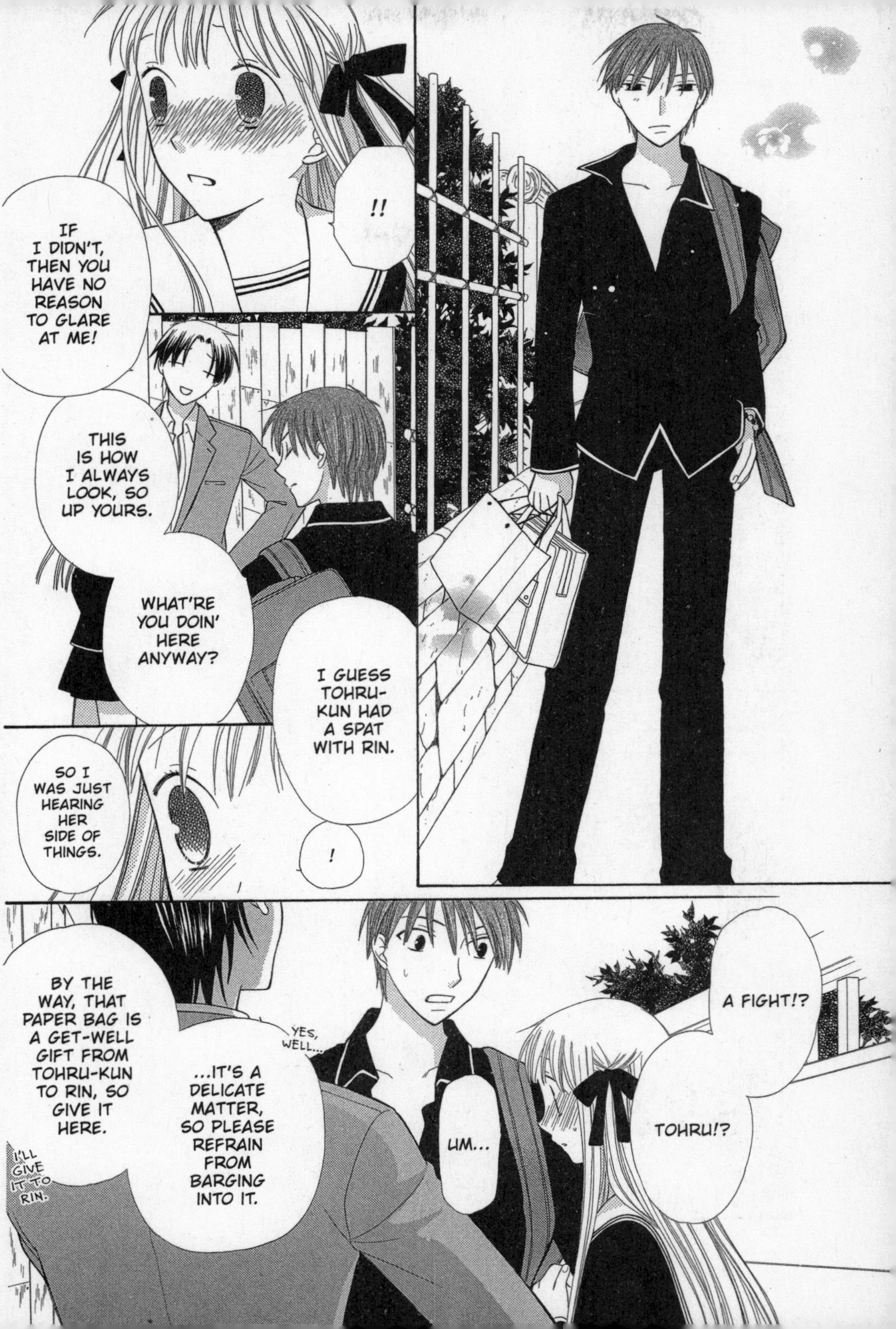
!!
IF I DIDN'T, THEN YOU HAVE NO REASON TO GLARE AT ME!
THIS IS HOW I ALWAYS LOOK, SO UP YOURS.
WHAT'RE YOU DOIN' HERE ANYWAY?
I GUESS TOHRU-KUN HAD A SPAT WITH RIN.
!
SO I WAS JUST HEARING HER SIDE OF THINGS.
A FIGHT!?
TOHRU!?
UM...
YES, WELL...
...IT'S A DELICATE MATTER, SO PLEASE REFRAIN FROM BARGING INTO IT.
BY THE WAY, THAT PAPER BAG IS A GET-WELL GIFT FROM TOHRU-KUN TO RIN, SO GIVE IT HERE.
I'LL GIVE IT TO RIN.

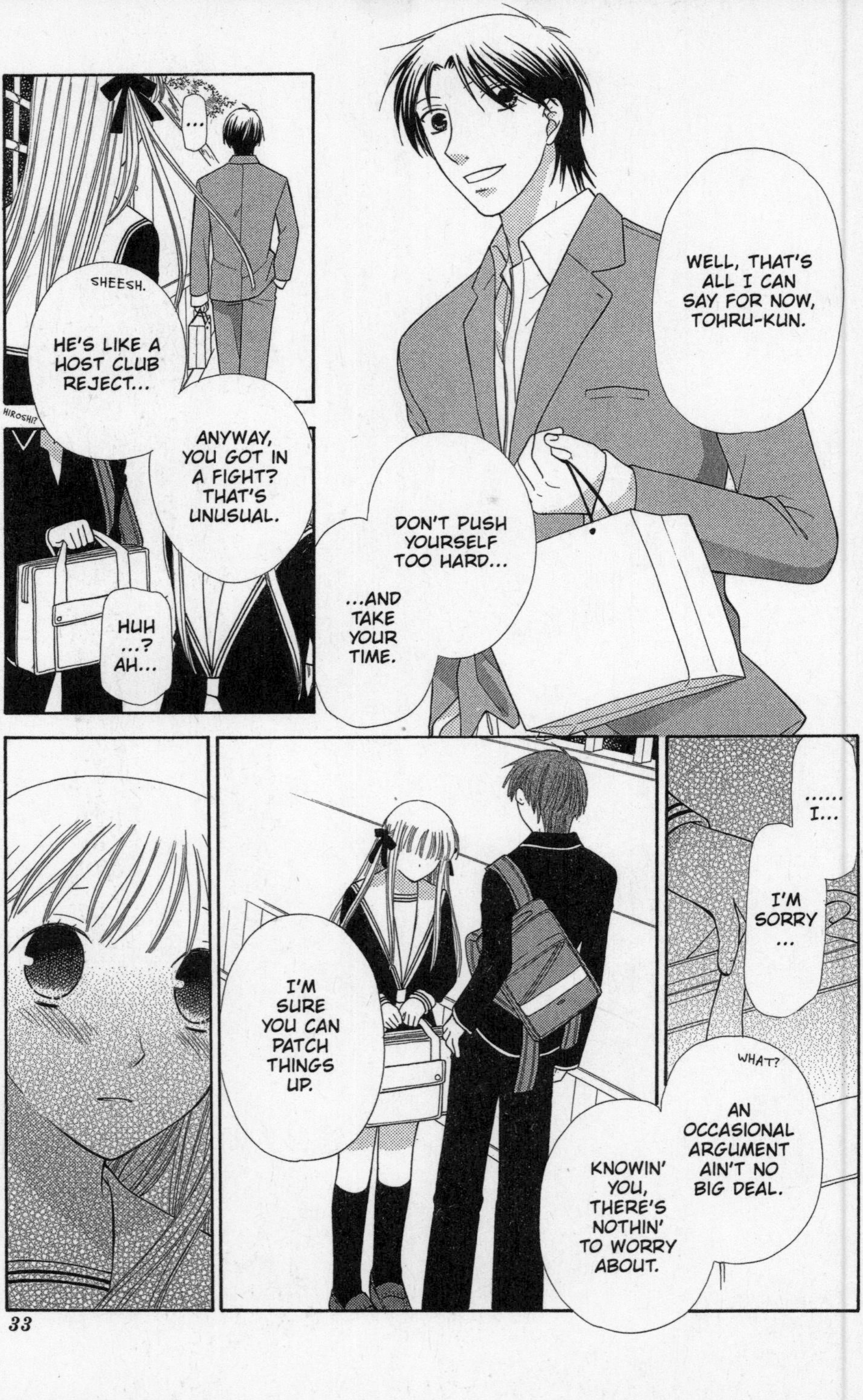
WELL, THAT'S ALL I CAN SAY FOR NOW, TOHRU-KUN.
DON'T PUSH YOURSELF TOO HARD...
...AND TAKE YOUR TIME.
...
SHEESH.
HE'S LIKE A HOST CLUB REJECT...
HIROSHI?
ANYWAY, YOU GOT IN A FIGHT? THAT'S UNUSUAL.
HUH ...? AH...
...... I...
I'M SORRY ...
WHAT?
AN OCCASIONAL ARGUMENT AIN'T NO BIG DEAL.
KNOWIN' YOU, THERE'S NOTHIN' TO WORRY ABOUT.
I'M SURE YOU CAN PATCH THINGS UP.

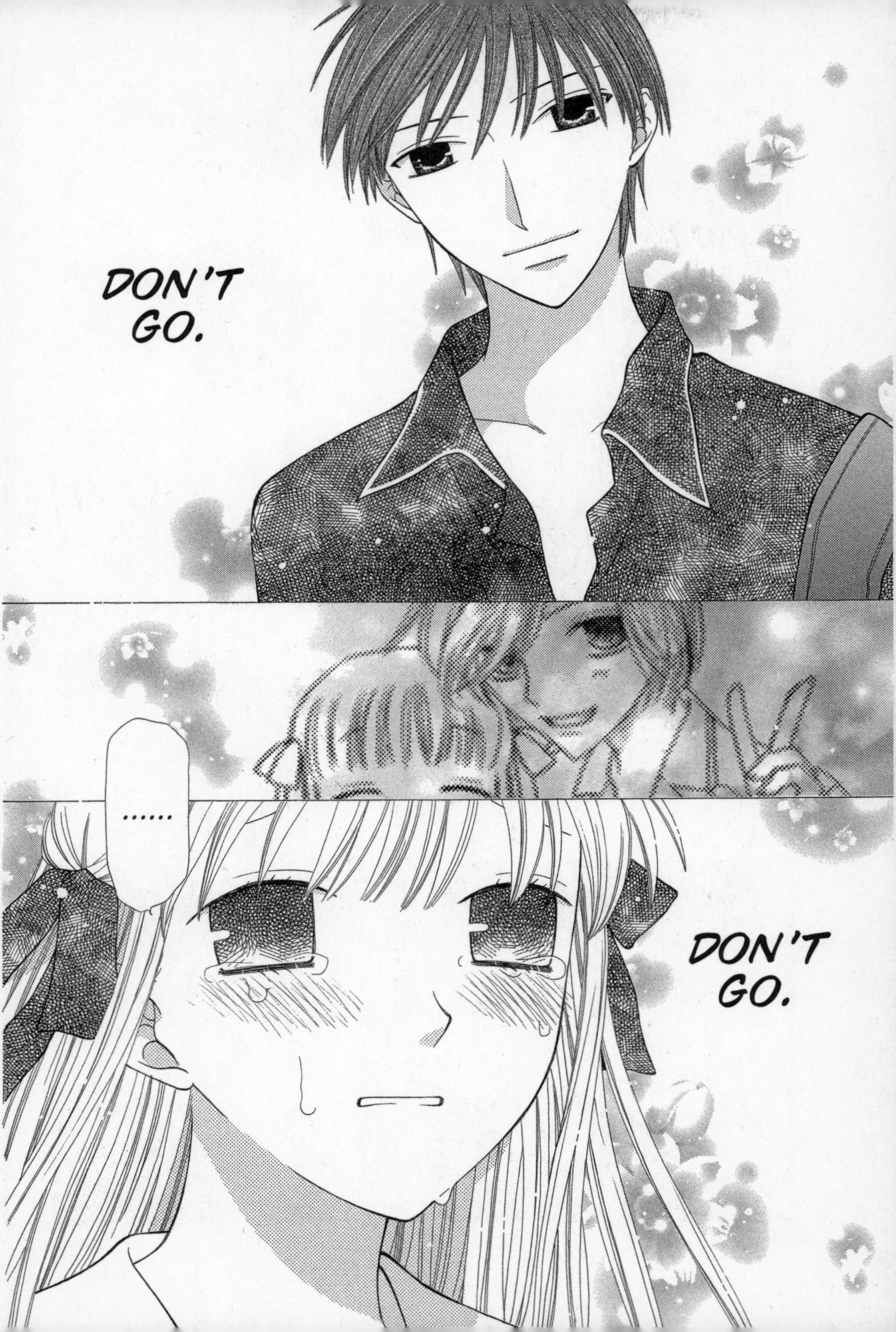
DON'T GO.
DON'T GO.
......

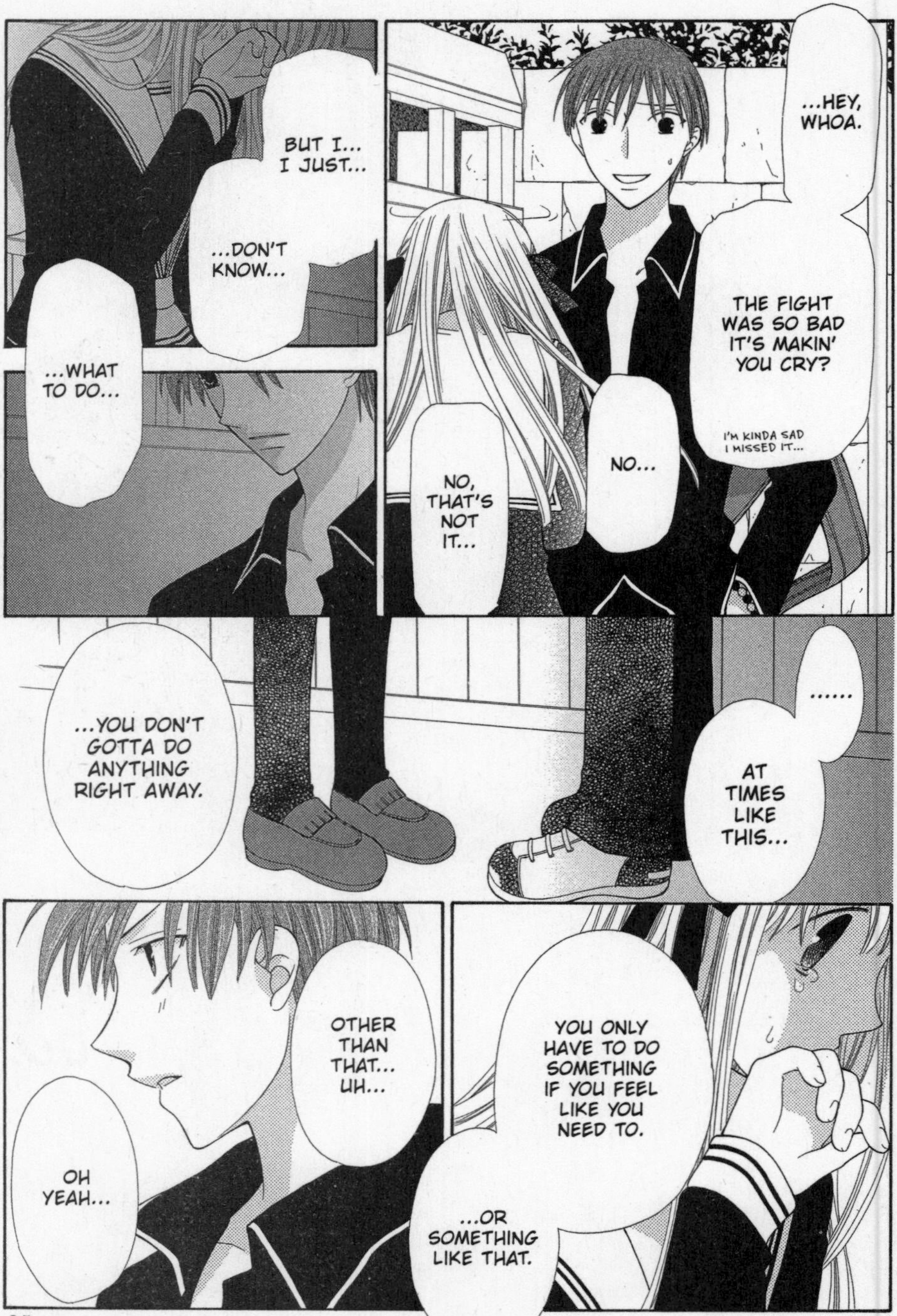
...HEY, WHOA.
THE FIGHT WAS SO BAD IT'S MAKIN' YOU CRY?
I'M KINDA SAD I MISSED IT...
NO...
NO, THAT'S NOT IT...
BUT I... I JUST...
...DON'T KNOW...
...WHAT TO DO...
......
AT TIMES LIKE THIS...
...YOU DON'T GOTTA DO ANYTHING RIGHT AWAY.
YOU ONLY HAVE TO DO SOMETHING IF YOU FEEL LIKE YOU NEED TO.
...OR SOMETHING LIKE THAT.
OTHER THAN THAT... UH...
OH YEAH...

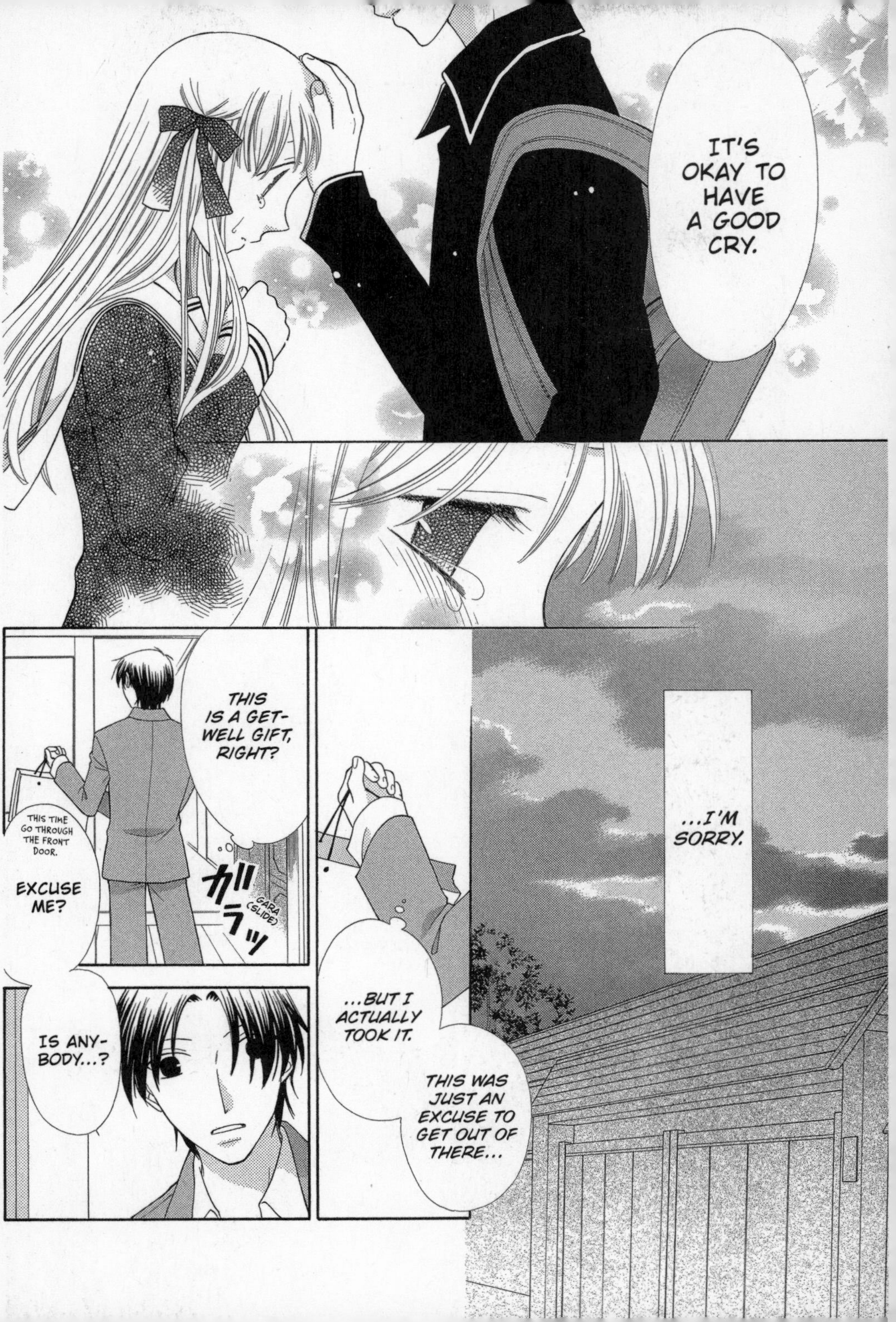
IT'S OKAY TO HAVE A GOOD CRY.
...I'M SORRY.
THIS IS A GET-WELL GIFT, RIGHT?
...BUT I ACTUALLY TOOK IT.
THIS WAS JUST AN EXCUSE TO GET OUT OF THERE...
ガラッ
GARA (SLIDE)
EXCUSE ME?
THIS TIME GO THROUGH THE FRONT DOOR.
IS ANY-BODY...?

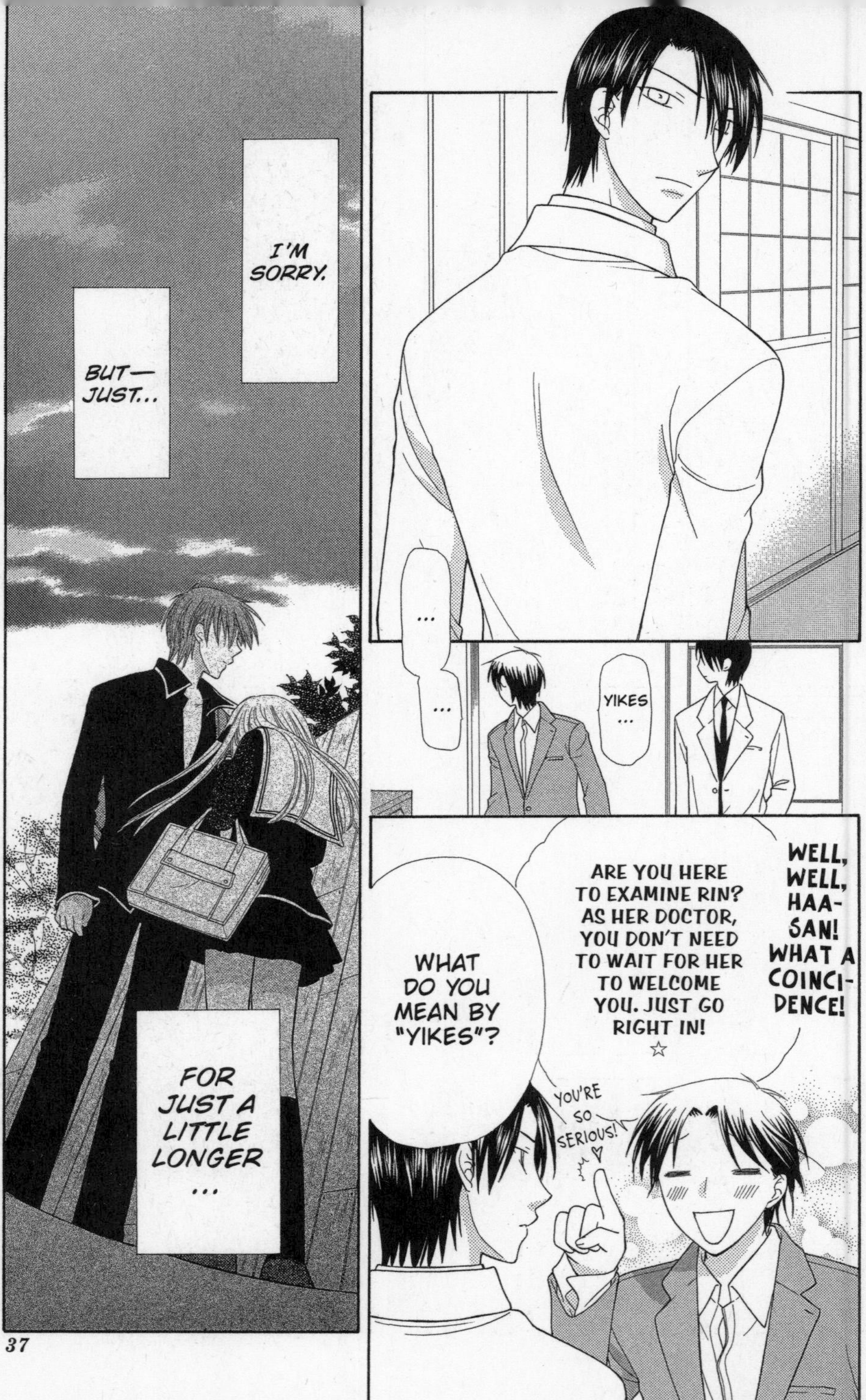
...
...
YIKES ...
WELL, WELL, HAA-SAN! WHAT A COINCIDENCE!
ARE YOU HERE TO EXAMINE RIN? AS HER DOCTOR, YOU DON'T NEED TO WAIT FOR HER TO WELCOME YOU. JUST GO RIGHT IN! ☆
WHAT DO YOU MEAN BY "YIKES"?
YOU'RE SO SERIOUS! ♥
I'M SORRY.
BUT— JUST...
FOR JUST A LITTLE LONGER ...

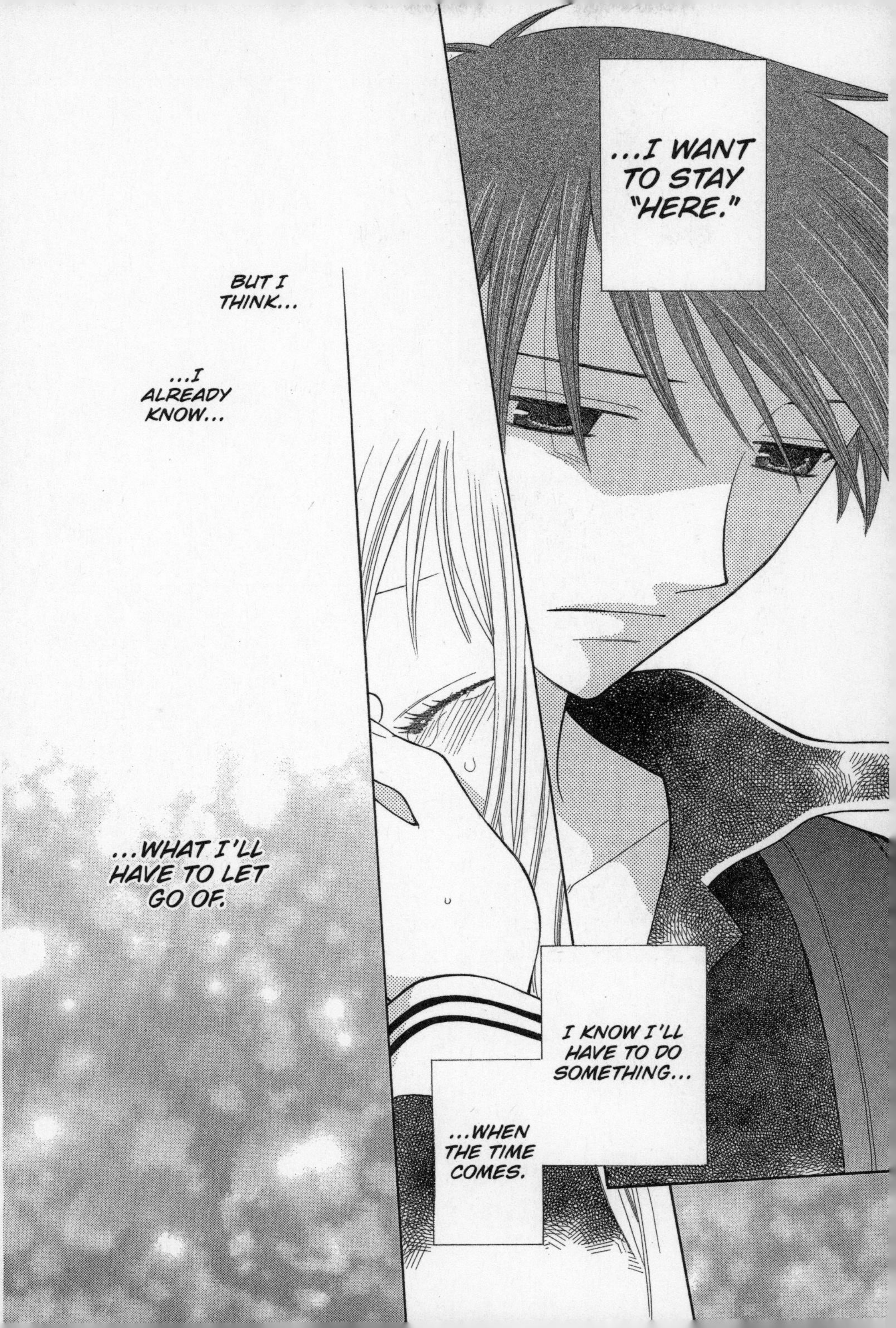
...I WANT TO STAY "HERE."
BUT I THINK...
...I ALREADY KNOW...
...WHAT I'LL HAVE TO LET GO OF.
I KNOW I'LL HAVE TO DO SOMETHING...
...WHEN THE TIME COMES.

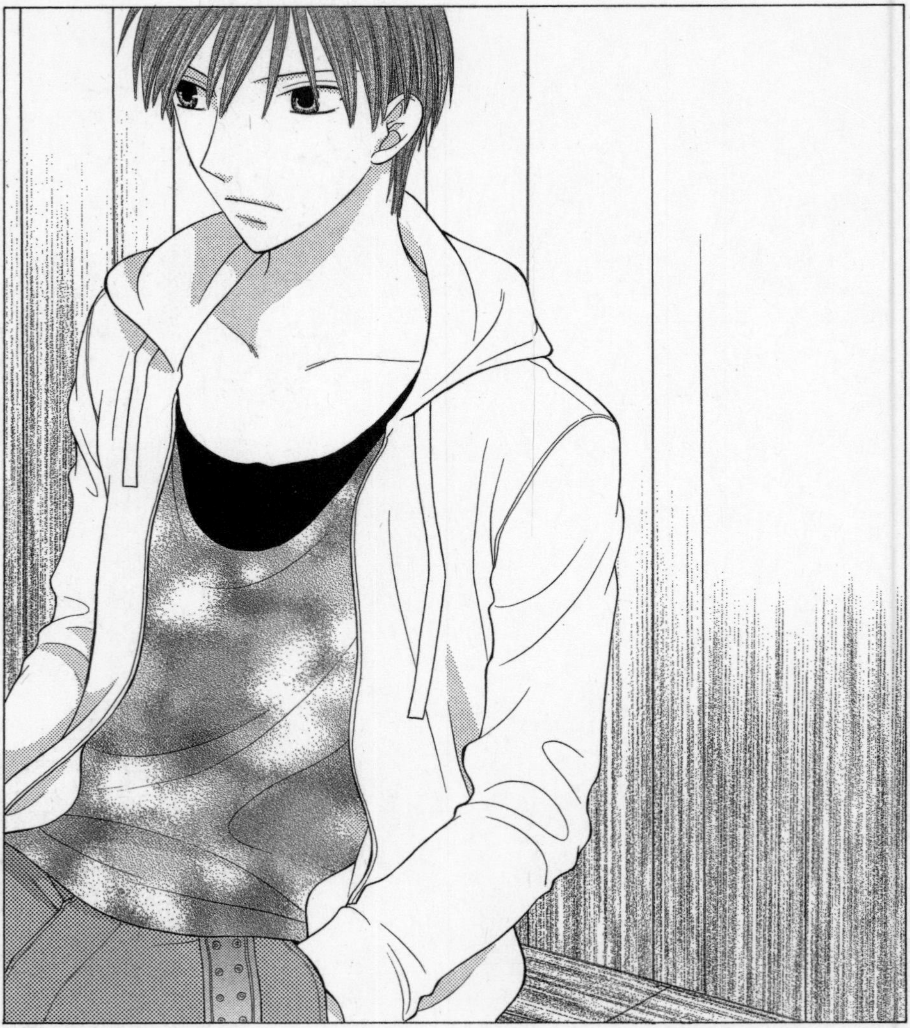

Chapter 109

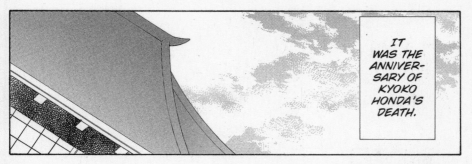

IT WAS THE ANNIVERSARY OF KYOKO HONDA'S DEATH.

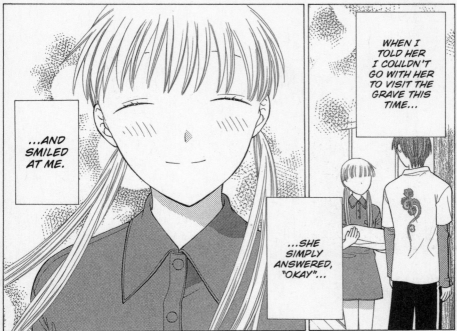

WHEN I TOLD HER I COULDN'T GO WITH HER TO VISIT THE GRAVE THIS TIME...

...SHE SIMPLY ANSWERED, "OKAY"...

...AND SMILED AT ME.

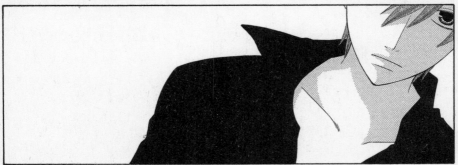

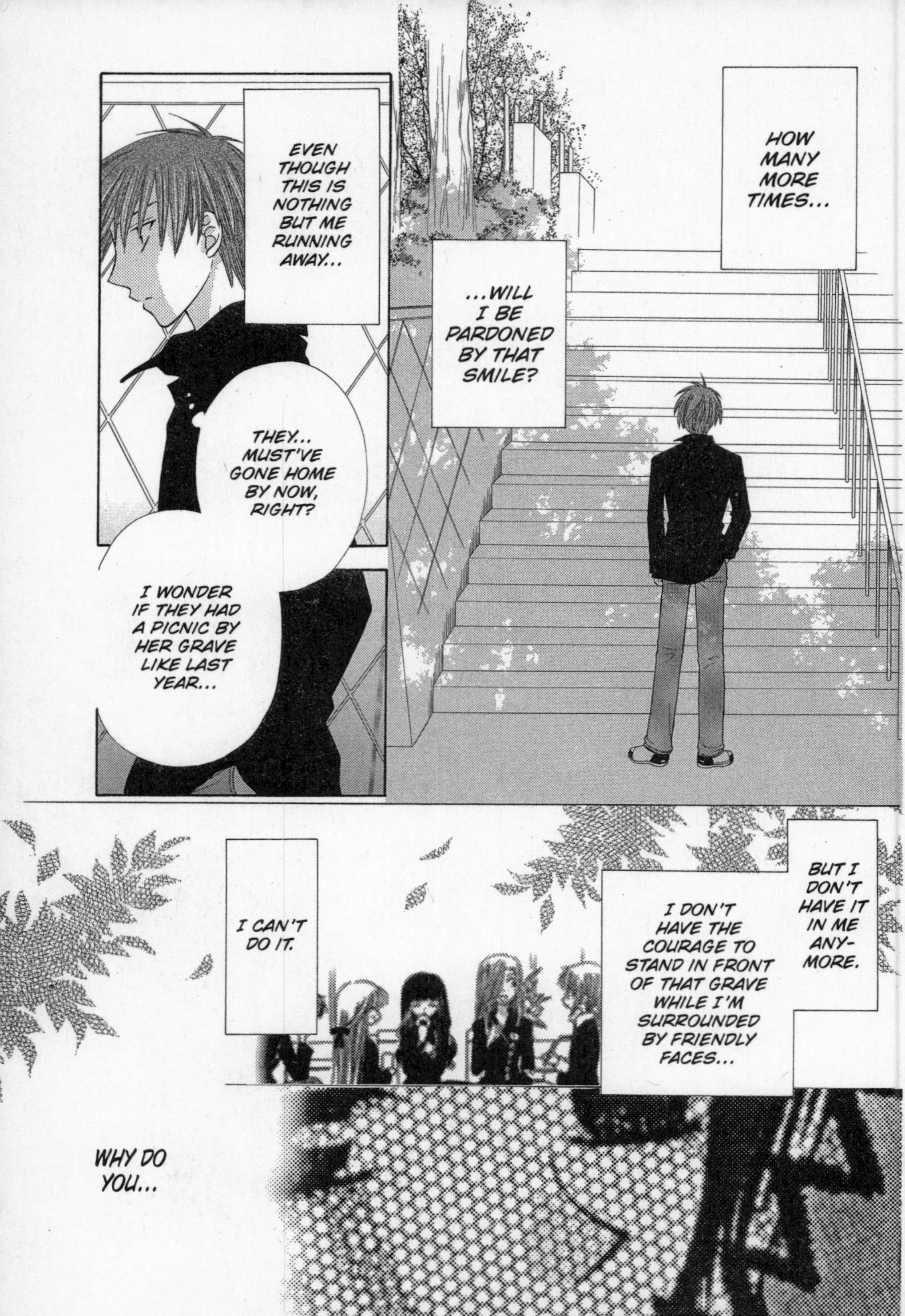
HOW MANY MORE TIMES...
...WILL I BE PARDONED BY THAT SMILE?
EVEN THOUGH THIS IS NOTHING BUT ME RUNNING AWAY...
THEY... MUST'VE GONE HOME BY NOW, RIGHT?
I WONDER IF THEY HAD A PICNIC BY HER GRAVE LIKE LAST YEAR...
BUT I DON'T HAVE IT IN ME ANY-MORE.
I DON'T HAVE THE COURAGE TO STAND IN FRONT OF THAT GRAVE WHILE I'M SURROUNDED BY FRIENDLY FACES...
I CAN'T DO IT.
WHY DO YOU...

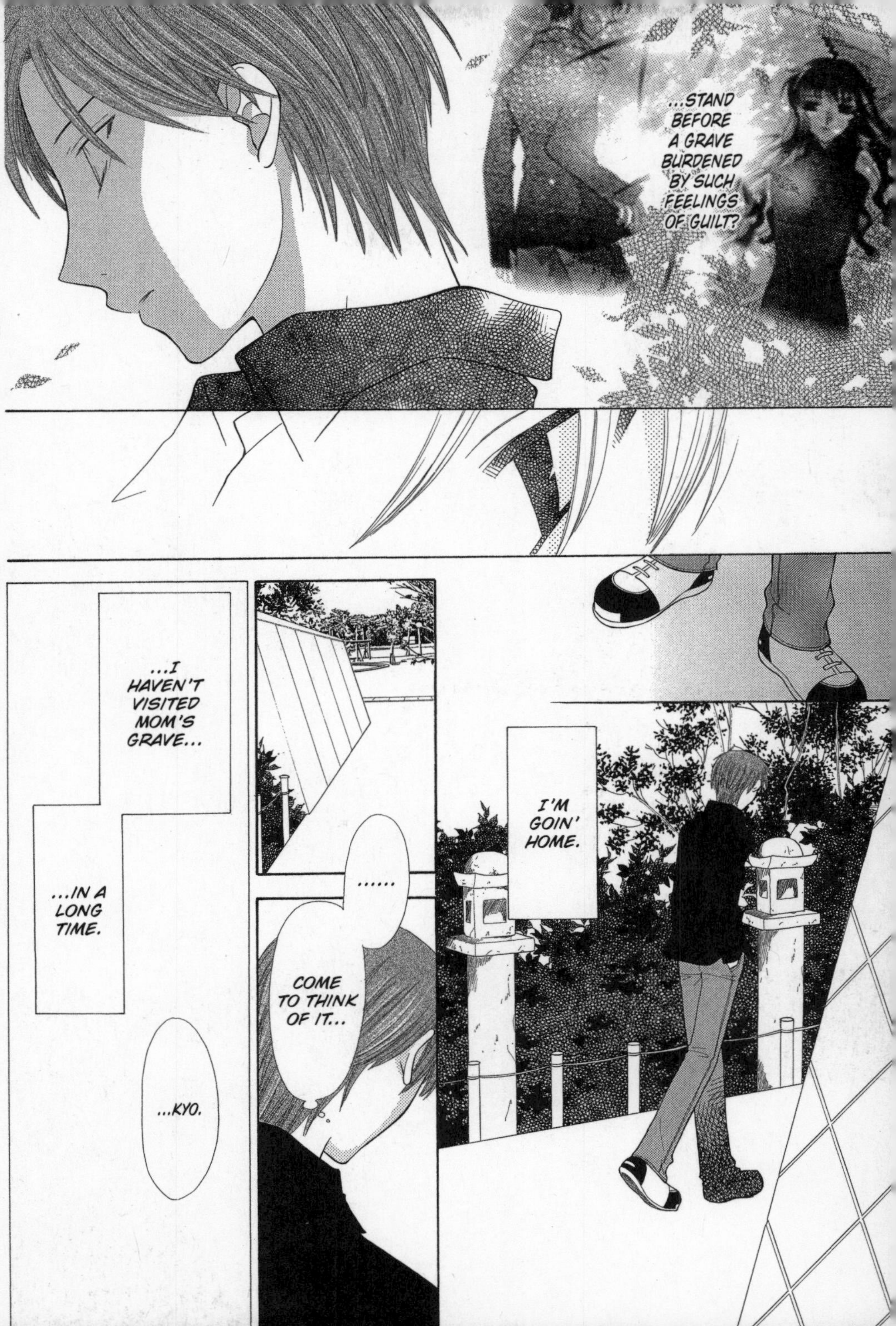
...STAND BEFORE A GRAVE BURDENED BY SUCH FEELINGS OF GUILT?
I'M GOIN' HOME.
......
COME TO THINK OF IT...
...KYO.
...I HAVEN'T VISITED MOM'S GRAVE...
...IN A LONG TIME.

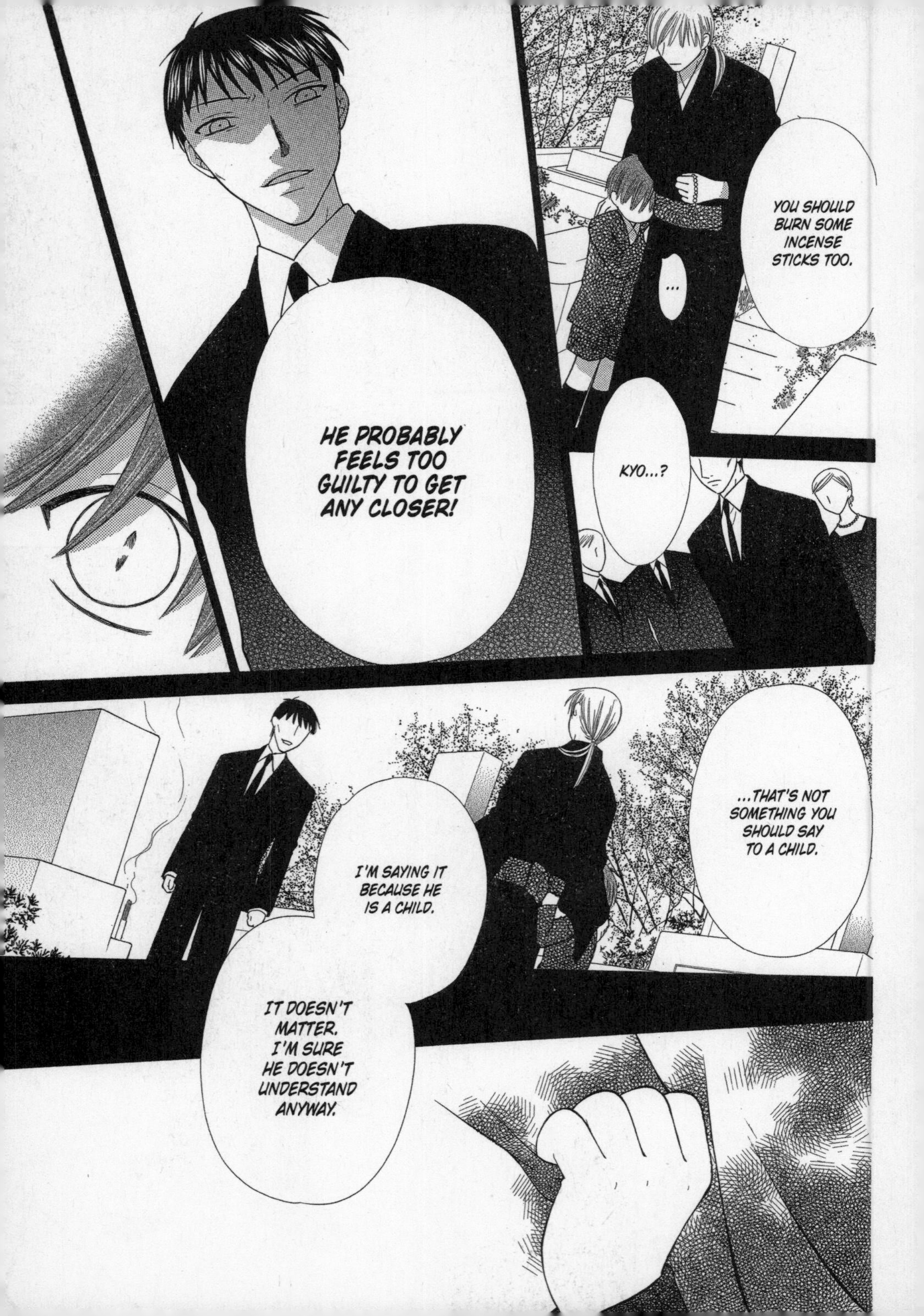
YOU SHOULD BURN SOME INCENSE STICKS TOO.
...
KYO...?
HE PROBABLY FEELS TOO GUILTY TO GET ANY CLOSER!
...THAT'S NOT SOMETHING YOU SHOULD SAY TO A CHILD.
I'M SAYING IT BECAUSE HE IS A CHILD.
IT DOESN'T MATTER. I'M SURE HE DOESN'T UNDERSTAND ANYWAY.

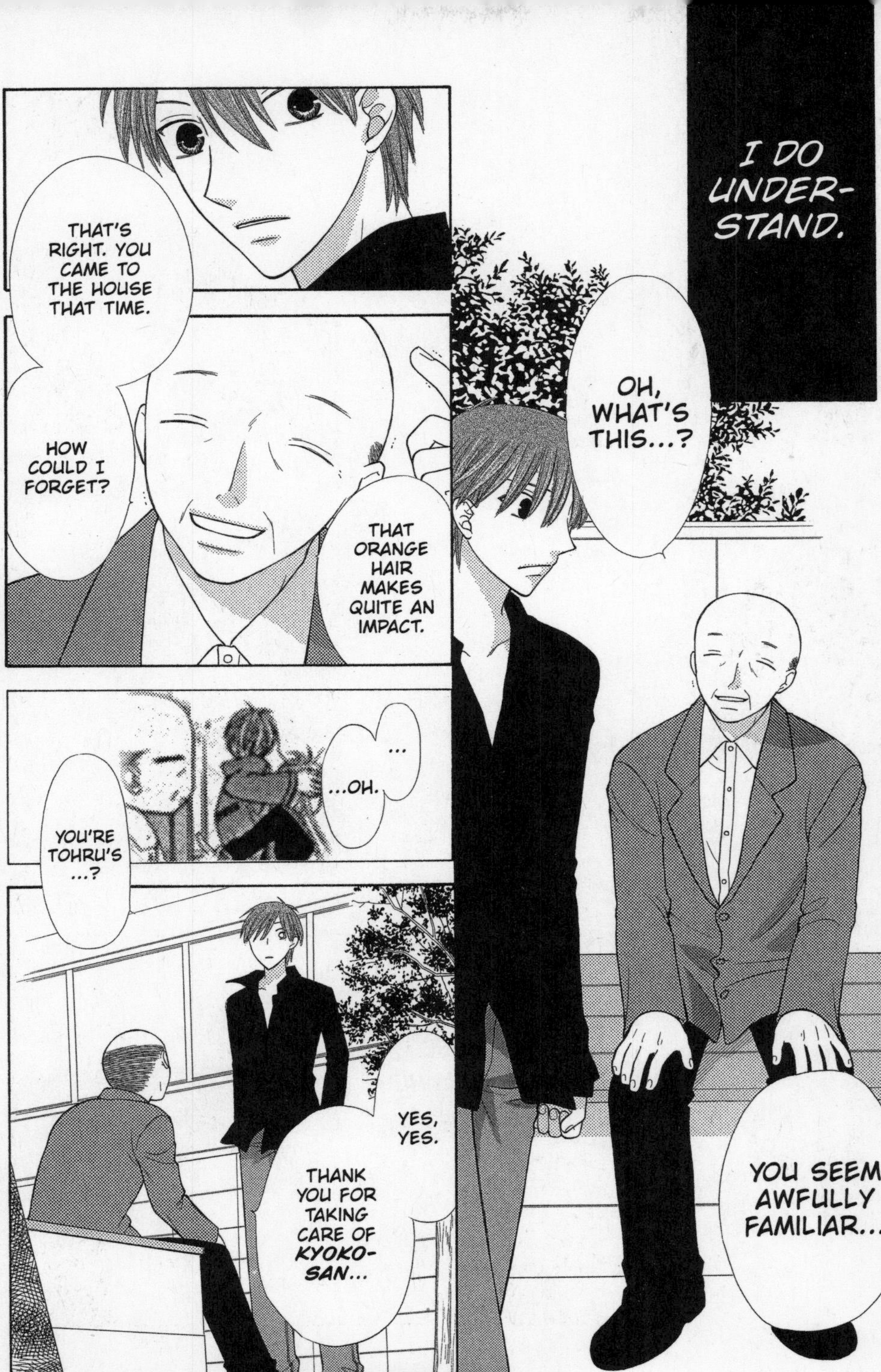
I DO UNDER-STAND.
OH, WHAT'S THIS...?
YOU SEEM AWFULLY FAMILIAR...
THAT'S RIGHT. YOU CAME TO THE HOUSE THAT TIME.
THAT ORANGE HAIR MAKES QUITE AN IMPACT.
HOW COULD I FORGET?
...
...OH.
YOU'RE TOHRU'S ...?
YES, YES.
THANK YOU FOR TAKING CARE OF *KYOKO-SAN*...

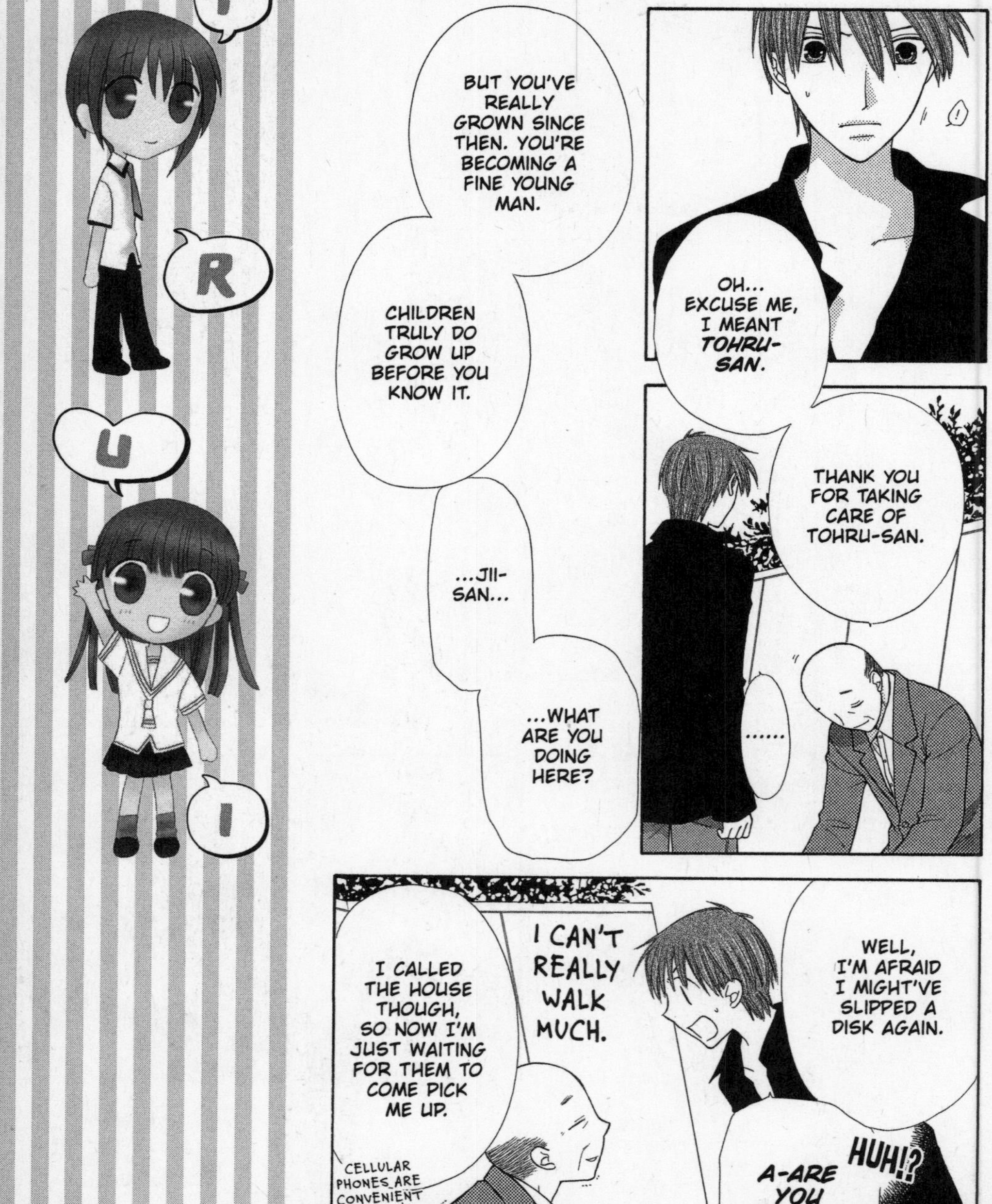
F
R
U
I
!
BUT YOU'VE REALLY GROWN SINCE THEN. YOU'RE BECOMING A FINE YOUNG MAN.
CHILDREN TRULY DO GROW UP BEFORE YOU KNOW IT.
...JII-SAN...
OH... EXCUSE ME, I MEANT *TOHRU-SAN*.
THANK YOU FOR TAKING CARE OF TOHRU-SAN.
......
...WHAT ARE YOU DOING HERE?
WELL, I'M AFRAID I MIGHT'VE SLIPPED A DISK AGAIN.
HUH!?
A-ARE YOU OKAY!?
I CAN'T REALLY WALK MUCH.
I CALLED THE HOUSE THOUGH, SO NOW I'M JUST WAITING FOR THEM TO COME PICK ME UP.
CELLULAR PHONES ARE CONVENIENT DEVICES, AREN'T THEY?

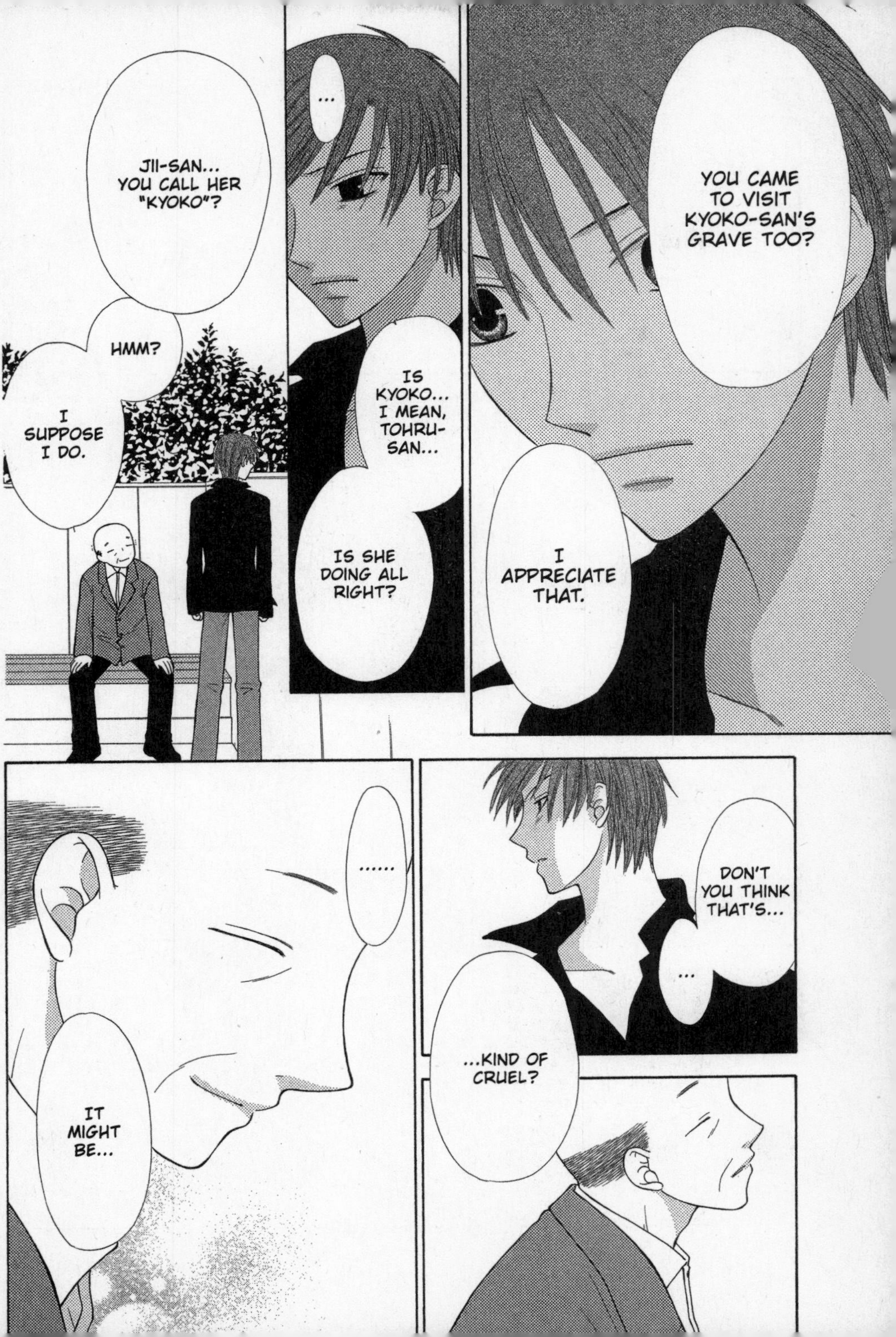
YOU CAME TO VISIT KYOKO-SAN'S GRAVE TOO?
I APPRECIATE THAT.
...
IS KYOKO... I MEAN, TOHRU-SAN...
IS SHE DOING ALL RIGHT?
JII-SAN... YOU CALL HER "KYOKO"?
HMM?
I SUPPOSE I DO.
DON'T YOU THINK THAT'S...
...
...KIND OF CRUEL?
......
IT MIGHT BE...

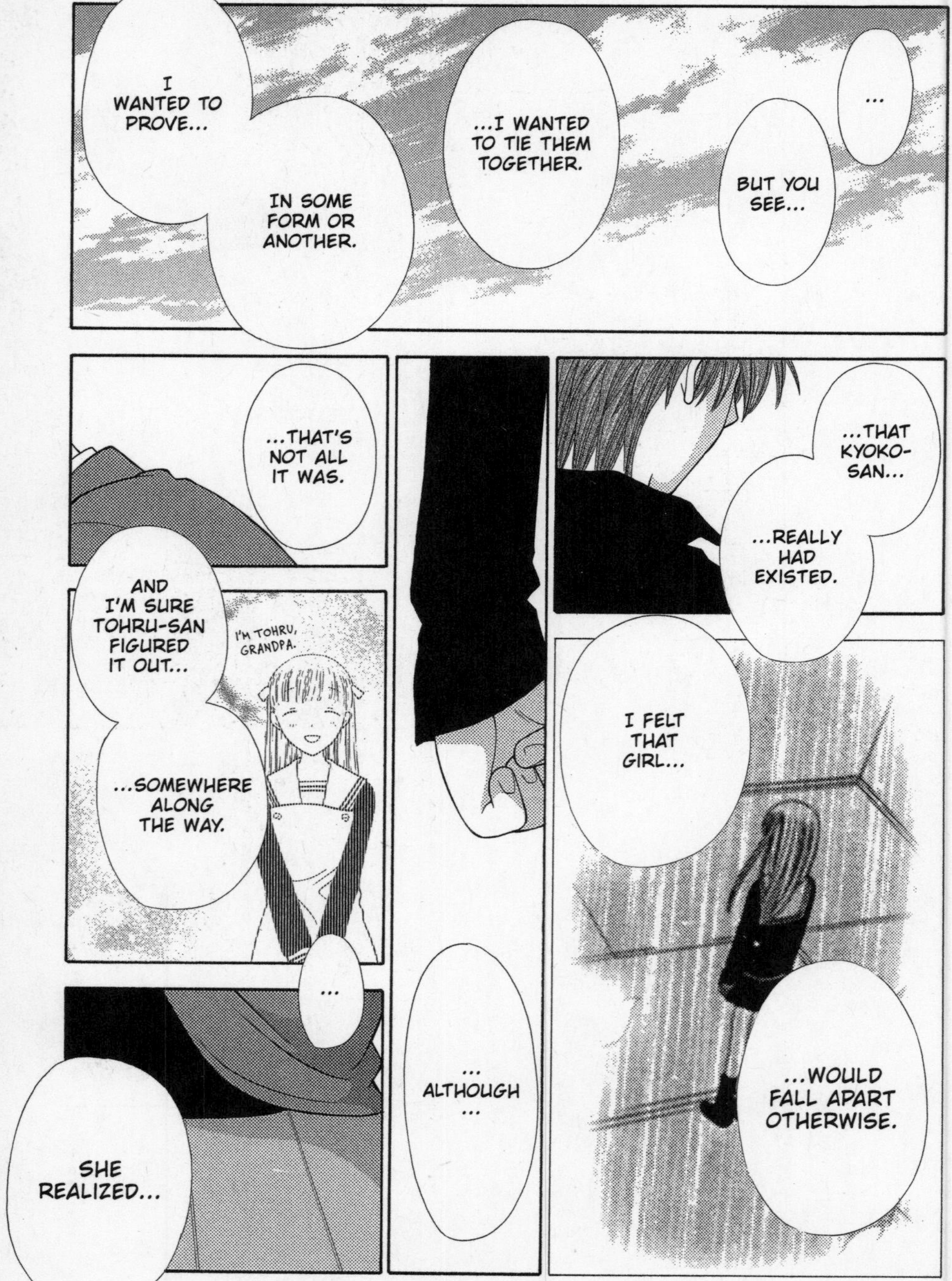
...
BUT YOU SEE...
...I WANTED TO TIE THEM TOGETHER.
I WANTED TO PROVE...
IN SOME FORM OR ANOTHER.
...THAT KYOKO-SAN...
...REALLY HAD EXISTED.
I FELT THAT GIRL...
...WOULD FALL APART OTHERWISE.
... ALTHOUGH ...
...THAT'S NOT ALL IT WAS.
AND I'M SURE TOHRU-SAN FIGURED IT OUT...
I'M TOHRU, GRANDPA.
...SOMEWHERE ALONG THE WAY.
...
SHE REALIZED...

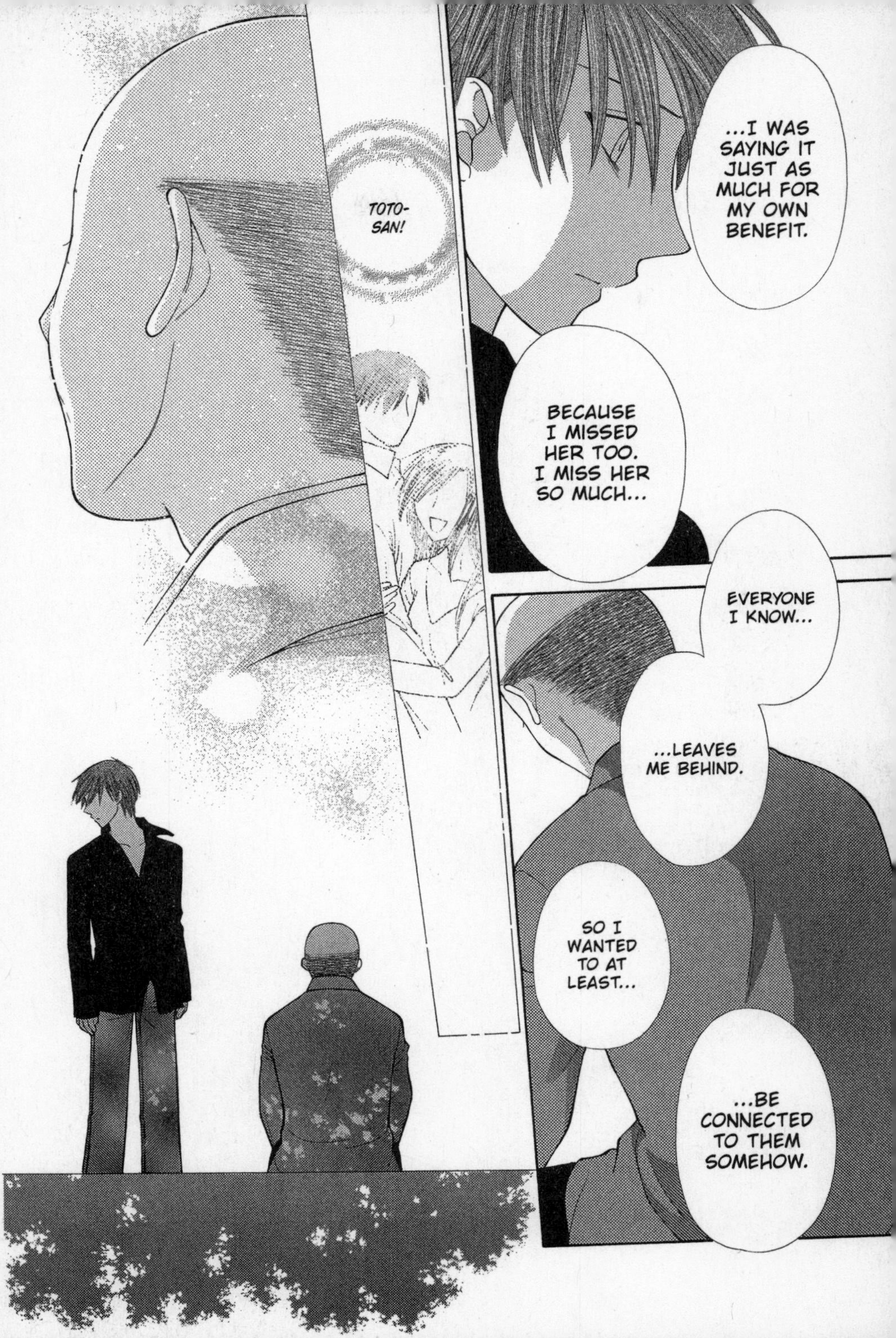
...I WAS SAYING IT JUST AS MUCH FOR MY OWN BENEFIT.
BECAUSE I MISSED HER TOO. I MISS HER SO MUCH...
EVERYONE I KNOW...
...LEAVES ME BEHIND.
SO I WANTED TO AT LEAST...
...BE CONNECTED TO THEM SOMEHOW.
TOTO-SAN!

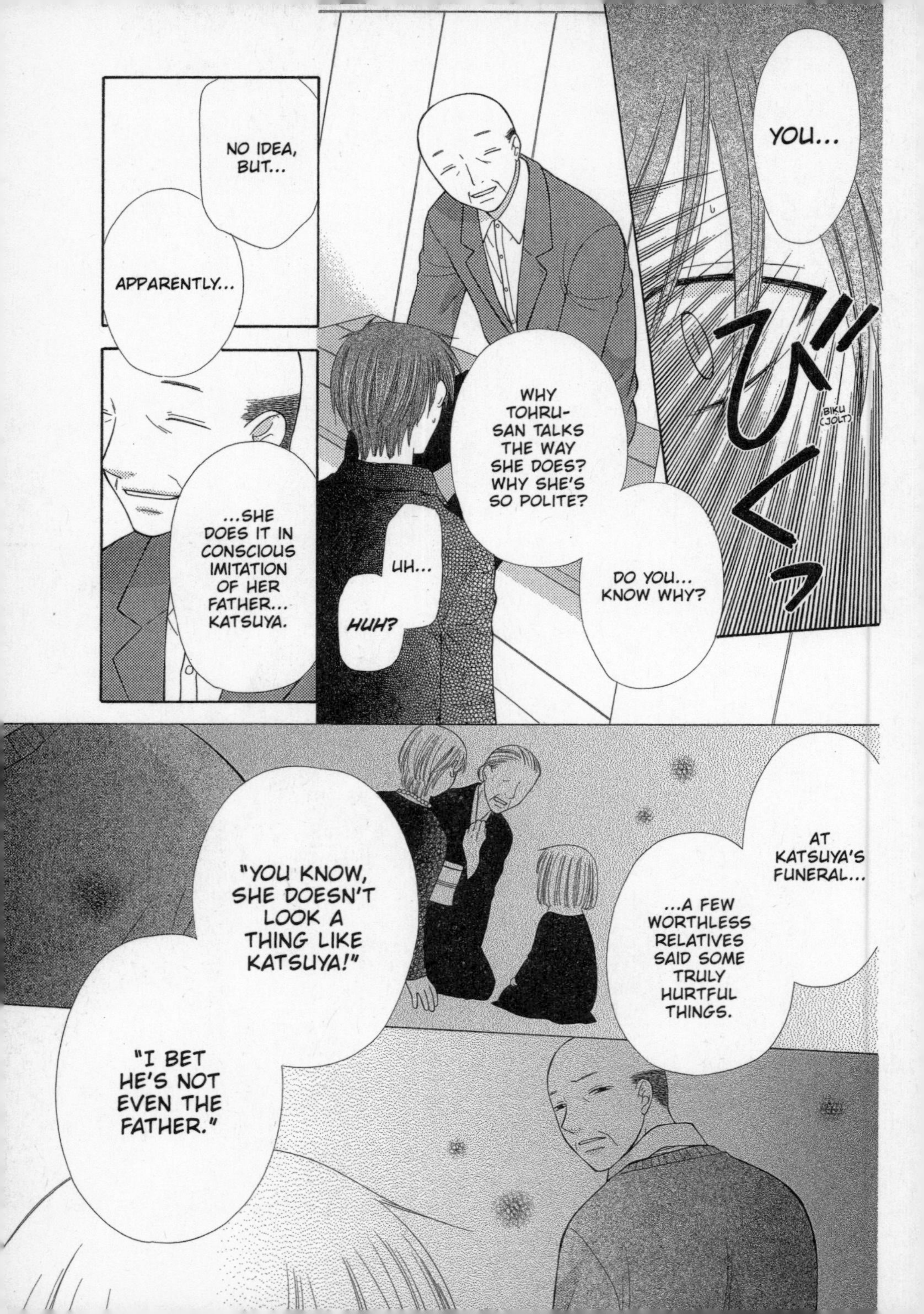
YOU...
びくっ
BIKU (JOLT)
WHY TOHRU-SAN TALKS THE WAY SHE DOES? WHY SHE'S SO POLITE?
DO YOU... KNOW WHY?
UH...
HUH?
NO IDEA, BUT...
APPARENTLY...
...SHE DOES IT IN CONSCIOUS IMITATION OF HER FATHER... KATSUYA.
AT KATSUYA'S FUNERAL...
...A FEW WORTHLESS RELATIVES SAID SOME TRULY HURTFUL THINGS.
"YOU KNOW, SHE DOESN'T LOOK A THING LIKE KATSUYA!"
"I BET HE'S NOT EVEN THE FATHER."

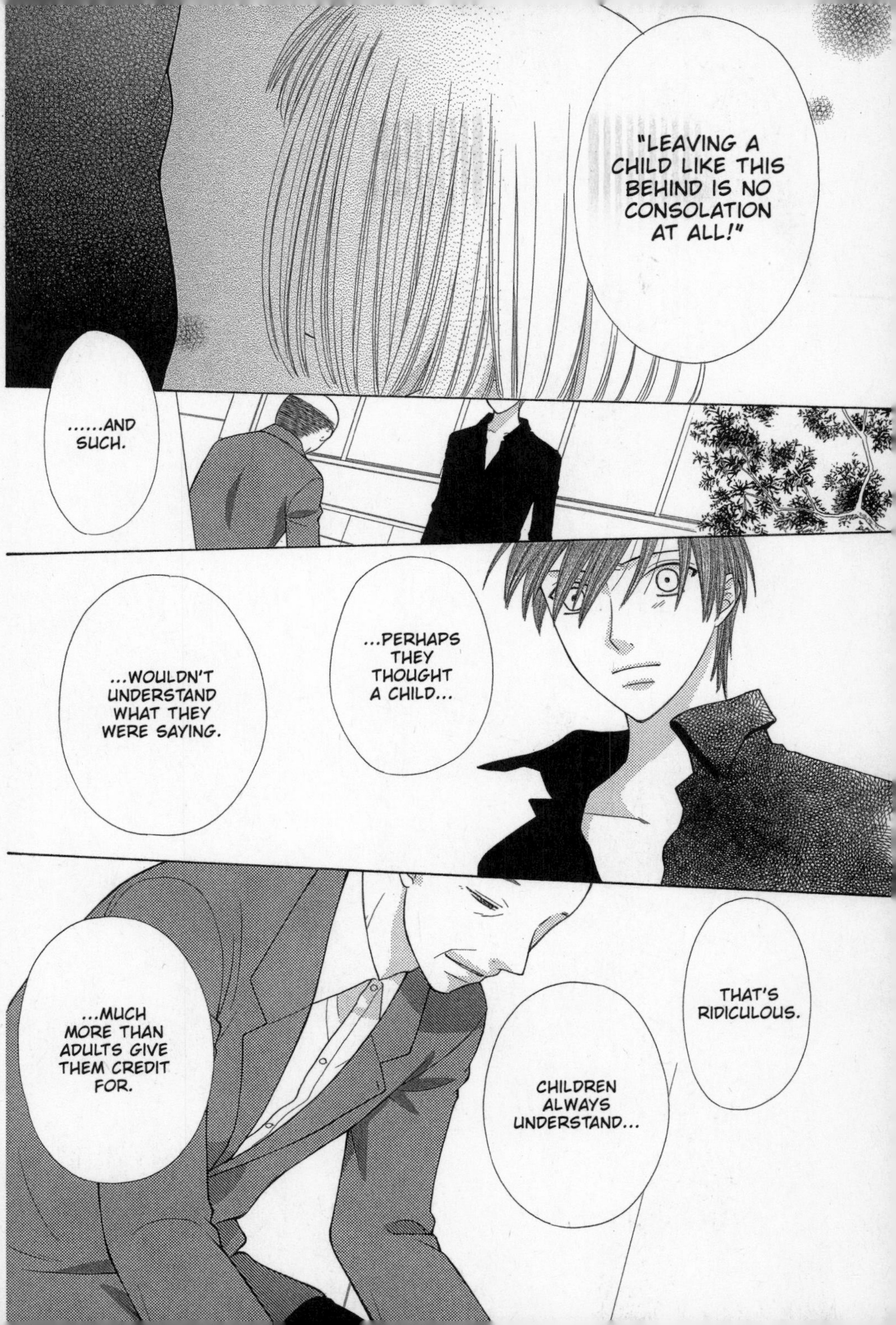
"LEAVING A CHILD LIKE THIS BEHIND IS NO CONSOLATION AT ALL!"
......AND SUCH.
...PERHAPS THEY THOUGHT A CHILD...
...WOULDN'T UNDERSTAND WHAT THEY WERE SAYING.
THAT'S RIDICULOUS.
CHILDREN ALWAYS UNDERSTAND...
...MUCH MORE THAN ADULTS GIVE THEM CREDIT FOR.

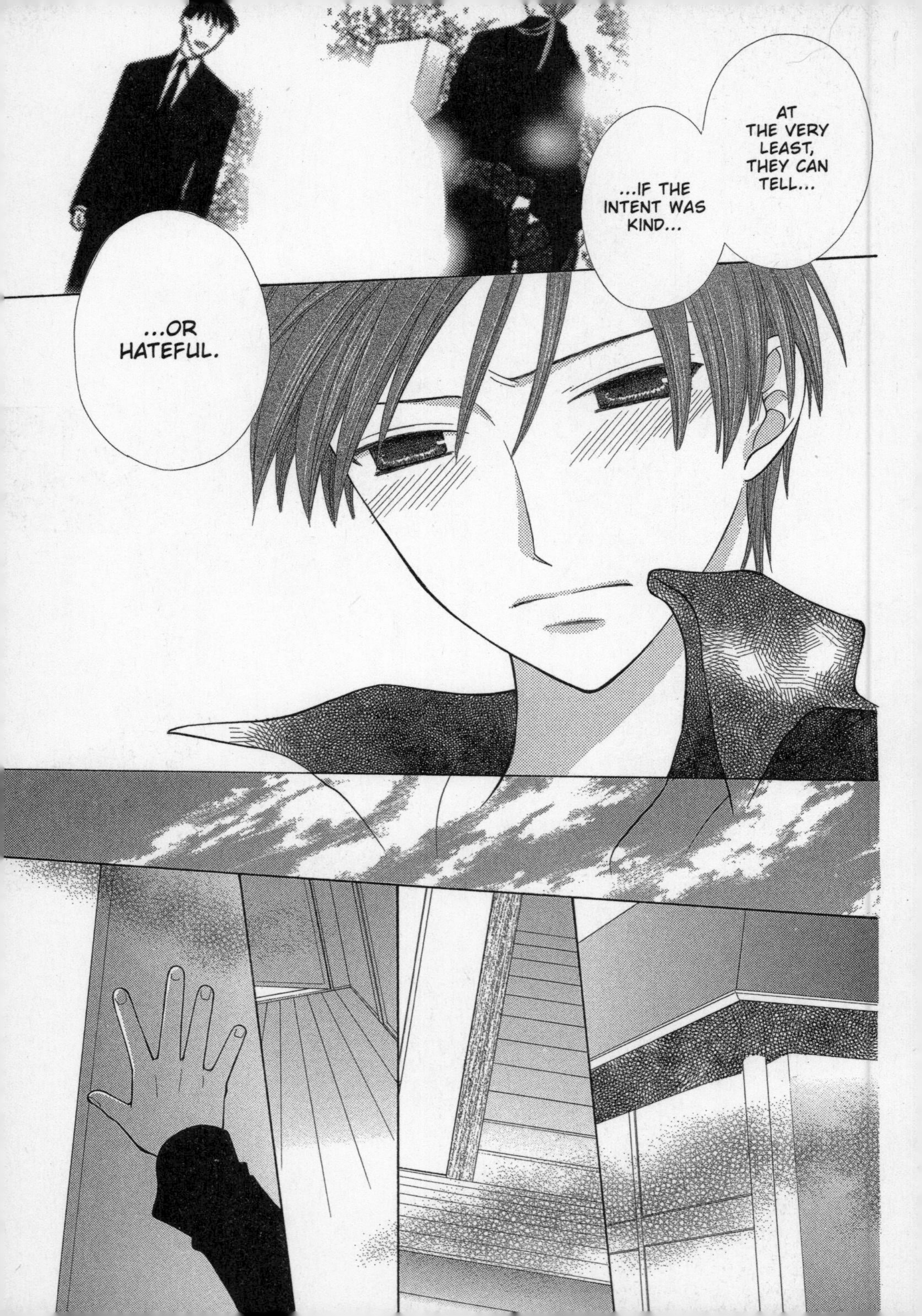
AT THE VERY LEAST, THEY CAN TELL...
...IF THE INTENT WAS KIND...
...OR HATEFUL.

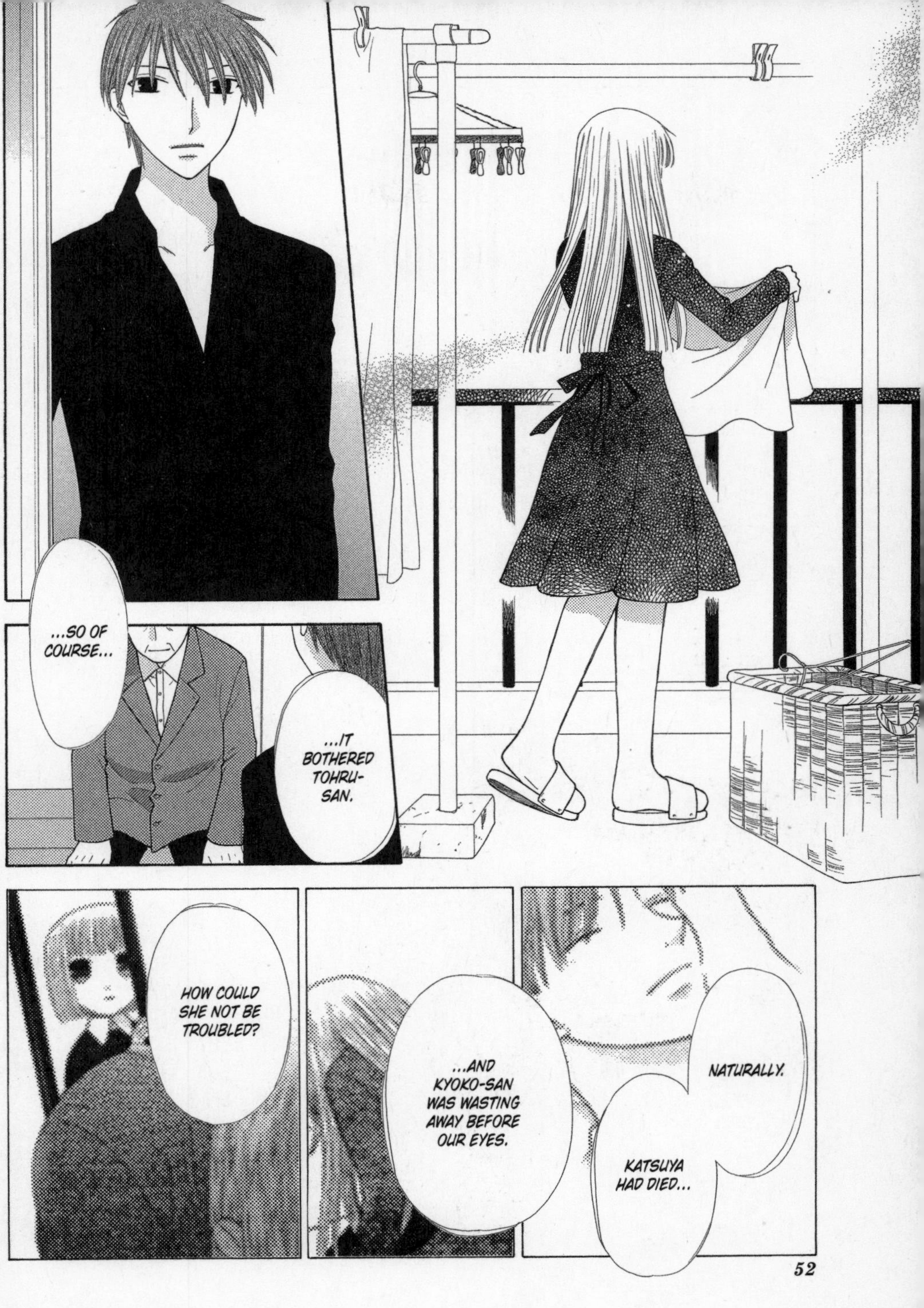
...SO OF COURSE...
...IT BOTHERED TOHRU-SAN.
NATURALLY.
KATSUYA HAD DIED...
...AND KYOKO-SAN WAS WASTING AWAY BEFORE OUR EYES.
HOW COULD SHE NOT BE TROUBLED?

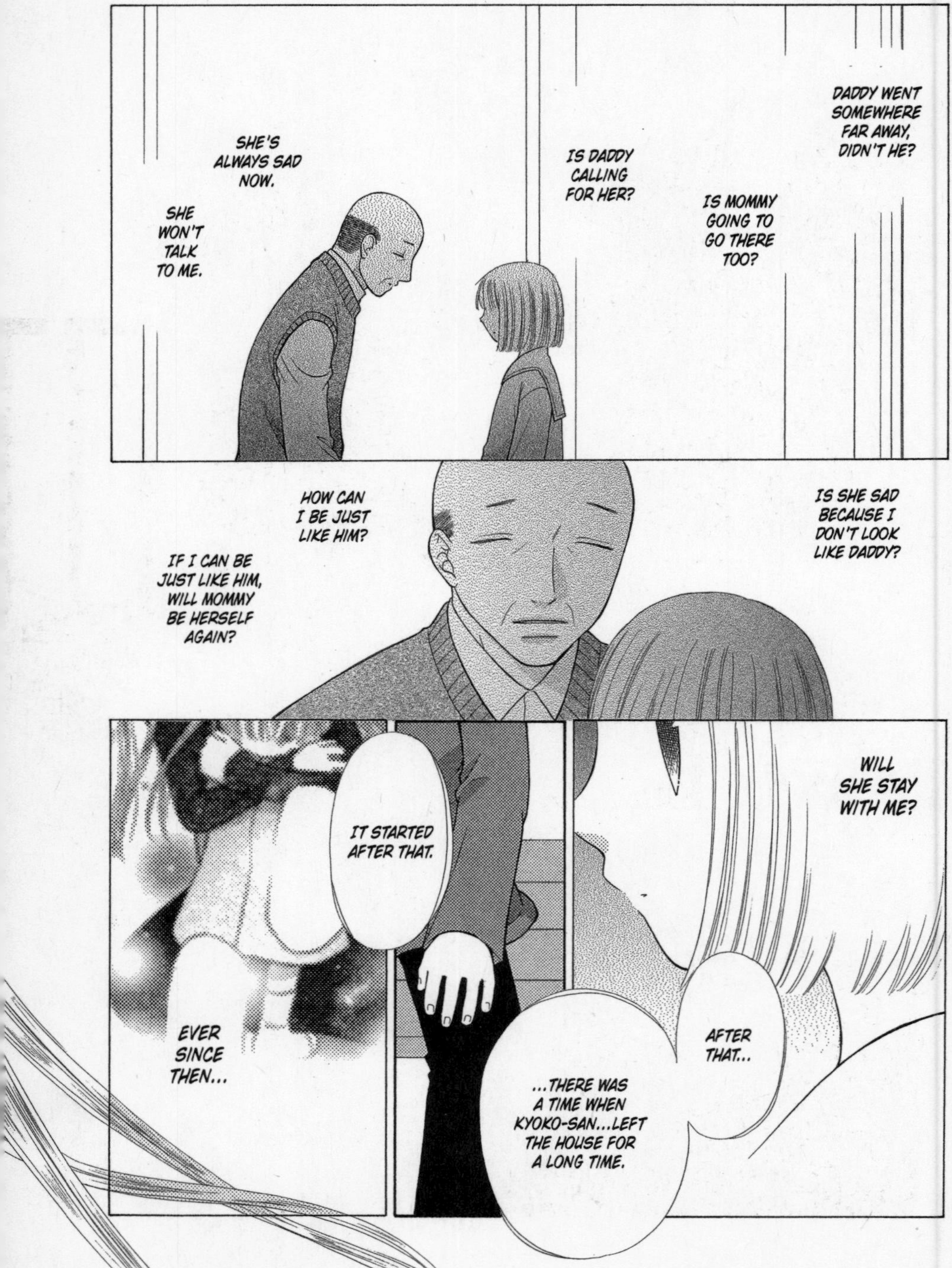
DADDY WENT SOMEWHERE FAR AWAY, DIDN'T HE?
IS MOMMY GOING TO GO THERE TOO?
IS DADDY CALLING FOR HER?
SHE'S ALWAYS SAD NOW.
SHE WON'T TALK TO ME.
IS SHE SAD BECAUSE I DON'T LOOK LIKE DADDY?
HOW CAN I BE JUST LIKE HIM?
IF I CAN BE JUST LIKE HIM, WILL MOMMY BE HERSELF AGAIN?
WILL SHE STAY WITH ME?
AFTER THAT...
...THERE WAS A TIME WHEN KYOKO-SAN...LEFT THE HOUSE FOR A LONG TIME.
IT STARTED AFTER THAT.
EVER SINCE THEN...

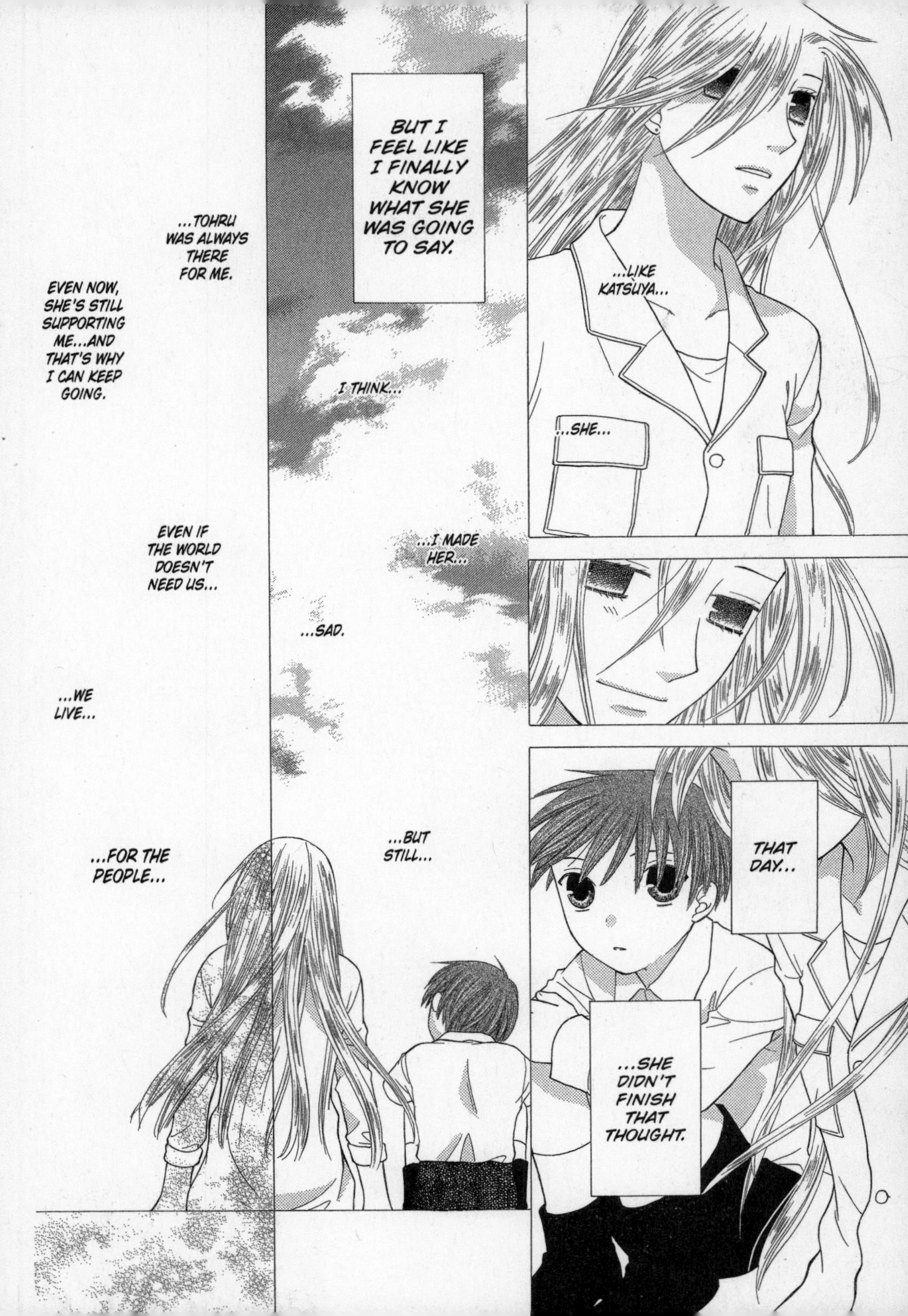
...LIKE KATSUYA...
...SHE...
THAT DAY...
...SHE DIDN'T FINISH THAT THOUGHT.
BUT I FEEL LIKE I FINALLY KNOW WHAT SHE WAS GOING TO SAY.
I THINK...
...I MADE HER...
...SAD.
...BUT STILL...
...TOHRU WAS ALWAYS THERE FOR ME.
EVEN NOW, SHE'S STILL SUPPORTING ME...AND THAT'S WHY I CAN KEEP GOING.
EVEN IF THE WORLD DOESN'T NEED US...
...WE LIVE...
...FOR THE PEOPLE...

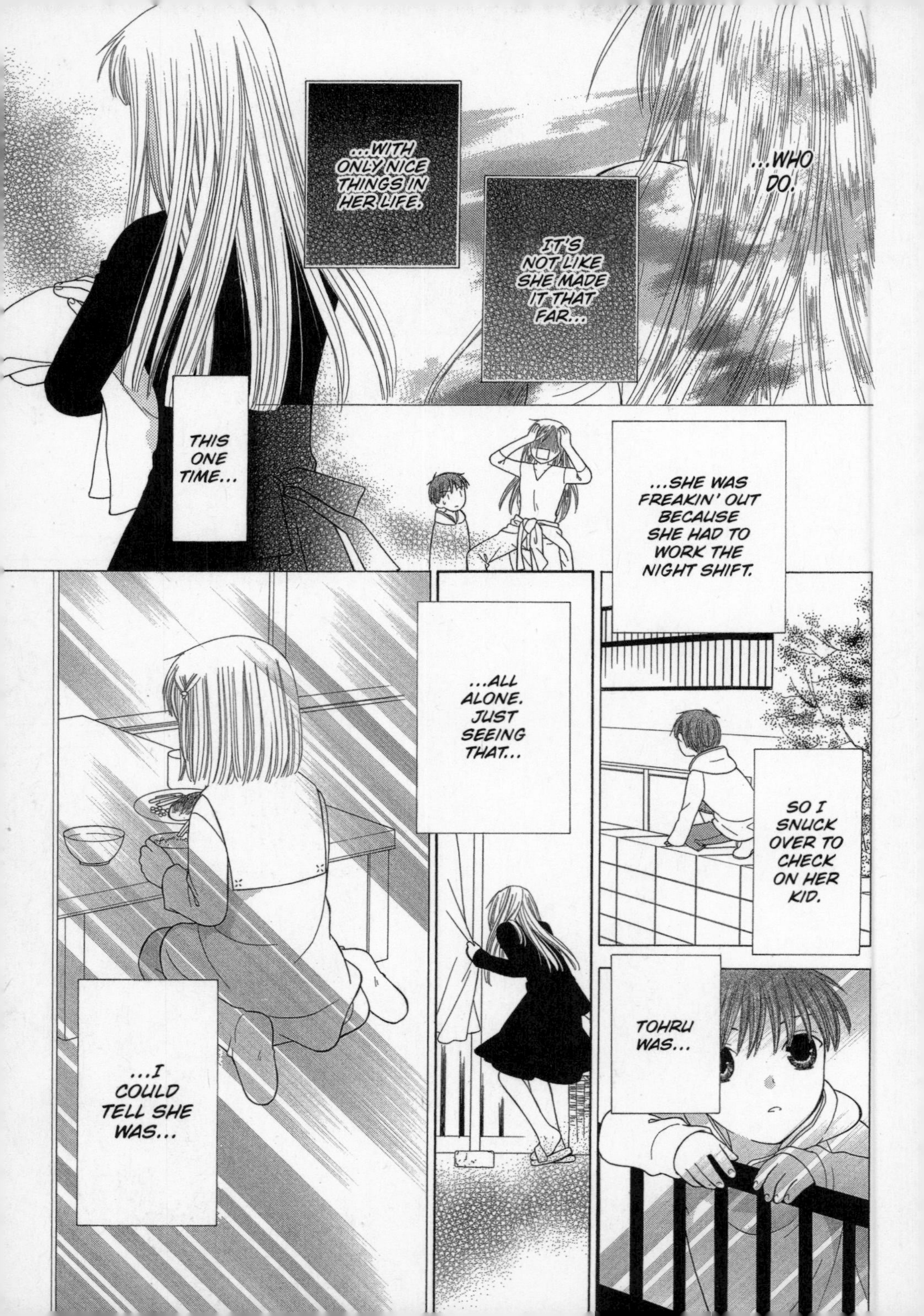

...WHO DO.
IT'S NOT LIKE SHE MADE IT THAT FAR...
...WITH ONLY NICE THINGS IN HER LIFE.
THIS ONE TIME...
...SHE WAS FREAKIN' OUT BECAUSE SHE HAD TO WORK THE NIGHT SHIFT.
SO I SNUCK OVER TO CHECK ON HER KID.
TOHRU WAS...
...ALL ALONE. JUST SEEING THAT...
...I COULD TELL SHE WAS...

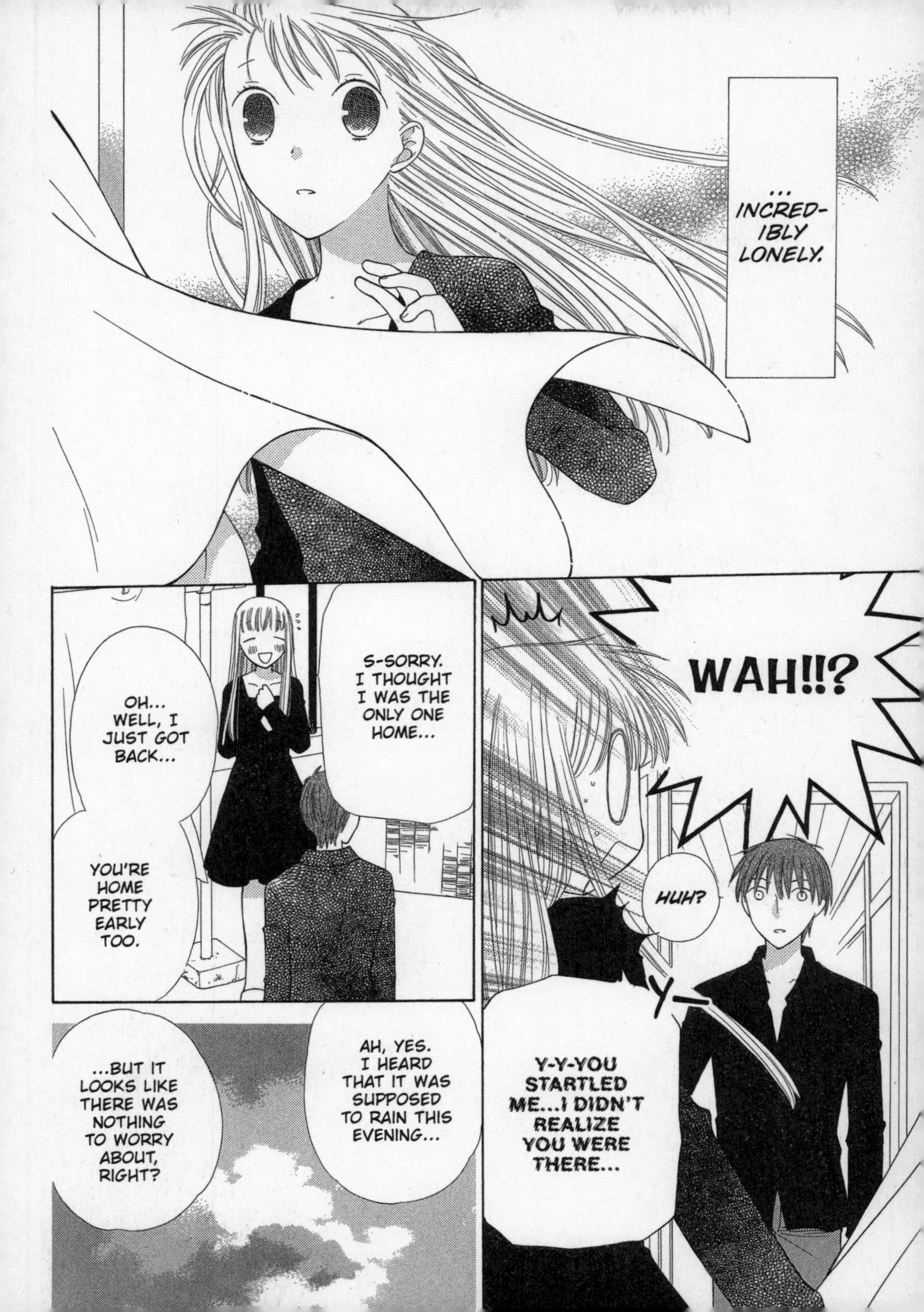
...INCRED-IBLY LONELY.
WAH!!?
HUH?
Y—
Y-Y-YOU STARTLED ME...I DIDN'T REALIZE YOU WERE THERE...
S-SORRY. I THOUGHT I WAS THE ONLY ONE HOME...
OH... WELL, I JUST GOT BACK...
YOU'RE HOME PRETTY EARLY TOO.
AH, YES. I HEARD THAT IT WAS SUPPOSED TO RAIN THIS EVENING...
...BUT IT LOOKS LIKE THERE WAS NOTHING TO WORRY ABOUT, RIGHT?

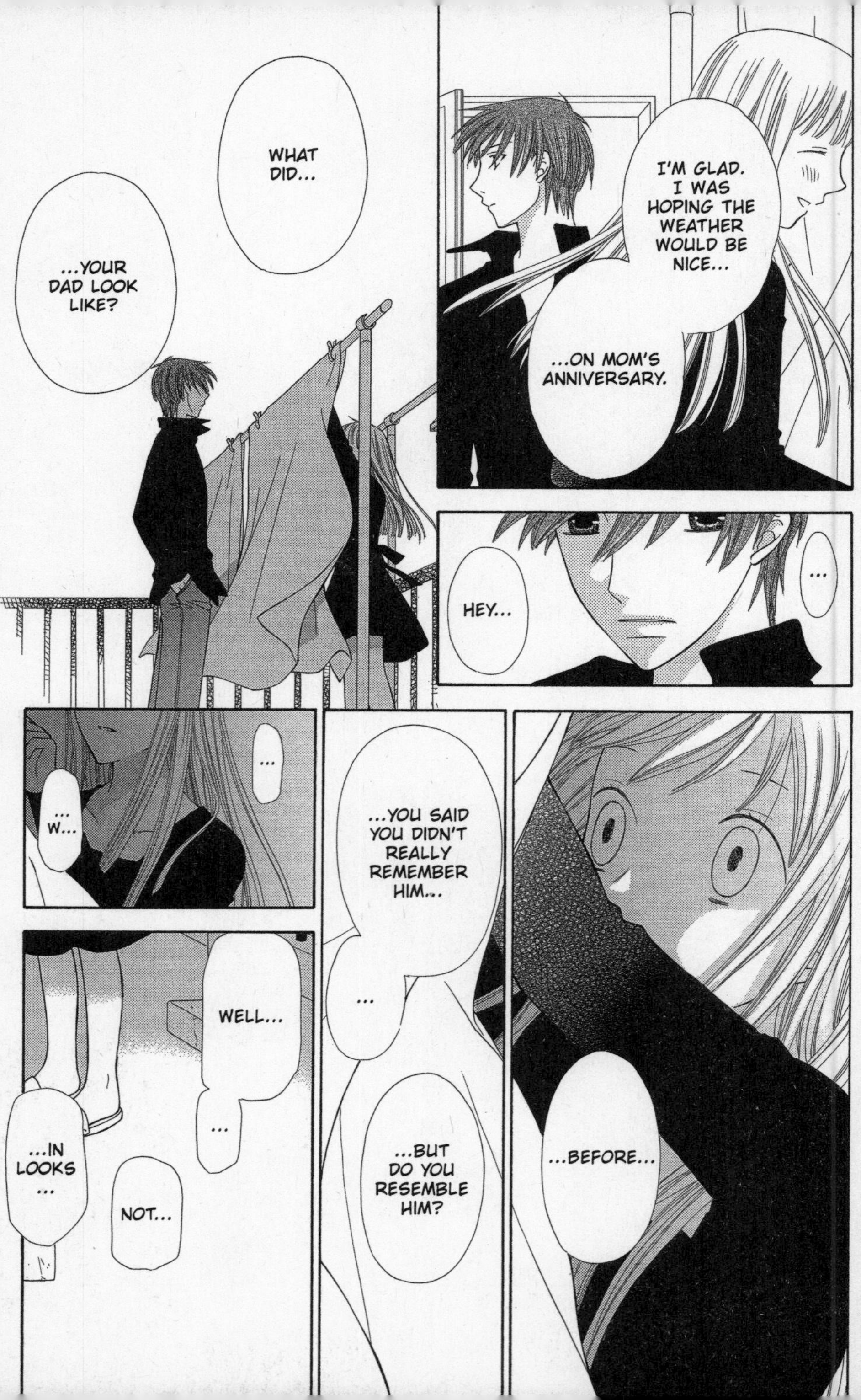
I'M GLAD. I WAS HOPING THE WEATHER WOULD BE NICE...
...ON MOM'S ANNIVERSARY.
...
HEY...
WHAT DID...
...YOUR DAD LOOK LIKE?
...YOU SAID YOU DIDN'T REALLY REMEMBER HIM...
...
...BEFORE...
...BUT DO YOU RESEMBLE HIM?
...
... W...
WELL...
...
...IN LOOKS ...
NOT...

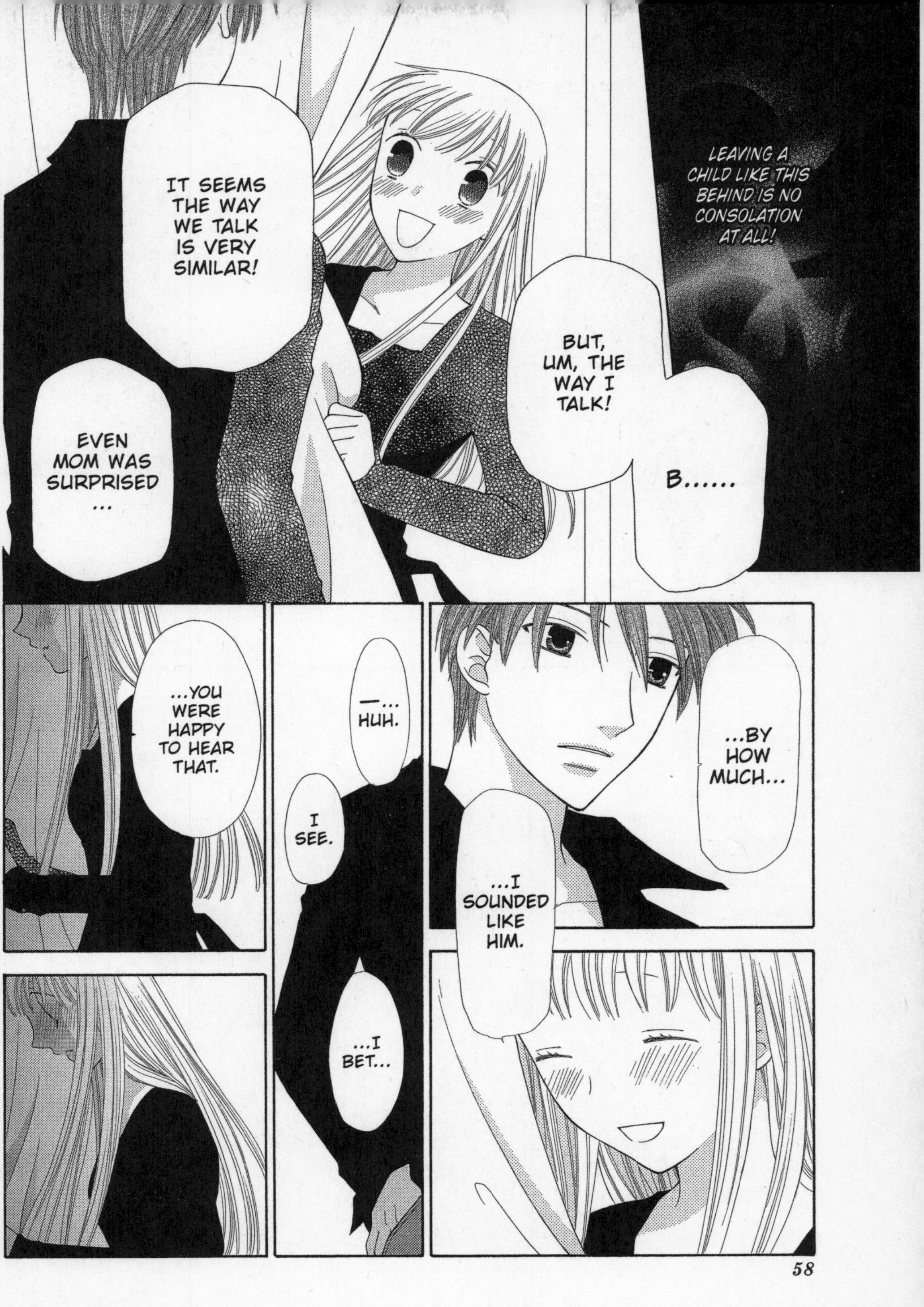
LEAVING A CHILD LIKE THIS BEHIND IS NO CONSOLATION AT ALL!
B......
BUT, UM, THE WAY I TALK!
IT SEEMS THE WAY WE TALK IS VERY SIMILAR!
EVEN MOM WAS SURPRISED...
...BY HOW MUCH...
...I SOUNDED LIKE HIM.
—... HUH.
I SEE.
...YOU WERE HAPPY TO HEAR THAT.
...I BET...

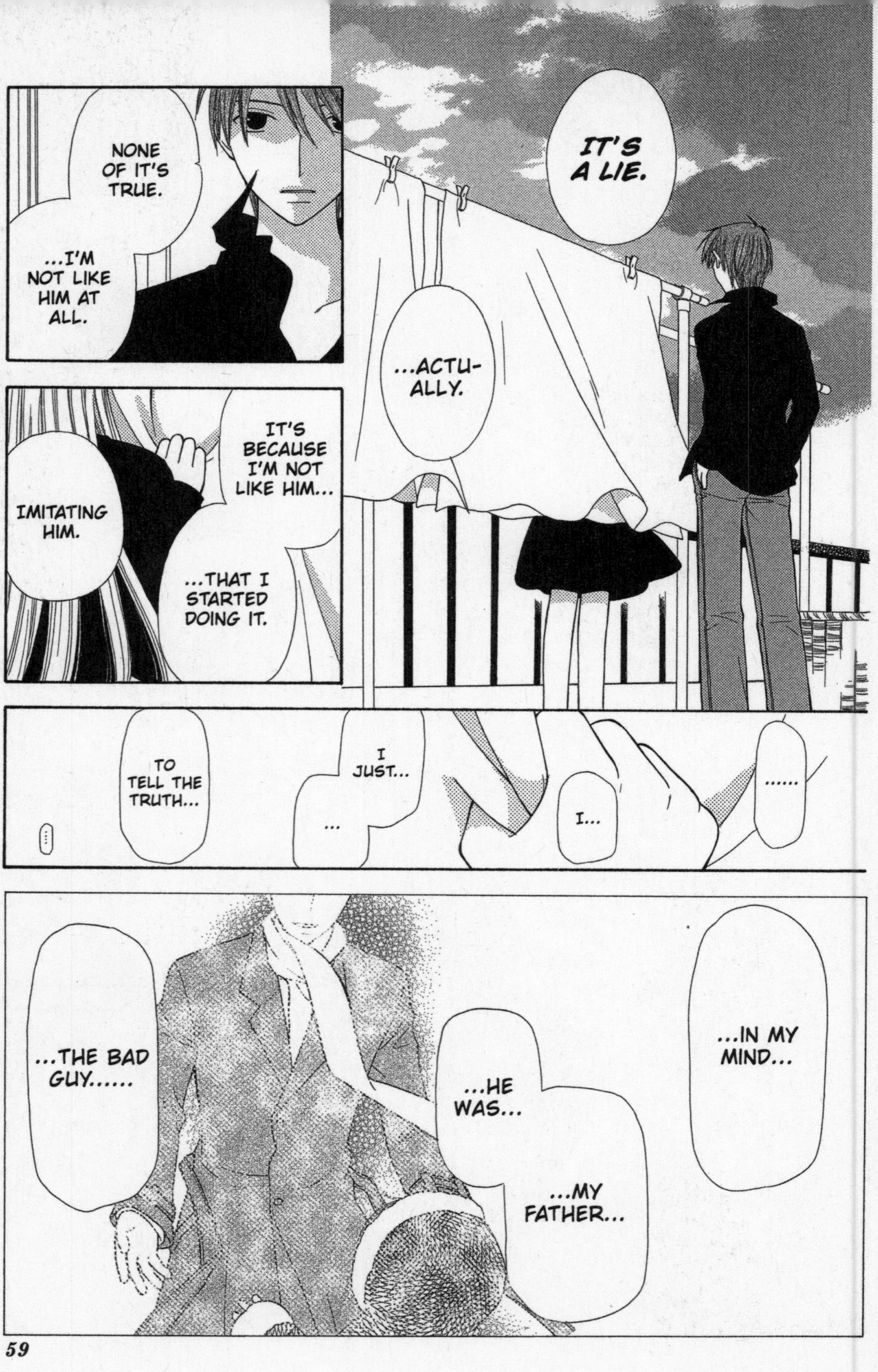
IT'S A LIE.
...ACTU-ALLY.
NONE OF IT'S TRUE.
...I'M NOT LIKE HIM AT ALL.
IT'S BECAUSE I'M NOT LIKE HIM...
...THAT I STARTED DOING IT.
IMITATING HIM.
......
I...
I JUST...
...
TO TELL THE TRUTH...
...
...IN MY MIND...
...HE WAS...
...MY FATHER...
...THE BAD GUY......

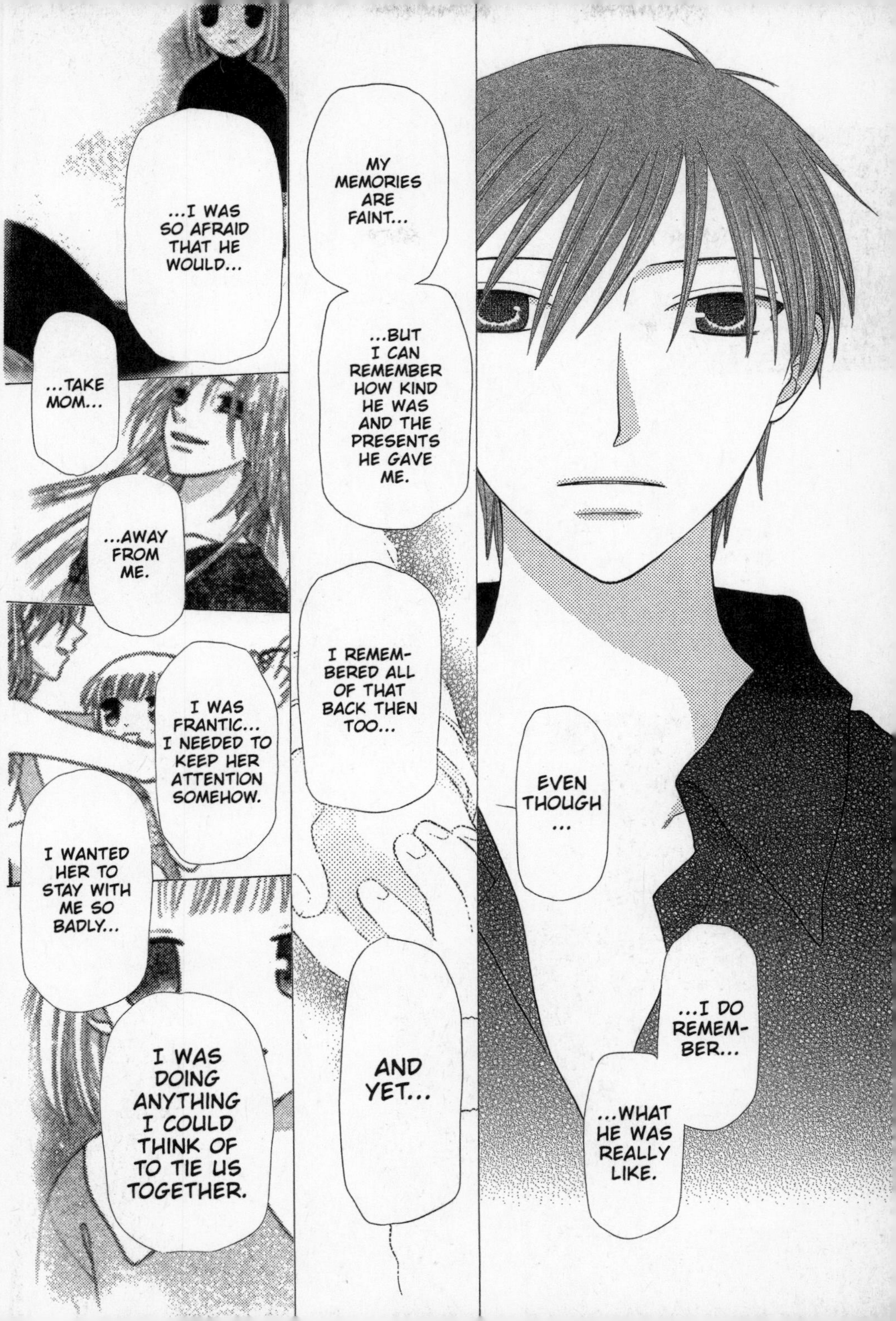
EVEN THOUGH...
...I DO REMEMBER...
...WHAT HE WAS REALLY LIKE.
MY MEMORIES ARE FAINT...
...BUT I CAN REMEMBER HOW KIND HE WAS AND THE PRESENTS HE GAVE ME.
I REMEMBERED ALL OF THAT BACK THEN TOO...
AND YET...
...I WAS SO AFRAID THAT HE WOULD...
...TAKE MOM...
...AWAY FROM ME.
I WAS FRANTIC... I NEEDED TO KEEP HER ATTENTION SOMEHOW.
I WANTED HER TO STAY WITH ME SO BADLY...
I WAS DOING ANYTHING I COULD THINK OF TO TIE US TOGETHER.

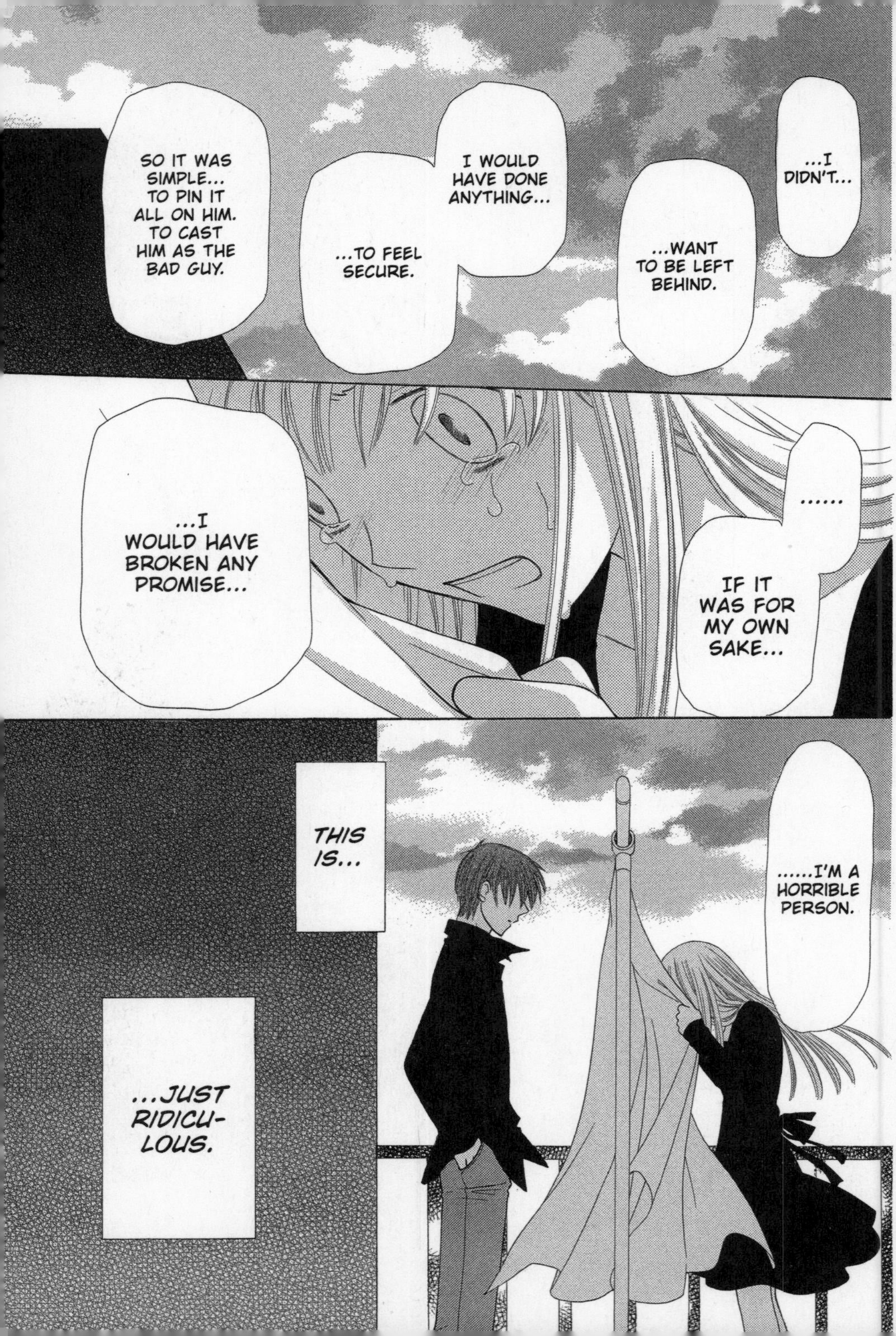
...I DIDN'T...
...WANT TO BE LEFT BEHIND.
I WOULD HAVE DONE ANYTHING...
...TO FEEL SECURE.
SO IT WAS SIMPLE... TO PIN IT ALL ON HIM. TO CAST HIM AS THE BAD GUY.
......
IF IT WAS FOR MY OWN SAKE...
...I WOULD HAVE BROKEN ANY PROMISE...
......I'M A HORRIBLE PERSON.
THIS IS...
...JUST RIDICU-LOUS.

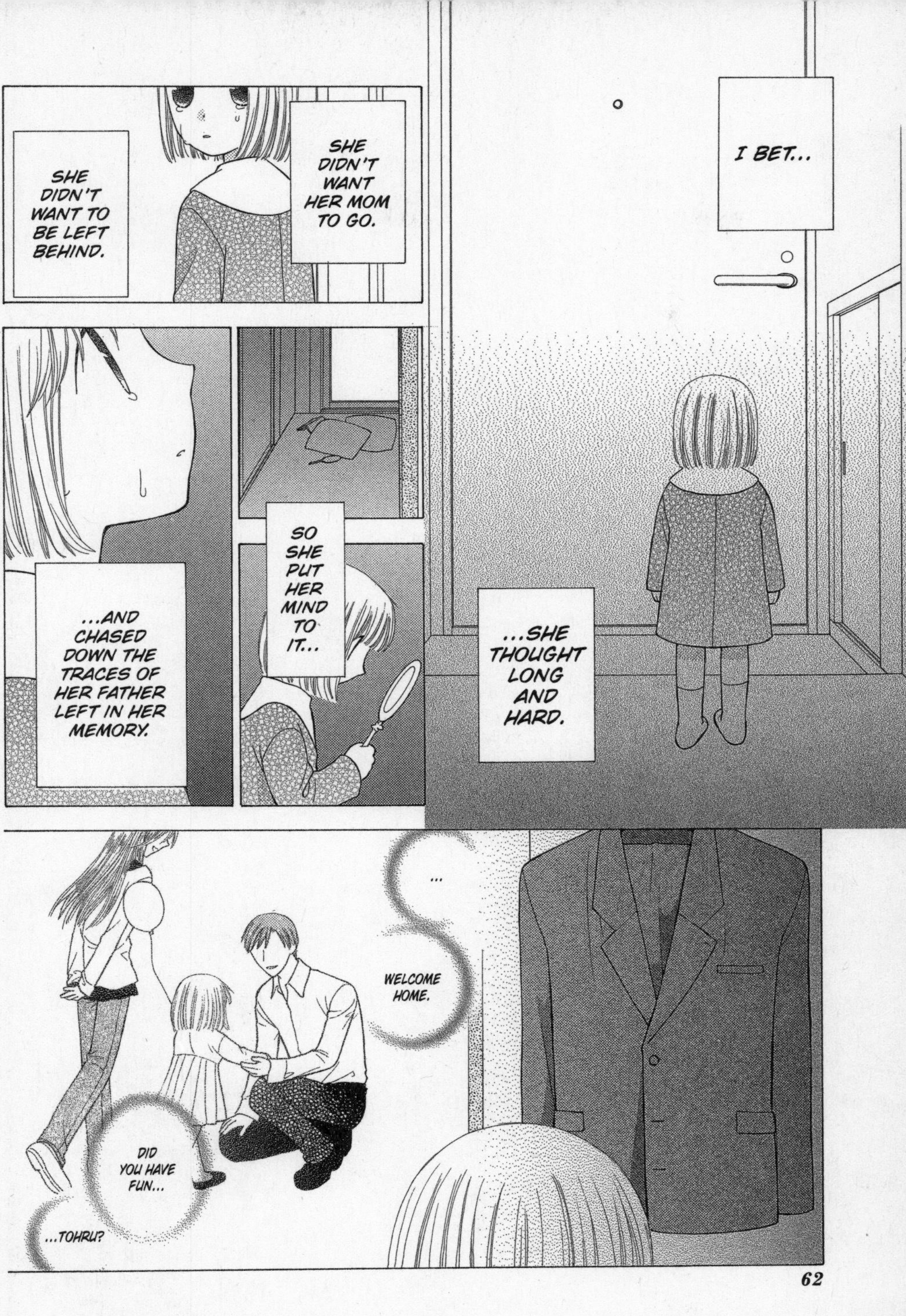
I BET...
...SHE THOUGHT LONG AND HARD.
SHE DIDN'T WANT HER MOM TO GO.
SHE DIDN'T WANT TO BE LEFT BEHIND.
SO SHE PUT HER MIND TO IT...
...AND CHASED DOWN THE TRACES OF HER FATHER LEFT IN HER MEMORY.
...
WELCOME HOME.
DID YOU HAVE FUN...
...TOHRU?

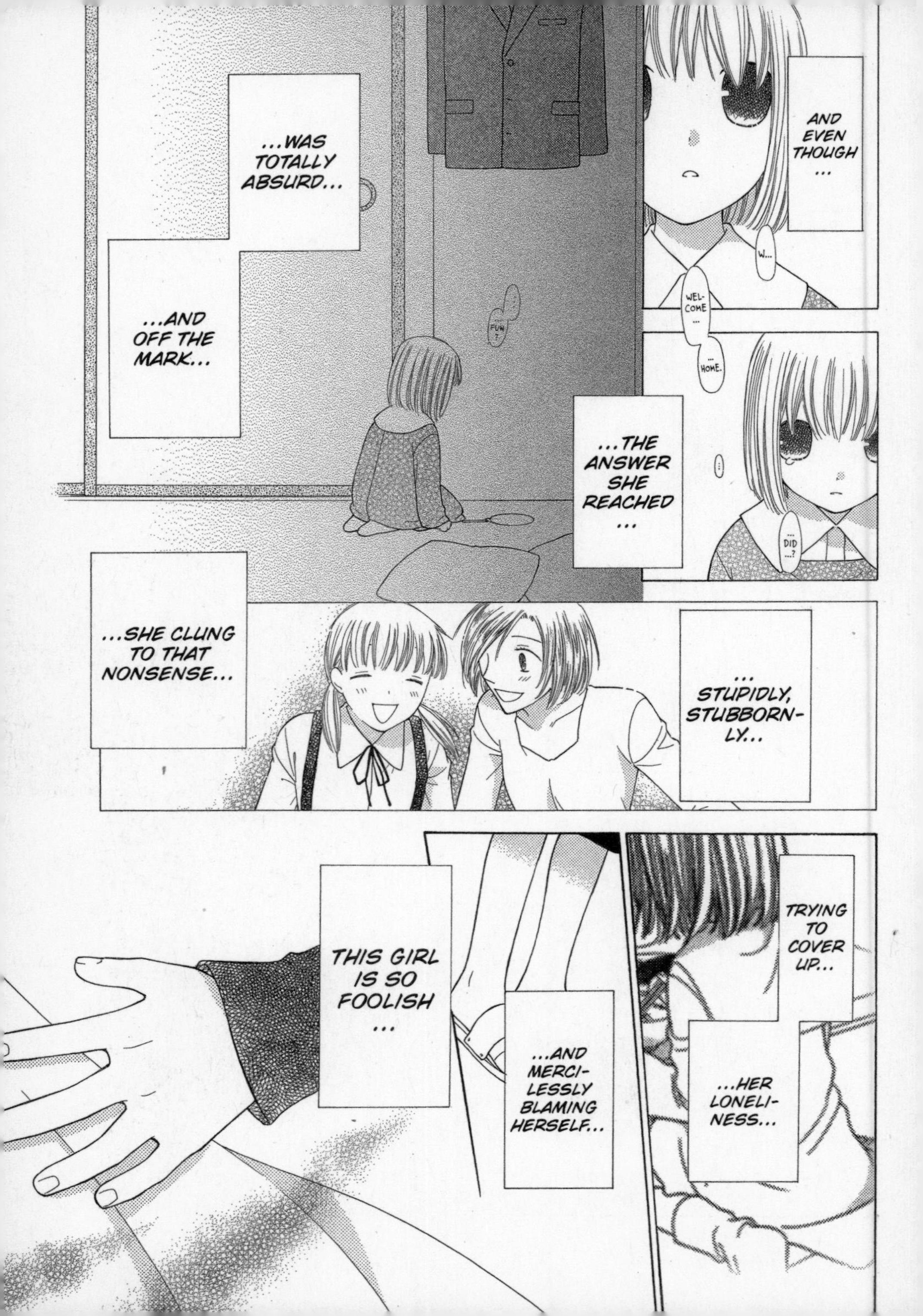
AND EVEN THOUGH...
W...
WEL-COME...
...HOME.
...!
...DID...?
...THE ANSWER SHE REACHED...
...WAS TOTALLY ABSURD...
...AND OFF THE MARK...
...FUN?
...STUPIDLY, STUBBORN-LY...
...SHE CLUNG TO THAT NONSENSE...
TRYING TO COVER UP...
...HER LONELI-NESS...
...AND MERCI-LESSLY BLAMING HERSELF...
THIS GIRL IS SO FOOLISH...

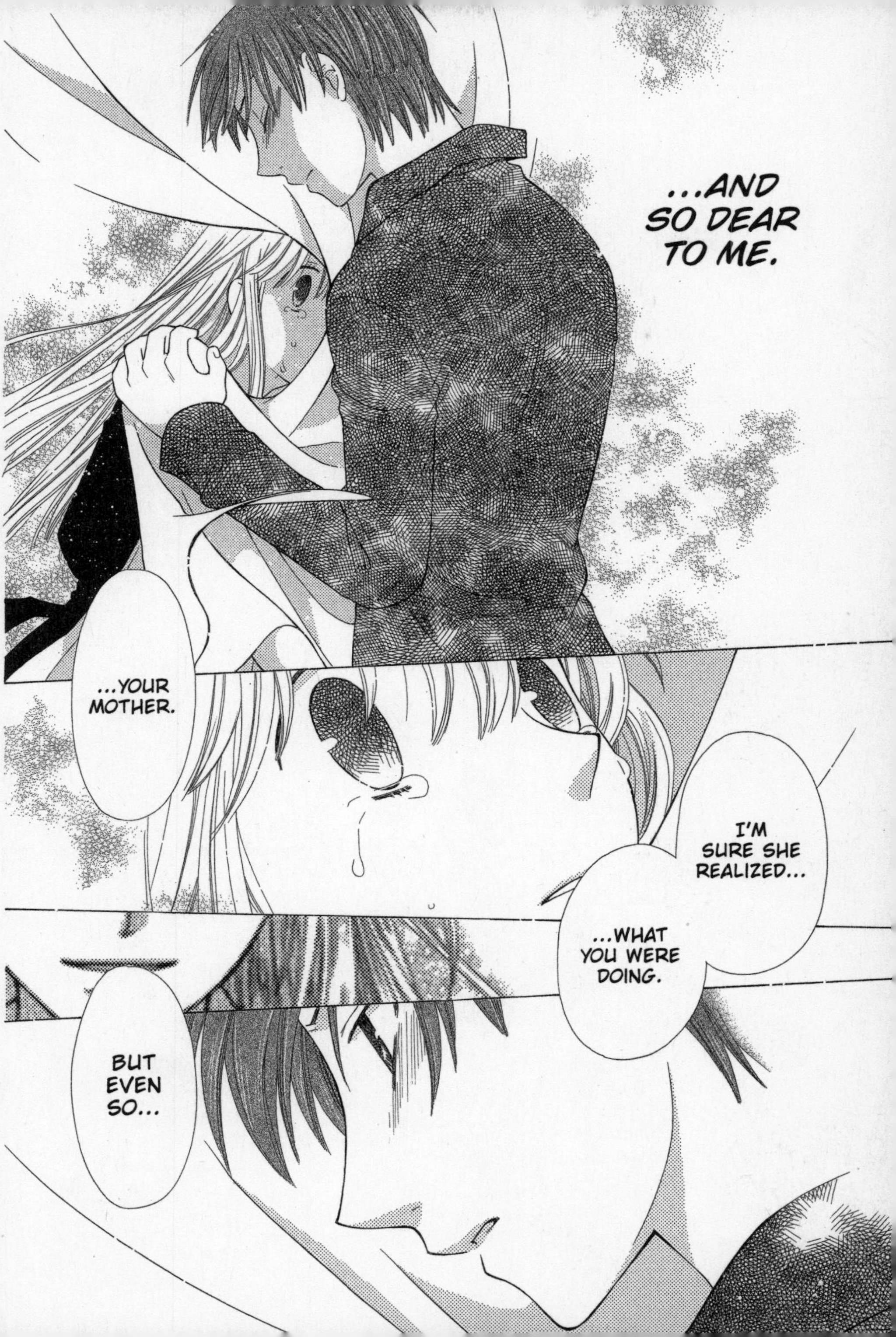
...AND SO DEAR TO ME.
...YOUR MOTHER.
I'M SURE SHE REALIZED...
...WHAT YOU WERE DOING.
BUT EVEN SO...

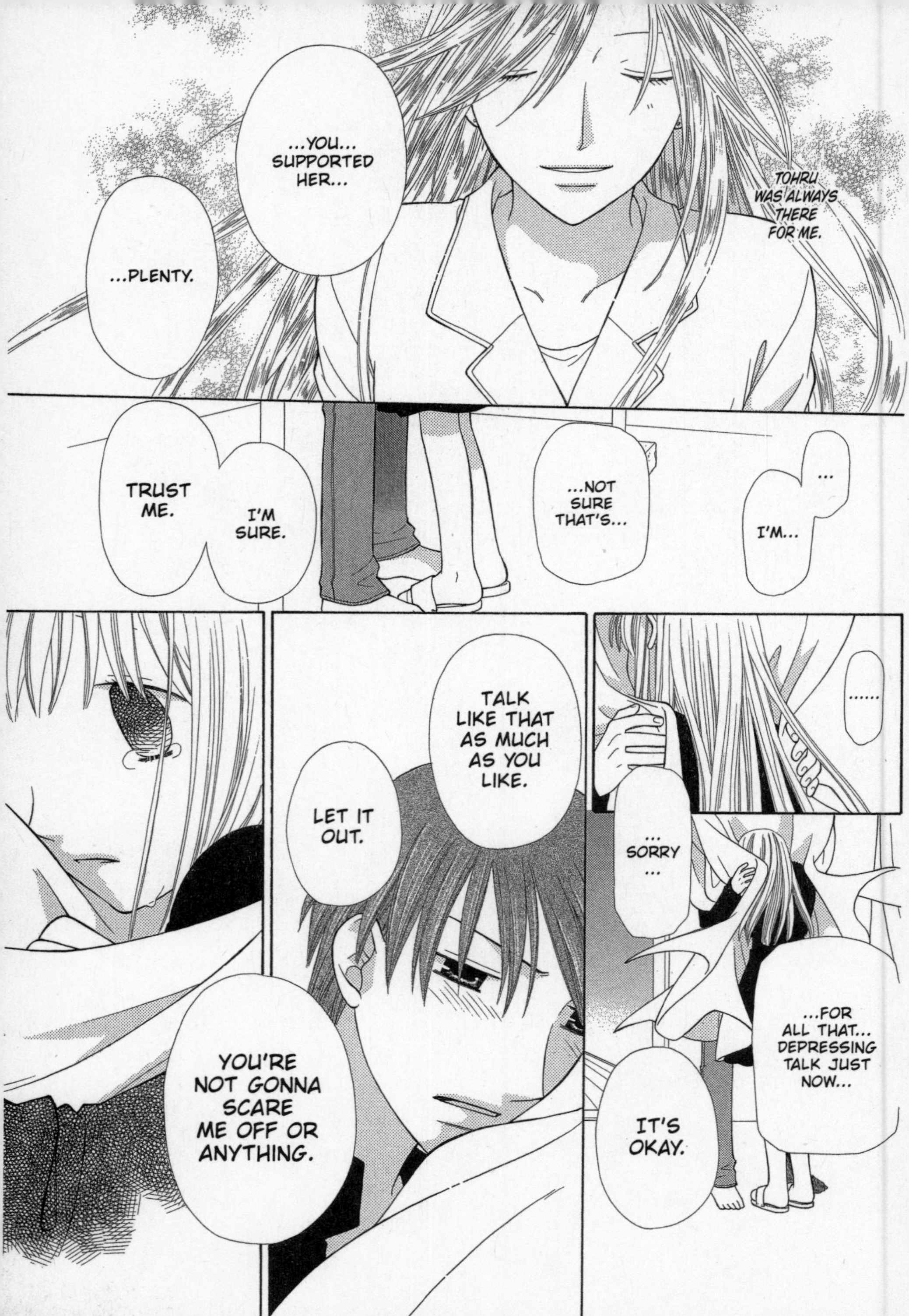
TOHRU WAS ALWAYS THERE FOR ME.
...YOU... SUPPORTED HER...
...PLENTY.
... I'M...
...NOT SURE THAT'S...
I'M SURE.
TRUST ME.
......
... SORRY ...
...FOR ALL THAT... DEPRESSING TALK JUST NOW...
IT'S OKAY.
TALK LIKE THAT AS MUCH AS YOU LIKE.
LET IT OUT.
YOU'RE NOT GONNA SCARE ME OFF OR ANYTHING.

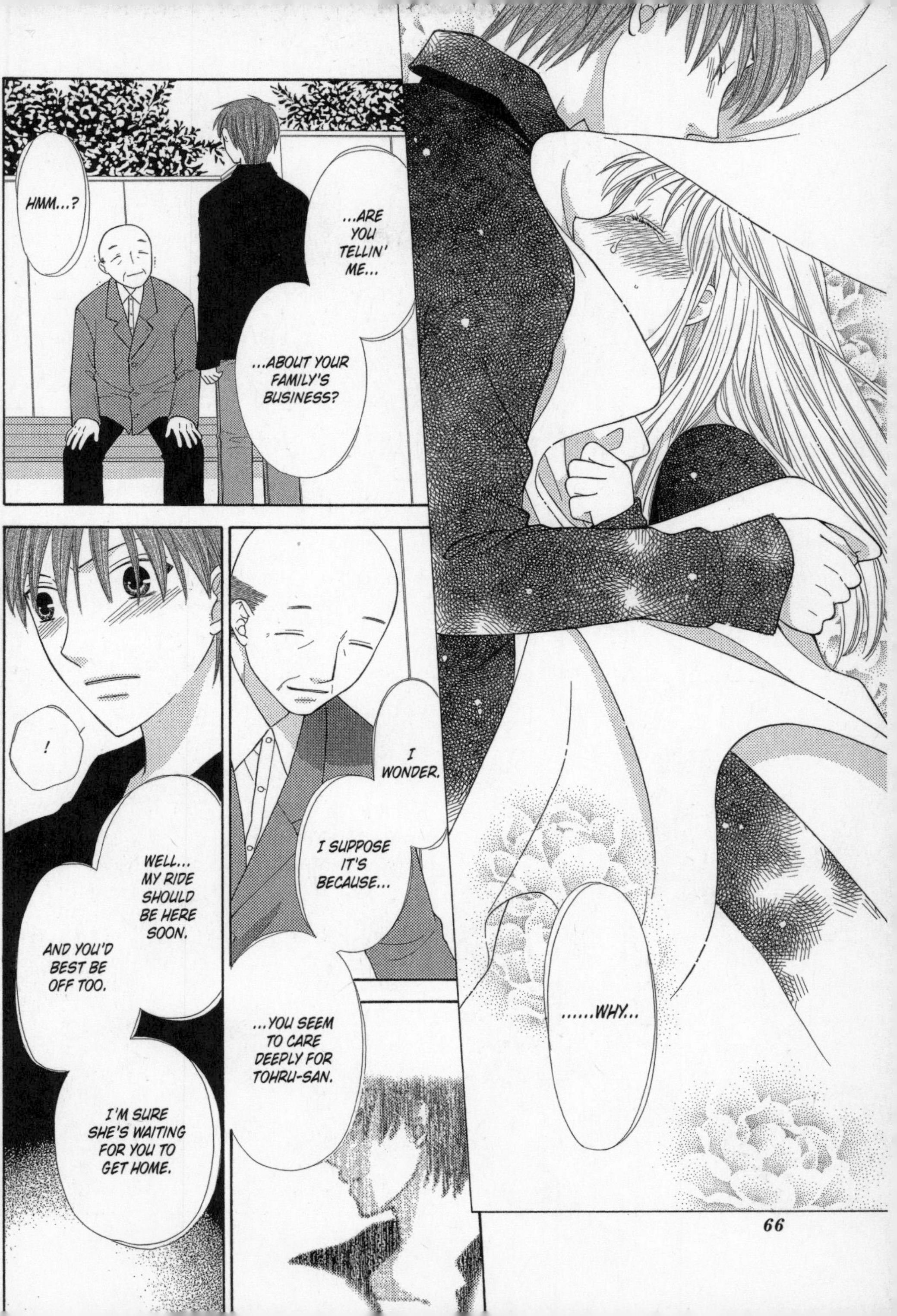

......WHY...
...ARE YOU TELLIN' ME...
...ABOUT YOUR FAMILY'S BUSINESS?
HMM...?
I WONDER.
I SUPPOSE IT'S BECAUSE...
...YOU SEEM TO CARE DEEPLY FOR TOHRU-SAN.
!
WELL... MY RIDE SHOULD BE HERE SOON.
AND YOU'D BEST BE OFF TOO.
I'M SURE SHE'S WAITING FOR YOU TO GET HOME.

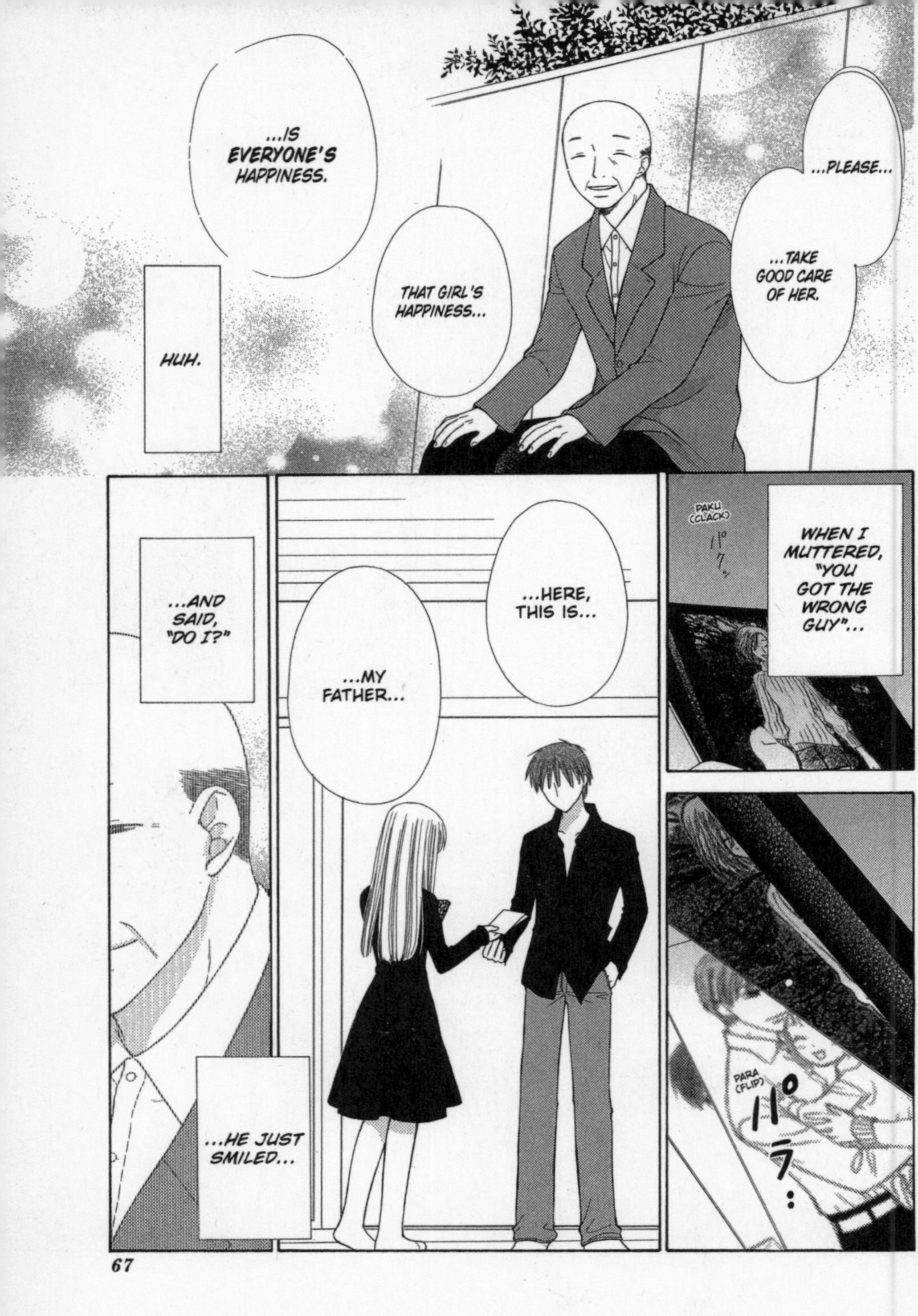
...PLEASE...
...TAKE GOOD CARE OF HER.
THAT GIRL'S HAPPINESS...
...IS EVERYONE'S HAPPINESS.
HUH.
WHEN I MUTTERED, "YOU GOT THE WRONG GUY"...
PAKU (CLACK)
パクッ
PARA (FLIP)
パラ…
...HERE, THIS IS...
...MY FATHER...
...AND SAID, "DO I?"
...HE JUST SMILED...

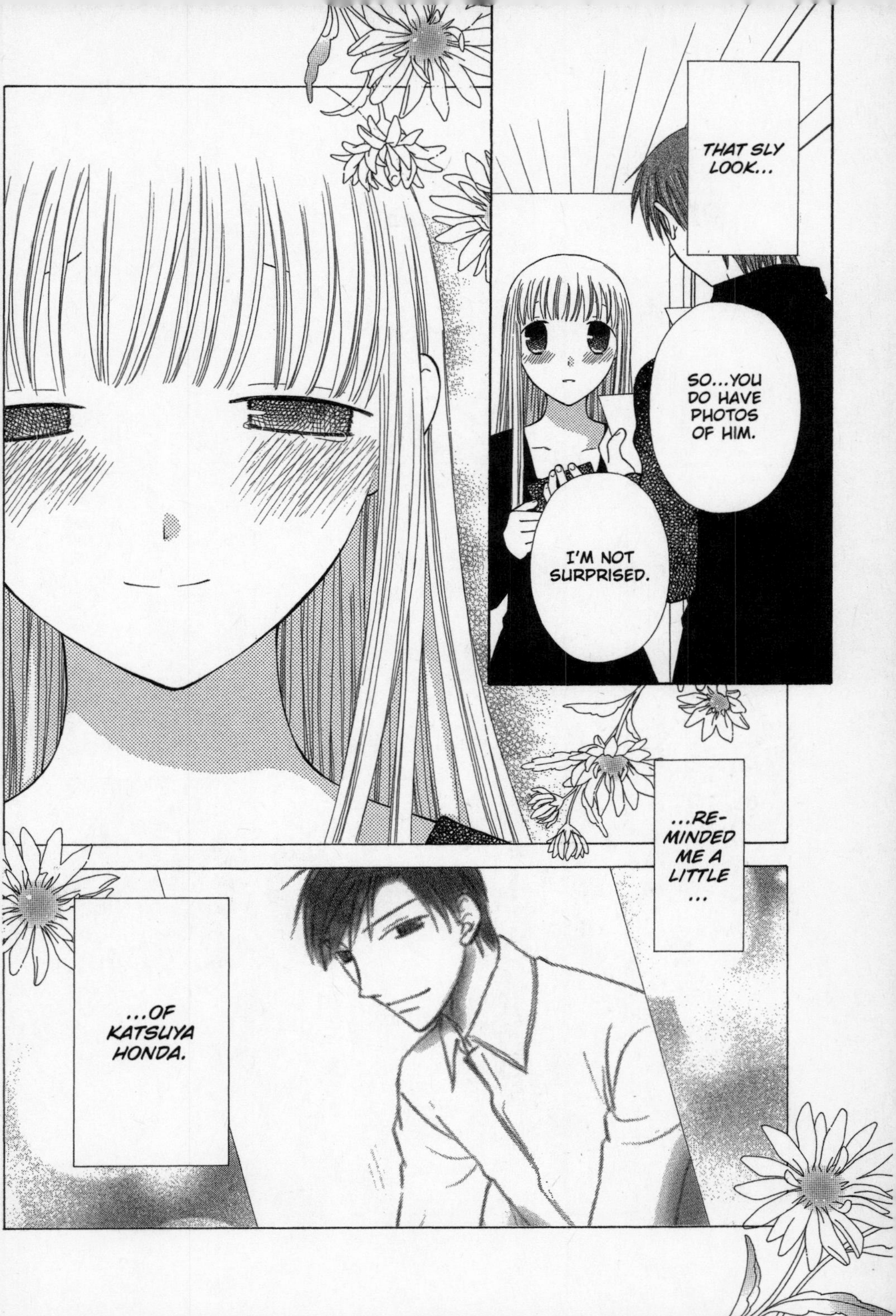
THAT SLY LOOK...
SO...YOU DO HAVE PHOTOS OF HIM.
I'M NOT SURPRISED.
...RE-MINDED ME A LITTLE...
...OF KATSUYA HONDA.

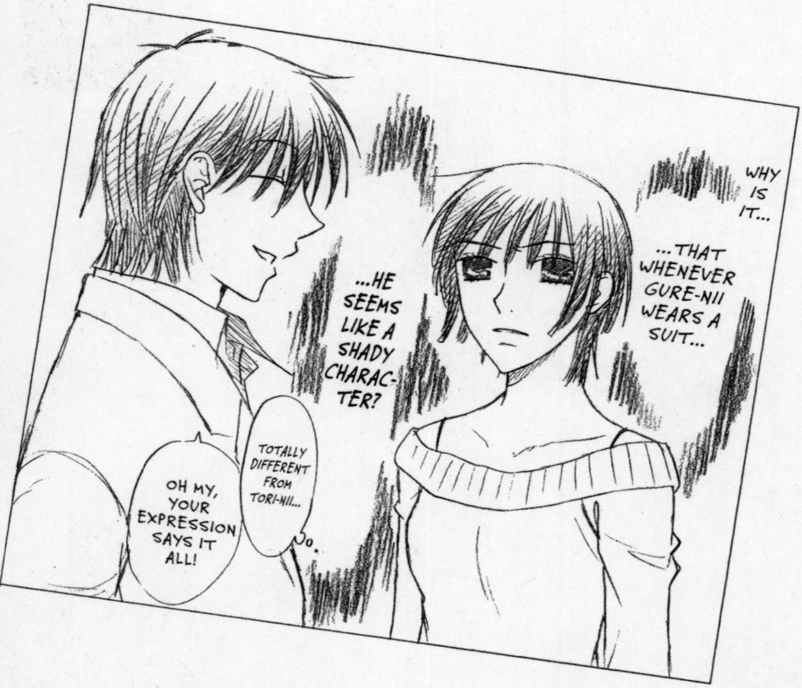
WHY IS IT...
...THAT WHENEVER GURE-NII WEARS A SUIT...
...HE SEEMS LIKE A SHADY CHARAC-TER?
TOTALLY DIFFERENT FROM TORI-NII...
OH MY, YOUR EXPRESSION SAYS IT ALL!

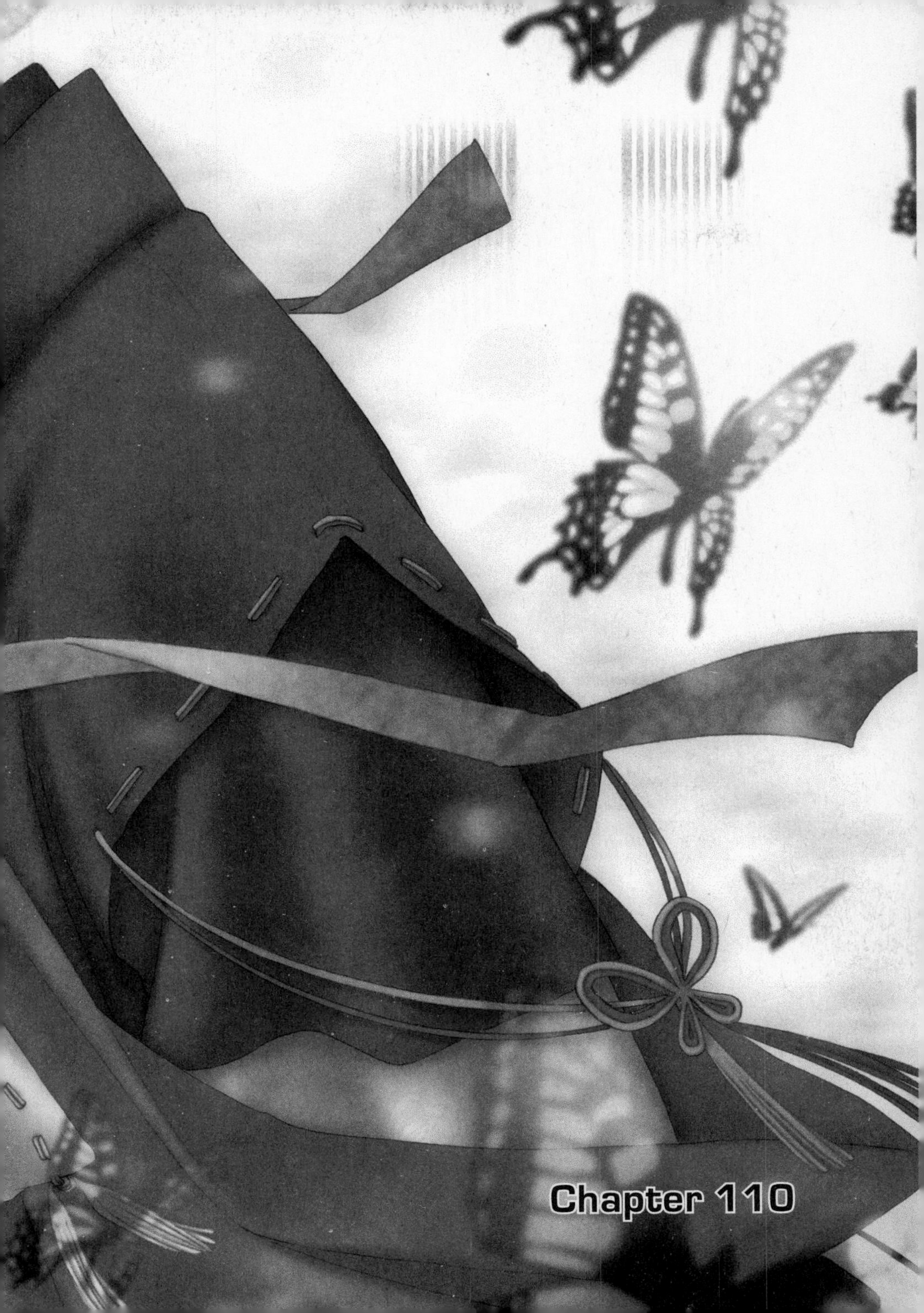
Chapter 110

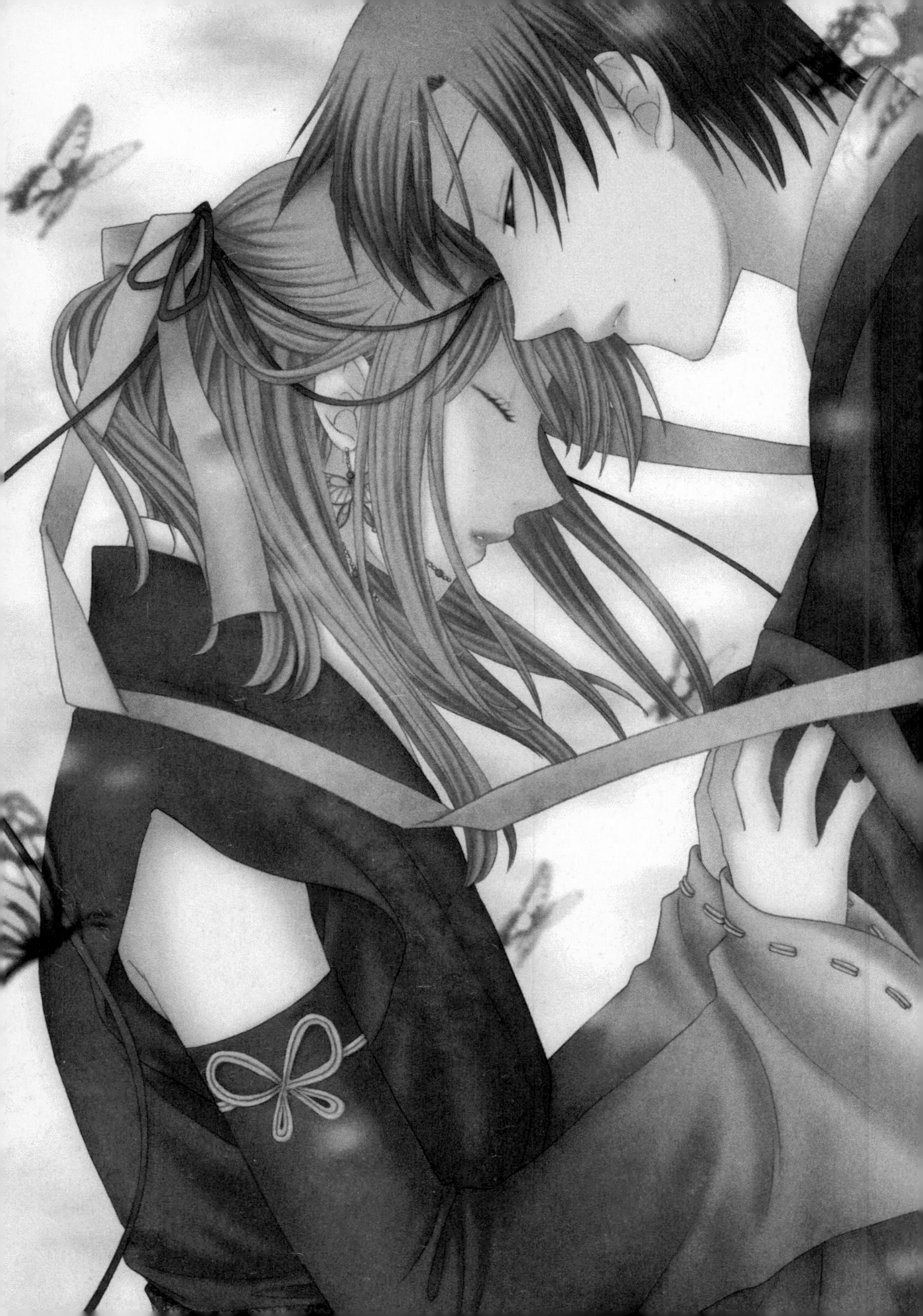

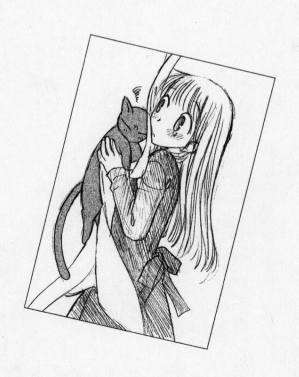

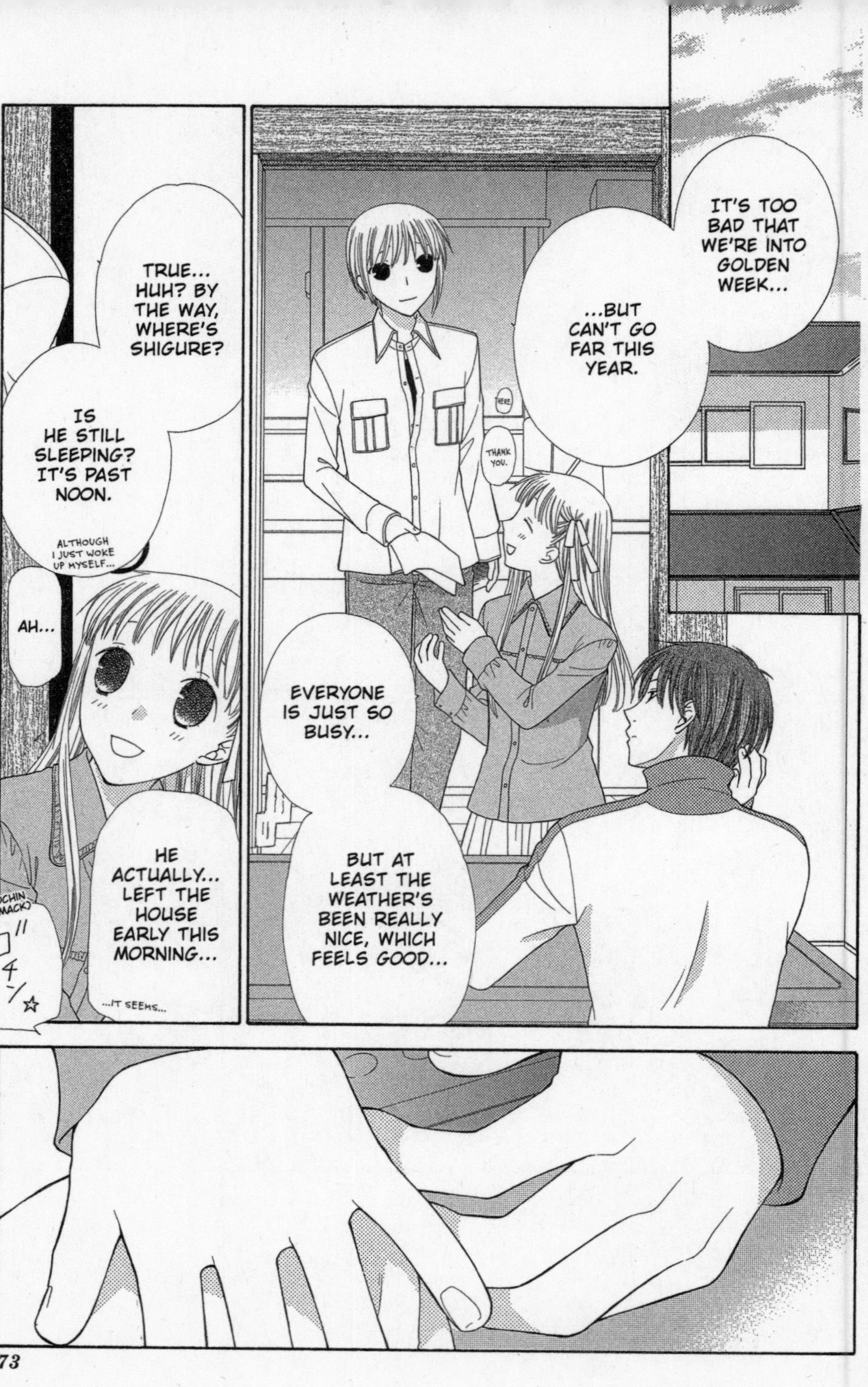
IT'S TOO BAD THAT WE'RE INTO GOLDEN WEEK...
...BUT CAN'T GO FAR THIS YEAR.
THERE.
THANK YOU.
EVERYONE IS JUST SO BUSY...
BUT AT LEAST THE WEATHER'S BEEN REALLY NICE, WHICH FEELS GOOD...
TRUE... HUH? BY THE WAY, WHERE'S SHIGURE?
IS HE STILL SLEEPING? IT'S PAST NOON.
ALTHOUGH I JUST WOKE UP MYSELF...
AH...
HE ACTUALLY... LEFT THE HOUSE EARLY THIS MORNING...
...IT SEEMS...
GOCHIN (SMACK)
ゴチーン☆

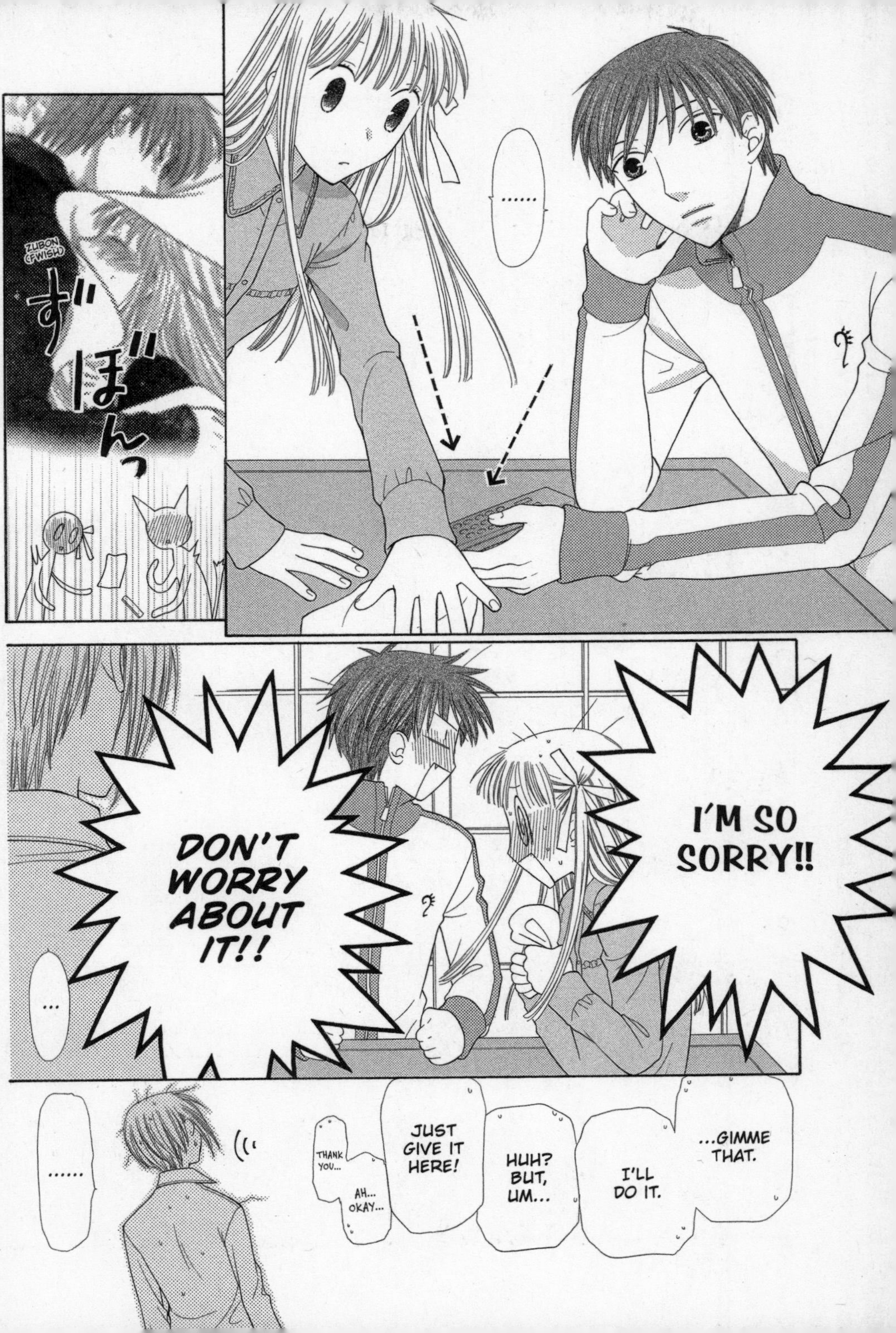

......
ZUBON (FWISH)
ずぼんっ
I'M SO SORRY!!
DON'T WORRY ABOUT IT!!
...
...GIMME THAT.
I'LL DO IT.
HUH? BUT, UM...
JUST GIVE IT HERE!
AH... OKAY...
THANK YOU...
......

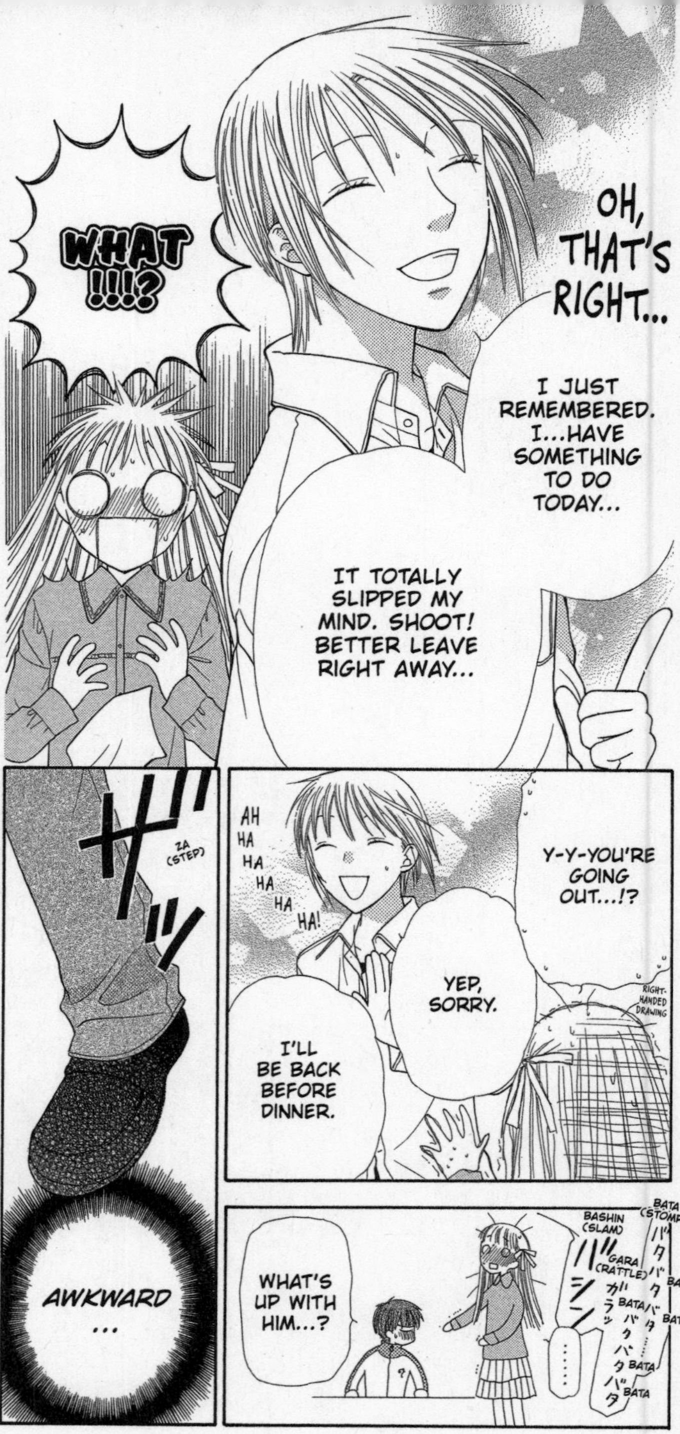
OH, THAT'S RIGHT...
I JUST REMEMBERED. I...HAVE SOMETHING TO DO TODAY...
IT TOTALLY SLIPPED MY MIND. SHOOT! BETTER LEAVE RIGHT AWAY...
WHAT!!!?
Y-Y-YOU'RE GOING OUT...!?
RIGHT-HANDED DRAWING
YEP, SORRY.
AH HA HA HA HA HA!
I'LL BE BACK BEFORE DINNER.
BATA (STOMP) BATA BATA BATA BATA BATA
BASHIN (SLAM)
GARA (RATTLE)
......
WHAT'S UP WITH HIM...?
ZA (STEP)
AWKWARD ...

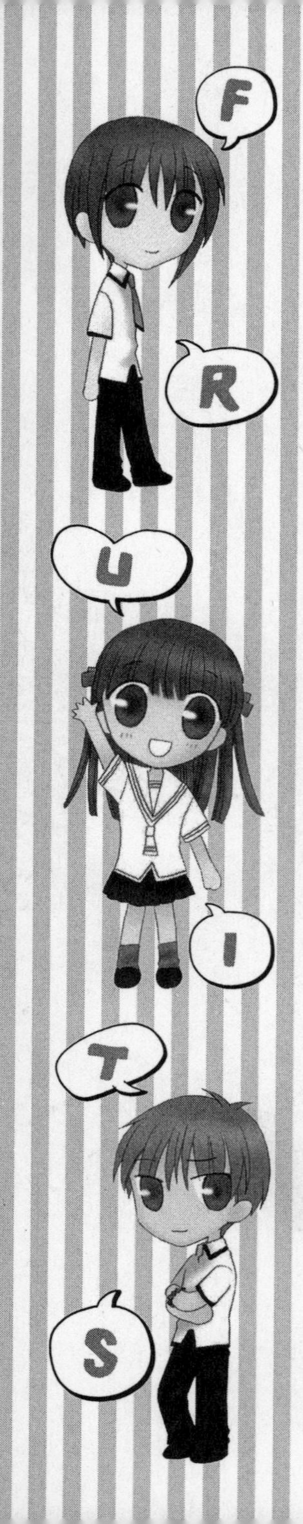
F
R
U
I
T
S

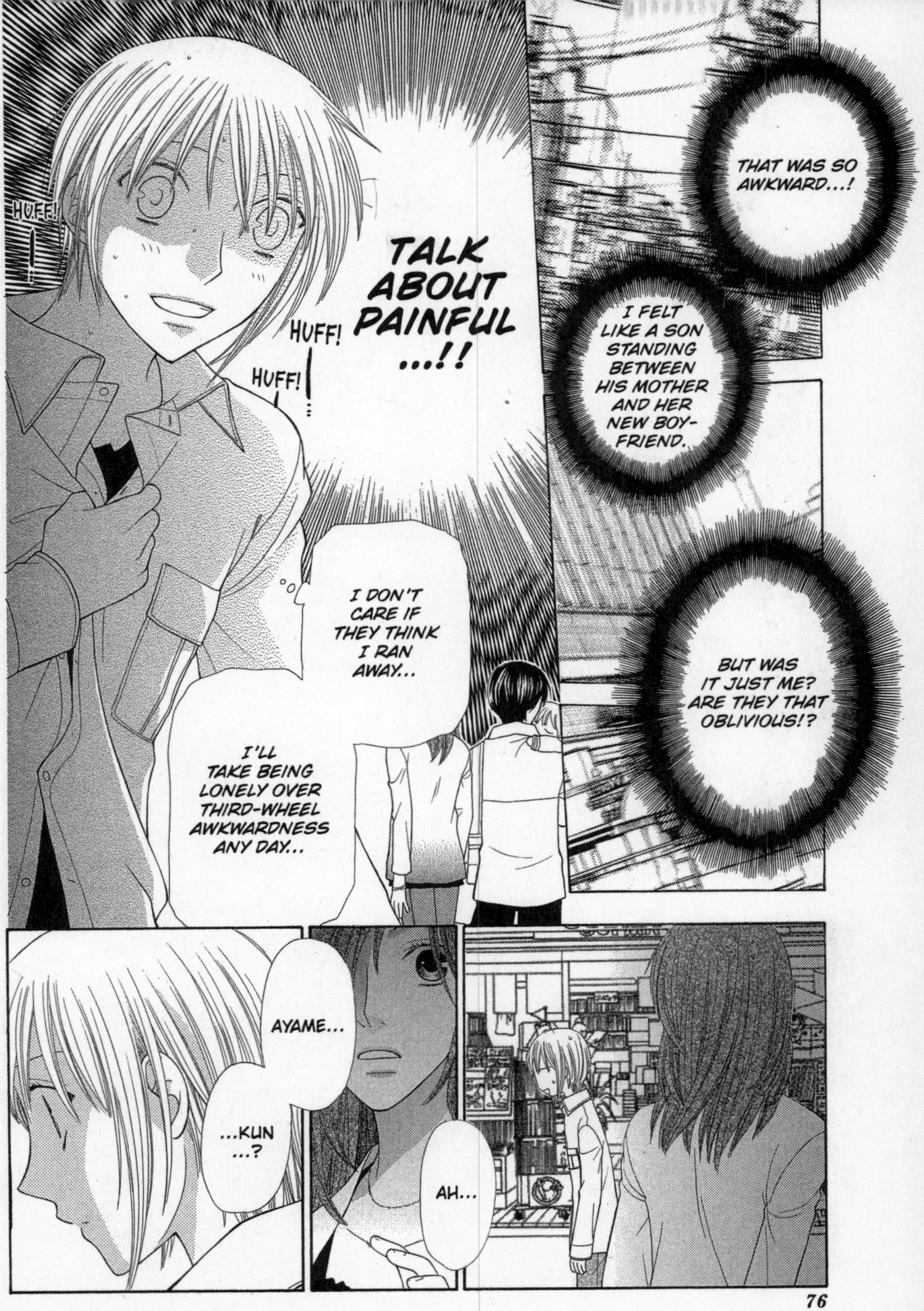
THAT WAS SO AWKWARD...!
I FELT LIKE A SON STANDING BETWEEN HIS MOTHER AND HER NEW BOY-FRIEND.
BUT WAS IT JUST ME? ARE THEY THAT OBLIVIOUS!?
HUFF!
HUFF!
HUFF!
TALK ABOUT PAINFUL ...!!
I DON'T CARE IF THEY THINK I RAN AWAY...
I'LL TAKE BEING LONELY OVER THIRD-WHEEL AWKWARDNESS ANY DAY...
AYAME...
...KUN ...?
AH...

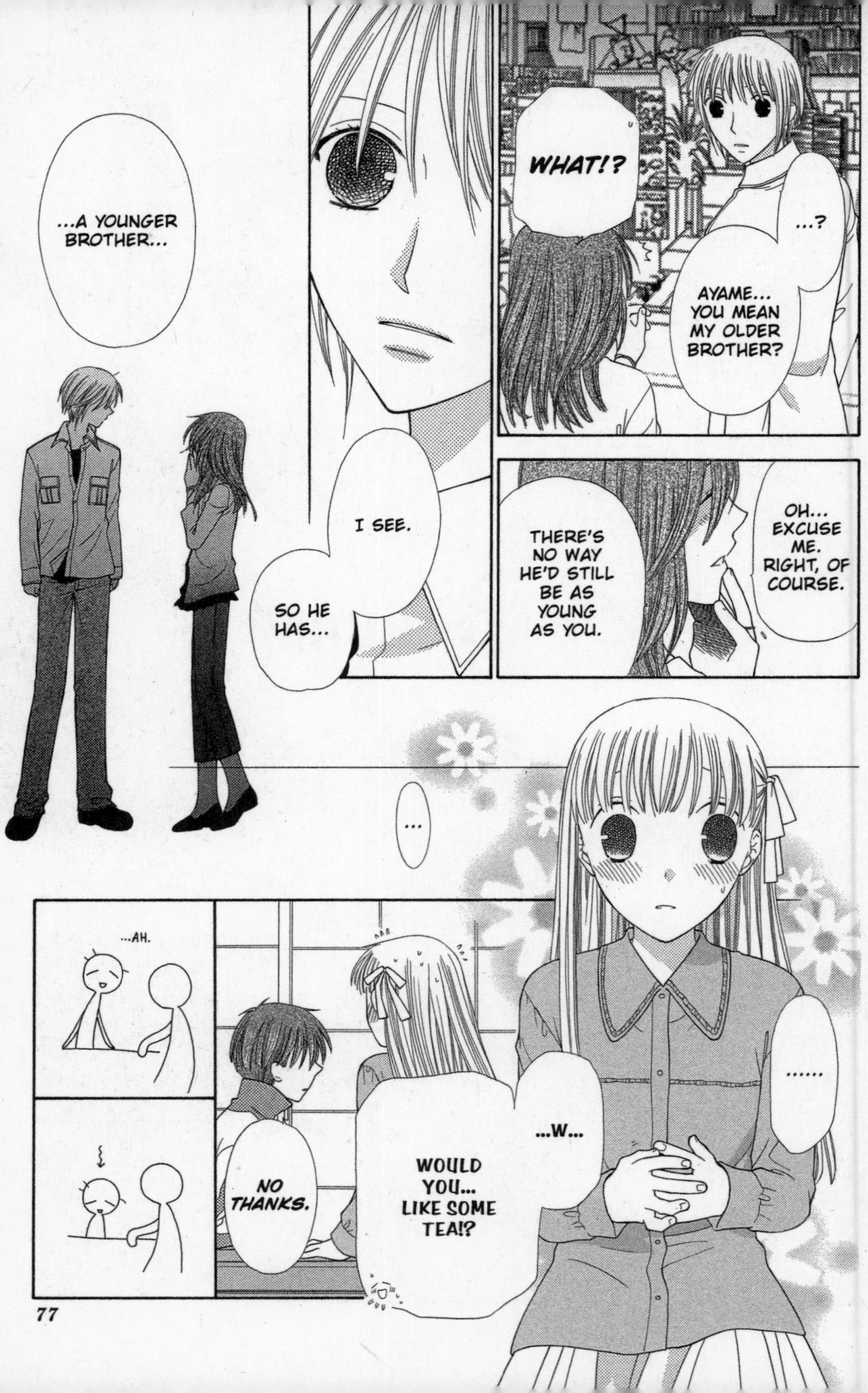
...?
AYAME... YOU MEAN MY OLDER BROTHER?
WHAT!?
OH... EXCUSE ME. RIGHT, OF COURSE.
THERE'S NO WAY HE'D STILL BE AS YOUNG AS YOU.
I SEE.
SO HE HAS...
...A YOUNGER BROTHER...
...
......
...W...
WOULD YOU... LIKE SOME TEA!?
NO THANKS.
...AH.

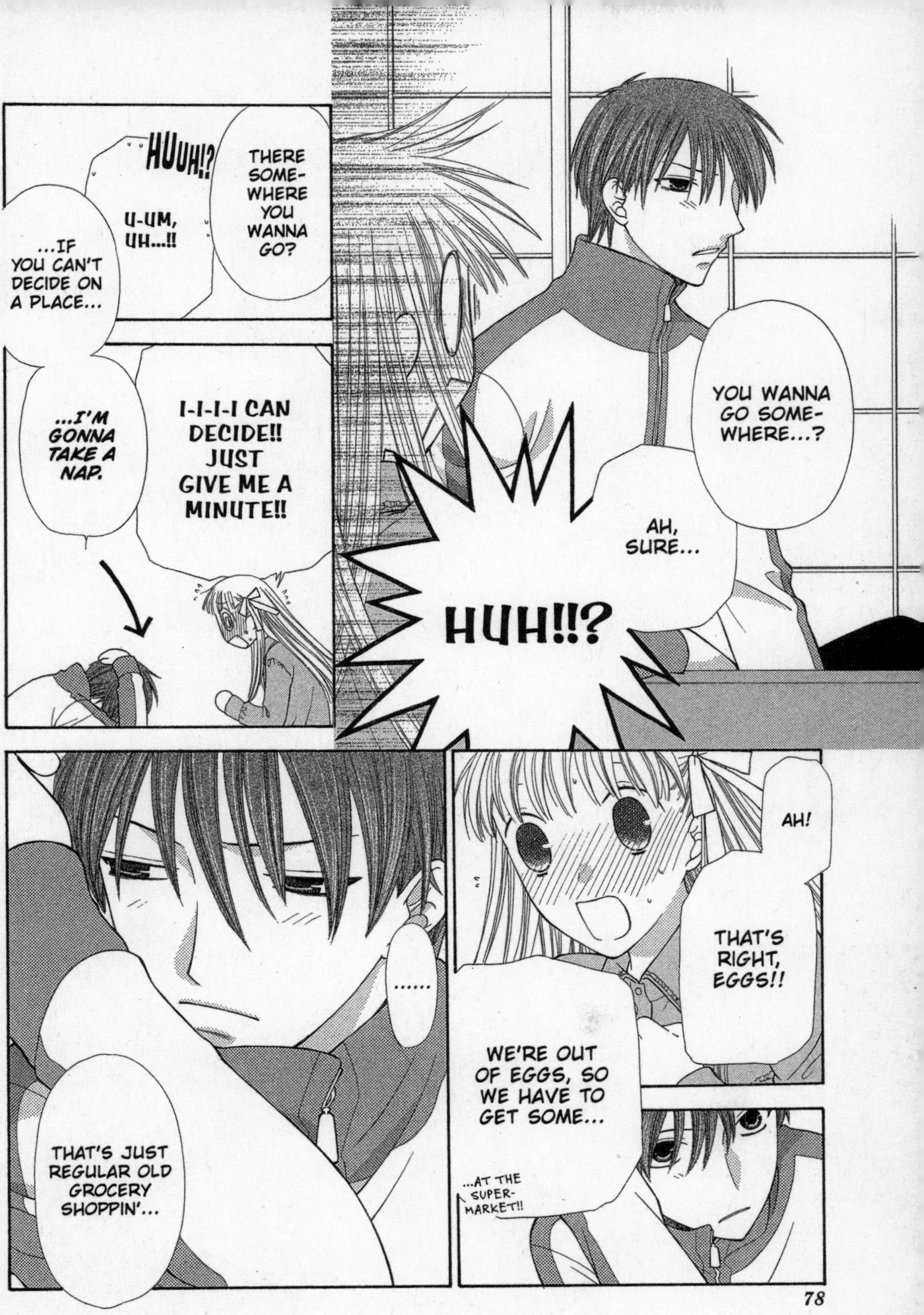
YOU WANNA GO SOME-WHERE...?
AH, SURE...
HUH!!?
THERE SOME-WHERE YOU WANNA GO?
HUUH!?
U-UM, UH...!!
...IF YOU CAN'T DECIDE ON A PLACE...
...I'M GONNA TAKE A NAP.
I-I-I-I CAN DECIDE!! JUST GIVE ME A MINUTE!!
AH!
THAT'S RIGHT, EGGS!!
WE'RE OUT OF EGGS, SO WE HAVE TO GET SOME...
...AT THE SUPER-MARKET!!
......
THAT'S JUST REGULAR OLD GROCERY SHOPPIN'...

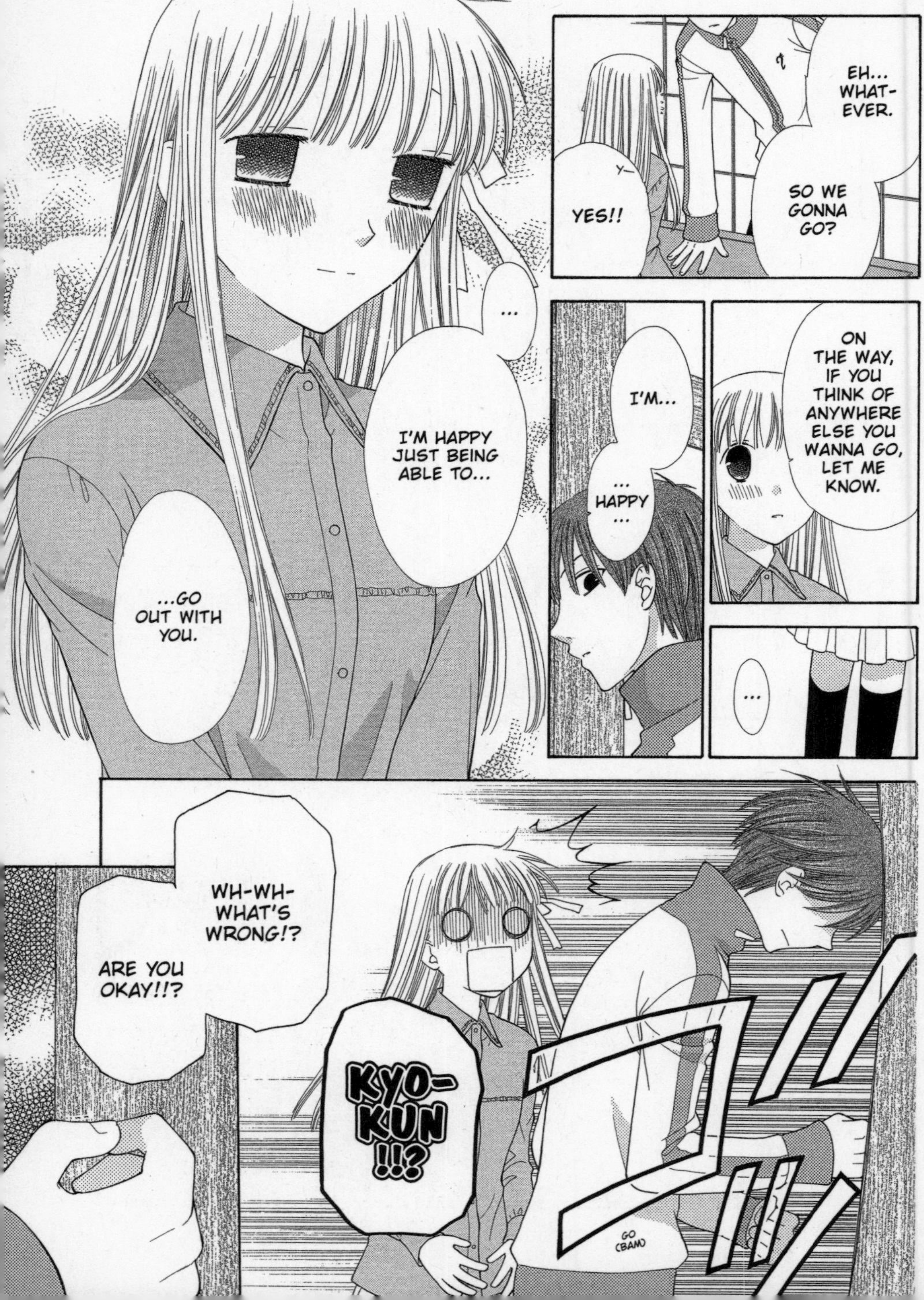
EH... WHAT-EVER.
SO WE GONNA GO?
Y— YES!!
ON THE WAY, IF YOU THINK OF ANYWHERE ELSE YOU WANNA GO, LET ME KNOW.
...
I'M...
...HAPPY...
...
I'M HAPPY JUST BEING ABLE TO...
...GO OUT WITH YOU.
GO (BAM)
KYO-KUN!!?
WH-WH-WHAT'S WRONG!?
ARE YOU OKAY!!?

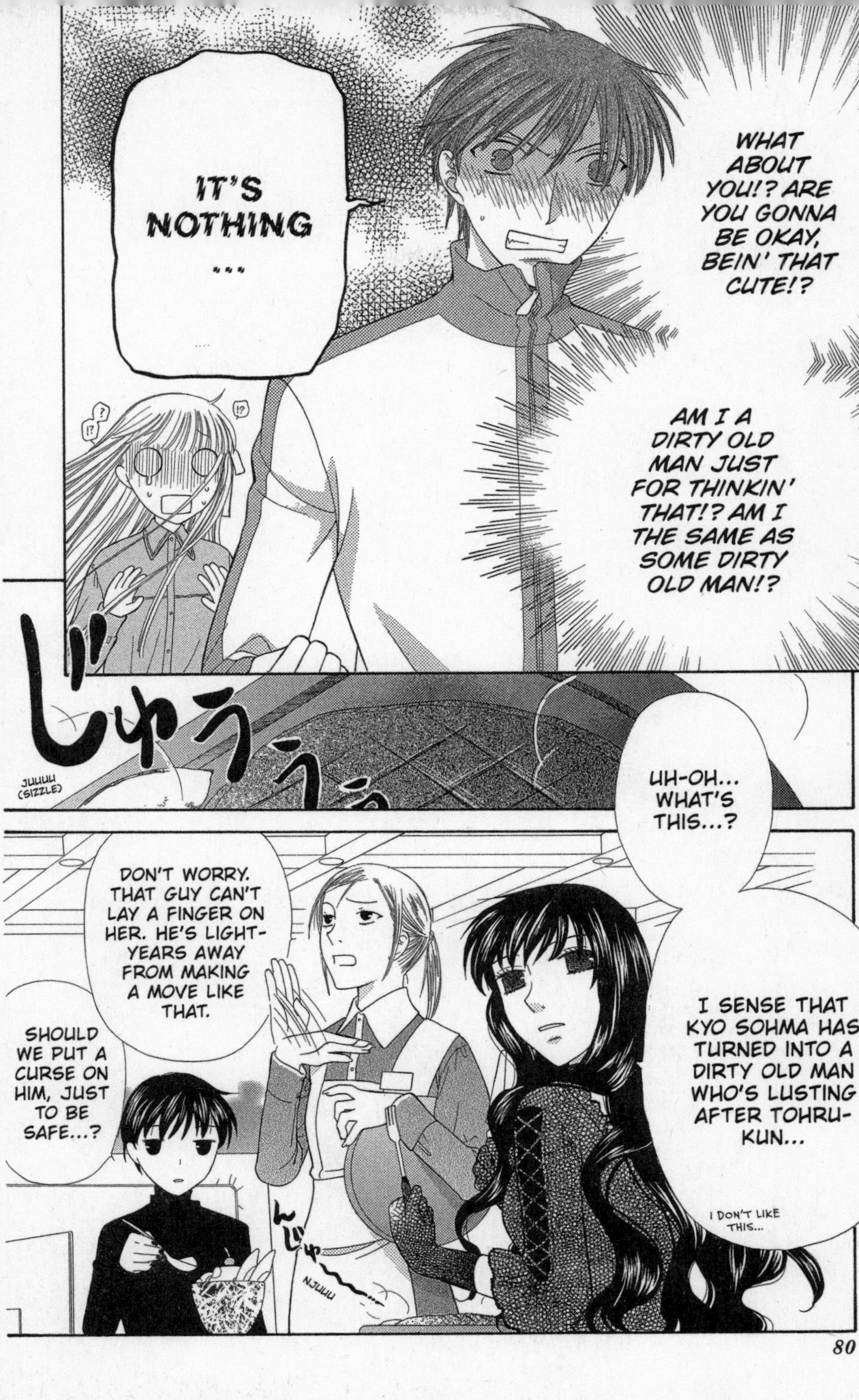
WHAT ABOUT YOU!? ARE YOU GONNA BE OKAY, BEIN' THAT CUTE!?
AM I A DIRTY OLD MAN JUST FOR THINKIN' THAT!? AM I THE SAME AS SOME DIRTY OLD MAN!?
IT'S NOTHING ...
!?
!?
!?
JUUUU (SIZZLE)
UH-OH... WHAT'S THIS...?
I SENSE THAT KYO SOHMA HAS TURNED INTO A DIRTY OLD MAN WHO'S LUSTING AFTER TOHRU-KUN...
I DON'T LIKE THIS...
DON'T WORRY. THAT GUY CAN'T LAY A FINGER ON HER. HE'S LIGHT-YEARS AWAY FROM MAKING A MOVE LIKE THAT.
SHOULD WE PUT A CURSE ON HIM, JUST TO BE SAFE...?
NJUUU

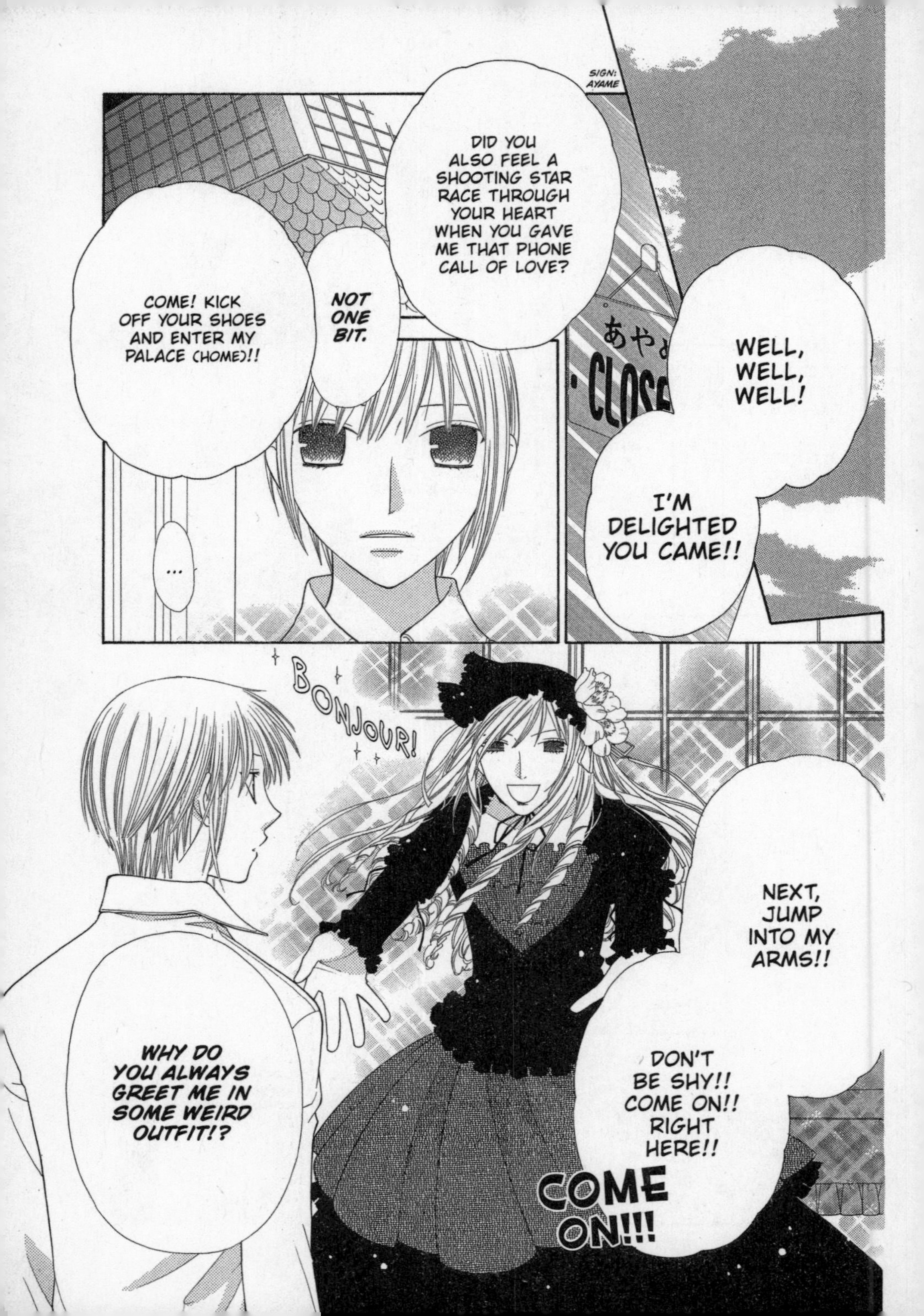
SIGN: AYAME
WELL, WELL, WELL!
I'M DELIGHTED YOU CAME!!
DID YOU ALSO FEEL A SHOOTING STAR RACE THROUGH YOUR HEART WHEN YOU GAVE ME THAT PHONE CALL OF LOVE?
NOT ONE BIT.
COME! KICK OFF YOUR SHOES AND ENTER MY PALACE (HOME)!!
...
BONJOUR!
NEXT, JUMP INTO MY ARMS!!
DON'T BE SHY!! COME ON!! RIGHT HERE!!
COME ON!!!
WHY DO YOU ALWAYS GREET ME IN SOME WEIRD OUTFIT!?

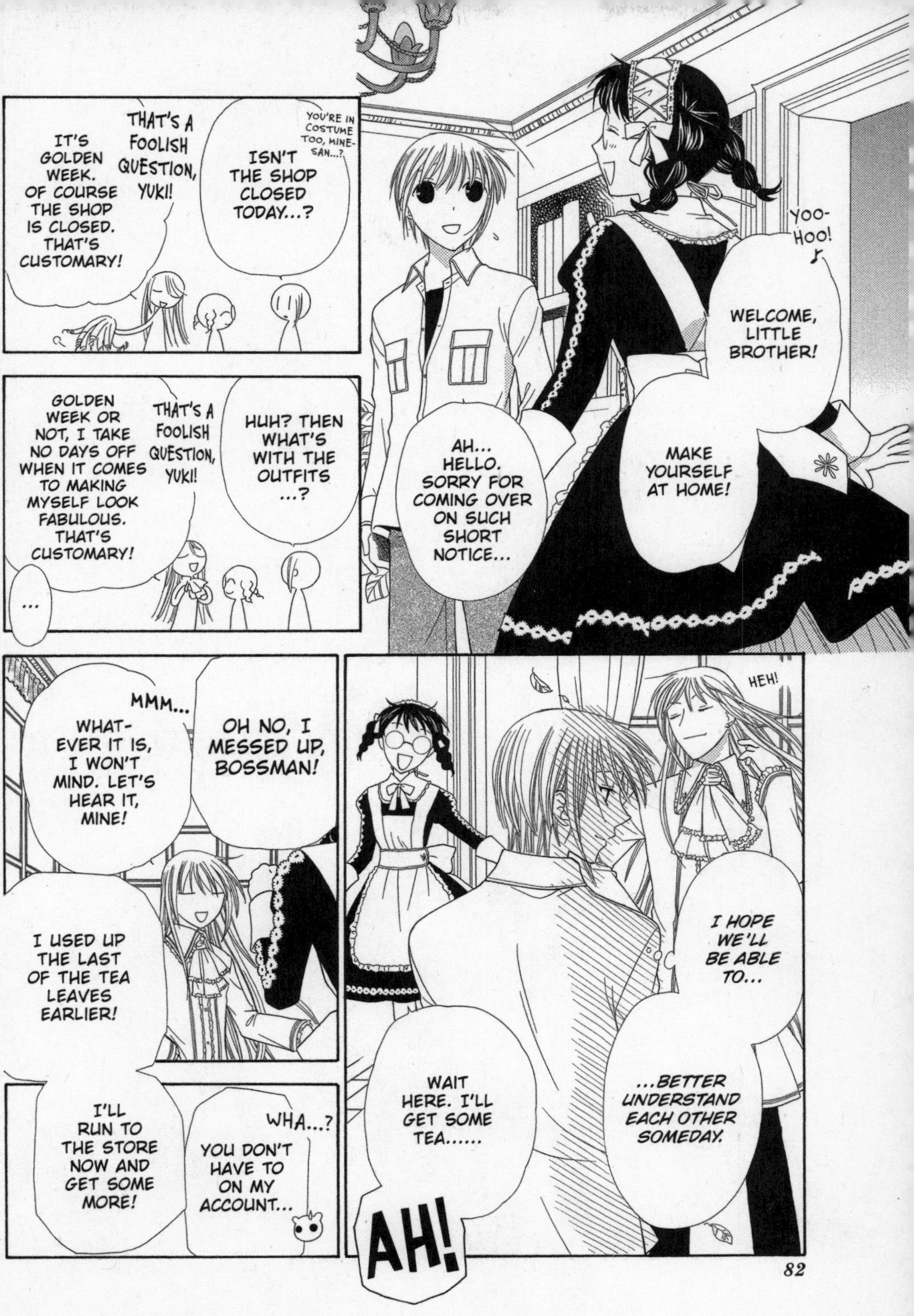
YOO-HOO! ♪
WELCOME, LITTLE BROTHER!
MAKE YOURSELF AT HOME!
AH... HELLO. SORRY FOR COMING OVER ON SUCH SHORT NOTICE...
YOU'RE IN COSTUME TOO, MINE-SAN...?
ISN'T THE SHOP CLOSED TODAY...?
THAT'S A FOOLISH QUESTION, YUKI!
IT'S GOLDEN WEEK. OF COURSE THE SHOP IS CLOSED. THAT'S CUSTOMARY!
HUH? THEN WHAT'S WITH THE OUTFITS ...?
THAT'S A FOOLISH QUESTION, YUKI!
GOLDEN WEEK OR NOT, I TAKE NO DAYS OFF WHEN IT COMES TO MAKING MYSELF LOOK FABULOUS. THAT'S CUSTOMARY!
...
HEH!
I HOPE WE'LL BE ABLE TO...
...BETTER UNDERSTAND EACH OTHER SOMEDAY.
WAIT HERE. I'LL GET SOME TEA......
AH!
OH NO, I MESSED UP, BOSSMAN!
MMM... WHAT-EVER IT IS, I WON'T MIND. LET'S HEAR IT, MINE!
I USED UP THE LAST OF THE TEA LEAVES EARLIER!
WHA...?
YOU DON'T HAVE TO ON MY ACCOUNT...
I'LL RUN TO THE STORE NOW AND GET SOME MORE!

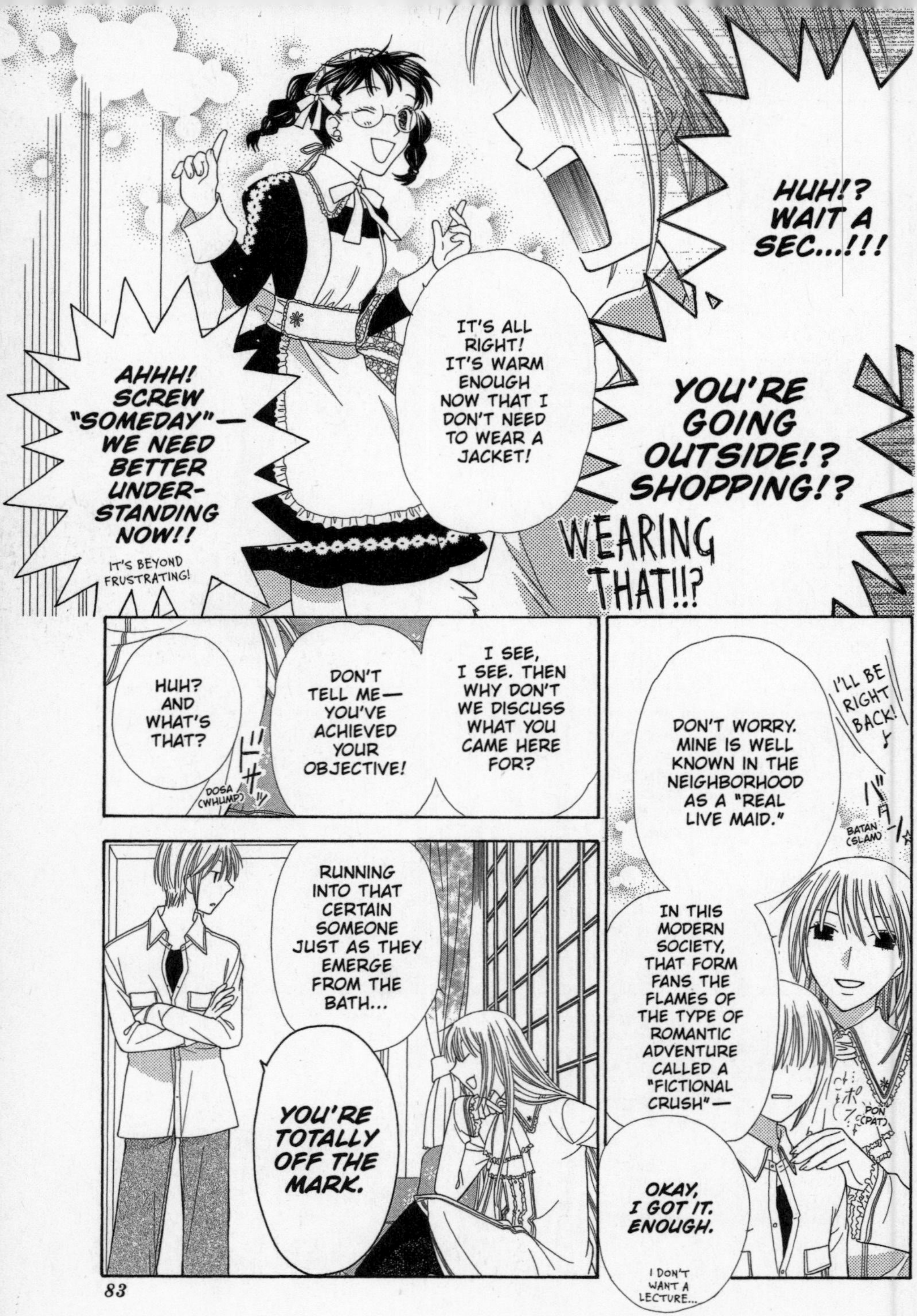
HUH!? WAIT A SEC...!!!
YOU'RE GOING OUTSIDE!? SHOPPING!?
WEARING THAT!!?
IT'S ALL RIGHT! IT'S WARM ENOUGH NOW THAT I DON'T NEED TO WEAR A JACKET!
AHHH! SCREW "SOMEDAY"— WE NEED BETTER UNDER-STANDING NOW!!
IT'S BEYOND FRUSTRATING!
I'LL BE RIGHT BACK! ♪
DON'T WORRY. MINE IS WELL KNOWN IN THE NEIGHBORHOOD AS A "REAL LIVE MAID."
BATAN (SLAM)
IN THIS MODERN SOCIETY, THAT FORM FANS THE FLAMES OF THE TYPE OF ROMANTIC ADVENTURE CALLED A "FICTIONAL CRUSH"—
PON (PAT)
OKAY, I GOT IT. ENOUGH.
I DON'T WANT A LECTURE...
I SEE, I SEE. THEN WHY DON'T WE DISCUSS WHAT YOU CAME HERE FOR?
DON'T TELL ME— YOU'VE ACHIEVED YOUR OBJECTIVE!
DOSA (WHUMP)
HUH? AND WHAT'S THAT?
RUNNING INTO THAT CERTAIN SOMEONE JUST AS THEY EMERGE FROM THE BATH...
YOU'RE TOTALLY OFF THE MARK.

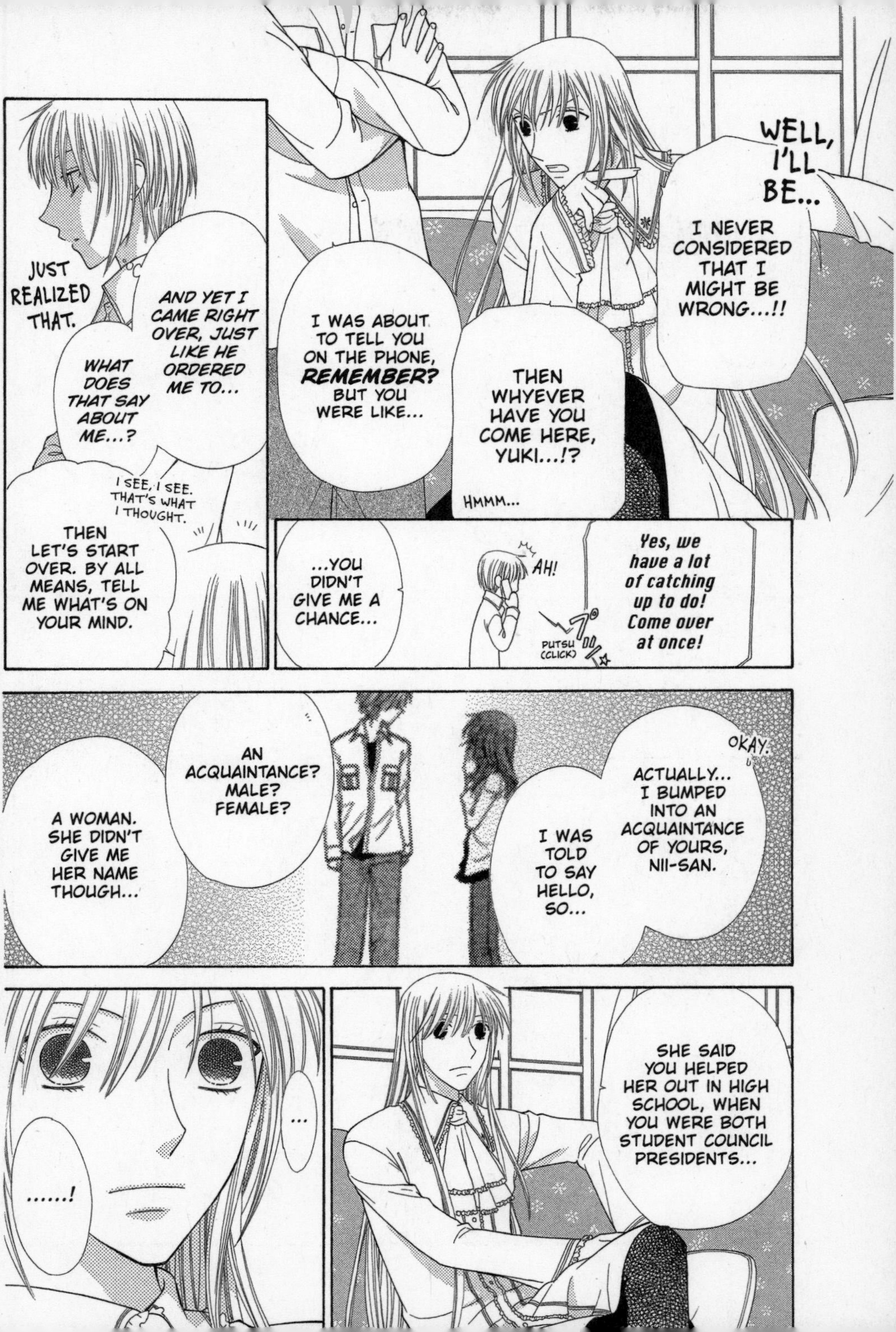
WELL, I'LL BE...
I NEVER CONSIDERED THAT I MIGHT BE WRONG...!!
THEN WHYEVER HAVE YOU COME HERE, YUKI...!?
HMMM...
I WAS ABOUT TO TELL YOU ON THE PHONE, **REMEMBER?** BUT YOU WERE LIKE...
Yes, we have a lot of catching up to do! Come over at once!
PUTSU (CLICK)
AH!
...YOU DIDN'T GIVE ME A CHANCE...
JUST REALIZED THAT.
AND YET I CAME RIGHT OVER, JUST LIKE HE ORDERED ME TO...
WHAT DOES THAT SAY ABOUT ME...?
I SEE, I SEE. THAT'S WHAT I THOUGHT.
THEN LET'S START OVER. BY ALL MEANS, TELL ME WHAT'S ON YOUR MIND.
OKAY.
ACTUALLY... I BUMPED INTO AN ACQUAINTANCE OF YOURS, NII-SAN.
I WAS TOLD TO SAY HELLO, SO...
AN ACQUAINTANCE? MALE? FEMALE?
A WOMAN. SHE DIDN'T GIVE ME HER NAME THOUGH...
SHE SAID YOU HELPED HER OUT IN HIGH SCHOOL, WHEN YOU WERE BOTH STUDENT COUNCIL PRESIDENTS...
...
......!

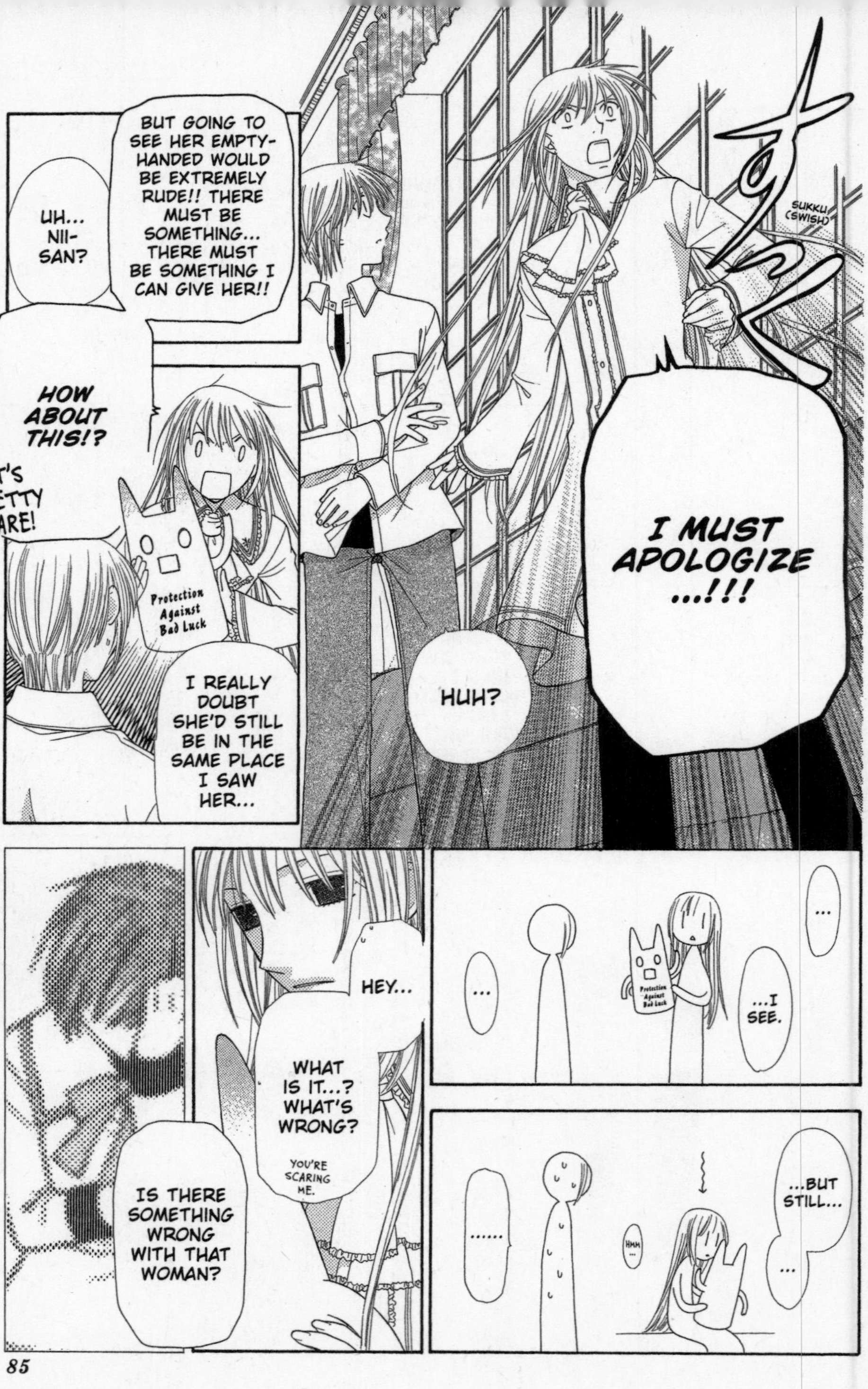
SUKKU (SWISH)
I MUST APOLOGIZE ...!!!
HUH?
BUT GOING TO SEE HER EMPTY-HANDED WOULD BE EXTREMELY RUDE!! THERE MUST BE SOMETHING... THERE MUST BE SOMETHING I CAN GIVE HER!!
UH... NII-SAN?
HOW ABOUT THIS!?
IT'S PRETTY RARE!
Protection Against Bad Luck
I REALLY DOUBT SHE'D STILL BE IN THE SAME PLACE I SAW HER...
...
...I SEE.
...
Protection Against Bad Luck
...BUT STILL...
...
HMM...
......
HEY...
WHAT IS IT...? WHAT'S WRONG?
YOU'RE SCARING ME.
IS THERE SOMETHING WRONG WITH THAT WOMAN?

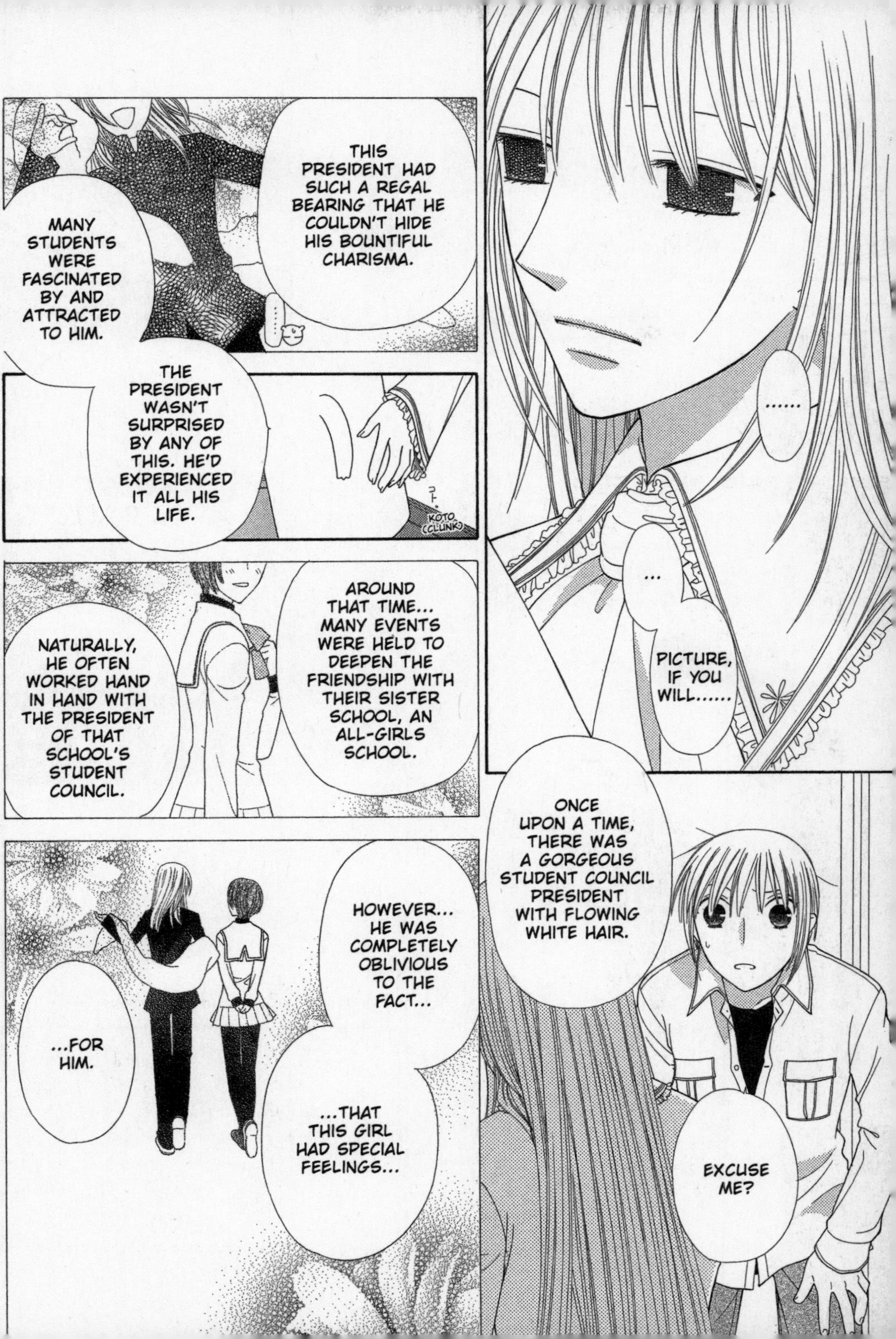
......
...
PICTURE, IF YOU WILL......
ONCE UPON A TIME, THERE WAS A GORGEOUS STUDENT COUNCIL PRESIDENT WITH FLOWING WHITE HAIR.
EXCUSE ME?
THIS PRESIDENT HAD SUCH A REGAL BEARING THAT HE COULDN'T HIDE HIS BOUNTIFUL CHARISMA.
MANY STUDENTS WERE FASCINATED BY AND ATTRACTED TO HIM.
THE PRESIDENT WASN'T SURPRISED BY ANY OF THIS. HE'D EXPERIENCED IT ALL HIS LIFE.
KOTO (CLUNK)
AROUND THAT TIME... MANY EVENTS WERE HELD TO DEEPEN THE FRIENDSHIP WITH THEIR SISTER SCHOOL, AN ALL-GIRLS SCHOOL.
NATURALLY, HE OFTEN WORKED HAND IN HAND WITH THE PRESIDENT OF THAT SCHOOL'S STUDENT COUNCIL.
HOWEVER... HE WAS COMPLETELY OBLIVIOUS TO THE FACT...
...THAT THIS GIRL HAD SPECIAL FEELINGS...
...FOR HIM.

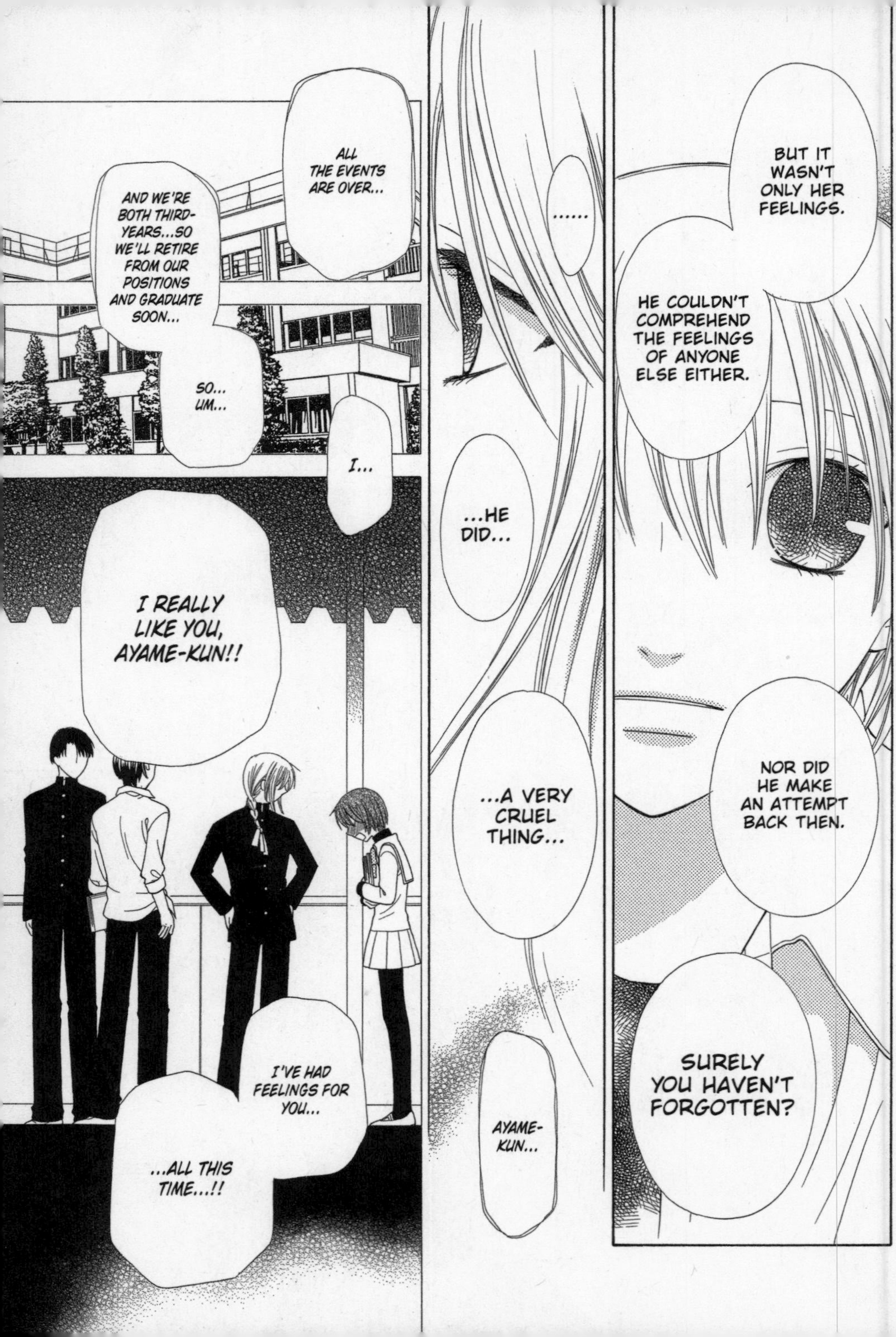
BUT IT WASN'T ONLY HER FEELINGS.
HE COULDN'T COMPREHEND THE FEELINGS OF ANYONE ELSE EITHER.
NOR DID HE MAKE AN ATTEMPT BACK THEN.
SURELY YOU HAVEN'T FORGOTTEN?
......
...HE DID...
...A VERY CRUEL THING...
AYAME-KUN...
ALL THE EVENTS ARE OVER...
AND WE'RE BOTH THIRD-YEARS...SO WE'LL RETIRE FROM OUR POSITIONS AND GRADUATE SOON...
SO... UM...
I...
I REALLY LIKE YOU, AYAME-KUN!!
I'VE HAD FEELINGS FOR YOU...
...ALL THIS TIME...!!

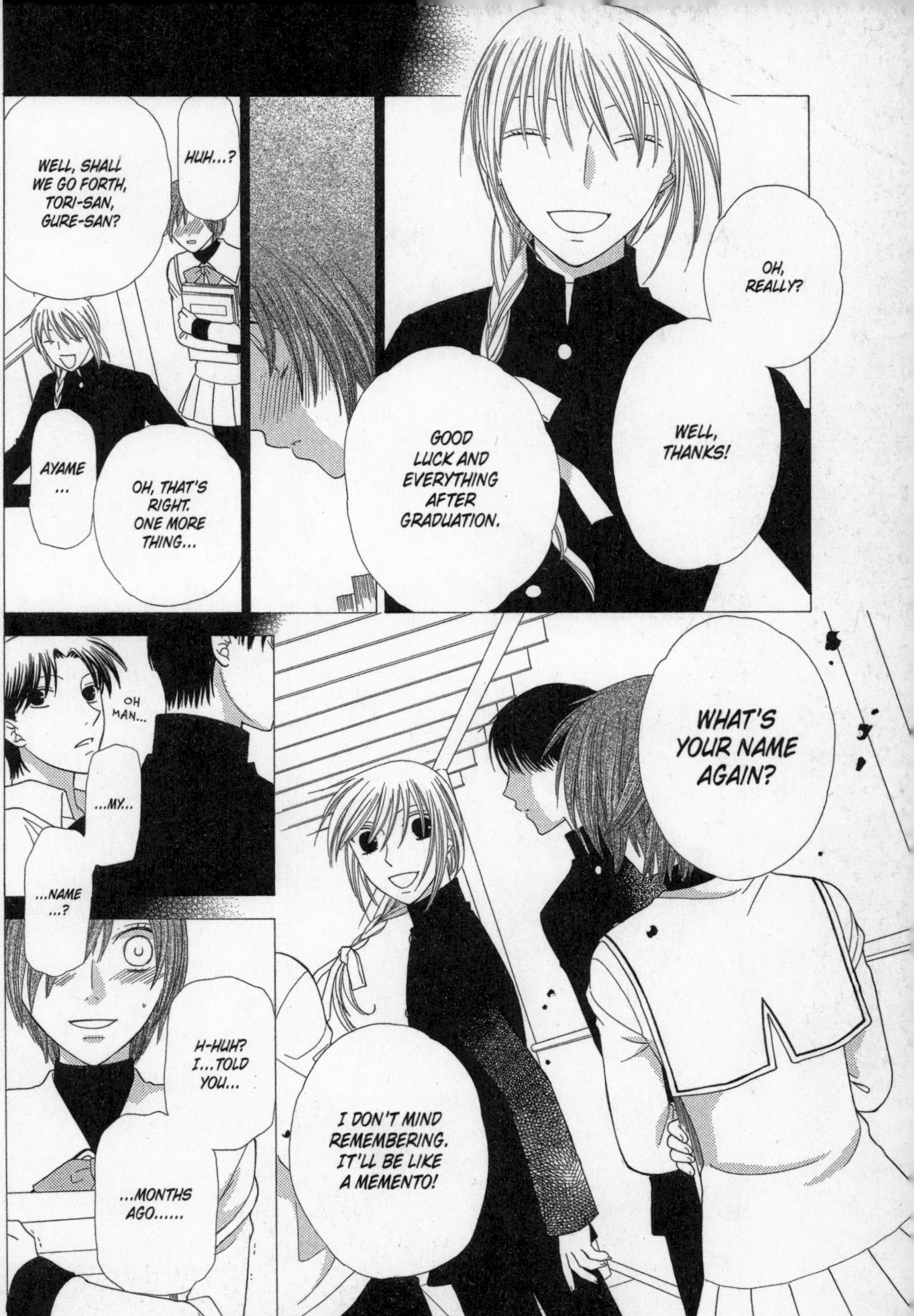
OH, REALLY?
WELL, THANKS!
GOOD LUCK AND EVERYTHING AFTER GRADUATION.
HUH...?
WELL, SHALL WE GO FORTH, TORI-SAN, GURE-SAN?
OH, THAT'S RIGHT. ONE MORE THING...
AYAME ...
WHAT'S YOUR NAME AGAIN?
I DON'T MIND REMEMBERING. IT'LL BE LIKE A MEMENTO!
OH MAN...
...MY...
...NAME ...?
H-HUH? I...TOLD YOU...
...MONTHS AGO......

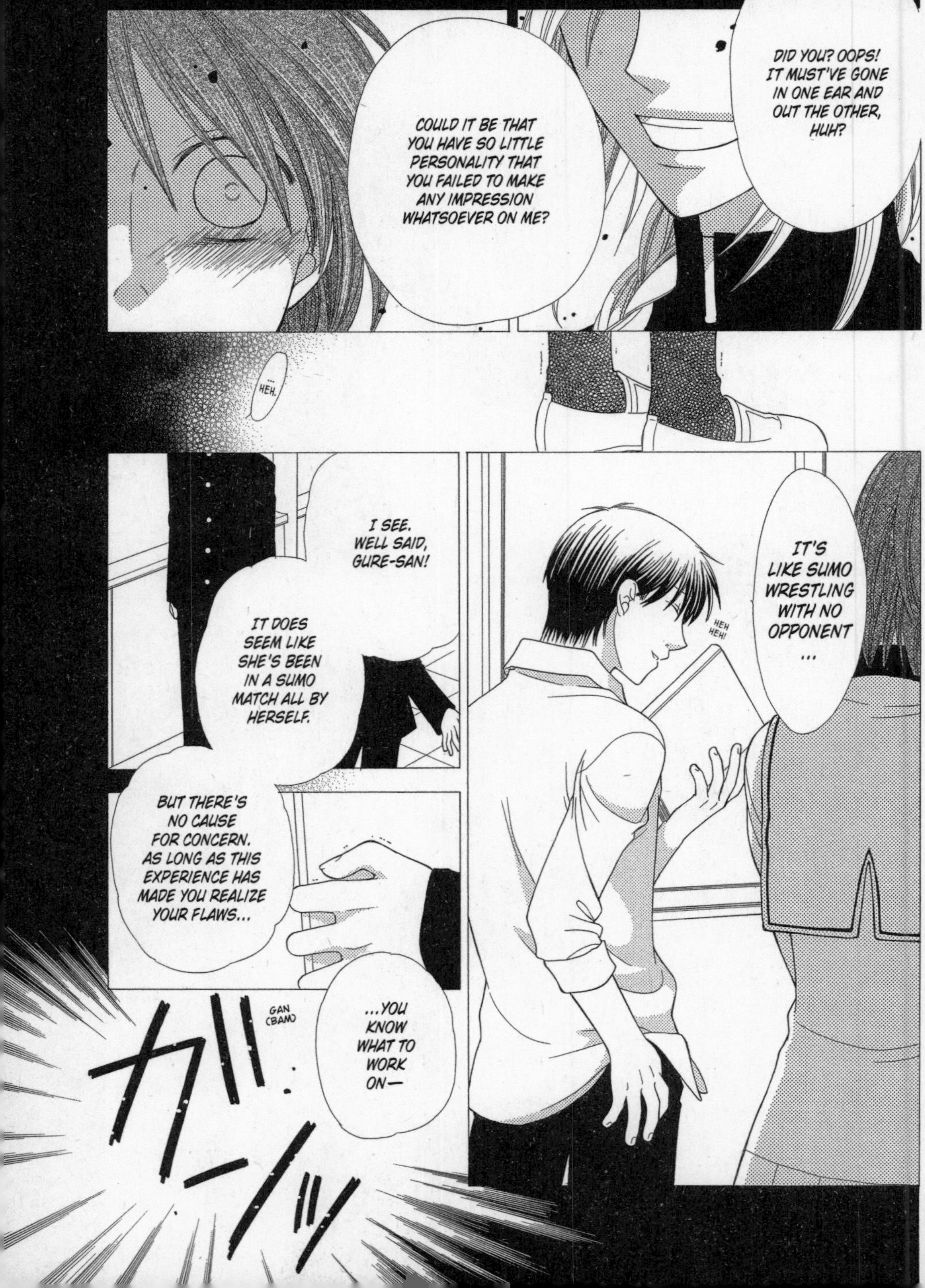
DID YOU? OOPS! IT MUST'VE GONE IN ONE EAR AND OUT THE OTHER, HUH?
COULD IT BE THAT YOU HAVE SO LITTLE PERSONALITY THAT YOU FAILED TO MAKE ANY IMPRESSION WHATSOEVER ON ME?
...HEH.
IT'S LIKE SUMO WRESTLING WITH NO OPPONENT...
HEH HEH!
I SEE. WELL SAID, GURE-SAN!
IT DOES SEEM LIKE SHE'S BEEN IN A SUMO MATCH ALL BY HERSELF.
BUT THERE'S NO CAUSE FOR CONCERN. AS LONG AS THIS EXPERIENCE HAS MADE YOU REALIZE YOUR FLAWS...
...YOU KNOW WHAT TO WORK ON—
GAN (BAM)

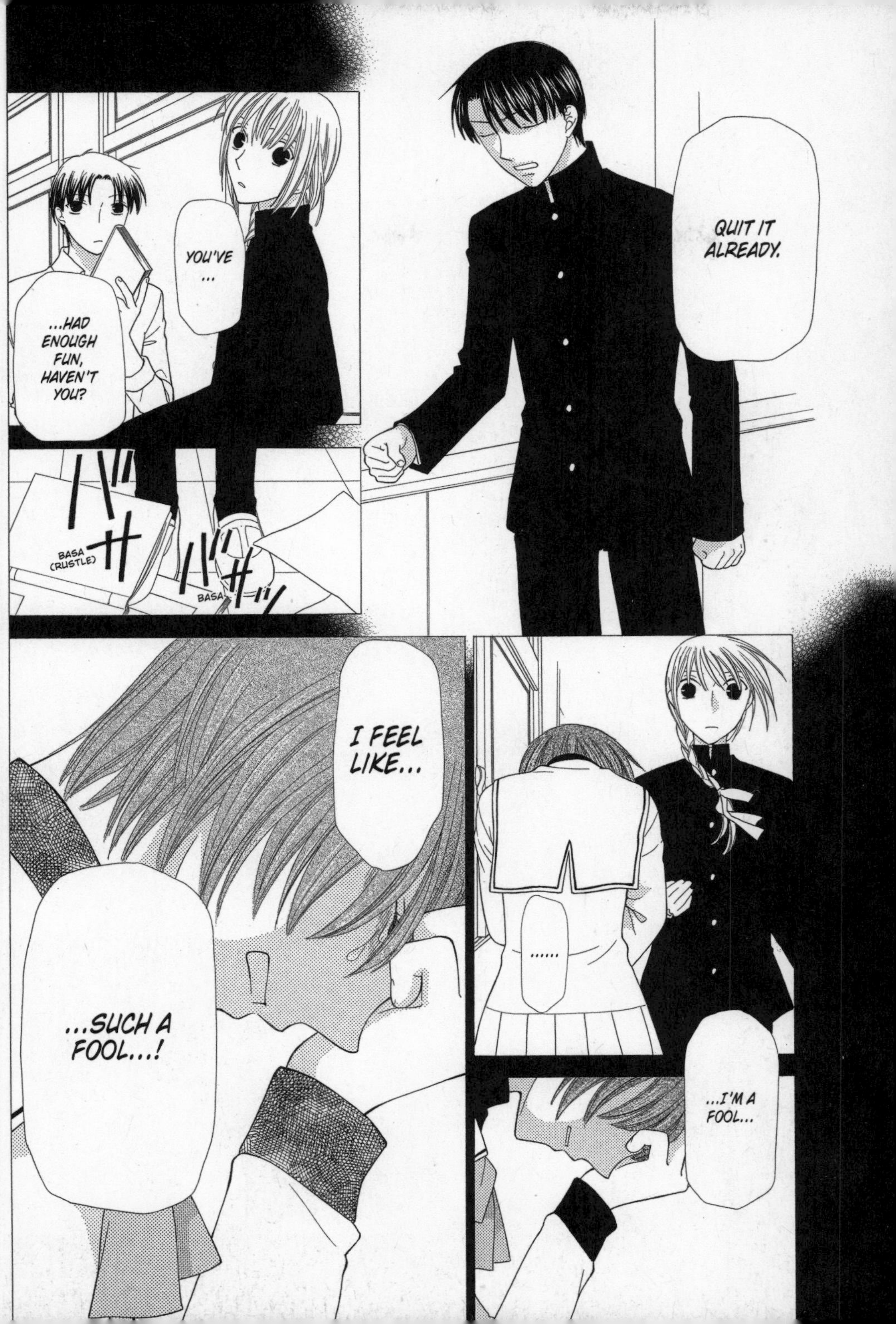
QUIT IT ALREADY.
YOU'VE ...
...HAD ENOUGH FUN, HAVEN'T YOU?
BASA (RUSTLE)
BASA
......
...I'M A FOOL...
I FEEL LIKE...
...SUCH A FOOL...!

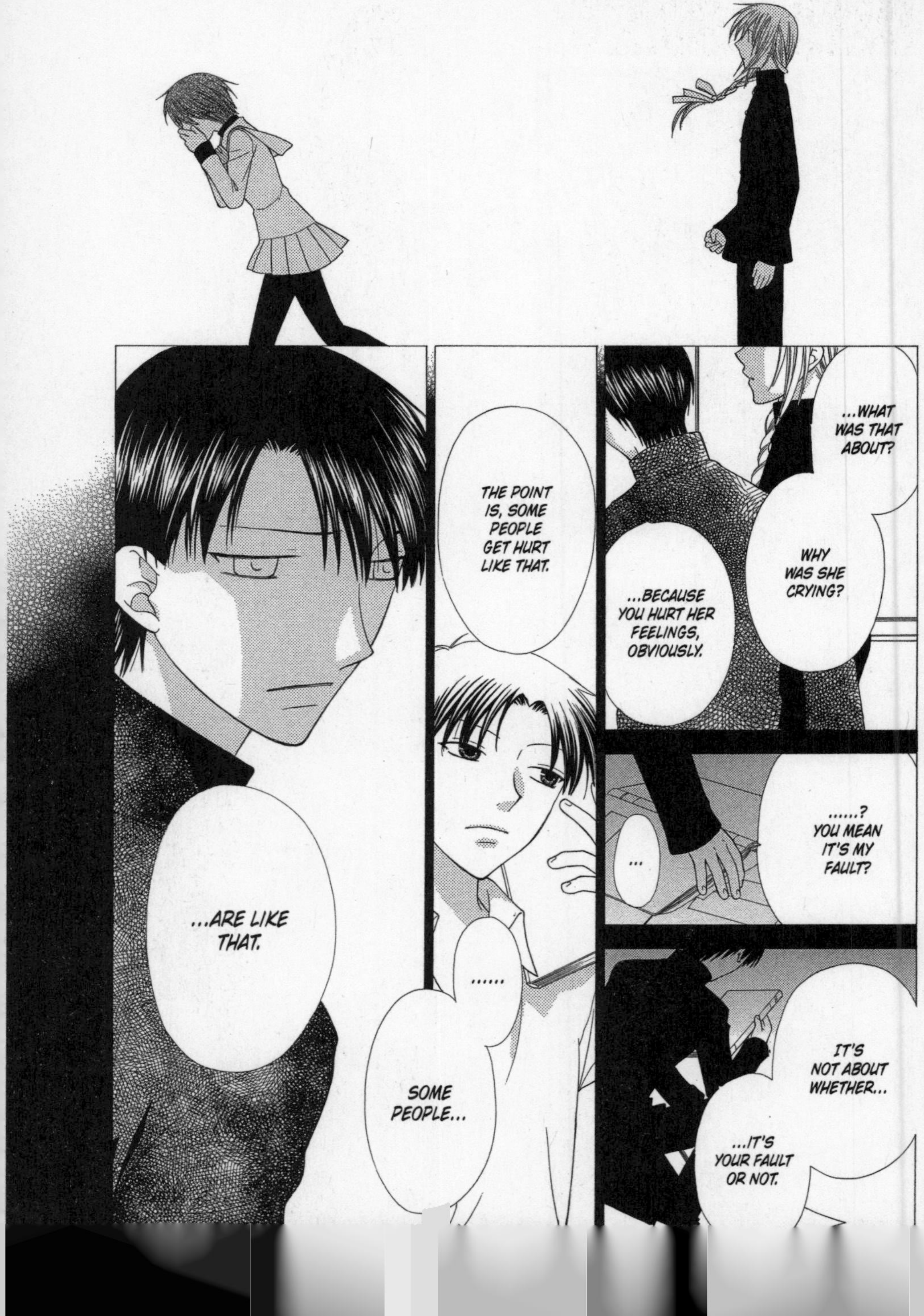
...WHAT WAS THAT ABOUT?
WHY WAS SHE CRYING?
...BECAUSE YOU HURT HER FEELINGS, OBVIOUSLY.
......? YOU MEAN IT'S MY FAULT?
...
IT'S NOT ABOUT WHETHER...
...IT'S YOUR FAULT OR NOT.
THE POINT IS, SOME PEOPLE GET HURT LIKE THAT.
......
SOME PEOPLE...
...ARE LIKE THAT.

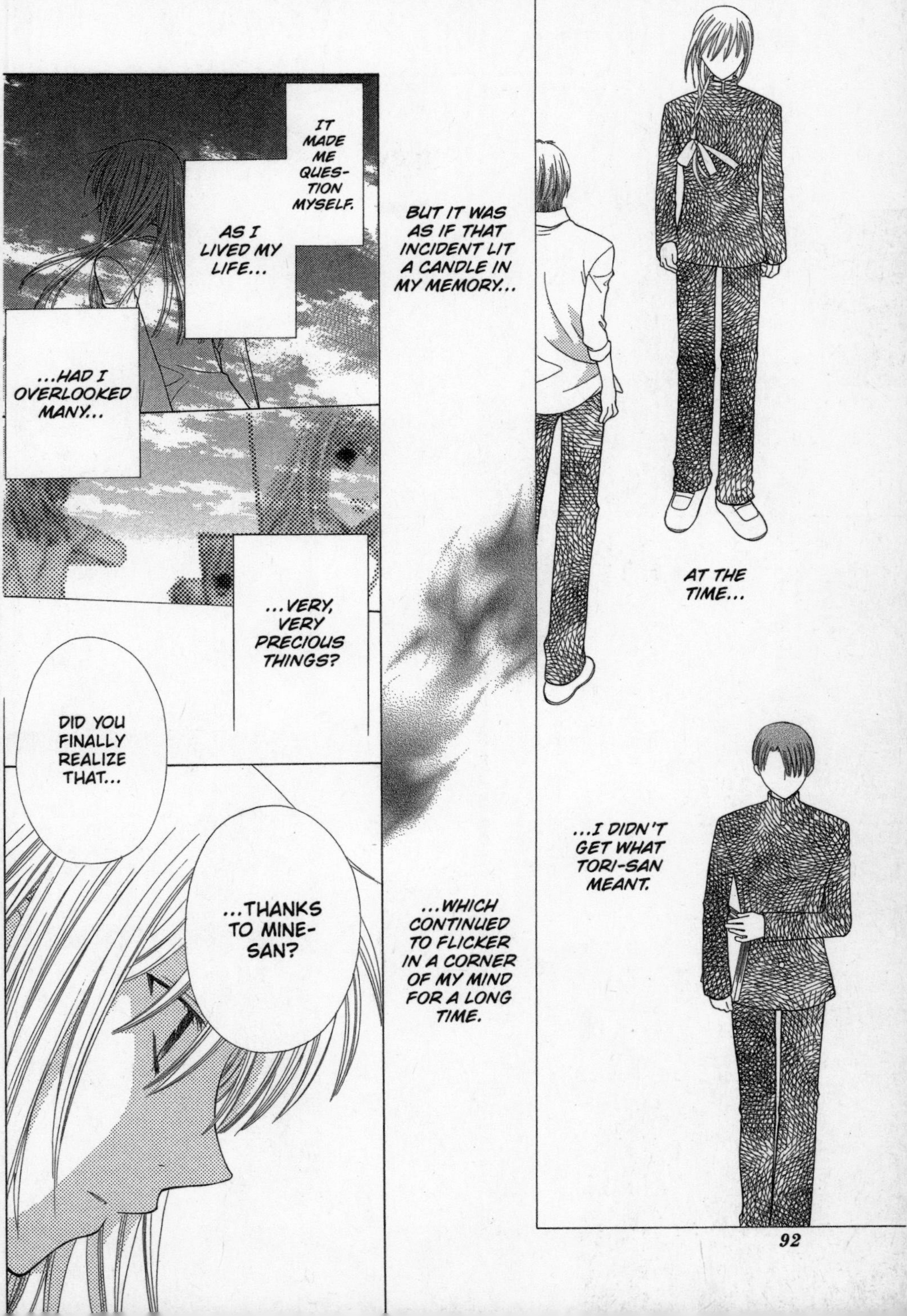
AT THE TIME...
...I DIDN'T GET WHAT TORI-SAN MEANT.
BUT IT WAS AS IF THAT INCIDENT LIT A CANDLE IN MY MEMORY...
...WHICH CONTINUED TO FLICKER IN A CORNER OF MY MIND FOR A LONG TIME.
IT MADE ME QUES-TION MYSELF.
AS I LIVED MY LIFE...
...HAD I OVERLOOKED MANY...
...VERY, VERY PRECIOUS THINGS?
DID YOU FINALLY REALIZE THAT...
...THANKS TO MINE-SAN?

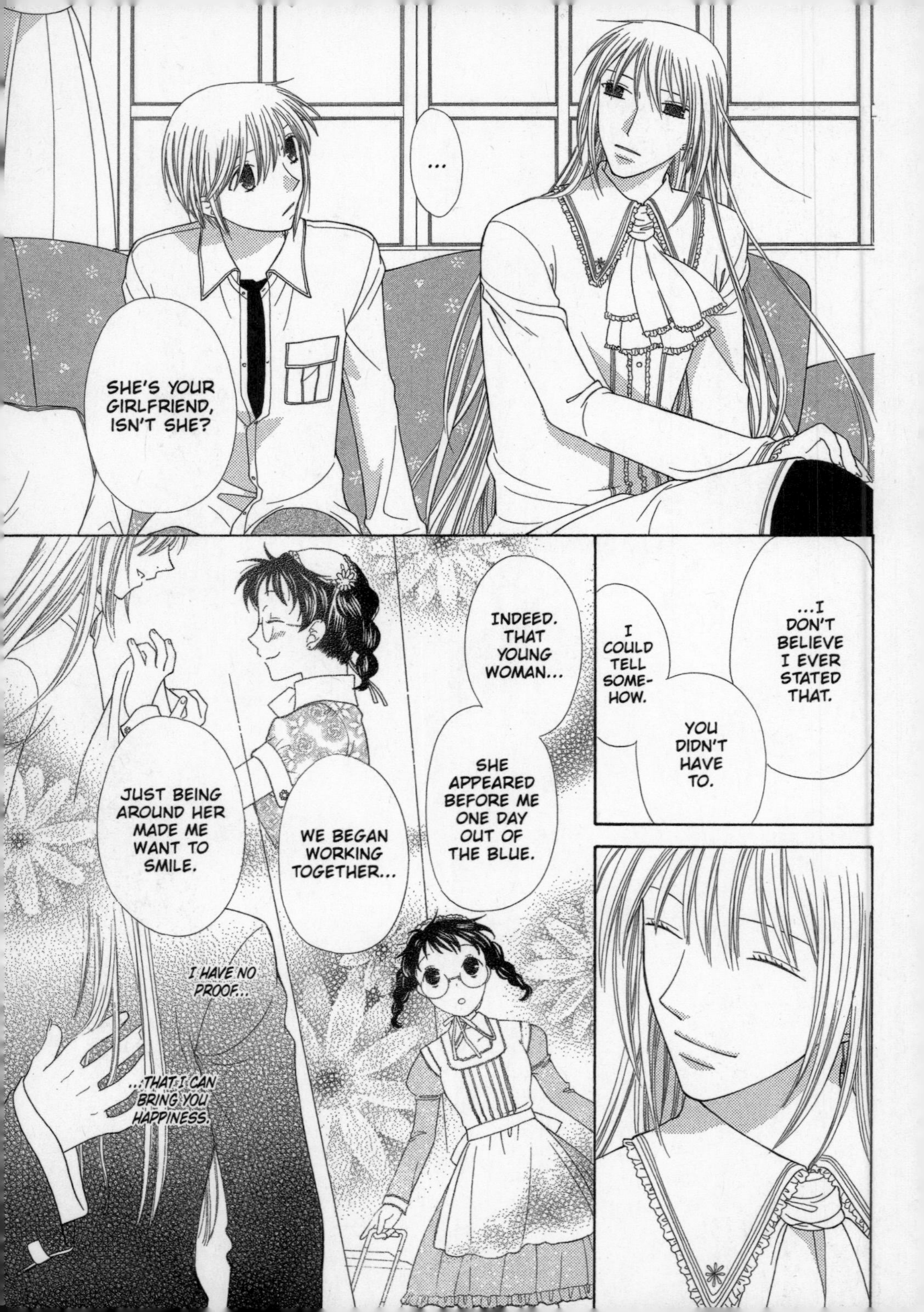
...
SHE'S YOUR GIRLFRIEND, ISN'T SHE?
...I DON'T BELIEVE I EVER STATED THAT.
YOU DIDN'T HAVE TO.
I COULD TELL SOME-HOW.
INDEED. THAT YOUNG WOMAN...
SHE APPEARED BEFORE ME ONE DAY OUT OF THE BLUE.
WE BEGAN WORKING TOGETHER...
JUST BEING AROUND HER MADE ME WANT TO SMILE.
I HAVE NO PROOF...
...THAT I CAN BRING YOU HAPPINESS.

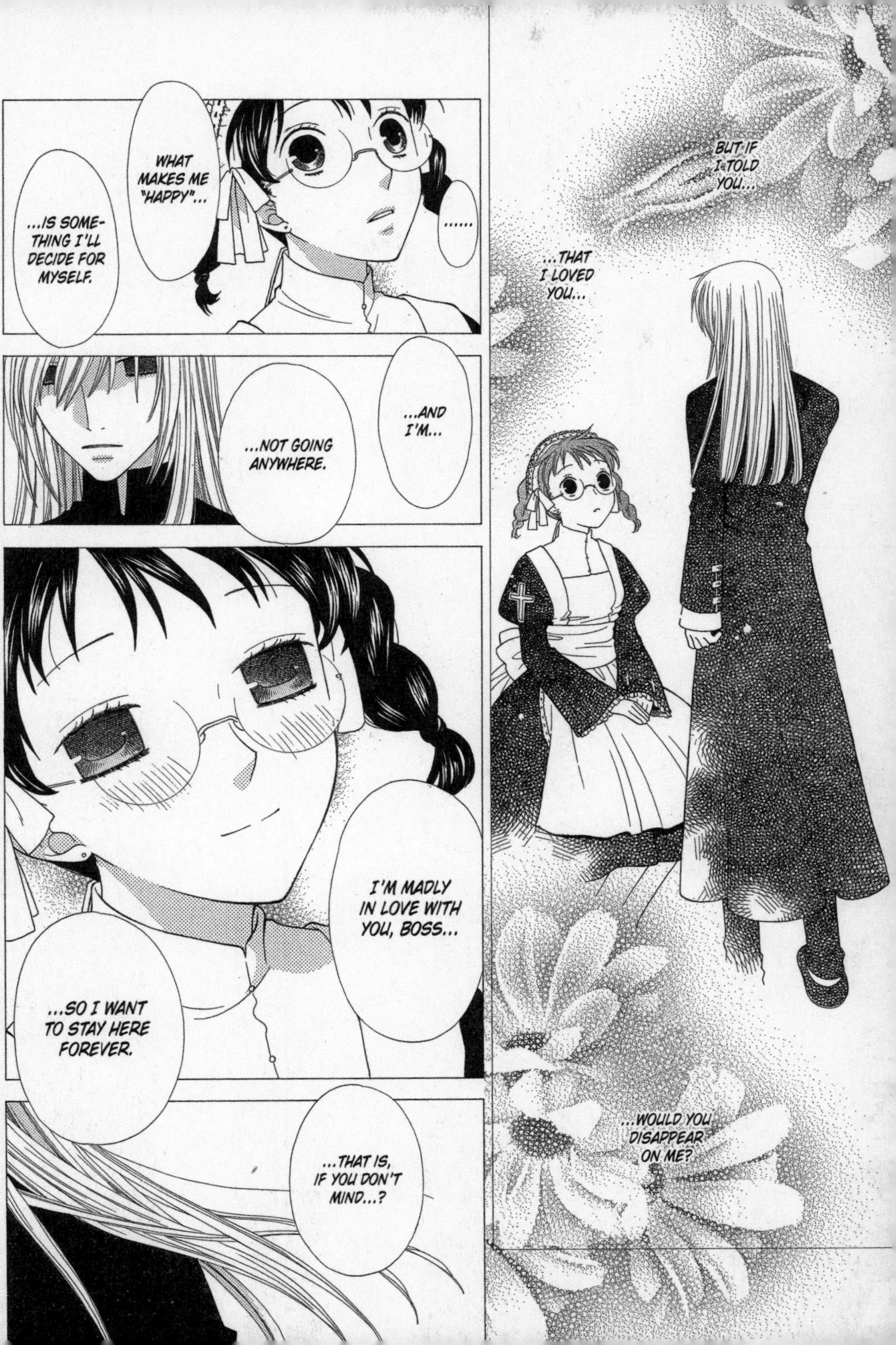
BUT IF I TOLD YOU...
...THAT I LOVED YOU...
...WOULD YOU DISAPPEAR ON ME?
......
WHAT MAKES ME "HAPPY"...
...IS SOMETHING I'LL DECIDE FOR MYSELF.
...AND I'M...
...NOT GOING ANYWHERE.
I'M MADLY IN LOVE WITH YOU, BOSS...
...SO I WANT TO STAY HERE FOREVER.
...THAT IS, IF YOU DON'T MIND...?

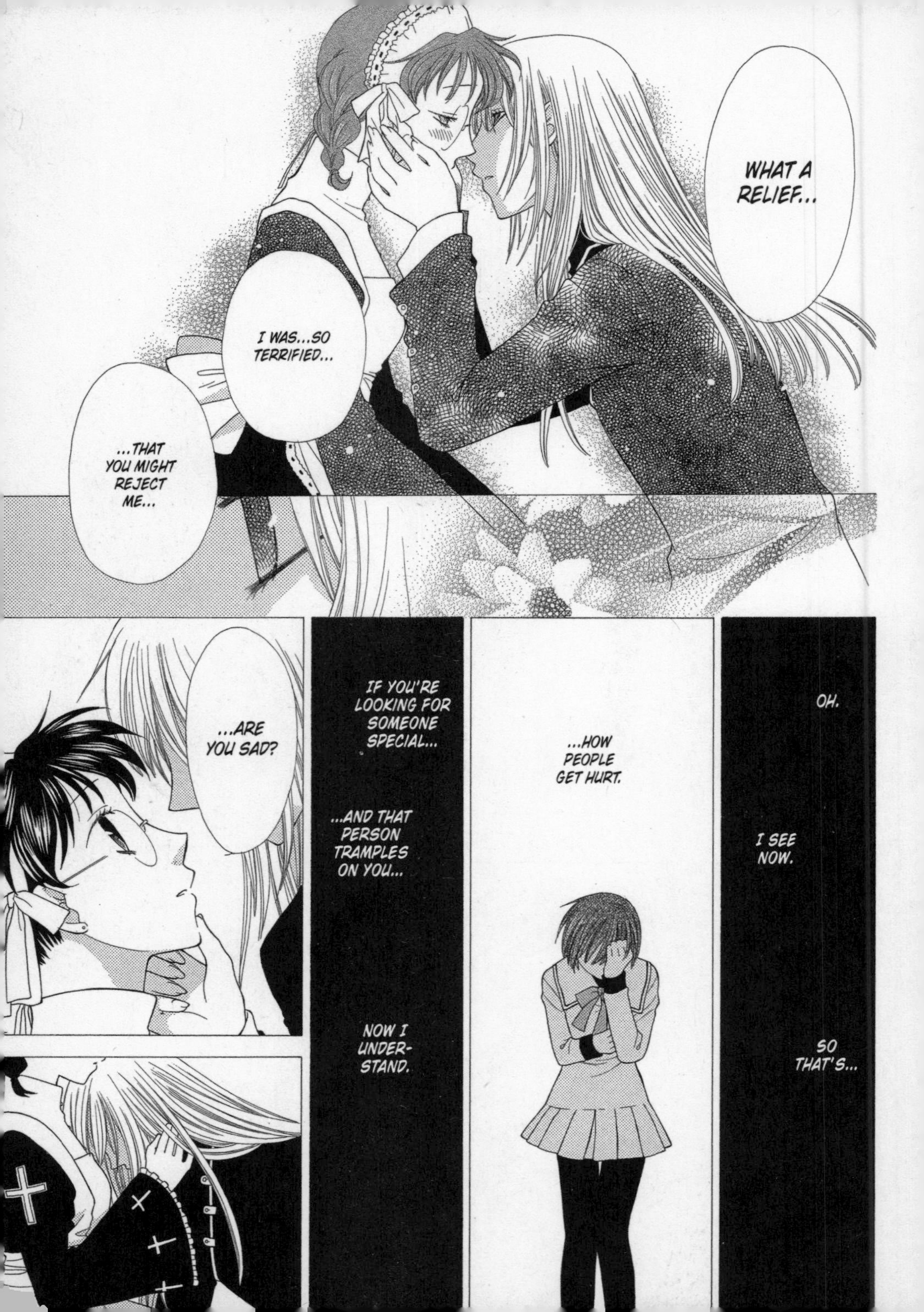
WHAT A RELIEF...
I WAS...SO TERRIFIED...
...THAT YOU MIGHT REJECT ME...
OH.
I SEE NOW.
SO THAT'S...
...HOW PEOPLE GET HURT.
IF YOU'RE LOOKING FOR SOMEONE SPECIAL...
...AND THAT PERSON TRAMPLES ON YOU...
NOW I UNDER-STAND.
...ARE YOU SAD?

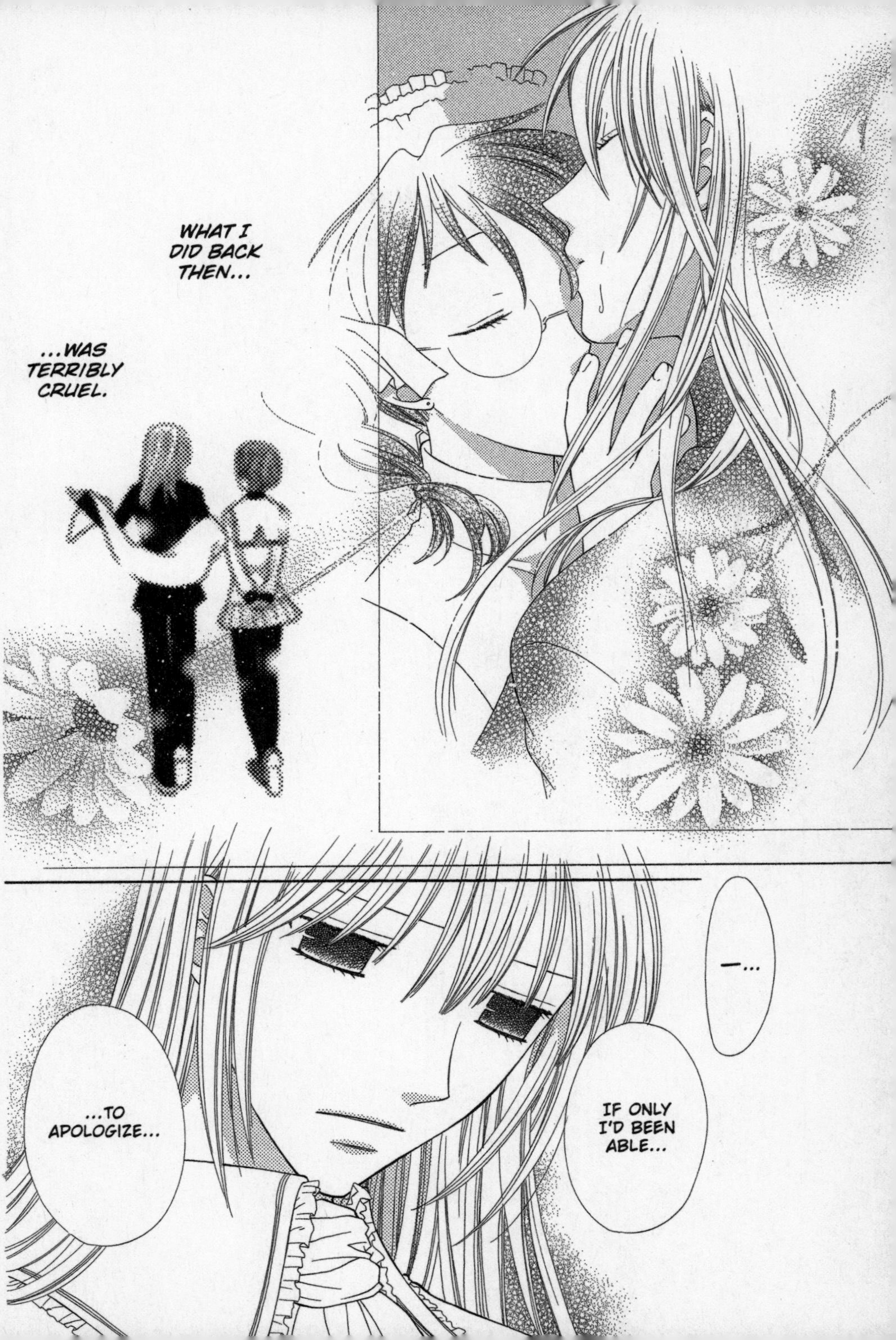
WHAT I DID BACK THEN...
...WAS TERRIBLY CRUEL.
—...
IF ONLY I'D BEEN ABLE...
...TO APOLOGIZE...

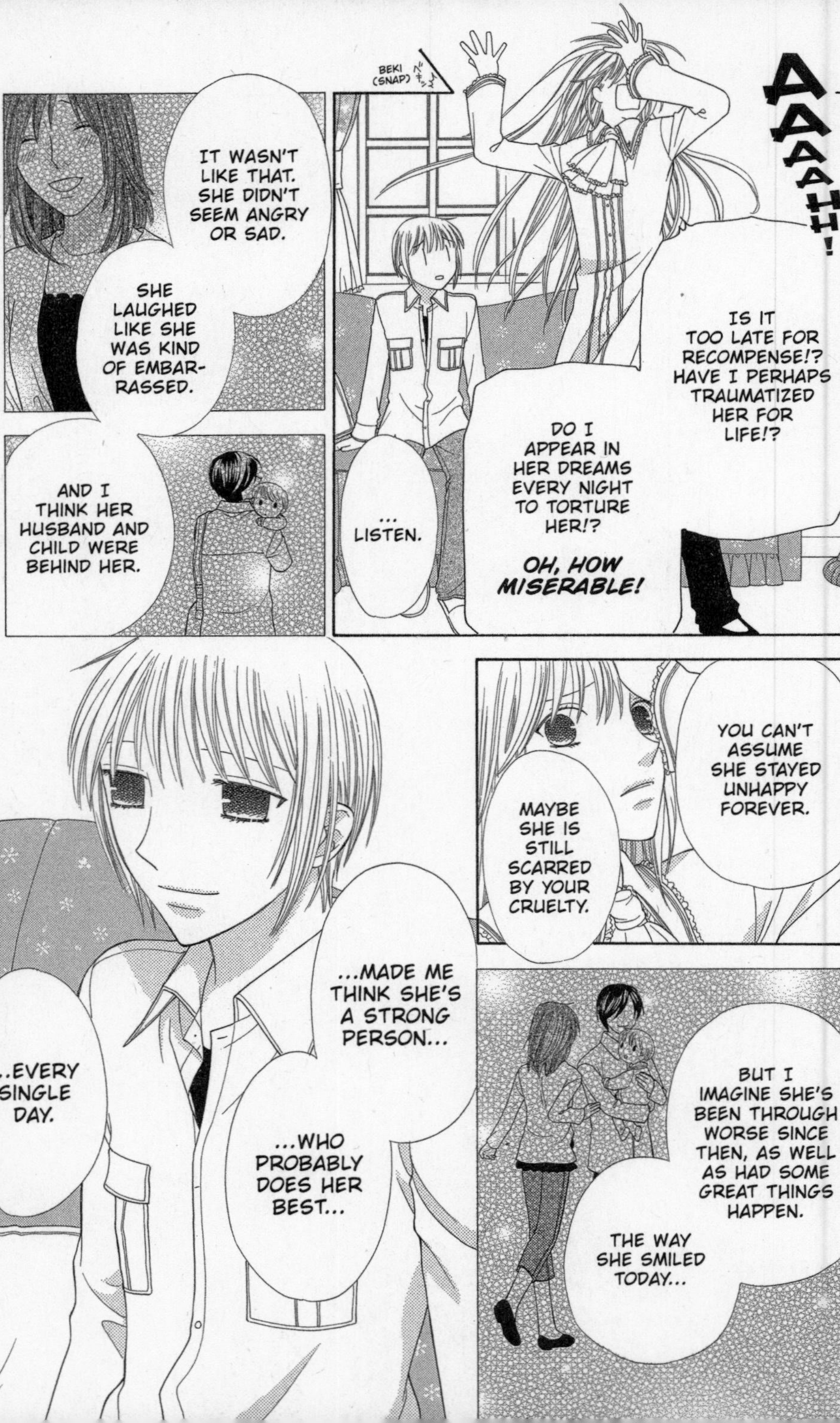
AAAAHH!
BEKI (SNAP)
IS IT TOO LATE FOR RECOMPENSE!? HAVE I PERHAPS TRAUMATIZED HER FOR LIFE!?
DO I APPEAR IN HER DREAMS EVERY NIGHT TO TORTURE HER!?
OH, HOW MISERABLE!
...LISTEN.
IT WASN'T LIKE THAT. SHE DIDN'T SEEM ANGRY OR SAD.
SHE LAUGHED LIKE SHE WAS KIND OF EMBARRASSED.
AND I THINK HER HUSBAND AND CHILD WERE BEHIND HER.
YOU CAN'T ASSUME SHE STAYED UNHAPPY FOREVER.
MAYBE SHE IS STILL SCARRED BY YOUR CRUELTY.
BUT I IMAGINE SHE'S BEEN THROUGH WORSE SINCE THEN, AS WELL AS HAD SOME GREAT THINGS HAPPEN.
THE WAY SHE SMILED TODAY...
...MADE ME THINK SHE'S A STRONG PERSON...
...WHO PROBABLY DOES HER BEST...
...EVERY SINGLE DAY.

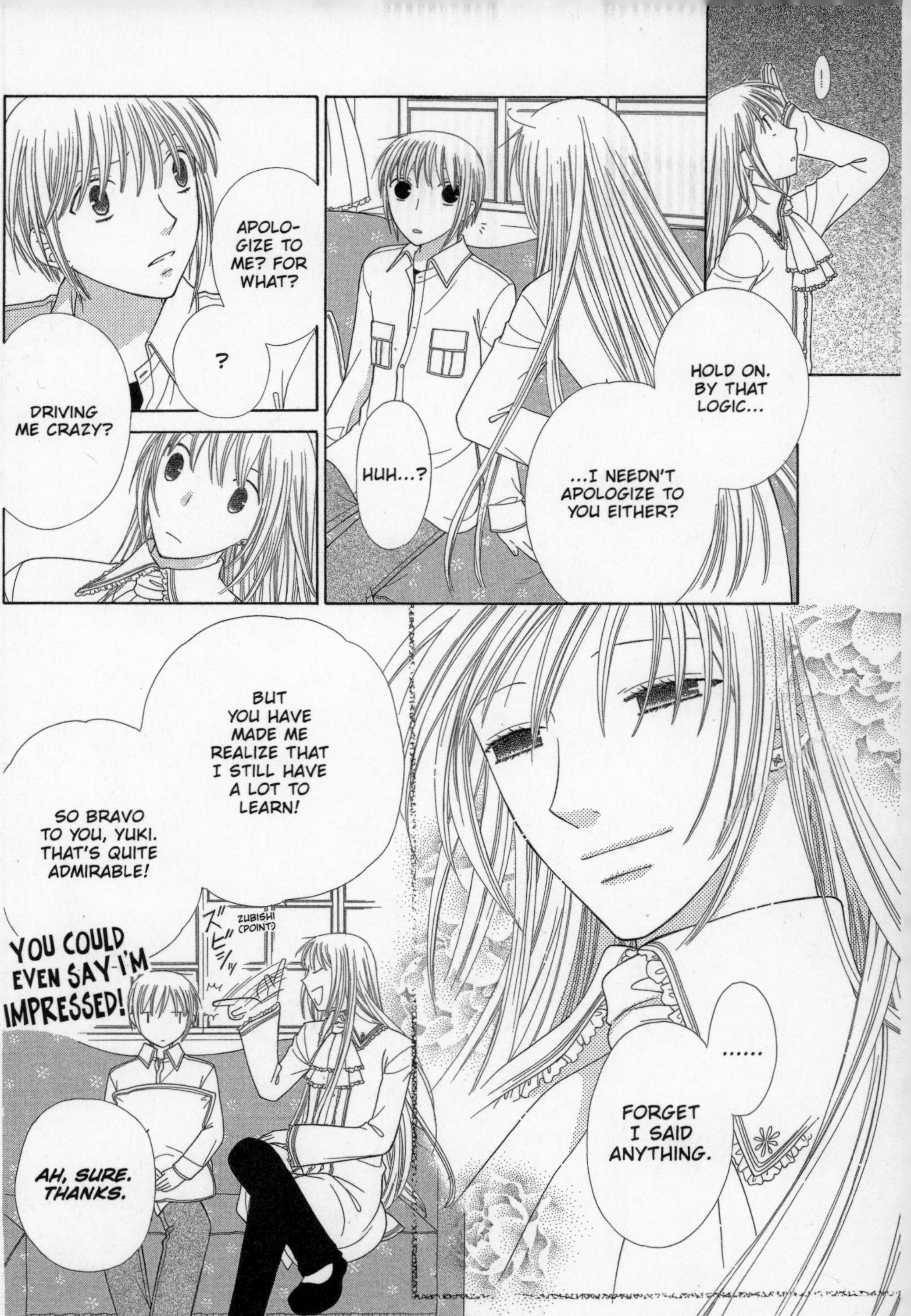
!
HOLD ON. BY THAT LOGIC...
...I NEEDN'T APOLOGIZE TO YOU EITHER?
HUH...?
APOLOGIZE TO ME? FOR WHAT?
?
DRIVING ME CRAZY?
......
FORGET I SAID ANYTHING.
BUT YOU HAVE MADE ME REALIZE THAT I STILL HAVE A LOT TO LEARN!
SO BRAVO TO YOU, YUKI. THAT'S QUITE ADMIRABLE!
YOU COULD EVEN SAY I'M IMPRESSED!
ZUBISHI (POINT)
AH, SURE. THANKS.

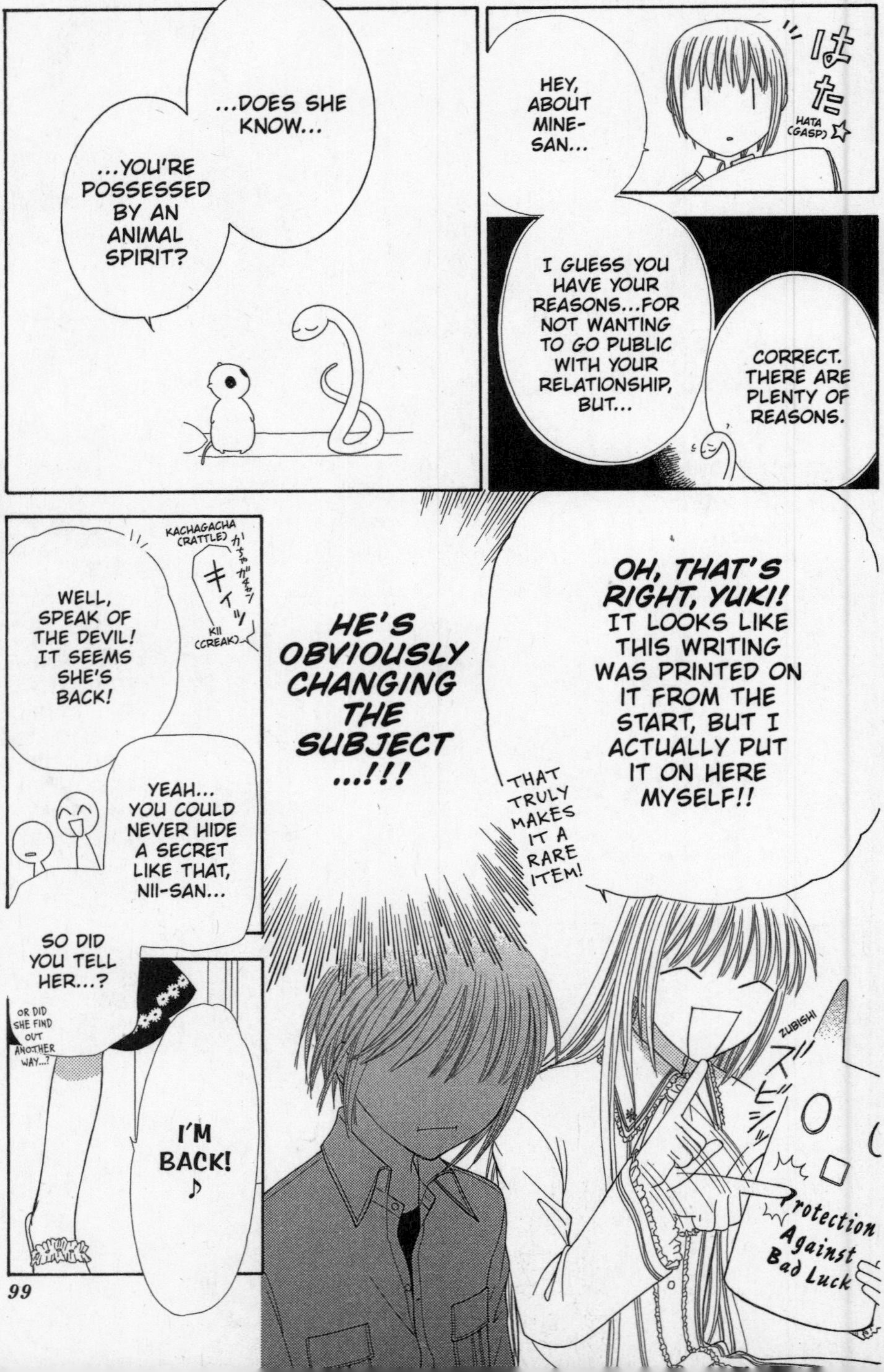
HEY, ABOUT MINE-SAN...
はた
HATA (GASP)
I GUESS YOU HAVE YOUR REASONS...FOR NOT WANTING TO GO PUBLIC WITH YOUR RELATIONSHIP, BUT...
CORRECT. THERE ARE PLENTY OF REASONS.
...DOES SHE KNOW...
...YOU'RE POSSESSED BY AN ANIMAL SPIRIT?
OH, THAT'S RIGHT, YUKI! IT LOOKS LIKE THIS WRITING WAS PRINTED ON IT FROM THE START, BUT I ACTUALLY PUT IT ON HERE MYSELF!!
THAT TRULY MAKES IT A RARE ITEM!
HE'S OBVIOUSLY CHANGING THE SUBJECT ...!!!
ZUBISHI
Protection Against Bad Luck
KACHAGACHA (RATTLE)
KII (CREAK)
WELL, SPEAK OF THE DEVIL! IT SEEMS SHE'S BACK!
YEAH... YOU COULD NEVER HIDE A SECRET LIKE THAT, NII-SAN...
SO DID YOU TELL HER...?
OR DID SHE FIND OUT ANOTHER WAY...?
I'M BACK! ♪

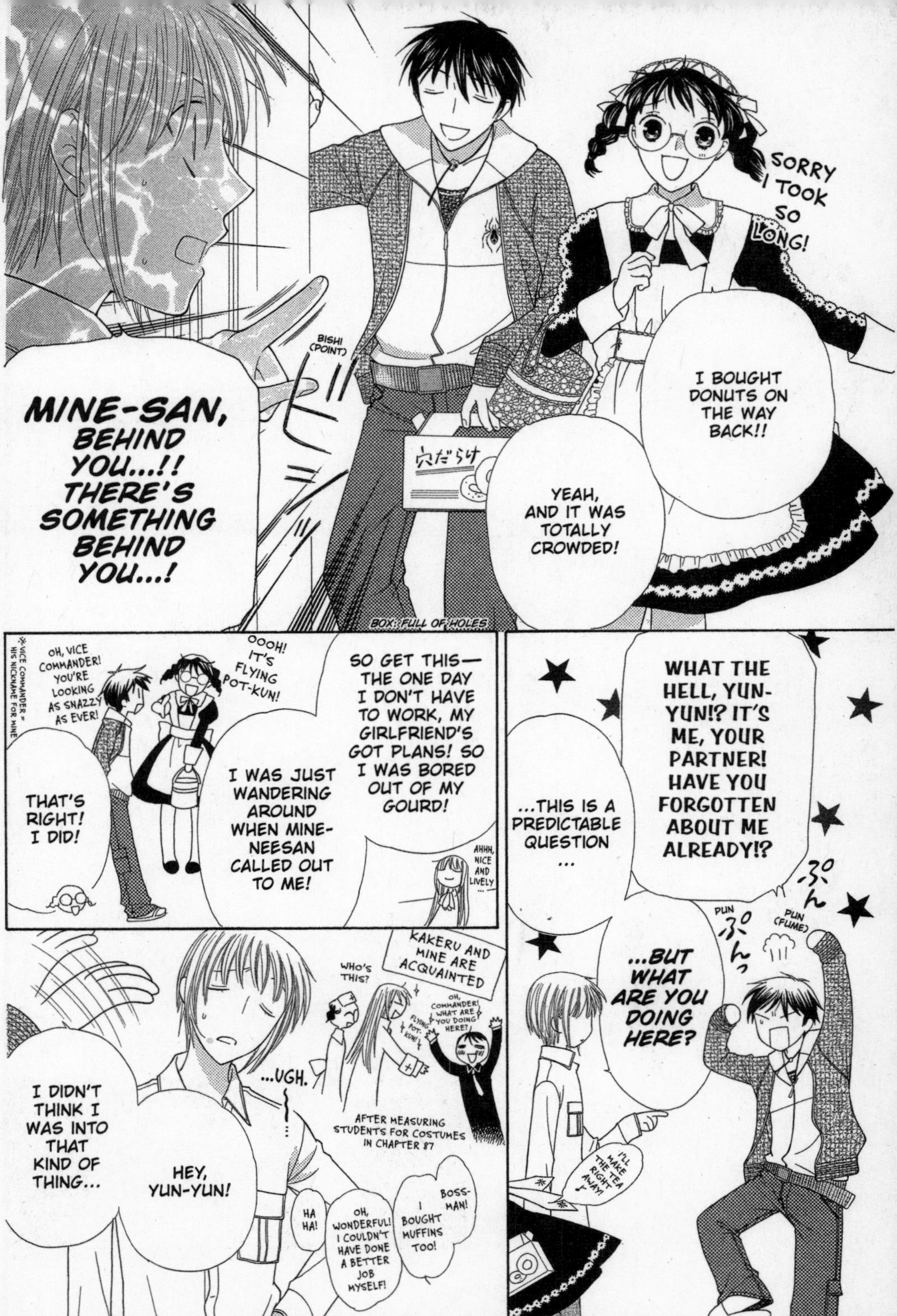
SORRY I TOOK SO LONG!
I BOUGHT DONUTS ON THE WAY BACK!!
YEAH, AND IT WAS TOTALLY CROWDED!
穴だらけ
BISHI (POINT)
MINE-SAN, BEHIND YOU...!! THERE'S SOMETHING BEHIND YOU...!
BOX: FULL OF HOLES
WHAT THE HELL, YUN-YUN!? IT'S ME, YOUR PARTNER! HAVE YOU FORGOTTEN ABOUT ME ALREADY!?
...THIS IS A PREDICTABLE QUESTION ...
ぷん
PUN (FUME)
ぷんっ
PUN
...BUT WHAT ARE YOU DOING HERE?
I'LL MAKE THE TEA RIGHT AWAY!
SO GET THIS— THE ONE DAY I DON'T HAVE TO WORK, MY GIRLFRIEND'S GOT PLANS! SO I WAS BORED OUT OF MY GOURD!
OOOH! IT'S FLYING POT-KUN!
I WAS JUST WANDERING AROUND WHEN MINE-NEESAN CALLED OUT TO ME!
AHHH, NICE AND LIVELY ...
OH, VICE COMMANDER! YOU'RE LOOKING AS SNAZZY AS EVER!
THAT'S RIGHT! I DID!
※VICE COMMANDER = HIS NICKNAME FOR MINE
KAKERU AND MINE ARE ACQUAINTED
OH, COMMANDER! WHAT ARE YOU DOING HERE?
FLYING POT-KUN!
WHO'S THIS?
...UGH.
AFTER MEASURING STUDENTS FOR COSTUMES IN CHAPTER 87
BOSS-MAN! I BOUGHT MUFFINS TOO!
OH, WONDERFUL! I COULDN'T HAVE DONE A BETTER JOB MYSELF!
HA HA!
HEY, YUN-YUN!
I DIDN'T THINK I WAS INTO THAT KIND OF THING...

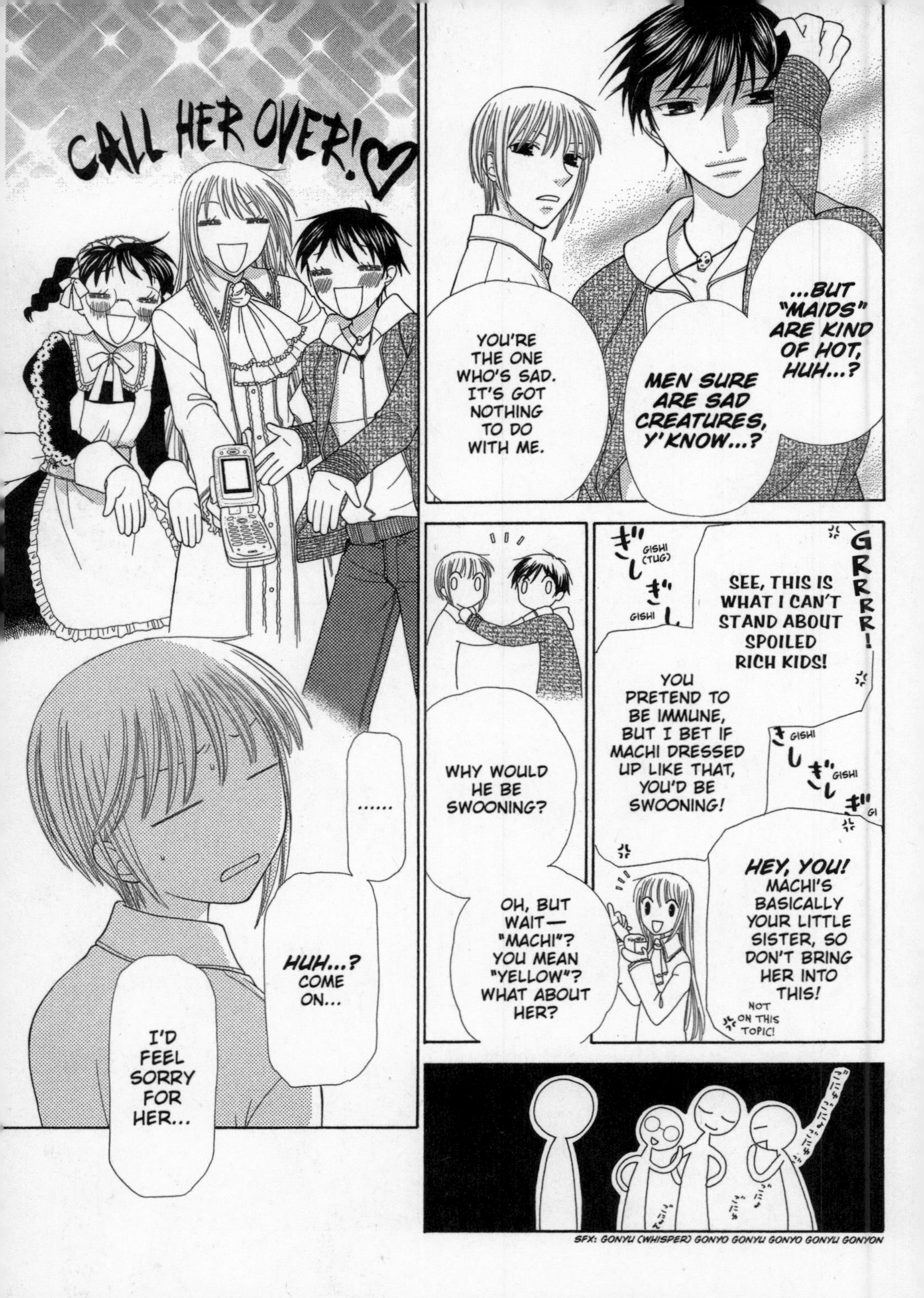
...BUT "MAIDS" ARE KIND OF HOT, HUH...?
MEN SURE ARE SAD CREATURES, Y'KNOW...?
YOU'RE THE ONE WHO'S SAD. IT'S GOT NOTHING TO DO WITH ME.
GRRRR!
ぎし GISHI (TUG) ぎし GISHI
SEE, THIS IS WHAT I CAN'T STAND ABOUT SPOILED RICH KIDS!
YOU PRETEND TO BE IMMUNE, BUT I BET IF MACHI DRESSED UP LIKE THAT, YOU'D BE SWOONING!
ぎし GISHI ぎし GISHI ぎ GI
HEY, YOU! MACHI'S BASICALLY YOUR LITTLE SISTER, SO DON'T BRING HER INTO THIS!
NOT ON THIS TOPIC!
WHY WOULD HE BE SWOONING?
OH, BUT WAIT— "MACHI"? YOU MEAN "YELLOW"? WHAT ABOUT HER?
SFX: GONYU (WHISPER) GONYO GONYU GONYO GONYU GONYON
CALL HER OVER!♡
......
HUH...? COME ON...
I'D FEEL SORRY FOR HER...

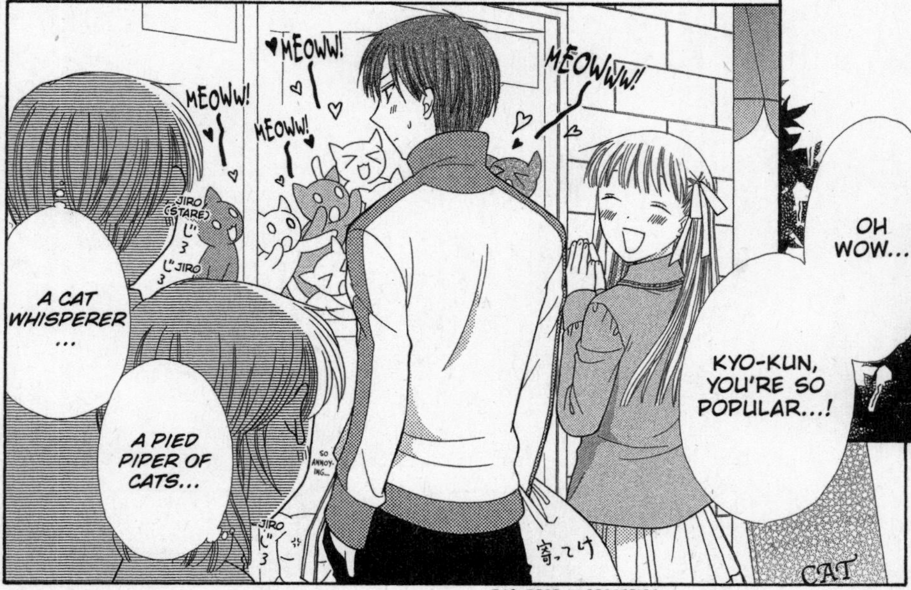
OH WOW...
KYO-KUN, YOU'RE SO POPULAR...!
MEOWWW!
MEOWW!
MEOWW!
MEOWW!
JIRO (STARE)
JIRO
A CAT WHISPERER...
A PIED PIPER OF CATS...
SO ANNOYING...
JIRO
寄ってけ
CAT

BAG: DROP-IN GROCERIES

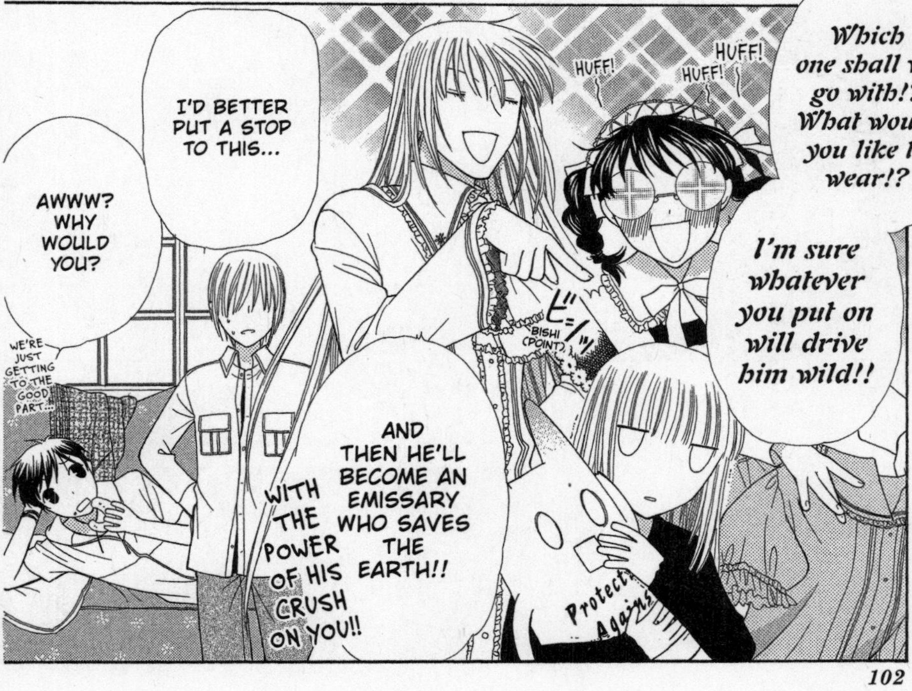
Which one shall we go with!? What would you like to wear!?
I'm sure whatever you put on will drive him wild!!
HUFF!
HUFF!
HUFF!
I'D BETTER PUT A STOP TO THIS...
BISHI (POINT)
AND THEN HE'LL BECOME AN EMISSARY WHO SAVES THE EARTH!!
WITH THE POWER OF HIS CRUSH ON YOU!!
AWWW? WHY WOULD YOU?
WE'RE JUST GETTING TO THE GOOD PART...

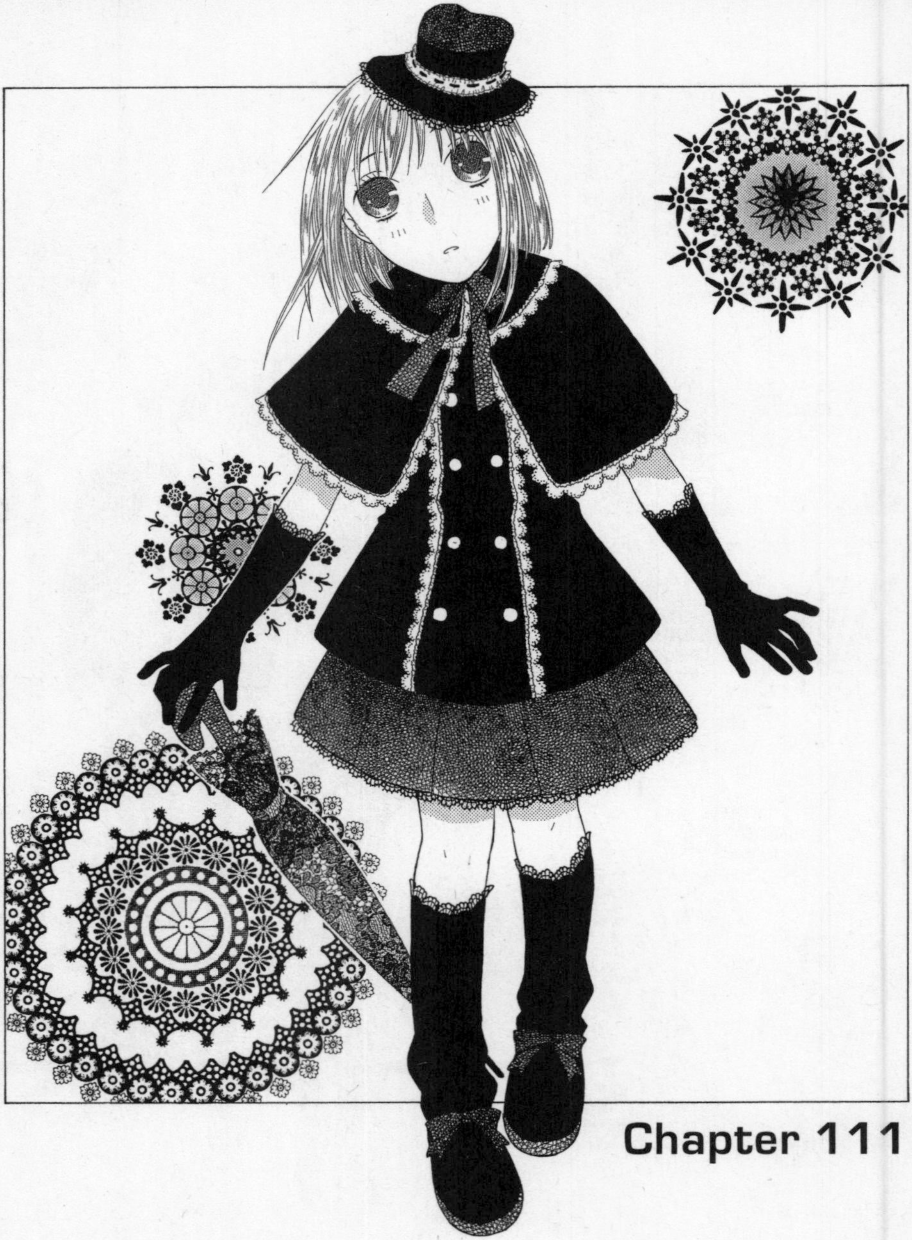

Chapter 111

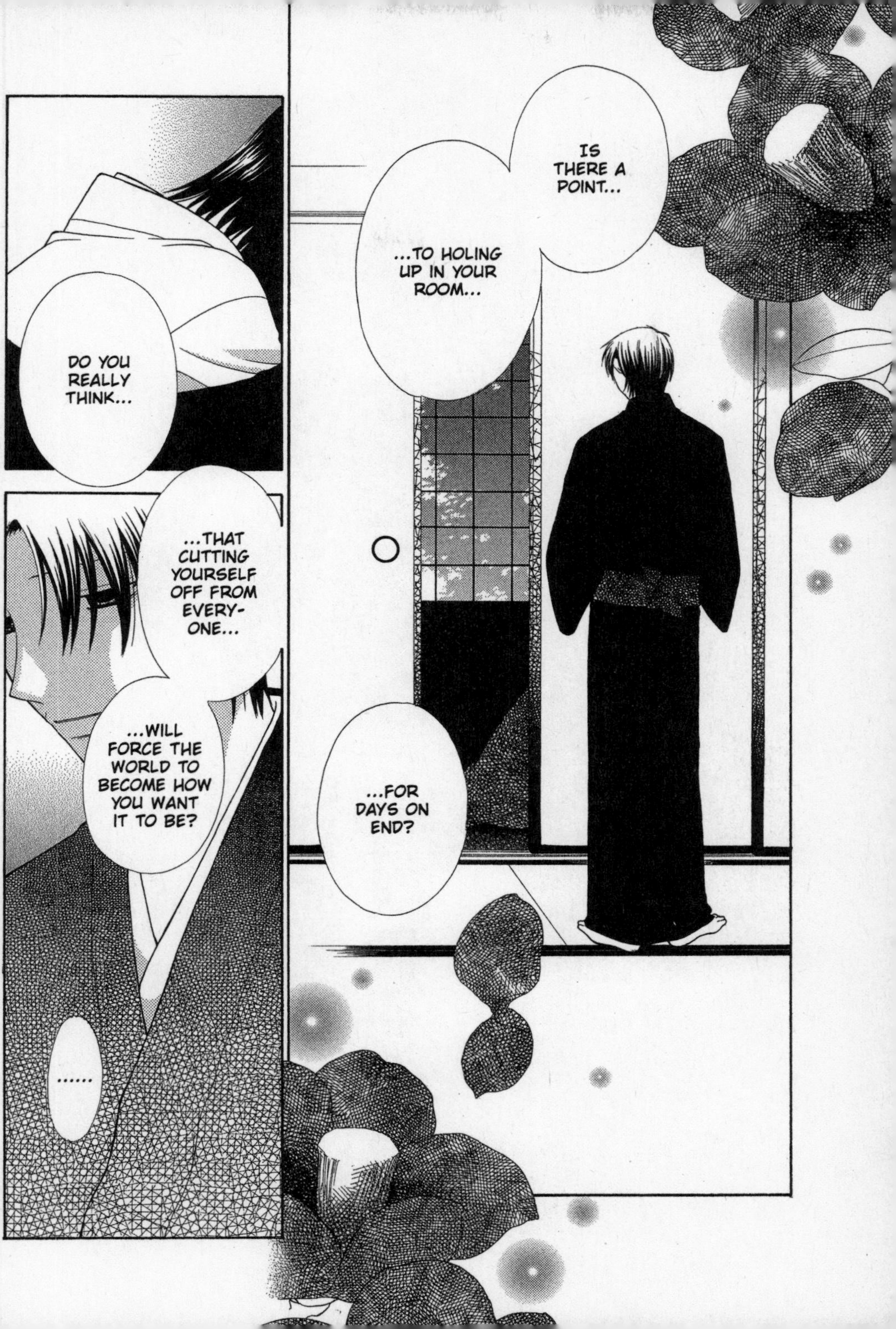
IS THERE A POINT...
...TO HOLING UP IN YOUR ROOM...
...FOR DAYS ON END?
DO YOU REALLY THINK...
...THAT CUTTING YOURSELF OFF FROM EVERY-ONE...
...WILL FORCE THE WORLD TO BECOME HOW YOU WANT IT TO BE?
......

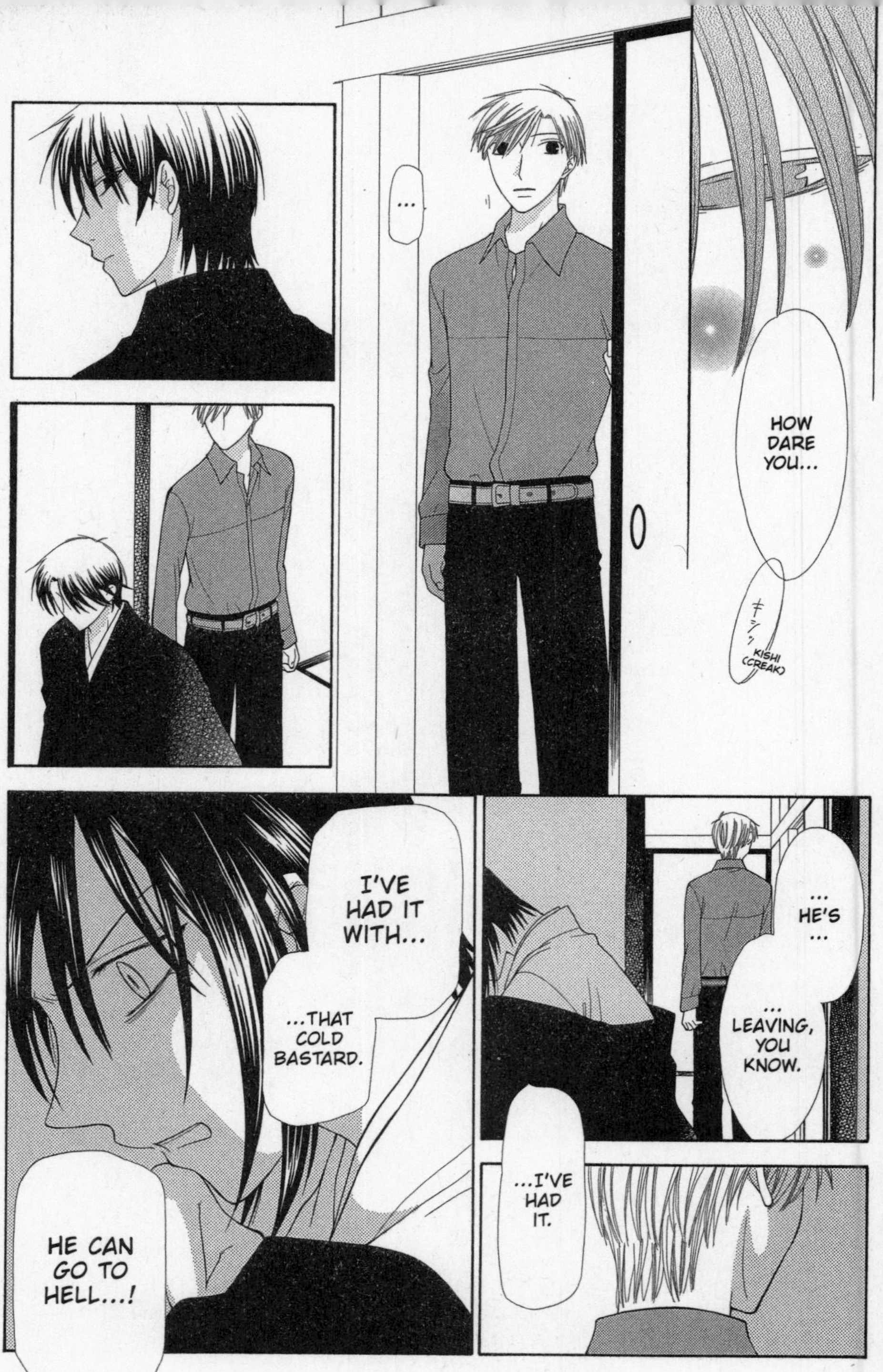
HOW DARE YOU...
キシッ
KISHI (CREAK)
...
... HE'S ...
... LEAVING, YOU KNOW.
...I'VE HAD IT.
I'VE HAD IT WITH...
...THAT COLD BASTARD.
HE CAN GO TO HELL...!

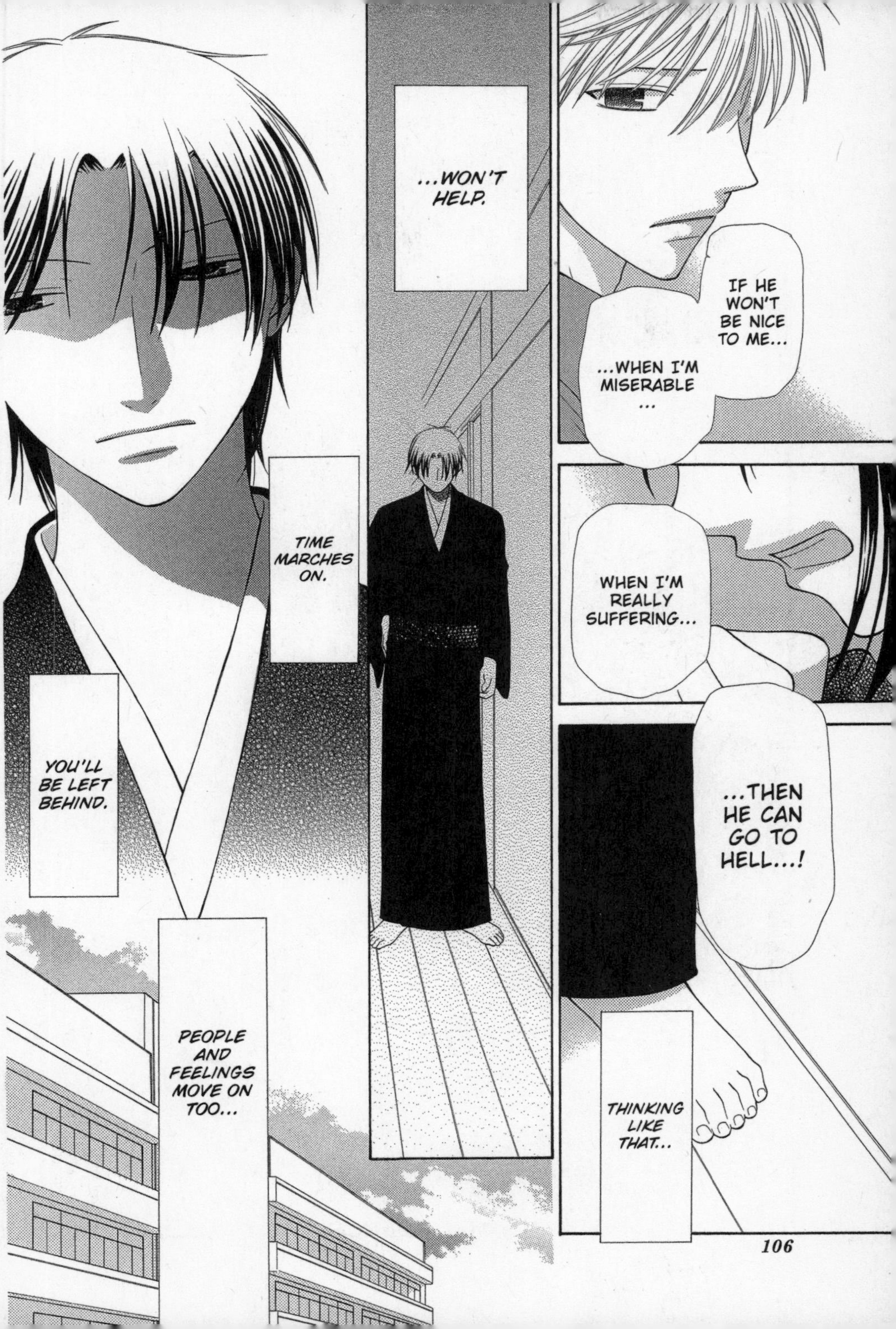
IF HE WON'T BE NICE TO ME...
...WHEN I'M MISERABLE ...
WHEN I'M REALLY SUFFERING...
...THEN HE CAN GO TO HELL...!
THINKING LIKE THAT...
...WON'T HELP.
TIME MARCHES ON.
YOU'LL BE LEFT BEHIND.
PEOPLE AND FEELINGS MOVE ON TOO...

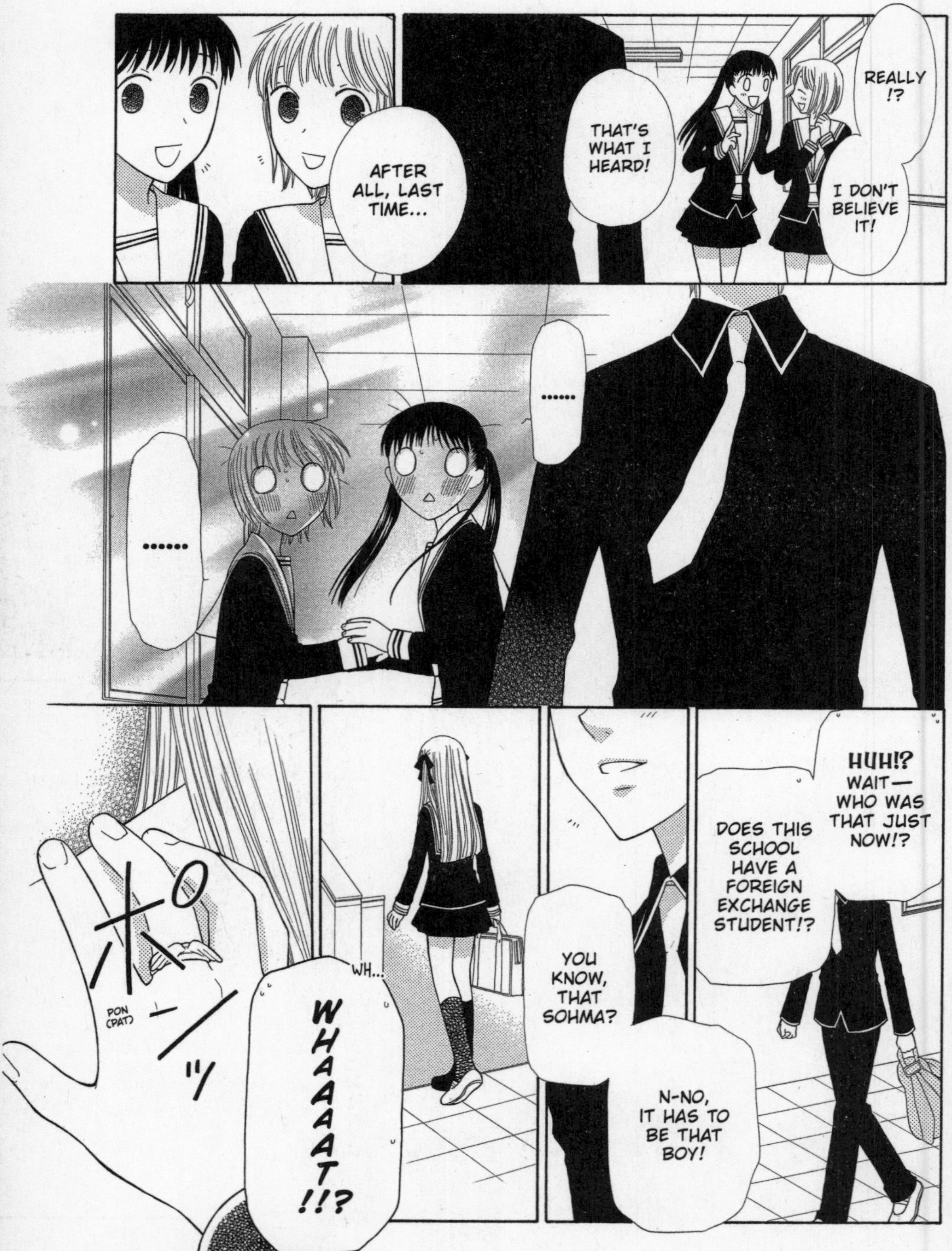
REALLY !?
I DON'T BELIEVE IT!
THAT'S WHAT I HEARD!
AFTER ALL, LAST TIME...
......
......
HUH!? WAIT— WHO WAS THAT JUST NOW!?
DOES THIS SCHOOL HAVE A FOREIGN EXCHANGE STUDENT!?
YOU KNOW, THAT SOHMA?
N-NO, IT HAS TO BE THAT BOY!
WH...
WHAAAAAT!!?
ポン
PON (PAT)

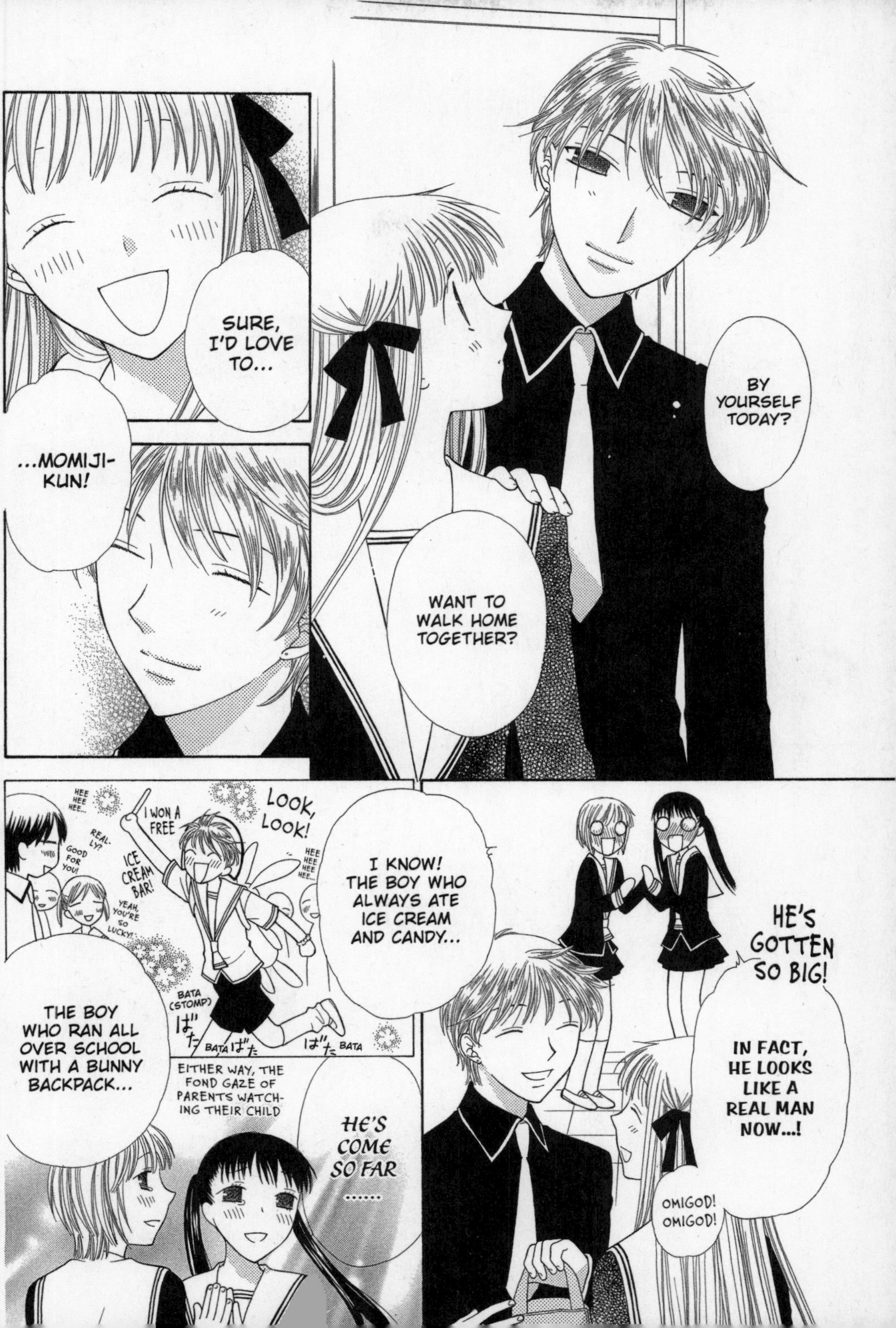
BY YOURSELF TODAY?
WANT TO WALK HOME TOGETHER?
SURE, I'D LOVE TO...
...MOMIJI-KUN!
HE'S GOTTEN SO BIG!
IN FACT, HE LOOKS LIKE A REAL MAN NOW...!
OMIGOD! OMIGOD!
I KNOW! THE BOY WHO ALWAYS ATE ICE CREAM AND CANDY...
LOOK, LOOK!
I WON A FREE ICE CREAM BAR!
HEE HEE HEE HEE...
REAL- LY?
GOOD FOR YOU!
HEE HEE HEE...
YEAH, YOU'RE SO LUCKY!
BATA (STOMP) ばた
BATA ばた
ばた BATA
THE BOY WHO RAN ALL OVER SCHOOL WITH A BUNNY BACKPACK...
EITHER WAY, THE FOND GAZE OF PARENTS WATCHING THEIR CHILD
HE'S COME SO FAR ......

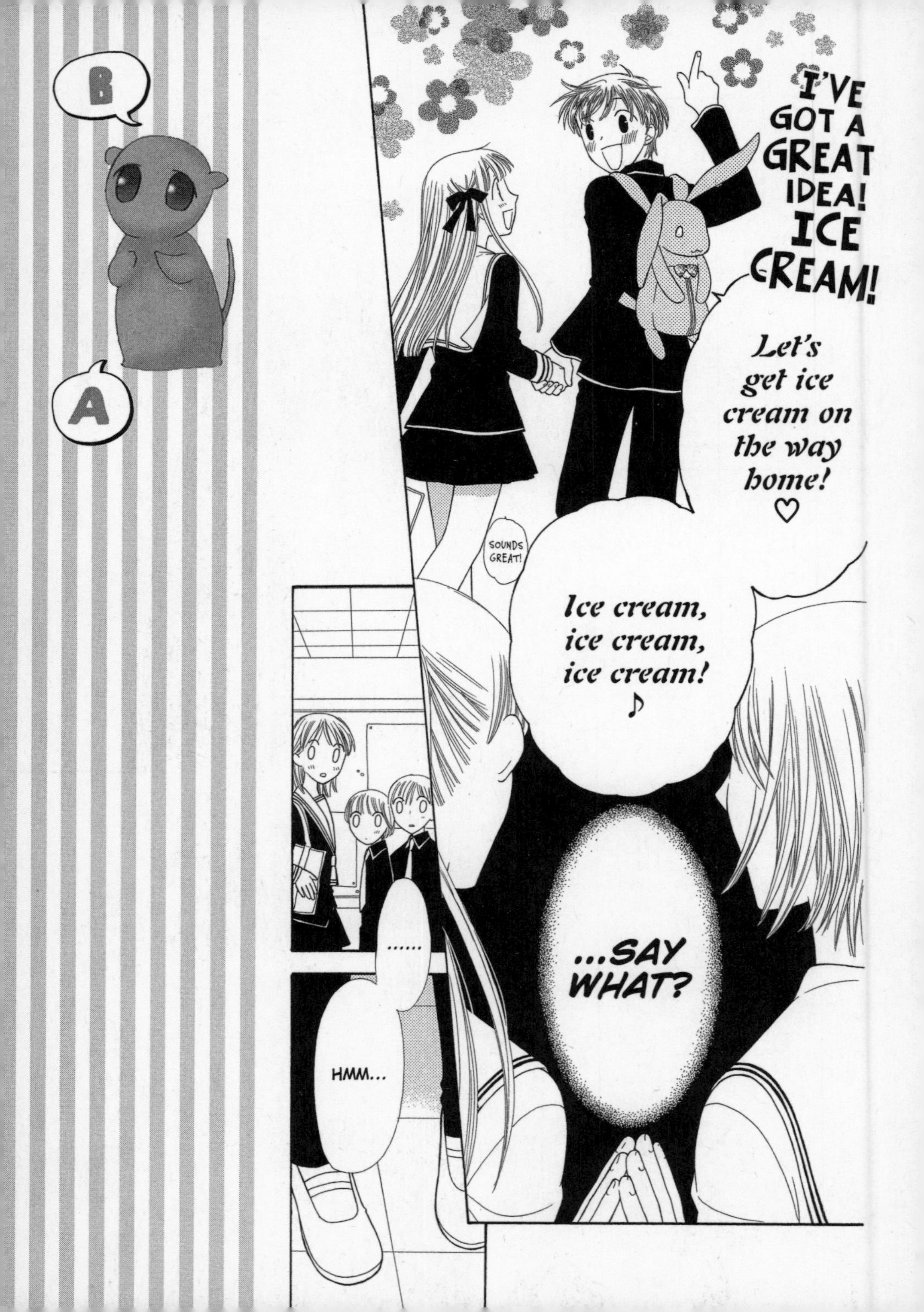
I'VE GOT A GREAT IDEA! ICE CREAM!
Let's get ice cream on the way home! ♡
SOUNDS GREAT!
Ice cream, ice cream, ice cream! ♪
...SAY WHAT?
......
HMM...
B
A

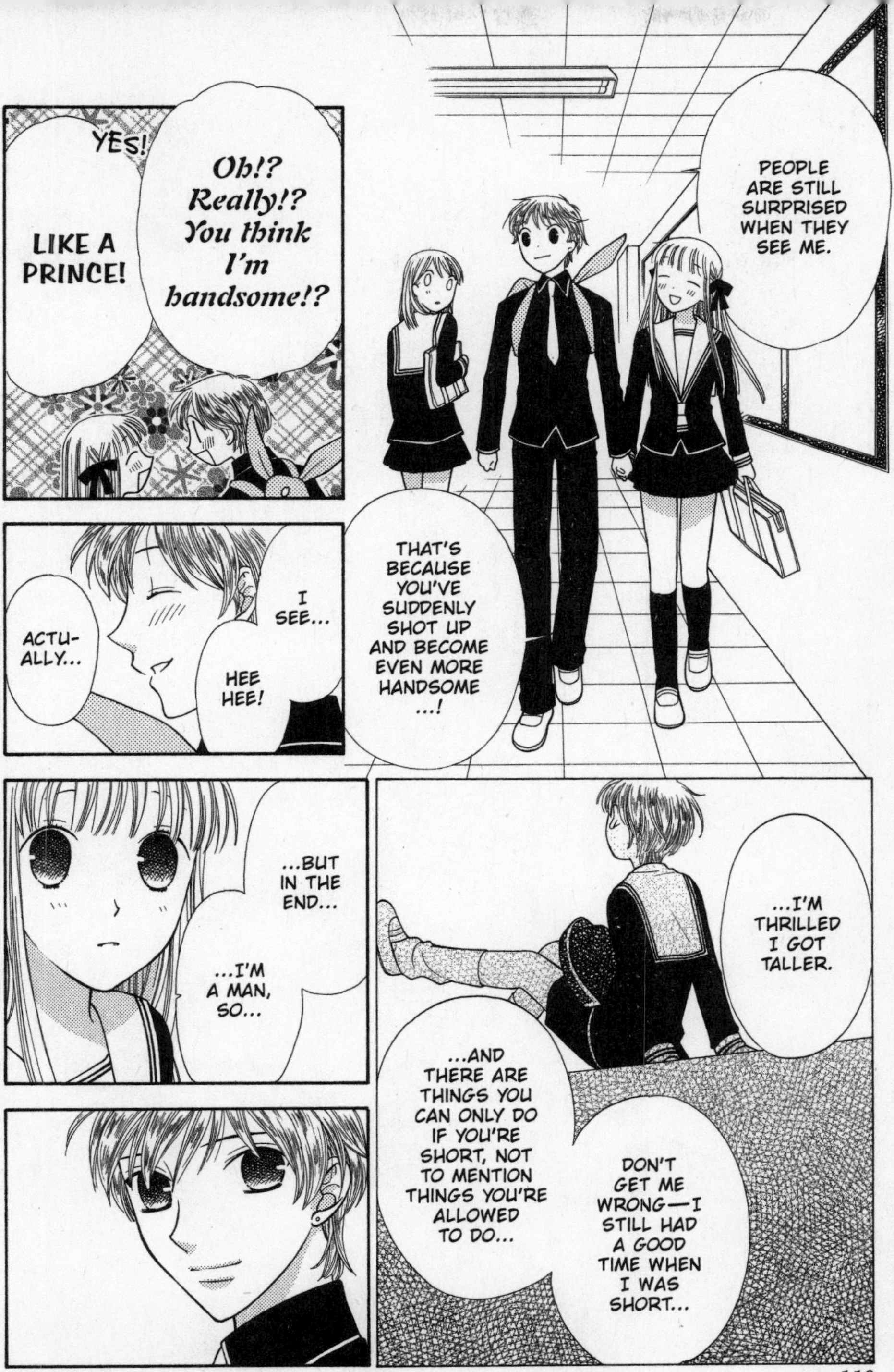
PEOPLE ARE STILL SURPRISED WHEN THEY SEE ME.
THAT'S BECAUSE YOU'VE SUDDENLY SHOT UP AND BECOME EVEN MORE HANDSOME ...!
Oh!? Really!? You think I'm handsome!?
YES!
LIKE A PRINCE!
I SEE...
HEE HEE!
ACTU-ALLY...
...I'M THRILLED I GOT TALLER.
DON'T GET ME WRONG—I STILL HAD A GOOD TIME WHEN I WAS SHORT...
...AND THERE ARE THINGS YOU CAN ONLY DO IF YOU'RE SHORT, NOT TO MENTION THINGS YOU'RE ALLOWED TO DO...
...BUT IN THE END...
...I'M A MAN, SO...

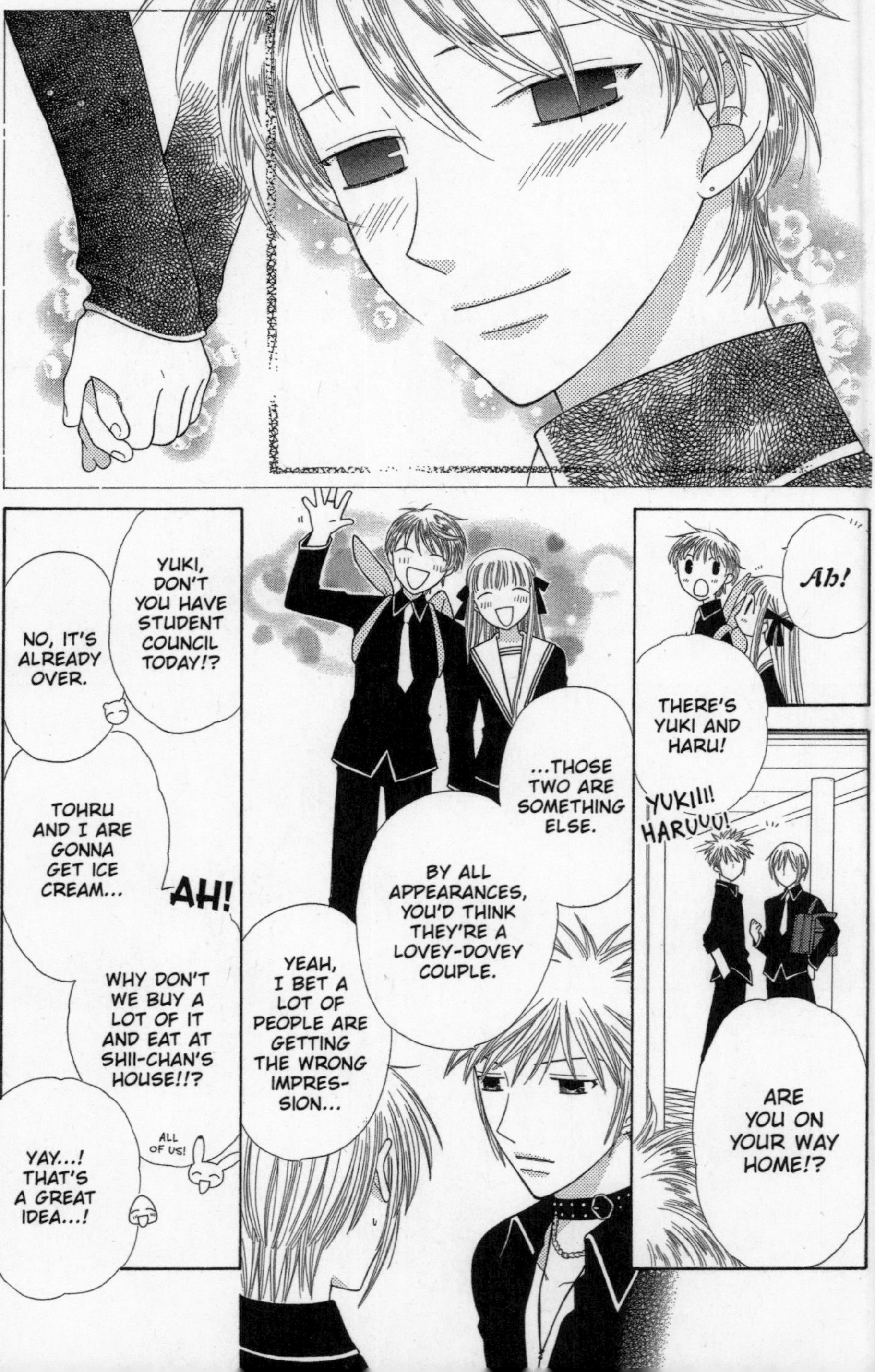
Ah!
THERE'S YUKI AND HARU!
YUKIII! HARUUU!
ARE YOU ON YOUR WAY HOME!?
...THOSE TWO ARE SOMETHING ELSE.
BY ALL APPEARANCES, YOU'D THINK THEY'RE A LOVEY-DOVEY COUPLE.
YEAH, I BET A LOT OF PEOPLE ARE GETTING THE WRONG IMPRESSION...
YUKI, DON'T YOU HAVE STUDENT COUNCIL TODAY!?
NO, IT'S ALREADY OVER.
TOHRU AND I ARE GONNA GET ICE CREAM...
AH!
WHY DON'T WE BUY A LOT OF IT AND EAT AT SHII-CHAN'S HOUSE!!?
ALL OF US!
YAY...! THAT'S A GREAT IDEA...!

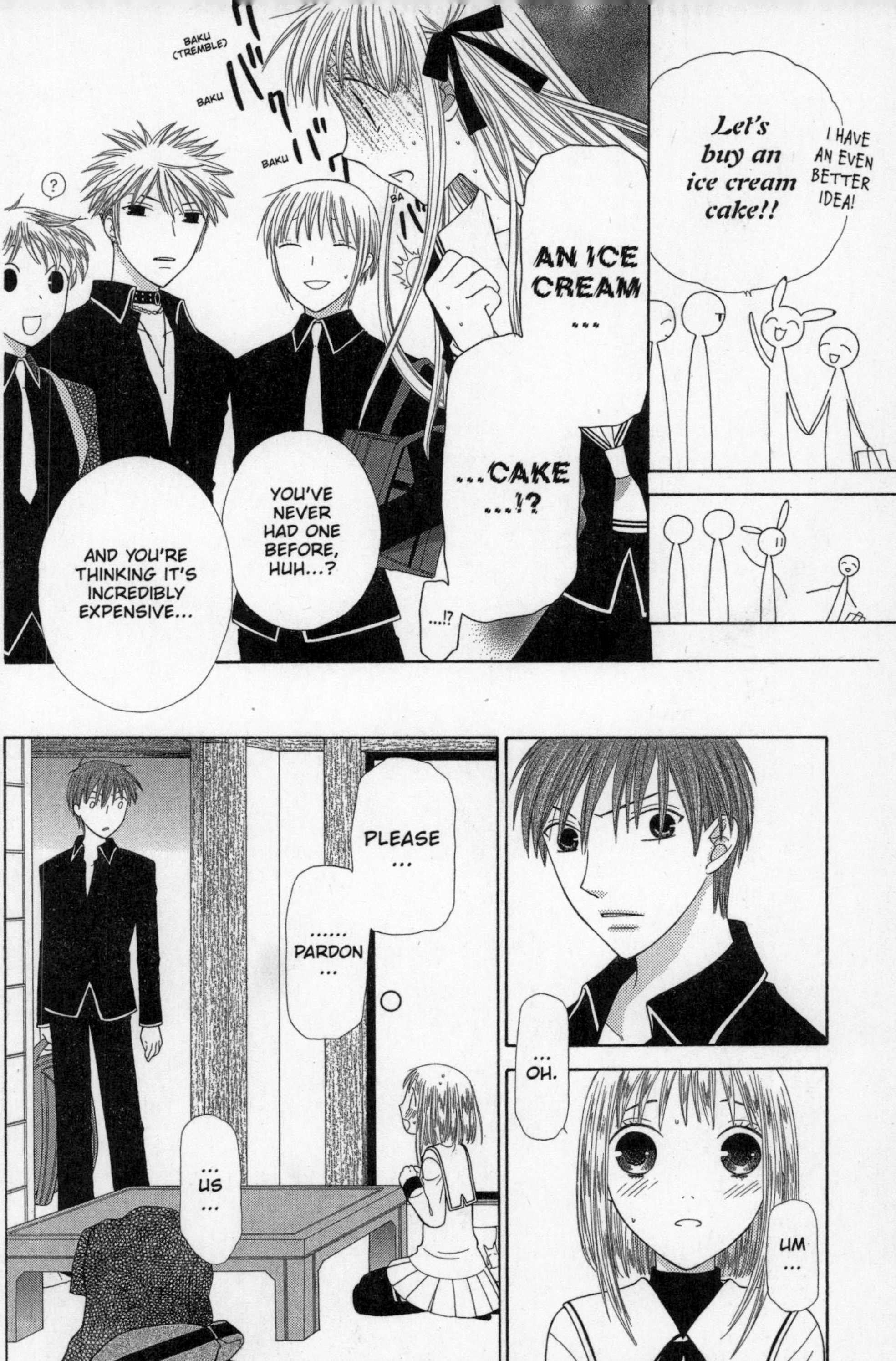
I HAVE AN EVEN BETTER IDEA!
Let's buy an ice cream cake!!
AN ICE CREAM ...
...CAKE ...!?
BAKU (TREMBLE)
BAKU
BAKU
BA
...!?
YOU'VE NEVER HAD ONE BEFORE, HUH...?
AND YOU'RE THINKING IT'S INCREDIBLY EXPENSIVE...
... OH.
UM ...
PLEASE ...
...... PARDON ...
... US ...

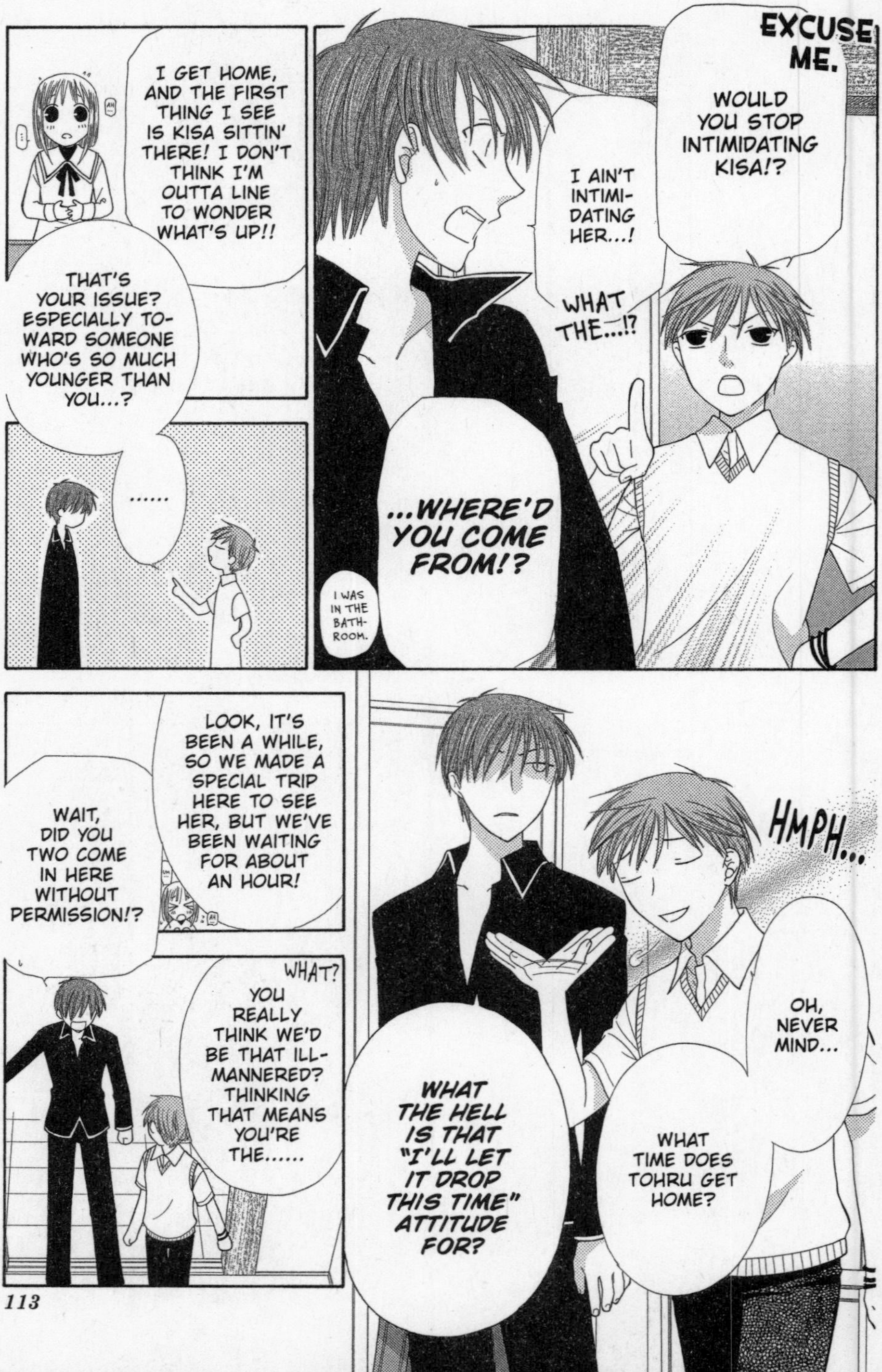
EXCUSE ME.
WOULD YOU STOP INTIMIDATING KISA!?
I AIN'T INTIMIDATING HER...!
WHAT THE...!?
...WHERE'D YOU COME FROM!?
I WAS IN THE BATHROOM.
I GET HOME, AND THE FIRST THING I SEE IS KISA SITTIN' THERE! I DON'T THINK I'M OUTTA LINE TO WONDER WHAT'S UP!!
THAT'S YOUR ISSUE? ESPECIALLY TO-WARD SOMEONE WHO'S SO MUCH YOUNGER THAN YOU...?
......
HMPH...
OH, NEVER MIND...
WHAT TIME DOES TOHRU GET HOME?
WHAT THE HELL IS THAT "I'LL LET IT DROP THIS TIME" ATTITUDE FOR?
LOOK, IT'S BEEN A WHILE, SO WE MADE A SPECIAL TRIP HERE TO SEE HER, BUT WE'VE BEEN WAITING FOR ABOUT AN HOUR!
WAIT, DID YOU TWO COME IN HERE WITHOUT PERMISSION!?
WHAT?
YOU REALLY THINK WE'D BE THAT ILL-MANNERED? THINKING THAT MEANS YOU'RE THE......

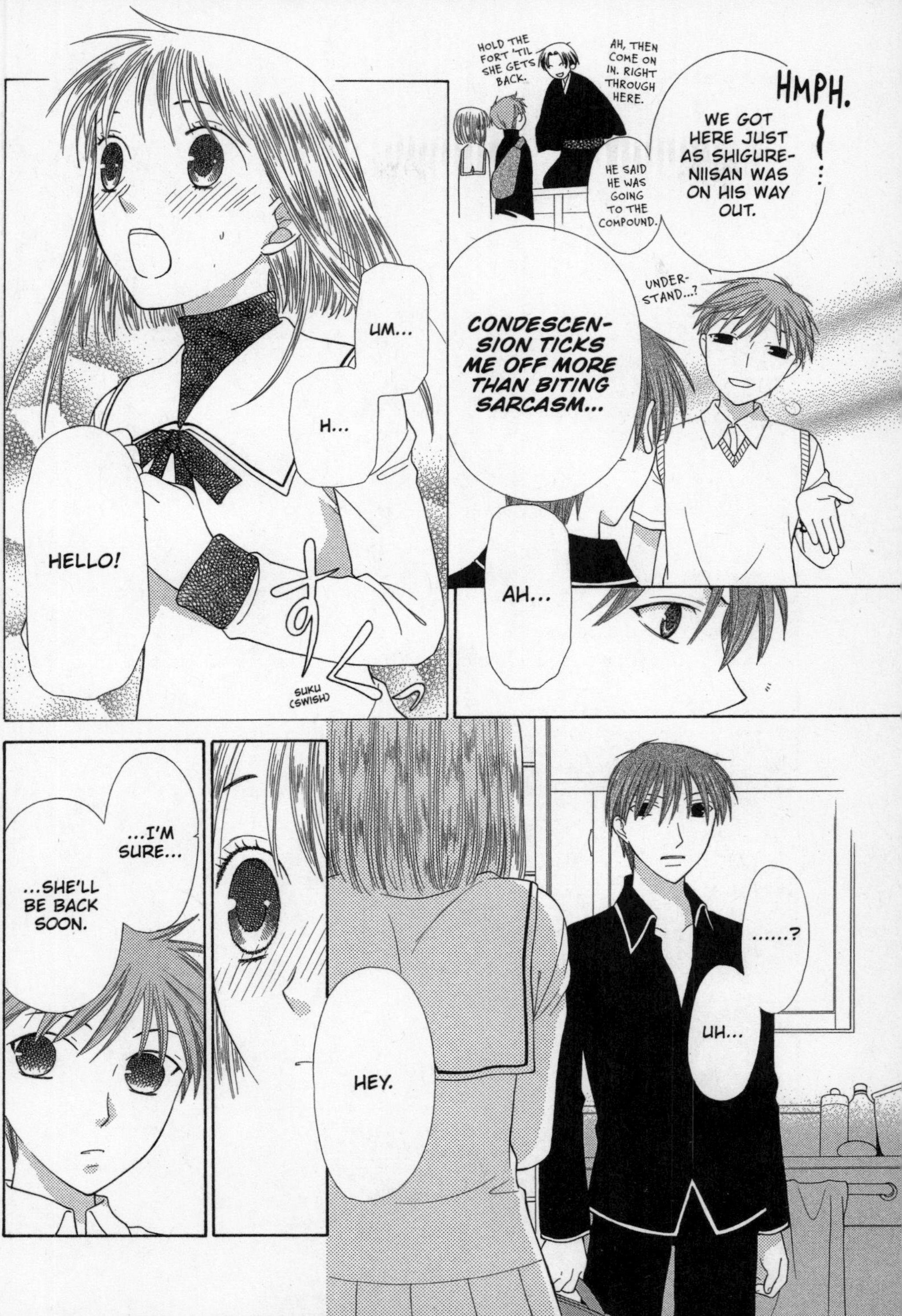
HMPH.
AH, THEN COME ON IN. RIGHT THROUGH HERE.
HOLD THE FORT 'TIL SHE GETS BACK.
WE GOT HERE JUST AS SHIGURE-NIISAN WAS ON HIS WAY OUT.
HE SAID HE WAS GOING TO THE COMPOUND.
UNDER-STAND...?
CONDESCEN-SION TICKS ME OFF MORE THAN BITING SARCASM...
AH...
UM...
H...
HELLO!
SUKU (SWISH)
......?
UH...
HEY.
...I'M SURE...
...SHE'LL BE BACK SOON.

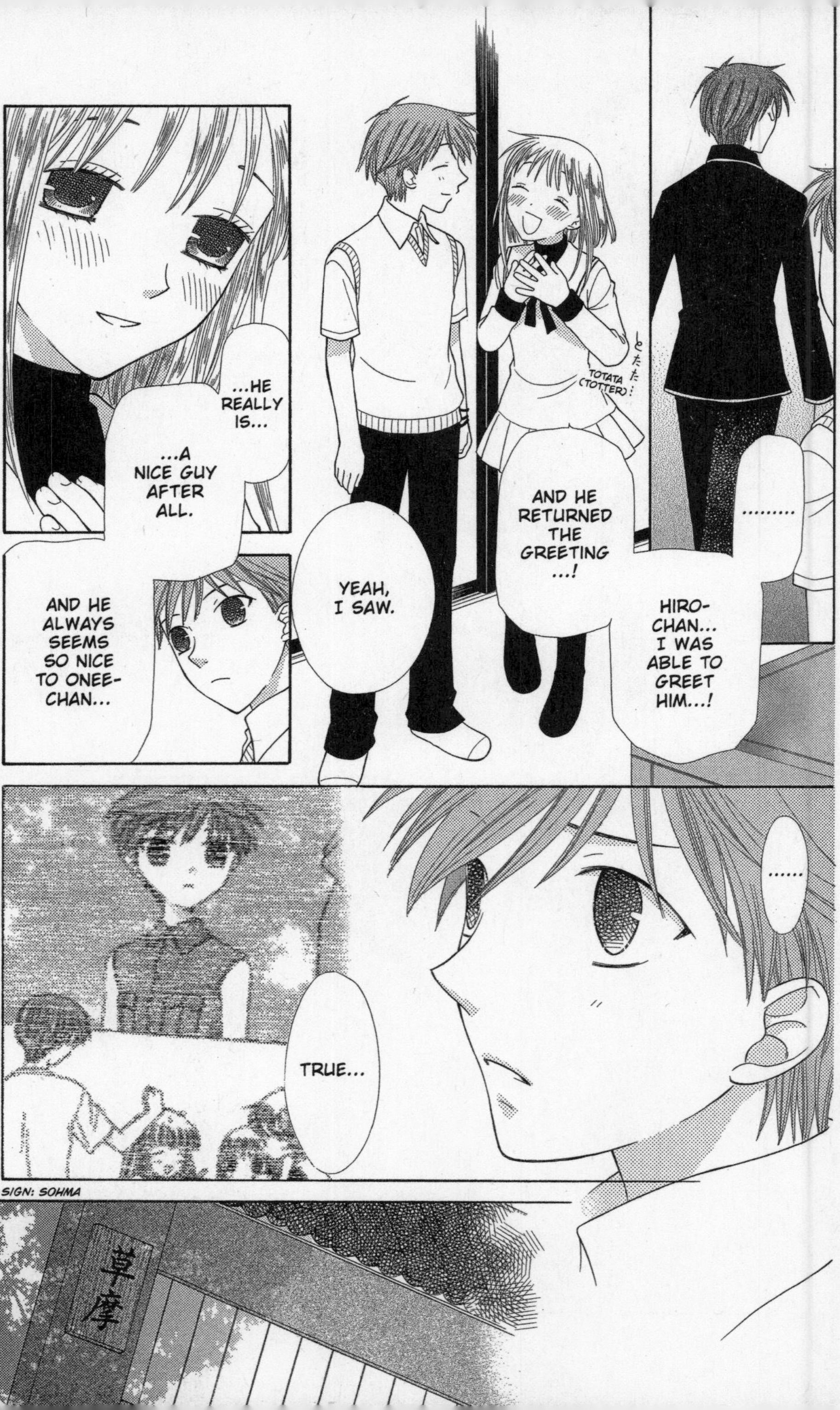
とたた
TOTATA (TOTTER)
....
HIRO-CHAN... I WAS ABLE TO GREET HIM...!
AND HE RETURNED THE GREETING...!
YEAH, I SAW.
...HE REALLY IS...
...A NICE GUY AFTER ALL.
AND HE ALWAYS SEEMS SO NICE TO ONEE-CHAN...
......
TRUE...
SIGN: SOHMA
草摩

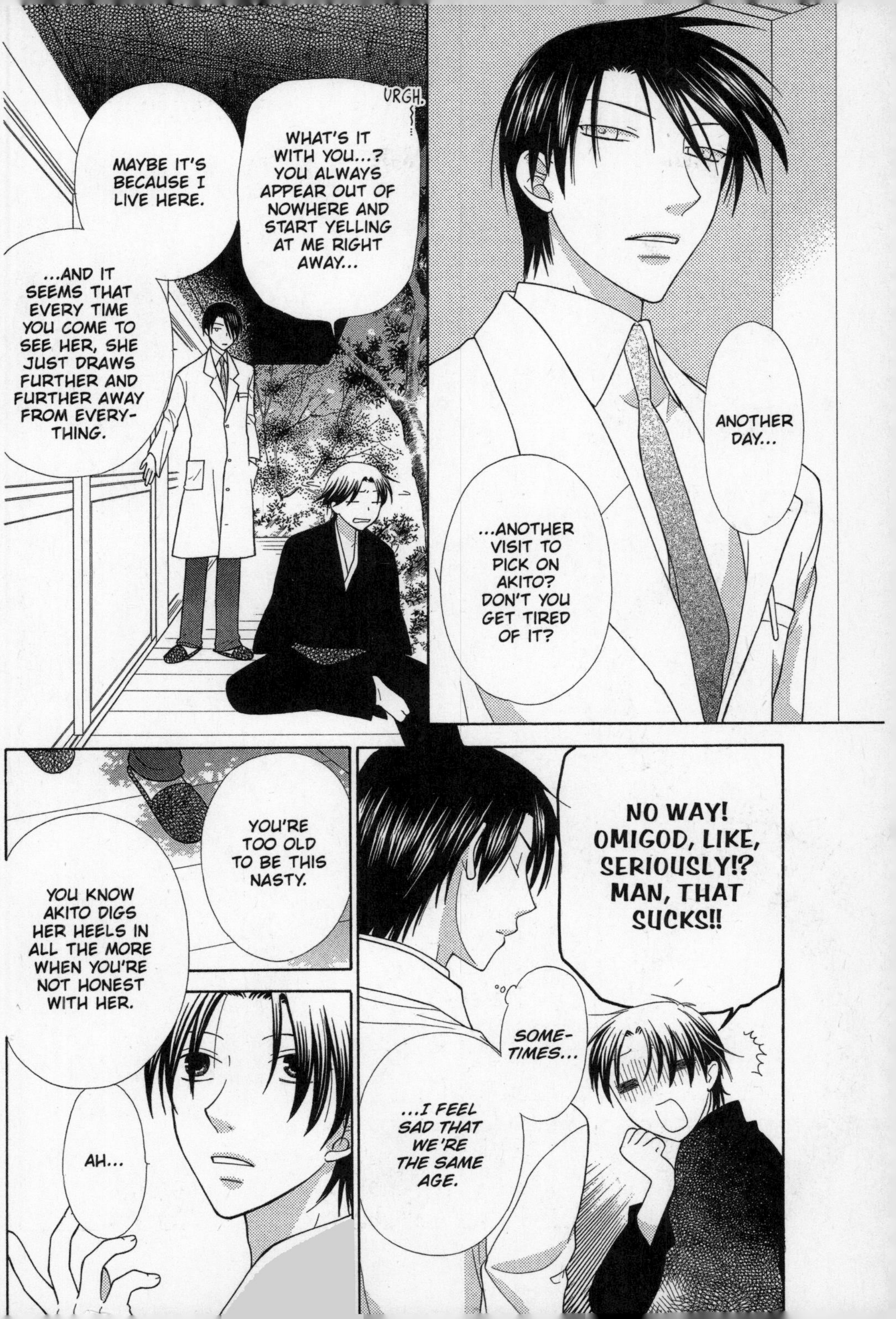
ANOTHER DAY...
...ANOTHER VISIT TO PICK ON AKITO? DON'T YOU GET TIRED OF IT?
URGH.
WHAT'S IT WITH YOU...? YOU ALWAYS APPEAR OUT OF NOWHERE AND START YELLING AT ME RIGHT AWAY...
MAYBE IT'S BECAUSE I LIVE HERE.
...AND IT SEEMS THAT EVERY TIME YOU COME TO SEE HER, SHE JUST DRAWS FURTHER AND FURTHER AWAY FROM EVERY-THING.
NO WAY! OMIGOD, LIKE, SERIOUSLY!? MAN, THAT SUCKS!!
SOME-TIMES...
...I FEEL SAD THAT WE'RE THE SAME AGE.
YOU'RE TOO OLD TO BE THIS NASTY.
YOU KNOW AKITO DIGS HER HEELS IN ALL THE MORE WHEN YOU'RE NOT HONEST WITH HER.
AH...

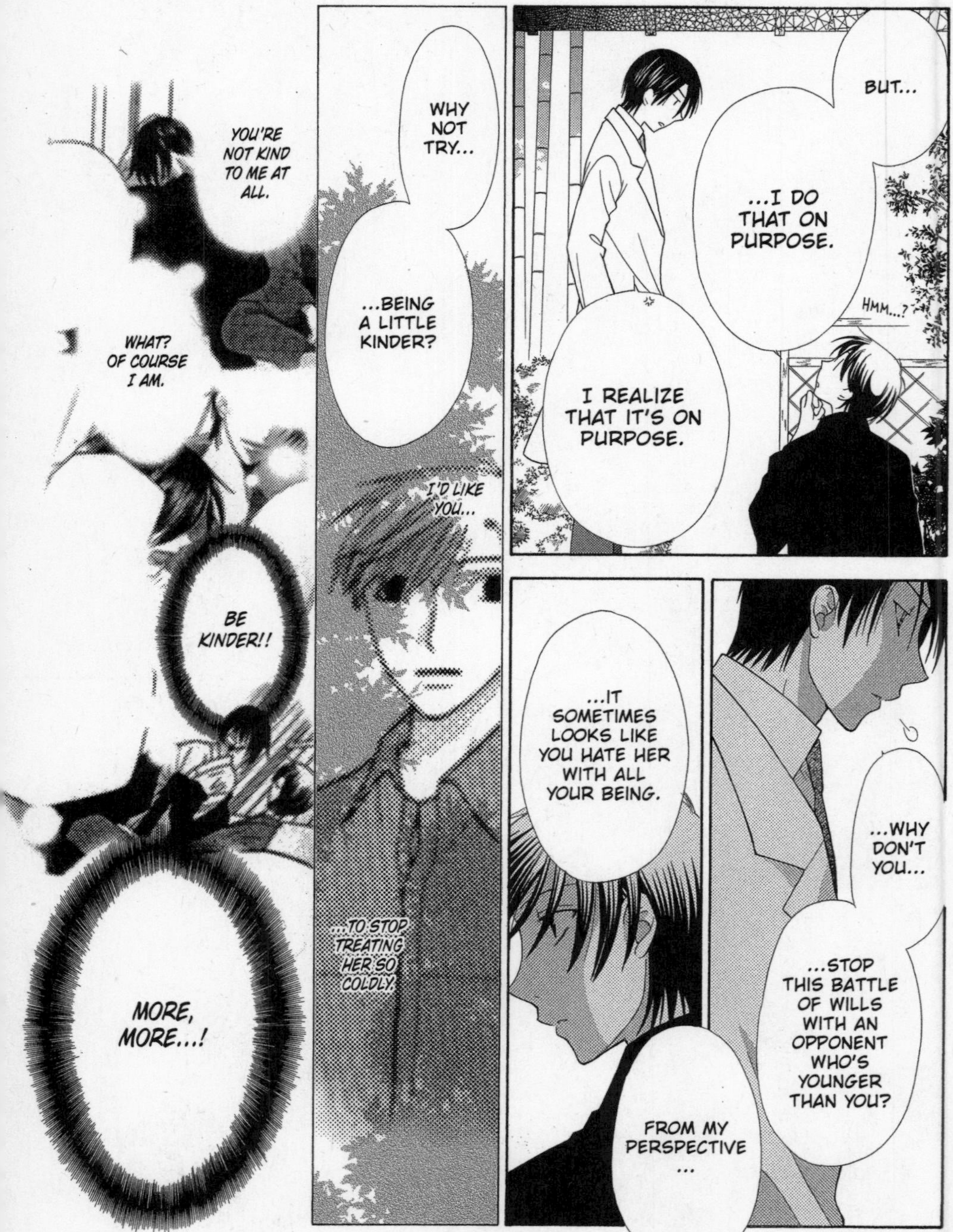
BUT...
...I DO THAT ON PURPOSE.
HMM...?
I REALIZE THAT IT'S ON PURPOSE.
...WHY DON'T YOU...
...STOP THIS BATTLE OF WILLS WITH AN OPPONENT WHO'S YOUNGER THAN YOU?
...IT SOMETIMES LOOKS LIKE YOU HATE HER WITH ALL YOUR BEING.
FROM MY PERSPECTIVE ...
WHY NOT TRY...
...BEING A LITTLE KINDER?
I'D LIKE YOU...
...TO STOP TREATING HER SO COLDLY.
YOU'RE NOT KIND TO ME AT ALL.
WHAT? OF COURSE I AM.
BE KINDER!!
MORE, MORE...!

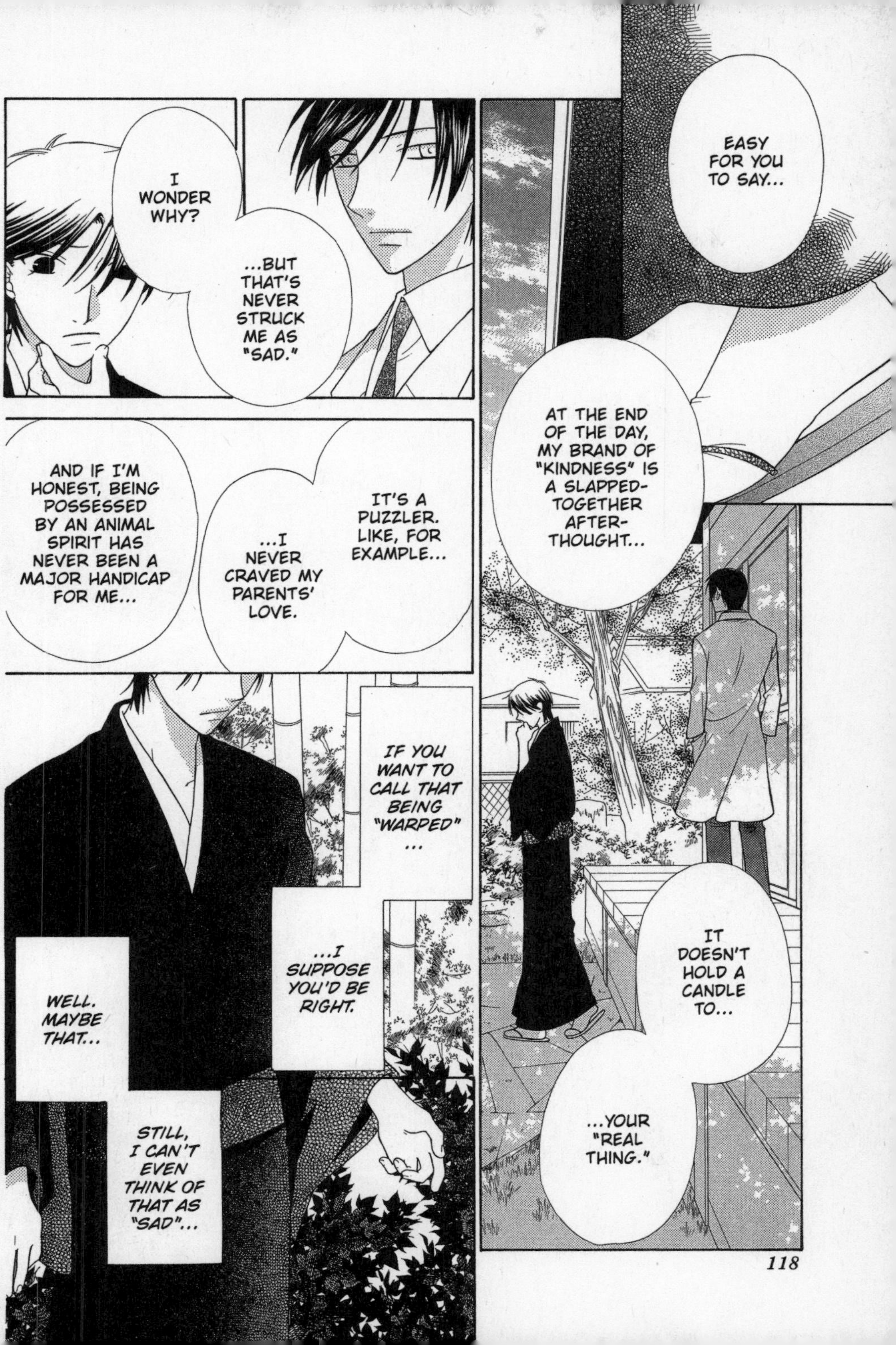
EASY FOR YOU TO SAY...
AT THE END OF THE DAY, MY BRAND OF "KINDNESS" IS A SLAPPED-TOGETHER AFTER-THOUGHT...
IT DOESN'T HOLD A CANDLE TO...
...YOUR "REAL THING."
...BUT THAT'S NEVER STRUCK ME AS "SAD."
I WONDER WHY?
IT'S A PUZZLER. LIKE, FOR EXAMPLE...
...I NEVER CRAVED MY PARENTS' LOVE.
AND IF I'M HONEST, BEING POSSESSED BY AN ANIMAL SPIRIT HAS NEVER BEEN A MAJOR HANDICAP FOR ME...
IF YOU WANT TO CALL THAT BEING "WARPED"...
...I SUPPOSE YOU'D BE RIGHT.
WELL. MAYBE THAT...
STILL, I CAN'T EVEN THINK OF THAT AS "SAD"...

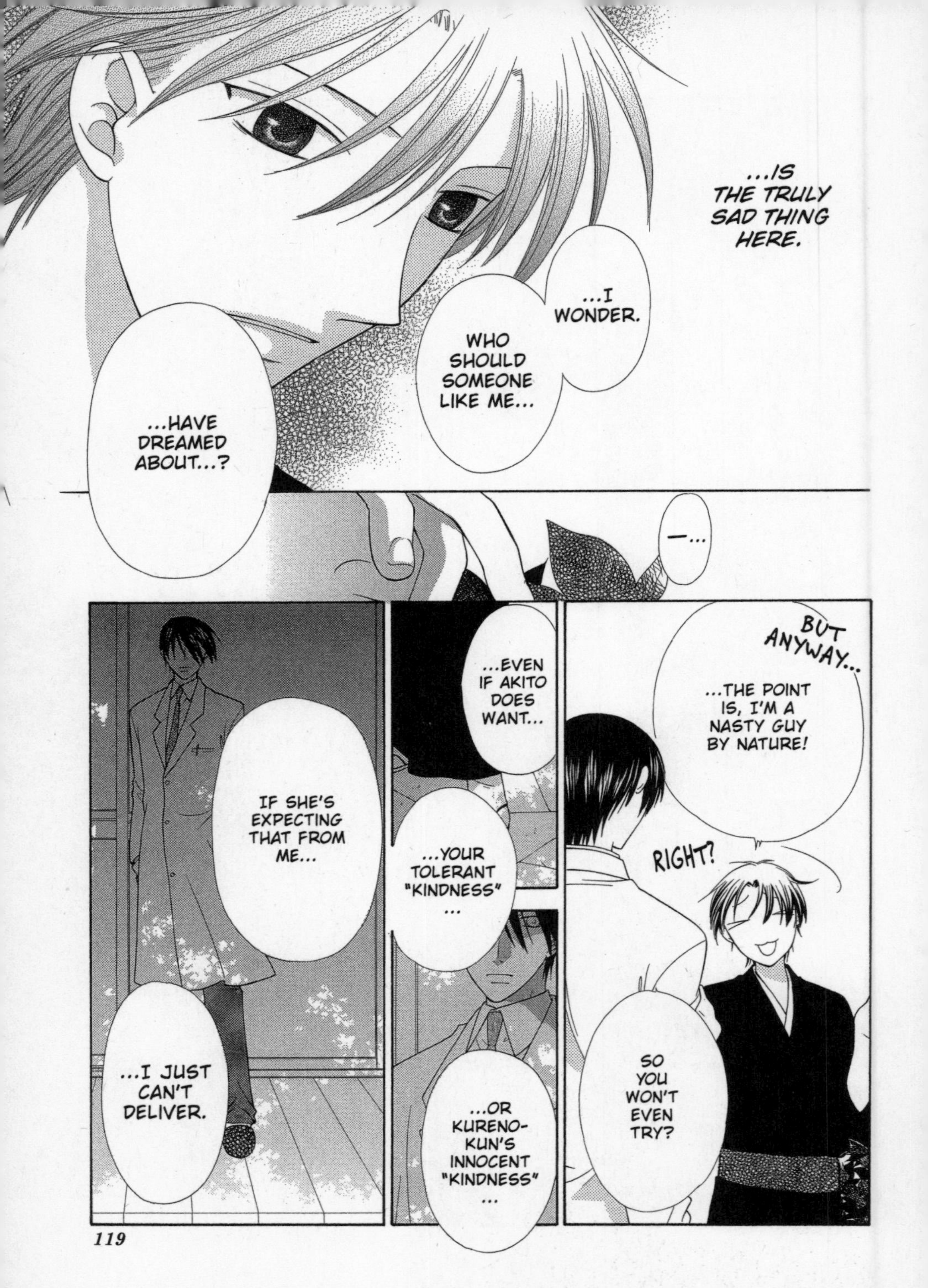
...IS THE TRULY SAD THING HERE.
...I WONDER.
WHO SHOULD SOMEONE LIKE ME...
...HAVE DREAMED ABOUT...?
—...
BUT ANYWAY...
...THE POINT IS, I'M A NASTY GUY BY NATURE!
RIGHT?
SO YOU WON'T EVEN TRY?
...EVEN IF AKITO DOES WANT...
...YOUR TOLERANT "KINDNESS"...
...OR KURENO-KUN'S INNOCENT "KINDNESS"...
IF SHE'S EXPECTING THAT FROM ME...
...I JUST CAN'T DELIVER.

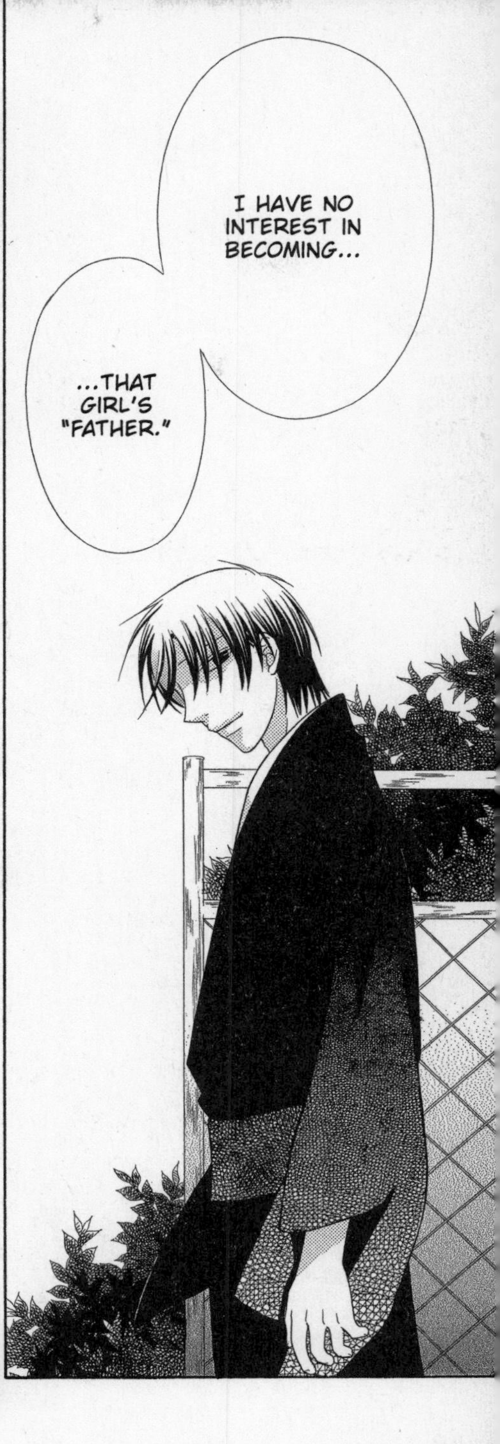
I HAVE NO INTEREST IN BECOMING...
...THAT GIRL'S "FATHER."

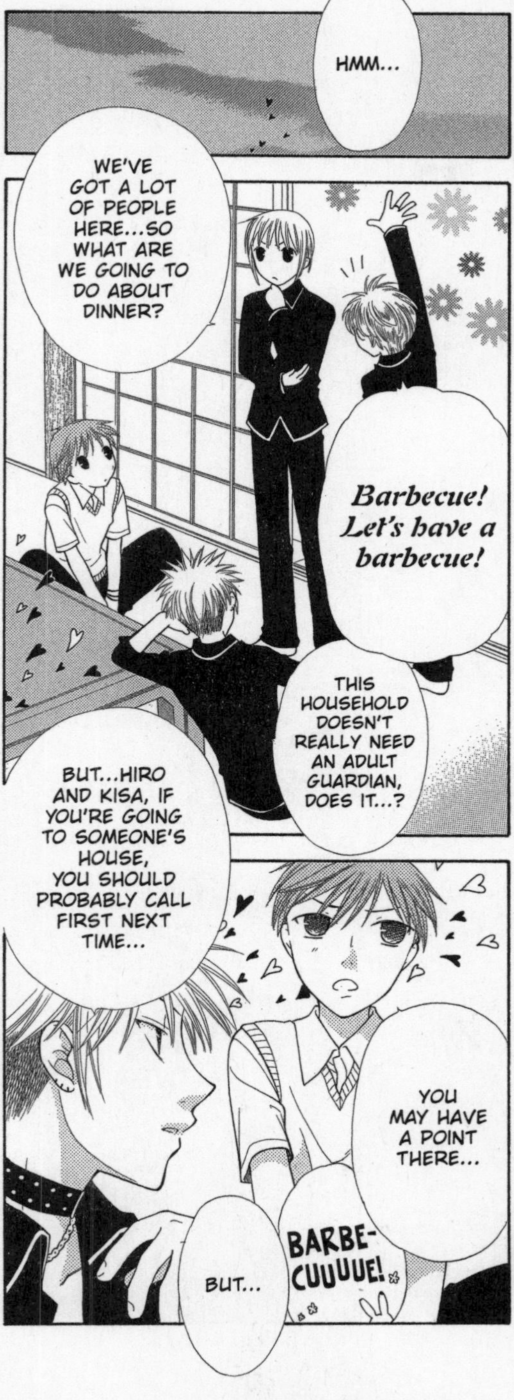
HMM...
WE'VE GOT A LOT OF PEOPLE HERE...SO WHAT ARE WE GOING TO DO ABOUT DINNER?
Barbecue! Let's have a barbecue!
THIS HOUSEHOLD DOESN'T REALLY NEED AN ADULT GUARDIAN, DOES IT...?
BUT...HIRO AND KISA, IF YOU'RE GOING TO SOMEONE'S HOUSE, YOU SHOULD PROBABLY CALL FIRST NEXT TIME...
YOU MAY HAVE A POINT THERE...
BARBE-CUUUUE!
BUT...

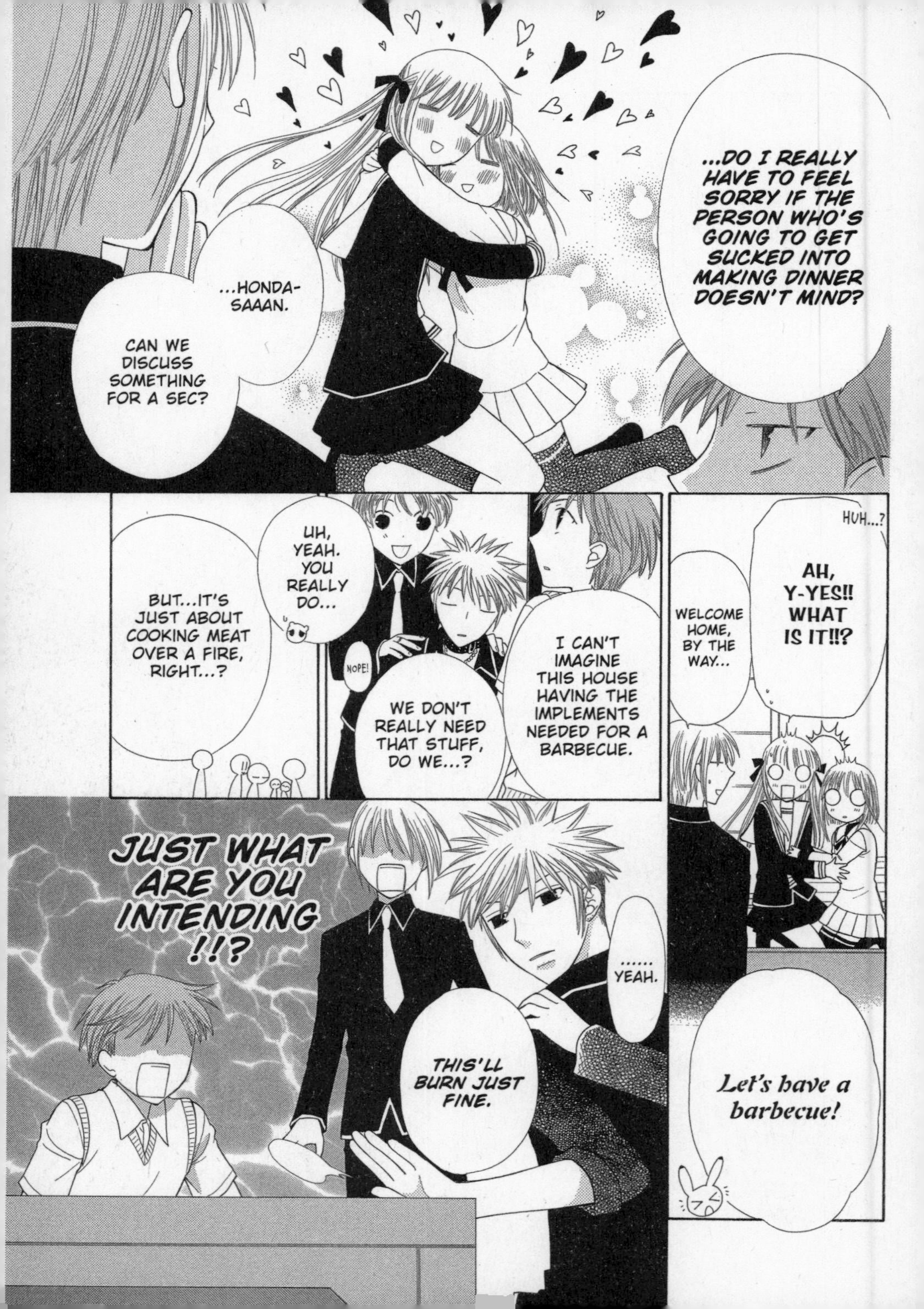
...DO I REALLY HAVE TO FEEL SORRY IF THE PERSON WHO'S GOING TO GET SUCKED INTO MAKING DINNER DOESN'T MIND?
...HONDA-SAAAN.
CAN WE DISCUSS SOMETHING FOR A SEC?
HUH...?
AH, Y-YES!! WHAT IS IT!!?
WELCOME HOME, BY THE WAY...
Let's have a barbecue!
I CAN'T IMAGINE THIS HOUSE HAVING THE IMPLEMENTS NEEDED FOR A BARBECUE.
WE DON'T REALLY NEED THAT STUFF, DO WE...?
NOPE!
UH, YEAH. YOU REALLY DO...
BUT...IT'S JUST ABOUT COOKING MEAT OVER A FIRE, RIGHT...?
......YEAH.
THIS'LL BURN JUST FINE.
JUST WHAT ARE YOU INTENDING!!?

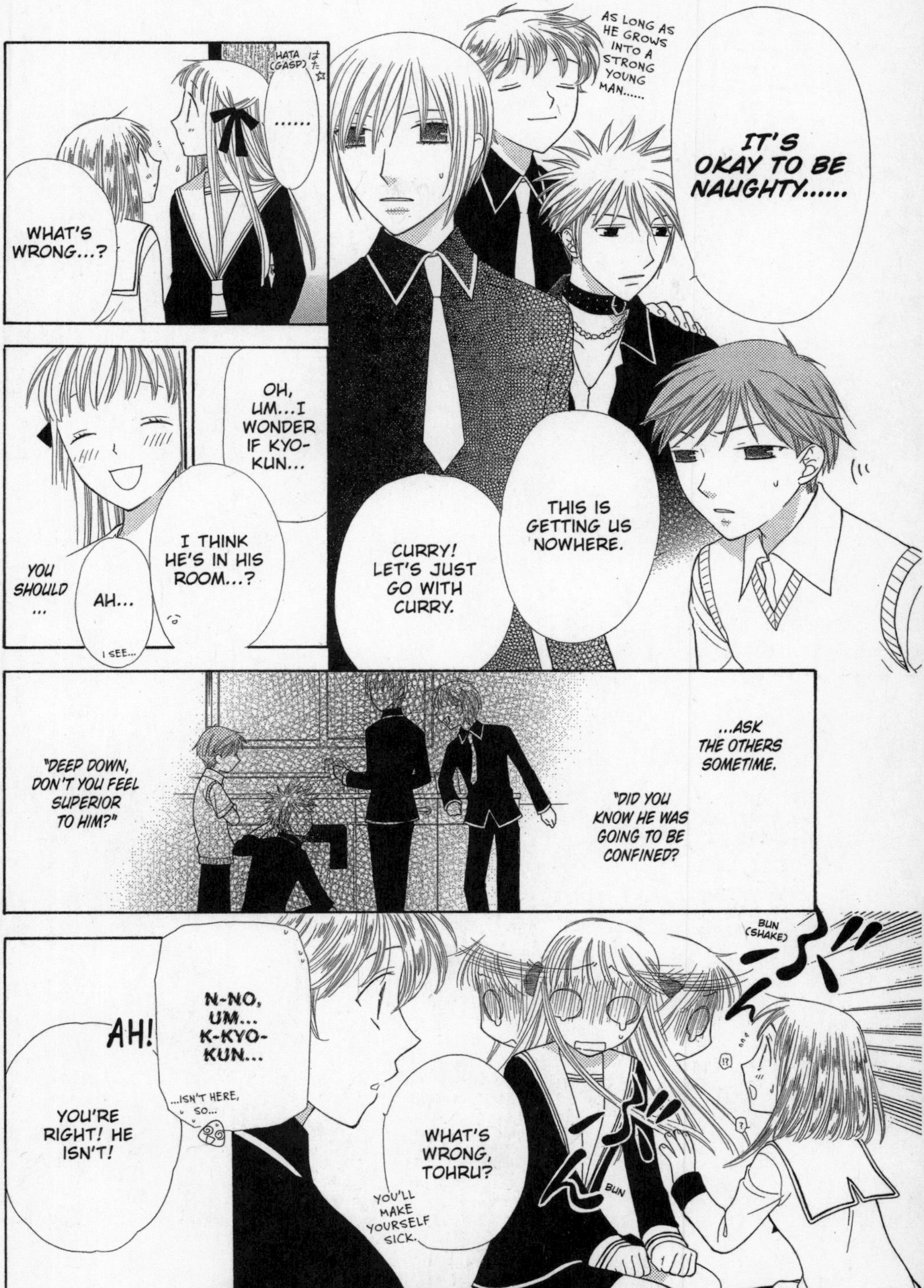
IT'S OKAY TO BE NAUGHTY......
AS LONG AS HE GROWS INTO A STRONG YOUNG MAN......
THIS IS GETTING US NOWHERE.
CURRY! LET'S JUST GO WITH CURRY.
HATA (GASP) はた☆
......
WHAT'S WRONG...?
OH, UM...I WONDER IF KYO-KUN...
I THINK HE'S IN HIS ROOM...?
AH...
I SEE...
YOU SHOULD ...
...ASK THE OTHERS SOMETIME.
"DID YOU KNOW HE WAS GOING TO BE CONFINED?
"DEEP DOWN, DON'T YOU FEEL SUPERIOR TO HIM?"
BUN (SHAKE)
BUN
WHAT'S WRONG, TOHRU?
YOU'LL MAKE YOURSELF SICK.
N-NO, UM... K-KYO-KUN...
...ISN'T HERE, SO...
AH!
YOU'RE RIGHT! HE ISN'T!

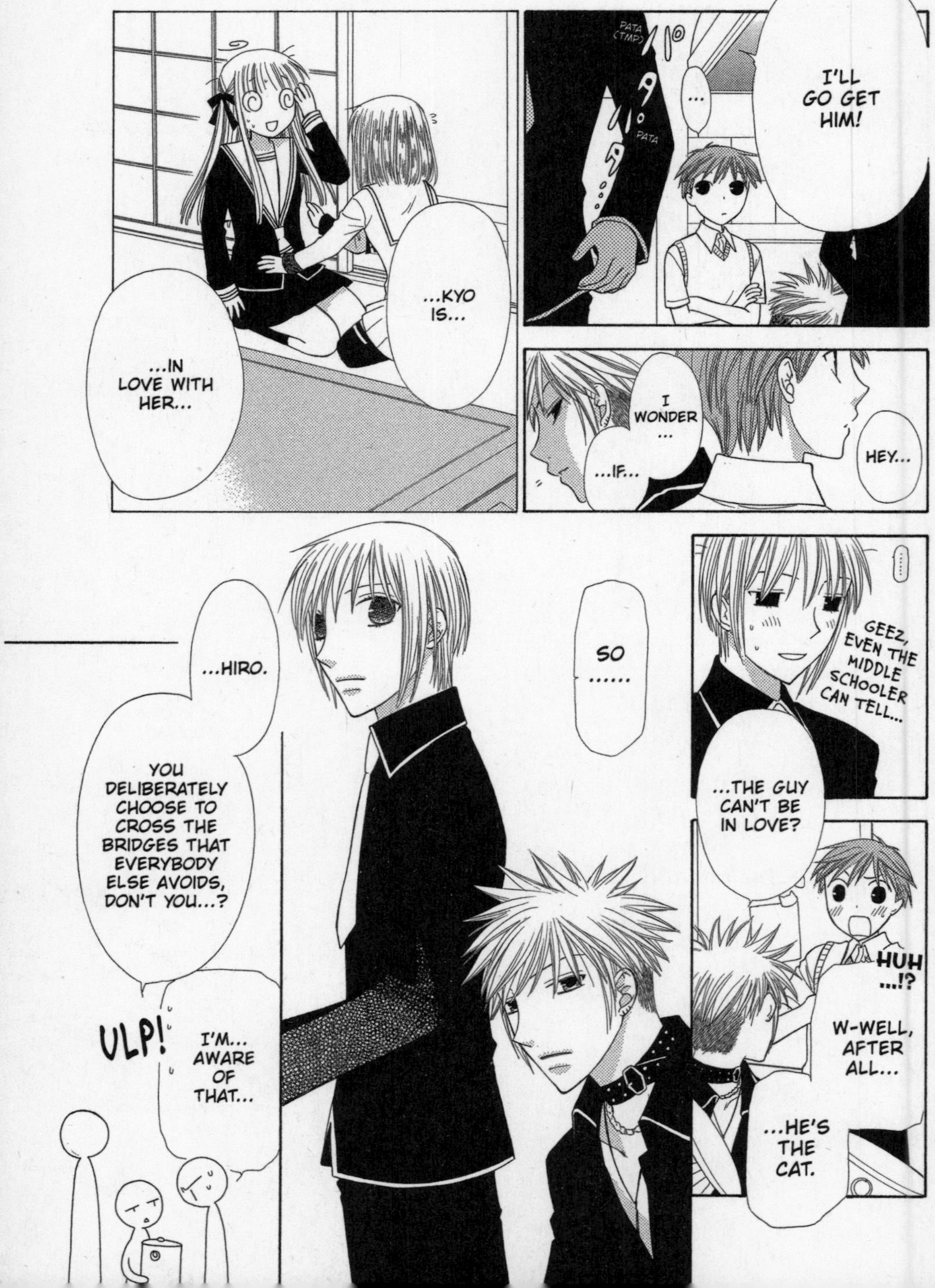

PATA (TMP) PATA
...
I'LL GO GET HIM!
HEY...
I WONDER ...
...IF...
...KYO IS...
...IN LOVE WITH HER...
!......
GEEZ, EVEN THE MIDDLE SCHOOLER CAN TELL...
SO ......
...THE GUY CAN'T BE IN LOVE?
HUH ...!?
W-WELL, AFTER ALL...
...HE'S THE CAT.
...HIRO.
YOU DELIBERATELY CHOOSE TO CROSS THE BRIDGES THAT EVERYBODY ELSE AVOIDS, DON'T YOU...?
ULP!
I'M... AWARE OF THAT...

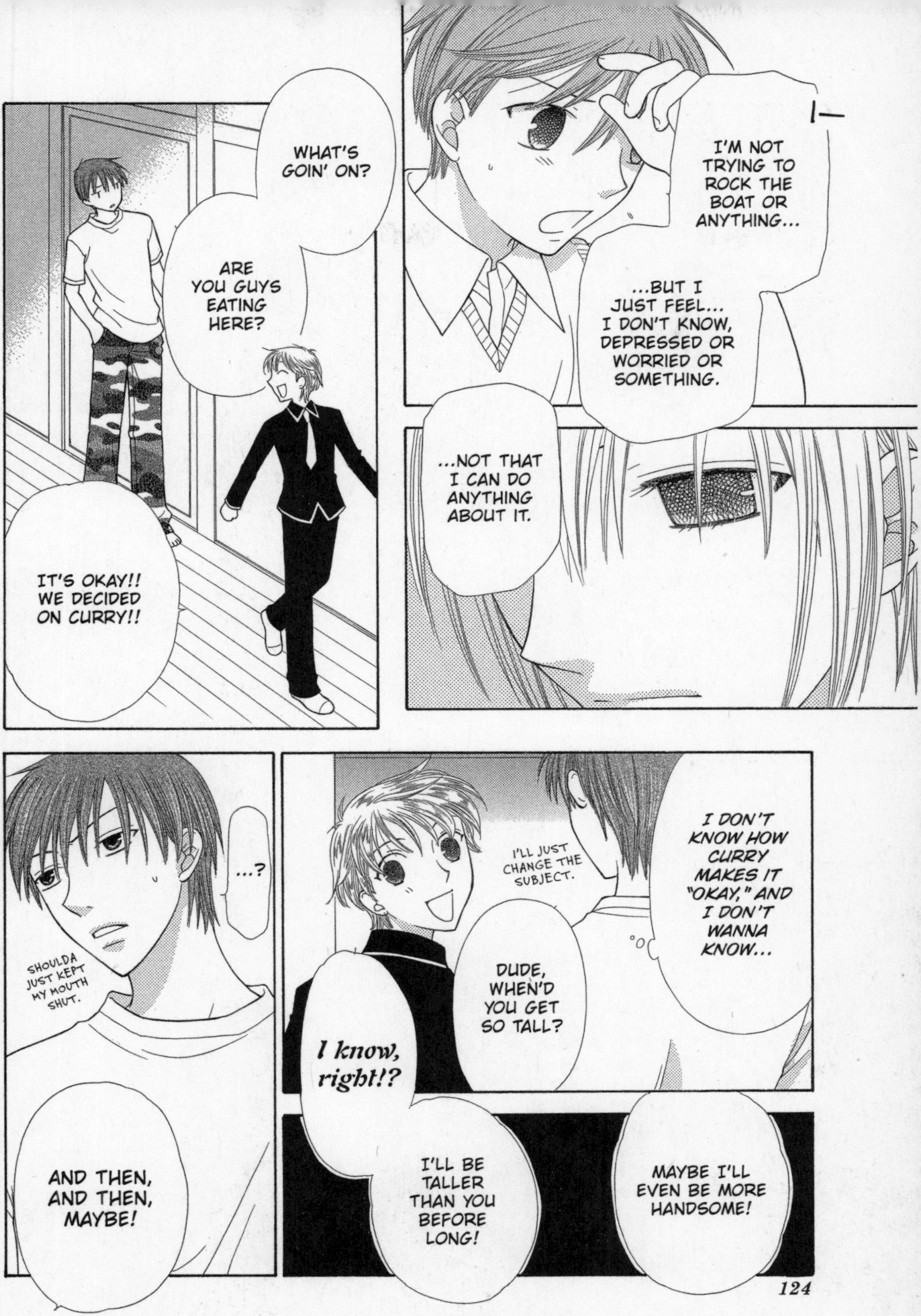
I–
I'M NOT TRYING TO ROCK THE BOAT OR ANYTHING...
...BUT I JUST FEEL... I DON'T KNOW, DEPRESSED OR WORRIED OR SOMETHING.
...NOT THAT I CAN DO ANYTHING ABOUT IT.
WHAT'S GOIN' ON?
ARE YOU GUYS EATING HERE?
IT'S OKAY!! WE DECIDED ON CURRY!!
I DON'T KNOW HOW CURRY MAKES IT "OKAY," AND I DON'T WANNA KNOW...
I'LL JUST CHANGE THE SUBJECT.
DUDE, WHEN'D YOU GET SO TALL?
I know, right!?
MAYBE I'LL EVEN BE MORE HANDSOME!
I'LL BE TALLER THAN YOU BEFORE LONG!
...?
SHOULDA JUST KEPT MY MOUTH SHUT.
AND THEN, AND THEN, MAYBE!

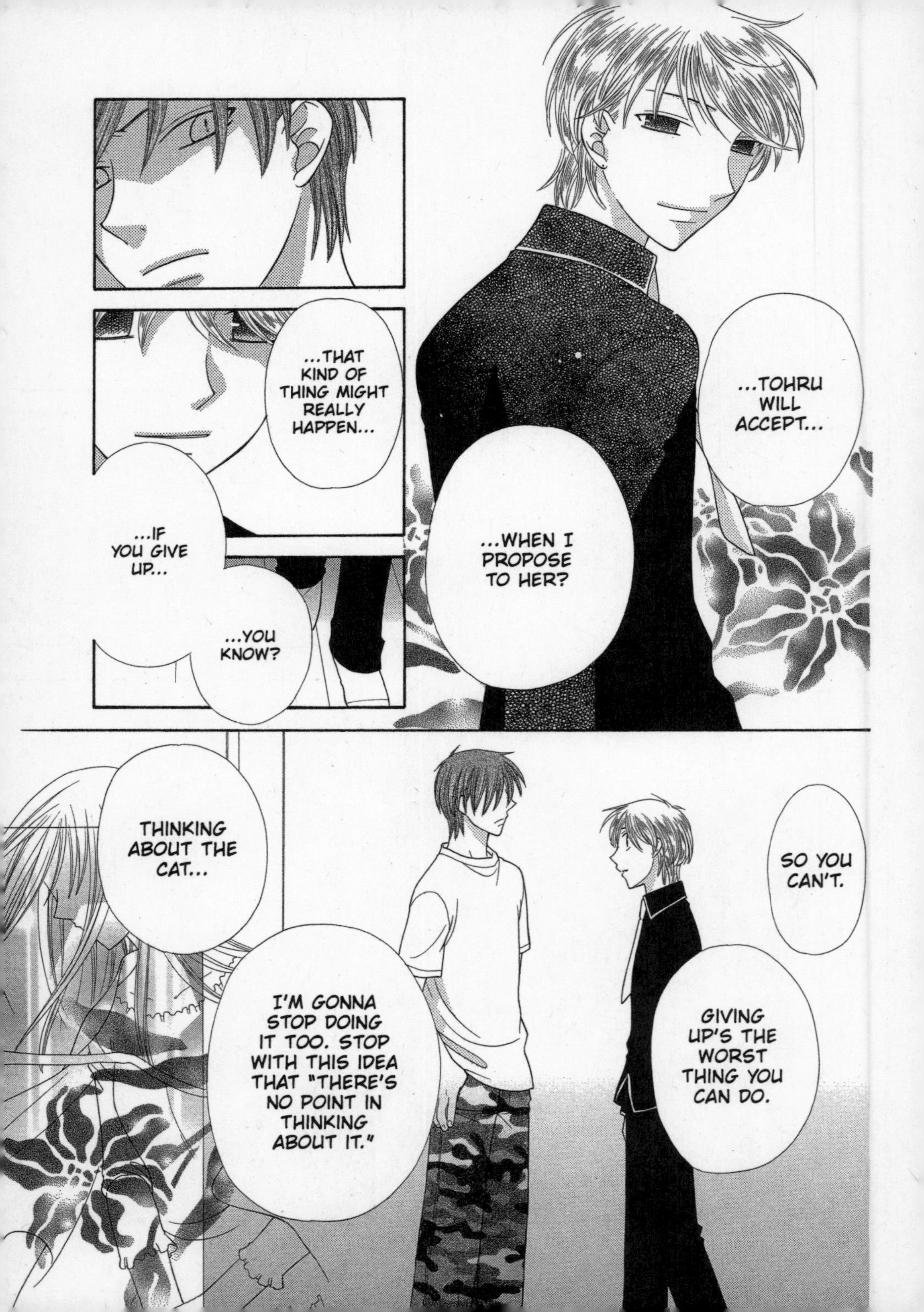
...TOHRU WILL ACCEPT...
...WHEN I PROPOSE TO HER?
...THAT KIND OF THING MIGHT REALLY HAPPEN...
...IF YOU GIVE UP...
...YOU KNOW?
SO YOU CAN'T.
GIVING UP'S THE WORST THING YOU CAN DO.
THINKING ABOUT THE CAT...
I'M GONNA STOP DOING IT TOO. STOP WITH THIS IDEA THAT "THERE'S NO POINT IN THINKING ABOUT IT."

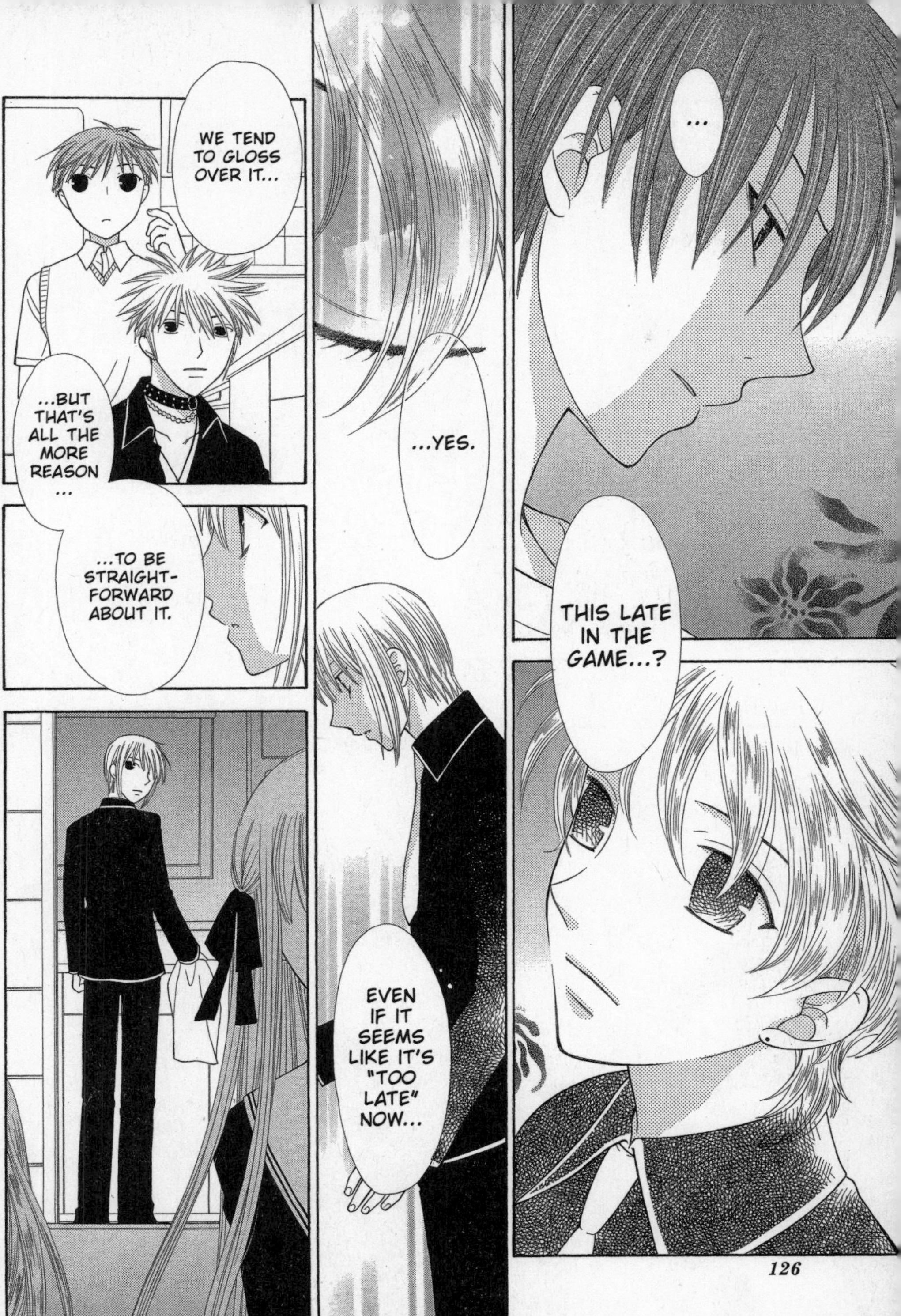
...
THIS LATE IN THE GAME...?
...YES.
EVEN IF IT SEEMS LIKE IT'S "TOO LATE" NOW...
WE TEND TO GLOSS OVER IT...
...BUT THAT'S ALL THE MORE REASON...
...TO BE STRAIGHTFORWARD ABOUT IT.

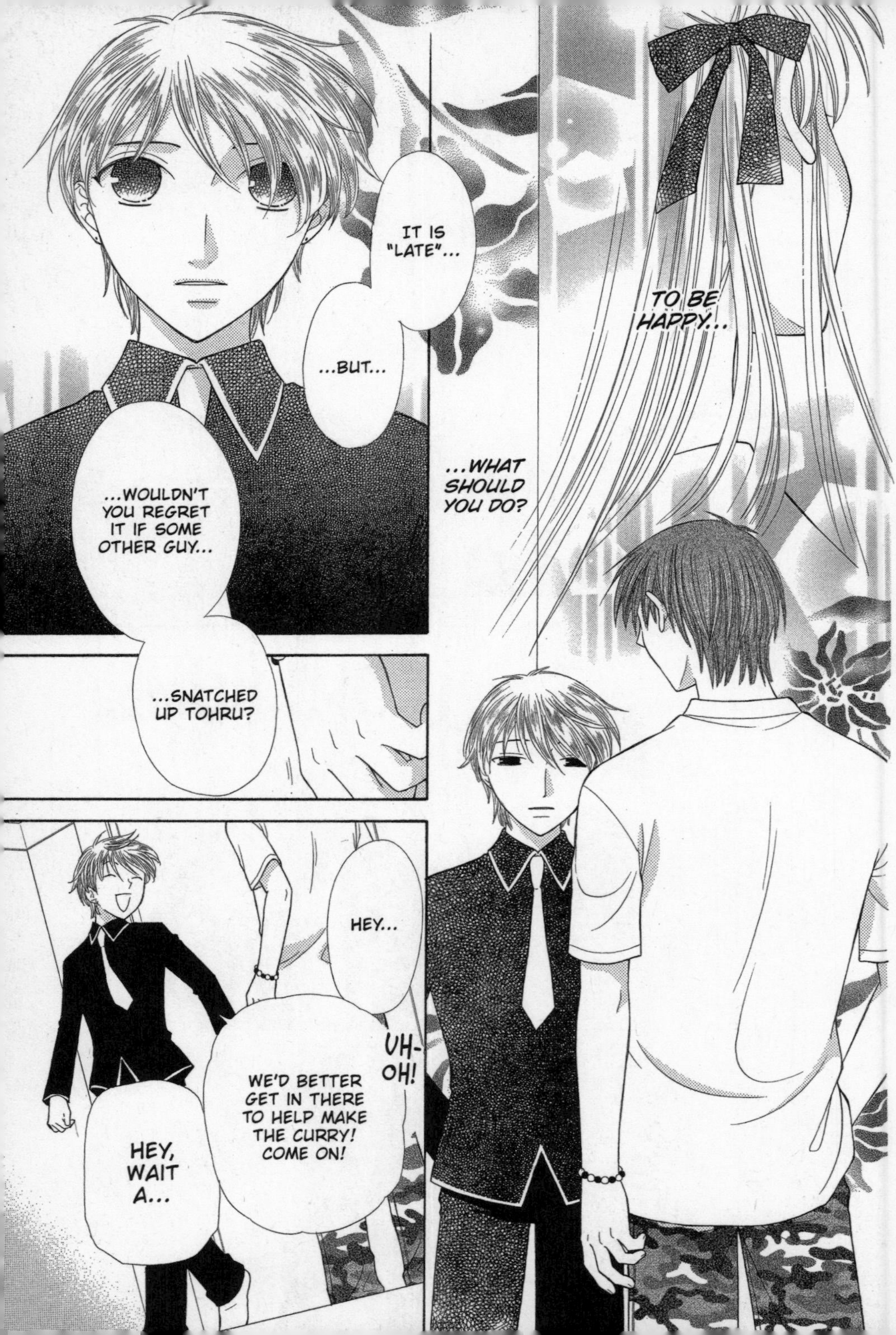

TO BE HAPPY...
...WHAT SHOULD YOU DO?
IT IS "LATE"...
...BUT...
...WOULDN'T YOU REGRET IT IF SOME OTHER GUY...
...SNATCHED UP TOHRU?
HEY...
UH-OH!
WE'D BETTER GET IN THERE TO HELP MAKE THE CURRY! COME ON!
HEY, WAIT A...

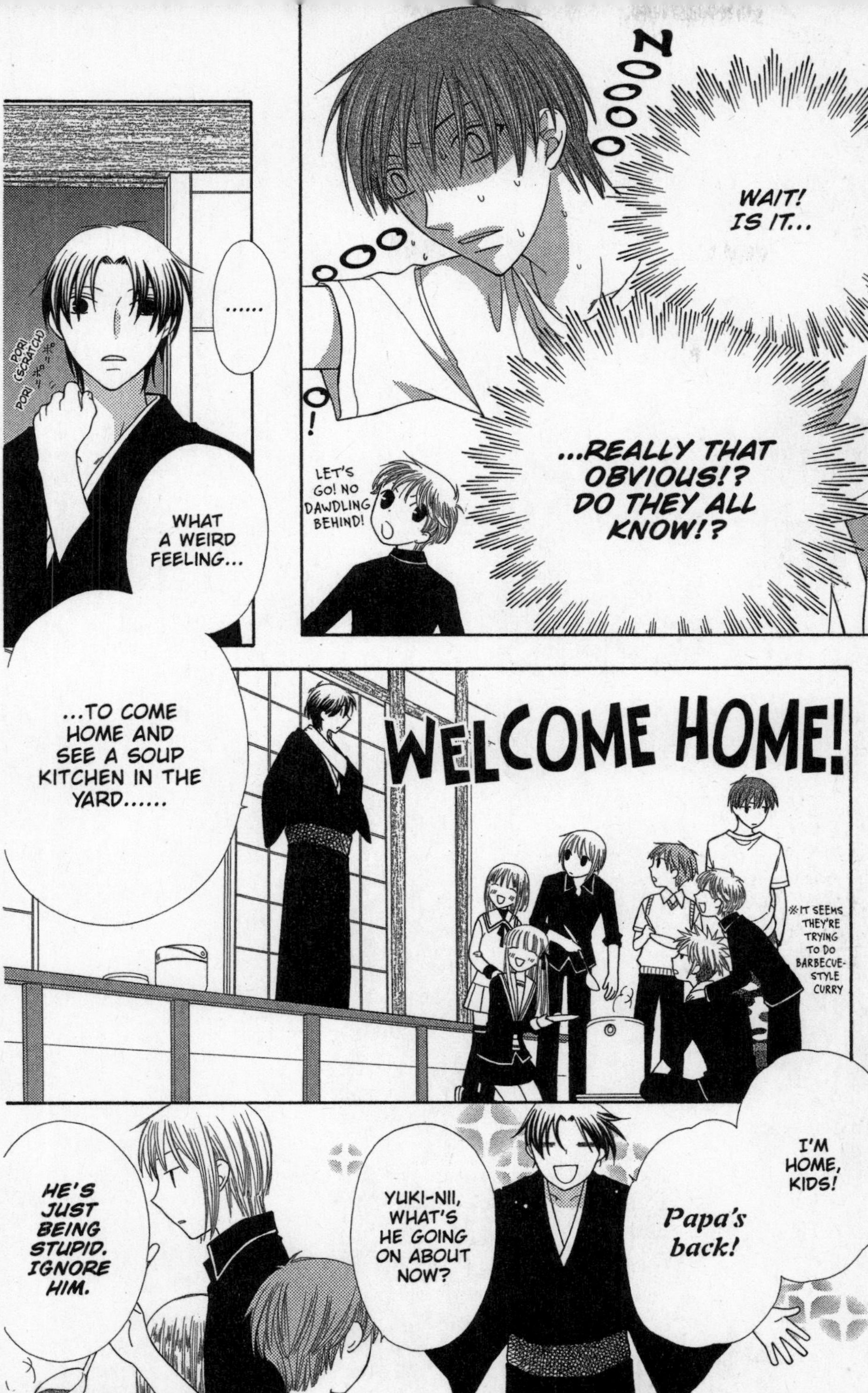
NOOOOOOOO!
WAIT! IS IT...
...REALLY THAT OBVIOUS!? DO THEY ALL KNOW!?
LET'S GO! NO DAWDLING BEHIND!
......
PORI PORI (SCRATCH)
WHAT A WEIRD FEELING...
...TO COME HOME AND SEE A SOUP KITCHEN IN THE YARD......
WELCOME HOME!
※IT SEEMS THEY'RE TRYING TO DO BARBECUE-STYLE CURRY
I'M HOME, KIDS!
Papa's back!
YUKI-NII, WHAT'S HE GOING ON ABOUT NOW?
HE'S JUST BEING STUPID. IGNORE HIM.

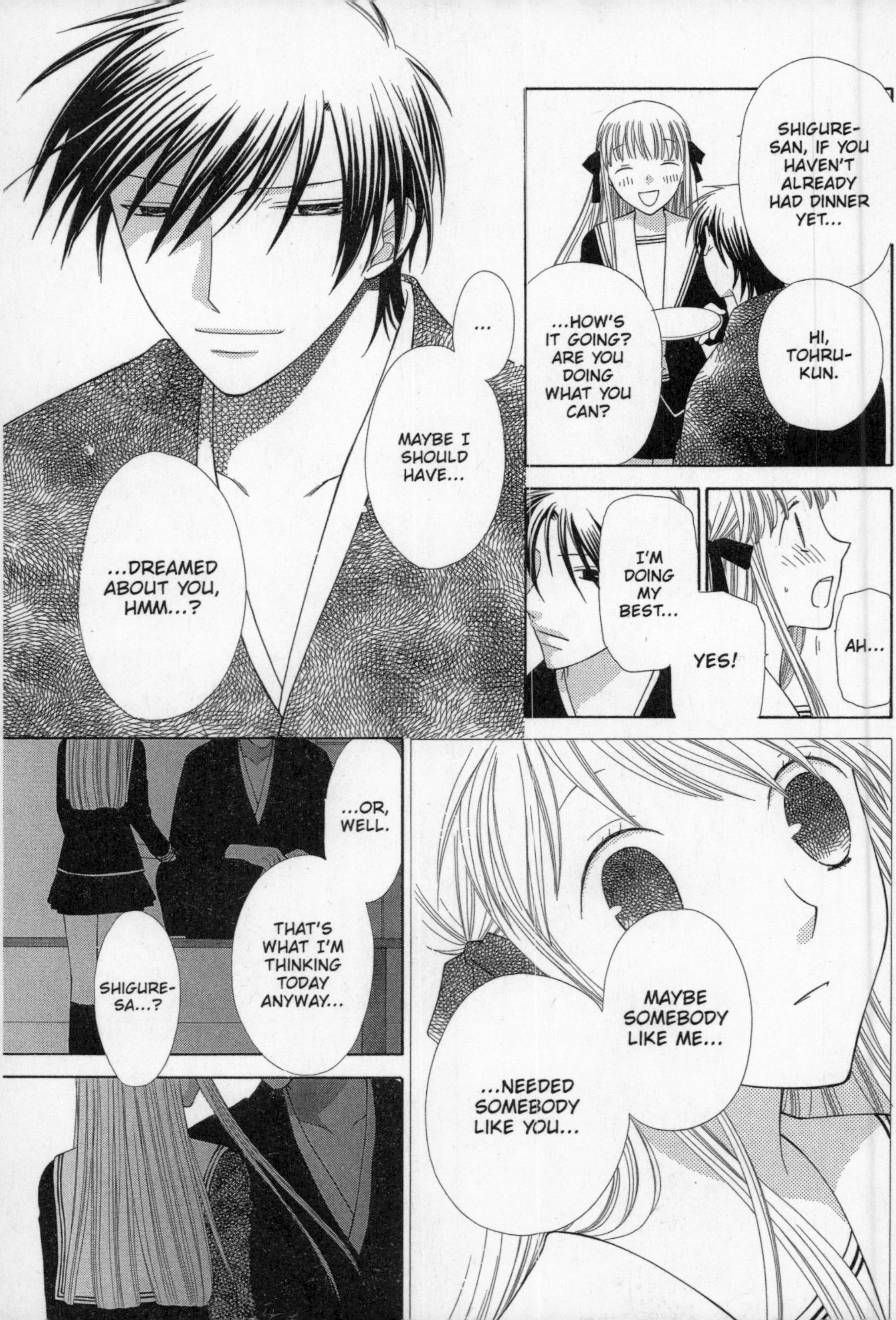
SHIGURE-SAN, IF YOU HAVEN'T ALREADY HAD DINNER YET...
HI, TOHRU-KUN.
...HOW'S IT GOING? ARE YOU DOING WHAT YOU CAN?
AH...
YES!
I'M DOING MY BEST...
...
MAYBE I SHOULD HAVE...
...DREAMED ABOUT YOU, HMM...?
MAYBE SOMEBODY LIKE ME...
...NEEDED SOMEBODY LIKE YOU...
...OR, WELL.
THAT'S WHAT I'M THINKING TODAY ANYWAY...
SHIGURE-SA...?

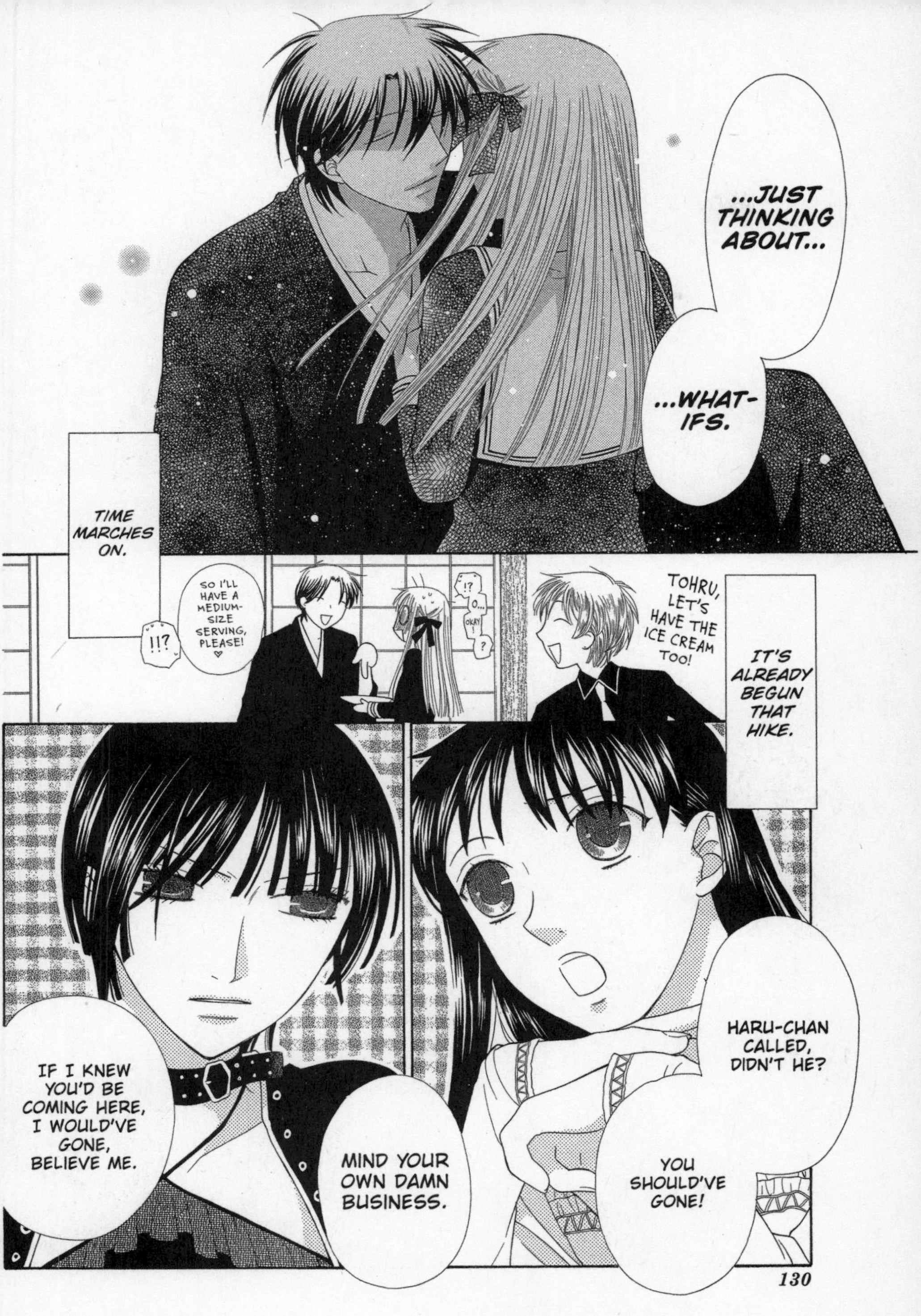
...JUST THINKING ABOUT...
...WHAT-IFS.
TIME MARCHES ON.
IT'S ALREADY BEGUN THAT HIKE.
TOHRU, LET'S HAVE THE ICE CREAM TOO!
!?
O... OKAY!
?
SO I'LL HAVE A MEDIUM-SIZE SERVING, PLEASE! ♡
!!?
HARU-CHAN CALLED, DIDN'T HE?
YOU SHOULD'VE GONE!
MIND YOUR OWN DAMN BUSINESS.
IF I KNEW YOU'D BE COMING HERE, I WOULD'VE GONE, BELIEVE ME.

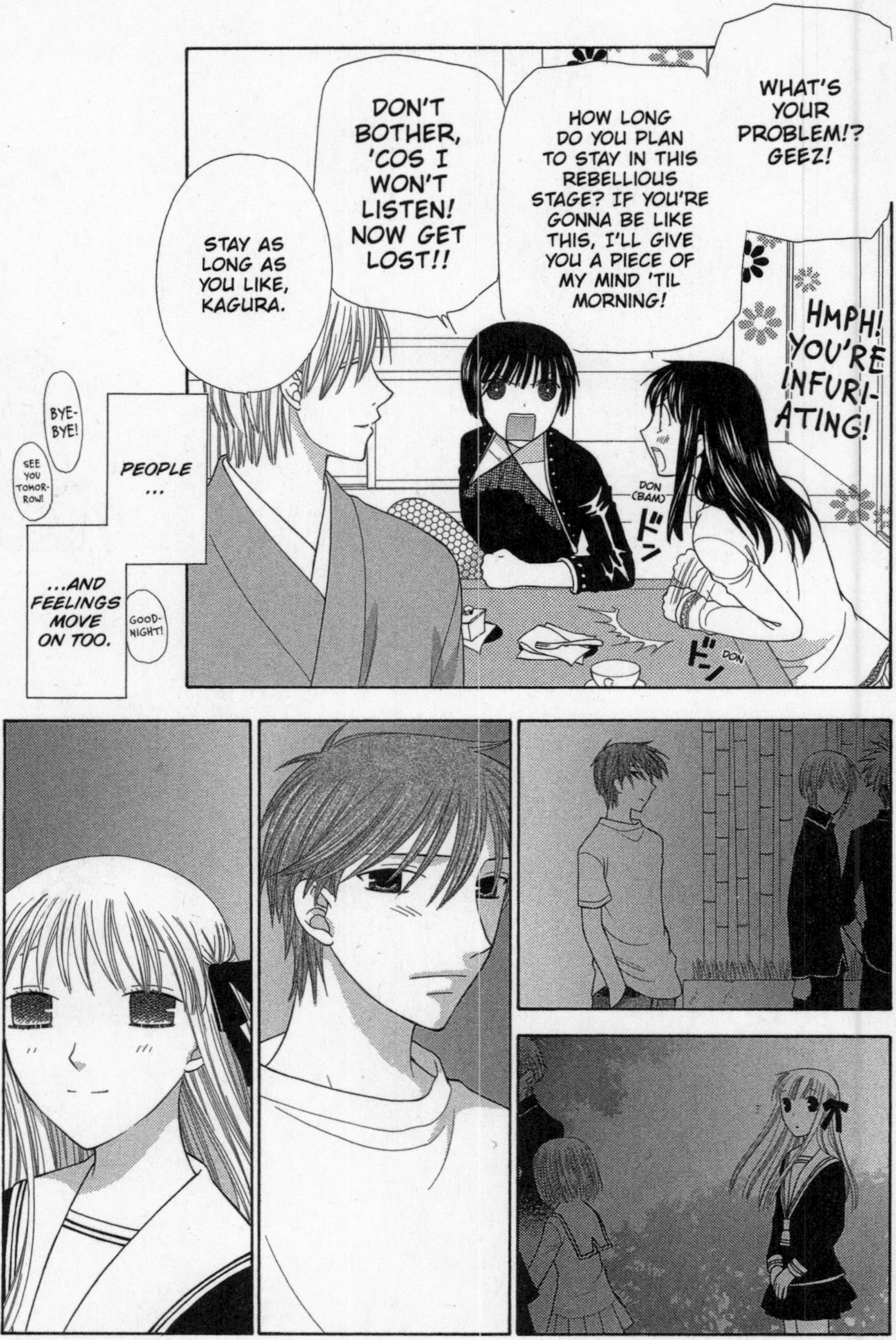

WHAT'S YOUR PROBLEM!? GEEZ!
HMPH! YOU'RE INFURIATING!
HOW LONG DO YOU PLAN TO STAY IN THIS REBELLIOUS STAGE? IF YOU'RE GONNA BE LIKE THIS, I'LL GIVE YOU A PIECE OF MY MIND 'TIL MORNING!
ドン
DON (BAM)
ドン
DON
DON'T BOTHER, 'COS I WON'T LISTEN! NOW GET LOST!!
STAY AS LONG AS YOU LIKE, KAGURA.
PEOPLE ...
BYE-BYE!
SEE YOU TOMOR-ROW!
...AND FEELINGS MOVE ON TOO.
GOOD-NIGHT!

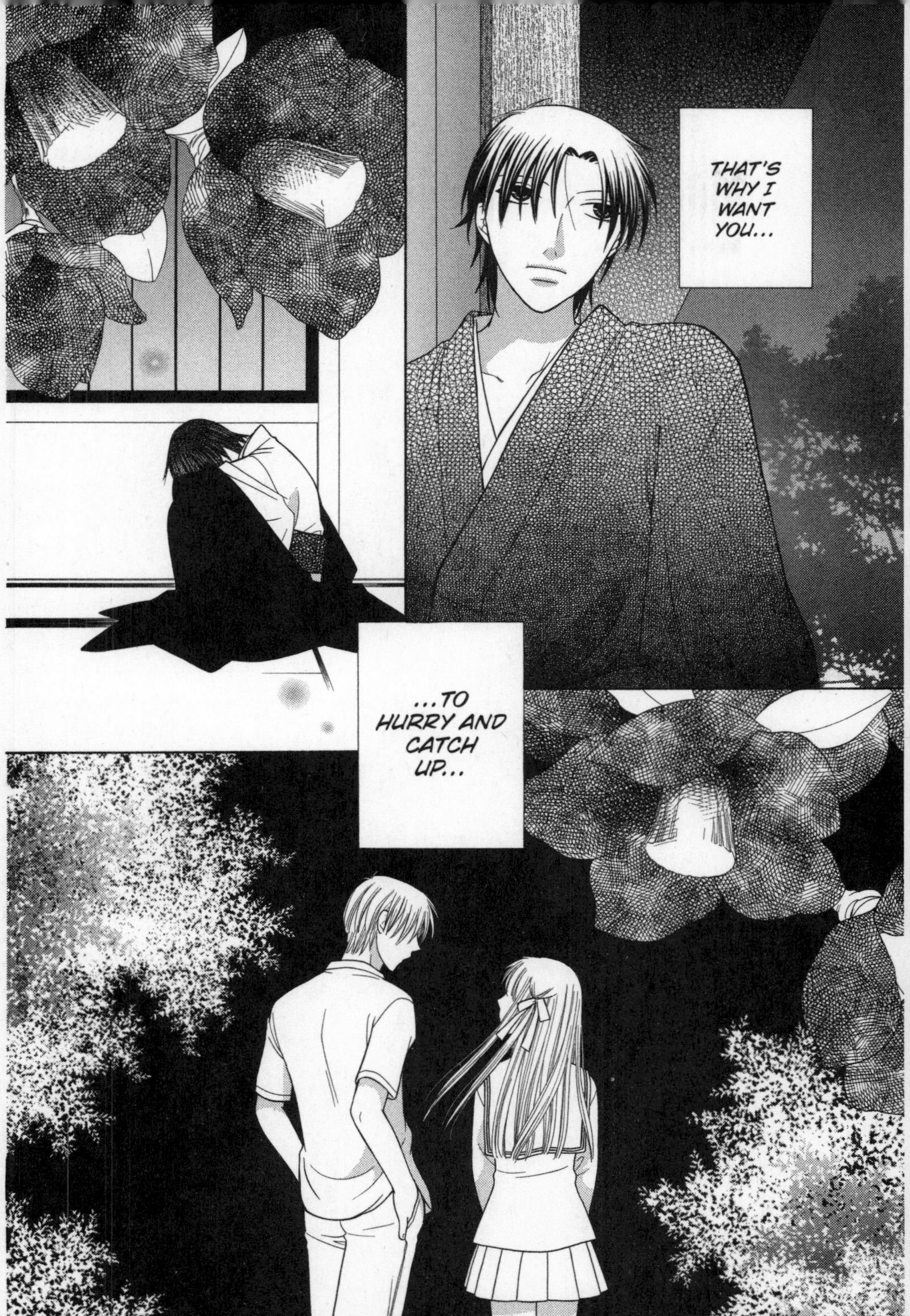
THAT'S WHY I WANT YOU...
...TO HURRY AND CATCH UP...

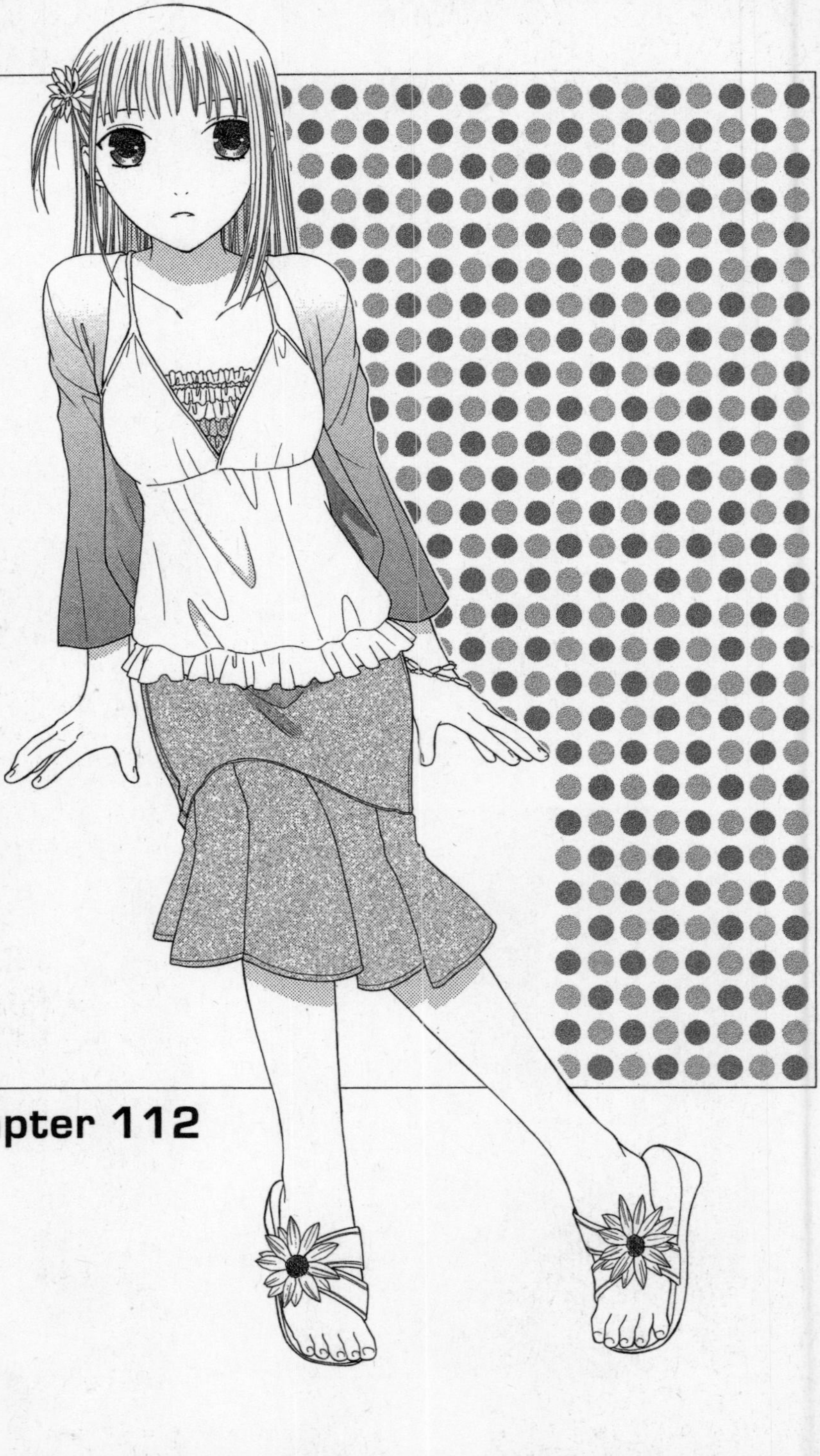

Chapter 112

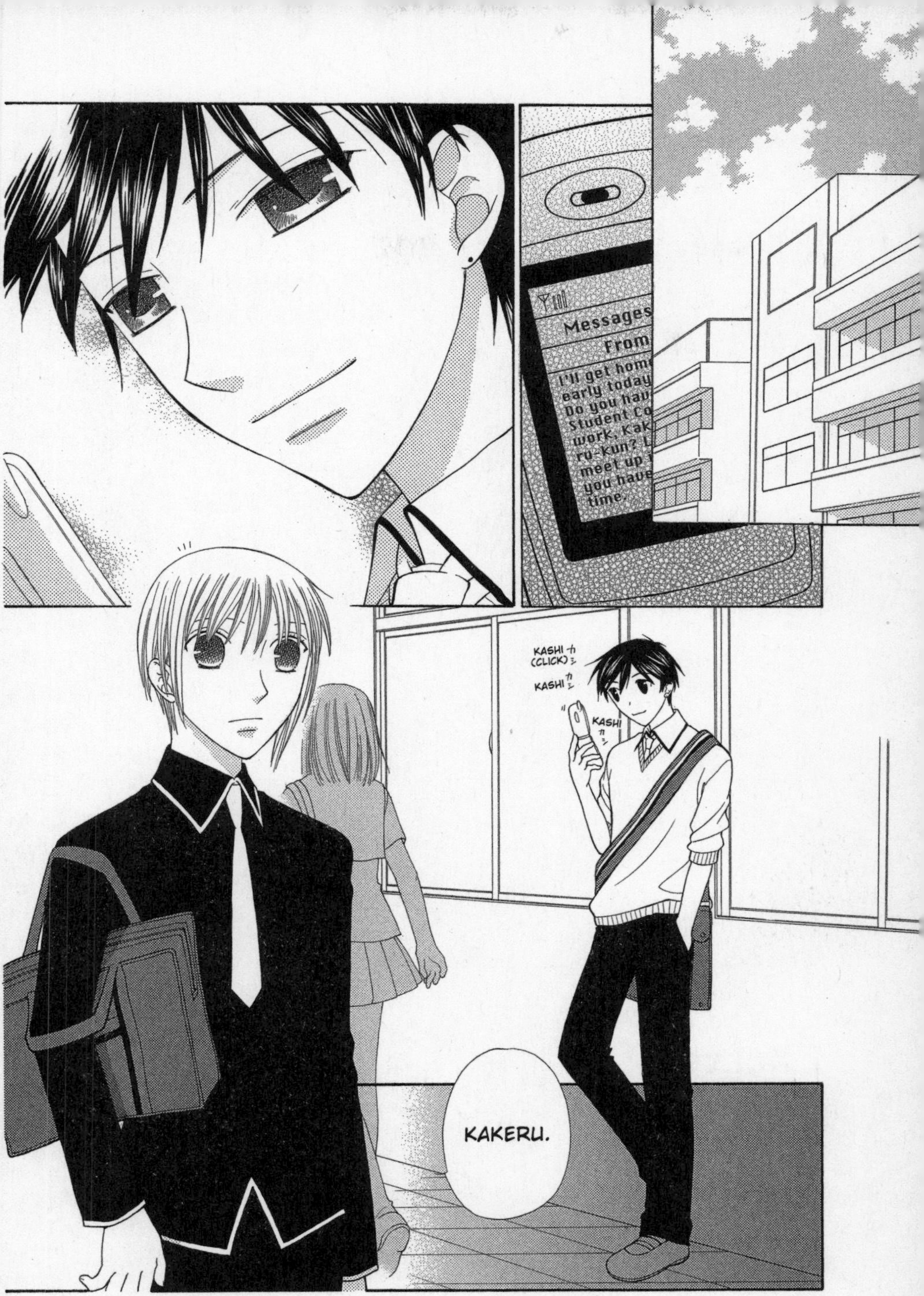

Messages
From
I'll get home
early today
Do you hav
Student Co
work, Kak
ru-kun? L
meet up i
you have
time.
KASHI (CLICK)
KASHI
KASHI
KAKERU.

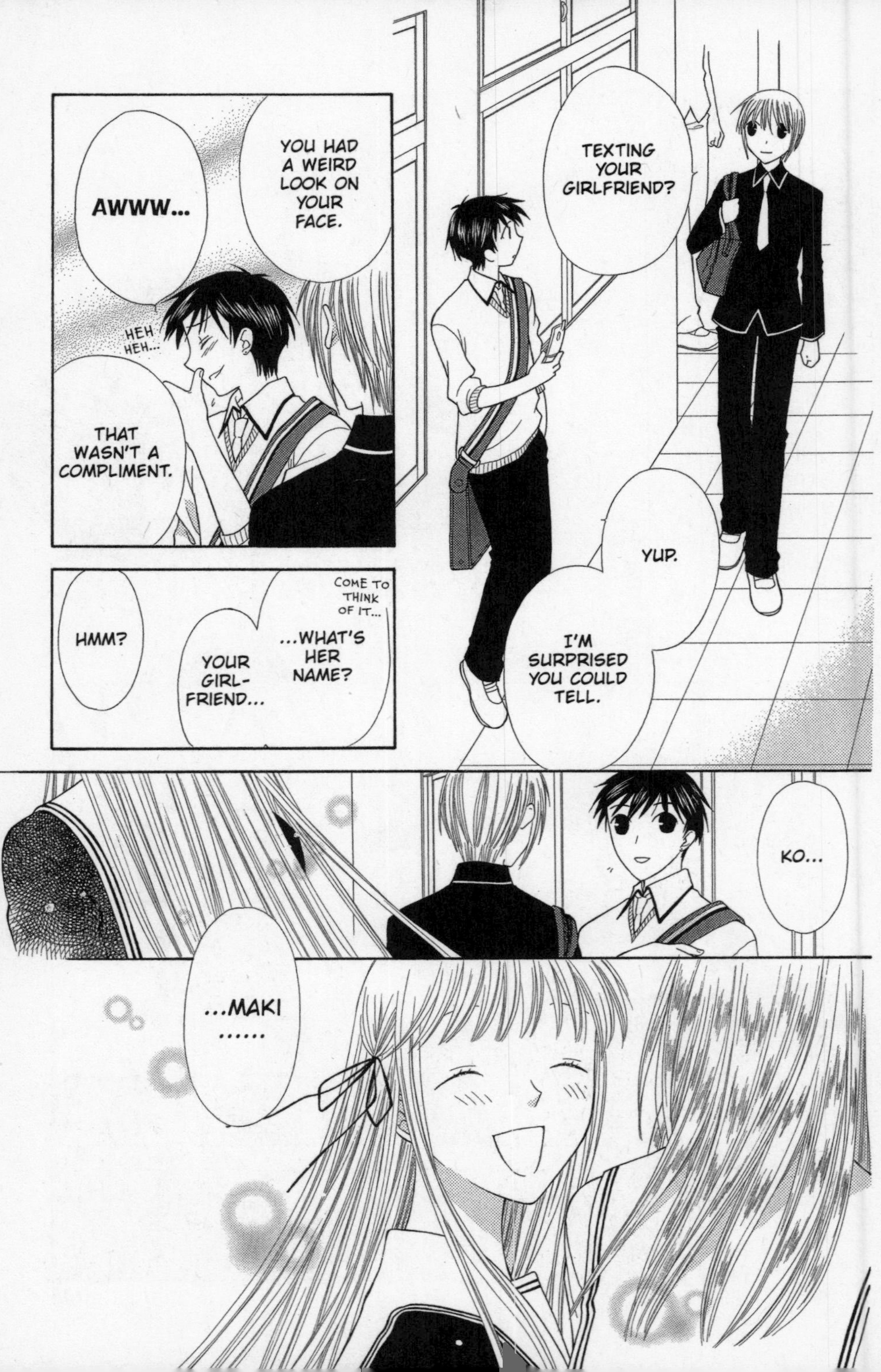
TEXTING YOUR GIRLFRIEND?
YUP.
I'M SURPRISED YOU COULD TELL.
YOU HAD A WEIRD LOOK ON YOUR FACE.
AWWW...
HEH HEH...
THAT WASN'T A COMPLIMENT.
COME TO THINK OF IT...
...WHAT'S HER NAME?
YOUR GIRL-FRIEND...
HMM?
KO...
...MAKI ......

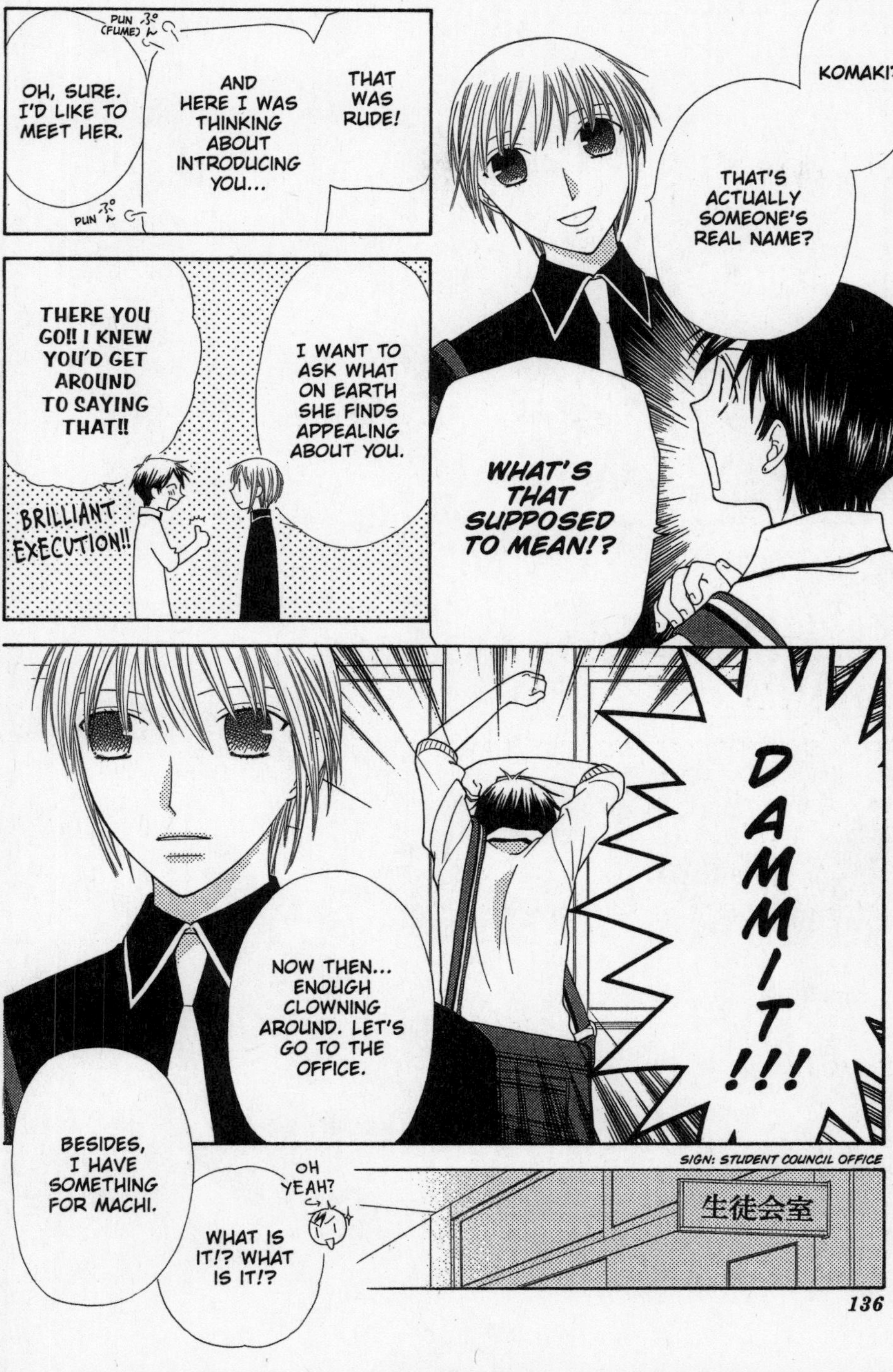
KOMAKI?
THAT'S ACTUALLY SOMEONE'S REAL NAME?
WHAT'S THAT SUPPOSED TO MEAN!?
THAT WAS RUDE!
AND HERE I WAS THINKING ABOUT INTRODUCING YOU...
PUN ぷん (FUME)
OH, SURE. I'D LIKE TO MEET HER.
PUN ぷん
I WANT TO ASK WHAT ON EARTH SHE FINDS APPEALING ABOUT YOU.
THERE YOU GO!! I KNEW YOU'D GET AROUND TO SAYING THAT!!
BRILLIANT EXECUTION!!
DAMMIT!!!
NOW THEN... ENOUGH CLOWNING AROUND. LET'S GO TO THE OFFICE.
BESIDES, I HAVE SOMETHING FOR MACHI.
SIGN: STUDENT COUNCIL OFFICE
生徒会室
OH YEAH?
WHAT IS IT!? WHAT IS IT!?

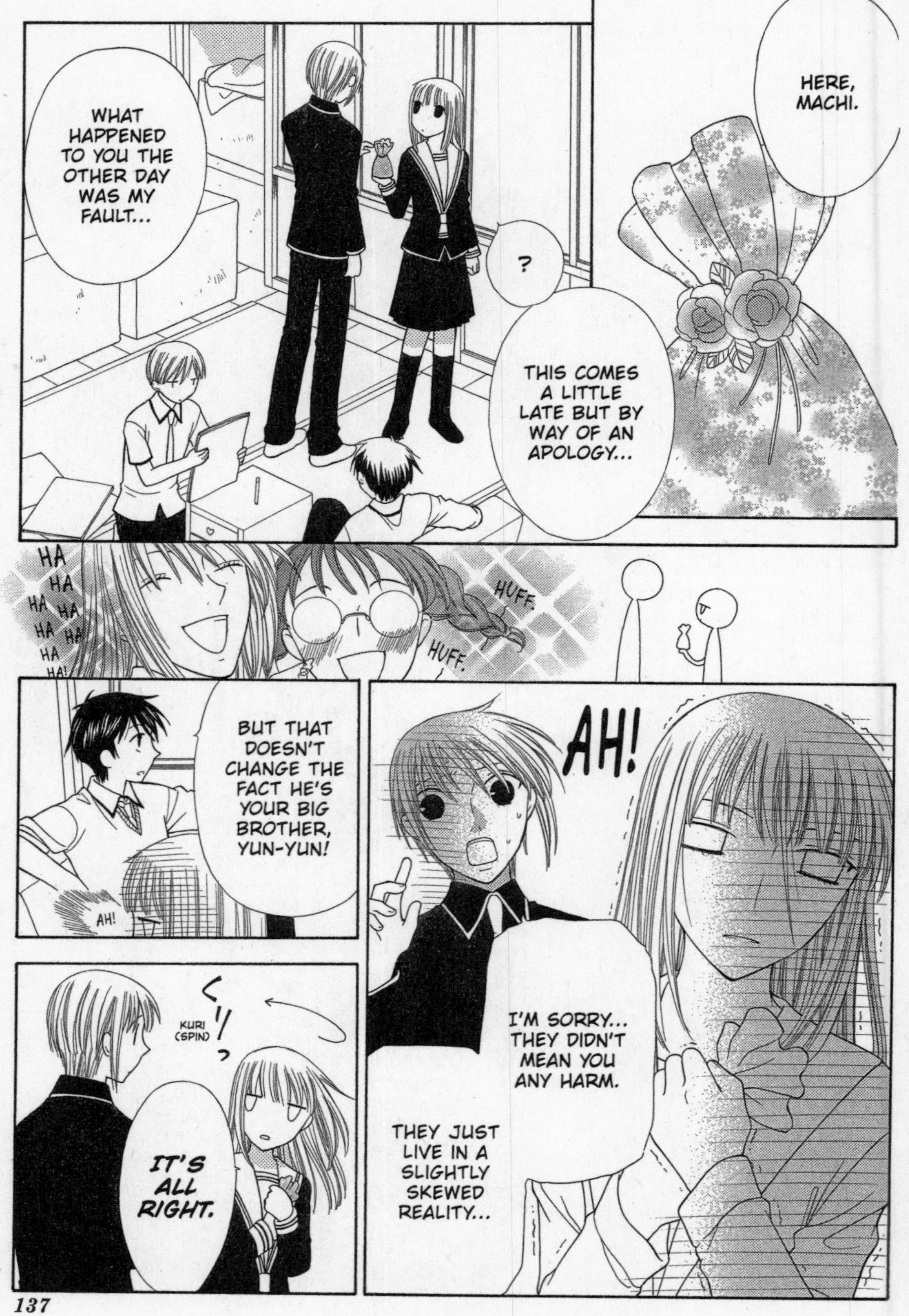
HERE, MACHI.
?
THIS COMES A LITTLE LATE BUT BY WAY OF AN APOLOGY...
WHAT HAPPENED TO YOU THE OTHER DAY WAS MY FAULT...
HUFF.
HUFF.
HA HA HA HA HA HA HA HA!
AH!
I'M SORRY... THEY DIDN'T MEAN YOU ANY HARM.
THEY JUST LIVE IN A SLIGHTLY SKEWED REALITY...
BUT THAT DOESN'T CHANGE THE FACT HE'S YOUR BIG BROTHER, YUN-YUN!
AH!
KURI (SPIN)
IT'S ALL RIGHT.

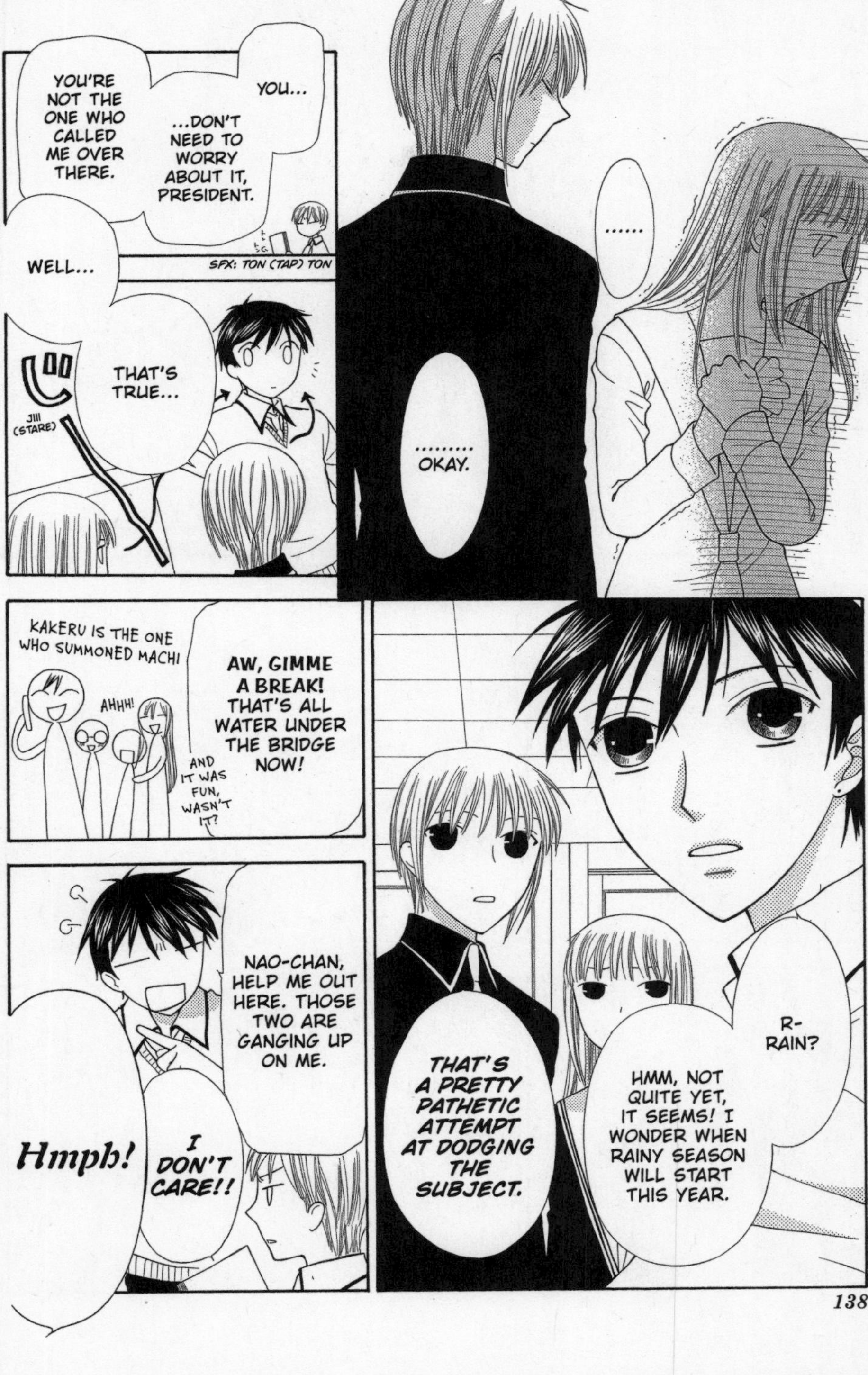
......
....
OKAY.
YOU...
...DON'T NEED TO WORRY ABOUT IT, PRESIDENT.
YOU'RE NOT THE ONE WHO CALLED ME OVER THERE.
SFX: TON (TAP) TON
WELL...
THAT'S TRUE...
JIII (STARE)
R-RAIN?
HMM, NOT QUITE YET, IT SEEMS! I WONDER WHEN RAINY SEASON WILL START THIS YEAR.
THAT'S A PRETTY PATHETIC ATTEMPT AT DODGING THE SUBJECT.
AW, GIMME A BREAK! THAT'S ALL WATER UNDER THE BRIDGE NOW!
KAKERU IS THE ONE WHO SUMMONED MACHI
AHHH!
AND IT WAS FUN, WASN'T IT?
NAO-CHAN, HELP ME OUT HERE. THOSE TWO ARE GANGING UP ON ME.
I DON'T CARE!!
Hmph!

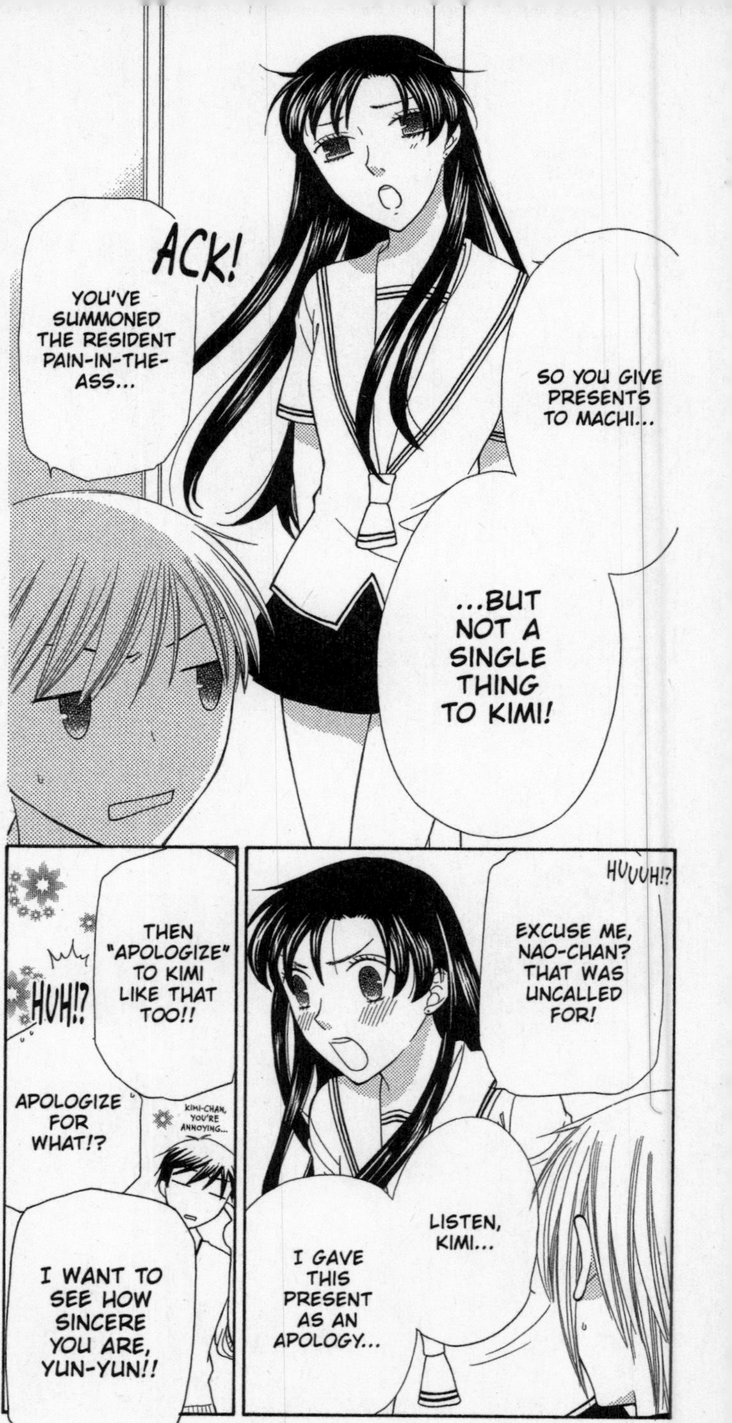
SO YOU GIVE PRESENTS TO MACHI...
...BUT NOT A SINGLE THING TO KIMI!
ACK!
YOU'VE SUMMONED THE RESIDENT PAIN-IN-THE-ASS...
HUUUH!?
EXCUSE ME, NAO-CHAN? THAT WAS UNCALLED FOR!
LISTEN, KIMI...
I GAVE THIS PRESENT AS AN APOLOGY...
THEN "APOLOGIZE" TO KIMI LIKE THAT TOO!!
HUH!?
KIMI-CHAN, YOU'RE ANNOYING...
APOLOGIZE FOR WHAT!?
I WANT TO SEE HOW SINCERE YOU ARE, YUN-YUN!!

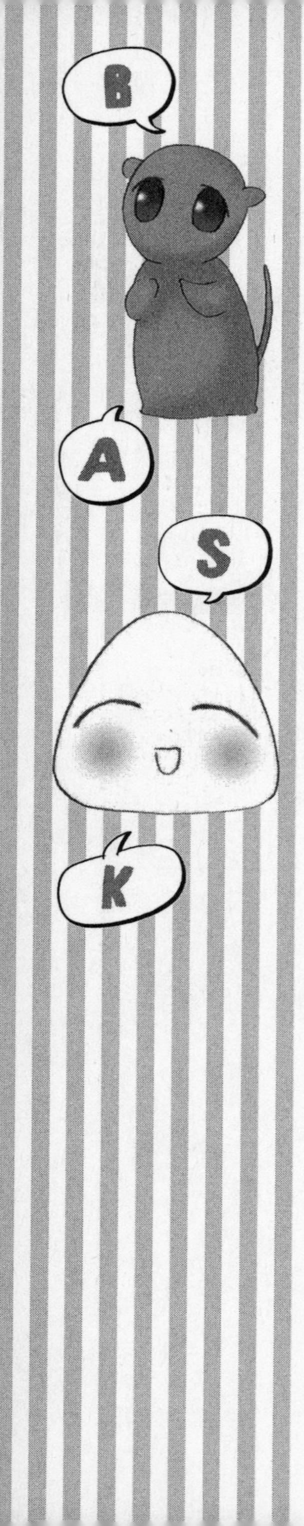
B
A
S
K

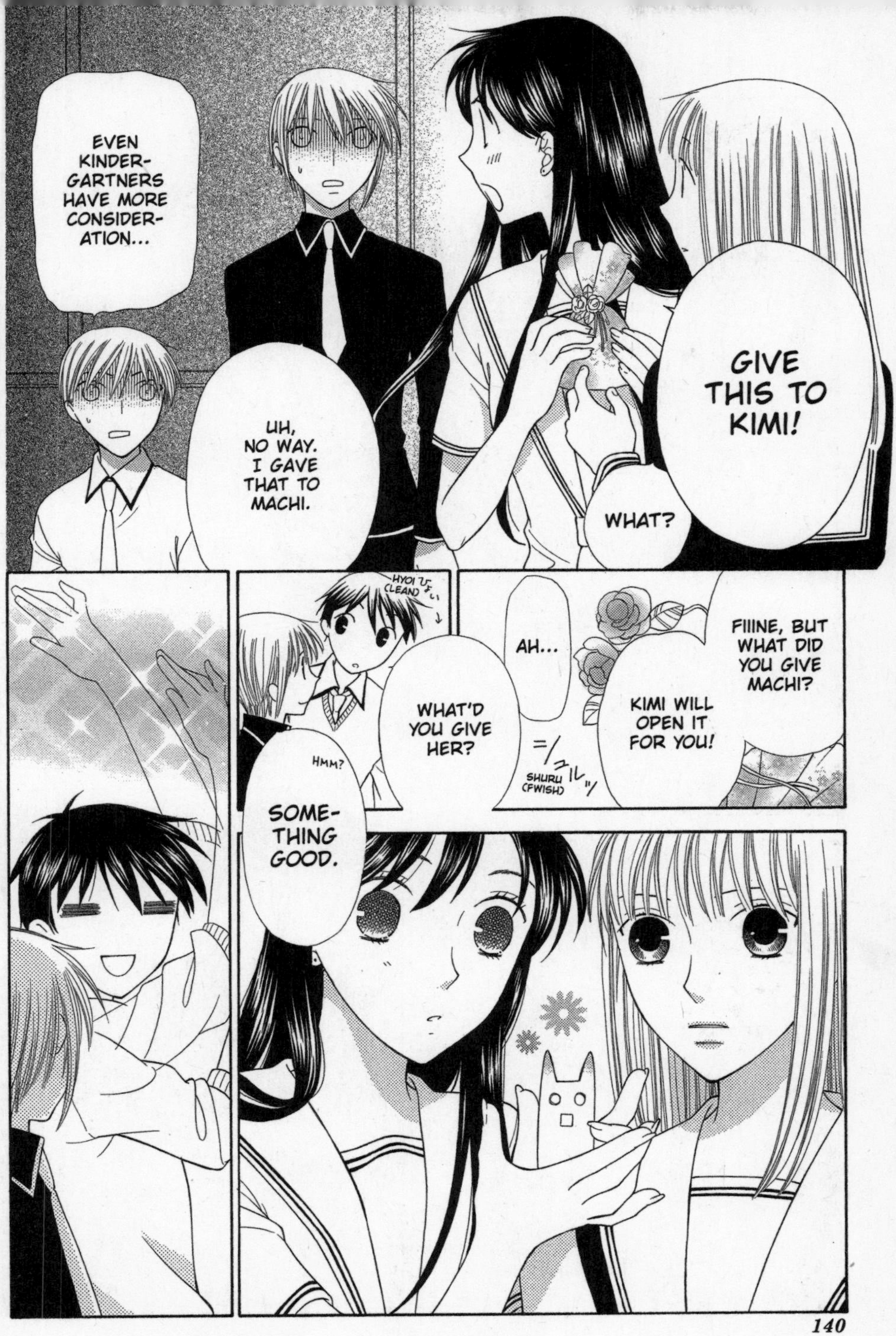
GIVE THIS TO KIMI!
WHAT?
UH, NO WAY. I GAVE THAT TO MACHI.
EVEN KINDER-GARTNERS HAVE MORE CONSIDER-ATION...
FIIINE, BUT WHAT DID YOU GIVE MACHI?
AH...
KIMI WILL OPEN IT FOR YOU!
SHURU (FWISH)
HYOI (LEAN)
WHAT'D YOU GIVE HER?
HMM?
SOME-THING GOOD.

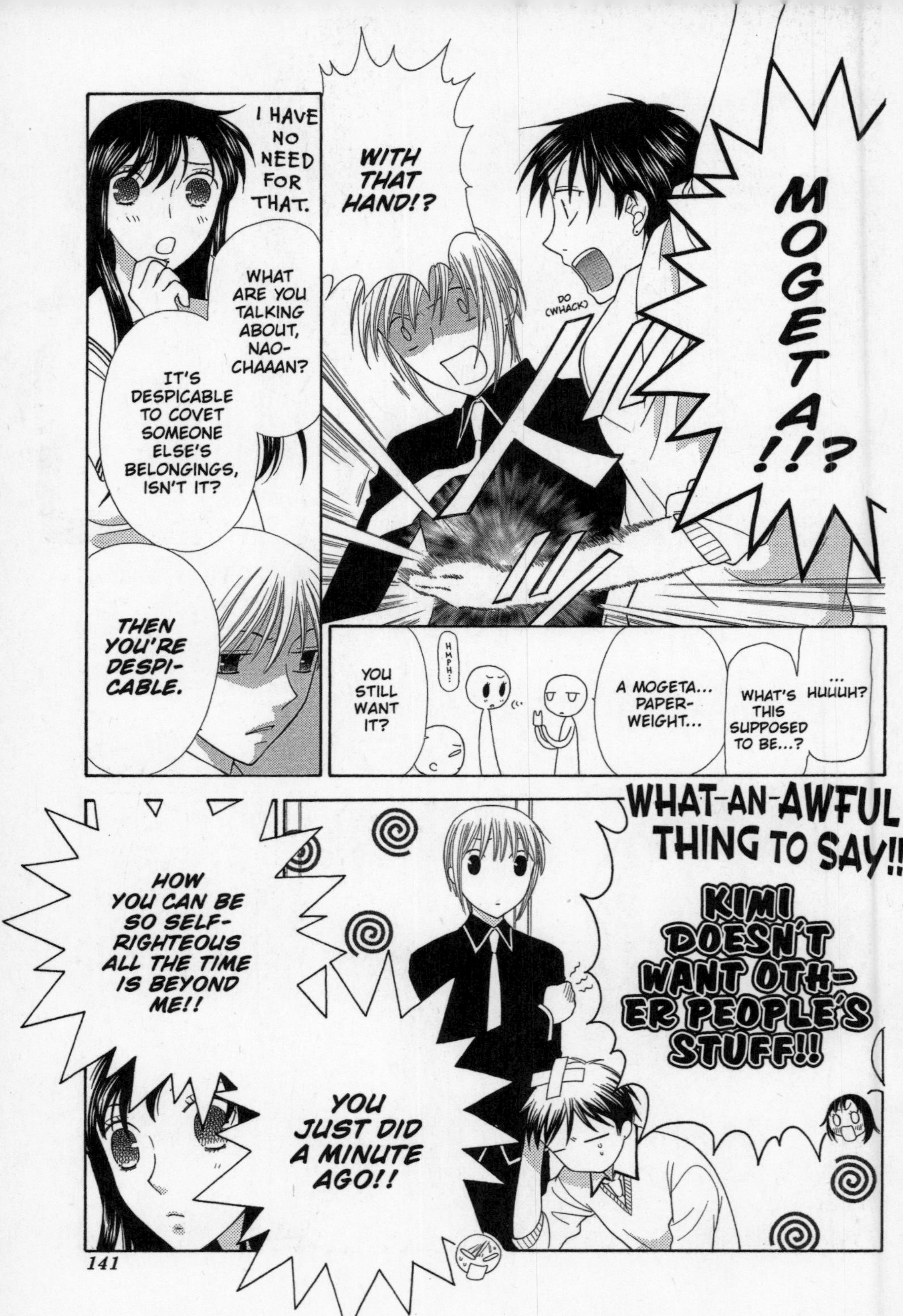

MOGETA!!?
WITH THAT HAND!?
DO (WHACK)
... HUUUH?
WHAT'S THIS SUPPOSED TO BE...?
A MOGETA... PAPER-WEIGHT...
HMPH...
YOU STILL WANT IT?
I HAVE NO NEED FOR THAT.
WHAT ARE YOU TALKING ABOUT, NAO-CHAAAN?
IT'S DESPICABLE TO COVET SOMEONE ELSE'S BELONGINGS, ISN'T IT?
THEN YOU'RE DESPI-CABLE.
WHAT-AN-AWFUL THING TO SAY!!!
KIMI DOESN'T WANT OTH-ER PEOPLE'S STUFF!!
HOW YOU CAN BE SO SELF-RIGHTEOUS ALL THE TIME IS BEYOND ME!!
YOU JUST DID A MINUTE AGO!!

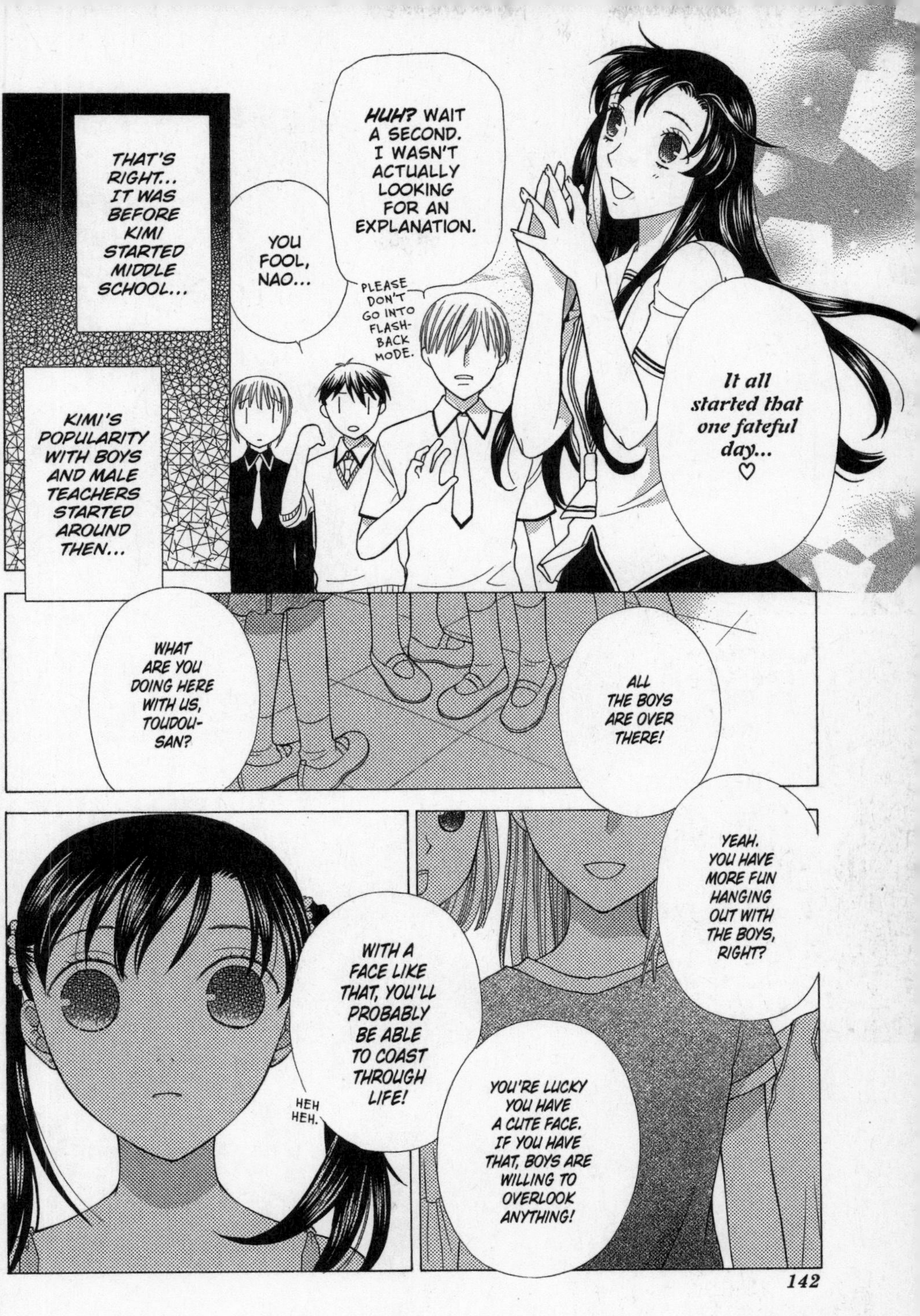
It all started that one fateful day... ♡
HUH? WAIT A SECOND. I WASN'T ACTUALLY LOOKING FOR AN EXPLANATION.
PLEASE DON'T GO INTO FLASH-BACK MODE.
YOU FOOL, NAO...
THAT'S RIGHT... IT WAS BEFORE KIMI STARTED MIDDLE SCHOOL...
KIMI'S POPULARITY WITH BOYS AND MALE TEACHERS STARTED AROUND THEN...
ALL THE BOYS ARE OVER THERE!
WHAT ARE YOU DOING HERE WITH US, TOUDOU-SAN?
YEAH. YOU HAVE MORE FUN HANGING OUT WITH THE BOYS, RIGHT?
YOU'RE LUCKY YOU HAVE A CUTE FACE. IF YOU HAVE THAT, BOYS ARE WILLING TO OVERLOOK ANYTHING!
WITH A FACE LIKE THAT, YOU'LL PROBABLY BE ABLE TO COAST THROUGH LIFE!
HEH HEH.

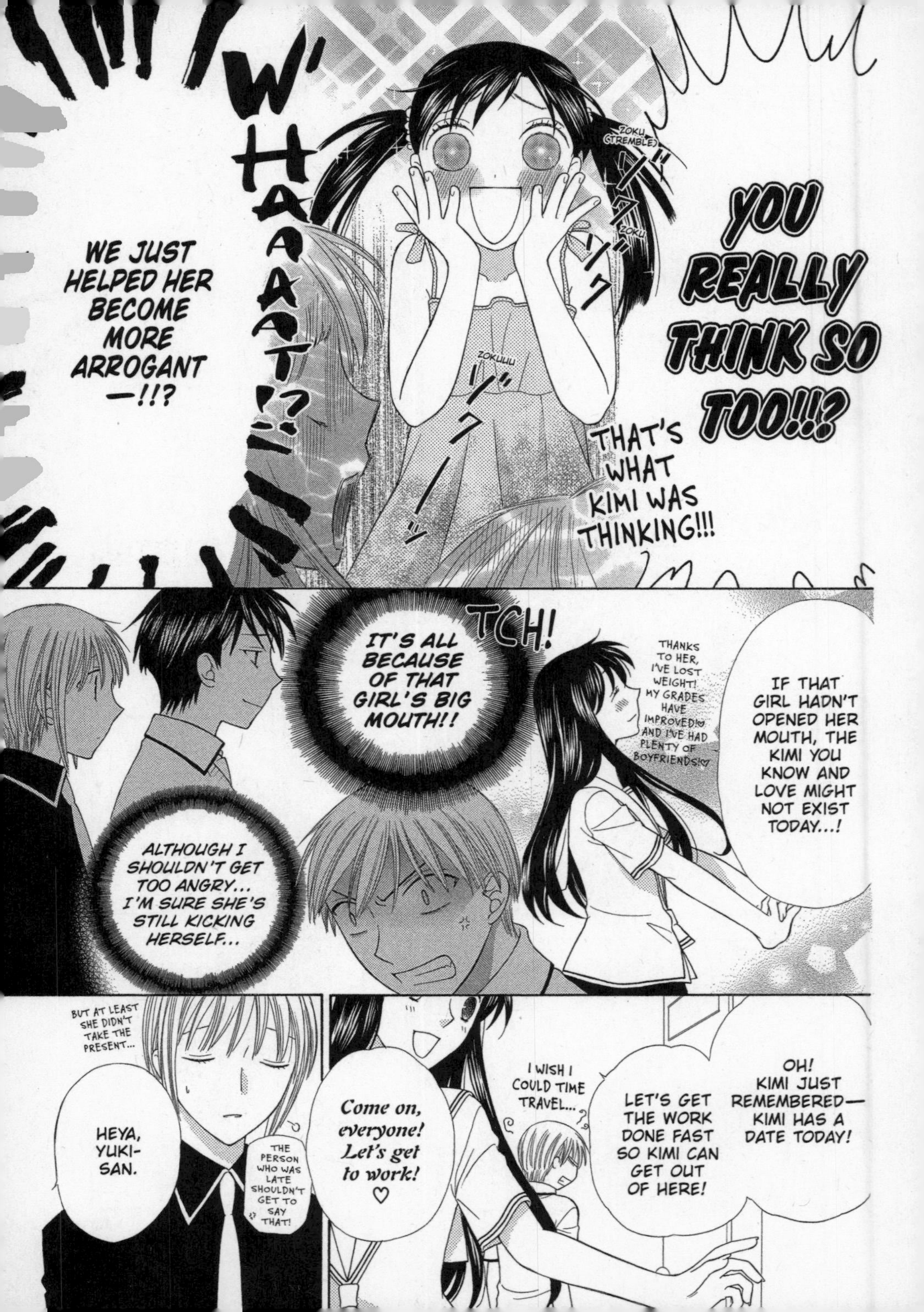
YOU REALLY THINK SO TOO!!!?
ZOKU (TREMBLE)
ZOKU
ZOKUUU
THAT'S WHAT KIMI WAS THINKING!!!
W'HAAAAT!!?
WE JUST HELPED HER BECOME MORE ARROGANT—!!?
IF THAT GIRL HADN'T OPENED HER MOUTH, THE KIMI YOU KNOW AND LOVE MIGHT NOT EXIST TODAY...!
THANKS TO HER, I'VE LOST WEIGHT! MY GRADES HAVE IMPROVED!♥ AND I'VE HAD PLENTY OF BOYFRIENDS!♥
TCH!
IT'S ALL BECAUSE OF THAT GIRL'S BIG MOUTH!!
ALTHOUGH I SHOULDN'T GET TOO ANGRY... I'M SURE SHE'S STILL KICKING HERSELF...
OH! KIMI JUST REMEMBERED— KIMI HAS A DATE TODAY!
LET'S GET THE WORK DONE FAST SO KIMI CAN GET OUT OF HERE!
I WISH I COULD TIME TRAVEL...
Come on, everyone! Let's get to work! ♡
BUT AT LEAST SHE DIDN'T TAKE THE PRESENT...
THE PERSON WHO WAS LATE SHOULDN'T GET TO SAY THAT!
HEYA, YUKI-SAN.

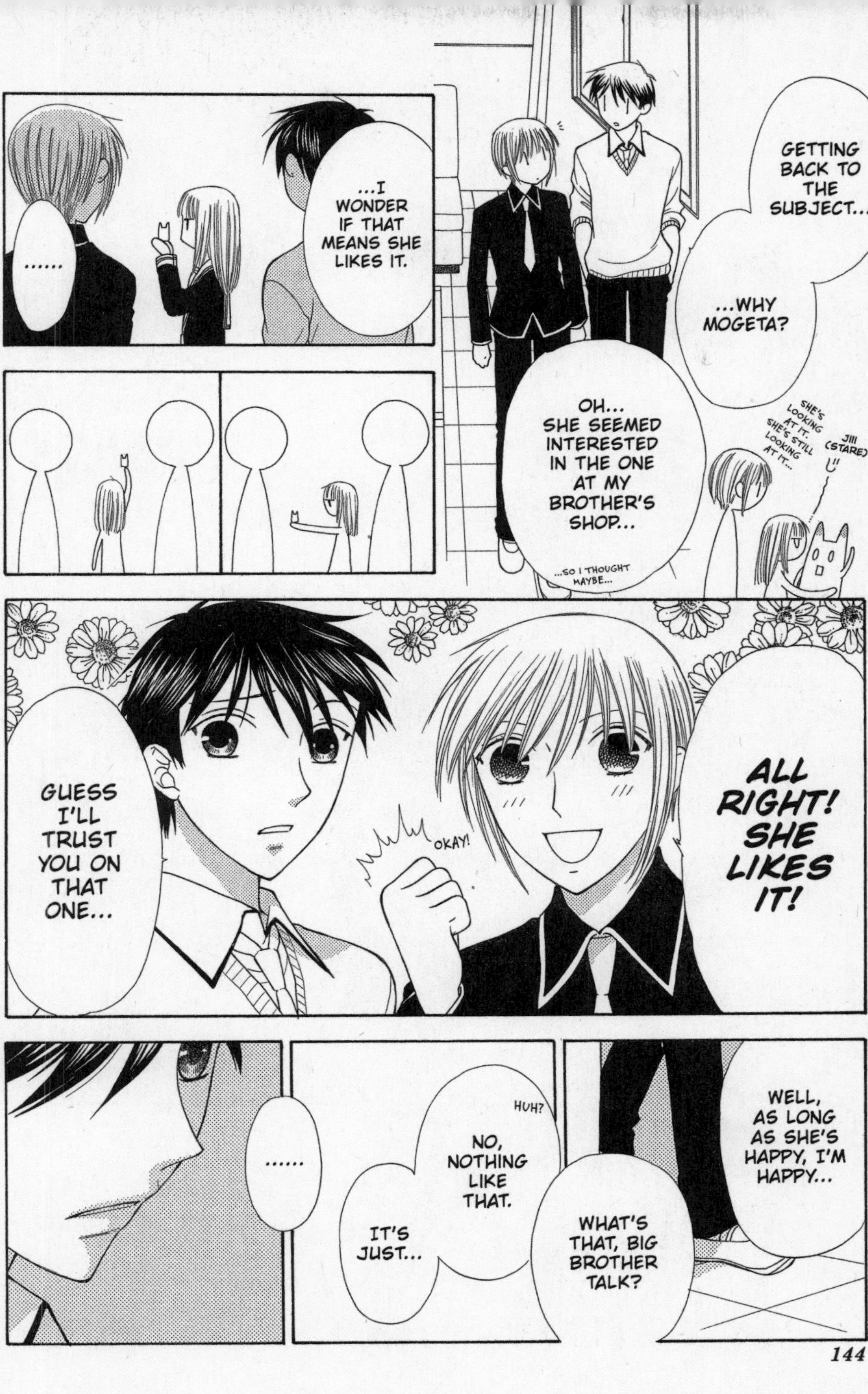
GETTING BACK TO THE SUBJECT...
...WHY MOGETA?
SHE'S LOOKING AT IT. SHE'S STILL LOOKING AT IT...
JIII (STARE)
OH... SHE SEEMED INTERESTED IN THE ONE AT MY BROTHER'S SHOP...
...SO I THOUGHT MAYBE...
...I WONDER IF THAT MEANS SHE LIKES IT.
......
ALL RIGHT! SHE LIKES IT!
OKAY!
GUESS I'LL TRUST YOU ON THAT ONE...
WELL, AS LONG AS SHE'S HAPPY, I'M HAPPY...
WHAT'S THAT, BIG BROTHER TALK?
HUH?
NO, NOTHING LIKE THAT.
IT'S JUST...
......

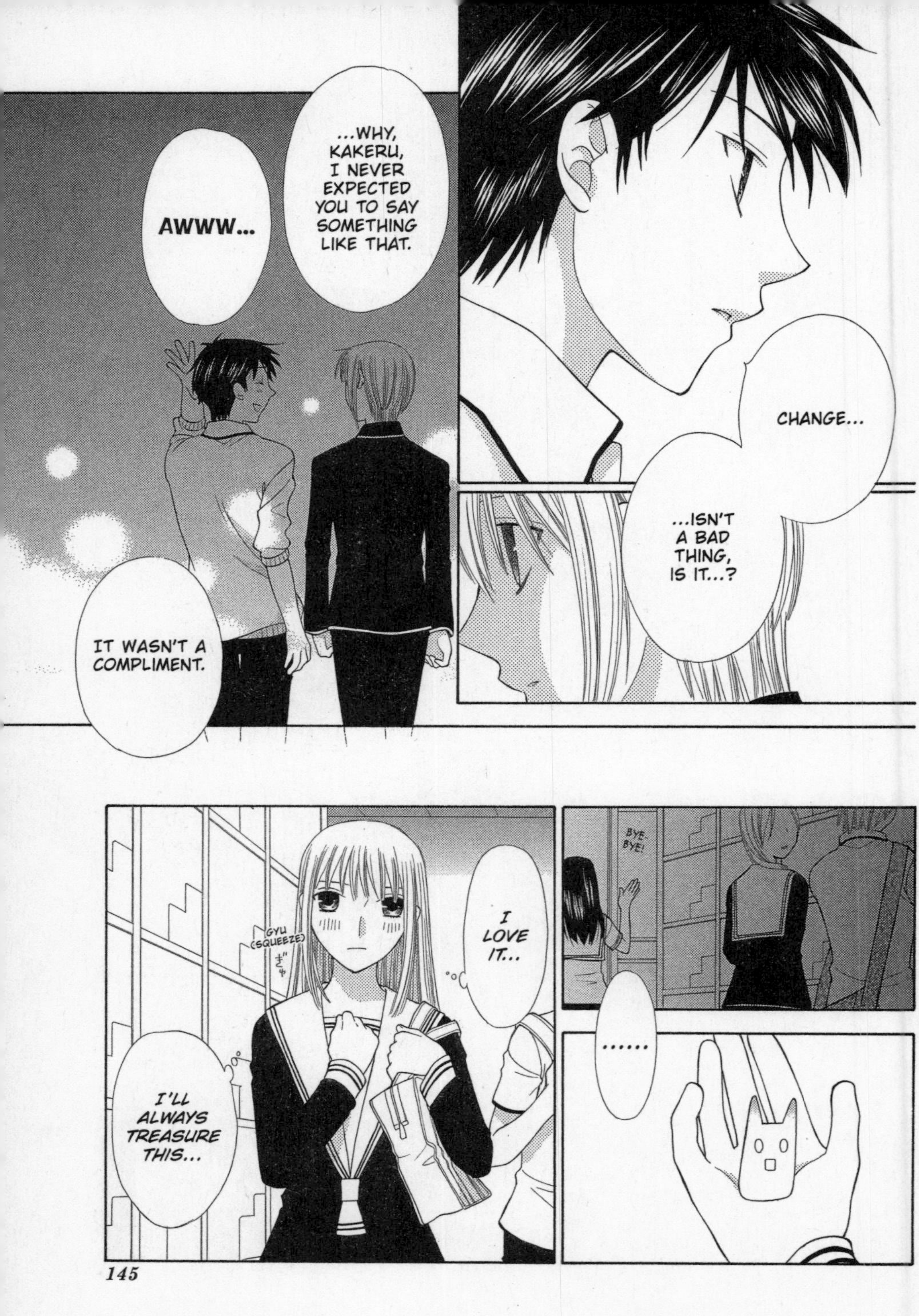
CHANGE...
...ISN'T A BAD THING, IS IT...?
...WHY, KAKERU, I NEVER EXPECTED YOU TO SAY SOMETHING LIKE THAT.
AWWW...
IT WASN'T A COMPLIMENT.
BYE-BYE!
......
I LOVE IT...
GYU (SQUEEZE)
ぎゅ
I'LL ALWAYS TREASURE THIS...

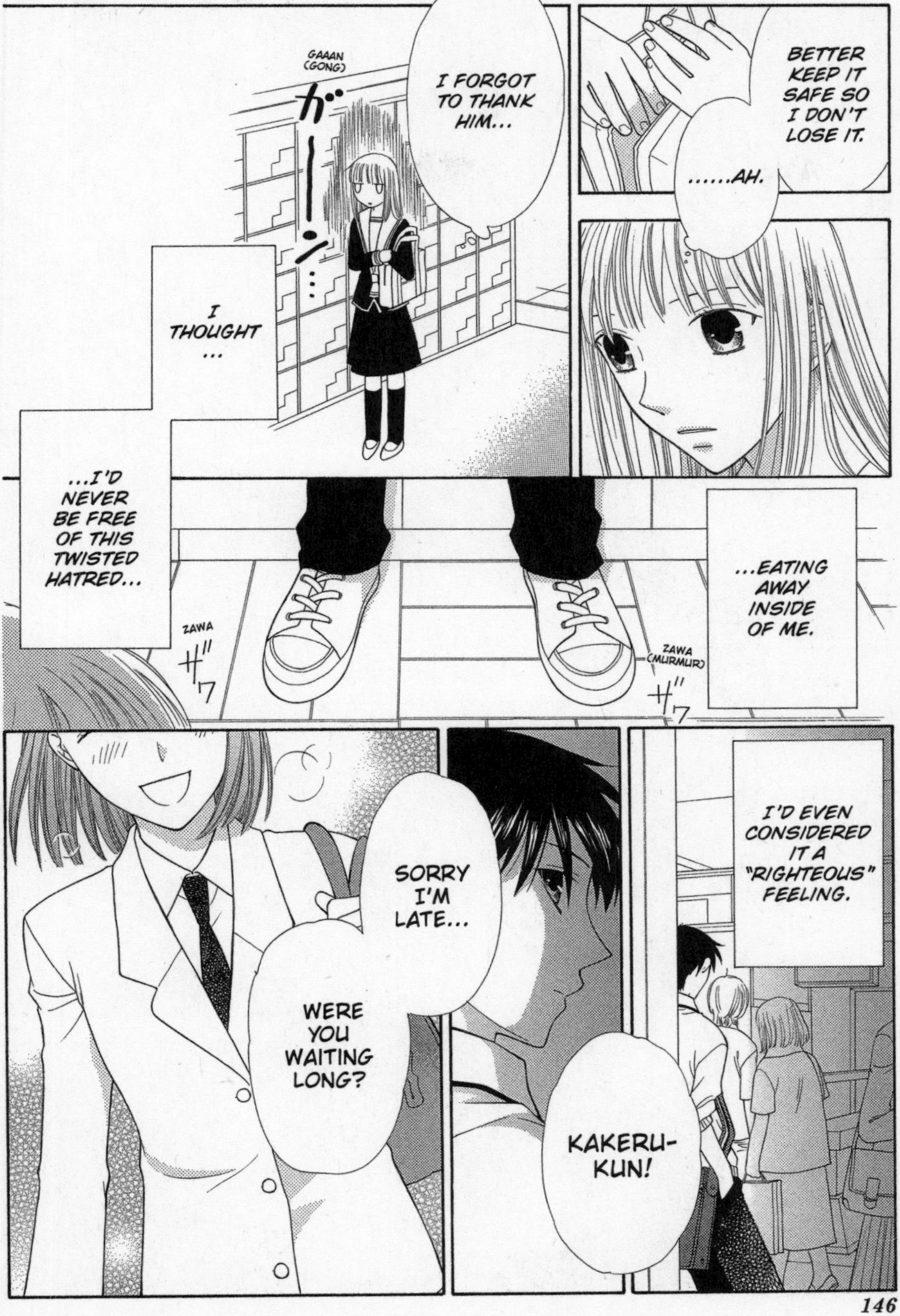
BETTER KEEP IT SAFE SO I DON'T LOSE IT.
......AH.
I FORGOT TO THANK HIM...
GAAAN (GONG)
ガーン…
I THOUGHT...
...I'D NEVER BE FREE OF THIS TWISTED HATRED...
...EATING AWAY INSIDE OF ME.
ZAWA (MURMUR)
ザワ
ZAWA
ザワ
I'D EVEN CONSIDERED IT A "RIGHTEOUS" FEELING.
KAKERU-KUN!
SORRY I'M LATE...
WERE YOU WAITING LONG?

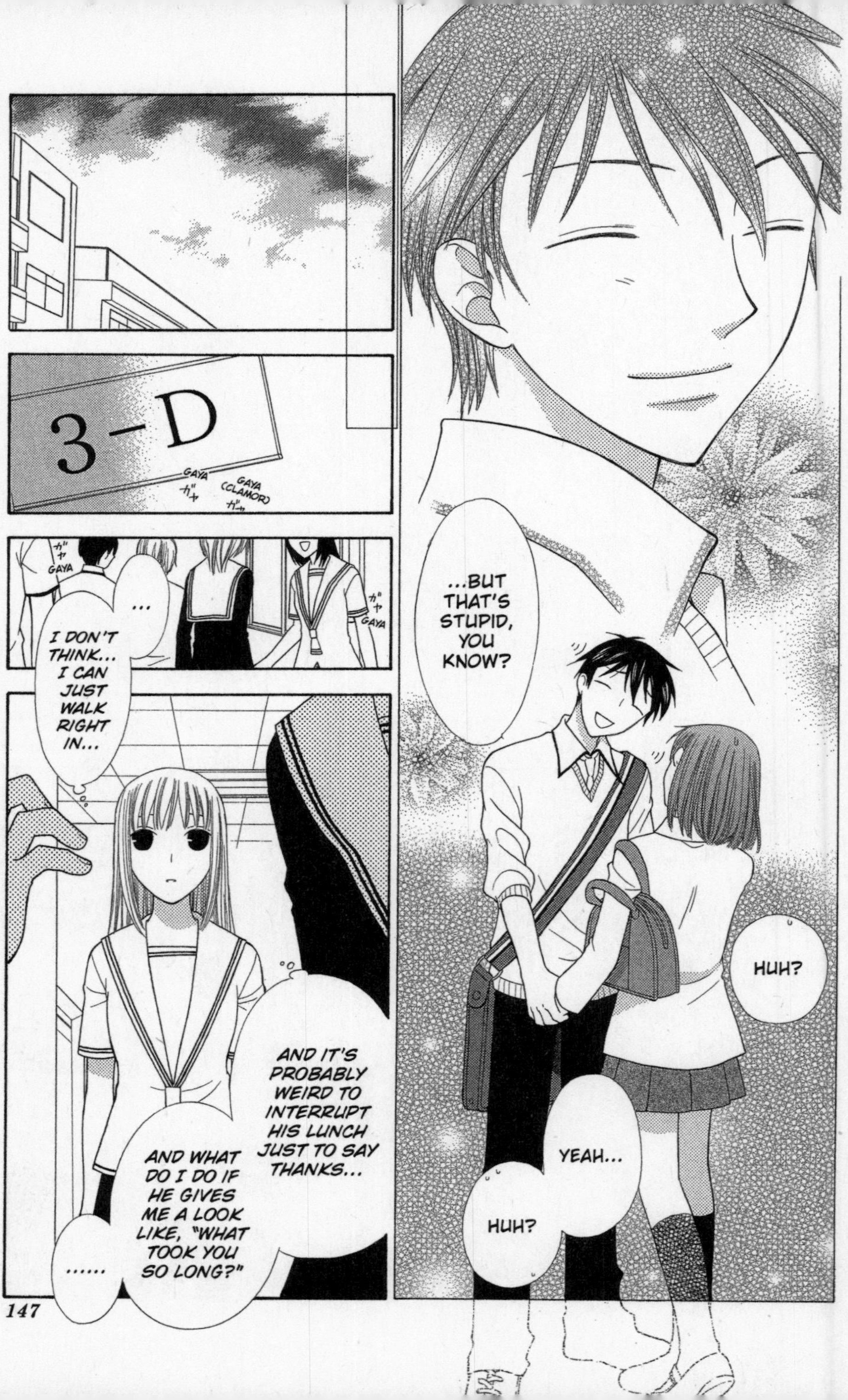
...BUT THAT'S STUPID, YOU KNOW?
HUH?
YEAH...
HUH?
3-D
GAYA ガヤ
GAYA (CLAMOR) ガヤ
ガヤ GAYA
...
I DON'T THINK... I CAN JUST WALK RIGHT IN...
ガヤ GAYA
AND IT'S PROBABLY WEIRD TO INTERRUPT HIS LUNCH JUST TO SAY THANKS...
AND WHAT DO I DO IF HE GIVES ME A LOOK LIKE, "WHAT TOOK YOU SO LONG?"
......

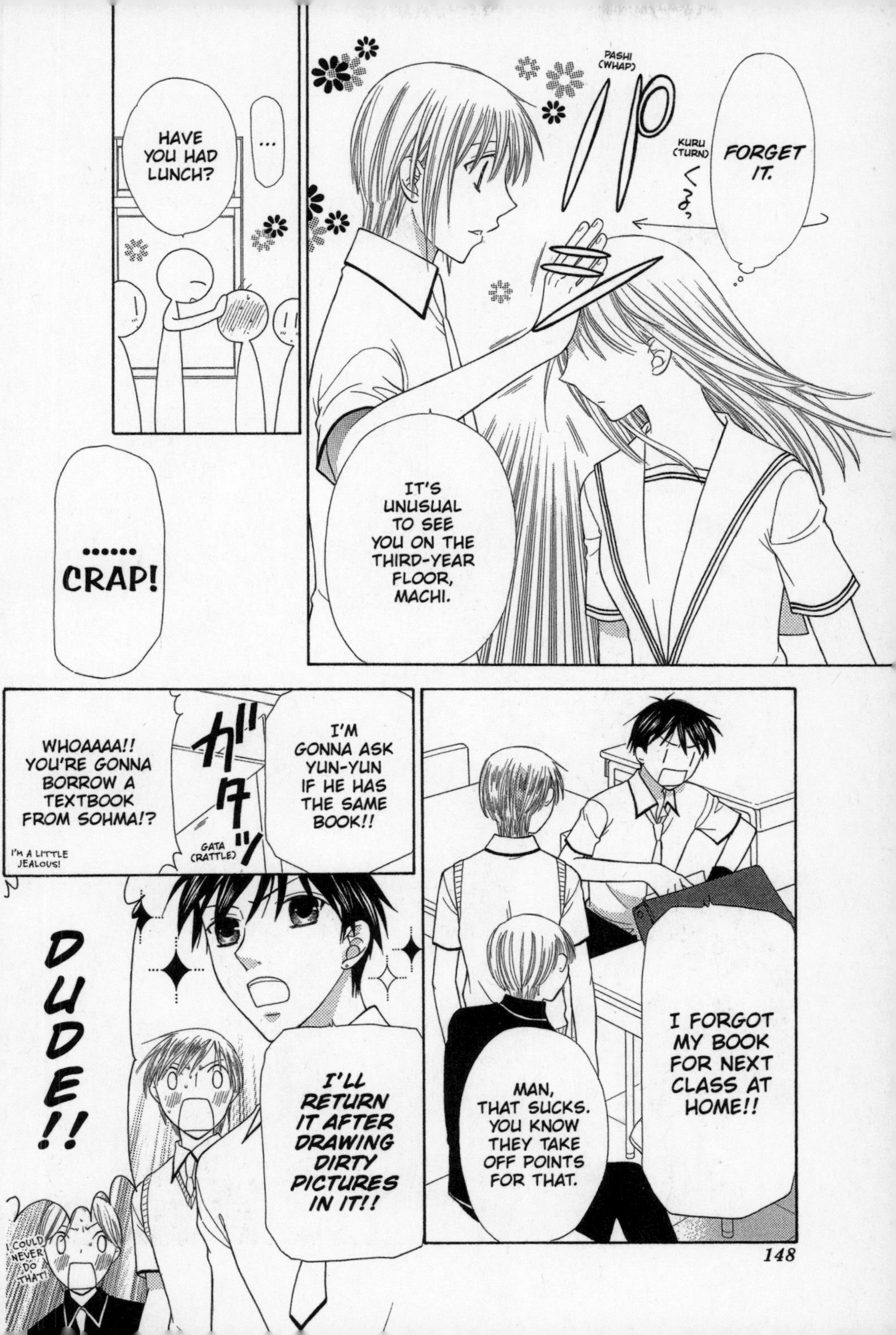

FORGET IT.
PASHI (WHAP)
KURU (TURN)
くる
IT'S UNUSUAL TO SEE YOU ON THE THIRD-YEAR FLOOR, MACHI.
...
HAVE YOU HAD LUNCH?
......CRAP!
I FORGOT MY BOOK FOR NEXT CLASS AT HOME!!
MAN, THAT SUCKS. YOU KNOW THEY TAKE OFF POINTS FOR THAT.
I'M GONNA ASK YUN-YUN IF HE HAS THE SAME BOOK!!
ガタッ
GATA (RATTLE)
WHOAAAA!! YOU'RE GONNA BORROW A TEXTBOOK FROM SOHMA!?
I'M A LITTLE JEALOUS!
I'LL RETURN IT AFTER DRAWING DIRTY PICTURES IN IT!!
DUDE!!
I COULD NEVER DO THAT!

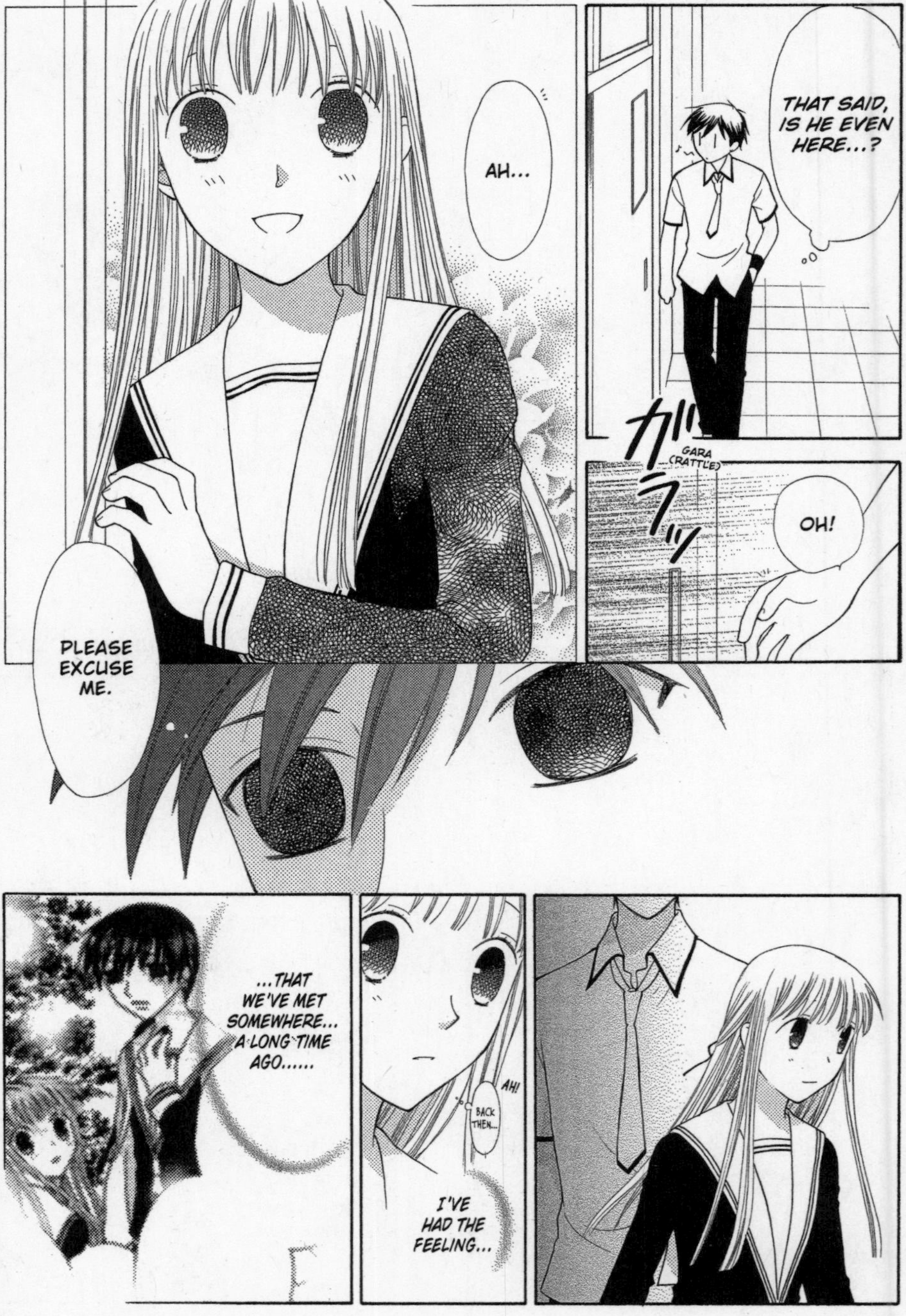
THAT SAID, IS HE EVEN HERE...?
GARA (RATTLE)
OH!
AH...
PLEASE EXCUSE ME.
AH! BACK THEN...
I'VE HAD THE FEELING...
...THAT WE'VE MET SOMEWHERE... A LONG TIME AGO......

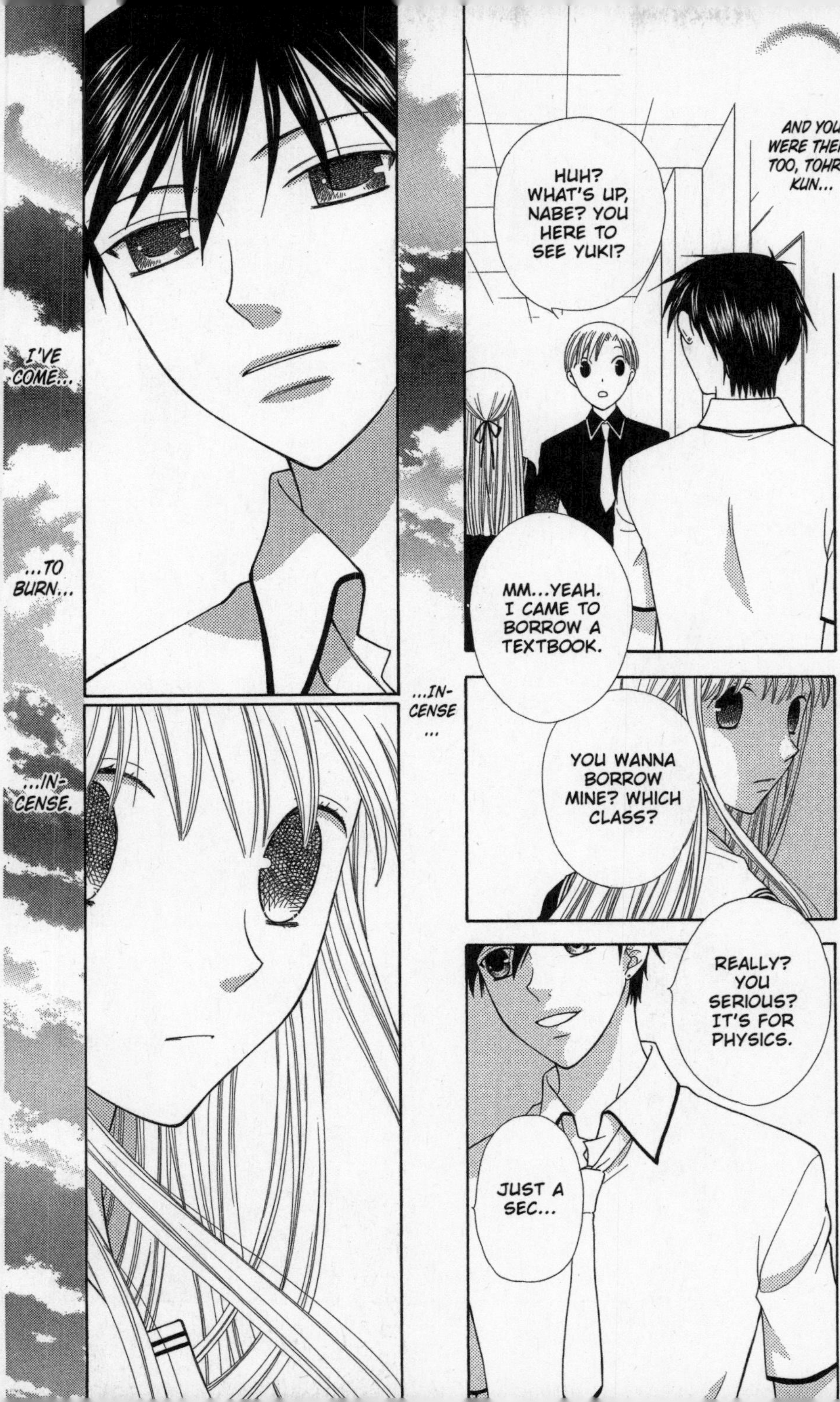
AND YOU WERE THERE TOO, TOHRU-KUN...
HUH? WHAT'S UP, NABE? YOU HERE TO SEE YUKI?
MM...YEAH. I CAME TO BORROW A TEXTBOOK.
YOU WANNA BORROW MINE? WHICH CLASS?
REALLY? YOU SERIOUS? IT'S FOR PHYSICS.
JUST A SEC...
...IN-CENSE...
I'VE COME...
...TO BURN...
...IN-CENSE.

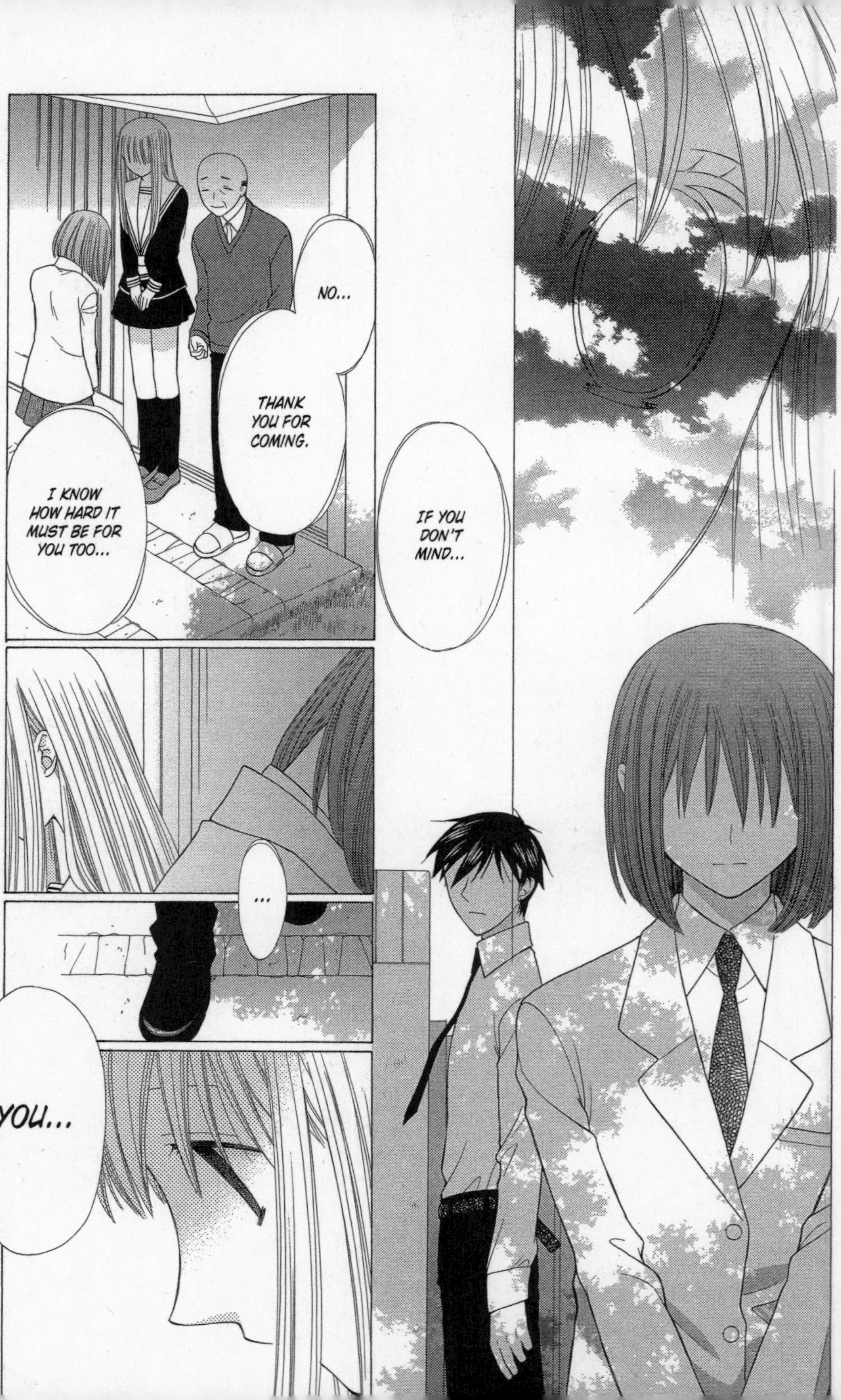
NO...
THANK YOU FOR COMING.
I KNOW HOW HARD IT MUST BE FOR YOU TOO...
IF YOU DON'T MIND...
...
YOU...

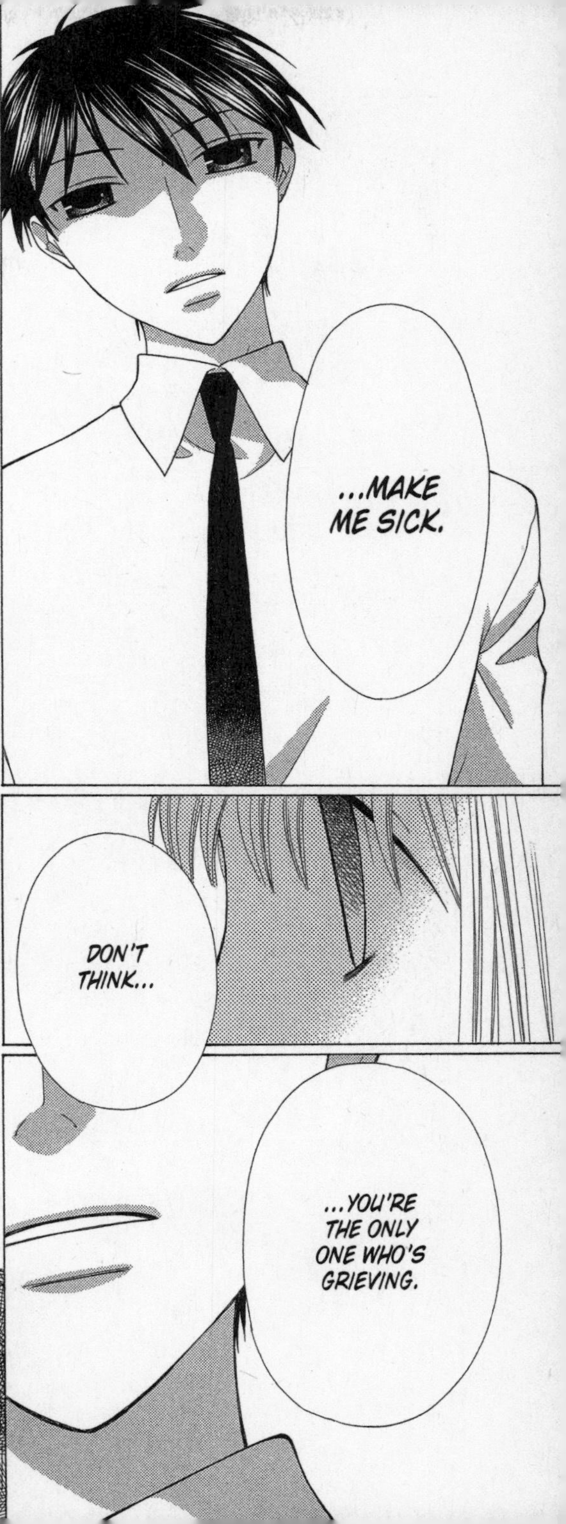
...MAKE ME SICK.
DON'T THINK...
...YOU'RE THE ONLY ONE WHO'S GRIEVING.
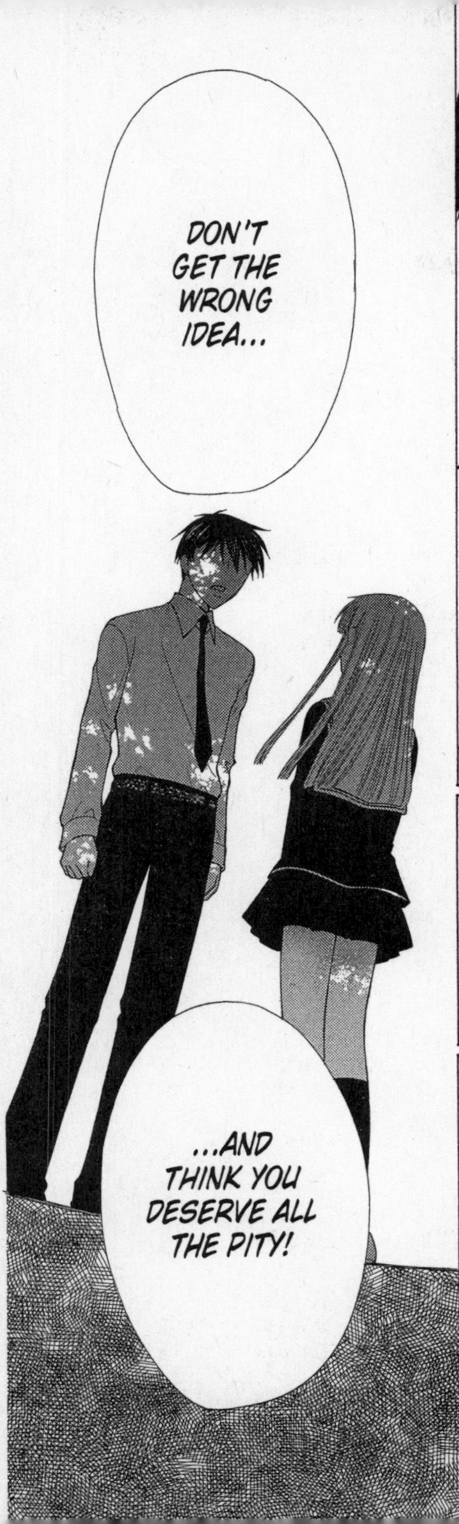
DON'T GET THE WRONG IDEA...
...AND THINK YOU DESERVE ALL THE PITY!

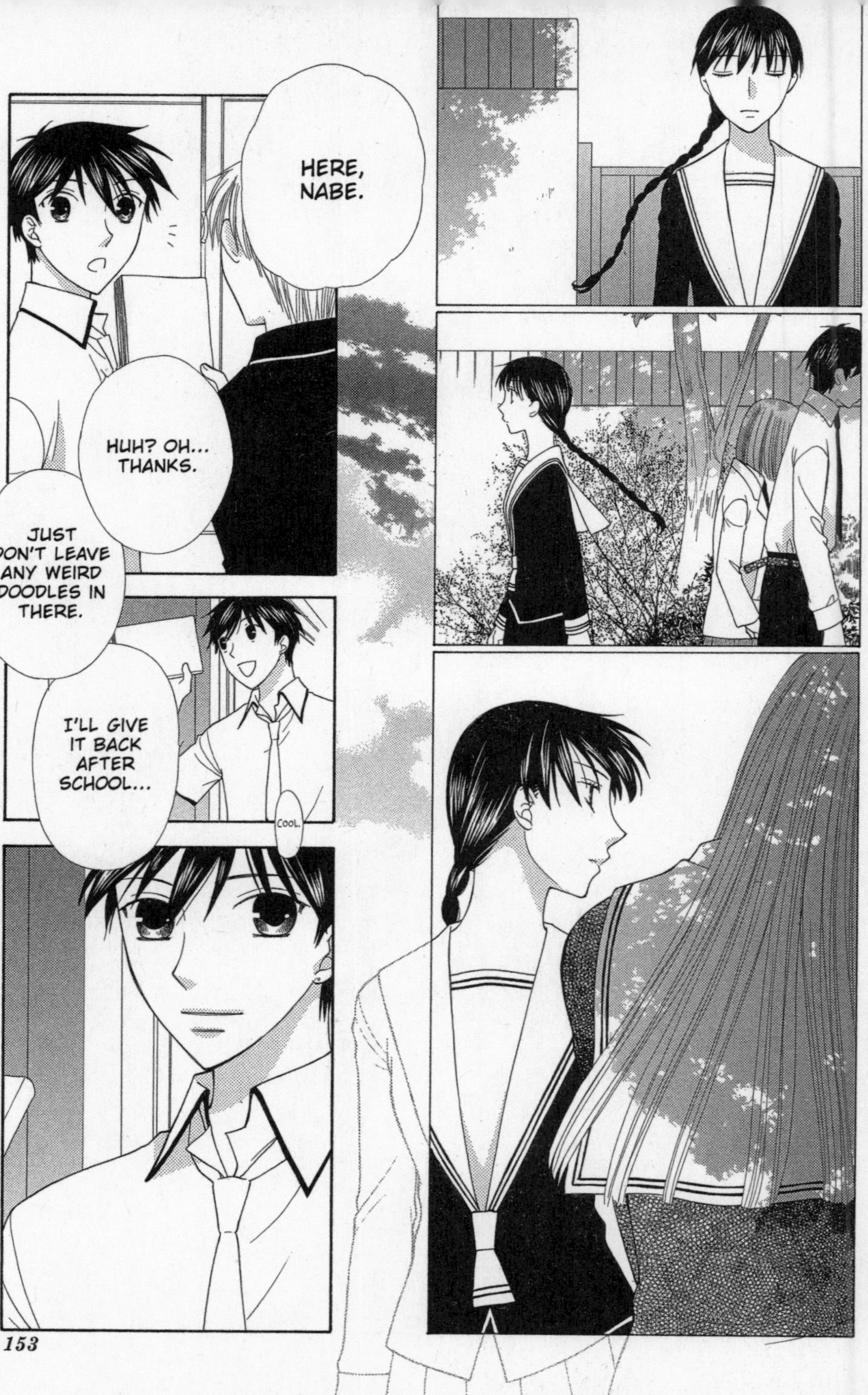
HERE, NABE.
HUH? OH... THANKS.
JUST DON'T LEAVE ANY WEIRD DOODLES IN THERE.
I'LL GIVE IT BACK AFTER SCHOOL...
COOL.

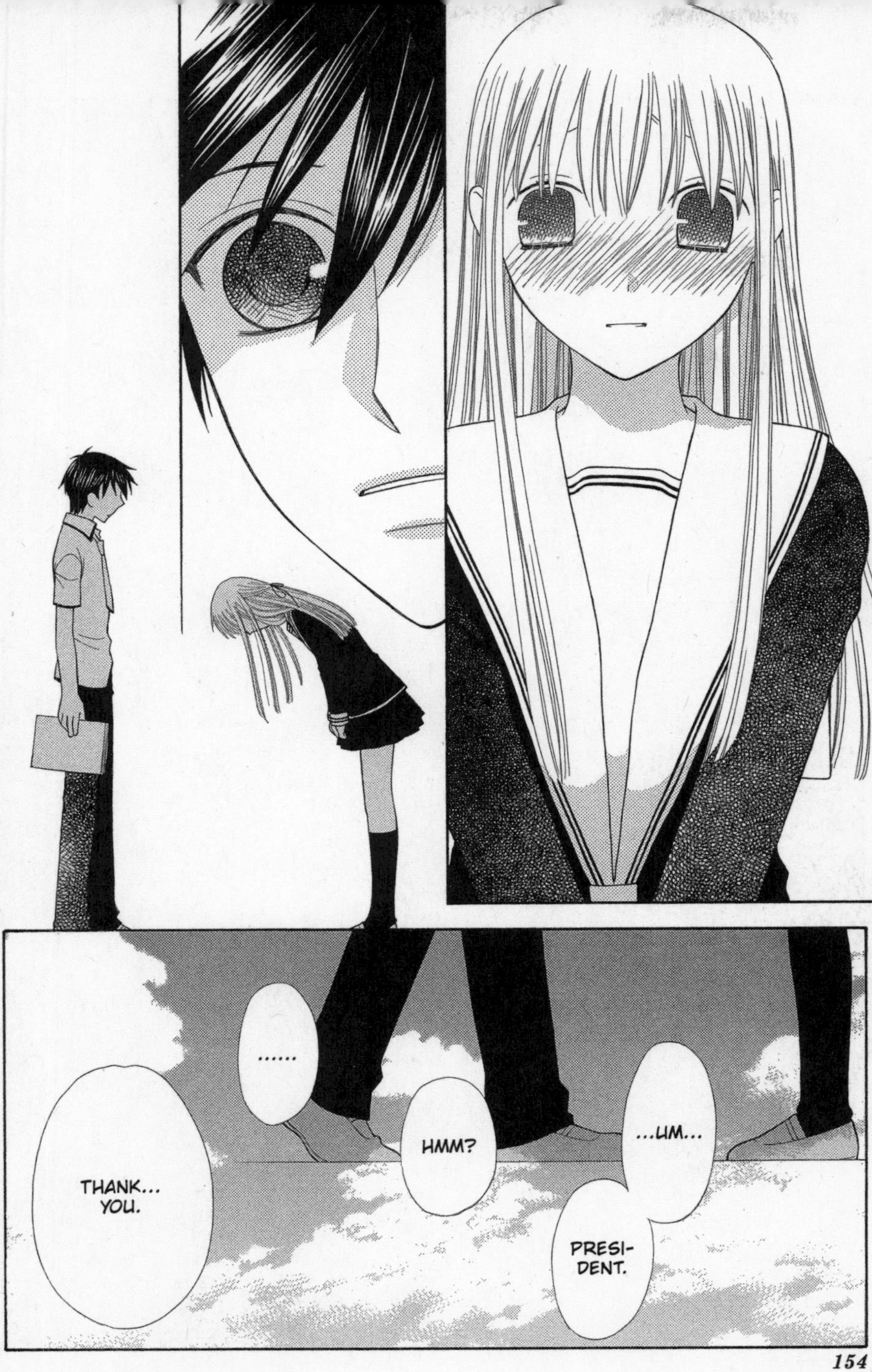
...UM...
PRESI-DENT.
HMM?
......
THANK... YOU.

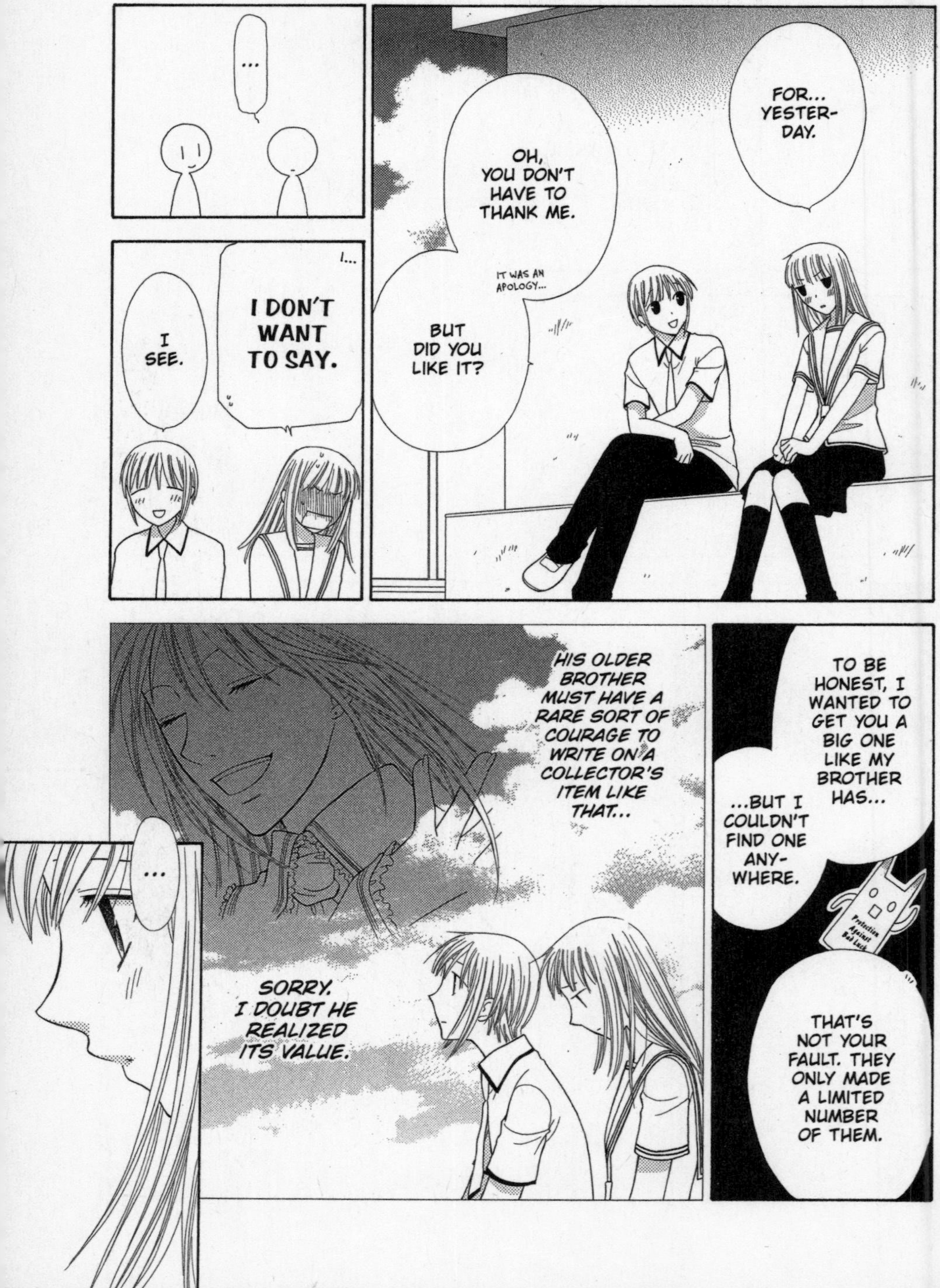
FOR... YESTER-DAY.
OH, YOU DON'T HAVE TO THANK ME.
IT WAS AN APOLOGY...
BUT DID YOU LIKE IT?
...
I...
I DON'T WANT TO SAY.
I SEE.
TO BE HONEST, I WANTED TO GET YOU A BIG ONE LIKE MY BROTHER HAS...
...BUT I COULDN'T FIND ONE ANY-WHERE.
Protection Against Bad Luck
THAT'S NOT YOUR FAULT. THEY ONLY MADE A LIMITED NUMBER OF THEM.
HIS OLDER BROTHER MUST HAVE A RARE SORT OF COURAGE TO WRITE ON A COLLECTOR'S ITEM LIKE THAT...
SORRY. I DOUBT HE REALIZED ITS VALUE.
...

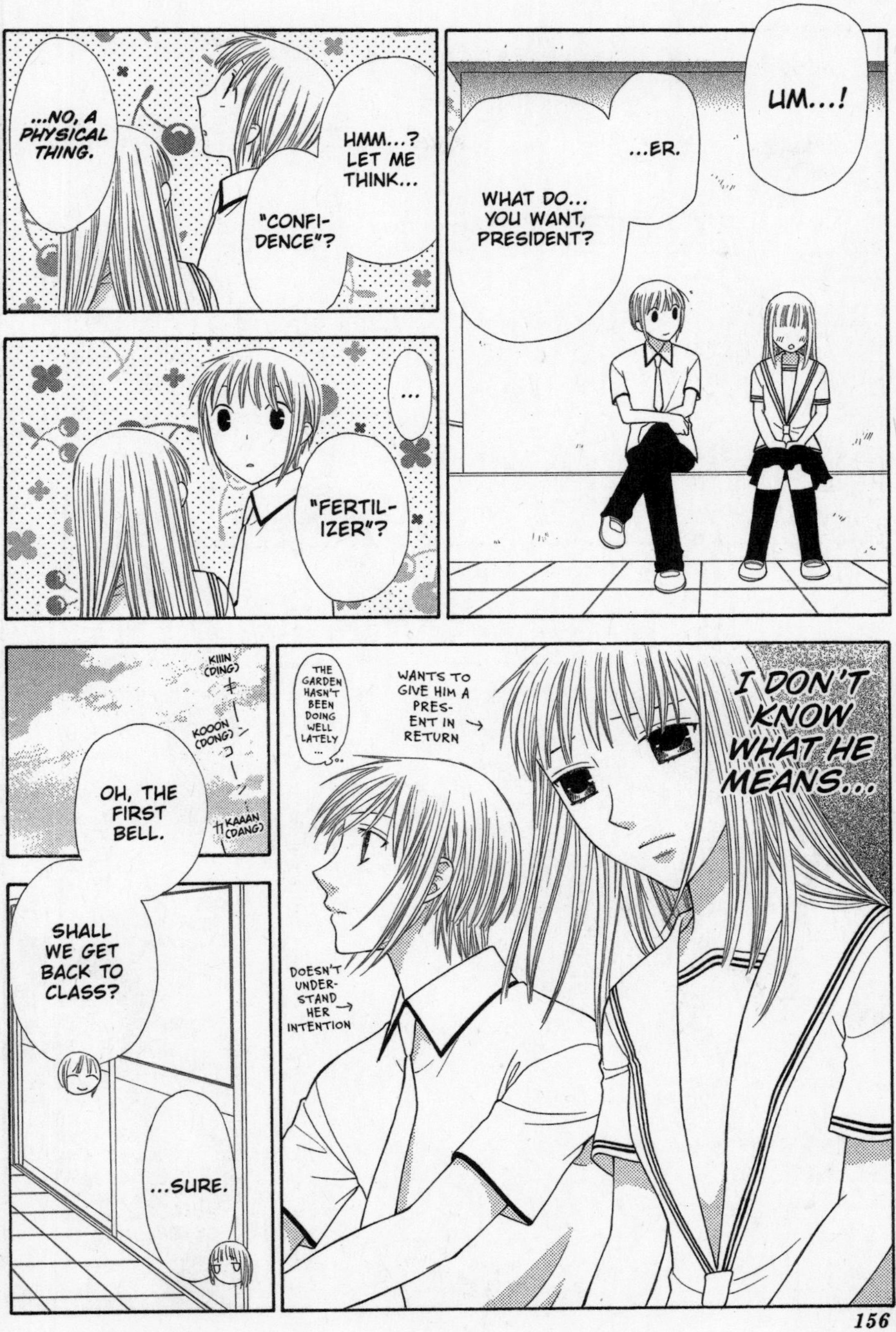

UM...!
...ER.
WHAT DO... YOU WANT, PRESIDENT?
HMM...? LET ME THINK...
"CONFI-DENCE"?
...NO, A PHYSICAL THING.
...
"FERTIL-IZER"?
I DON'T KNOW WHAT HE MEANS...
WANTS TO GIVE HIM A PRES-ENT IN RETURN →
THE GARDEN HASN'T BEEN DOING WELL LATELY...
DOESN'T UNDER-STAND HER INTENTION →
KIIIN (DING)
KOOON (DONG)
KAAAN (DANG)
OH, THE FIRST BELL.
SHALL WE GET BACK TO CLASS?
...SURE.

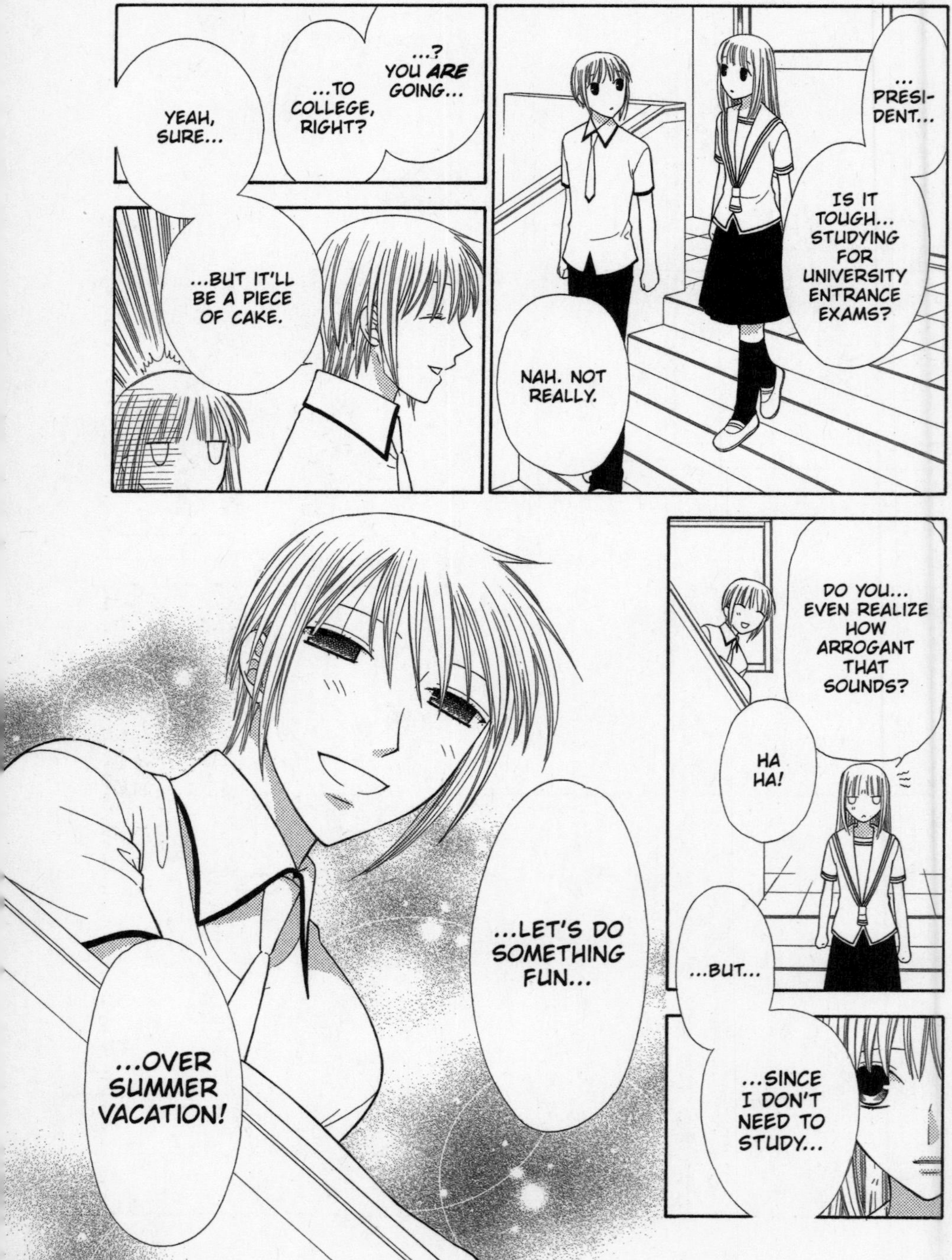
...PRESIDENT...
IS IT TOUGH... STUDYING FOR UNIVERSITY ENTRANCE EXAMS?
NAH. NOT REALLY.
...? YOU *ARE* GOING...
...TO COLLEGE, RIGHT?
YEAH, SURE...
...BUT IT'LL BE A PIECE OF CAKE.
DO YOU... EVEN REALIZE HOW ARROGANT THAT SOUNDS?
HA HA!
...BUT...
...SINCE I DON'T NEED TO STUDY...
...LET'S DO SOMETHING FUN...
...OVER SUMMER VACATION!

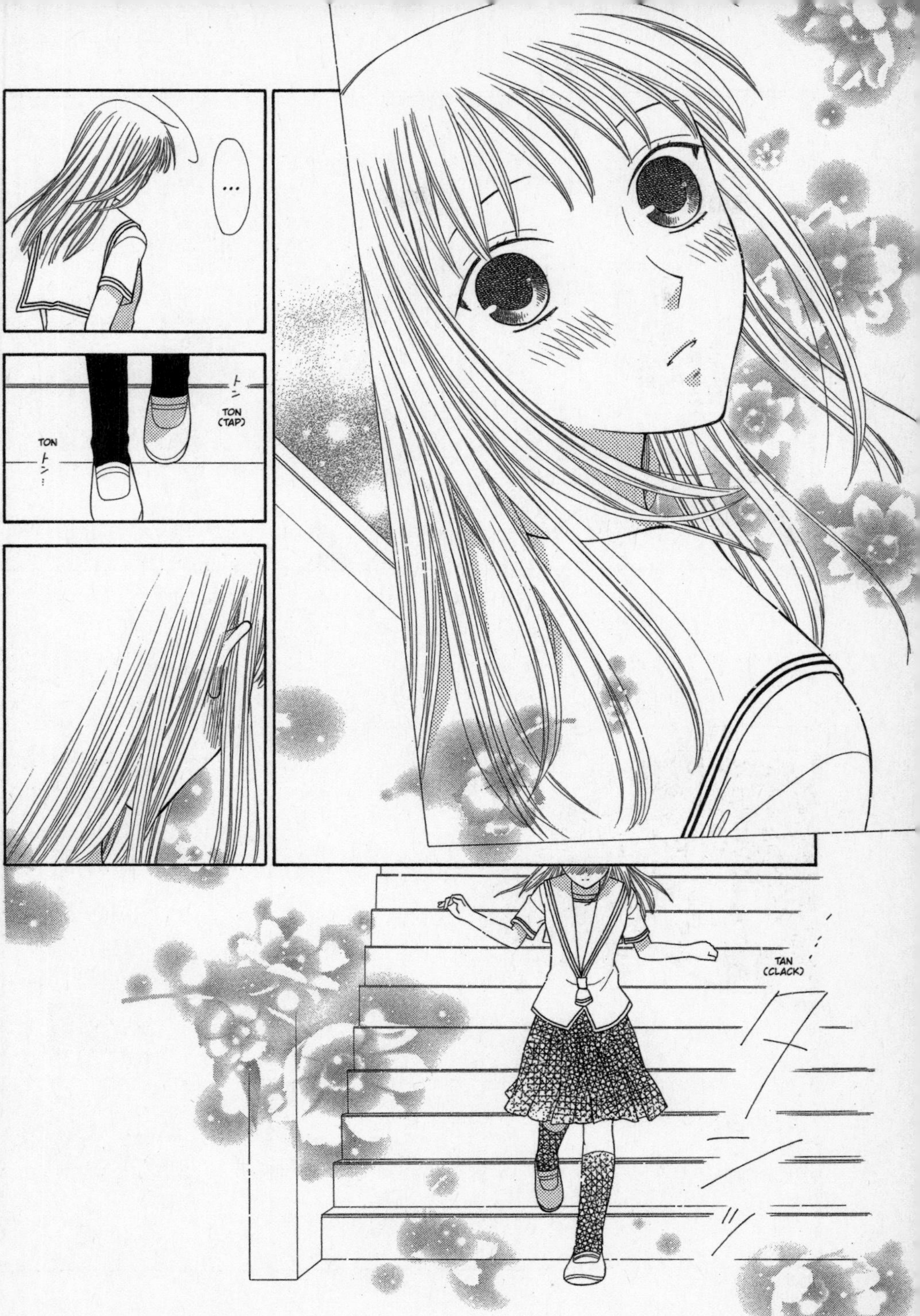
...
トン
TON
(TAP)
TON
トン…
TAN
(CLACK)

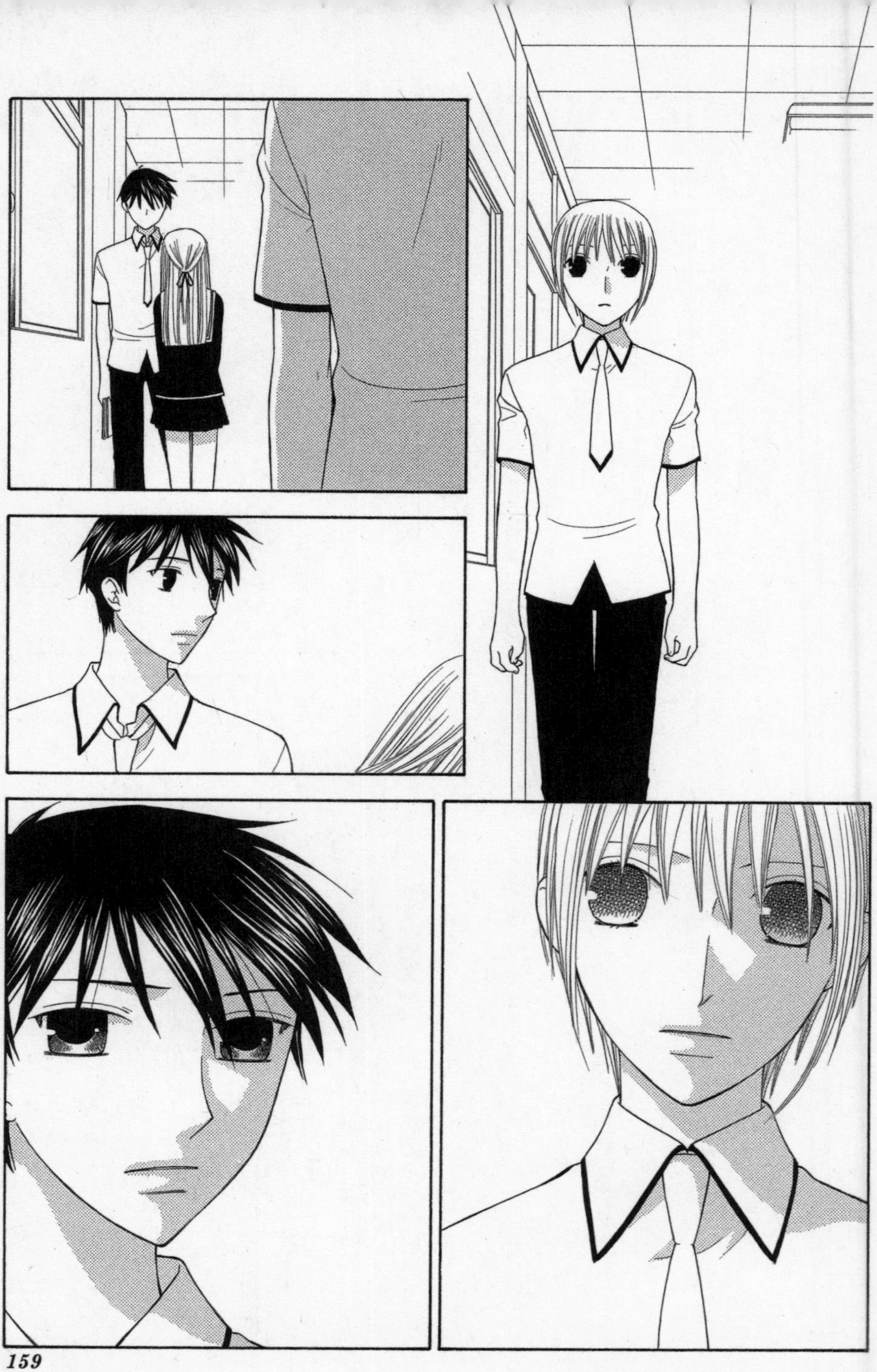

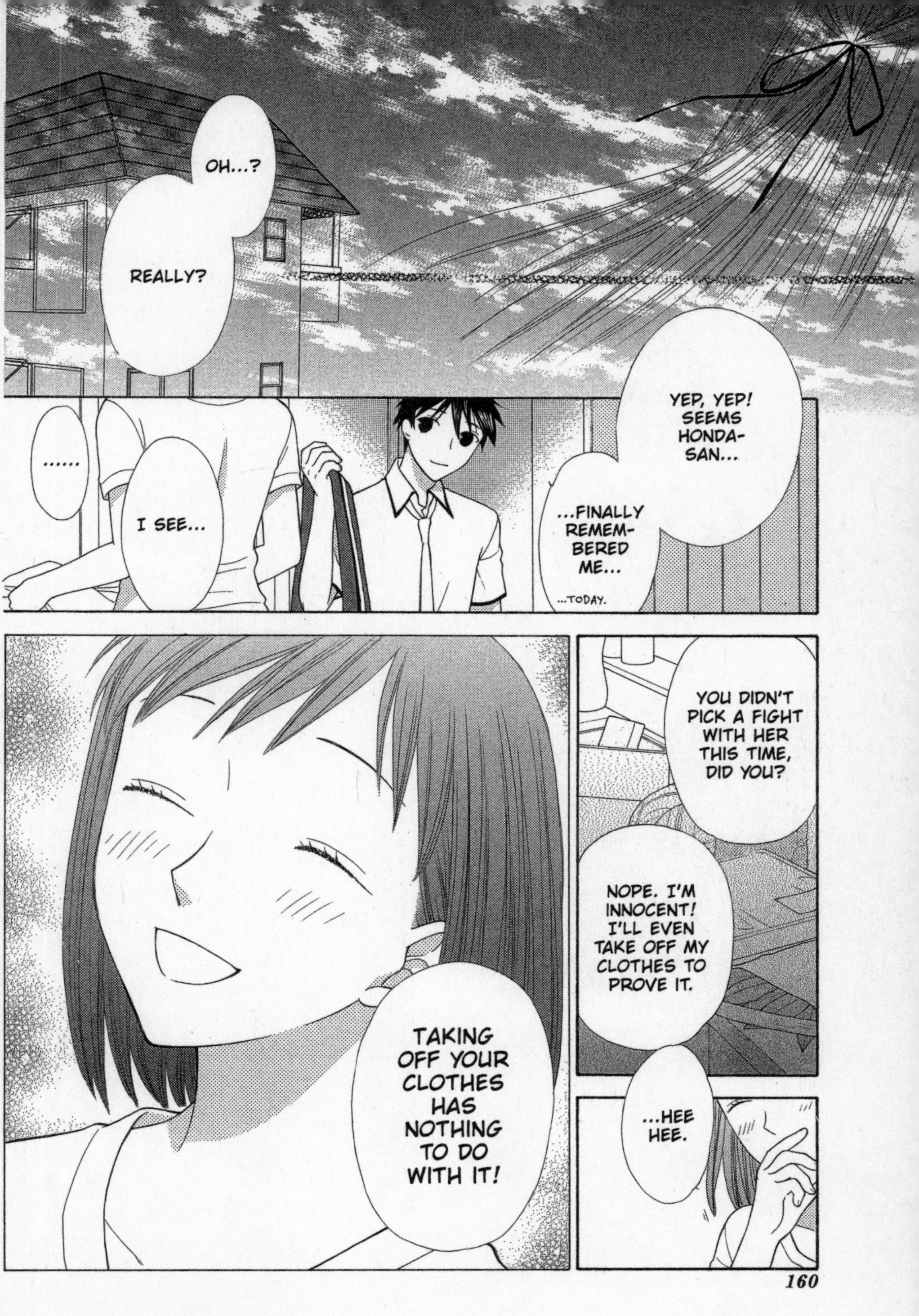
OH...?
REALLY?
YEP, YEP! SEEMS HONDA-SAN...
...FINALLY REMEMBERED ME...
...TODAY.
......
I SEE...
YOU DIDN'T PICK A FIGHT WITH HER THIS TIME, DID YOU?
NOPE. I'M INNOCENT! I'LL EVEN TAKE OFF MY CLOTHES TO PROVE IT.
...HEE HEE.
TAKING OFF YOUR CLOTHES HAS NOTHING TO DO WITH IT!

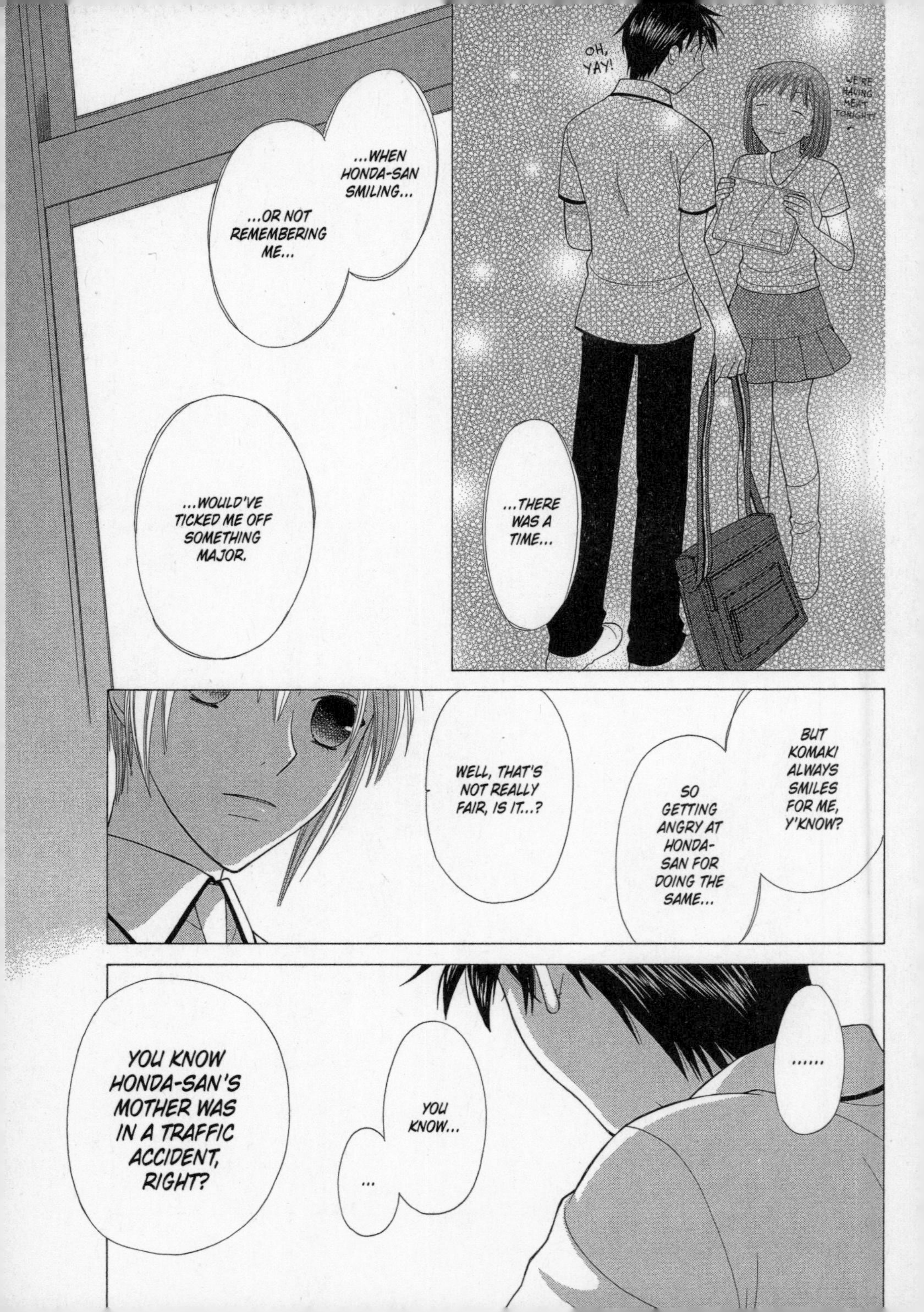
WE'RE HAVING MEAT TONIGHT!
OH, YAY!
...THERE WAS A TIME...
...WHEN HONDA-SAN SMILING...
...OR NOT REMEMBERING ME...
...WOULD'VE TICKED ME OFF SOMETHING MAJOR.
BUT KOMAKI ALWAYS SMILES FOR ME, Y'KNOW?
SO GETTING ANGRY AT HONDA-SAN FOR DOING THE SAME...
WELL, THAT'S NOT REALLY FAIR, IS IT...?
......
YOU KNOW...
...
YOU KNOW HONDA-SAN'S MOTHER WAS IN A TRAFFIC ACCIDENT, RIGHT?

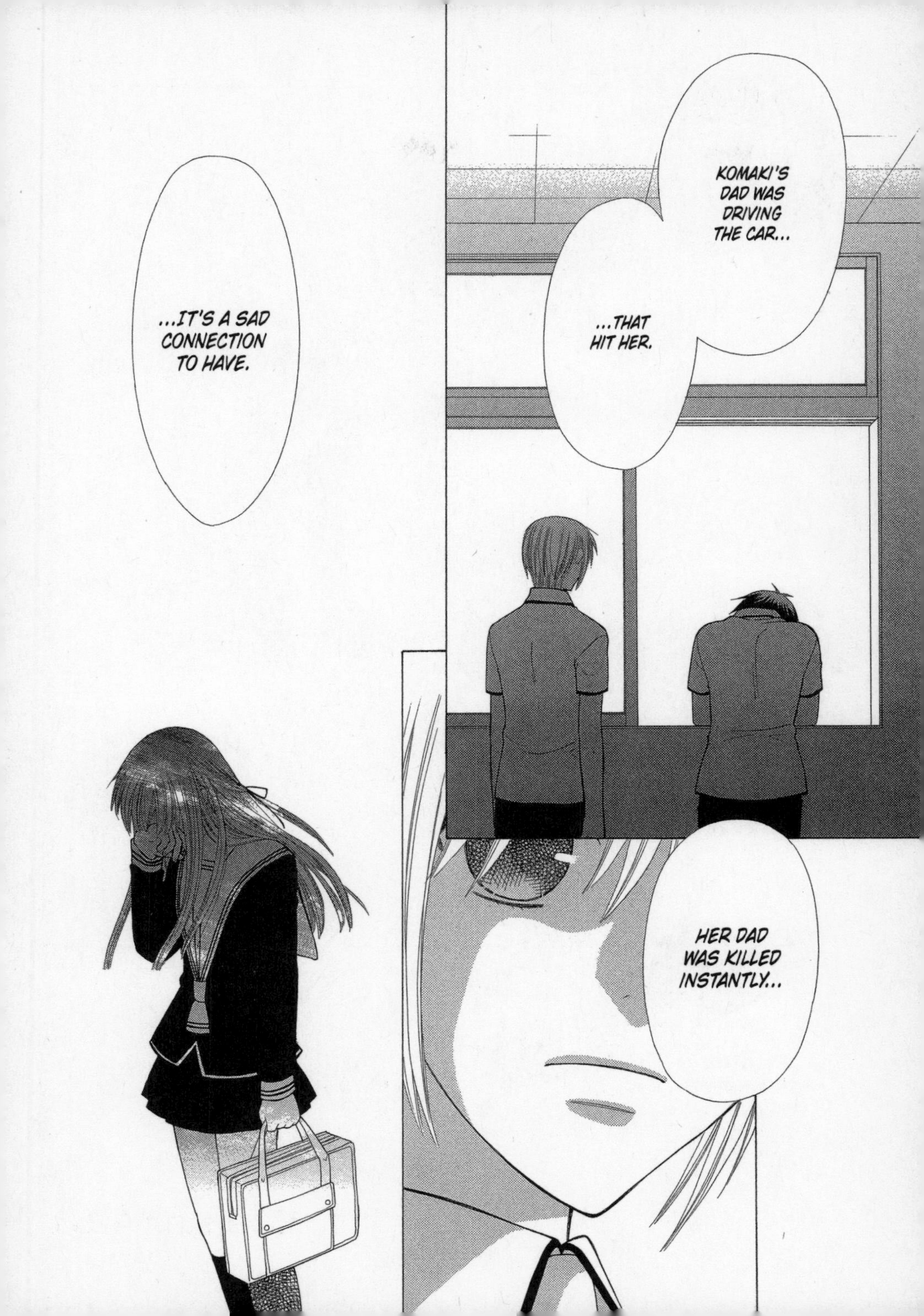
KOMAKI'S DAD WAS DRIVING THE CAR...
...THAT HIT HER.
HER DAD WAS KILLED INSTANTLY...
...IT'S A SAD CONNECTION TO HAVE.

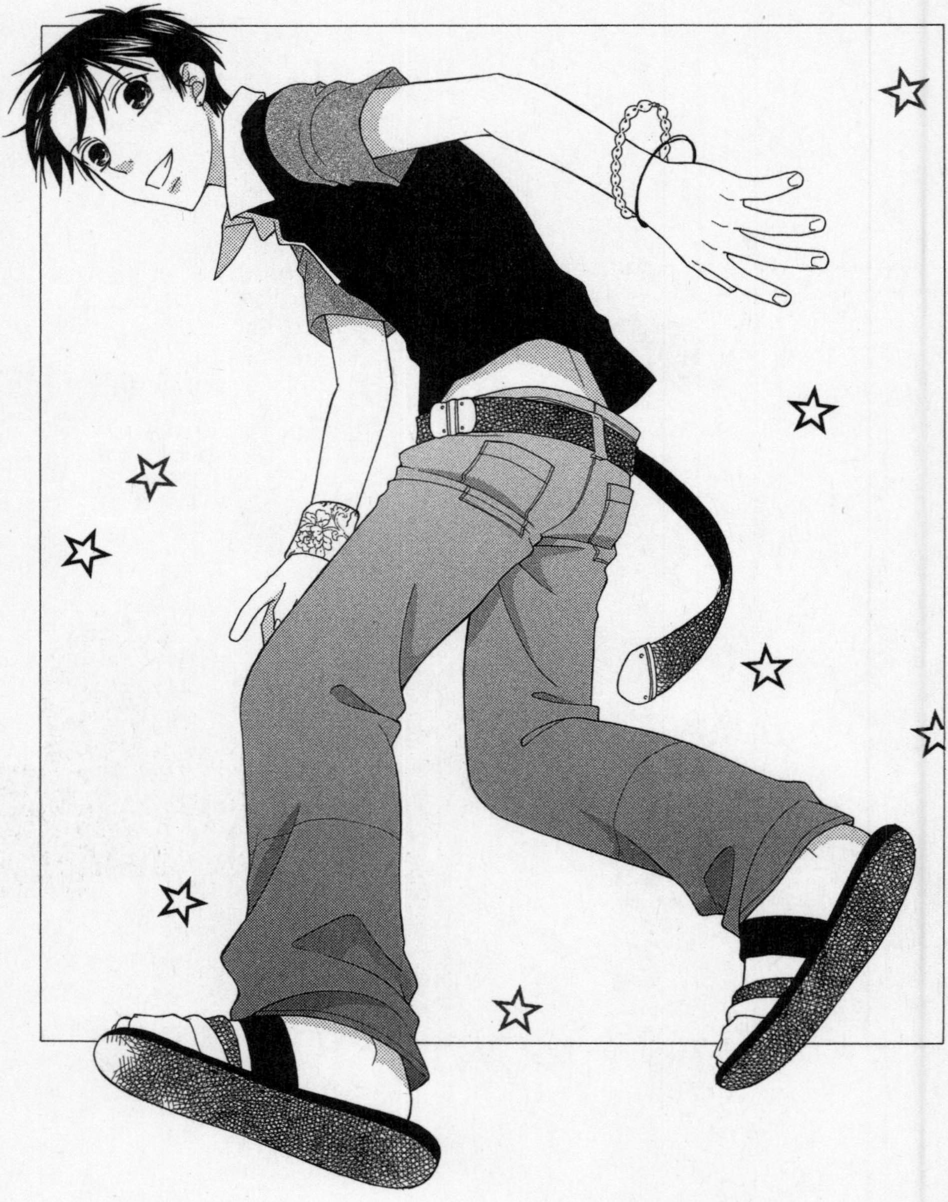

Chapter 113

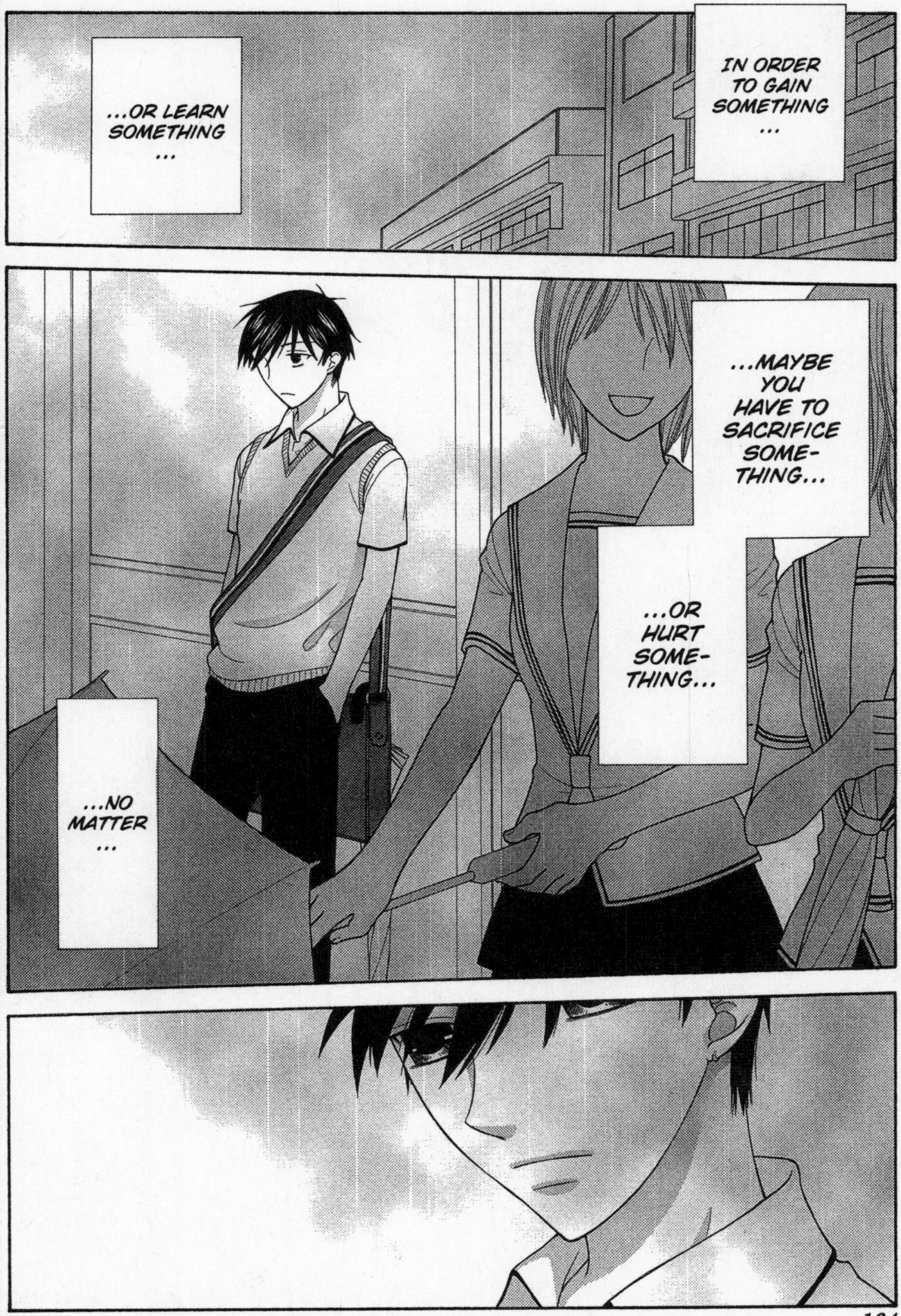
IN ORDER TO GAIN SOMETHING ...
...OR LEARN SOMETHING ...
...MAYBE YOU HAVE TO SACRIFICE SOME-THING...
...OR HURT SOME-THING...
...NO MATTER ...

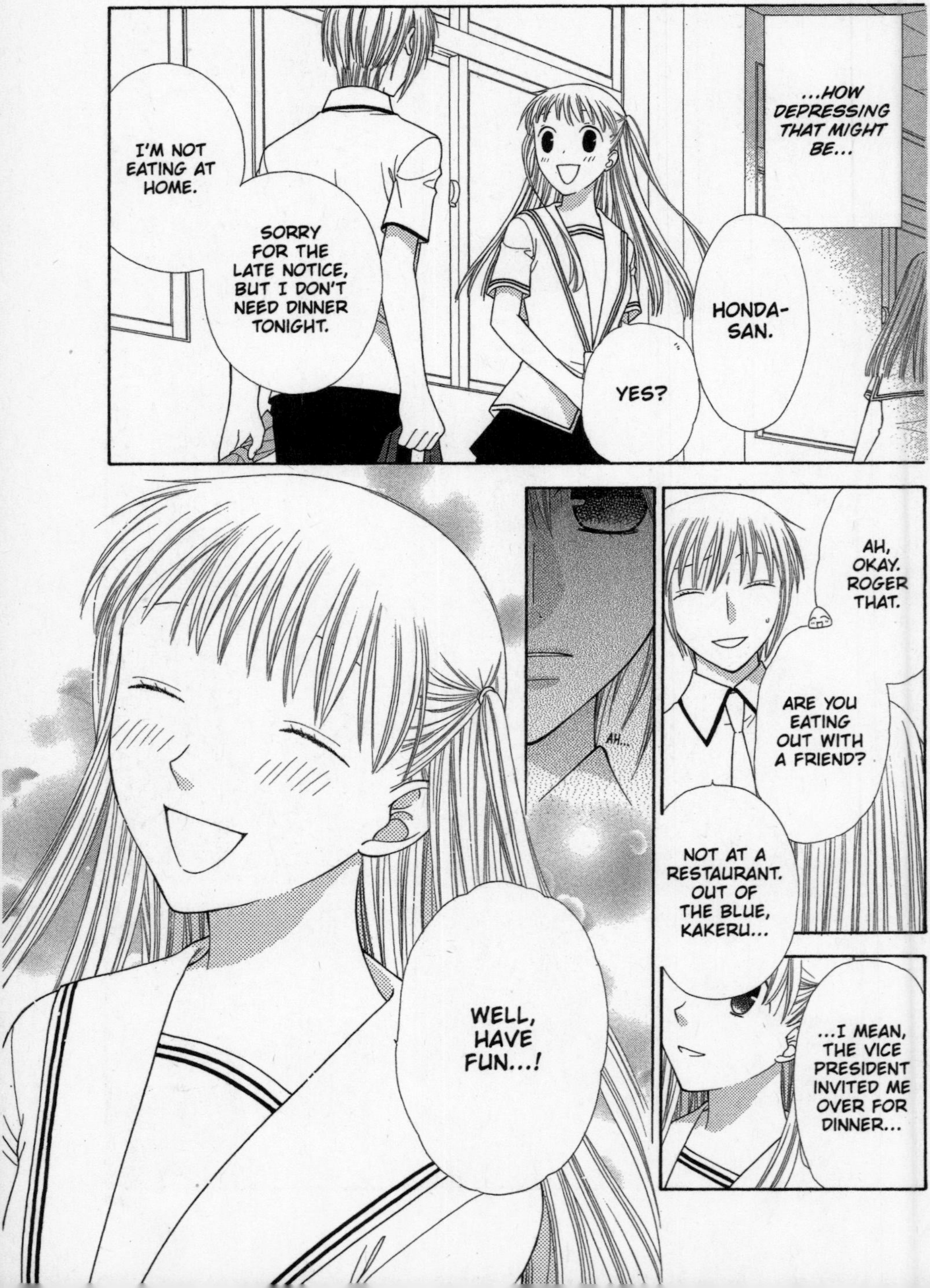
...HOW DEPRESSING THAT MIGHT BE...
HONDA-SAN.
YES?
I'M NOT EATING AT HOME.
SORRY FOR THE LATE NOTICE, BUT I DON'T NEED DINNER TONIGHT.
AH, OKAY. ROGER THAT.
ARE YOU EATING OUT WITH A FRIEND?
NOT AT A RESTAURANT. OUT OF THE BLUE, KAKERU...
...I MEAN, THE VICE PRESIDENT INVITED ME OVER FOR DINNER...
AH...
WELL, HAVE FUN...!

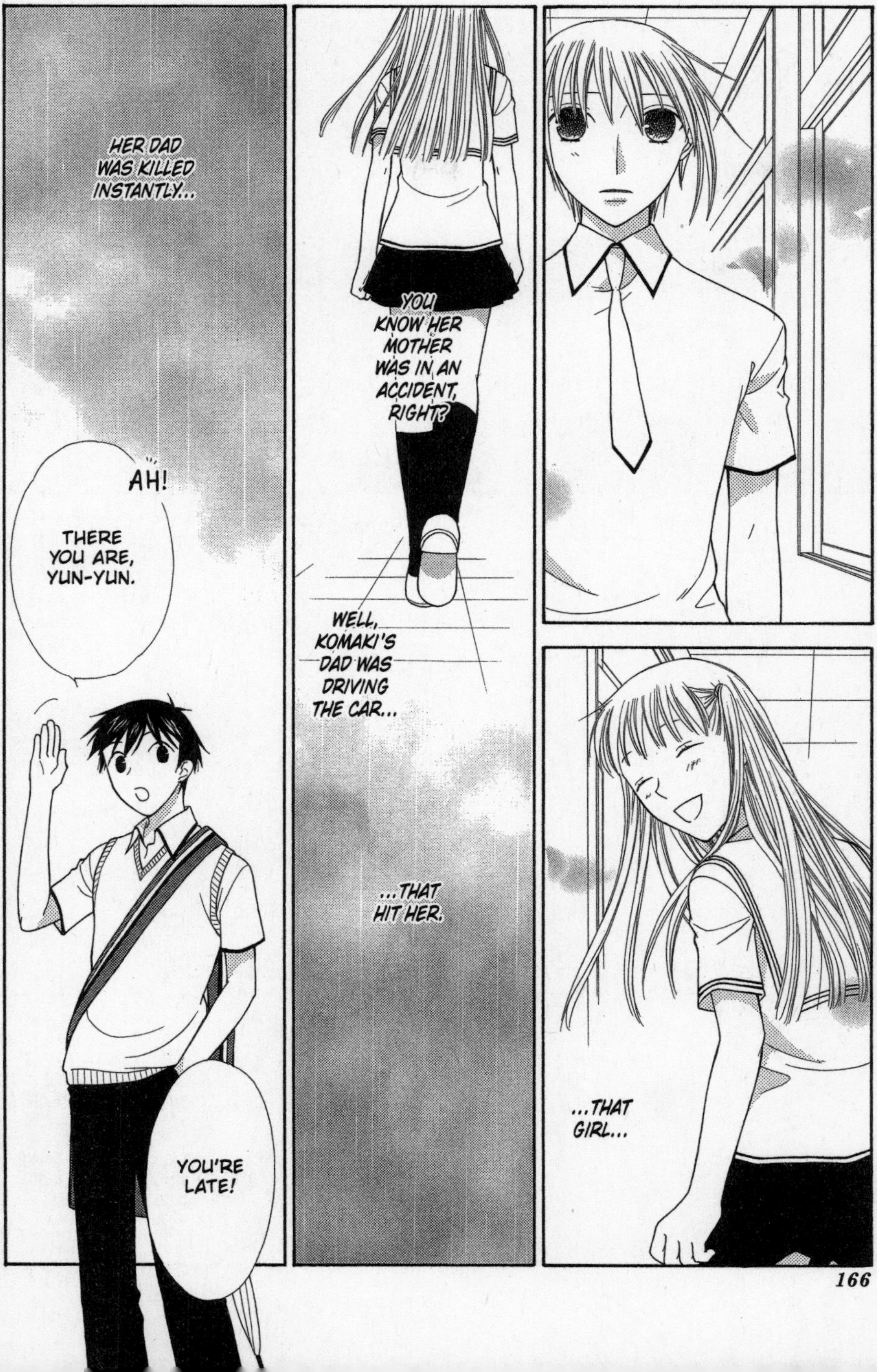
...THAT GIRL...
YOU KNOW HER MOTHER WAS IN AN ACCIDENT, RIGHT?
WELL, KOMAKI'S DAD WAS DRIVING THE CAR...
...THAT HIT HER.
HER DAD WAS KILLED INSTANTLY...
AH!
THERE YOU ARE, YUN-YUN.
YOU'RE LATE!

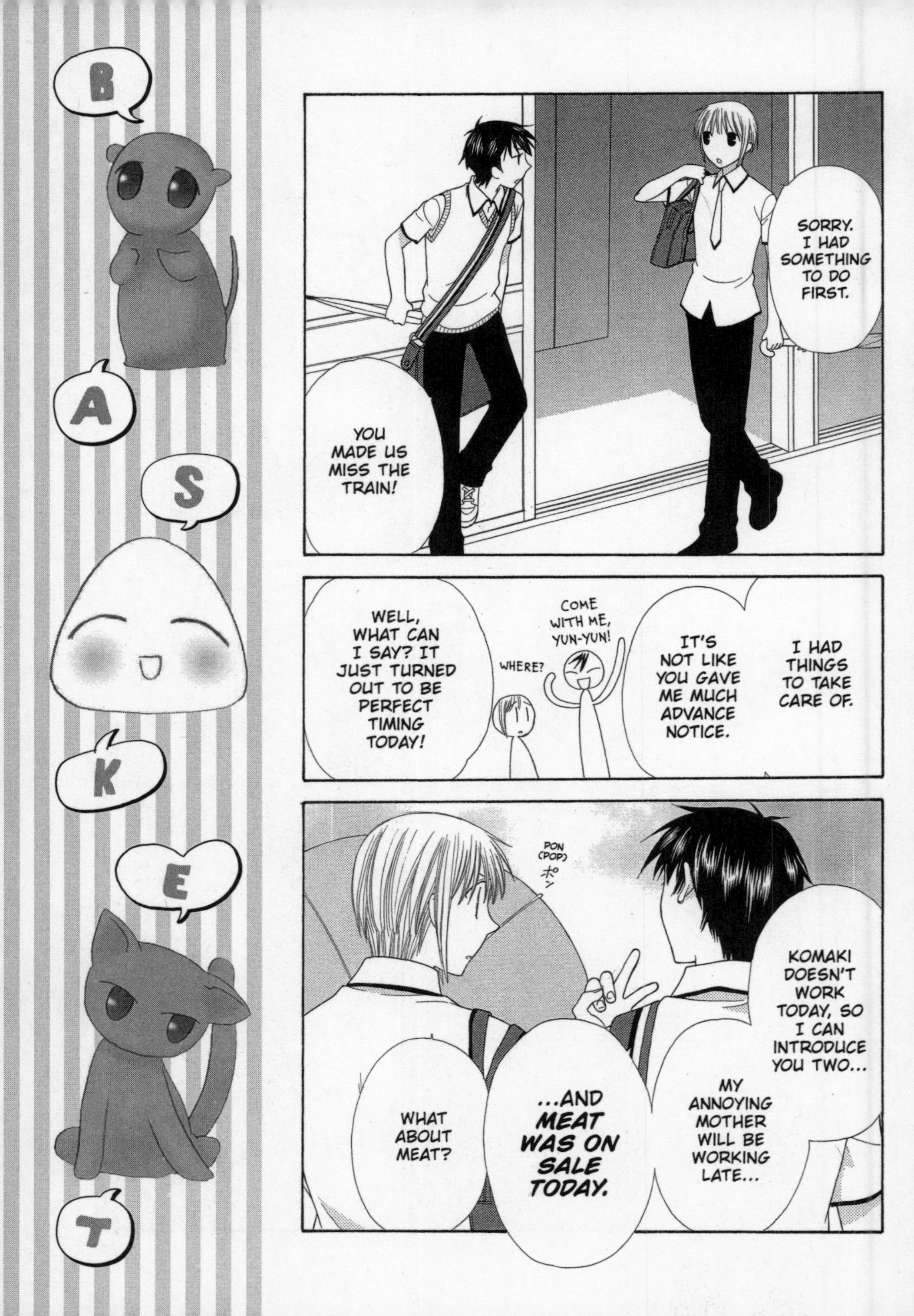
SORRY. I HAD SOMETHING TO DO FIRST.
YOU MADE US MISS THE TRAIN!
I HAD THINGS TO TAKE CARE OF.
IT'S NOT LIKE YOU GAVE ME MUCH ADVANCE NOTICE.
COME WITH ME, YUN-YUN!
WHERE?
WELL, WHAT CAN I SAY? IT JUST TURNED OUT TO BE PERFECT TIMING TODAY!
PON (POP) ポン
KOMAKI DOESN'T WORK TODAY, SO I CAN INTRODUCE YOU TWO...
MY ANNOYING MOTHER WILL BE WORKING LATE...
...AND MEAT WAS ON SALE TODAY.
WHAT ABOUT MEAT?
B
A
S
K
E
T

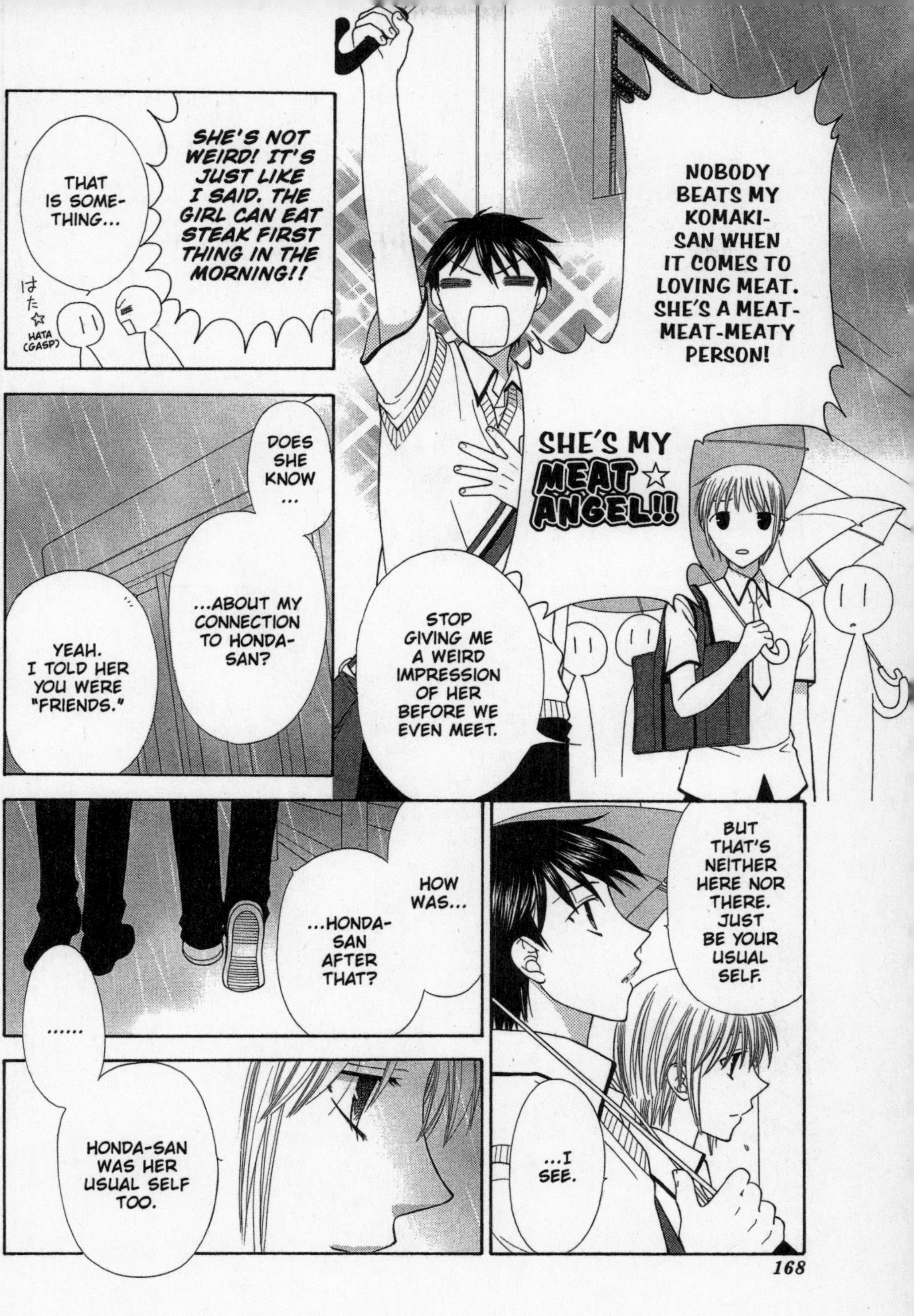
NOBODY BEATS MY KOMAKI-SAN WHEN IT COMES TO LOVING MEAT. SHE'S A MEAT-MEAT-MEATY PERSON!
SHE'S MY MEAT☆ANGEL!!
STOP GIVING ME A WEIRD IMPRESSION OF HER BEFORE WE EVEN MEET.
SHE'S NOT WEIRD! IT'S JUST LIKE I SAID. THE GIRL CAN EAT STEAK FIRST THING IN THE MORNING!!
THAT IS SOME-THING...
はた☆
HATA (GASP)
DOES SHE KNOW...
...ABOUT MY CONNECTION TO HONDA-SAN?
YEAH. I TOLD HER YOU WERE "FRIENDS."
BUT THAT'S NEITHER HERE NOR THERE. JUST BE YOUR USUAL SELF.
HOW WAS...
...HONDA-SAN AFTER THAT?
......
...I SEE.
HONDA-SAN WAS HER USUAL SELF TOO.

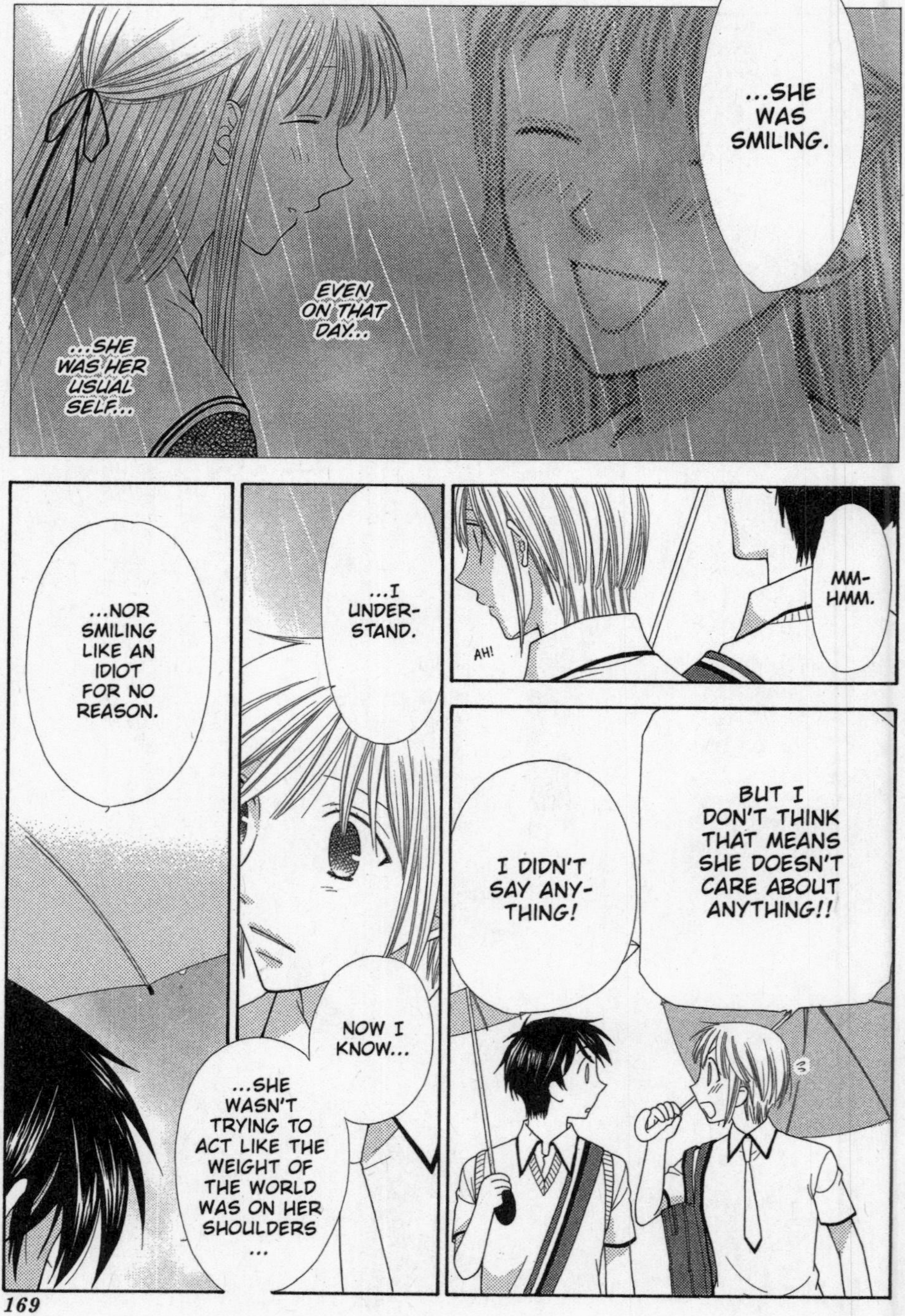
...SHE WAS SMILING.
EVEN ON THAT DAY...
...SHE WAS HER USUAL SELF...
MM-HMM.
AH!
BUT I DON'T THINK THAT MEANS SHE DOESN'T CARE ABOUT ANYTHING!!
I DIDN'T SAY ANY-THING!
...I UNDER-STAND.
NOW I KNOW...
...SHE WASN'T TRYING TO ACT LIKE THE WEIGHT OF THE WORLD WAS ON HER SHOULDERS ...
...NOR SMILING LIKE AN IDIOT FOR NO REASON.

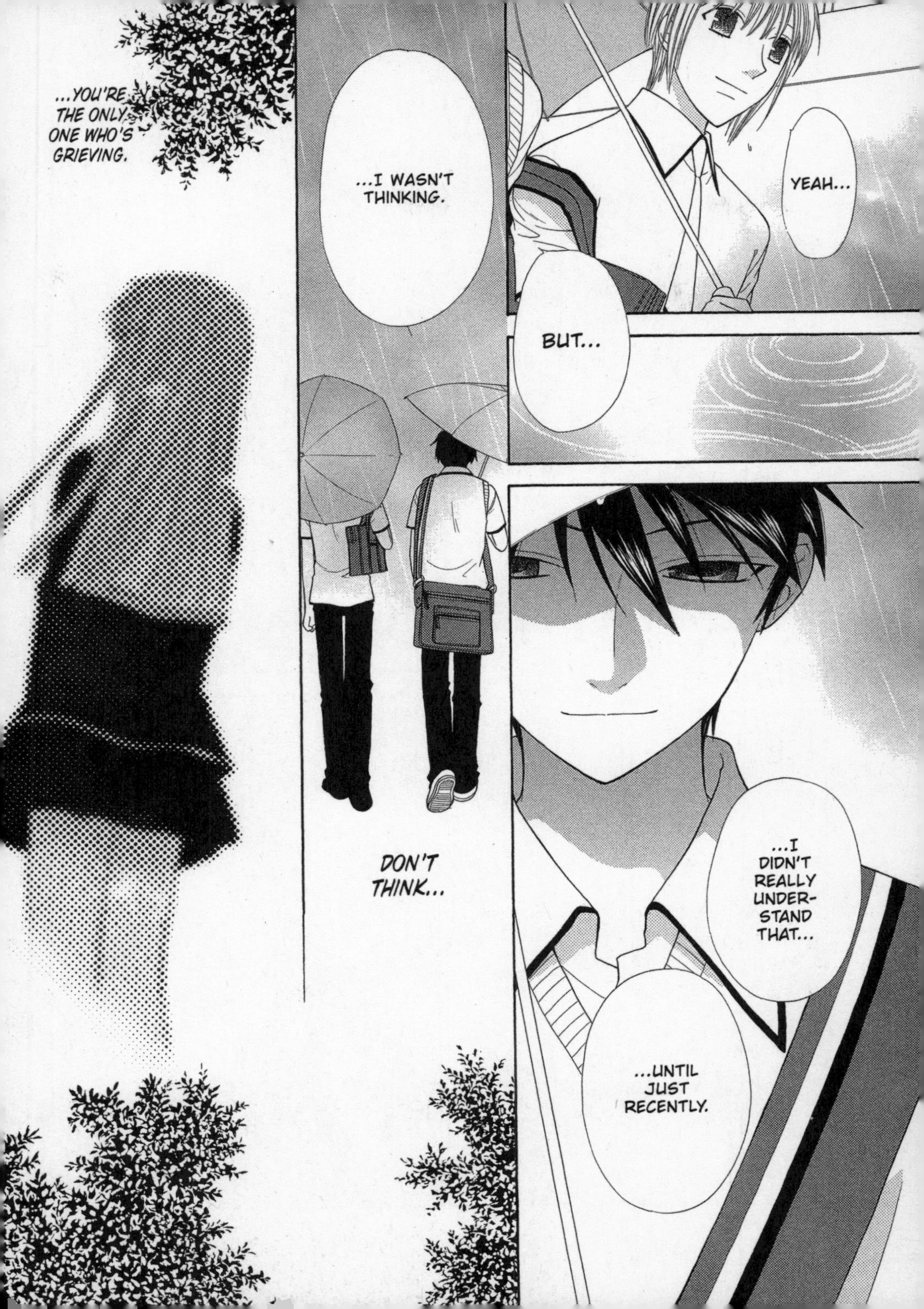
YEAH...
BUT...
...I DIDN'T REALLY UNDER-STAND THAT...
...UNTIL JUST RECENTLY.
...I WASN'T THINKING.
DON'T THINK...
...YOU'RE THE ONLY ONE WHO'S GRIEVING.

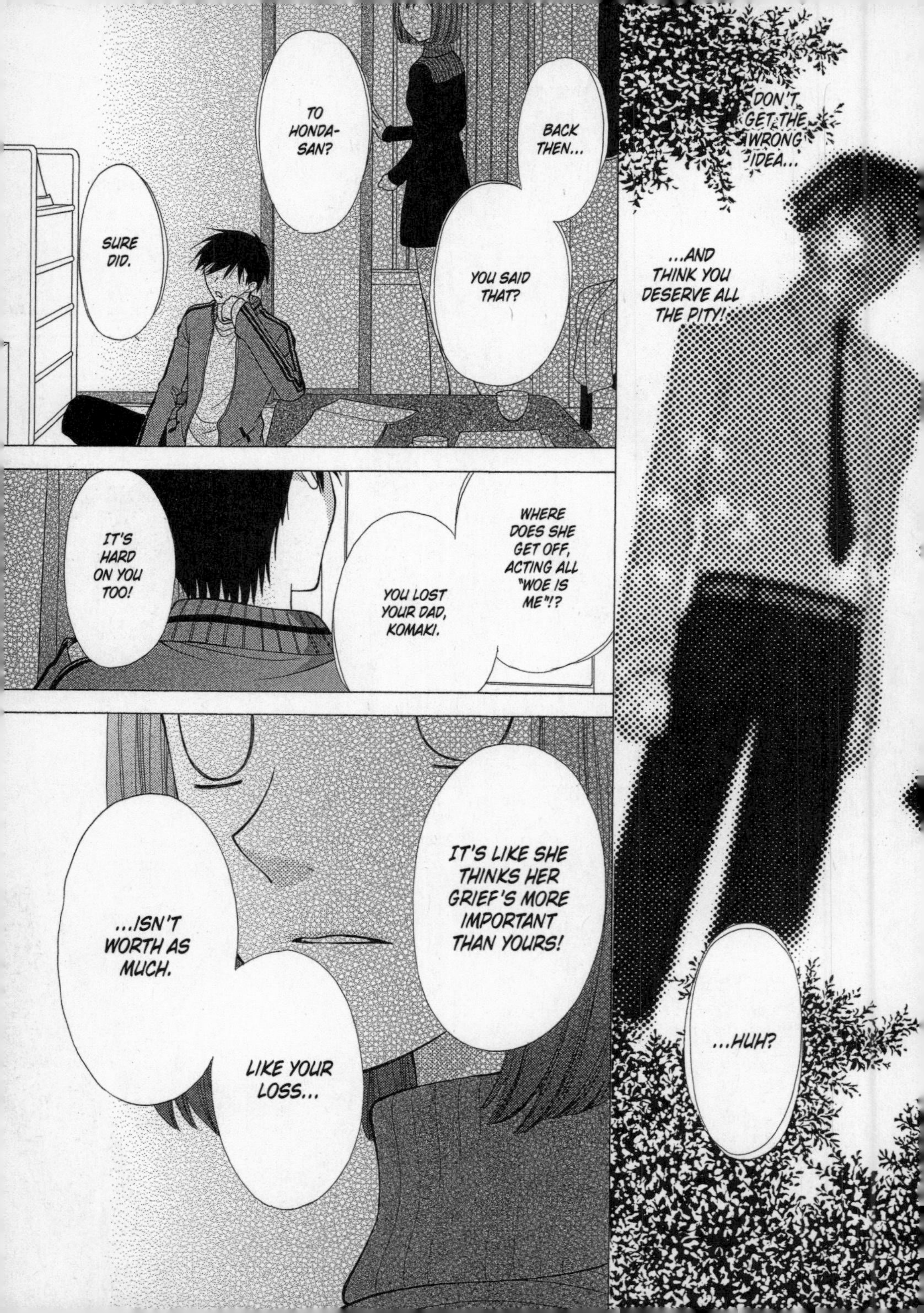
DON'T GET THE WRONG IDEA...
...AND THINK YOU DESERVE ALL THE PITY!
...HUH?
BACK THEN...
YOU SAID THAT?
TO HONDA-SAN?
SURE DID.
WHERE DOES SHE GET OFF, ACTING ALL "WOE IS ME"!?
YOU LOST YOUR DAD, KOMAKI.
IT'S HARD ON YOU TOO!
IT'S LIKE SHE THINKS HER GRIEF'S MORE IMPORTANT THAN YOURS!
LIKE YOUR LOSS...
...ISN'T WORTH AS MUCH.

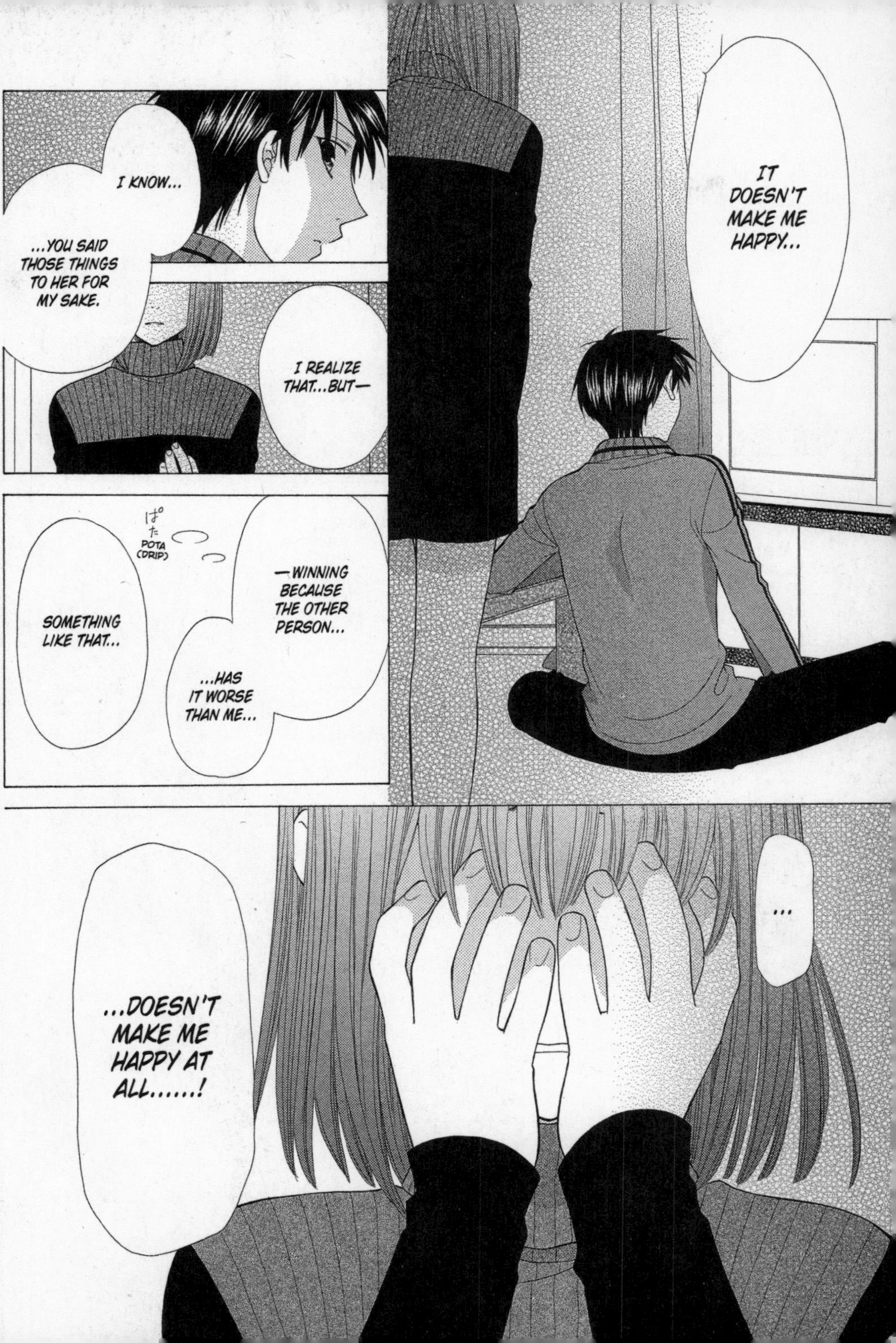
IT DOESN'T MAKE ME HAPPY...
I KNOW...
...YOU SAID THOSE THINGS TO HER FOR MY SAKE.
I REALIZE THAT...BUT—
—WINNING BECAUSE THE OTHER PERSON...
...HAS IT WORSE THAN ME...
ぱた
POTA (DRIP)
SOMETHING LIKE THAT...
...
...DOESN'T MAKE ME HAPPY AT ALL......!

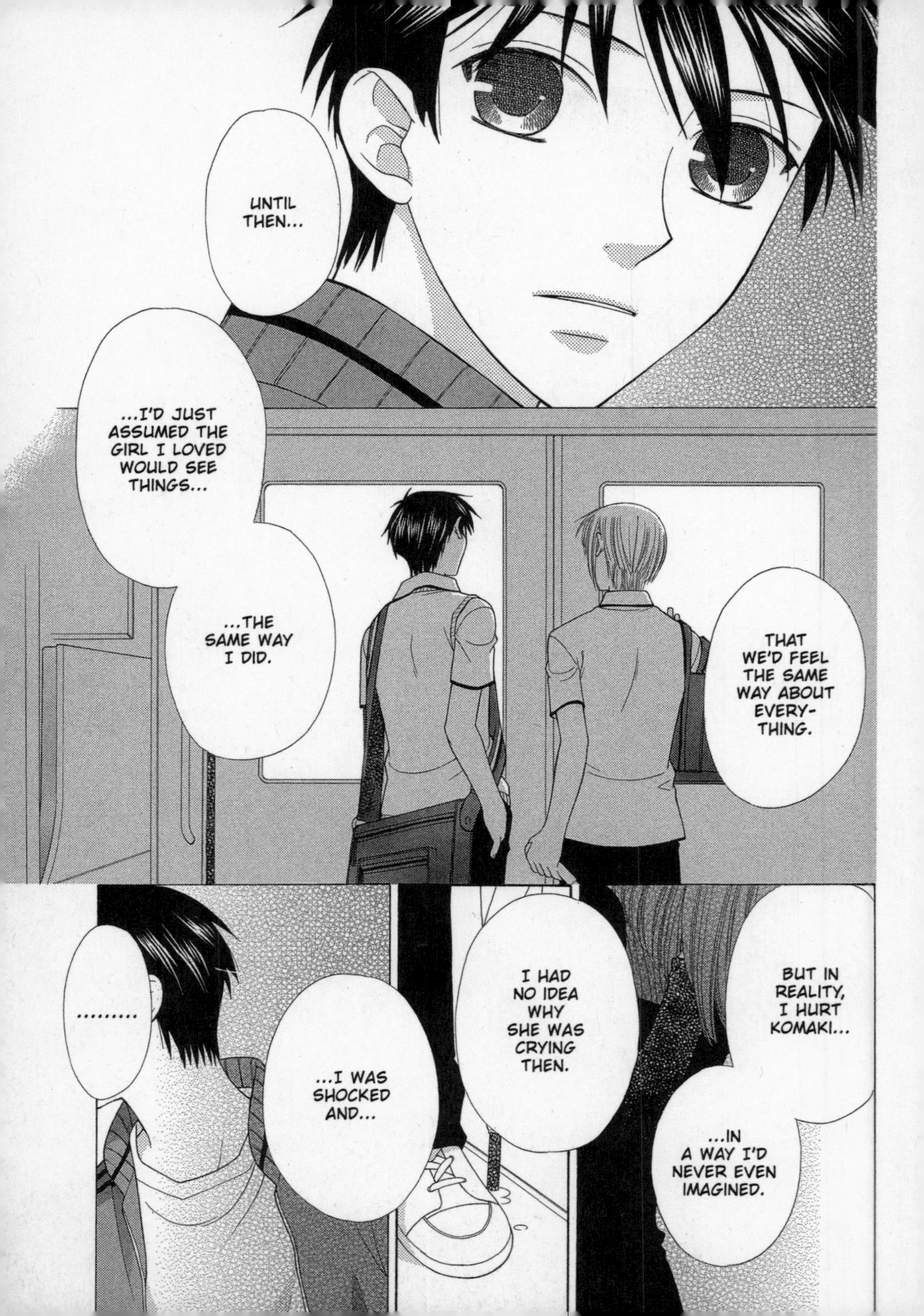
UNTIL THEN...
...I'D JUST ASSUMED THE GIRL I LOVED WOULD SEE THINGS...
...THE SAME WAY I DID.
THAT WE'D FEEL THE SAME WAY ABOUT EVERY-THING.
BUT IN REALITY, I HURT KOMAKI...
...IN A WAY I'D NEVER EVEN IMAGINED.
I HAD NO IDEA WHY SHE WAS CRYING THEN.
...I WAS SHOCKED AND...
....

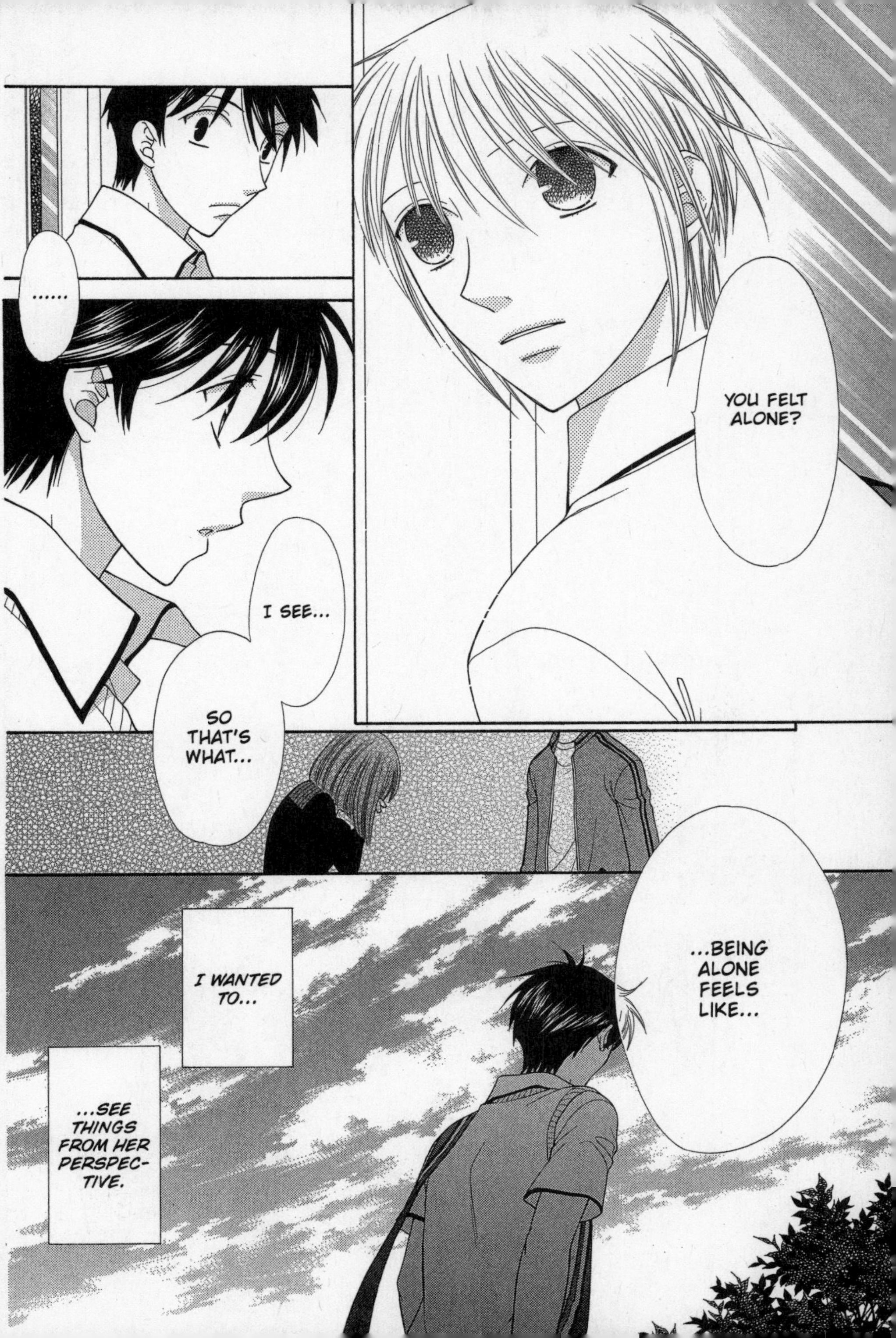
YOU FELT ALONE?
......
I SEE...
SO THAT'S WHAT...
...BEING ALONE FEELS LIKE...
I WANTED TO...
...SEE THINGS FROM HER PERSPEC-TIVE.

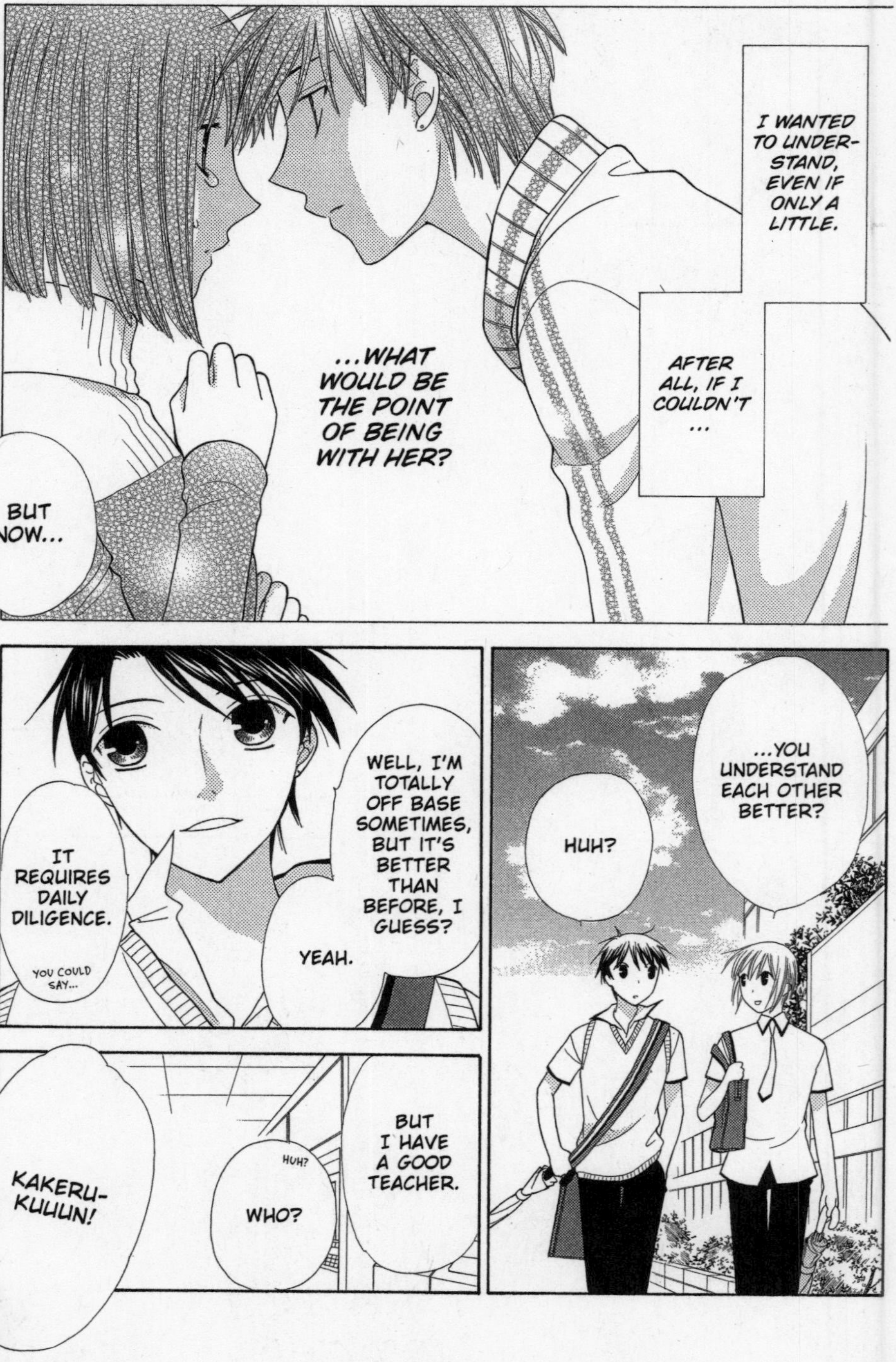
I WANTED TO UNDER-STAND, EVEN IF ONLY A LITTLE.
AFTER ALL, IF I COULDN'T ...
...WHAT WOULD BE THE POINT OF BEING WITH HER?
BUT NOW...
...YOU UNDERSTAND EACH OTHER BETTER?
HUH?
WELL, I'M TOTALLY OFF BASE SOMETIMES, BUT IT'S BETTER THAN BEFORE, I GUESS?
YEAH.
IT REQUIRES DAILY DILIGENCE.
YOU COULD SAY...
BUT I HAVE A GOOD TEACHER.
HUH?
WHO?
KAKERU-KUUUN!

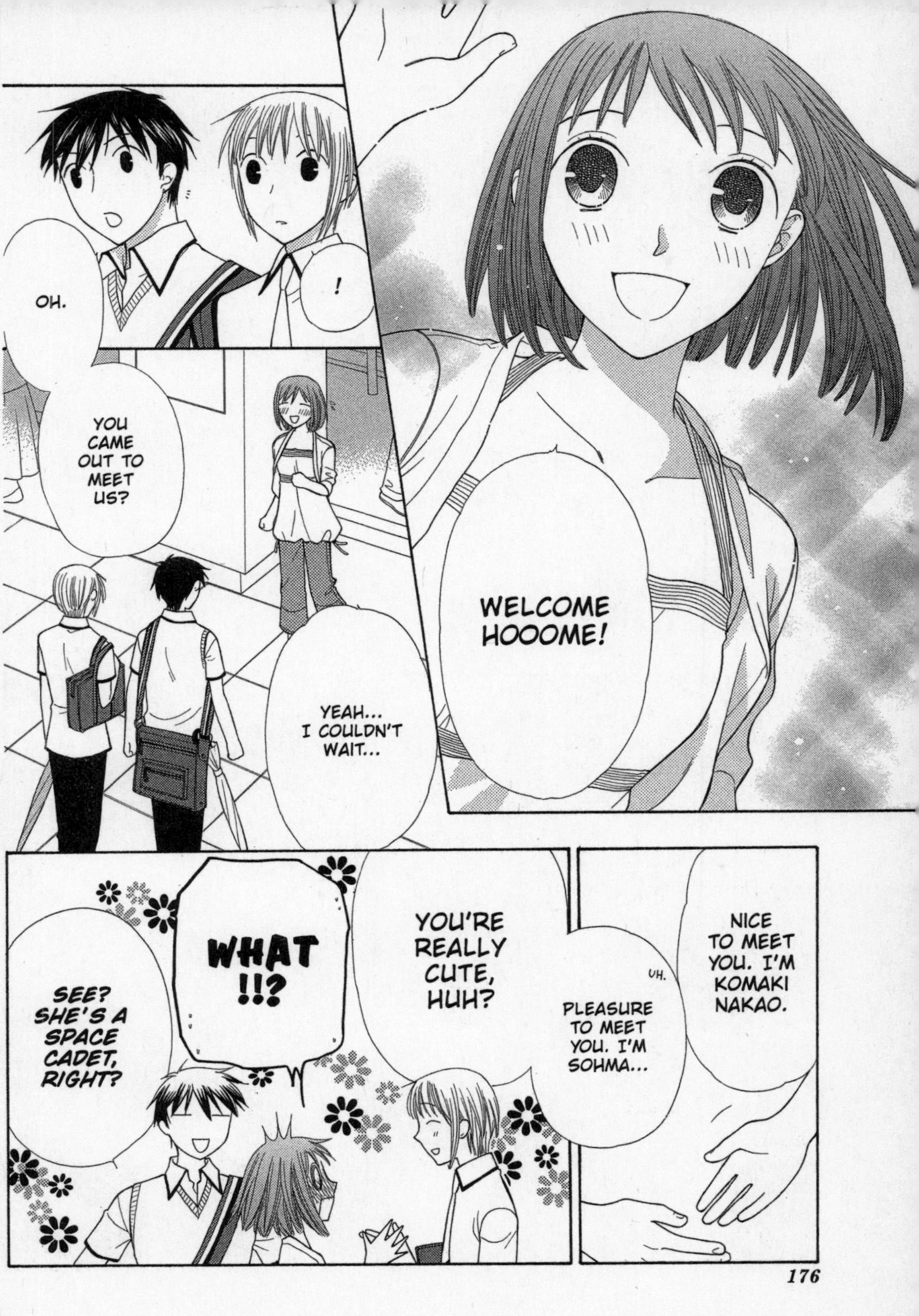
WELCOME HOOOME!
!
OH.
YOU CAME OUT TO MEET US?
YEAH... I COULDN'T WAIT...
NICE TO MEET YOU. I'M KOMAKI NAKAO.
UH.
PLEASURE TO MEET YOU. I'M SOHMA...
YOU'RE REALLY CUTE, HUH?
WHAT!!?
SEE? SHE'S A SPACE CADET, RIGHT?

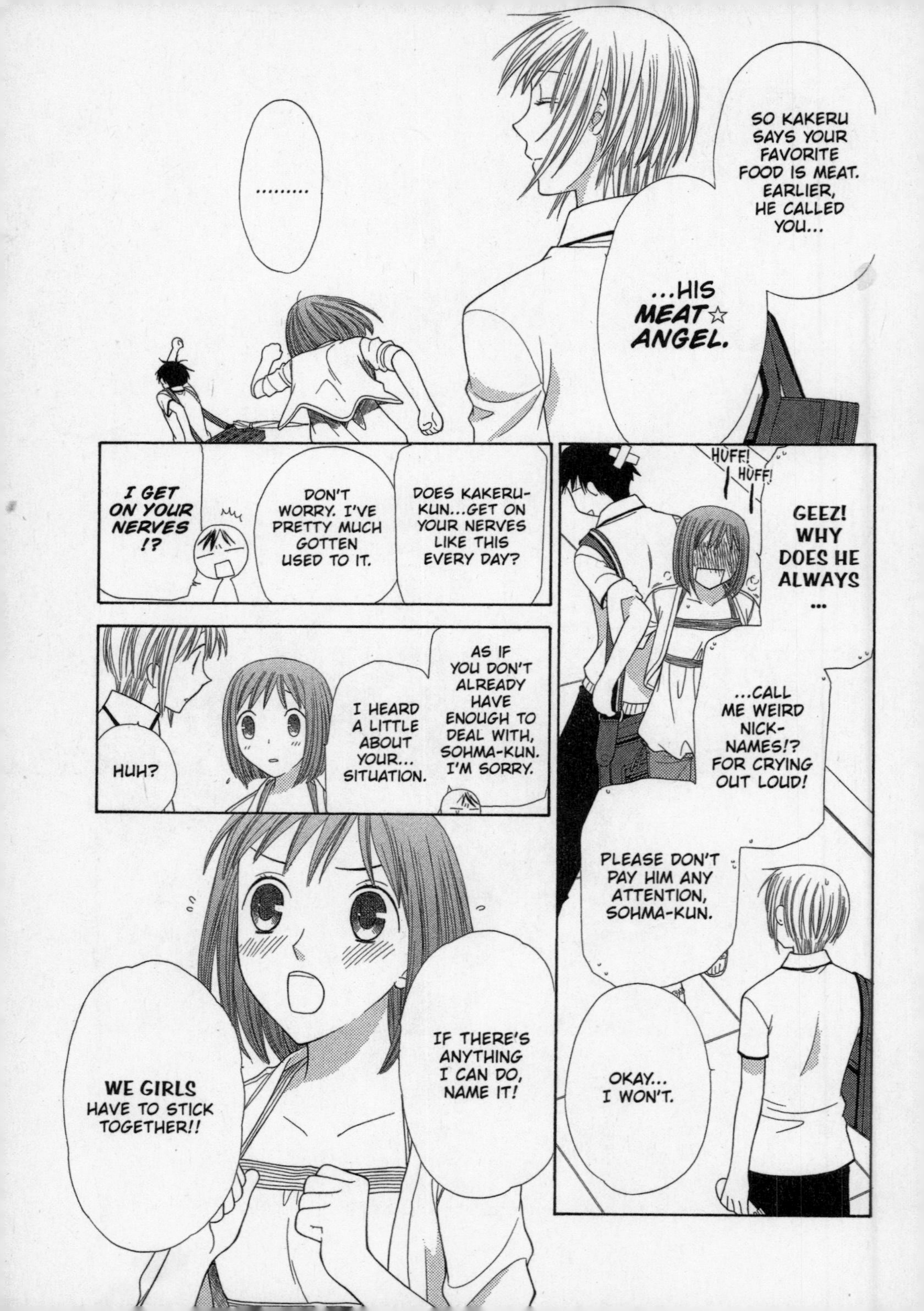
SO KAKERU SAYS YOUR FAVORITE FOOD IS MEAT. EARLIER, HE CALLED YOU...
...HIS MEAT☆ ANGEL.
....
HUFF! HUFF!
GEEZ! WHY DOES HE ALWAYS ...
...CALL ME WEIRD NICK-NAMES!? FOR CRYING OUT LOUD!
PLEASE DON'T PAY HIM ANY ATTENTION, SOHMA-KUN.
OKAY... I WON'T.
DOES KAKERU-KUN...GET ON YOUR NERVES LIKE THIS EVERY DAY?
DON'T WORRY. I'VE PRETTY MUCH GOTTEN USED TO IT.
I GET ON YOUR NERVES!?
AS IF YOU DON'T ALREADY HAVE ENOUGH TO DEAL WITH, SOHMA-KUN. I'M SORRY.
I HEARD A LITTLE ABOUT YOUR... SITUATION.
HUH?
IF THERE'S ANYTHING I CAN DO, NAME IT!
WE GIRLS HAVE TO STICK TOGETHER!!

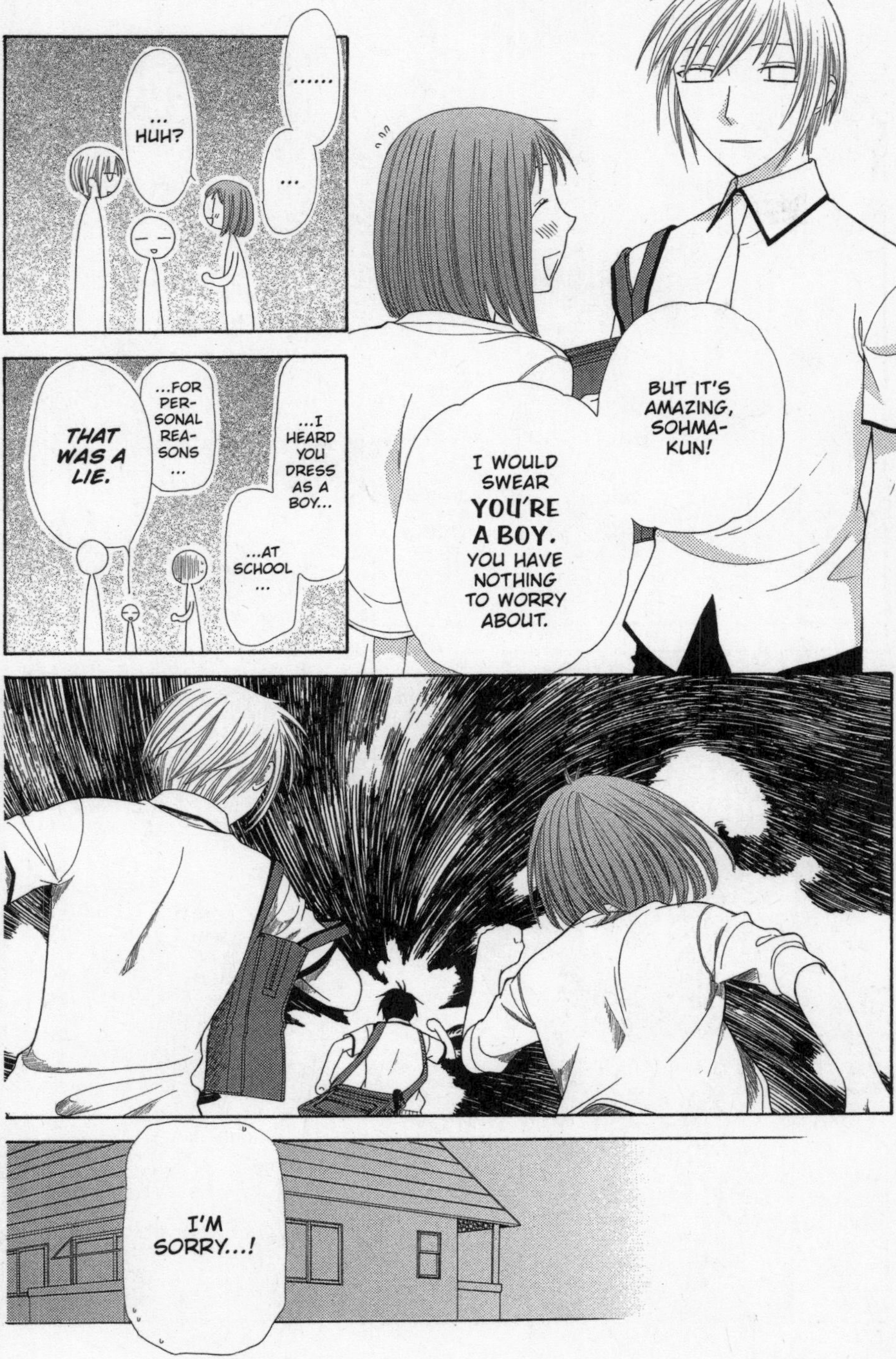
BUT IT'S AMAZING, SOHMA-KUN!
I WOULD SWEAR YOU'RE A BOY. YOU HAVE NOTHING TO WORRY ABOUT.
......
...
... HUH?
...I HEARD YOU DRESS AS A BOY...
...AT SCHOOL ...
...FOR PERSONAL REASONS ...
THAT WAS A LIE.
I'M SORRY...!

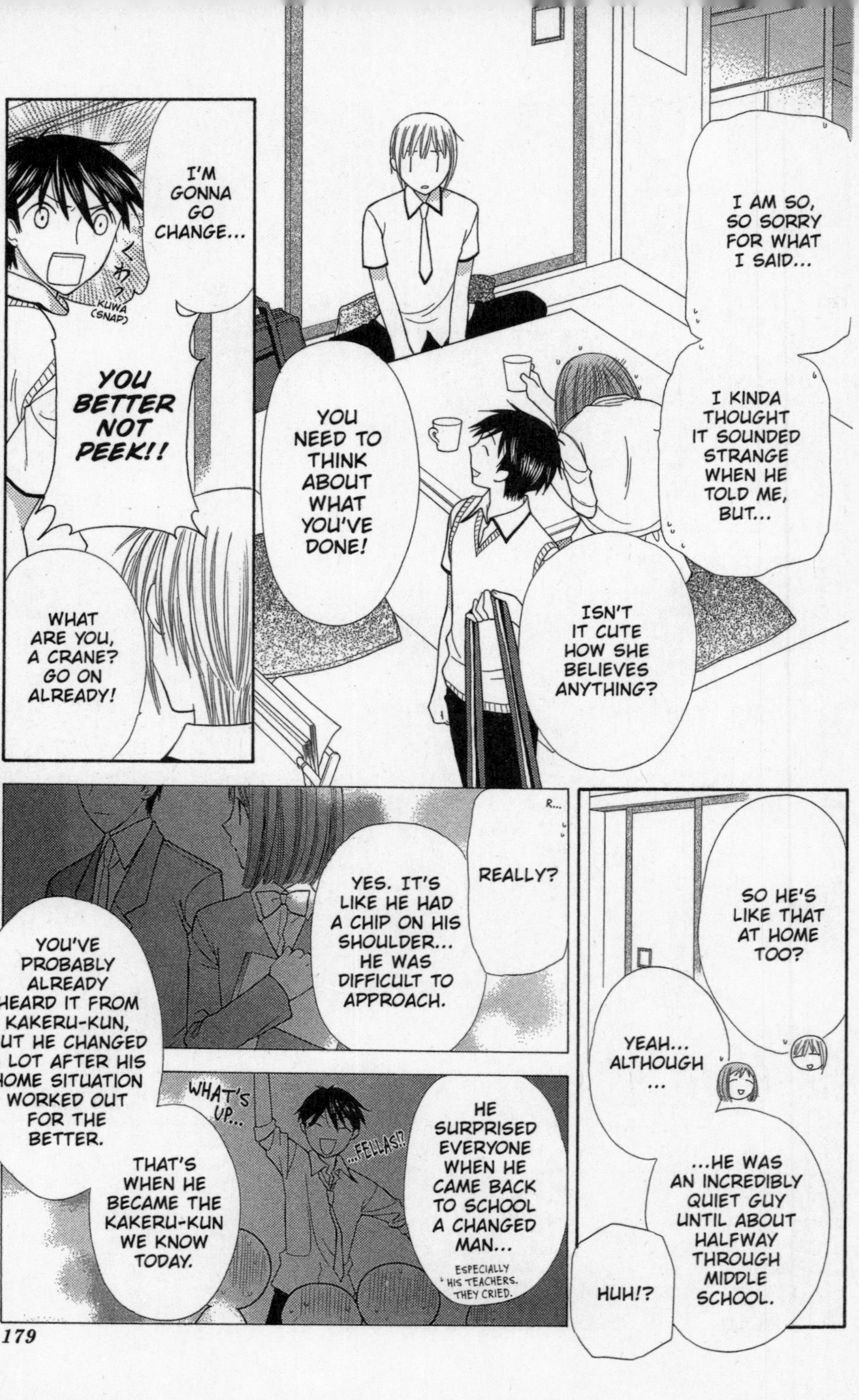
I AM SO, SO SORRY FOR WHAT I SAID...
I KINDA THOUGHT IT SOUNDED STRANGE WHEN HE TOLD ME, BUT...
YOU NEED TO THINK ABOUT WHAT YOU'VE DONE!
ISN'T IT CUTE HOW SHE BELIEVES ANYTHING?
I'M GONNA GO CHANGE...
KUWA (SNAP)
YOU BETTER NOT PEEK!!
WHAT ARE YOU, A CRANE? GO ON ALREADY!
SO HE'S LIKE THAT AT HOME TOO?
YEAH... ALTHOUGH...
...HE WAS AN INCREDIBLY QUIET GUY UNTIL ABOUT HALFWAY THROUGH MIDDLE SCHOOL.
HUH!?
R...
REALLY?
YES. IT'S LIKE HE HAD A CHIP ON HIS SHOULDER... HE WAS DIFFICULT TO APPROACH.
YOU'VE PROBABLY ALREADY HEARD IT FROM KAKERU-KUN, BUT HE CHANGED A LOT AFTER HIS HOME SITUATION WORKED OUT FOR THE BETTER.
HE SURPRISED EVERYONE WHEN HE CAME BACK TO SCHOOL A CHANGED MAN...
ESPECIALLY HIS TEACHERS. THEY CRIED.
WHAT'S UP...
...FELLAS!?
THAT'S WHEN HE BECAME THE KAKERU-KUN WE KNOW TODAY.

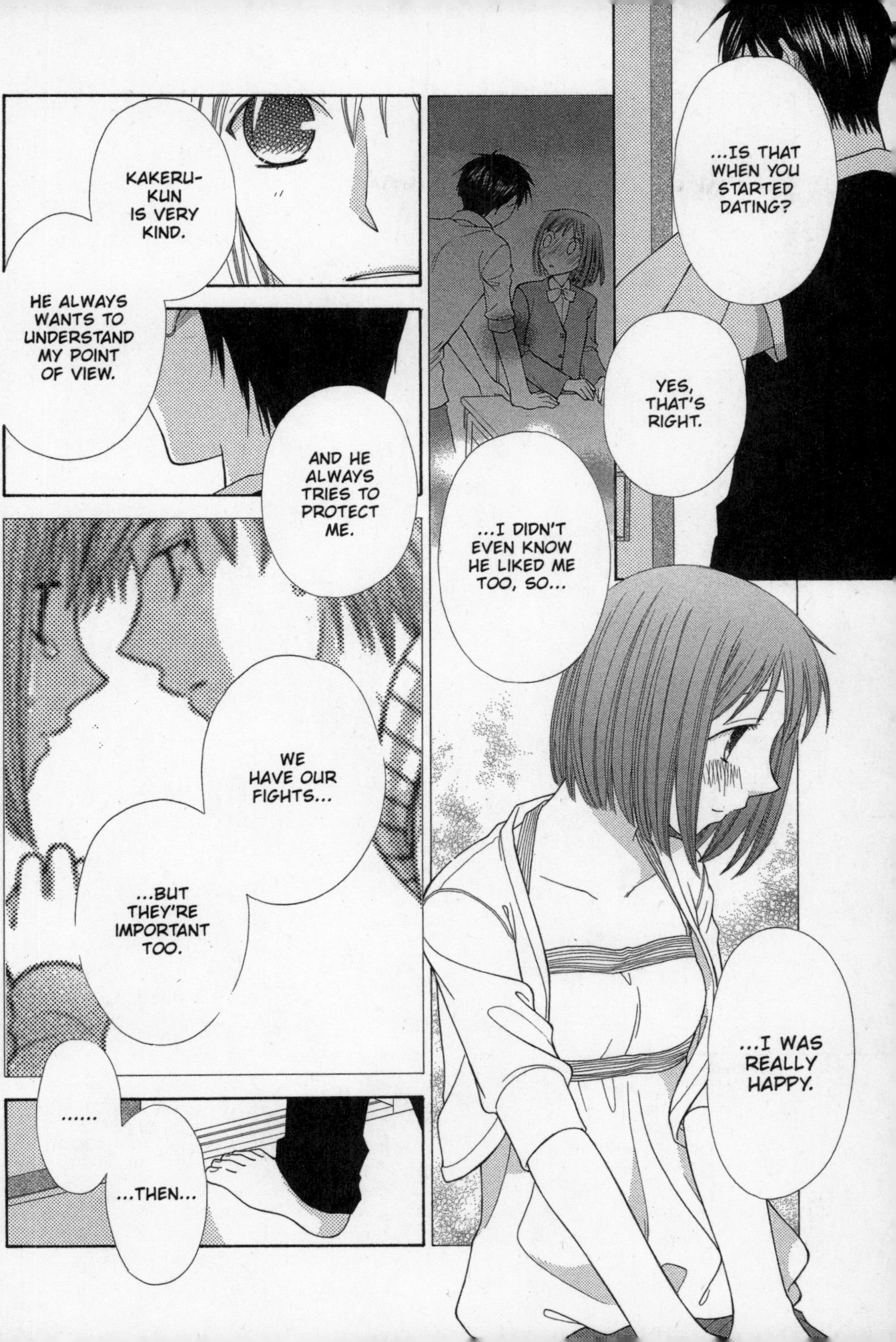
...IS THAT WHEN YOU STARTED DATING?
YES, THAT'S RIGHT.
...I DIDN'T EVEN KNOW HE LIKED ME TOO, SO...
...I WAS REALLY HAPPY.
KAKERU-KUN IS VERY KIND.
HE ALWAYS WANTS TO UNDERSTAND MY POINT OF VIEW.
AND HE ALWAYS TRIES TO PROTECT ME.
WE HAVE OUR FIGHTS...
...BUT THEY'RE IMPORTANT TOO.
......
...THEN...

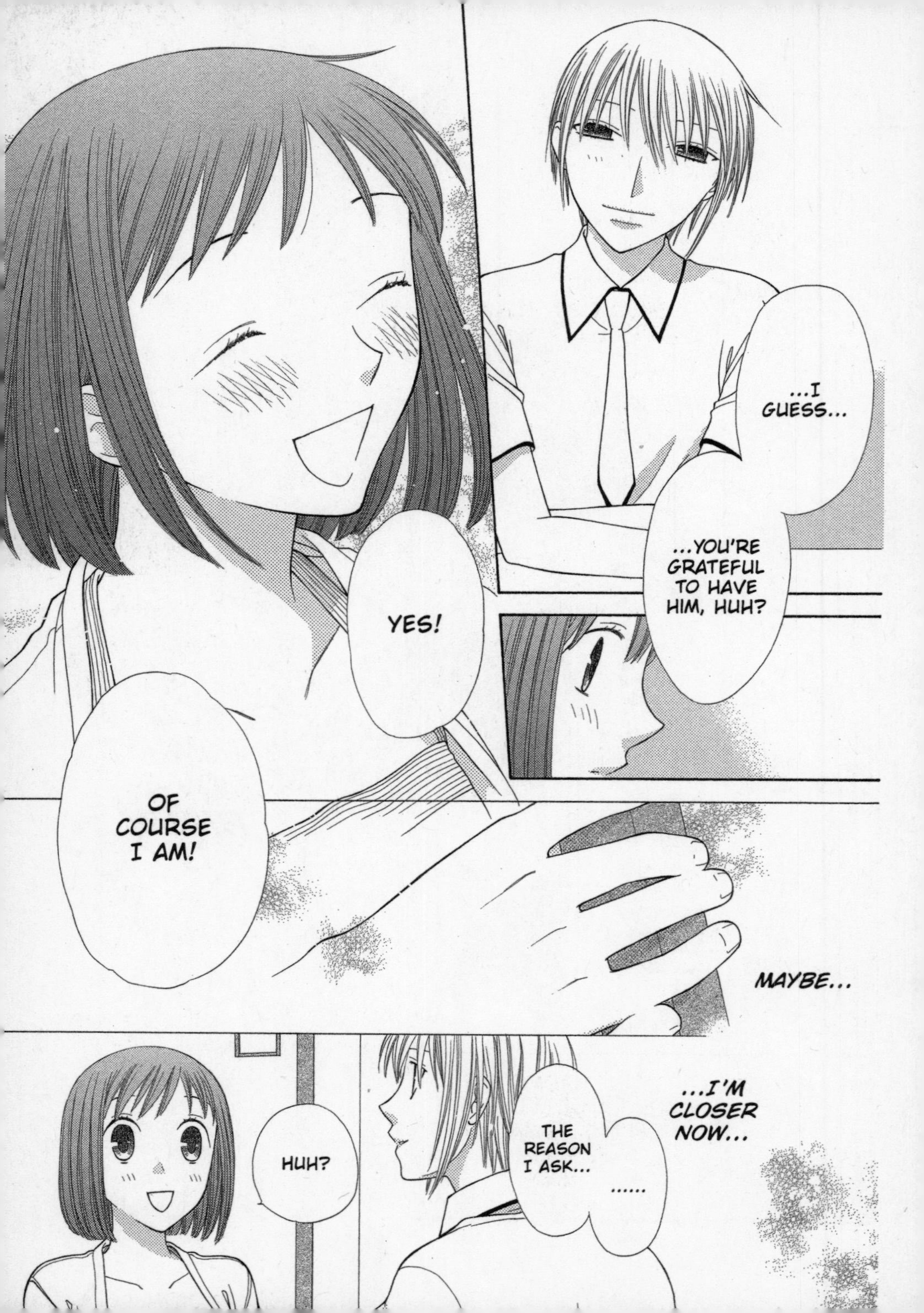

...I GUESS...
...YOU'RE GRATEFUL TO HAVE HIM, HUH?
YES!
OF COURSE I AM!
MAYBE...
...I'M CLOSER NOW...
......
THE REASON I ASK...
HUH?

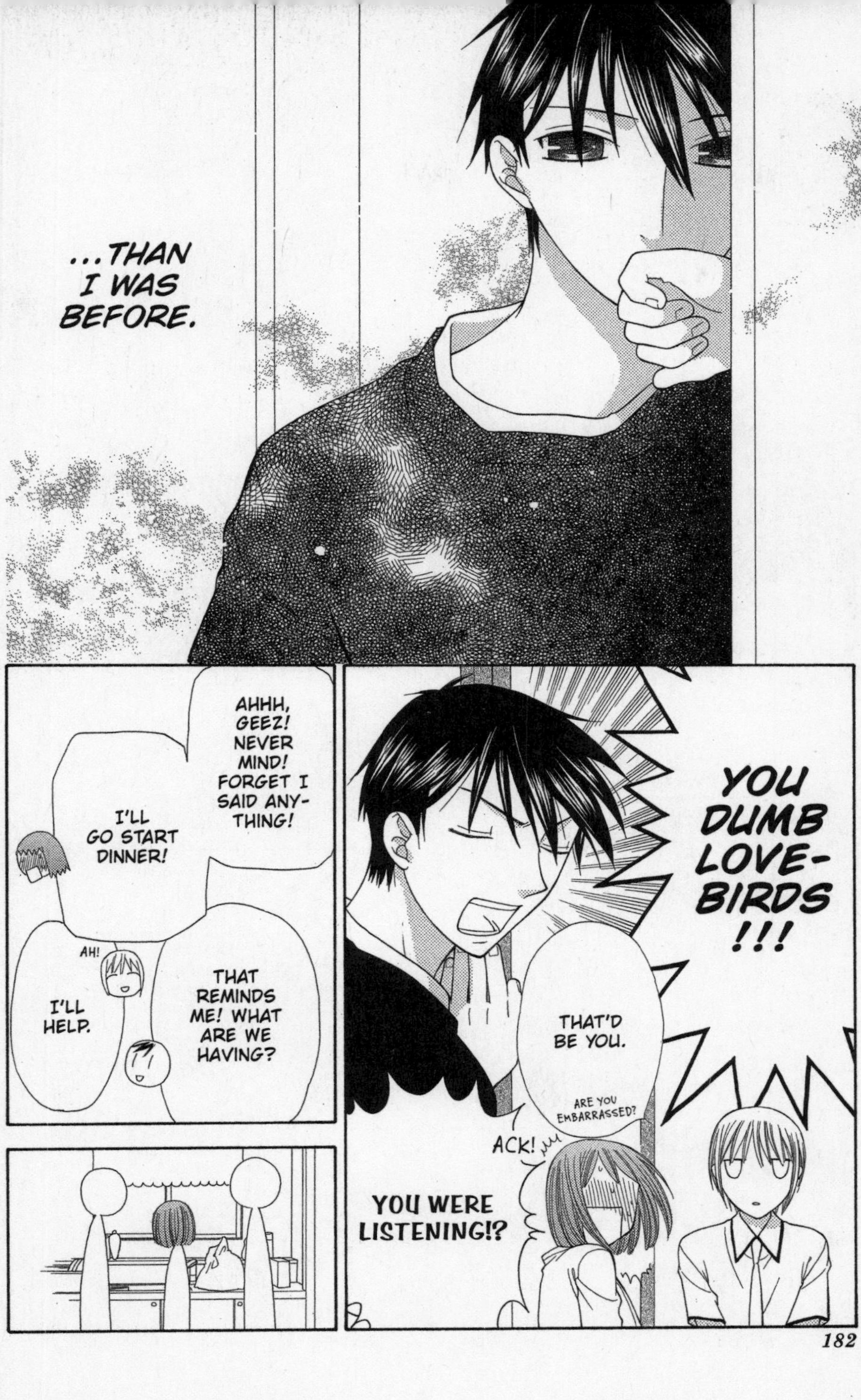
...THAN I WAS BEFORE.
YOU DUMB LOVE-BIRDS!!!
THAT'D BE YOU.
ARE YOU EMBARRASSED?
ACK!
YOU WERE LISTENING!?
AHHH, GEEZ! NEVER MIND! FORGET I SAID ANY-THING!
I'LL GO START DINNER!
THAT REMINDS ME! WHAT ARE WE HAVING?
AH!
I'LL HELP.

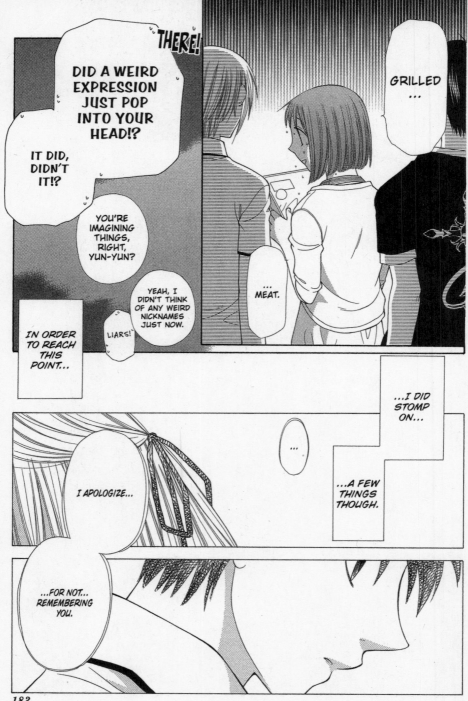

THERE!

DID A WEIRD EXPRESSION JUST POP INTO YOUR HEAD!?

IT DID, DIDN'T IT!?

YOU'RE IMAGINING THINGS, RIGHT, YUN-YUN?

YEAH, I DIDN'T THINK OF ANY WEIRD NICKNAMES JUST NOW.

LIARS!

IN ORDER TO REACH THIS POINT...

GRILLED...

... MEAT.

...I DID STOMP ON...

...

...A FEW THINGS THOUGH.

I APOLOGIZE...

...FOR NOT... REMEMBERING YOU.

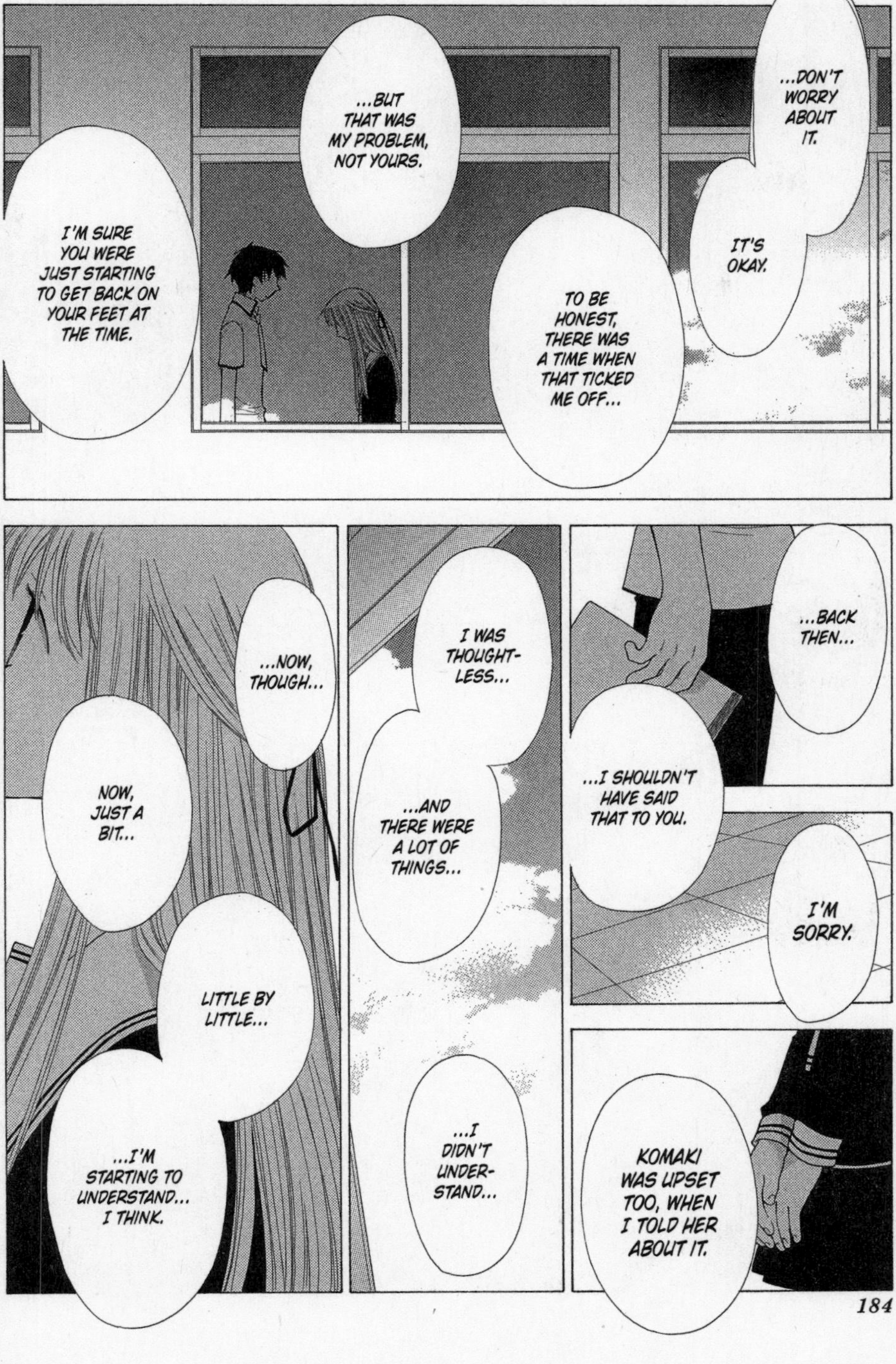
...DON'T WORRY ABOUT IT.
IT'S OKAY.
TO BE HONEST, THERE WAS A TIME WHEN THAT TICKED ME OFF...
...BUT THAT WAS MY PROBLEM, NOT YOURS.
I'M SURE YOU WERE JUST STARTING TO GET BACK ON YOUR FEET AT THE TIME.
...BACK THEN...
...I SHOULDN'T HAVE SAID THAT TO YOU.
I'M SORRY.
KOMAKI WAS UPSET TOO, WHEN I TOLD HER ABOUT IT.
I WAS THOUGHT-LESS...
...AND THERE WERE A LOT OF THINGS...
...I DIDN'T UNDER-STAND...
...NOW, THOUGH...
NOW, JUST A BIT...
LITTLE BY LITTLE...
...I'M STARTING TO UNDERSTAND... I THINK.

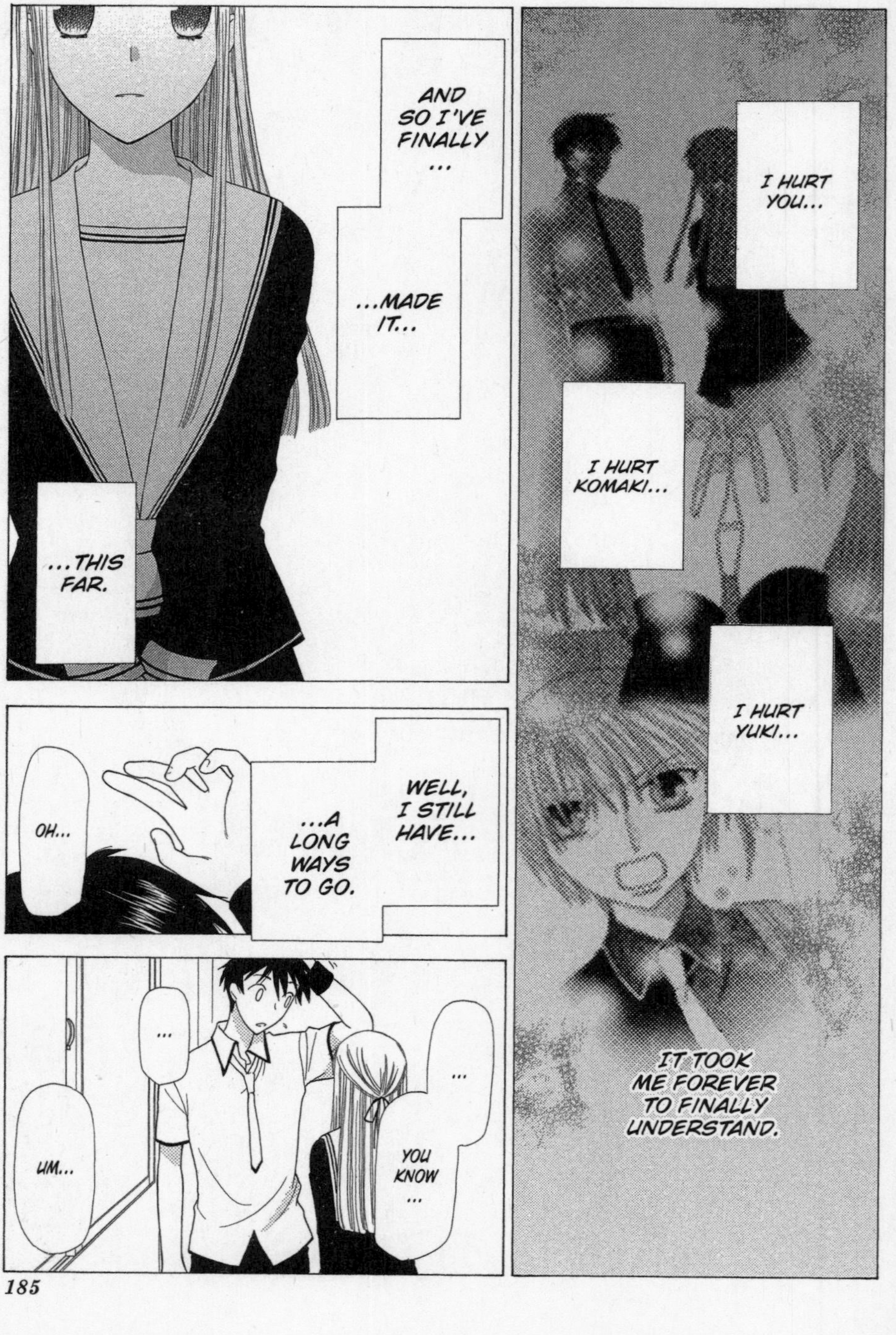
I HURT YOU...
I HURT KOMAKI...
I HURT YUKI...
IT TOOK ME FOREVER TO FINALLY UNDERSTAND.
AND SO I'VE FINALLY ...
...MADE IT...
...THIS FAR.
WELL, I STILL HAVE...
...A LONG WAYS TO GO.
OH...
...
YOU KNOW ...
...
UM...

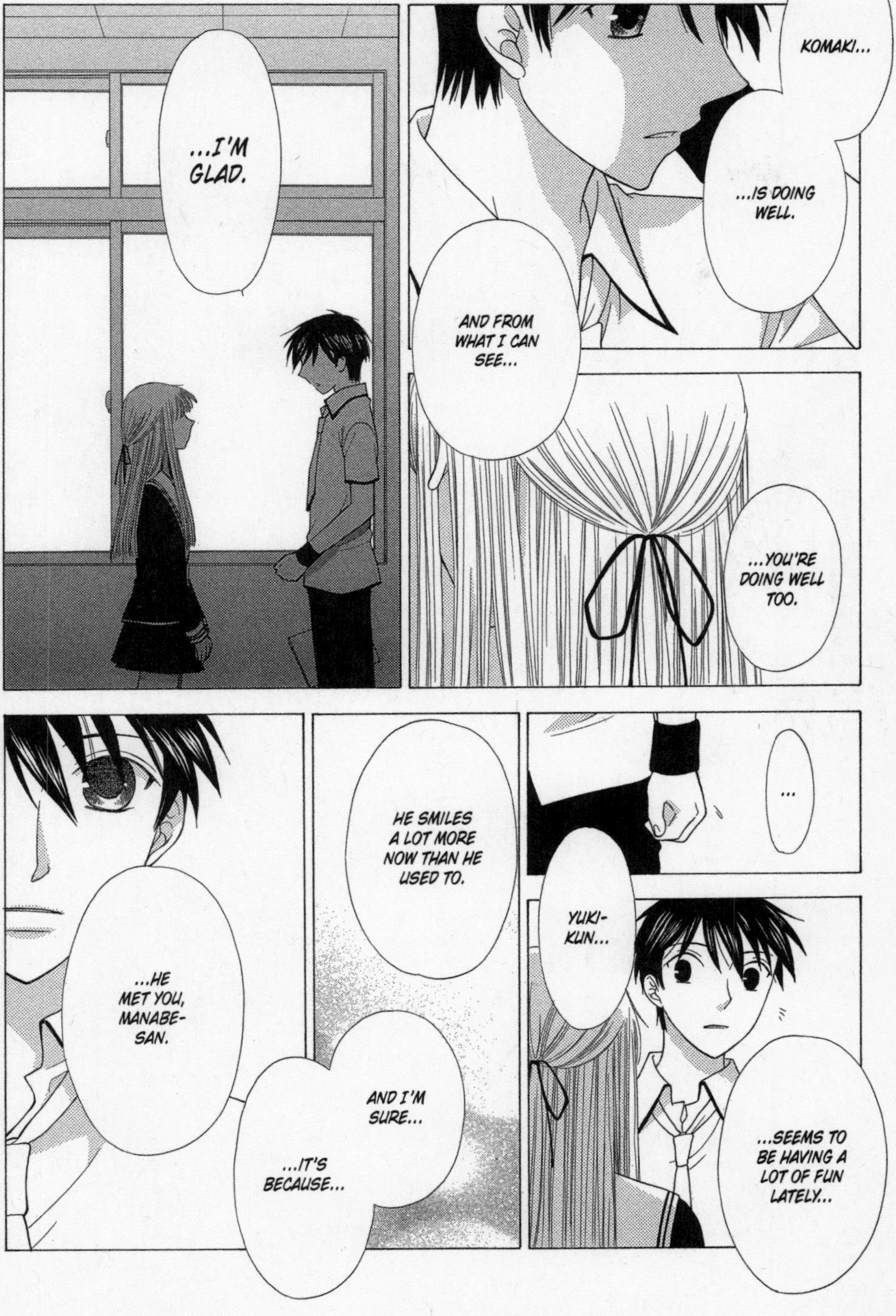
KOMAKI...
...IS DOING WELL.
AND FROM WHAT I CAN SEE...
...YOU'RE DOING WELL TOO.
...I'M GLAD.
...
YUKI-KUN...
...SEEMS TO BE HAVING A LOT OF FUN LATELY...
HE SMILES A LOT MORE NOW THAN HE USED TO.
AND I'M SURE...
...IT'S BECAUSE...
...HE MET YOU, MANABE-SAN.

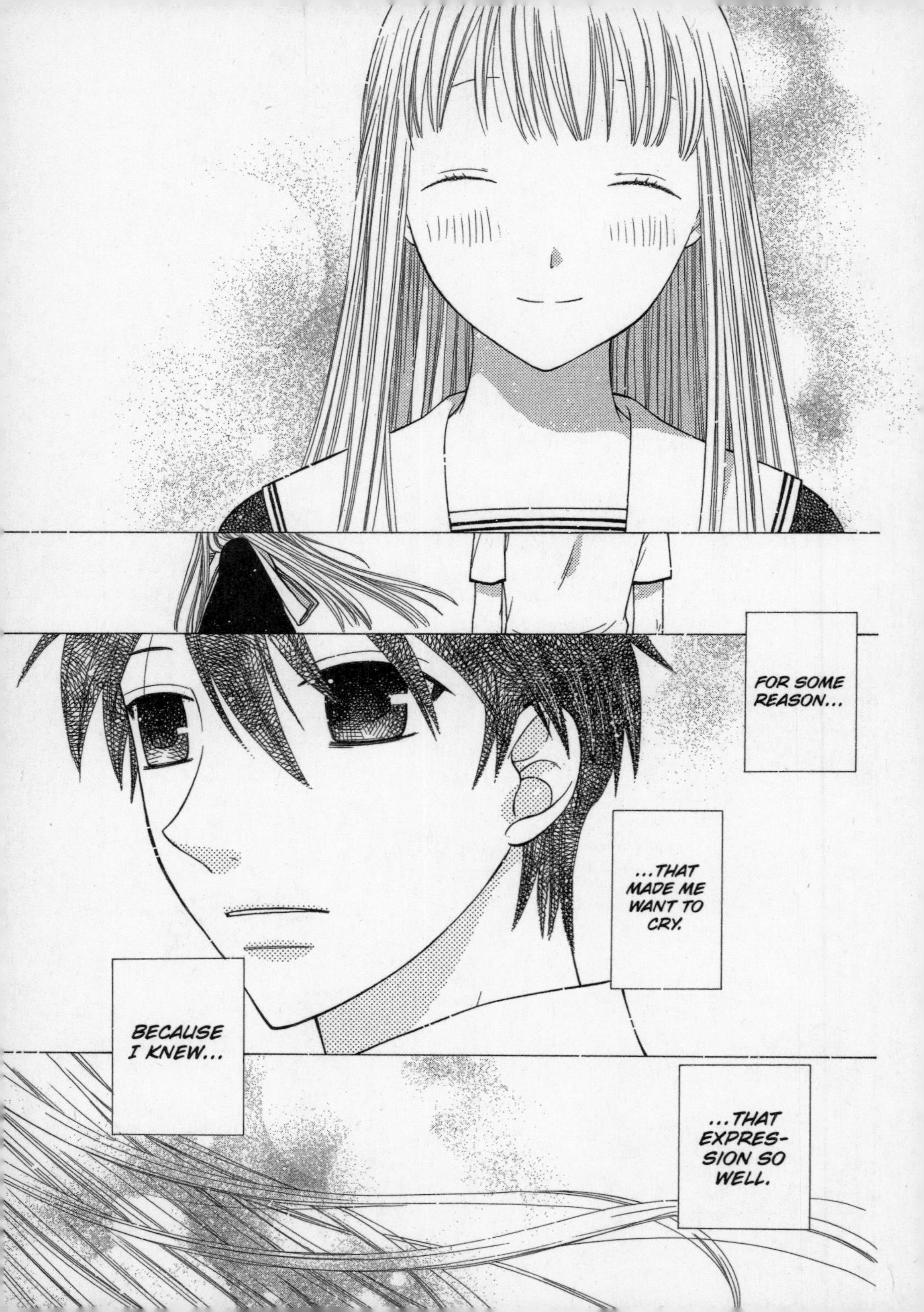
FOR SOME REASON...
...THAT MADE ME WANT TO CRY.
BECAUSE I KNEW...
...THAT EXPRES-SION SO WELL.

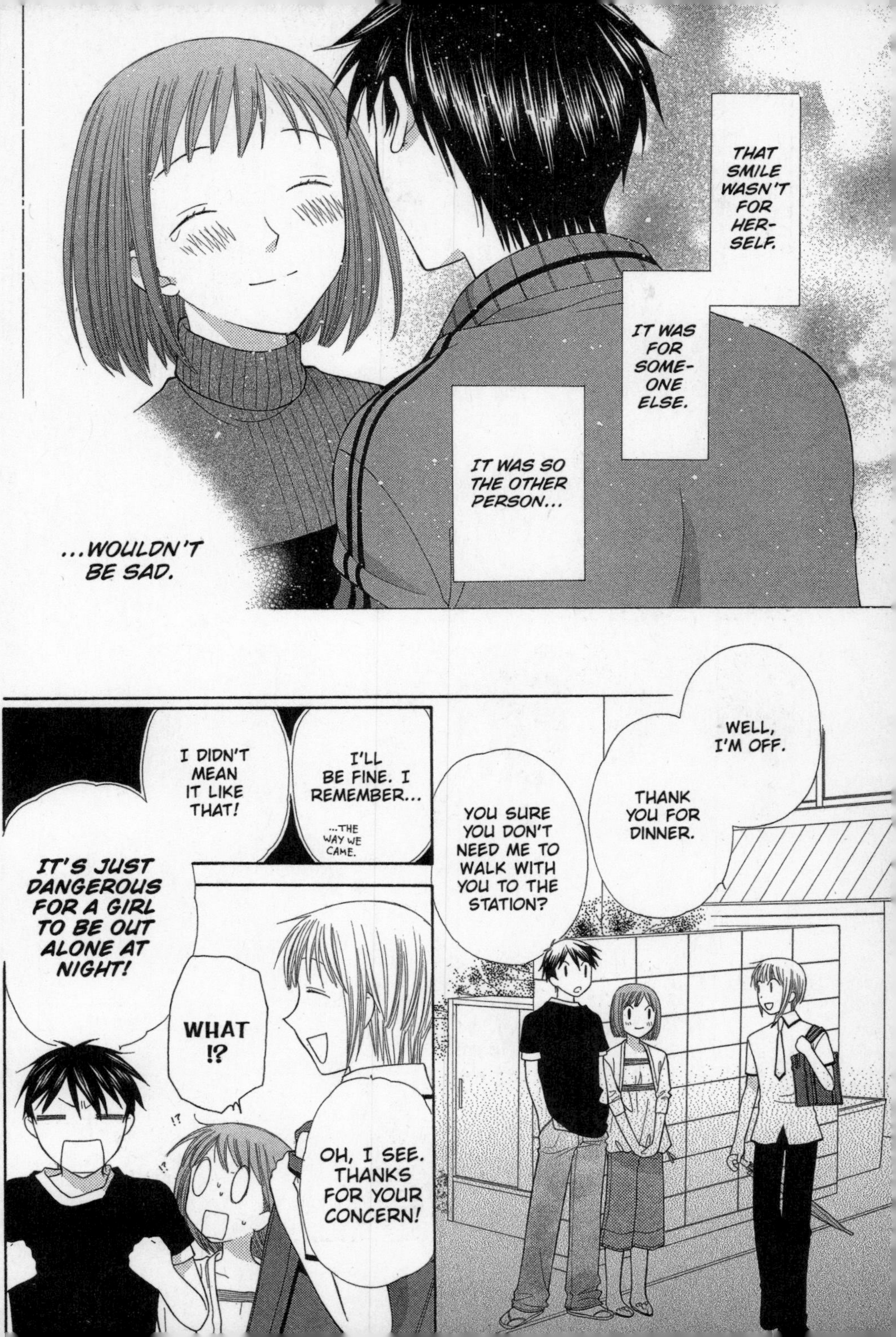
THAT SMILE WASN'T FOR HER-SELF.
IT WAS FOR SOME-ONE ELSE.
IT WAS SO THE OTHER PERSON...
...WOULDN'T BE SAD.
WELL, I'M OFF.
THANK YOU FOR DINNER.
YOU SURE YOU DON'T NEED ME TO WALK WITH YOU TO THE STATION?
I'LL BE FINE. I REMEMBER...
...THE WAY WE CAME.
I DIDN'T MEAN IT LIKE THAT!
IT'S JUST DANGEROUS FOR A GIRL TO BE OUT ALONE AT NIGHT!
WHAT !?
OH, I SEE. THANKS FOR YOUR CONCERN!

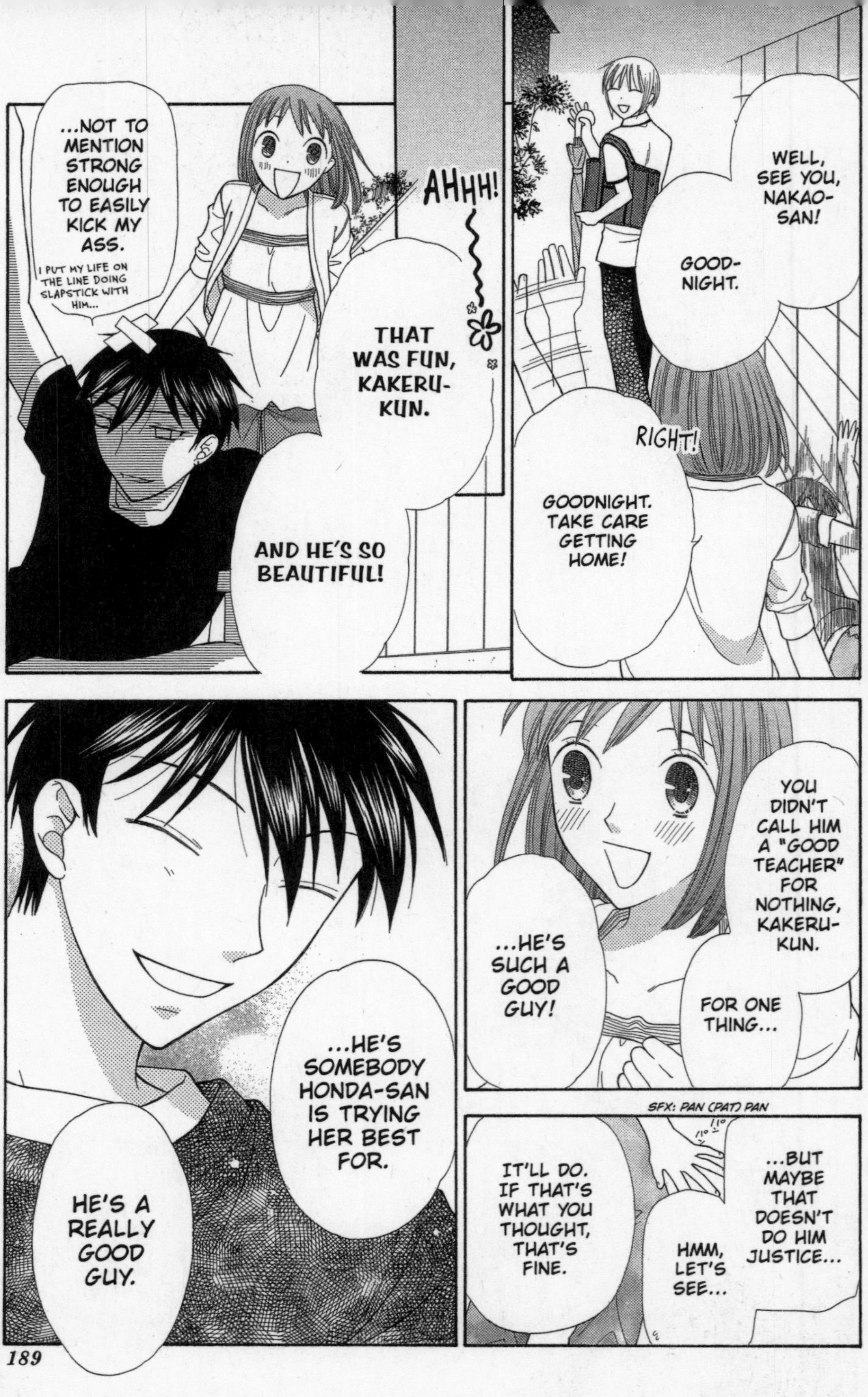
WELL, SEE YOU, NAKAO-SAN!
GOOD-NIGHT.
RIGHT!
GOODNIGHT. TAKE CARE GETTING HOME!
AHHH!
THAT WAS FUN, KAKERU-KUN.
AND HE'S SO BEAUTIFUL!
...NOT TO MENTION STRONG ENOUGH TO EASILY KICK MY ASS.
I PUT MY LIFE ON THE LINE DOING SLAPSTICK WITH HIM...
YOU DIDN'T CALL HIM A "GOOD TEACHER" FOR NOTHING, KAKERU-KUN.
FOR ONE THING...
...HE'S SUCH A GOOD GUY!
SFX: PAN (PAT) PAN
...BUT MAYBE THAT DOESN'T DO HIM JUSTICE...
HMM, LET'S SEE...
IT'LL DO. IF THAT'S WHAT YOU THOUGHT, THAT'S FINE.
...HE'S SOMEBODY HONDA-SAN IS TRYING HER BEST FOR.
HE'S A REALLY GOOD GUY.

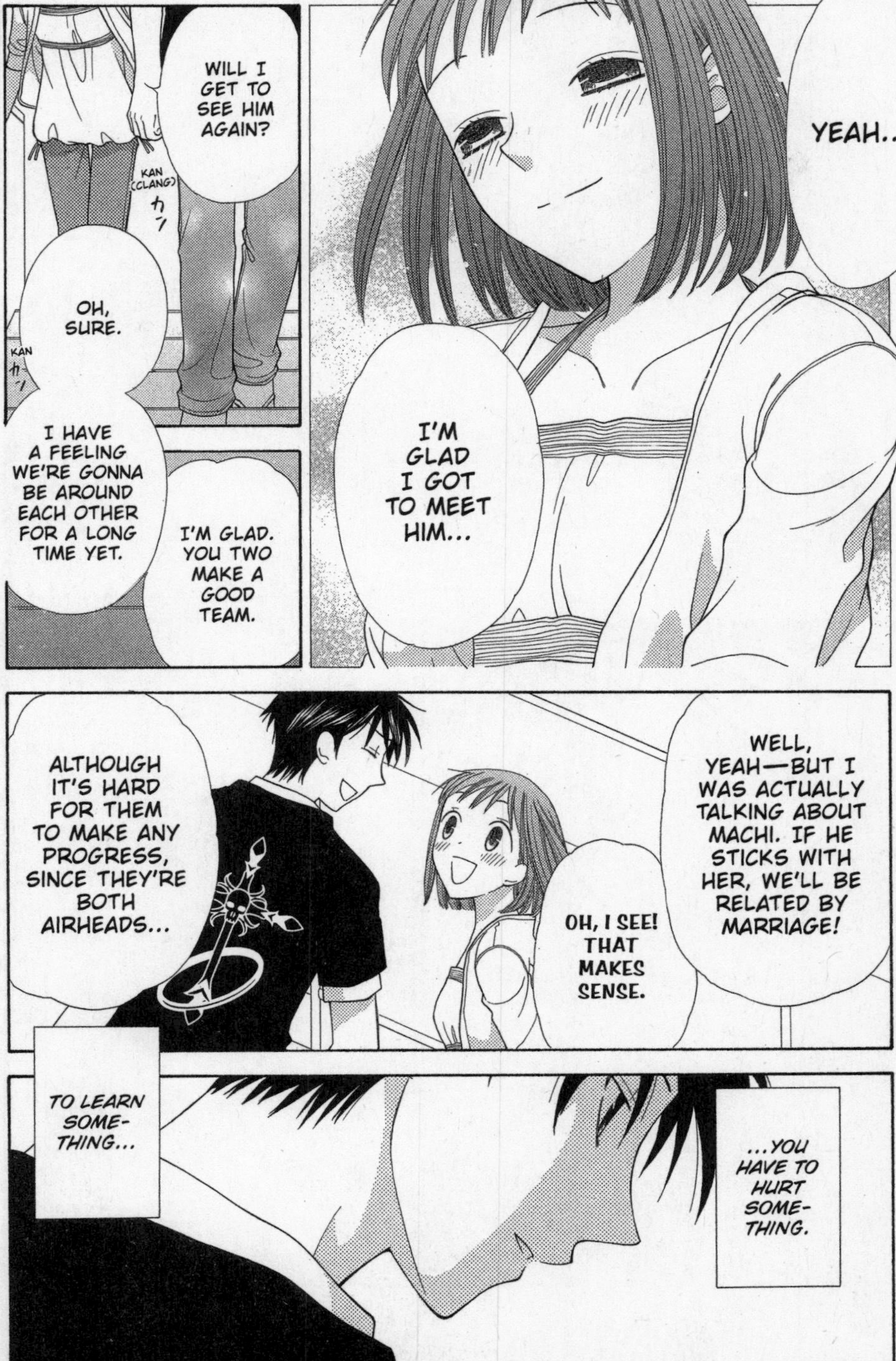
YEAH...
I'M GLAD I GOT TO MEET HIM...
WILL I GET TO SEE HIM AGAIN?
KAN (CLANG)
カン
OH, SURE.
KAN
カン
I HAVE A FEELING WE'RE GONNA BE AROUND EACH OTHER FOR A LONG TIME YET.
I'M GLAD. YOU TWO MAKE A GOOD TEAM.
WELL, YEAH—BUT I WAS ACTUALLY TALKING ABOUT MACHI. IF HE STICKS WITH HER, WE'LL BE RELATED BY MARRIAGE!
OH, I SEE! THAT MAKES SENSE.
ALTHOUGH IT'S HARD FOR THEM TO MAKE ANY PROGRESS, SINCE THEY'RE BOTH AIRHEADS...
TO LEARN SOME-THING...
...YOU HAVE TO HURT SOME-THING.

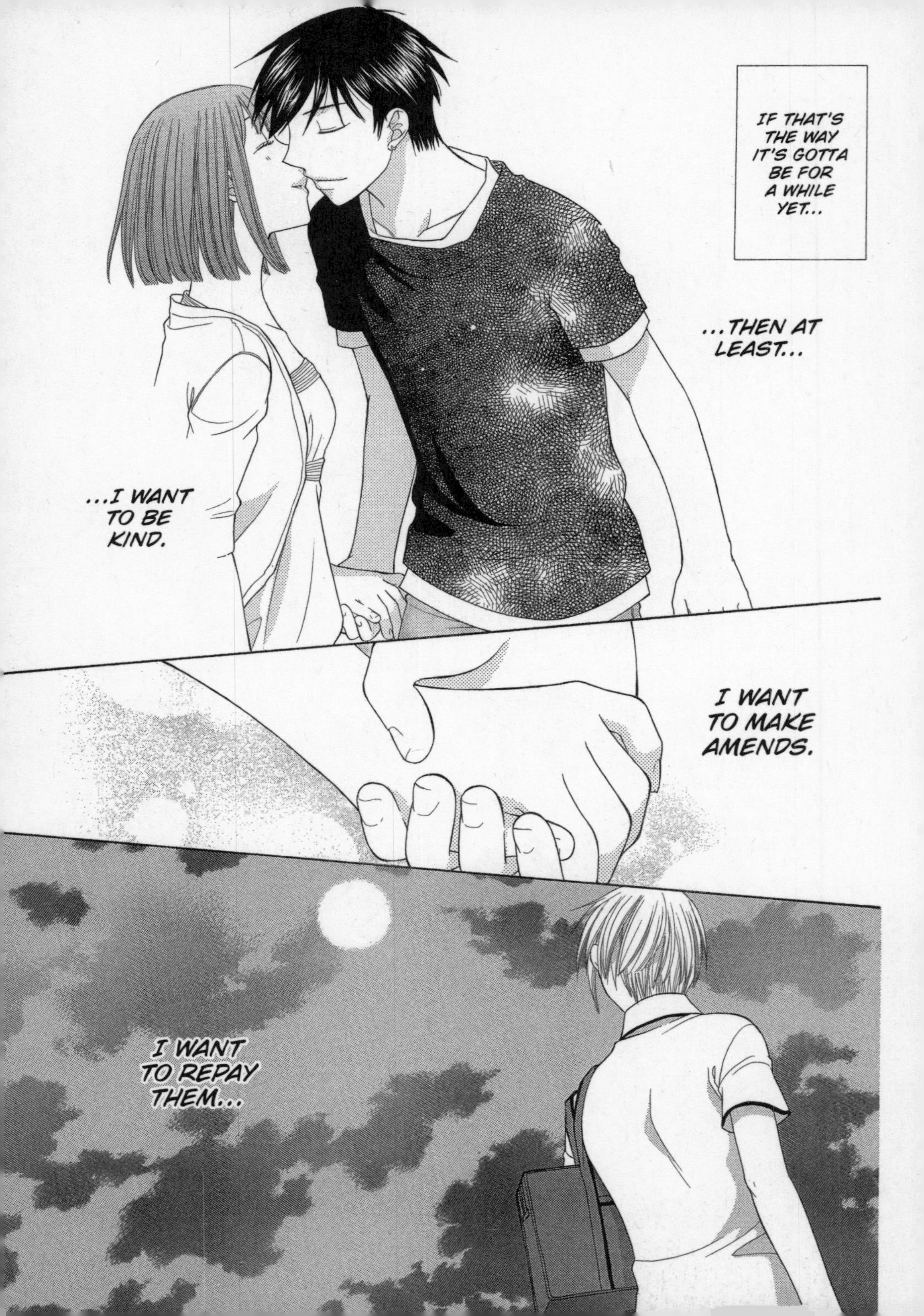
IF THAT'S THE WAY IT'S GOTTA BE FOR A WHILE YET...
...THEN AT LEAST...
...I WANT TO BE KIND.
I WANT TO MAKE AMENDS.
I WANT TO REPAY THEM...

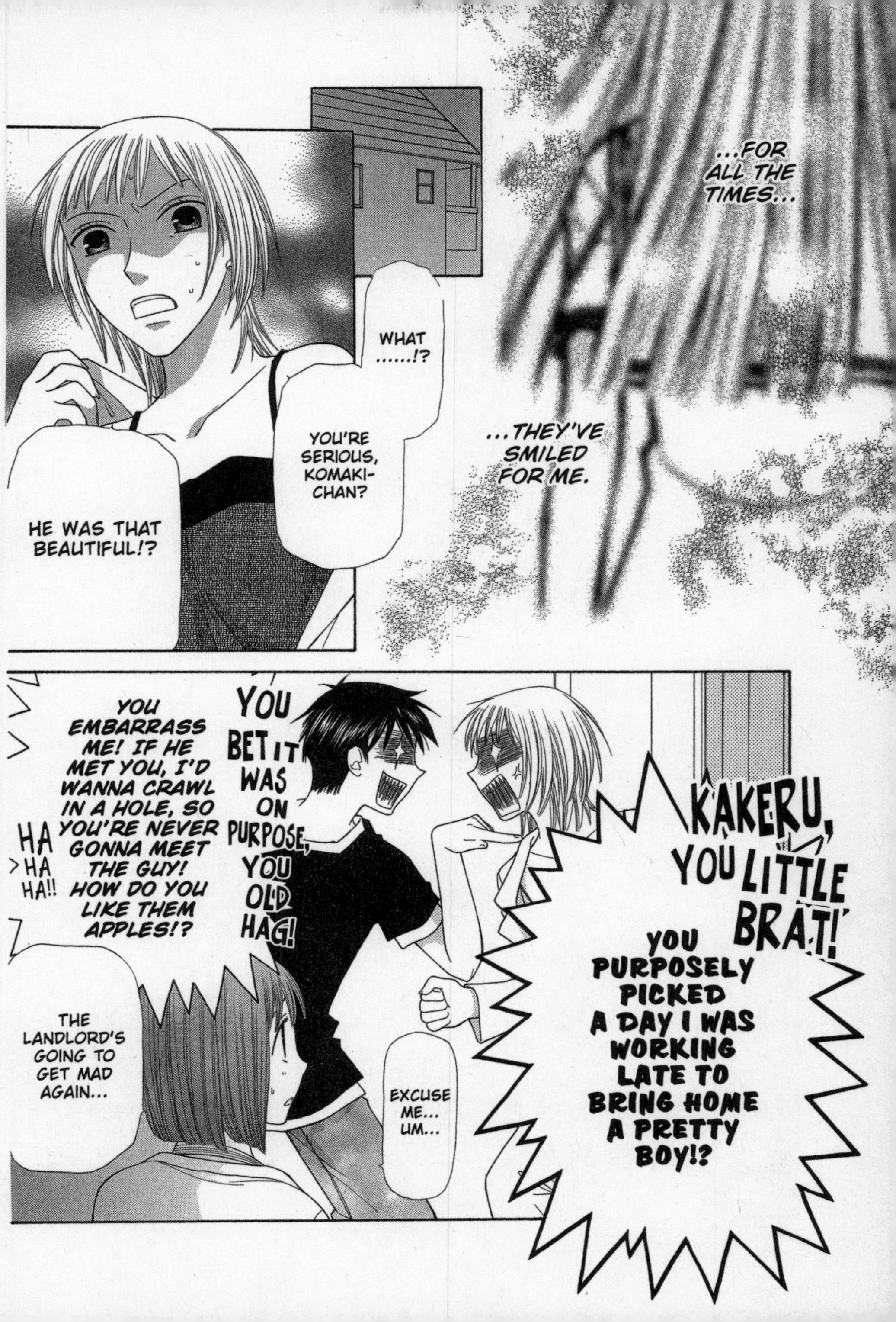
...FOR ALL THE TIMES...
...THEY'VE SMILED FOR ME.
WHAT ......!?
YOU'RE SERIOUS, KOMAKI-CHAN?
HE WAS THAT BEAUTIFUL!?
KAKERU, YOU LITTLE BRAT!
YOU PURPOSELY PICKED A DAY I WAS WORKING LATE TO BRING HOME A PRETTY BOY!?
YOU BET IT WAS ON PURPOSE, YOU OLD HAG!
YOU EMBARRASS ME! IF HE MET YOU, I'D WANNA CRAWL IN A HOLE, SO YOU'RE NEVER GONNA MEET THE GUY! HOW DO YOU LIKE THEM APPLES!?
HA HA HA!!
EXCUSE ME... UM...
THE LANDLORD'S GOING TO GET MAD AGAIN...

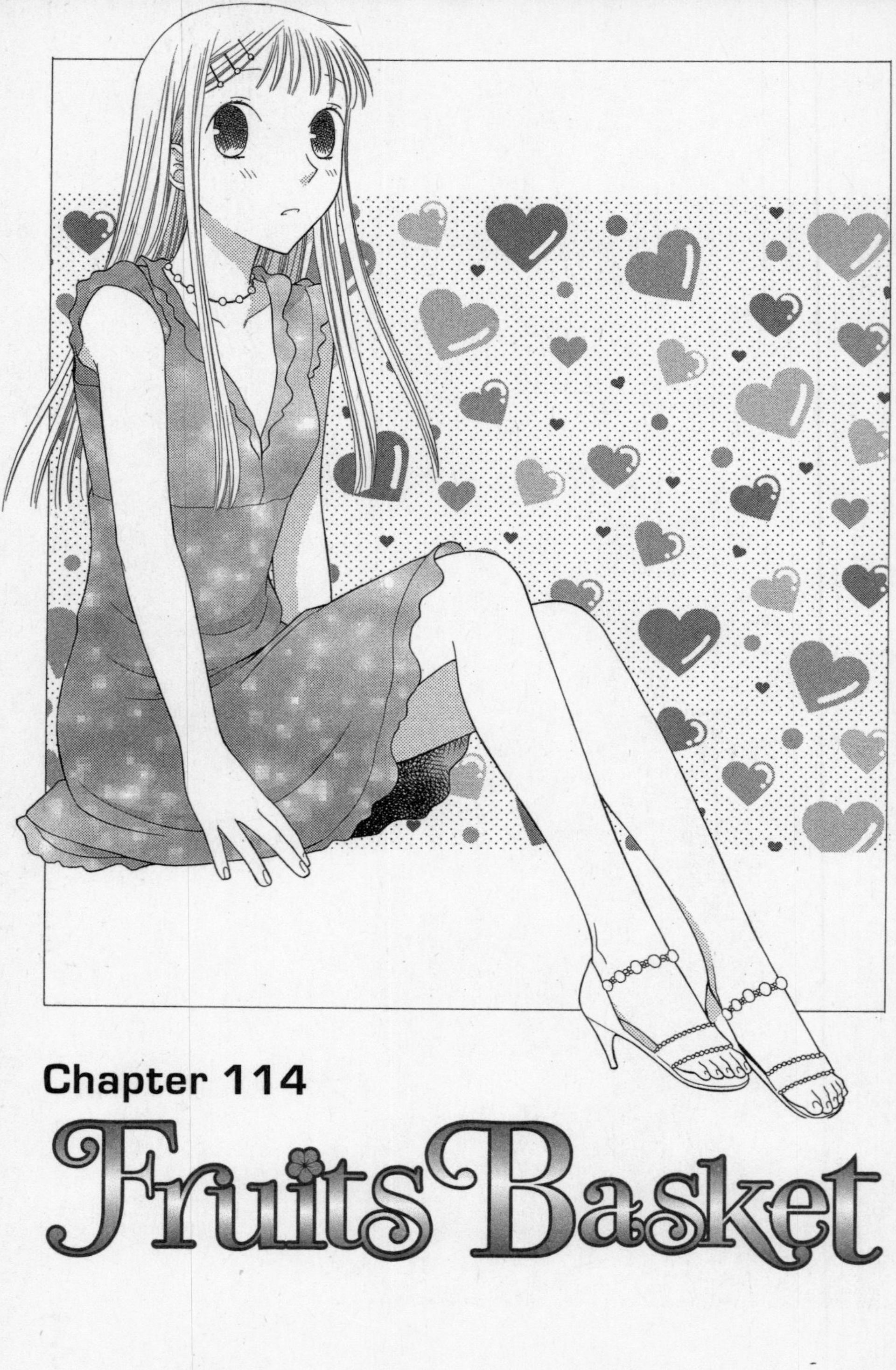

Chapter 114

Fruits Basket

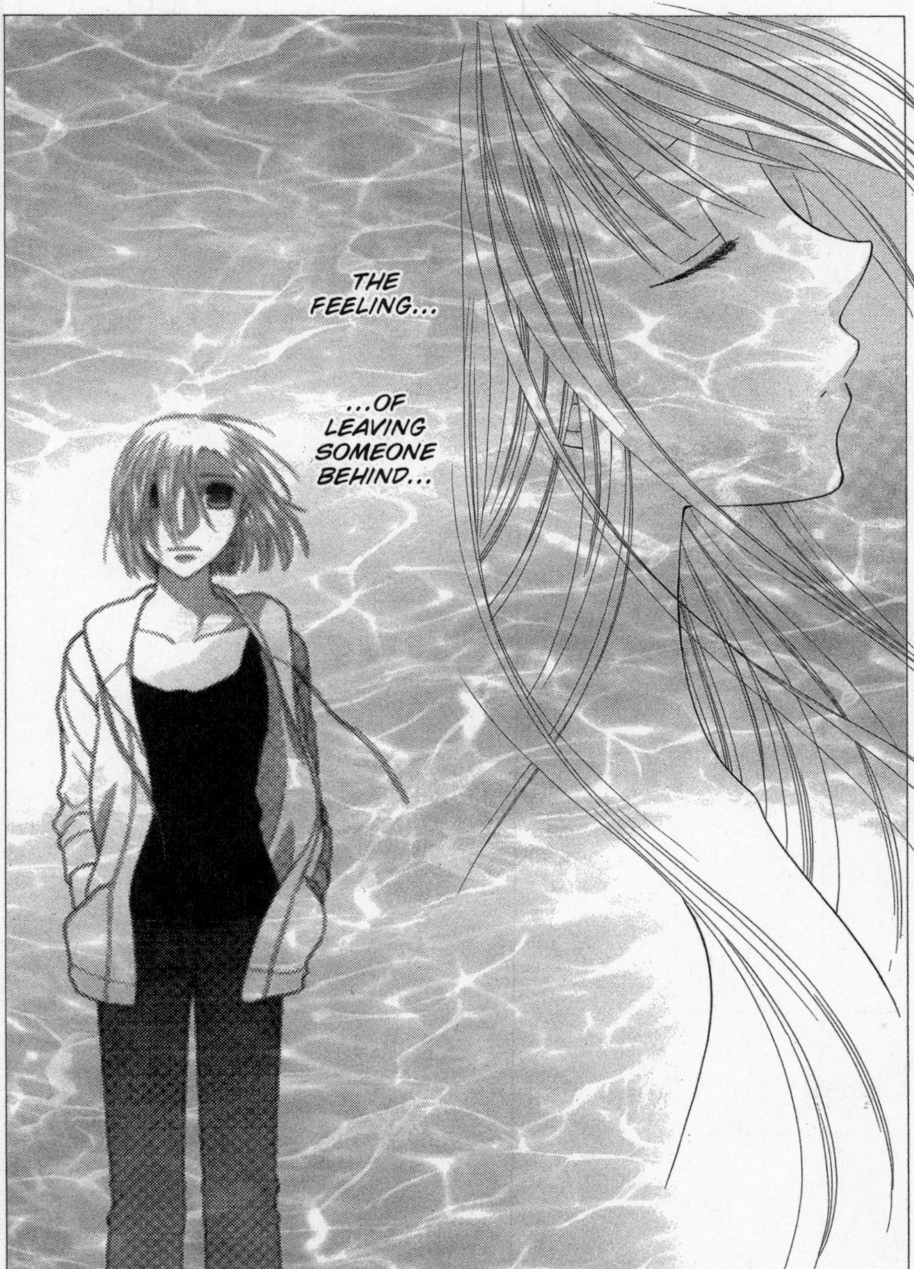
THE FEELING...
...OF LEAVING SOMEONE BEHIND...

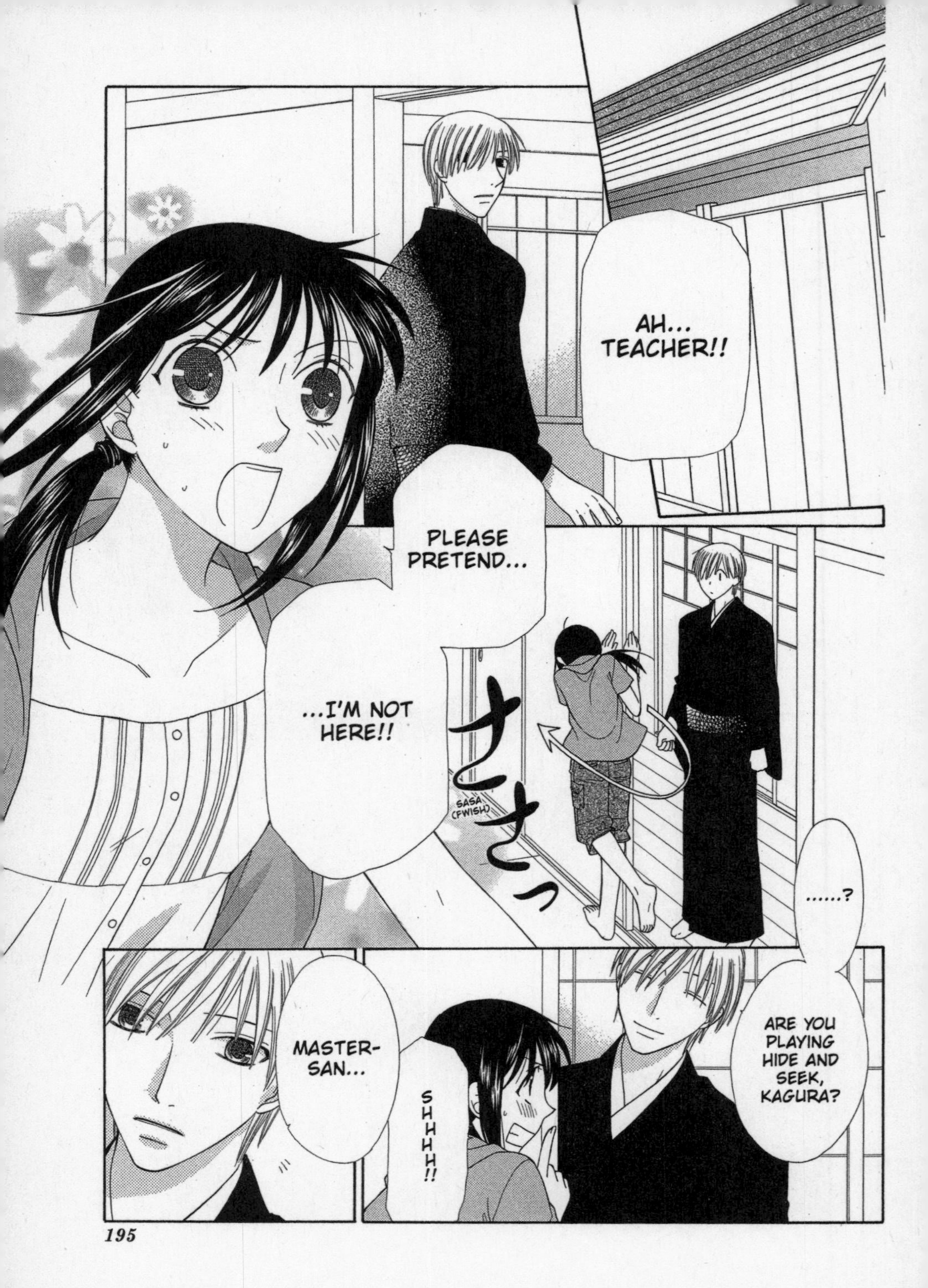
AH... TEACHER!!
PLEASE PRETEND...
...I'M NOT HERE!!
SASA (FWISH)
......?
ARE YOU PLAYING HIDE AND SEEK, KAGURA?
SHHHH!!
MASTER-SAN...

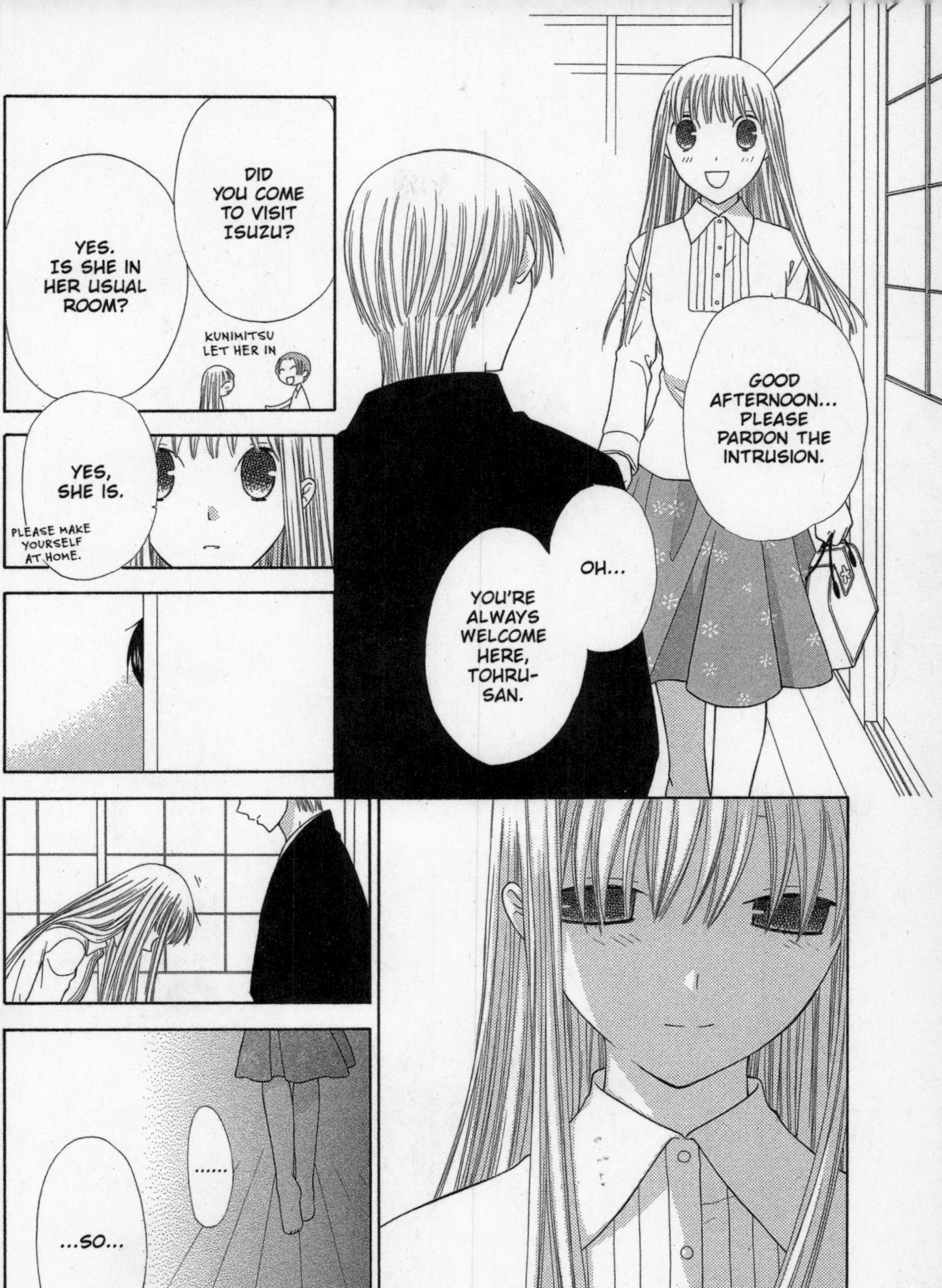
GOOD AFTERNOON... PLEASE PARDON THE INTRUSION.
OH...
YOU'RE ALWAYS WELCOME HERE, TOHRU-SAN.
DID YOU COME TO VISIT ISUZU?
YES. IS SHE IN HER USUAL ROOM?
KUNIMITSU LET HER IN
YES, SHE IS.
PLEASE MAKE YOURSELF AT HOME.
......
...SO...

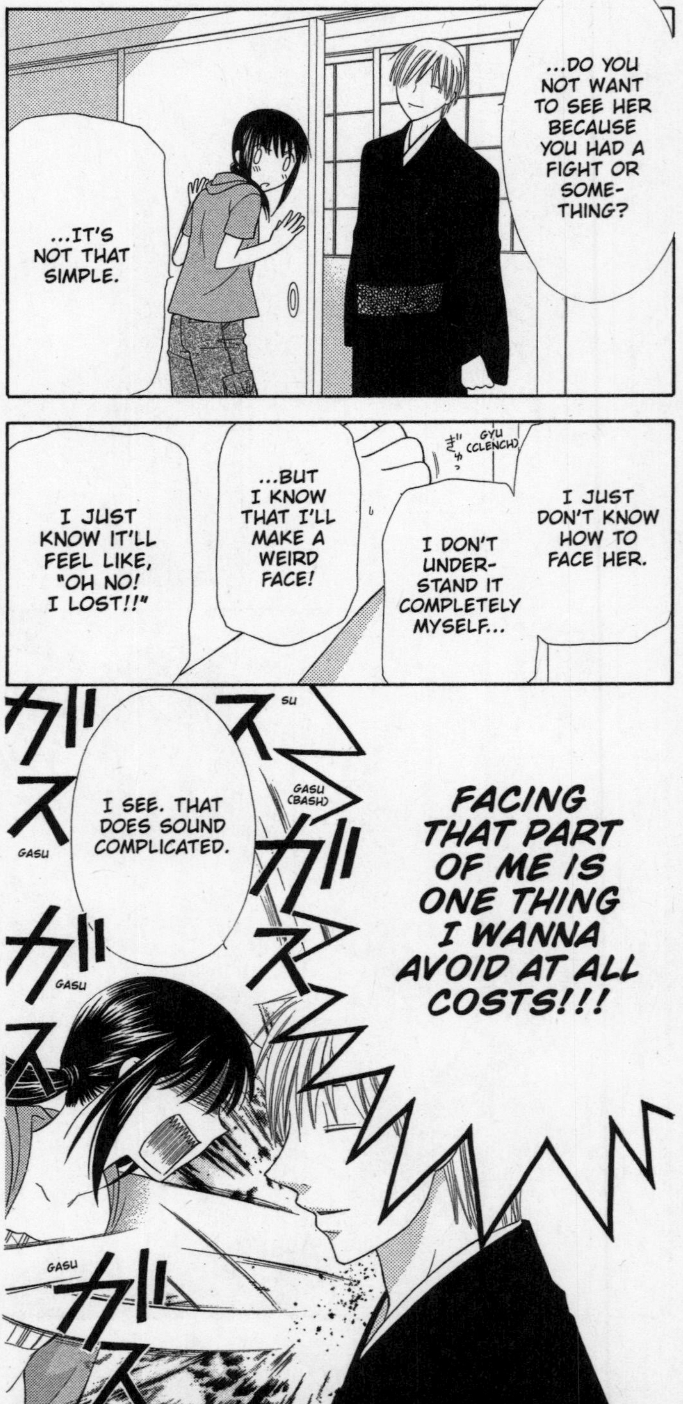
...DO YOU NOT WANT TO SEE HER BECAUSE YOU HAD A FIGHT OR SOME-THING?
...IT'S NOT THAT SIMPLE.
ぎゅっ
GYU (CLENCH)
I JUST DON'T KNOW HOW TO FACE HER.
I DON'T UNDER-STAND IT COMPLETELY MYSELF...
...BUT I KNOW THAT I'LL MAKE A WEIRD FACE!
I JUST KNOW IT'LL FEEL LIKE, "OH NO! I LOST!!"
FACING THAT PART OF ME IS ONE THING I WANNA AVOID AT ALL COSTS!!!
SU
GASU (BASH)
I SEE. THAT DOES SOUND COMPLICATED.
GASU
GASU
GASU

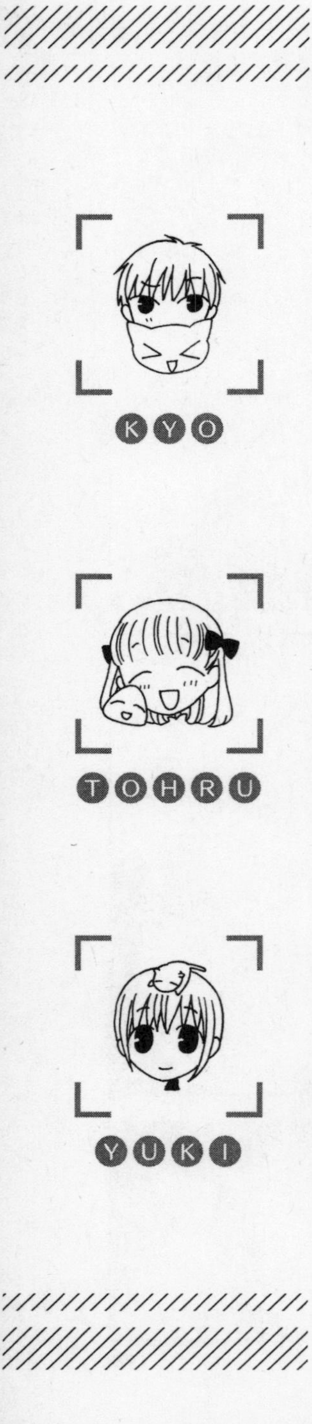
KYO
TOHRU
YUKI

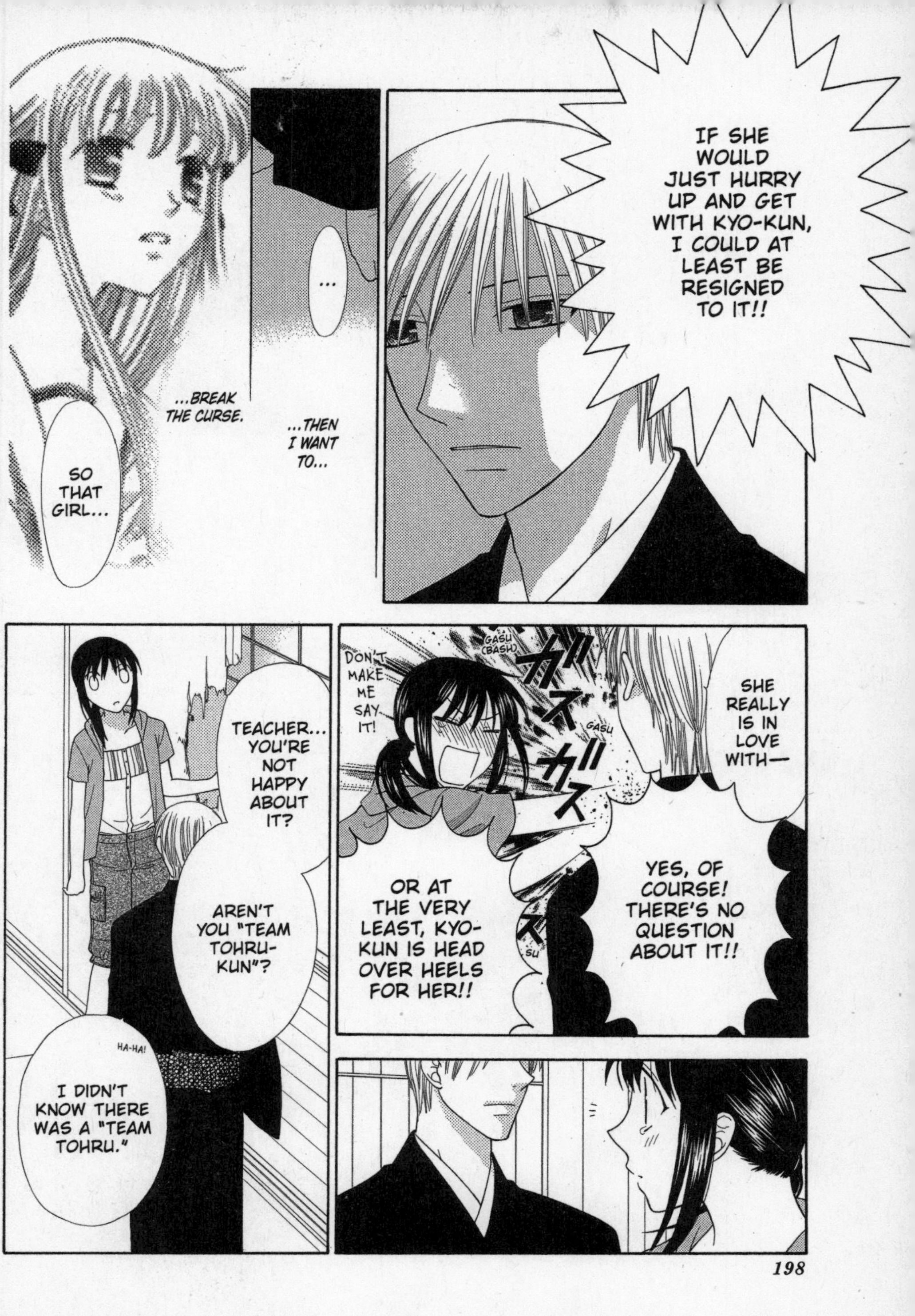
IF SHE WOULD JUST HURRY UP AND GET WITH KYO-KUN, I COULD AT LEAST BE RESIGNED TO IT!!
...
...THEN I WANT TO...
...BREAK THE CURSE.
SO THAT GIRL...
SHE REALLY IS IN LOVE WITH—
YES, OF COURSE! THERE'S NO QUESTION ABOUT IT!!
GASU (BASH)
GASU
SU
OR AT THE VERY LEAST, KYO-KUN IS HEAD OVER HEELS FOR HER!!
DON'T MAKE ME SAY IT!
TEACHER... YOU'RE NOT HAPPY ABOUT IT?
AREN'T YOU "TEAM TOHRU-KUN"?
HA-HA!
I DIDN'T KNOW THERE WAS A "TEAM TOHRU."

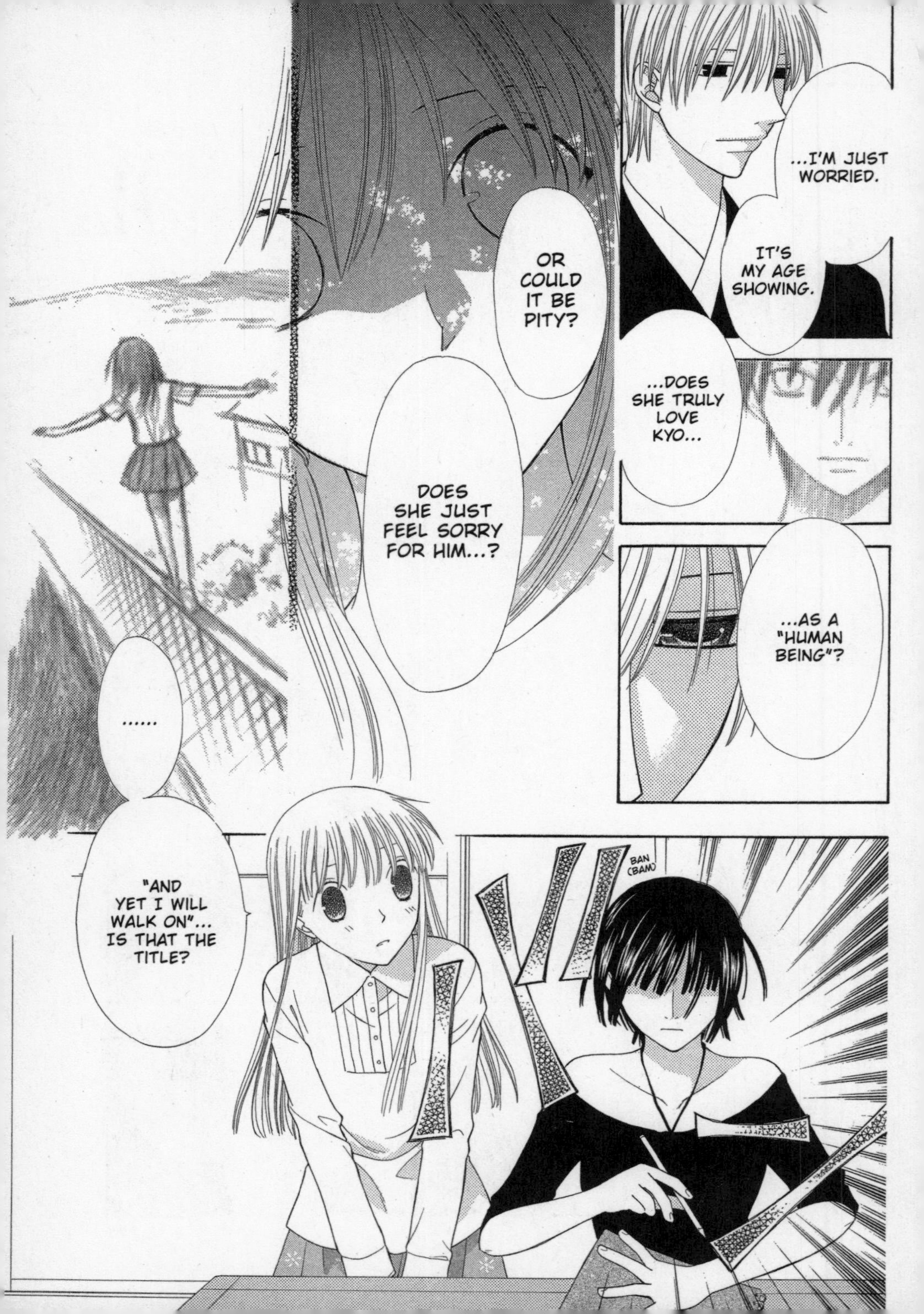
...I'M JUST WORRIED.
IT'S MY AGE SHOWING.
...DOES SHE TRULY LOVE KYO...
...AS A "HUMAN BEING"?
OR COULD IT BE PITY?
DOES SHE JUST FEEL SORRY FOR HIM...?
......
BAN (BAM)
"AND YET I WILL WALK ON"... IS THAT THE TITLE?

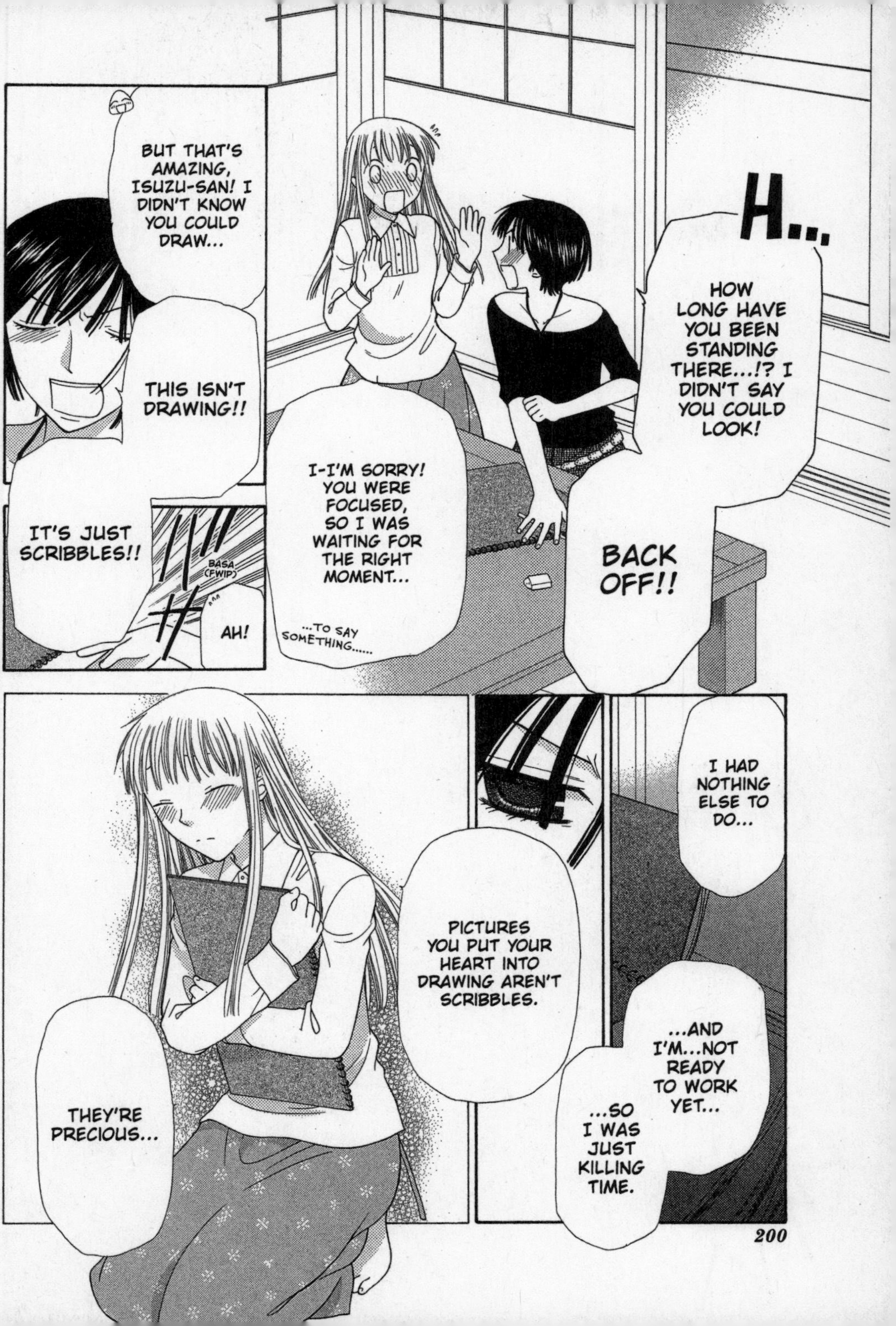
H...
HOW LONG HAVE YOU BEEN STANDING THERE...!? I DIDN'T SAY YOU COULD LOOK!
BACK OFF!!
I-I'M SORRY! YOU WERE FOCUSED, SO I WAS WAITING FOR THE RIGHT MOMENT...
...TO SAY SOMETHING......
BUT THAT'S AMAZING, ISUZU-SAN! I DIDN'T KNOW YOU COULD DRAW...
THIS ISN'T DRAWING!!
IT'S JUST SCRIBBLES!!
BASA (FWIP)
AH!
I HAD NOTHING ELSE TO DO...
...AND I'M...NOT READY TO WORK YET...
...SO I WAS JUST KILLING TIME.
PICTURES YOU PUT YOUR HEART INTO DRAWING AREN'T SCRIBBLES.
THEY'RE PRECIOUS...

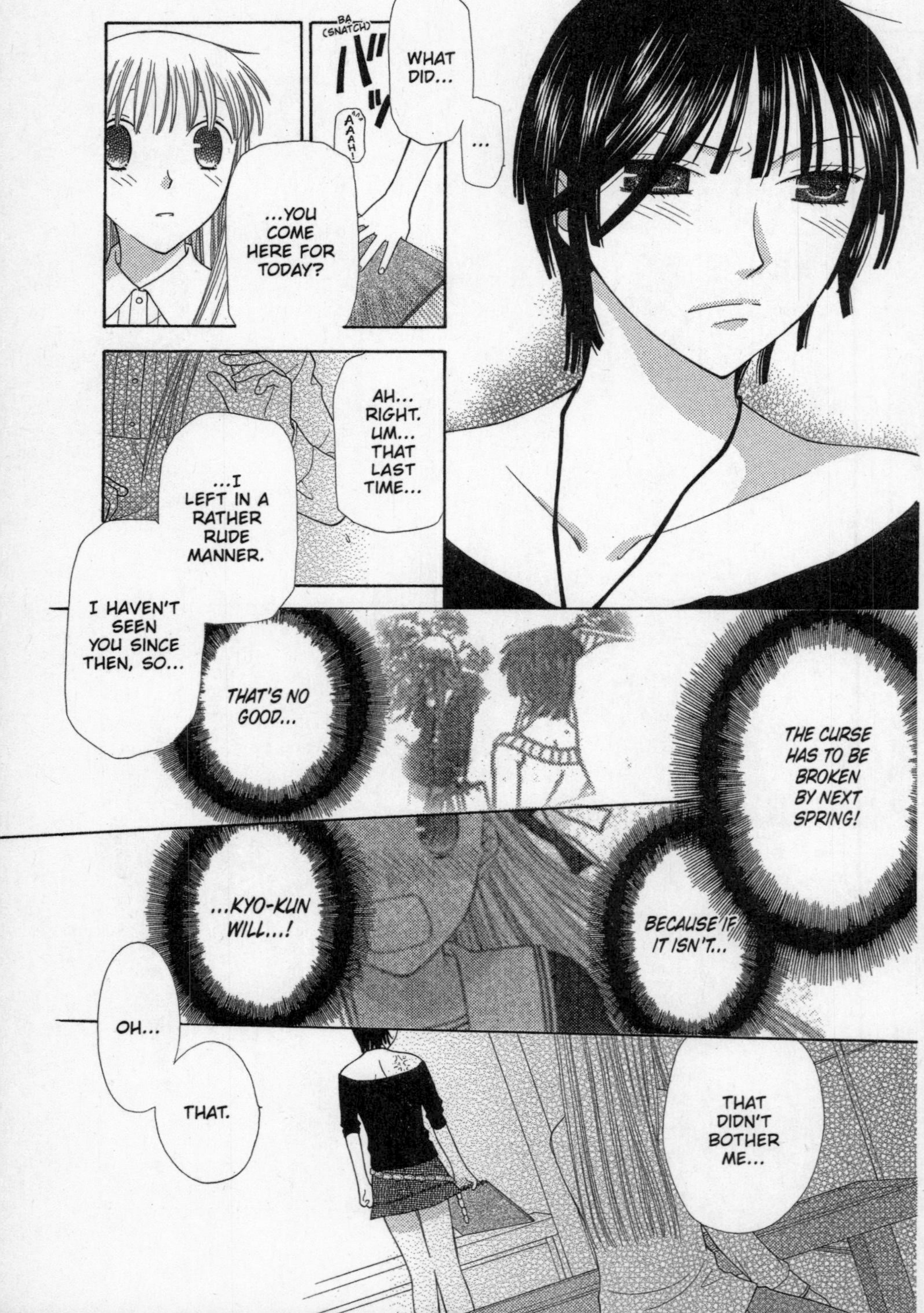
...
BA (SNATCH)
バッ
WHAT DID...
AAAH!
...YOU COME HERE FOR TODAY?
AH... RIGHT. UM... THAT LAST TIME...
...I LEFT IN A RATHER RUDE MANNER.
I HAVEN'T SEEN YOU SINCE THEN, SO...
THE CURSE HAS TO BE BROKEN BY NEXT SPRING!
THAT'S NO GOOD...
BECAUSE IF IT ISN'T...
...KYO-KUN WILL...!
OH...
THAT.
THAT DIDN'T BOTHER ME...

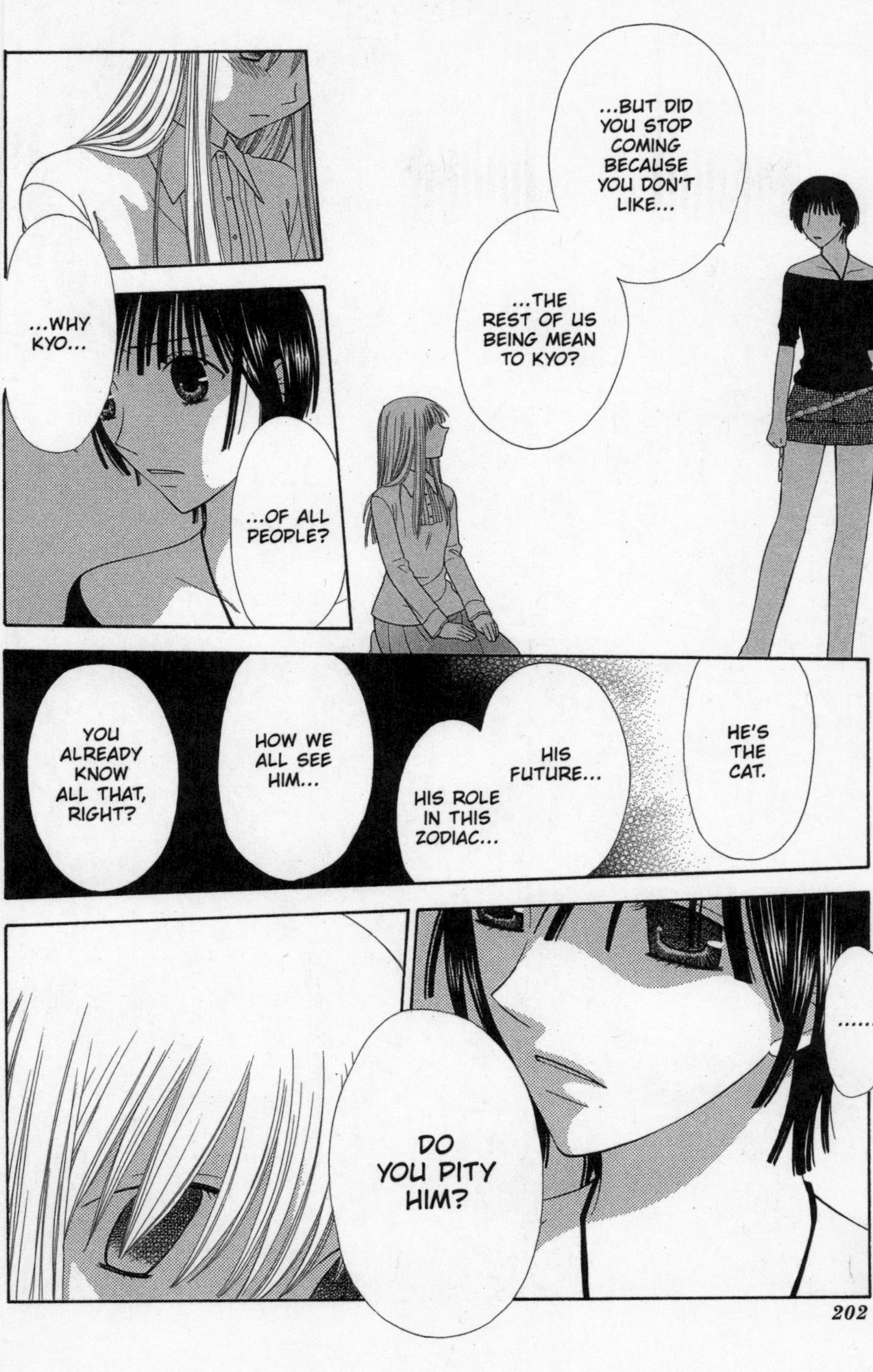
...BUT DID YOU STOP COMING BECAUSE YOU DON'T LIKE...
...THE REST OF US BEING MEAN TO KYO?
...WHY KYO...
...OF ALL PEOPLE?
HE'S THE CAT.
HIS FUTURE...
HIS ROLE IN THIS ZODIAC...
HOW WE ALL SEE HIM...
YOU ALREADY KNOW ALL THAT, RIGHT?
......
DO YOU PITY HIM?

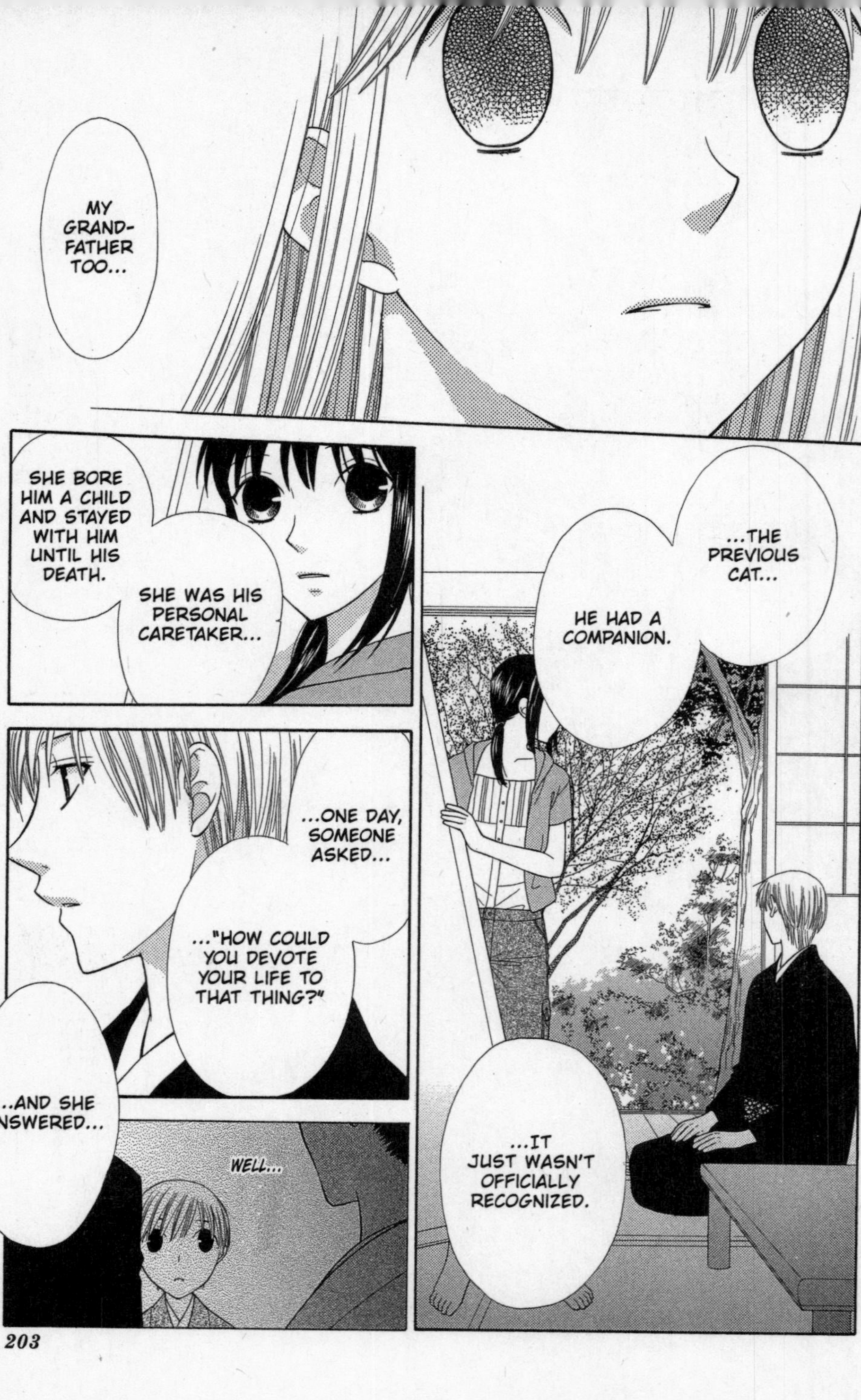
MY GRAND-FATHER TOO...
...THE PREVIOUS CAT...
HE HAD A COMPANION.
...IT JUST WASN'T OFFICIALLY RECOGNIZED.
SHE WAS HIS PERSONAL CARETAKER...
SHE BORE HIM A CHILD AND STAYED WITH HIM UNTIL HIS DEATH.
...ONE DAY, SOMEONE ASKED...
..."HOW COULD YOU DEVOTE YOUR LIFE TO THAT THING?"
...AND SHE ANSWERED...
WELL...

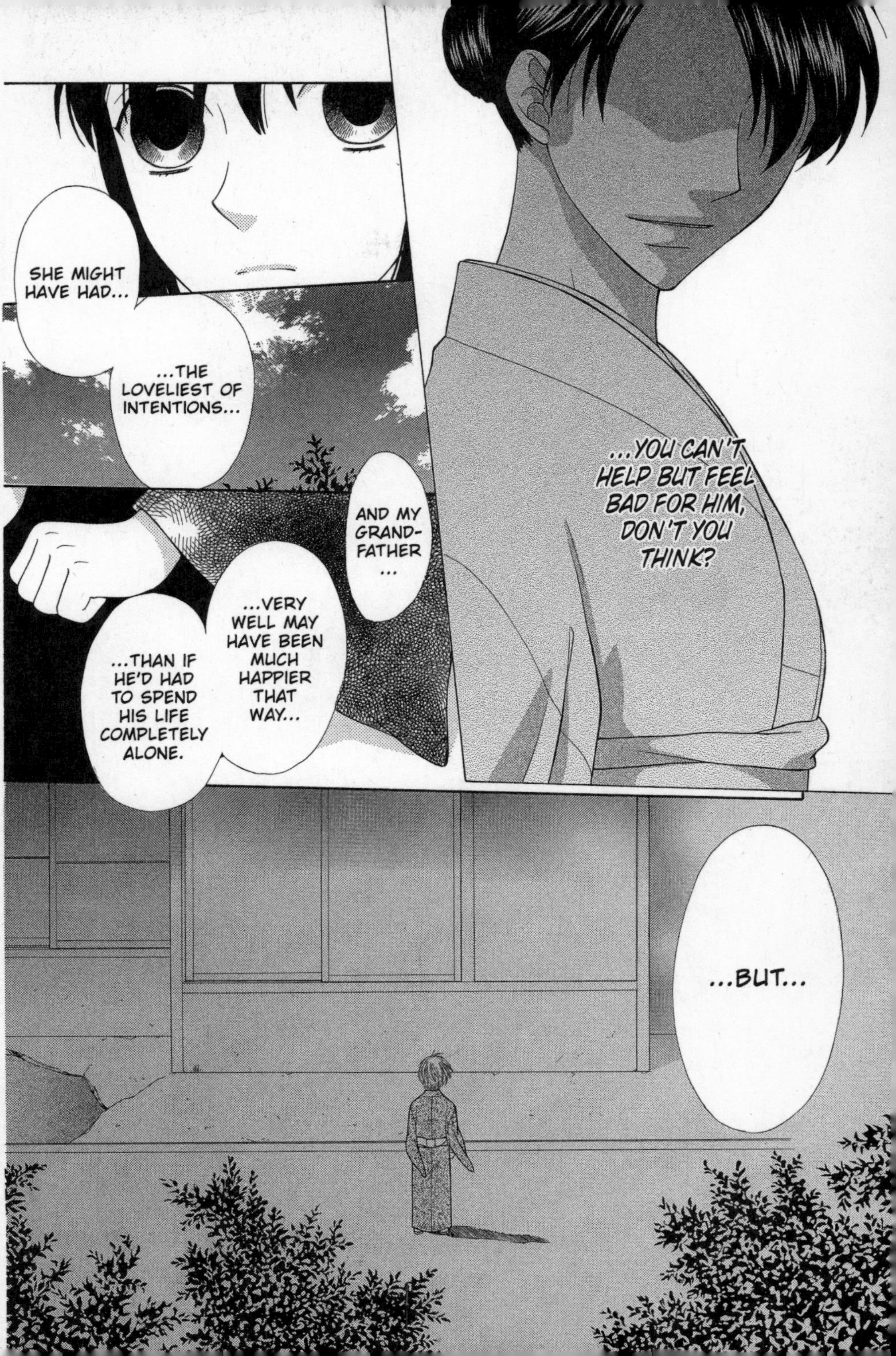
...YOU CAN'T HELP BUT FEEL BAD FOR HIM, DON'T YOU THINK?
SHE MIGHT HAVE HAD...
...THE LOVELIEST OF INTENTIONS...
AND MY GRAND-FATHER...
...VERY WELL MAY HAVE BEEN MUCH HAPPIER THAT WAY...
...THAN IF HE'D HAD TO SPEND HIS LIFE COMPLETELY ALONE.
...BUT...

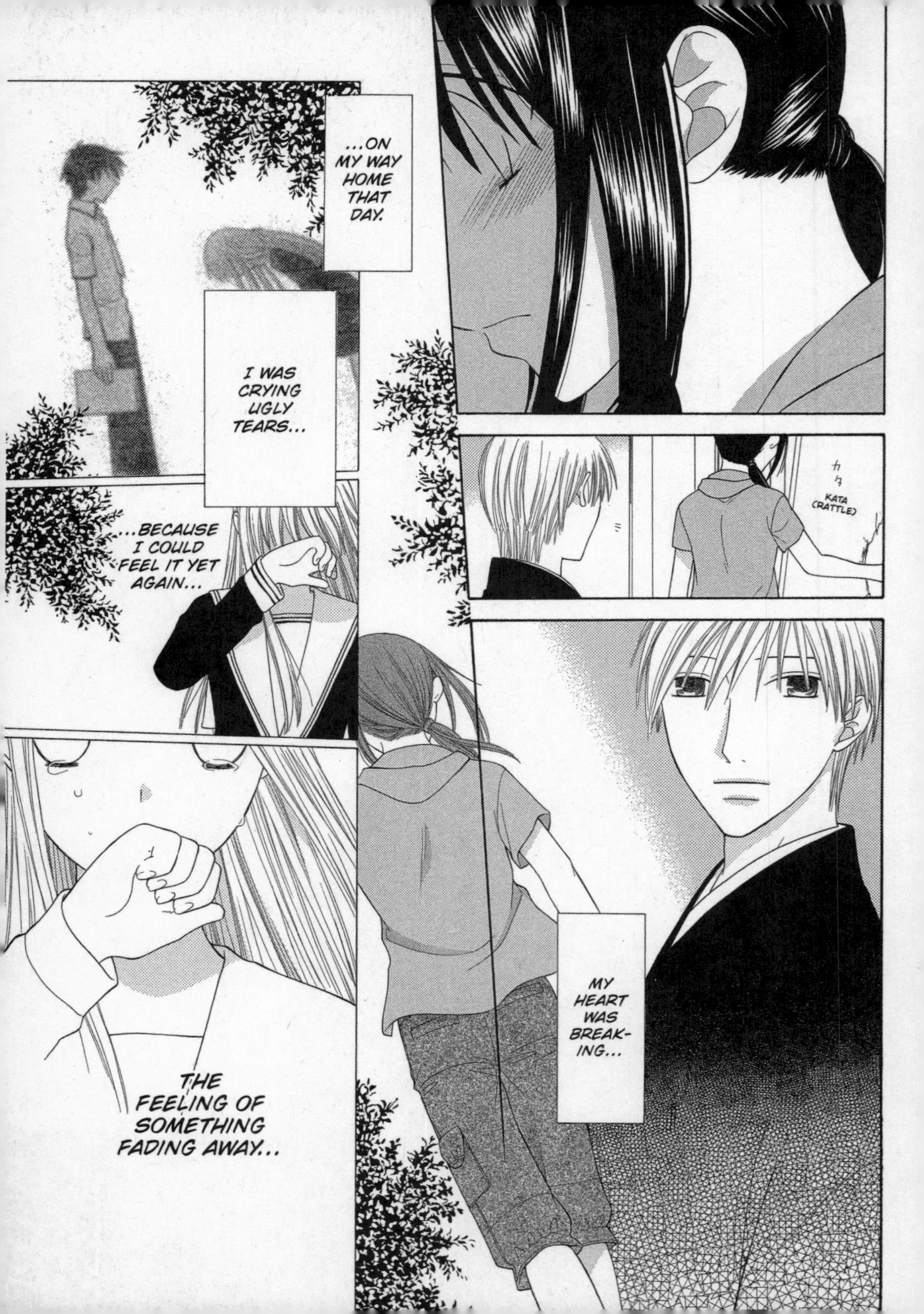
カタ
KATA (RATTLE)
MY HEART WAS BREAK-ING...
...ON MY WAY HOME THAT DAY.
I WAS CRYING UGLY TEARS...
...BECAUSE I COULD FEEL IT YET AGAIN...
THE FEELING OF SOMETHING FADING AWAY...

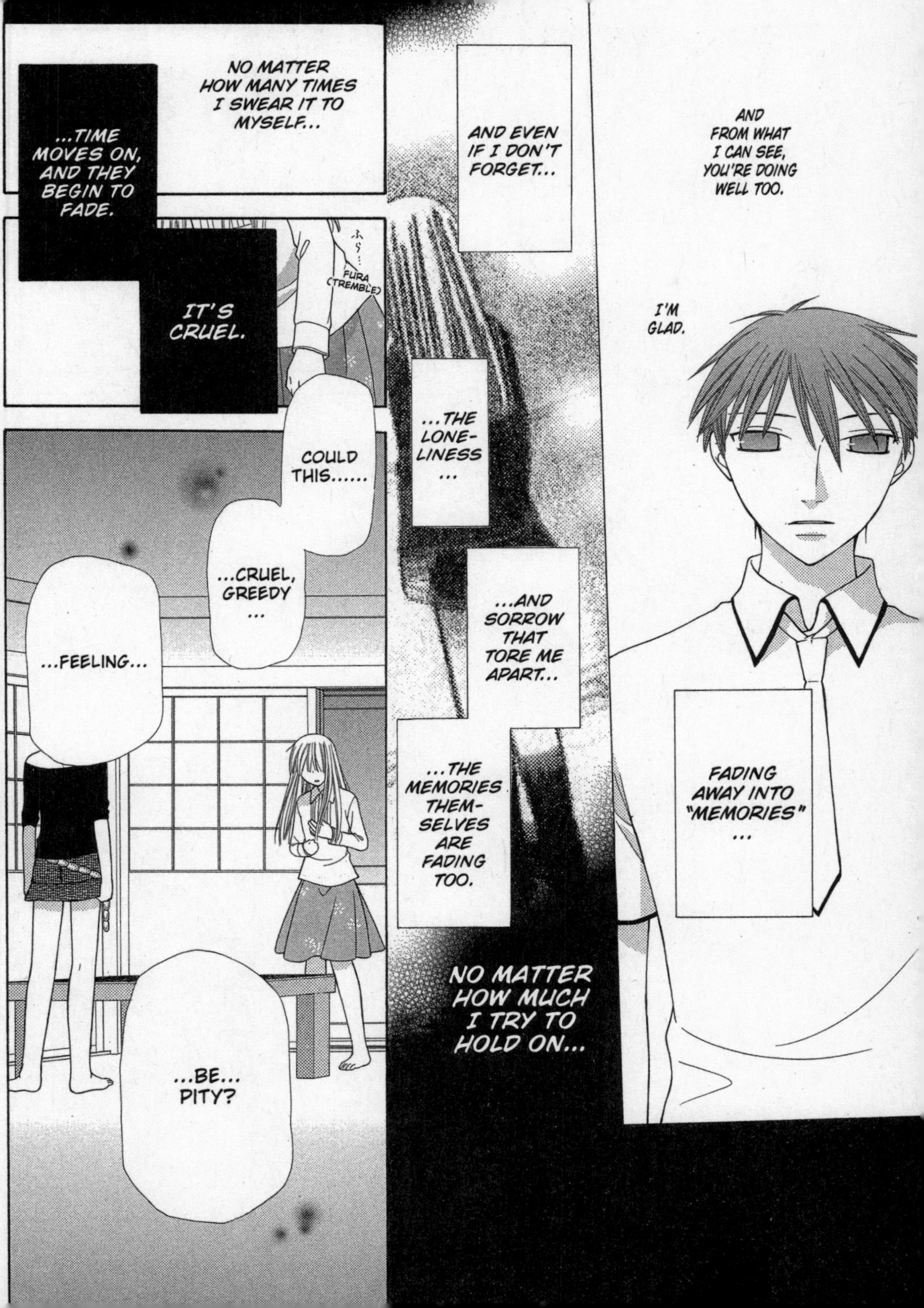
AND FROM WHAT I CAN SEE, YOU'RE DOING WELL TOO.
I'M GLAD.
FADING AWAY INTO "MEMORIES"...
AND EVEN IF I DON'T FORGET...
...THE LONELINESS...
...AND SORROW THAT TORE ME APART...
...THE MEMORIES THEMSELVES ARE FADING TOO.
NO MATTER HOW MUCH I TRY TO HOLD ON...
NO MATTER HOW MANY TIMES I SWEAR IT TO MYSELF...
...TIME MOVES ON, AND THEY BEGIN TO FADE.
ふら…
FURA (TREMBLE)
IT'S CRUEL.
COULD THIS......
...CRUEL, GREEDY...
...FEELING...
...BE... PITY?

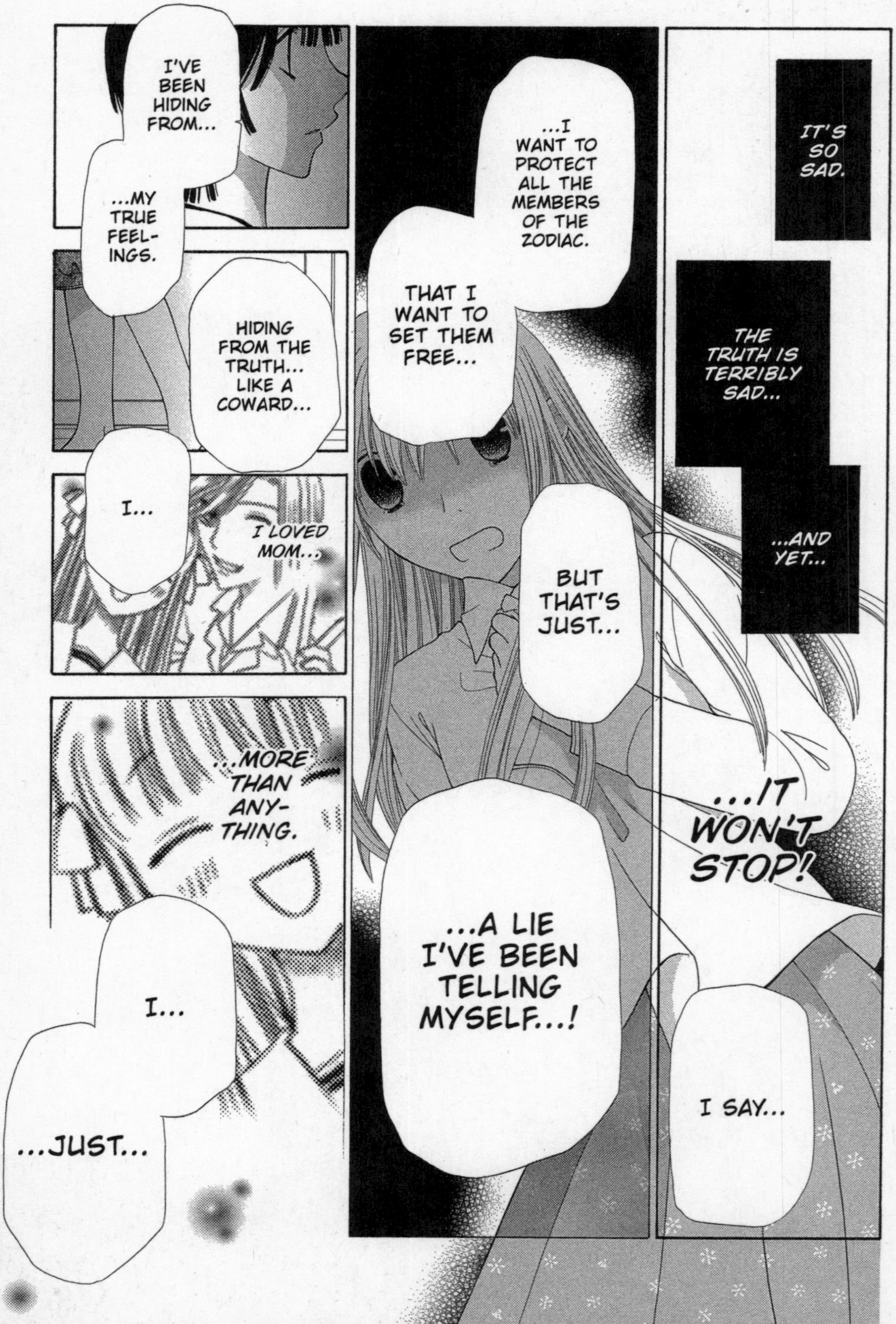
IT'S SO SAD.
THE TRUTH IS TERRIBLY SAD...
...AND YET...
...IT WON'T STOP!
I SAY...
...I WANT TO PROTECT ALL THE MEMBERS OF THE ZODIAC.
THAT I WANT TO SET THEM FREE...
BUT THAT'S JUST...
...A LIE I'VE BEEN TELLING MYSELF...!
I'VE BEEN HIDING FROM...
...MY TRUE FEEL-INGS.
HIDING FROM THE TRUTH... LIKE A COWARD...
I...
I LOVED MOM...
...MORE THAN ANY-THING.
I...
...JUST...

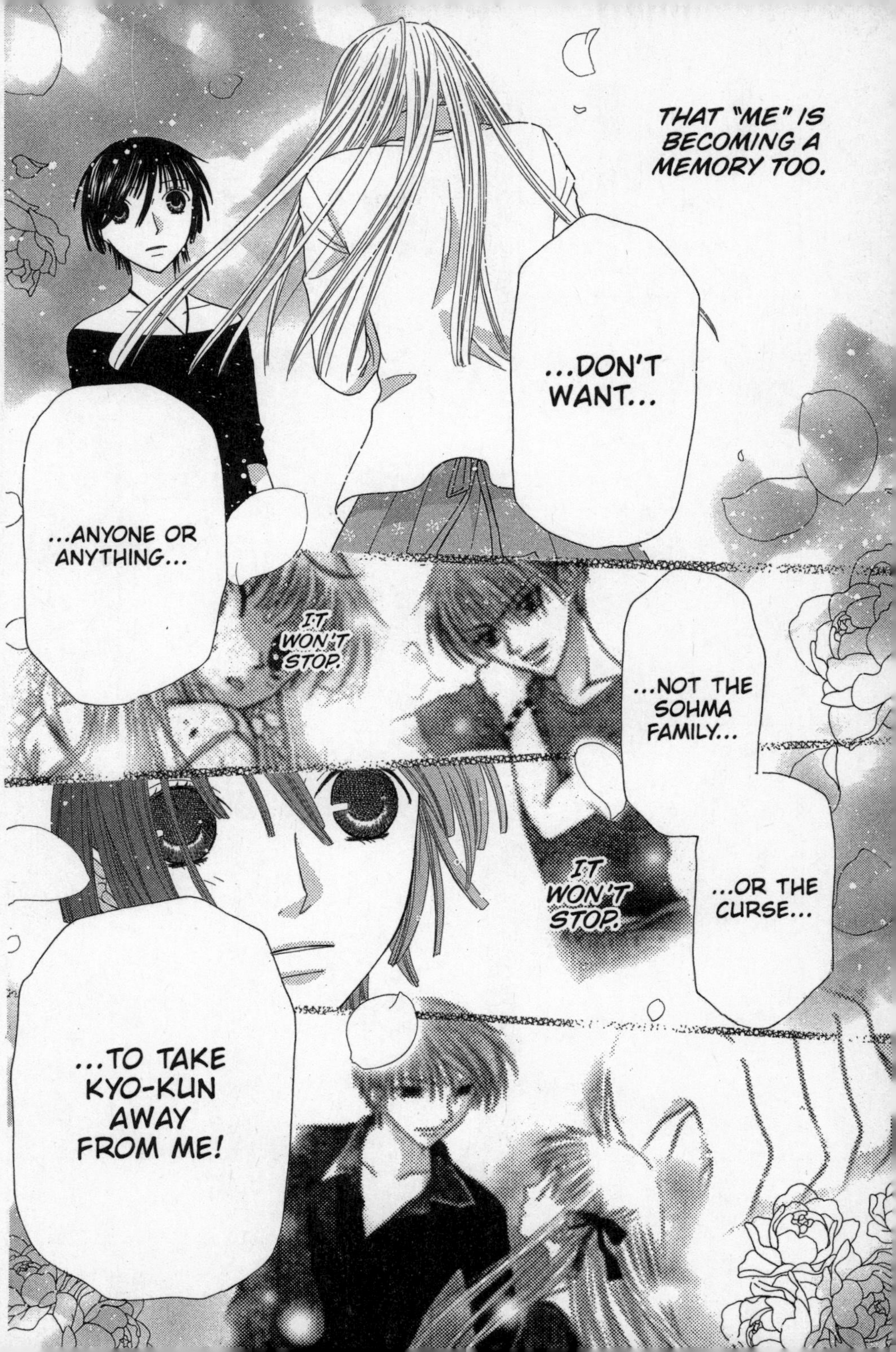
THAT "ME" IS BECOMING A MEMORY TOO.
...DON'T WANT...
...ANYONE OR ANYTHING...
...NOT THE SOHMA FAMILY...
IT WON'T STOP.
...OR THE CURSE...
IT WON'T STOP.
...TO TAKE KYO-KUN AWAY FROM ME!

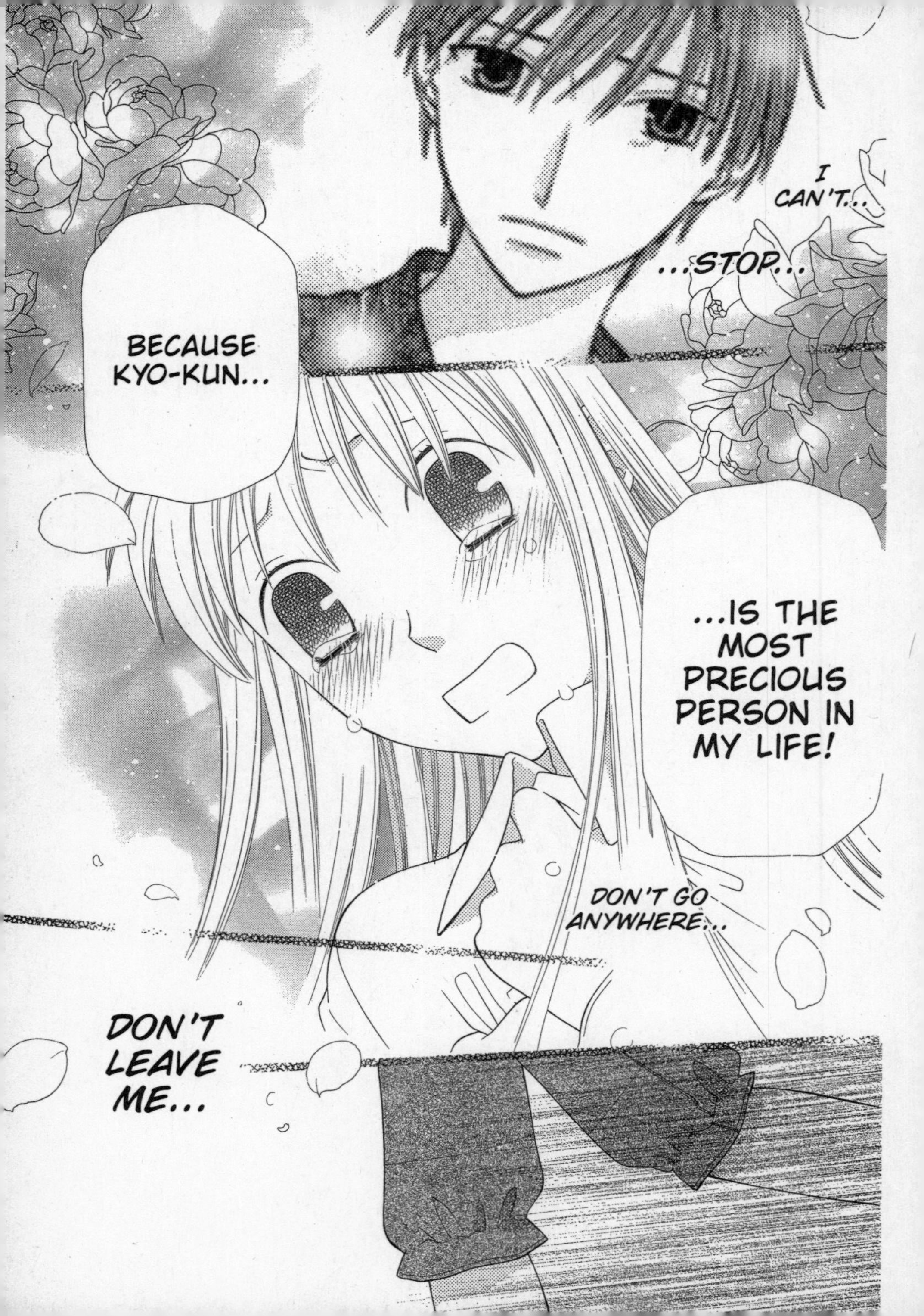
I CAN'T...
...STOP...
BECAUSE KYO-KUN...
...IS THE MOST PRECIOUS PERSON IN MY LIFE!
DON'T GO ANYWHERE...
DON'T LEAVE ME...

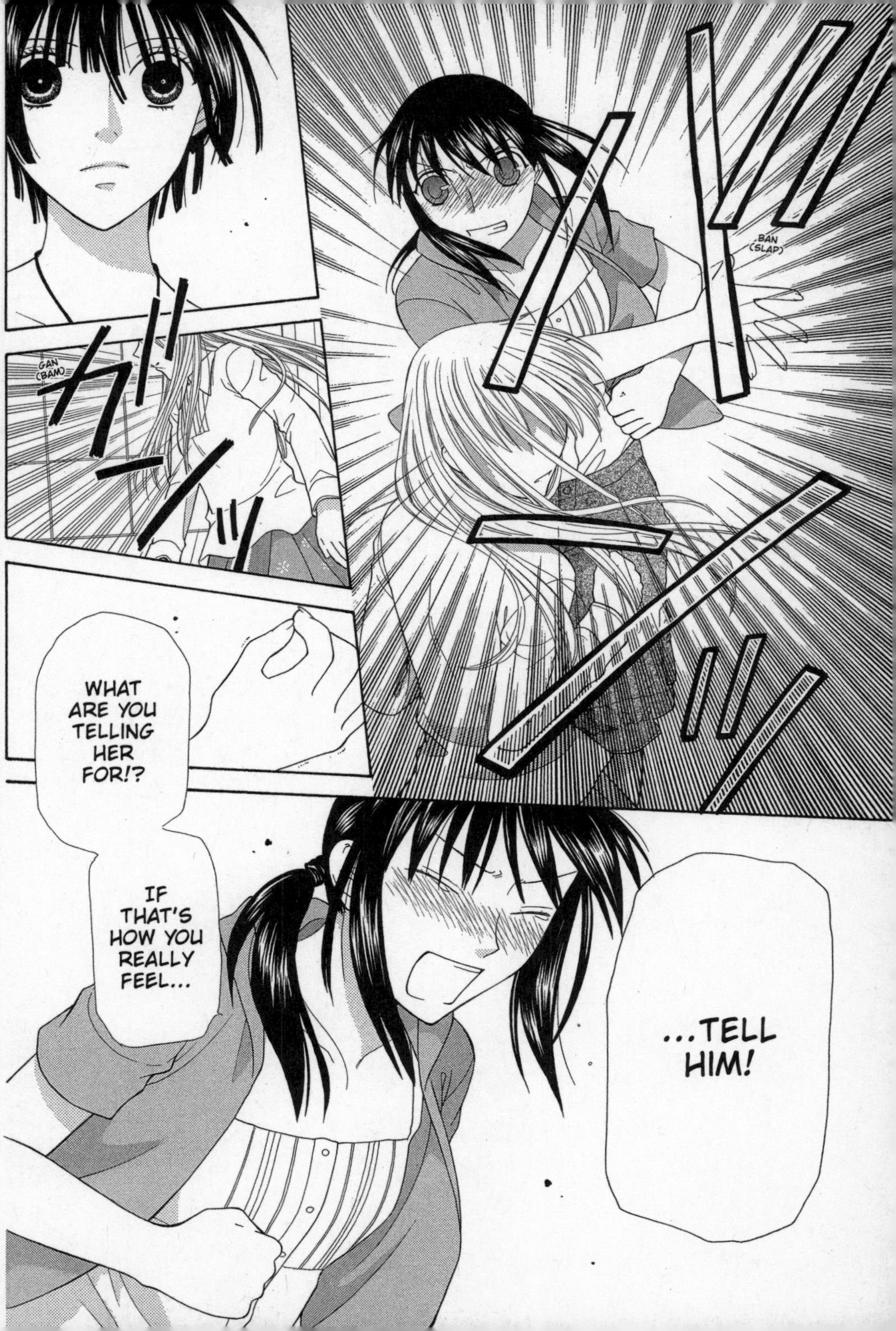
BAN (SLAP)
GAN (BAM)
WHAT ARE YOU TELLING HER FOR!?
IF THAT'S HOW YOU REALLY FEEL...
...TELL HIM!

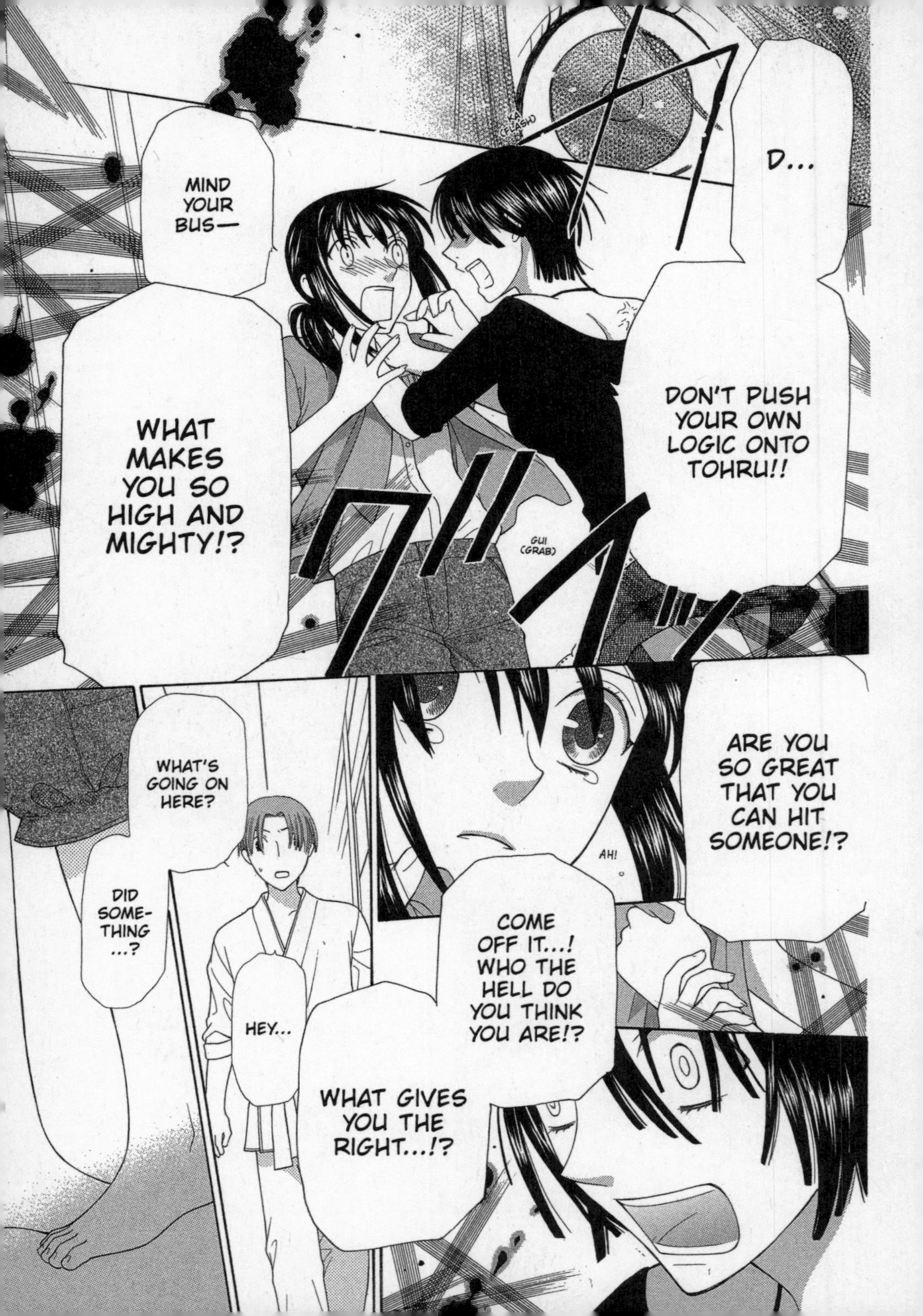
D...
DON'T PUSH YOUR OWN LOGIC ONTO TOHRU!!
KA (FLASH)
MIND YOUR BUS—
WHAT MAKES YOU SO HIGH AND MIGHTY!?
GUI (GRAB)
ARE YOU SO GREAT THAT YOU CAN HIT SOMEONE!?
AH!
COME OFF IT...! WHO THE HELL DO YOU THINK YOU ARE!?
WHAT GIVES YOU THE RIGHT...!?
WHAT'S GOING ON HERE?
DID SOME-THING ...?
HEY...

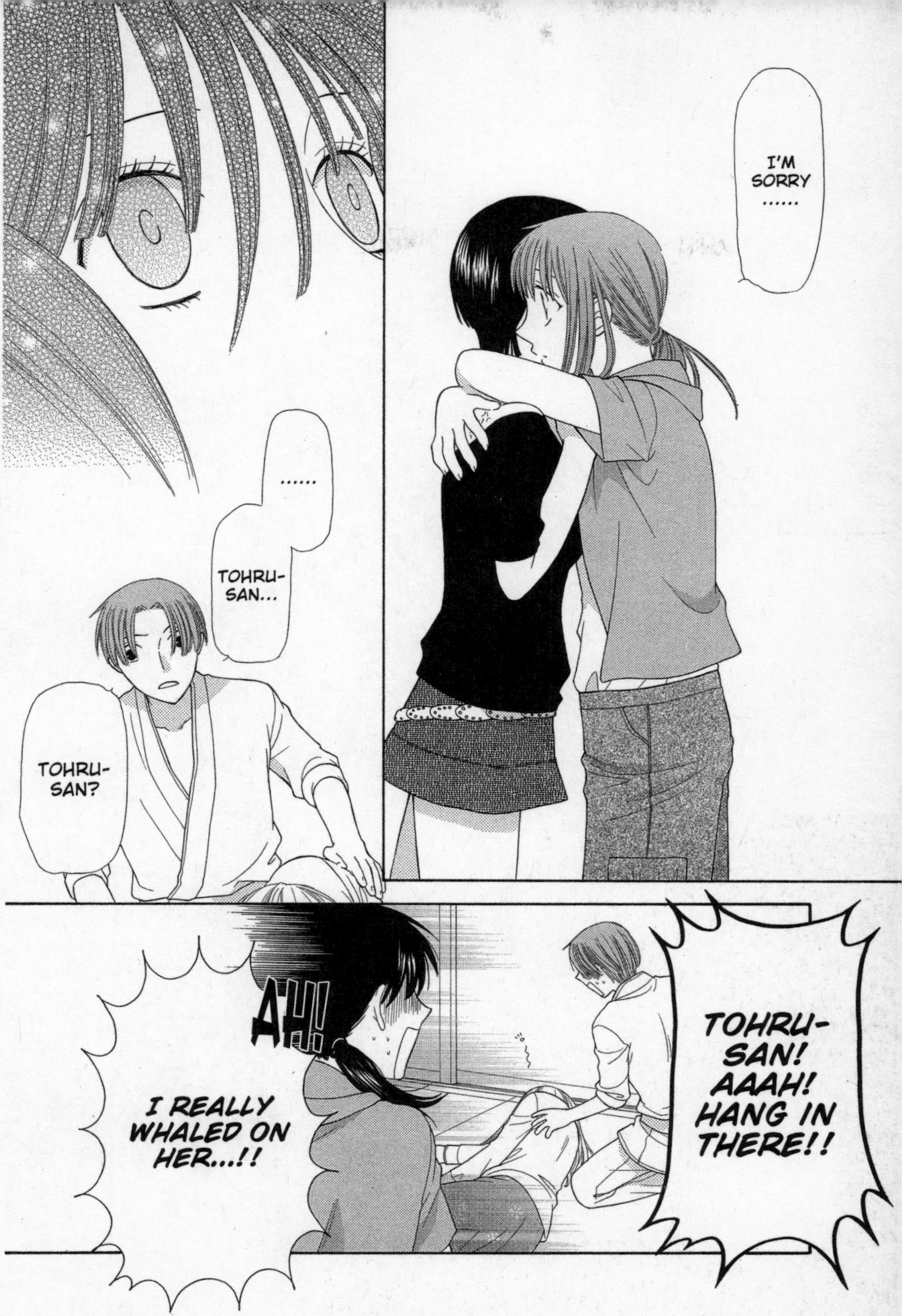
I'M SORRY ......
......
TOHRU-SAN...
TOHRU-SAN?
TOHRU-SAN! AAAH! HANG IN THERE!!
AH!
I REALLY WHALED ON HER...!!

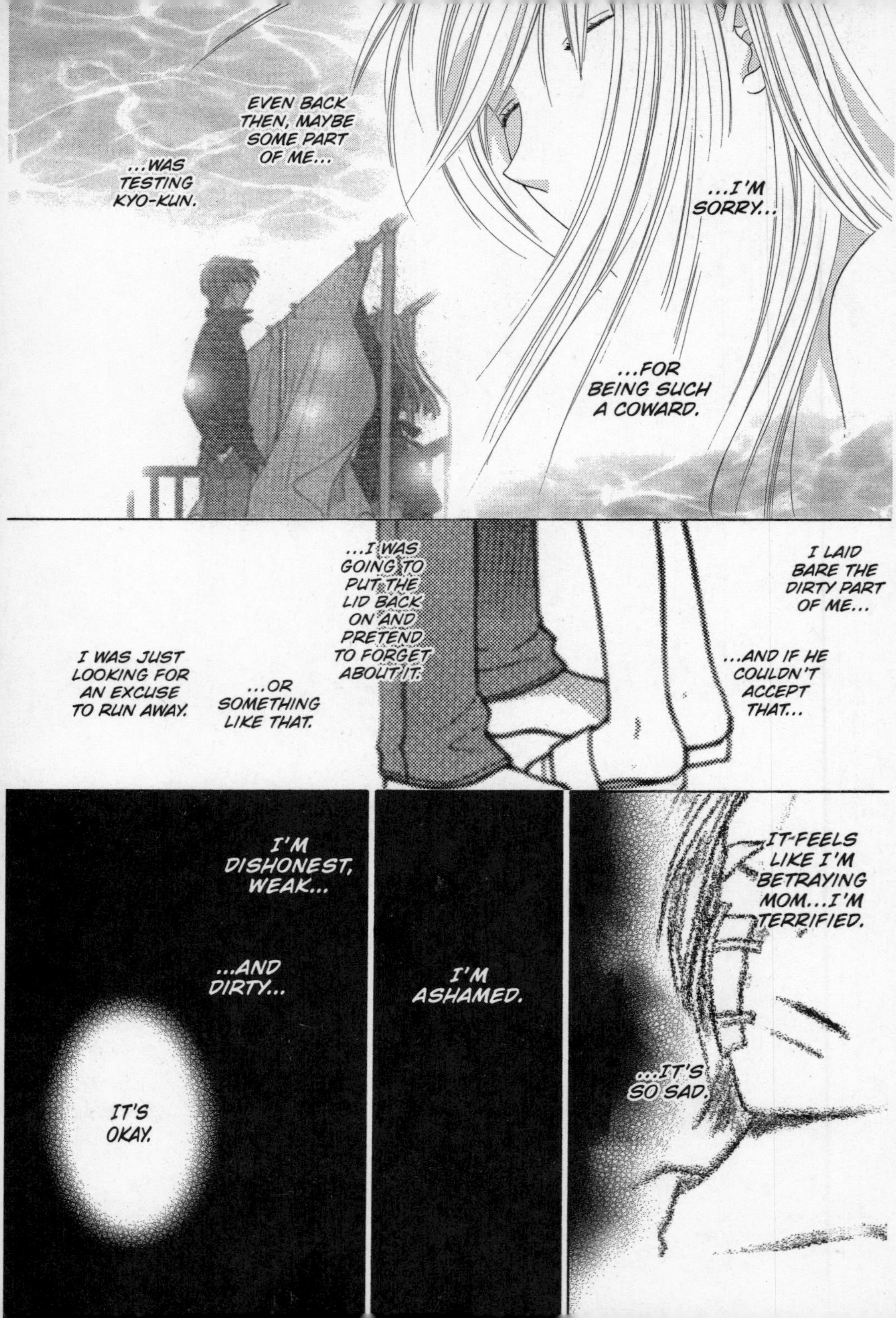
EVEN BACK THEN, MAYBE SOME PART OF ME...
...WAS TESTING KYO-KUN.
...I'M SORRY...
...FOR BEING SUCH A COWARD.
I LAID BARE THE DIRTY PART OF ME...
...AND IF HE COULDN'T ACCEPT THAT...
...I WAS GOING TO PUT THE LID BACK ON AND PRETEND TO FORGET ABOUT IT.
...OR SOMETHING LIKE THAT.
I WAS JUST LOOKING FOR AN EXCUSE TO RUN AWAY.
IT-FEELS LIKE I'M BETRAYING MOM...I'M TERRIFIED.
...IT'S SO SAD.
I'M ASHAMED.
I'M DISHONEST, WEAK...
...AND DIRTY...
IT'S OKAY.

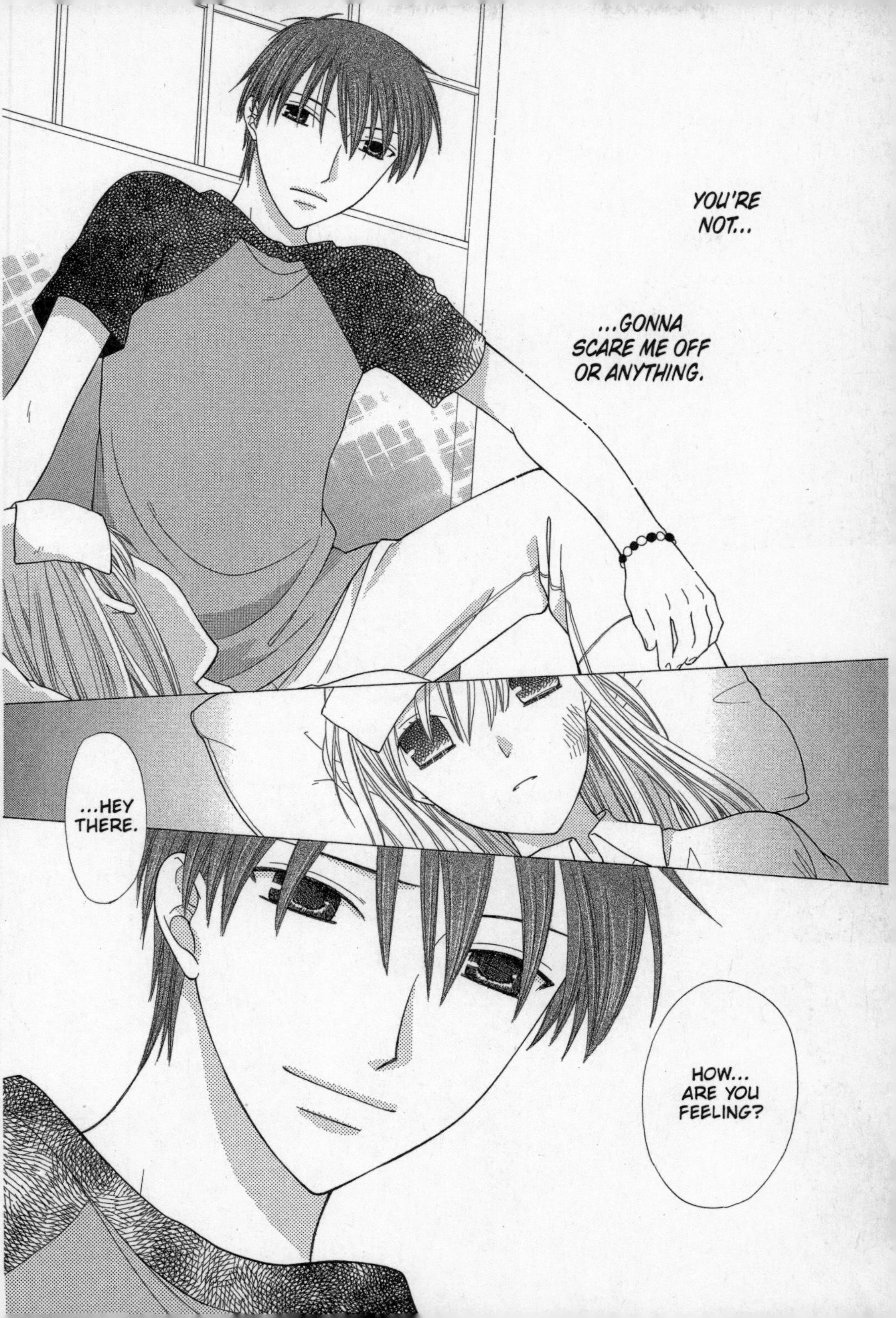
YOU'RE NOT...
...GONNA SCARE ME OFF OR ANYTHING.
...HEY THERE.
HOW... ARE YOU FEELING?

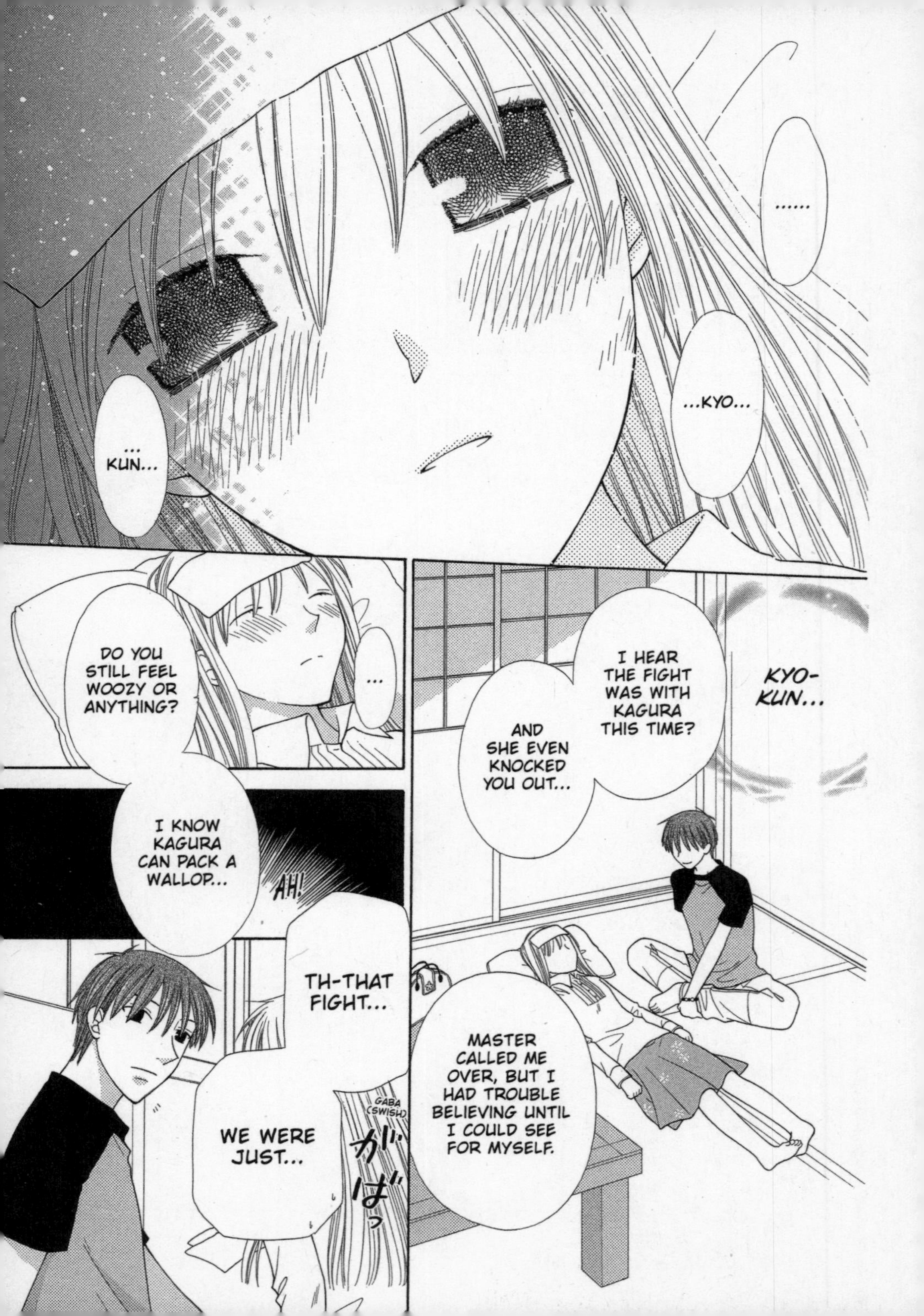

......
...KYO...
...
KUN...
KYO-KUN...
I HEAR THE FIGHT WAS WITH KAGURA THIS TIME?
AND SHE EVEN KNOCKED YOU OUT...
MASTER CALLED ME OVER, BUT I HAD TROUBLE BELIEVING UNTIL I COULD SEE FOR MYSELF.
...
DO YOU STILL FEEL WOOZY OR ANYTHING?
I KNOW KAGURA CAN PACK A WALLOP...
AH!
TH-THAT FIGHT...
WE WERE JUST...
GABA (SWISH)
がばっ

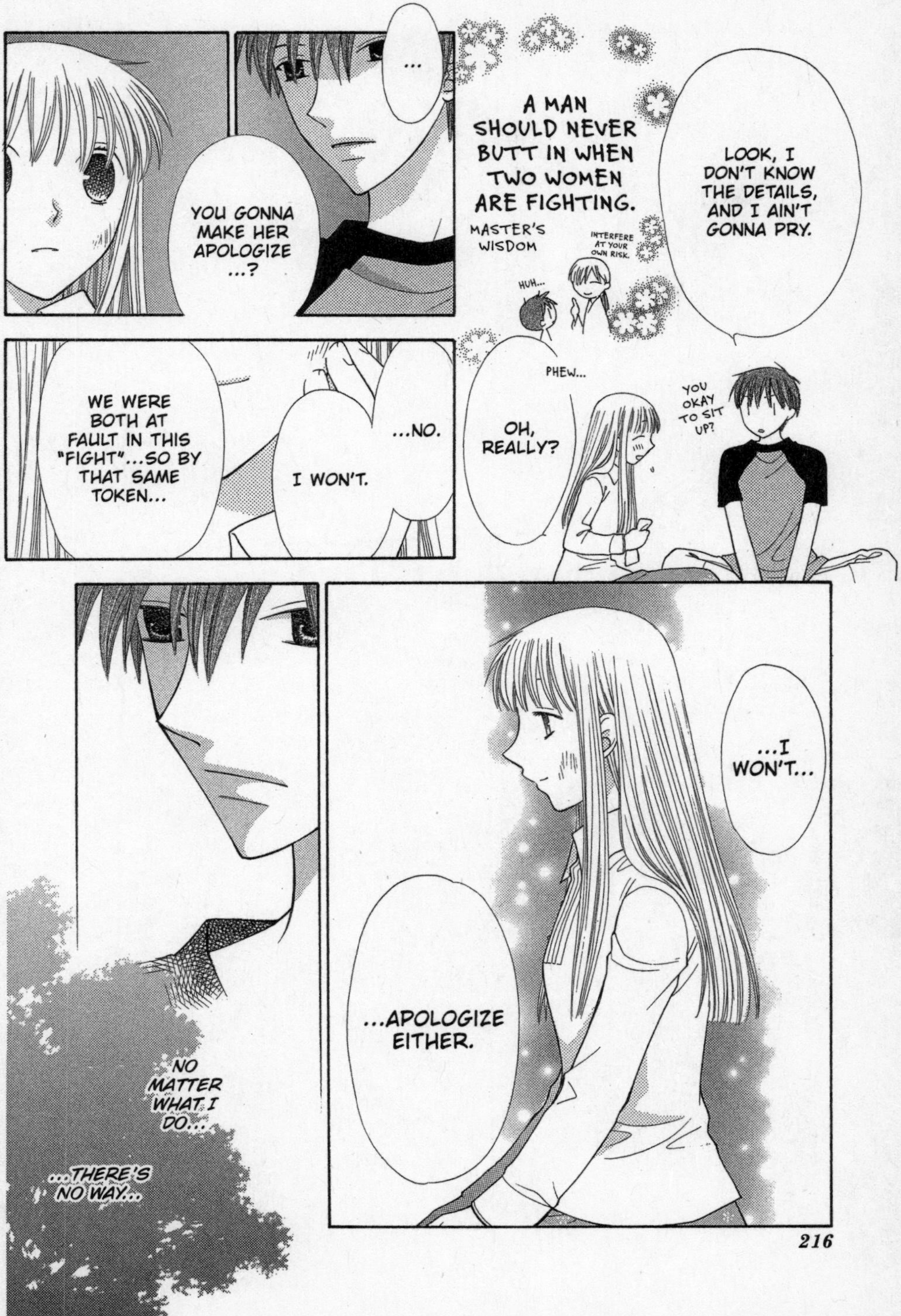
LOOK, I DON'T KNOW THE DETAILS, AND I AIN'T GONNA PRY.
A MAN SHOULD NEVER BUTT IN WHEN TWO WOMEN ARE FIGHTING.
MASTER'S WISDOM
INTERFERE AT YOUR OWN RISK.
HUH...
PHEW...
OH, REALLY?
YOU OKAY TO SIT UP?
...
YOU GONNA MAKE HER APOLOGIZE ...?
...NO.
I WON'T.
WE WERE BOTH AT FAULT IN THIS "FIGHT"...SO BY THAT SAME TOKEN...
...I WON'T...
...APOLOGIZE EITHER.
NO MATTER WHAT I DO...
...THERE'S NO WAY...

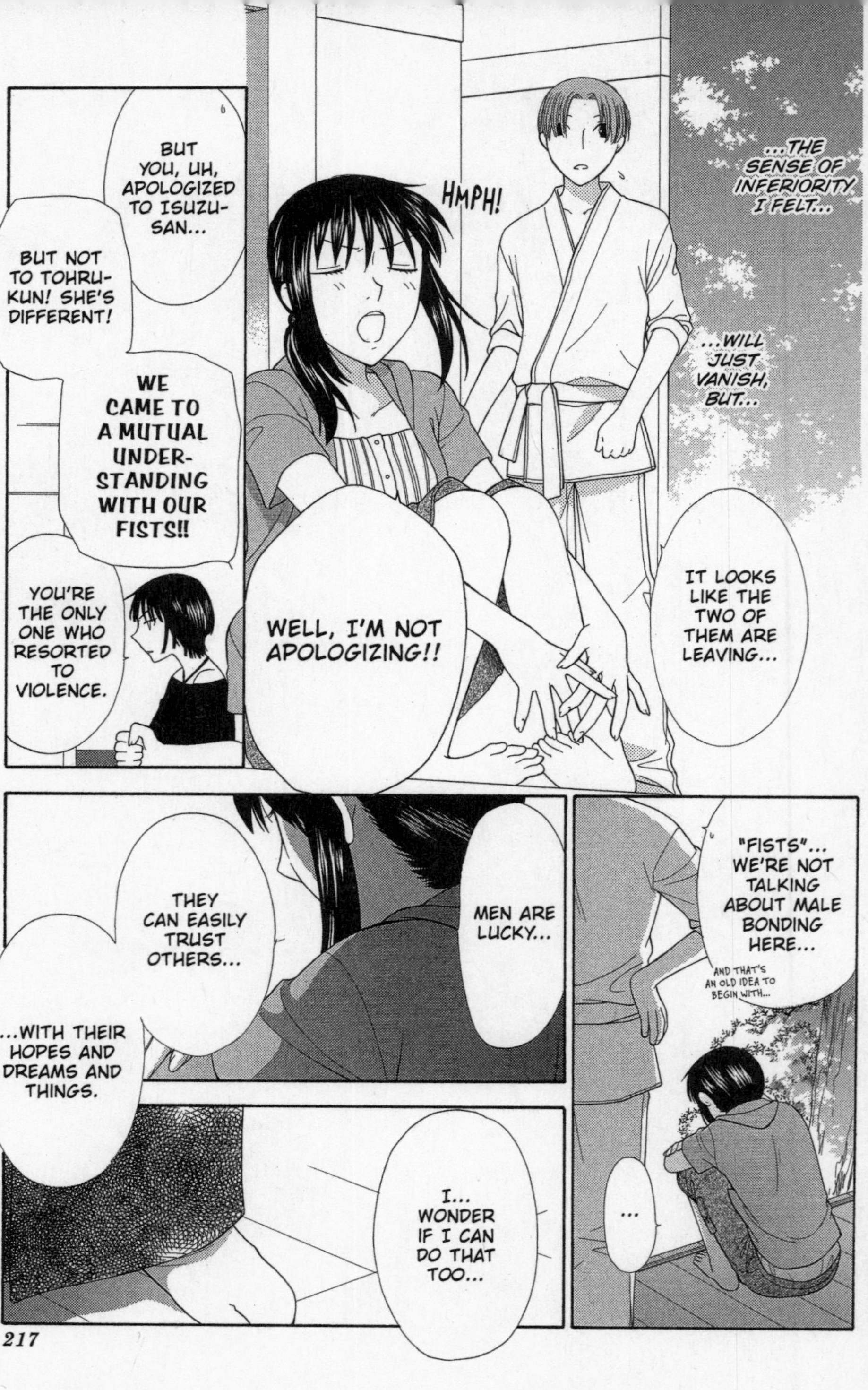
...THE SENSE OF INFERIORITY I FELT...
...WILL JUST VANISH, BUT...
IT LOOKS LIKE THE TWO OF THEM ARE LEAVING...
HMPH!
WELL, I'M NOT APOLOGIZING!!
BUT YOU, UH, APOLOGIZED TO ISUZU-SAN...
BUT NOT TO TOHRU-KUN! SHE'S DIFFERENT!
WE CAME TO A MUTUAL UNDER-STANDING WITH OUR FISTS!!
YOU'RE THE ONLY ONE WHO RESORTED TO VIOLENCE.
"FISTS"... WE'RE NOT TALKING ABOUT MALE BONDING HERE...
AND THAT'S AN OLD IDEA TO BEGIN WITH...
...
MEN ARE LUCKY...
THEY CAN EASILY TRUST OTHERS...
...WITH THEIR HOPES AND DREAMS AND THINGS.
I... WONDER IF I CAN DO THAT TOO...

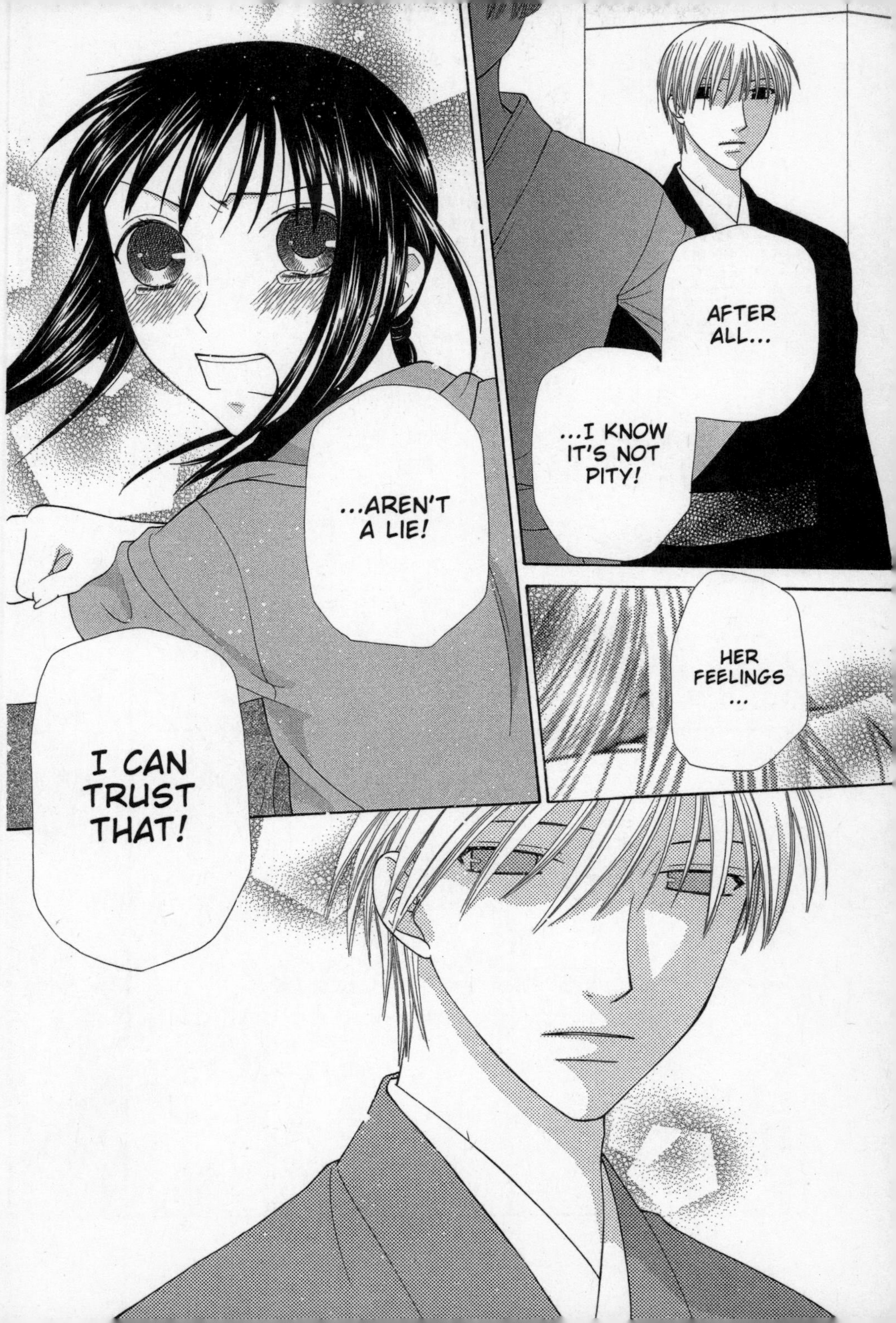
AFTER ALL...
...I KNOW IT'S NOT PITY!
HER FEELINGS...
...AREN'T A LIE!
I CAN TRUST THAT!

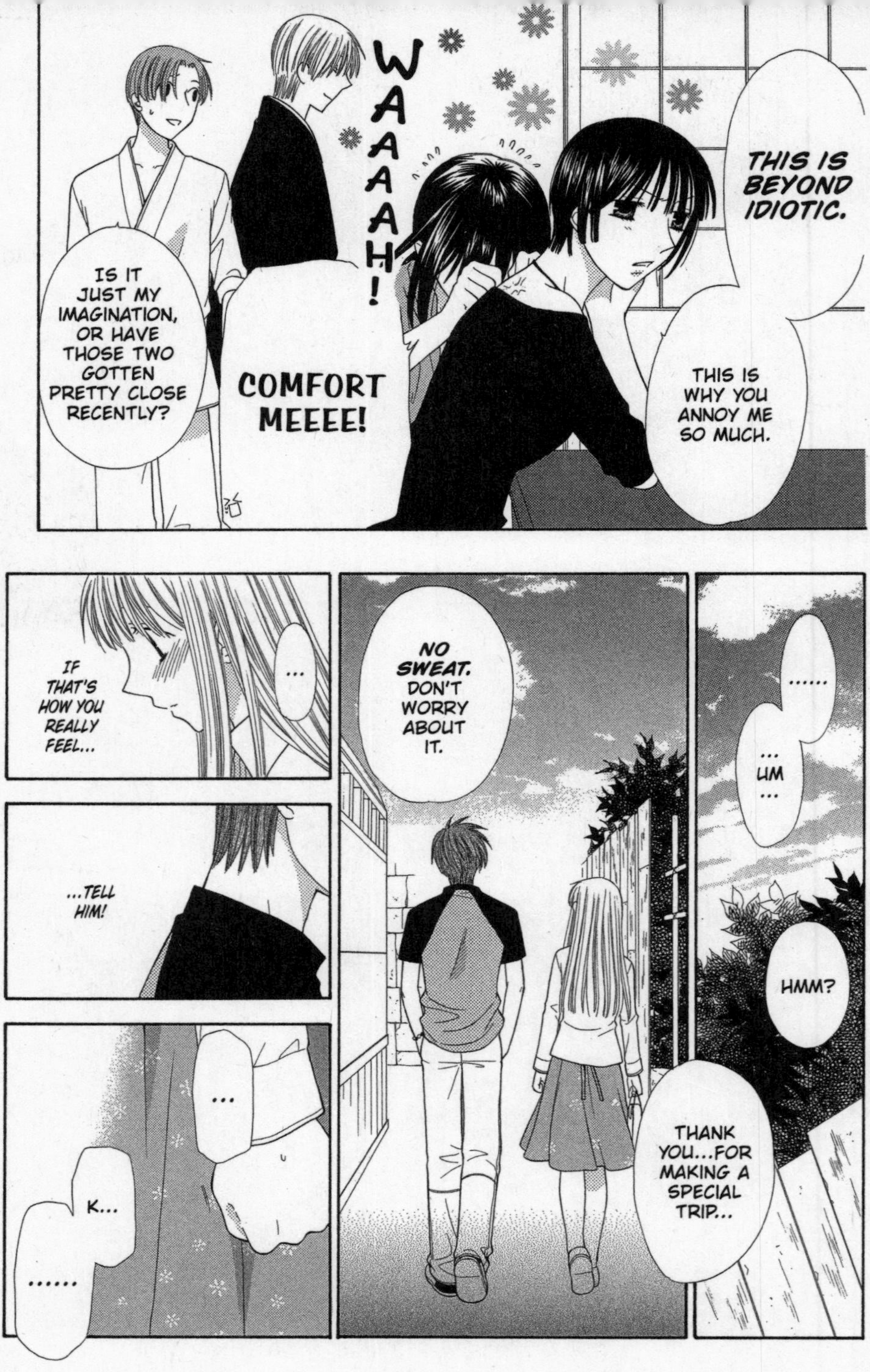
THIS IS BEYOND IDIOTIC.
THIS IS WHY YOU ANNOY ME SO MUCH.
WAAAAAH!
COMFORT MEEEE!
IS IT JUST MY IMAGINATION, OR HAVE THOSE TWO GOTTEN PRETTY CLOSE RECENTLY?
......
...UM...
HMM?
THANK YOU...FOR MAKING A SPECIAL TRIP...
NO SWEAT. DON'T WORRY ABOUT IT.
...
IF THAT'S HOW YOU REALLY FEEL...
...TELL HIM!
...
K...
....

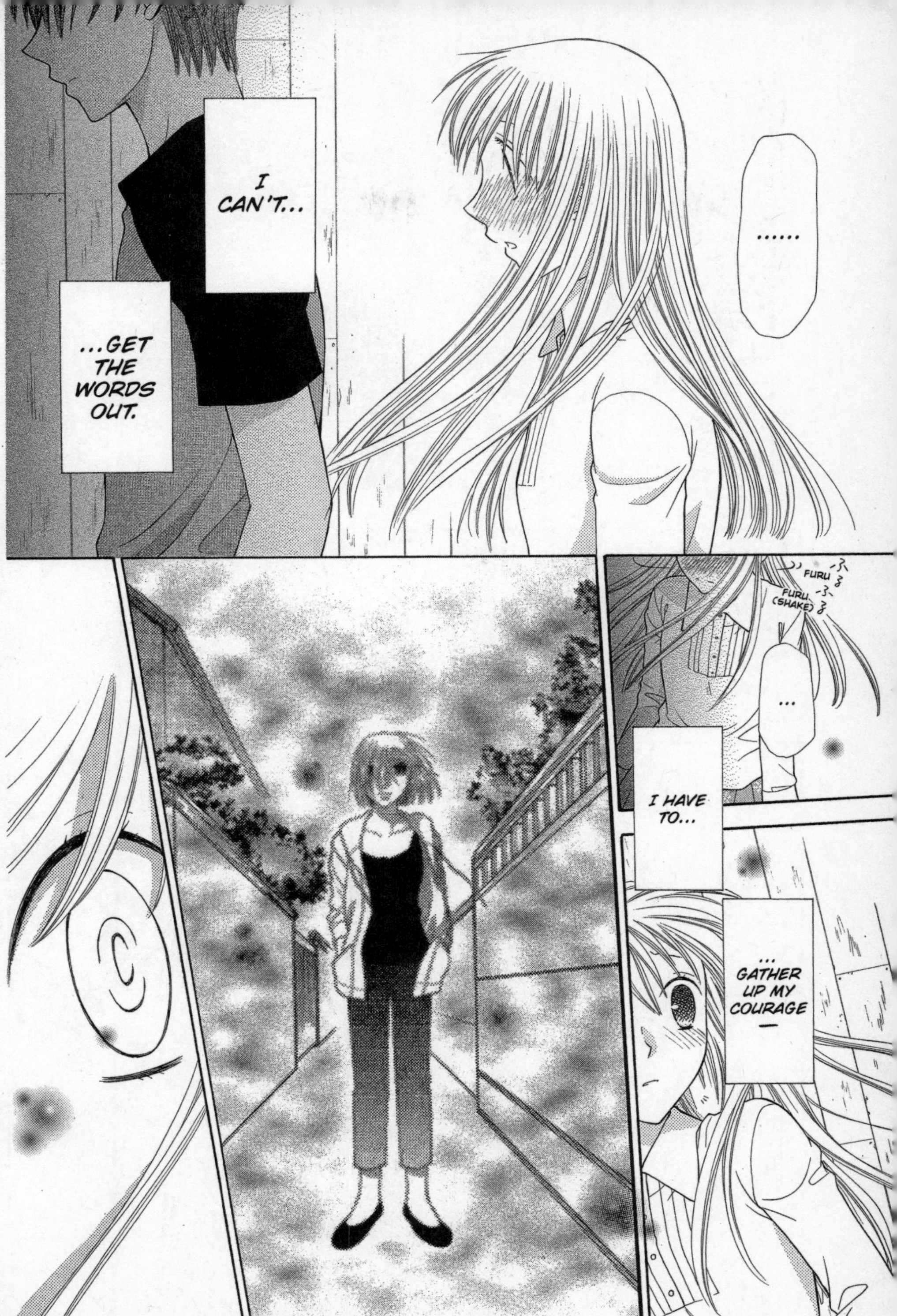
......
I CAN'T...
...GET THE WORDS OUT.
FURU FURU (SHAKE)
...
I HAVE TO...
...GATHER UP MY COURAGE—

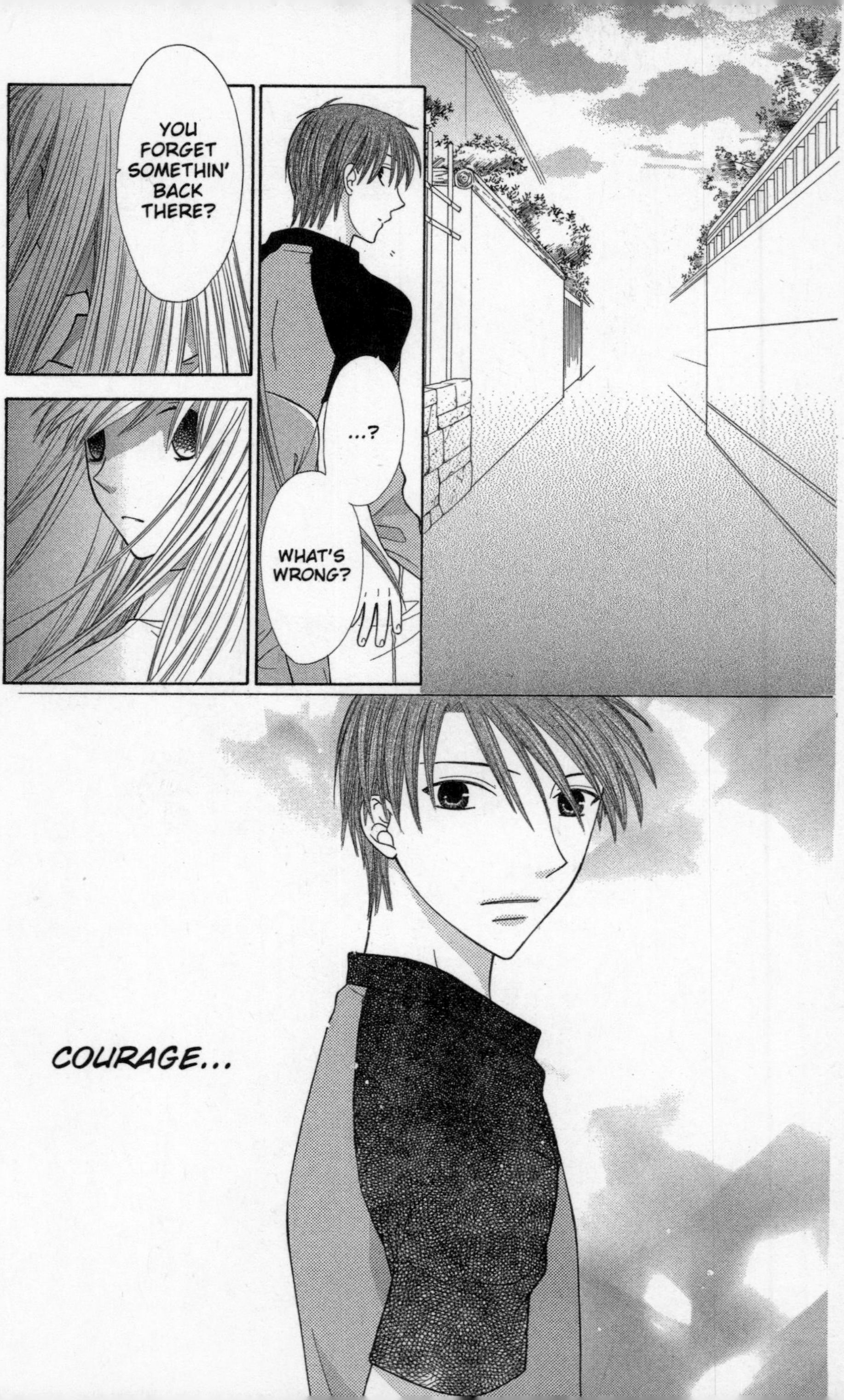
YOU FORGET SOMETHIN' BACK THERE?
...?
WHAT'S WRONG?
COURAGE...

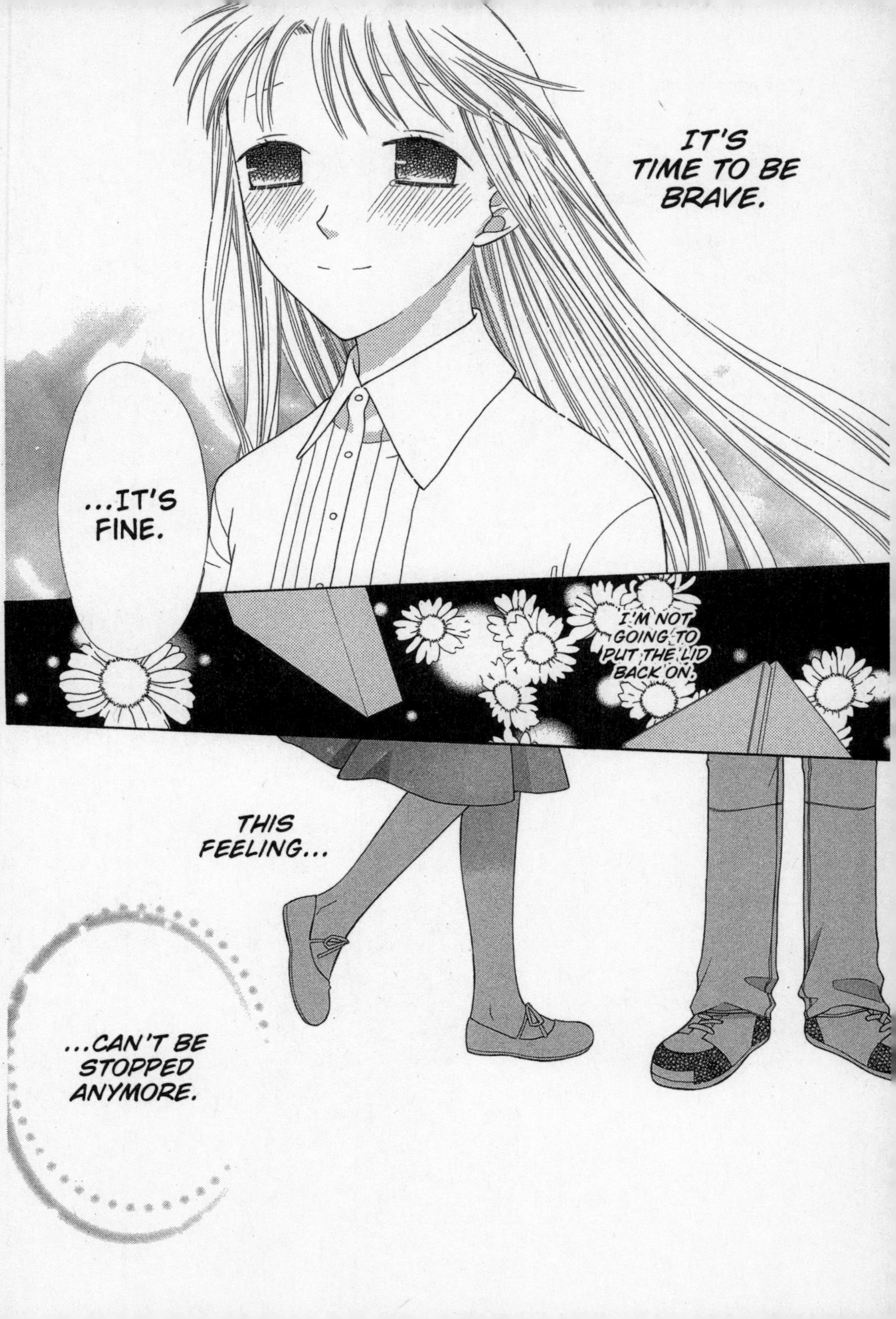
IT'S TIME TO BE BRAVE.
...IT'S FINE.
I'M NOT GOING TO PUT THE LID BACK ON.
THIS FEELING...
...CAN'T BE STOPPED ANYMORE.

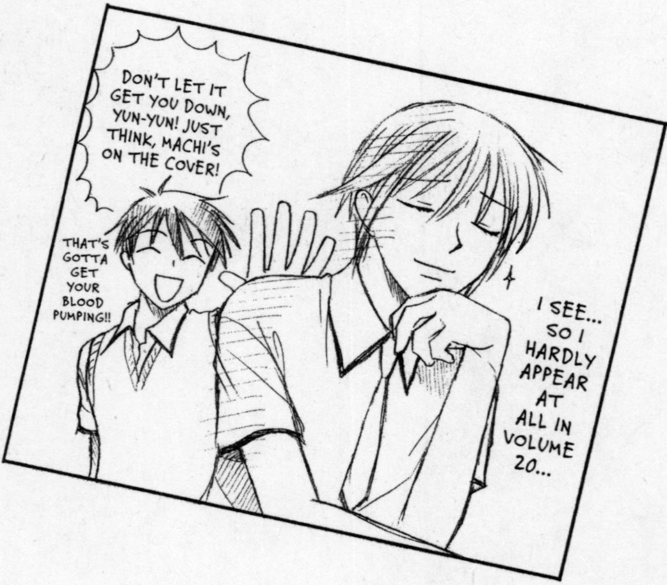
DON'T LET IT GET YOU DOWN, YUN-YUN! JUST THINK, MACHI'S ON THE COVER!
I SEE... SO I HARDLY APPEAR AT ALL IN VOLUME 20...
THAT'S GOTTA GET YOUR BLOOD PUMPING!!

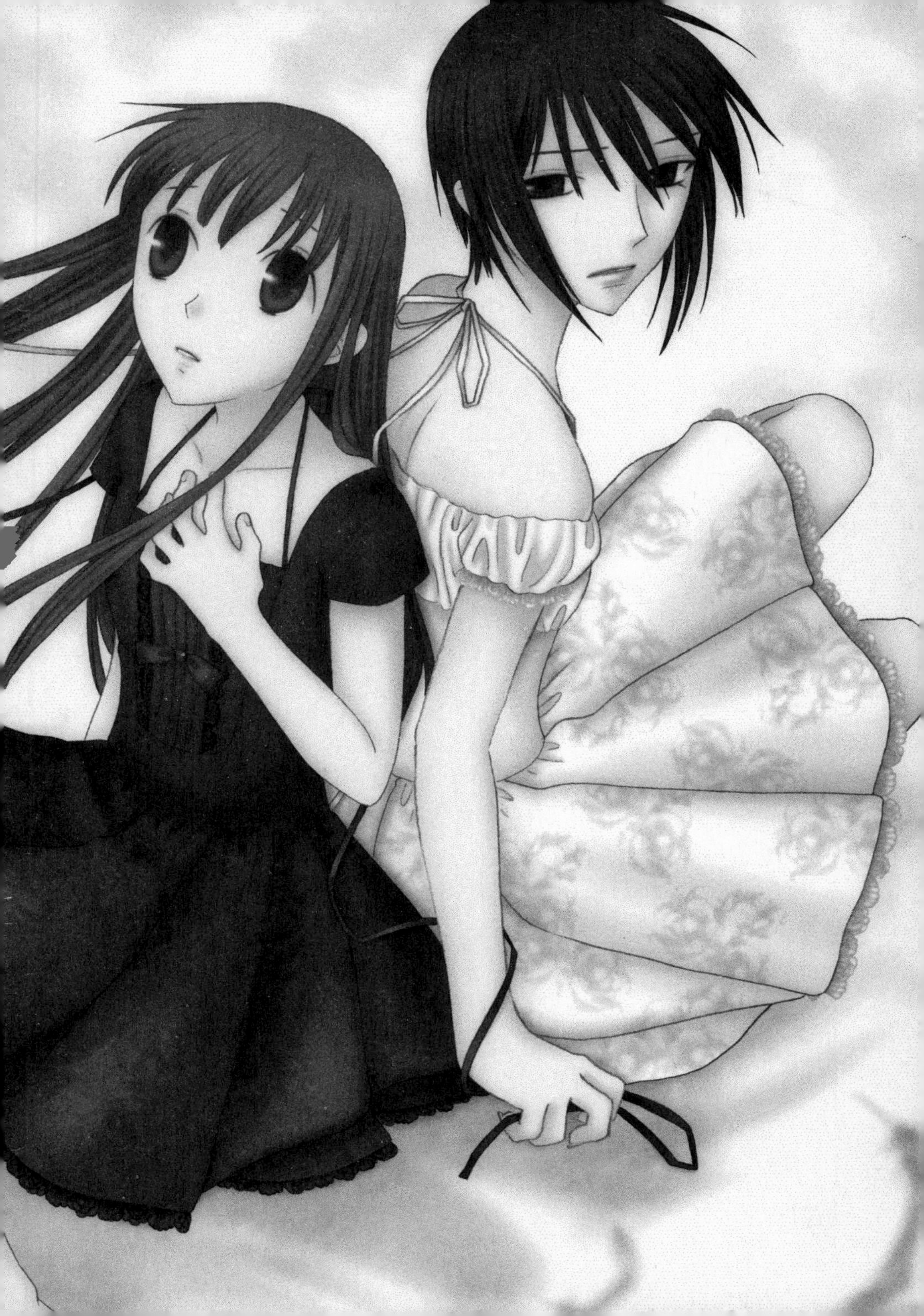

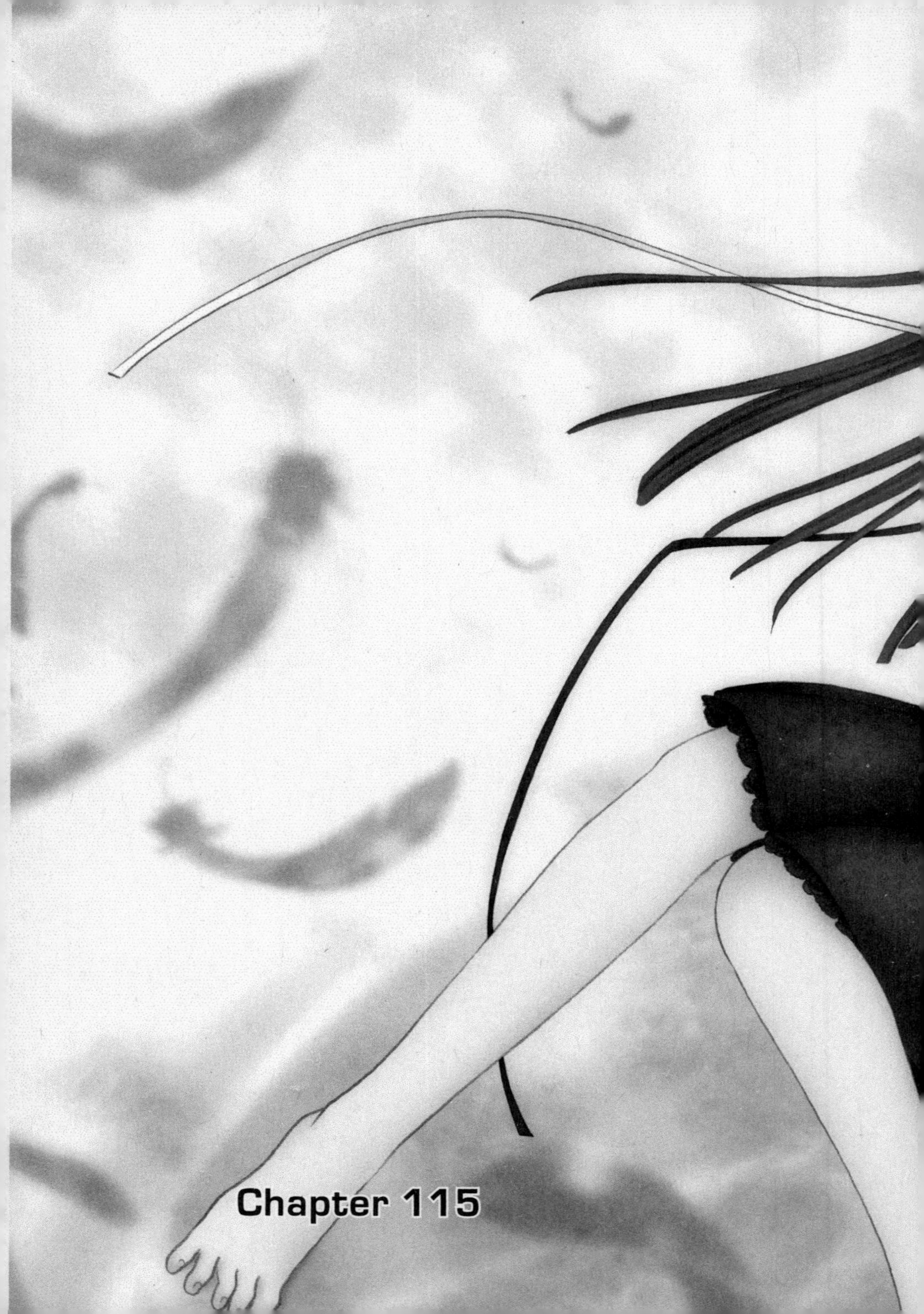

Chapter 115

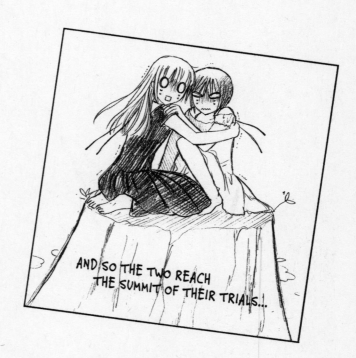

AND SO THE TWO REACH
THE SUMMIT OF THEIR TRIALS...

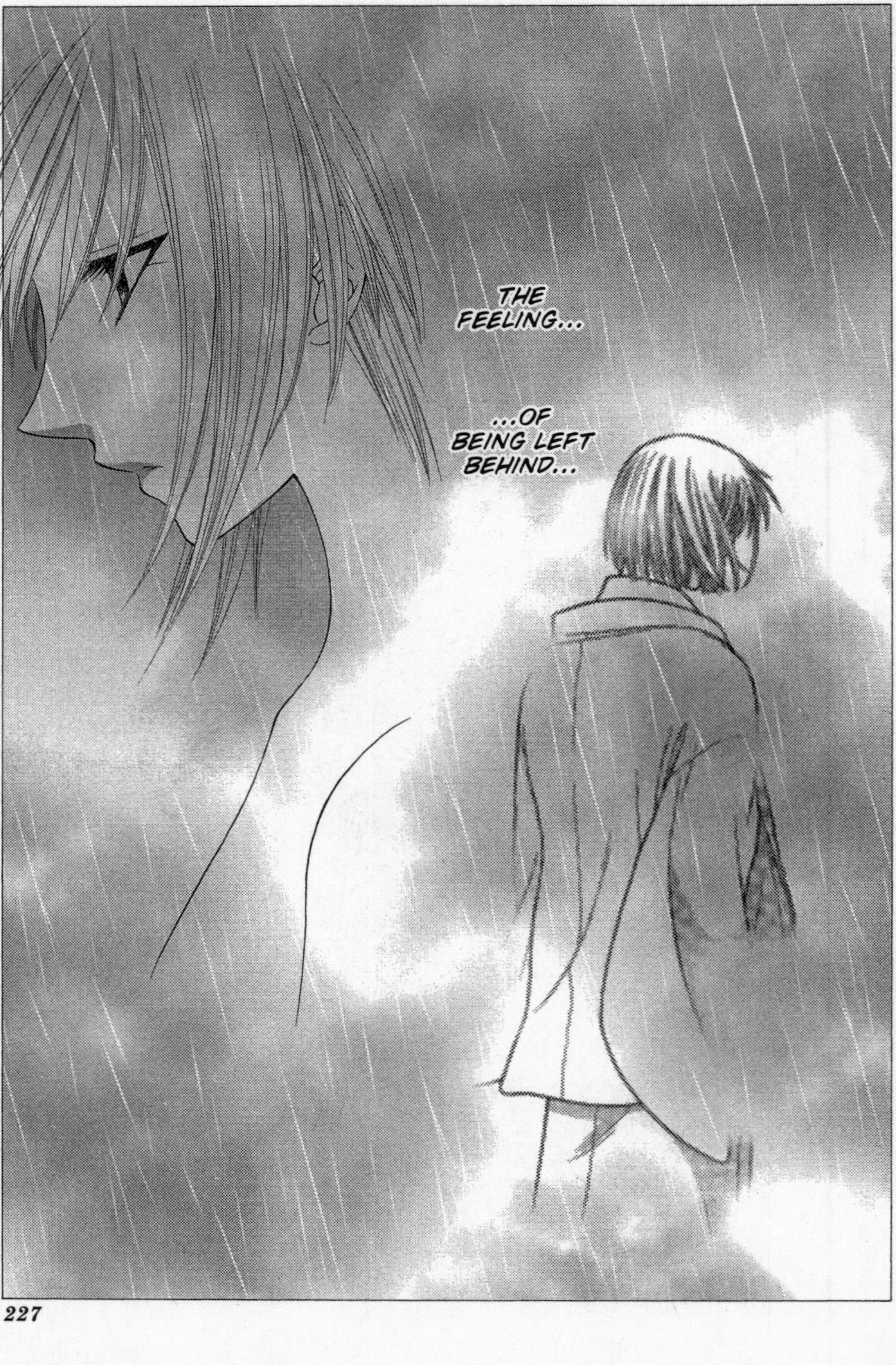
THE FEELING...
...OF BEING LEFT BEHIND...

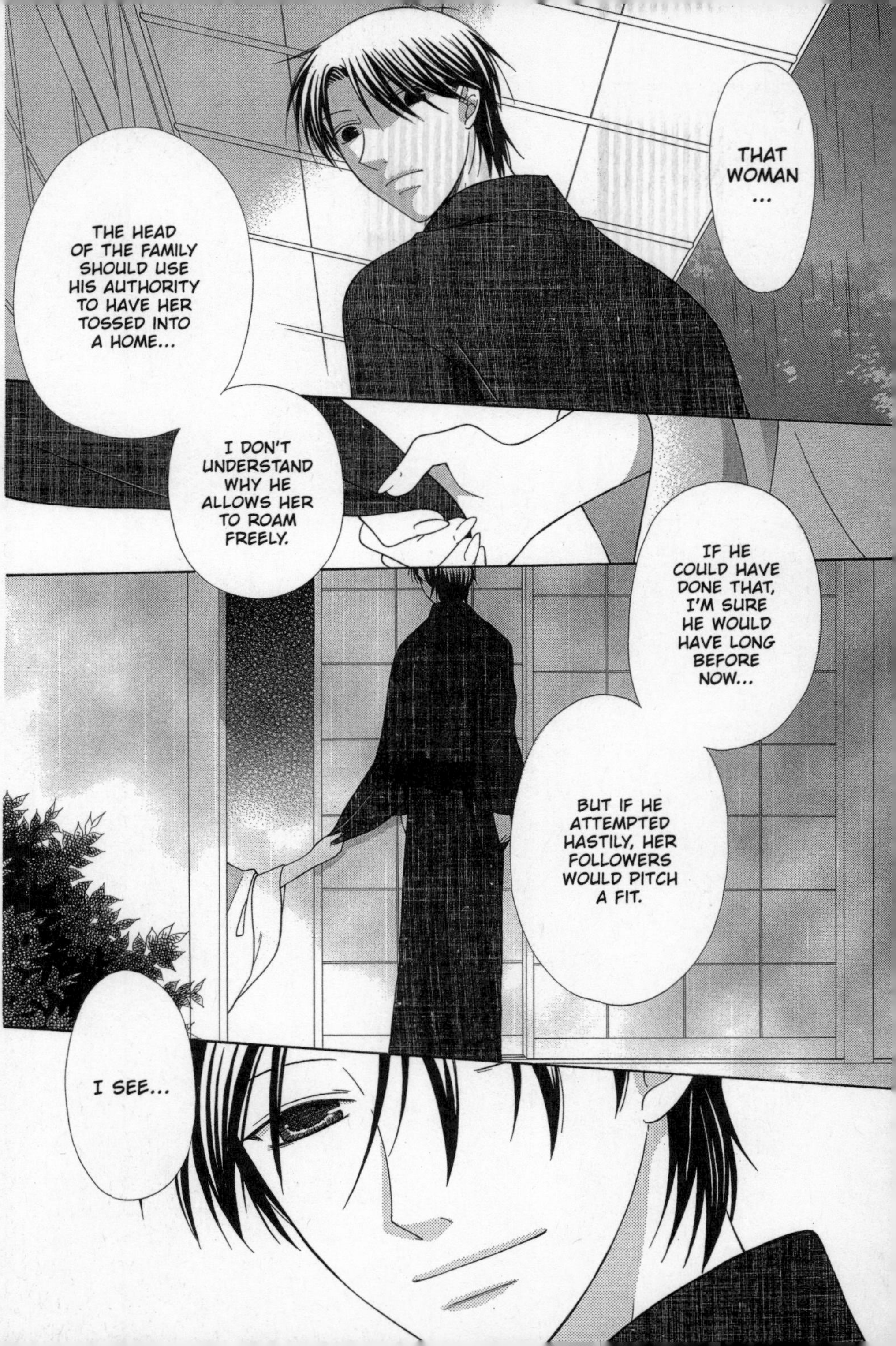
THAT WOMAN...
THE HEAD OF THE FAMILY SHOULD USE HIS AUTHORITY TO HAVE HER TOSSED INTO A HOME...
I DON'T UNDERSTAND WHY HE ALLOWS HER TO ROAM FREELY.
IF HE COULD HAVE DONE THAT, I'M SURE HE WOULD HAVE LONG BEFORE NOW...
BUT IF HE ATTEMPTED HASTILY, HER FOLLOWERS WOULD PITCH A FIT.
I SEE...

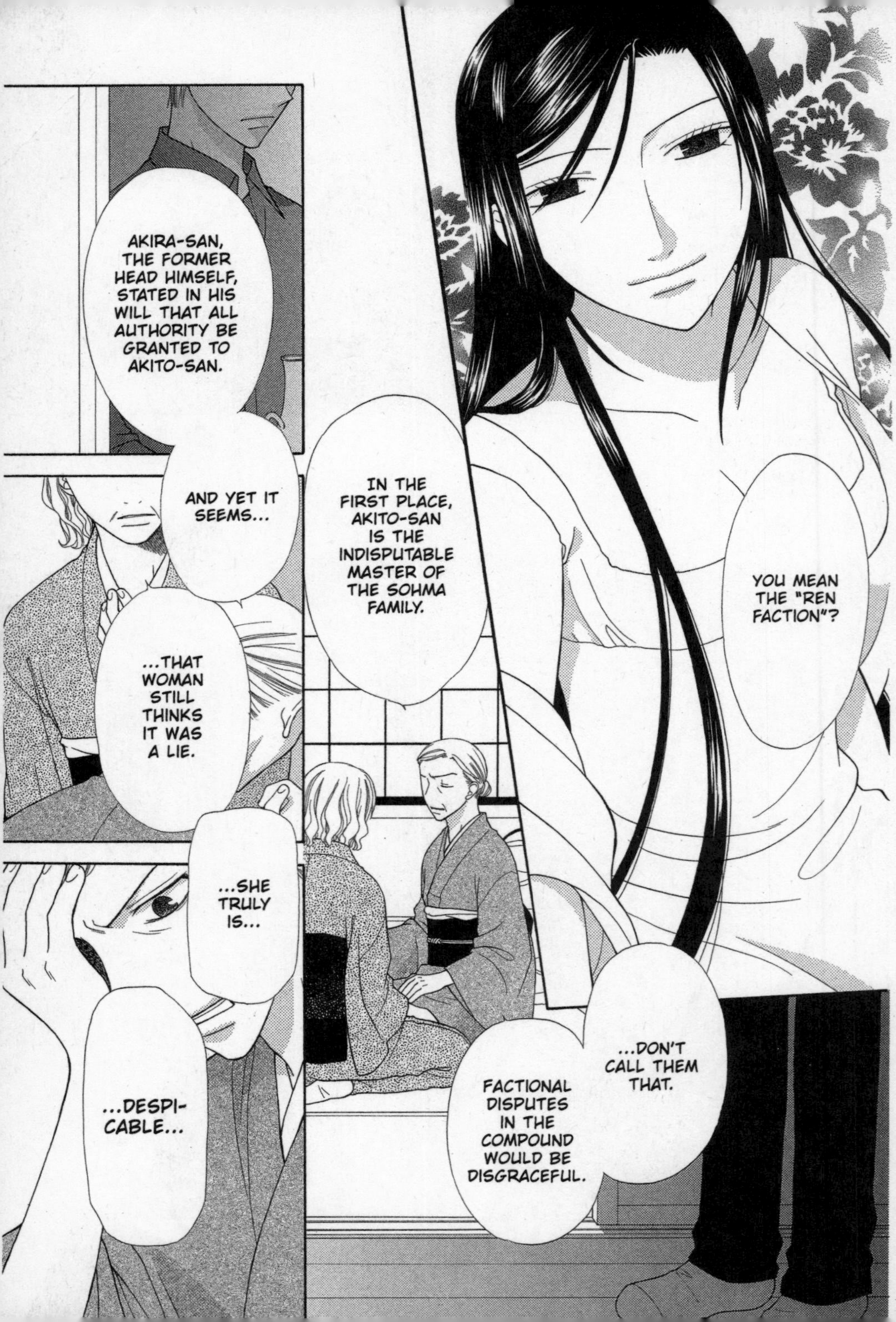
AKIRA-SAN, THE FORMER HEAD HIMSELF, STATED IN HIS WILL THAT ALL AUTHORITY BE GRANTED TO AKITO-SAN.
IN THE FIRST PLACE, AKITO-SAN IS THE INDISPUTABLE MASTER OF THE SOHMA FAMILY.
AND YET IT SEEMS...
...THAT WOMAN STILL THINKS IT WAS A LIE.
...SHE TRULY IS...
...DESPI-CABLE...
YOU MEAN THE "REN FACTION"?
...DON'T CALL THEM THAT.
FACTIONAL DISPUTES IN THE COMPOUND WOULD BE DISGRACEFUL.

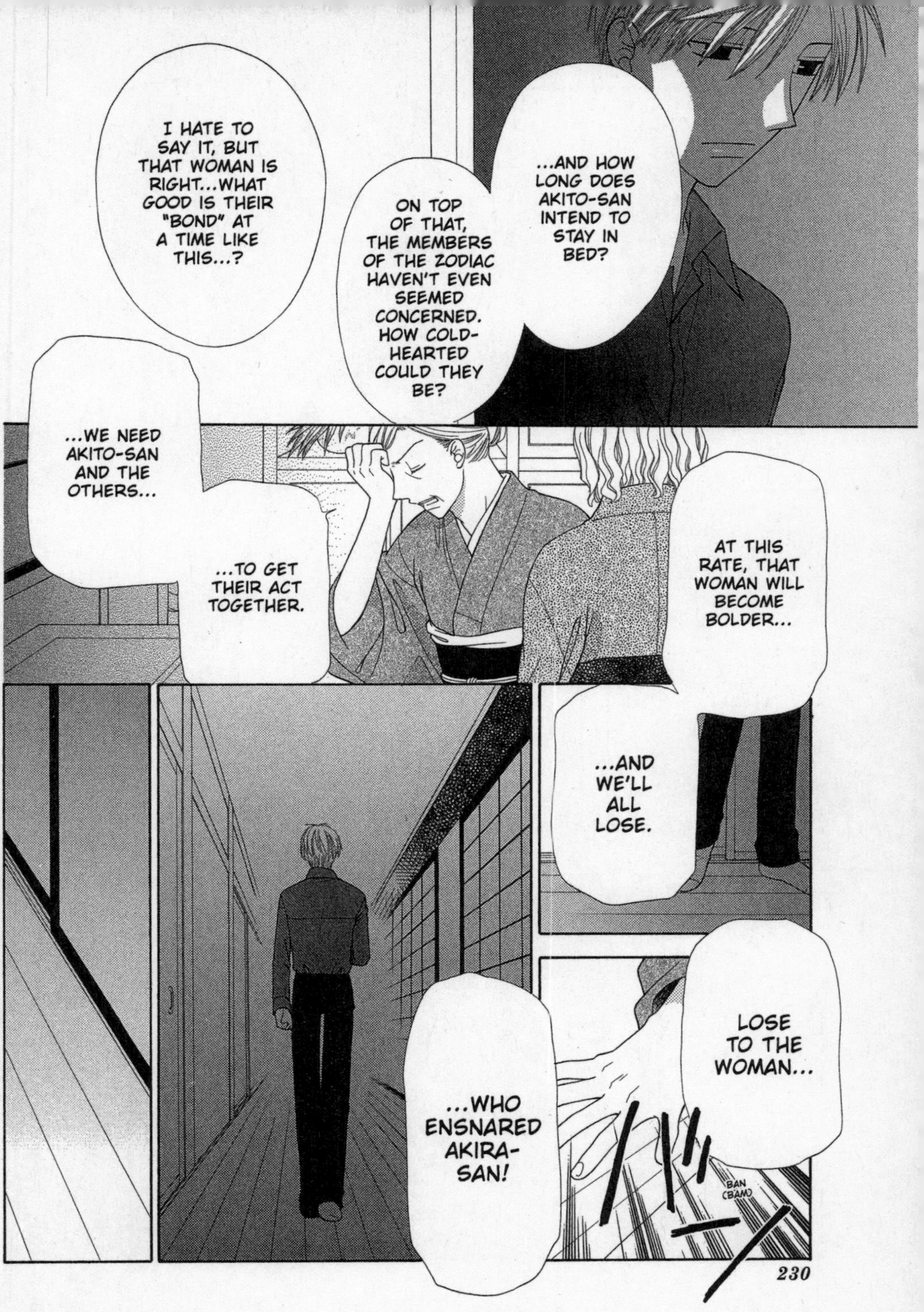
...AND HOW LONG DOES AKITO-SAN INTEND TO STAY IN BED?
ON TOP OF THAT, THE MEMBERS OF THE ZODIAC HAVEN'T EVEN SEEMED CONCERNED. HOW COLD-HEARTED COULD THEY BE?
I HATE TO SAY IT, BUT THAT WOMAN IS RIGHT...WHAT GOOD IS THEIR "BOND" AT A TIME LIKE THIS...?
AT THIS RATE, THAT WOMAN WILL BECOME BOLDER...
...WE NEED AKITO-SAN AND THE OTHERS...
...TO GET THEIR ACT TOGETHER.
...AND WE'LL ALL LOSE.
LOSE TO THE WOMAN...
...WHO ENSNARED AKIRA-SAN!
BAN (BAM)

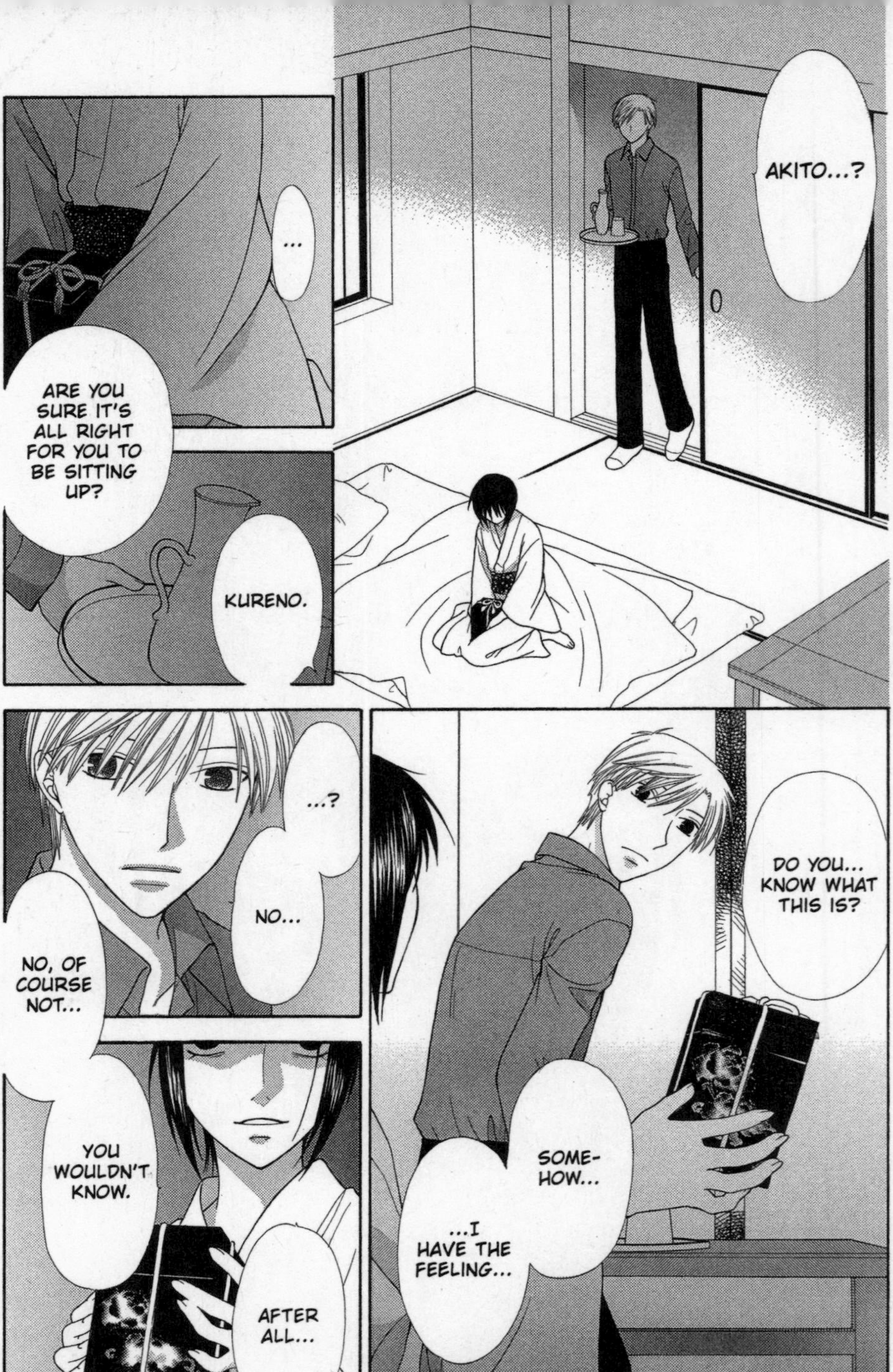

AKITO...?
...
ARE YOU SURE IT'S ALL RIGHT FOR YOU TO BE SITTING UP?
KURENO.
DO YOU... KNOW WHAT THIS IS?
SOME-HOW...
...I HAVE THE FEELING...
...?
NO...
NO, OF COURSE NOT...
YOU WOULDN'T KNOW.
AFTER ALL...

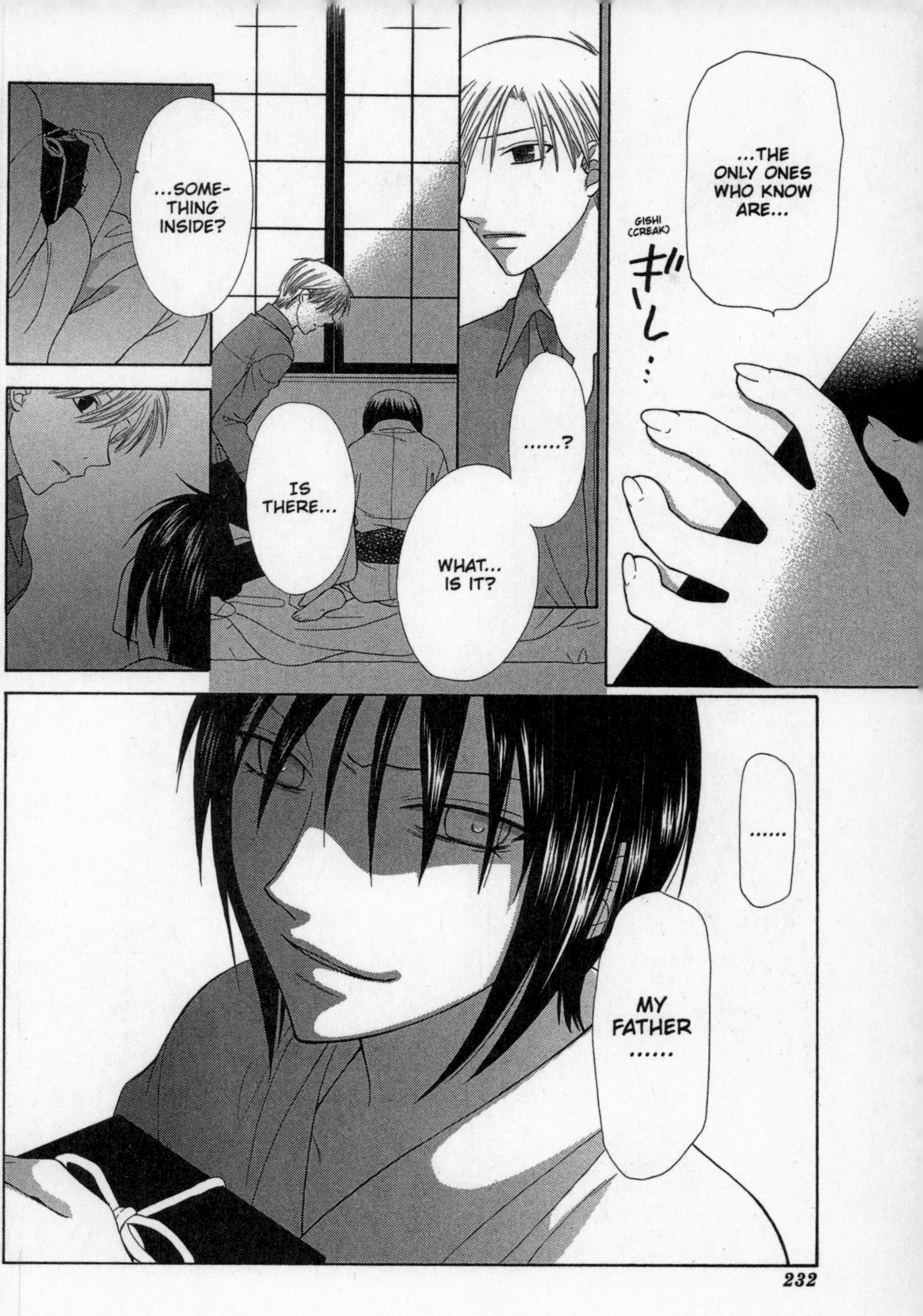
...THE ONLY ONES WHO KNOW ARE...
GISHI (CREAK)
......?
WHAT... IS IT?
IS THERE...
...SOME-THING INSIDE?
......
MY FATHER ......

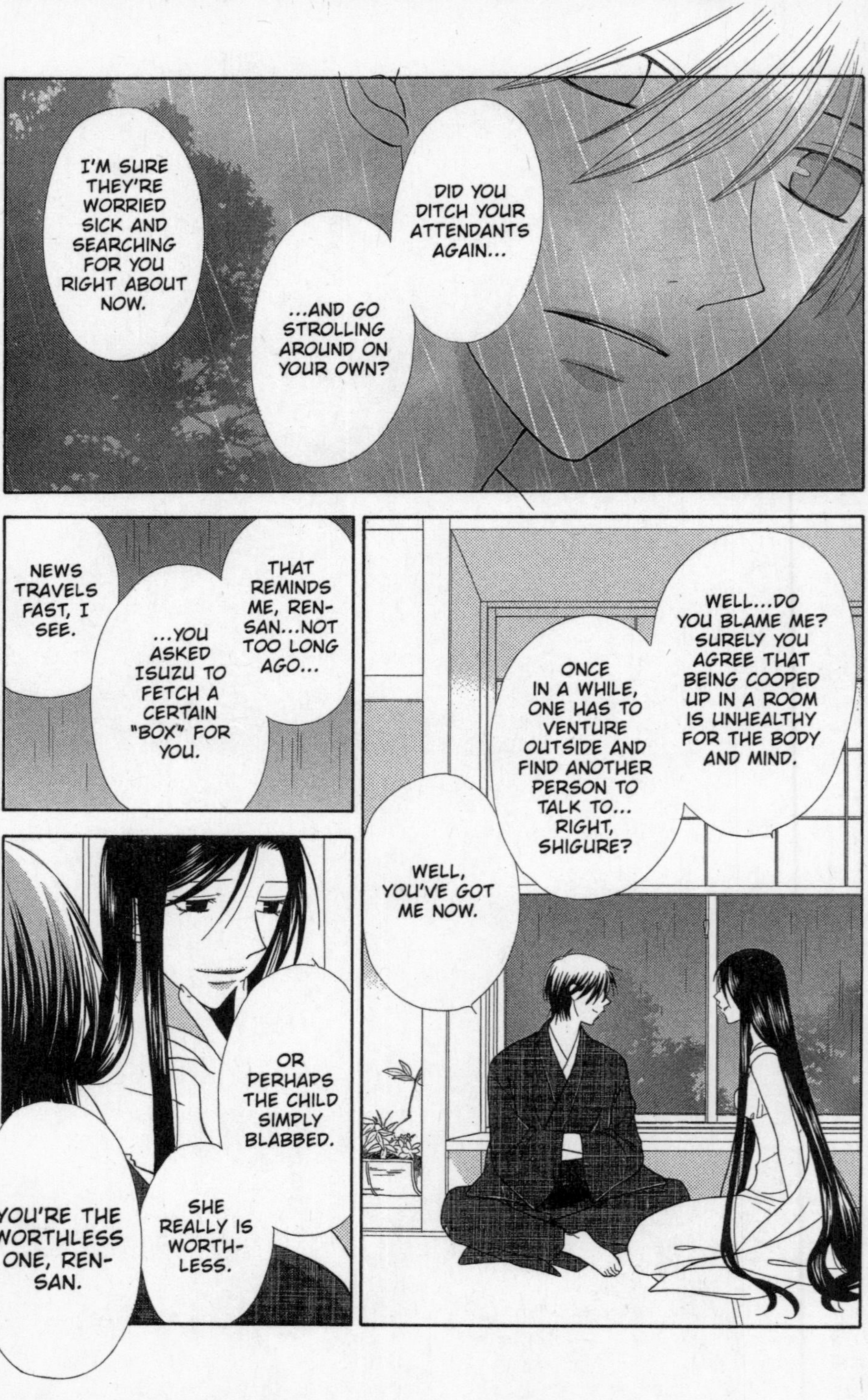
DID YOU DITCH YOUR ATTENDANTS AGAIN...
...AND GO STROLLING AROUND ON YOUR OWN?
I'M SURE THEY'RE WORRIED SICK AND SEARCHING FOR YOU RIGHT ABOUT NOW.
WELL...DO YOU BLAME ME? SURELY YOU AGREE THAT BEING COOPED UP IN A ROOM IS UNHEALTHY FOR THE BODY AND MIND.
ONCE IN A WHILE, ONE HAS TO VENTURE OUTSIDE AND FIND ANOTHER PERSON TO TALK TO... RIGHT, SHIGURE?
WELL, YOU'VE GOT ME NOW.
THAT REMINDS ME, REN-SAN...NOT TOO LONG AGO...
...YOU ASKED ISUZU TO FETCH A CERTAIN "BOX" FOR YOU.
NEWS TRAVELS FAST, I SEE.
OR PERHAPS THE CHILD SIMPLY BLABBED.
SHE REALLY IS WORTH-LESS.
YOU'RE THE WORTHLESS ONE, REN-SAN.

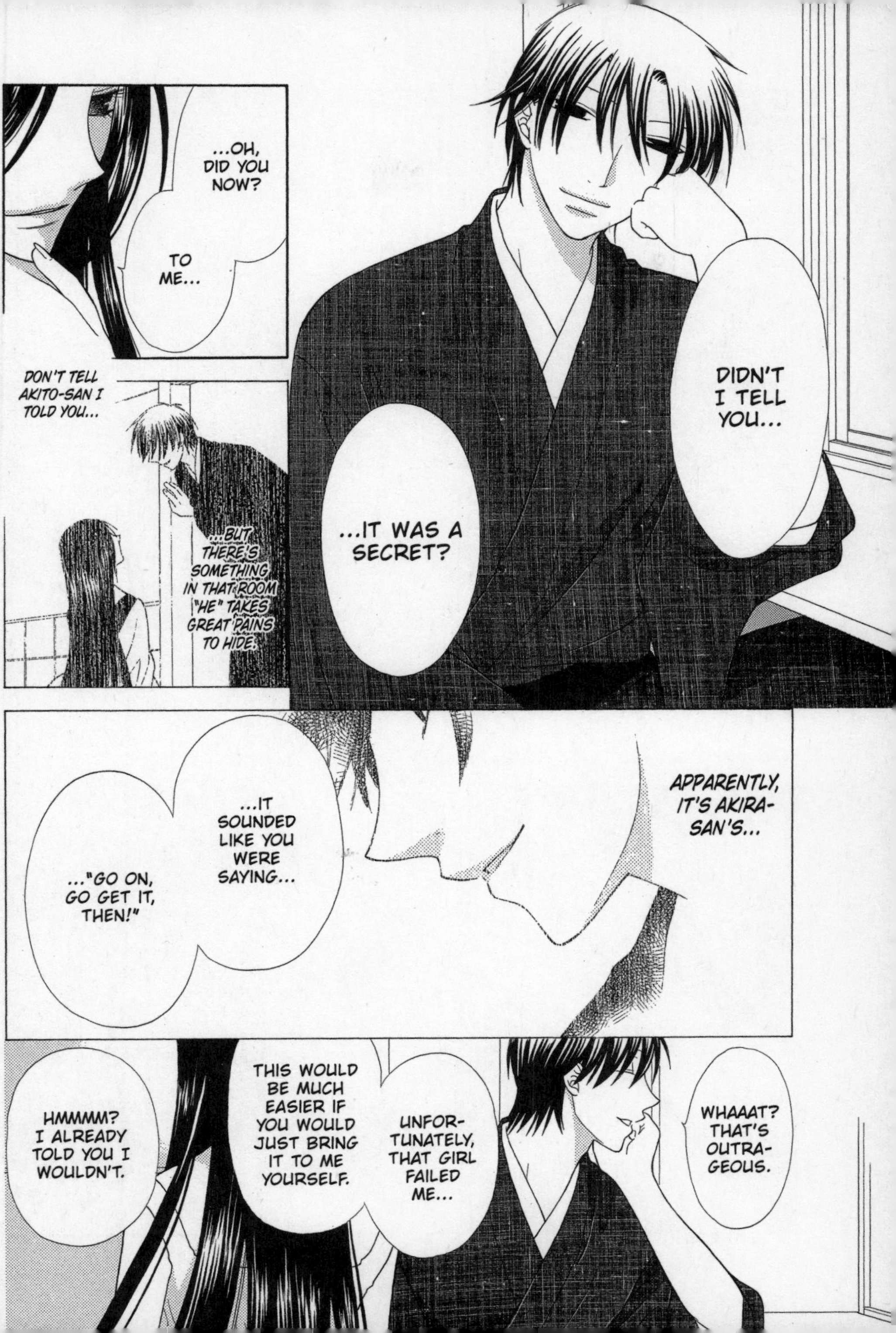
DIDN'T I TELL YOU...
...IT WAS A SECRET?
...OH, DID YOU NOW?
TO ME...
DON'T TELL AKITO-SAN I TOLD YOU...
...BUT THERE'S SOMETHING IN THAT ROOM "HE" TAKES GREAT PAINS TO HIDE.
APPARENTLY, IT'S AKIRA-SAN'S...
...IT SOUNDED LIKE YOU WERE SAYING...
..."GO ON, GO GET IT, THEN!"
WHAAAT? THAT'S OUTRA-GEOUS.
UNFOR-TUNATELY, THAT GIRL FAILED ME...
THIS WOULD BE MUCH EASIER IF YOU WOULD JUST BRING IT TO ME YOURSELF.
HMMMM? I ALREADY TOLD YOU I WOULDN'T.

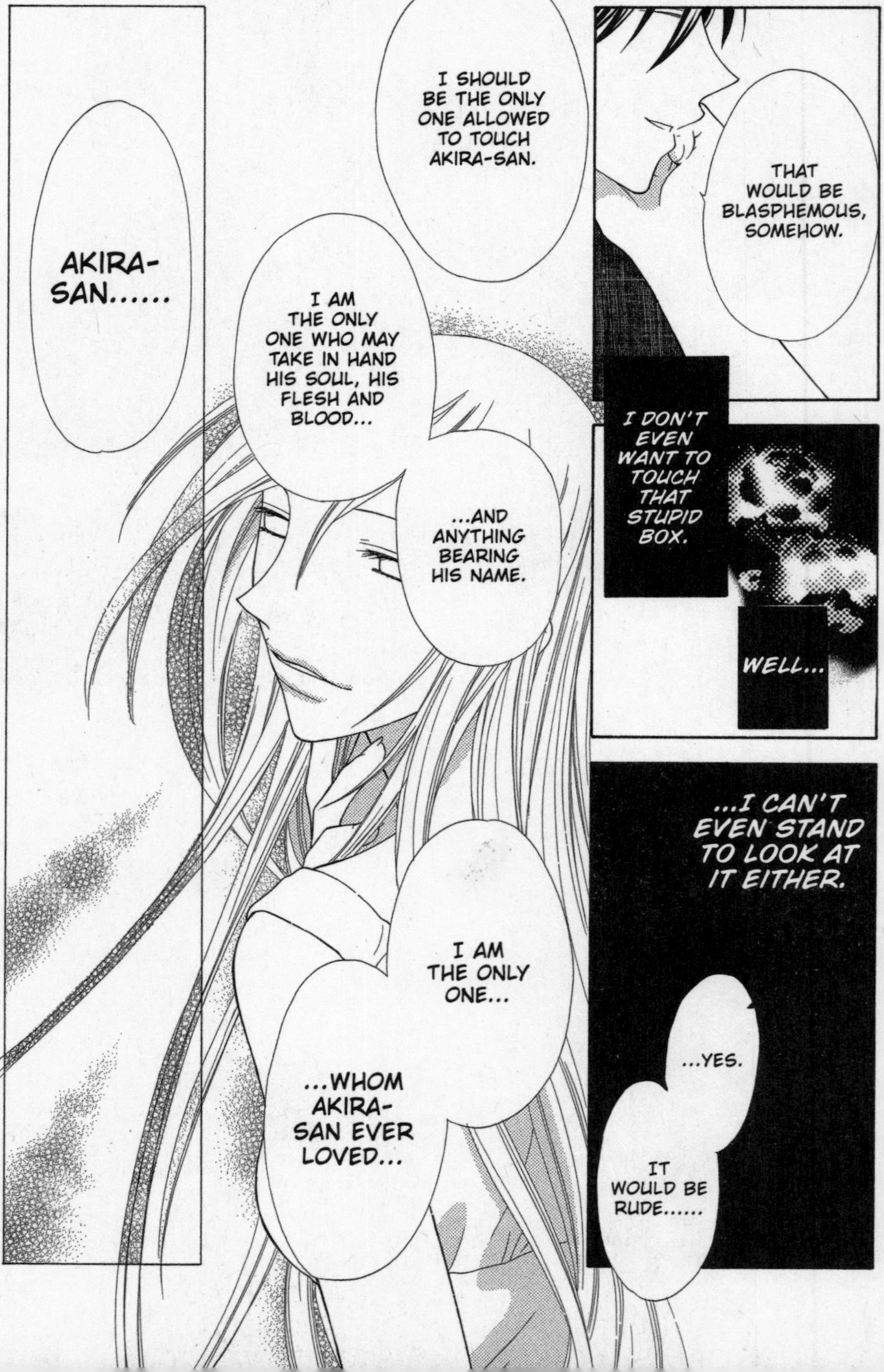
THAT WOULD BE BLASPHEMOUS, SOMEHOW.
I DON'T EVEN WANT TO TOUCH THAT STUPID BOX.
WELL...
...I CAN'T EVEN STAND TO LOOK AT IT EITHER.
...YES.
IT WOULD BE RUDE......
I SHOULD BE THE ONLY ONE ALLOWED TO TOUCH AKIRA-SAN.
I AM THE ONLY ONE WHO MAY TAKE IN HAND HIS SOUL, HIS FLESH AND BLOOD...
...AND ANYTHING BEARING HIS NAME.
I AM THE ONLY ONE...
...WHOM AKIRA-SAN EVER LOVED...
AKIRA-SAN......

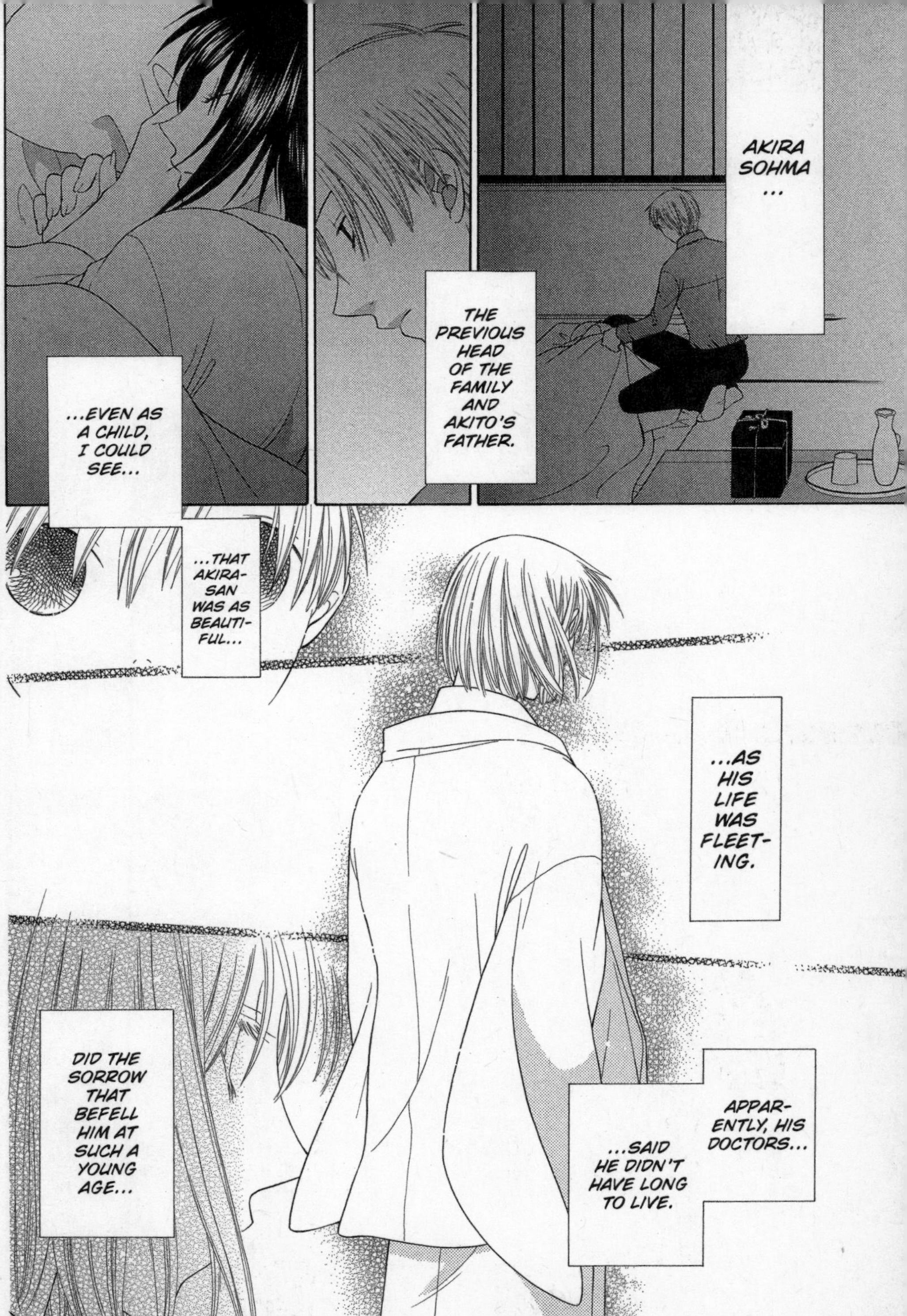
AKIRA SOHMA...
THE PREVIOUS HEAD OF THE FAMILY AND AKITO'S FATHER.
...EVEN AS A CHILD, I COULD SEE...
...THAT AKIRA-SAN WAS AS BEAUTIFUL...
...AS HIS LIFE WAS FLEETING.
APPARENTLY, HIS DOCTORS...
...SAID HE DIDN'T HAVE LONG TO LIVE.
DID THE SORROW THAT BEFELL HIM AT SUCH A YOUNG AGE...

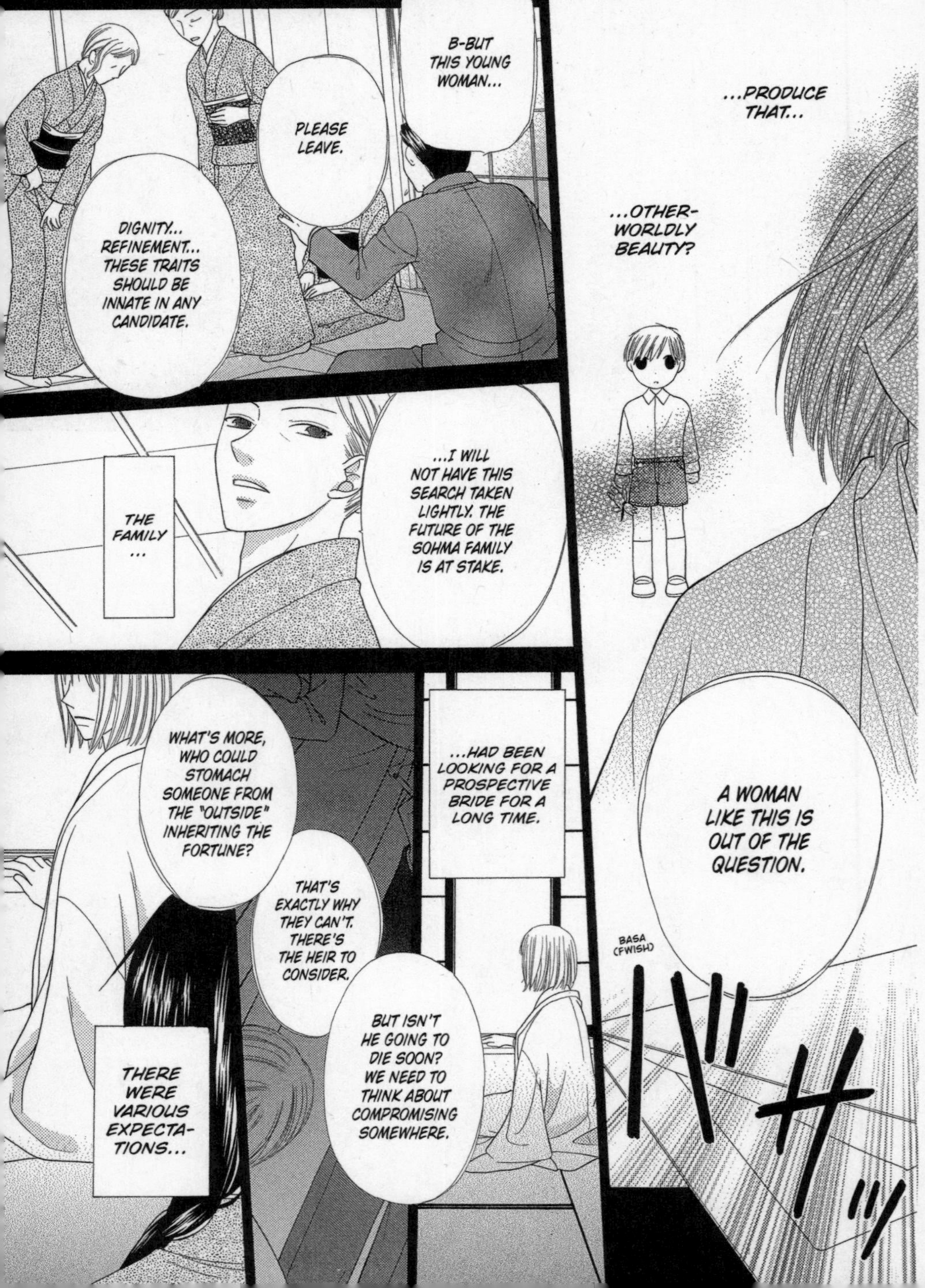
...PRODUCE THAT...
...OTHER-WORLDLY BEAUTY?
A WOMAN LIKE THIS IS OUT OF THE QUESTION.
BASA (FWISH)
B-BUT THIS YOUNG WOMAN...
PLEASE LEAVE.
DIGNITY... REFINEMENT... THESE TRAITS SHOULD BE INNATE IN ANY CANDIDATE.
...I WILL NOT HAVE THIS SEARCH TAKEN LIGHTLY. THE FUTURE OF THE SOHMA FAMILY IS AT STAKE.
THE FAMILY...
...HAD BEEN LOOKING FOR A PROSPECTIVE BRIDE FOR A LONG TIME.
WHAT'S MORE, WHO COULD STOMACH SOMEONE FROM THE "OUTSIDE" INHERITING THE FORTUNE?
THAT'S EXACTLY WHY THEY CAN'T. THERE'S THE HEIR TO CONSIDER.
BUT ISN'T HE GOING TO DIE SOON? WE NEED TO THINK ABOUT COMPROMISING SOMEWHERE.
THERE WERE VARIOUS EXPECTA-TIONS...

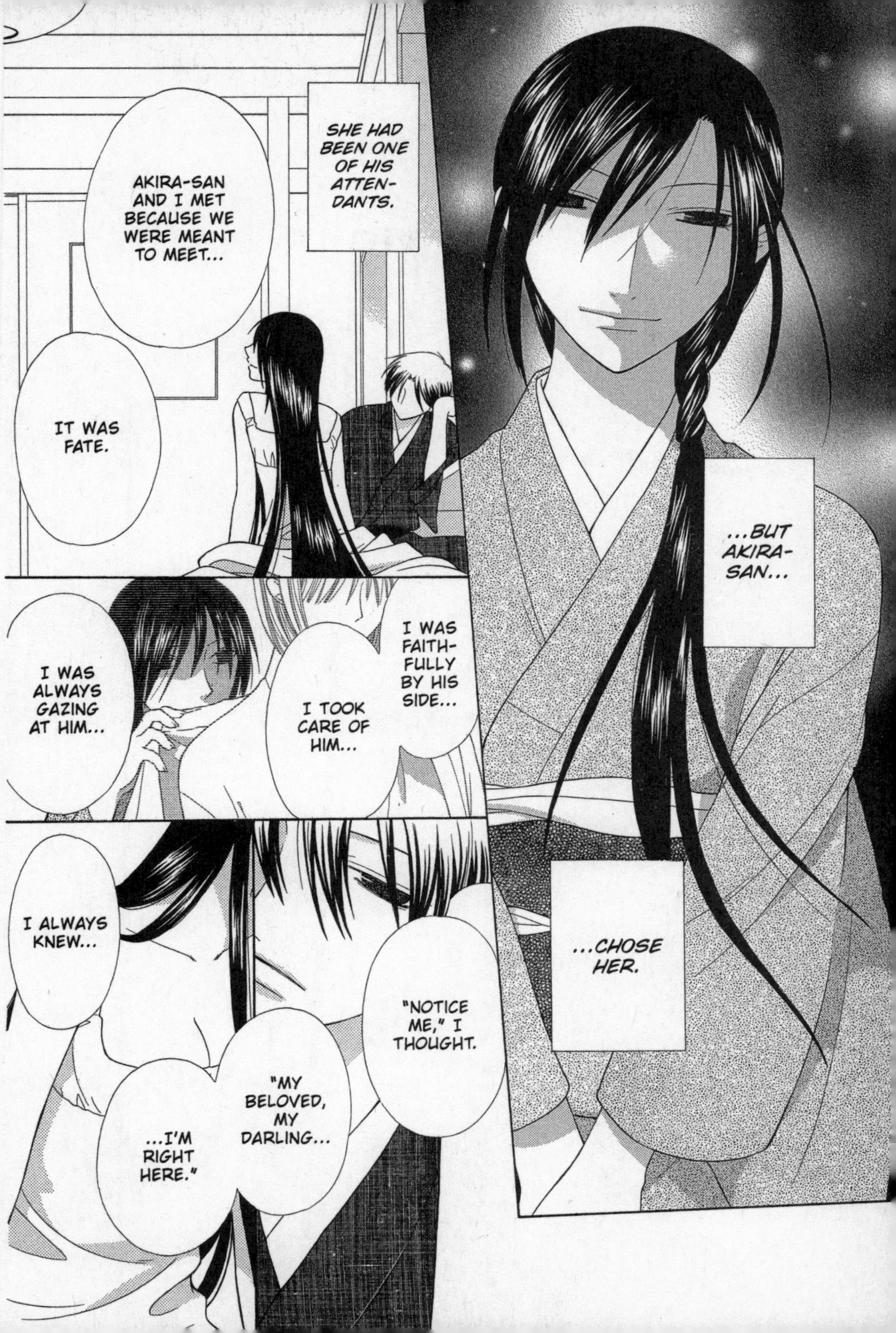
...BUT AKIRA-SAN...
...CHOSE HER.
SHE HAD BEEN ONE OF HIS ATTENDANTS.
AKIRA-SAN AND I MET BECAUSE WE WERE MEANT TO MEET...
IT WAS FATE.
I WAS FAITHFULLY BY HIS SIDE...
I TOOK CARE OF HIM...
I WAS ALWAYS GAZING AT HIM...
"NOTICE ME," I THOUGHT.
I ALWAYS KNEW...
"MY BELOVED, MY DARLING...
...I'M RIGHT HERE."

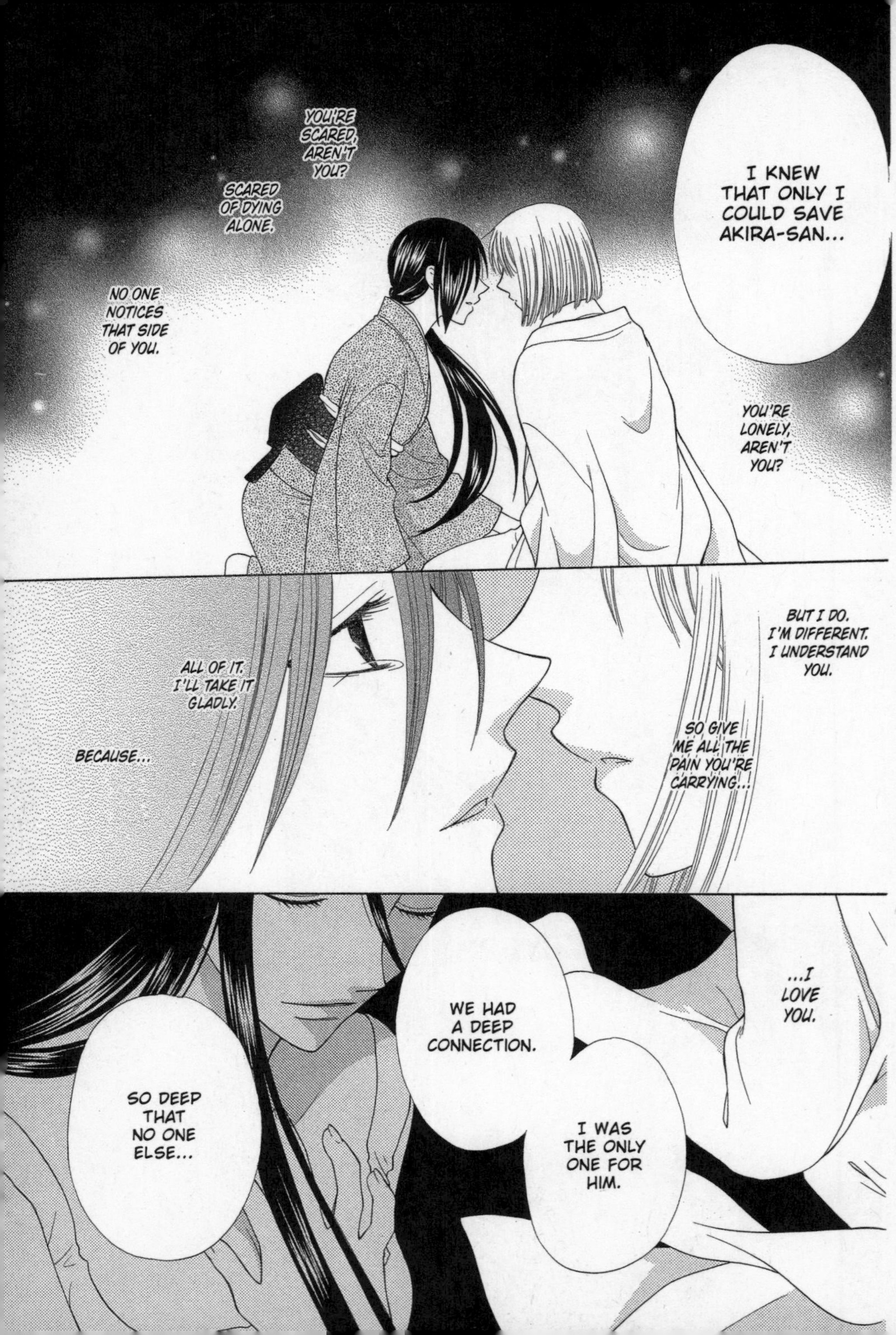
I KNEW THAT ONLY I COULD SAVE AKIRA-SAN...
YOU'RE LONELY, AREN'T YOU?
YOU'RE SCARED, AREN'T YOU?
SCARED OF DYING ALONE.
NO ONE NOTICES THAT SIDE OF YOU.
BUT I DO. I'M DIFFERENT. I UNDERSTAND YOU.
SO GIVE ME ALL THE PAIN YOU'RE CARRYING...
ALL OF IT. I'LL TAKE IT GLADLY.
BECAUSE...
...I LOVE YOU.
WE HAD A DEEP CONNECTION.
I WAS THE ONLY ONE FOR HIM.
SO DEEP THAT NO ONE ELSE...

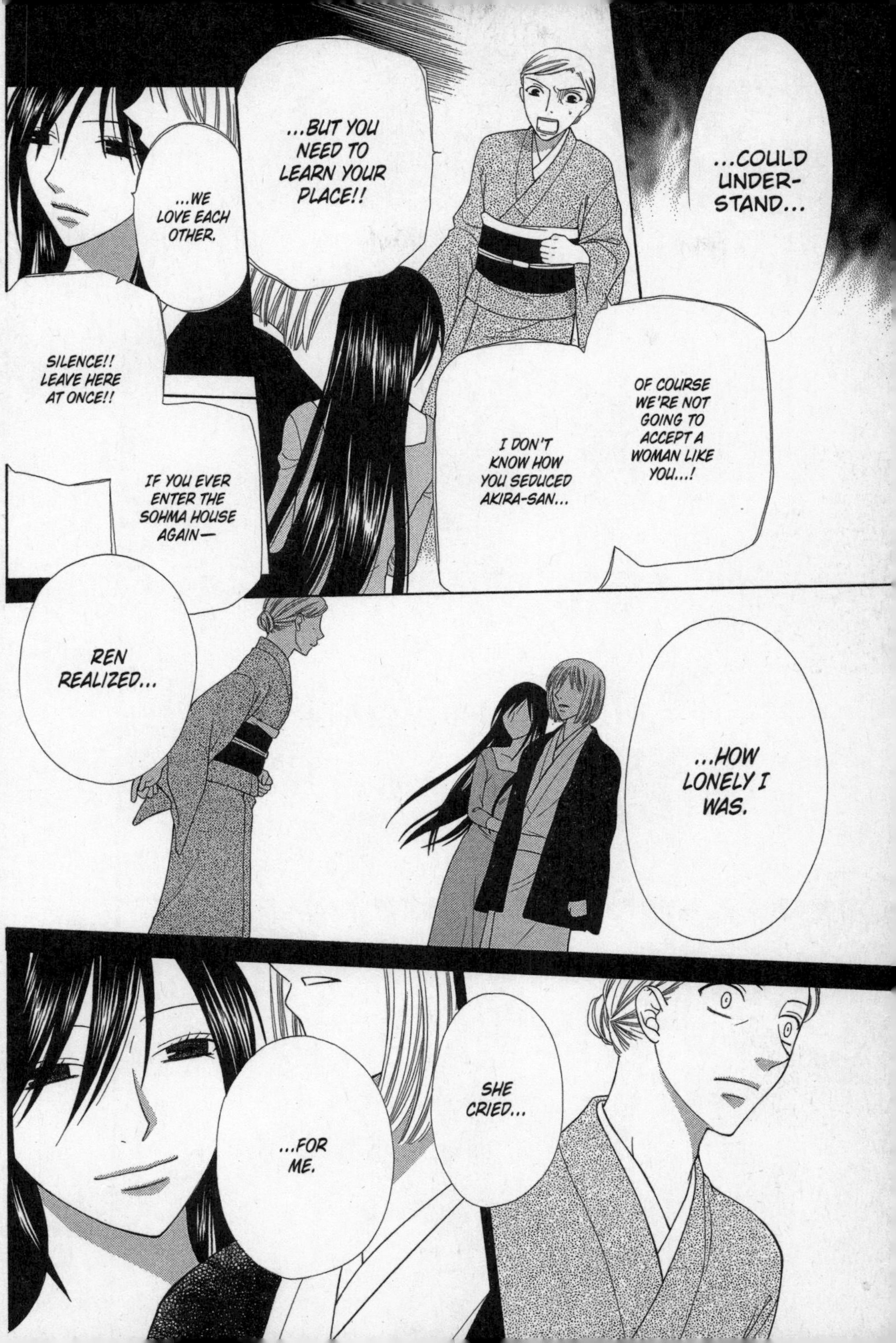
...COULD UNDER-STAND...
OF COURSE WE'RE NOT GOING TO ACCEPT A WOMAN LIKE YOU...!
I DON'T KNOW HOW YOU SEDUCED AKIRA-SAN...
...BUT YOU NEED TO LEARN YOUR PLACE!!
...WE LOVE EACH OTHER.
SILENCE!! LEAVE HERE AT ONCE!!
IF YOU EVER ENTER THE SOHMA HOUSE AGAIN—
...HOW LONELY I WAS.
REN REALIZED...
SHE CRIED...
...FOR ME.

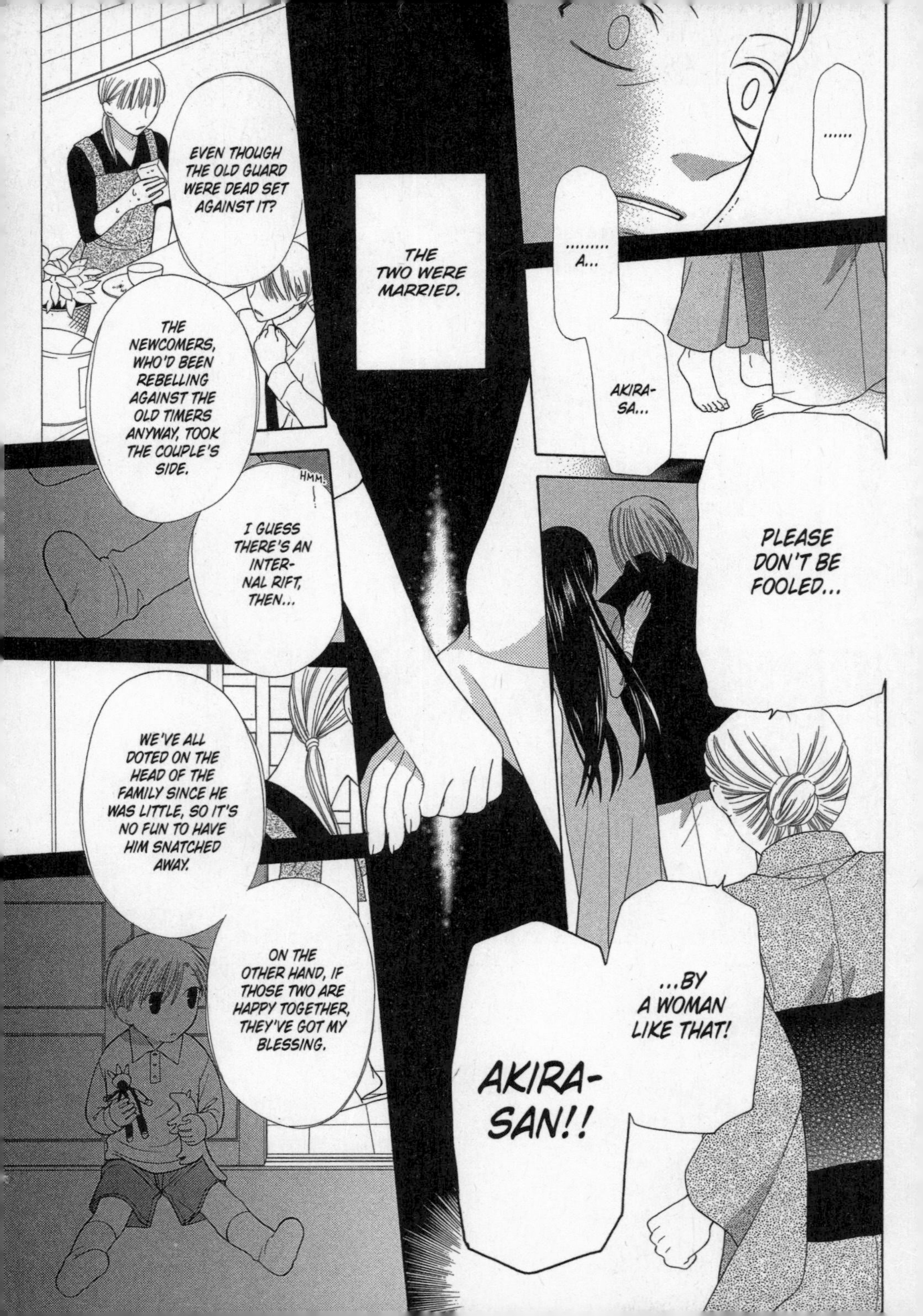
......
....
A...
AKIRA-SA...
PLEASE DON'T BE FOOLED...
...BY A WOMAN LIKE THAT!
AKIRA-SAN!!
THE TWO WERE MARRIED.
EVEN THOUGH THE OLD GUARD WERE DEAD SET AGAINST IT?
THE NEWCOMERS, WHO'D BEEN REBELLING AGAINST THE OLD TIMERS ANYWAY, TOOK THE COUPLE'S SIDE.
HMM.
I GUESS THERE'S AN INTER-NAL RIFT, THEN...
WE'VE ALL DOTED ON THE HEAD OF THE FAMILY SINCE HE WAS LITTLE, SO IT'S NO FUN TO HAVE HIM SNATCHED AWAY.
ON THE OTHER HAND, IF THOSE TWO ARE HAPPY TOGETHER, THEY'VE GOT MY BLESSING.

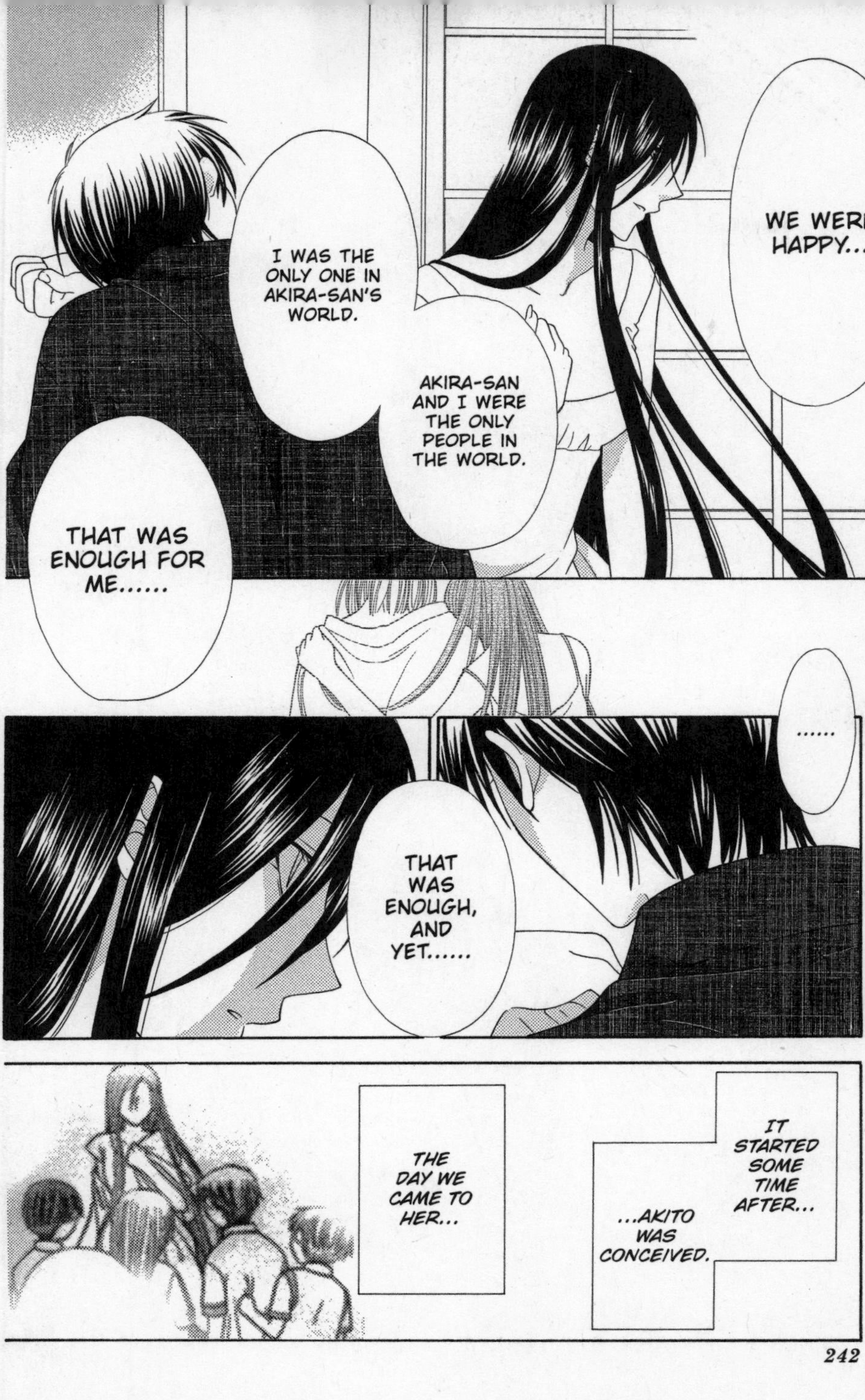
WE WERE HAPPY...
I WAS THE ONLY ONE IN AKIRA-SAN'S WORLD.
AKIRA-SAN AND I WERE THE ONLY PEOPLE IN THE WORLD.
THAT WAS ENOUGH FOR ME......
......
THAT WAS ENOUGH, AND YET......
IT STARTED SOME TIME AFTER...
...AKITO WAS CONCEIVED.
THE DAY WE CAME TO HER...

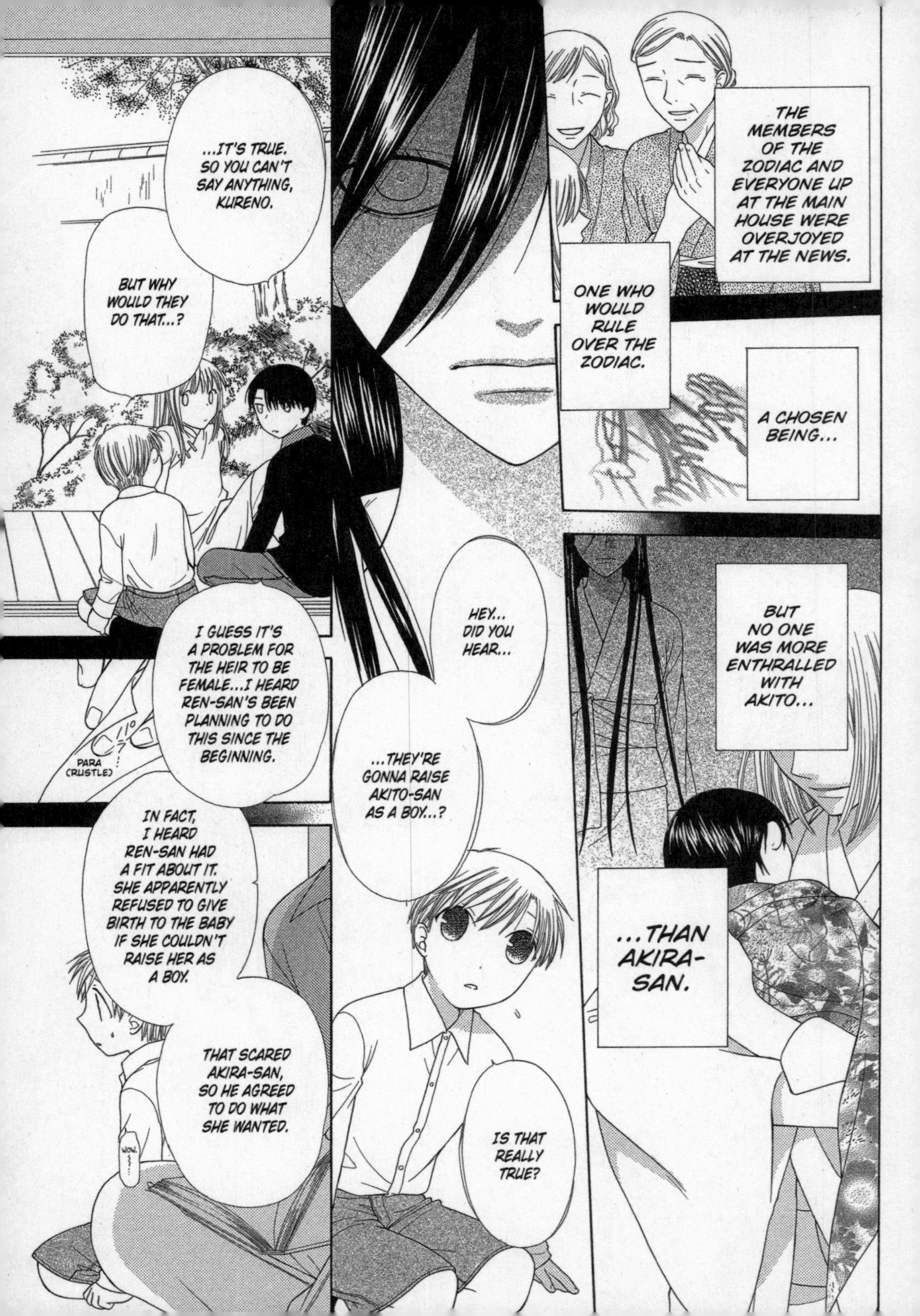
THE MEMBERS OF THE ZODIAC AND EVERYONE UP AT THE MAIN HOUSE WERE OVERJOYED AT THE NEWS.
ONE WHO WOULD RULE OVER THE ZODIAC.
A CHOSEN BEING...
...IT'S TRUE. SO YOU CAN'T SAY ANYTHING, KURENO.
BUT WHY WOULD THEY DO THAT...?
BUT NO ONE WAS MORE ENTHRALLED WITH AKITO...
...THAN AKIRA-SAN.
HEY... DID YOU HEAR...
...THEY'RE GONNA RAISE AKITO-SAN AS A BOY...?
I GUESS IT'S A PROBLEM FOR THE HEIR TO BE FEMALE...I HEARD REN-SAN'S BEEN PLANNING TO DO THIS SINCE THE BEGINNING.
PARA (RUSTLE)
IN FACT, I HEARD REN-SAN HAD A FIT ABOUT IT. SHE APPARENTLY REFUSED TO GIVE BIRTH TO THE BABY IF SHE COULDN'T RAISE HER AS A BOY.
THAT SCARED AKIRA-SAN, SO HE AGREED TO DO WHAT SHE WANTED.
IS THAT REALLY TRUE?
WOW...

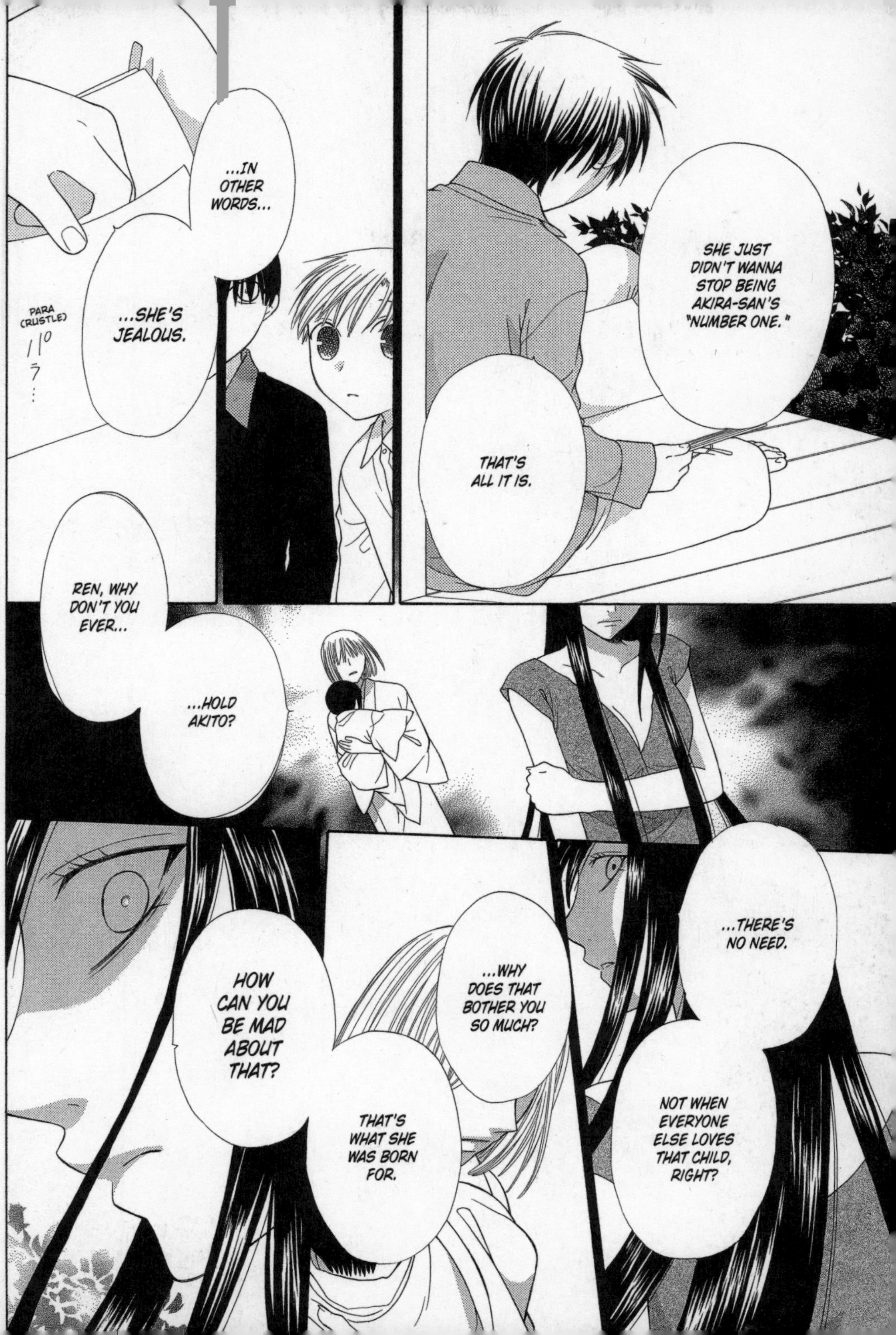
SHE JUST DIDN'T WANNA STOP BEING AKIRA-SAN'S "NUMBER ONE."
THAT'S ALL IT IS.
...IN OTHER WORDS...
...SHE'S JEALOUS.
PARA (RUSTLE)
REN, WHY DON'T YOU EVER...
...HOLD AKITO?
...THERE'S NO NEED.
NOT WHEN EVERYONE ELSE LOVES THAT CHILD, RIGHT?
...WHY DOES THAT BOTHER YOU SO MUCH?
HOW CAN YOU BE MAD ABOUT THAT?
THAT'S WHAT SHE WAS BORN FOR.

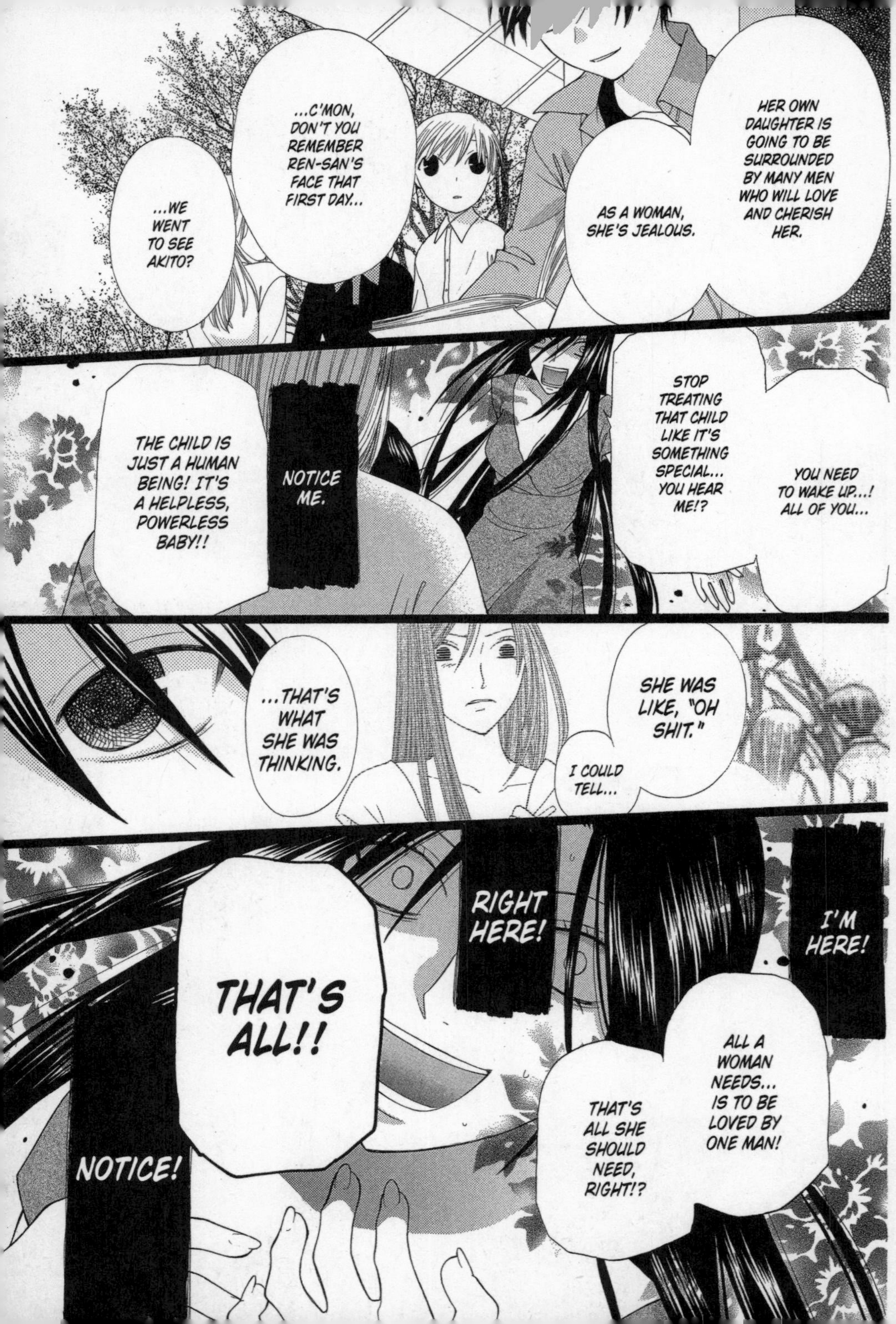
HER OWN DAUGHTER IS GOING TO BE SURROUNDED BY MANY MEN WHO WILL LOVE AND CHERISH HER.
AS A WOMAN, SHE'S JEALOUS.
...C'MON, DON'T YOU REMEMBER REN-SAN'S FACE THAT FIRST DAY...
...WE WENT TO SEE AKITO?
YOU NEED TO WAKE UP...! ALL OF YOU...
STOP TREATING THAT CHILD LIKE IT'S SOMETHING SPECIAL... YOU HEAR ME!?
NOTICE ME.
THE CHILD IS JUST A HUMAN BEING! IT'S A HELPLESS, POWERLESS BABY!!
SHE WAS LIKE, "OH SHIT."
I COULD TELL...
...THAT'S WHAT SHE WAS THINKING.
I'M HERE!
RIGHT HERE!
ALL A WOMAN NEEDS... IS TO BE LOVED BY ONE MAN!
THAT'S ALL SHE SHOULD NEED, RIGHT!?
THAT'S ALL!!
NOTICE!

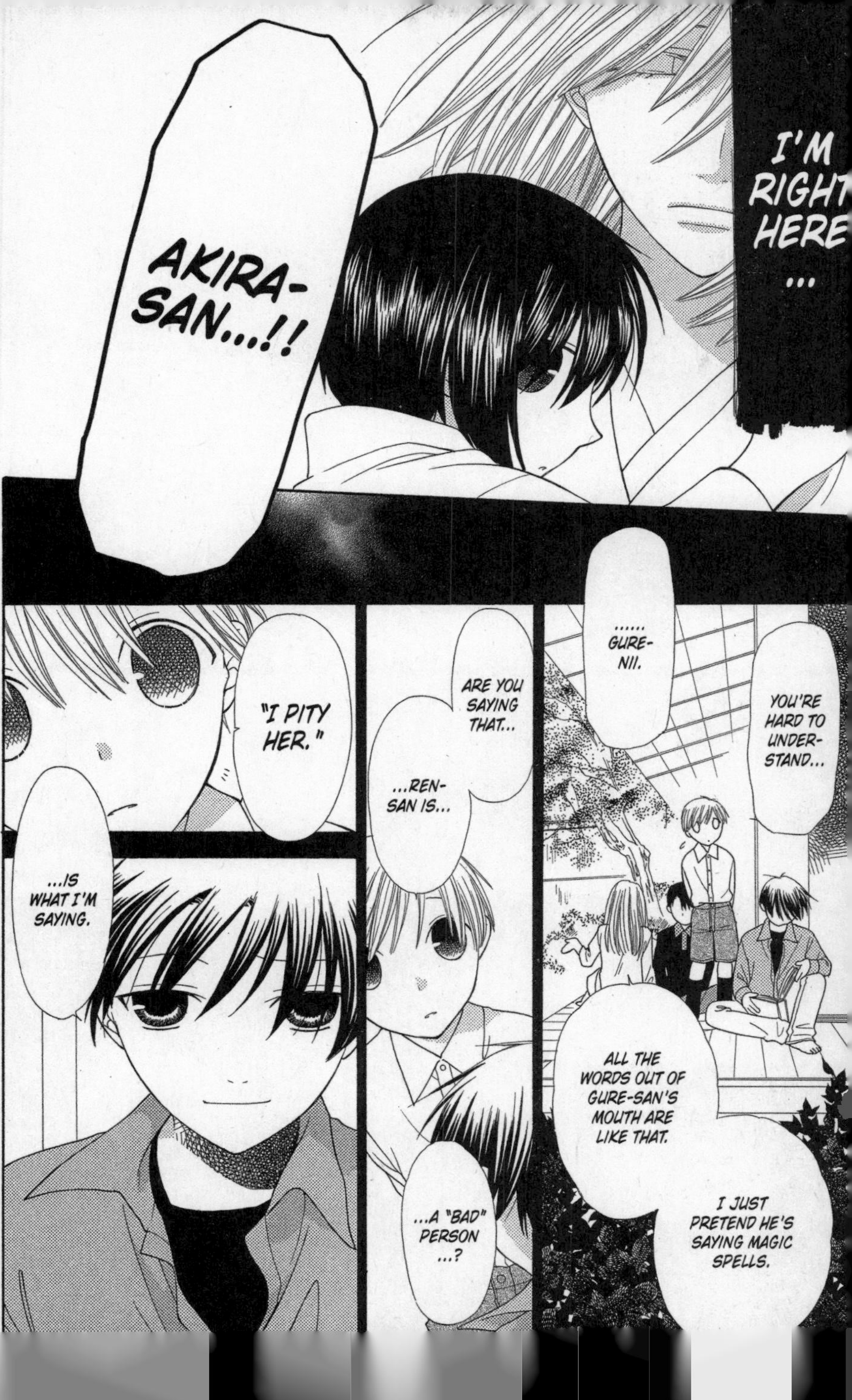
I'M RIGHT HERE...
AKIRA-SAN...!!
......GURE-NII.
YOU'RE HARD TO UNDERSTAND...
ALL THE WORDS OUT OF GURE-SAN'S MOUTH ARE LIKE THAT.
I JUST PRETEND HE'S SAYING MAGIC SPELLS.
ARE YOU SAYING THAT...
...REN-SAN IS...
...A "BAD" PERSON...?
"I PITY HER."
...IS WHAT I'M SAYING.

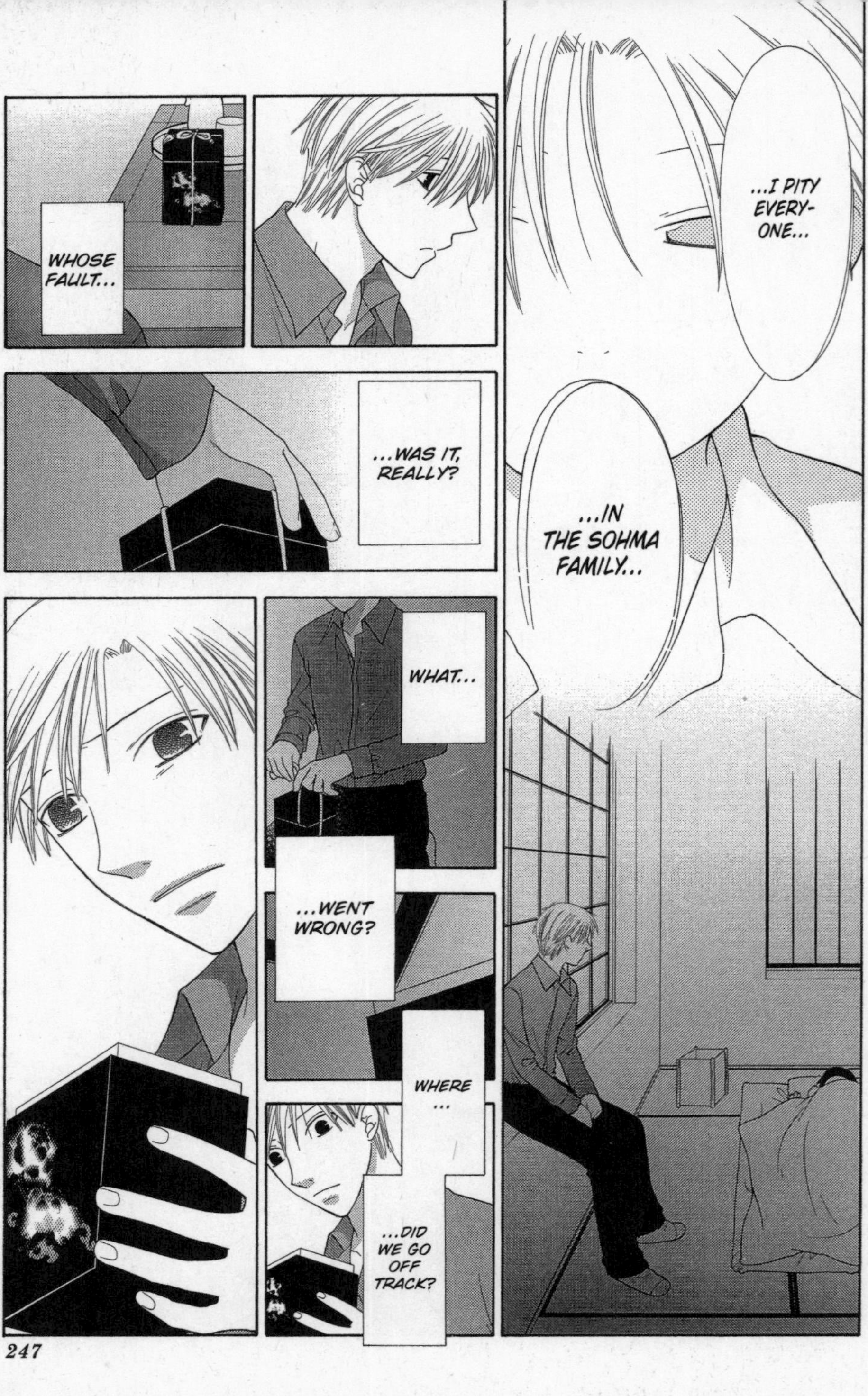
...I PITY EVERY-ONE...
...IN THE SOHMA FAMILY...
WHOSE FAULT...
...WAS IT, REALLY?
WHAT...
...WENT WRONG?
WHERE ...
...DID WE GO OFF TRACK?

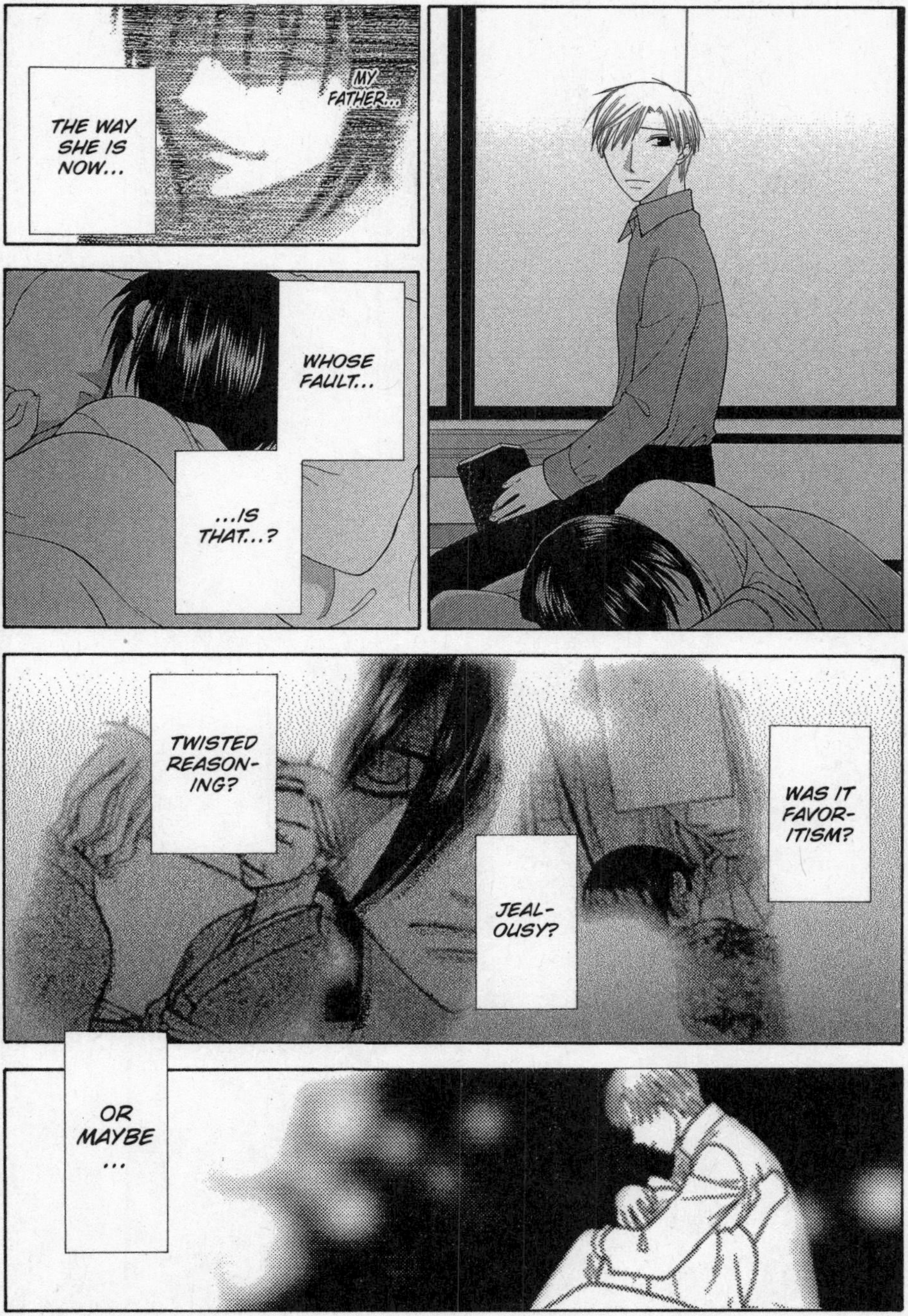
MY FATHER...
THE WAY SHE IS NOW...
WHOSE FAULT...
...IS THAT...?
WAS IT FAVOR-ITISM?
JEAL-OUSY?
TWISTED REASON-ING?
OR MAYBE ...

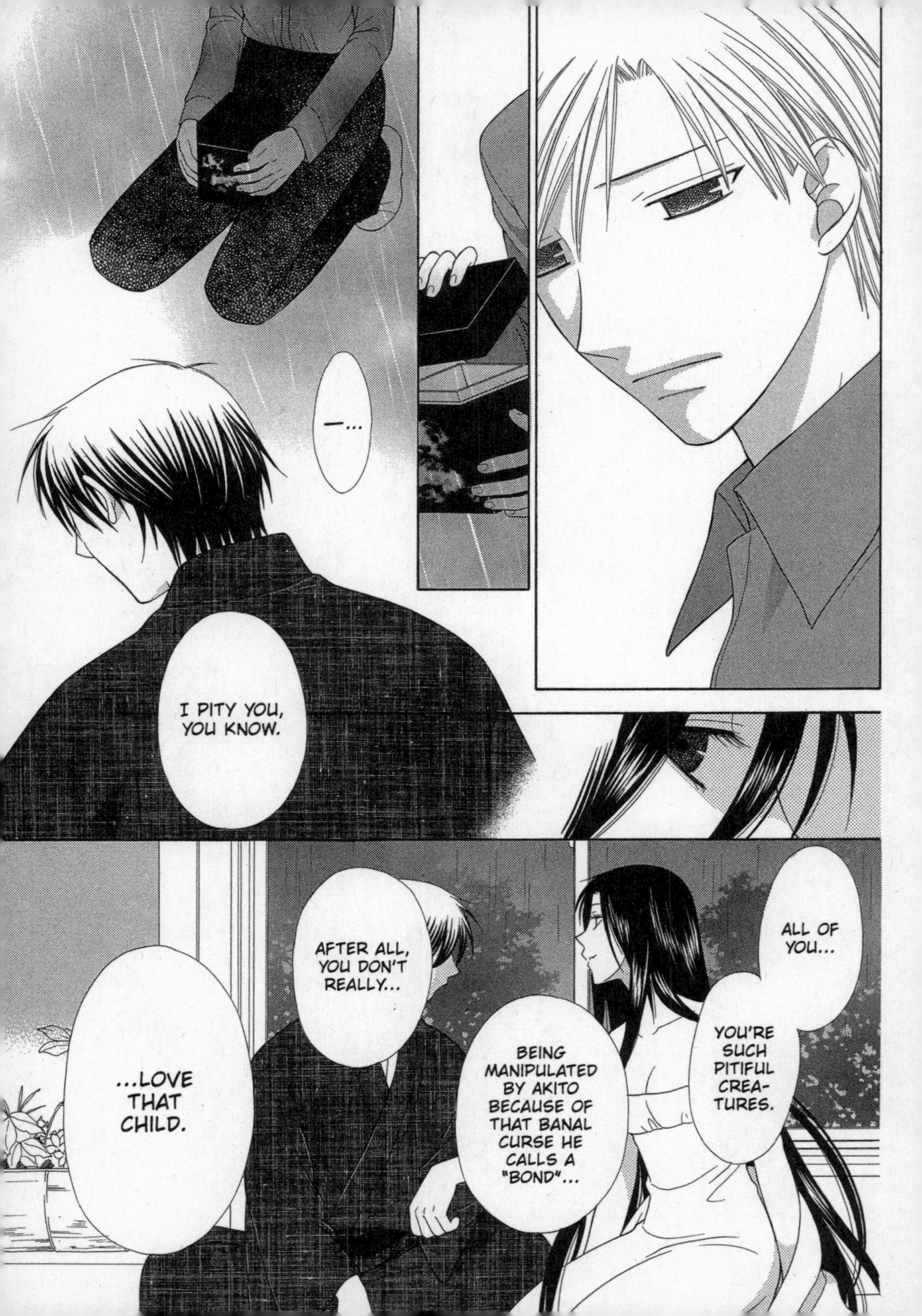
—...
I PITY YOU, YOU KNOW.
ALL OF YOU...
YOU'RE SUCH PITIFUL CREA-TURES.
BEING MANIPULATED BY AKITO BECAUSE OF THAT BANAL CURSE HE CALLS A "BOND"...
AFTER ALL, YOU DON'T REALLY...
...LOVE THAT CHILD.

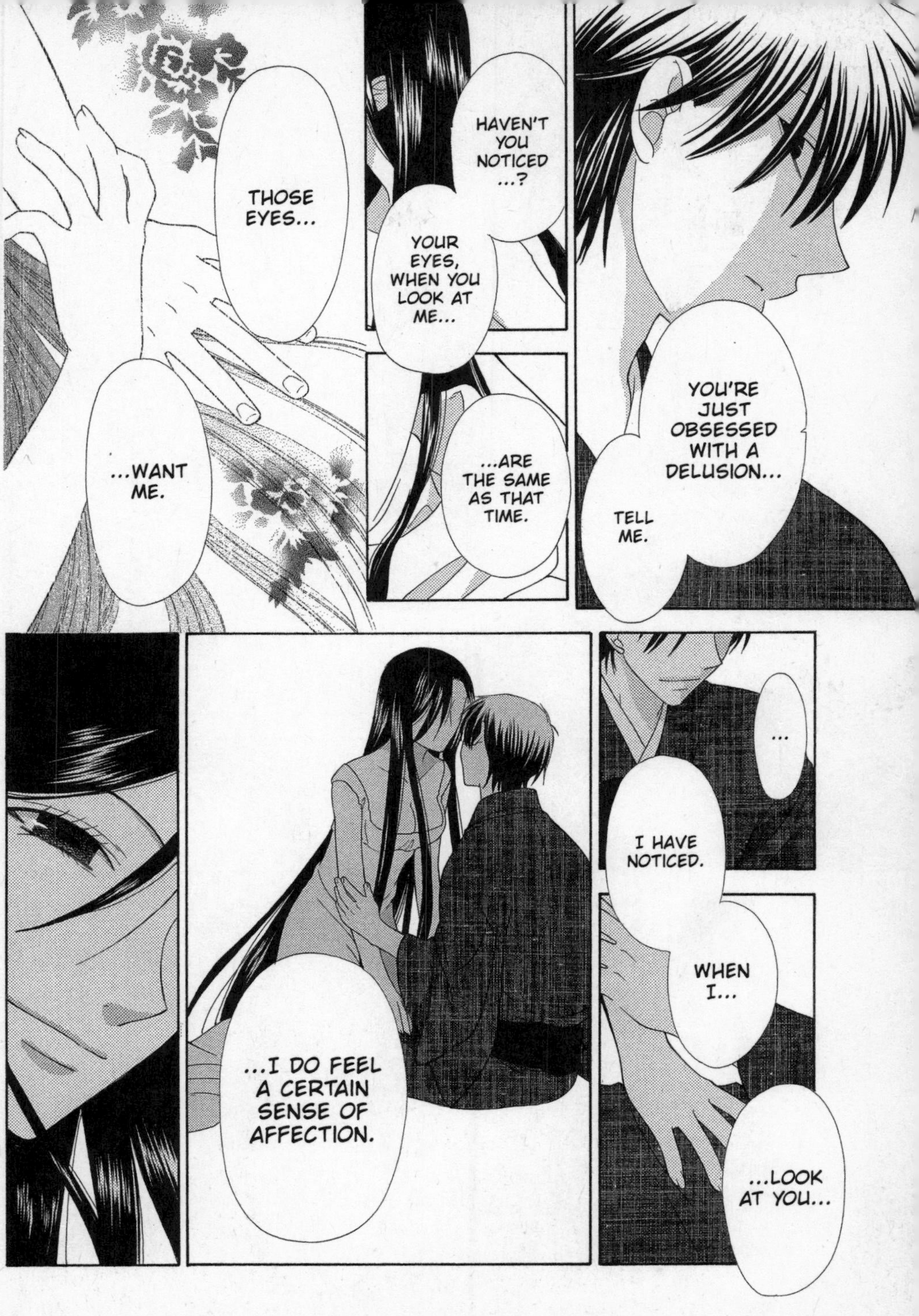
YOU'RE JUST OBSESSED WITH A DELUSION...
TELL ME.
HAVEN'T YOU NOTICED ...?
YOUR EYES, WHEN YOU LOOK AT ME...
...ARE THE SAME AS THAT TIME.
THOSE EYES...
...WANT ME.
...
I HAVE NOTICED.
WHEN I...
...LOOK AT YOU...
...I DO FEEL A CERTAIN SENSE OF AFFECTION.

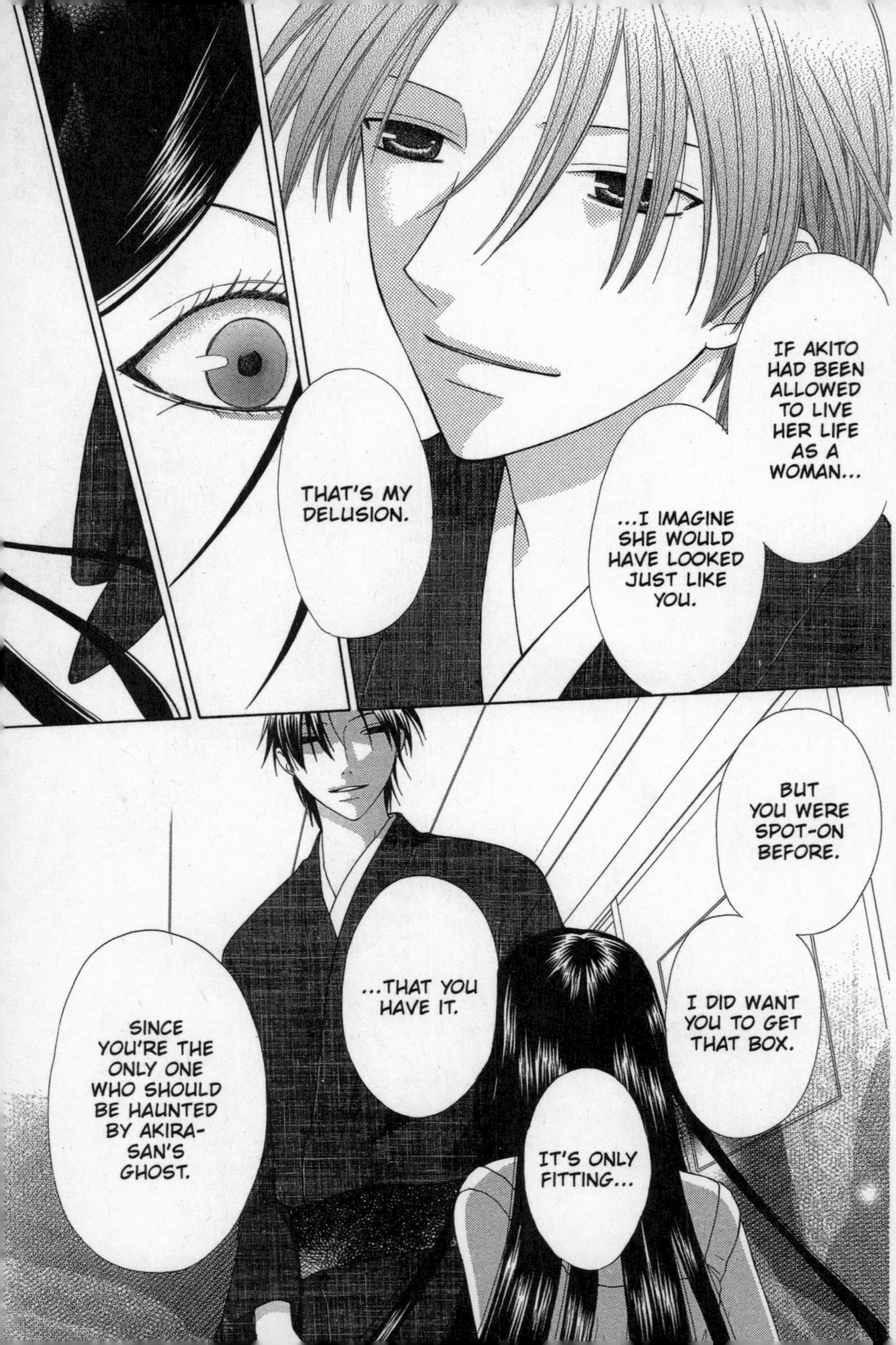
IF AKITO HAD BEEN ALLOWED TO LIVE HER LIFE AS A WOMAN...
...I IMAGINE SHE WOULD HAVE LOOKED JUST LIKE YOU.
THAT'S MY DELUSION.
BUT YOU WERE SPOT-ON BEFORE.
I DID WANT YOU TO GET THAT BOX.
IT'S ONLY FITTING...
...THAT YOU HAVE IT.
SINCE YOU'RE THE ONLY ONE WHO SHOULD BE HAUNTED BY AKIRA-SAN'S GHOST.

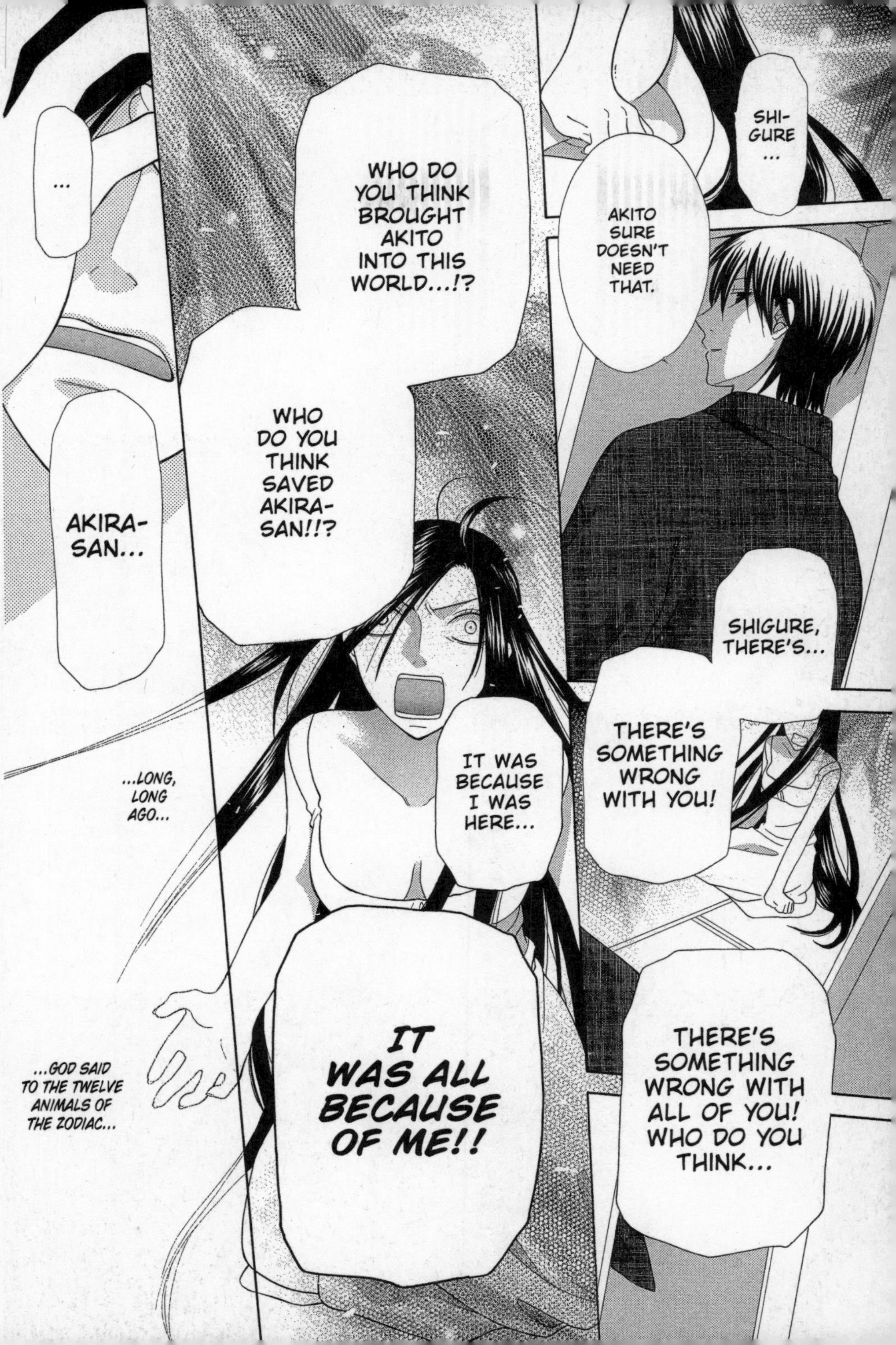
SHIGURE ...
AKITO SURE DOESN'T NEED THAT.
SHIGURE, THERE'S...
THERE'S SOMETHING WRONG WITH YOU!
THERE'S SOMETHING WRONG WITH ALL OF YOU! WHO DO YOU THINK...
WHO DO YOU THINK BROUGHT AKITO INTO THIS WORLD...!?
WHO DO YOU THINK SAVED AKIRA-SAN!!?
IT WAS BECAUSE I WAS HERE...
IT WAS ALL BECAUSE OF ME!!
...
AKIRA-SAN...
...LONG, LONG AGO...
...GOD SAID TO THE TWELVE ANIMALS OF THE ZODIAC...

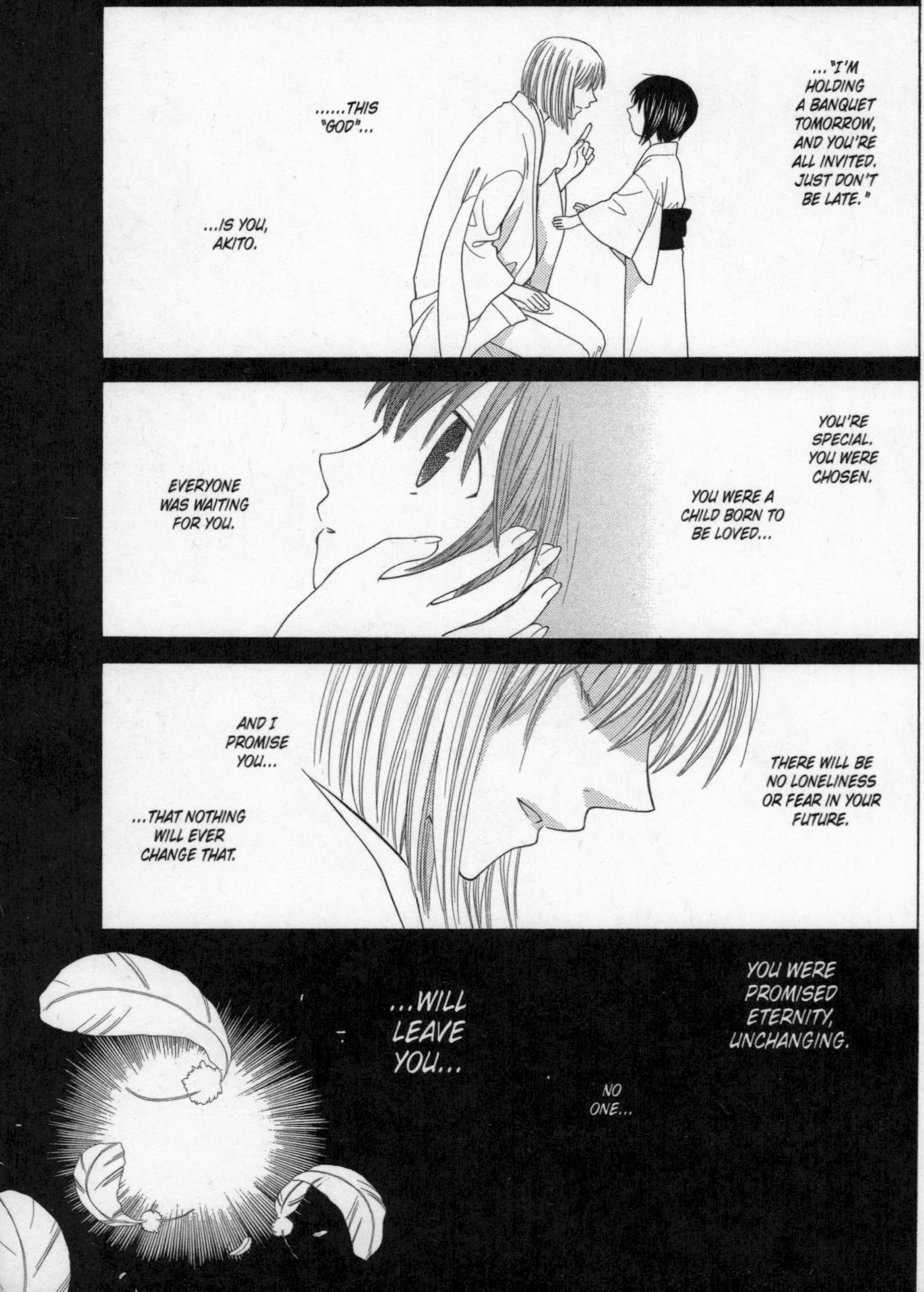
..."I'M HOLDING A BANQUET TOMORROW, AND YOU'RE ALL INVITED. JUST DON'T BE LATE."
......THIS "GOD"...
...IS YOU, AKITO.
YOU'RE SPECIAL. YOU WERE CHOSEN.
YOU WERE A CHILD BORN TO BE LOVED...
EVERYONE WAS WAITING FOR YOU.
THERE WILL BE NO LONELINESS OR FEAR IN YOUR FUTURE.
AND I PROMISE YOU...
...THAT NOTHING WILL EVER CHANGE THAT.
YOU WERE PROMISED ETERNITY, UNCHANGING.
NO ONE...
...WILL LEAVE YOU...

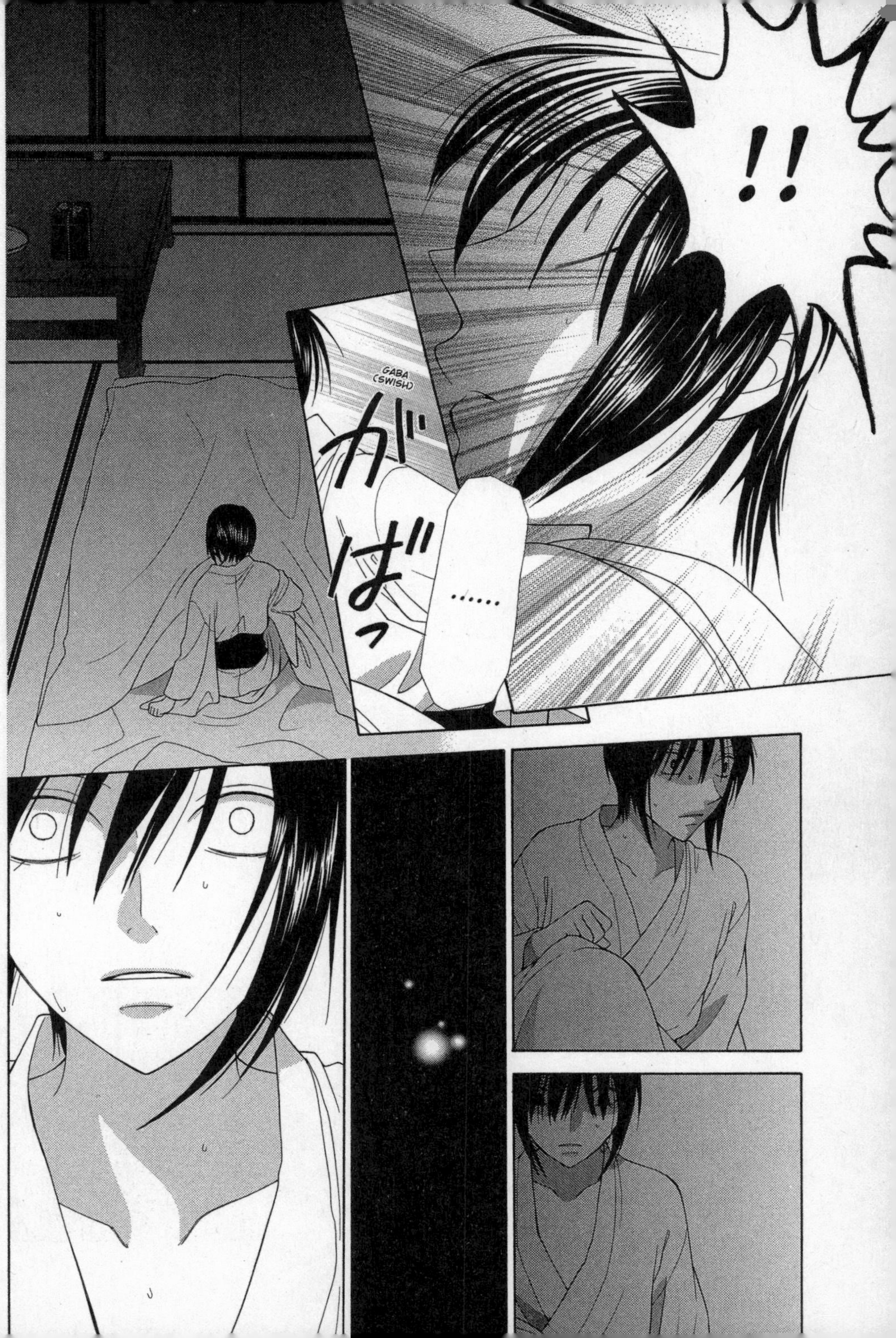
!!
GABA (SWISH)
がばっ
......

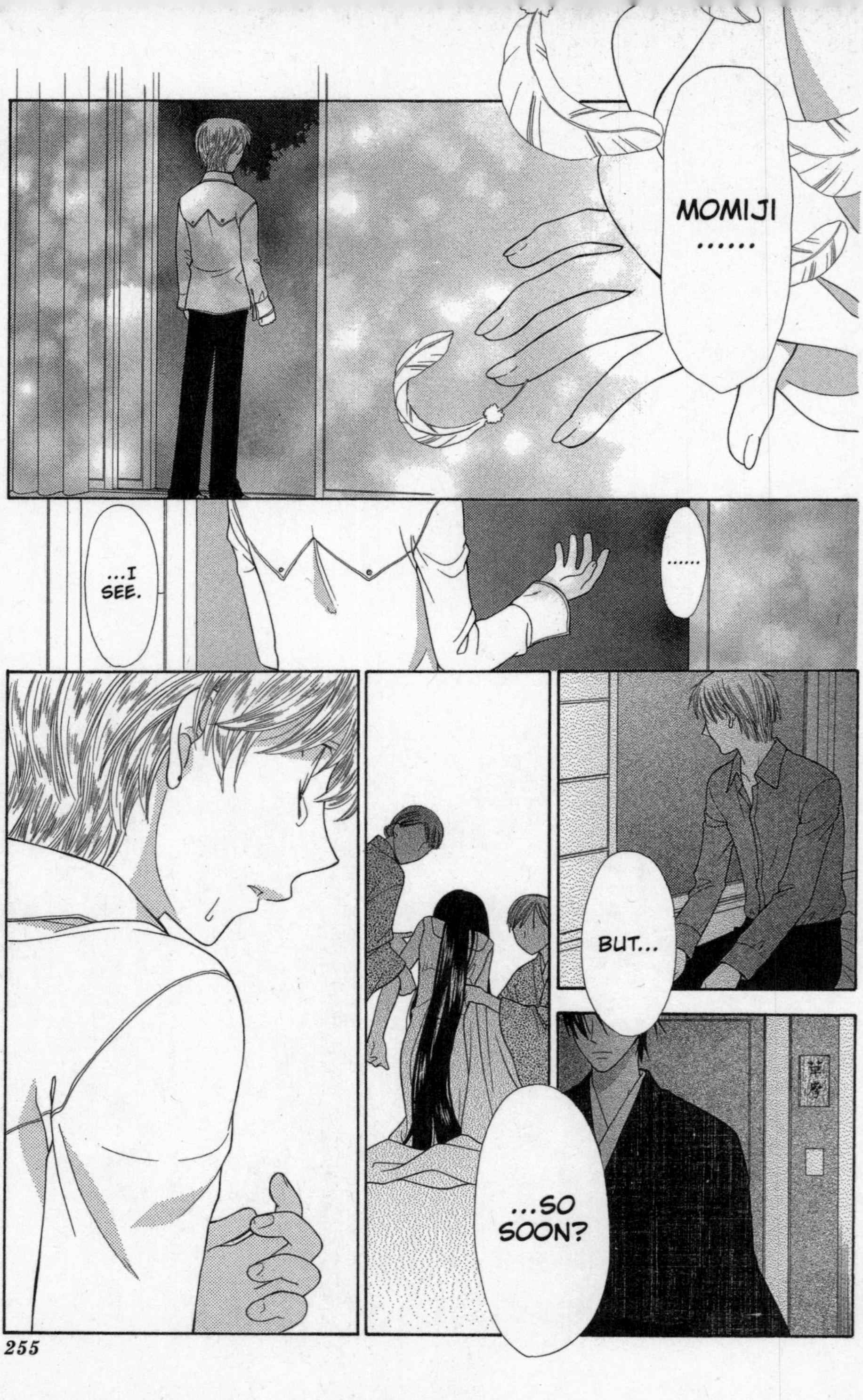
MOMIJI ......
......
...I SEE.
BUT...
...SO SOON?

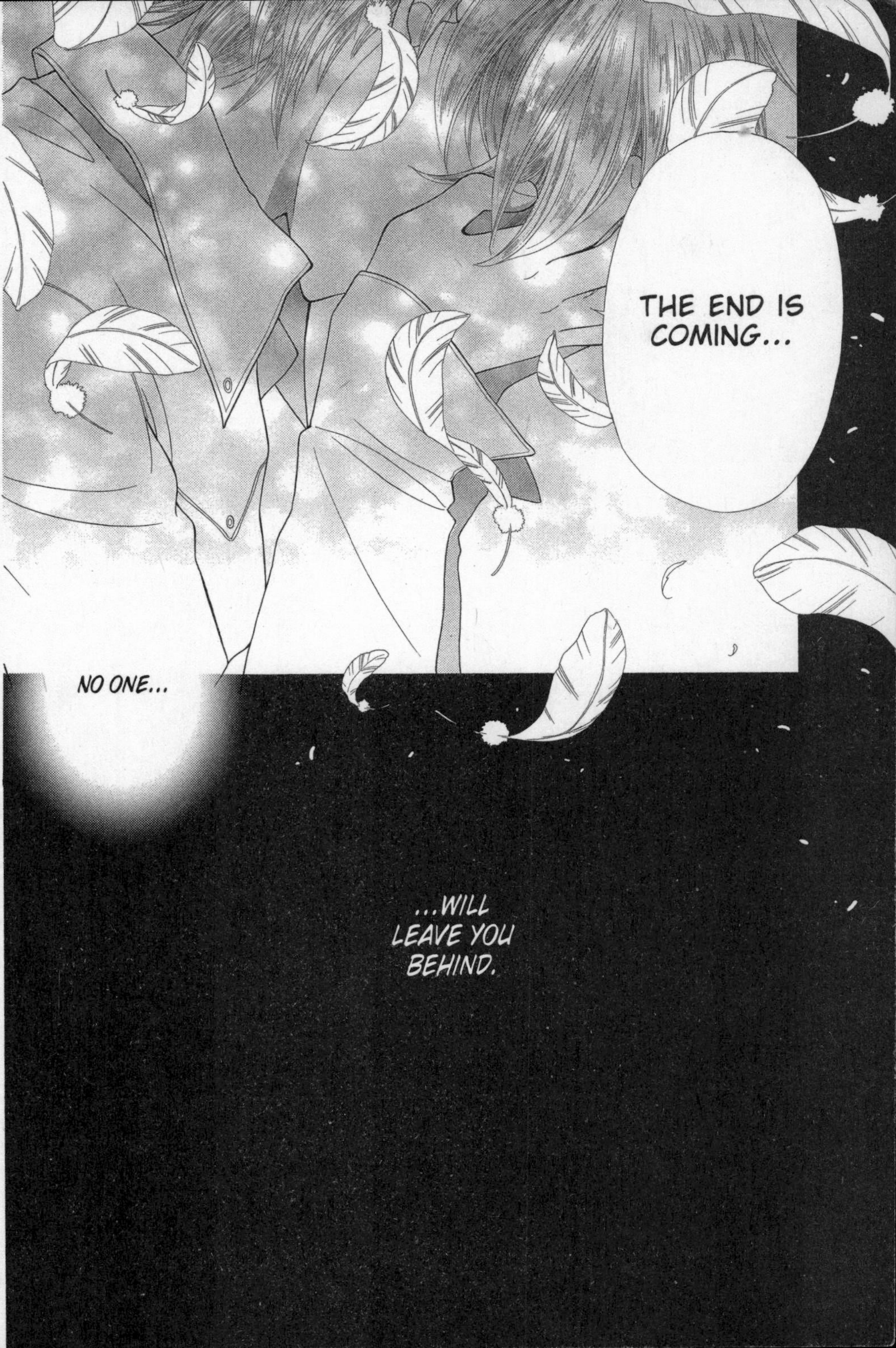
THE END IS COMING...
NO ONE...
...WILL LEAVE YOU BEHIND.

Chapter 116

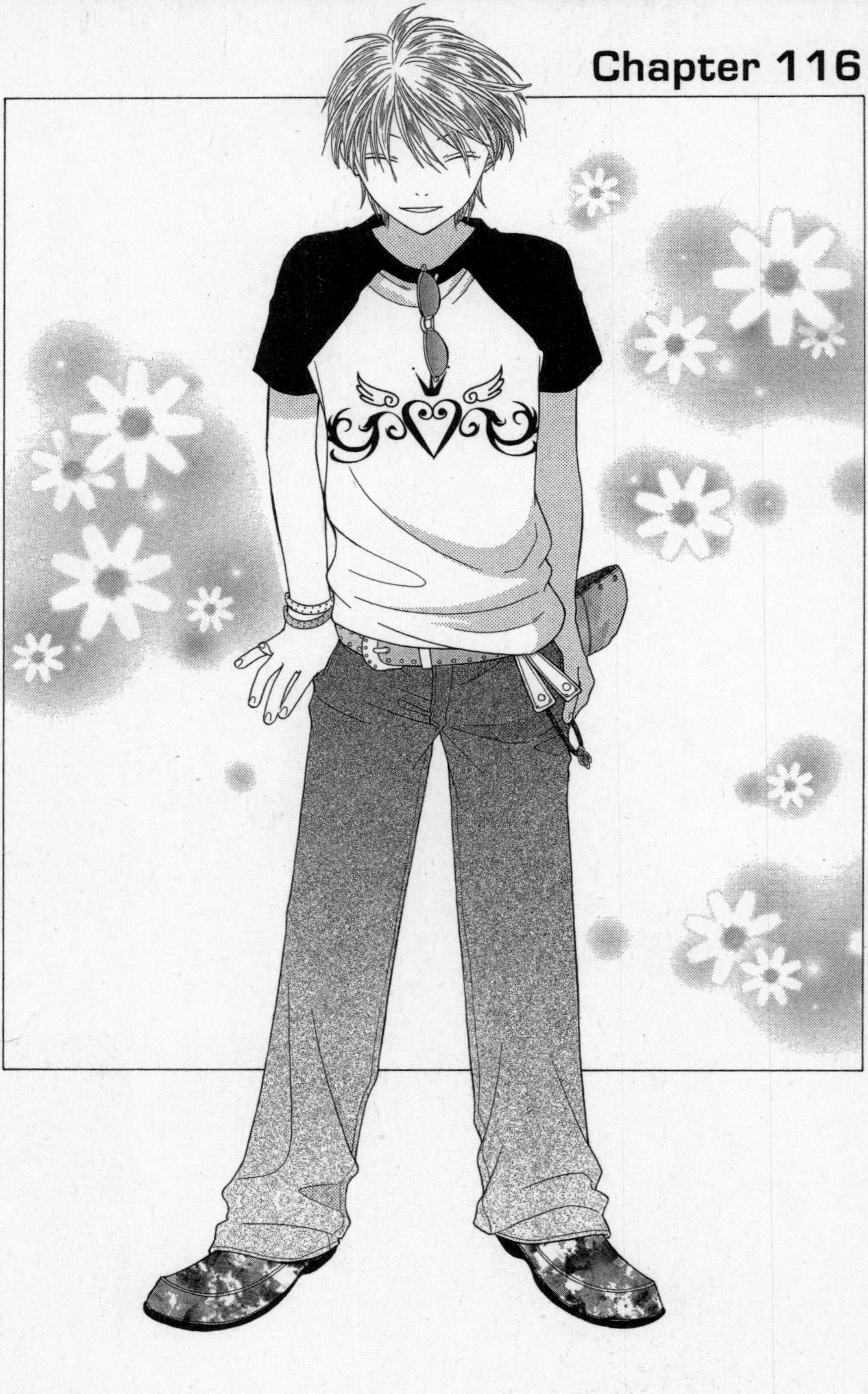

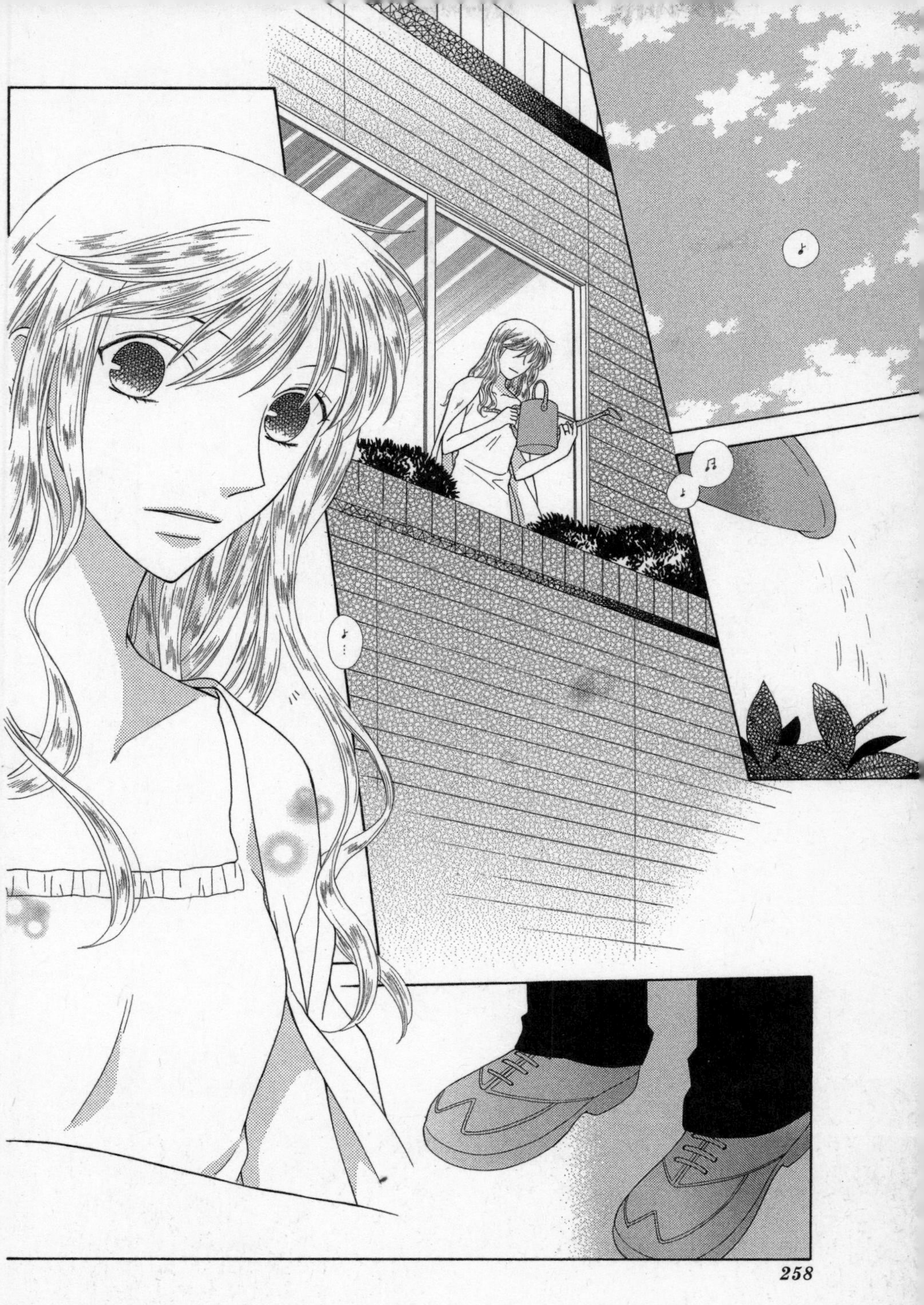
♪
♫
♪
♪…

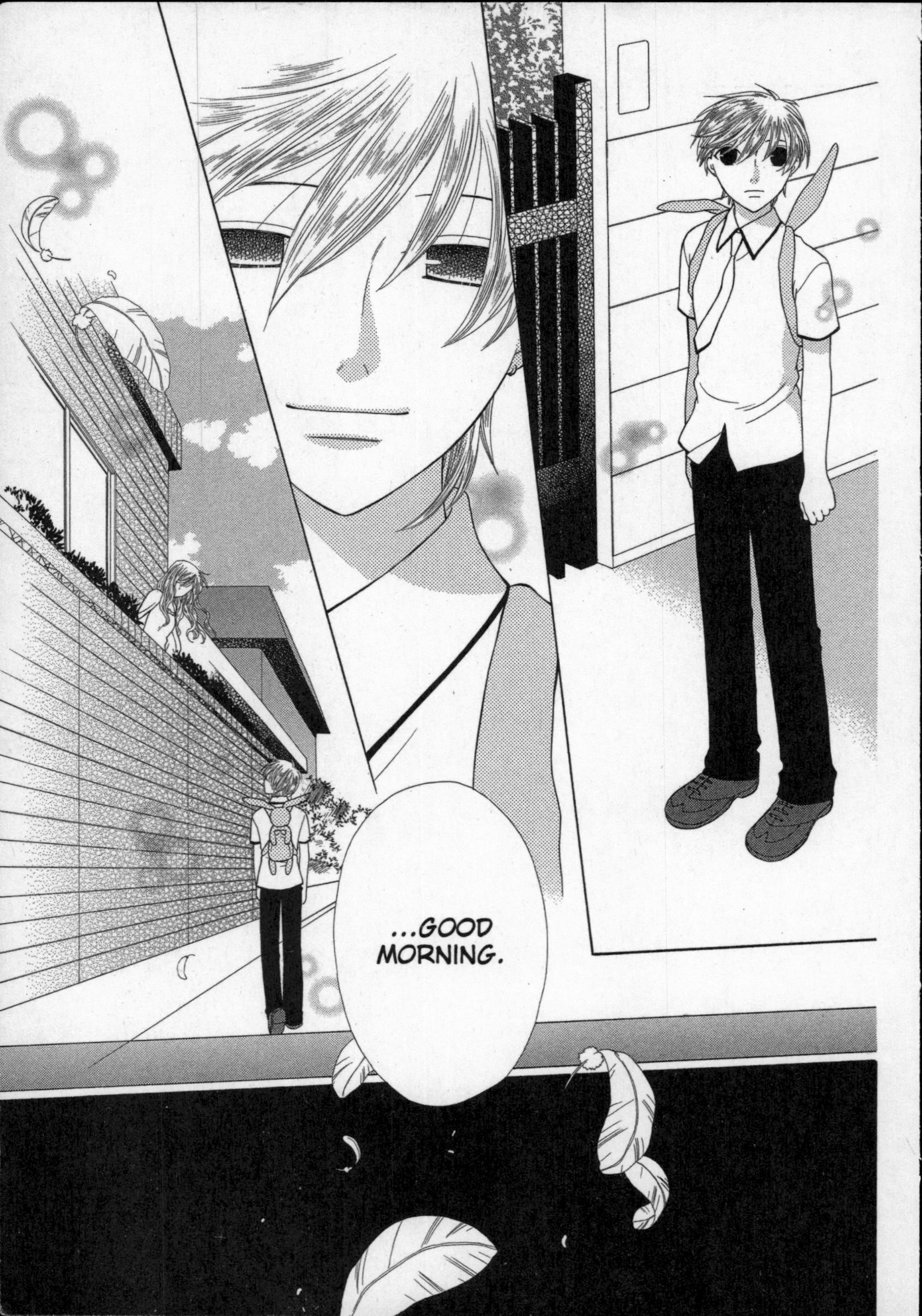
...GOOD MORNING.

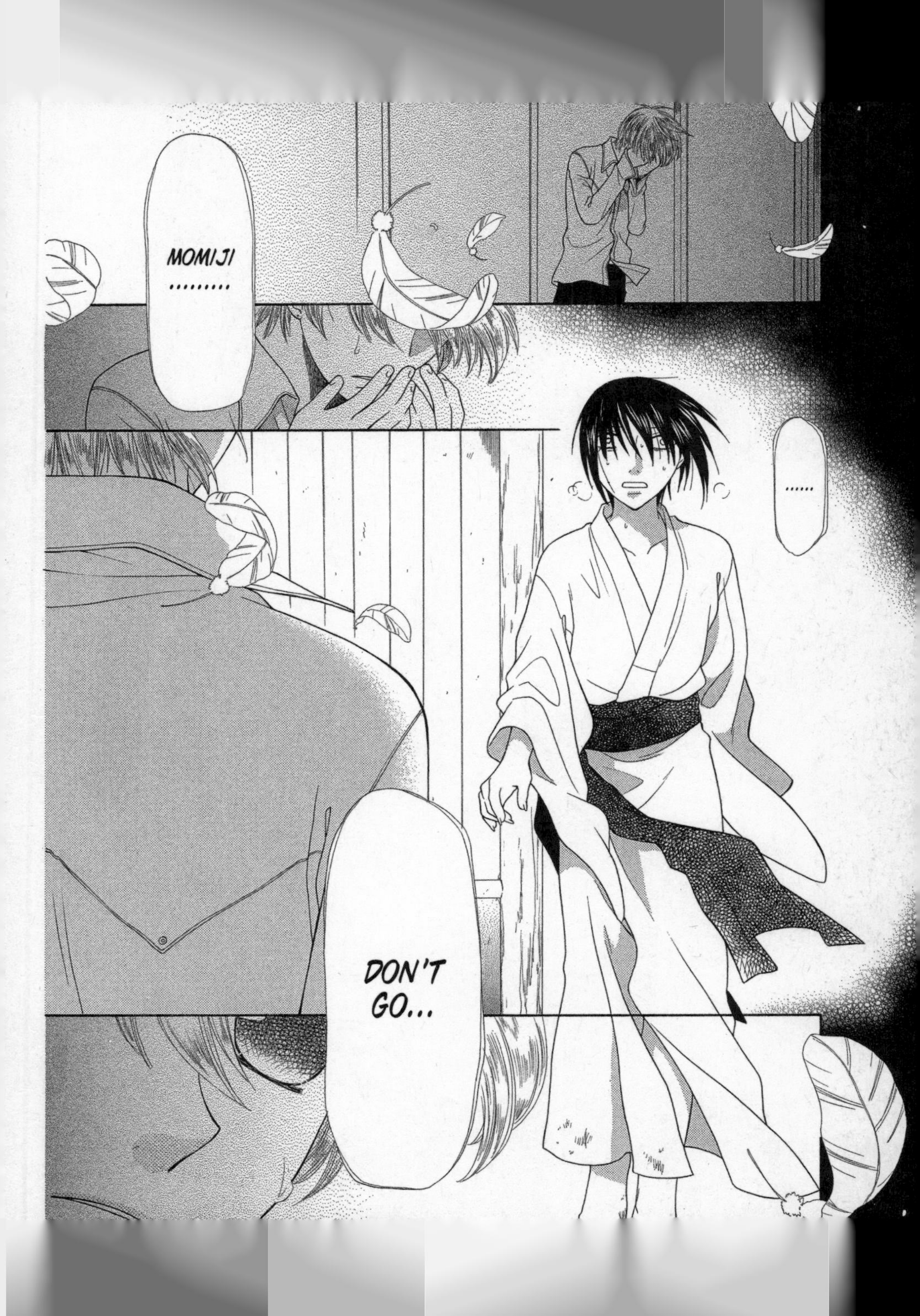
MOMIJI ....
......
DON'T GO...

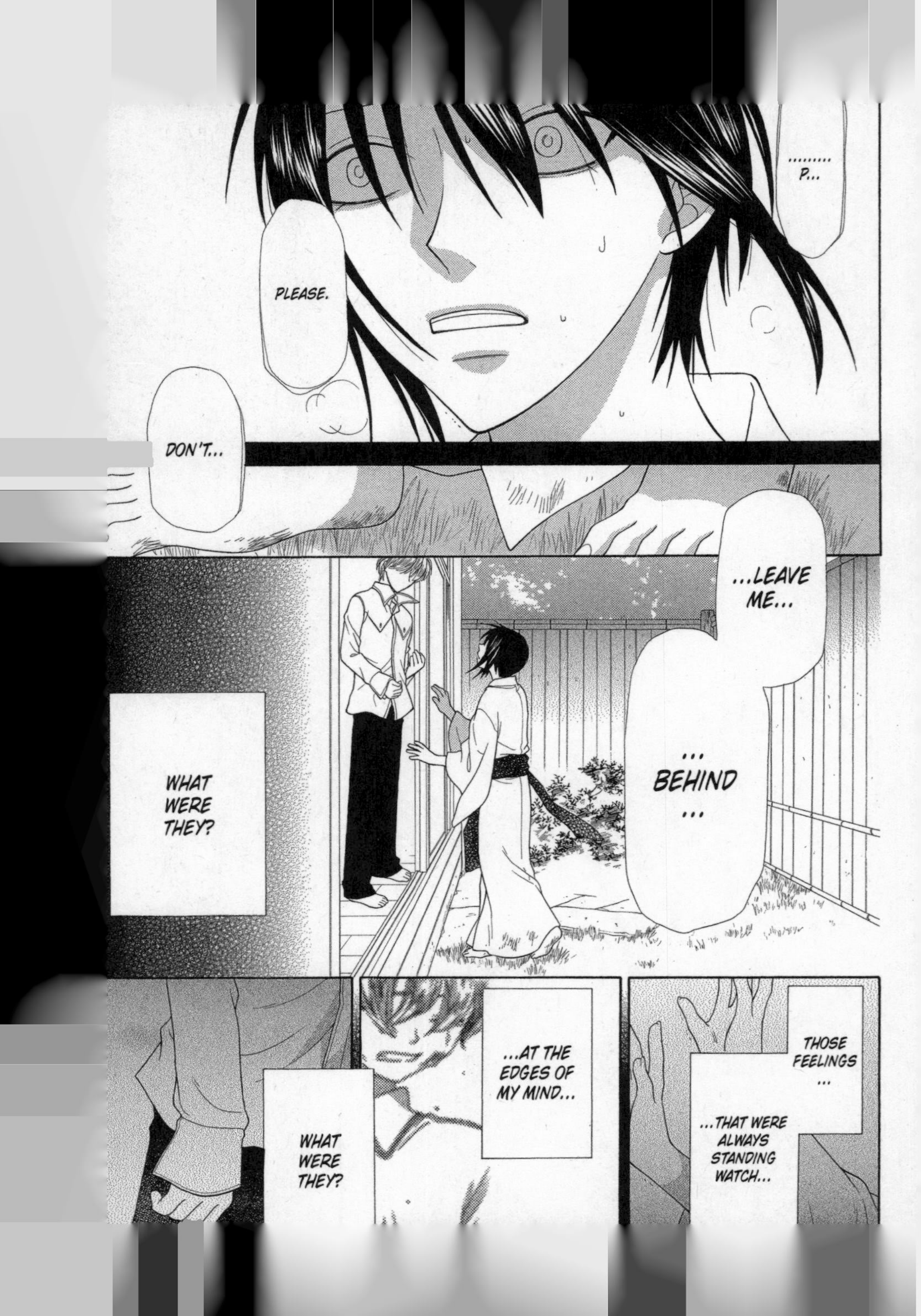
.... P...
PLEASE.
DON'T...
...LEAVE ME...
... BEHIND ...
WHAT WERE THEY?
THOSE FEELINGS ...
...THAT WERE ALWAYS STANDING WATCH...
...AT THE EDGES OF MY MIND...
WHAT WERE THEY?

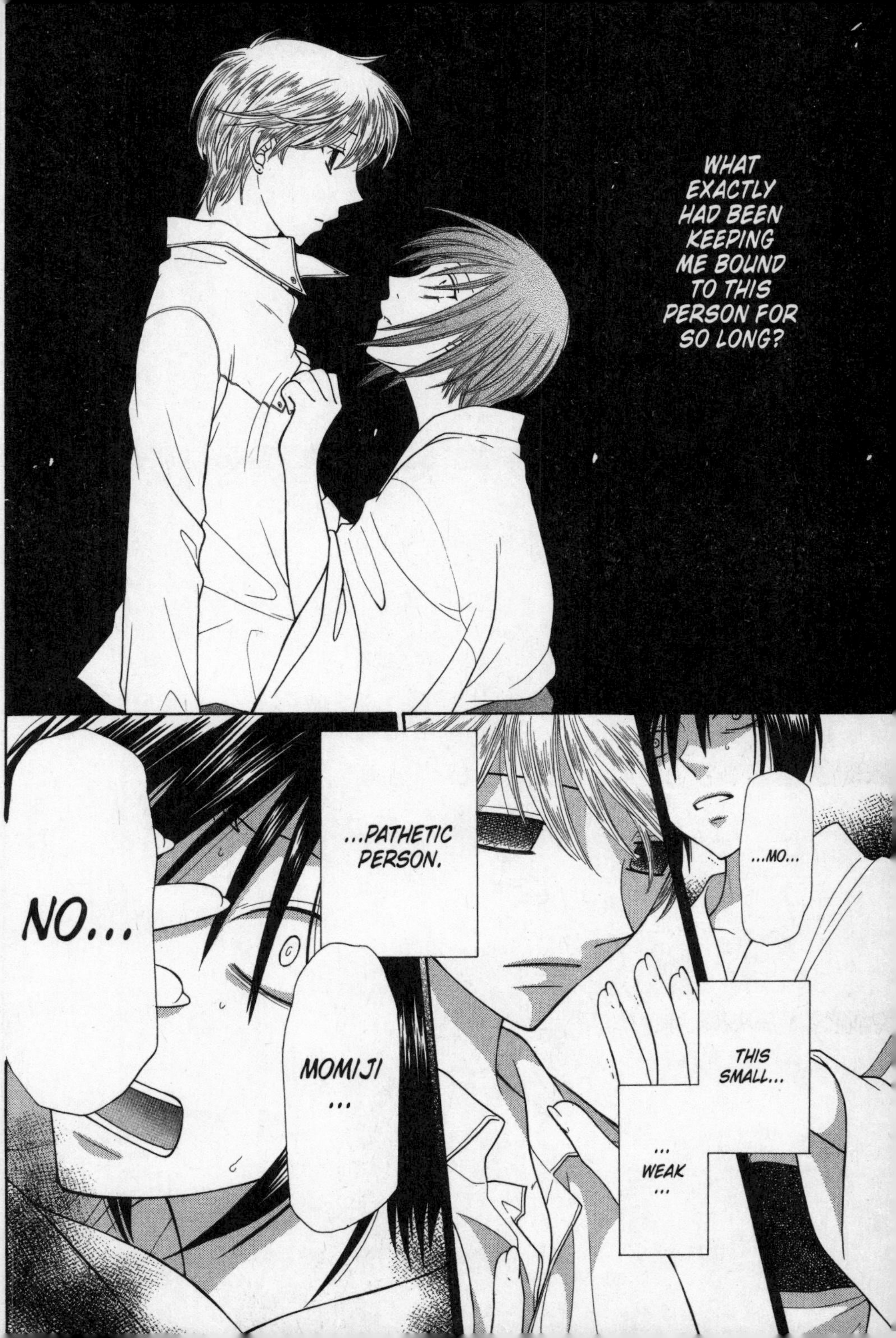
WHAT EXACTLY HAD BEEN KEEPING ME BOUND TO THIS PERSON FOR SO LONG?
...MO...
...PATHETIC PERSON.
NO...
THIS SMALL...
MOMIJI ...
... WEAK ...

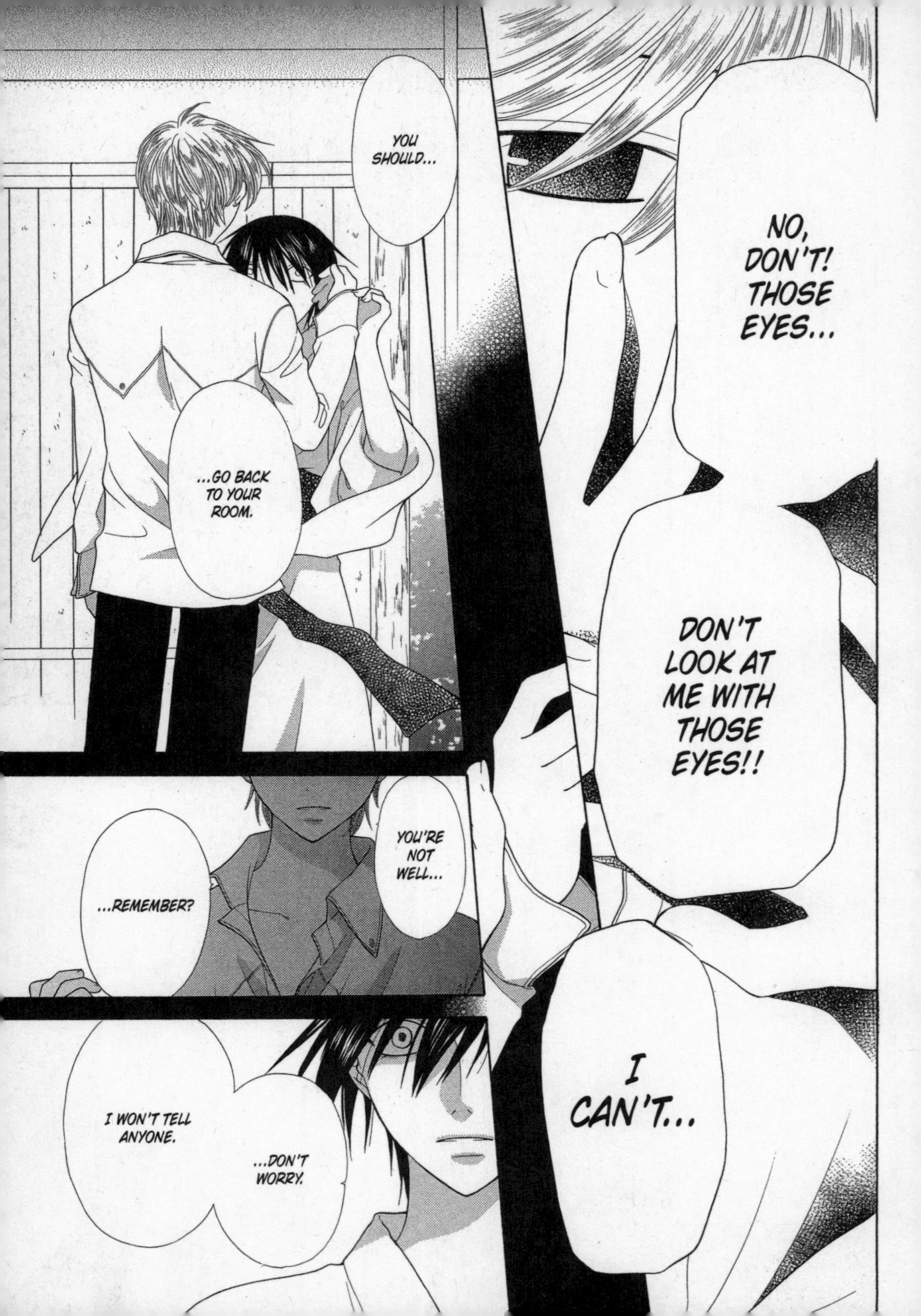
NO, DON'T! THOSE EYES...
DON'T LOOK AT ME WITH THOSE EYES!!
I CAN'T...
YOU SHOULD...
...GO BACK TO YOUR ROOM.
YOU'RE NOT WELL...
...REMEMBER?
I WON'T TELL ANYONE.
...DON'T WORRY.

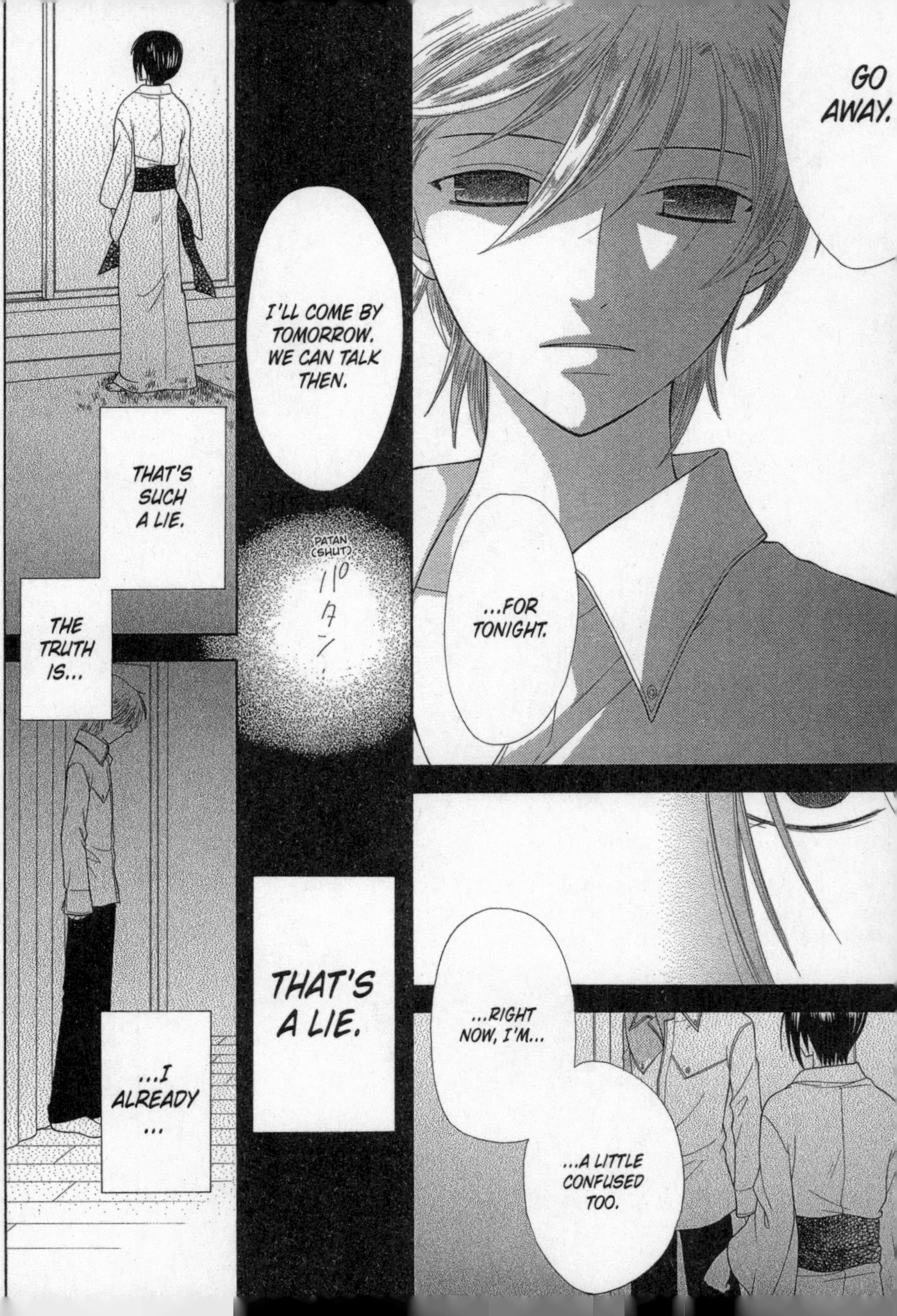
GO AWAY.
...FOR TONIGHT.
...RIGHT NOW, I'M...
...A LITTLE CONFUSED TOO.
I'LL COME BY TOMORROW. WE CAN TALK THEN.
PATAN (SHUT)
パタン
THAT'S A LIE.
THAT'S SUCH A LIE.
THE TRUTH IS...
...I ALREADY ...

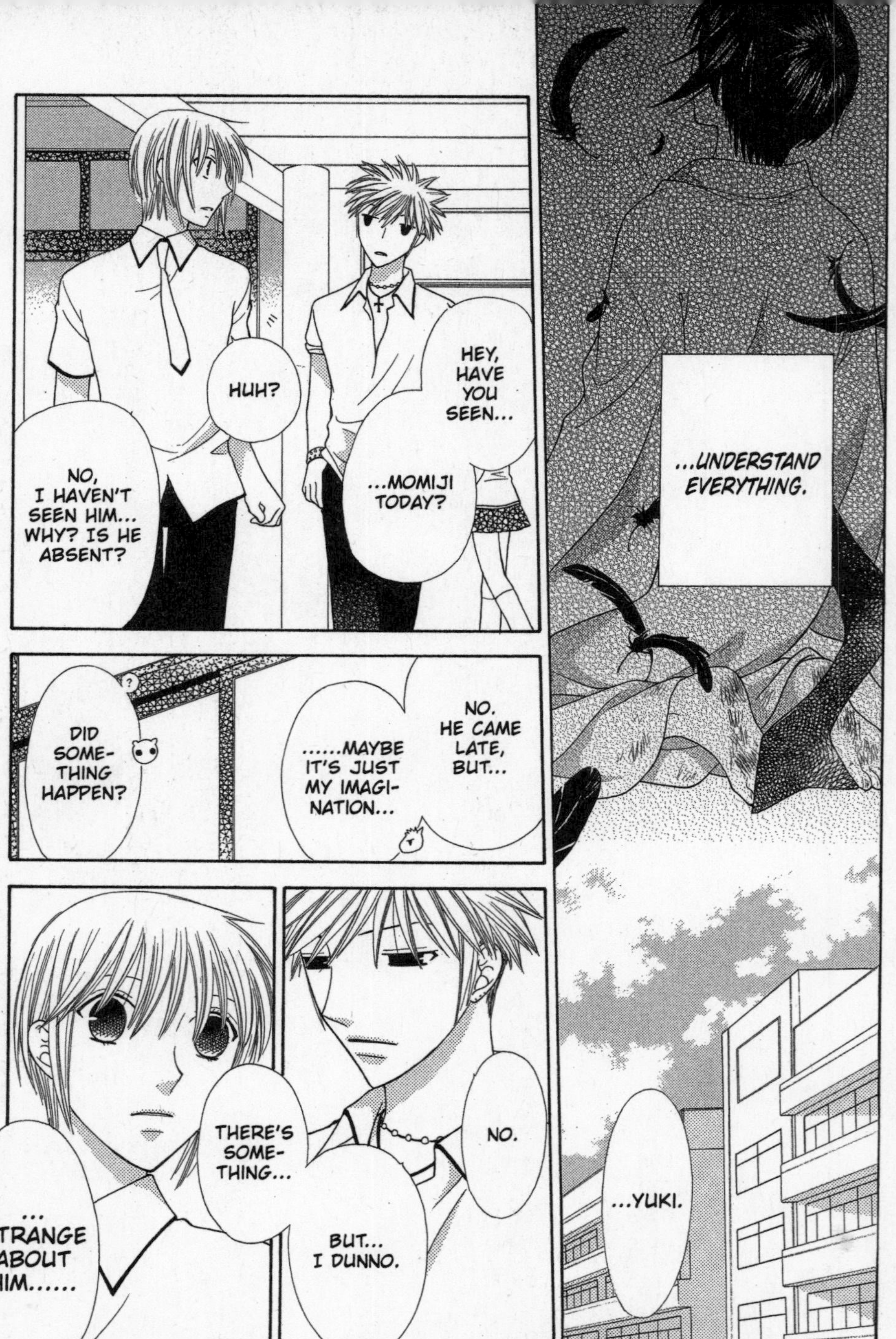
...UNDERSTAND EVERYTHING.
...YUKI.
HEY, HAVE YOU SEEN...
...MOMIJI TODAY?
HUH?
NO, I HAVEN'T SEEN HIM... WHY? IS HE ABSENT?
NO. HE CAME LATE, BUT...
......MAYBE IT'S JUST MY IMAGINATION...
DID SOME-THING HAPPEN?
NO.
BUT... I DUNNO.
THERE'S SOME-THING...
... STRANGE ABOUT HIM......

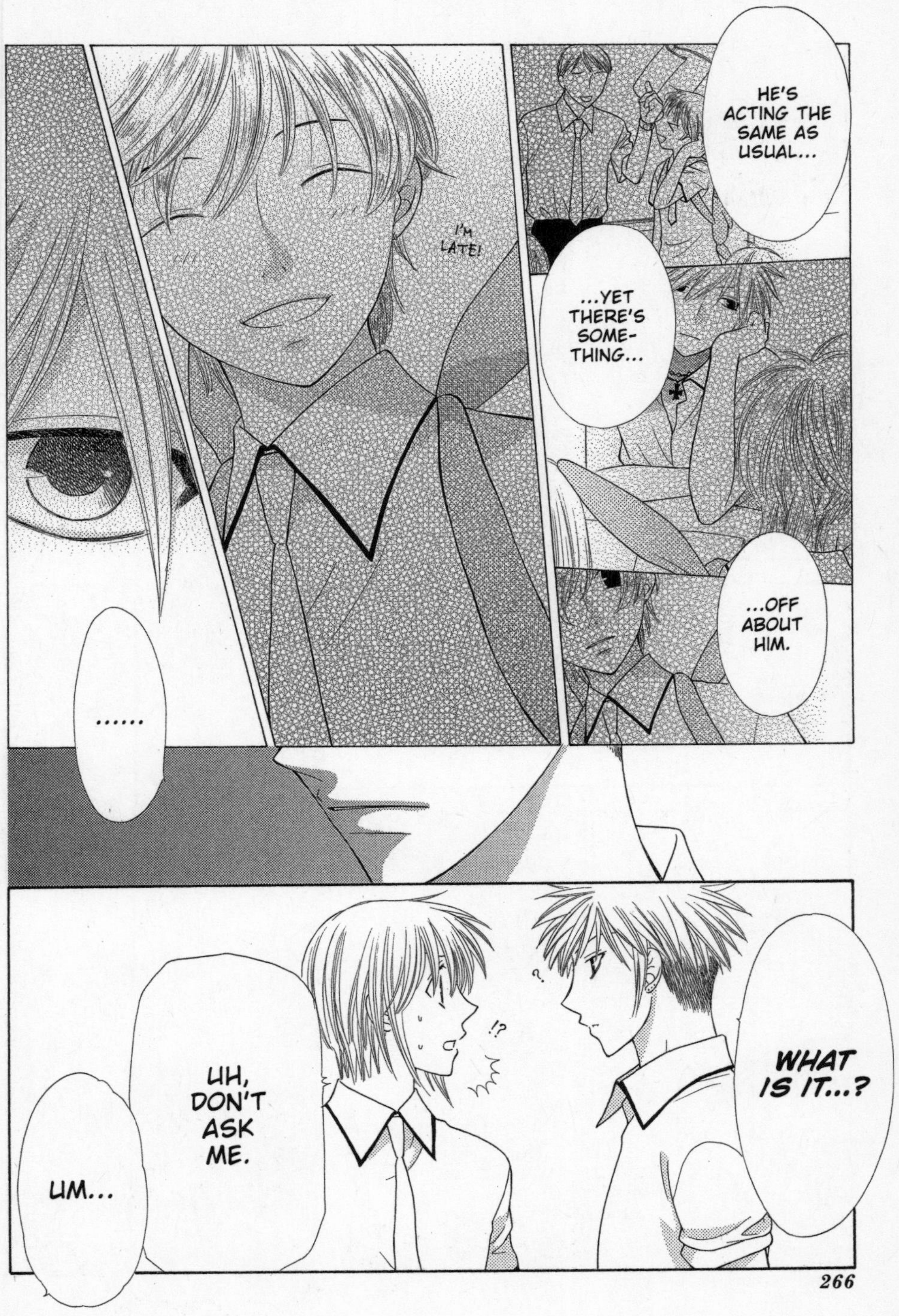
HE'S ACTING THE SAME AS USUAL...
...YET THERE'S SOME-THING...
...OFF ABOUT HIM.
I'M LATE!
......
WHAT IS IT...?
?
!?
UH, DON'T ASK ME.
UM...

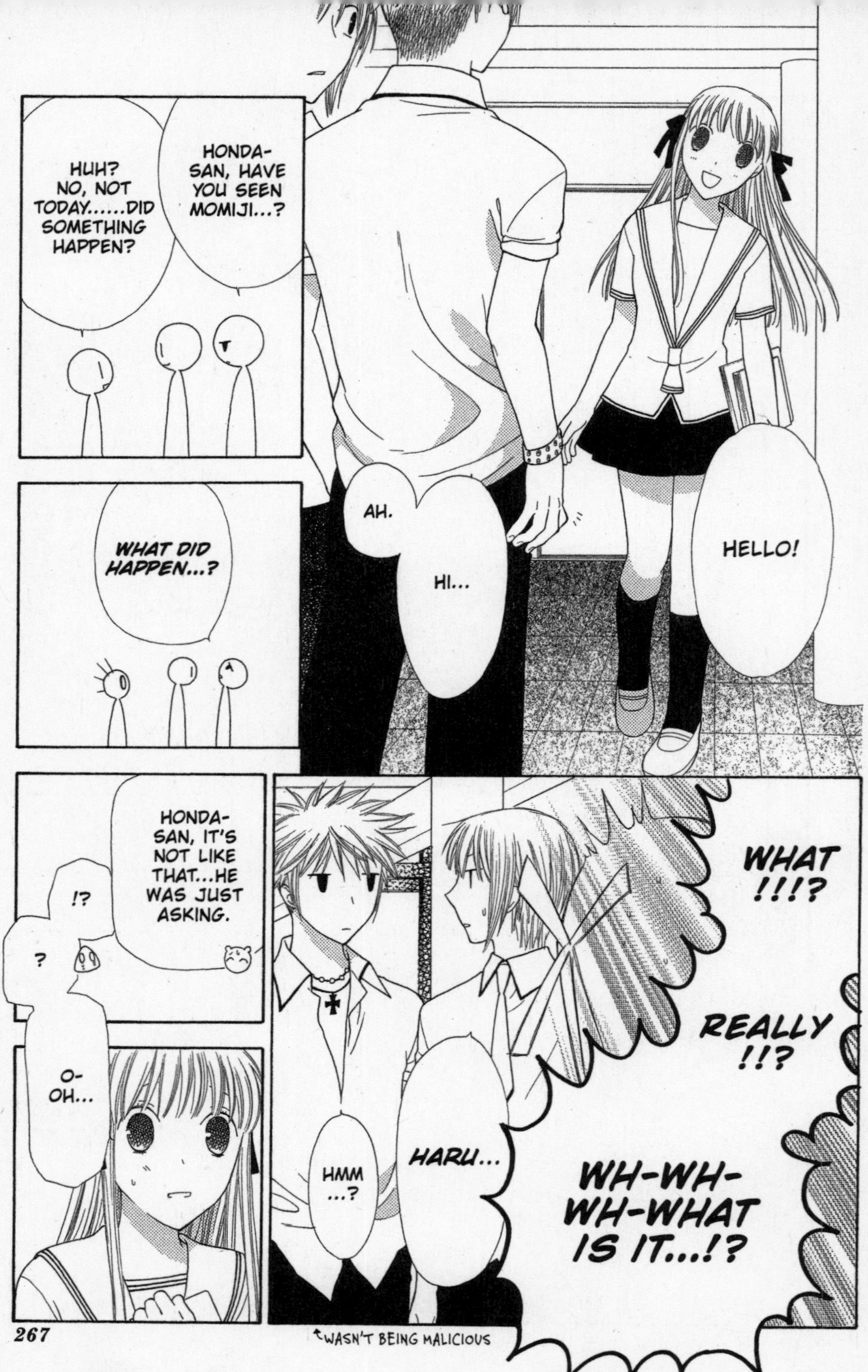
HELLO!
AH.
HI...
HONDA-SAN, HAVE YOU SEEN MOMIJI...?
HUH? NO, NOT TODAY......DID SOMETHING HAPPEN?
WHAT DID HAPPEN...?
WHAT!!!?
REALLY!!?
WH-WH-WH-WHAT IS IT...!?
HARU...
HMM...?
HONDA-SAN, IT'S NOT LIKE THAT...HE WAS JUST ASKING.
!?
?
O-OH...
WASN'T BEING MALICIOUS

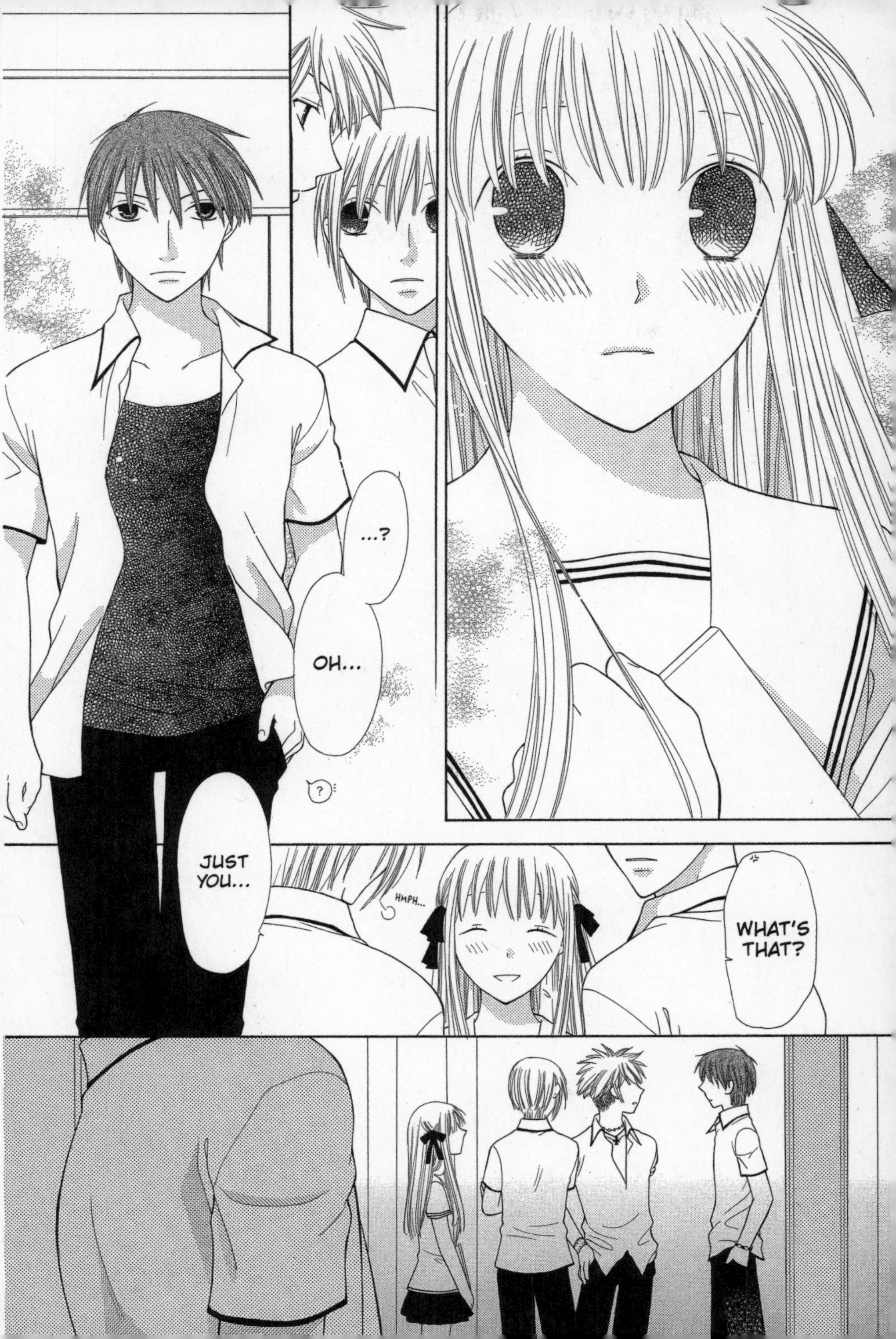
WHAT'S THAT?
HMPH...
...?
OH...
?
JUST YOU...

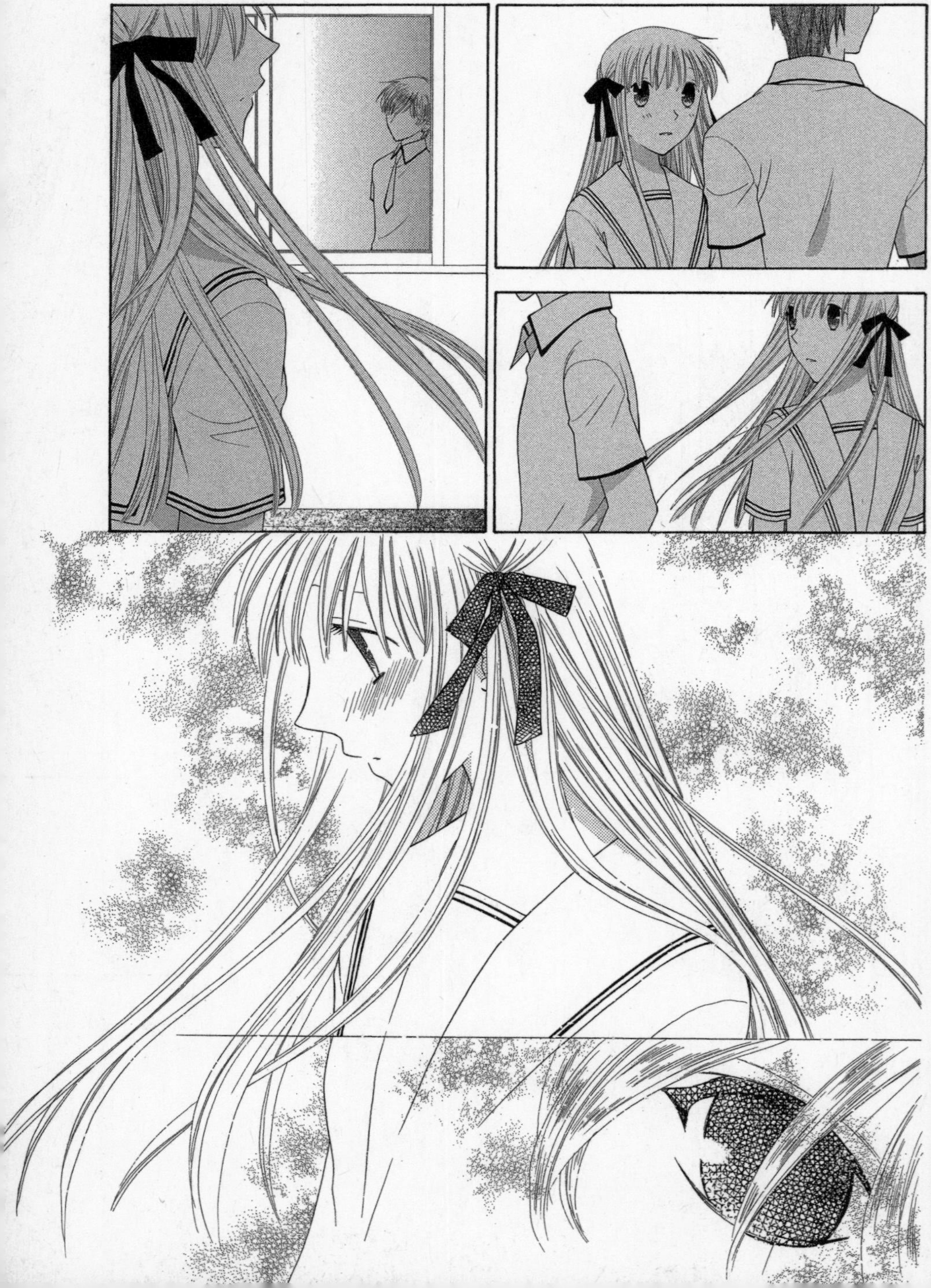

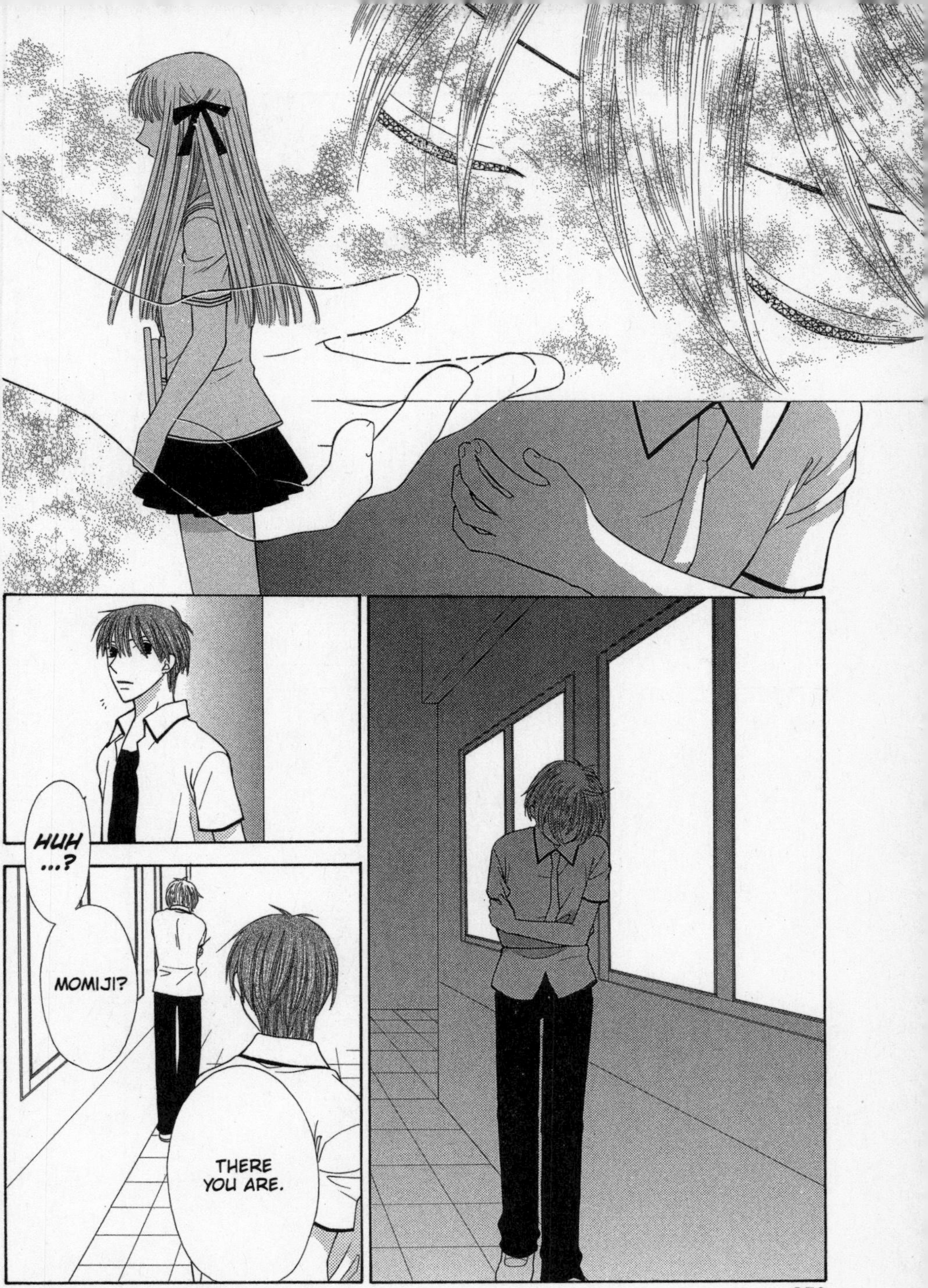
HUH ...?
MOMIJI?
THERE YOU ARE.

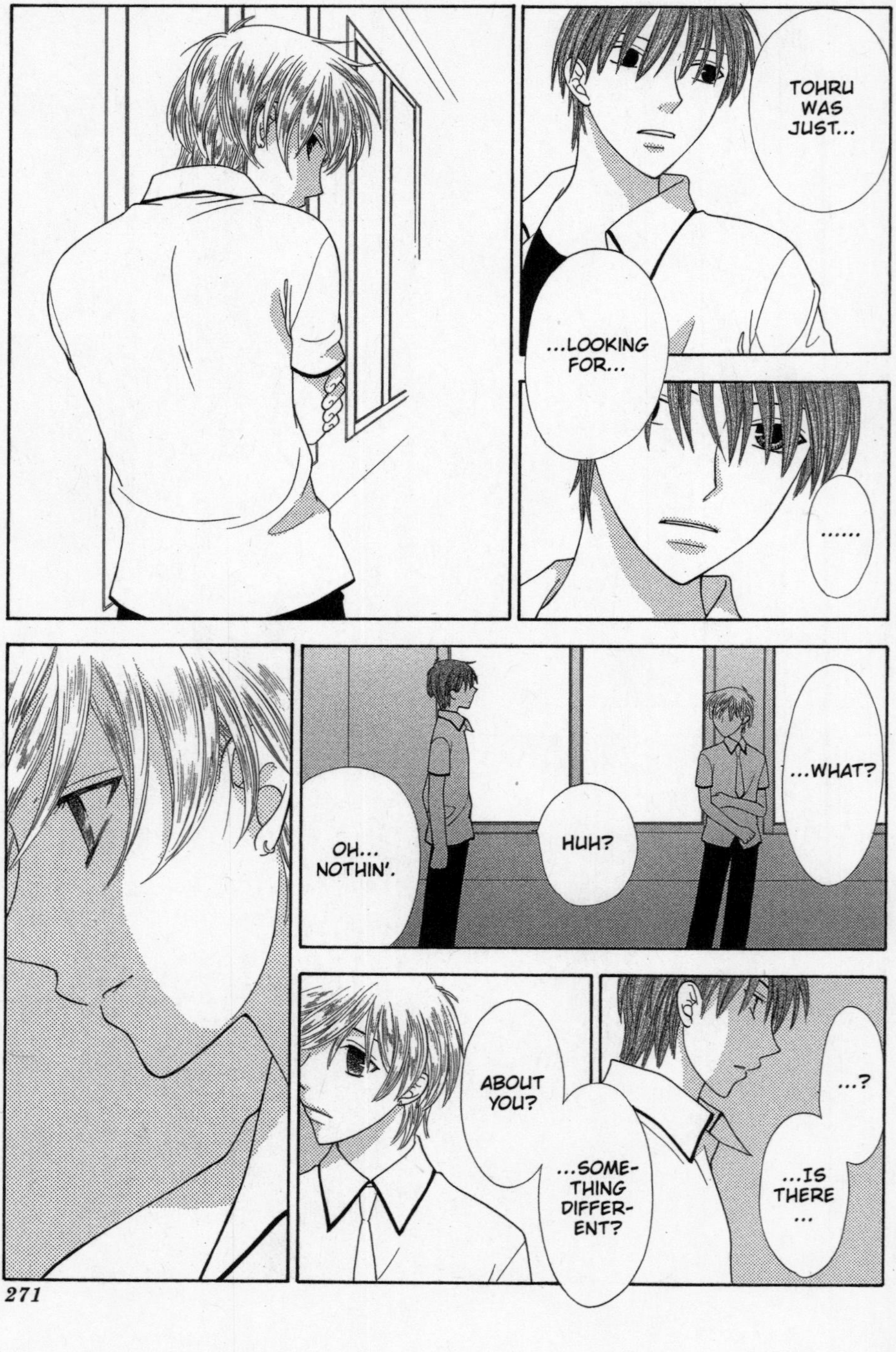
TOHRU WAS JUST...
...LOOKING FOR...
......
...WHAT?
HUH?
OH... NOTHIN'.
...?
...IS THERE ...
...SOME-THING DIFFER-ENT?
ABOUT YOU?

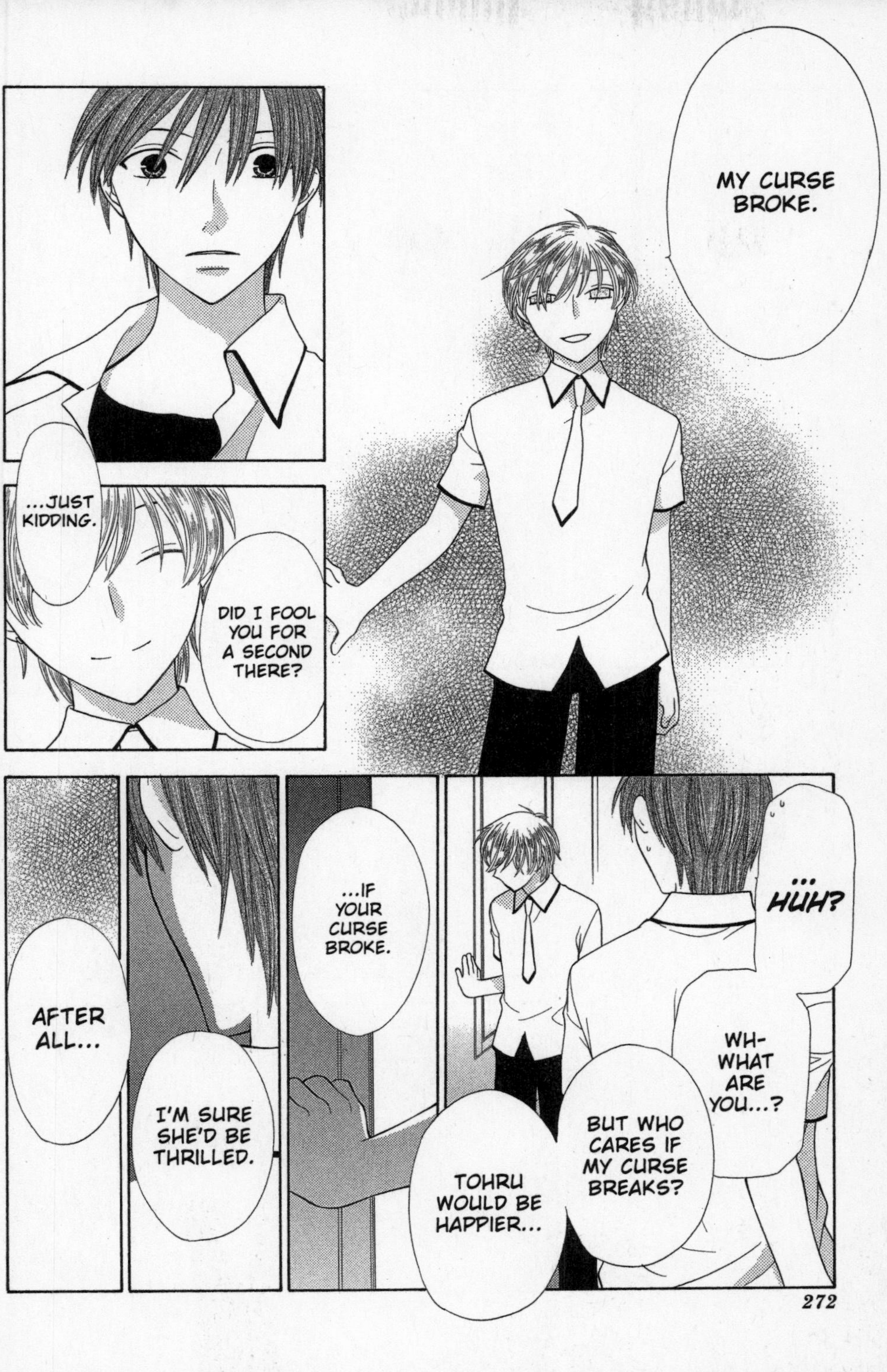
MY CURSE BROKE.
...JUST KIDDING.
DID I FOOL YOU FOR A SECOND THERE?
...HÜH?
WH-WHAT ARE YOU...?
BUT WHO CARES IF MY CURSE BREAKS?
TOHRU WOULD BE HAPPIER...
...IF YOUR CURSE BROKE.
AFTER ALL...
I'M SURE SHE'D BE THRILLED.

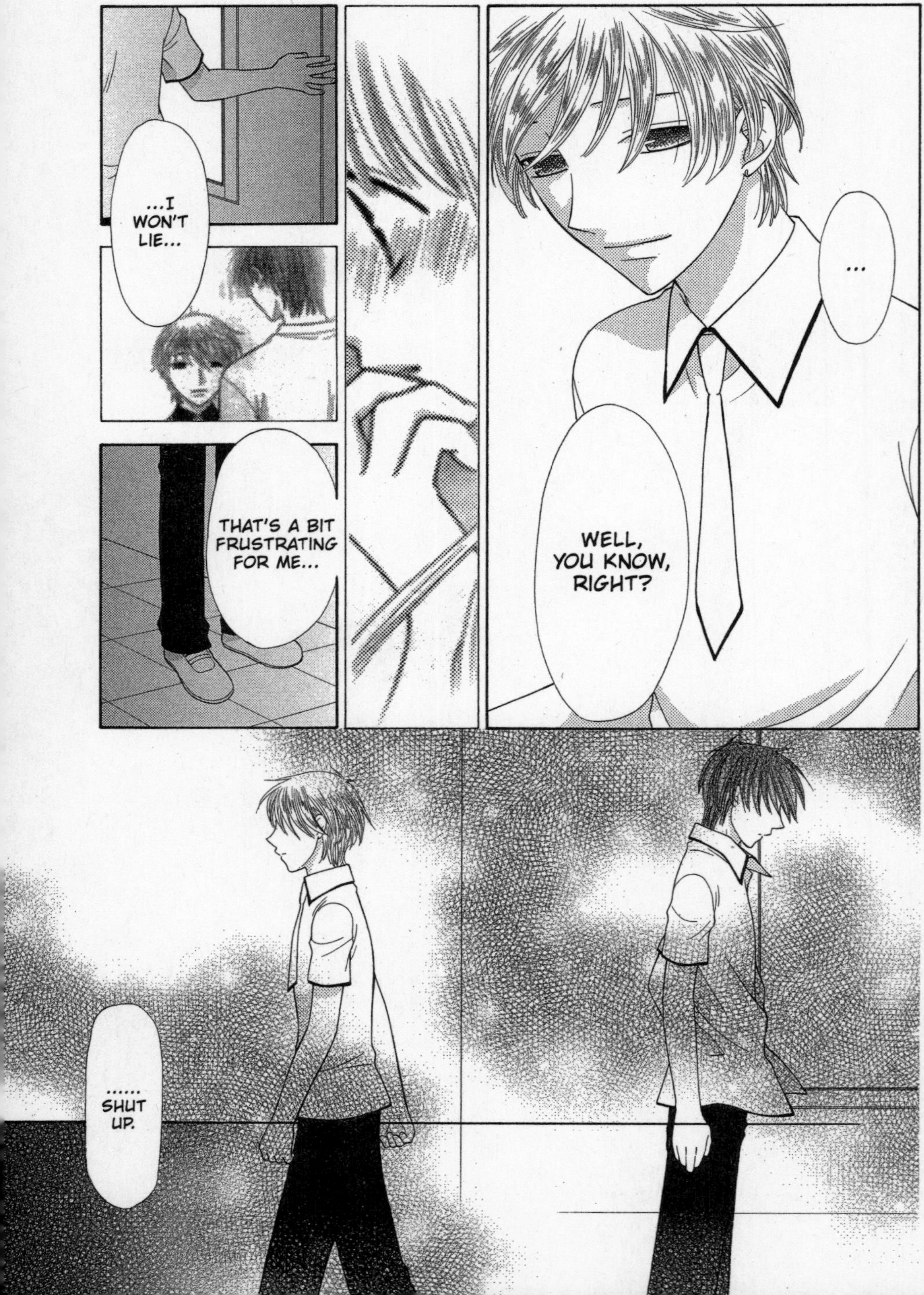
...
WELL, YOU KNOW, RIGHT?
...I WON'T LIE...
THAT'S A BIT FRUSTRATING FOR ME...
...... SHUT UP.

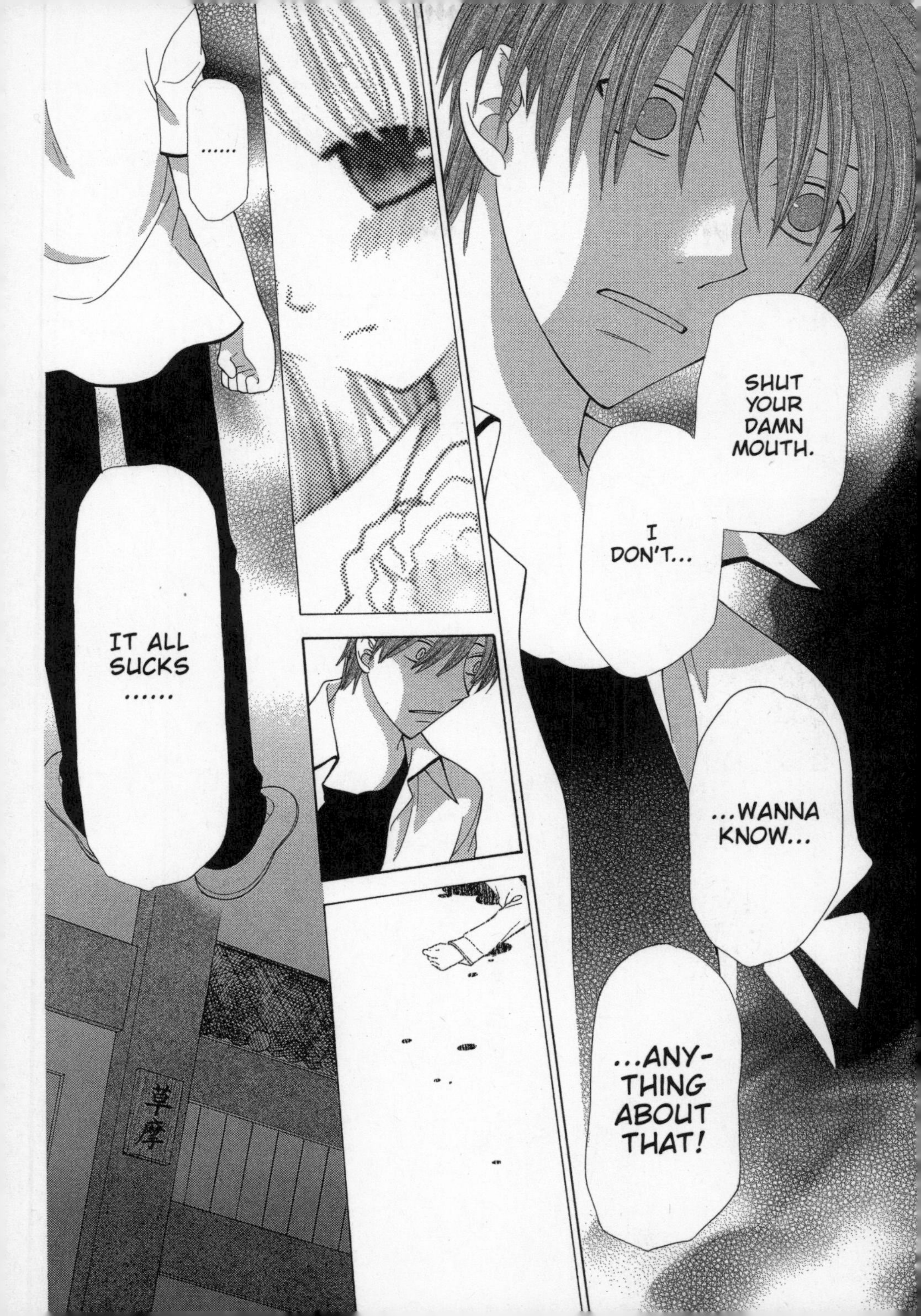
SHUT YOUR DAMN MOUTH.
I DON'T...
...WANNA KNOW...
...ANY-THING ABOUT THAT!
......
IT ALL SUCKS ......
草摩

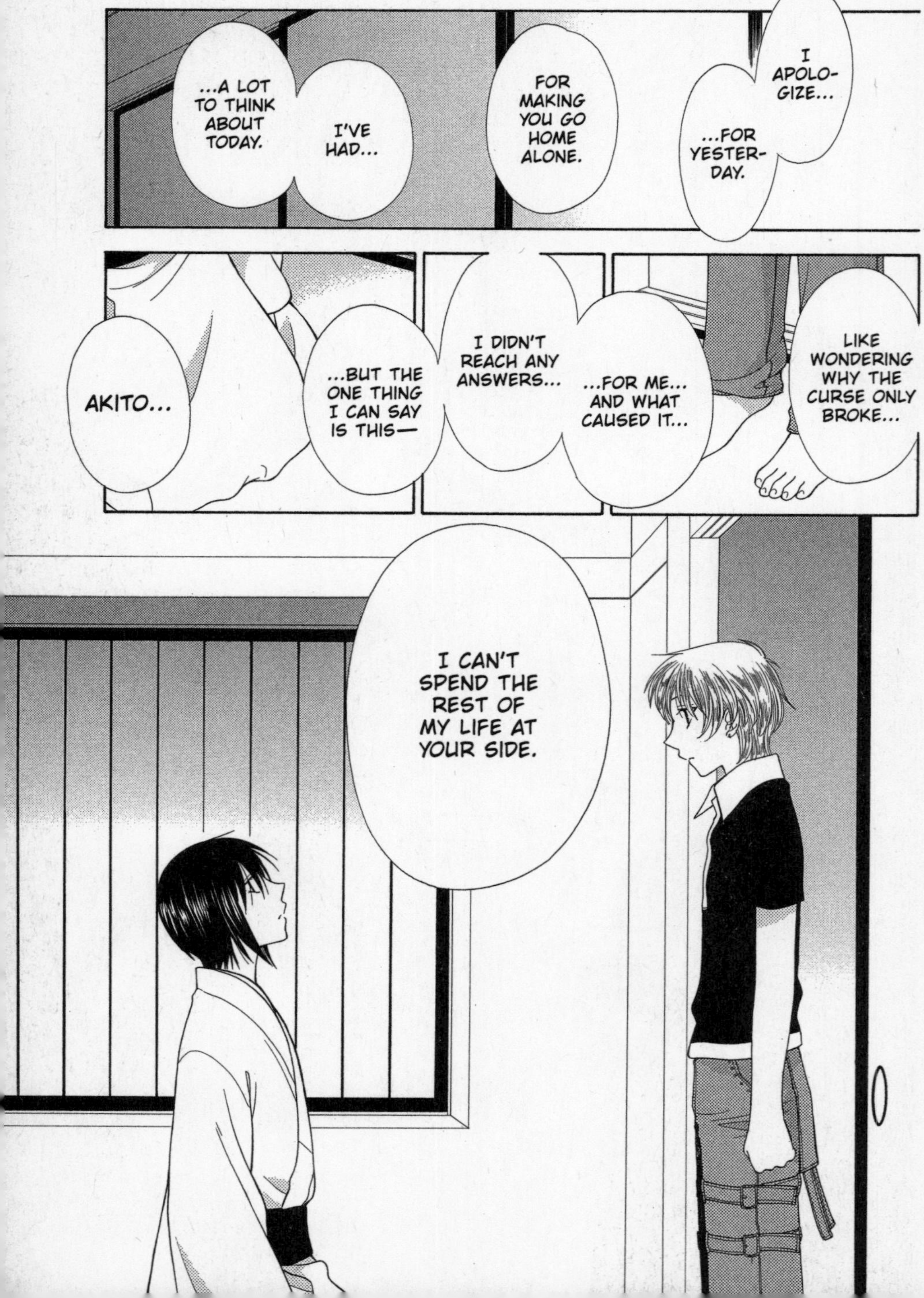
I APOLOGIZE...
...FOR YESTERDAY.
FOR MAKING YOU GO HOME ALONE.
I'VE HAD...
...A LOT TO THINK ABOUT TODAY.
LIKE WONDERING WHY THE CURSE ONLY BROKE...
...FOR ME... AND WHAT CAUSED IT...
I DIDN'T REACH ANY ANSWERS...
...BUT THE ONE THING I CAN SAY IS THIS—
AKITO...
I CAN'T SPEND THE REST OF MY LIFE AT YOUR SIDE.

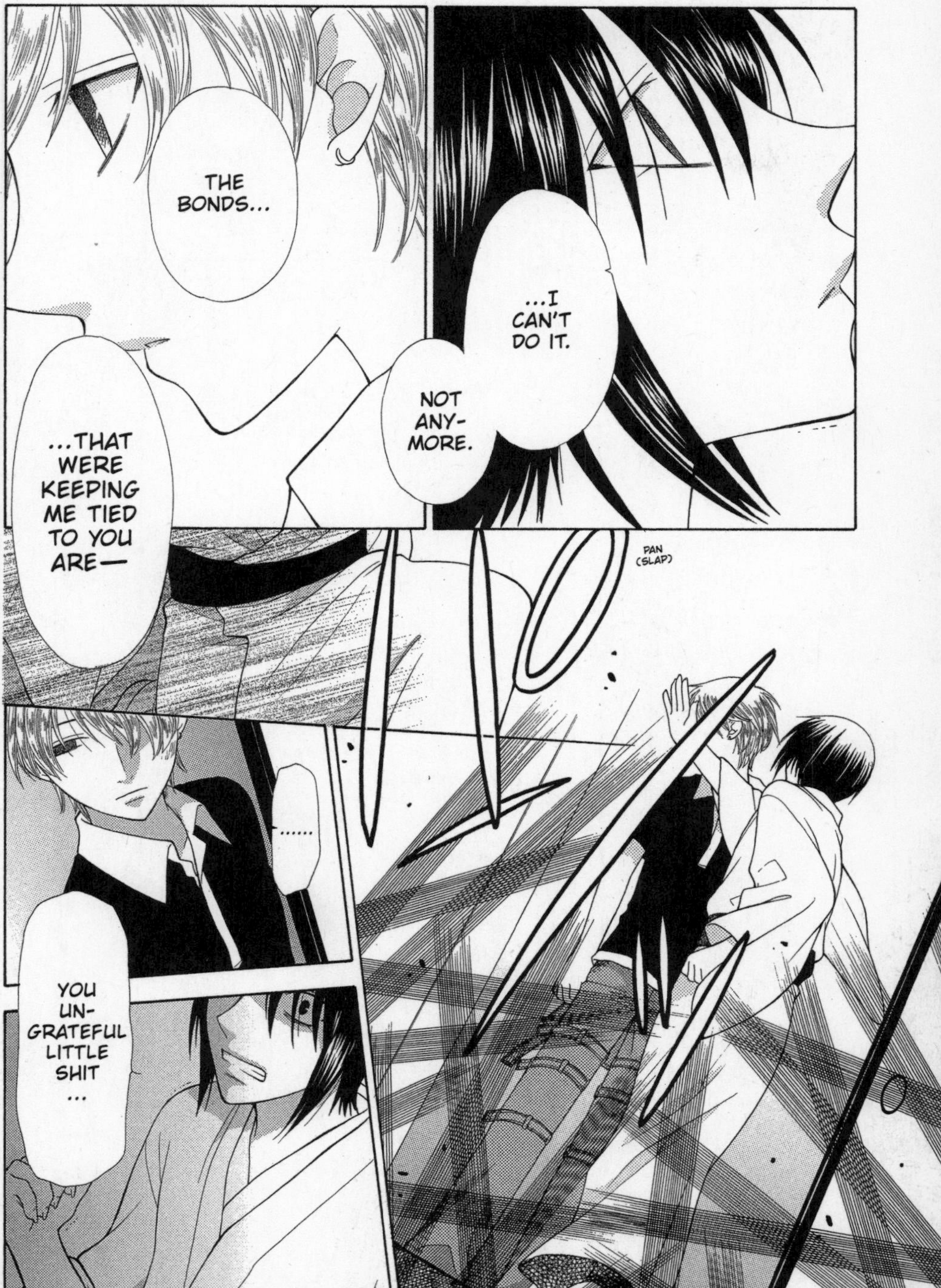
...I CAN'T DO IT.
NOT ANYMORE.
THE BONDS...
...THAT WERE KEEPING ME TIED TO YOU ARE—
PAN (SLAP)
......
YOU UN-GRATEFUL LITTLE SHIT ...

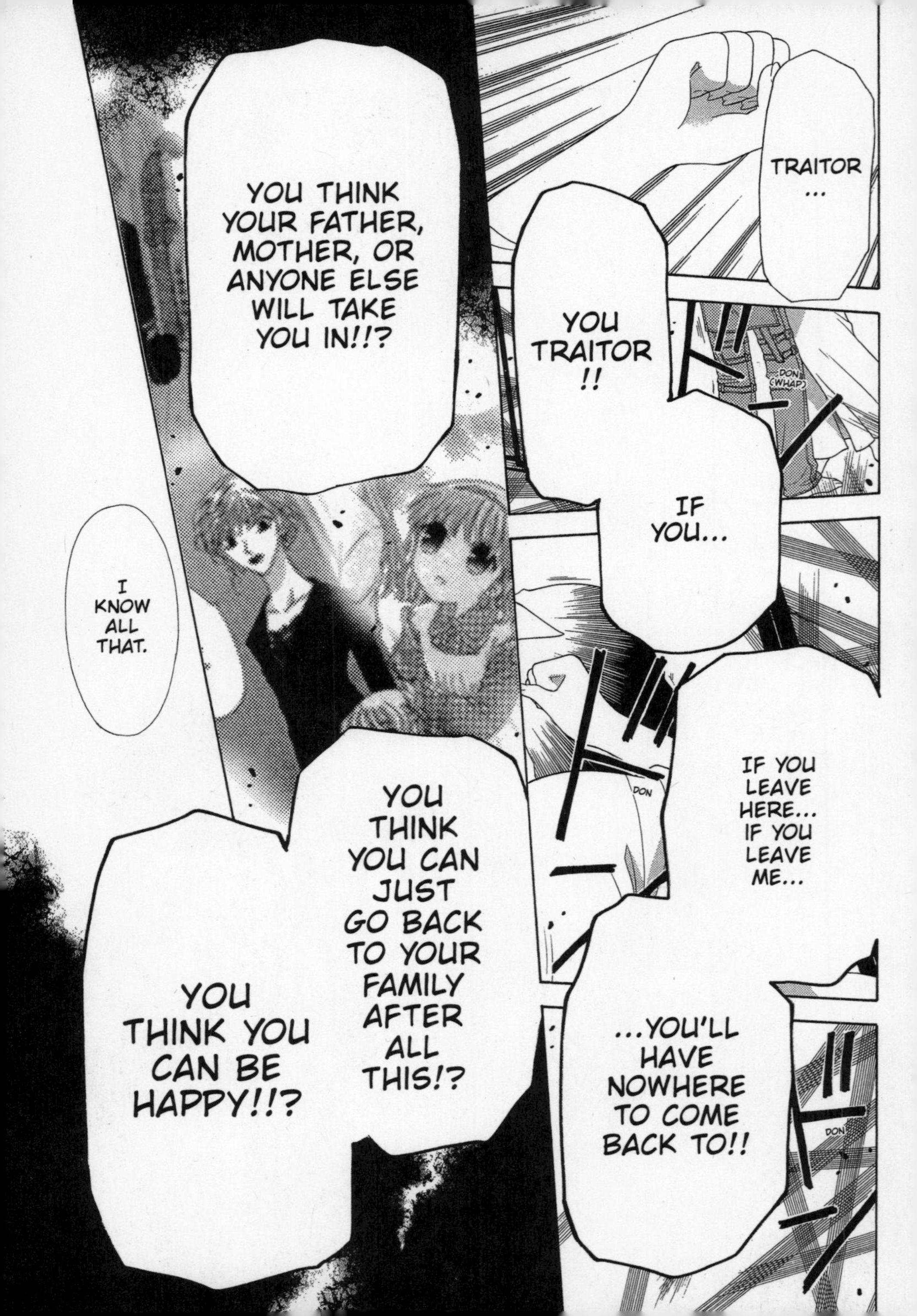
TRAITOR ...
YOU TRAITOR !!
DON (WHAP)
IF YOU...
DON
IF YOU LEAVE HERE... IF YOU LEAVE ME...
...YOU'LL HAVE NOWHERE TO COME BACK TO!!
DON
YOU THINK YOUR FATHER, MOTHER, OR ANYONE ELSE WILL TAKE YOU IN!!?
I KNOW ALL THAT.
YOU THINK YOU CAN JUST GO BACK TO YOUR FAMILY AFTER ALL THIS!?
YOU THINK YOU CAN BE HAPPY!!?

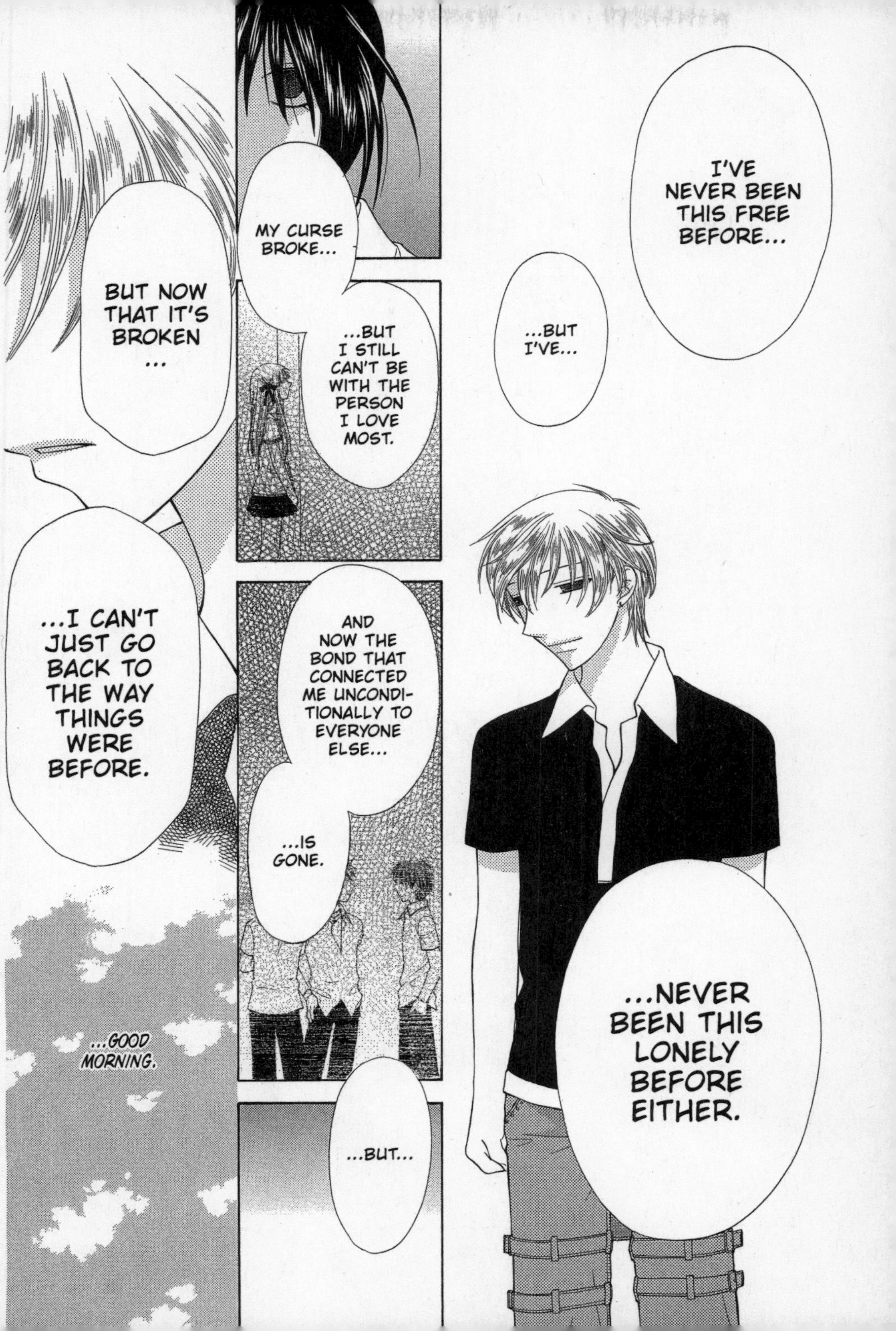
I'VE NEVER BEEN THIS FREE BEFORE...
...BUT I'VE...
...NEVER BEEN THIS LONELY BEFORE EITHER.
MY CURSE BROKE...
...BUT I STILL CAN'T BE WITH THE PERSON I LOVE MOST.
AND NOW THE BOND THAT CONNECTED ME UNCONDI-TIONALLY TO EVERYONE ELSE...
...IS GONE.
...BUT...
BUT NOW THAT IT'S BROKEN ...
...I CAN'T JUST GO BACK TO THE WAY THINGS WERE BEFORE.
...GOOD MORNING.

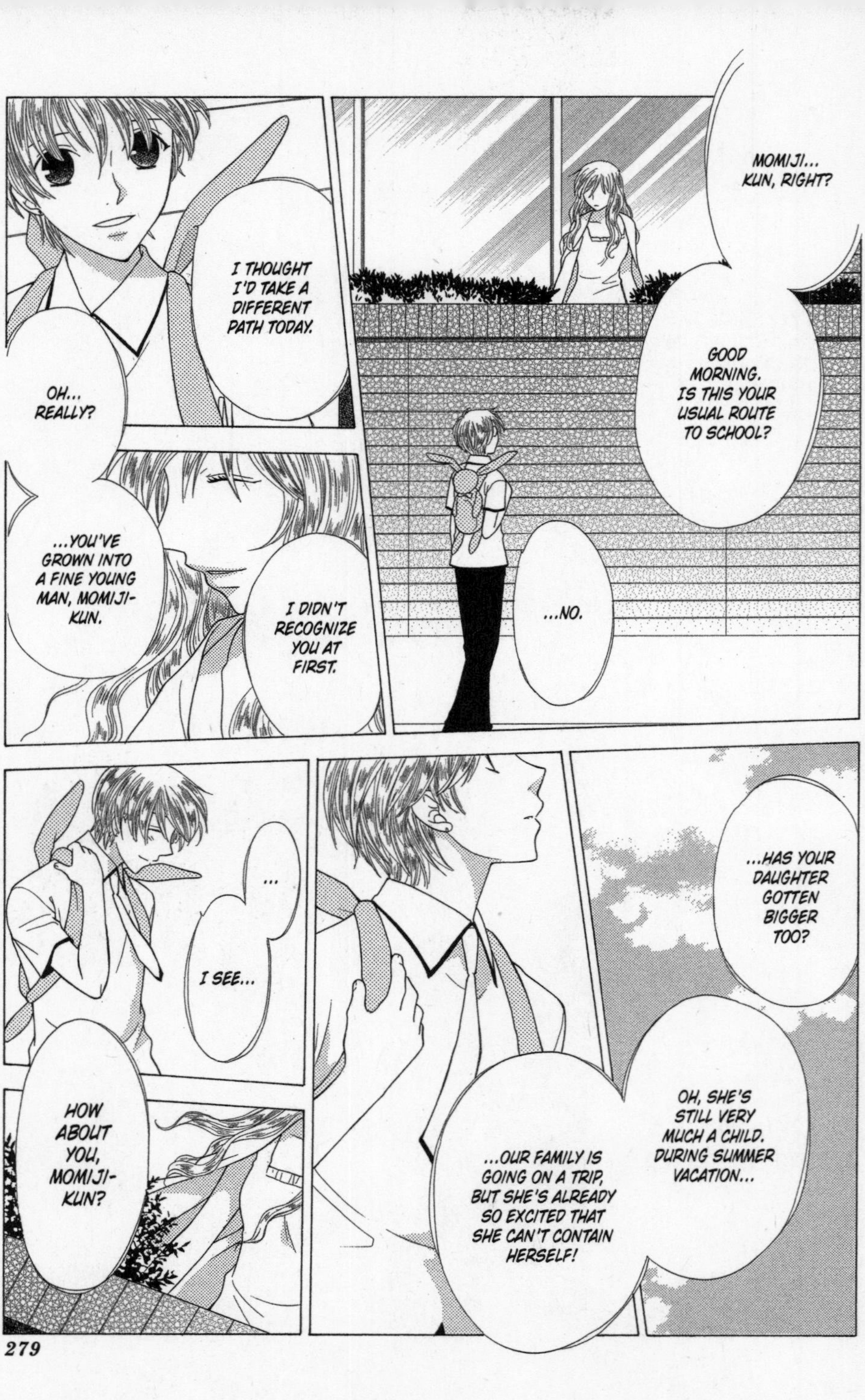
MOMIJI... KUN, RIGHT?
GOOD MORNING. IS THIS YOUR USUAL ROUTE TO SCHOOL?
...NO.
I THOUGHT I'D TAKE A DIFFERENT PATH TODAY.
OH... REALLY?
I DIDN'T RECOGNIZE YOU AT FIRST.
...YOU'VE GROWN INTO A FINE YOUNG MAN, MOMIJI-KUN.
...HAS YOUR DAUGHTER GOTTEN BIGGER TOO?
OH, SHE'S STILL VERY MUCH A CHILD. DURING SUMMER VACATION...
...OUR FAMILY IS GOING ON A TRIP, BUT SHE'S ALREADY SO EXCITED THAT SHE CAN'T CONTAIN HERSELF!
...
I SEE...
HOW ABOUT YOU, MOMIJI-KUN?

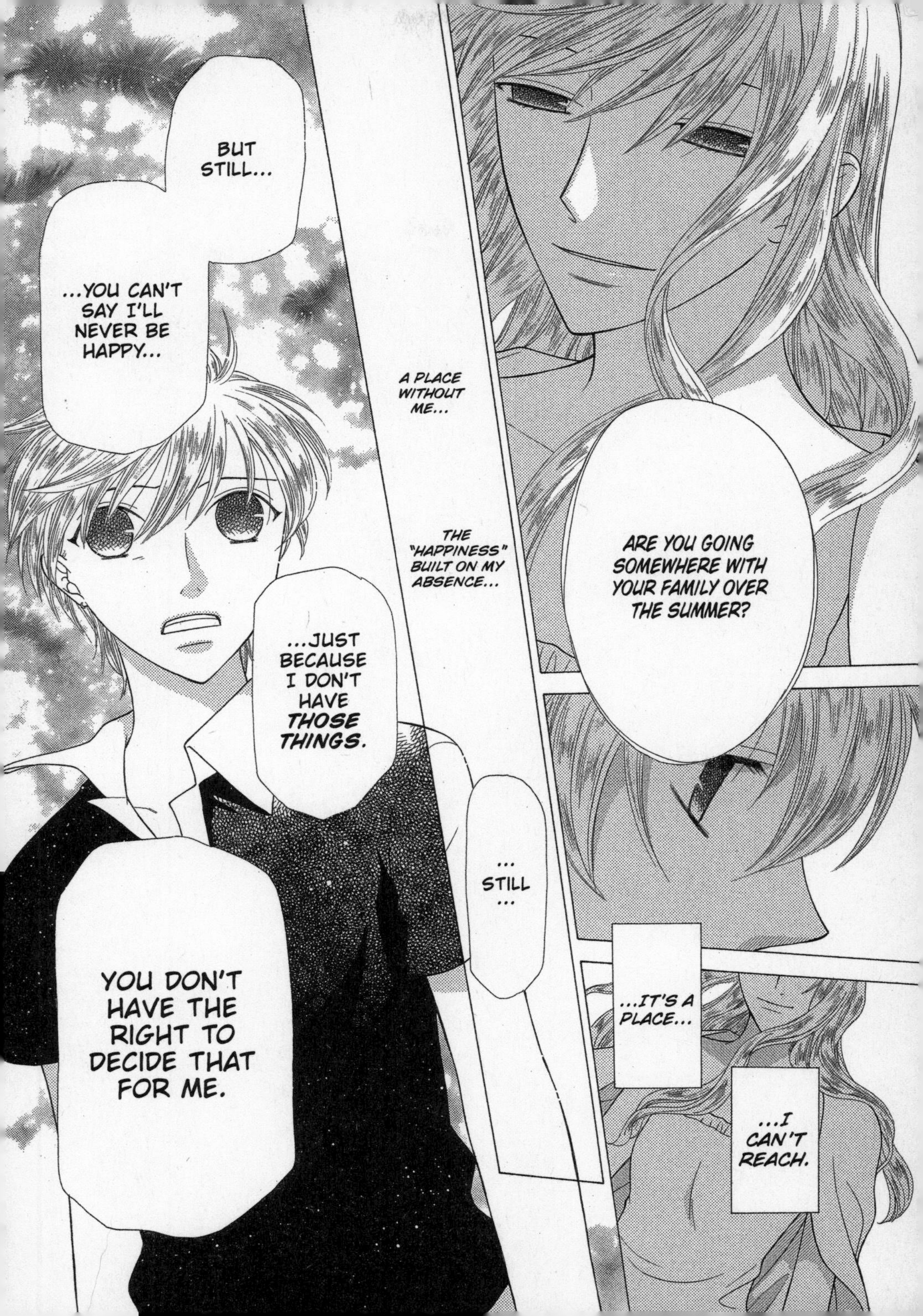
ARE YOU GOING SOMEWHERE WITH YOUR FAMILY OVER THE SUMMER?
...IT'S A PLACE...
...I CAN'T REACH.
A PLACE WITHOUT ME...
THE "HAPPINESS" BUILT ON MY ABSENCE...
...STILL...
BUT STILL...
...YOU CAN'T SAY I'LL NEVER BE HAPPY...
...JUST BECAUSE I DON'T HAVE *THOSE THINGS*.
YOU DON'T HAVE THE RIGHT TO DECIDE THAT FOR ME.

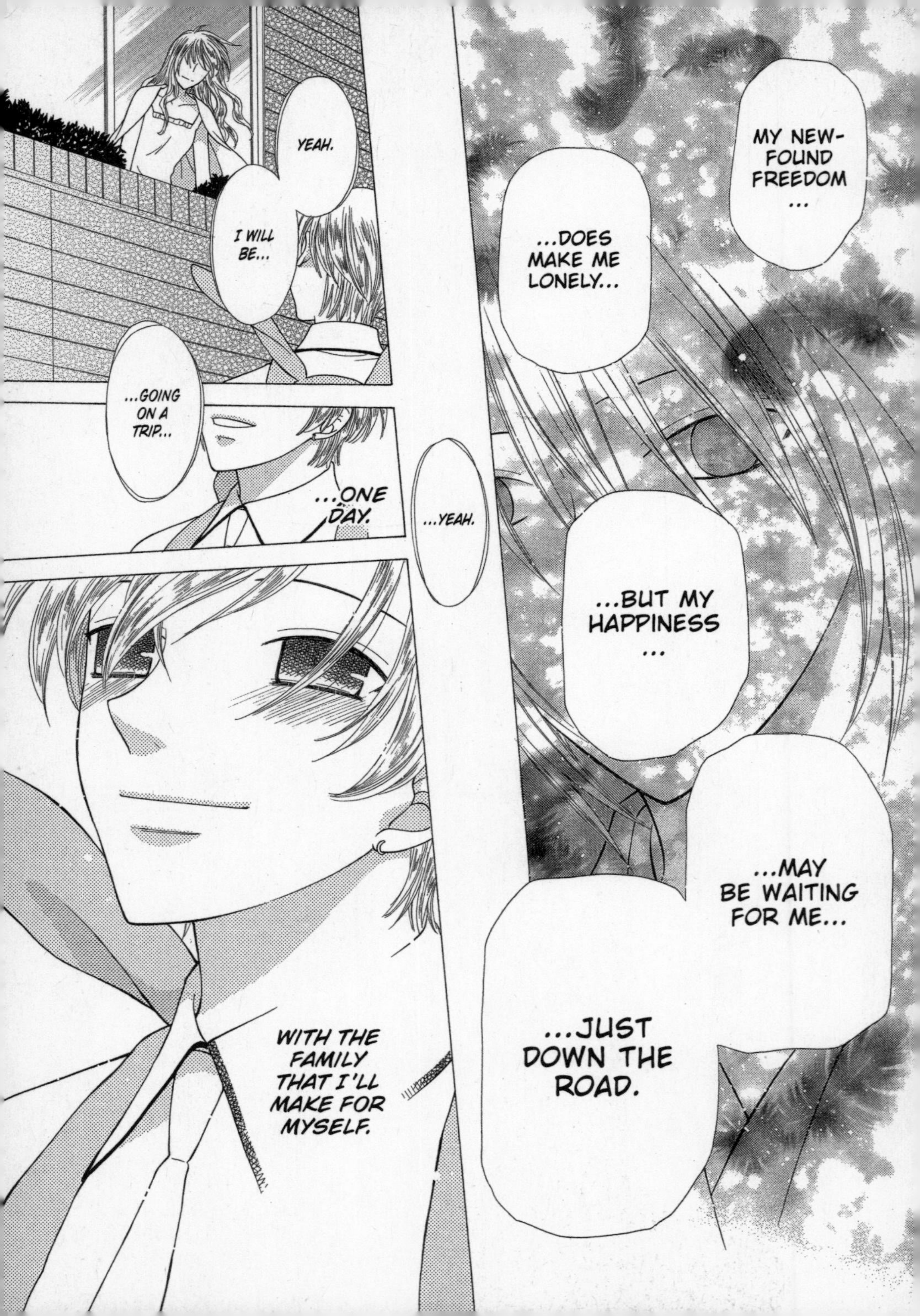
MY NEW-FOUND FREEDOM...
...DOES MAKE ME LONELY...
...BUT MY HAPPINESS...
...MAY BE WAITING FOR ME...
...JUST DOWN THE ROAD.
YEAH.
I WILL BE...
...GOING ON A TRIP...
...ONE DAY.
...YEAH.
WITH THE FAMILY THAT I'LL MAKE FOR MYSELF.

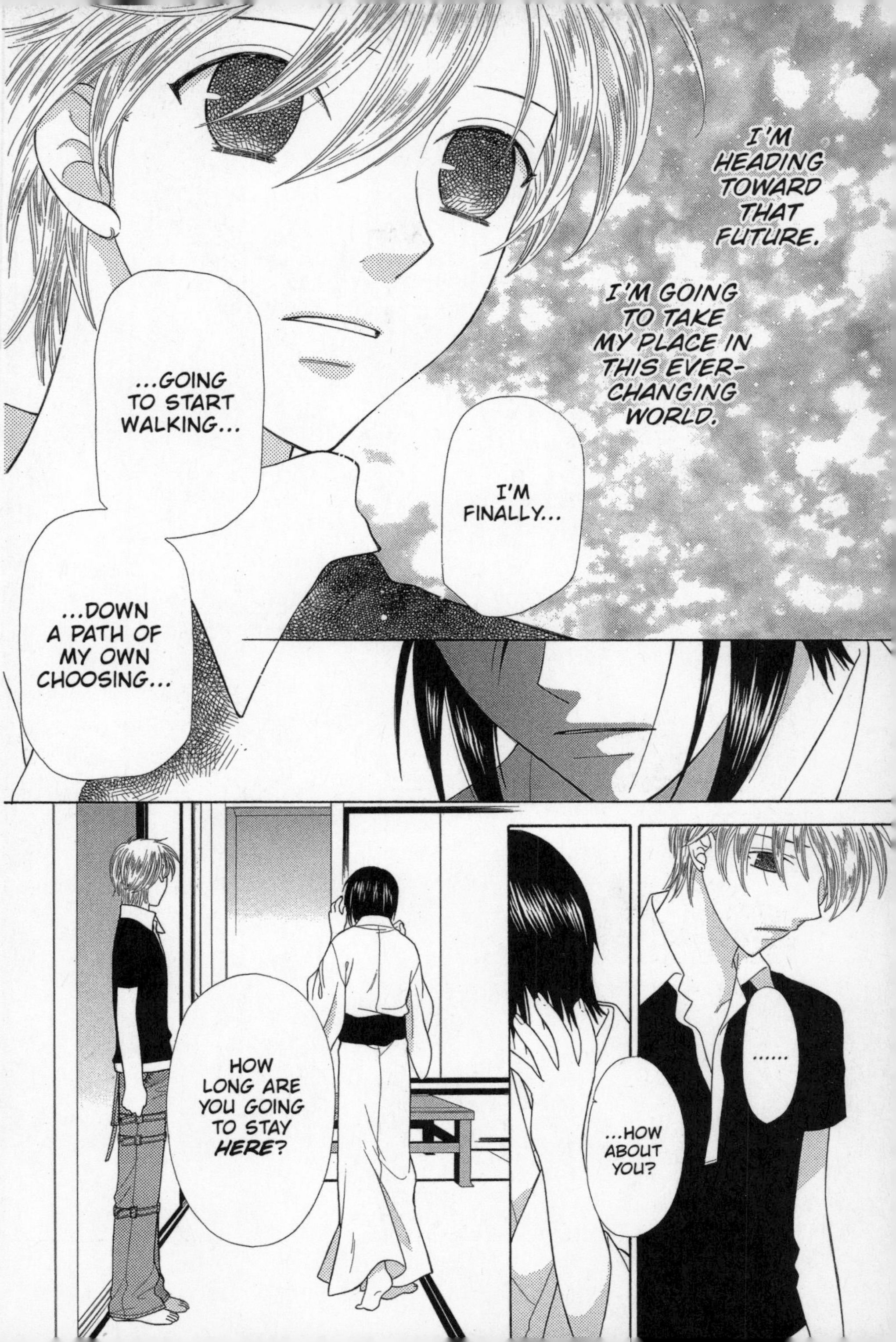
I'M HEADING TOWARD THAT FUTURE.
I'M GOING TO TAKE MY PLACE IN THIS EVER-CHANGING WORLD.
I'M FINALLY...
...GOING TO START WALKING...
...DOWN A PATH OF MY OWN CHOOSING...
......
...HOW ABOUT YOU?
HOW LONG ARE YOU GOING TO STAY *HERE*?

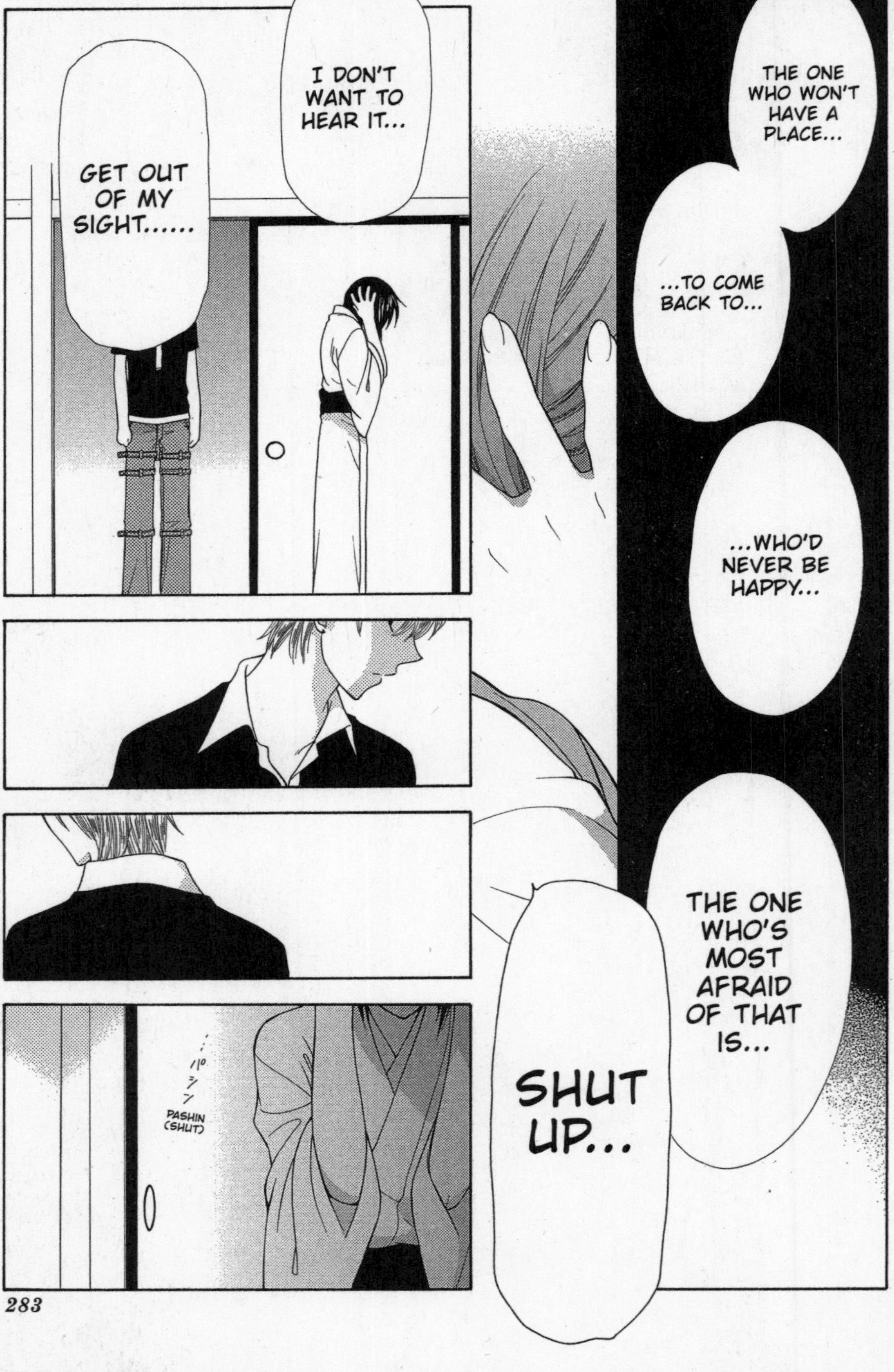
THE ONE WHO WON'T HAVE A PLACE...
...TO COME BACK TO...
...WHO'D NEVER BE HAPPY...
THE ONE WHO'S MOST AFRAID OF THAT IS...
SHUT UP...
I DON'T WANT TO HEAR IT...
GET OUT OF MY SIGHT......
パシン
PASHIN (SHUT)

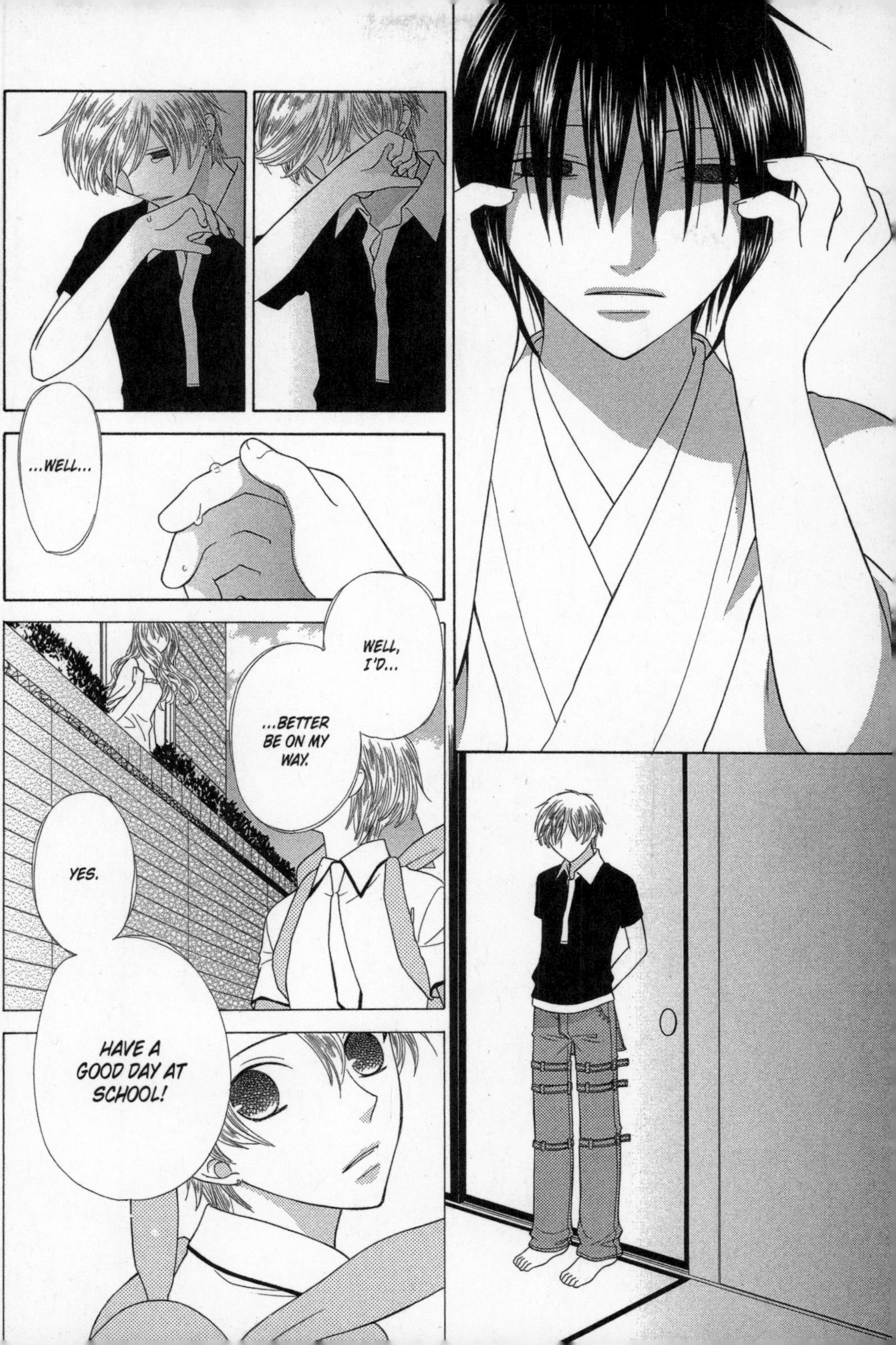
...WELL...
WELL, I'D...
...BETTER BE ON MY WAY.
YES.
HAVE A GOOD DAY AT SCHOOL!

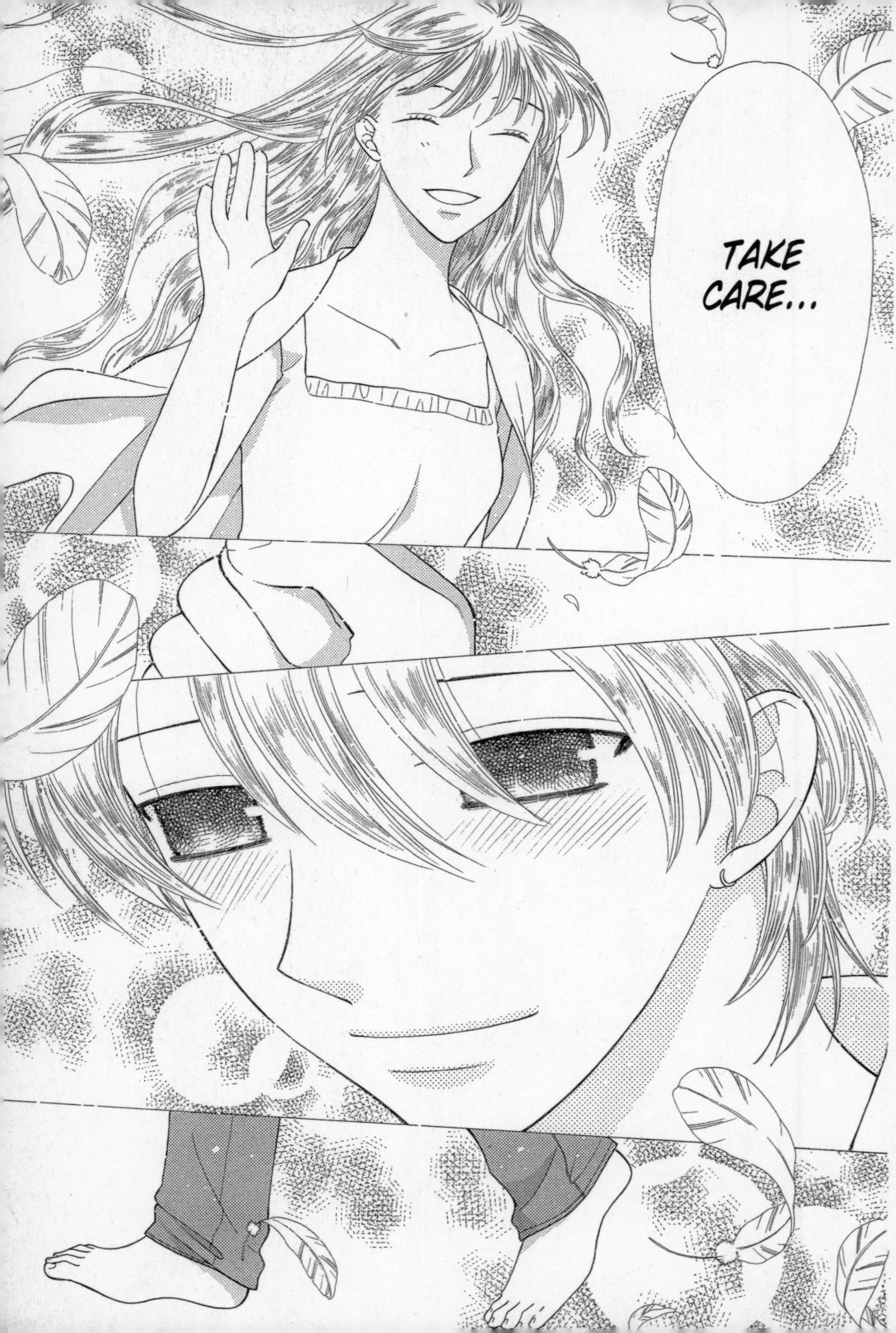
TAKE CARE...

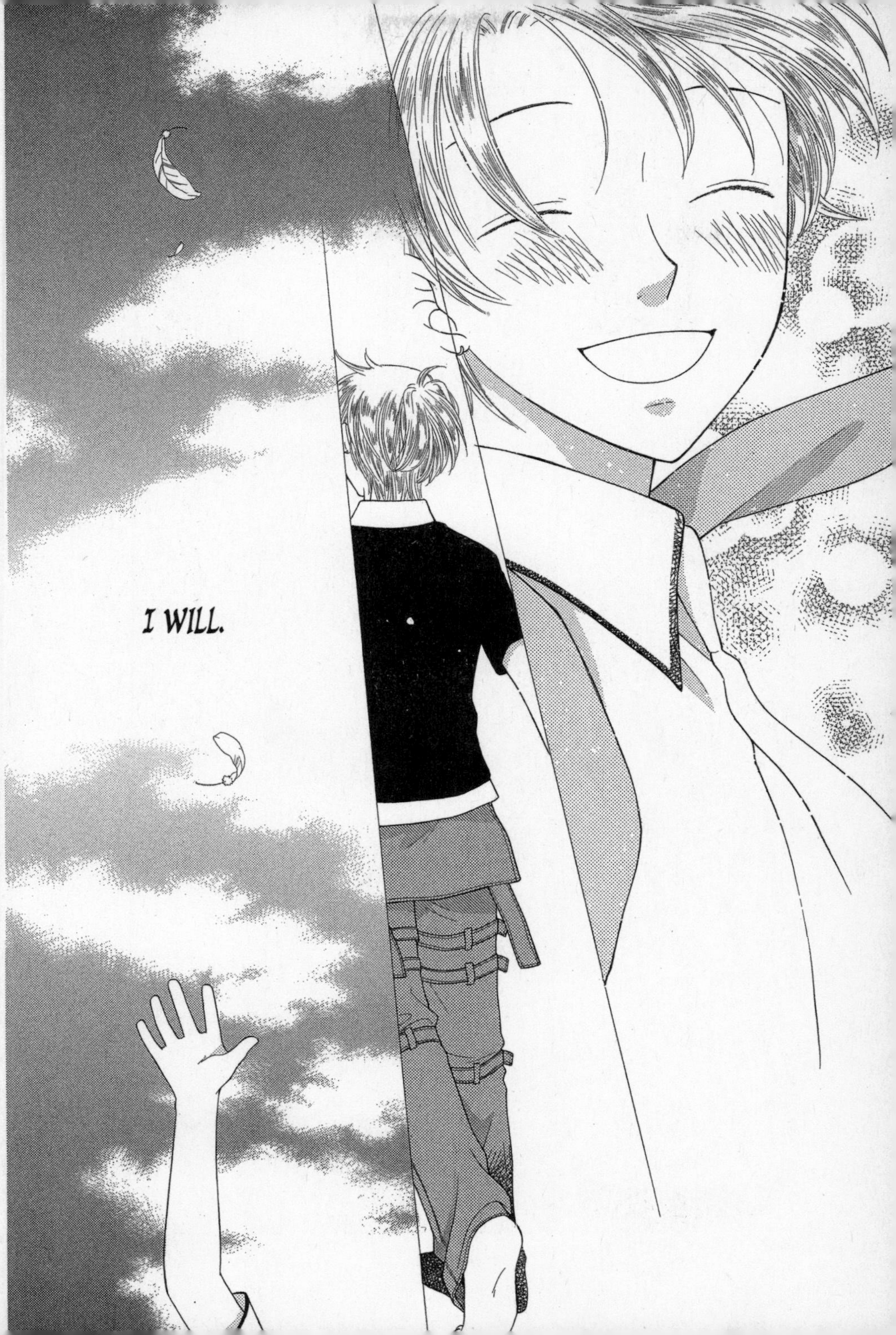
I WILL.

Chapter 117

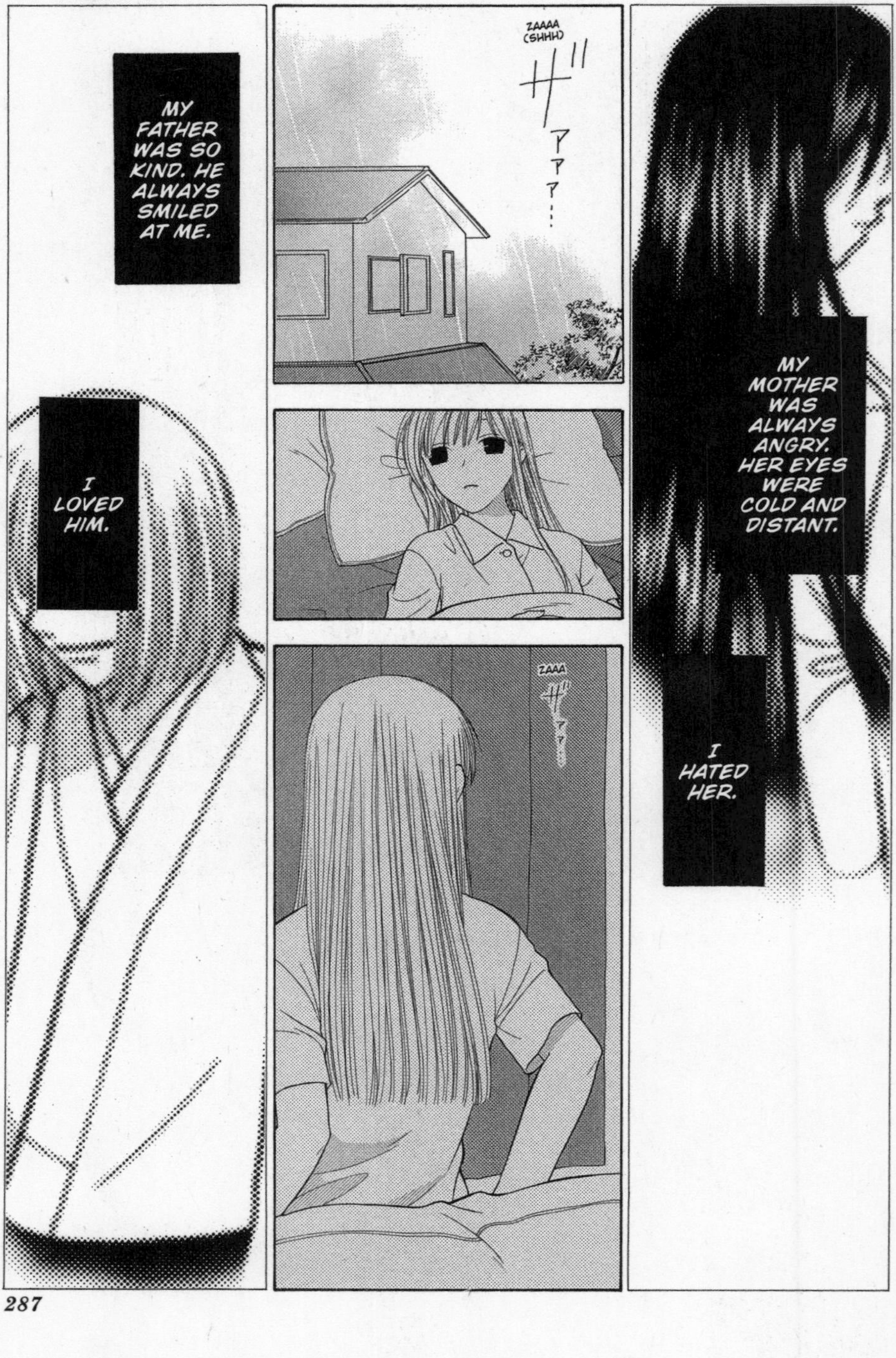

MY MOTHER WAS ALWAYS ANGRY. HER EYES WERE COLD AND DISTANT.
I HATED HER.
ZAAAA (SHHH)
ZAAA
MY FATHER WAS SO KIND. HE ALWAYS SMILED AT ME.
I LOVED HIM.

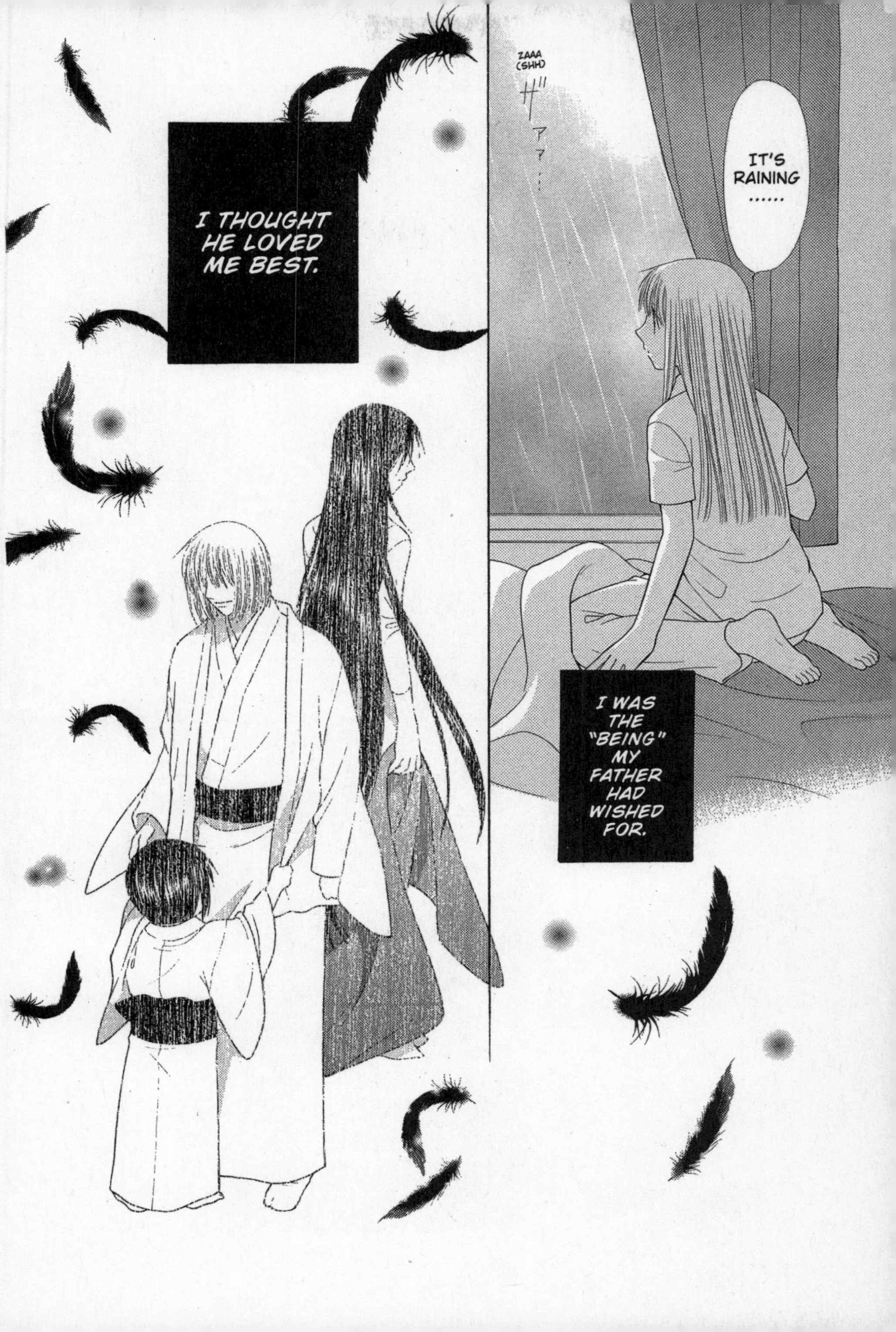
ZAAA (SHH)
IT'S RAINING ......
I WAS THE "BEING" MY FATHER HAD WISHED FOR.
I THOUGHT HE LOVED ME BEST.

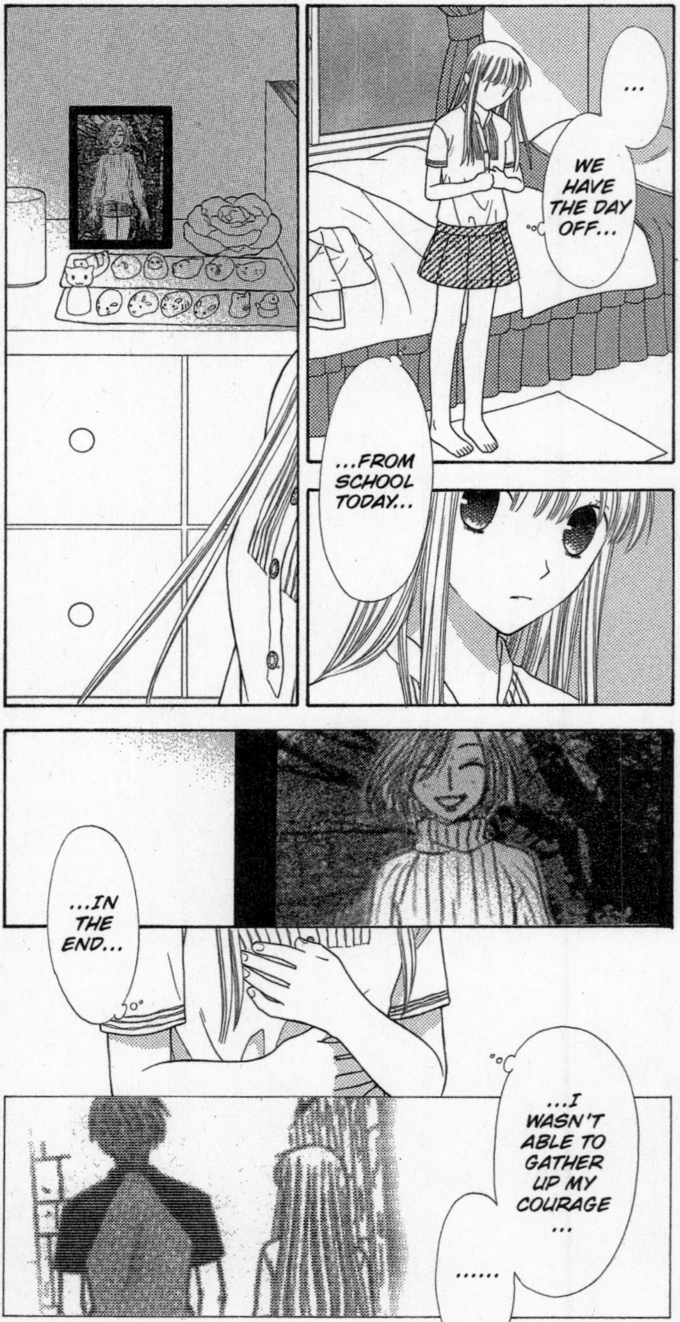
...
WE HAVE THE DAY OFF...
...FROM SCHOOL TODAY...
...IN THE END...
...I WASN'T ABLE TO GATHER UP MY COURAGE ...
......
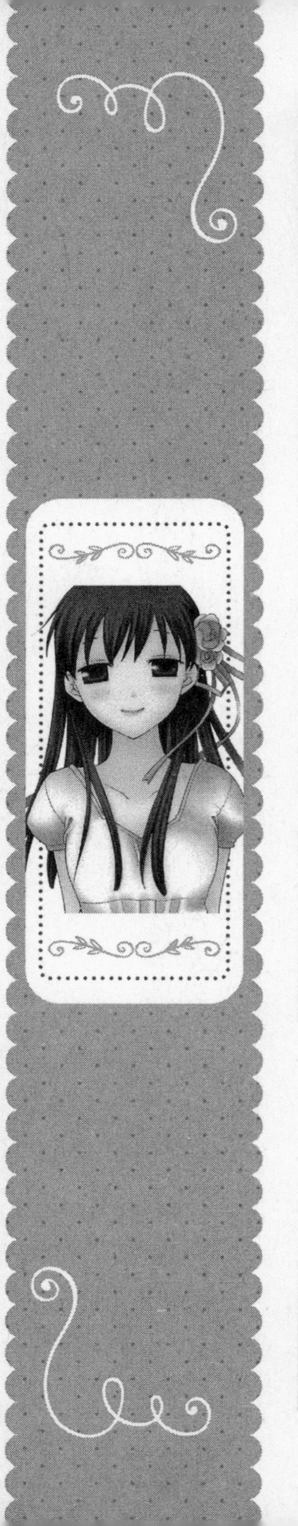

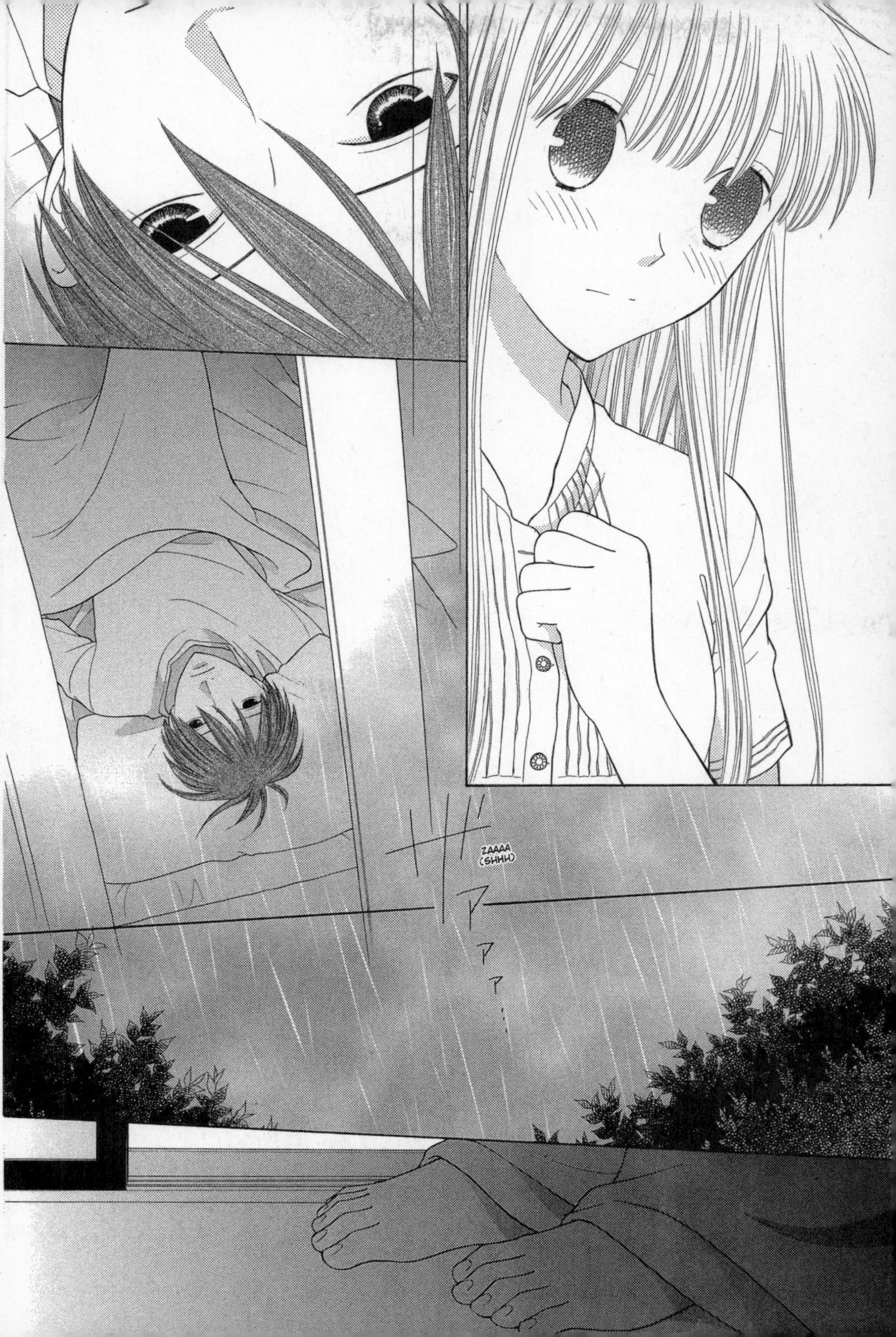
ZAAAA
(SHHH)

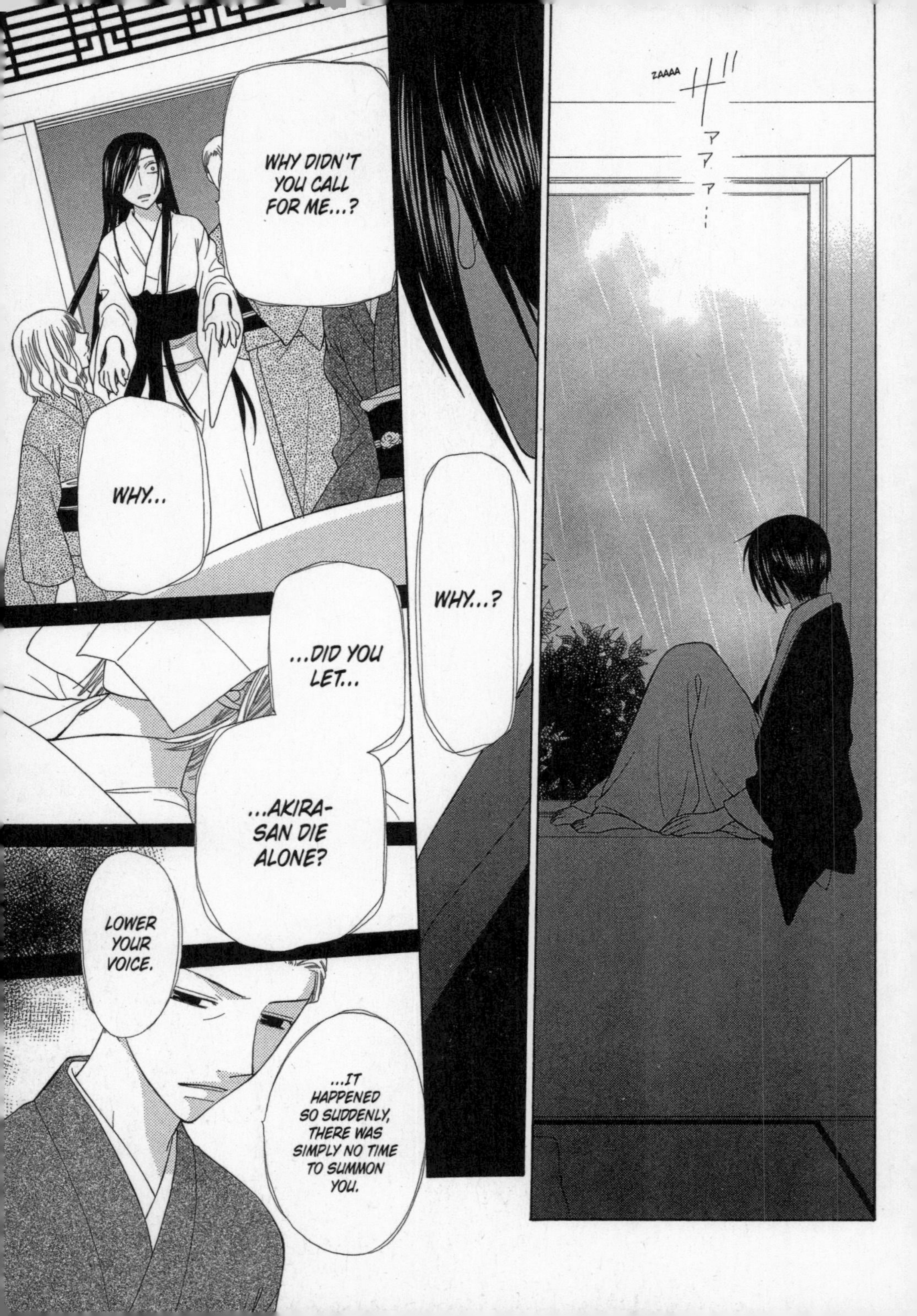
ZAAAA
ザァァァ…
WHY DIDN'T YOU CALL FOR ME...?
WHY...
WHY...?
...DID YOU LET...
...AKIRA-SAN DIE ALONE?
LOWER YOUR VOICE.
...IT HAPPENED SO SUDDENLY, THERE WAS SIMPLY NO TIME TO SUMMON YOU.

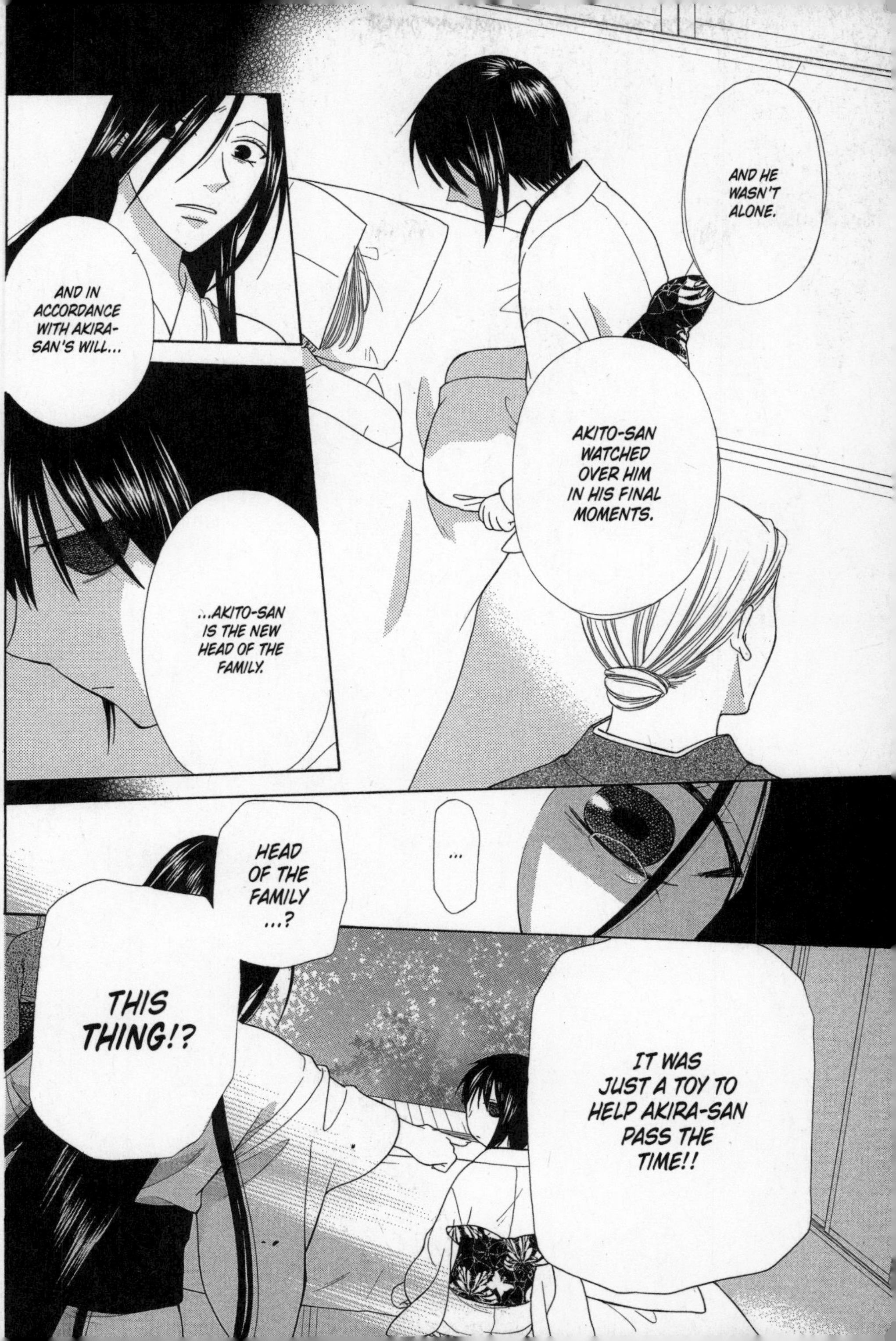
AND HE WASN'T ALONE.
AKITO-SAN WATCHED OVER HIM IN HIS FINAL MOMENTS.
AND IN ACCORDANCE WITH AKIRA-SAN'S WILL...
...AKITO-SAN IS THE NEW HEAD OF THE FAMILY.
...
HEAD OF THE FAMILY ...?
THIS THING!?
IT WAS JUST A TOY TO HELP AKIRA-SAN PASS THE TIME!!

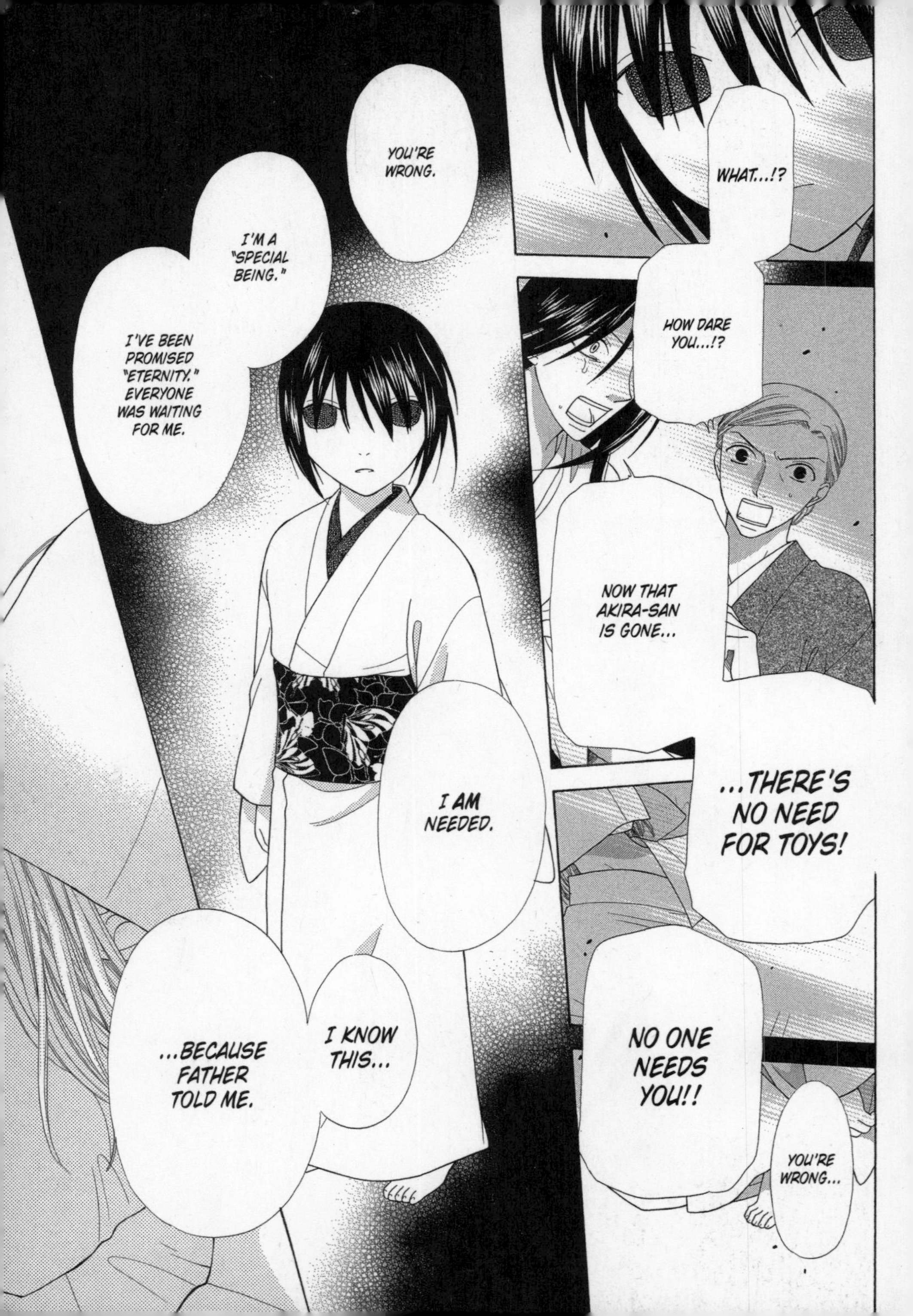
WHAT...!?
HOW DARE YOU...!?
NOW THAT AKIRA-SAN IS GONE...
...THERE'S NO NEED FOR TOYS!
NO ONE NEEDS YOU!!
YOU'RE WRONG...
YOU'RE WRONG.
I'M A "SPECIAL BEING."
I'VE BEEN PROMISED "ETERNITY." EVERYONE WAS WAITING FOR ME.
I AM NEEDED.
I KNOW THIS...
...BECAUSE FATHER TOLD ME.

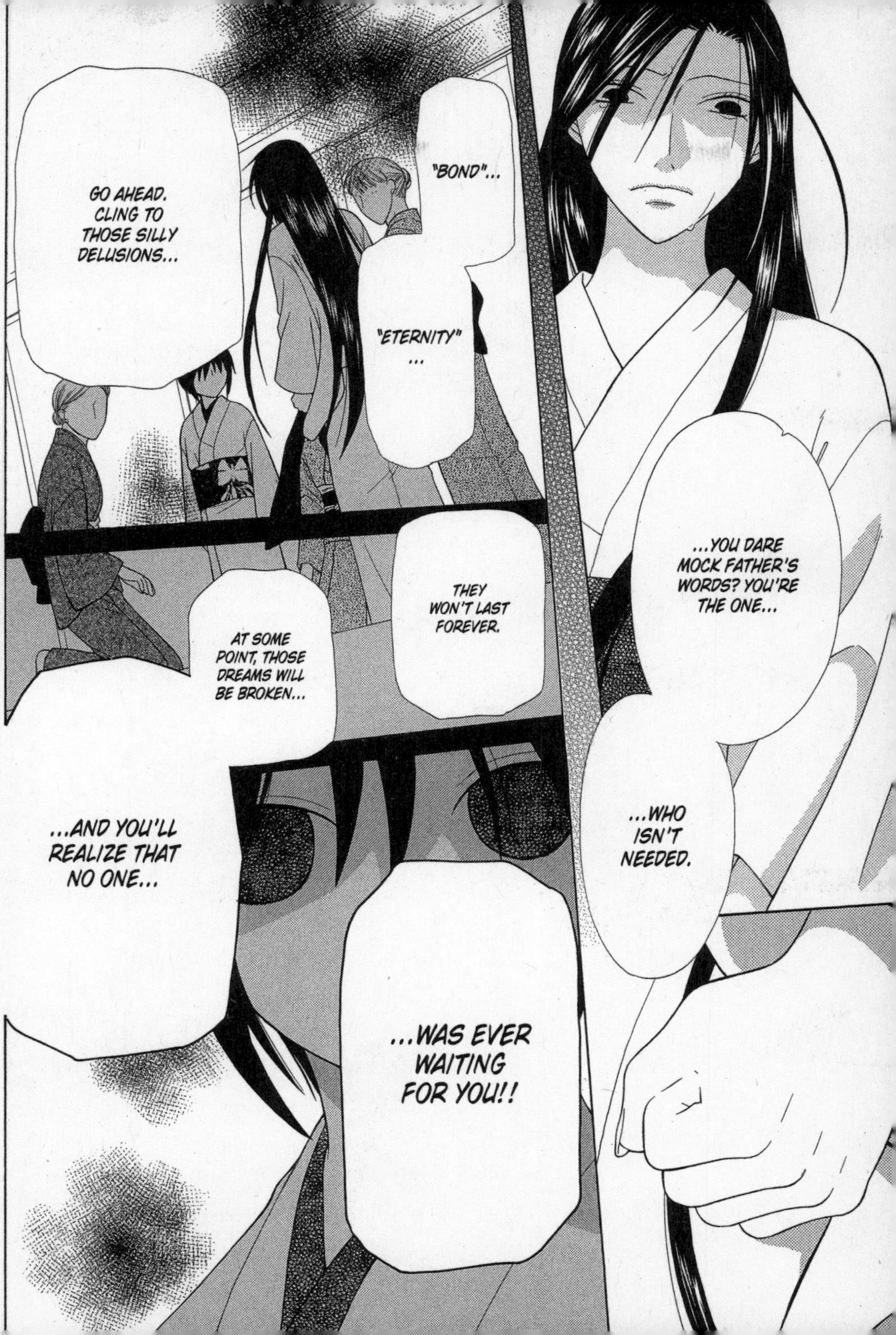
...YOU DARE MOCK FATHER'S WORDS? YOU'RE THE ONE...
...WHO ISN'T NEEDED.
"BOND"...
"ETERNITY" ...
GO AHEAD. CLING TO THOSE SILLY DELUSIONS...
THEY WON'T LAST FOREVER.
AT SOME POINT, THOSE DREAMS WILL BE BROKEN...
...AND YOU'LL REALIZE THAT NO ONE...
...WAS EVER WAITING FOR YOU!!

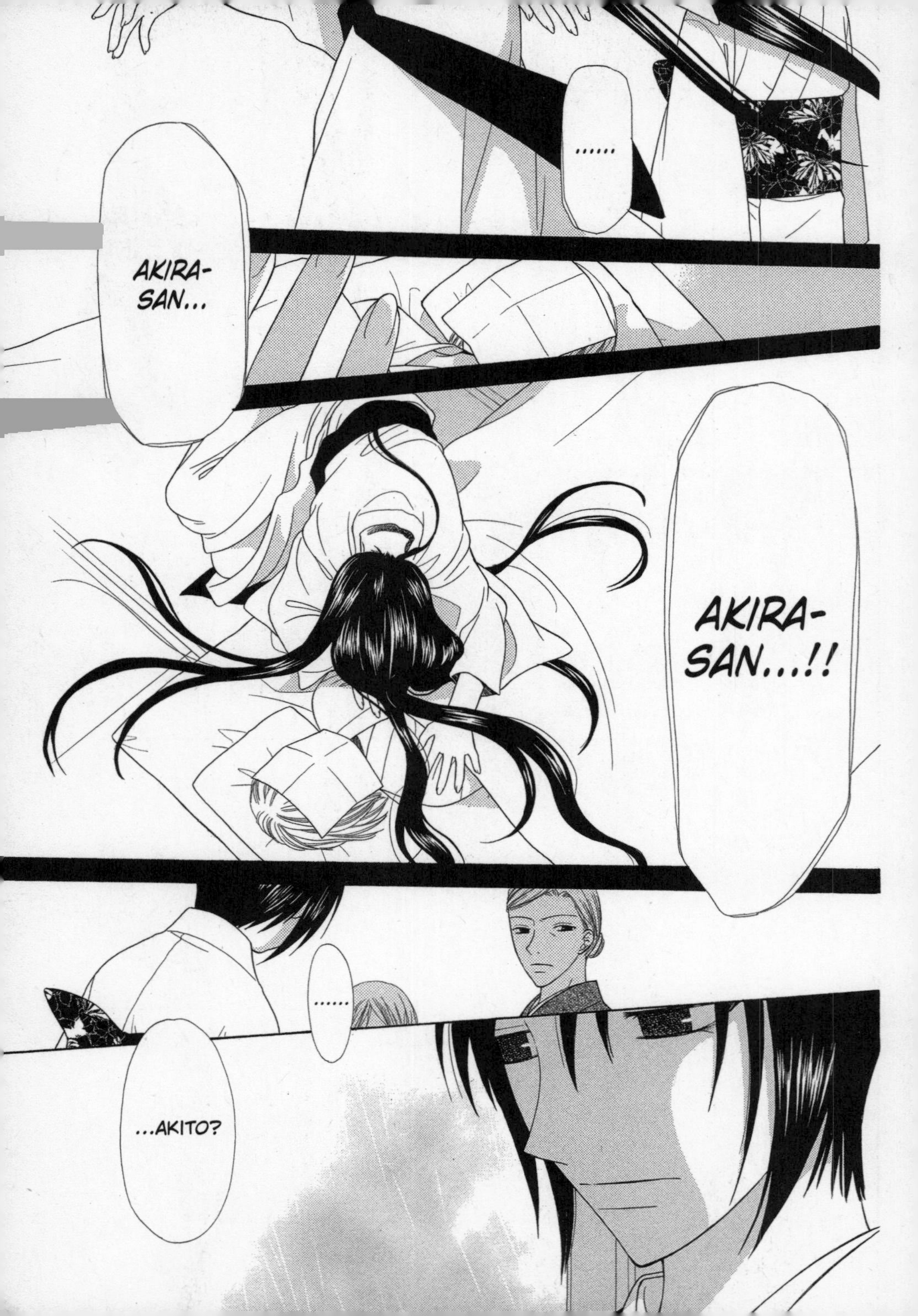
......
AKIRA-SAN...
AKIRA-SAN...!!
......
...AKITO?

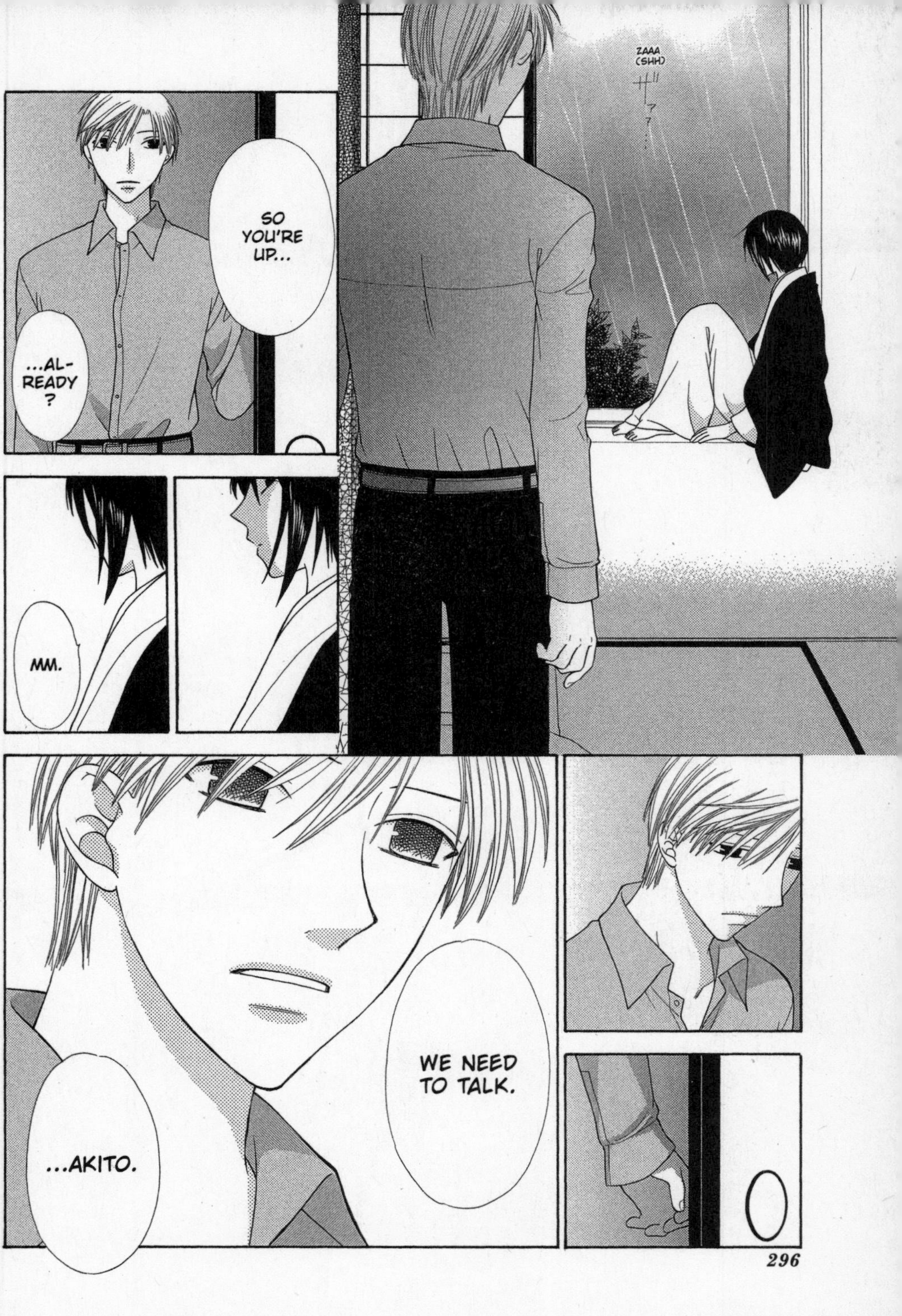
ZAAA (SHH)
SO YOU'RE UP...
...AL-READY?
MM.
WE NEED TO TALK.
...AKITO.

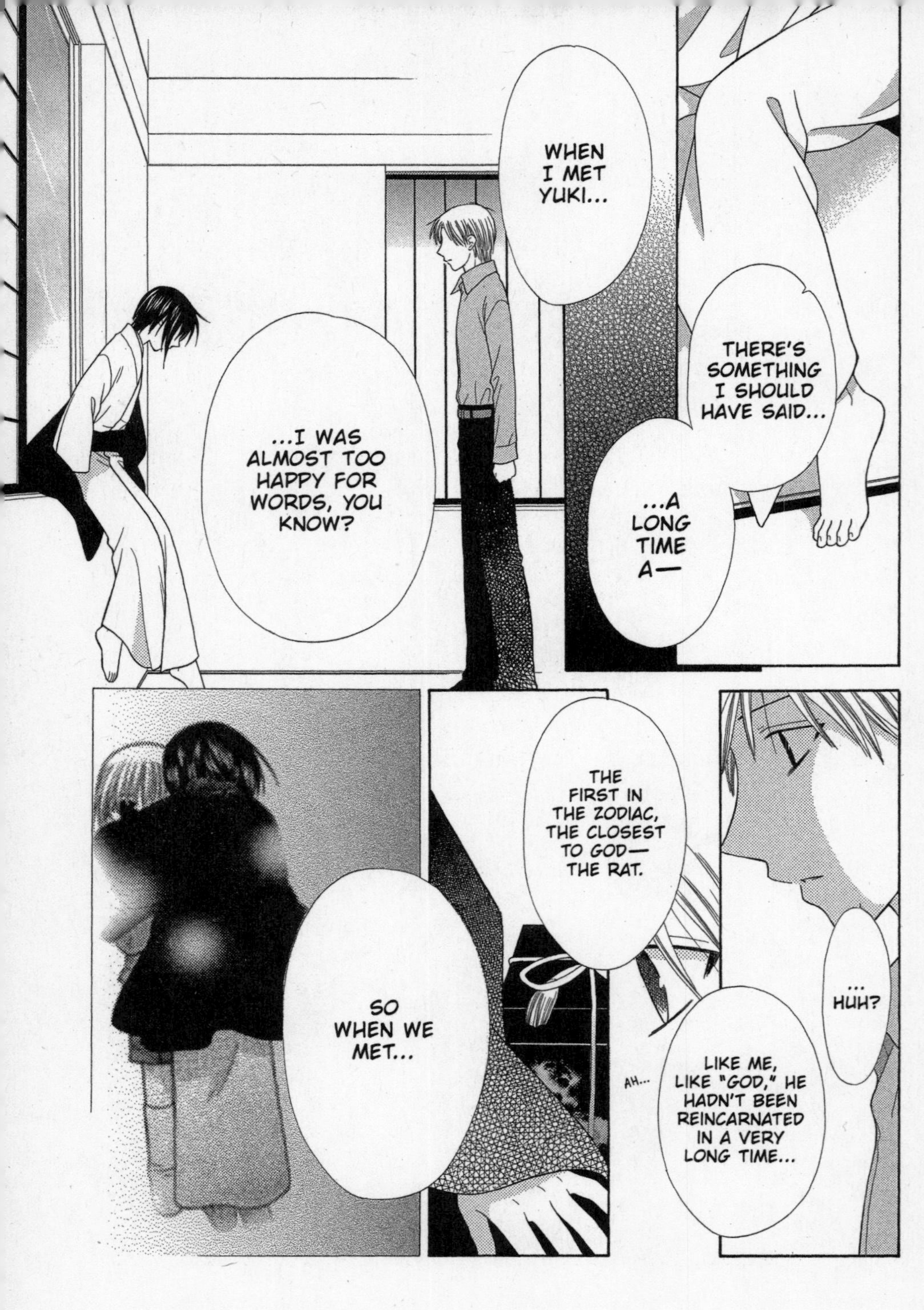
THERE'S SOMETHING I SHOULD HAVE SAID...
...A LONG TIME A—
WHEN I MET YUKI...
...I WAS ALMOST TOO HAPPY FOR WORDS, YOU KNOW?
...HUH?
LIKE ME, LIKE "GOD," HE HADN'T BEEN REINCARNATED IN A VERY LONG TIME...
AH...
THE FIRST IN THE ZODIAC, THE CLOSEST TO GOD— THE RAT.
SO WHEN WE MET...

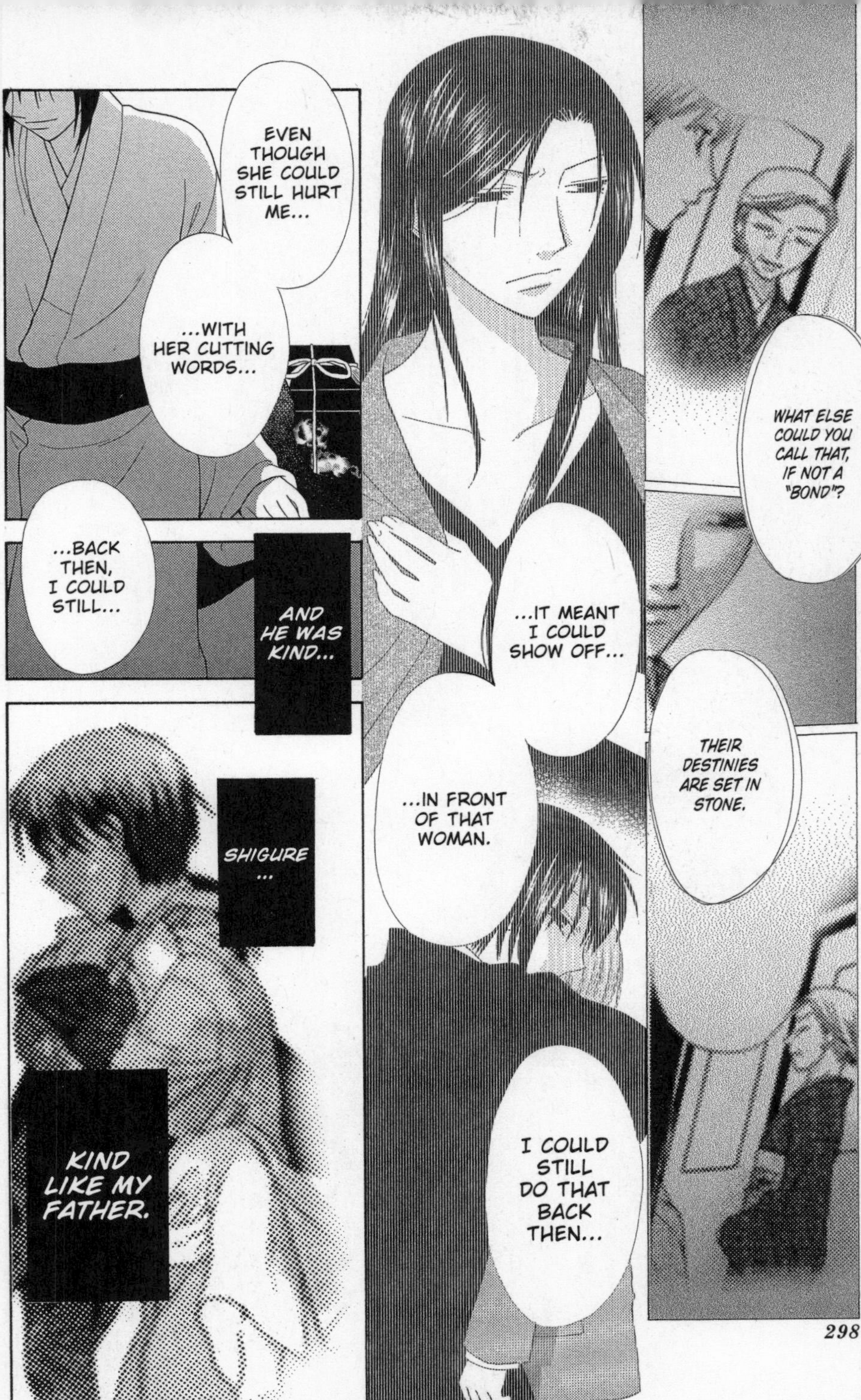
WHAT ELSE COULD YOU CALL THAT, IF NOT A "BOND"?
THEIR DESTINIES ARE SET IN STONE.
...IT MEANT I COULD SHOW OFF...
...IN FRONT OF THAT WOMAN.
I COULD STILL DO THAT BACK THEN...
EVEN THOUGH SHE COULD STILL HURT ME...
...WITH HER CUTTING WORDS...
...BACK THEN, I COULD STILL...
AND HE WAS KIND...
SHIGURE ...
KIND LIKE MY FATHER.

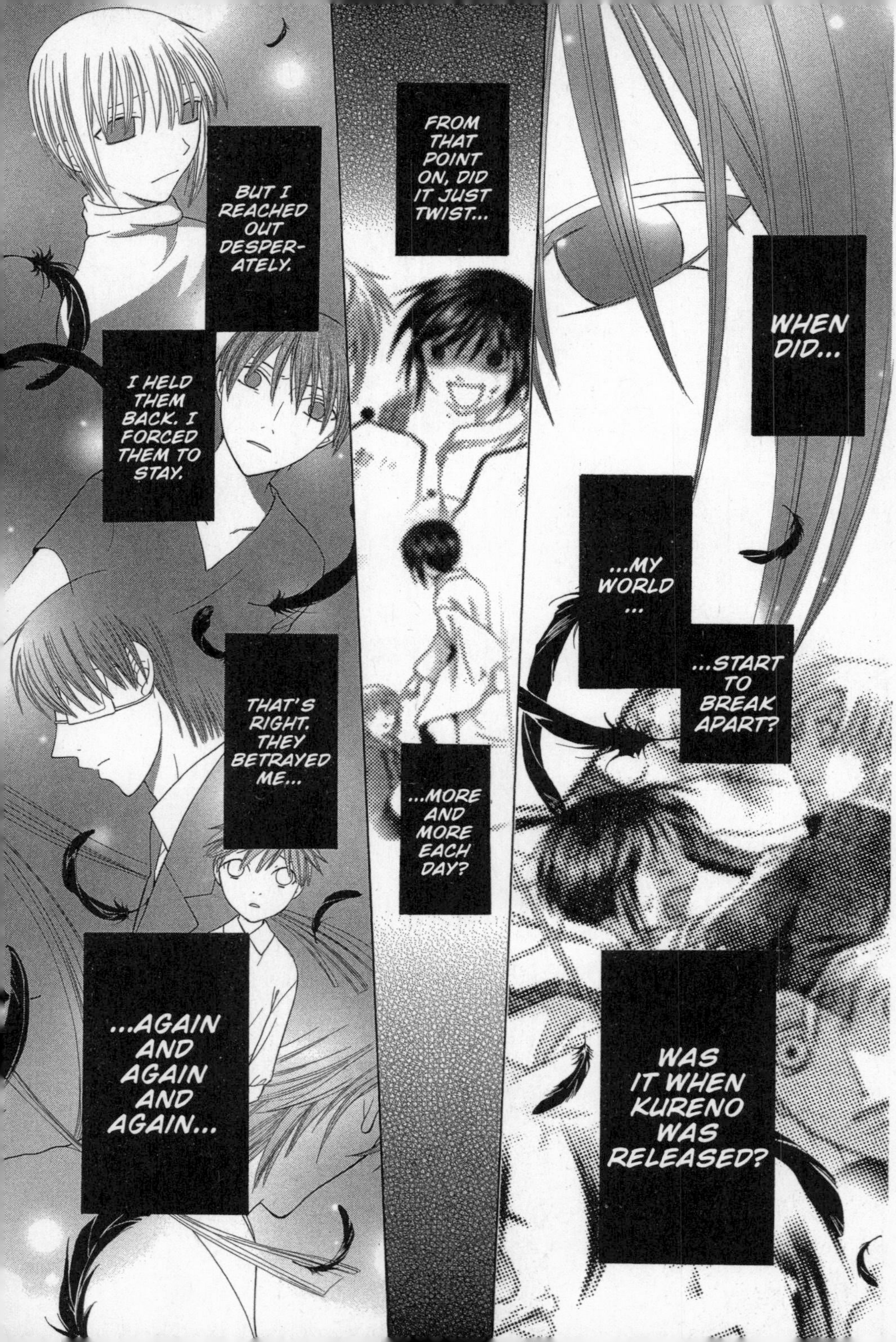
WHEN DID...
...MY WORLD ...
...START TO BREAK APART?
WAS IT WHEN KURENO WAS RELEASED?
FROM THAT POINT ON, DID IT JUST TWIST...
...MORE AND MORE EACH DAY?
BUT I REACHED OUT DESPERATELY.
I HELD THEM BACK. I FORCED THEM TO STAY.
THAT'S RIGHT. THEY BETRAYED ME...
...AGAIN AND AGAIN AND AGAIN...

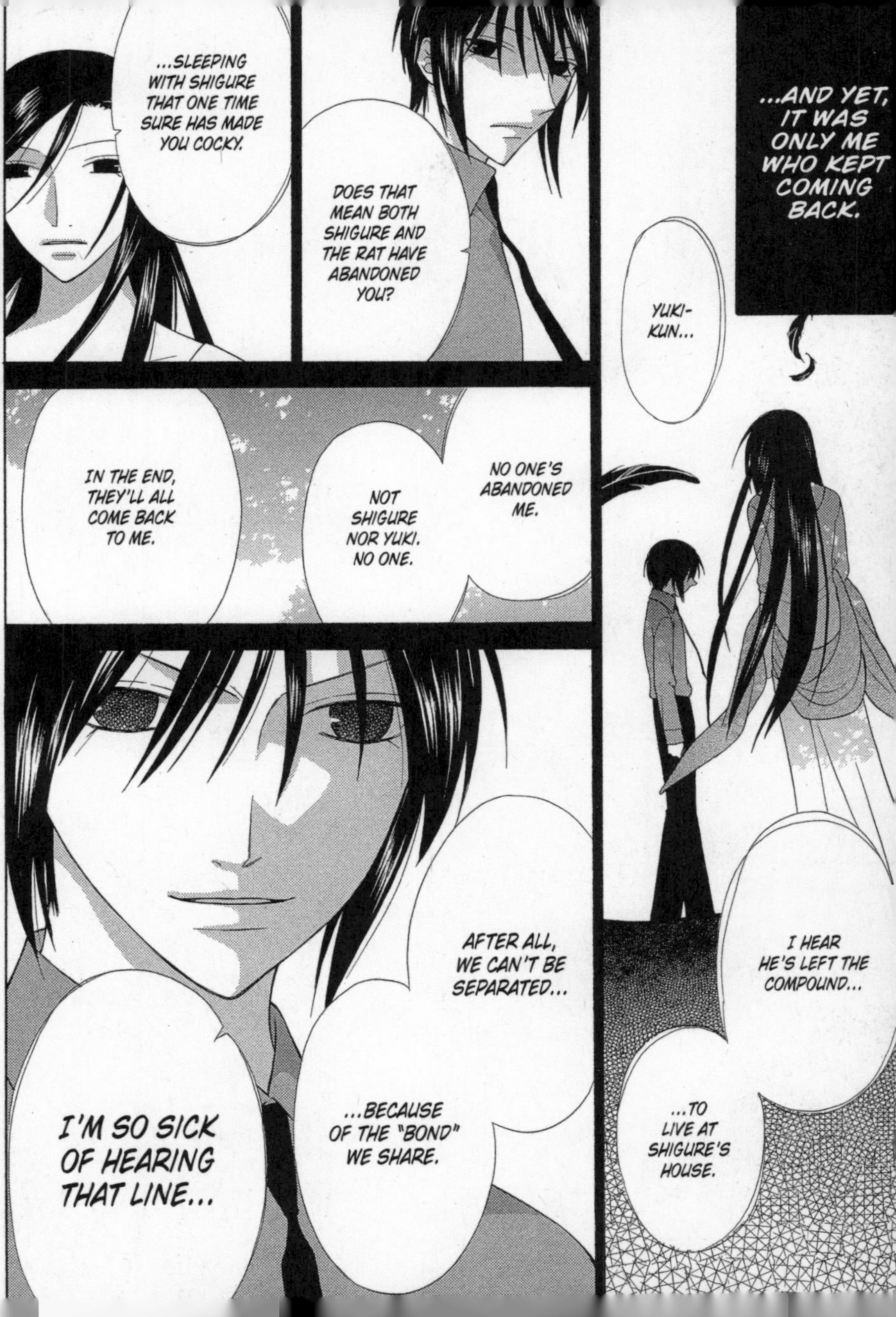
...AND YET, IT WAS ONLY ME WHO KEPT COMING BACK.
YUKI-KUN...
I HEAR HE'S LEFT THE COMPOUND...
...TO LIVE AT SHIGURE'S HOUSE.
DOES THAT MEAN BOTH SHIGURE AND THE RAT HAVE ABANDONED YOU?
...SLEEPING WITH SHIGURE THAT ONE TIME SURE HAS MADE YOU COCKY.
NO ONE'S ABANDONED ME.
NOT SHIGURE NOR YUKI. NO ONE.
IN THE END, THEY'LL ALL COME BACK TO ME.
AFTER ALL, WE CAN'T BE SEPARATED...
...BECAUSE OF THE "BOND" WE SHARE.
I'M SO SICK OF HEARING THAT LINE...

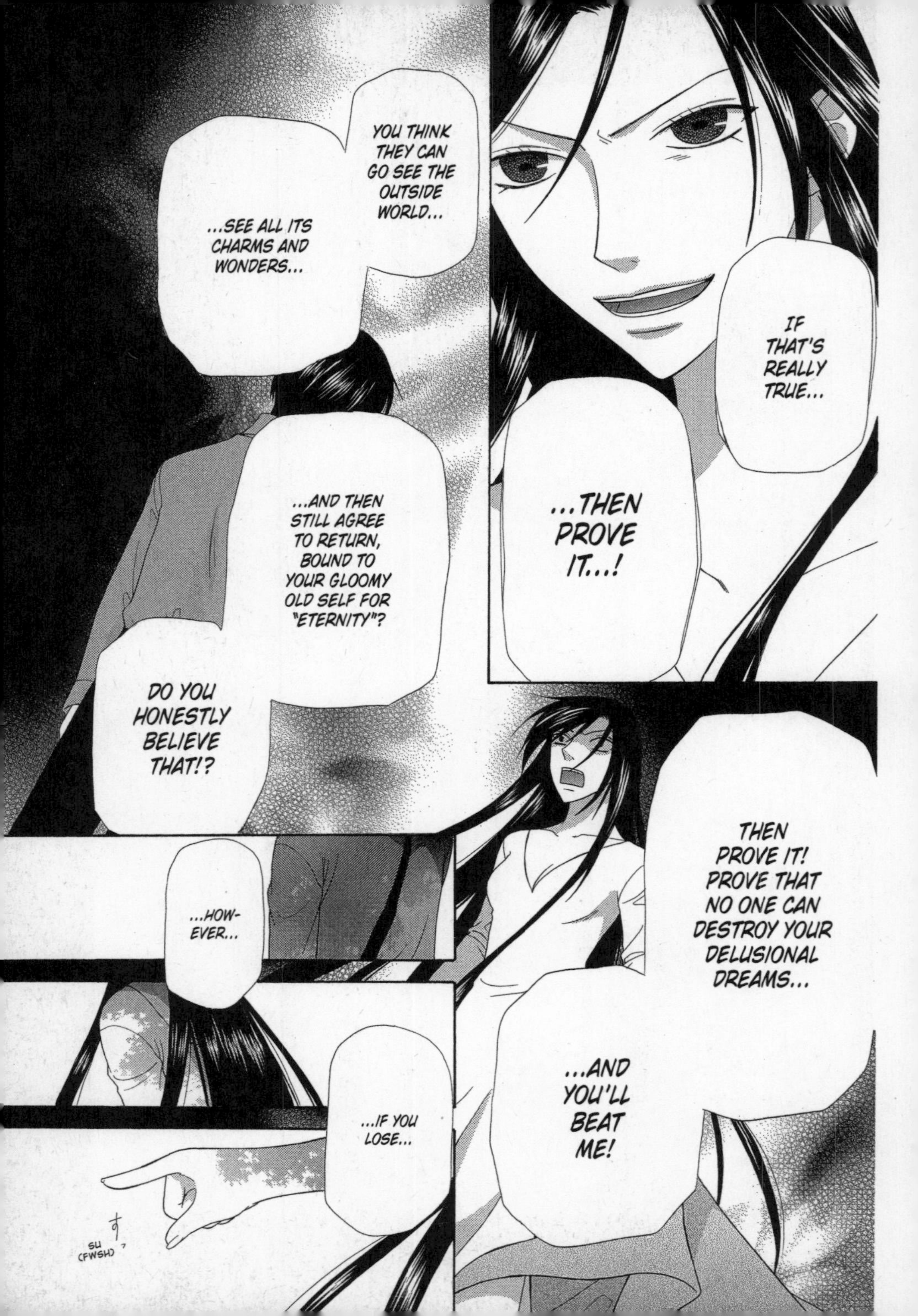
IF THAT'S REALLY TRUE...
...THEN PROVE IT...!
YOU THINK THEY CAN GO SEE THE OUTSIDE WORLD...
...SEE ALL ITS CHARMS AND WONDERS...
...AND THEN STILL AGREE TO RETURN, BOUND TO YOUR GLOOMY OLD SELF FOR "ETERNITY"?
DO YOU HONESTLY BELIEVE THAT!?
THEN PROVE IT! PROVE THAT NO ONE CAN DESTROY YOUR DELUSIONAL DREAMS...
...AND YOU'LL BEAT ME!
...HOW-EVER...
...IF YOU LOSE...
す
SU (FWSH)

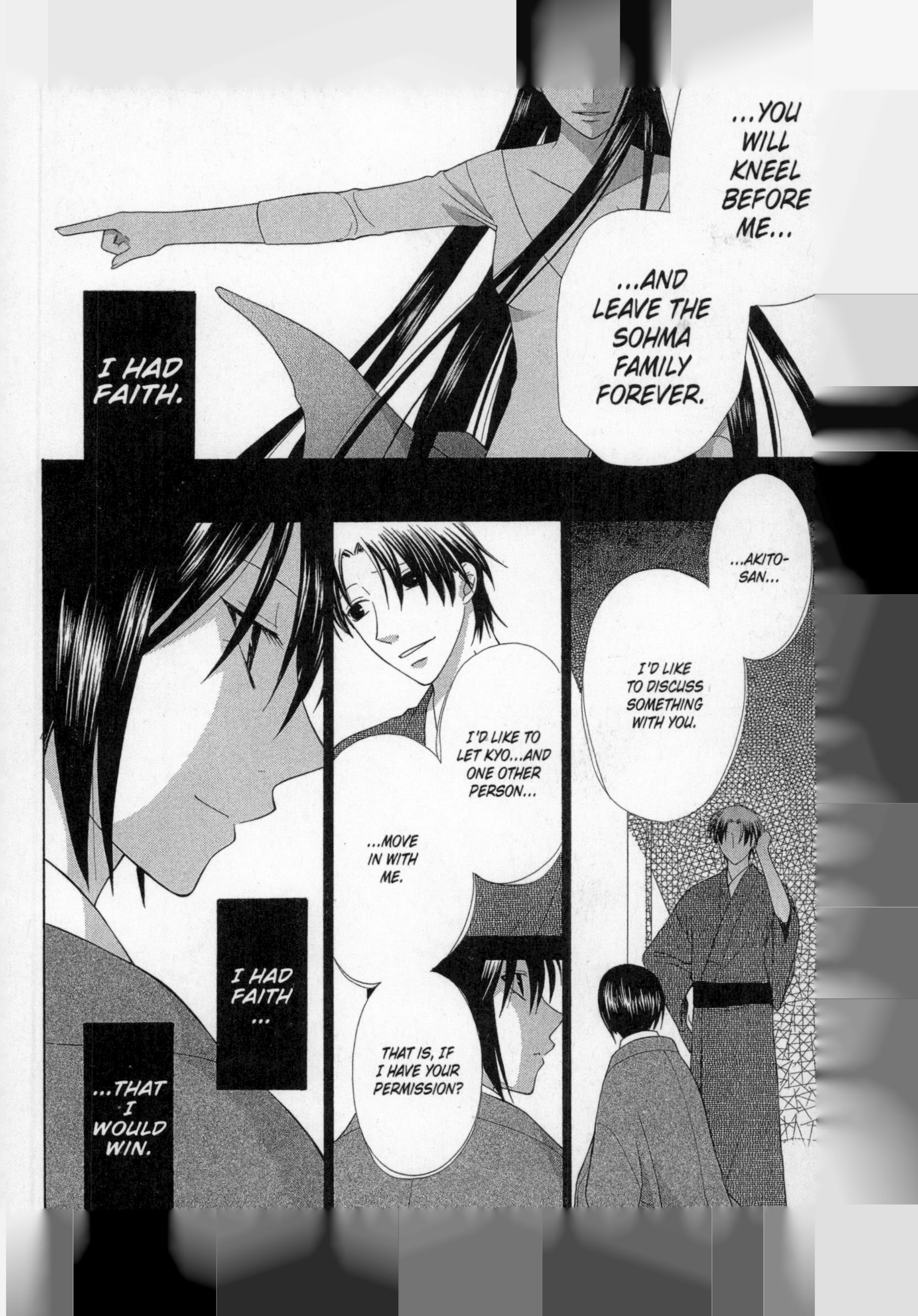
...YOU WILL KNEEL BEFORE ME...
...AND LEAVE THE SOHMA FAMILY FOREVER.
I HAD FAITH.
...AKITO-SAN...
I'D LIKE TO DISCUSS SOMETHING WITH YOU.
I'D LIKE TO LET KYO...AND ONE OTHER PERSON...
...MOVE IN WITH ME.
THAT IS, IF I HAVE YOUR PERMISSION?
I HAD FAITH...
...THAT I WOULD WIN.

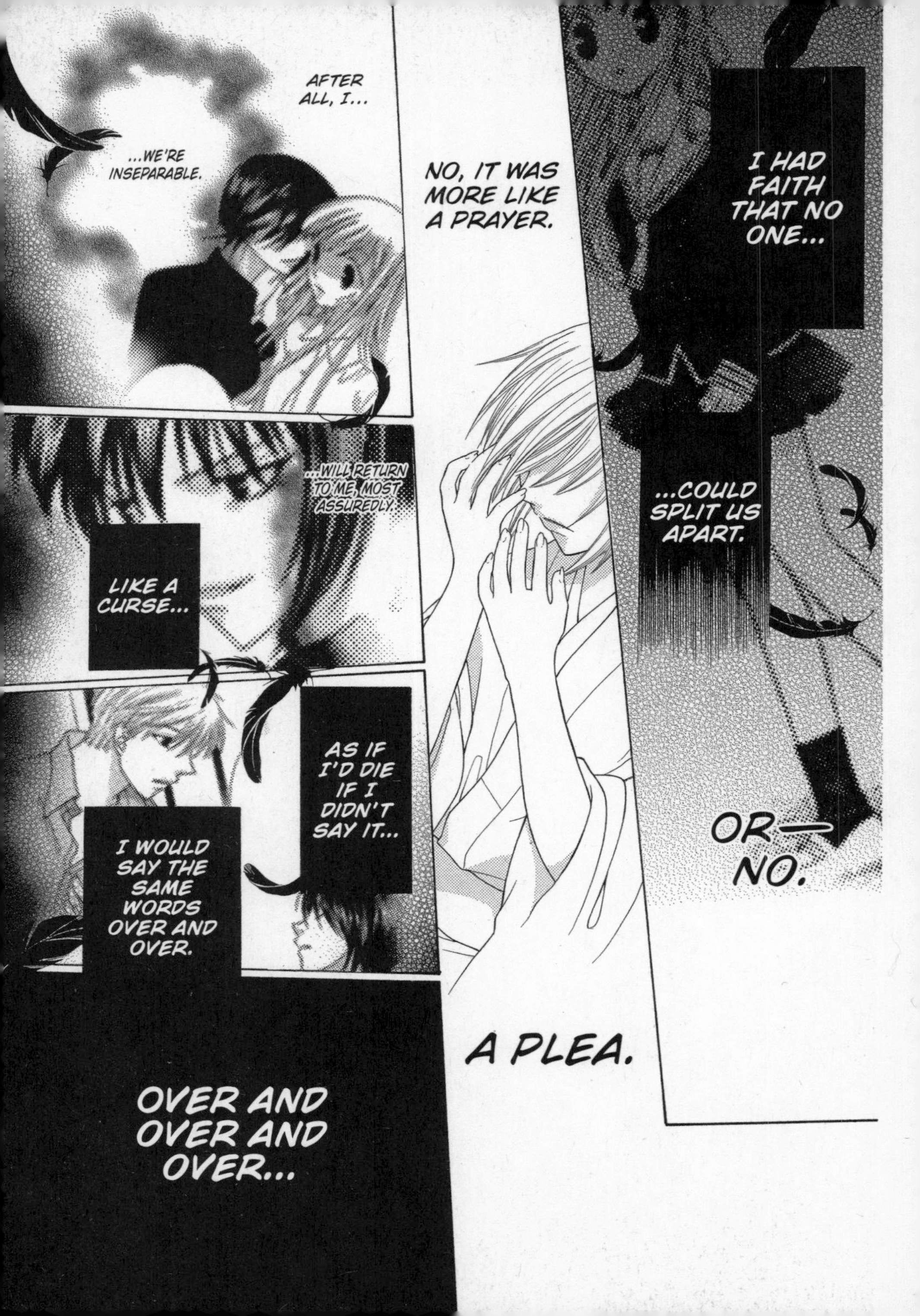
I HAD FAITH THAT NO ONE...
...COULD SPLIT US APART.
OR— NO.
NO, IT WAS MORE LIKE A PRAYER.
A PLEA.
AFTER ALL, I...
...WE'RE INSEPARABLE.
...WILL RETURN TO ME, MOST ASSUREDLY.
LIKE A CURSE...
AS IF I'D DIE IF I DIDN'T SAY IT...
I WOULD SAY THE SAME WORDS OVER AND OVER.
OVER AND OVER AND OVER...

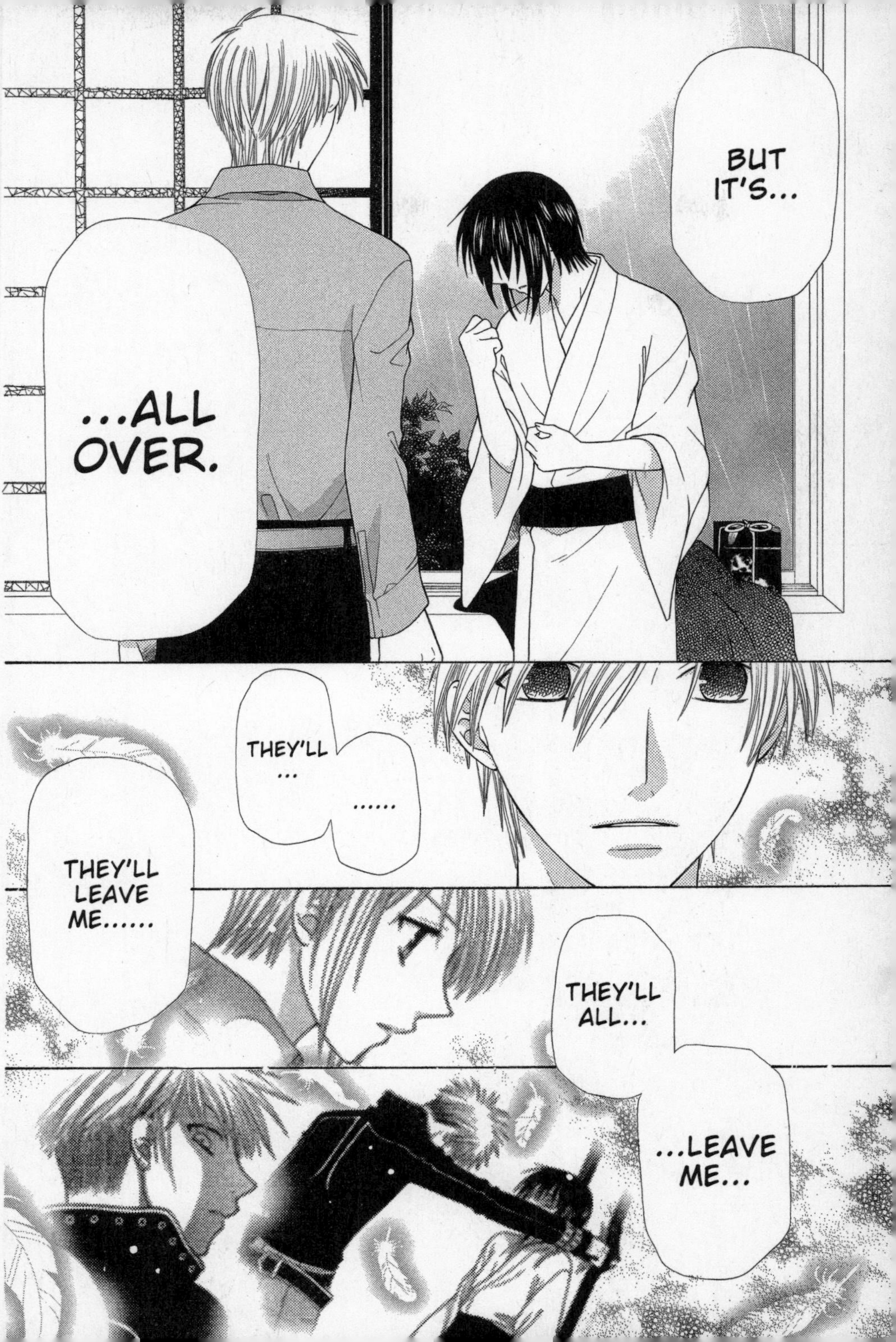
BUT IT'S...
...ALL OVER.
THEY'LL...
......
THEY'LL LEAVE ME......
THEY'LL ALL...
...LEAVE ME...

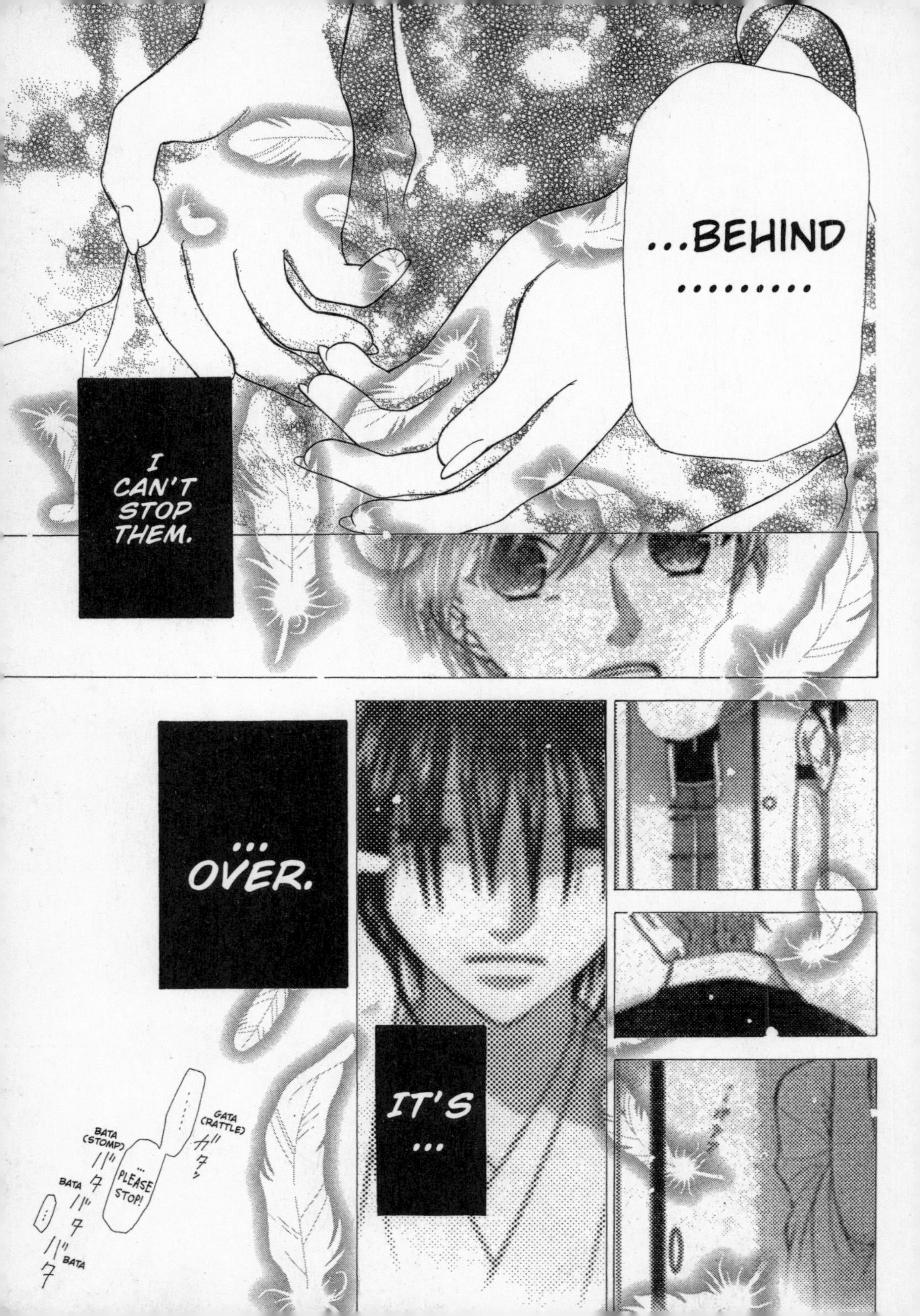

...BEHIND
....
I CAN'T STOP THEM.
IT'S ...
... OVER.
......
GATA (RATTLE)
... PLEASE STOP!
BATA (STOMP)
BATA
BATA
...

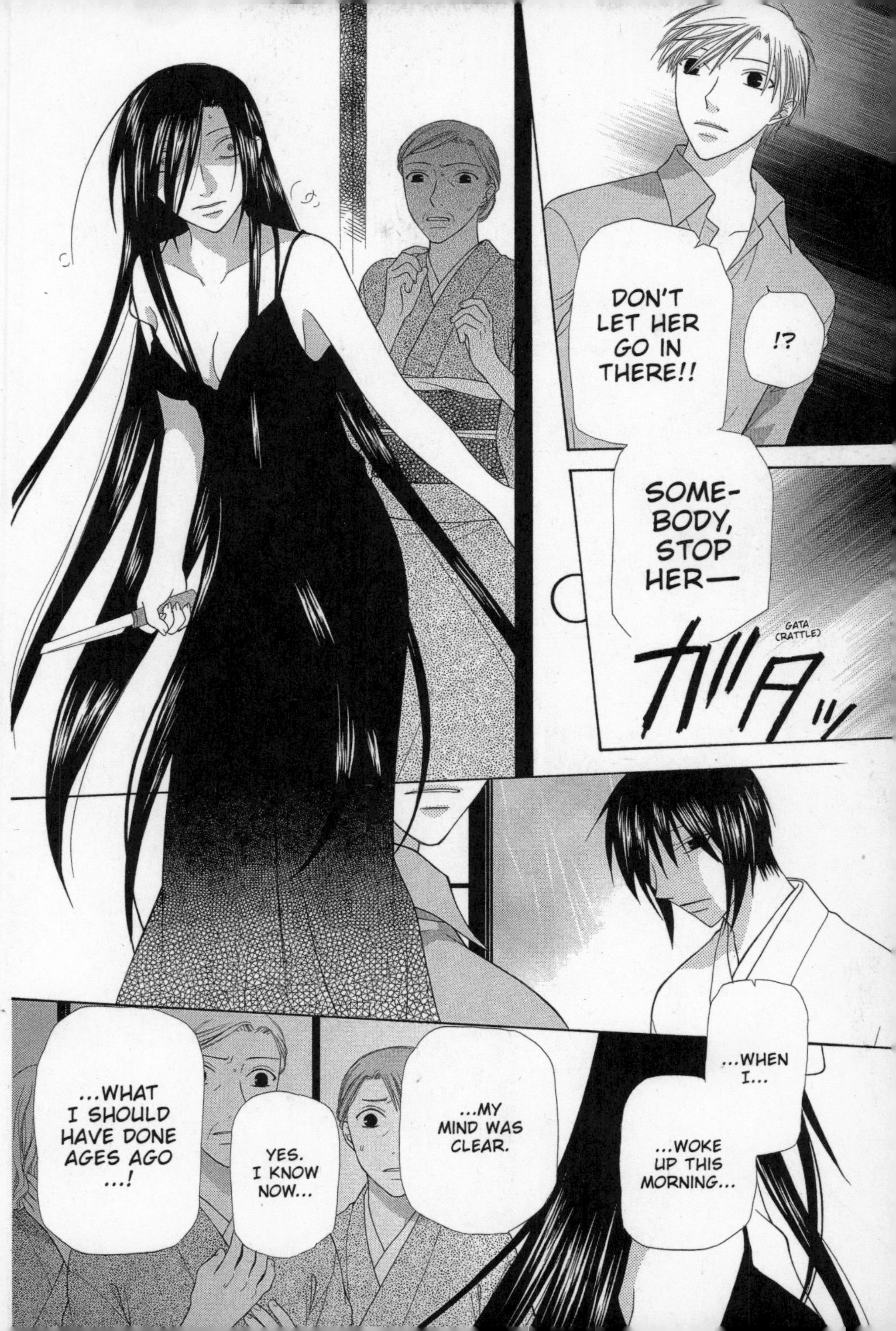
!?
DON'T LET HER GO IN THERE!!
SOMEBODY, STOP HER—
GATA (RATTLE)
...WHEN I...
...WOKE UP THIS MORNING...
...MY MIND WAS CLEAR.
YES. I KNOW NOW...
...WHAT I SHOULD HAVE DONE AGES AGO...!

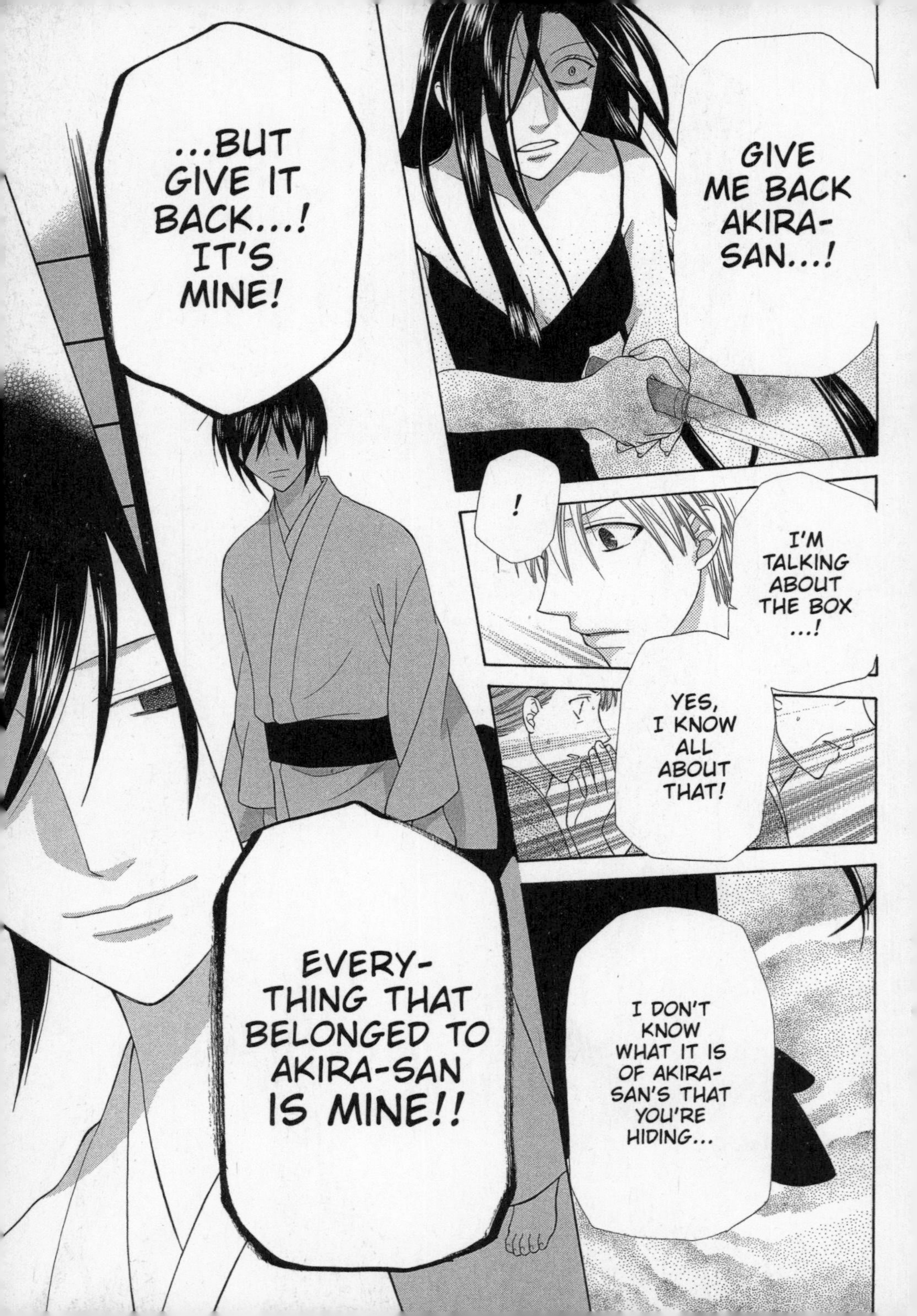
GIVE ME BACK AKIRA-SAN...!
I'M TALKING ABOUT THE BOX ...!
!
YES, I KNOW ALL ABOUT THAT!
I DON'T KNOW WHAT IT IS OF AKIRA-SAN'S THAT YOU'RE HIDING...
...BUT GIVE IT BACK...! IT'S MINE!
EVERY-THING THAT BELONGED TO AKIRA-SAN IS MINE!!

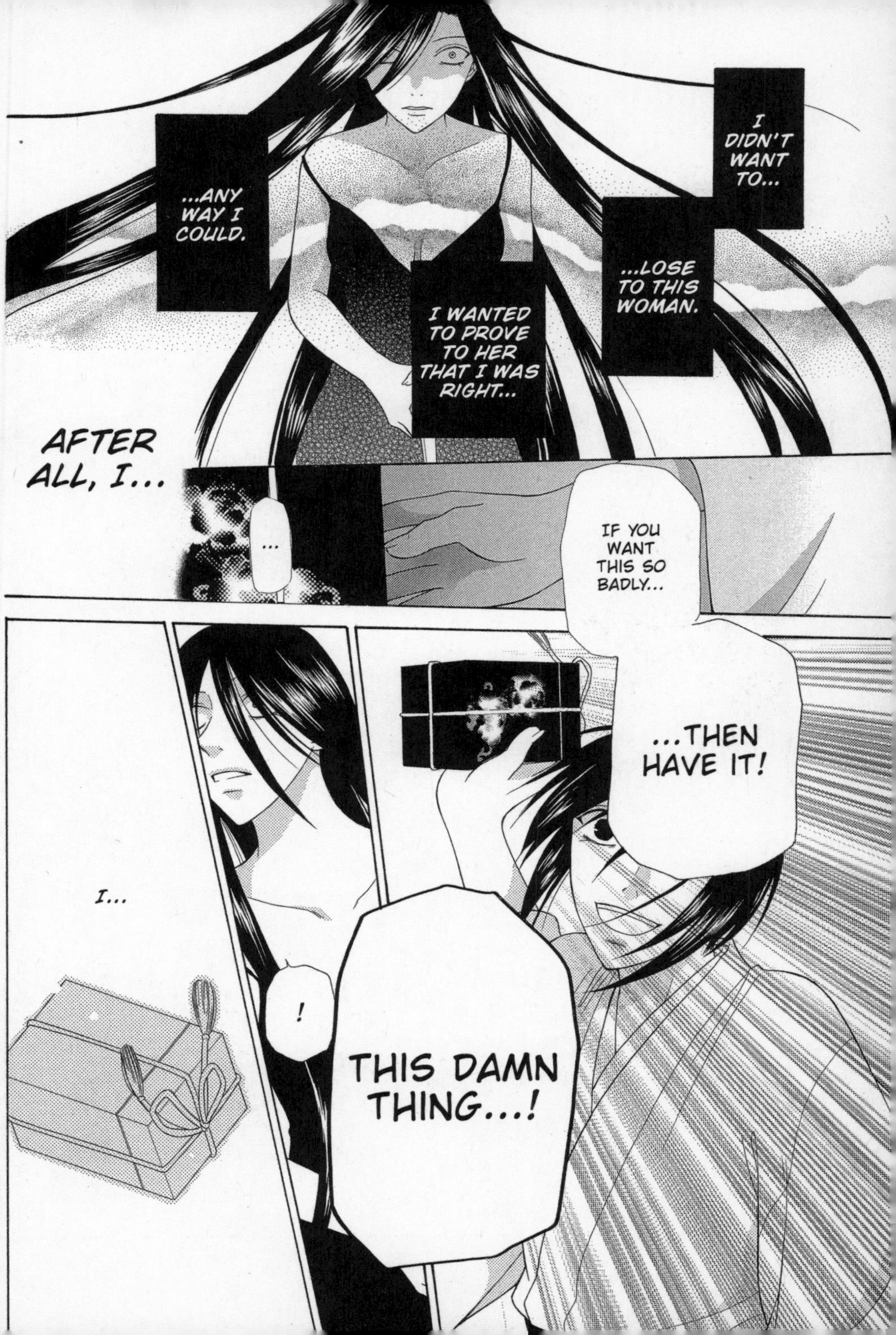
I DIDN'T WANT TO...
...LOSE TO THIS WOMAN.
I WANTED TO PROVE TO HER THAT I WAS RIGHT...
...ANY WAY I COULD.
AFTER ALL, I...
IF YOU WANT THIS SO BADLY...
...
...THEN HAVE IT!
THIS DAMN THING...!
!
I...

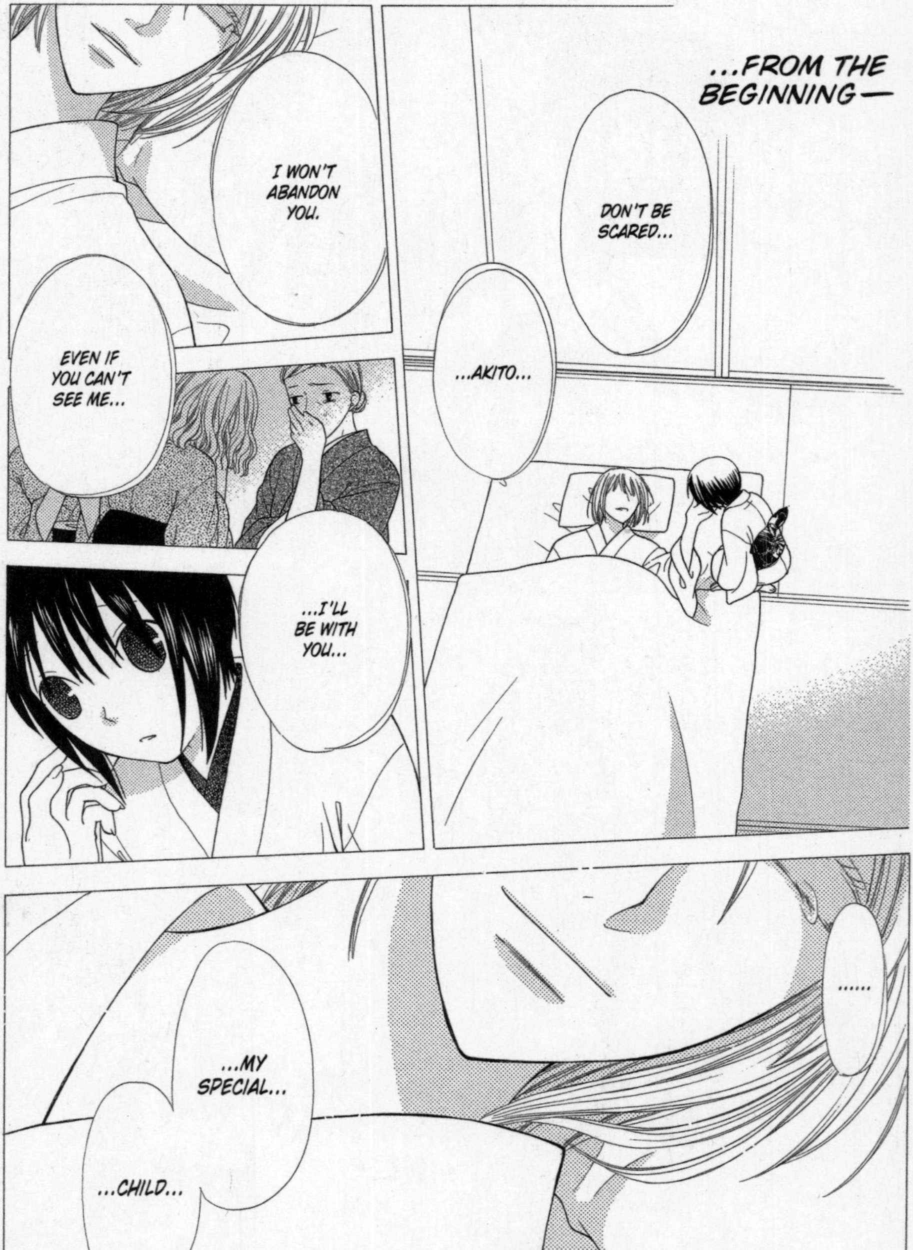
...FROM THE BEGINNING—
DON'T BE SCARED...
...AKITO...
I WON'T ABANDON YOU.
EVEN IF YOU CAN'T SEE ME...
...I'LL BE WITH YOU...
......
...MY SPECIAL...
...CHILD...

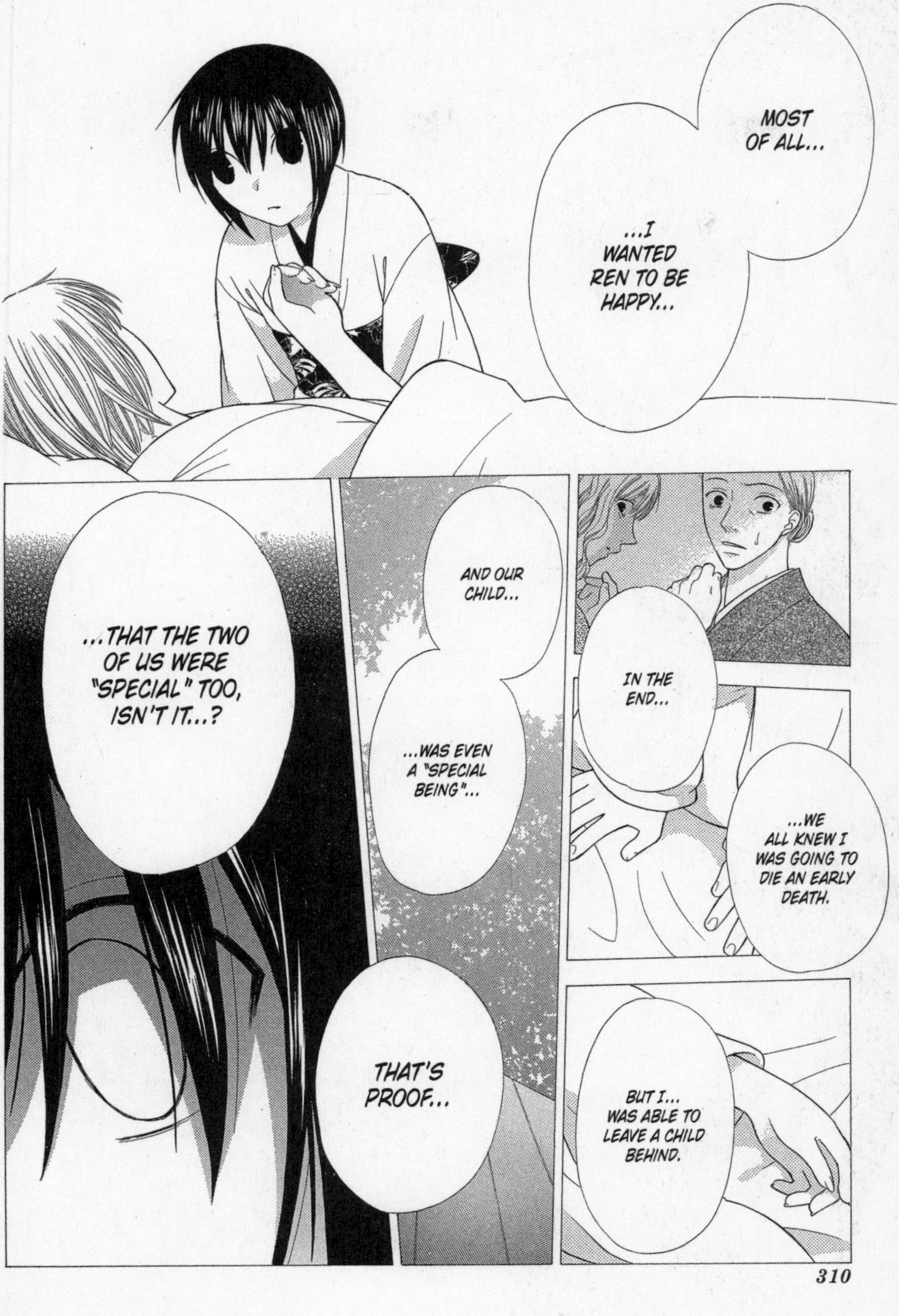

MOST OF ALL...
...I WANTED REN TO BE HAPPY...
IN THE END...
...WE ALL KNEW I WAS GOING TO DIE AN EARLY DEATH.
BUT I... WAS ABLE TO LEAVE A CHILD BEHIND.
AND OUR CHILD...
...WAS EVEN A "SPECIAL BEING"...
THAT'S PROOF...
...THAT THE TWO OF US WERE "SPECIAL" TOO, ISN'T IT...?

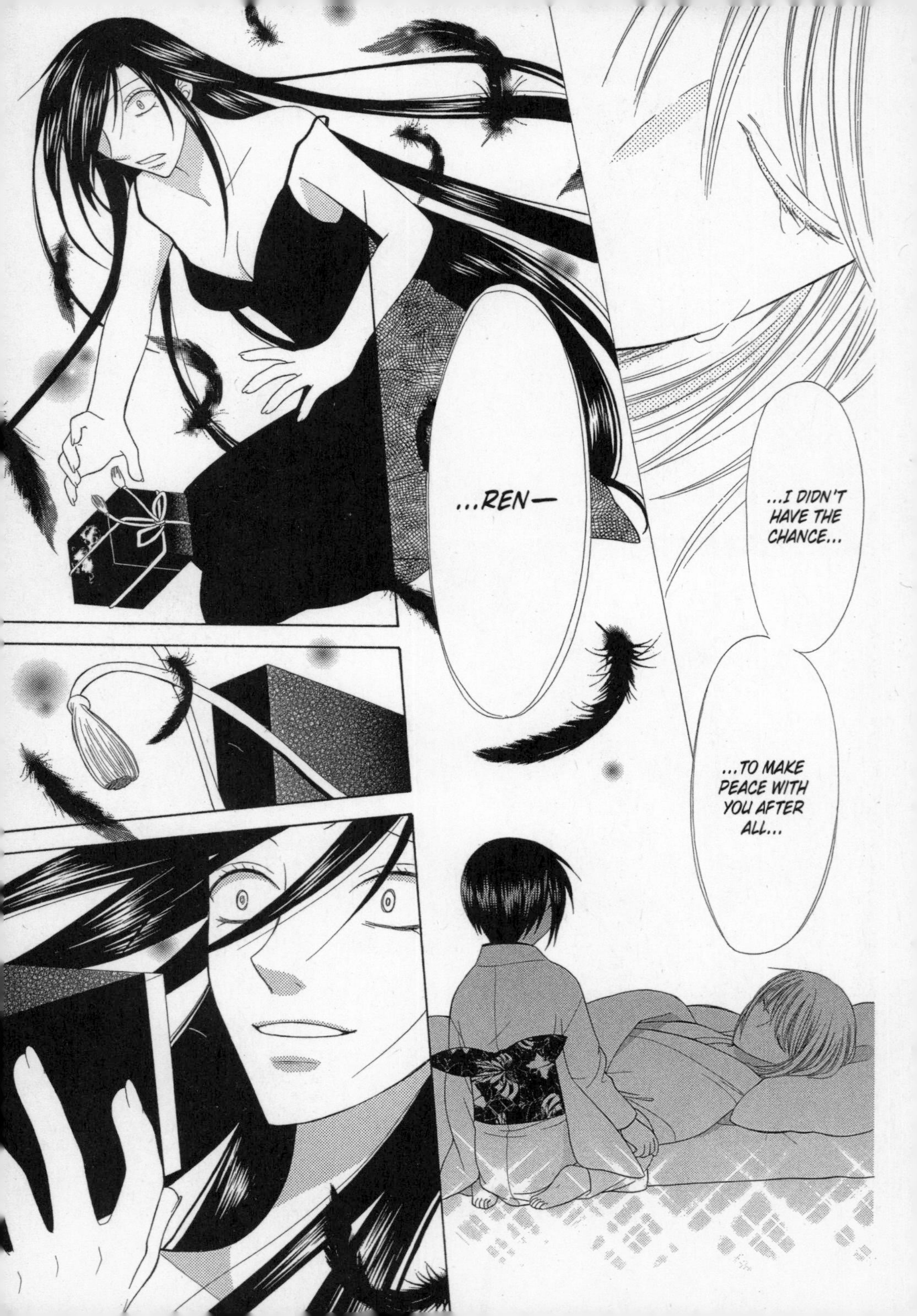
...I DIDN'T HAVE THE CHANCE...
...TO MAKE PEACE WITH YOU AFTER ALL...
...REN—

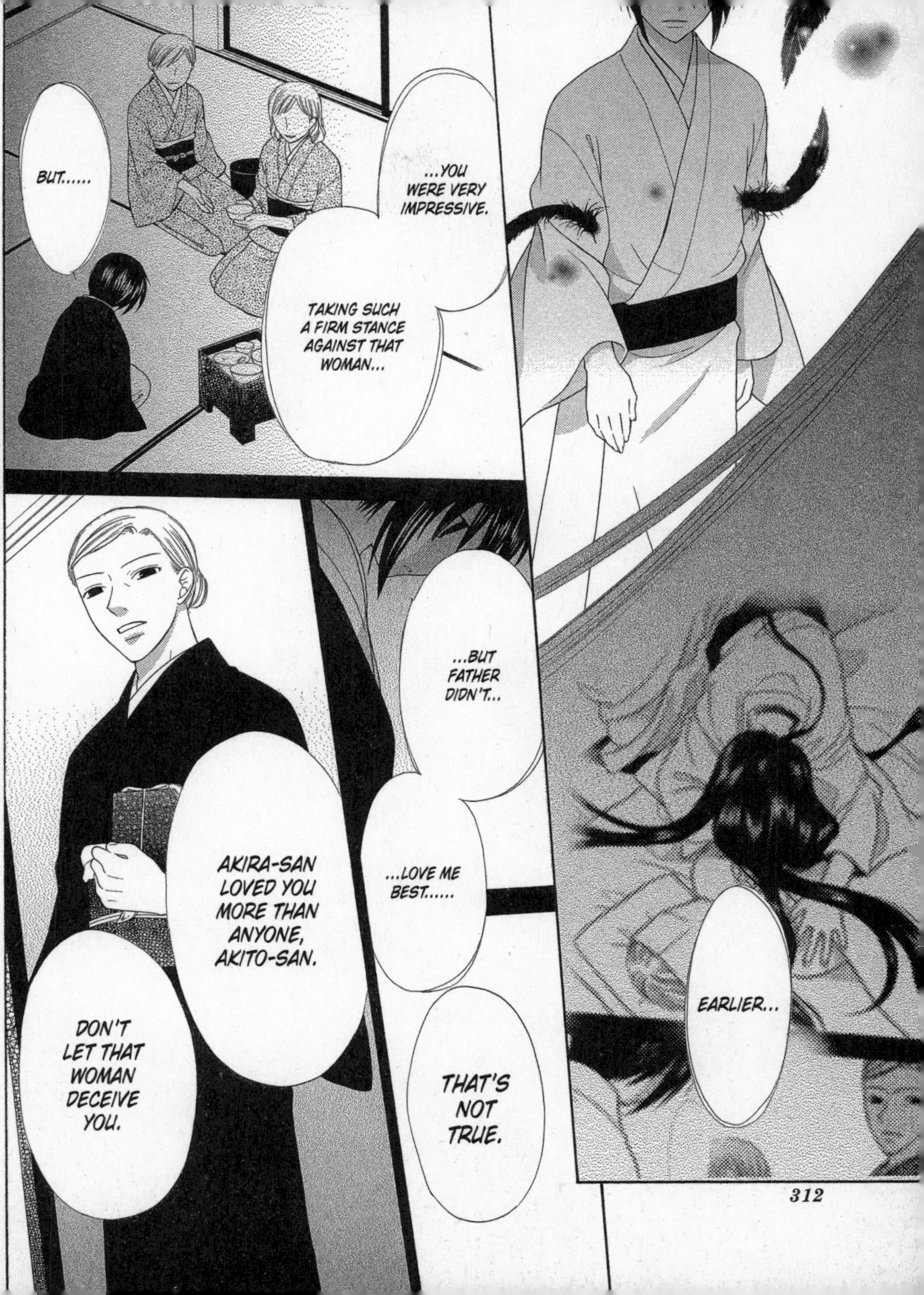
...YOU WERE VERY IMPRESSIVE.
TAKING SUCH A FIRM STANCE AGAINST THAT WOMAN...
BUT......
EARLIER...
...BUT FATHER DIDN'T...
...LOVE ME BEST......
THAT'S NOT TRUE.
AKIRA-SAN LOVED YOU MORE THAN ANYONE, AKITO-SAN.
DON'T LET THAT WOMAN DECEIVE YOU.

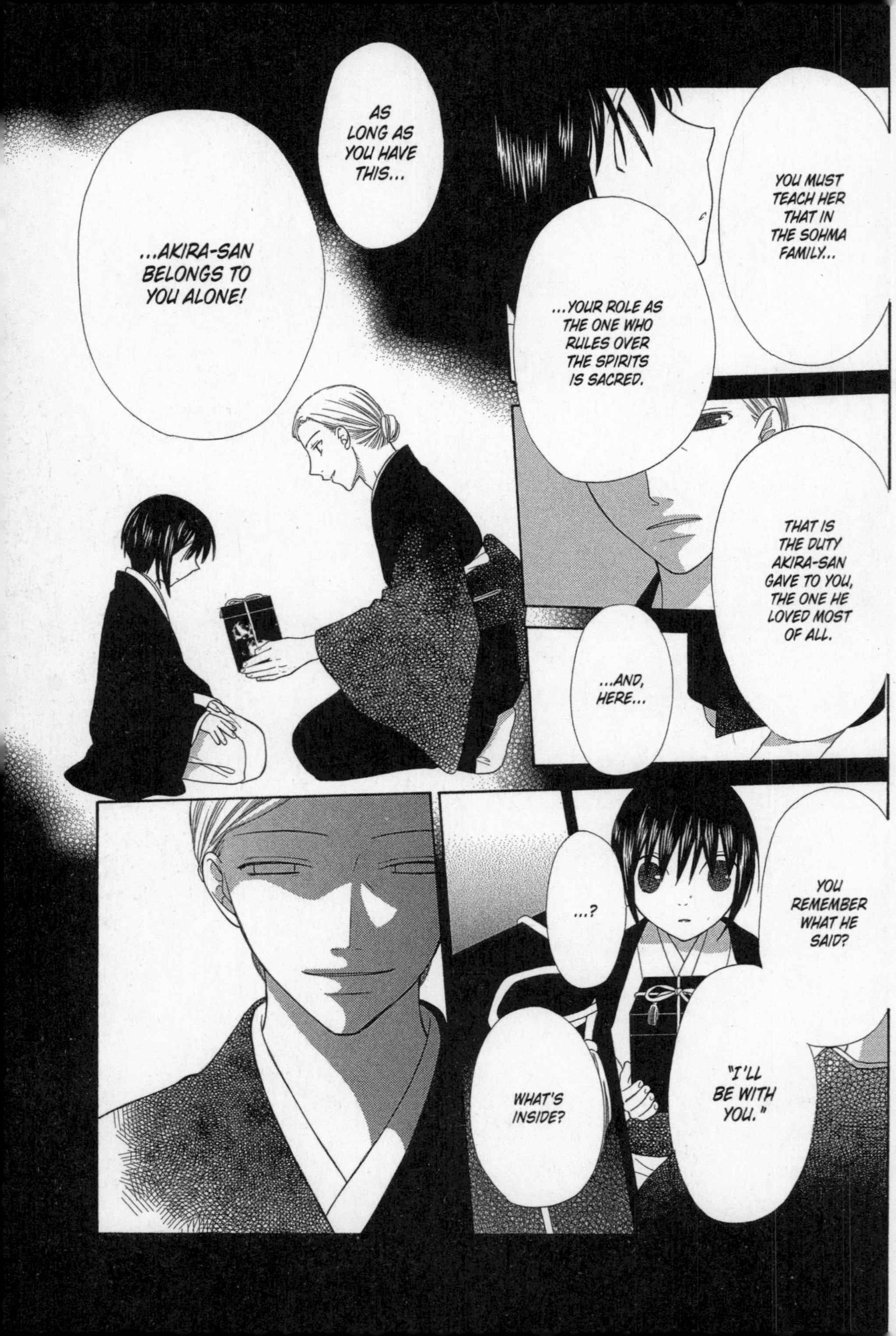
YOU MUST TEACH HER THAT IN THE SOHMA FAMILY...
...YOUR ROLE AS THE ONE WHO RULES OVER THE SPIRITS IS SACRED.
THAT IS THE DUTY AKIRA-SAN GAVE TO YOU, THE ONE HE LOVED MOST OF ALL.
...AND, HERE...
AS LONG AS YOU HAVE THIS...
...AKIRA-SAN BELONGS TO YOU ALONE!
YOU REMEMBER WHAT HE SAID?
"I'LL BE WITH YOU."
...?
WHAT'S INSIDE?

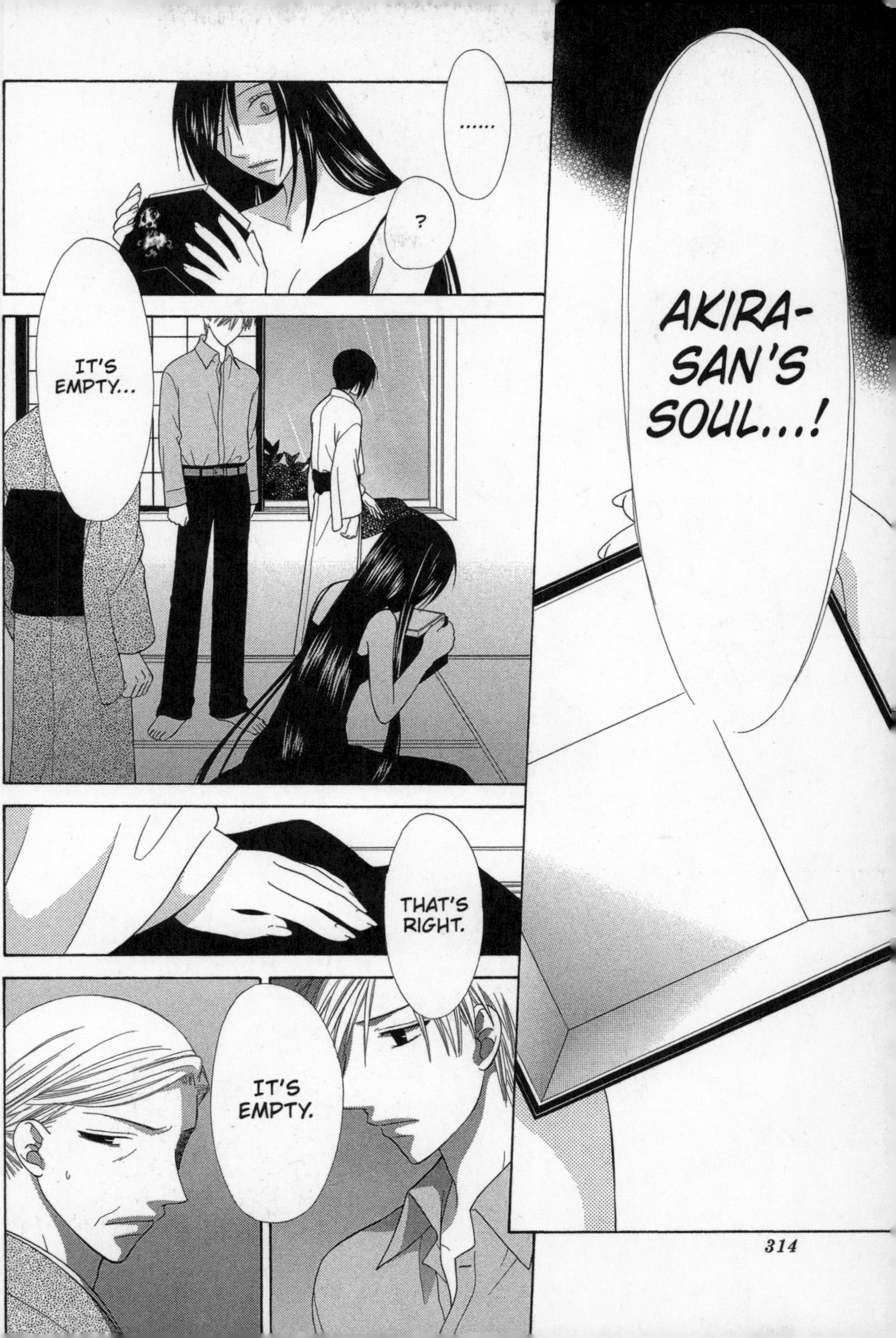

AKIRA-SAN'S SOUL...!
......
?
IT'S EMPTY...
THAT'S RIGHT.
IT'S EMPTY.

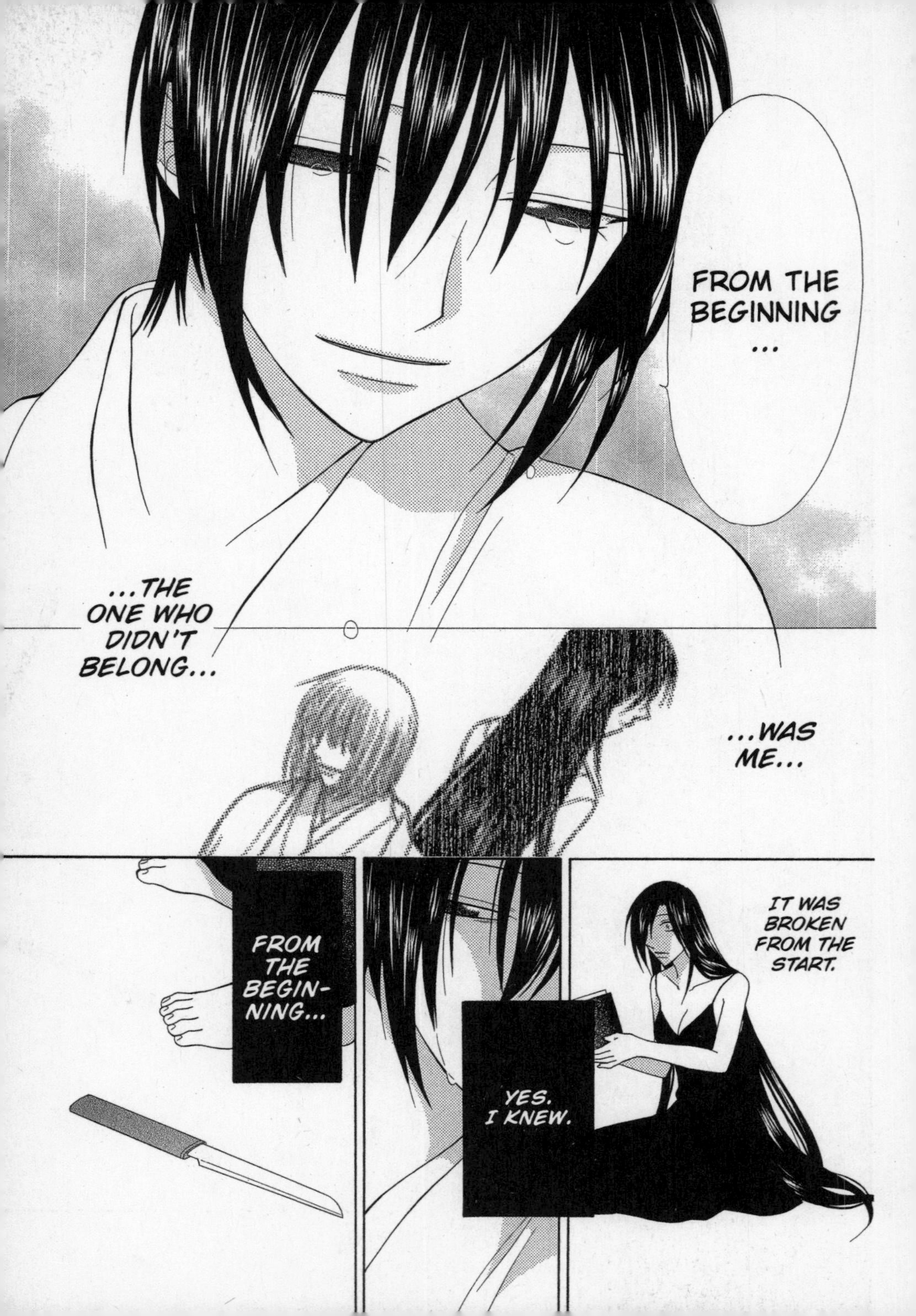
FROM THE BEGINNING ...
...THE ONE WHO DIDN'T BELONG...
...WAS ME...
IT WAS BROKEN FROM THE START.
YES. I KNEW.
FROM THE BEGIN-NING...

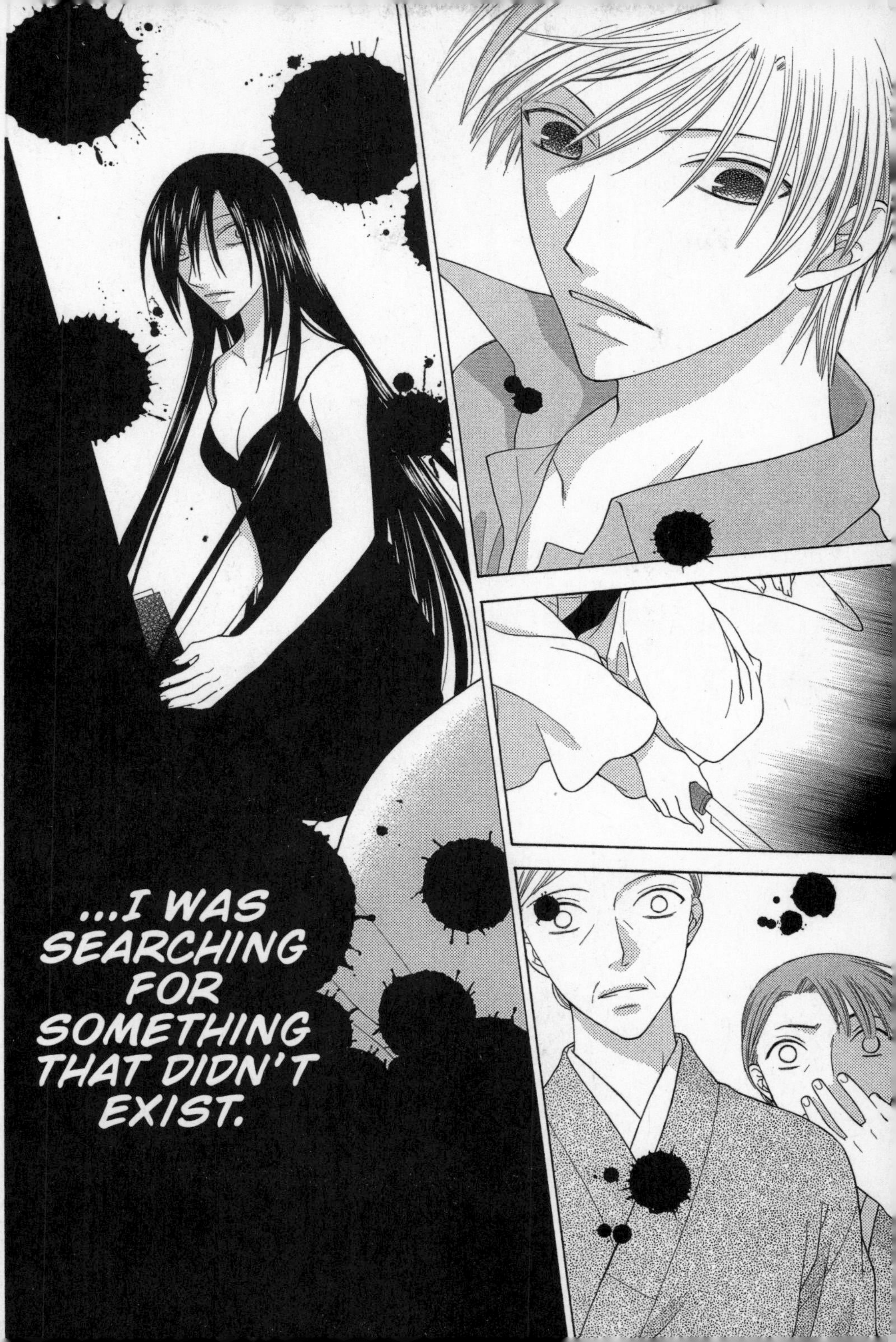
...I WAS SEARCHING FOR SOMETHING THAT DIDN'T EXIST.

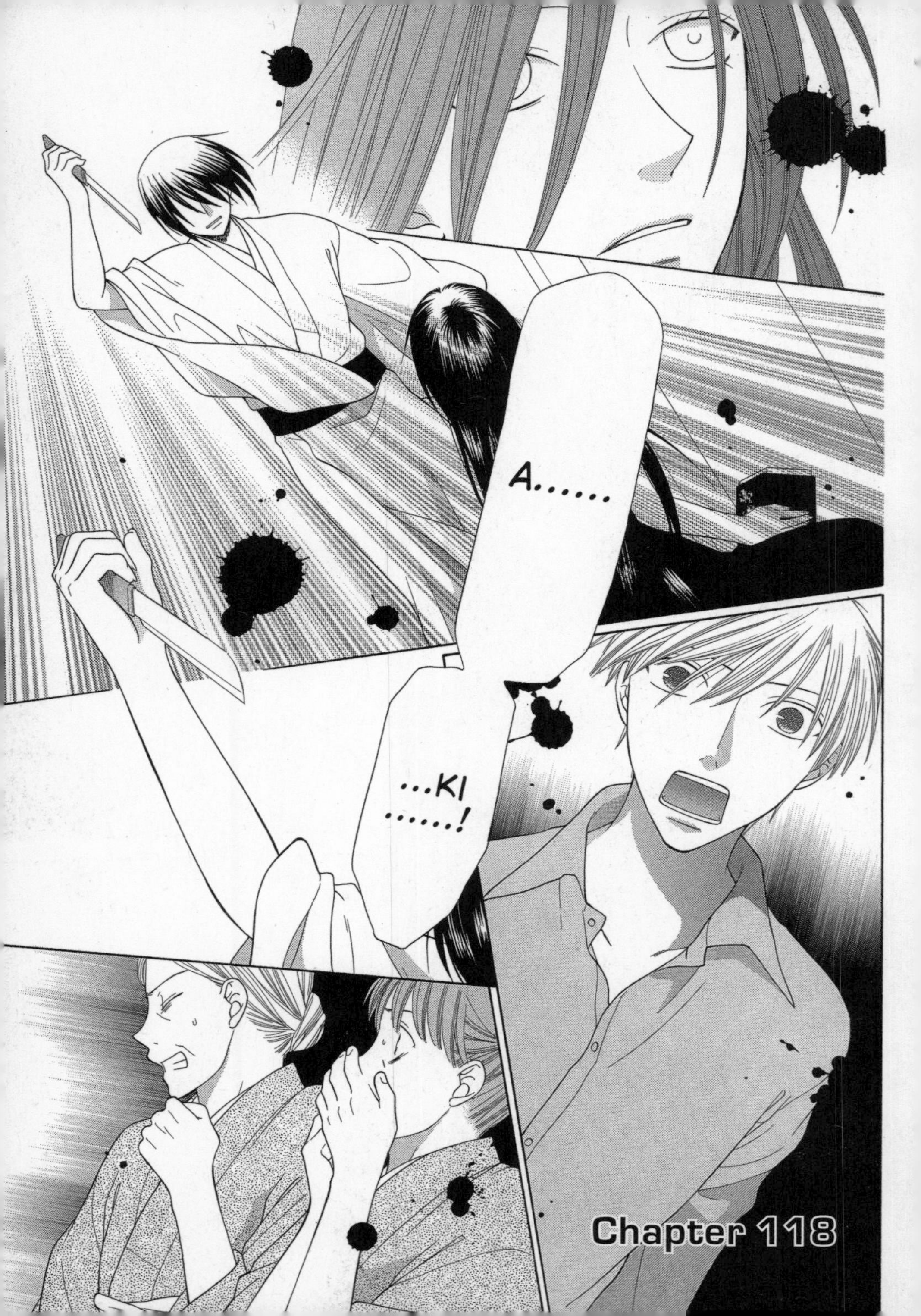
A......
...KI
......!
Chapter 118

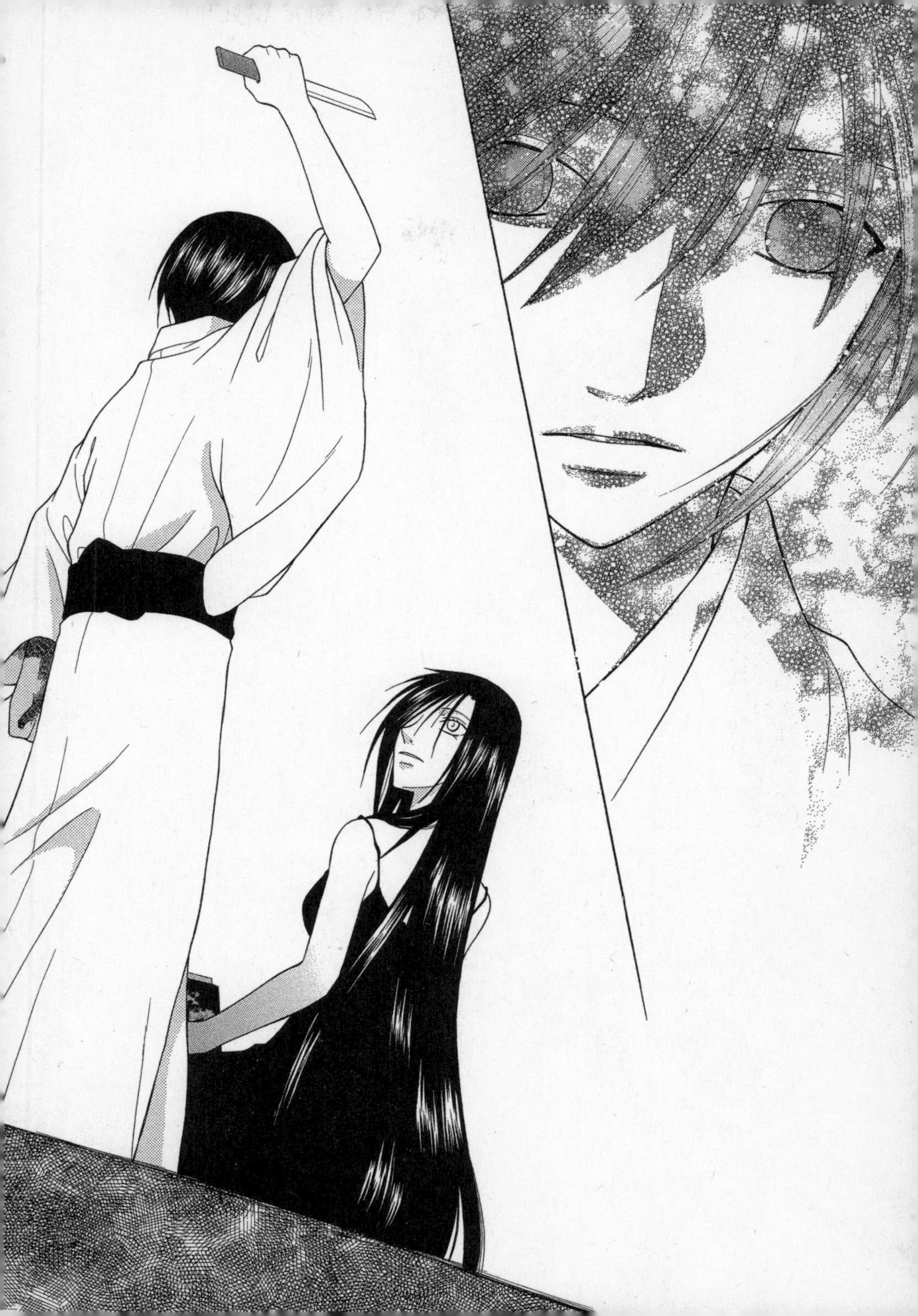

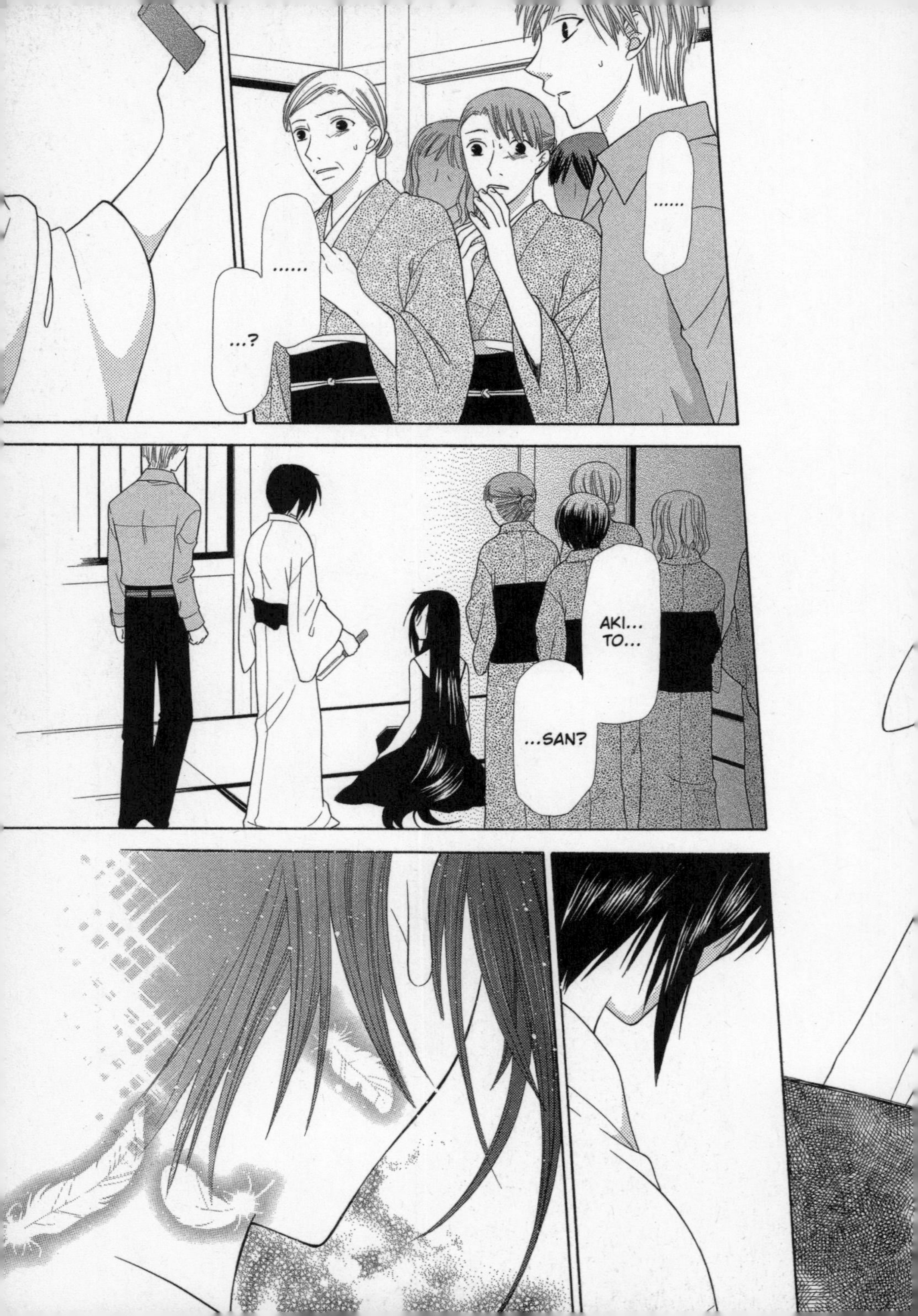
......
......
...?
AKI... TO...
...SAN?

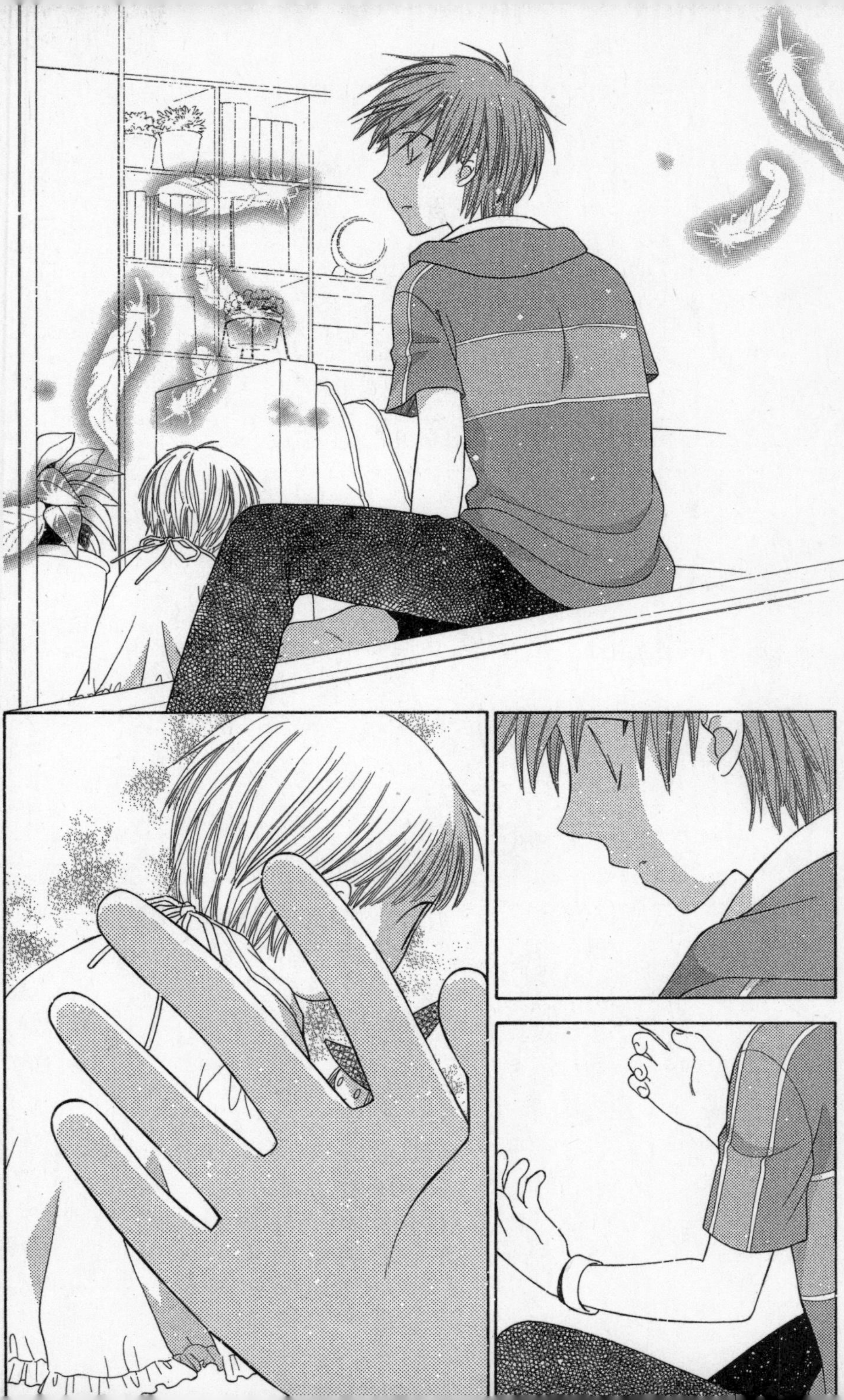

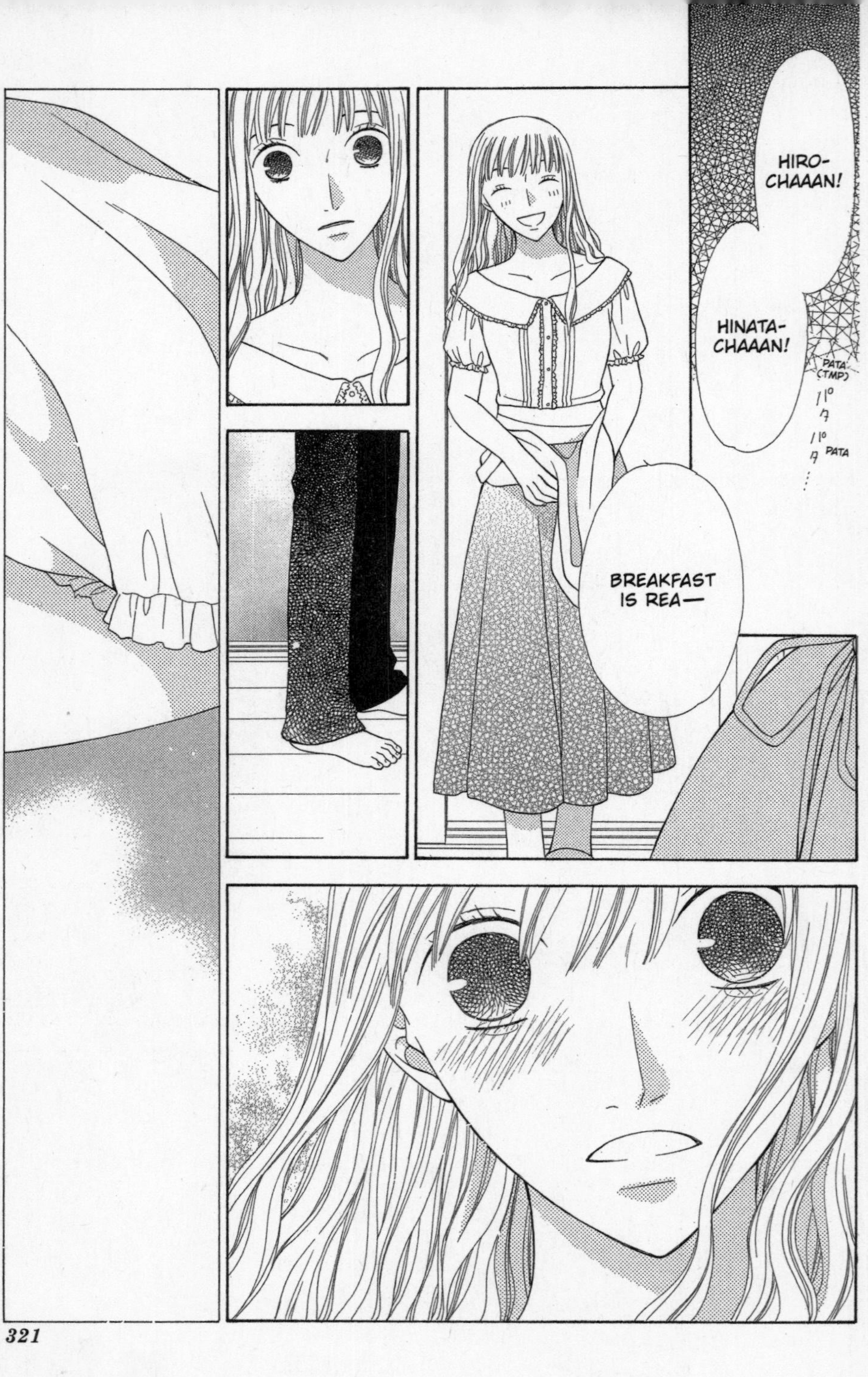
HIRO-CHAAAN!
HINATA-CHAAAN!
PATA (TMP)
パタ
パタ
PATA
BREAKFAST IS REA—

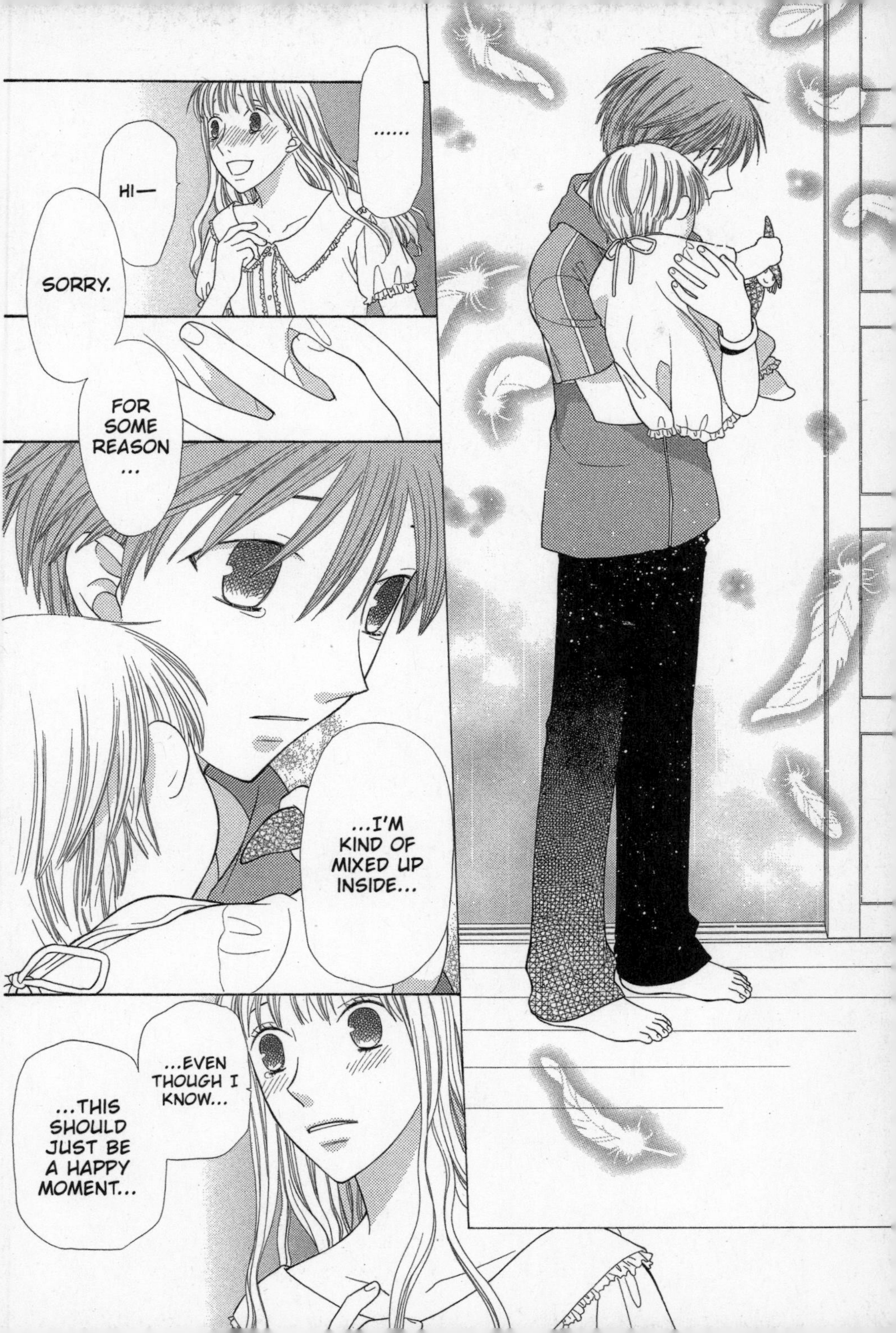
......
HI—
SORRY.
FOR SOME REASON...
...I'M KIND OF MIXED UP INSIDE...
...EVEN THOUGH I KNOW...
...THIS SHOULD JUST BE A HAPPY MOMENT...

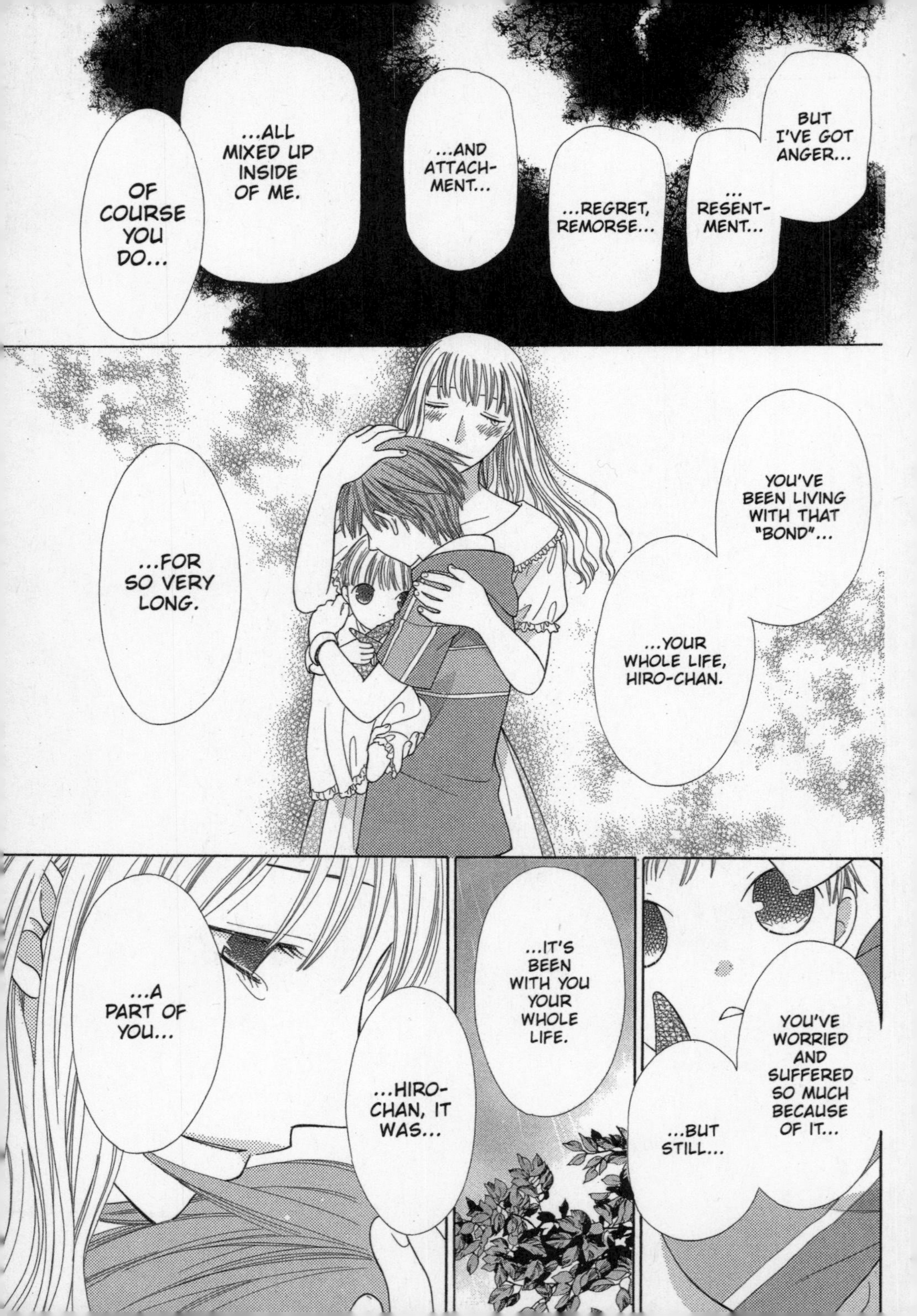
BUT I'VE GOT ANGER...
...RESENTMENT...
...REGRET, REMORSE...
...AND ATTACHMENT...
...ALL MIXED UP INSIDE OF ME.
OF COURSE YOU DO...
YOU'VE BEEN LIVING WITH THAT "BOND"...
...YOUR WHOLE LIFE, HIRO-CHAN.
...FOR SO VERY LONG.
YOU'VE WORRIED AND SUFFERED SO MUCH BECAUSE OF IT...
...BUT STILL...
...IT'S BEEN WITH YOU YOUR WHOLE LIFE.
...HIRO-CHAN, IT WAS...
...A PART OF YOU...

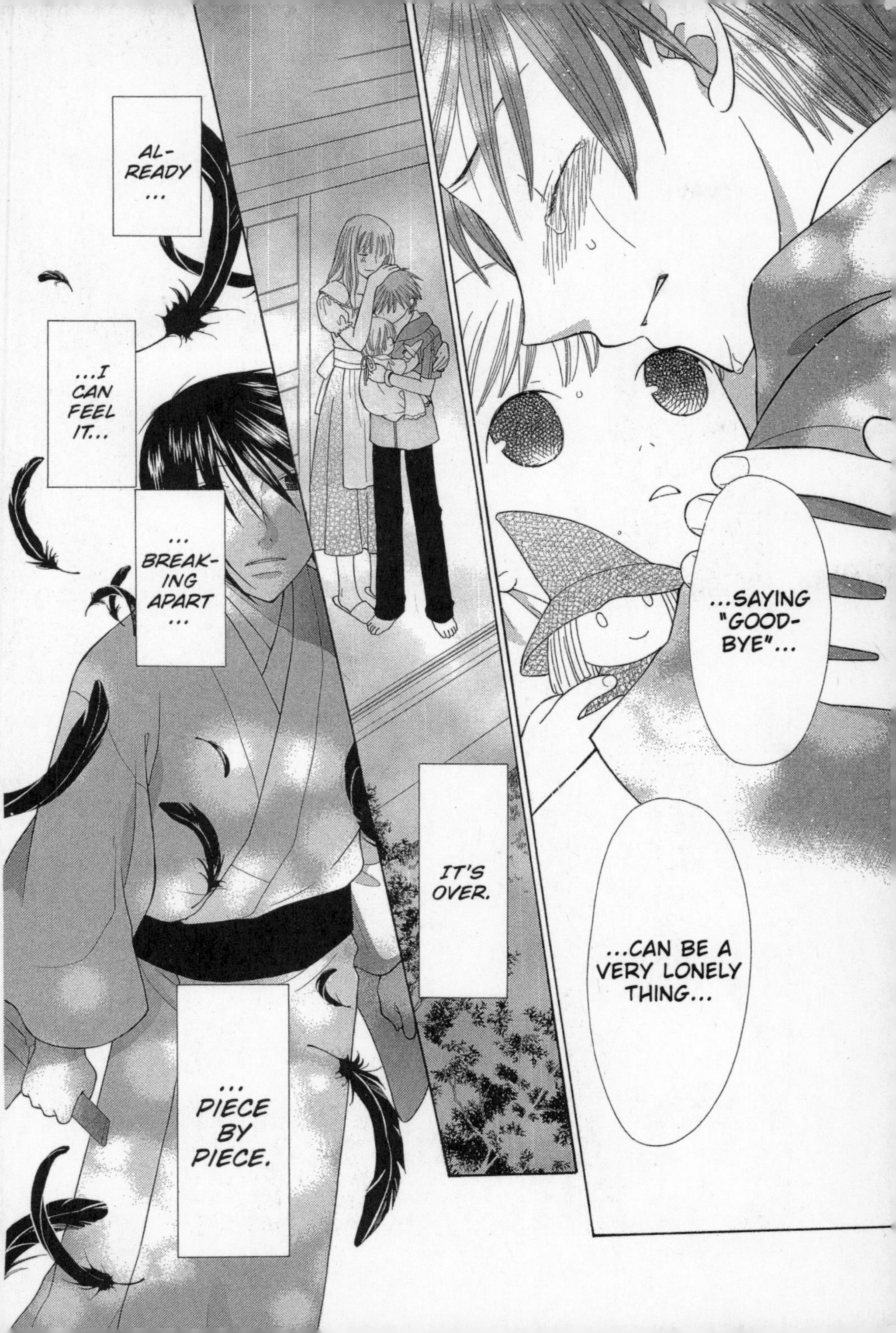

...SAYING "GOOD-BYE"...
...CAN BE A VERY LONELY THING...
IT'S OVER.
AL-READY...
...I CAN FEEL IT...
...BREAKING APART...
...PIECE BY PIECE.

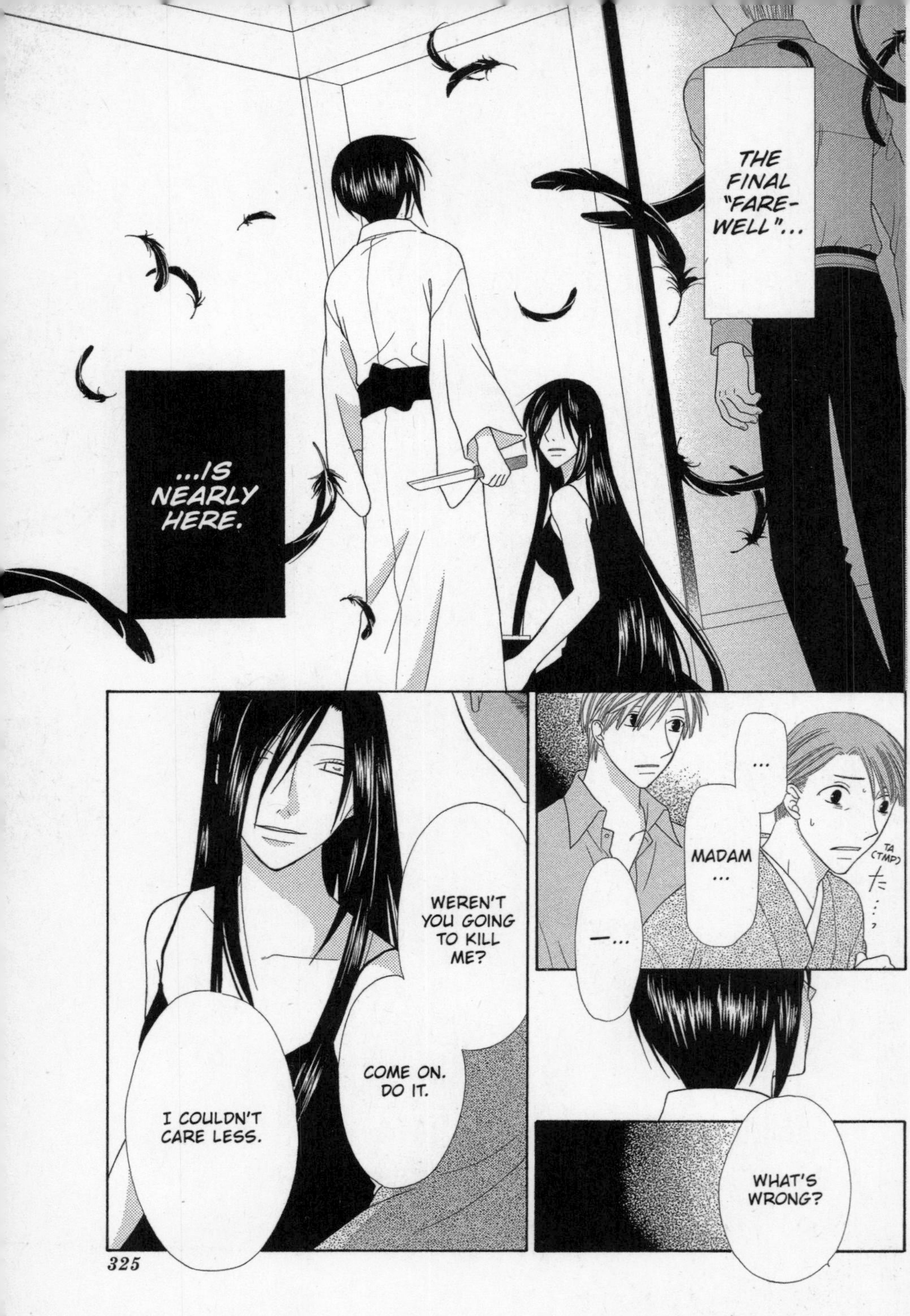
THE FINAL "FARE-WELL"...
...IS NEARLY HERE.
...
TA (TMP)
MADAM ...
—...
WHAT'S WRONG?
WEREN'T YOU GOING TO KILL ME?
COME ON. DO IT.
I COULDN'T CARE LESS.

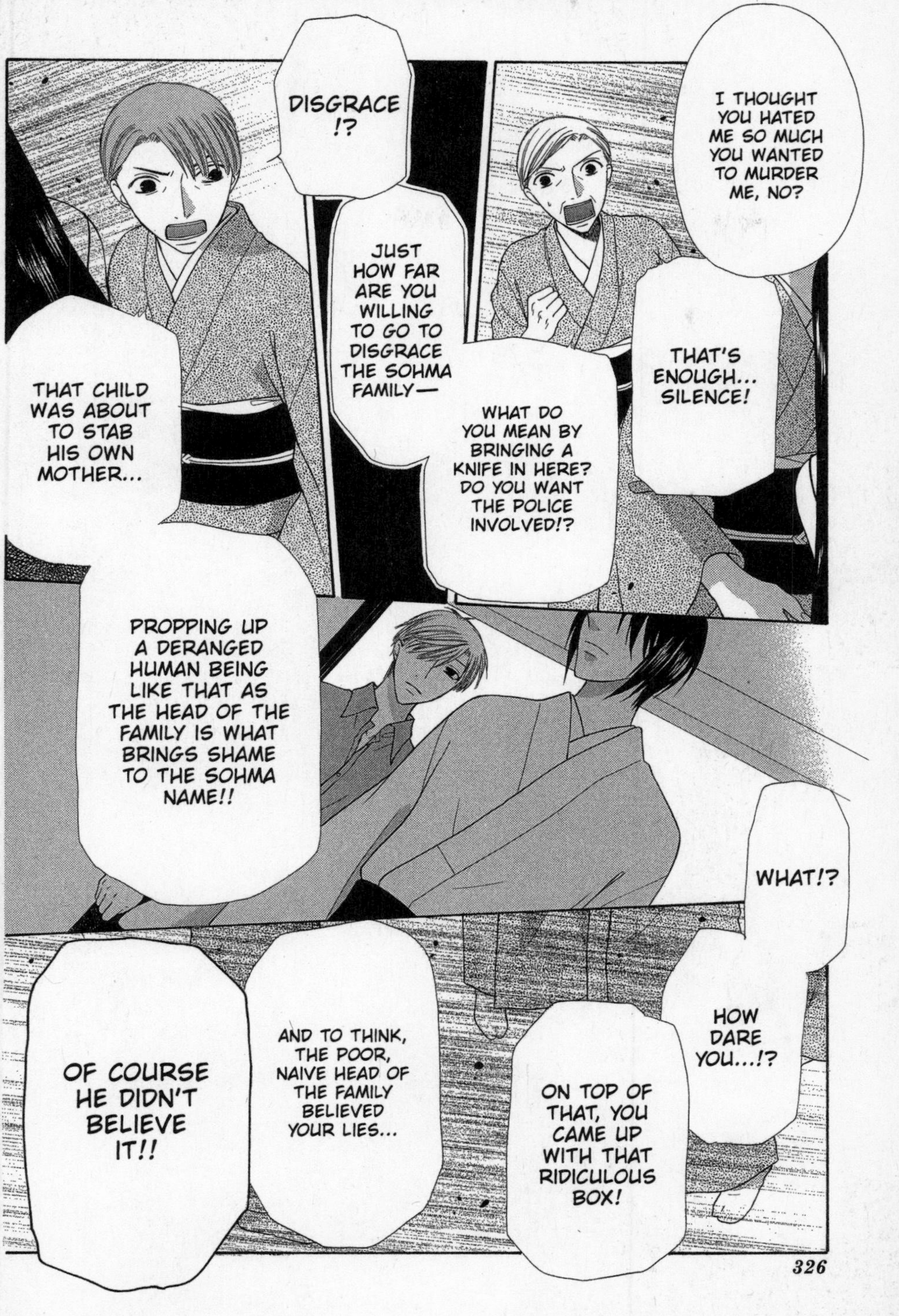
I THOUGHT YOU HATED ME SO MUCH YOU WANTED TO MURDER ME, NO?
THAT'S ENOUGH... SILENCE!
WHAT DO YOU MEAN BY BRINGING A KNIFE IN HERE? DO YOU WANT THE POLICE INVOLVED!?
JUST HOW FAR ARE YOU WILLING TO GO TO DISGRACE THE SOHMA FAMILY—
DISGRACE !?
THAT CHILD WAS ABOUT TO STAB HIS OWN MOTHER...
PROPPING UP A DERANGED HUMAN BEING LIKE THAT AS THE HEAD OF THE FAMILY IS WHAT BRINGS SHAME TO THE SOHMA NAME!!
WHAT!?
HOW DARE YOU...!?
ON TOP OF THAT, YOU CAME UP WITH THAT RIDICULOUS BOX!
AND TO THINK, THE POOR, NAIVE HEAD OF THE FAMILY BELIEVED YOUR LIES...
OF COURSE HE DIDN'T BELIEVE IT!!

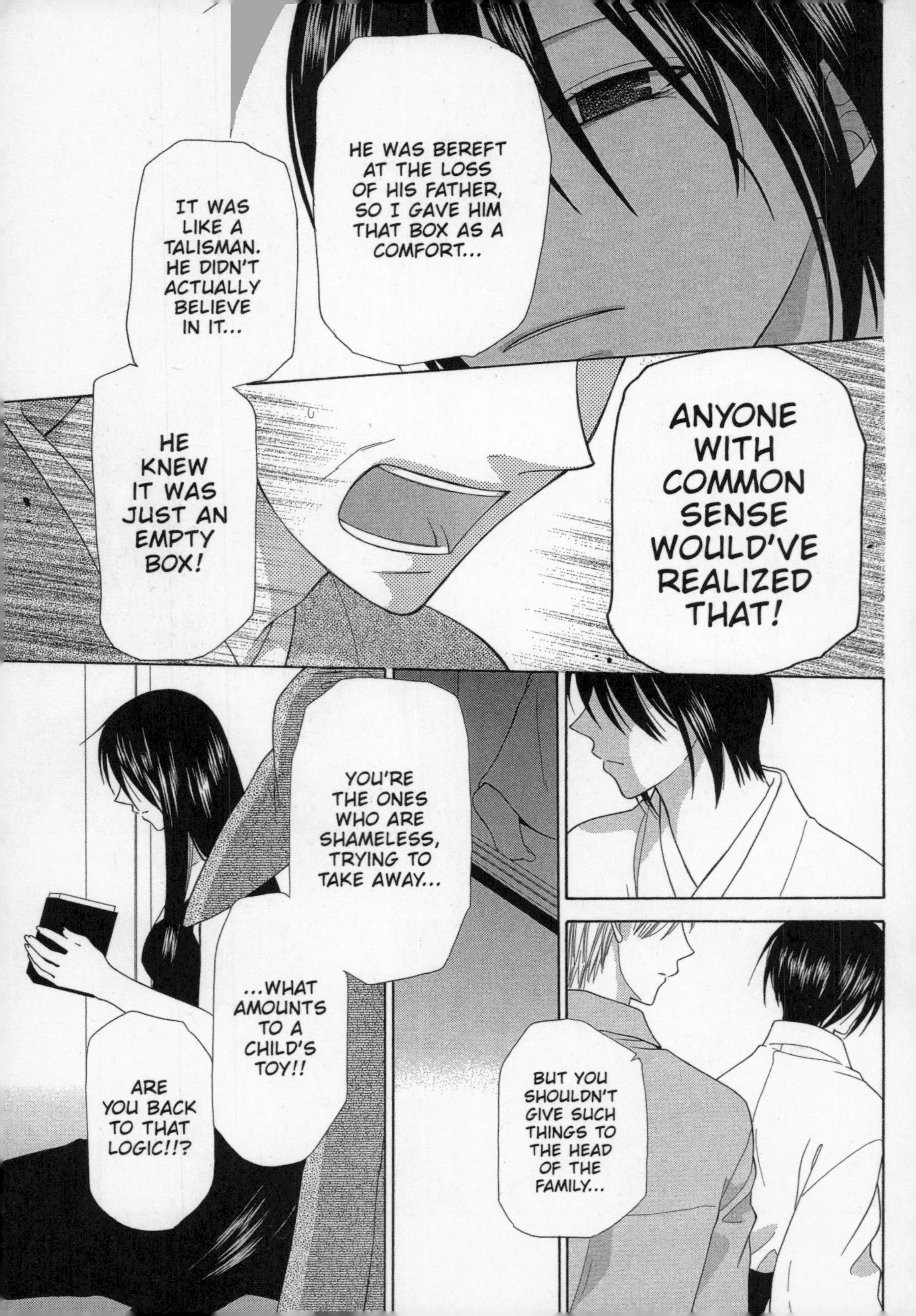
HE WAS BEREFT AT THE LOSS OF HIS FATHER, SO I GAVE HIM THAT BOX AS A COMFORT...
IT WAS LIKE A TALISMAN. HE DIDN'T ACTUALLY BELIEVE IN IT...
ANYONE WITH COMMON SENSE WOULD'VE REALIZED THAT!
HE KNEW IT WAS JUST AN EMPTY BOX!
BUT YOU SHOULDN'T GIVE SUCH THINGS TO THE HEAD OF THE FAMILY...
YOU'RE THE ONES WHO ARE SHAMELESS, TRYING TO TAKE AWAY...
...WHAT AMOUNTS TO A CHILD'S TOY!!
ARE YOU BACK TO THAT LOGIC!!?

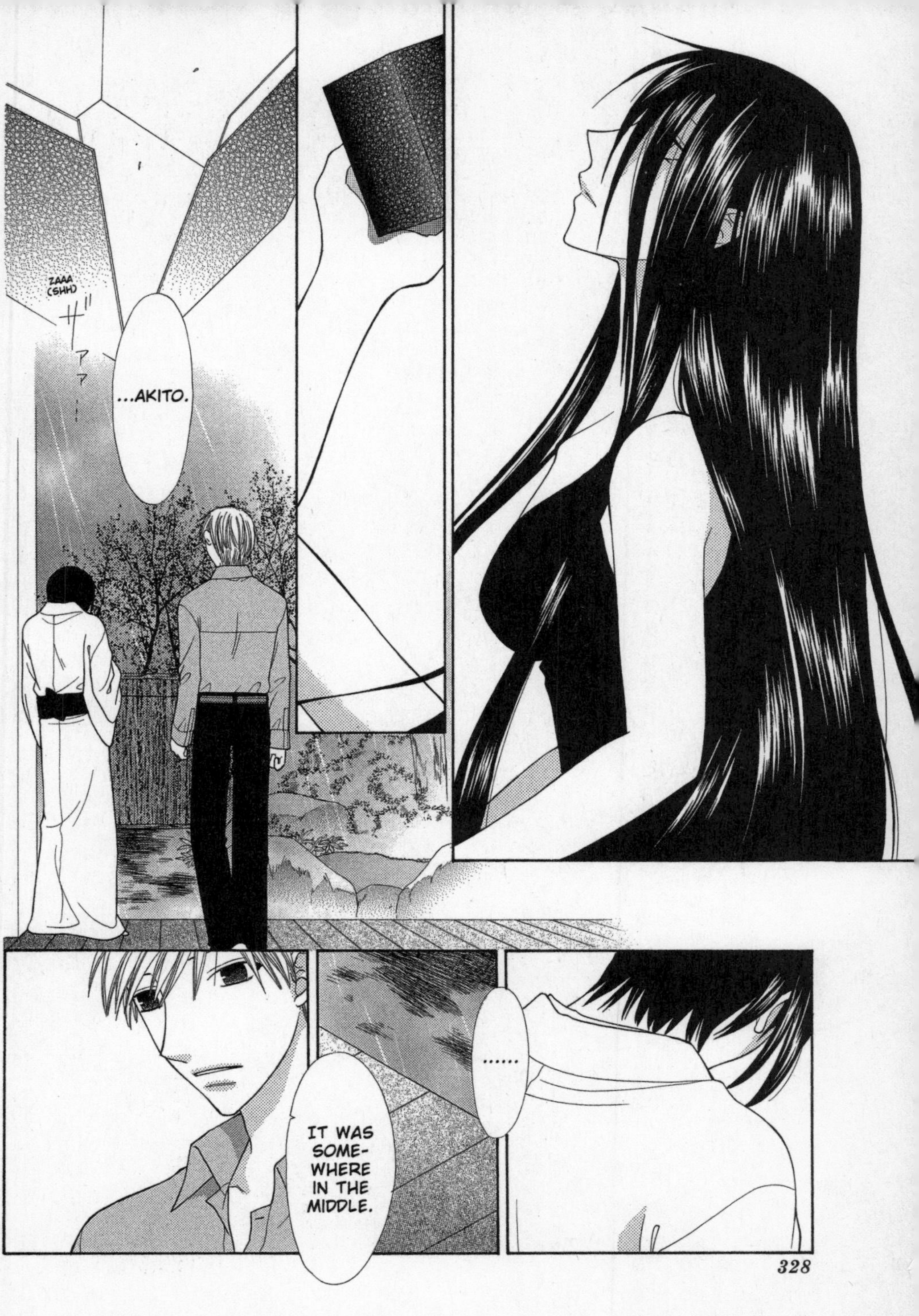
...AKITO.
ZAAA (SHH)
......
IT WAS SOMEWHERE IN THE MIDDLE.

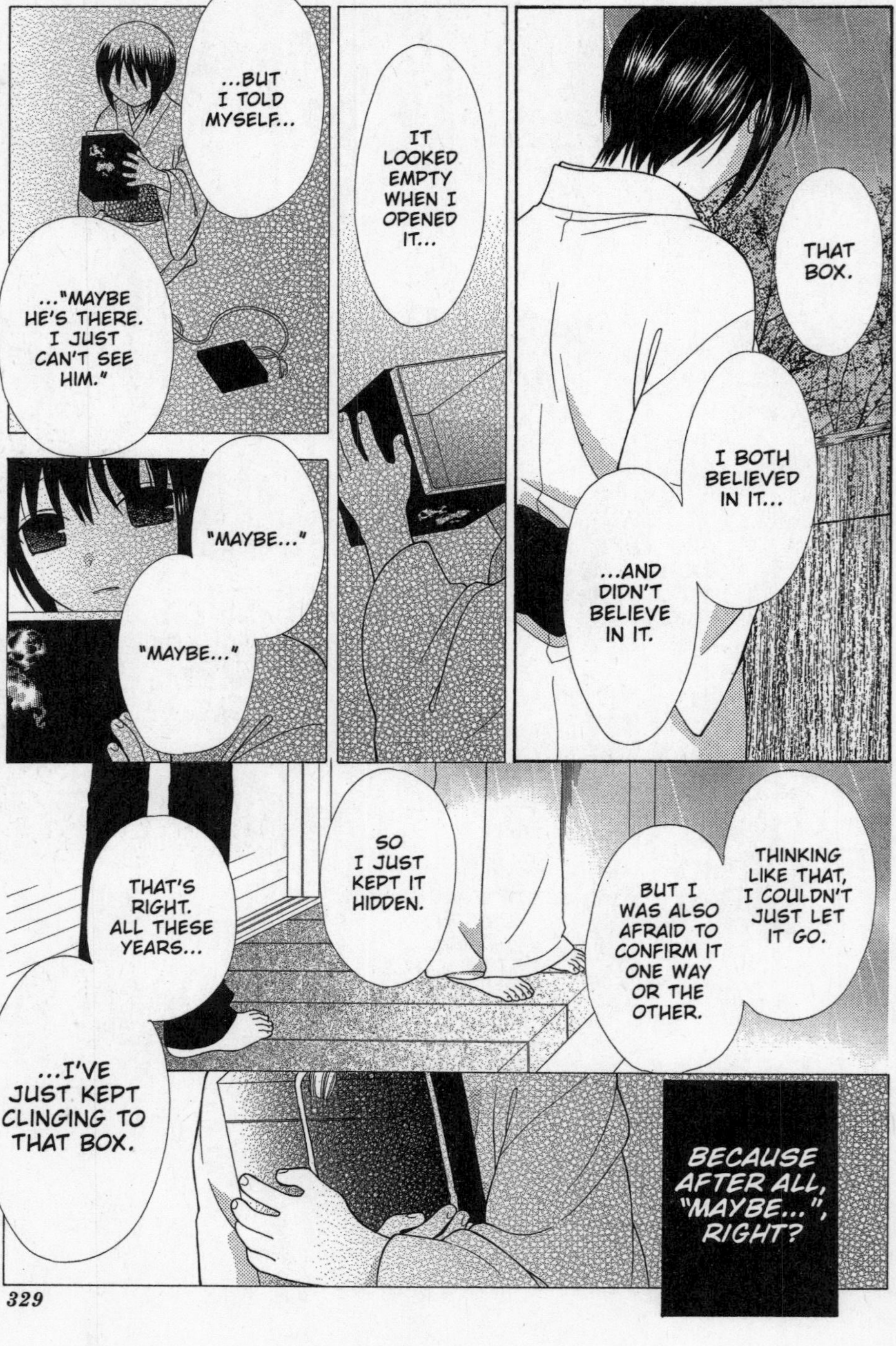
THAT BOX.
I BOTH BELIEVED IN IT...
...AND DIDN'T BELIEVE IN IT.
IT LOOKED EMPTY WHEN I OPENED IT...
...BUT I TOLD MYSELF...
..."MAYBE HE'S THERE. I JUST CAN'T SEE HIM."
"MAYBE..."
"MAYBE..."
THINKING LIKE THAT, I COULDN'T JUST LET IT GO.
BUT I WAS ALSO AFRAID TO CONFIRM IT ONE WAY OR THE OTHER.
SO I JUST KEPT IT HIDDEN.
THAT'S RIGHT. ALL THESE YEARS...
...I'VE JUST KEPT CLINGING TO THAT BOX.
BECAUSE AFTER ALL, "MAYBE...", RIGHT?

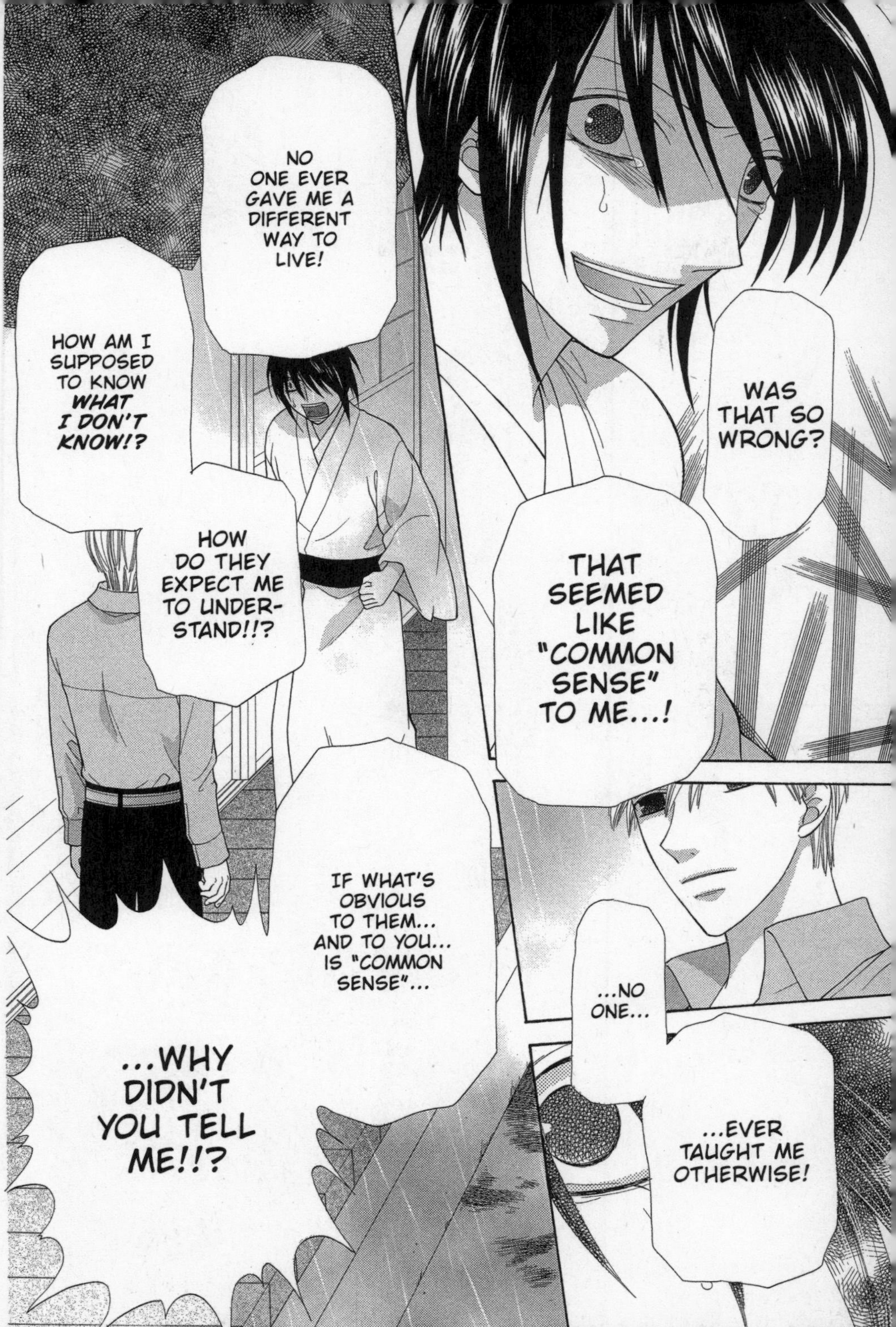
WAS THAT SO WRONG?
THAT SEEMED LIKE "COMMON SENSE" TO ME...!
...NO ONE...
...EVER TAUGHT ME OTHERWISE!
NO ONE EVER GAVE ME A DIFFERENT WAY TO LIVE!
HOW AM I SUPPOSED TO KNOW *WHAT I DON'T KNOW!?*
HOW DO THEY EXPECT ME TO UNDER-STAND!!?
IF WHAT'S OBVIOUS TO THEM... AND TO YOU... IS "COMMON SENSE"...
...WHY DIDN'T YOU TELL ME!!?

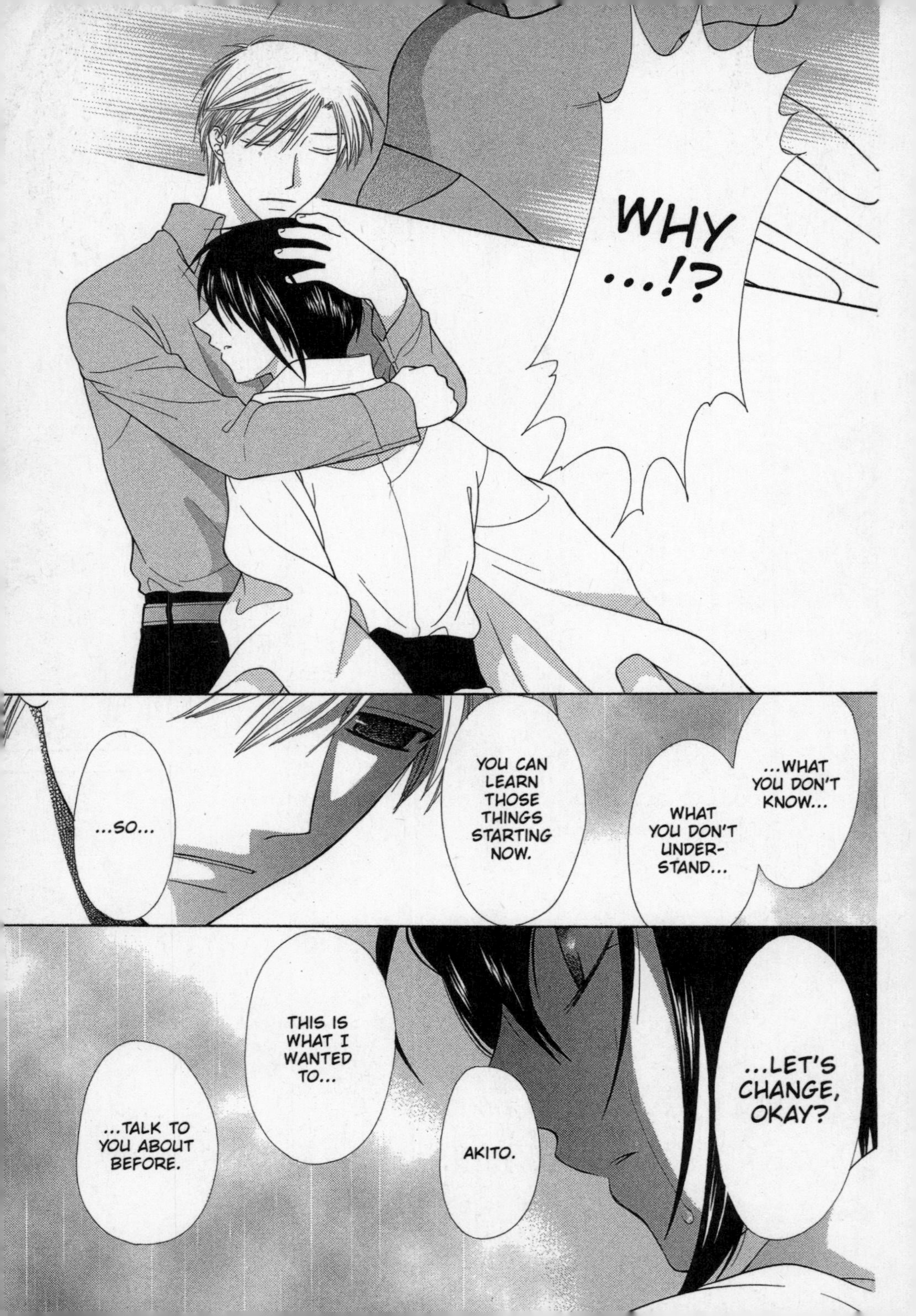
WHY ...!?
...WHAT YOU DON'T KNOW...
WHAT YOU DON'T UNDER-STAND...
YOU CAN LEARN THOSE THINGS STARTING NOW.
...SO...
...LET'S CHANGE, OKAY?
AKITO.
THIS IS WHAT I WANTED TO...
...TALK TO YOU ABOUT BEFORE.

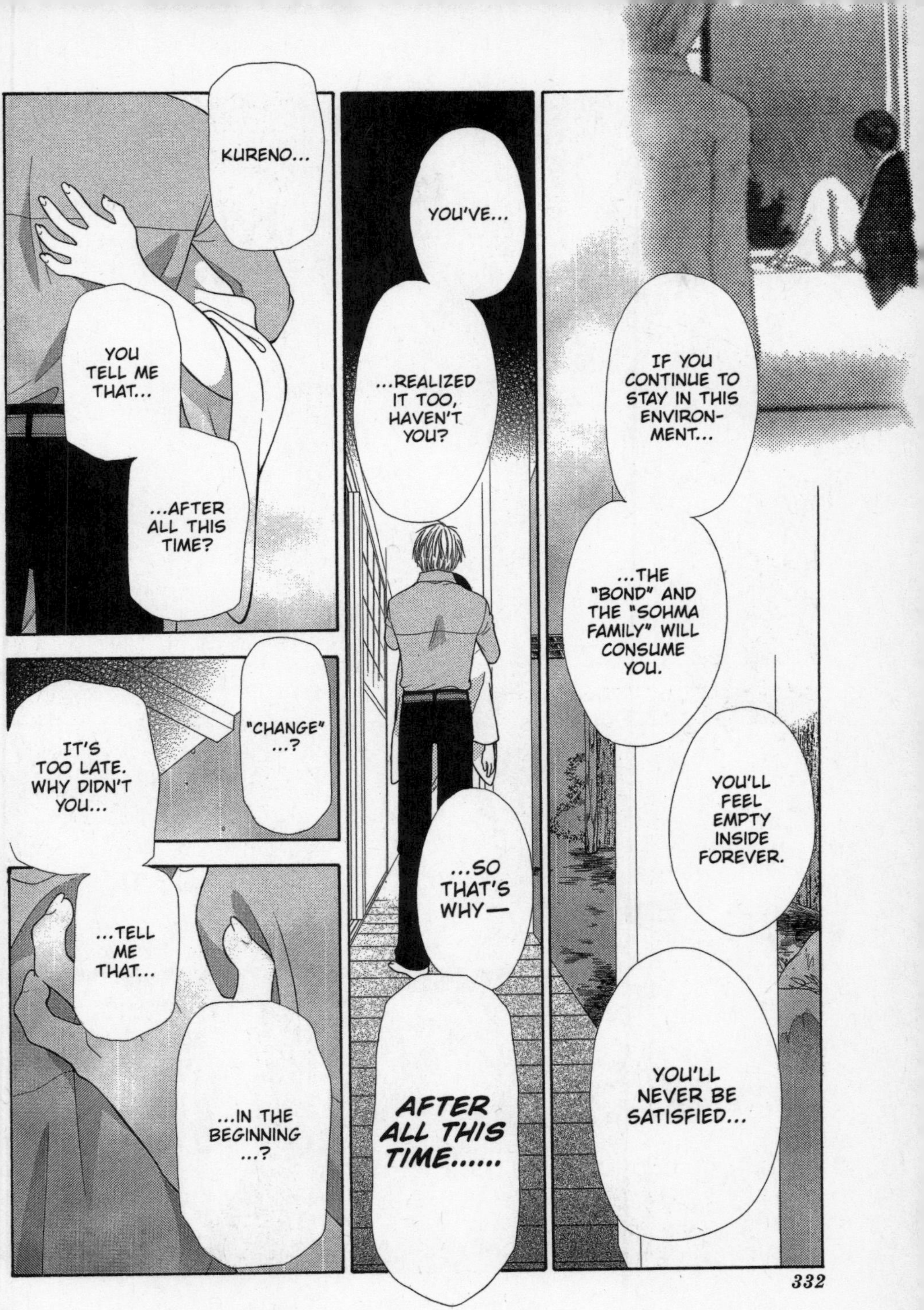
IF YOU CONTINUE TO STAY IN THIS ENVIRONMENT...
...THE "BOND" AND THE "SOHMA FAMILY" WILL CONSUME YOU.
YOU'LL FEEL EMPTY INSIDE FOREVER.
YOU'LL NEVER BE SATISFIED...
YOU'VE...
...REALIZED IT TOO, HAVEN'T YOU?
...SO THAT'S WHY—
AFTER ALL THIS TIME......
KURENO...
YOU TELL ME THAT...
...AFTER ALL THIS TIME?
"CHANGE" ...?
IT'S TOO LATE. WHY DIDN'T YOU...
...TELL ME THAT...
...IN THE BEGINNING ...?

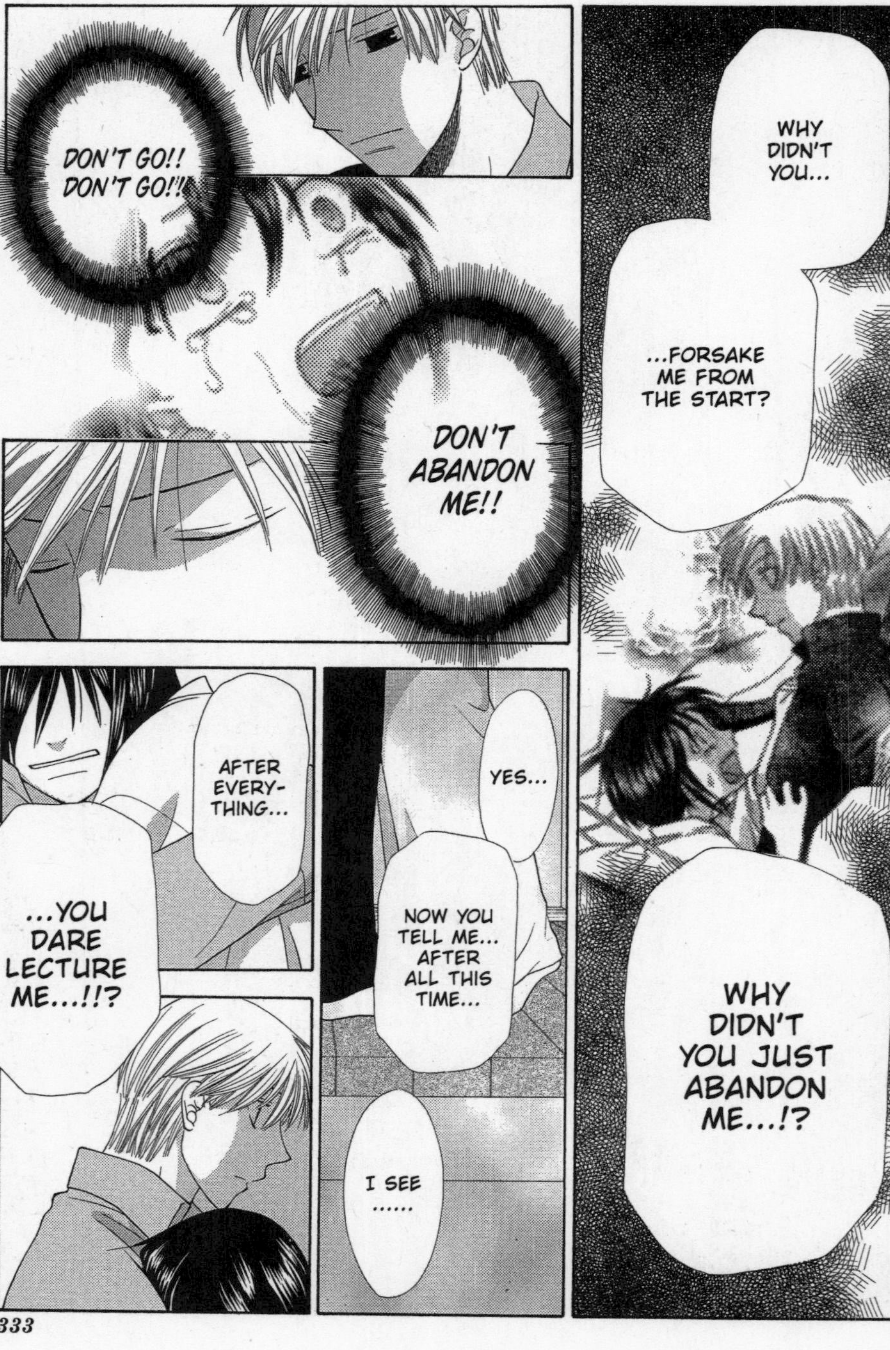
WHY DIDN'T YOU...
...FORSAKE ME FROM THE START?
WHY DIDN'T YOU JUST ABANDON ME...!?
DON'T GO!! DON'T GO!!
DON'T ABANDON ME!!
YES...
NOW YOU TELL ME... AFTER ALL THIS TIME...
I SEE ......
AFTER EVERY-THING...
...YOU DARE LECTURE ME...!!?

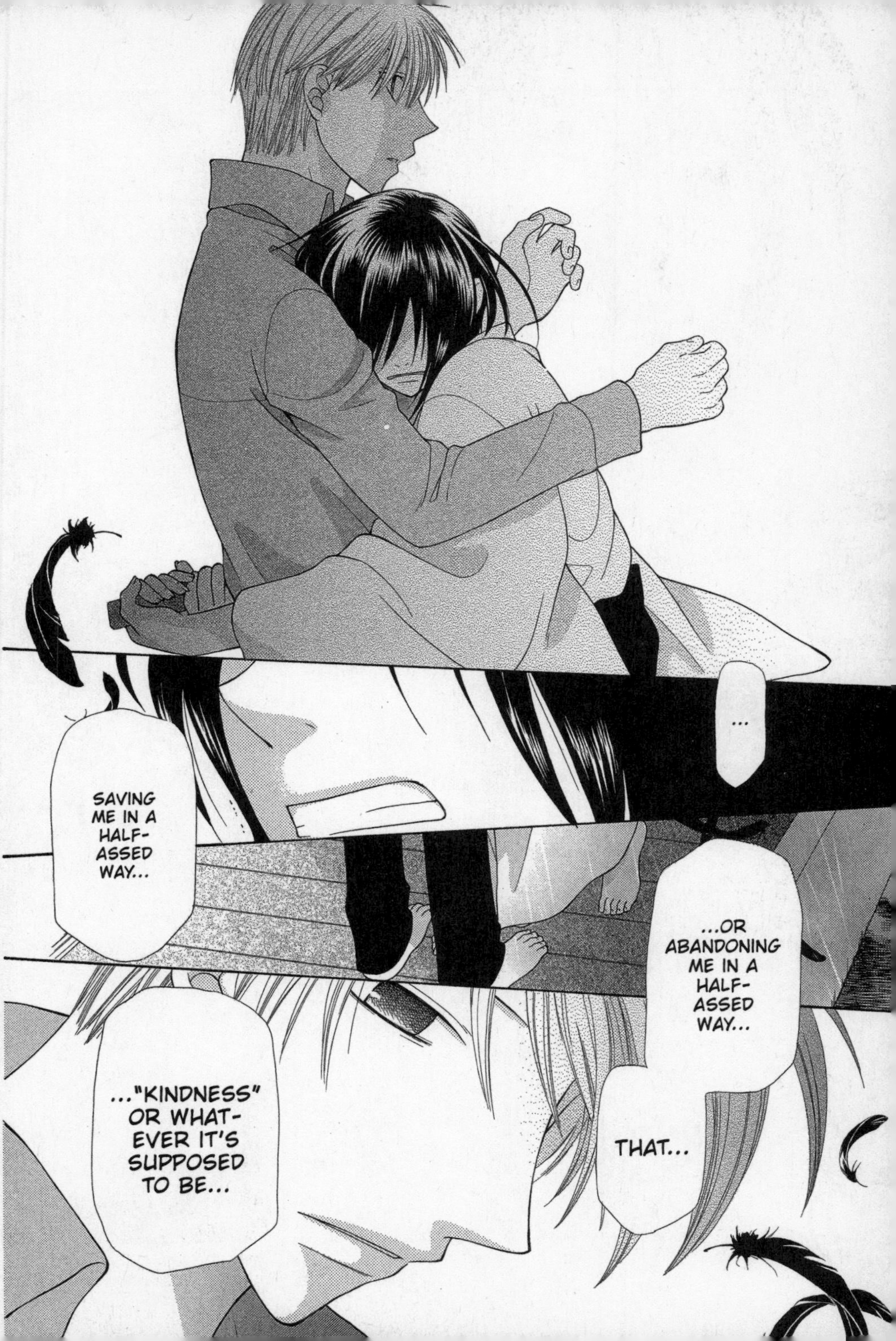
...
SAVING ME IN A HALF-ASSED WAY...
...OR ABANDONING ME IN A HALF-ASSED WAY...
THAT...
..."KINDNESS" OR WHAT-EVER IT'S SUPPOSED TO BE...

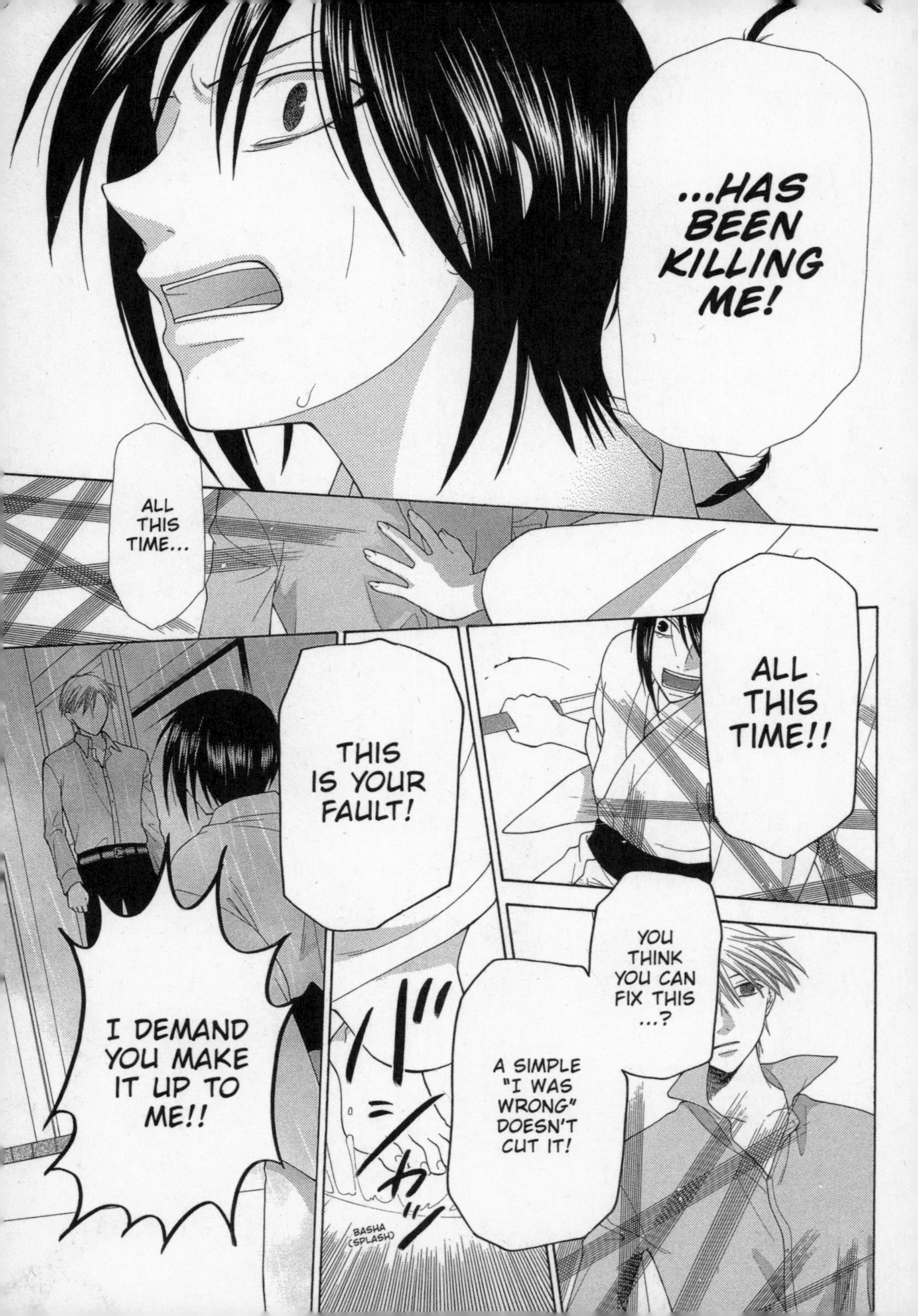
...HAS BEEN KILLING ME!
ALL THIS TIME...
ALL THIS TIME!!
YOU THINK YOU CAN FIX THIS ...?
A SIMPLE "I WAS WRONG" DOESN'T CUT IT!
THIS IS YOUR FAULT!
BASHA (SPLASH)
I DEMAND YOU MAKE IT UP TO ME!!

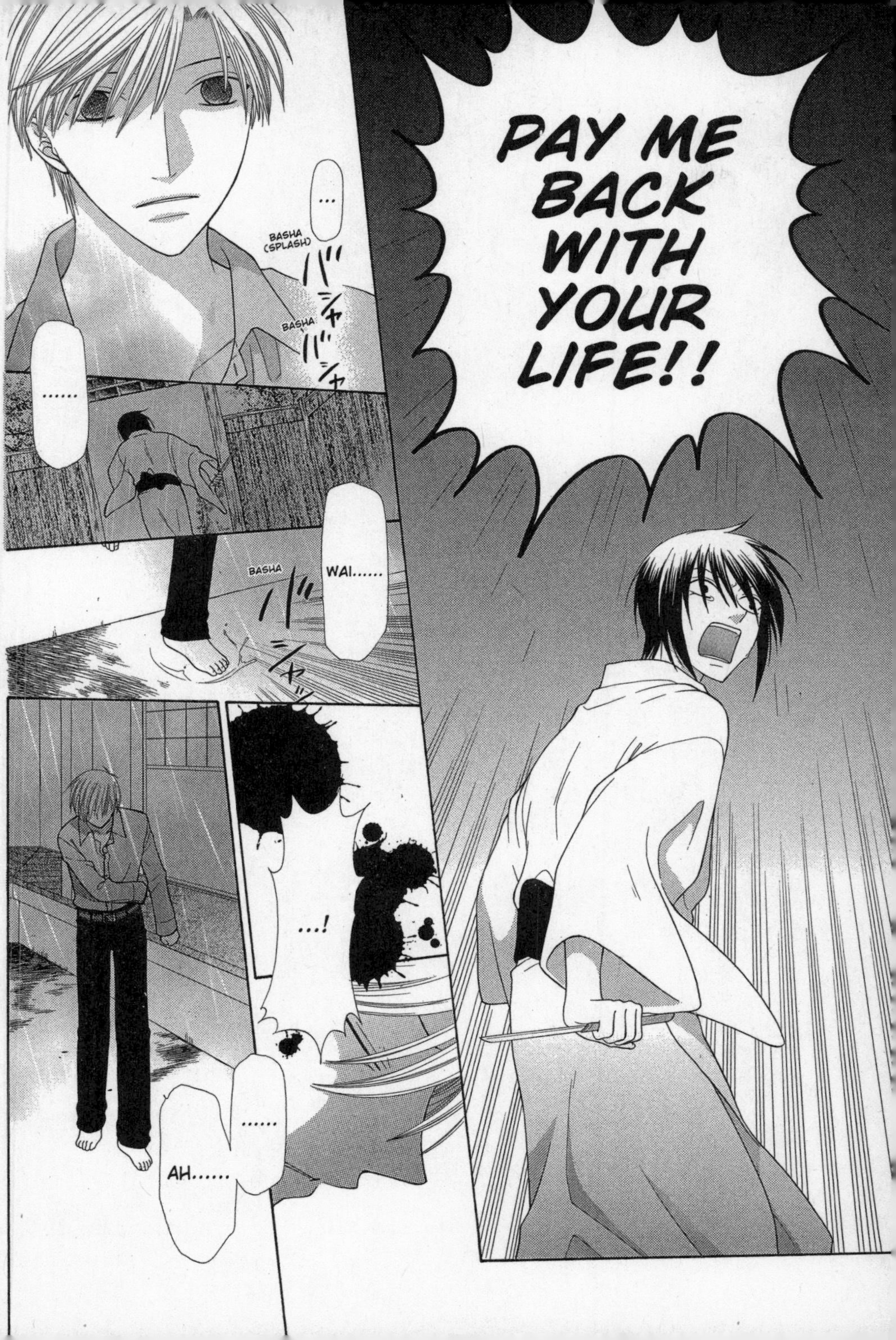
PAY ME BACK WITH YOUR LIFE!!
...
BASHA (SPLASH)
バシャ
BASHA
バシャ
......
BASHA
バシャ
WAI......
...!
......
AH......

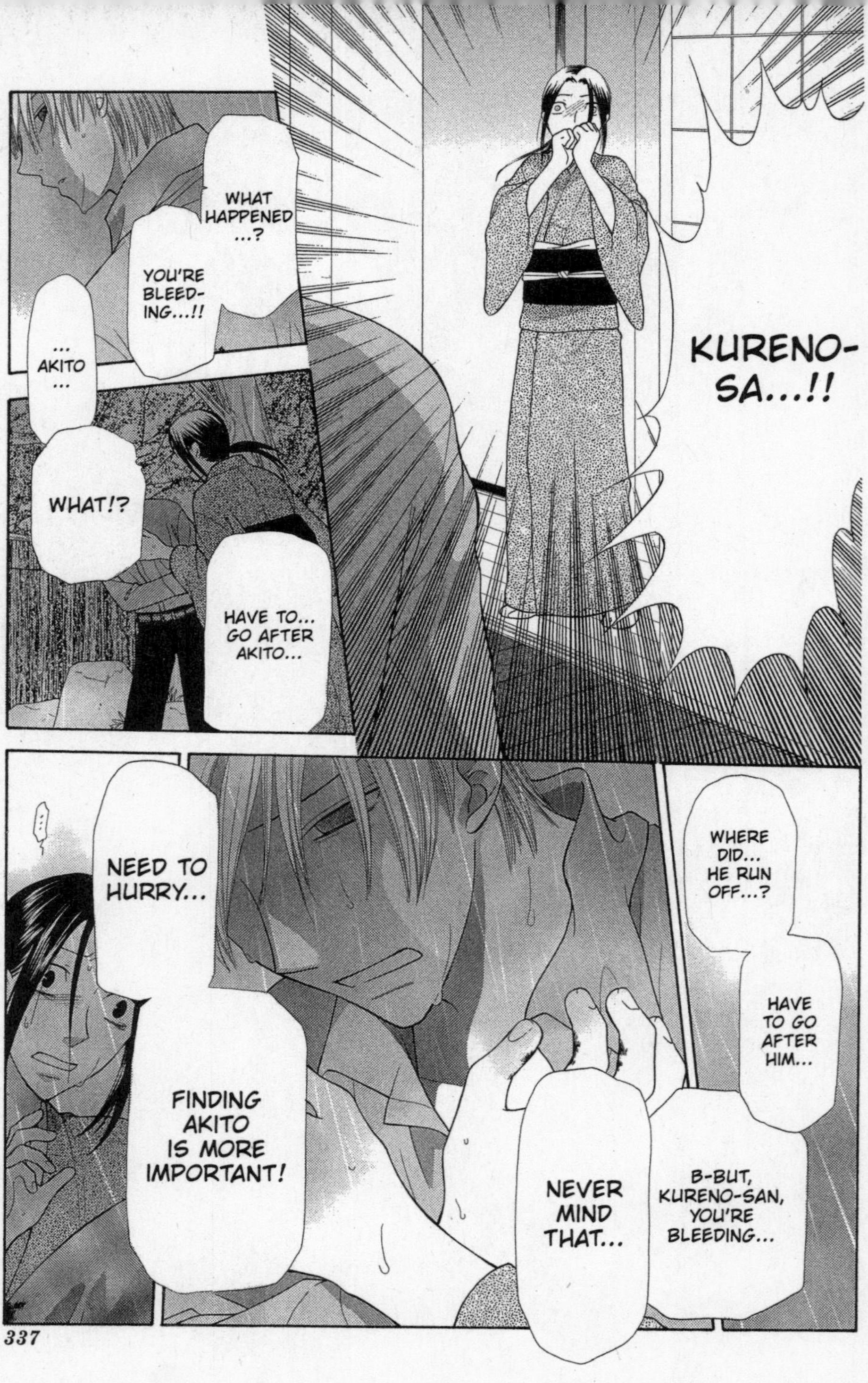
KURENO-SA...!!
WHAT HAPPENED...?
YOU'RE BLEEDING...!!
...AKITO...
WHAT!?
HAVE TO... GO AFTER AKITO...
WHERE DID... HE RUN OFF...?
HAVE TO GO AFTER HIM...
B-BUT, KURENO-SAN, YOU'RE BLEEDING...
NEVER MIND THAT...
NEED TO HURRY...
FINDING AKITO IS MORE IMPORTANT!
...!

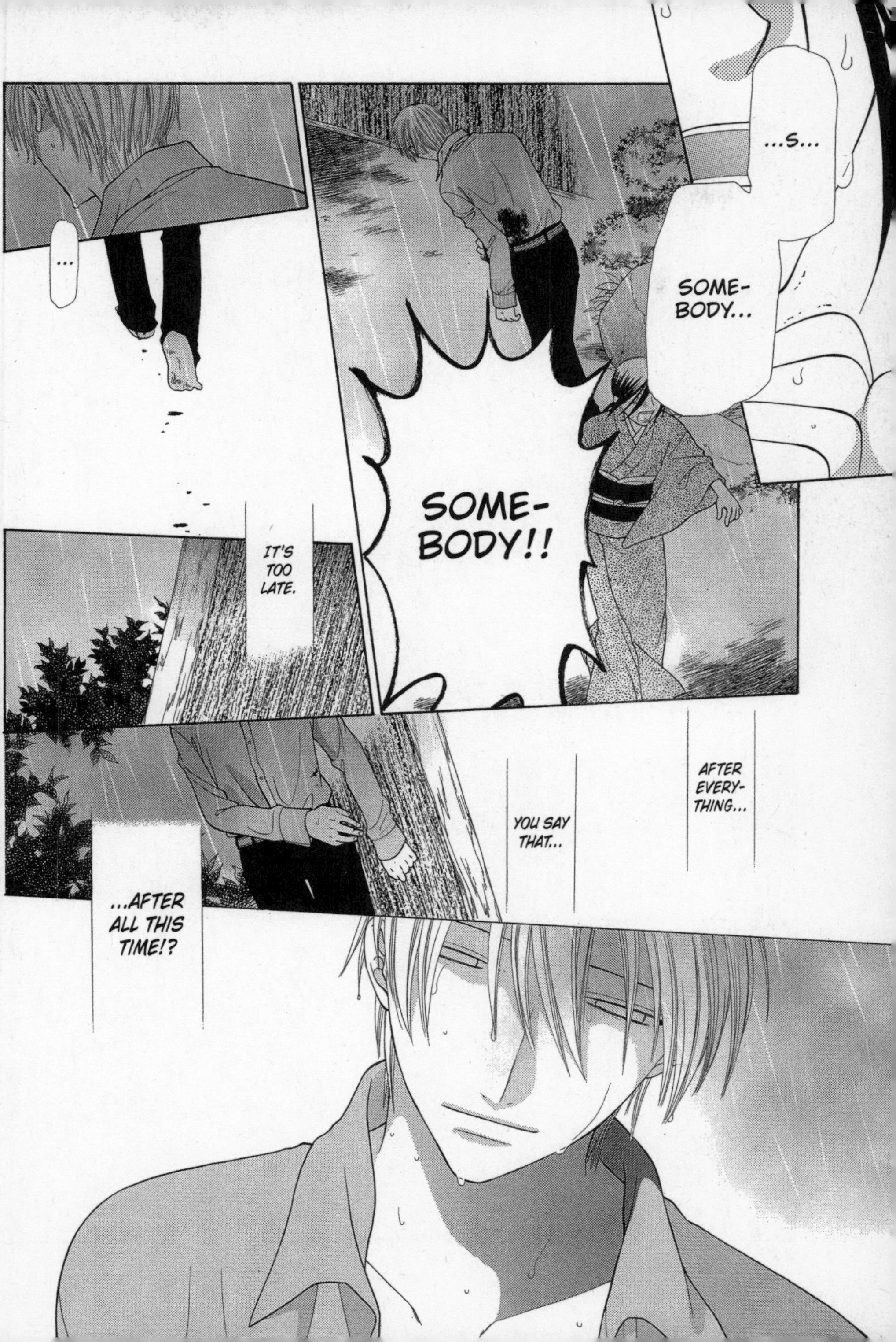
...S...
SOME-BODY...
SOME-BODY!!
...
IT'S TOO LATE.
AFTER EVERY-THING...
YOU SAY THAT...
...AFTER ALL THIS TIME!?

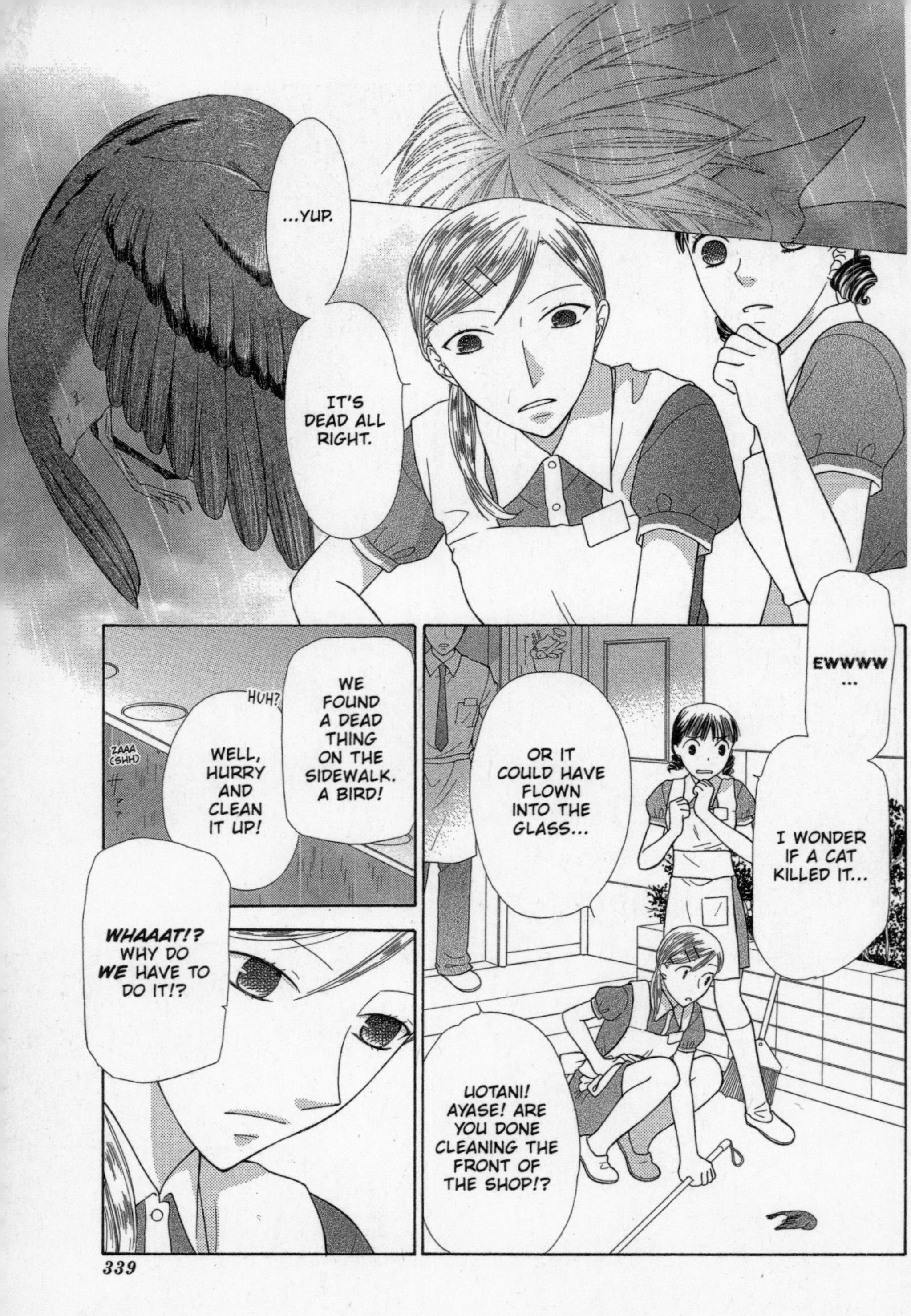
...YUP.
IT'S DEAD ALL RIGHT.
EWWWW...
I WONDER IF A CAT KILLED IT...
OR IT COULD HAVE FLOWN INTO THE GLASS...
UOTANI! AYASE! ARE YOU DONE CLEANING THE FRONT OF THE SHOP!?
WE FOUND A DEAD THING ON THE SIDEWALK. A BIRD!
HUH?
WELL, HURRY AND CLEAN IT UP!
ZAAA (SHH)
WHAAAT!? WHY DO *WE* HAVE TO DO IT!?

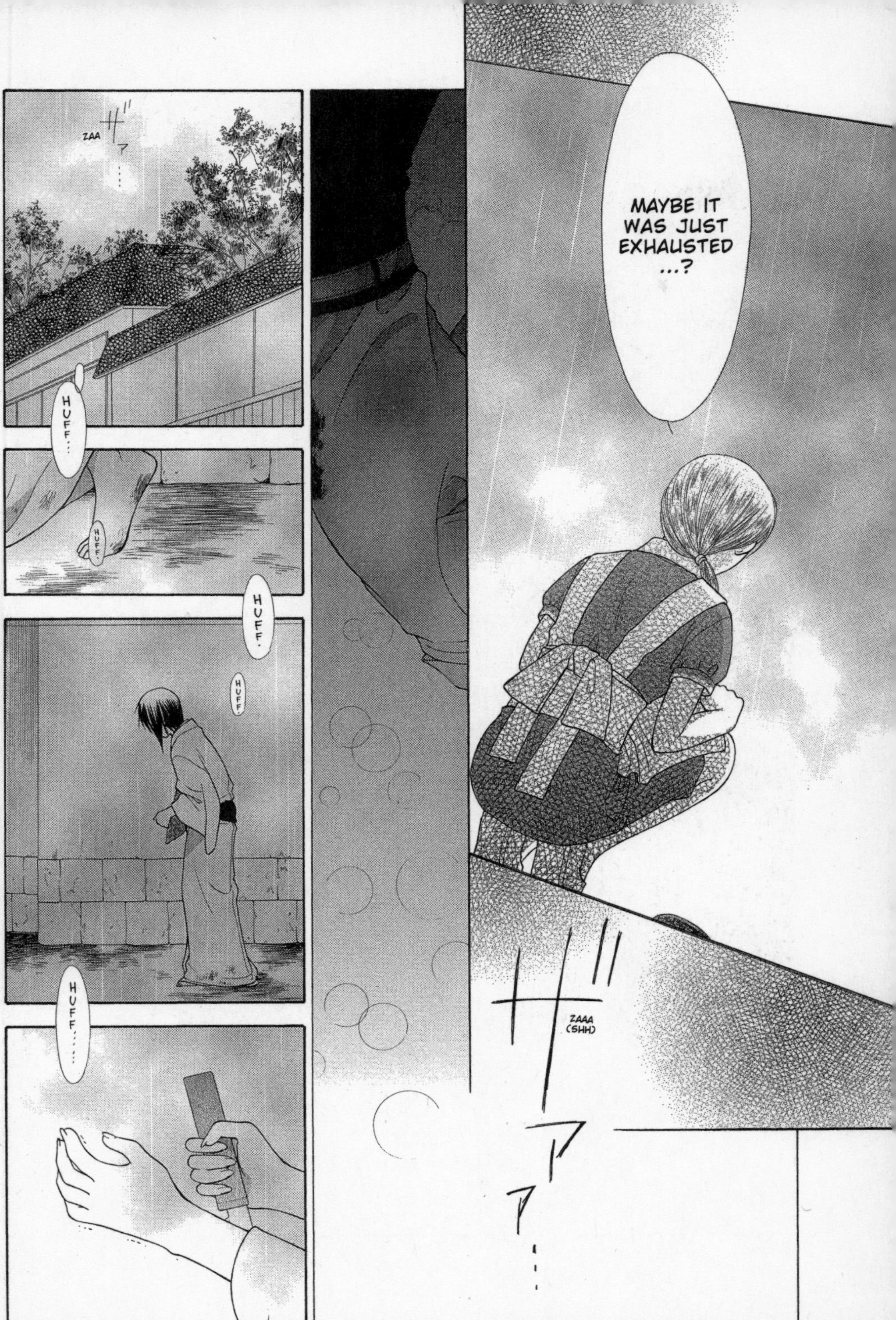
MAYBE IT WAS JUST EXHAUSTED ...?
ZAAA (SHH)
ZAA
HUFF...
HUFF.
HUFF.
HUFF.
HUFF.....

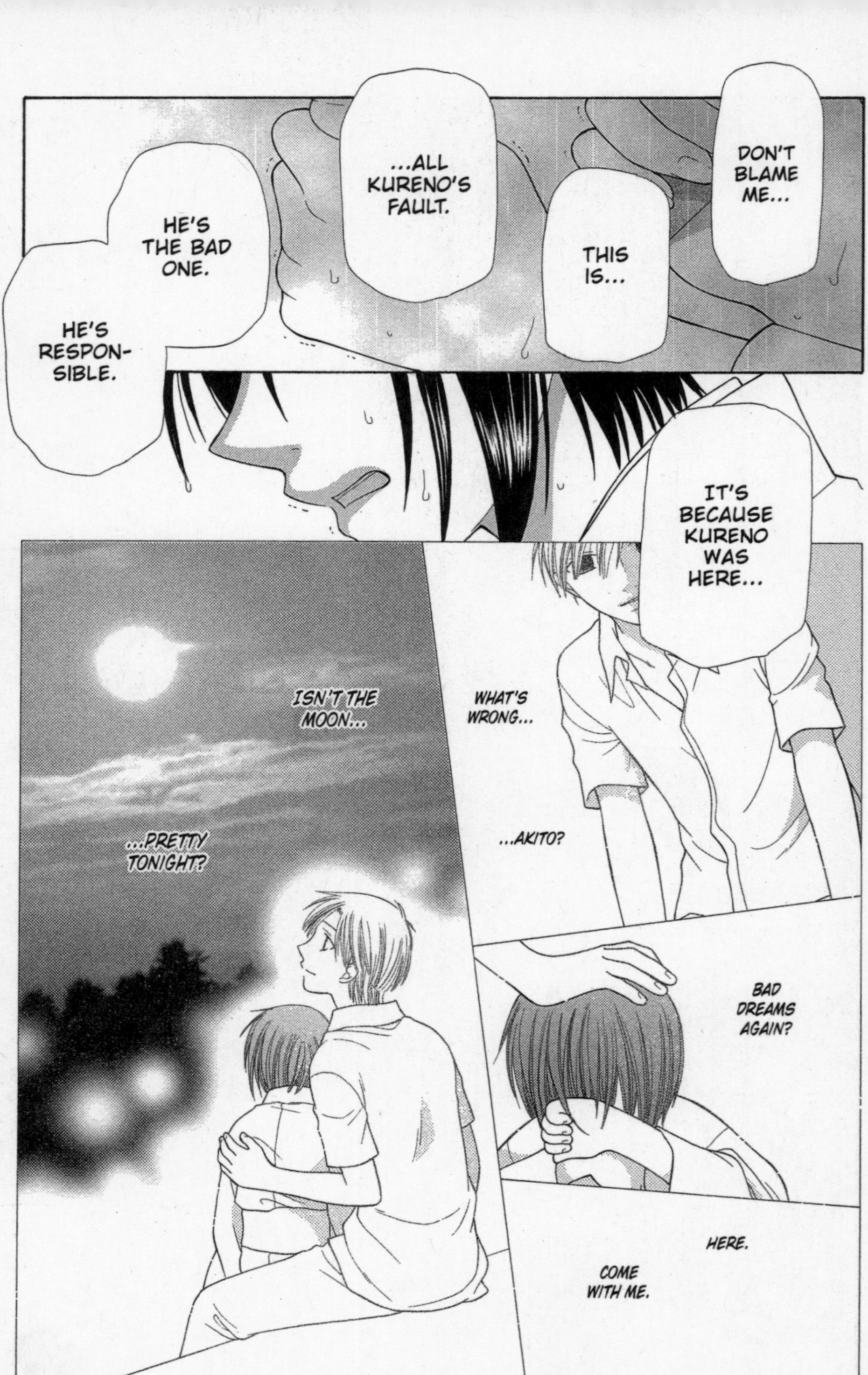
DON'T BLAME ME...
THIS IS...
...ALL KURENO'S FAULT.
HE'S THE BAD ONE.
HE'S RESPON-SIBLE.
IT'S BECAUSE KURENO WAS HERE...
WHAT'S WRONG...
...AKITO?
BAD DREAMS AGAIN?
HERE.
COME WITH ME.
ISN'T THE MOON...
...PRETTY TONIGHT?

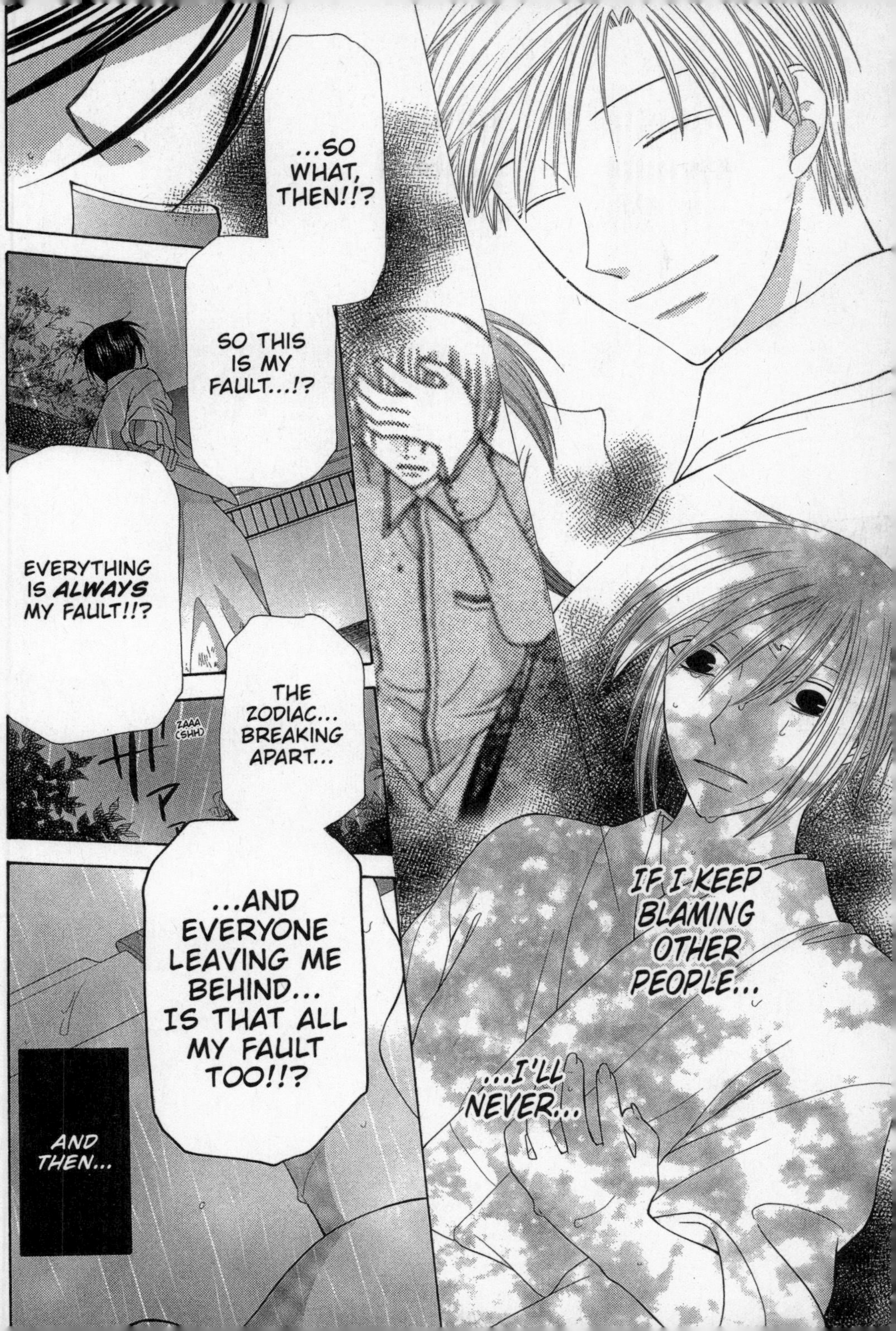
...SO WHAT, THEN!!?
SO THIS IS MY FAULT...!?
EVERYTHING IS ALWAYS MY FAULT!!?
THE ZODIAC... BREAKING APART...
ZAAA (SHHH)
...AND EVERYONE LEAVING ME BEHIND... IS THAT ALL MY FAULT TOO!!?
IF I KEEP BLAMING OTHER PEOPLE...
...I'LL NEVER...
AND THEN...

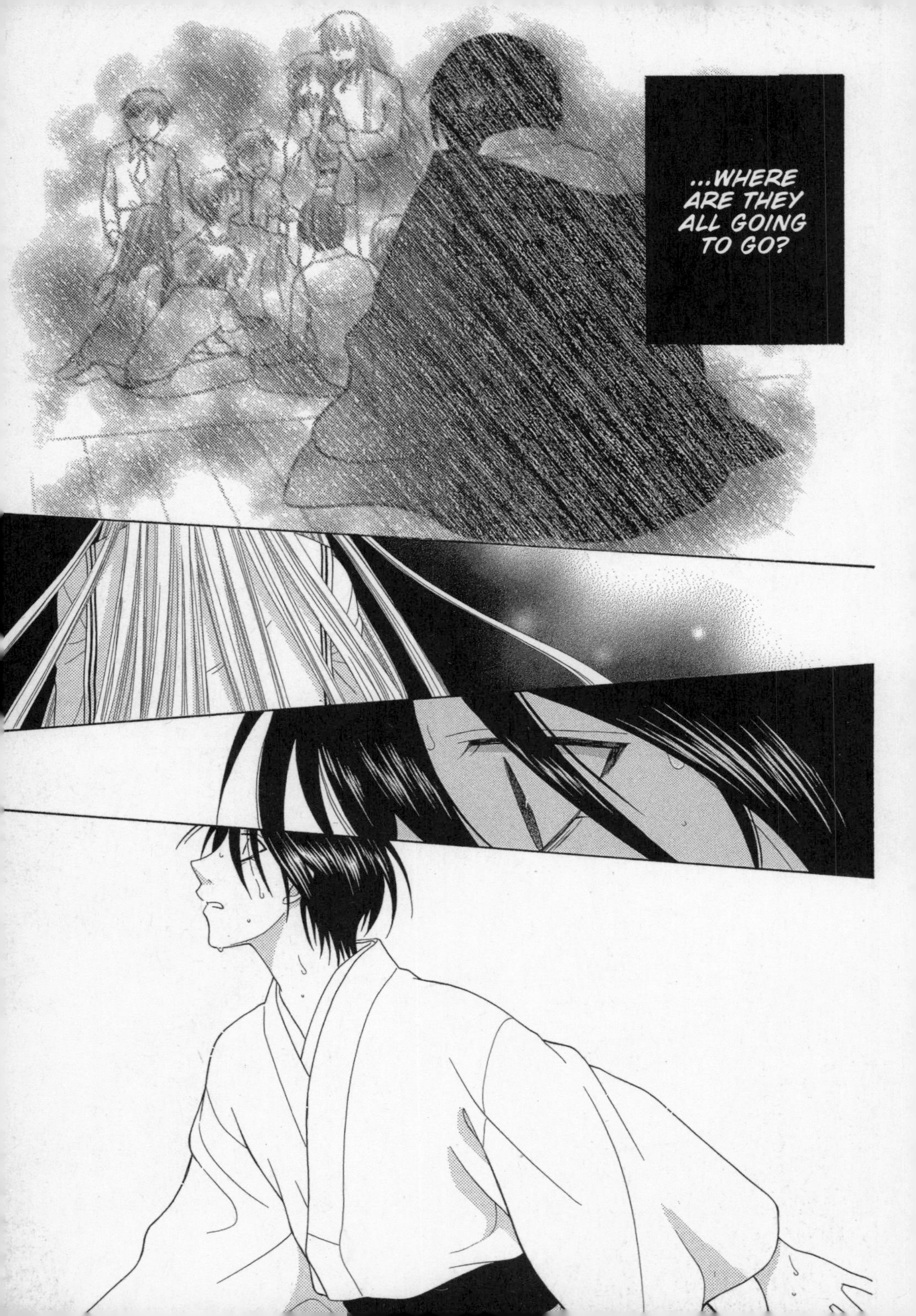
...WHERE ARE THEY ALL GOING TO GO?

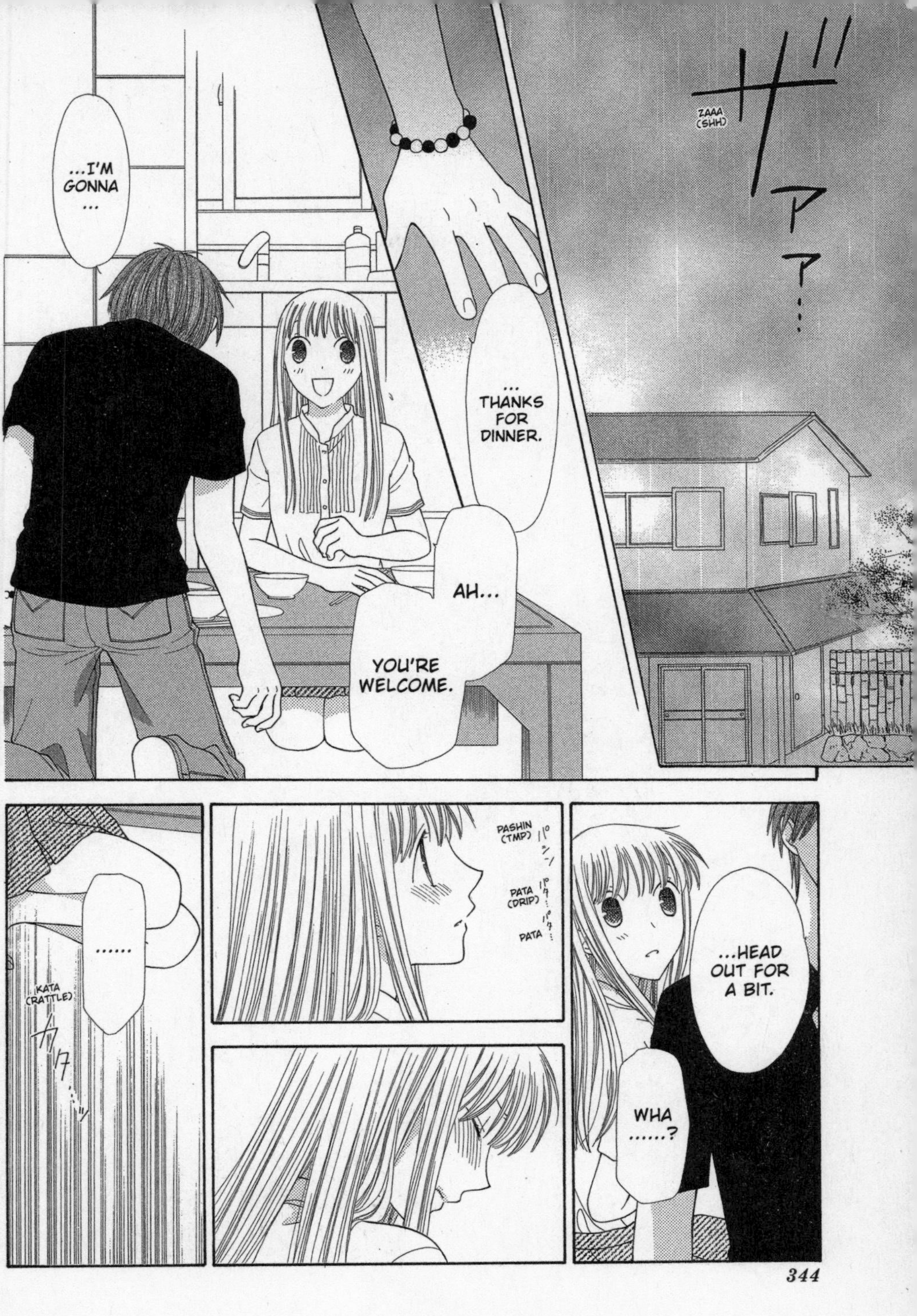
ZAAA (SHH)
...THANKS FOR DINNER.
AH...
YOU'RE WELCOME.
...I'M GONNA ...
...HEAD OUT FOR A BIT.
WHA ......?
PASHIN (TMP)
PATA (DRIP)
PATA
......
KATA (RATTLE)

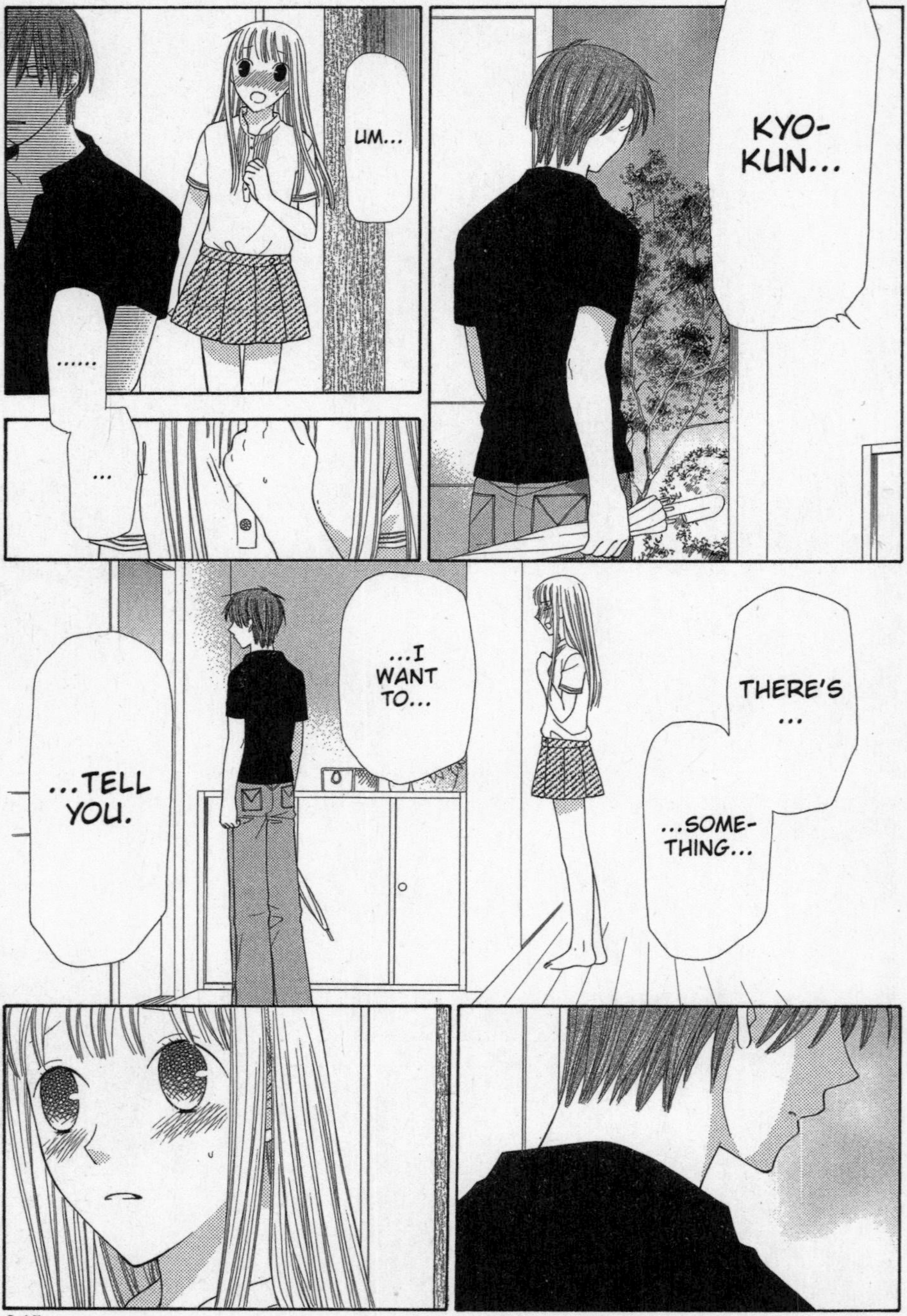
KYO-KUN...
UM...
......
...
THERE'S ...
...SOME-THING...
...I WANT TO...
...TELL YOU.

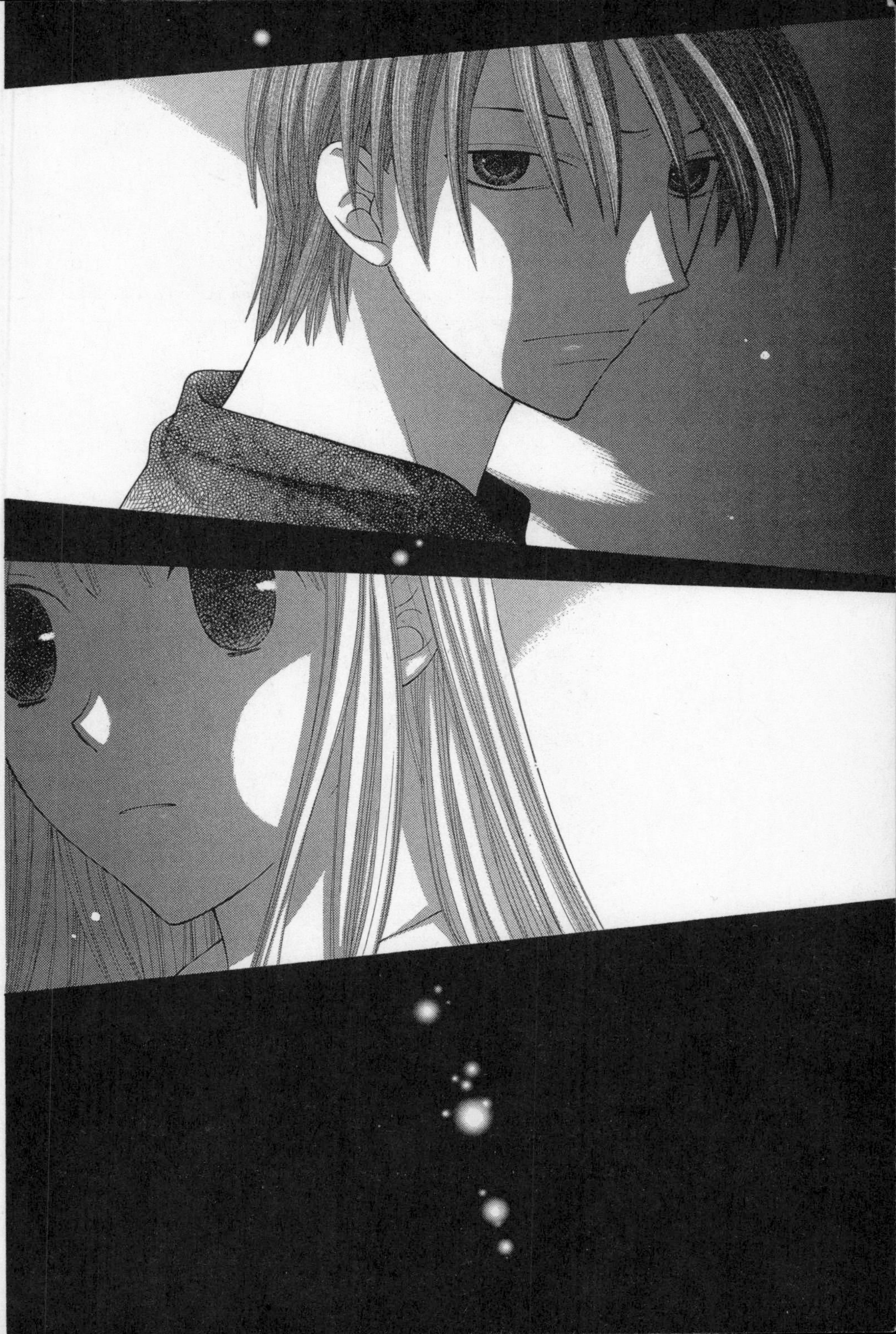

Chapter 119

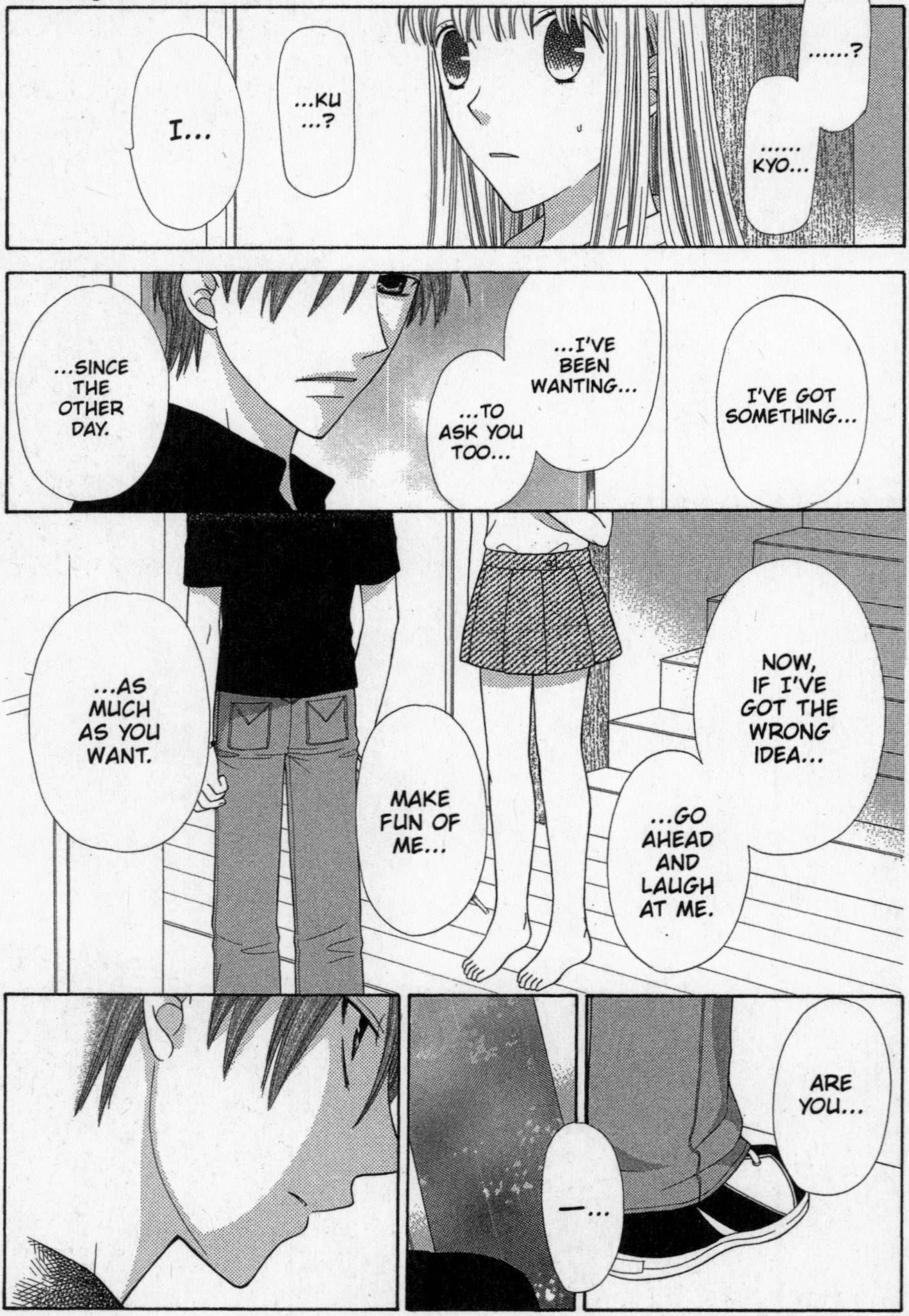
......?
...... KYO...
...KU ...?
I...
I'VE GOT SOMETHING...
...I'VE BEEN WANTING...
...TO ASK YOU TOO...
...SINCE THE OTHER DAY.
NOW, IF I'VE GOT THE WRONG IDEA...
...GO AHEAD AND LAUGH AT ME.
MAKE FUN OF ME...
...AS MUCH AS YOU WANT.
ARE YOU...
—...

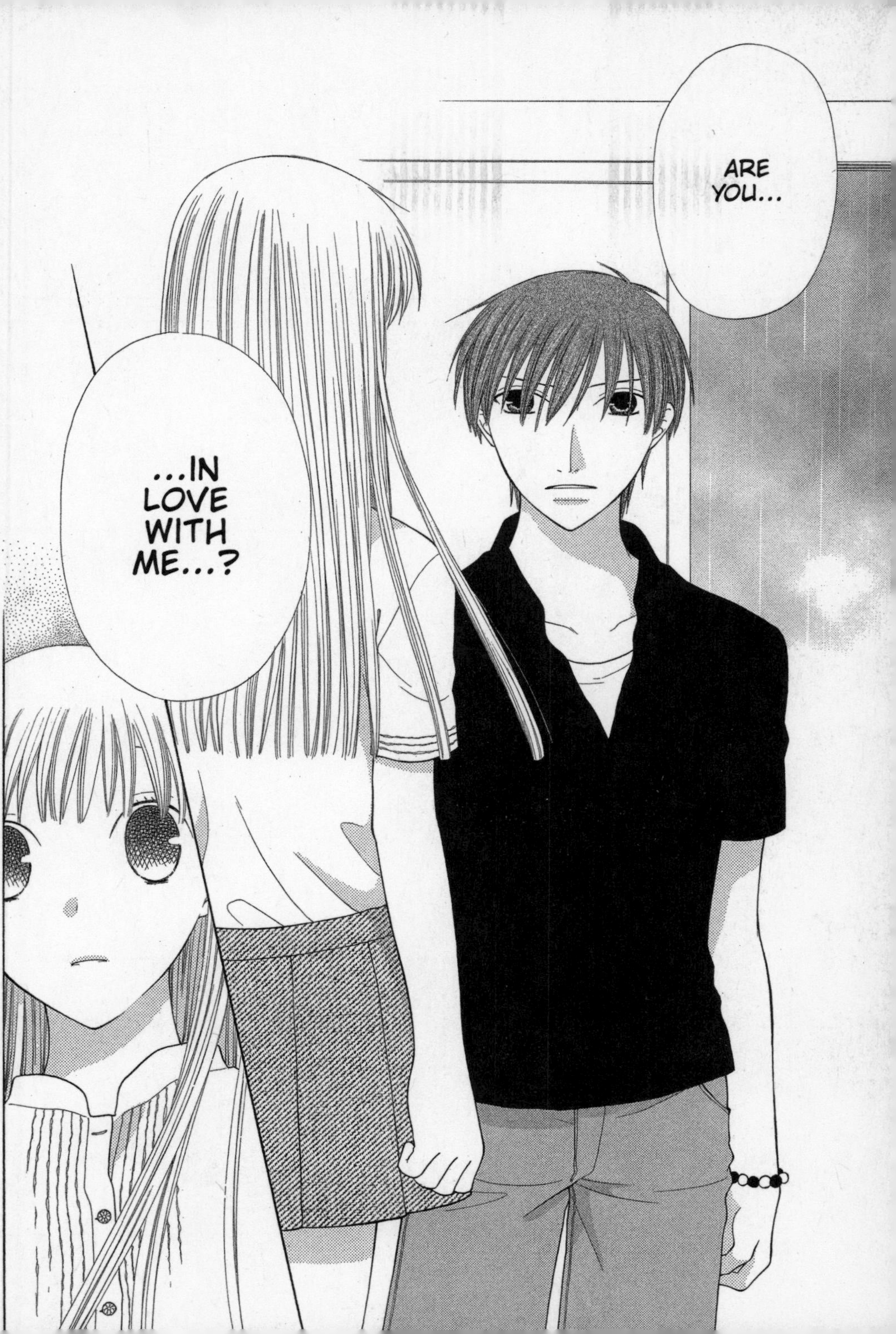
ARE YOU...
...IN LOVE WITH ME...?

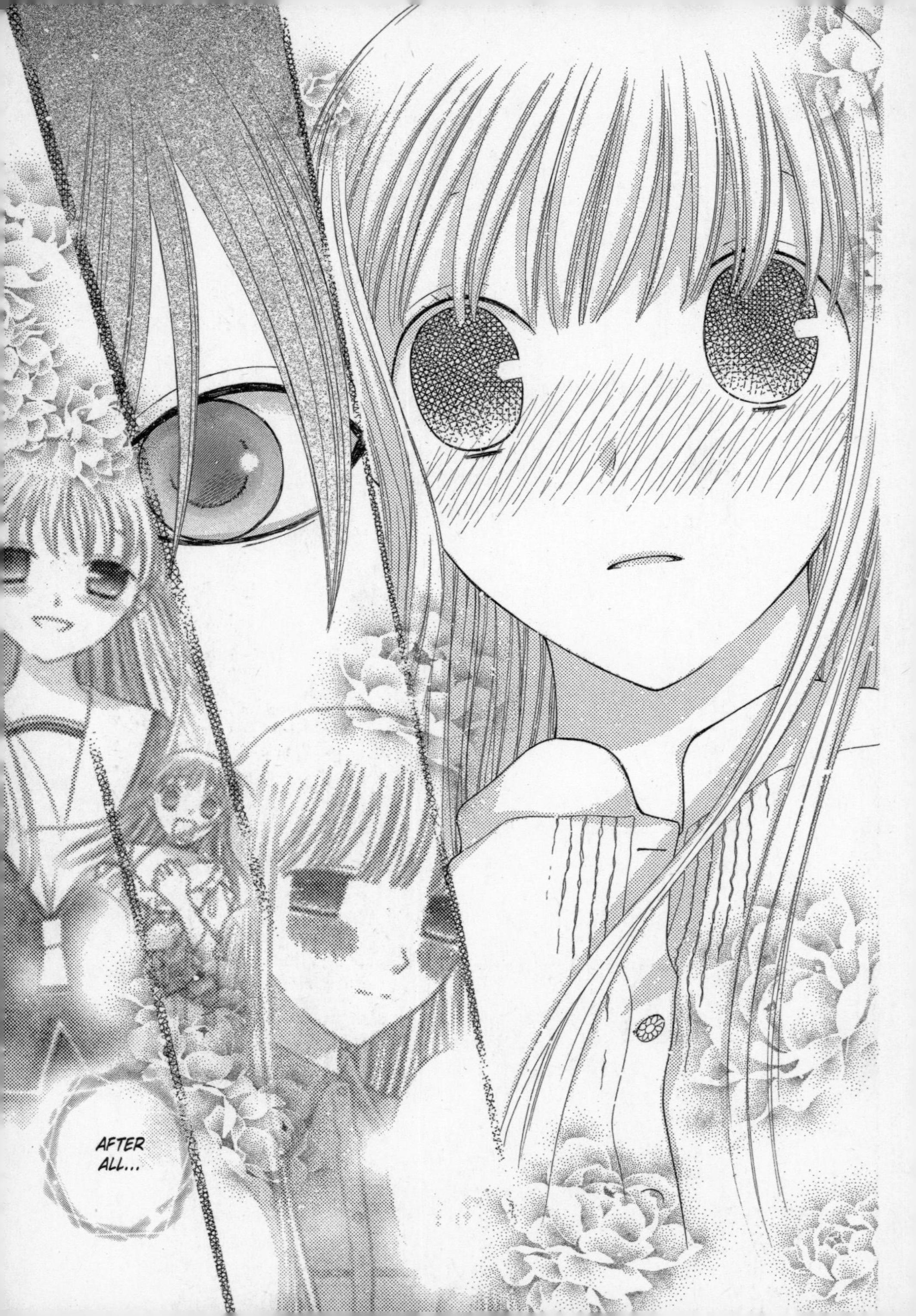
AFTER ALL...

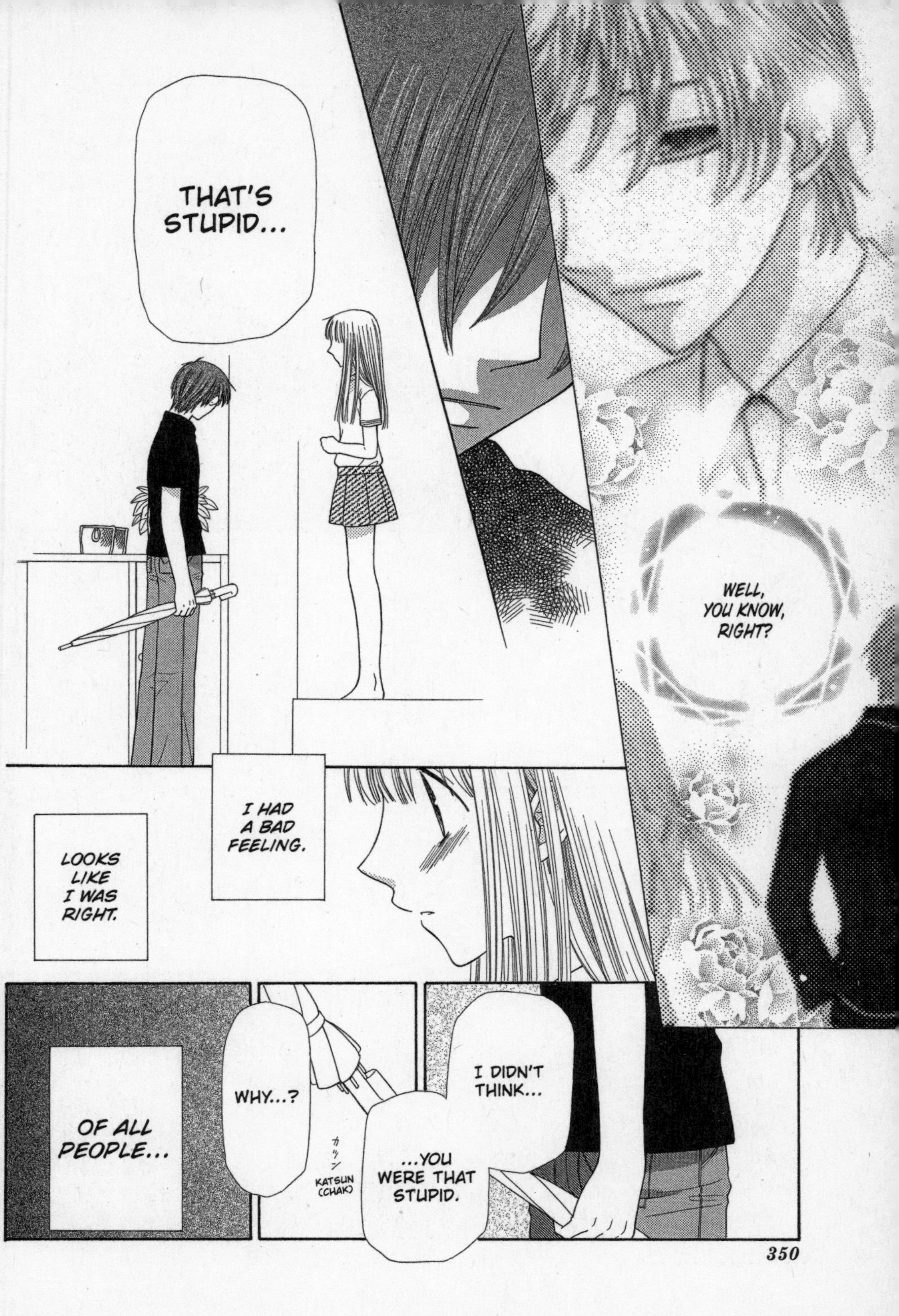
WELL, YOU KNOW, RIGHT?
THAT'S STUPID...
I HAD A BAD FEELING.
LOOKS LIKE I WAS RIGHT.
I DIDN'T THINK...
...YOU WERE THAT STUPID.
WHY...?
カツン
KATSUN (CHAK)
OF ALL PEOPLE...

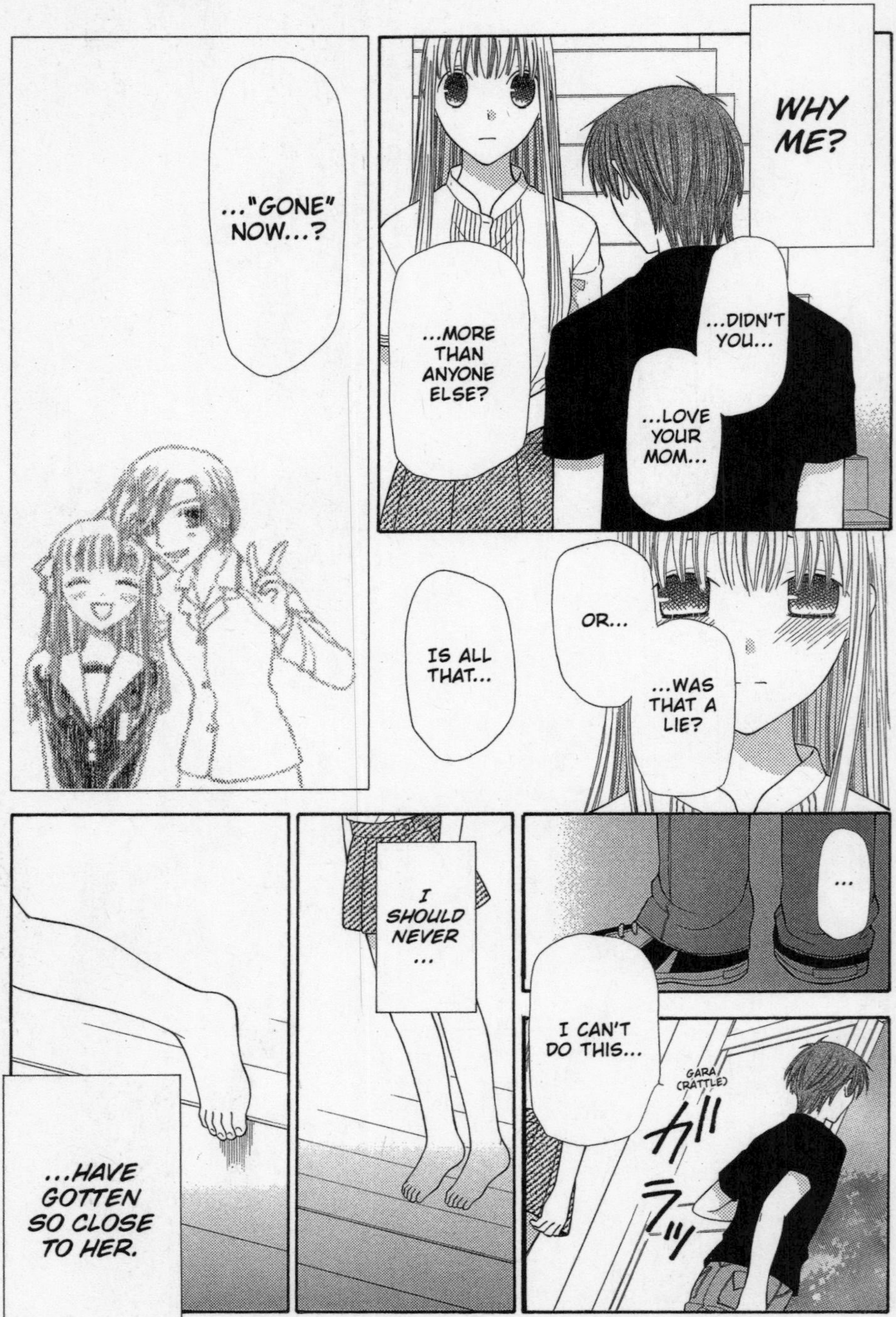
WHY ME?
...DIDN'T YOU...
...LOVE YOUR MOM...
...MORE THAN ANYONE ELSE?
OR...
...WAS THAT A LIE?
IS ALL THAT...
..."GONE" NOW...?
...
I CAN'T DO THIS...
GARA (RATTLE)
I SHOULD NEVER ...
...HAVE GOTTEN SO CLOSE TO HER.

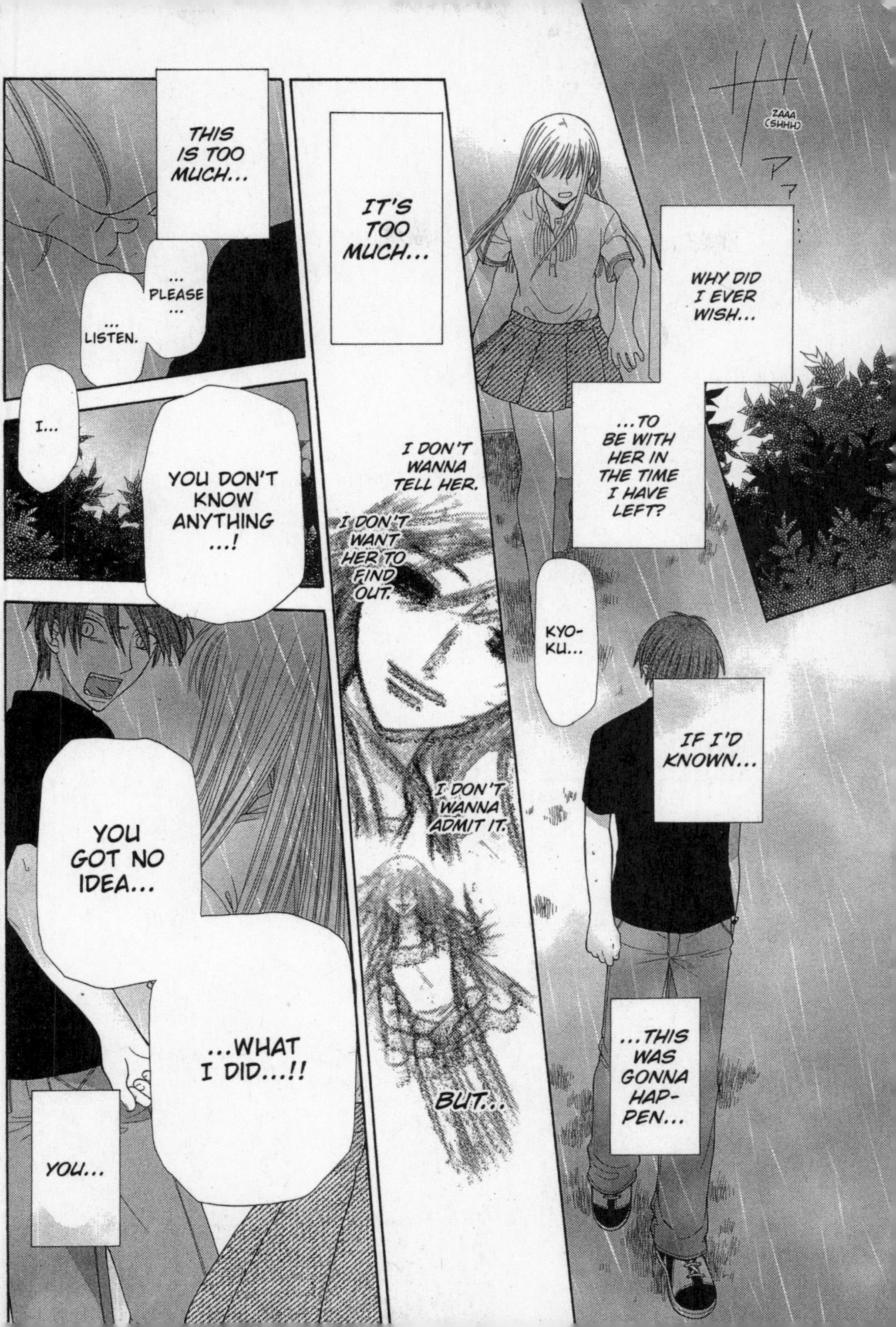
ZAAA (SHHH)
WHY DID I EVER WISH...
...TO BE WITH HER IN THE TIME I HAVE LEFT?
KYO-KU...
IF I'D KNOWN...
...THIS WAS GONNA HAPPEN...
IT'S TOO MUCH...
I DON'T WANNA TELL HER.
I DON'T WANT HER TO FIND OUT.
I DON'T WANNA ADMIT IT.
BUT...
THIS IS TOO MUCH...
...PLEASE...
...LISTEN.
I...
YOU DON'T KNOW ANYTHING...!
YOU GOT NO IDEA...
...WHAT I DID...!!
YOU...

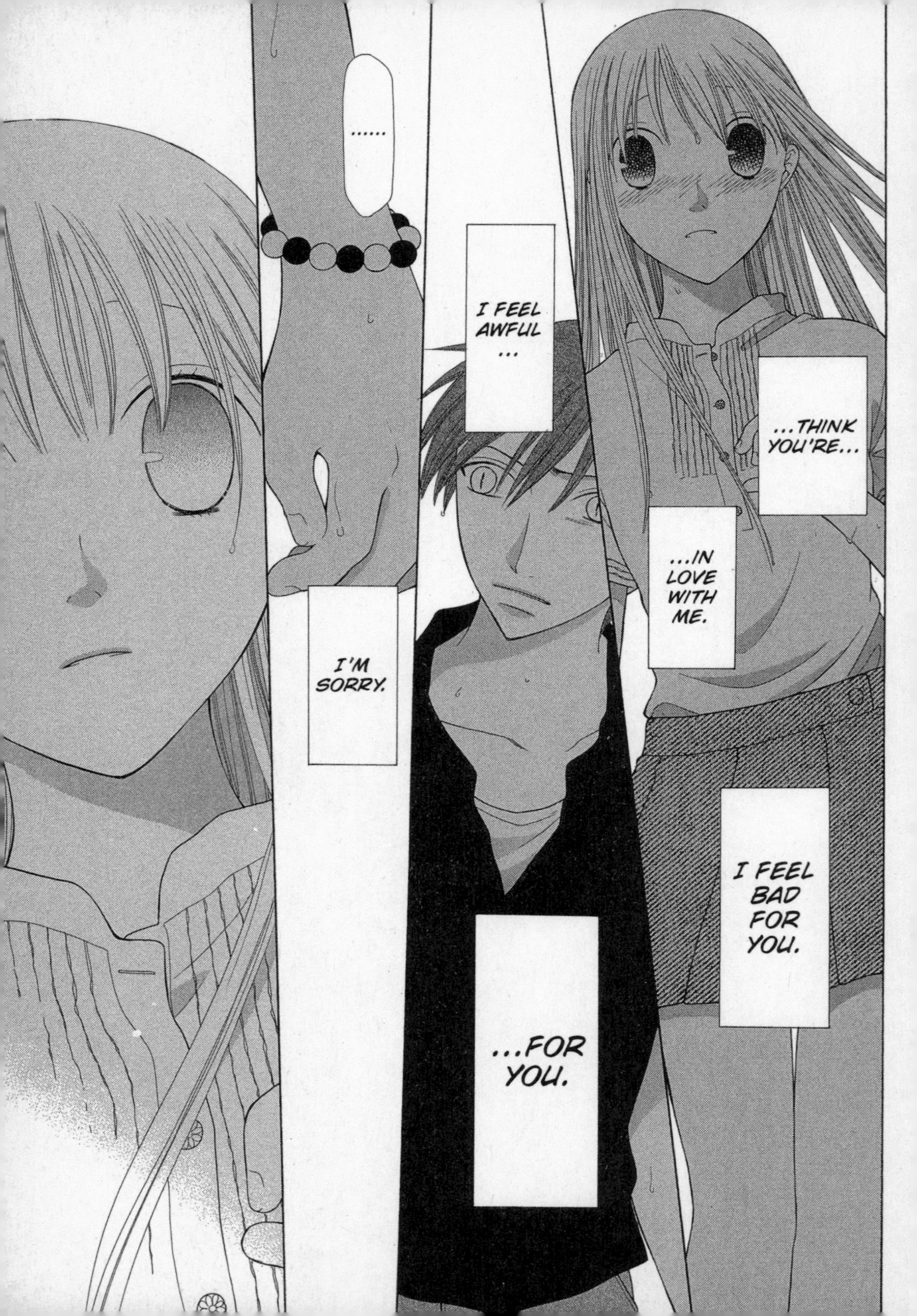
...THINK YOU'RE...
...IN LOVE WITH ME.
I FEEL BAD FOR YOU.
I FEEL AWFUL ...
...FOR YOU.
......
I'M SORRY.

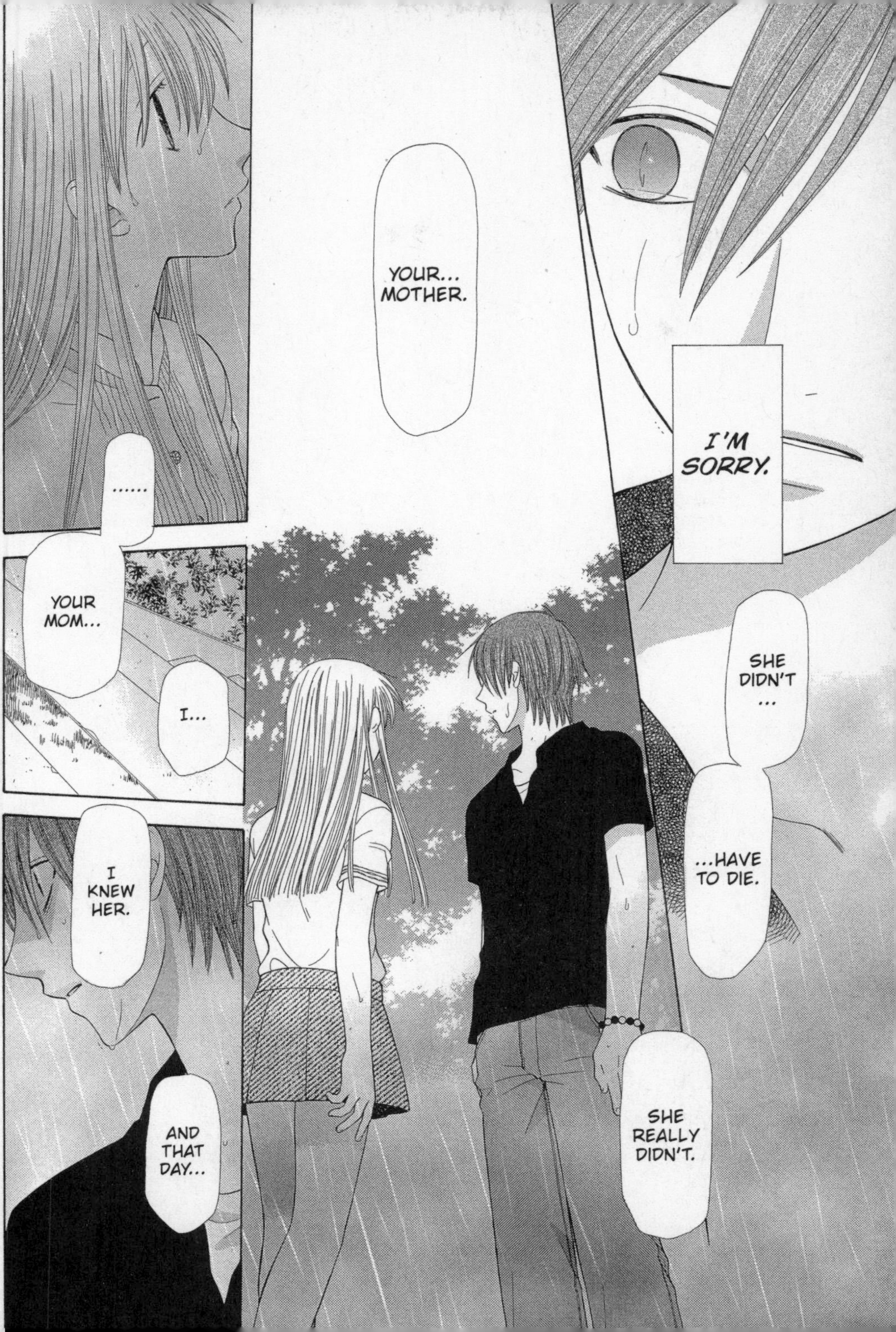
YOUR... MOTHER.
I'M SORRY.
SHE DIDN'T ...
...HAVE TO DIE.
SHE REALLY DIDN'T.
......
YOUR MOM...
I...
I KNEW HER.
AND THAT DAY...

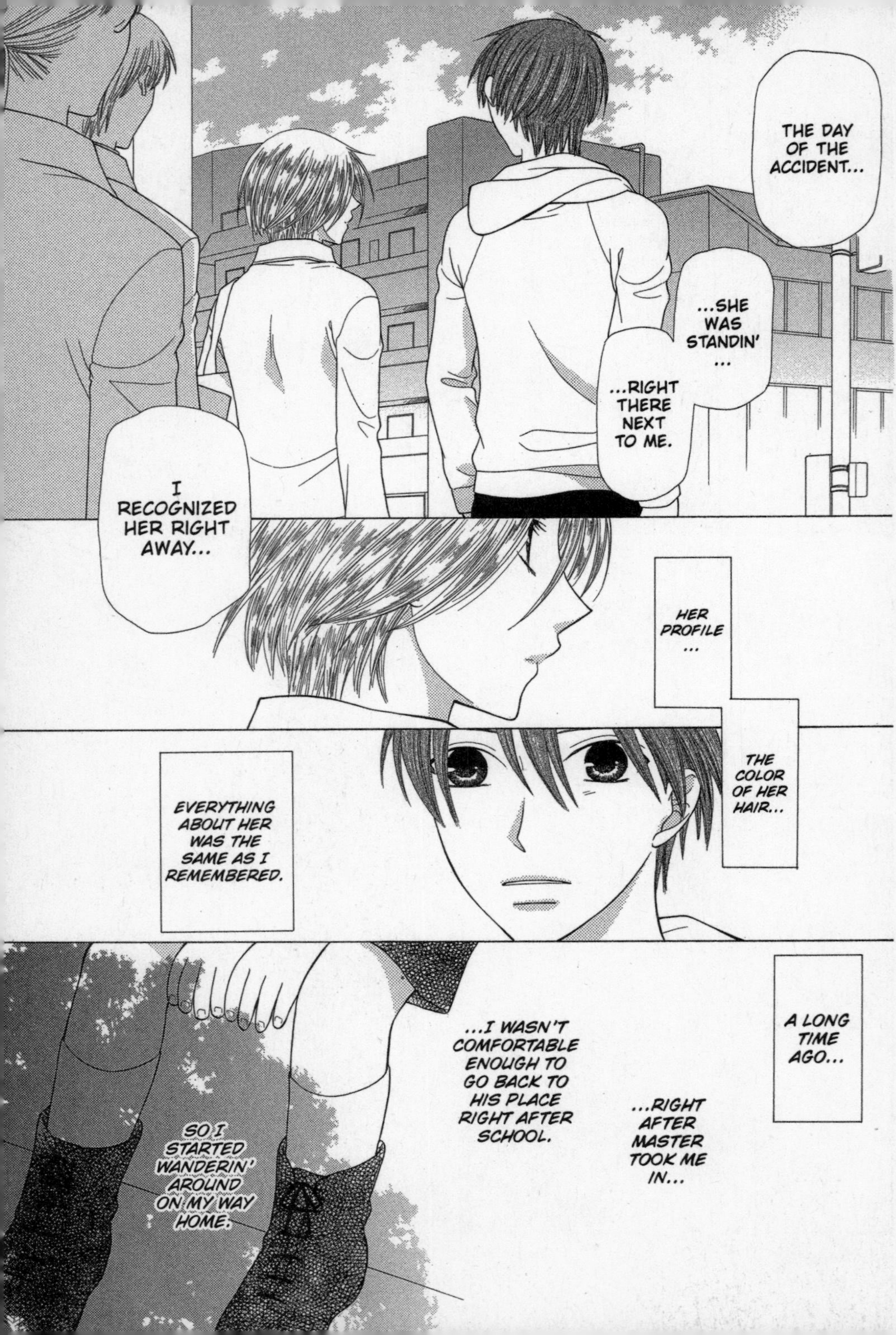
THE DAY OF THE ACCIDENT...
...SHE WAS STANDIN' ...
...RIGHT THERE NEXT TO ME.
I RECOGNIZED HER RIGHT AWAY...
HER PROFILE ...
THE COLOR OF HER HAIR...
EVERYTHING ABOUT HER WAS THE SAME AS I REMEMBERED.
A LONG TIME AGO...
...RIGHT AFTER MASTER TOOK ME IN...
...I WASN'T COMFORTABLE ENOUGH TO GO BACK TO HIS PLACE RIGHT AFTER SCHOOL.
SO I STARTED WANDERIN' AROUND ON MY WAY HOME.

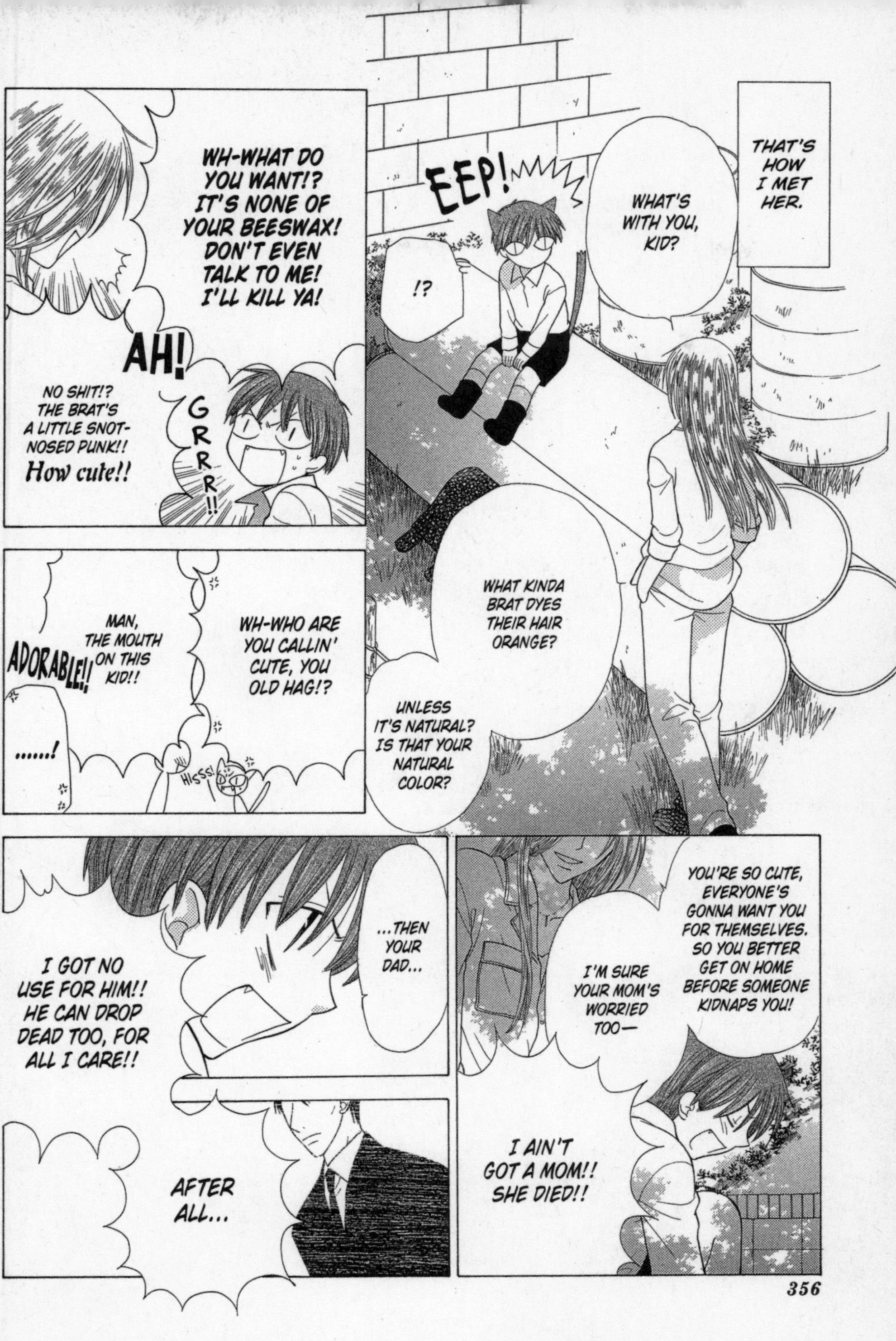
THAT'S HOW I MET HER.
WHAT'S WITH YOU, KID?
EEP!
!?
WHAT KINDA BRAT DYES THEIR HAIR ORANGE?
UNLESS IT'S NATURAL? IS THAT YOUR NATURAL COLOR?
WH-WHAT DO YOU WANT!? IT'S NONE OF YOUR BEESWAX! DON'T EVEN TALK TO ME! I'LL KILL YA!
AH!
GRRR!!
NO SHIT!? THE BRAT'S A LITTLE SNOT-NOSED PUNK!! How cute!!
WH-WHO ARE YOU CALLIN' CUTE, YOU OLD HAG!?
MAN, THE MOUTH ON THIS KID!!
ADORABLE!!
......!
HISSS!
YOU'RE SO CUTE, EVERYONE'S GONNA WANT YOU FOR THEMSELVES. SO YOU BETTER GET ON HOME BEFORE SOMEONE KIDNAPS YOU!
I'M SURE YOUR MOM'S WORRIED TOO—
I AIN'T GOT A MOM!! SHE DIED!!
...THEN YOUR DAD...
I GOT NO USE FOR HIM!! HE CAN DROP DEAD TOO, FOR ALL I CARE!!
AFTER ALL...

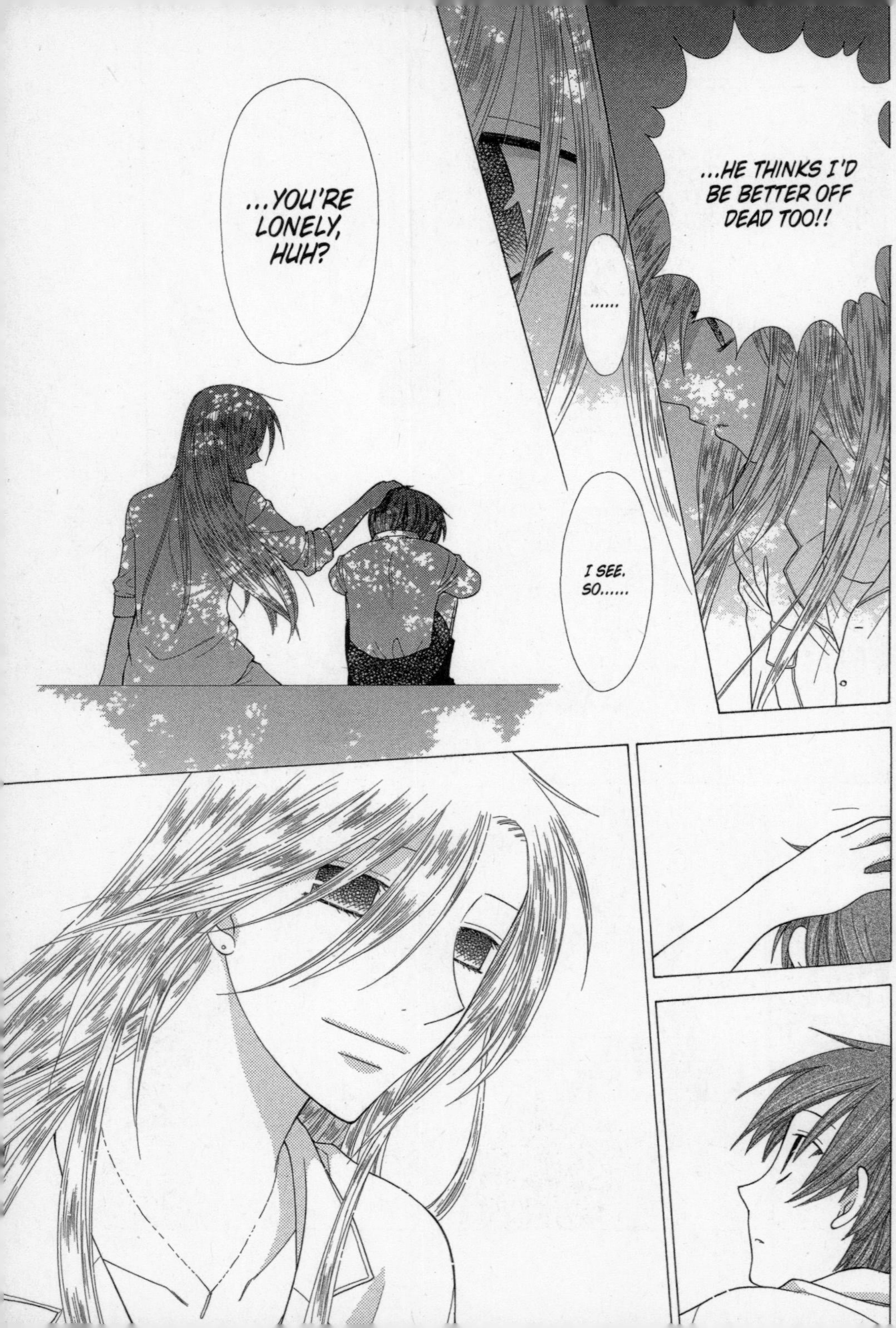
...HE THINKS I'D BE BETTER OFF DEAD TOO!!
......
I SEE. SO......
...YOU'RE LONELY, HUH?

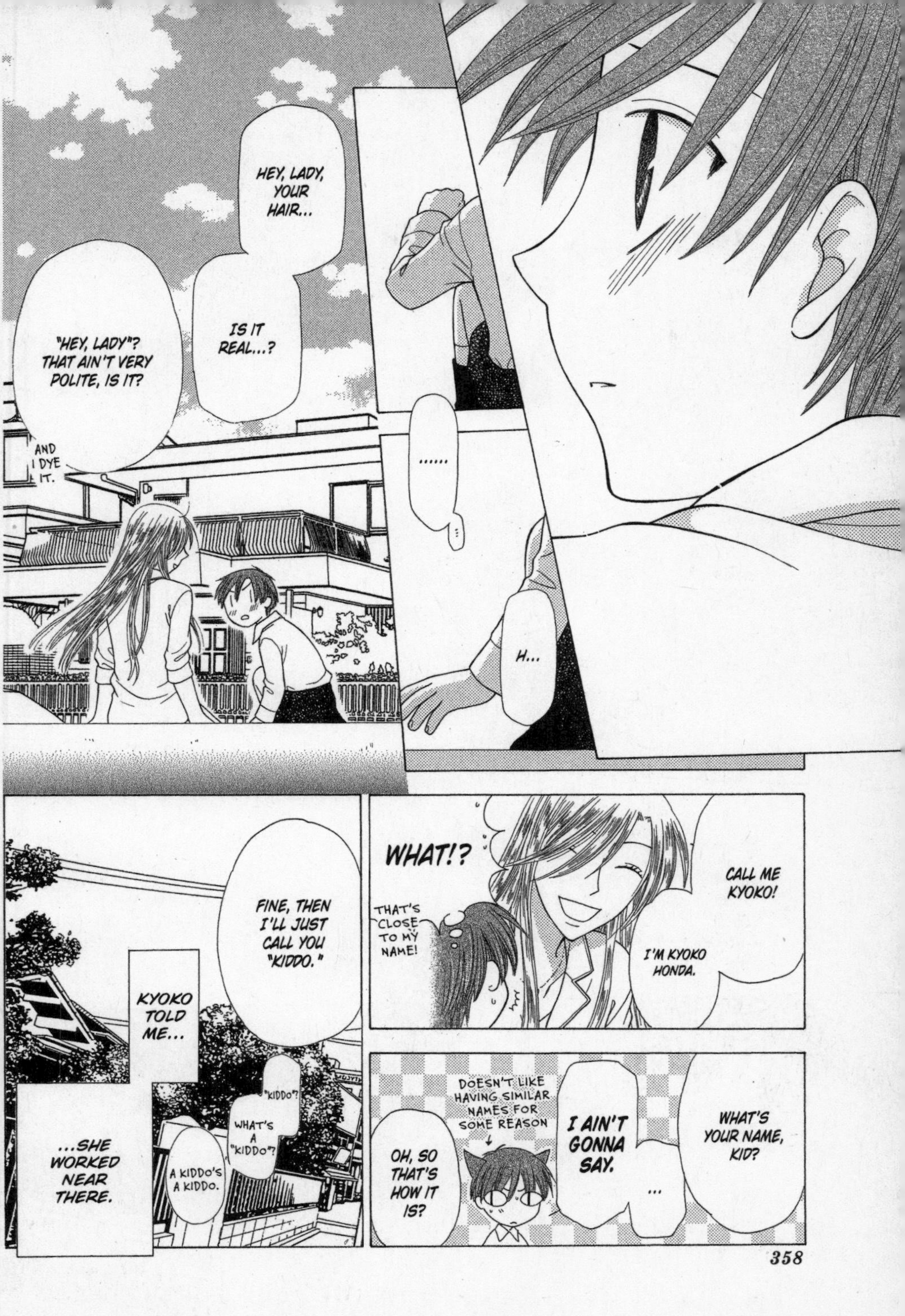
......
H...
HEY, LADY, YOUR HAIR...
IS IT REAL...?
"HEY, LADY"? THAT AIN'T VERY POLITE, IS IT?
AND I DYE IT.
CALL ME KYOKO!
I'M KYOKO HONDA.
WHAT!?
THAT'S CLOSE TO MY NAME!
WHAT'S YOUR NAME, KID?
...
I AIN'T GONNA SAY.
DOESN'T LIKE HAVING SIMILAR NAMES FOR SOME REASON
OH, SO THAT'S HOW IT IS?
FINE, THEN I'LL JUST CALL YOU "KIDDO."
"KIDDO"?
WHAT'S A "KIDDO"?
A KIDDO'S A KIDDO.
KYOKO TOLD ME...
...SHE WORKED NEAR THERE.

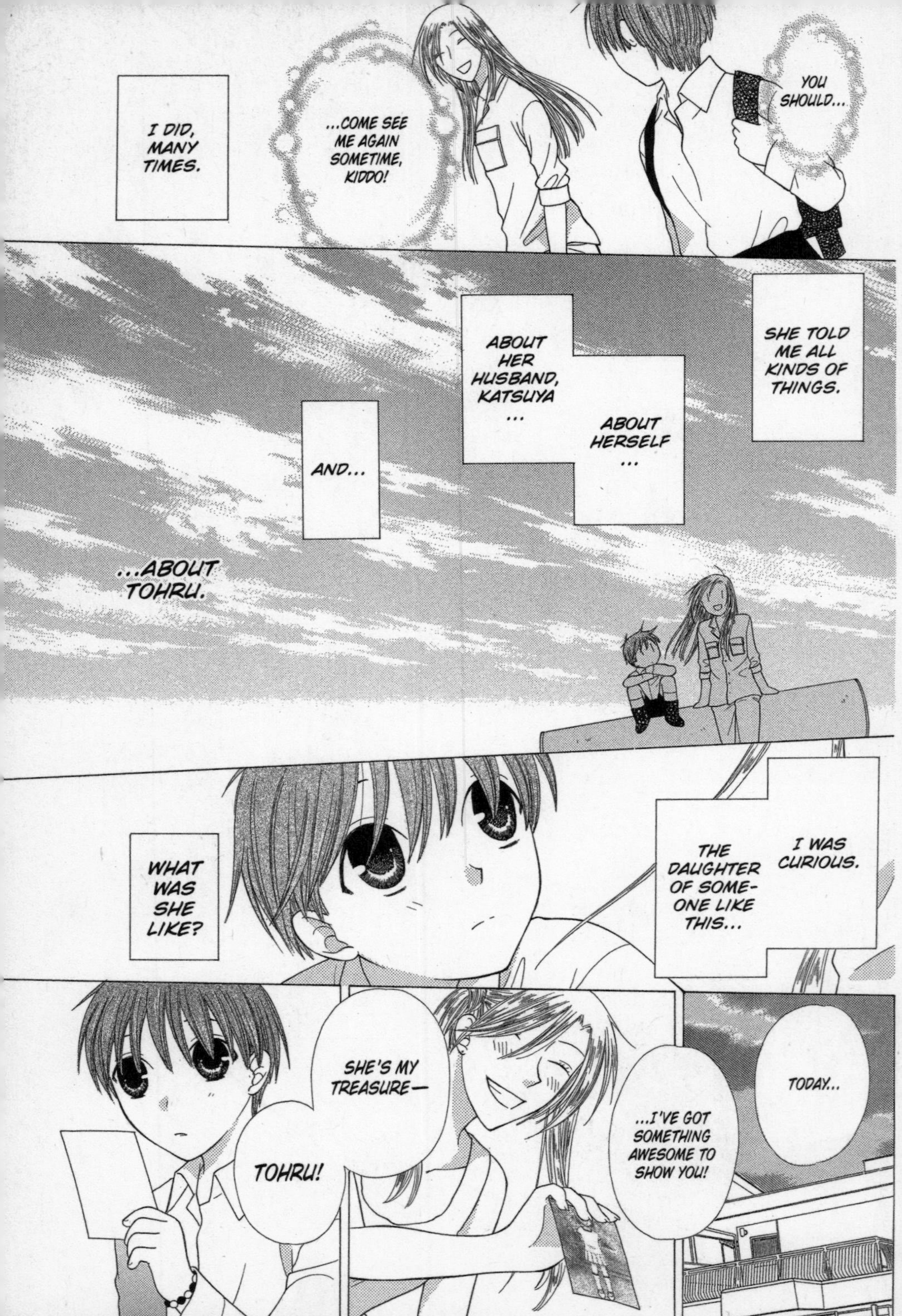
YOU SHOULD...
...COME SEE ME AGAIN SOMETIME, KIDDO!
I DID, MANY TIMES.
SHE TOLD ME ALL KINDS OF THINGS.
ABOUT HER HUSBAND, KATSUYA...
ABOUT HERSELF...
AND...
...ABOUT TOHRU.
I WAS CURIOUS.
THE DAUGHTER OF SOME-ONE LIKE THIS...
WHAT WAS SHE LIKE?
TODAY...
...I'VE GOT SOMETHING AWESOME TO SHOW YOU!
SHE'S MY TREASURE—
TOHRU!

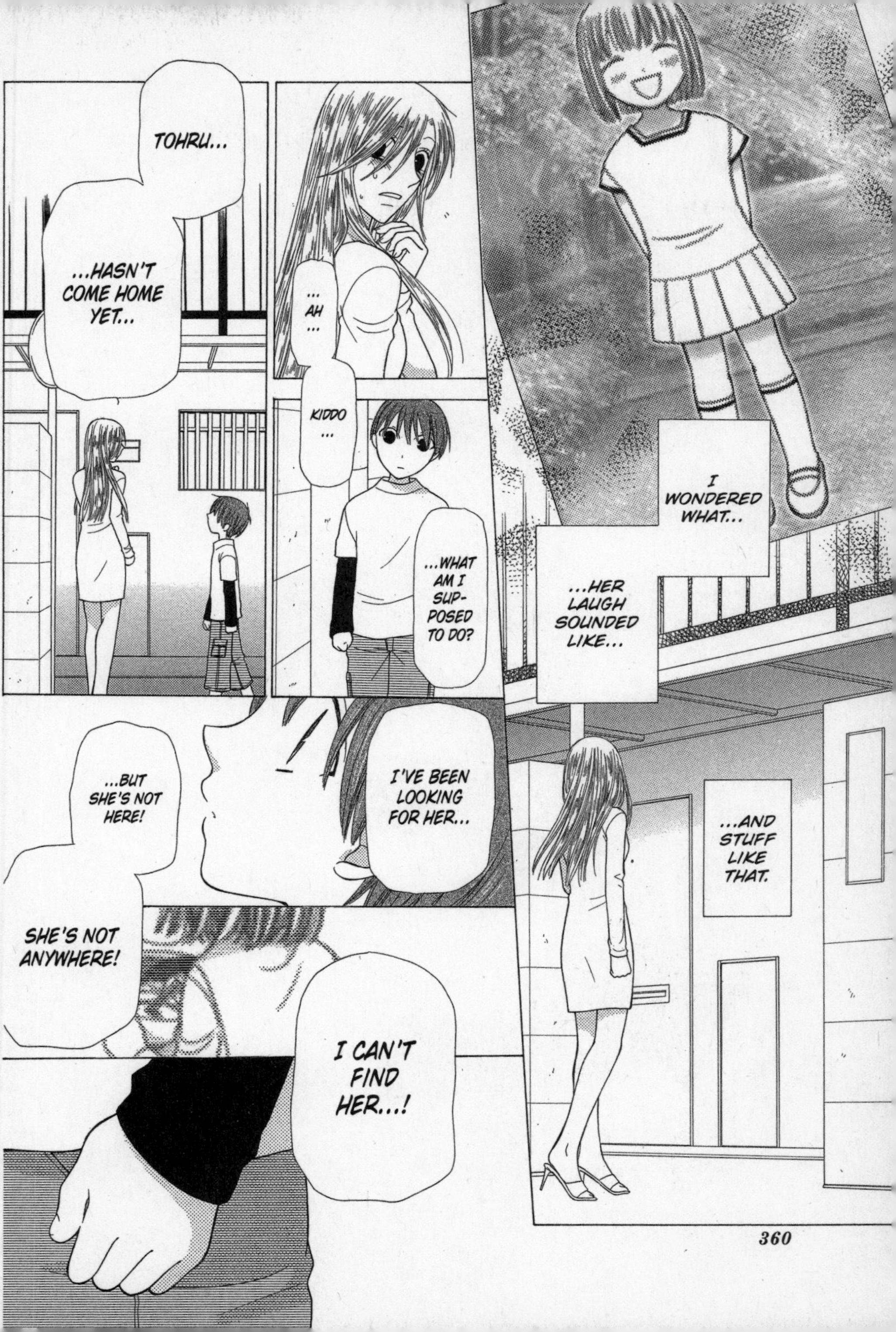
I WONDERED WHAT...
...HER LAUGH SOUNDED LIKE...
...AND STUFF LIKE THAT.
...AH...
KIDDO...
...WHAT AM I SUPPOSED TO DO?
TOHRU...
...HASN'T COME HOME YET...
I'VE BEEN LOOKING FOR HER...
...BUT SHE'S NOT HERE!
I CAN'T FIND HER...!
SHE'S NOT ANYWHERE!

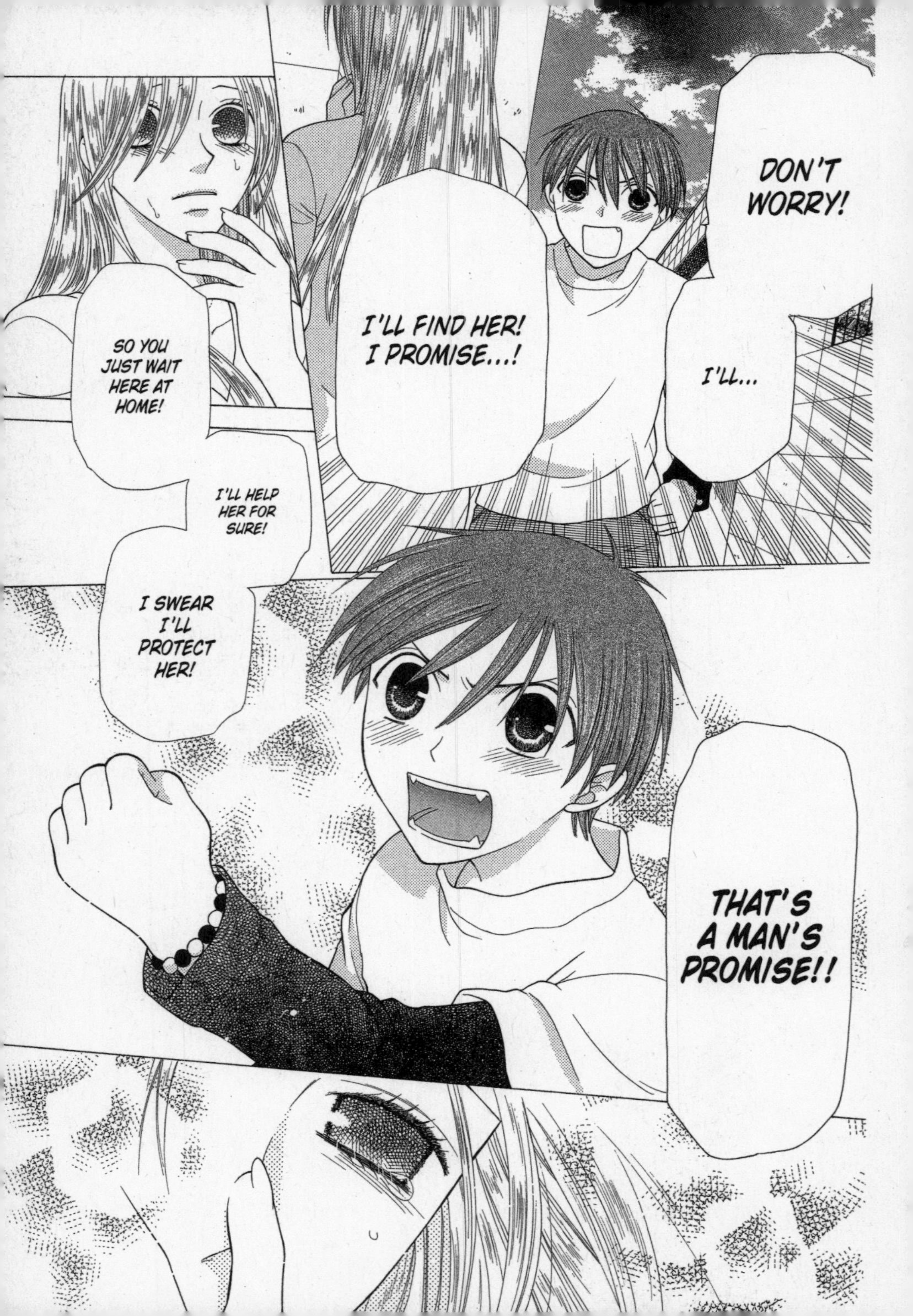
DON'T WORRY!
I'LL...
I'LL FIND HER! I PROMISE...!
SO YOU JUST WAIT HERE AT HOME!
I'LL HELP HER FOR SURE!
I SWEAR I'LL PROTECT HER!
THAT'S A MAN'S PROMISE!!

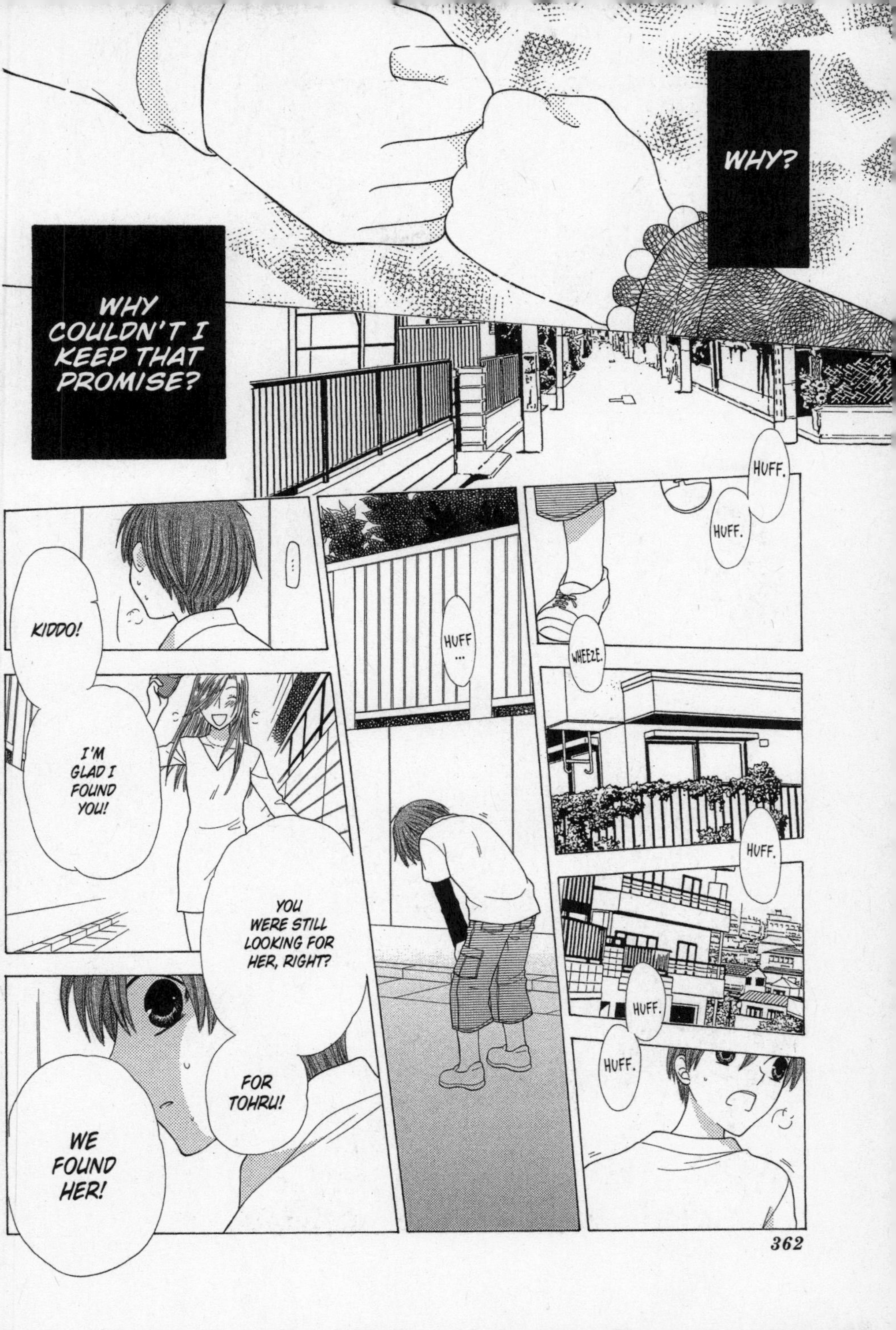
WHY?
WHY COULDN'T I KEEP THAT PROMISE?
HUFF.
HUFF.
WHEEZE.
HUFF.
HUFF.
HUFF.
HUFF...
...
KIDDO!
I'M GLAD I FOUND YOU!
YOU WERE STILL LOOKING FOR HER, RIGHT?
FOR TOHRU!
WE FOUND HER!

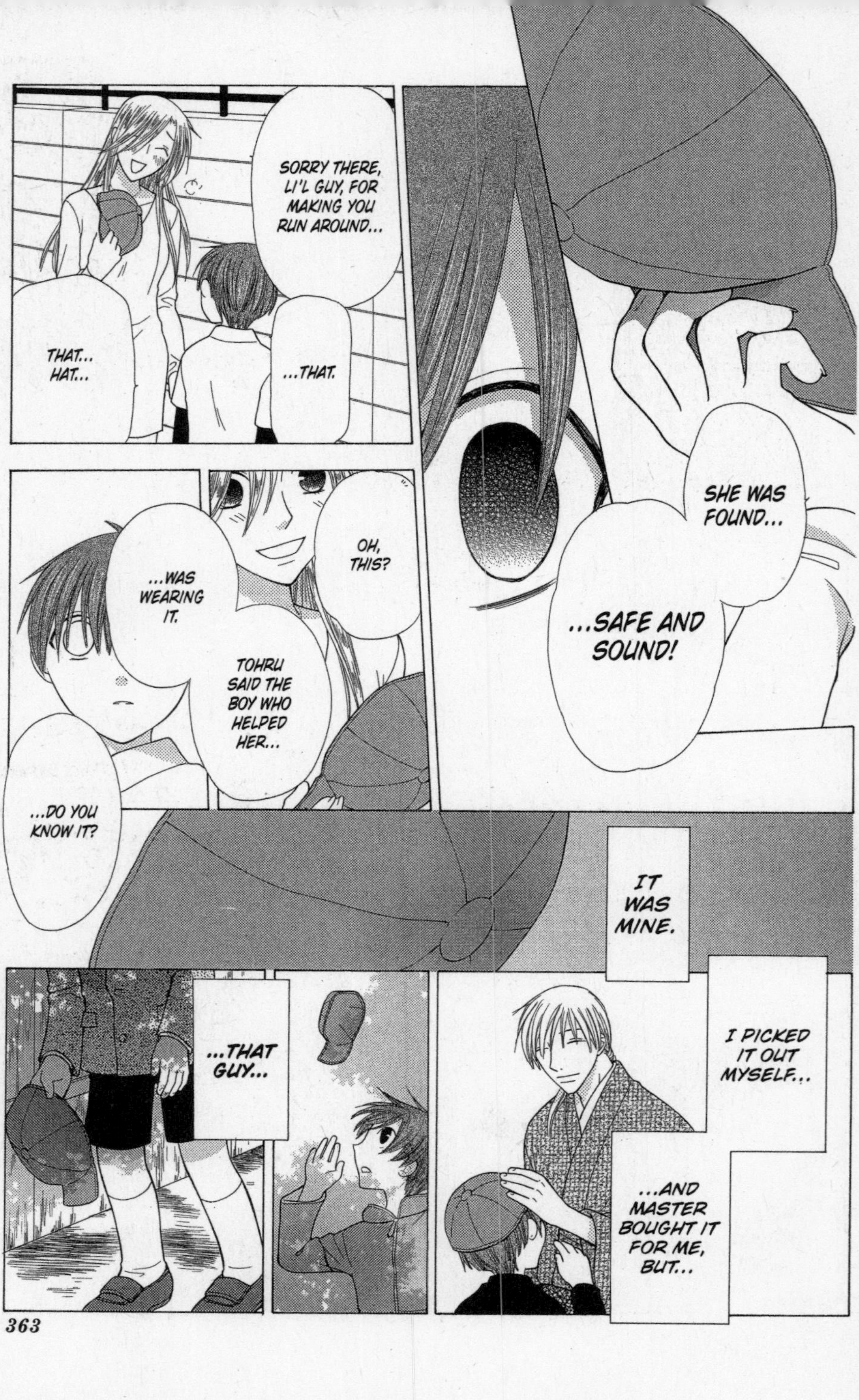
SHE WAS FOUND...
...SAFE AND SOUND!
SORRY THERE, LI'L GUY, FOR MAKING YOU RUN AROUND...
THAT... HAT...
...THAT.
OH, THIS?
TOHRU SAID THE BOY WHO HELPED HER...
...WAS WEARING IT.
...DO YOU KNOW IT?
IT WAS MINE.
I PICKED IT OUT MYSELF...
...AND MASTER BOUGHT IT FOR ME, BUT...
...THAT GUY...

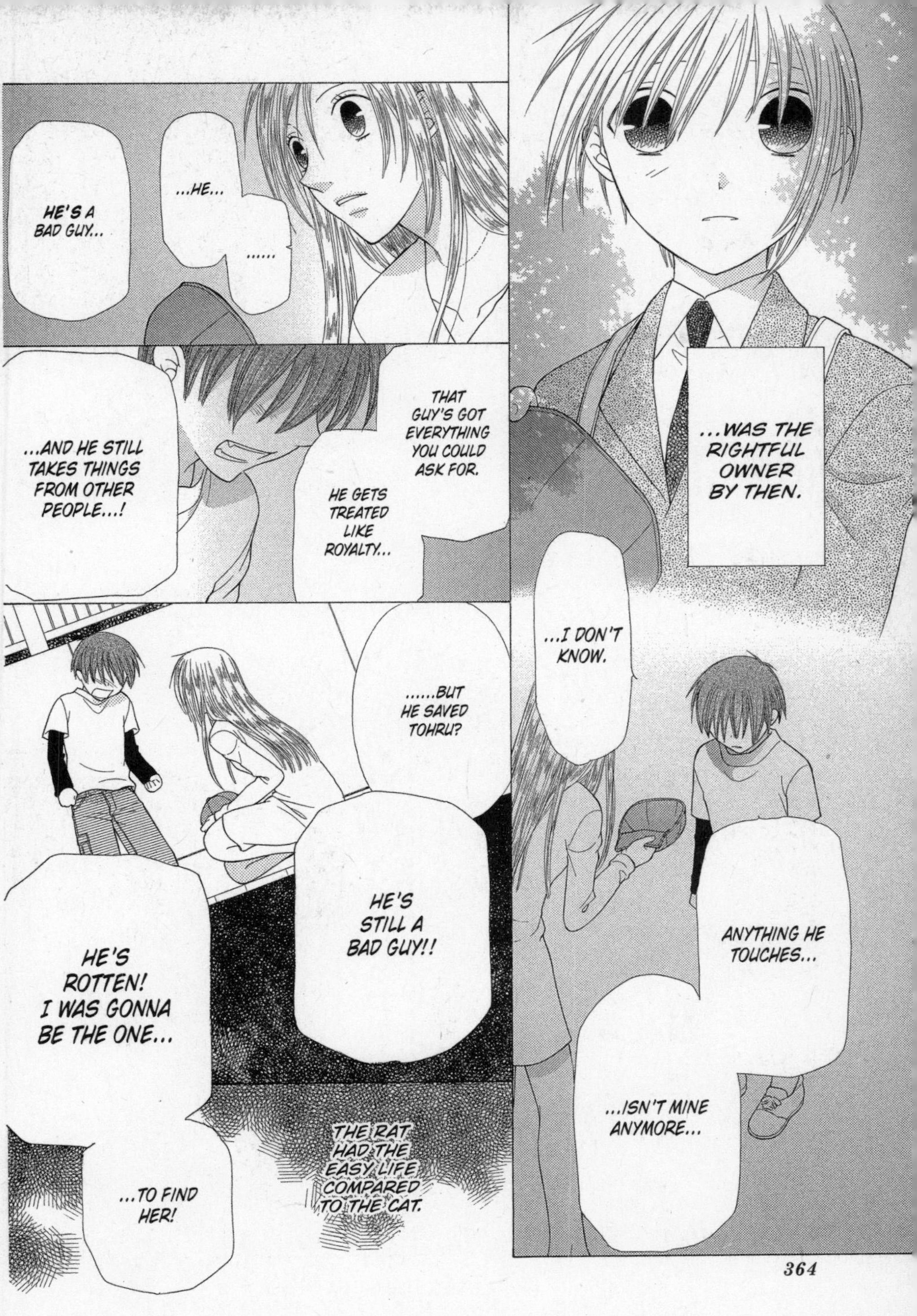
...WAS THE RIGHTFUL OWNER BY THEN.
HE'S A BAD GUY...
...HE...
......
THAT GUY'S GOT EVERYTHING YOU COULD ASK FOR.
HE GETS TREATED LIKE ROYALTY...
...AND HE STILL TAKES THINGS FROM OTHER PEOPLE...!
...I DON'T KNOW.
ANYTHING HE TOUCHES...
...ISN'T MINE ANYMORE...
......BUT HE SAVED TOHRU?
HE'S STILL A BAD GUY!!
HE'S ROTTEN! I WAS GONNA BE THE ONE...
...TO FIND HER!
THE RAT HAD THE EASY LIFE COMPARED TO THE CAT.

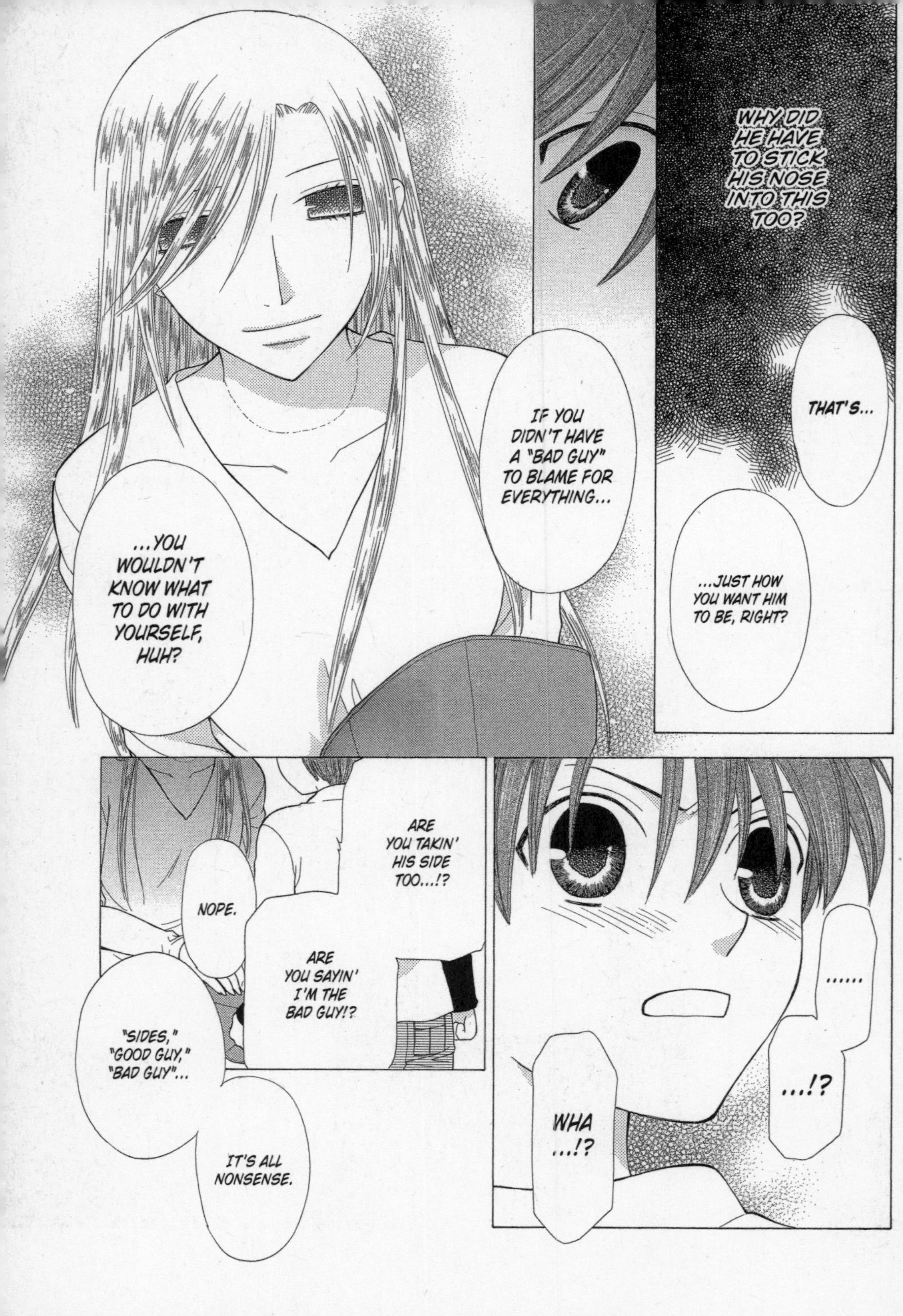
WHY DID HE HAVE TO STICK HIS NOSE INTO THIS TOO?
THAT'S...
...JUST HOW YOU WANT HIM TO BE, RIGHT?
IF YOU DIDN'T HAVE A "BAD GUY" TO BLAME FOR EVERYTHING...
...YOU WOULDN'T KNOW WHAT TO DO WITH YOURSELF, HUH?
......
...!?
WHA ...!?
ARE YOU TAKIN' HIS SIDE TOO...!?
NOPE.
ARE YOU SAYIN' I'M THE BAD GUY!?
"SIDES," "GOOD GUY," "BAD GUY"...
IT'S ALL NONSENSE.

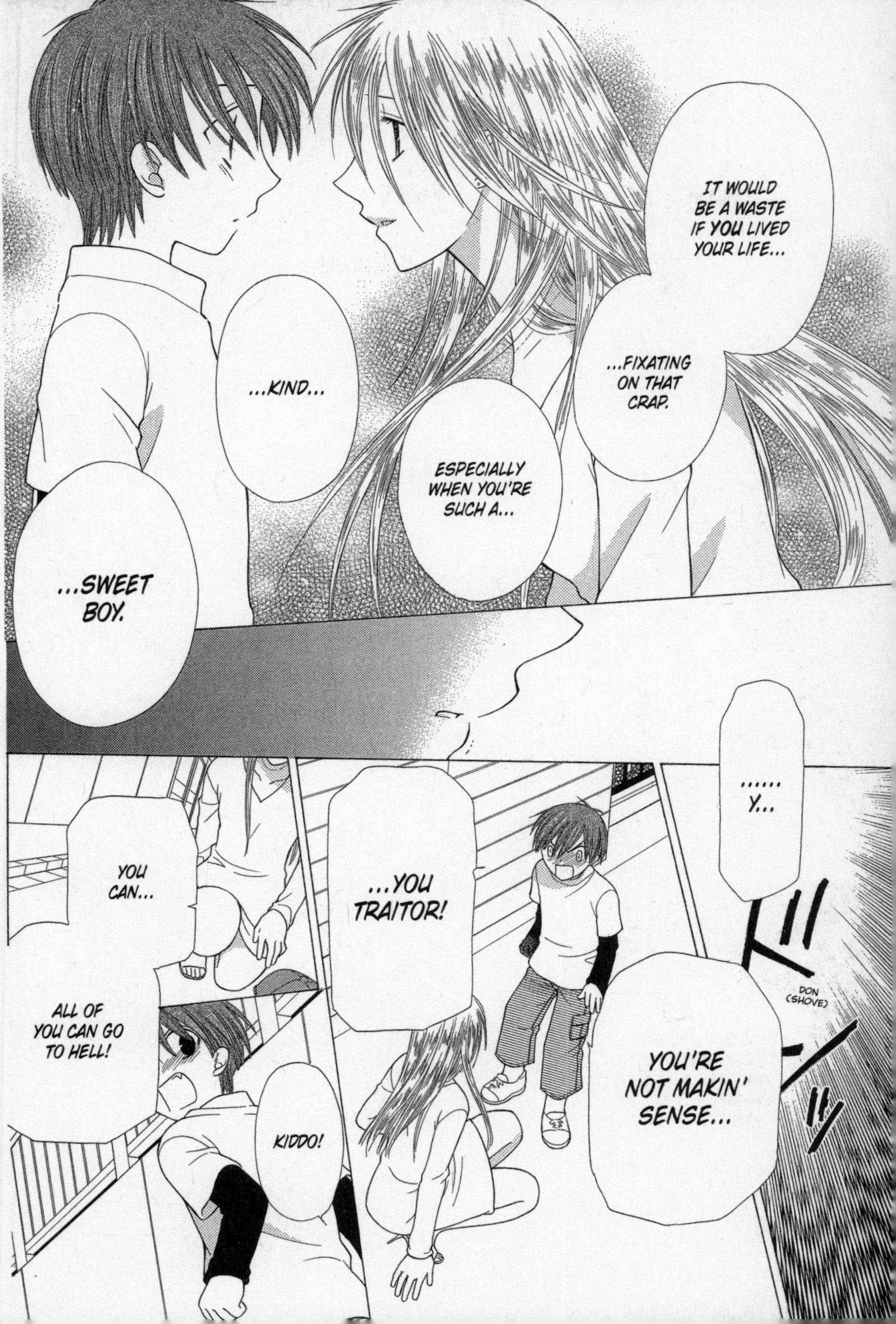
IT WOULD BE A WASTE IF YOU LIVED YOUR LIFE...
...FIXATING ON THAT CRAP.
ESPECIALLY WHEN YOU'RE SUCH A...
...KIND...
...SWEET BOY.
...... Y...
DON (SHOVE)
YOU'RE NOT MAKIN' SENSE...
...YOU TRAITOR!
KIDDO!
YOU CAN...
ALL OF YOU CAN GO TO HELL!

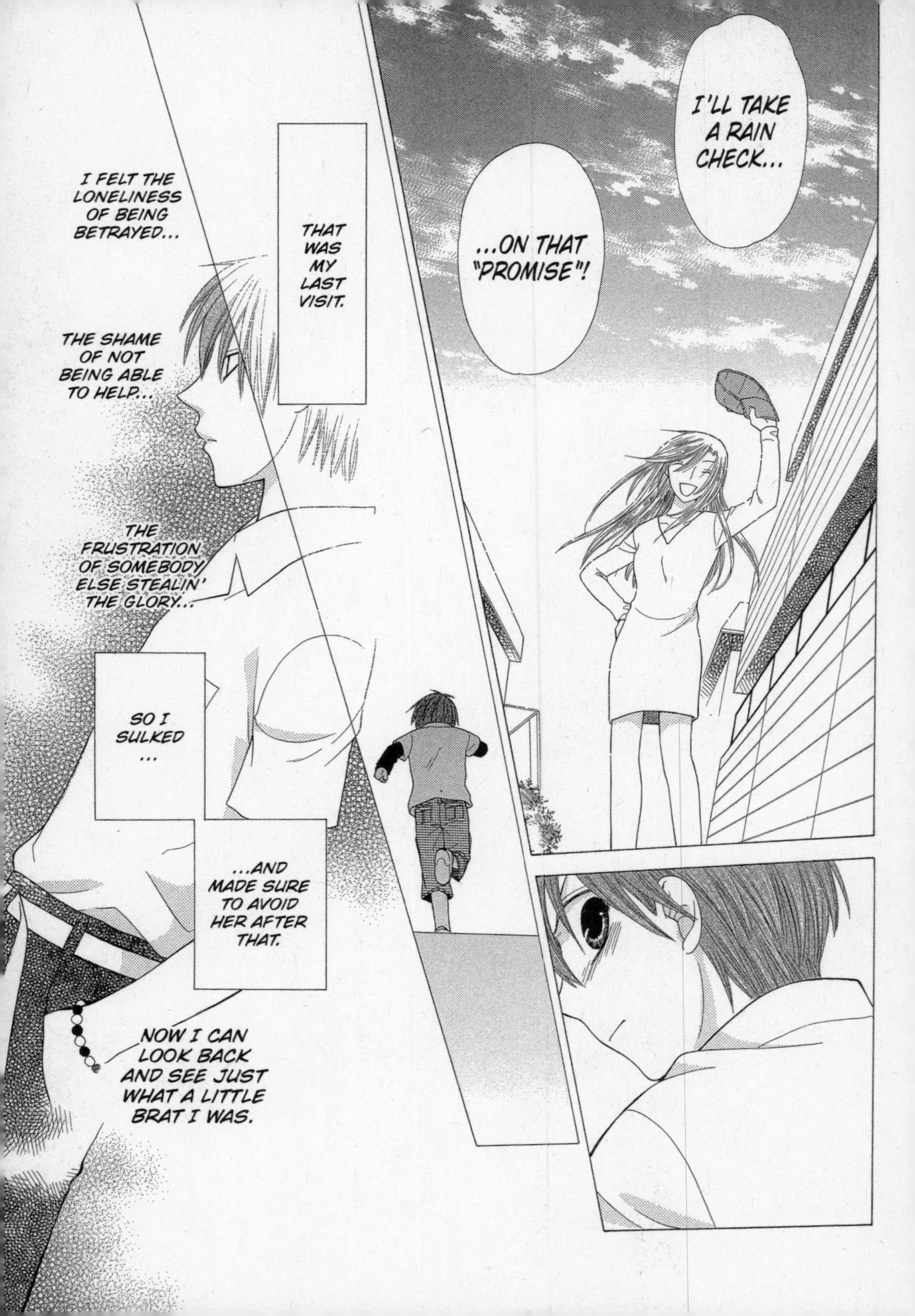
I'LL TAKE A RAIN CHECK...
...ON THAT "PROMISE"!
THAT WAS MY LAST VISIT.
I FELT THE LONELINESS OF BEING BETRAYED...
THE SHAME OF NOT BEING ABLE TO HELP...
THE FRUSTRATION OF SOMEBODY ELSE STEALIN' THE GLORY...
SO I SULKED ...
...AND MADE SURE TO AVOID HER AFTER THAT.
NOW I CAN LOOK BACK AND SEE JUST WHAT A LITTLE BRAT I WAS.

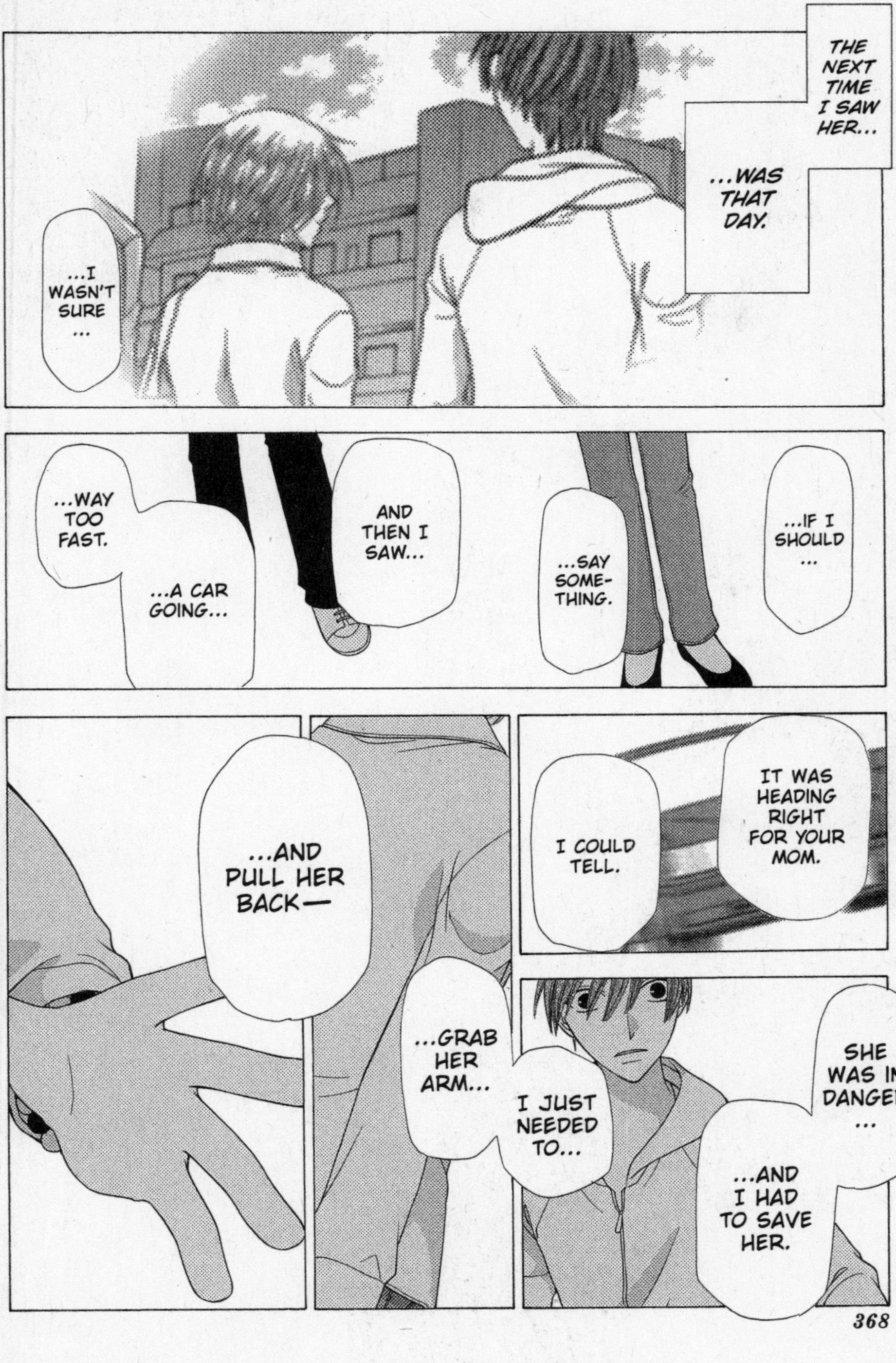
THE NEXT TIME I SAW HER...
...WAS THAT DAY.
...I WASN'T SURE...
...IF I SHOULD...
...SAY SOMETHING.
AND THEN I SAW...
...A CAR GOING...
...WAY TOO FAST.
IT WAS HEADING RIGHT FOR YOUR MOM.
I COULD TELL.
SHE WAS IN DANGER...
...AND I HAD TO SAVE HER.
I JUST NEEDED TO...
...GRAB HER ARM...
...AND PULL HER BACK—

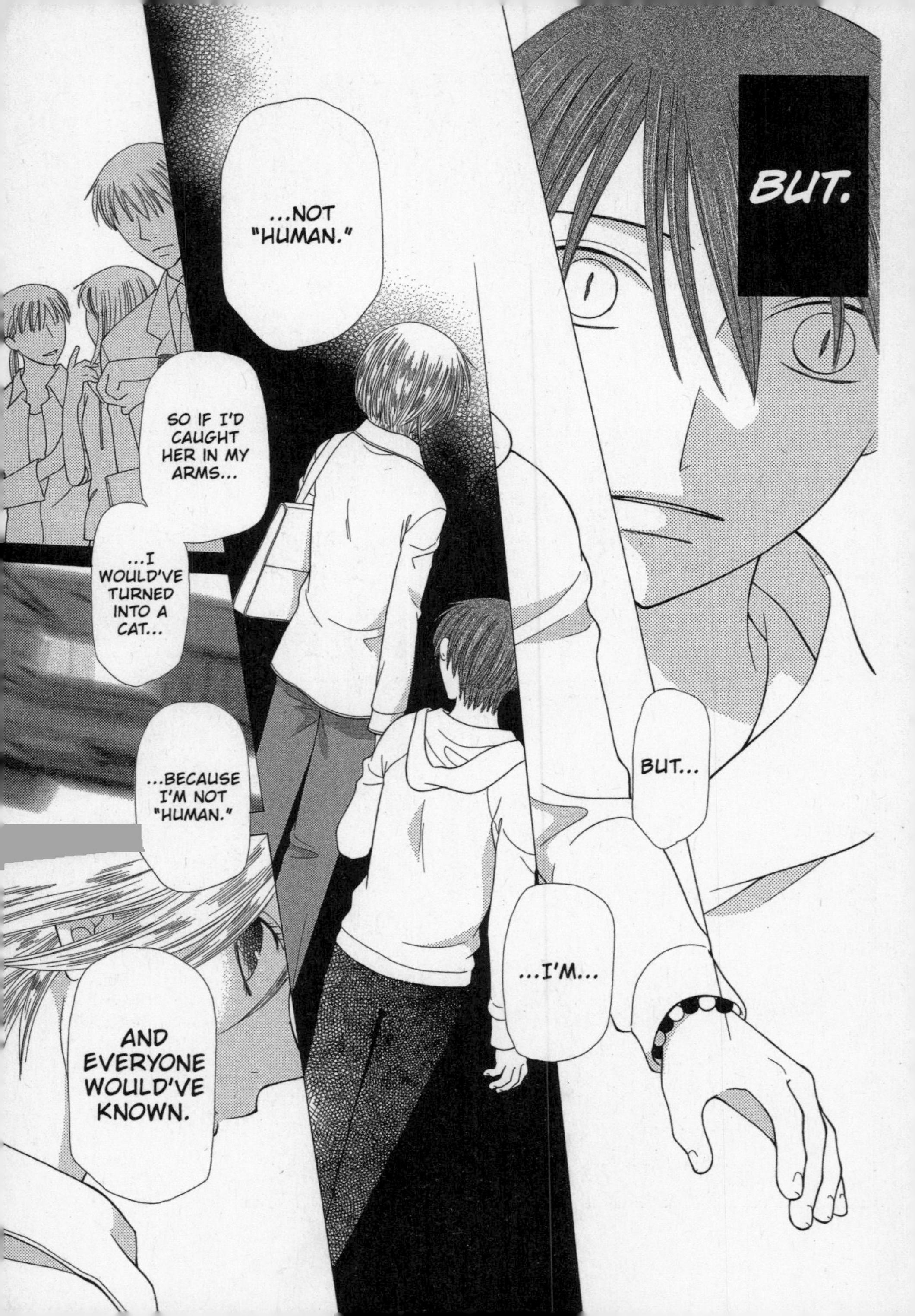
BUT.
BUT...
...I'M...
...NOT "HUMAN."
SO IF I'D CAUGHT HER IN MY ARMS...
...I WOULD'VE TURNED INTO A CAT...
...BECAUSE I'M NOT "HUMAN."
AND EVERYONE WOULD'VE KNOWN.

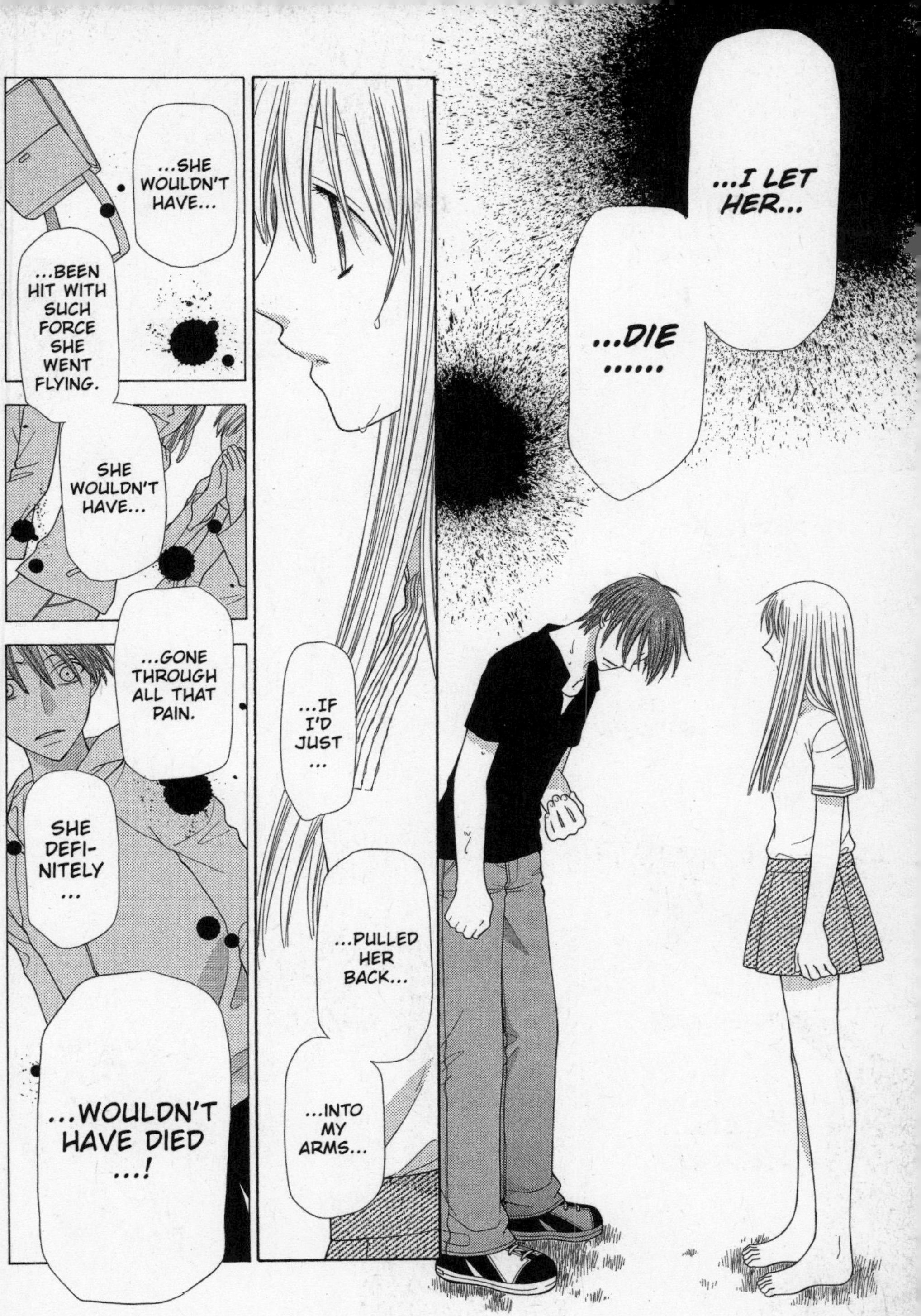
...I LET HER...
...DIE ......
...IF I'D JUST ...
...PULLED HER BACK...
...INTO MY ARMS...
...SHE WOULDN'T HAVE...
...BEEN HIT WITH SUCH FORCE SHE WENT FLYING.
SHE WOULDN'T HAVE...
...GONE THROUGH ALL THAT PAIN.
SHE DEFINITELY ...
...WOULDN'T HAVE DIED ...!

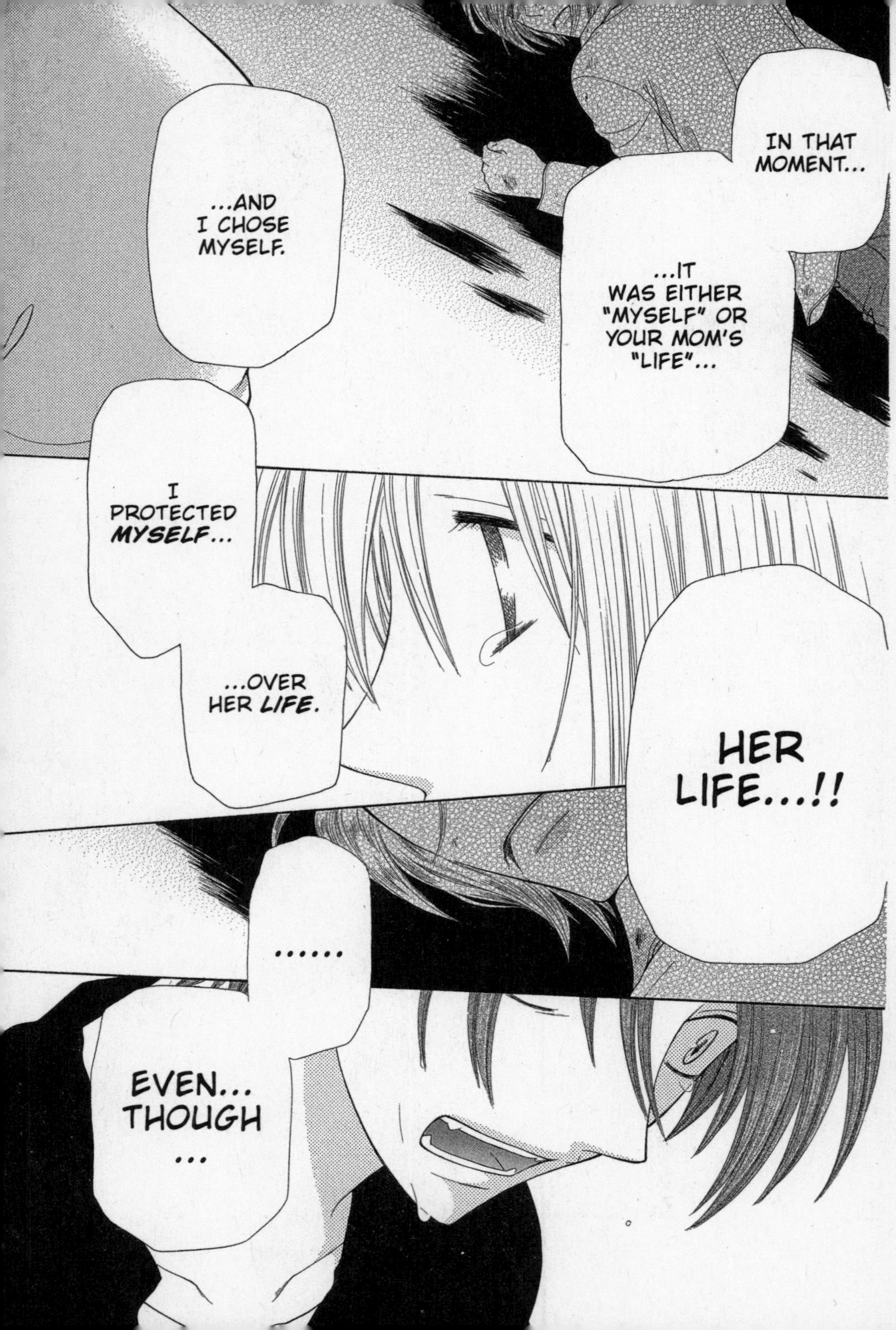
IN THAT MOMENT...
...IT WAS EITHER "MYSELF" OR YOUR MOM'S "LIFE"...
...AND I CHOSE MYSELF.
I PROTECTED *MYSELF*...
...OVER HER *LIFE*.
HER LIFE...!!
......
EVEN... THOUGH ...

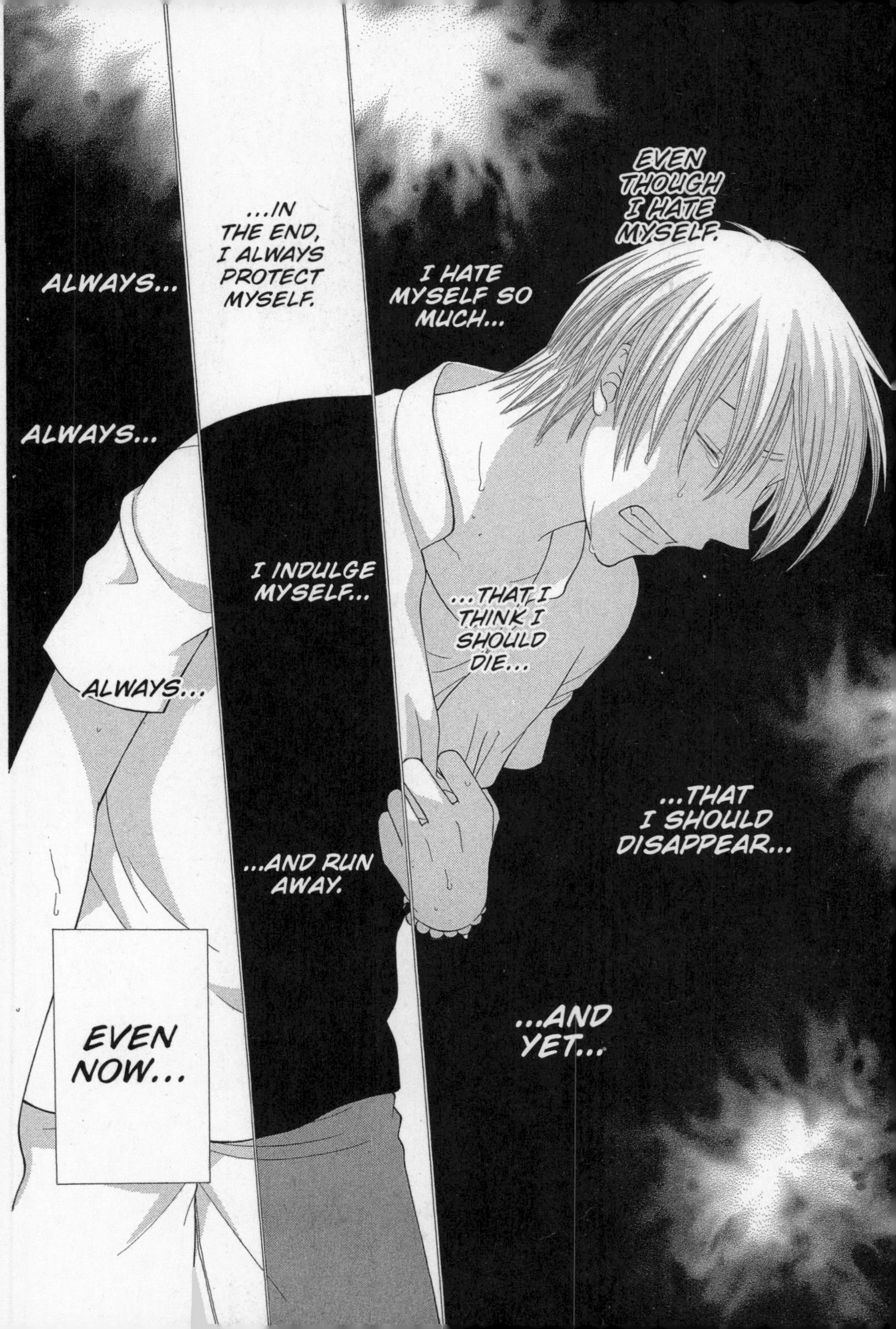
EVEN THOUGH I HATE MYSELF.
I HATE MYSELF SO MUCH...
...THAT I THINK I SHOULD DIE...
...THAT I SHOULD DISAPPEAR...
...AND YET...
...IN THE END, I ALWAYS PROTECT MYSELF.
I INDULGE MYSELF...
...AND RUN AWAY.
ALWAYS...
ALWAYS...
ALWAYS...
EVEN NOW...

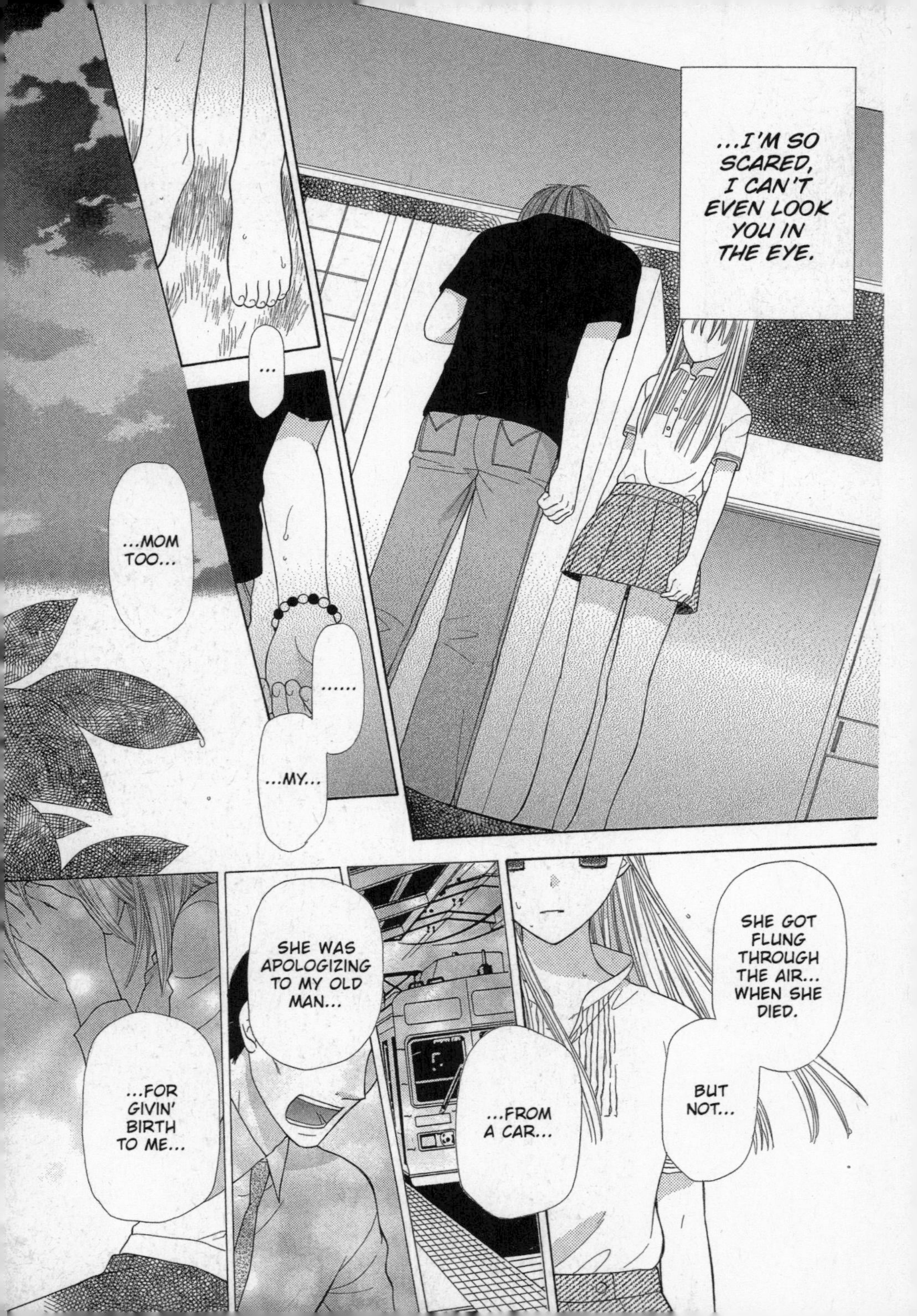

...I'M SO SCARED, I CAN'T EVEN LOOK YOU IN THE EYE.
...
......
...MY...
...MOM TOO...
SHE GOT FLUNG THROUGH THE AIR... WHEN SHE DIED.
BUT NOT...
...FROM A CAR...
SHE WAS APOLOGIZING TO MY OLD MAN...
...FOR GIVIN' BIRTH TO ME...

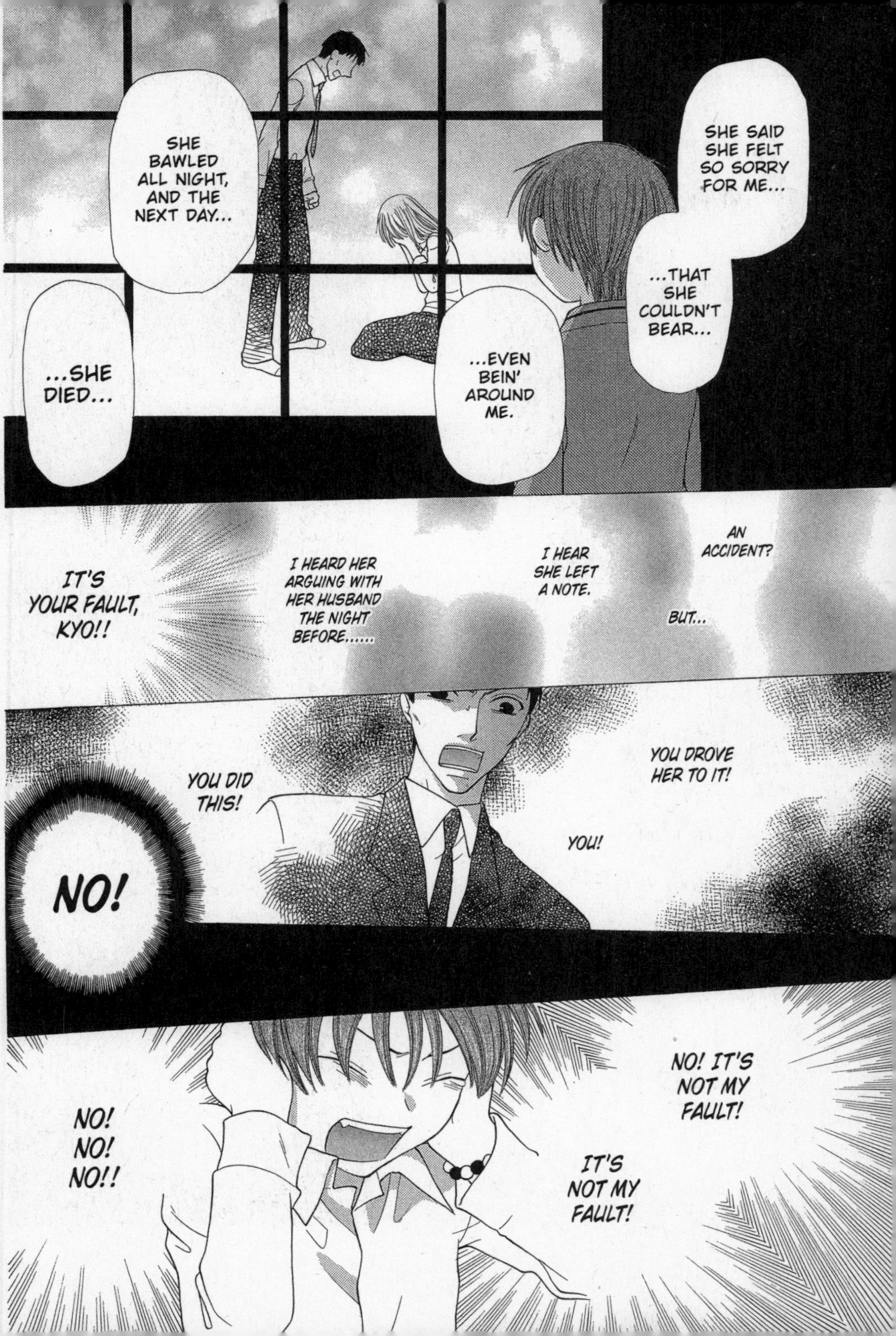
SHE SAID SHE FELT SO SORRY FOR ME...
...THAT SHE COULDN'T BEAR...
...EVEN BEIN' AROUND ME.
SHE BAWLED ALL NIGHT, AND THE NEXT DAY...
...SHE DIED...
AN ACCIDENT?
BUT...
I HEAR SHE LEFT A NOTE.
I HEARD HER ARGUING WITH HER HUSBAND THE NIGHT BEFORE......
IT'S YOUR FAULT, KYO!!
YOU DROVE HER TO IT!
YOU!
YOU DID THIS!
NO!
NO! IT'S NOT MY FAULT!
IT'S NOT MY FAULT!
NO! NO! NO!!

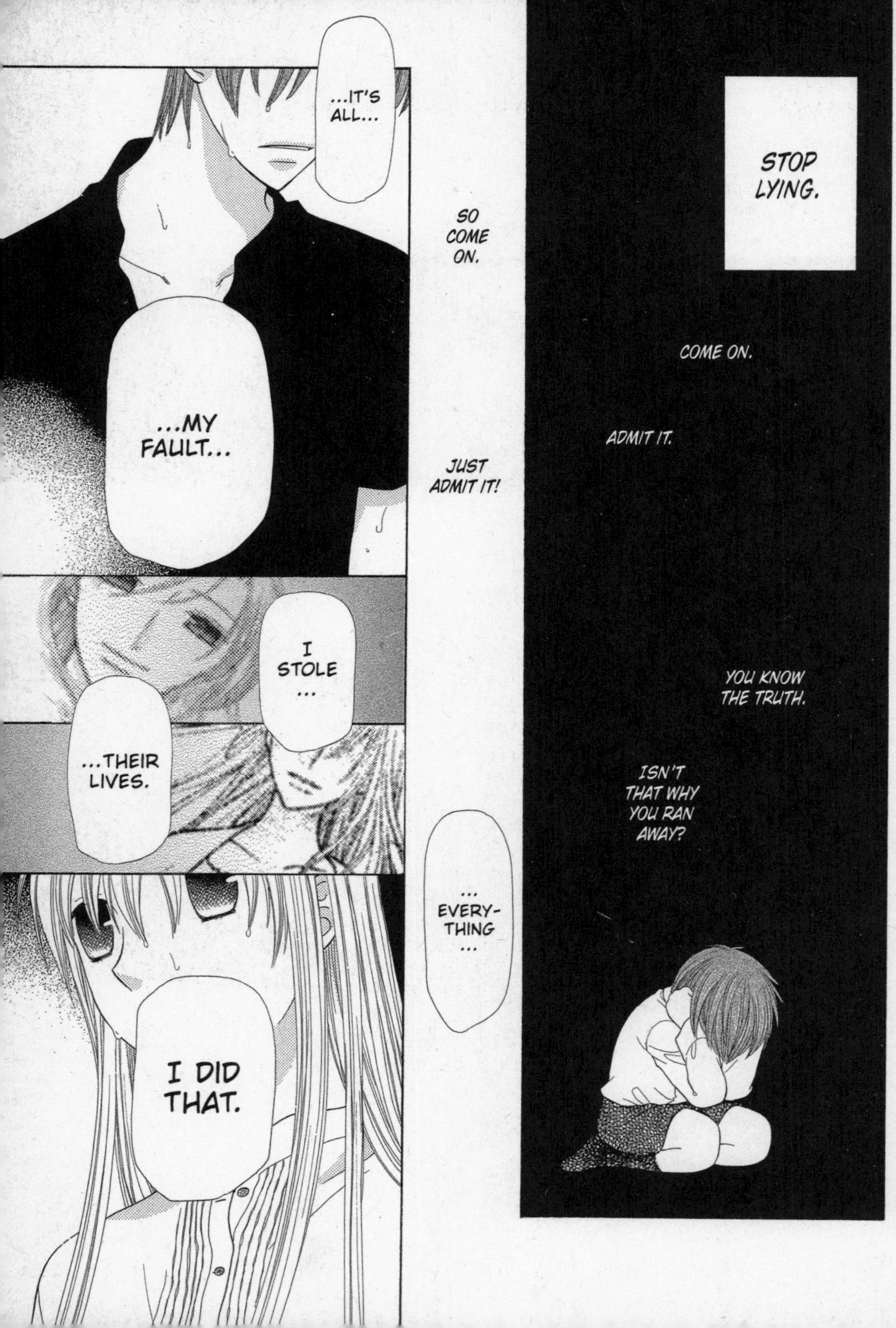
STOP LYING.
COME ON.
ADMIT IT.
YOU KNOW THE TRUTH.
ISN'T THAT WHY YOU RAN AWAY?
SO COME ON.
...IT'S ALL...
JUST ADMIT IT!
...MY FAULT...
I STOLE ...
...THEIR LIVES.
... EVERY-THING ...
I DID THAT.

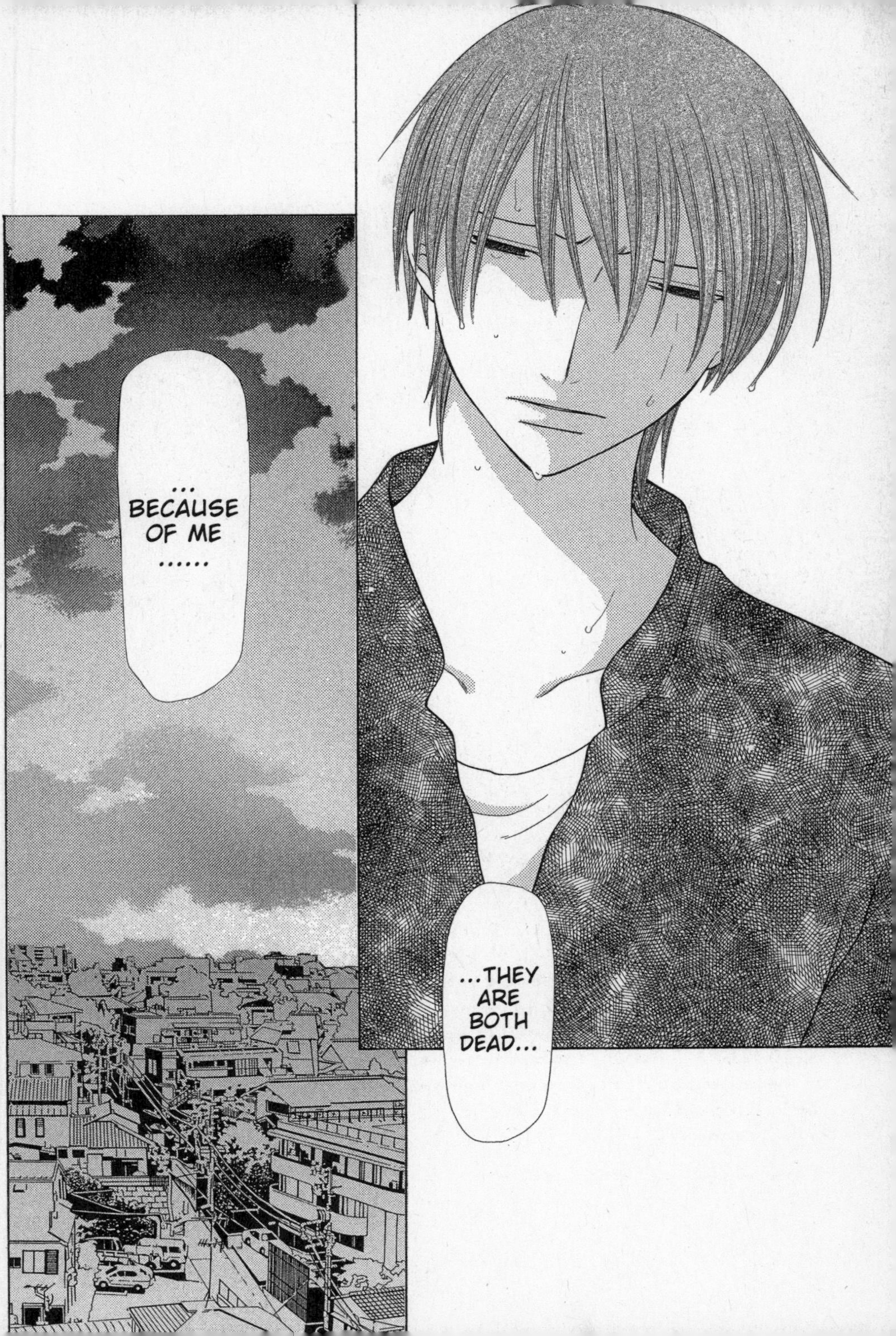
...THEY ARE BOTH DEAD...
...BECAUSE OF ME ......

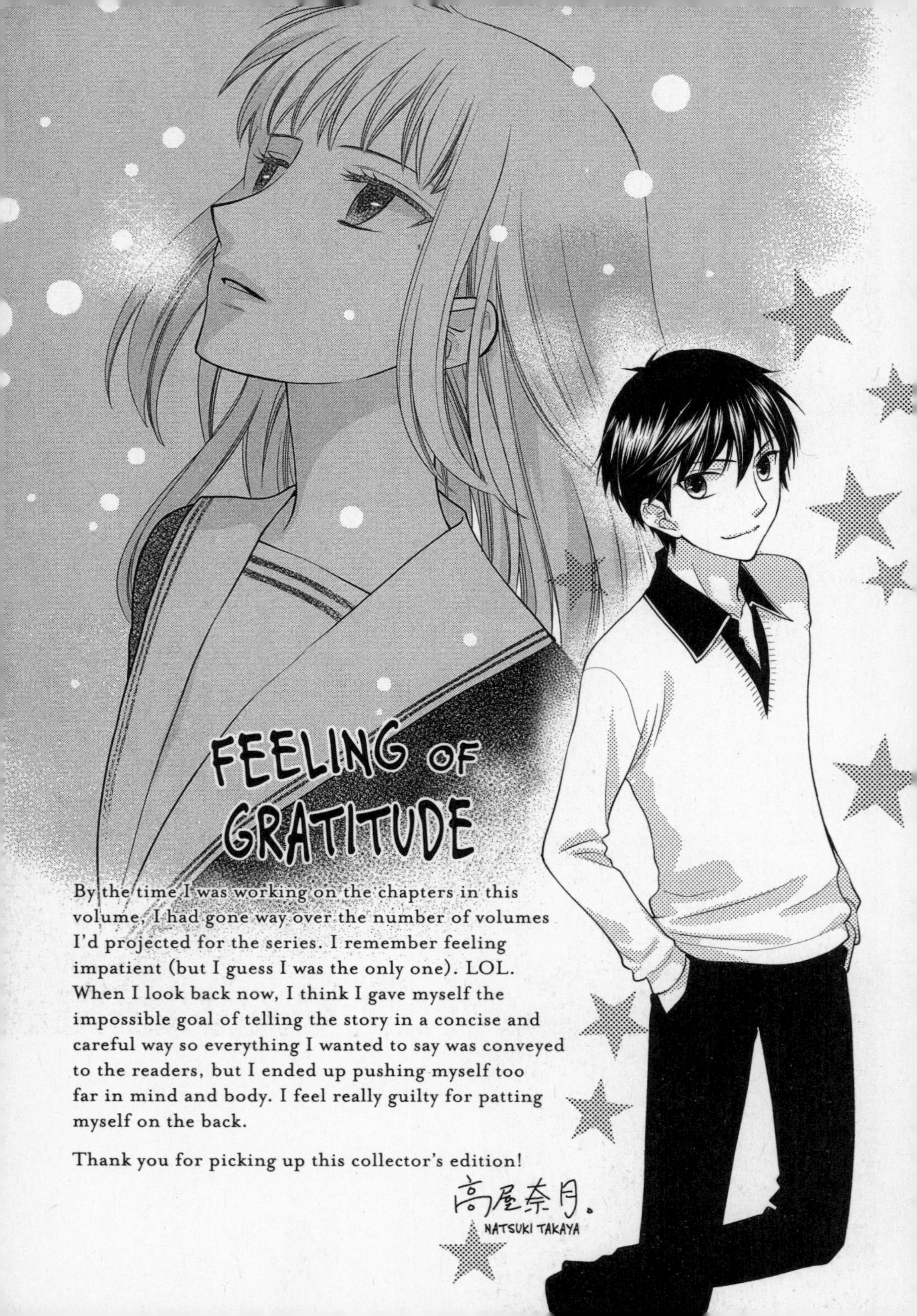

FEELING OF GRATITUDE

By the time I was working on the chapters in this volume, I had gone way over the number of volumes I'd projected for the series. I remember feeling impatient (but I guess I was the only one). LOL. When I look back now, I think I gave myself the impossible goal of telling the story in a concise and careful way so everything I wanted to say was conveyed to the readers, but I ended up pushing myself too far in mind and body. I feel really guilty for patting myself on the back.

Thank you for picking up this collector's edition!

高屋奈月。
NATSUKI TAKAYA

TRANSLATION NOTES

COMMON HONORIFICS

no honorific: Indicates familiarity or closeness; if used without permission or reason, addressing someone in this manner would constitute an insult.

-san: The Japanese equivalent of Mr./Mrs./Miss. If a situation calls for politeness, this is the fail-safe honorific.

-sama: Conveys great respect; may also indicate that the social status of the speaker is lower than that of the addressee.

-kun: Used most often when referring to boys, this indicates affection or familiarity. Occasionally used by older men among their peers, but it may also be used by anyone referring to a person of lower standing.

-chan: An affectionate honorific indicating familiarity used mostly in reference to girls; also used in reference to cute persons or animals of either gender.

-senpai: A suffix used to address upperclassmen or more experienced coworkers.

-kouhai: A suffix used to address underclassmen or less experienced coworkers.

-sensei: A respectful term for teachers, artists, or high-level professionals.

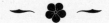

Page 33
Host club reject: A reference to Hiroshi (real name Kenichi Saito), a stand-up comedian known for his portrayal of a depressed host club host who recounts his various failures in life.

Page 43
Burn incense sticks: Incense is often left as an offering for the dead at gravesites and also at Shinto shrines and Buddhist temples to please the local spirits.

Page 45
Jii-san: Polite form for a grandfather (although adding an *o* at the beginning would make it more polite, while using *-chan* instead of *-san* would make it more casual). Also used, as Kyo does here, to mean a male senior citizen.

Page 84
Nii-san: "Big brother" in Japanese, this is a respectful form of address for an older brother or a young man who is older than the speaker.

Page 100
Nee-san: The female equivalent to *nii-san*.

Page 122
"It's okay to be naughty...as long as he grows into a strong young man......": This is the tagline from the series of Marudai Boneless Ham commercials in the 1970s.

Page 136
"That's actually someone's real name?": *Komaki* sounds like a nickname. In Japan, nicknames are sometimes formed by putting the first part of a surname before the given name. For example, *Gomaki*, the nickname of former Morning Musume idol Maki Goto—the Japanese order of her name, *Goto Maki*, makes this naming scheme more obvious.

Page 179
"What are you, a crane?": A reference to the Japanese folktale "Tsuru no Ongaeshi" ("The Crane Returns a Favor"). One day, an old man helps a crane out of a trap; later, a beautiful young girl appears to him and his wife and becomes their adopted daughter. She asks them to bring her yarn so that she may make cloth—and also warns them not to peek in her room while she does so. However, curiosity eventually overcomes the couple, and they spy on her. They see that she is actually the crane the old man saved in the beginning, plucking feathers from her wings to weave into the cloth! But now that they have seen her true form, she has to leave. She turns back into a crane for good and flies off into the sky.

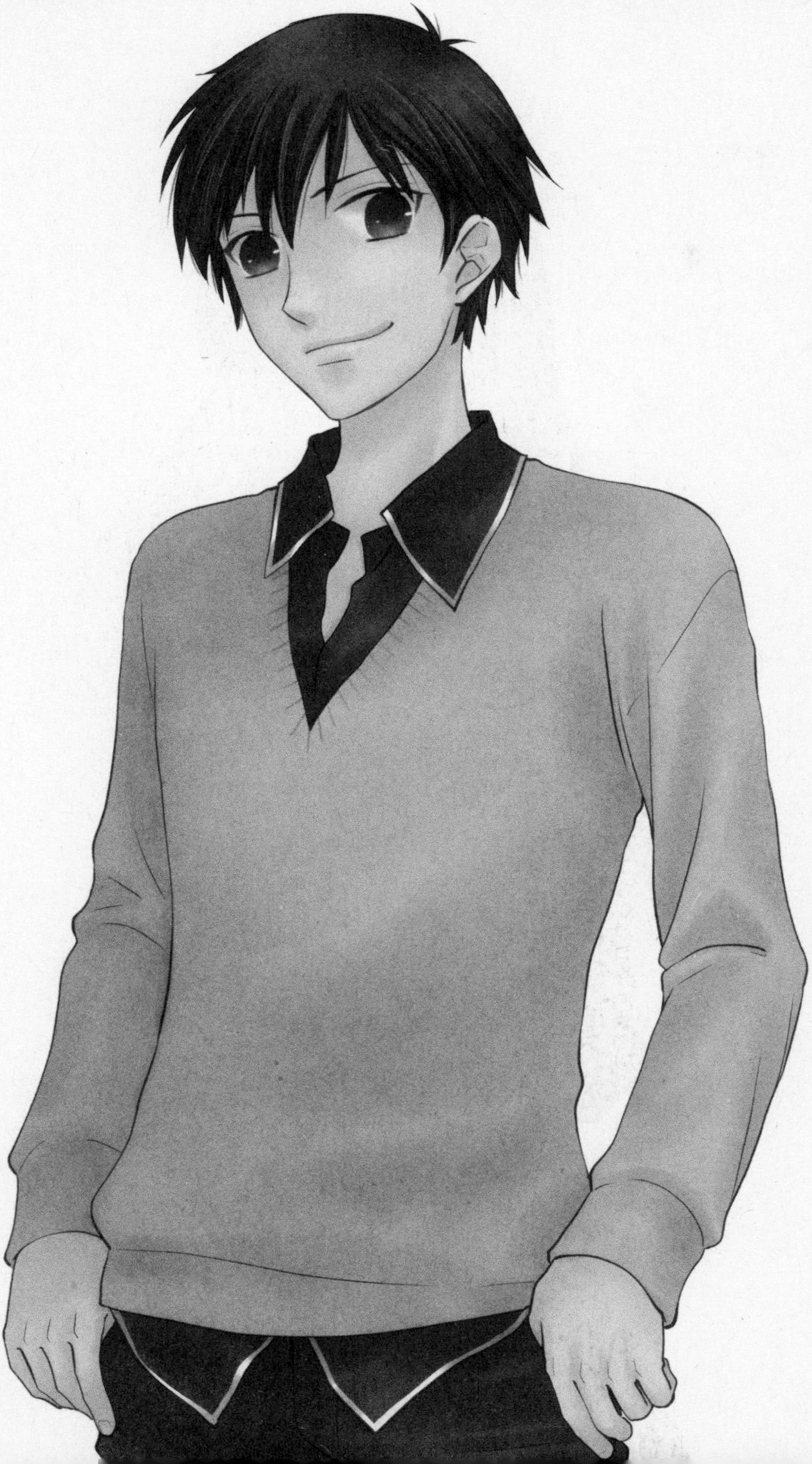

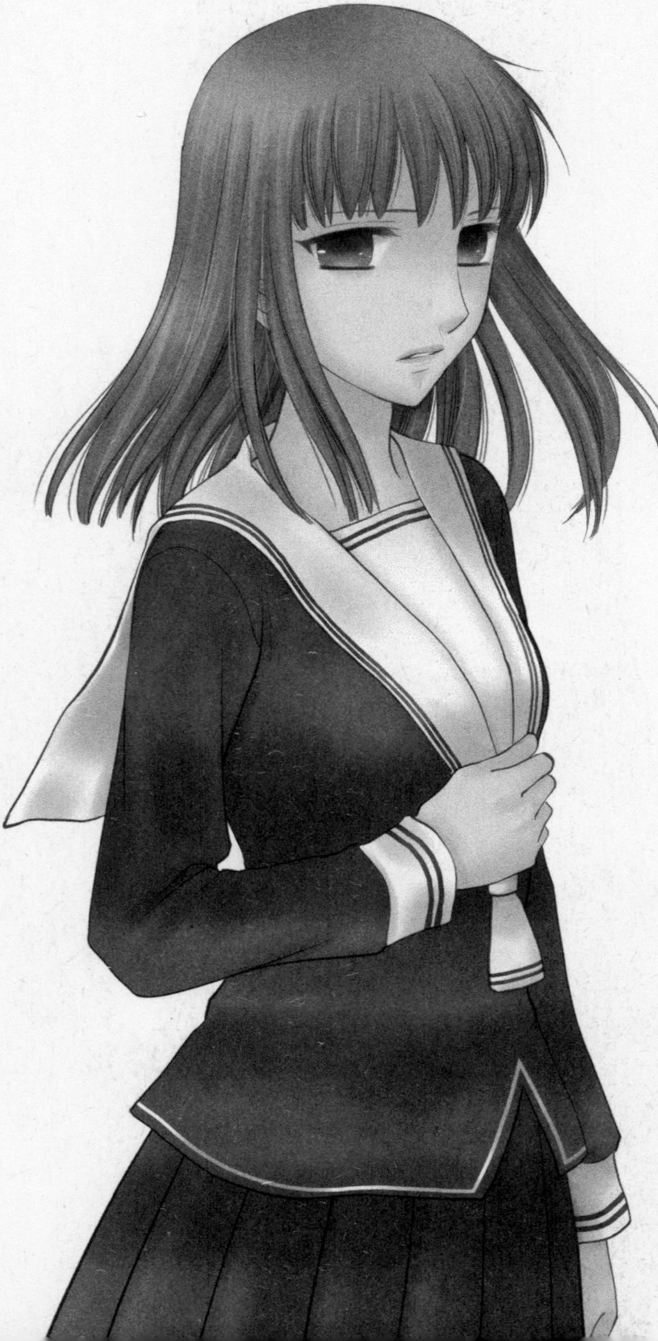

COLLECTOR'S EDITION

Fruits Basket

Read on for an early look at Volume 11,
coming March 2017.

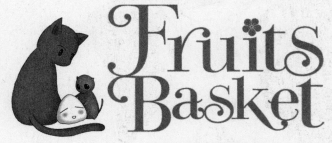

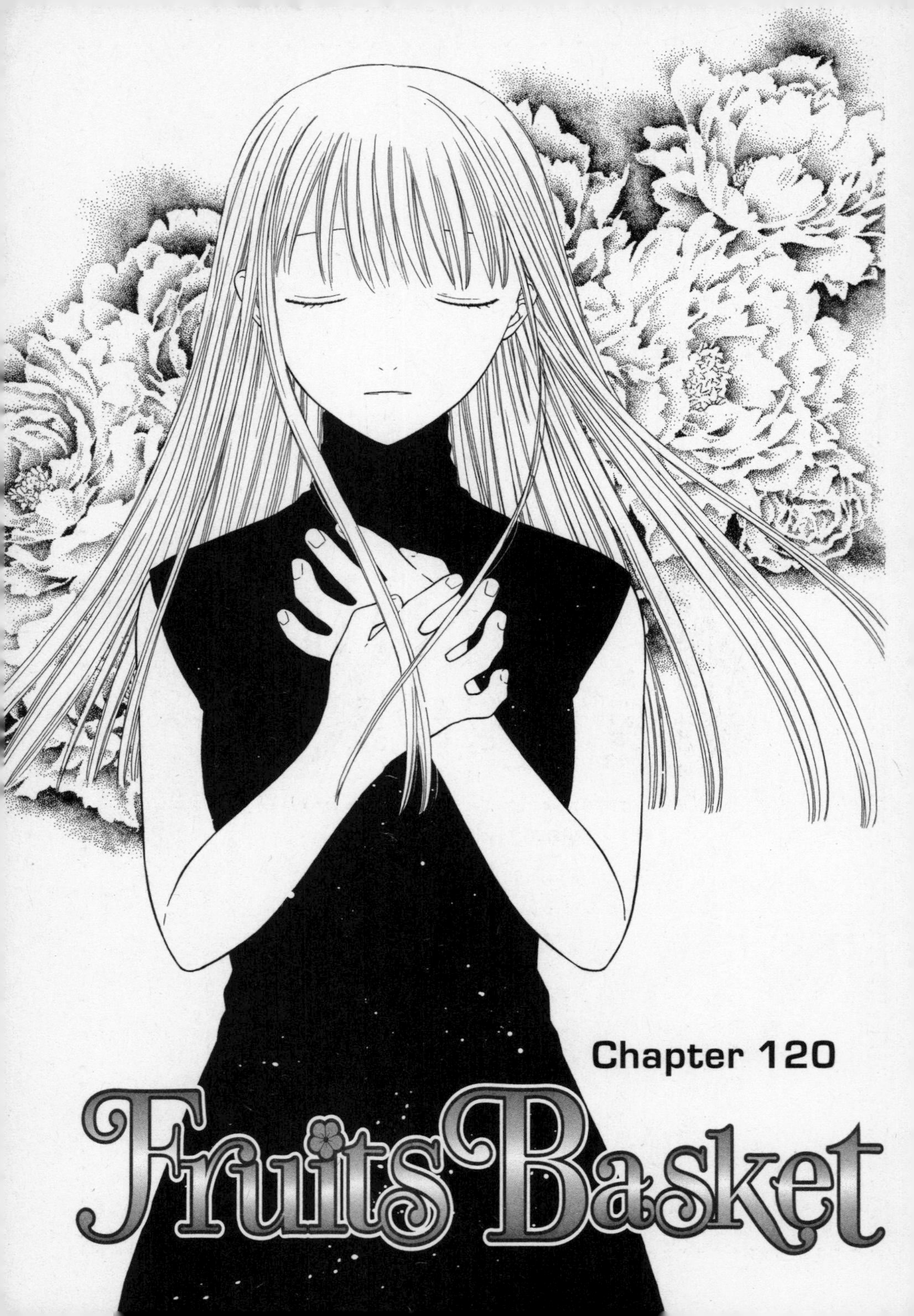
Chapter 120
Fruits Basket

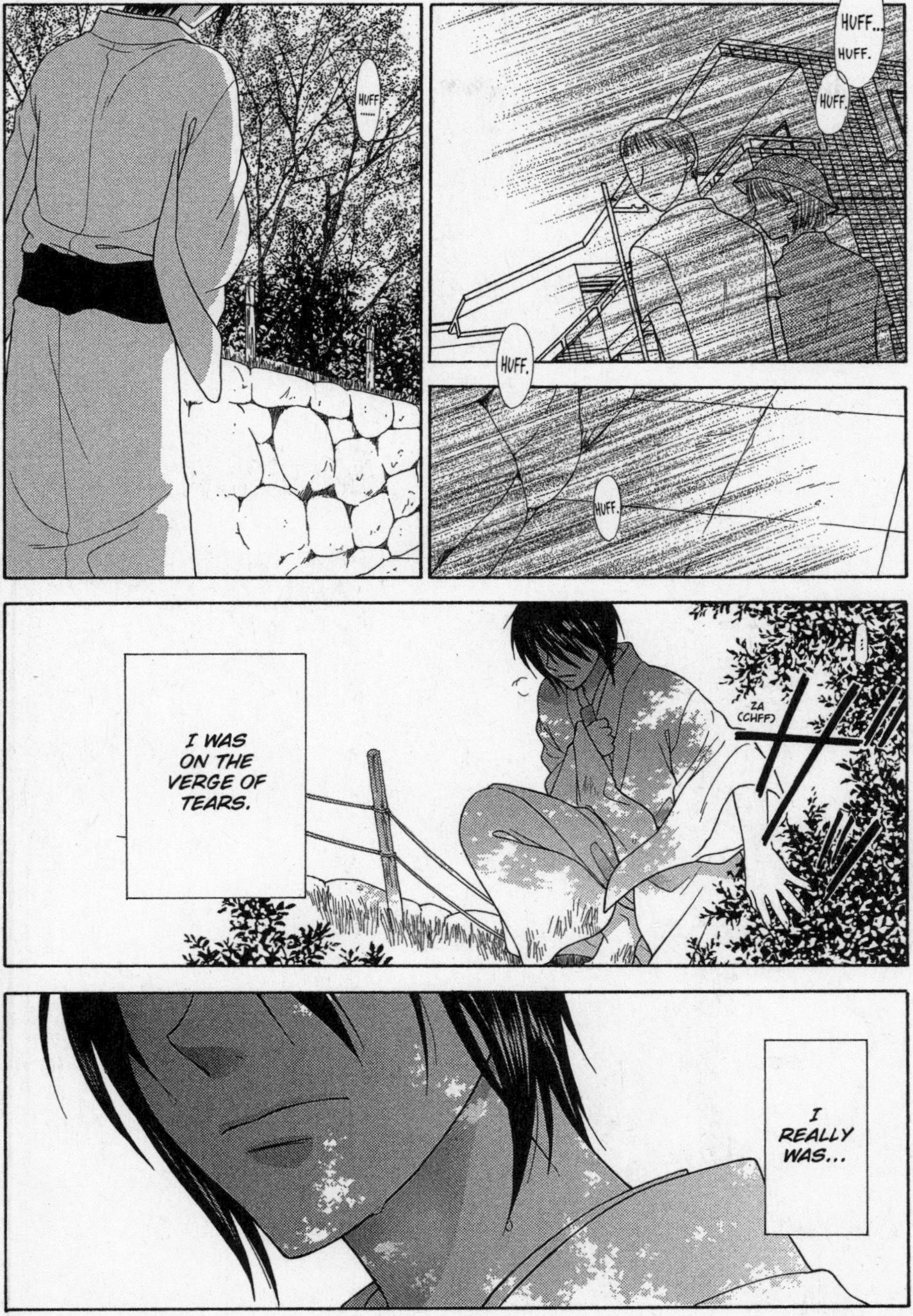
HUFF...
HUFF.
HUFF.
HUFF.
HUFF.
HUFF......
...
ZA (CHFF)
I WAS ON THE VERGE OF TEARS.
I REALLY WAS...

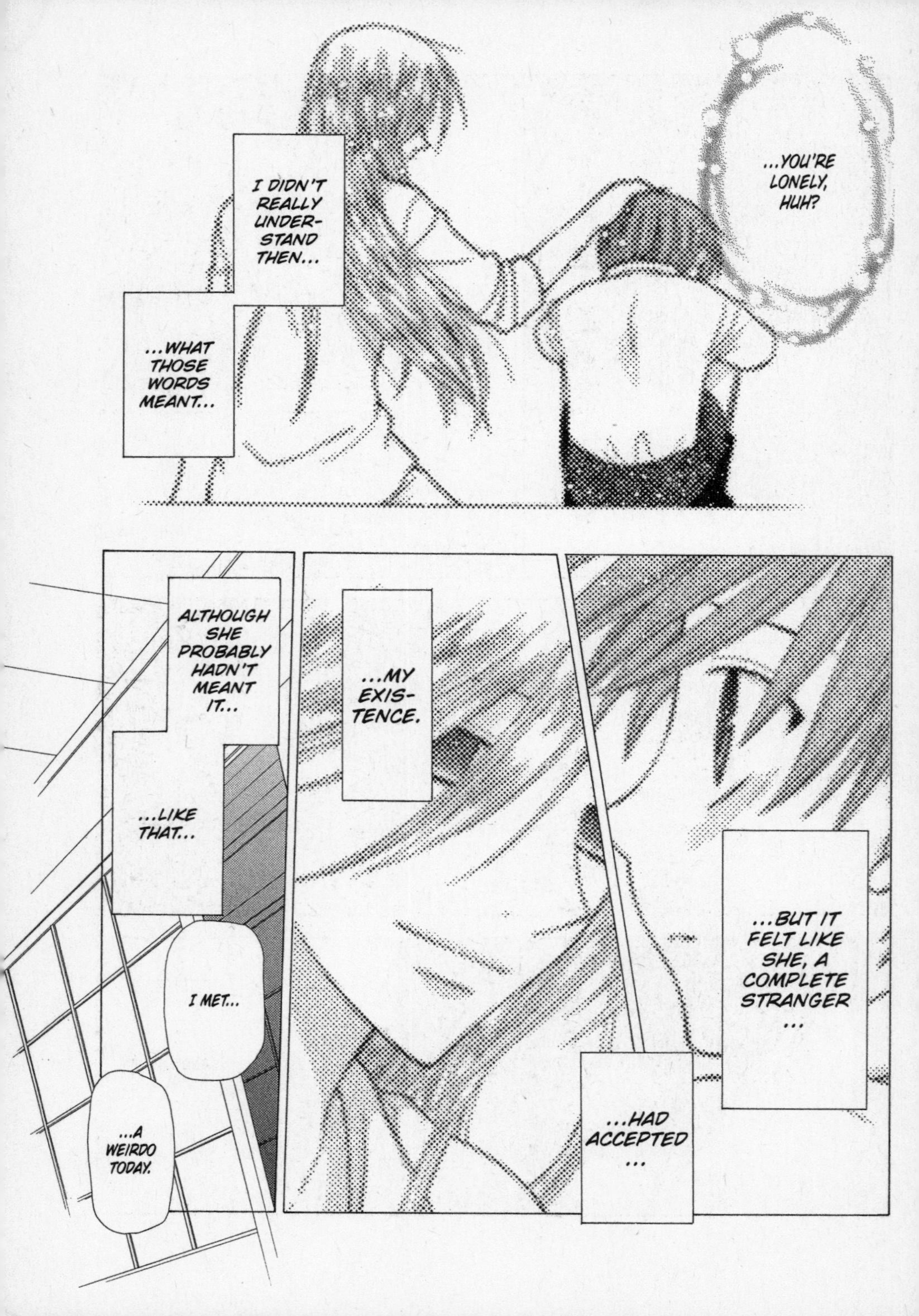
...YOU'RE LONELY, HUH?
I DIDN'T REALLY UNDER-STAND THEN...
...WHAT THOSE WORDS MEANT...
...BUT IT FELT LIKE SHE, A COMPLETE STRANGER...
...HAD ACCEPTED...
...MY EXIS-TENCE.
ALTHOUGH SHE PROBABLY HADN'T MEANT IT...
...LIKE THAT...
I MET...
...A WEIRDO TODAY.

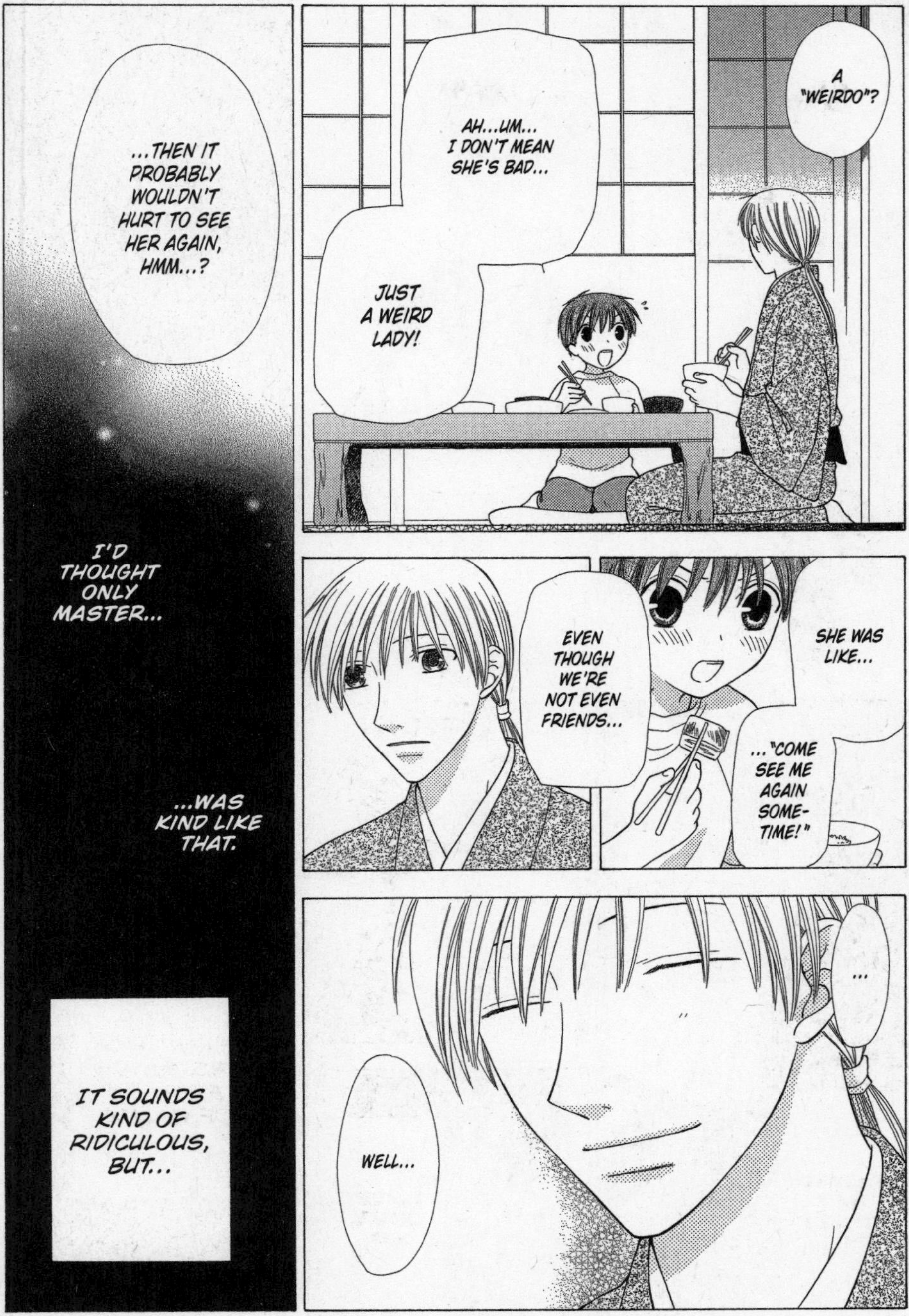
A "WEIRDO"?
AH...UM... I DON'T MEAN SHE'S BAD...
JUST A WEIRD LADY!
SHE WAS LIKE...
..."COME SEE ME AGAIN SOME-TIME!"
EVEN THOUGH WE'RE NOT EVEN FRIENDS...
...
WELL...
...THEN IT PROBABLY WOULDN'T HURT TO SEE HER AGAIN, HMM...?
I'D THOUGHT ONLY MASTER...
...WAS KIND LIKE THAT.
IT SOUNDS KIND OF RIDICULOUS, BUT...

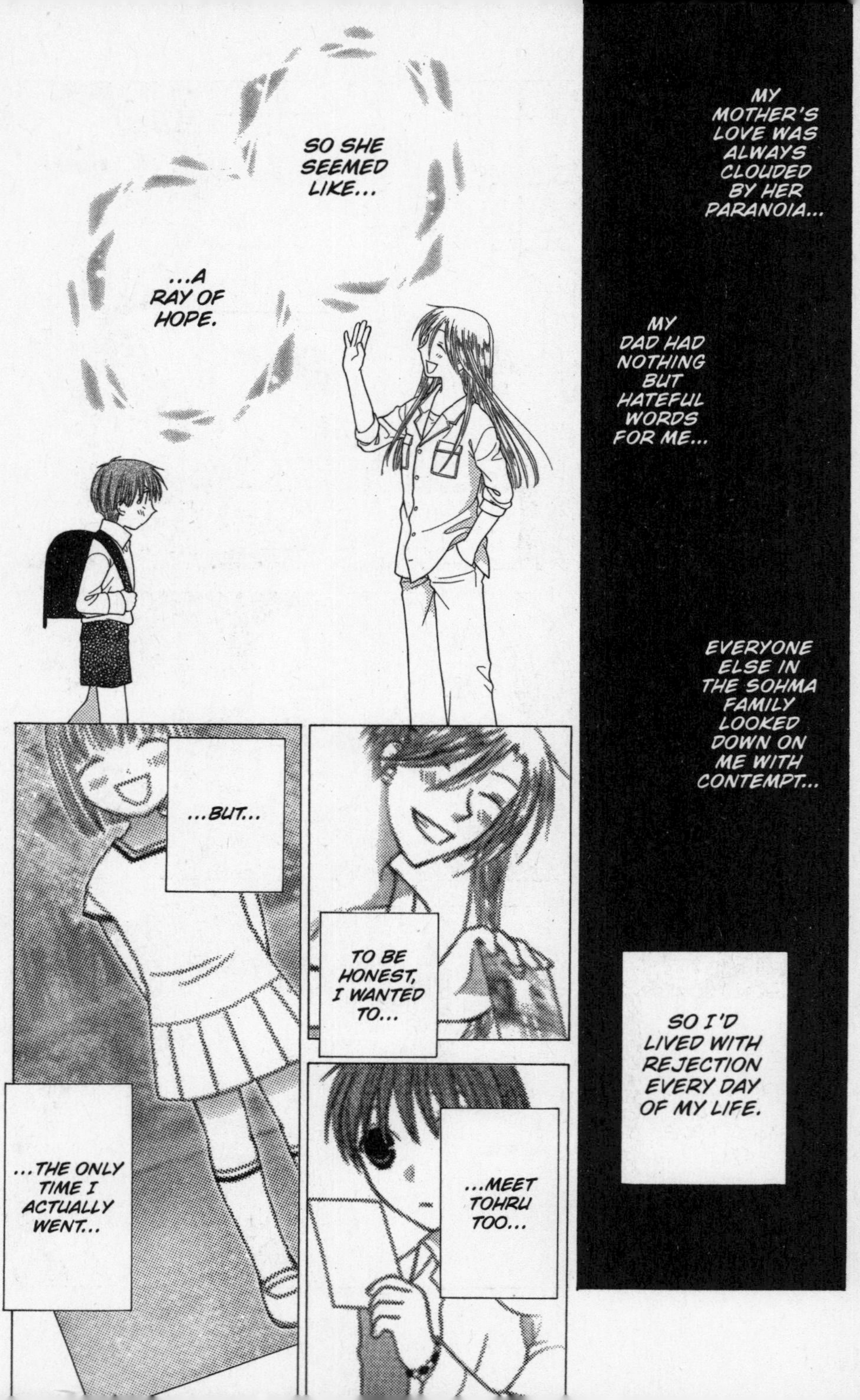
MY MOTHER'S LOVE WAS ALWAYS CLOUDED BY HER PARANOIA...
MY DAD HAD NOTHING BUT HATEFUL WORDS FOR ME...
EVERYONE ELSE IN THE SOHMA FAMILY LOOKED DOWN ON ME WITH CONTEMPT...
SO I'D LIVED WITH REJECTION EVERY DAY OF MY LIFE.
SO SHE SEEMED LIKE...
...A RAY OF HOPE.
TO BE HONEST, I WANTED TO...
...MEET TOHRU TOO...
...BUT...
...THE ONLY TIME I ACTUALLY WENT...

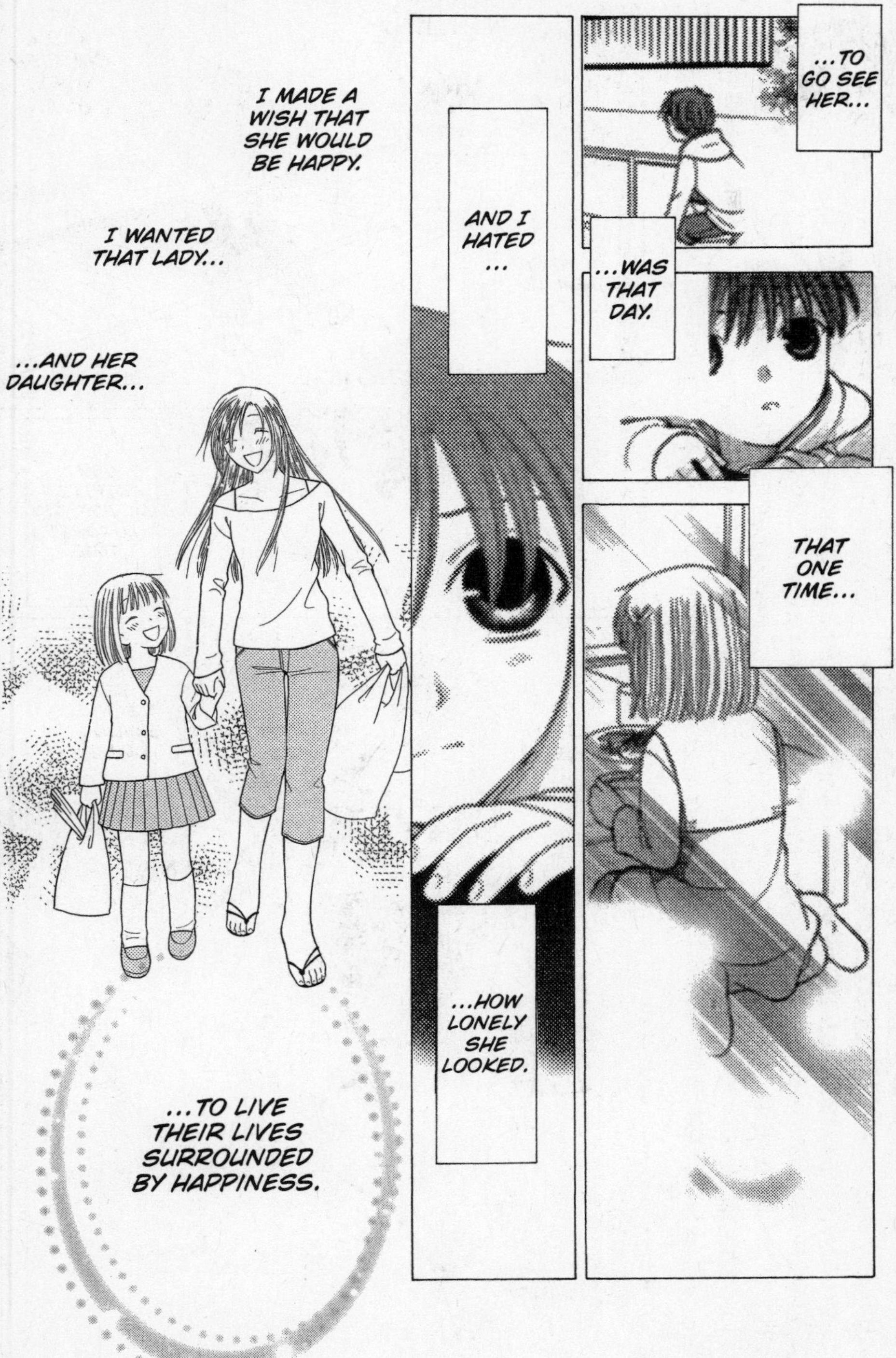
...TO GO SEE HER...
...WAS THAT DAY.
THAT ONE TIME...
AND I HATED...
...HOW LONELY SHE LOOKED.
I MADE A WISH THAT SHE WOULD BE HAPPY.
I WANTED THAT LADY...
...AND HER DAUGHTER...
...TO LIVE THEIR LIVES SURROUNDED BY HAPPINESS.

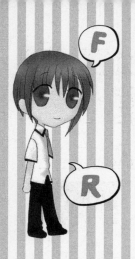

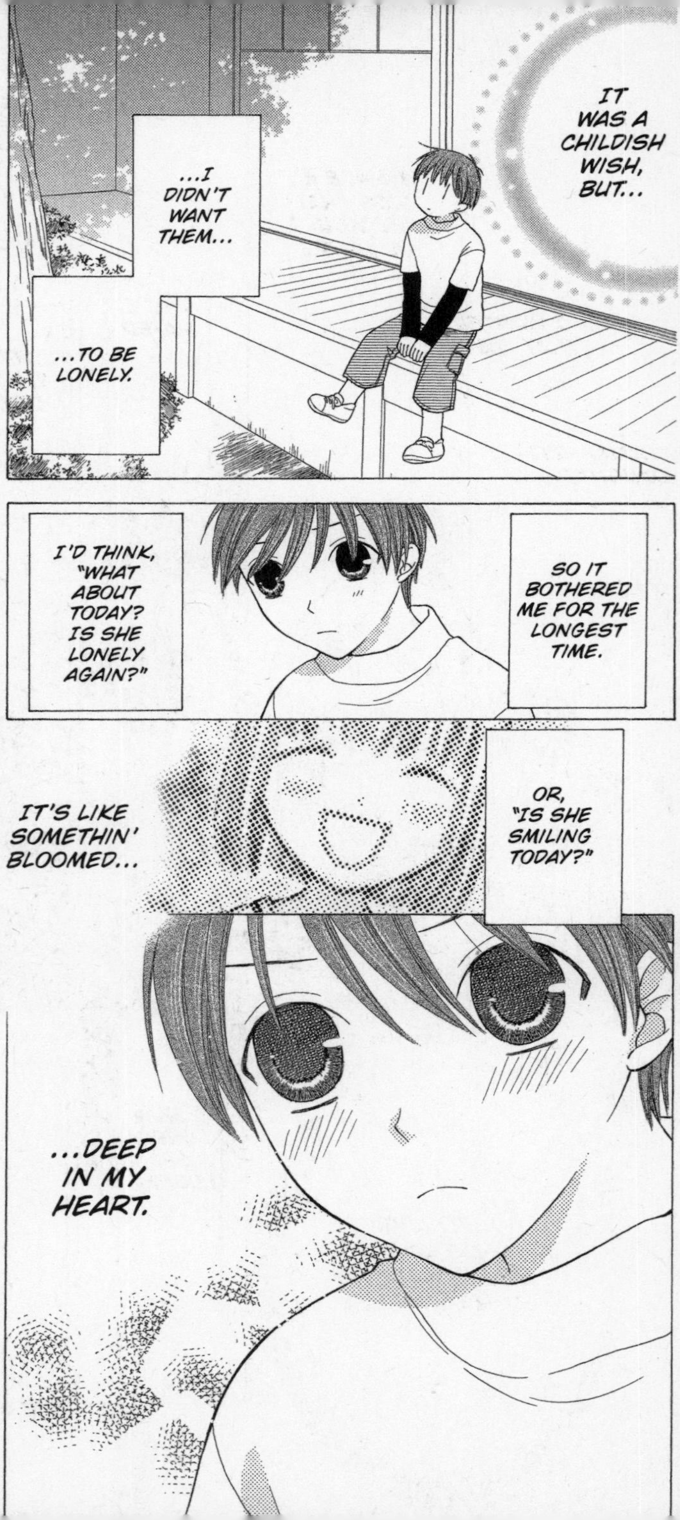
IT WAS A CHILDISH WISH, BUT...
...I DIDN'T WANT THEM...
...TO BE LONELY.
SO IT BOTHERED ME FOR THE LONGEST TIME.
I'D THINK, "WHAT ABOUT TODAY? IS SHE LONELY AGAIN?"
OR, "IS SHE SMILING TODAY?"
IT'S LIKE SOMETHIN' BLOOMED...
...DEEP IN MY HEART.

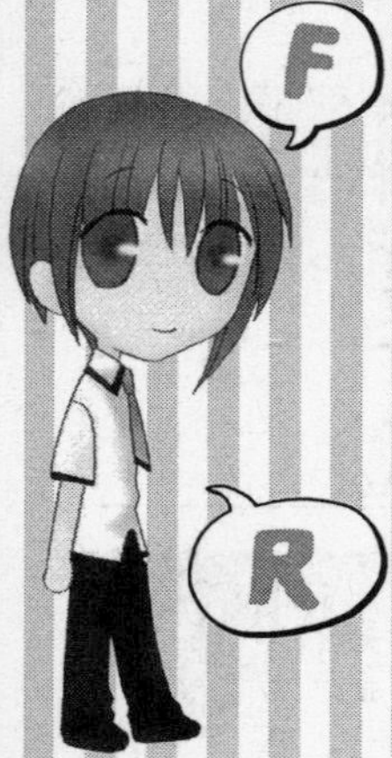
F
R

TO BE CONTINUED IN VOLUME ⑪

Love Natsuki Takaya?
Don't forget to check out her other works
also available from Yen Press!

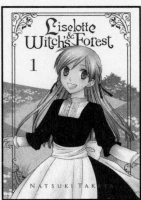

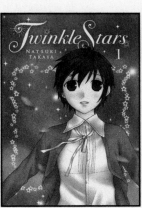

**Volumes 1-3,
available now.**

**Volume 1 and 2,
available now.**

COLLECTOR'S EDITION

Fruits Basket

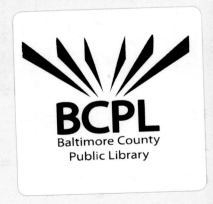

COLLECTOR'S EDITION

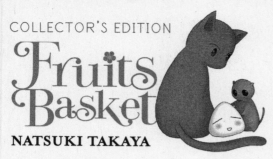

Fruits Basket

NATSUKI TAKAYA

Translation: Sheldon Drzka • Lettering: Lys Blakeslee

Fruits Basket Collector's Edition, Vol. 10 by Natsuki Takaya
© Natsuki Takaya 2016
All rights reserved.
First published in Japan in 2016 by HAKUSENSHA, INC., Tokyo.
English language translation rights in U.S.A., Canada and U.K. arranged with
HAKUSENSHA, INC., Tokyo through Tuttle-Mori Agency, Inc., Tokyo.

English Translation © 2017 by Yen Press, LLC

Yen Press
1290 Avenue of the Americas
New York, NY 10104

Visit us at yenpress.com
facebook.com/yenpress
twitter.com/yenpress
yenpress.tumblr.com
instagram.com/yenpress

First Yen Press Edition: February 2017

Yen Press is an imprint of Yen Press, LLC.
The Yen Press name and logo are trademarks of Yen Press, LLC.

The publisher is not responsible for websites (or their content) that are not owned by the publisher.

Library of Congress Control Number: 2016932692

ISBN: 978-0-316-50164-4

10 9 8 7 6 5 4 3 2 1

BVG

Printed in the United States of America

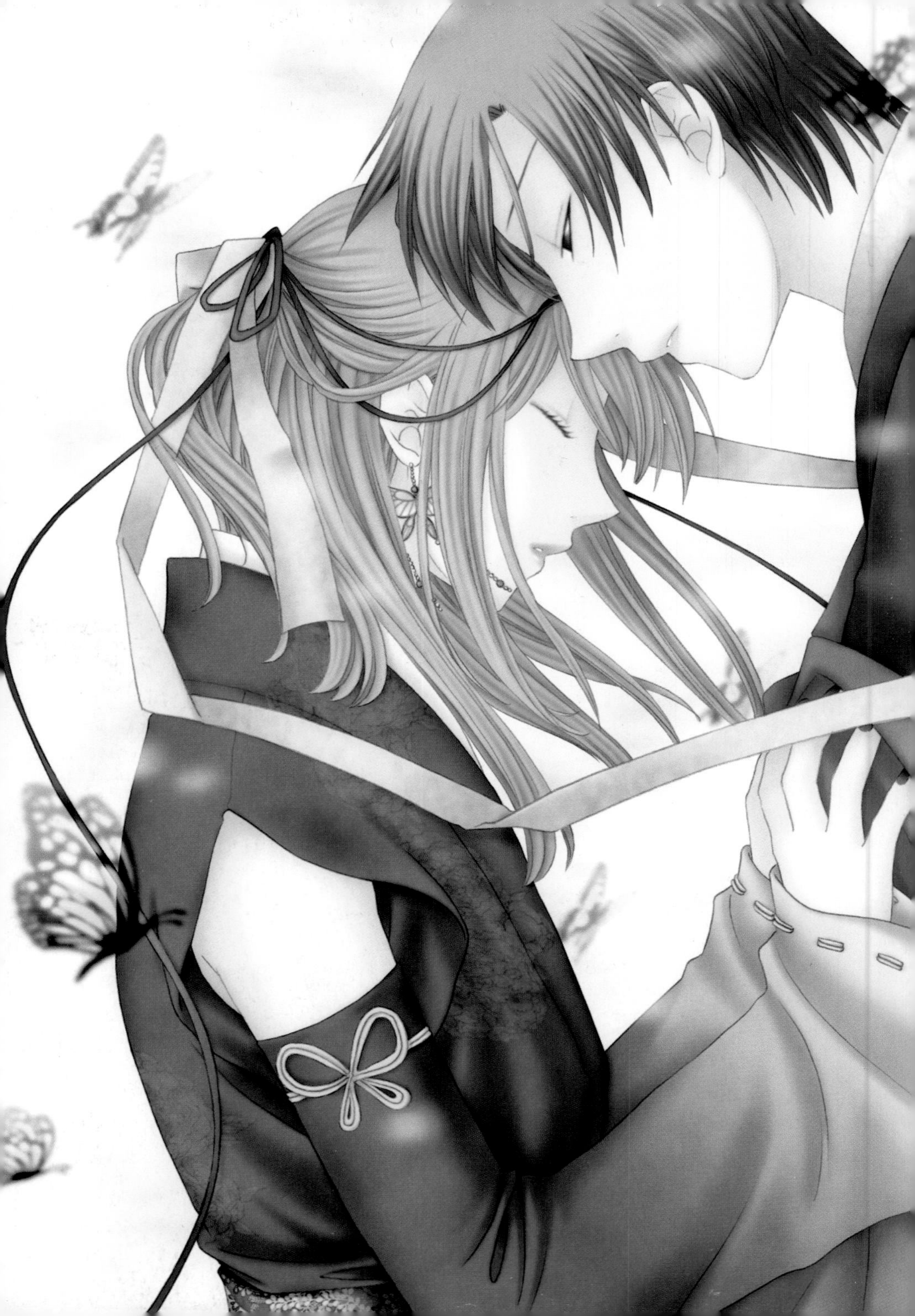

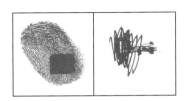

DISCARD

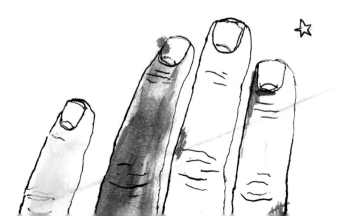

My name
is Jason.

Mine too.

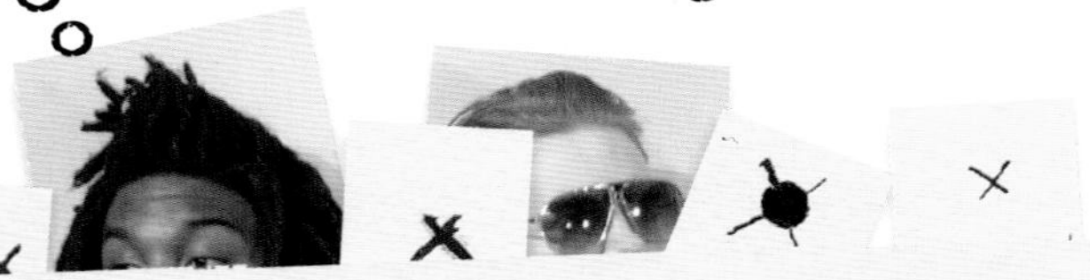

OUR STORY.

OUR WAY.

by
Jason
Reynolds
and
Jason
Griffin

atheneum

NEW YORK   LONDON   TORONTO
SYDNEY   NEW DELHI

A very special shout-out of thanks goes to Joanna Cutler, Alyson Day, Karen Nagel, Lydia Wills, Jason Yarn, Charles Yuen, Carla Weise, Ruiko Tokunaga, Dorothy Pietrewicz, Christopher Baily, Jenny Rozbruch, and Kathryn Silsand.

atheneum

ATHENEUM BOOKS FOR YOUNG READERS
An imprint of Simon & Schuster Children's Publishing Division
1230 Avenue of the Americas, New York, New York 10020
This work is a memoir. It reflects the author's present recollections of his experiences over a period of years.
© 2009 by Jason Reynolds and Jason Griffin
Cover illustration © 2009 by Jason Griffin
Back panel photographs © 2021 by Adedayo "Dayo" Kosoko
Back panel design © 2022 by Simon & Schuster, Inc.
Book design by Charles Yuen
For information about special discounts for bulk purchases, please contact Simon & Schuster Special Sales at 1-866-506-1949 or business@simonandschuster.com.
The Simon & Schuster Speakers Bureau can bring authors to your live event. For more information or to book an event, contact the Simon & Schuster Speakers Bureau at 1-866-248-3049 or visit our website at www.simonspeakers.com.
Also available in an Atheneum Books for Young Readers hardcover edition
The illustrations for this book were rendered in various physical and digital media.
Manufactured in China
First Atheneum Books for Young Readers paperback edition June 2022
10 9 8 7 6 5 4 3 2 1
Library of Congress Cataloging-in-Publication Data
Names: Reynolds, Jason, author. | Griffin, Jason, illustrator.
Title: My name is Jason. Mine too : our story, our way / Jason Reynolds ; illustrated by Jason Griffin.
Description: New York : Atheneum Books for Young Readers 2022. | "This work is a memoir. It reflects the authors present recollections of his experiences over a period of years."—Copyright page. | Audience: Ages 12 and Up | Audience: Grades 7-9 | Summary: "Jason Reynolds. Jason Griffin. One a poet. One an artist. One Black. One white. Two voices. One journey. To move to New York, and make it in New York. Best friends willing to have a hard life if it meant a happy life. All they needed was a chance. A reissue of a memoir of a moment in time within a lifetime of friendship"—Provided by publisher.
Identifiers: LCCN 2021049639 (print) | LCCN 2021049640 (ebook) | ISBN 9781534478237 (hardcover) | ISBN 9781534478220 (paperback) | ISBN 9781534478244 (ebook)
Classification: LCC PS3618.E9753 M9 2022 (print) | LCC PS3618.E9753 (ebook) | DDC 811/.6—dc23
LC record available at https://lccn.loc.gov/2021049639
LC ebook record available at https://lccn.loc.gov/2021049640

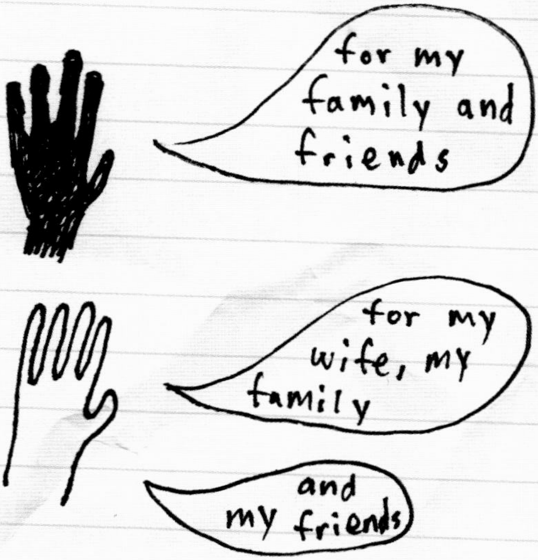
for my family and friends
for my wife, my family
and my friends

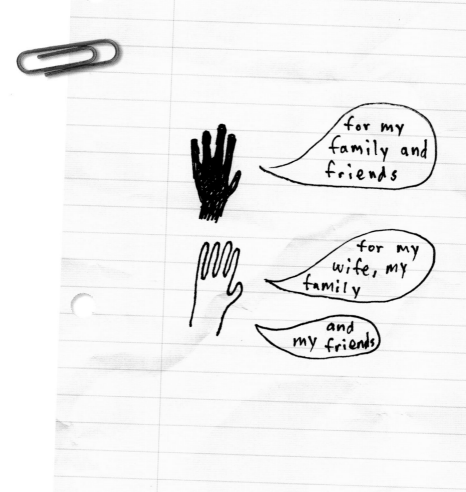

A poet. An artist. Black. white. we were college roommates. Now, close friends.

I could taste graduation. Tasted like freedom. No clue of what to do with that freedom. worked at a bookstore. At the checkout counter I wrote poems.

Dropped out of school. felt like freedom . I was a business major but only took art classes. I just wanted to paint. without the lecture. so I left and I did. with all the free time, I started working with jason. I did the art. He wrote drafts of poems at work.

At night we met at jason's house. I shared my poems. He shared his paintings. we shared similar pain, similar happiness, similar fear. we made the poems and paintings share space, just as we'd learned to.

A poet. An artist. Black. white. SELF .

Not SELVES. SELF.

I wasn't quite satisfied. Needed room to grow . Decided to move to New York city. Figured it would be easier to make it there with a friend, so I asked jason to come. Idea: sell SELF there.

I felt like a second grader. Like if I said no he wouldn't be my friend anymore. started packing my bags. Had to tell my mom. she loathes New York.

I was glad he said yes. I knew he was nervous about it. I insisted.

The ride seemed to last forever. Didn't think we'd ever get there. Secretly, I hoped we'd never get there.

New home. New hope. Brooklyn. Beautiful Bed-Stuy. A plastic plant, a wicker couch, a couple of mattresses, and boxes upon boxes of books.

And a TV. The one we had in college.

No sweat.

Shortly after arriving we learned the rules. NO money. NO name. NO chance.

No food. For the first six months we only ate cereal, peanut butter toast.

Tuna. Fried tuna. Tuna and rice. Rice and soup.

The hungrier we got, the closer we became. Within months we were family. Brothers.

Forced to lean on each other.

Couldn't afford not to.

Couldn't afford canvas. Jason painted on abandoned wooden doors, old checkbooks, milk cartons, and whatever else he could find. Visitors, beware.

Jason sat in the window of a coffee shop every single day for about three months, writing a collection of poems. Poems about friendship, growth, creativity. He drank coffee.

Lots of coffee.

It was time to take a huge risk. If I failed, at least Jason would be there to fail with me. I had an art show.

My mom got sick. I live in New York. I never should've left home.

Hundreds of people came to the show.

Really cool people. Jason's mom was there. She asked about my mother. I said she was fine. I lied.

I didn't sell a single piece. A failure. Men pretend not to cry. I did. Rent's due.

All those people came to see Jason's work. A success. My mother sent her love from the hospital.

Rent's late. There's always something.

So tired. So worried. So many questions. I needed to write.

Somehow I had to make it work. Somehow we had to make it work. I hoped.

what do people think of us? what are we
being perceived as? irresponsible or passionate?
probably stupid.

why be an artist? was dropping out of school a
bad decision? should i hang up the brush? why are my
clothes too big?

why do we care? i'm having the time of my
life. good times. bad times. never laughed so loud.
never cried so hard. never actually thought risks were
worth it. changed my mind. let's make a book. i'll
start writing now.

rent's paid. again. we always seem to make it. they
never seem to understand us. that's ok.
they never seem to stop us either.

a poet. an artist. black. white. regular guys.
survivors. friends. brothers.

pretty cool.

by the way, to all those reading, my name is
jason.

mine too.

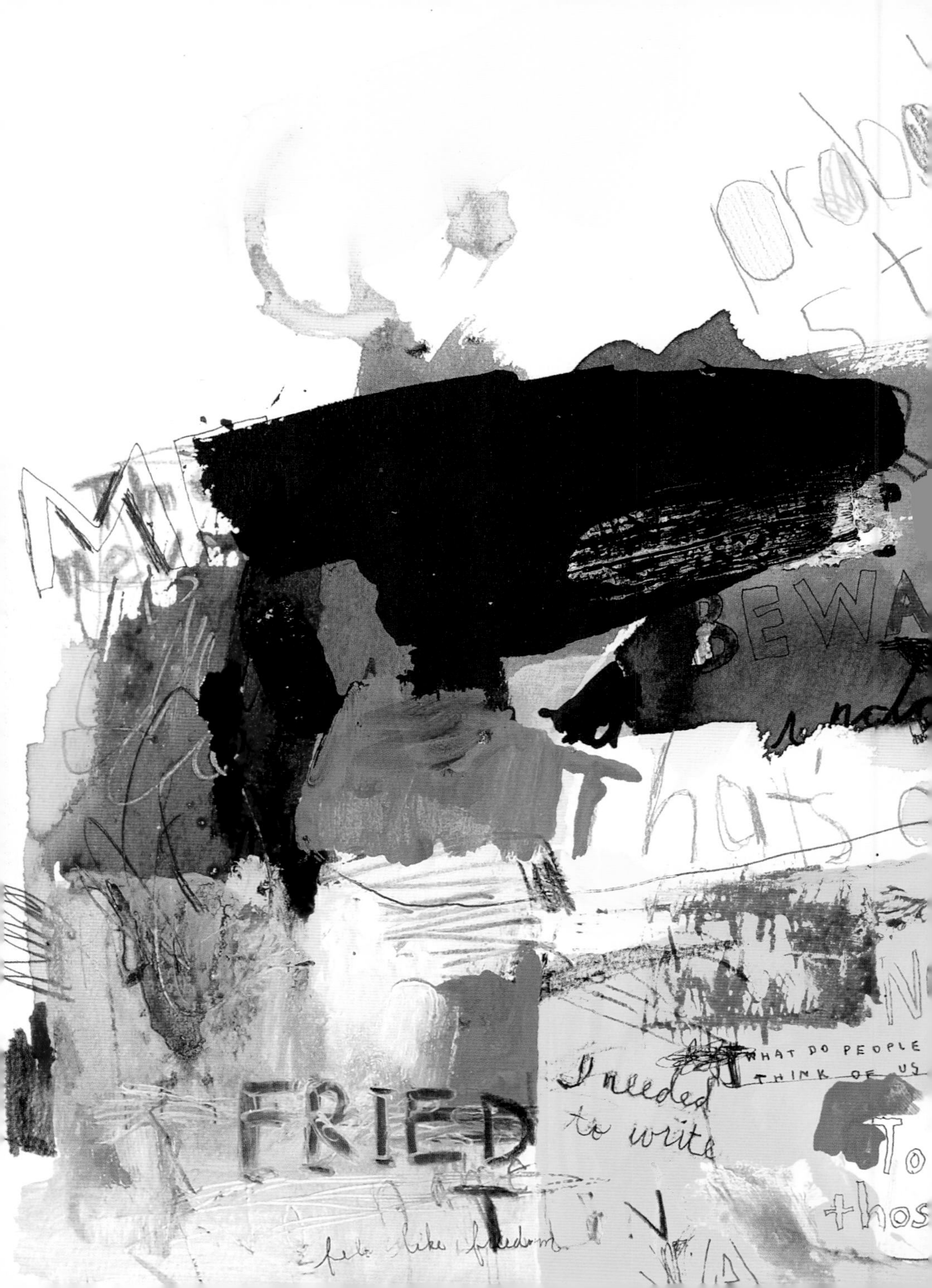
BEWA
That's
WHAT DO PEOPLE
THINK OF US
I needed
to write
To
thos
FRIED
felt like freedom

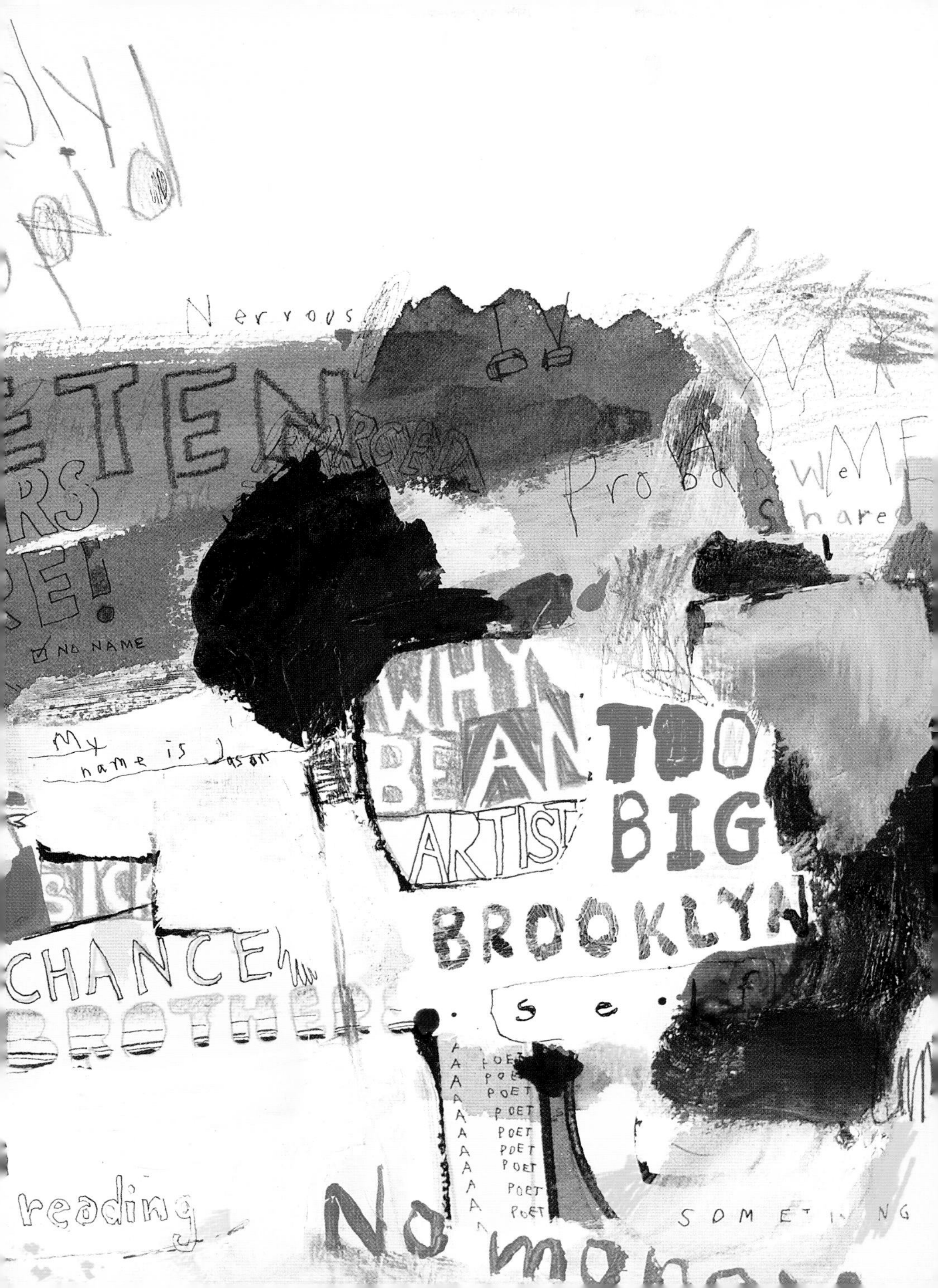

Nervous

TV

TEN

Probably WE

Shared

RS

E!

☑ NO NAME

My name is Jason

WHY
BE AN
ARTIST

TOO
BIG

BROOKLYN

CHANCE

BROTHER

s e f

SICK

A
A
A
A
A
A
A
A
A
A

POET
POET
POET
POET
POET
POET
POET
POET
POET

reading

No money

SOMETHING

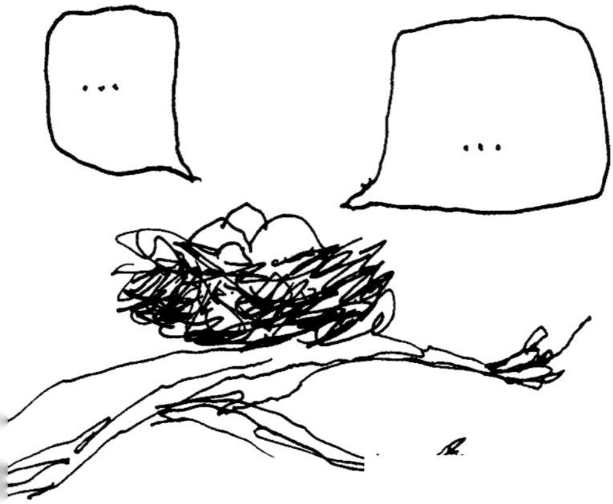

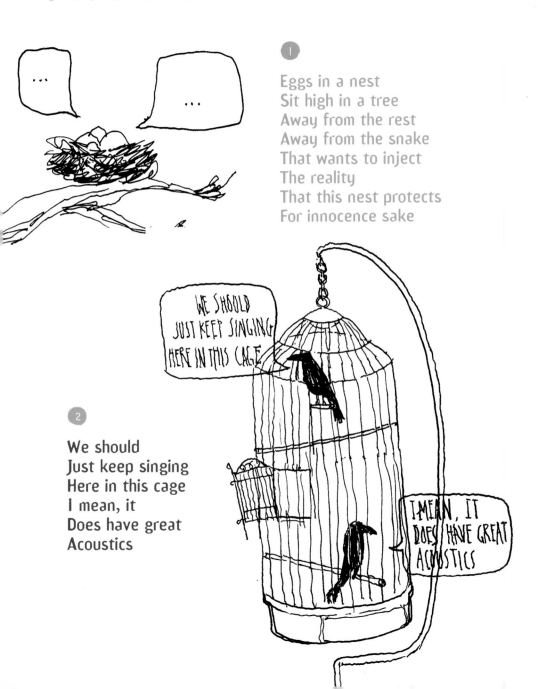

1

Eggs in a nest
Sit high in a tree
Away from the rest
Away from the snake
That wants to inject
The reality
That this nest protects
For innocence sake

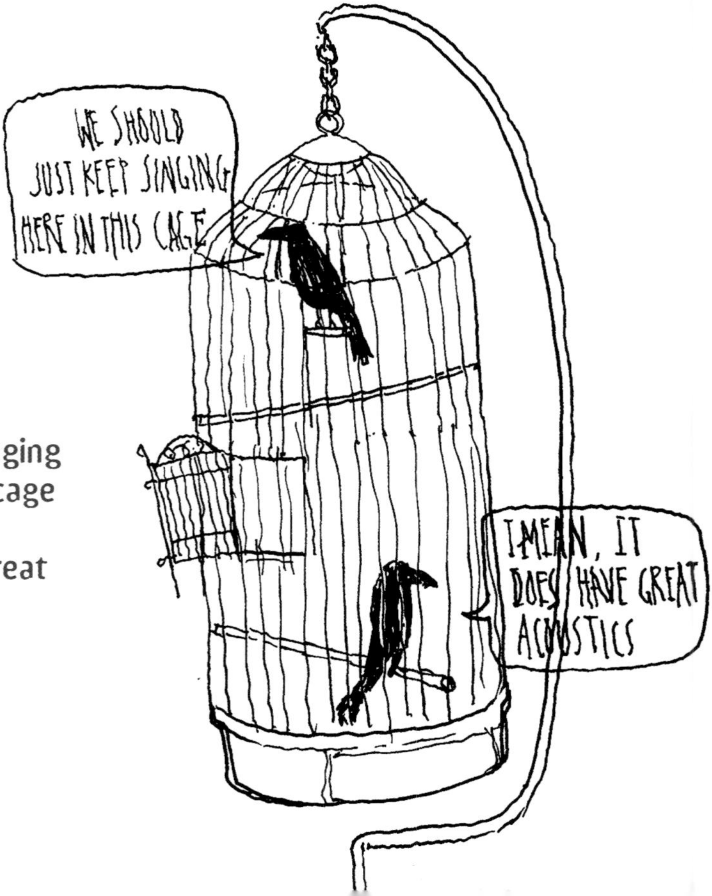
WE SHOULD JUST KEEP SINGING HERE IN THIS CAGE
I MEAN, IT DOES HAVE GREAT ACOUSTICS

2

We should
Just keep singing
Here in this cage
I mean, it
Does have great
Acoustics

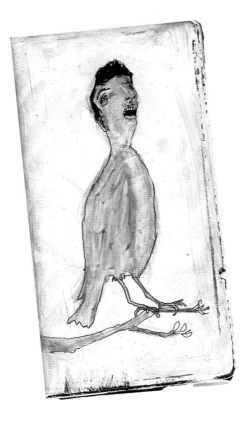

3

The early bird
Don't necessarily
Always catch
The worm
It just be
The first awake
To recognize
It's hungry
Should've slept in

4

An Epiphany:
There's gotta be
More
Than just cages
And worms
I gotta have wings
For a reason
I gotta have

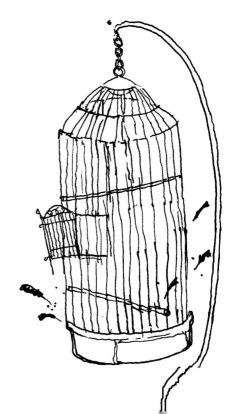

FELT

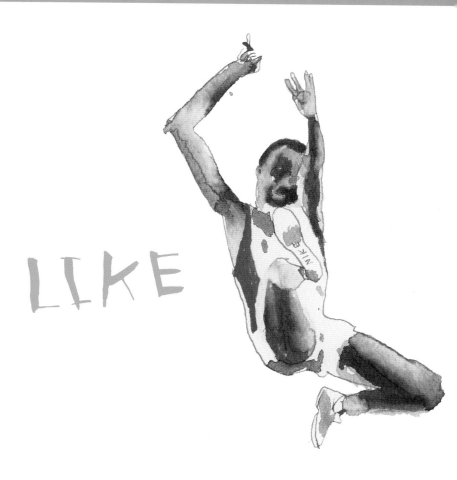

LIKE

FREEDOM

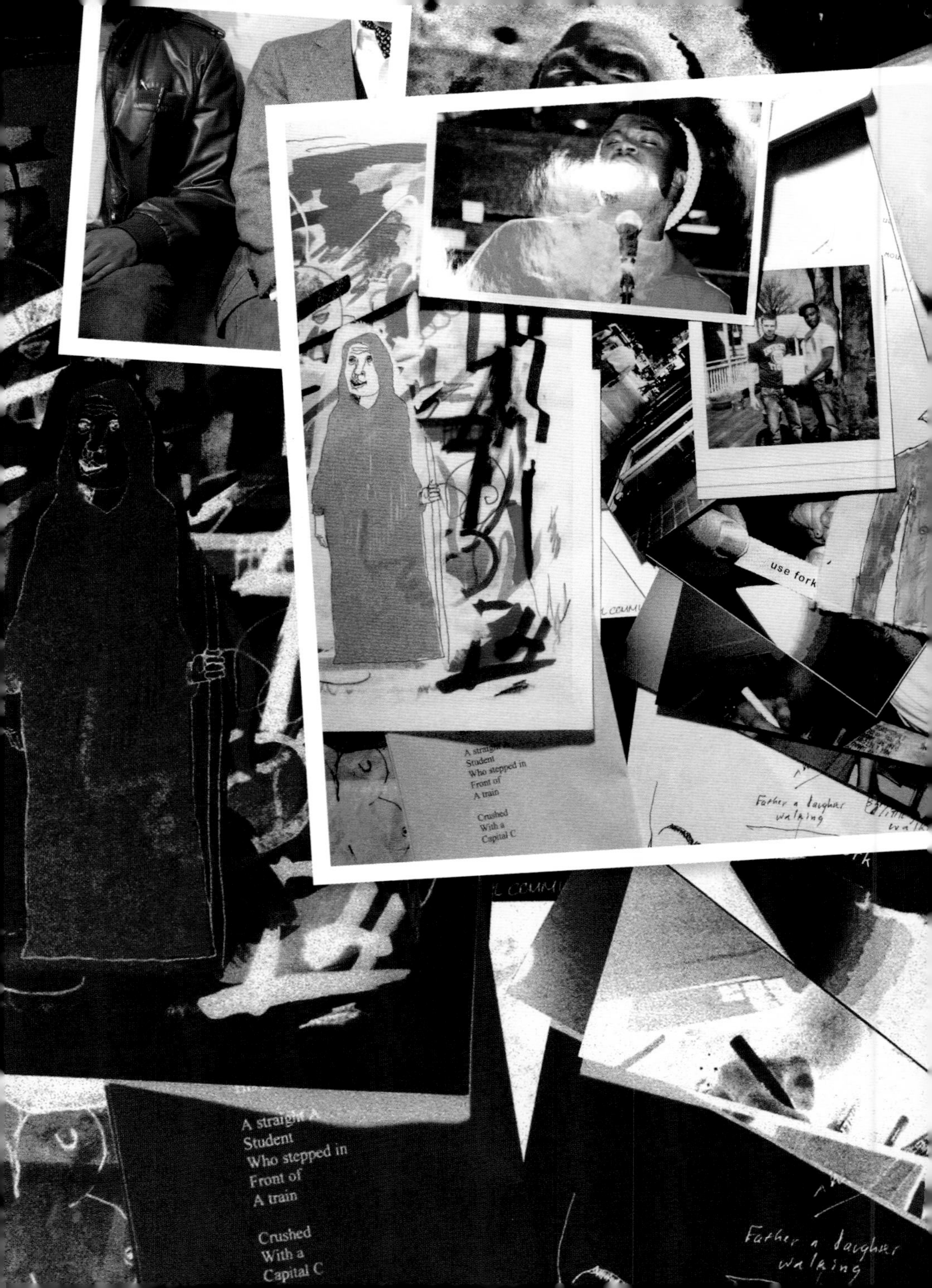
use fork
A straight A
Student
Who stepped in
Front of
A train
Crushed
With a
Capital C
Father a daugher
walking
A straight A
Student
Who stepped in
Front of
A train
Crushed
With a
Capital C
Father a daugher
walking

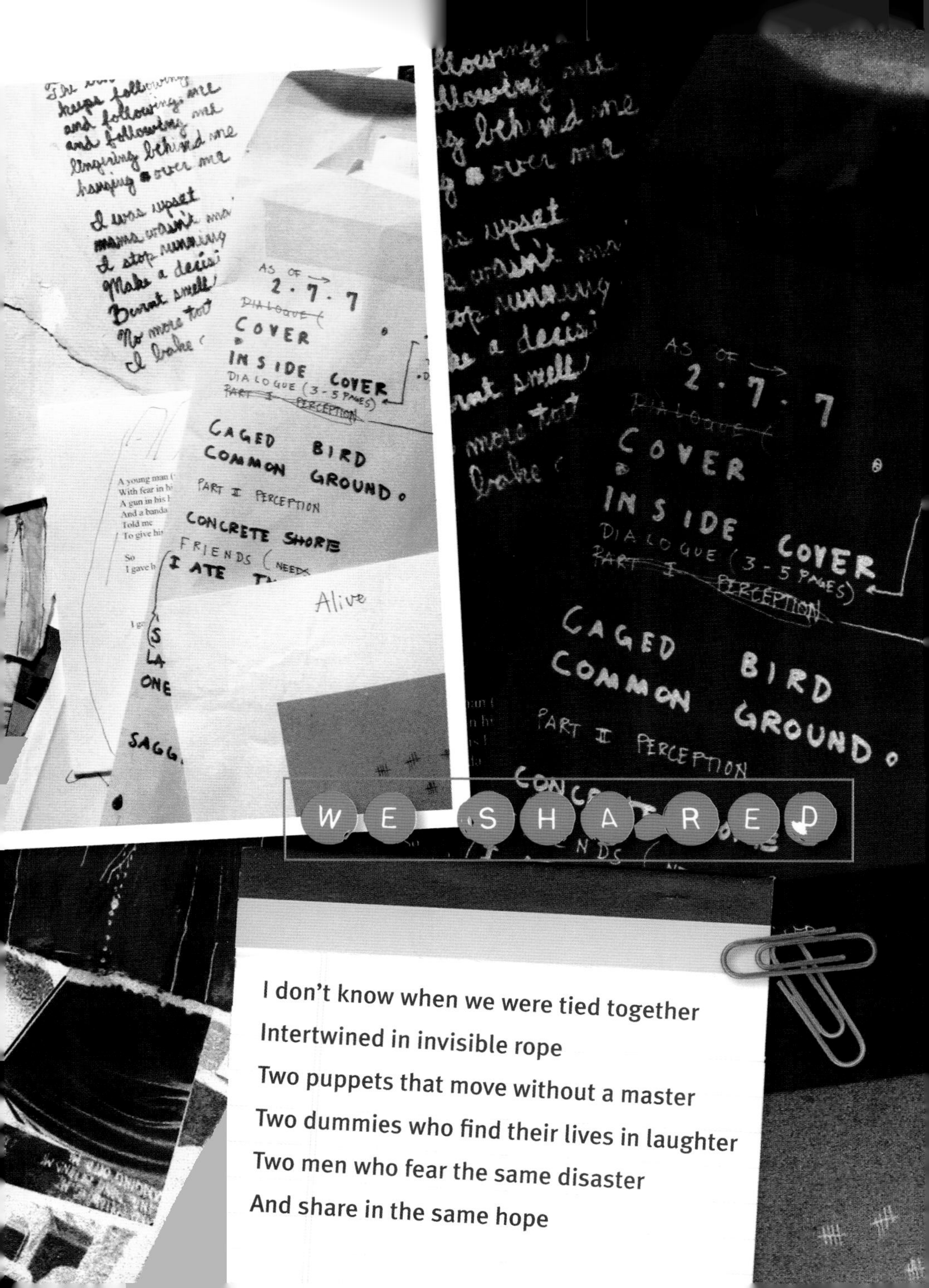
keeps following me
and following me
and following me
lingering behind me
hanging over me
I was upset
I stop running
Make a decisi
Burnt smell
No more
AS OF 2·7·7
DIALOGUE
COVER
INSIDE COVER
DIALOGUE (3-5 PAGES)
PART I PERCEPTION
CAGED BIRD
COMMON GROUND
PART II PERCEPTION
CONCRETE SHORE
FRIENDS (NEEDS
I ATE
Alive
A young man
With fear in hi
A gun in his h
And a banda
Told me
To give hi
So
I gave h
SAGG

WE SHARED

I don't know when we were tied together
Intertwined in invisible rope
Two puppets that move without a master
Two dummies who find their lives in laughter
Two men who fear the same disaster
And share in the same hope

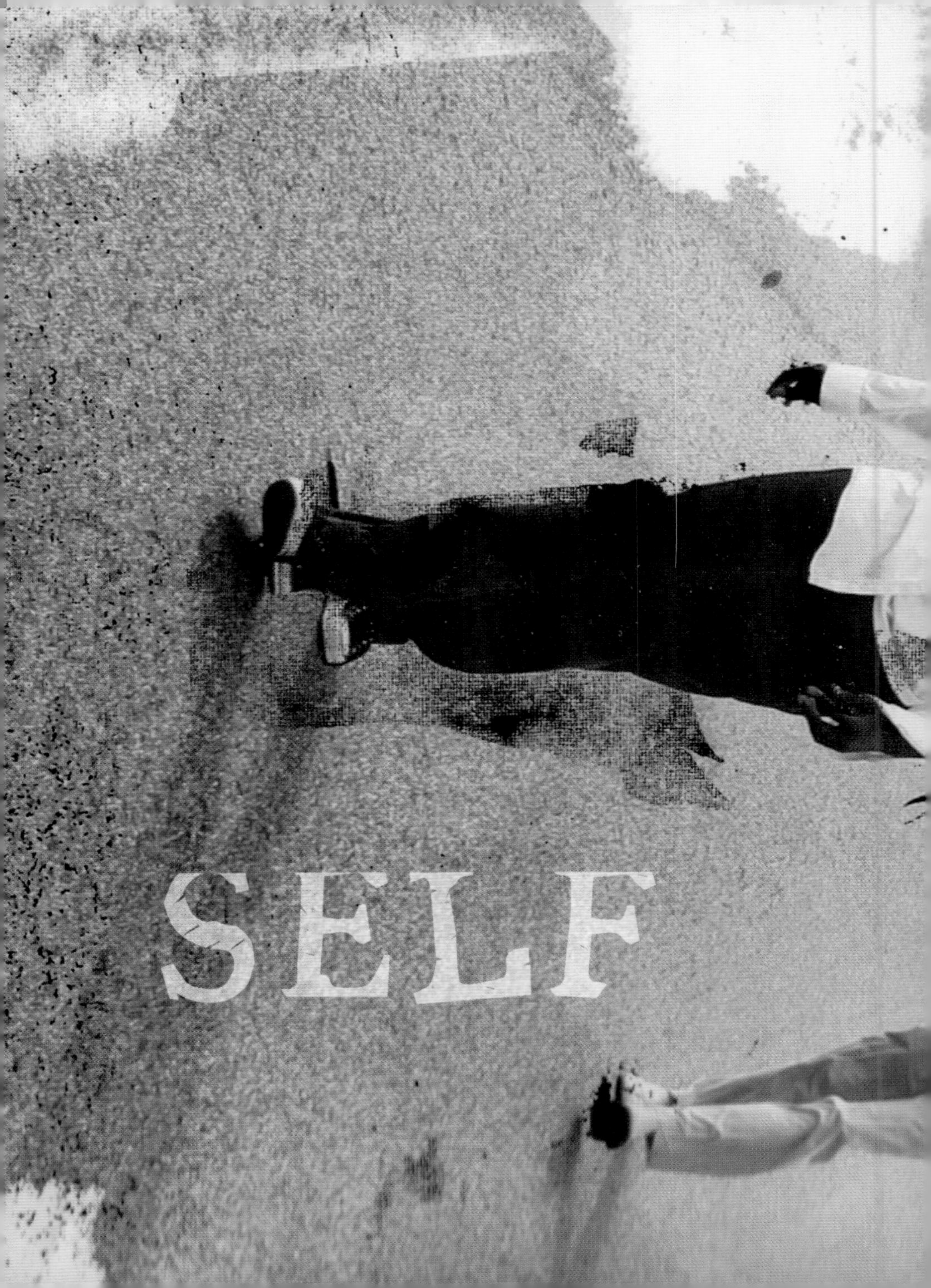
SELF

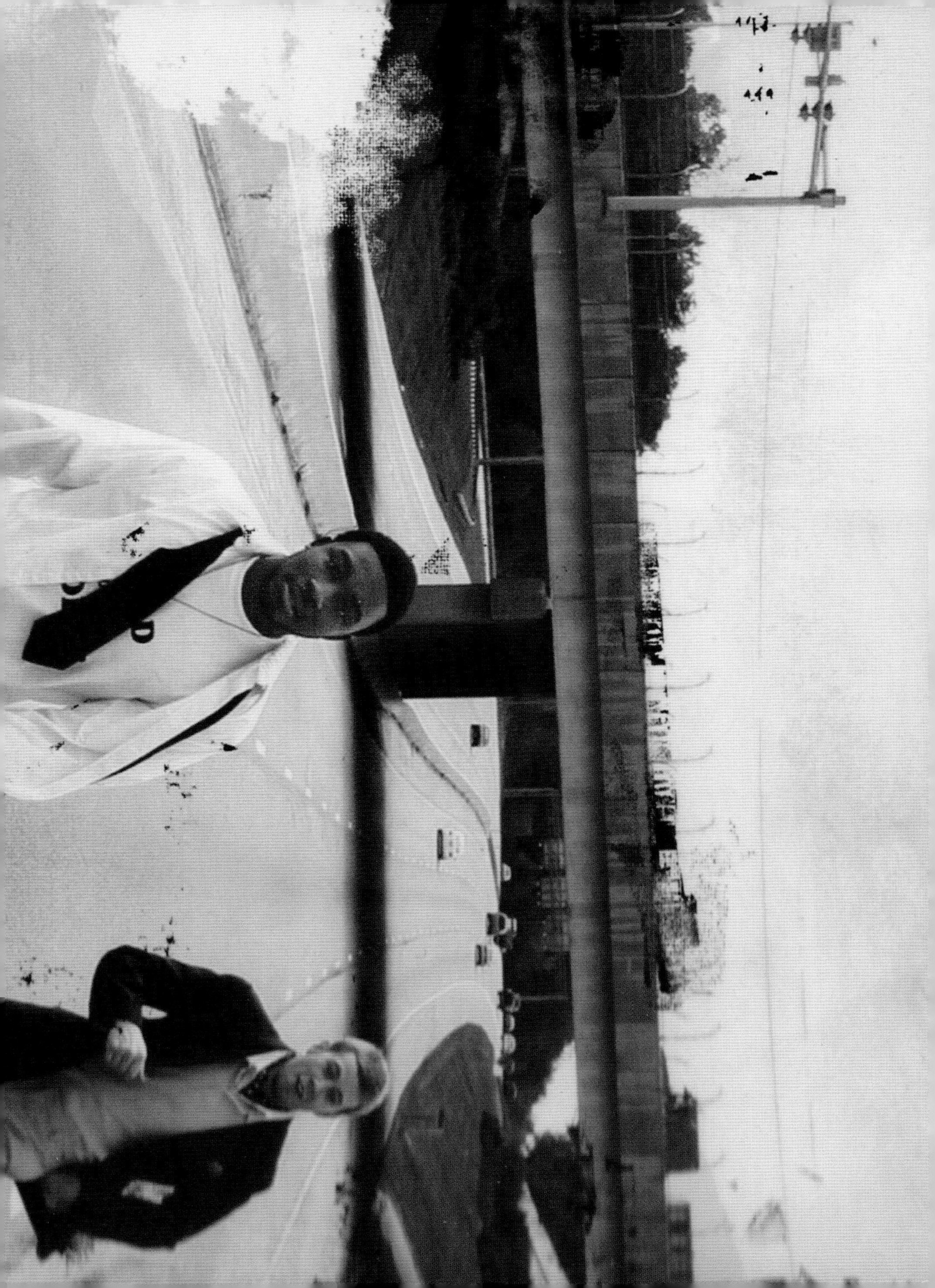

room to grow

art?

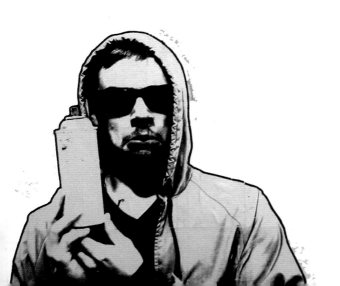

Here
Today
We change

Meet me at the
Railroad tracks
Bring your art supplies
And an extra handful
Of courage
Just in case the
Trains come

Just in case
Yesterday decides
To show its face

We'll create a piece of art
To bring forth peace of heart
And tell grandparents
With hate-stained memories   art.
To hold on to hope
For healing can happen
Before heaven

Here
Today
We stand

At the train tracks
That separate different
Parts of the same land

Paint and pen in hand
Feet planted on a
Ground now common
Praying painting poeting that blood
On this ground
Won't be

Anymore

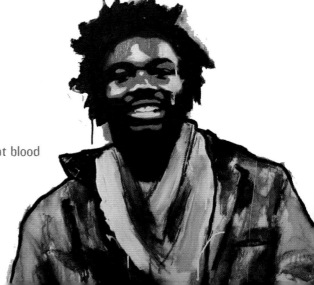

nervous

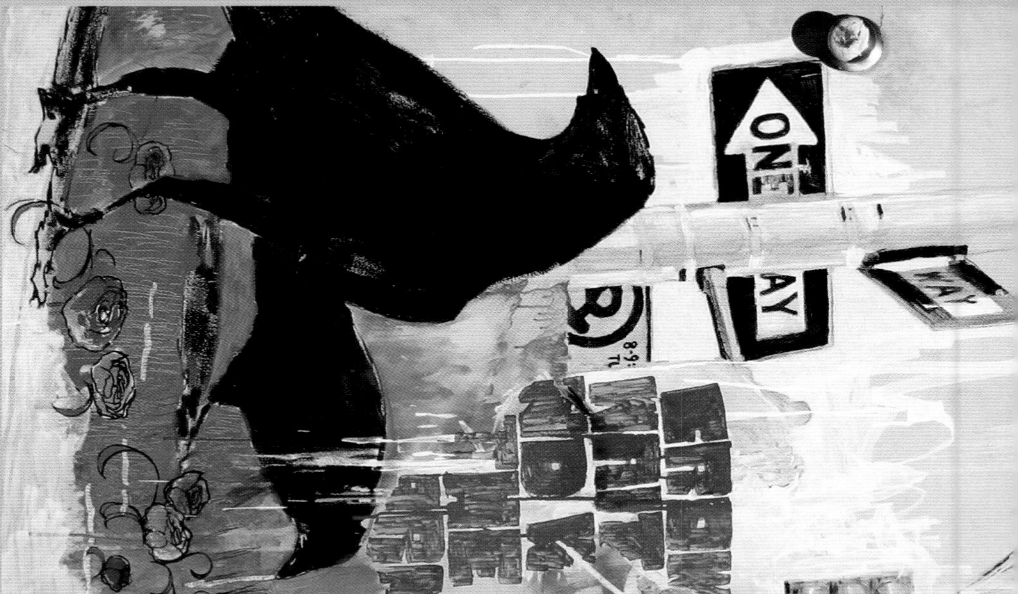
ONE WAY

Through the rearview
My house shrinks
My heart sinks
To the bottom
Of a spoiled
Stomach

I'm afraid
I'll miss dinner tonight
Mom

But I had to go
Find my appetite

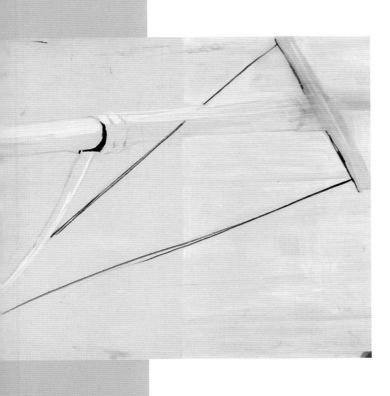

~~Decided to move~~

~~to borough~~

~~to borough crowde~~

Decided to move
to borough   crowded with dreams
hope there's room for mine

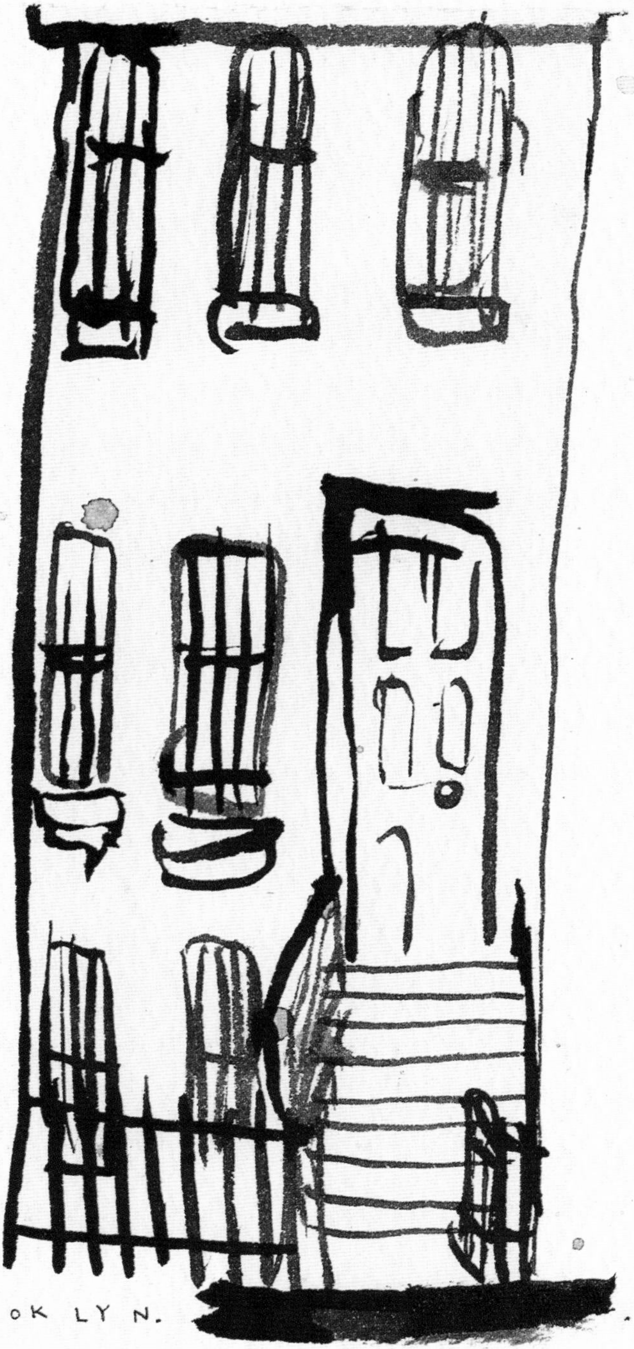

BROOKLYN.

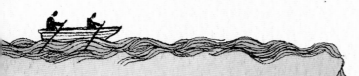

I was warned about this city
Told the tales of torturous time
A painful paradise for the unpretty
A week of work is worth a dime

Told to fear this savage land
If I desired my life spared
Give not and take not a hand
Sensitivity never shared

I have heard the rumors ring
Every person lives a lie
On the train don't say a thing
Look nobody in the eye

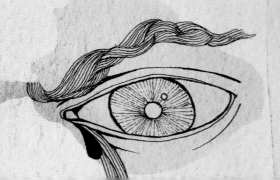

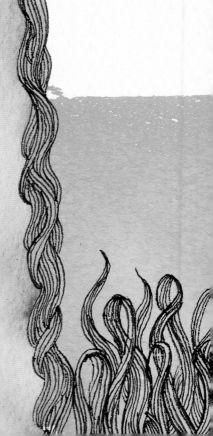

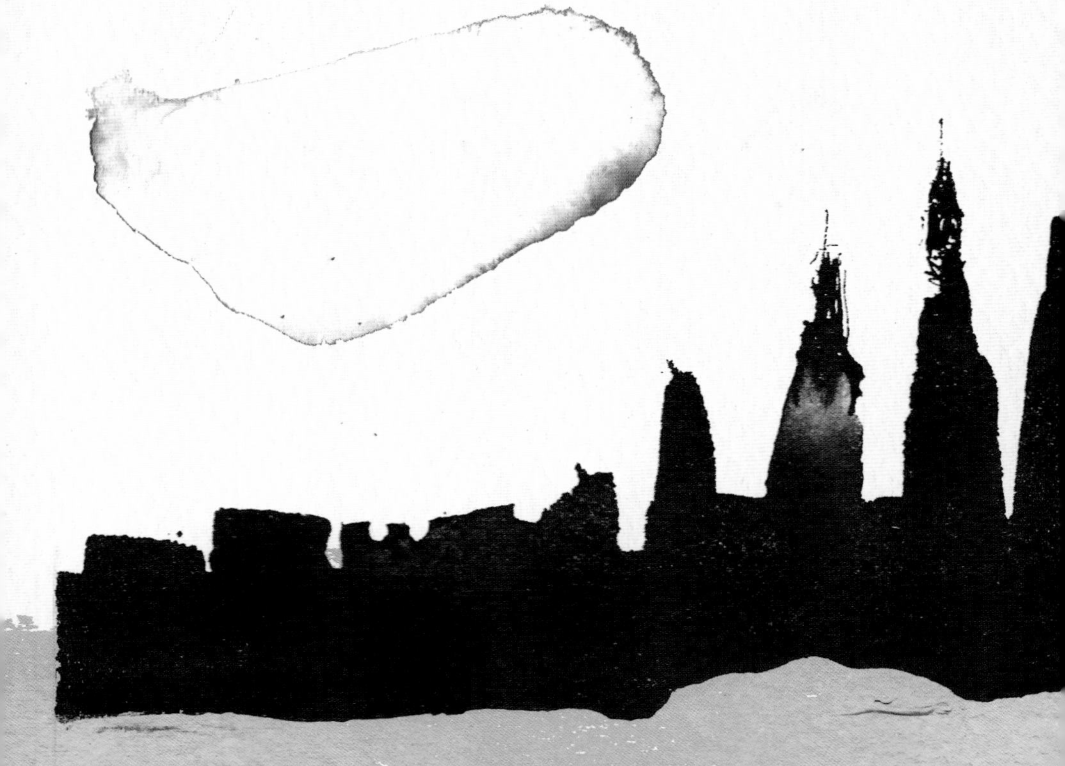

But I've learned
Ain't no heaven in this city
If all you do is hide

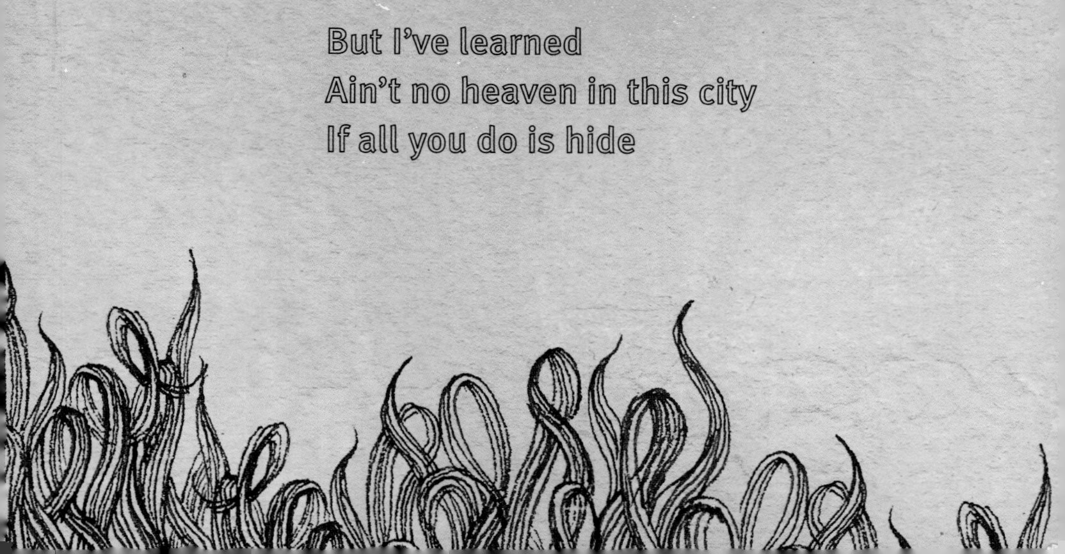

no money

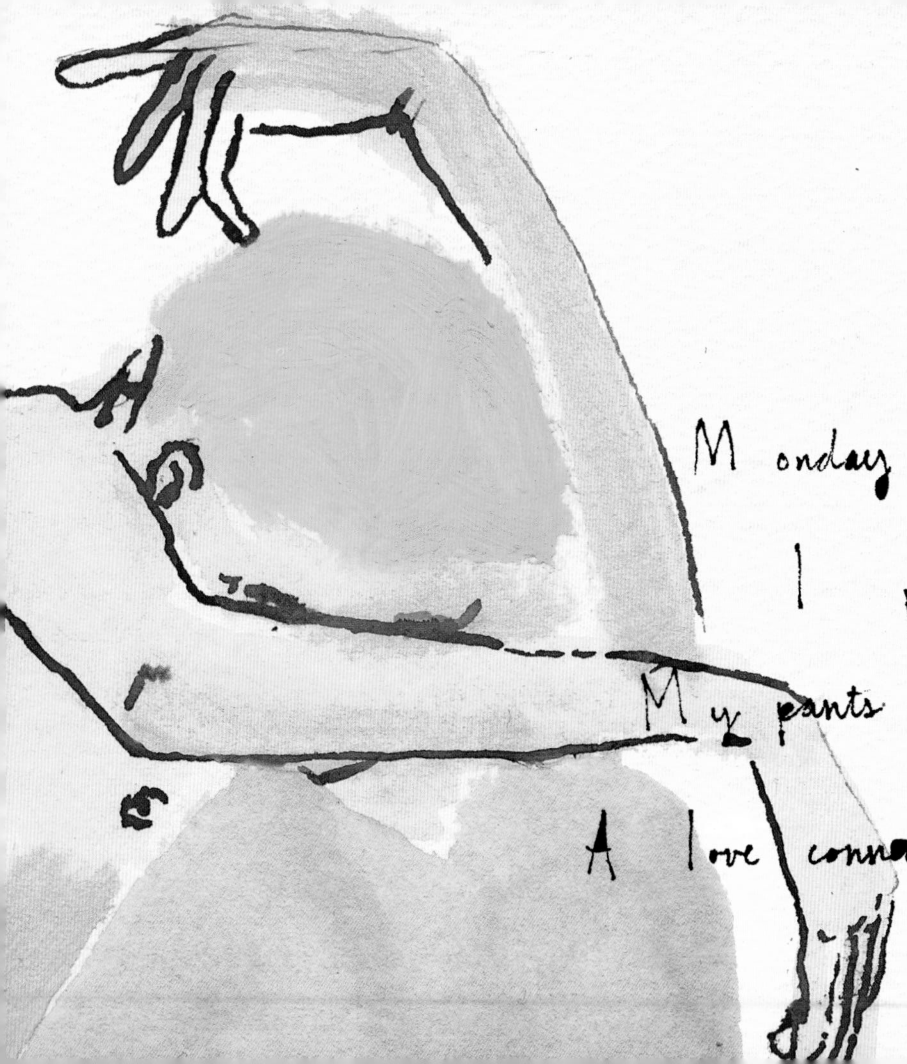
Monday morning
I promised
My pants pockets
A love connection soon

Monday morning

I promised

My pants pockets

A love connection soon

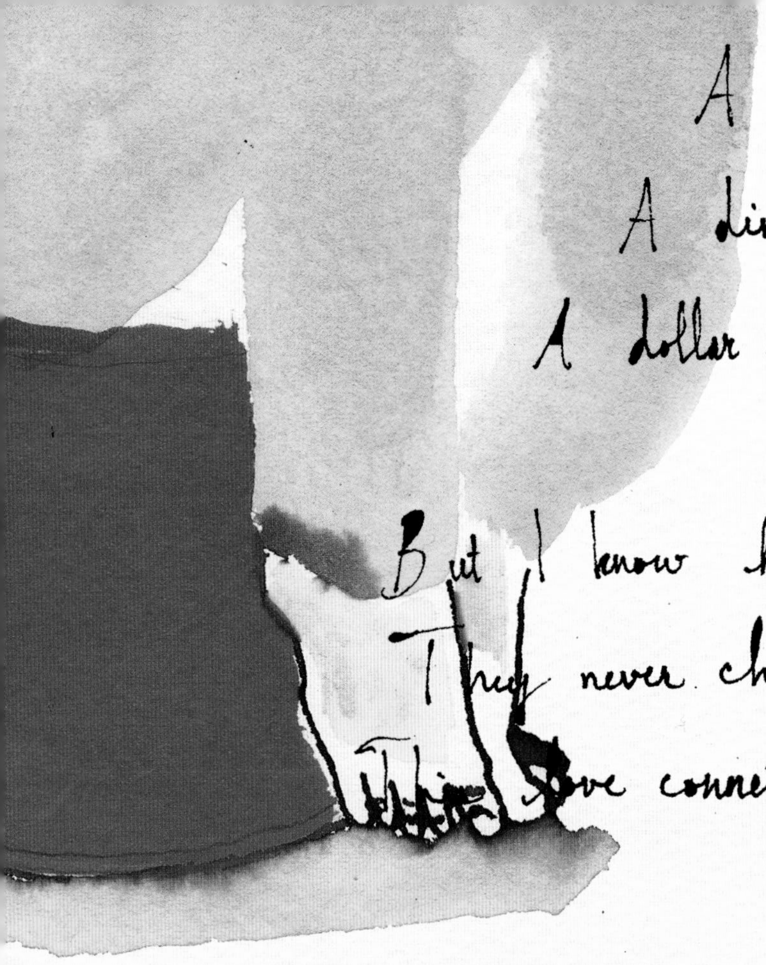

A nice nickel

A dime divine

A dollar dream to swoon

But I know how these pockets do

They never change, it's nothing new

This love connection will be through

By Tuesday afternoon

Sometimes I like to
Take taxis
To wherever the cool
People hang out
And get out
Wearing a huge hat
Sunglasses
And a scarf around
My mouth

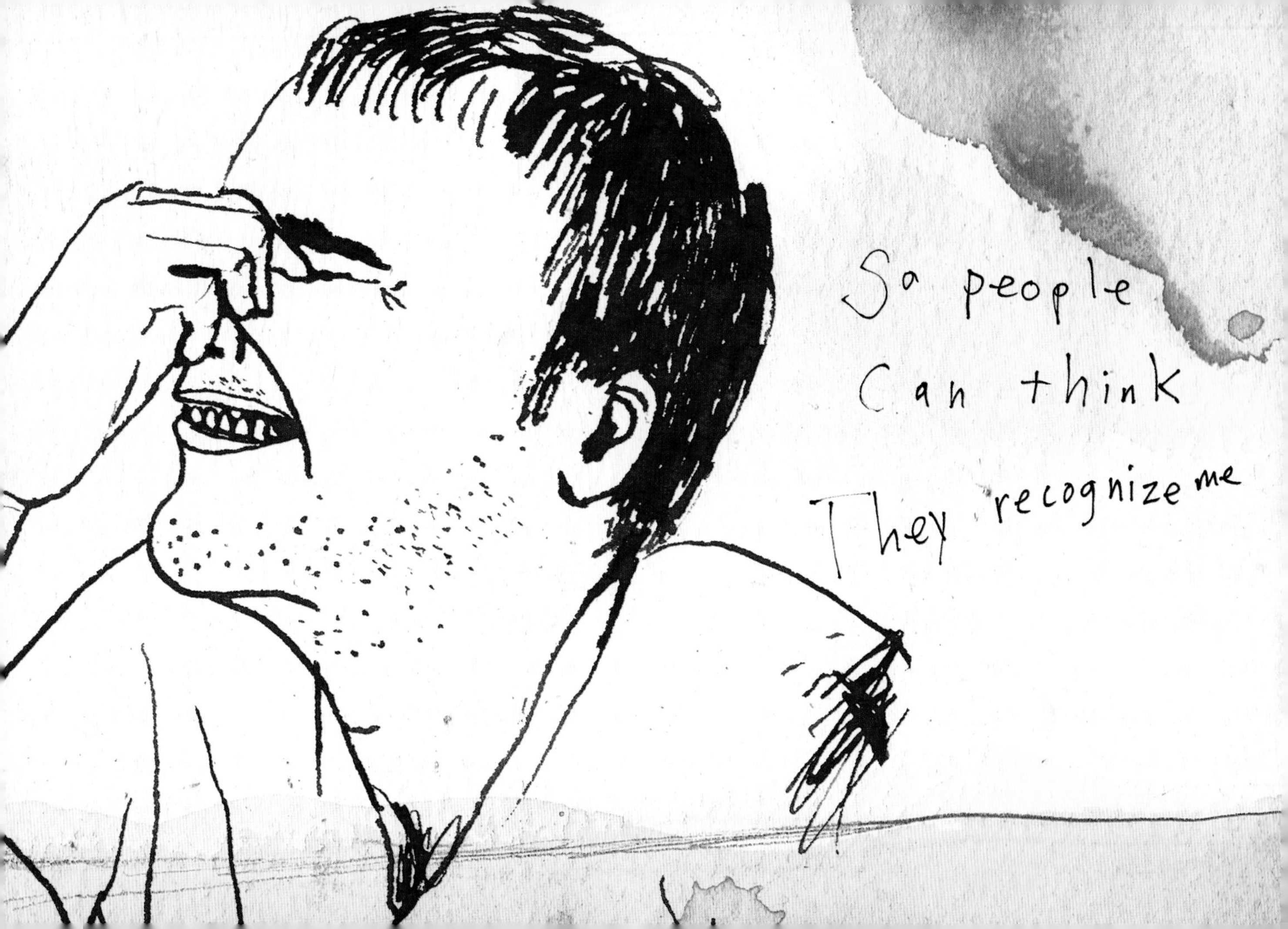
So people
Can think
They recognize me

I can see a child
Outside my window
Sitting on the
Concrete   shore
With feet in   an
Asphalt   sea
      crying
Fighting against the
Current

Pulling
Pulling him in

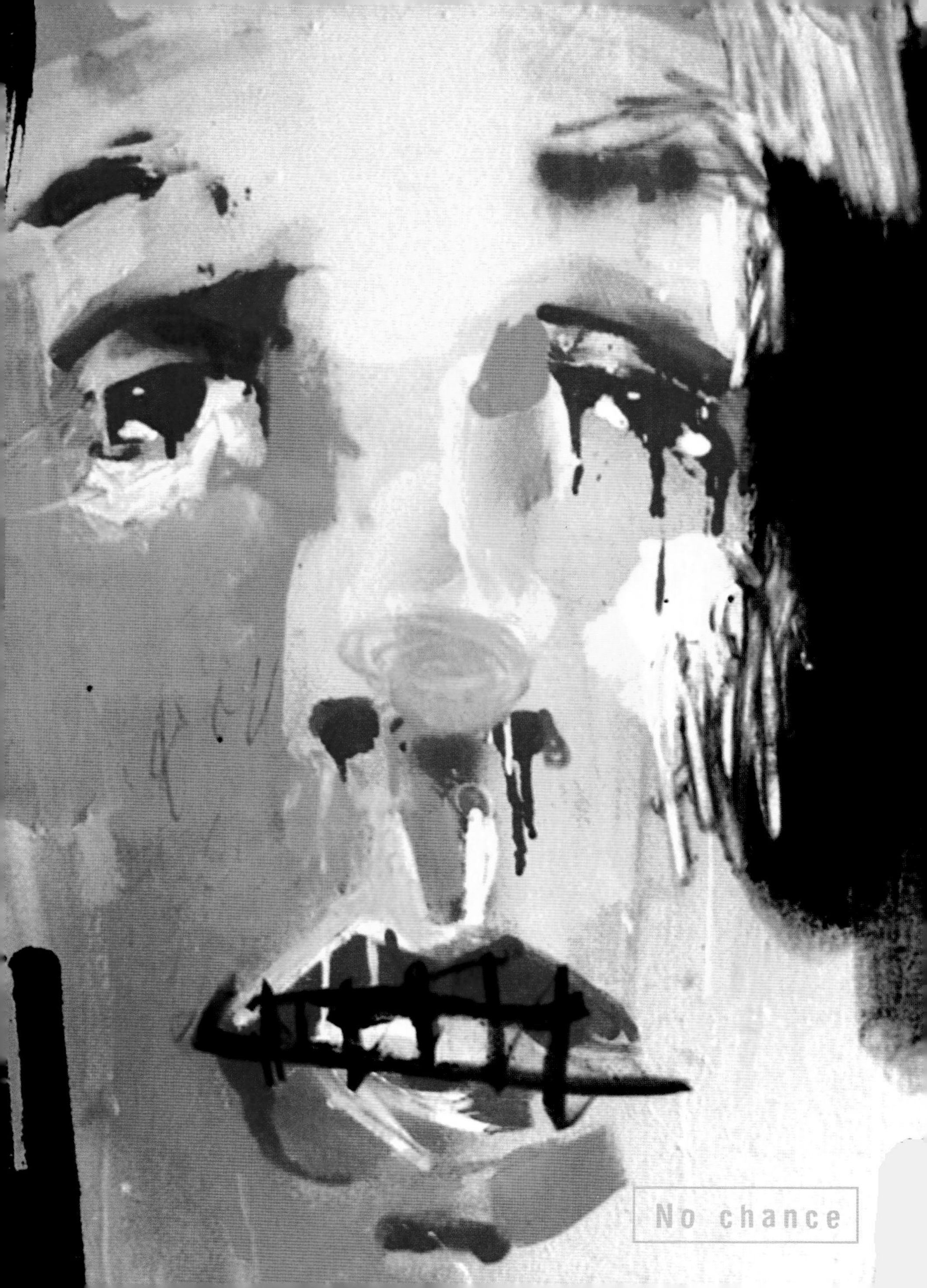
No chance

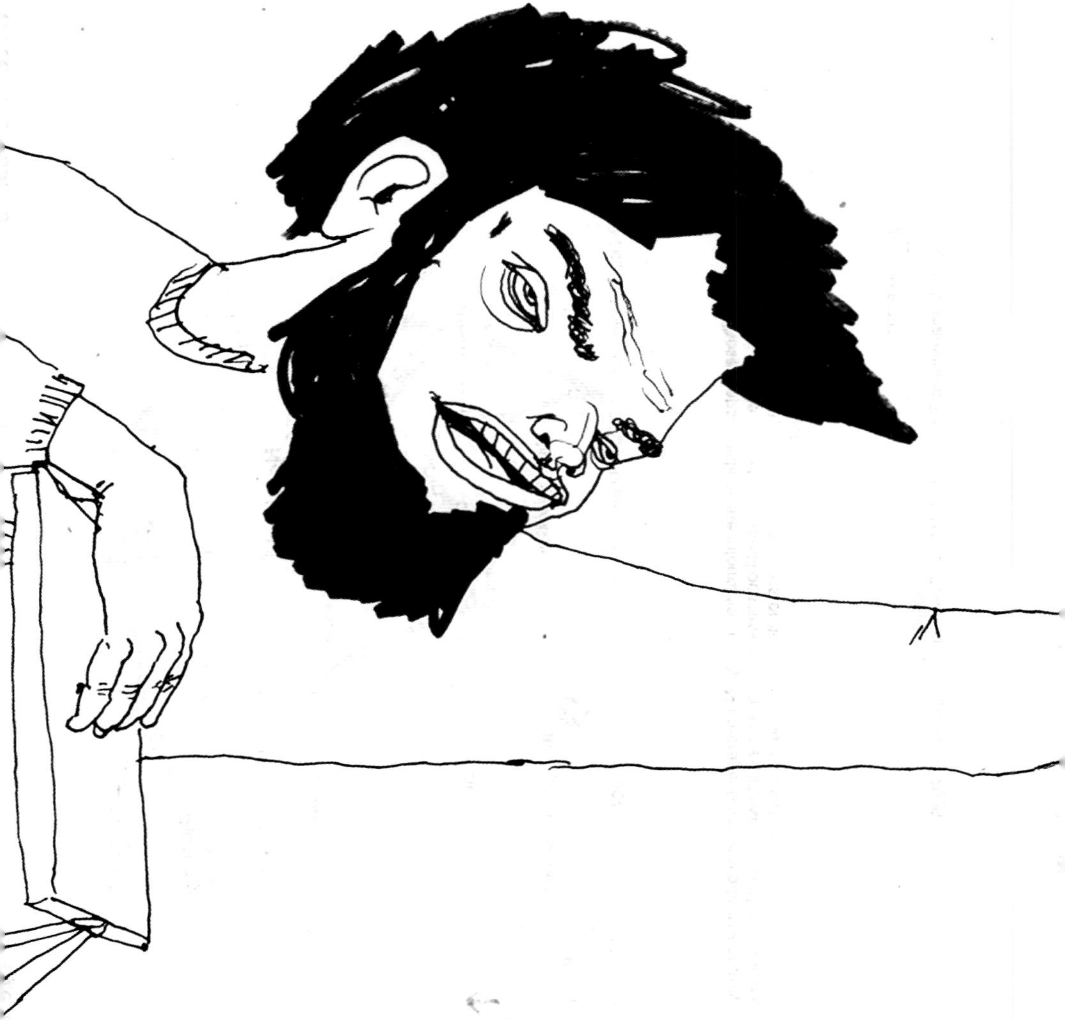

fried tuna

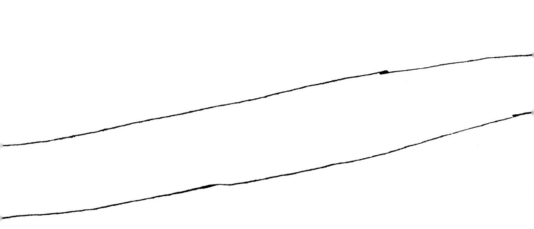

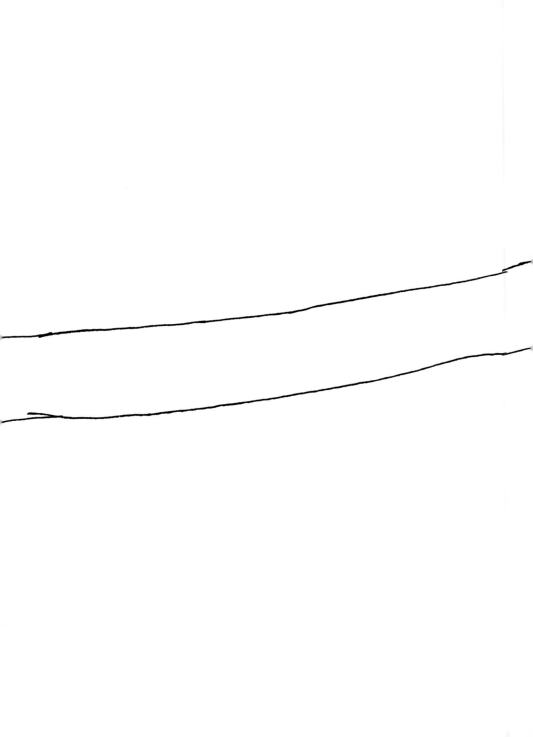

fried tuna

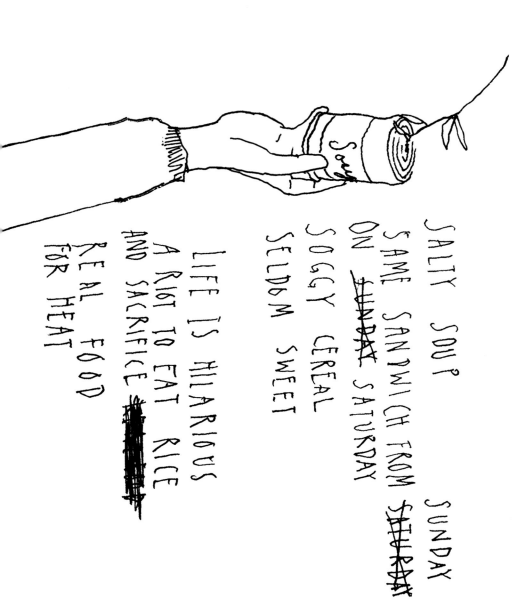

SALTY SOUP
SAME SANDWICH FROM
ON ~~SUNDAY~~ SATURDAY
SOGGY CEREAL
SELDOM SWEET

LIFE IS HILARIOUS
A RIOT TO EAT RICE
AND SACRIFICE
REAL FOOD
FOR HEAT

SUNDAY
~~SATURDAY~~

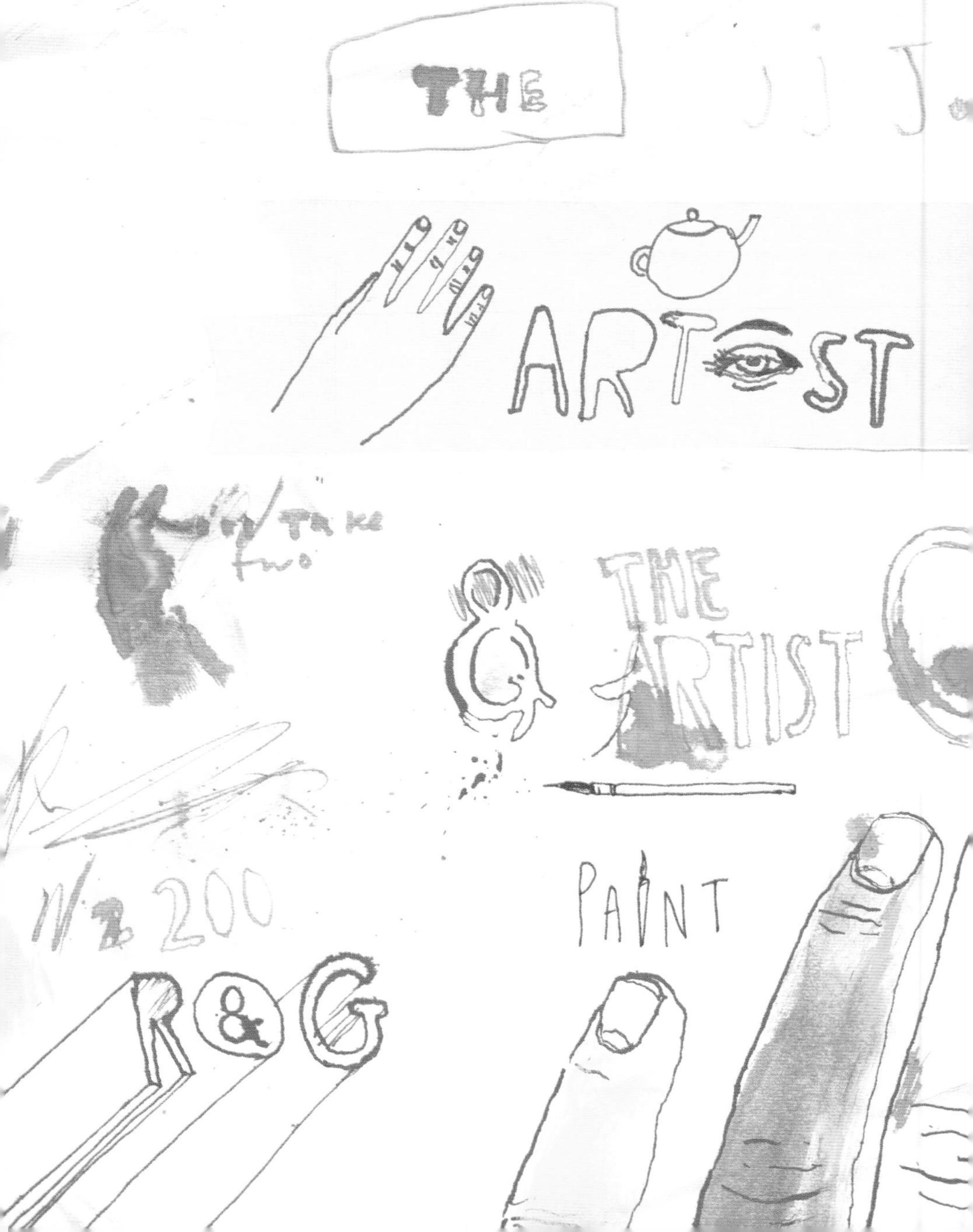
THE
ARTIST
TAKE two
& THE ARTIST
200
R&G
PAINT

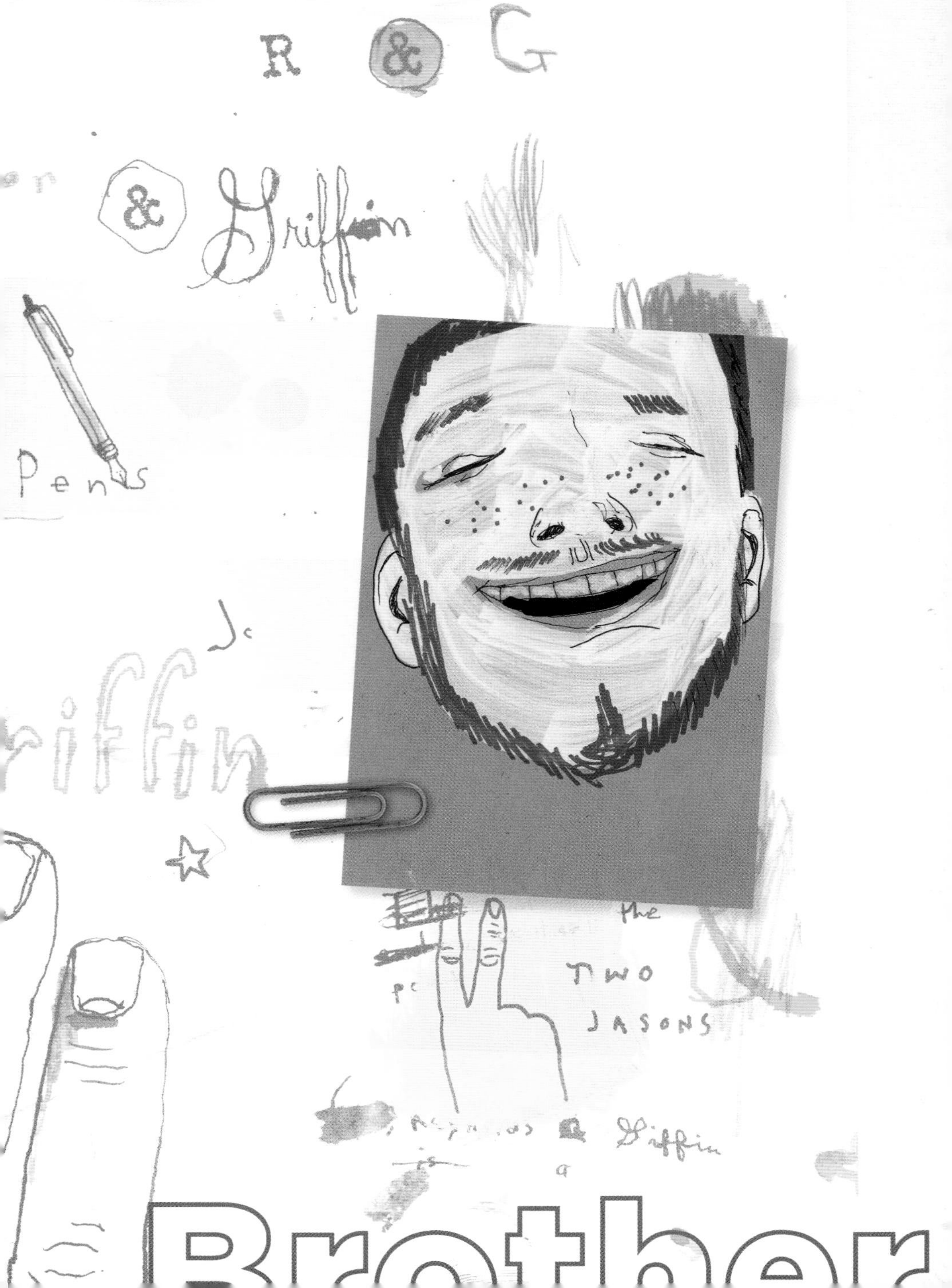
R & G
& Griffin
Pens
riffin
the
TWO
JASONS
& Griffin
a
Brother

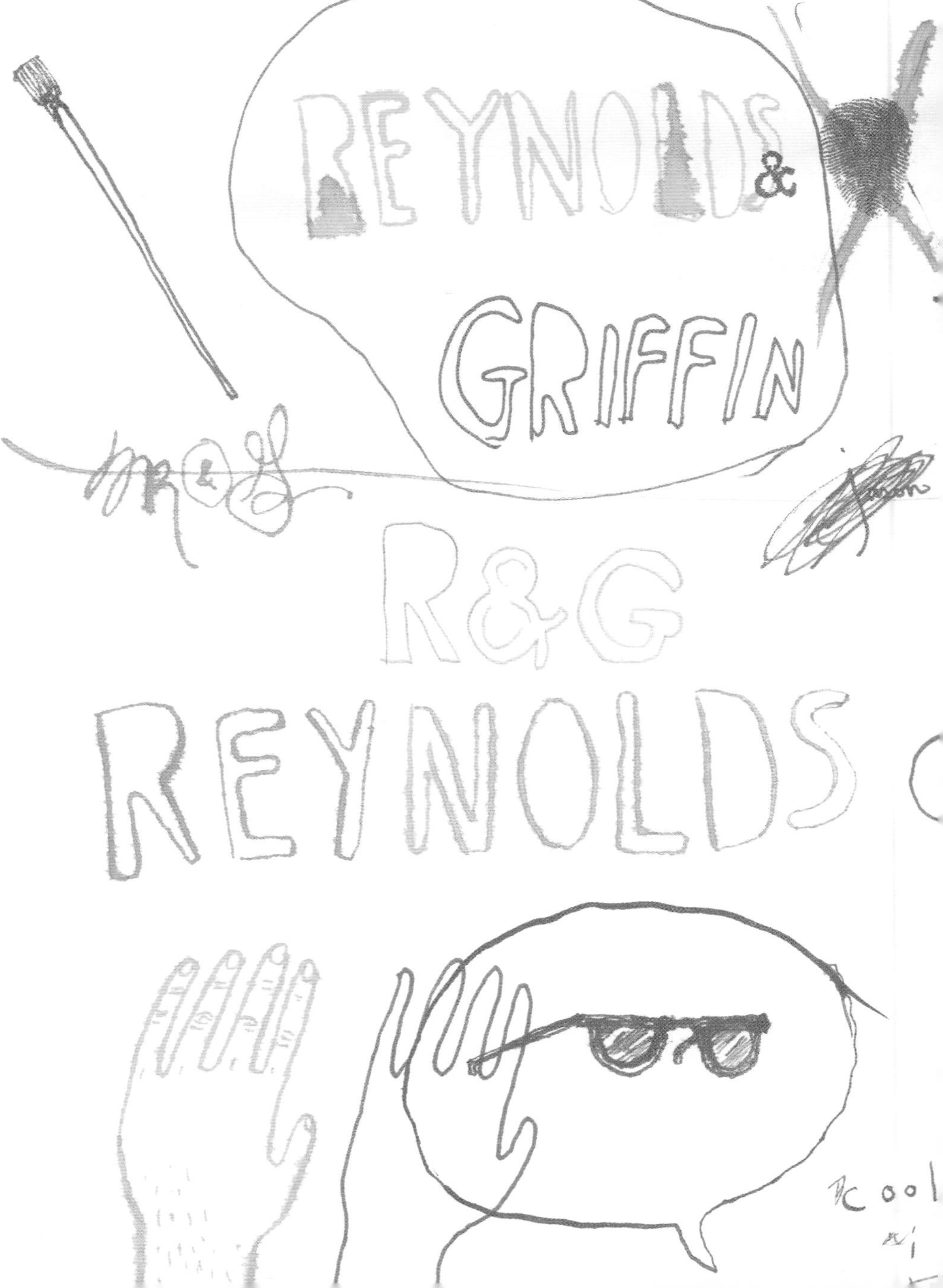
REYNOLDS &
GRIFFIN
R&G
REYNOLDS
cool

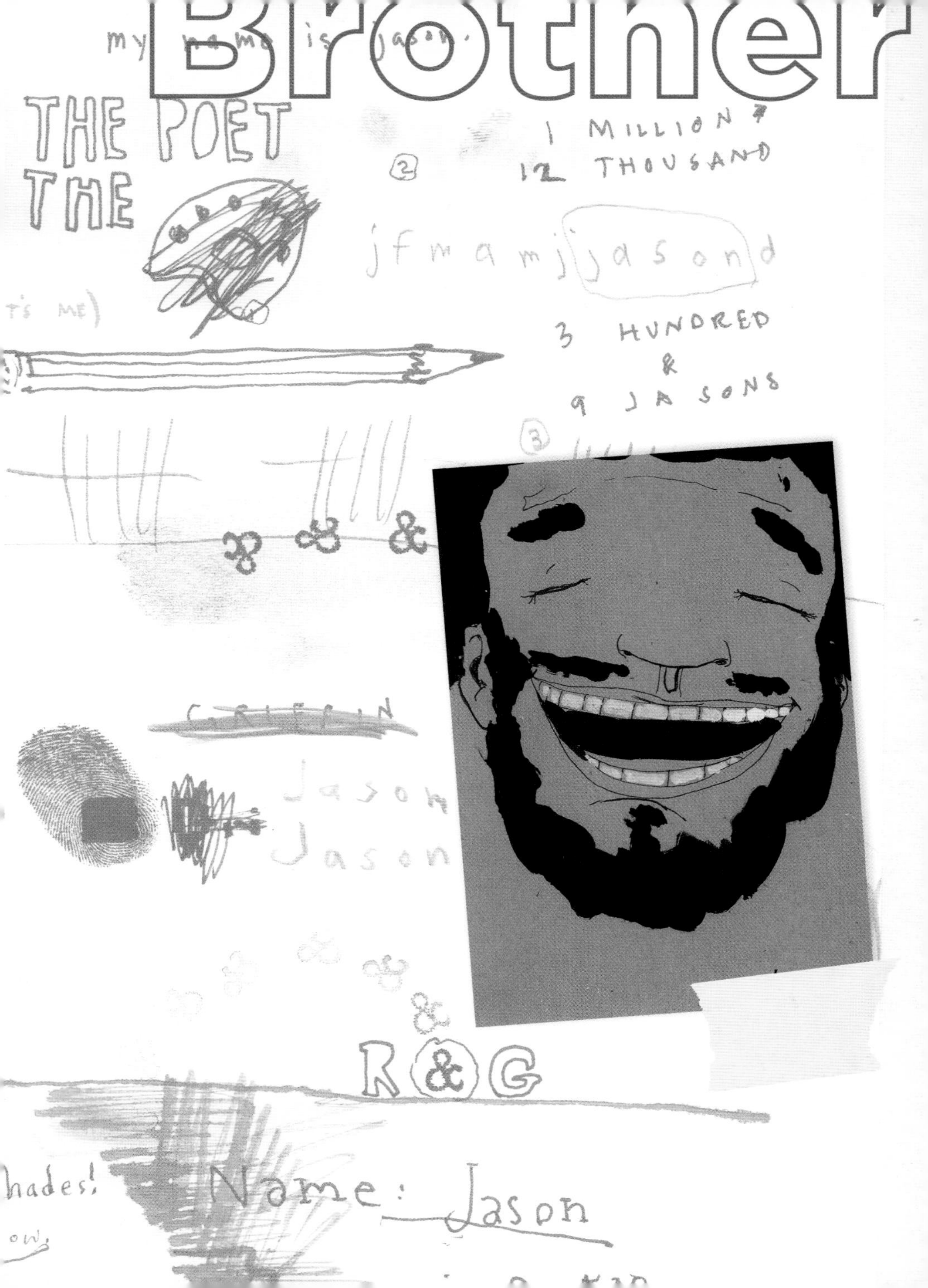

Brother

THE POET
THE

('s ME)

② 1 MILLION #
12 THOUSAND

j f m a m j j a s o n d

3 HUNDRED
&
9 JASONS

③

GRIFFIN

Jason
Jason

&

R & G

hades!

ow,

Name: Jason

I gotta friend whose hair is red
Looks like a fire atop his head
Mine is curly, thick and black
Pay it no mind I like it like that

And if anyone ever asks me why
I choose to hang out with this guy
I'll say we're different yes I know
But for us both hair does grow
So-and-so can carry on
For we'll be friends
            till hair is gone

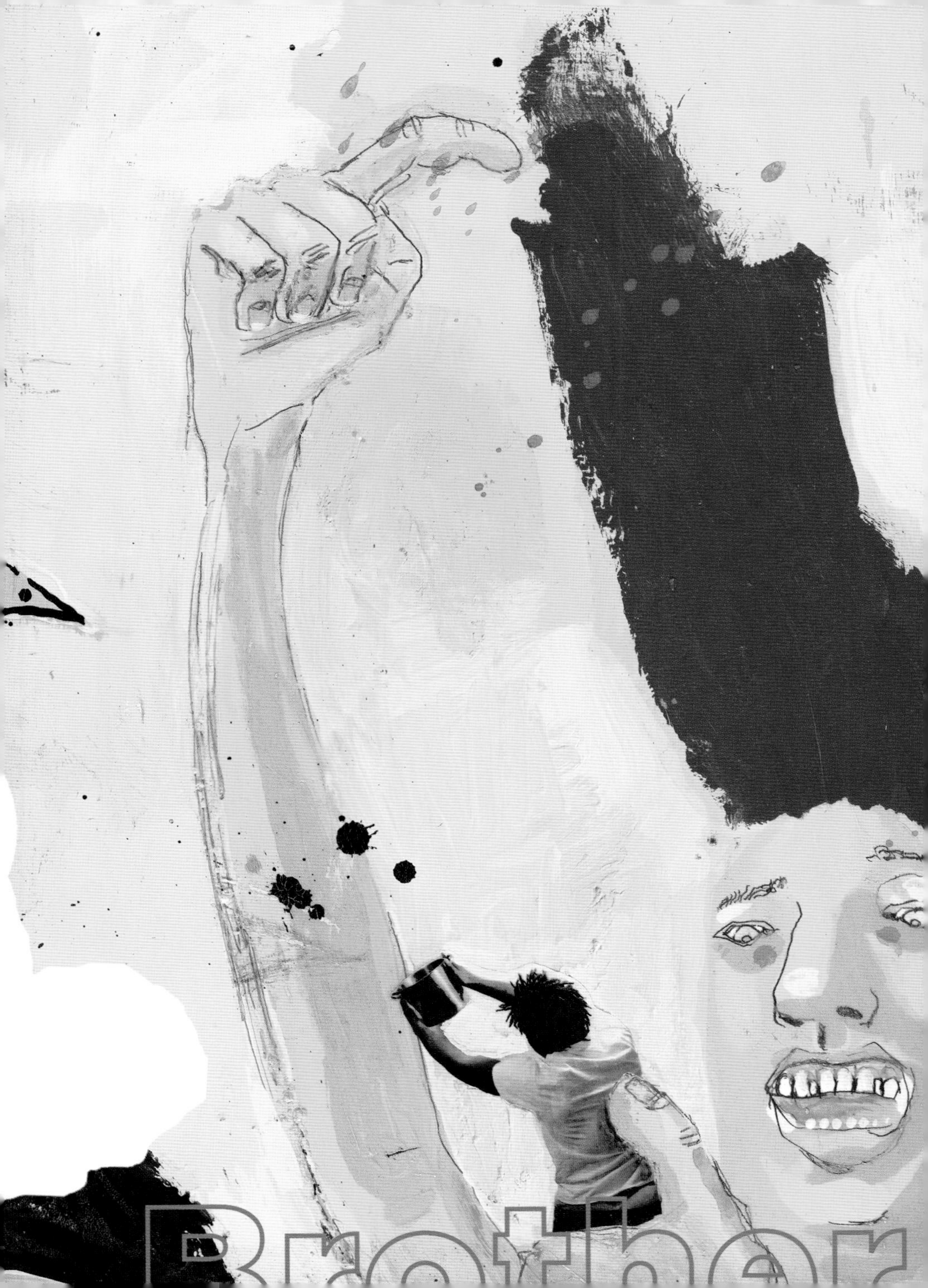
Brother

THIS WAS SUPPOSED TO BE
A CLICHÉD P O E M
ABOUT CLIMBING THE MOUNTAIN
OF LIFE ON MY OWN

BUT WHEN I SAT DOWN TO WRITE IT
I REALIZED T H A T
I HAD TO ASK A FRIEND OF MINE
FOR A PIECE OF PAPER

Forced to lean

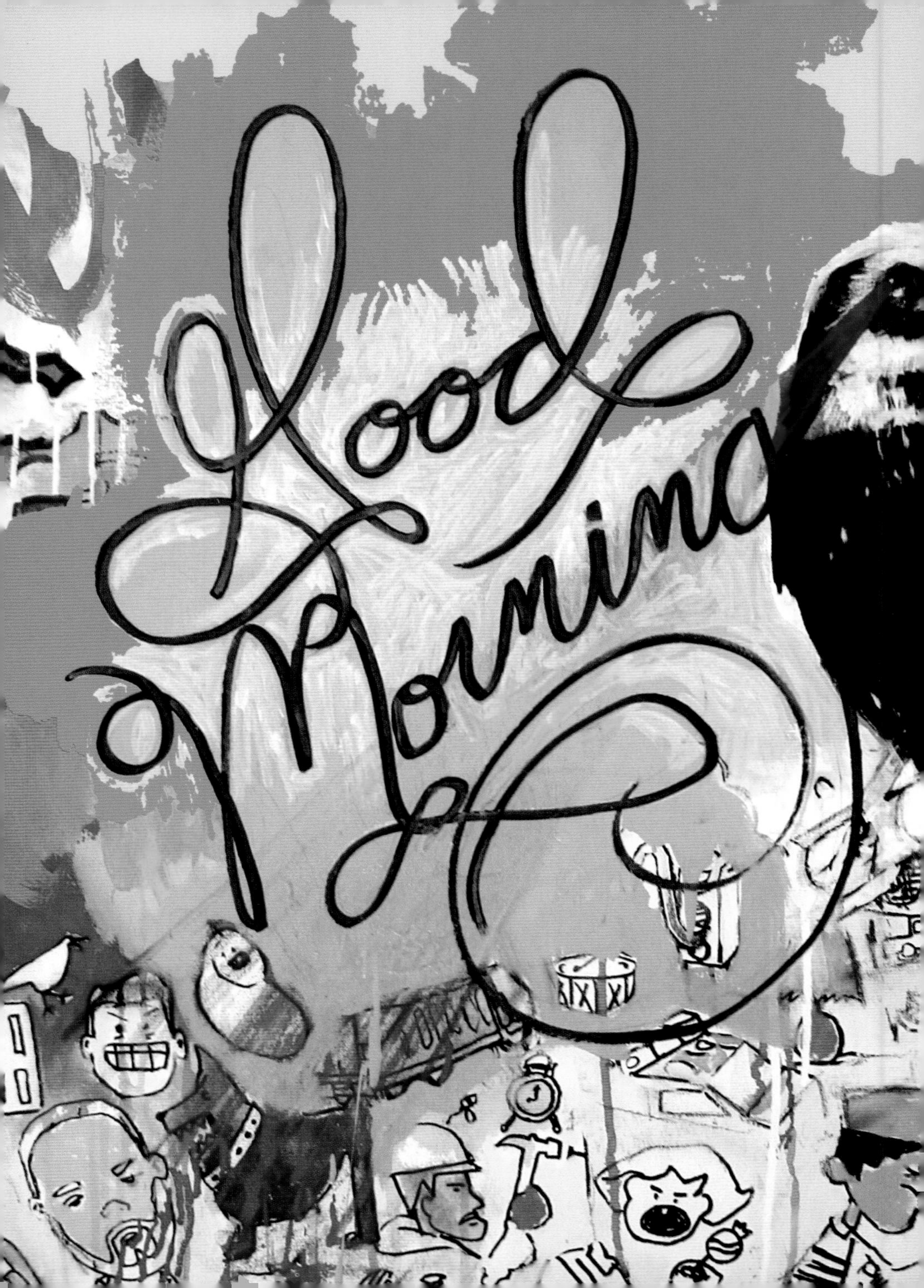
Good Morning

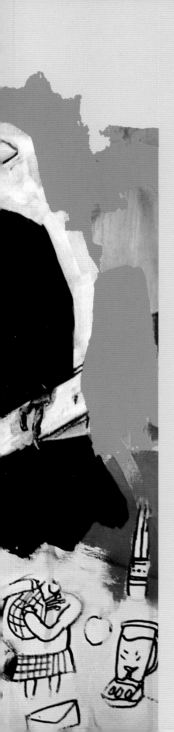

Visitors, beware

There's a guy on our couch

And a sink full of dishes

Hot water on the stove

And a fridge full of wishes

And paint has spilled all over

The kitchen floor

There's a stain on the rug

And a splat on the wall

And a half bag of chips

That is shared by us all

So it's funny to request

That each and every guest

Take their shoes off at the door

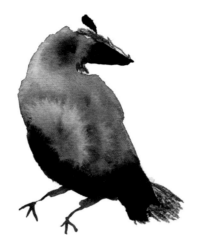

A BLACK BIRD LANDS AND TAKES A REST

FROM FLYING SO FREE

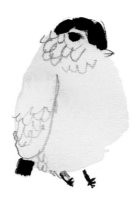

A YELLOW BIRD FROZEN

LIKE A VASE ON A SHELF

AFRAID TO FLY

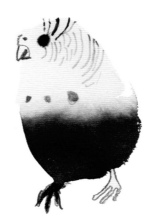

A BLUE BIRD SAD WITH BROKEN WINGS

HAS FALLEN FROM A TREE

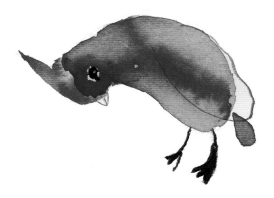

AND A RED BIRD WITH SO MUCH PASSION TO FLY

A RED BIRD KINDA LIKE ME

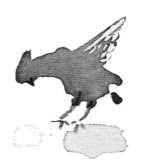

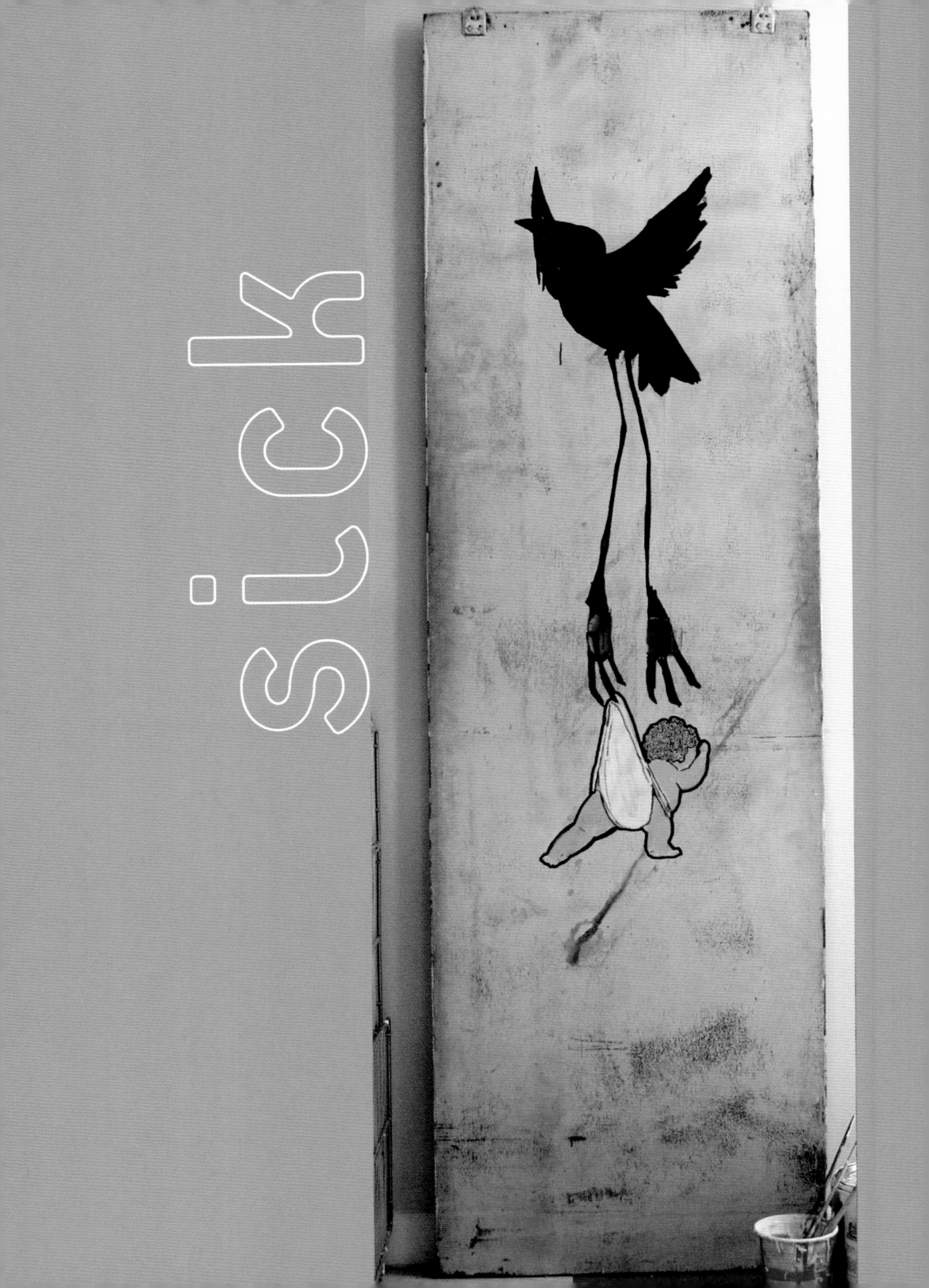
sick

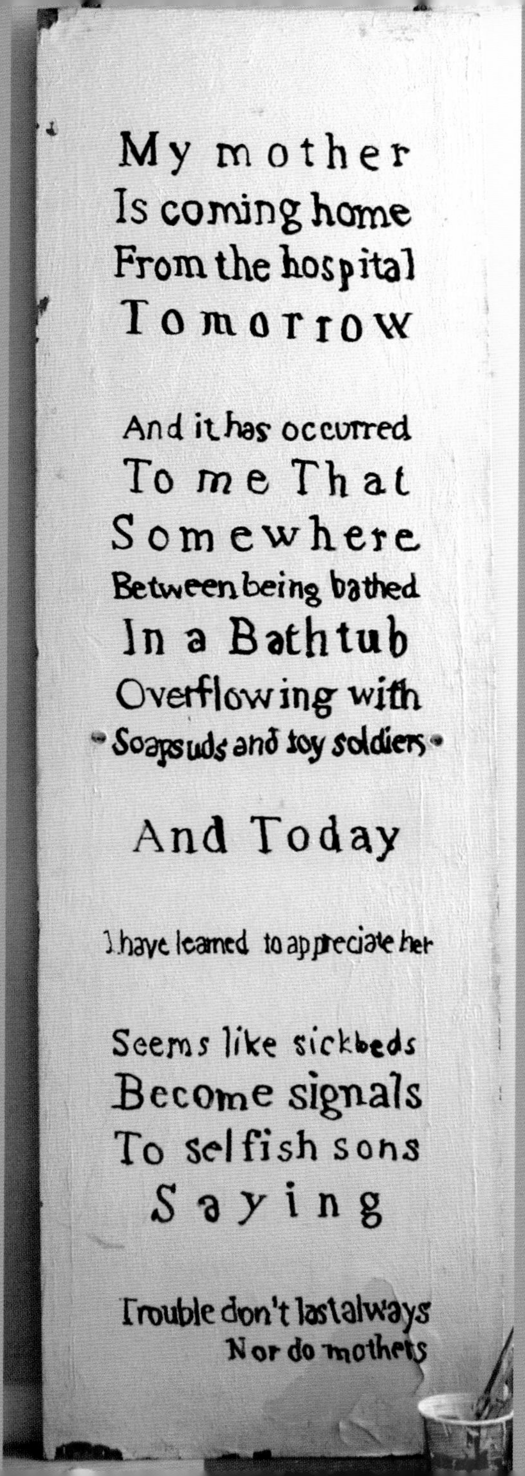
My mother
Is coming home
From the hospital
Tomorrow
And it has occurred
To me That
Somewhere
Between being bathed
In a Bathtub
Overflowing with
Soapsuds and toy soldiers
And Today
I have learned to appreciate her
Seems like sickbeds
Become signals
To selfish sons
Saying
Trouble don't last always
Nor do mothers

really cool people

chyanne

used to teach kindergarten

jealous of four-year-olds'

stick figures

made with crayon

on construction paper

she cried at their

creativity

and quit to become

a copycat

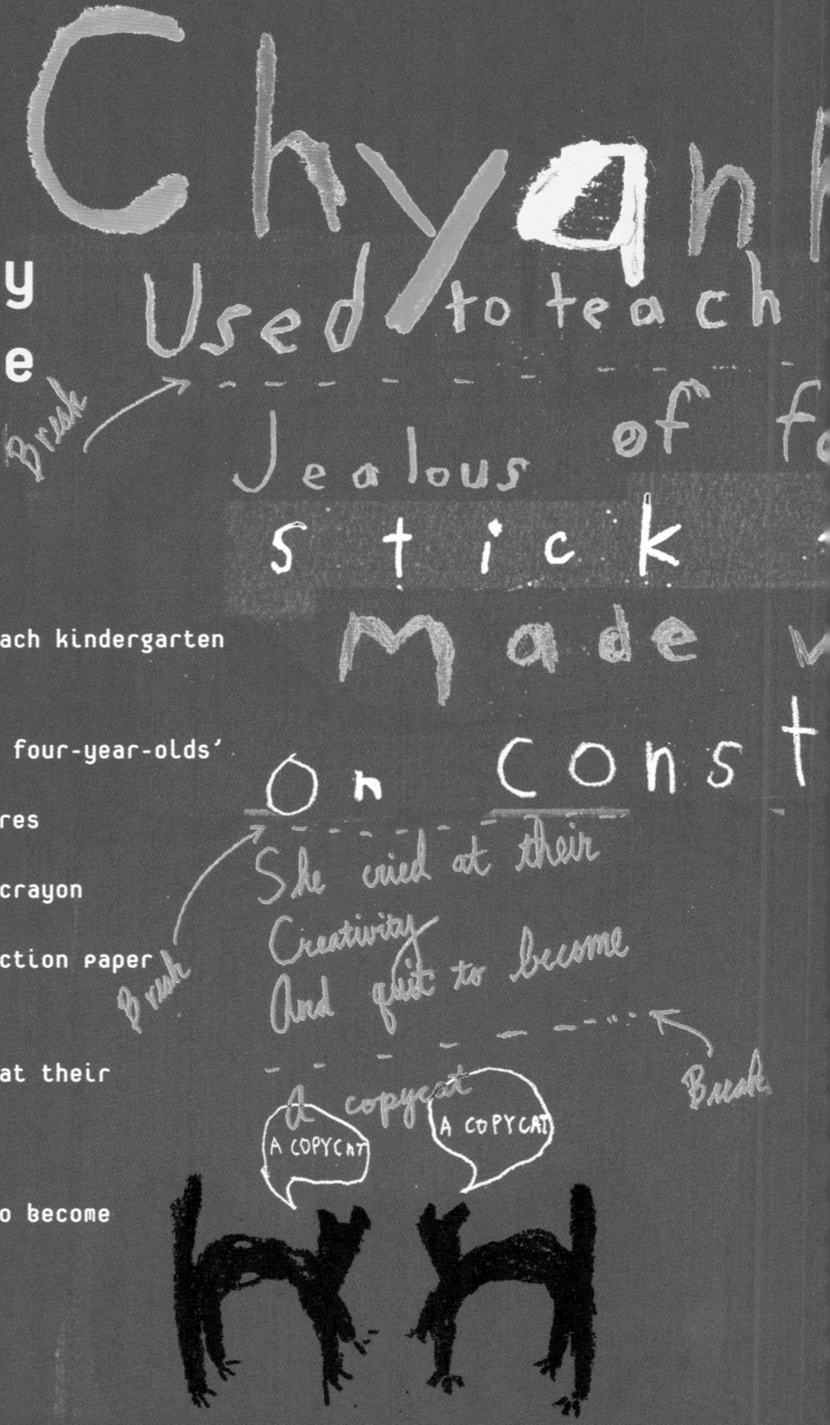

Chyan
Used to teach
Break
Jealous of
stick
Made
On const
Break
She cried at their
Creativity
And quit to become
Break
A copycat
A COPYCAT
A COPYCAT

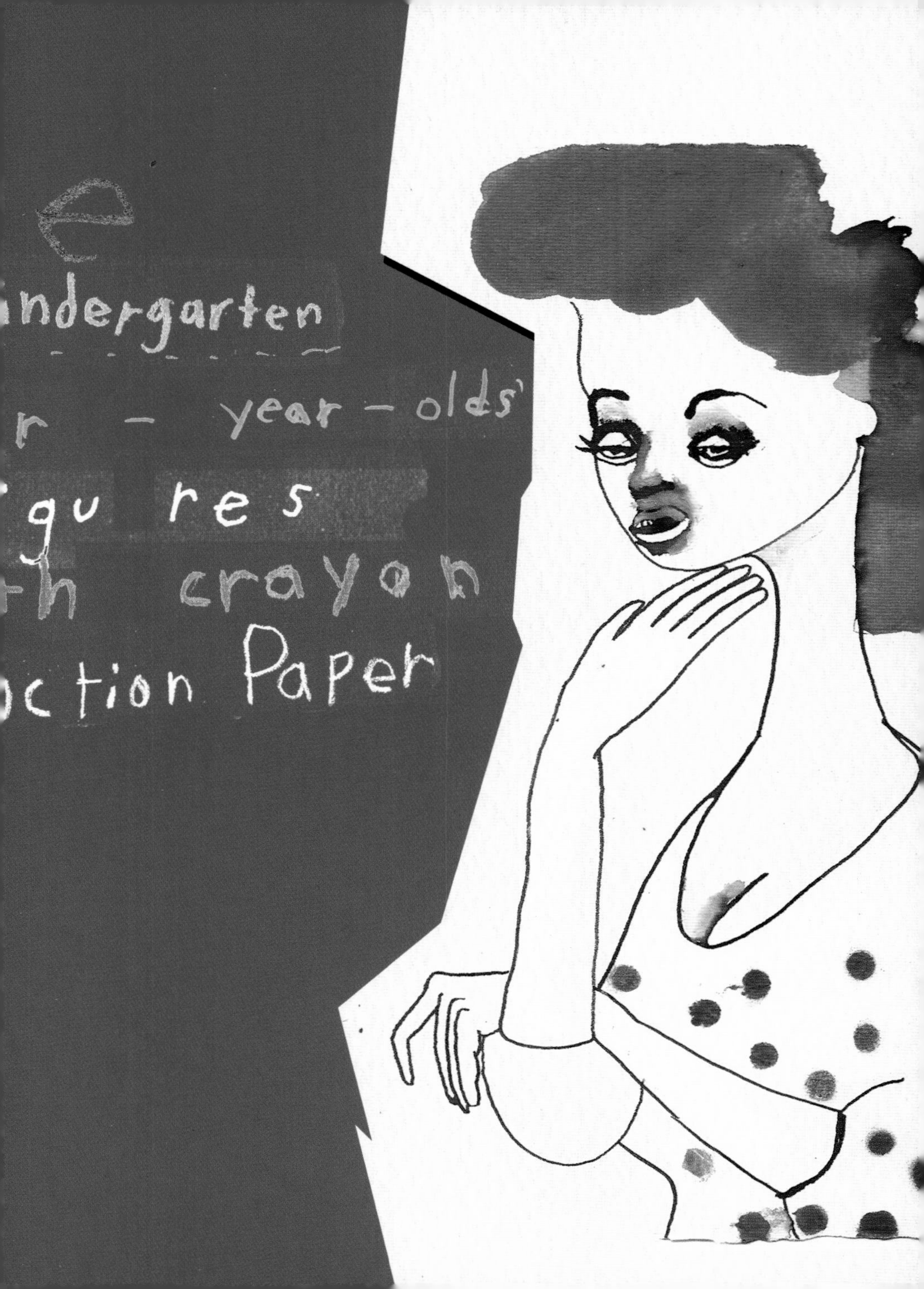

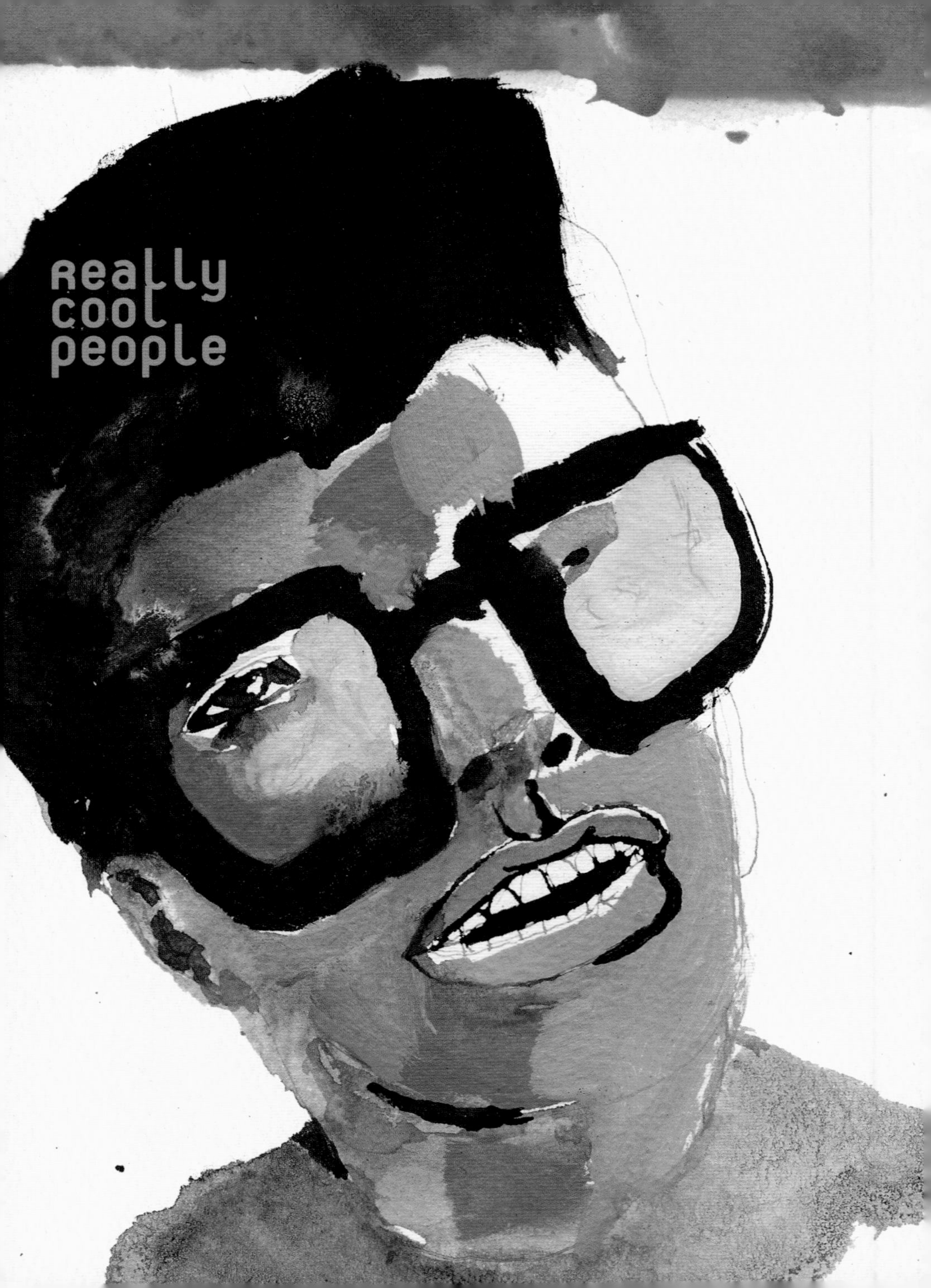
really
cool
people

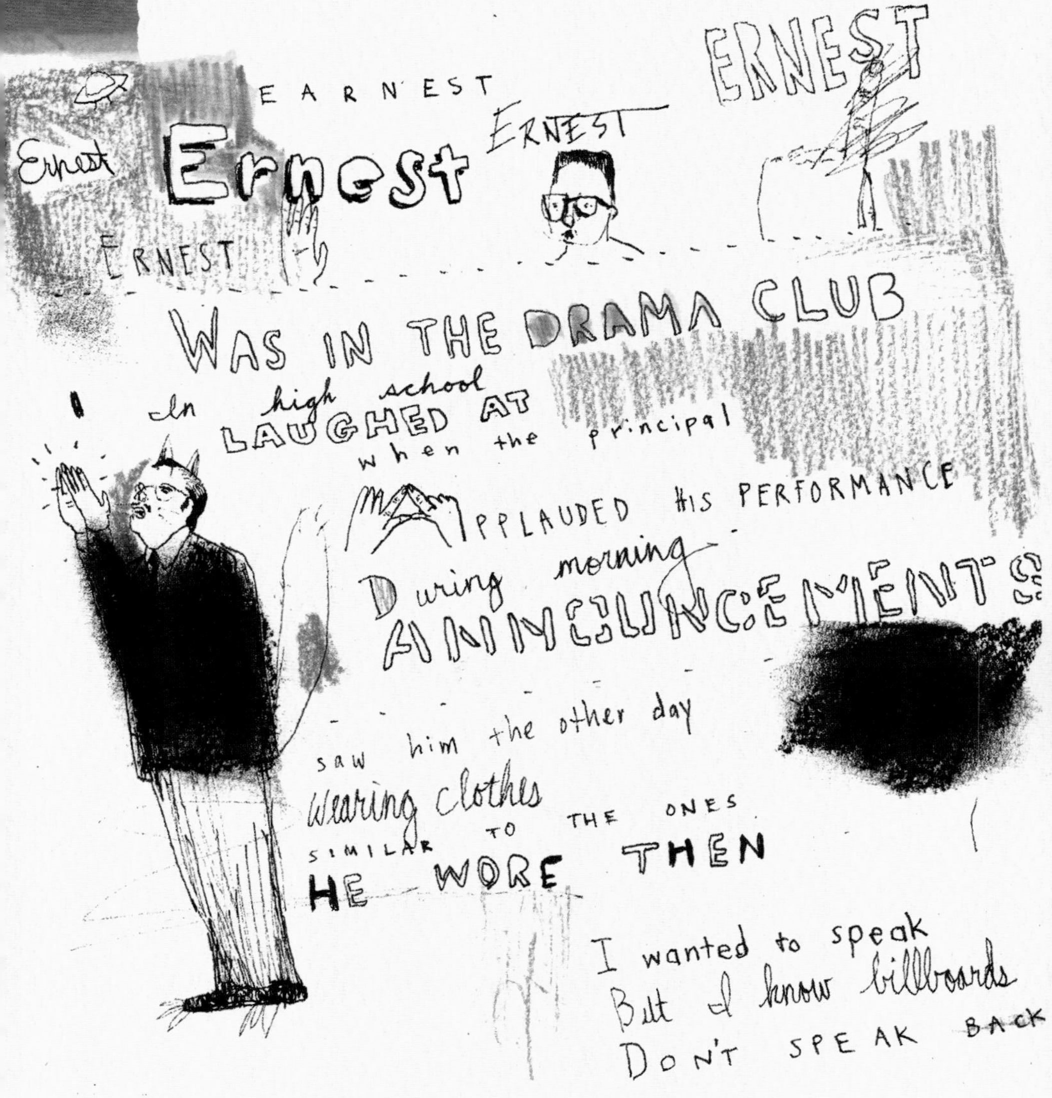

EARNEST
Ernest
Ernest
ERNEST
ERNEST
ERNEST
WAS IN THE DRAMA CLUB
In high school
I LAUGHED AT
when the principal
APPLAUDED HIS PERFORMANCE
During morning
ANNOUNCEMENTS
saw him the other day
wearing clothes
SIMILAR TO THE ONES
HE WORE THEN
I wanted to speak
But I know billboards
DON'T SPEAK BACK

Franco

really
cool
people

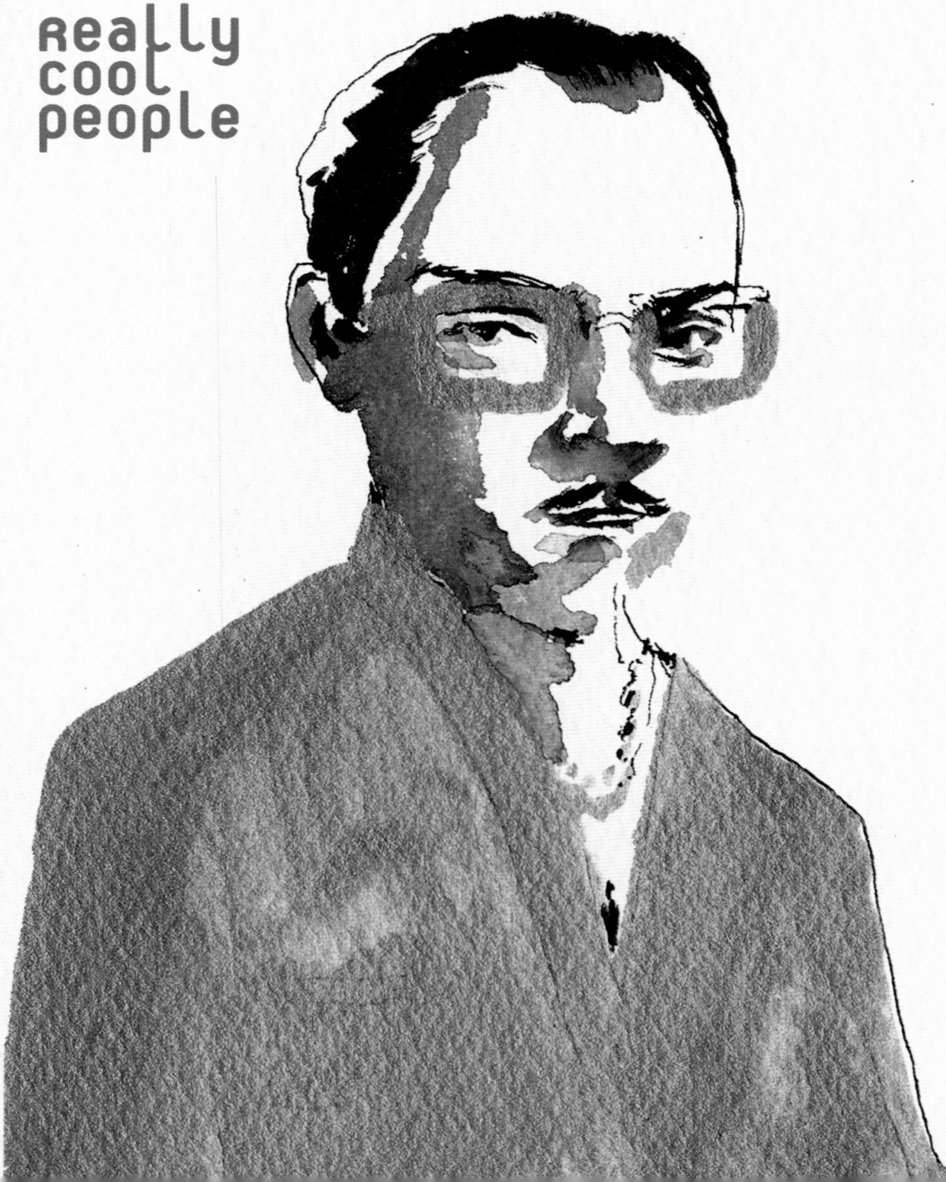

IN HIS TWENTIES
HE WAS SELLING
HOT DOGS TO
TOURISTS

FOUR FOR A FRANK
FIVE ~~——~~ WITH A BUN

~~IN HIS FIFTIES~~

IN HIS THIRTIES
HE WROTE A BOOK
~~ABOUT~~ ABOUT IT

Franks by Frank

SOLD A MILLION COPIES

IN HIS FORTIES
HE USED THE MONEY
TO BUY ART
REALLY
REALLY
REALLY
EXPENSIVE ART

~~NOW HE'S IN HIS~~

NOW HE'S IN HIS FIFTIES
AND THIS IS THE STORY
HE TELLS

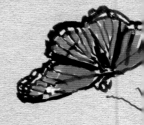

MEN PRETEND

Men don't cry
or write poetry
or paint
or dance
or hug
or kiss
or like
or love
or listen
I hear

I guess they pretend

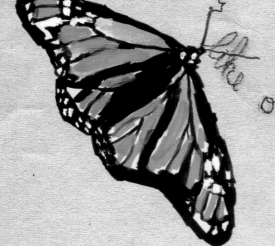

Men don't cry or write poetry or paint or dance or like or love or listen I...

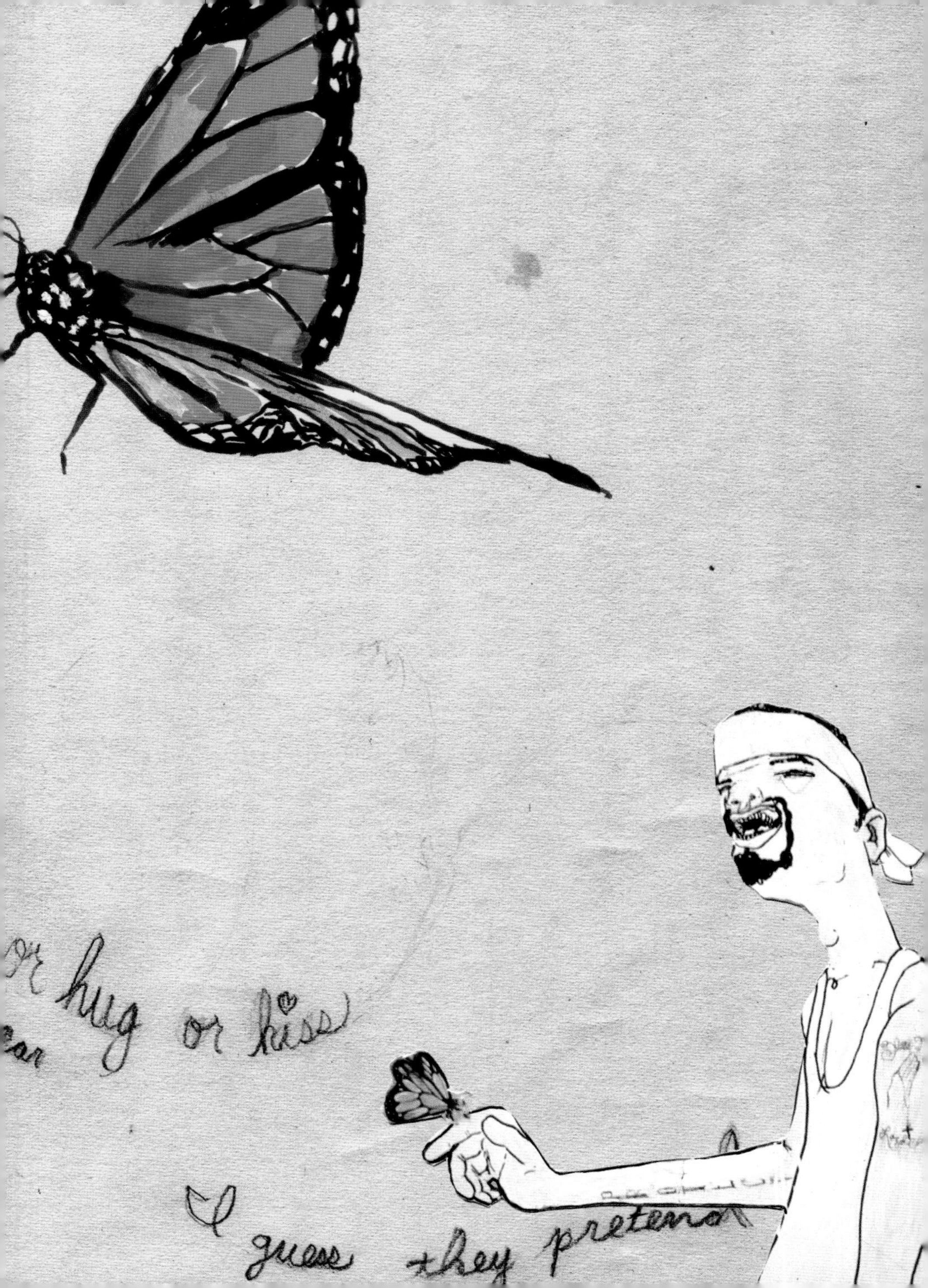
hug or kiss
I guess they pretend

There's something there
Something I have always had
Complicated and complex
Turn my happiness to sad
Keeping me from what is next

There's something there
Whispering in an open ear
Telling me to be afraid
When I sleep it reappears
Mashing up the things I've made

There's something there
With its hand around my heart
Squeezing till it does not beat
Stopping me before I start
Comfortable within defeat

There's something there
Something there I can't ignore
But I don't want it there for sure
For something there must leave
Before it scars me till my soul is sore

And I never get to something more

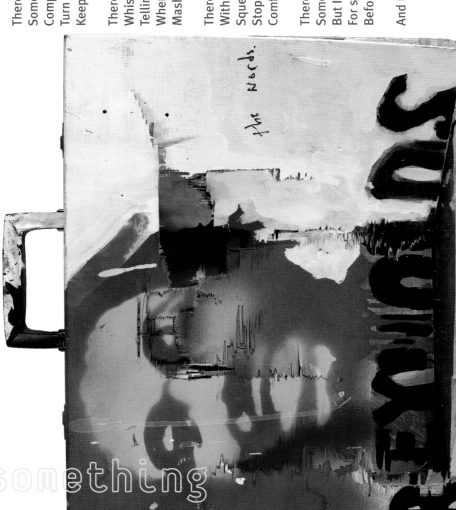

the words.

something

REYNOLDS

There's something there
Something I have always had
Complicated and complex
Turn my happiness to sad
Keeping me from what is next

There's something there
Whispering in an open ear
Telling me to be afraid
When I sleep it reappears
Mashing up the things I've made

There's something there
With its hand around my heart
Squeezing till it does not beat
Stopping me before I start
Comfortable within defeat

There's something there
Something there I can't ignore
But I don't want it there for sure
For something there must leave
Before it scars me till my soul is sore

And I never get to something more

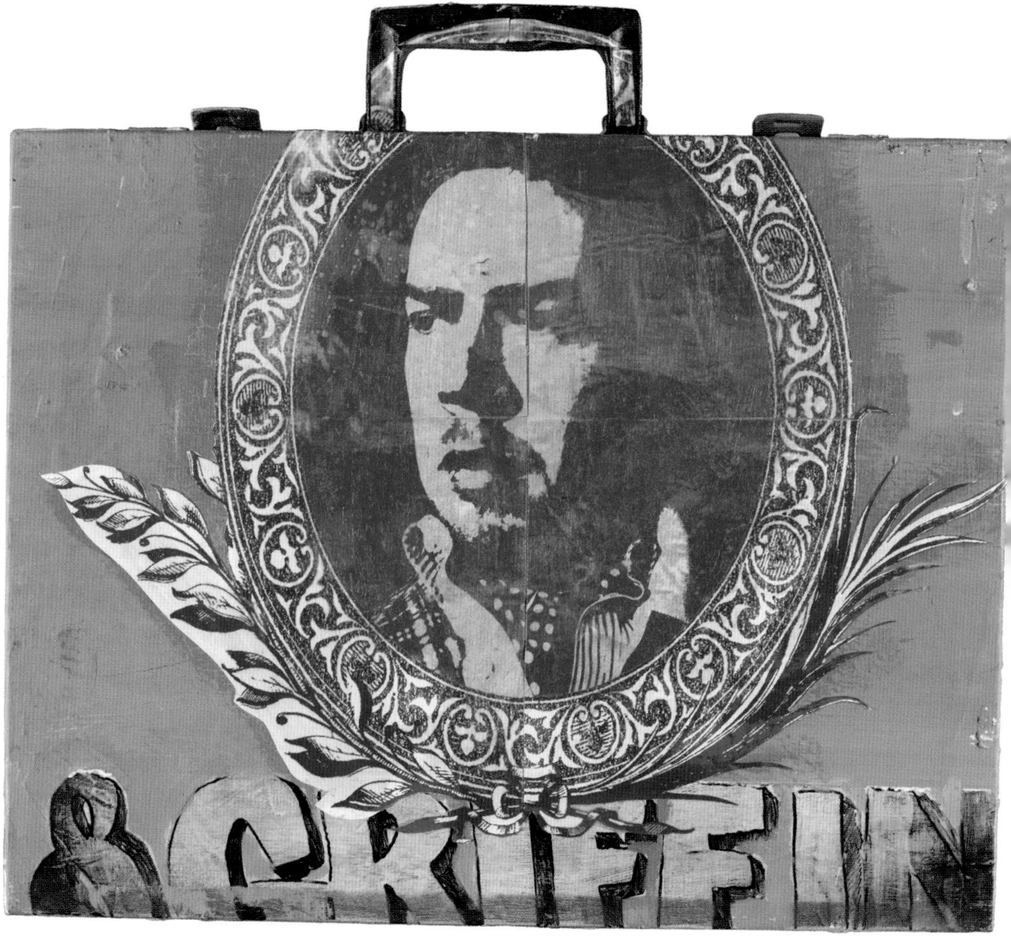
GRIFFIN

It's hard to walk
With my pants
Falling down
Saggin'

Blue jeans
With deep
Pockets packed
With pain

I just need
A moment

Some time
To rest

A moment
To pull
Out the
Poems

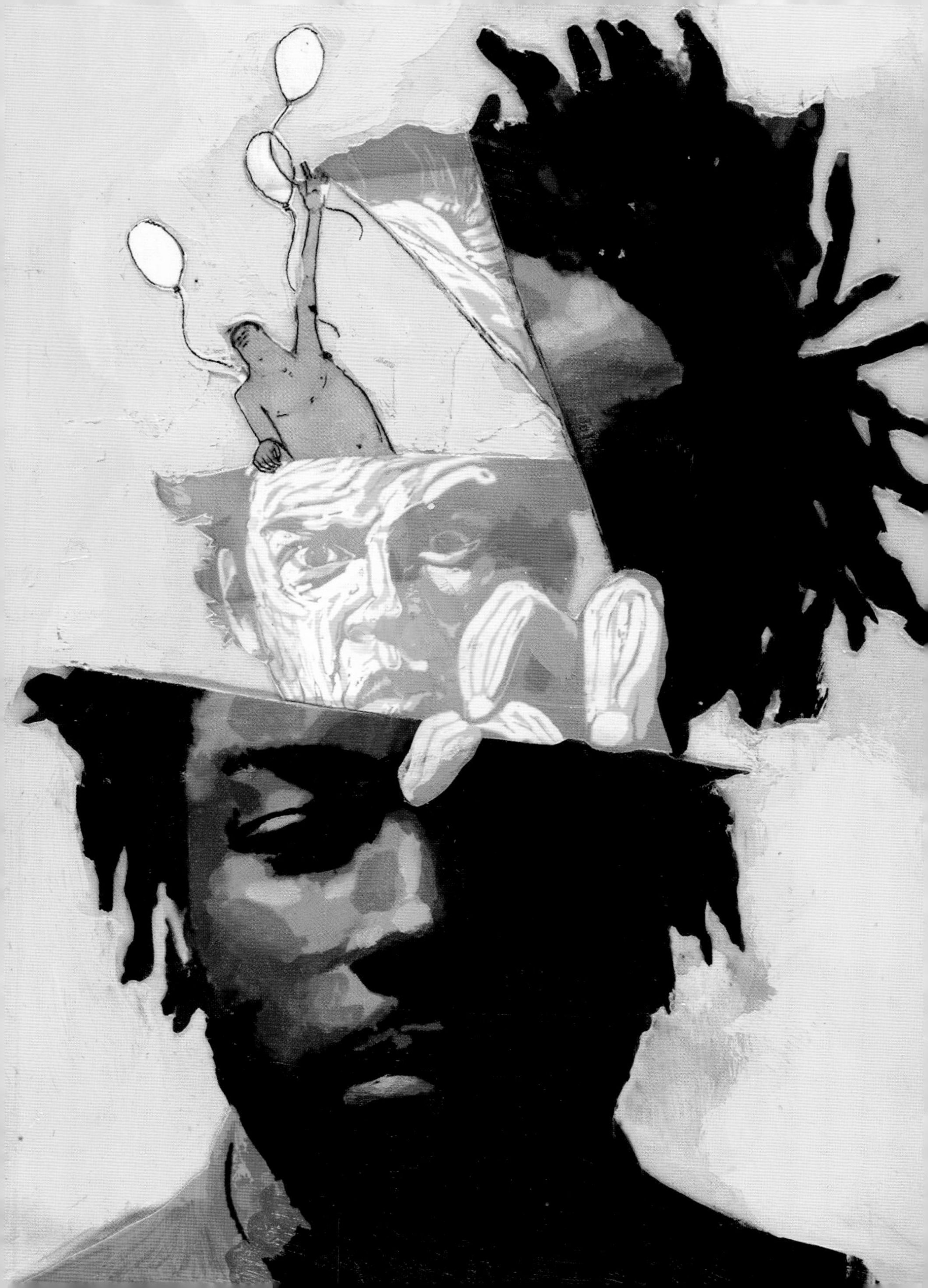

What do people think of us?

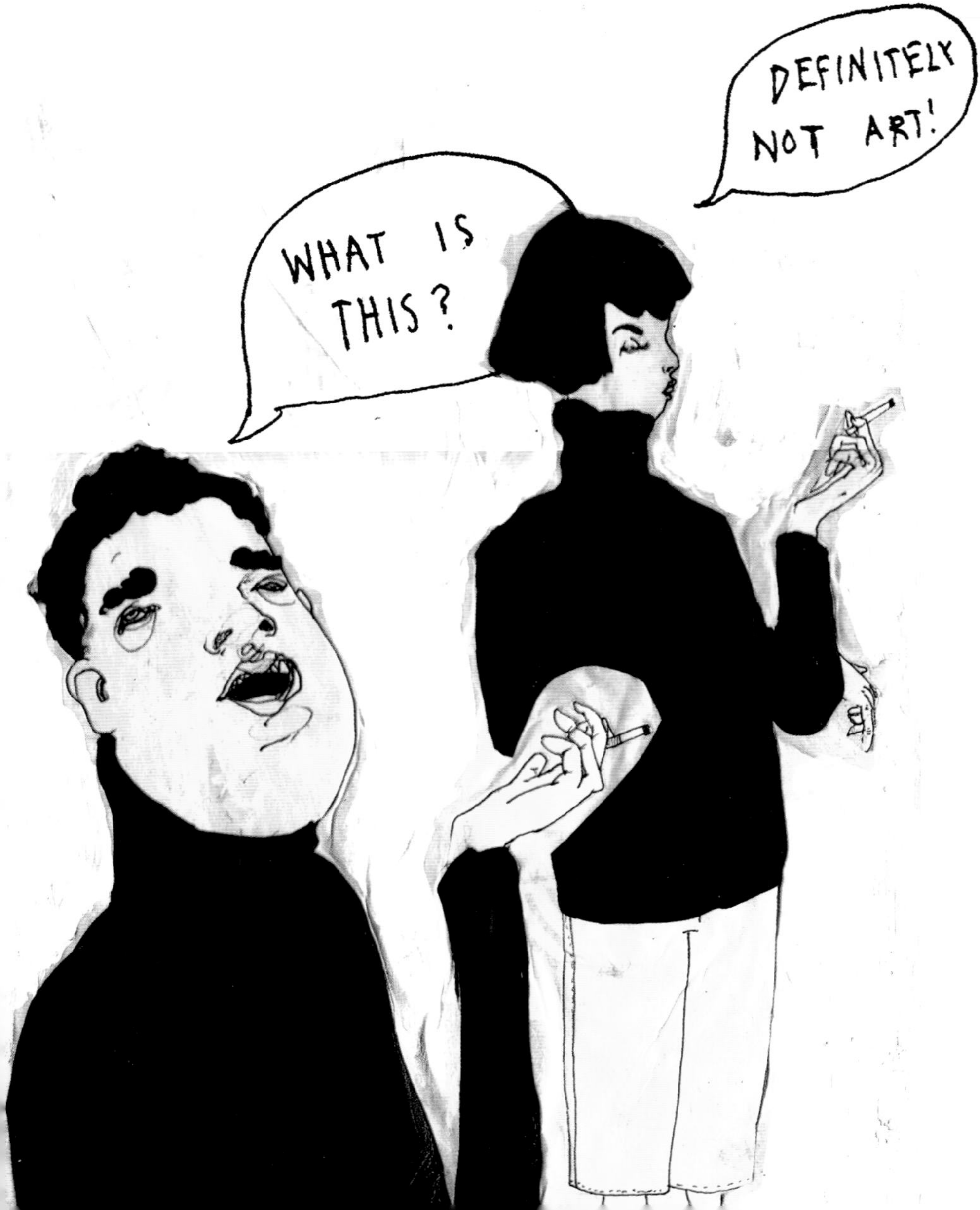
DEFINITELY NOT ART!
WHAT IS THIS?

If you can't eat the poem
And you can't drink the paint
Then a dummy you are
And an artist you ain't

Call me when you grow up
Or when you blow up

Whichever happens first

I LOVE YOU LOSER

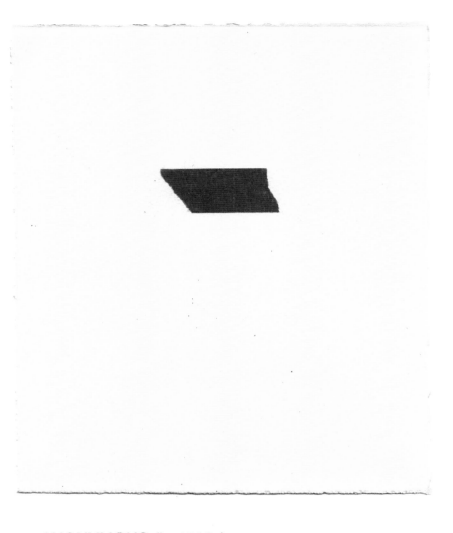

ANONYMOUS (b. 1980s)
Art
Blue masking tape on paper
2008
$100,000 – $150,000

I'd like to think ~~my~~
my poems are like
picnic potato chips.

Lightly salted slices of
heaven.
But there are always a few
burnt ones in the bag.

This is one of those.

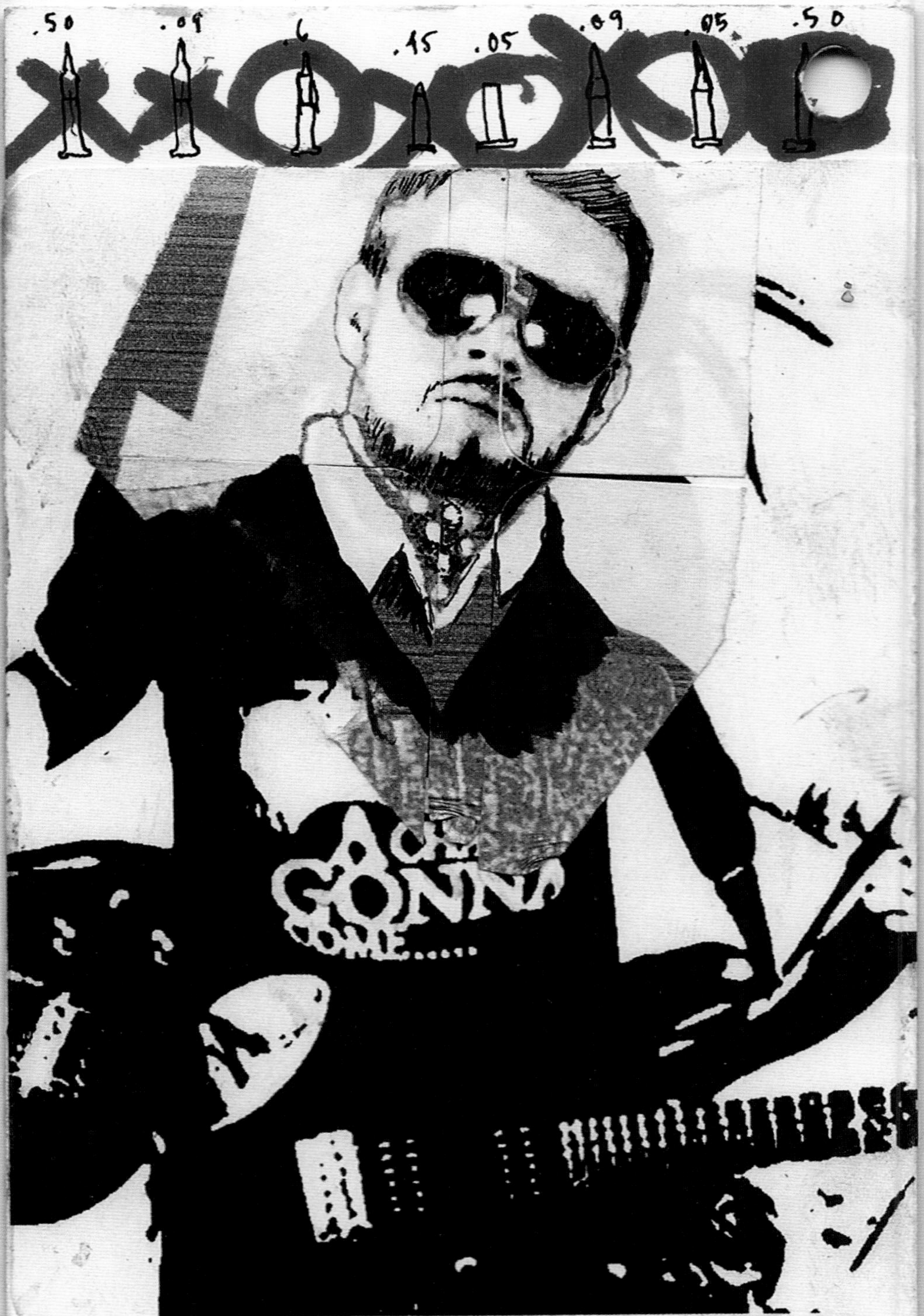
.50 .09 .6 .15 .05 .09 .05 .50
GONN

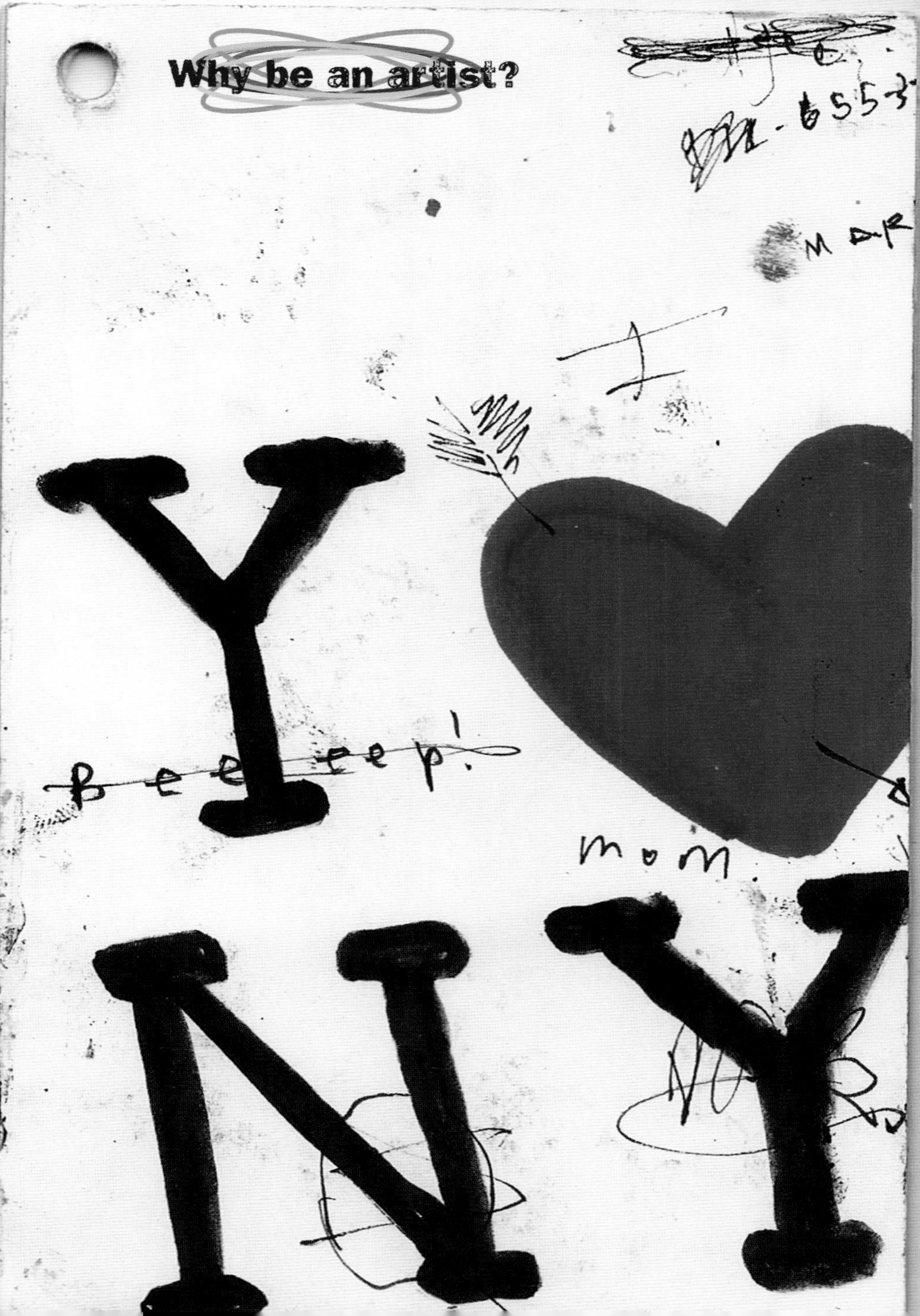
Why be an artist?
MAR
Beeeep!
mom
NY

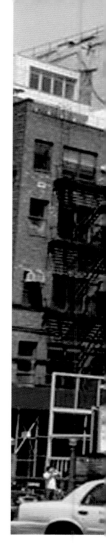

too

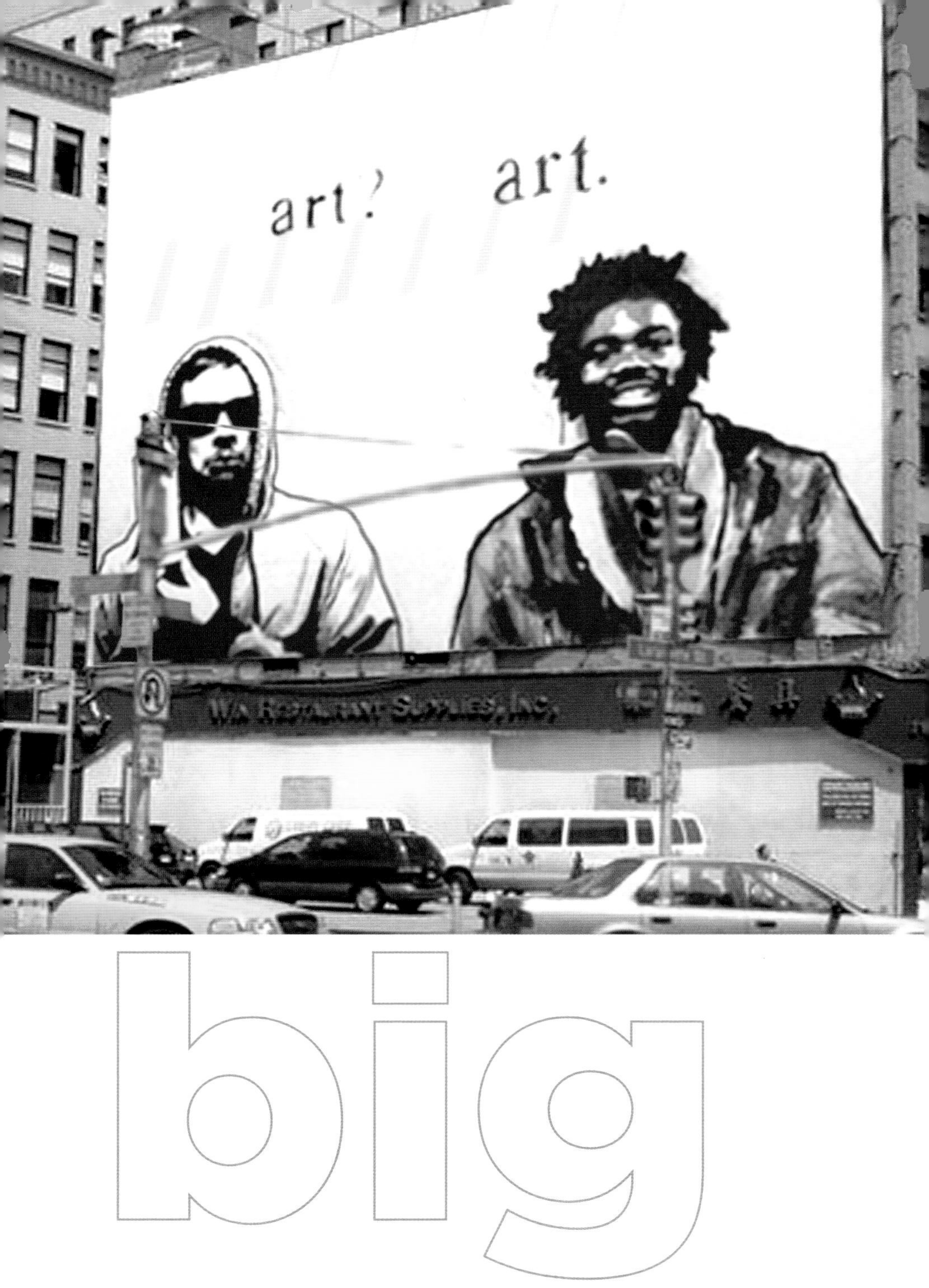
art? art.

big

New York has
Finally offered me
Importance

A gift I guess

Something nice to wear
To the totem pole party

Of course, I accepted it
But I refuse to wear it
Instead I gave it to
My mother

Why do we care?

Told her keep it
By her bed
By the picture of me
Framed in humility
For the nights
When she questions

Whether or not
This city is
Swallowing me whole

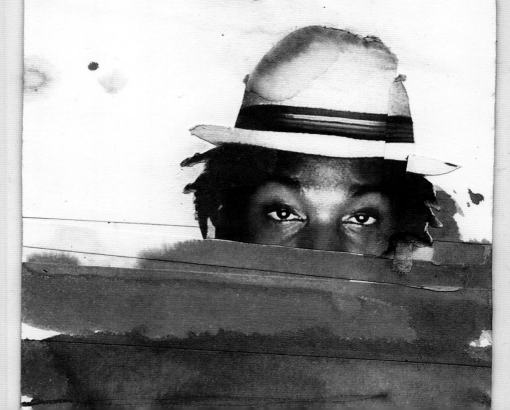

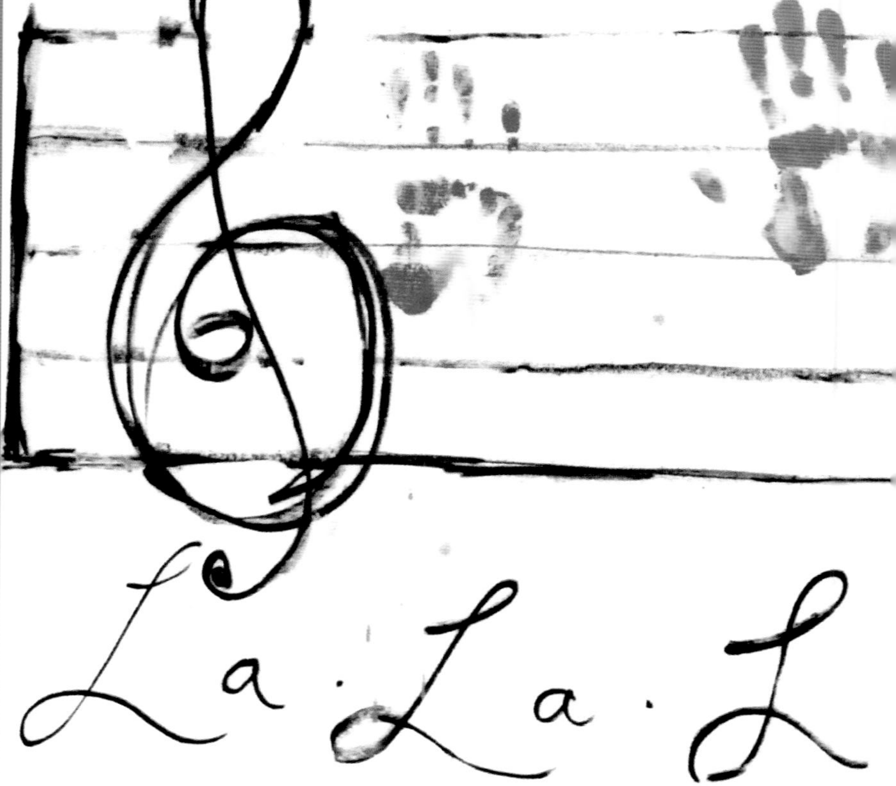
La·La·L

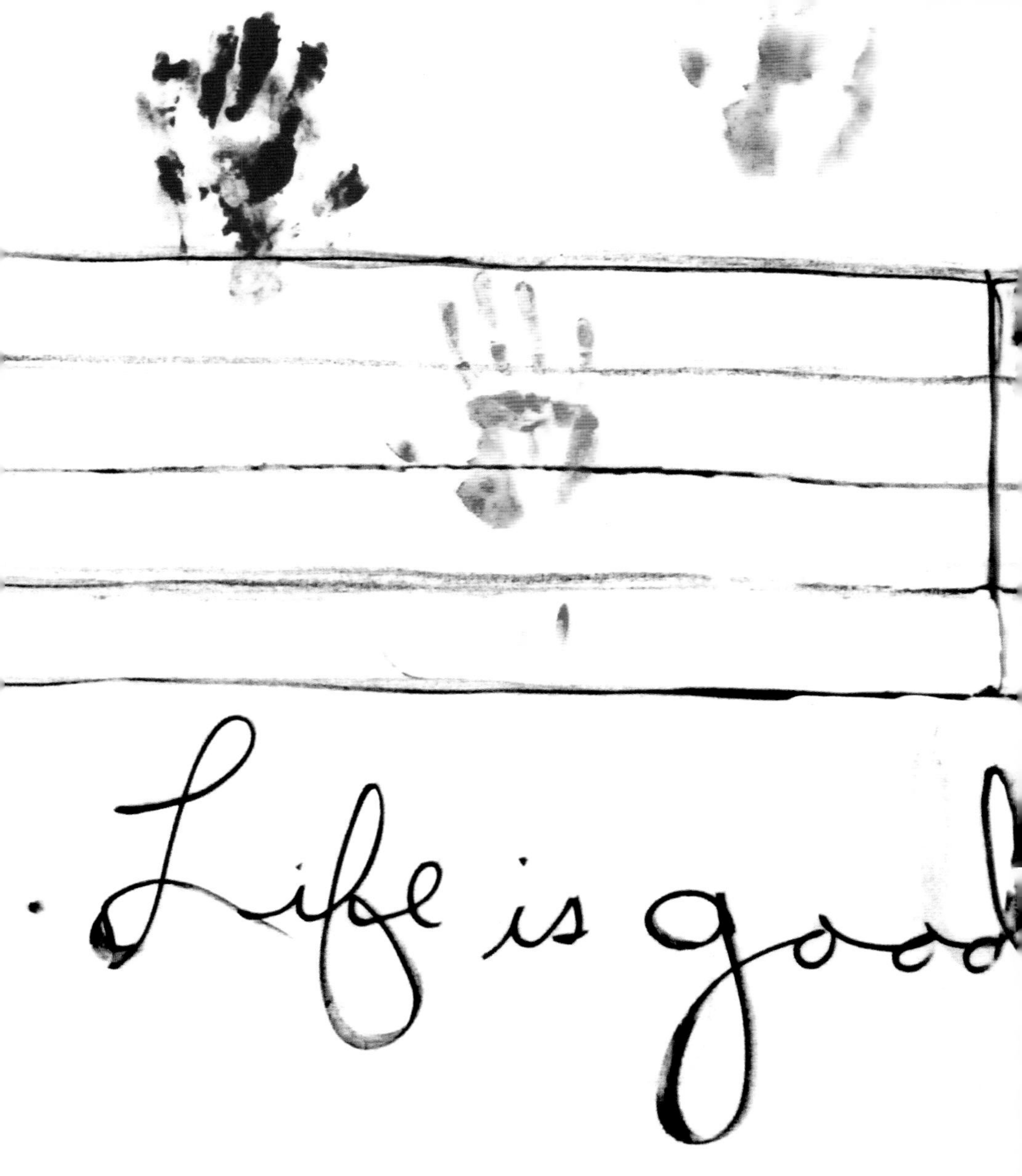
Life is good

life: Good

life: Good

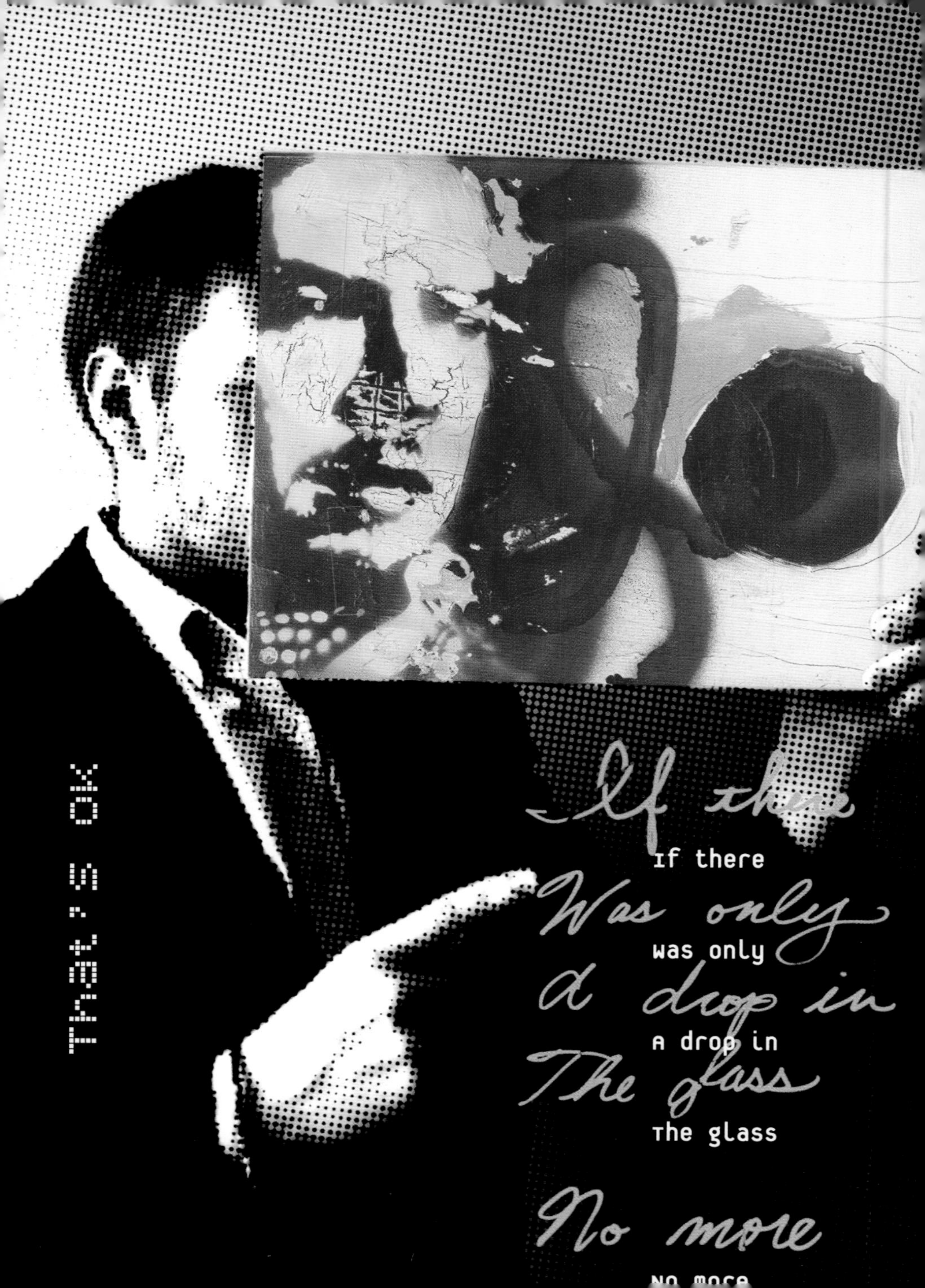
That's OK
If there
if there
Was only
was only
A drop in
a drop in
The glass
the glass
No more

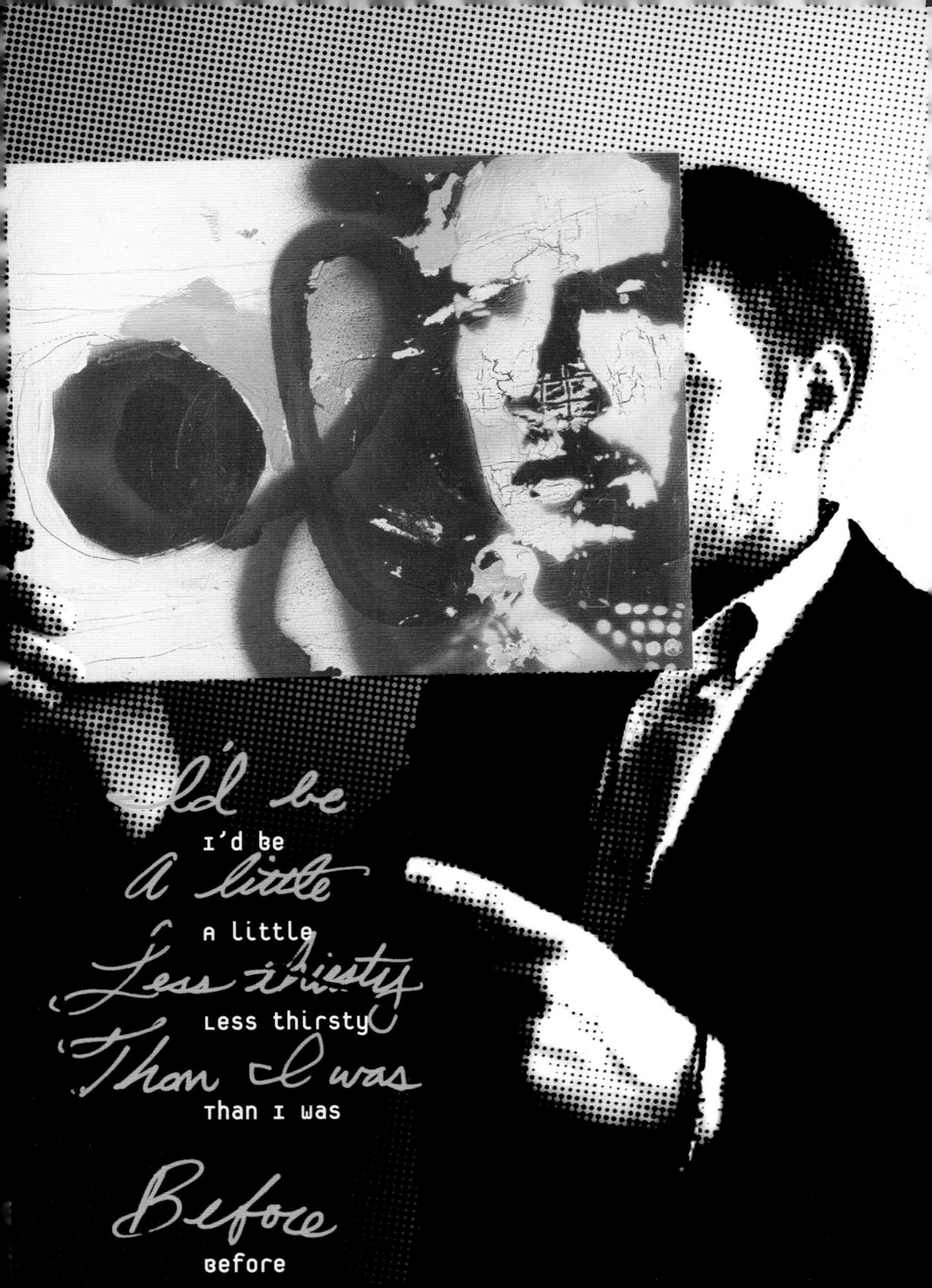
I'd be
I'd be
A little
A little
Less thirsty
Less thirsty
Than I was
Than I was
Before
Before

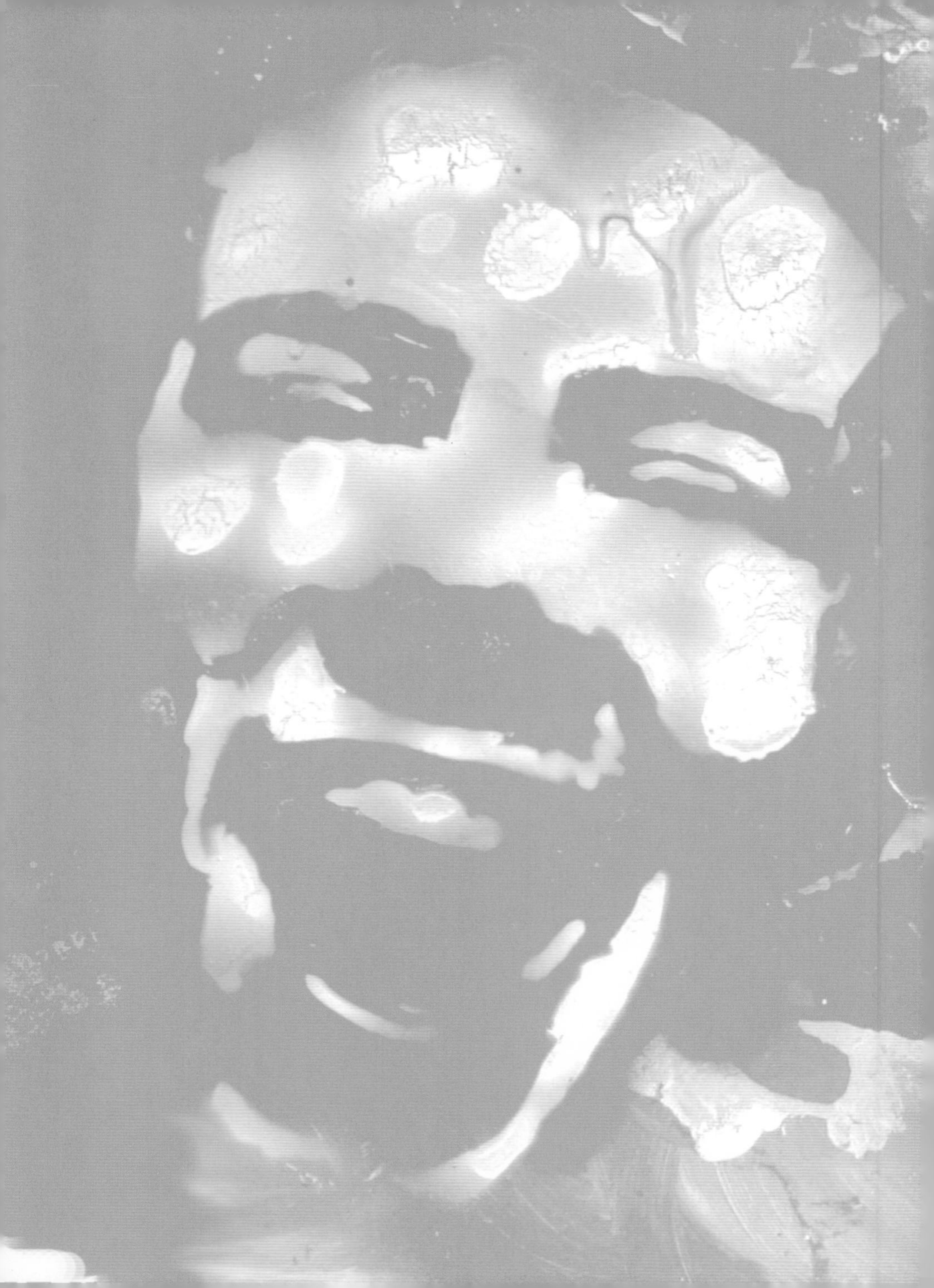

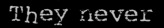

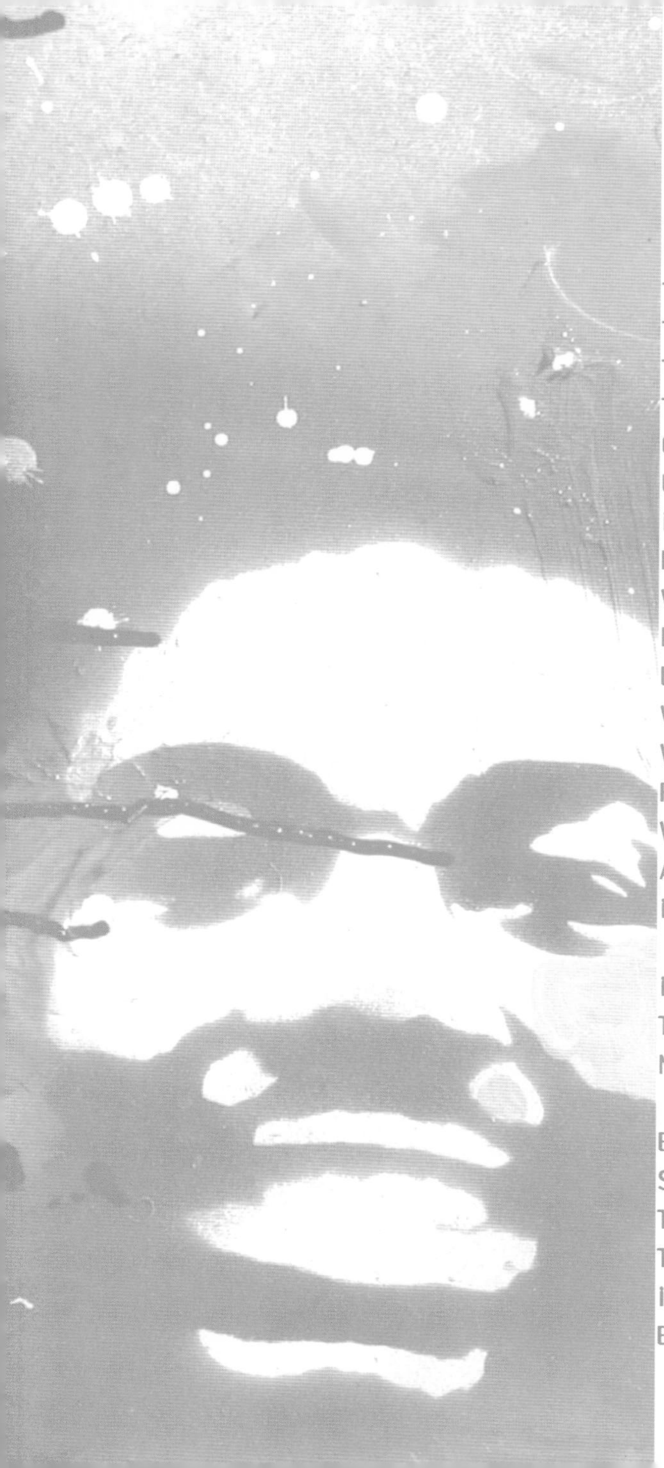

It's so hard
To explain to people
The beauty in brokenness
The scarring in sweet salvation
The lovely lacerations
Of the unlimited
Unlaminated
Illuminated
Few
Who dare to do don'ts
Miss a few meals
But will to do won'ts
While well-to-dos
Whisper questions
Regarding
Who I think I am
And who they think
I should be

I laugh and hope
They leave
Me alone

Because it's just
So hard
To explain to people
That my life
Is not unhard
But not unhappy

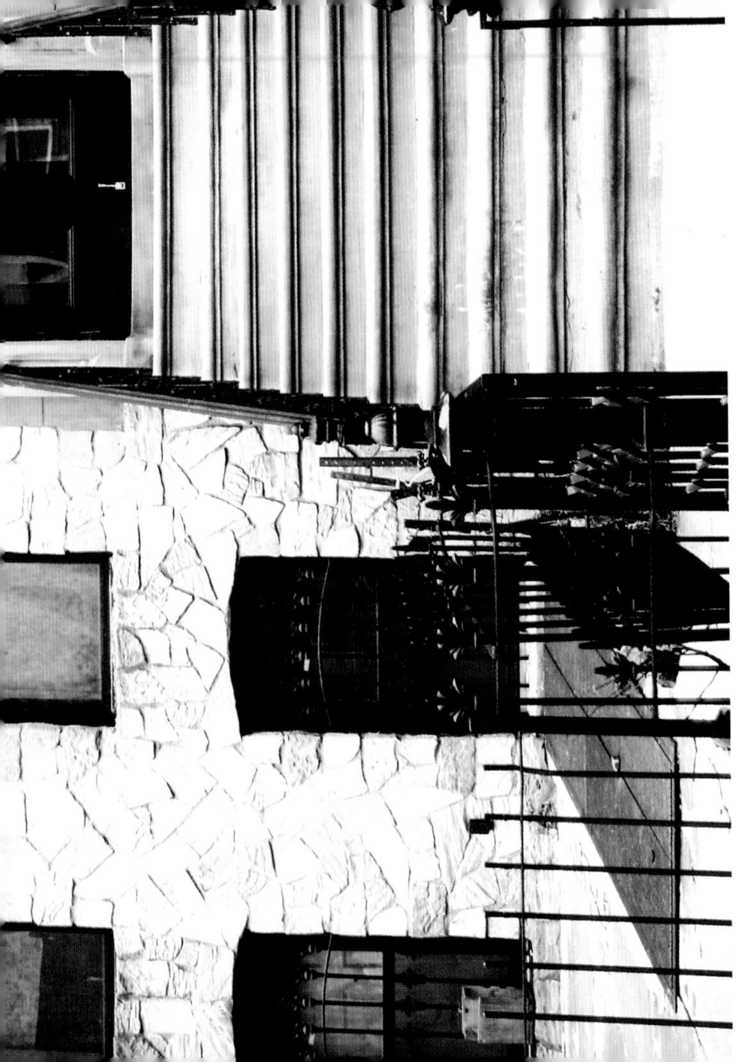

A poet

He walks in
His hair everywhere
His clothes not so neat
But he's comfortable and
He's confident

He walks in
Books in his hand
Words running around
His mind like children
Playing tag on a snow day
He's ready

He walks in
Introduces himself as a poet
And their professor

Each student wondering
Where his corduroy blazer was
Where his horn-rimmed glasses
And corncob pipe were
And when was his beard
Going to turn white

He walks in
As himself and
Teaches his first lesson
On cliché

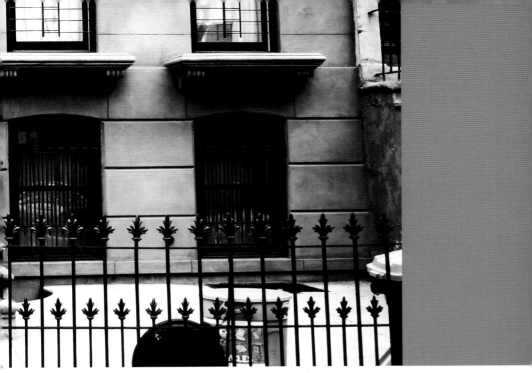

I wrote a poem once
About a poem that could
Do things

Like grow legs and walk
Grow arms and hold someone
Wrap them in wonderfuls
And other good words

A poem with a heart

A poem that could
Jump rope on the sidewalk
And high five
Five-year-olds for
Smiling and laughing

A poem that could smile
And laugh
And listen
To old ladies talk

About the poems
They're sick and tired of

A poem that could live forever
And give birth
To humans

And tell them how
Great they are

A poem with
No comma
Period
Or indentation
That could love
And love

I wrote a poem once
About a poem that could
Do things

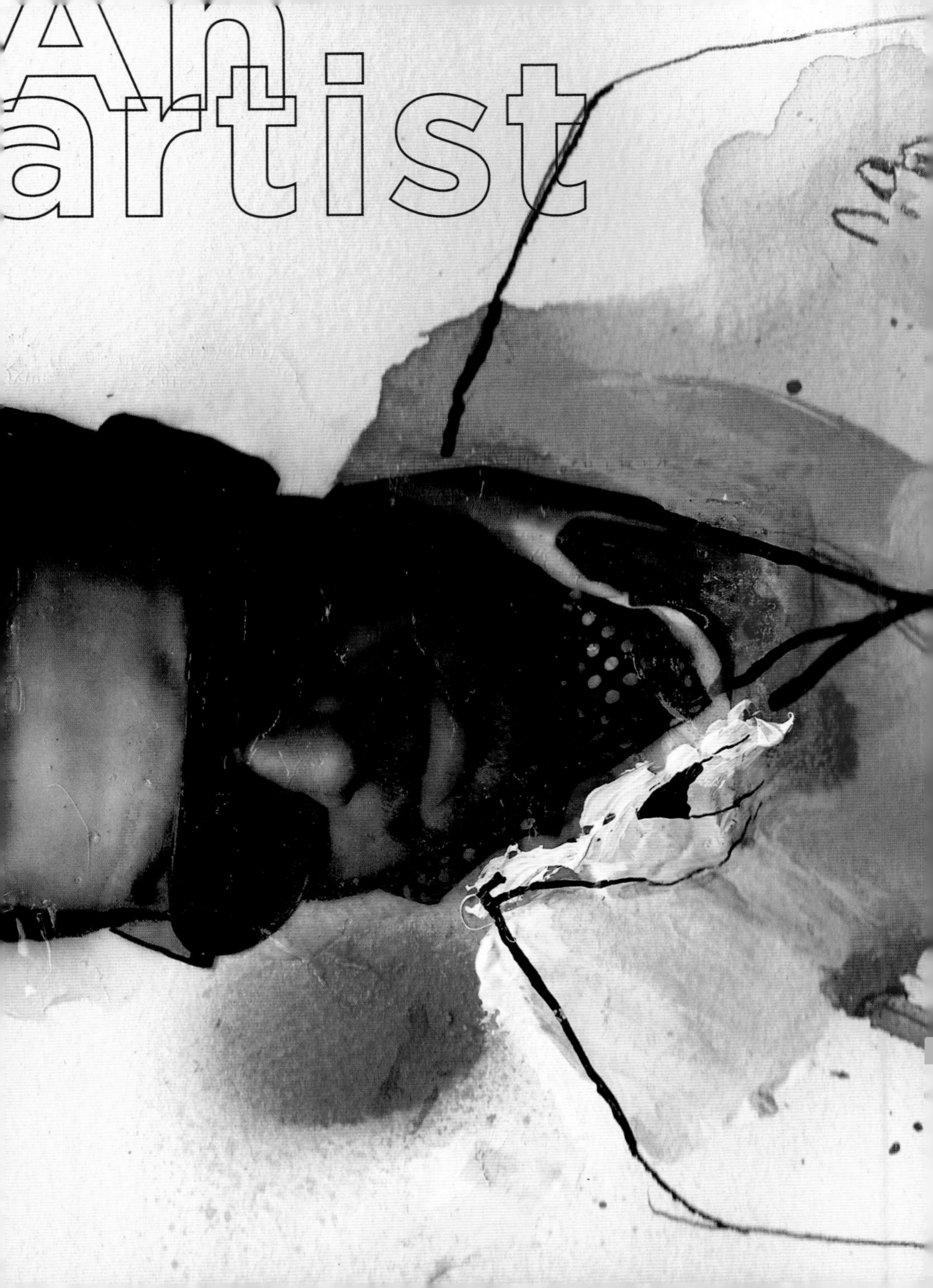
An
artist

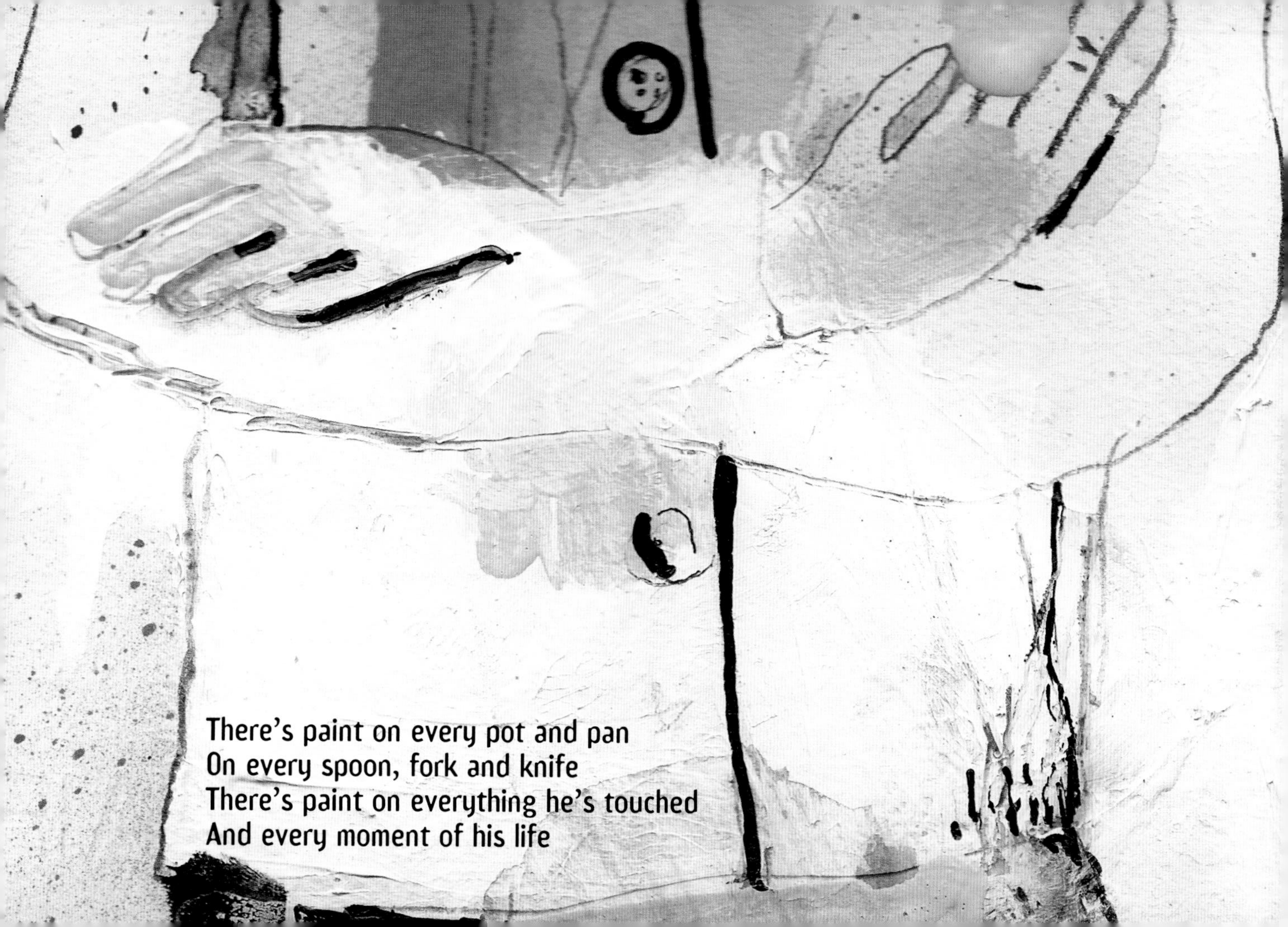

There's paint on every pot and pan
On every spoon, fork and knife
There's paint on everything he's touched
And every moment of his life

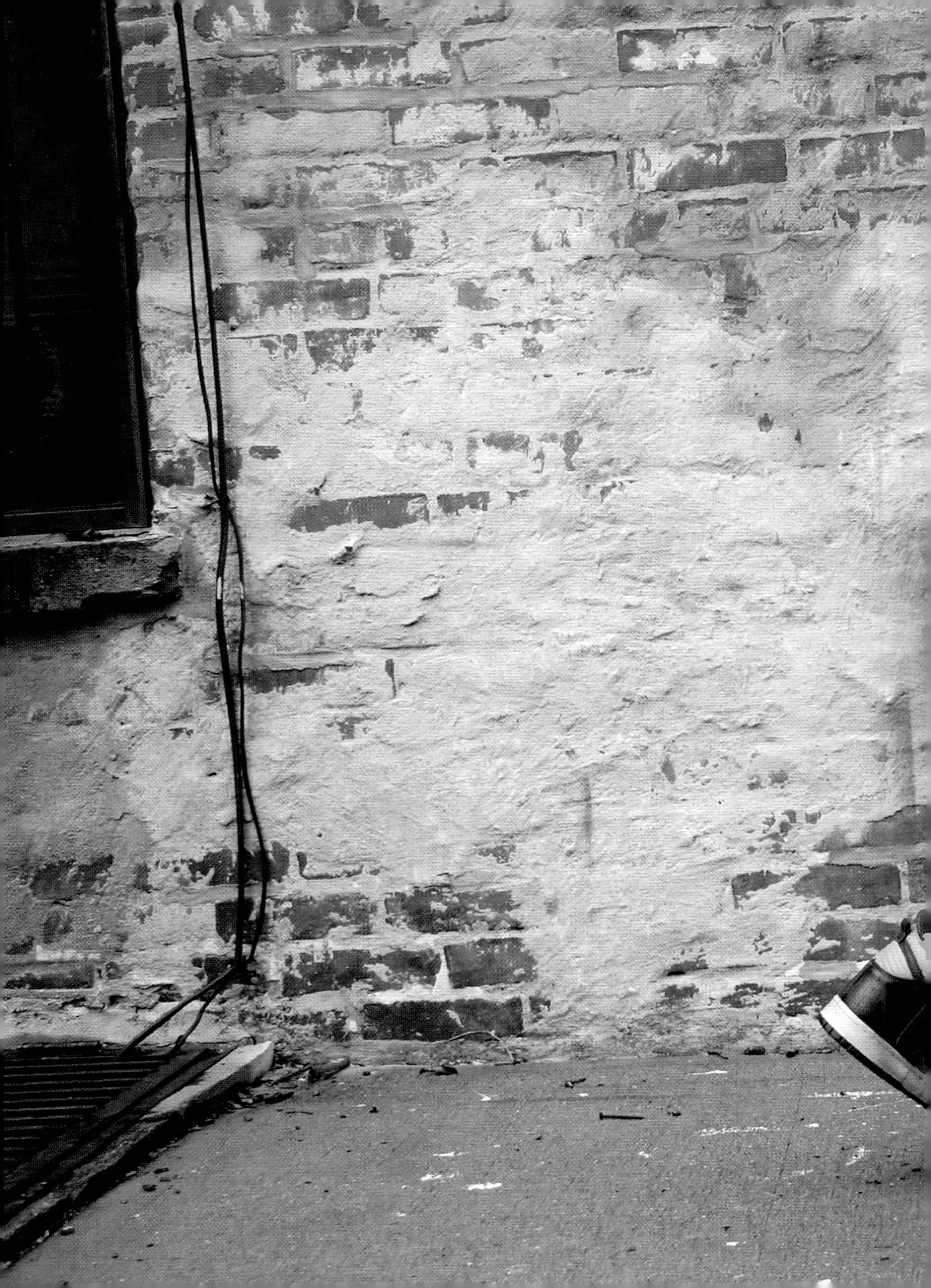

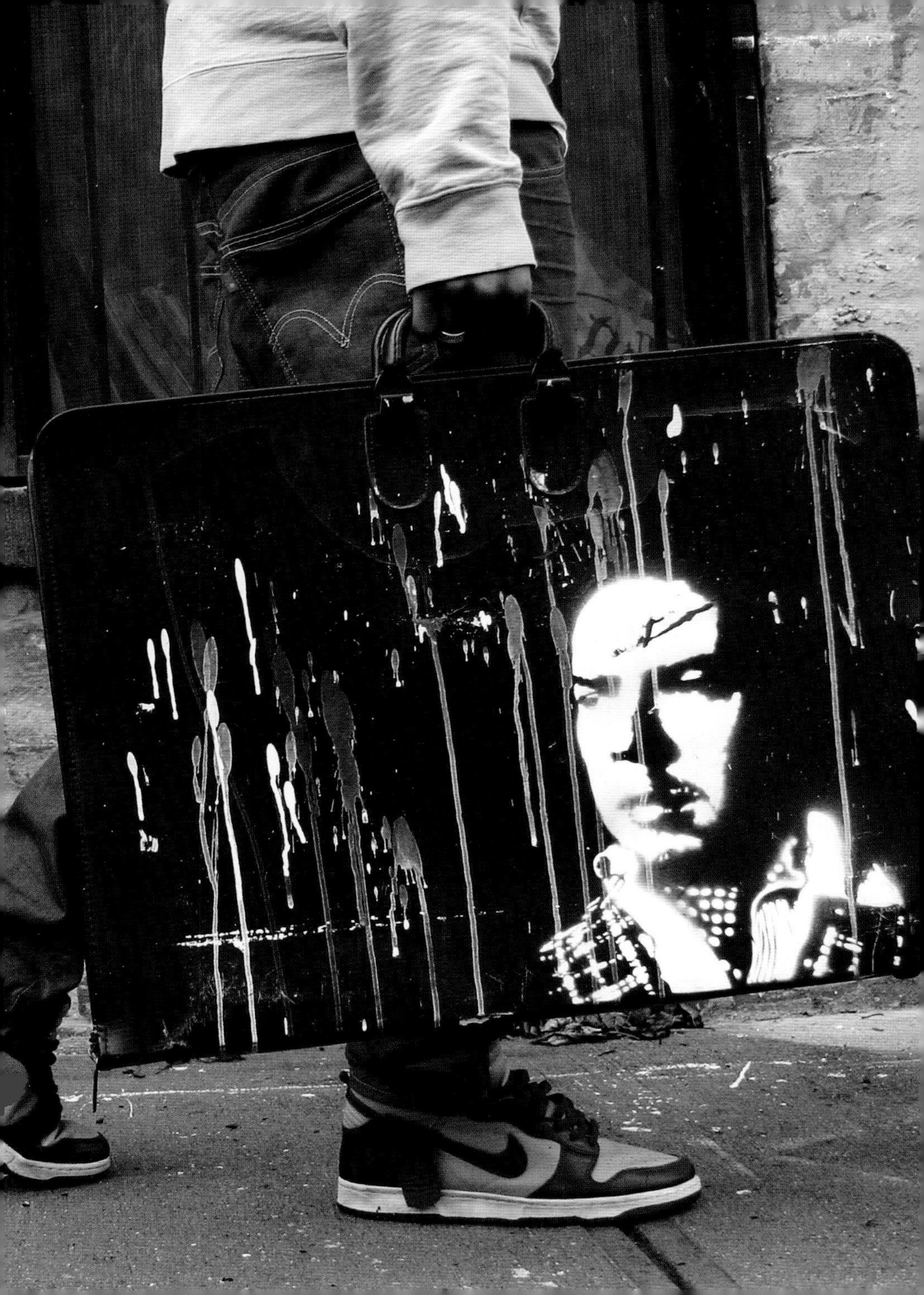

Question to a Friend

What happens if the pen runs dry
And the canvas doesn't stretch
Or if there was no more paper supply
And pencils didn't sketch?

What if my hands suddenly were numb
And there was nothing I could hold
Or if suddenly I was deaf and dumb
And no story could be told?

What if all I could paint was the color black
And the only word I could write was wrong?
What if my niche just wasn't my knack
And I was misled all along?

What if painting was a sin
And poetry became taboo
And no one ever clapped for me again
My question is, would you?

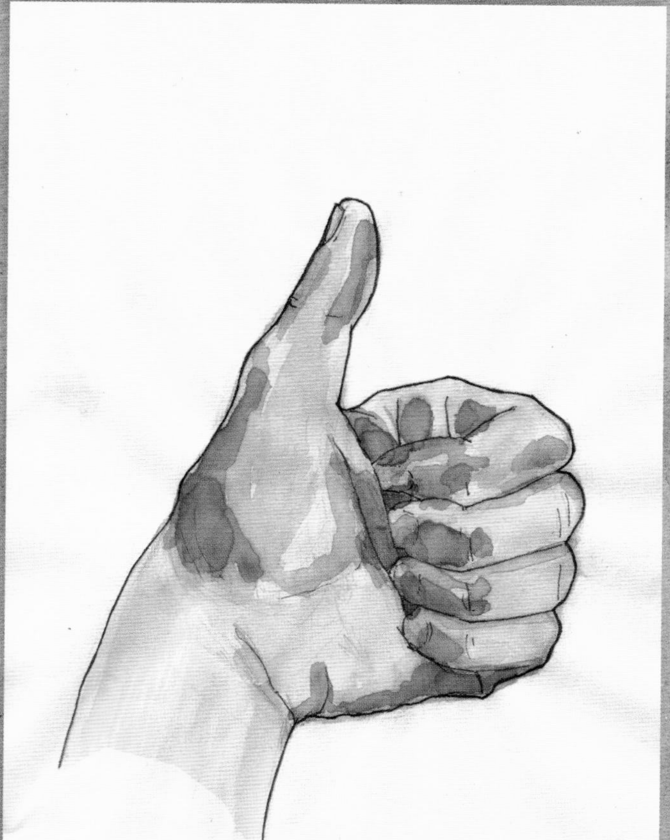

to all those reading

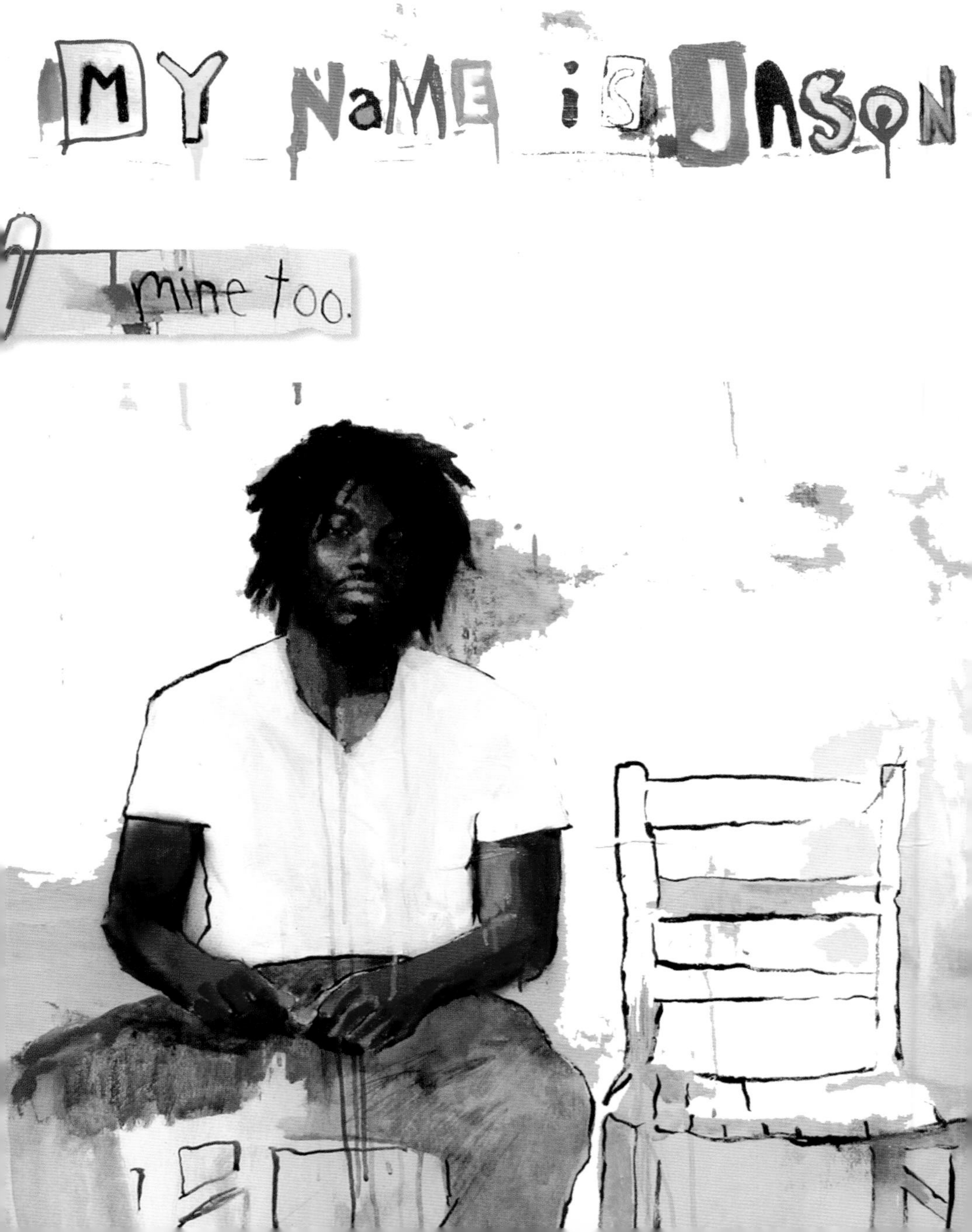
MY NaME iS JASON
mine too.

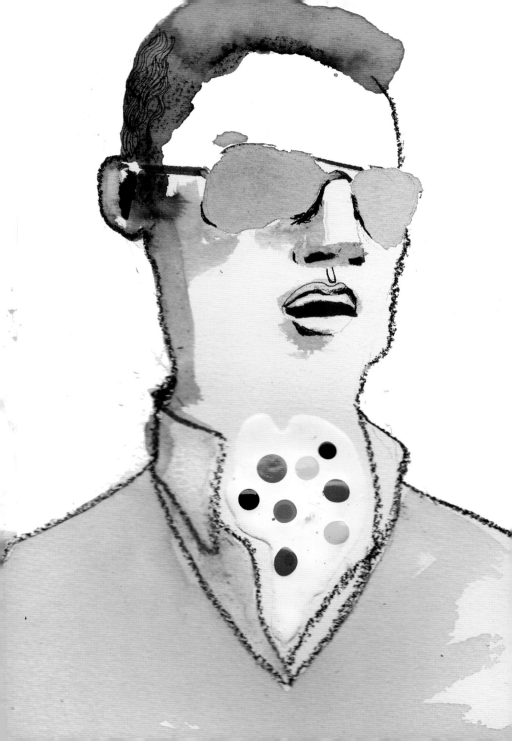

Thirteen years later...

Griffin: Thinking back, over a decade ago, when we were creating *My Name Is Jason. Mine Too.*, what memory stands out to you?

Reynolds: The fact that we seemed to never sleep! Seriously, when I think back, I remember the two of us moving to Brooklyn, unpacking everything—which wasn't much—and then eating Chinese food. After that . . . work. Just, work! I'd go to bed at like three a.m., leaving you awake painting on old doors we found on the street or whatever else you could get your hands on. I'd wake up and come downstairs at nine a.m., and you'd already be up, sitting on the floor in the kitchen, working. It was almost as if you never went to sleep. Like you were a machine!

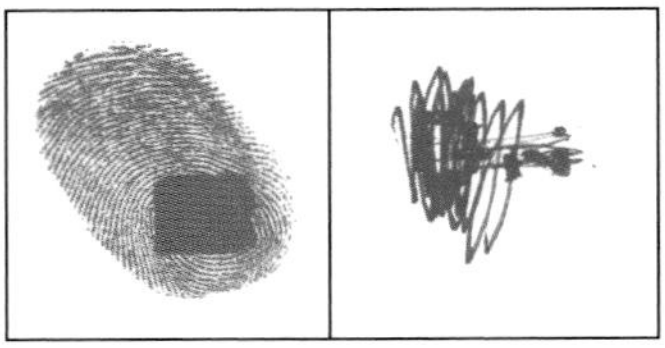

Griffin: Man, just thinking about that schedule makes me tired! But I appreciate that, J, especially coming from one of the hardest-working people I know. It's kinda cliché, but when you're doing what you love, it doesn't feel like work. That being said, I think there was also a bit of fear driving us. Or maybe the balancing act of ego and humility. Moving to the big city, and quickly realizing the big city wasn't waiting for us, definitely stands out as a moment. The work in this book reminds me of how we coped with that reality. And also how we were willing to bet it all because we felt we had no other choice. Like, *This is our shot—we can't slip up.*

Reynolds: There was definitely some fear there. And definitely a peculiar ego at that age. I was twenty. You were twenty-two. We really believed we were making something no one had ever seen and that we were reinventing what people thought of when they thought of books. I'm not sure we completely succeeded, and honestly, looking back, I'm not sure that even matters. But it definitely meant something that we wanted to push ourselves that way. That we were able to harness the moxie of youth to make whatever we wanted. Now we're almost twenty years older. Do y still feel that?

Griffin: Good point. And that's such an inte esting question. For me, I think it's alwa about truth—but how we find that truth is a d ferent story. And so if truth is the baromet then in some ways I have to work harder no It's almost like it becomes harder to be hones and I have to purposely unlearn certain thin to get to it. Such a strange concept. But a gre example of how we, adults, need to stop a thank our younger selves, and learn from the And in some ways, strive to be them.

Reynolds: I totally agre Because I miss the Jason th wrote this book. Well, act ally, that's not true. I hunt th Jason down every morning continue this work. And not ju the work of making art, becau this book ain't even about th But the work of being a friend to myself, and friend to others.

Griffin: And perhaps that requires exactly wh it required back then—working through em tional layers of excitement, insecurity, hope, name a few. Laughter definitely got us throu too. Remember that time I tried to hurdle t spiked iron fence?

Reynolds: Of course! You remember crashi parties just for food?

Griffin: Yooooo, that's right! Destroying t refreshments. You know how many little plat you gotta eat to get full?! They knew, bro. Th all knew.

Reynolds: They definitely knew! But we d whatever it took. And twenty years later, thou differently, we're still doing whatever it takes

Griffin: Some things never change.

—November 2(